30th ISSAT International Conference on Reliability and Quality in Design (ISSAT 2025)

Honolulu, Hawaii, USA
6 - 8 August 2025

ISBN: 979-8-3313-2573-2

Printed from e-media with permission by:

Curran Associates, Inc.
57 Morehouse Lane
Red Hook, NY 12571

Some format issues inherent in the e-media version may also appear in this print version.

International Society of Science & Applied Technologies (ISSAT)
Box 4134
Metuchen, NJ 08840
USA

www.issatconferences.org

Additional copies of this publication are available from:

Curran Associates, Inc.
57 Morehouse Lane
Red Hook, NY 12571 USA
Phone: 845-758-0400
Fax: 845-758-2633
Email: curran@proceedings.com
Web: www.proceedings.com

ISSAT

CONFERENCE PROCEEDINGS

30th ISSAT International Conference on Reliability and Quality in Design

Honolulu, Hawaii, U.S.A.

August 6-8, 2025

Editor HOANG PHAM

ISSAT
www.issatconferences.org

Conference Sponsor

The International Society of Science and Applied Technologies

In Cooperation with:

The Korean Reliability Society (KORAS)
Reliability Engineering Association of Japan (REAJ)
Reliability Society Japan Join Chapter (IEEE-RSJC)

Organizing Committee

Conference Chairs

Professor **Hoang Pham**
Rutgers University, USA

Professor **Shigeru Yamada**
Tottori University, Japan

Program Chairs

Professor **Yi-Kuei Lin**
National Yang Ming Chiao Tung University, Taiwan

Dr. **Feng-Bin Sun**
Tesla, Inc., USA

Professor **Xufeng Zhao**
Nanjing University of Aeronautics and Astronautics, China

International Program Committee

M. Z. Anis (India)
Mahmoud Boushaba (Algeria)
Antonio Casimiro Caputo (Italy)
Philippe Castagliola (France)
Antonella Certa (Italy)
In Hong Chang (Korea)
Ping-Chen Chang (Taiwan)
Chung-Ho Chen (Taiwan)
Kuen-Suan Chen (Taiwan)
Shin-Guang Chen (Taiwan)
Kuan-Jung Chung (Taiwan)
Maxim Finkelstein (South Africa)
Lance Fiondella (USA)
Kehan Gao (USA)
Feng Geng (UK)
Antoine Grall (France)
Xuefei Guan (China)
Cheng-Fu Huang (Taiwan)
Shinji Inoue (Japan)
Mingxiao Jiang (USA)
Taghi M. Khoshgoftaar (USA)
Mitsuhiro Kimura (Japan)
Debasis Kundu (India)
Tobias Leopold (Germany)
Anatoly Lisnianski (Israel)
Yu Liu (China)
Satoshi Mizutani (Japan)
N. V. R. Naidu (India)
Kazuhira Okumoto (USA)
Dong H. Park (Korea)
Minjae Park (Korea)
Alexander Parkhomovsky (USA)
Alessandro Persona (Italy)
Florin Popentiu Vladicescu (Romania)
Gordon J. Savage (Canada)
Shey-Huei Sheu (Taiwan)
Kazuyuki Suzuki (Japan)
Yoshinobu Tamura (Japan)
Loon-Ching Tang (Singapore)
Zhigang Tian (Canada)
Tzong-Ru Tsai (Taiwan)
Fugee Tsung (Hong Kong)
Nikola Vujanovic (Serbia)
Hongzhou Wang (USA)
Eric T. T. Wong (Hong Kong)
Liyang Xie (China)
Min Xie (Hong Kong)
Ruey Huei Yeh (Taiwan)
Songlin Zheng (China)
Mengmeng Zhu (USA)
Ming J. Zuo (Canada)

Table of Contents

SESSION 7: PRODUCT QUALITY: MODELS AND THEIR APPLICATIONS

SESSION 8: MODELING AND ANALYSIS WITH MACHINE LEARNING: METHODS AND APPLICATIONS

SESSION 9: ADVANCES IN DEEP LEARNING AND FEATURE SELECTION: METHODS AND APPLICATIONS

SESSION 10: RELIABILITY MODELING, OPTIMIZATION, AND THEIR APPLICATIONS

Socio-Economic Impact Assessment of the Company Value Chain System on the Local Economy: A Methodological Overview

KUSKOVA, Valentina V.,[1] ZAYTSEV, Dmitry[2]

[1] Lucy Family Institute for Data & Society, University of Notre Dame, Notre Dame, IN, USA, vkuskova@nd.edu
[2] Lucy Family Institute for Data & Society, University of Notre Dame, Notre Dame, IN, USA, dzaytsev@nd.edu

Keywords: economic impact assessment, social impact assessment, company system, contribution to economic development

Abstract - A socio-economic impact assessment (SEIA) requires a rigorous framework that encompasses both quantitative and qualitative indicators in order to capture a company's broader contributions to national and regional development. In an effort to expand the existing methodology of SEA to an entire value chain of a major company with multiple production cites and an extensive value chain, this study adopts an approach that integrates conventional economic metrics with input-output modeling, primary survey data, and extensive use of official statistics. The primary objective is to evaluate not only direct effects - such as the company's internal employment statistics, tax payments, and investments - but also the indirect and induced effects that arise as these expenditures ripple throughout the economy. By combining multiple data sources and using methodologies that have proven robust in prior research, in addition to developing proprietary methodologies, the study provides a comprehensive, methodologically sound account of the Coca-Cola System's total impact on Russia's socio-economic landscape. The purpose of this publication is to concentrate on the methodology of the assessment rather than the actual results.

1. Introduction

Socio-economic impact assessment is a methodological framework designed to analyze how a specific organization, project, or initiative influences the economic well-being and social fabric of a given region or country [1]. Its core premise is that any economic entity - whether a single factory or a multinational corporation - interacts with a wide range of stakeholders: employees, suppliers, local communities, and government institutions. These interactions give rise to measurable effects such as job creation, tax revenue, and investment flows, as well as more intangible social outcomes like community support, workforce development, and environmental management. A comprehensive assessment draws on both quantitative and qualitative techniques to capture this multifaceted influence, with an emphasis on tracing the interconnected chains of production and consumption that extend far beyond the entity's immediate operations [2].

All socio-economic impact assessments begin by defining the object of study and specifying the scope of analysis. Some assessments focus on a single plant in one region, while others examine national or even international operations [3]. The choice of scope determines the breadth of data collection and frames the analytical strategies employed. In most cases, the assessment considers three interrelated effects. Direct effects refer to the immediate outputs of the entity's operations, such as the wages it pays, the materials it purchases, and the taxes it remits. Indirect effects arise in the organization's supply chain: when a manufacturer buys machinery, packaging, or logistics services, those suppliers in turn must acquire inputs from further upstream firms, creating a network of economic dependencies. Induced effects, meanwhile, reflect how employees of both the focal organization and its suppliers spend their incomes in local communities, thereby stimulating broader consumer demand. Taken together, these three categories of impact help analysts move beyond straightforward indicators – such as total investment or headcount – and toward a richer understanding of how wealth creation and resource allocation radiate throughout the economy.

Input-output modeling is a key methodological pillar in capturing these effects. Originally developed by Wassily Leontief [4], this approach relies on inter-industry tables that map how goods and services flow among different sectors of an economy. By tracking each sector's imports, outputs, and dependencies on other industries, input-output modeling generates multipliers that show how initial spending in one area ripples outward through the supply chain. This is particularly useful for quantifying indirect and induced impacts because it can account for sector-specific nuances: in some regions, a particular input might be predominantly imported, while in others it can be supplied locally. The analyst first determines the entity's spending patterns across a range of goods and services, then applies these multipliers to estimate how many additional jobs, how much extra production, or how many added tax receipts this spending ultimately generates. Through this process, input-output analysis reveals the knock-on effects that a large company or project can have, providing a metric for gauging the degree to which an economy truly benefits from its presence.

Data collection occupies a central place in socio-economic impact assessment [5]. Because the analysis extends well beyond internal expenditures, researchers must gather information from multiple sources in order to build a credible picture of the total impact. Company records, including financial statements, procurement data, and human resources files, typically serve as the baseline for identifying direct effects, especially when those records have been subject to external audits or government verification. Official statistics from national or regional statistical agencies help contextualize these figures and supply average wage levels, total employment rates, and other macroeconomic indicators. Where the company's own data leave gaps - perhaps in identifying the precise composition of indirect supply chains -analysts may consult specialized market research databases or industry reports. They may also conduct original surveys and interviews with local suppliers or community stakeholders, which can yield practical insights into the chain of subcontractors that do not always appear in official documentation.

Once collected, data are subjected to a process of validation and triangulation [6]. It is not unusual, for instance, for the direct purchases a company reports to be cross-checked against suppliers' sales figures. Where input-output tables rely on average ratios of local production to imports, surveys of suppliers can confirm or refine these assumptions. If discrepancies arise, analysts can investigate whether the variation stems from something unique about the focal company's supply chain or from inaccuracies in official databases. By consolidating results across multiple sources, the final impact assessment avoids overreliance on any single dataset, thereby increasing both rigor and transparency.

Socio-economic impact assessments often span multiple years [9], particularly when the organization in question has made investments or expansions over a long period. To compare financial figures across time, researchers typically convert nominal values into a single base year's currency. This step accounts for inflation and exchange-rate fluctuations, which would otherwise make it difficult to discern real changes in the scale of operations. Historical exchange rates might be taken from a central bank or an international organization, and inflation adjustments are typically anchored by recognized indices such as the Consumer Price Index (CPI) or Producer Price Index (PPI). The resulting standardized time series allows analysts to see, for example, whether the ratio of local procurement to imports has risen or declined in real terms or whether the value of total investments has increased consistently, irrespective of currency shifts.

In addition to economic metrics, contemporary assessments frequently include social and environmental dimensions [7]. Although not as readily expressed in multiplier formats, these variables reflect significant considerations for community well-being. Workforce statistics - such as the proportion of women in managerial roles, average age, or workforce stability - indicate broader labor-market contributions and inclusivity policies. Similarly, data on safety performance, volunteer initiatives, and community-based educational programs offer insight into the overall quality of the corporate presence. Environmental indicators may include resource consumption, waste management, and compliance with international standards. In each instance, analysts strive to collect data in ways that match established frameworks, such as ISO certifications or the Global Reporting Initiative, so that the results can be compared with industry norms or best practices.

The final stage of socio-economic impact assessment is assembling these diverse findings into a cohesive narrative that both quantifies the magnitude of the company's impact and explains how it unfolds through specific economic linkages. Presentation strategies vary, but the goal is to demonstrate how direct spending leads to indirect supplier activity and, ultimately, the induced wave of consumer spending. By emphasizing the logic behind each step - how multipliers are derived, how surveys fill data gaps, and how inflation adjustments standardize monetary figures - analysts enhance the credibility of their conclusions. Any shortfalls in data or gaps in coverage can be acknowledged openly, clarifying which figures are precise calculations and which are approximations or estimates.

In essence, socio-economic impact assessment offers a structured way to move beyond superficial indicators - like total capital spent or tax paid - and to uncover the broader reach that an organization's operations can have on an economy and its communities. It achieves this by combining existing techniques, such as input-output modeling, with thorough data collection, careful cross-checking, and a methodology for exploring social and environmental factors alongside traditional economic metrics. The resulting picture is one in which a single entity's decisions to build, hire, procure, or partner resonate through multiple layers of society, highlighting both the tangible and less tangible pathways through which local and national development can occur. In this paper, we focus on the methodological aspects of the assessment, including the proprietary methodology developed for such an assessment of the Coca-Cola in Russia system ("the Company"), evaluated for the years 2013-2020.

2. Rationale and Scope of the Impact Assessment

An overarching rationale for the assessment lies in the Company's long history of direct investment in Russia and its extensive network of business relationships. These relationships, which involve suppliers, buyers, service providers, and local communities, often create complex multiplier effects. Traditional corporate reports tend to focus on direct indicators - such as a firm's capital spending or headcount - without fully accounting for the additional layers of value generated in local supply chains and labor markets. The Coca-Cola System's size and operational breadth in Russia make it an especially apt subject for a study that attempts to trace these broader dynamics. The time frame of 2013 to 2020 captures a period of both macroeconomic challenges and shifts in the domestic beverage market, thereby offering insight into how large multinational companies behave and adapt under varying conditions. While the study was conducted at the end of 2020, not all 2020 data were available, requiring some extrapolation.

Within this context, we define "impact" along three principal axes: economic (e.g., gross domestic product [GDP] contributions, tax revenues, investments, employment), social (e.g., workforce diversity, youth and community development programs, volunteerism), and environmental (e.g., resource usage, waste management, and labor safety standards). While the study is designed to detail these outcomes extensively, the methodological apparatus we report in this paper is centered on accurately measuring how the Company and its stakeholders interact across different spheres of the Russian economy.

3. Foundational Methodologies: Direct, Indirect, and Induced Effects

To structure the measurement of impact, we adopted a framework based on the standard distinction among direct, indirect, and induced effects. Direct effects represent the most immediate outcomes of the Company's own activities and are derived from its financial records, staffing data, and taxation figures. Such direct indicators are relatively straightforward: they reflect Coca-Cola's direct spending on wages, raw materials, facilities, equipment, and other operational expenses.

However, relying solely on direct effects would underestimate the overall magnitude of a large multinational's footprint on the host economy. For that reason, we calculated indirect effects by identifying the layers of business activities triggered by the Company's presence. In practice, this entails tracing how expenditures along the value chain, such as sugar, packaging materials, marketing services, transportation, and other inputs impact local suppliers, many of whom, in turn, purchase goods and services from additional tiers of producers. On the other end, the discounts provided to buyers (mostly wholesalers, though retailers working directly with the Company can also be included in the calculations) account for additional effects on the other end of the value chain. To do so credibly requires a methodology that can capture not only the immediate supplier relationships but also the extended networks of smaller firms and subcontractors further down the chain.

Once direct and indirect effects were estimated, we addressed induced effects. These arise from the spending patterns of individuals employed by both the Company and its suppliers and buyers. The wages they earn - whether at the Coca-Cola System itself or at upstream and downstream firms - are injected back into the local economy as households purchase goods and services. Such household spending, in turn, supports additional employment and further economic growth, creating a feedback loop of consumption and production. This iterative process ensures that the final impact figures go beyond a simple tally of plant investments or production line expansions, instead reflecting a multi-layered view of how the Company's economic activity reverberates across Russia.

4. Input-Output Analysis and Leontief's Multipliers

A key methodological pillar for capturing indirect and induced effects is the use of input-output analysis, which relies on tables originally conceptualized by Nobel Prize winner Wassily Leontief [4]. These input-output tables record the flows of goods and services among various industries within a national or regional economy. By linking each industry's outputs to its inputs from other industries, the tables yield multipliers that reflect how initial expenditures in one sector lead to incremental activity elsewhere.

For this study, we drew on data from international organizations - most notably the OECD [8] - and supplemented those figures with relevant Russian statistical publications (RosStat) to map industry interdependencies. In practical terms, we first isolated the direct spending of the Coca-Cola System, then distributed those expenditures across the relevant industries (e.g., agriculture, manufacturing, logistics, distribution) in proportion to publicly available procurement data. By applying Leontief's multipliers to each category of expenditure, it becomes possible to estimate the knock-on effects generated by intermediate suppliers, even when those secondary businesses are located several steps removed from the Company's immediate operations.

Because the Russian Federation has specific patterns of import dependence in certain sectors (for instance, specialized agricultural inputs may be partially imported), the input-output approach helps distinguish truly local production activities from what is ultimately imported. This distinction is crucial in quantifying the "local content" dimension of the Company's footprint. The methodology thus accounts for intermediate imports hidden at various stages of the supply chain, producing a more refined calculation of how much of the total value added is retained within Russia.

5. Data Collection and Triangulation

The study's design incorporates multiple streams of data to strengthen the validity of the results. First, internal Company data - such as official financial statements, tax filings, procurement records, and employment statistics - supply the foundational metrics for direct effects. Because Coca-Cola Russia holds official "major taxpayer" status, its tax reporting is subject to heightened scrutiny and is widely regarded as reliable, thereby providing a stable baseline for analysis.

Second, we used external databases to furnish important contextual and comparative data. The official Russian Federal Statistics Service (RosStat [10]) offers nationally representative statistics on employment, average wages, and industrial output, making it feasible to benchmark the Company's figures against broader industry or regional norms. Other sources, including SPARK [11], which provides financial information on all companies operating in Russia, Canadean [12], which offers market research for beverages industry, and Euromonitor [13], which conducts market research in multiple industries, yield additional insights into the performance of Russia's non-alcoholic beverage sector and its supply chains, allowing for a better approximation of how Coca-Cola's procurement and sales patterns fit within the overall marketplace.

Third, a primary data collection effort was undertaken specifically for this study. It comprised two main elements: (1) a standardized supplier survey of 311 businesses that supply goods and services to the Company, and (2) seventeen in-depth interviews with members of the Company's management. The standardized survey focused on procurement volumes, subcontracting practices, and local employment patterns, while the in-depth interviews helped clarify corporate procurement strategies, philanthropic initiatives, and internal human resource programs. These qualitative accounts offered nuance to the numerical data from official reports, especially in areas where supply chain relationships are particularly complex.

To ensure rigor, the research team triangulated these different sources. For instance, the input-output tables' multipliers were initially used to approximate indirect and induced employment generation; those estimates were then refined by comparing them with actual supplier employment figures reported through the survey. The alignment of these figures helped pinpoint any anomalies and establish more confidence in the final totals. A similar approach guided the assessment of tax payments down the supply chain, where official data from RosStat, combined with procurement distributions, indicated how much additional value - and thus tax revenue - was generated by second-tier or third-tier suppliers.

6. Standardizing Monetary Values and Temporal Coverage

A core analytical challenge lay in the effort to quantify historical and recent investments. Given the lengthy timeline of Coca-Cola's operations in Russia, we needed to present all capital expenditures in a standardized monetary unit to neutralize inflationary effects and exchange-rate fluctuations. For this purpose, we employed constant 2020 U.S. dollars. Where applicable, data from the Bank of Russia and the World Bank were used to compute annual exchange rates, ensuring consistency for earlier periods. Additionally, the study leveraged the U.S. Bureau of Labor Statistics' Producer Price Index (PPI) and Consumer Price Index (CPI) to convert nominal ruble values into inflation-adjusted dollars.

This conversion process allowed for more meaningful comparisons across years. Rather than simply noting that the Company invested a nominal sum in a decade when the ruble's value was dramatically different, we harmonized these figures into a single base year. This step is critical for avoiding distortions that might otherwise arise, for example, during periods of significant devaluation of the ruble or heightened inflation within Russia's domestic economy.

In terms of temporal scope, we concentrated primarily on the eight-year window of 2013 to 2020 for detailed analyses, while also incorporating broader historical information and trends whenever such data illuminate longer-term developments (e.g., early acquisitions of production facilities in the 1990s). Where external data sources did not provide statistics for the past years, we relied on 2019 figures to extrapolate 2020 levels. We used full information maximum likelihood approach for doing so, treating absent data as missing at random.

7. Integrating Social and Environmental Dimensions

Although the bulk of the methodology centers on economic indicators such as GDP contribution, employment, and tax revenues, the research design also includes a qualitative component for social and environmental impact. This aspect relies on document analysis of Company reporting, interviews with management, and external verification from industry benchmarks. For instance, data on workforce demographics (e.g., percentage of female managers, average age) were drawn from internal human resources reports, then contextualized using RosStat's labor force data. Similarly, environmental practices were evaluated through certifications like ISO 9001 [14], FSSC 22000 [15], or OHSAS 18001 [16], which offer standardized criteria for product quality, food safety, and workplace safety.

While such social and environmental indicators may not lend themselves as neatly to multiplier-based calculations, we still applied an evidence-based rationale wherever possible. For example, the methodological effort includes correlating changes in accident rates with the degree of training or safety protocols introduced, thus supplementing the more straightforward numbers (like accident counts) with an analysis of potential causes and improvements.

8. Concluding Reflections on the Methodological Approach

By adopting a multifaceted methodology, spanning direct financial data, input-output modeling, quantitative surveys, qualitative interviews, and standardized index adjustments, this paper presents a robust framework for measuring Coca-Cola Russia's socio-economic impact. The emphasis on triangulating multiple data sources helps ensure that the calculations of indirect and induced effects reflect reality rather than mere modeling assumptions. Moreover, the examination of environmental and social considerations, although at times less amenable to purely quantitative methods, aligns with international standards for integrated reporting and demonstrates how a large multinational can influence broad developmental outcomes.

The analytical design of our underscores the value of situating a single corporation's activities within the wider economic system. The reliance on tools such as Leontief multipliers and cost-output tables acknowledges the interconnectedness of modern supply chains. When combined with company-specific data, verified through tax records, surveys, and interviews, the final results can highlight the full reach of a company's contributions, capturing not just the immediate monetary outlays but also the deeper socio-economic currents propelled by corporate operations.

Such studies could be used not only as an analytical tool for policymakers and business leaders, but also as a powerful instrument for shaping public perception. By quantifying contributions such as job creation, local procurement, and tax revenues, an organization can demonstrate its positive influence on regional development and thereby strengthen its reputation among consumers, investors, and government agencies. This evidence-based narrative of community support, workforce development, and sustainable practices often becomes the cornerstone of public relations campaigns, helping an enterprise foster goodwill and secure social license to operate. In addition, the assessment's findings can be a basis for corporate social responsibility initiatives, stakeholder engagement, and brand positioning, as they offer concrete proof of an organization's commitment to the broader community and its stakeholders.

Despite the study's multi-layered design, several structural assumptions and data constraints inevitably shape its findings. First, the input-output framework rests on the premise that technical coefficients – the fixed ratios that link one sector's demand for another sector's outputs – remain stable over time. In reality, supply chains adjust continuously to shifts in technology, relative prices, and trade policy; treating those relationships as static may overstate or understate secondary and tertiary effects, particularly in the later years of the 2013-2020 window. For similar reasons, the Leontief multipliers employed here assume unlimited capacity in upstream industries and no price feedbacks, implicitly presuming that suppliers can meet additional demand without raising prices or displacing other customers. Where production bottlenecks or import constraints exist, the true multiplier would be lower than the model suggests.

Data availability introduces an additional layer of uncertainty. Internal Company accounts offer a robust record for direct spending and employment, yet they cannot fully capture informal subcontracting or off-balance-sheet transactions that sometimes characterize logistics and agricultural procurement in Russia. External statistics mitigate this blind spot, but official

Russian input-output tables are published with a lag and at aggregated industry resolutions; disaggregating them to match Coca-Cola's specific procurement profile required proportionality assumptions that may blur sector-specific nuances. Moreover, approximately one-fifth of the 2020 observations had to be extrapolated using 2019 patterns under a full-information maximum-likelihood approach, implicitly assuming that the pandemic and associated market disruptions did not alter the structure of spending or household consumption in ways the model cannot observe.

The primary survey of 311 suppliers and the seventeen management interviews bring valuable granularity, yet they are not strictly random samples. Participation skewed toward firms with long-standing relationships and toward managers predisposed to highlight positive spillovers, which could bias estimates upward if less-entrenched or struggling suppliers were under-represented. Although triangulation with SPARK, Euromonitor, and RosStat sources helped flag obvious outliers, the study still assumes that non-respondents resemble respondents after weighting for sector and size – an assumption that cannot be fully tested without additional fieldwork.

Household-level induced effects rely on national averages for the marginal propensity to consume and on representative budget surveys for spending composition. These parameters implicitly presume that employees of Coca-Cola and its supply chain behave like the median Russian household. If, for example, beverage-sector wages are systematically higher and savings rates lower than the national mean, the induced employment and GDP effects could be understated; the opposite holds if workers allocate a greater share of income to savings or imported goods.

Finally, social and environmental indicators are folded into the narrative alongside economic metrics, but they cannot be linked to the input-output structure with the same mathematical precision. The analysis therefore treats improvements in, say, workforce diversity or accident rates as concurrent developments rather than causally connected multipliers. This approach avoids overstating certainty, yet it also means the study cannot quantitatively apportion how much of a social or environmental gain stems directly from the Company's spending versus broader regulatory or cultural trends.

Taken together, these limitations do not invalidate the overall portrait of the Company's contribution; rather, they illuminate the bounds within which the results should be interpreted. The assessment offers a well-triangulated, best-available estimate of socio-economic reach, but its magnitudes should be read as indicative ranges conditioned on stable technical coefficients, representative survey responses, and average behavioral parameters – contingencies that future research can refine by expanding the temporal horizon, improving sampling frames, and integrating dynamic, price-sensitive modeling techniques.

9. References

[1] Glasson, J., 2017. Socio-economic impacts 1: overview and economic impacts. *Methods of environmental and social impact assessment*, pp.475-514.

[2] Vis, M., Dörnbrack, A.S. and Haye, S., 2014. Socio-economic impact assessment tools. In *Socio-Economic Impacts of Bioenergy Production* (pp. 1-16). Cham: Springer International Publishing.

[3] Holman, I.P., Rounsevell, M.D.A., Shackley, S., Harrison, P.A., Nicholls, R.J., Berry, P.M. and Audsley, E., 2005. A regional, multi-sectoral and integrated assessment of the impacts of climate and socio-economic change in the UK: Part I. Methodology. *Climatic Change*, *71*, pp.9-41.

[4] Leontief, W. ed., 1986. *Input-output economics*. Oxford University Press.

[5] Peersman, G., 2014. Overview: Data collection and analysis methods in impact evaluation.

[6] Santos, K.D.S., Ribeiro, M.C., Queiroga, D.E.U.D., Silva, I.A.P.D. and Ferreira, S.M.S., 2020. The use of multiple triangulations as a validation strategy in a qualitative study. *Ciencia & saude coletiva*, *25*, pp.655-664.

[7] Dendena, B. and Corsi, S., 2015. The Environmental and Social Impact Assessment: a further step towards an integrated assessment process. *Journal of cleaner production*, *108*, pp.965-977.

[8] https://www.oecd.org/en/data/datasets/input-output-tables.html

[9] Coker, C.C., Okonjo, C.U., Ajah, J.O., Odoemena, I. and Ibeakuzie, I., 2014. Longitudinal and Cross Sectional Mix Data Approach to Impact Assessment: A Case Study of Community Based Natural Resource Management Programme, Nigeria. *Ethiopian Journal of Environmental Studies and Management*, *7*(1), pp.731-743.

[10] https://eng.rosstat.gov.ru/

[11] https://spark-interfax.ru/

[12] https://www.just-food.com/contractors/training/canadean/

[13] https://www.euromonitor.com/

[14] https://www.iso.org/standards/popular/iso-9000-family

[15] https://www.fssc.com/schemes/fssc-22000/

[16] https://www.nqa.com/nl-nl/certification/standards/ohsas-18001

Reliability Allocation Using Importance-Weighted Geometric Mean based "Feasibility of Objectives" Method

Fengbin Sun

[1]Reliability Engineering, Tesla Inc., Palo Alto, California, U.S.A., franksun9999@gmail.com

Keywords: Reliability Allocation, Feasibility of Objectives, Importance-Weighted Geometric Mean,

Abstract - This paper proposes a novel reliability allocation algorithm by introducing an Importance-Weighted Geometric Mean approach to extend the traditional "Feasibility of Objectives" Method. This extension makes the allocation method more flexible and general to accommodate a wide range of engineering factors in real world reliability allocation.

1. Introduction

When engineers develop new products or enhance existing systems, they must design solutions that adhere to specific reliability requirements. This challenge often involves a strategic balancing act to determine how best to distribute reliability targets across the system's subsystems or components.

Reliability allocation involves establishing reliability targets for individual subsystems to ensure the overall system meets a specified reliability goal. It aims to balance hardware and software reliability objectives effectively. A well-balanced allocation typically means achieving a relative equilibrium in development time, complexity, risk, or minimizing total development costs.

This process often requires determining the optimal reliability, mean life, or failure rate of subsystems and components to achieve the system-level objectives for mission reliability, mean life, or failure rate:

$$f(R_1, R_2, \dots, R_n) \geq R_S$$

$$g(m_1, m_2, \dots, m_n) \geq m_S$$

$$h(\lambda_1, \lambda_2, \dots, \lambda_n) \leq \lambda_S$$

where:

R_S, m_S and λ_S are the system level target for mission reliability, mean life, and failure rate to be allocated to its subsystems/components.

R_i, m_i and λ_i are the reliability, mean life, and failure rate allocated to the ith subsystem/component.

f, g , and h are the reliability allocation transfer function between the subsystem/component and the system for reliability, mean life, and failure rate.

Over the years, many reliability allocation models and algorithms have been proposed including [1-10]:

- Equal apportionment method
- AGREE apportionment method
- ARINC apportionment method
- Feasibility of Objectives (FOO) apportionment method
- Bracha apportionment method
- Repairable Systems apportionment method
- AWM apportionment method
- MEOWA apportionment method
- ...

Each method has its own historical background, advantage and disadvantages. Some of the key features can be summarized as follows:

- **Equal Apportionment**: Simple but often unrealistic.
- **AGREE**: Iterative approach considering component interdependencies.
- **ARINC**: Focus on aerospace and mission-critical components.
- **FOO**: Balances goals with technological and economic feasibility.
- **Bracha**: Weighted approach based on subsystem importance.
- **Repairable Systems**: Focus on reliability with continuous maintenance.
- **AWM**: Balances cost, performance, and reliability through optimization.
- **MEOWA**: Multi-objective optimization, effective for conflicting goals.

The Feasibility of Objectives (FOO) Method is one of the widely used methods. However, the traditional FOO allocation method has limitations, such as assuming equal importance for all allocation factors, which does not accurately reflect real-world applications. This paper introduces a novel reliability allocation algorithm that incorporates importance weighting for each factor. It proposes an Importance-Weighted Geometric Mean approach as an enhancement to the traditional "Feasibility of Objectives" method. By assigning importance weights, the approach differentiates factors more effectively and refines factor scoring. This extension enhances flexibility and generalization, making the allocation method more adaptable to diverse engineering considerations in real-world reliability allocation.

The rest of the paper is arranged as follows. Section 2 provides a review of Classical Feasibility of Objectives (FOO) Method. Sections 3 presents the newly proposed Importance-Weighted Geometric Mean (IWGM) Method as an extension and generalization of the Classical FOO Method. Section 4 discusses the advantage of the new method as compared with the classical method. Section 5 gives a numerical example to illustrate the application of the model. Section 6 provides a further extension of the new method for product refresh (new generation). Section 7 wraps up the paper with additional insights on model applicability and important considerations.

2. Classical Feasibility of Objectives (FOO) Method

The classical FOO apportionment method was first introduced in 1976 and was included in the MIL-HDBK-338B Electronic Reliability Design Handbook [4] as a method to develop and implement reliability programs for generic military products. It is assumed that all subsystems are in series and have an exponential failure distribution.

Following the classical FOO method, the subsystem or component allocation factors are computed as a function of a numerical rating of the following factors:

- complexity (*Co*),
- state of the art (*St*),
- operating time (*Ot*), and
- environment condition (*En*).

Ratings for each factor range from a low of 1 to a high of 10 and are assigned based on the engineer's experience and judgment as shown in Table 1.

Table 1: Allocation Factors and Their Scoring for Classical Feasibility of Objectives (FOO) Method*.

Factor Names	Symbol	Scaling: 1 - 10
Intricacy / Complexity Factor	Cx	10: most complex => highest FR; 1: least complex => lowest FR
State-of-Arts Factor	Sa	10: least developed => highest FR; 1: most developed => lowest FR
Operating Time	Ot	10: operate entire mission & highest workload => highest FR; 1: operate least time and under lowest workload => lowest FR
Environment Factor	En	10: most severe => highest FR; 1: least severe => lowest FR

*Note: FR=failure rate

The rating values are then multiplied to achieve the partial weight factor for each subsystem or component, i , which has values ranging from 1 to 10,000:

$$S_i = (Cxi \times Sai \times Oti \times Eni) \quad (1)$$

The subsystem ratings are normalized so that their sum is equal to 1.0 [4]:

$$\omega_i = \frac{(Cxi \times Sai \times Oti \times Eni)}{\sum_{j=1}^{n}(Cxij \times Saj \times Otj \times Enj)} = \frac{S_i}{\sum_{j=1}^{n} S_j} \quad (2)$$

which is the allocation weighting factor for each subsystem or component. Then the allocated failure rate for each individual subsystem or component, i, is given by

$$\lambda_i = \omega_i \, \lambda_S \quad (3)$$

where

- λ_S is the system failure rate.
- λ_i is the allocated failure rate for subsystem *i*.

3. Extension and Generalization of the Classical FOO Method – the Importance-Weighted Geometric Mean (IWGM) Method

It may be seen that the classical FOO method is simple and straightforward. But it has some disadvantages and limitations including:

- The allocation factors considered are limited. For example, the failure severity, operating stress and cost, etc. are not considered.
- Each factor is treated equally in the model which is often not representative in engineering applications.

To overcome the above shortcomings, we propose the following:

1. Extend the allocation factor list and be open to other relevant factors.
2. Introduce the importance weighting for each allocation factor and modify the model structure to be more general and intuitive for engineering practitioners in both understanding and implementation.

Below are the high-level steps for the new approach:

Step #0: Identify the system reliability target metric, such as failure rate, mean life, mission reliability, unscheduled downtime, etc. Convert any non-failure-rate metric into its corresponding failure rate, λ_{System}, based on input information.

Step #1: Identify the relevant allocation factors, for example

- Failure Severity
- Design (Technology) Maturity
- Cost of Repair
- Design Complexity
- Usage Intensity

- Stress Level
- Current Reliability Performance
- ……

Step #2: Classify the identified allocation factors into two categories: "H" Category and "L" Category according to the following logic:

"H" Category - "higher rank demands **Higher** allocation metric, such as failure rate" category, for example

- **H1, say** Complexity (**Cx**): the higher the design complexity, the higher the allocated failure rate
- **H2**, say Usage (**Us**): the higher the field expected usage, the higher the allocated failure rate
- **H3**, say Stress (**St**): the higher the field expected stress, the higher the allocated failure rate

"L" Category - "higher rank demands **Lower** allocation metric, such as failure rate" category, for example

- **L1**, say Failure Severity (**Fs**): the higher the failure severity, the lower the allocated failure rate
- **L2**, say Design Maturity (**Dm**): the higher the design maturity, the lower the allocated failure rate
- **L3**, say Cost of Repair (**Cr**): the higher the failure repair cost, the lower the allocated failure rate.

Step #3: Assign the rating score for each factor following the natural language implication as shown in Column 2 of Table 2. For example, assign higher score for higher complexity, higher usage, higher stress, higher severity, higher maturity, higher cost, etc. Assign lower score for lower complexity, lower usage, lower stress, lower severity, lower maturity, lower cost, etc. The score value can be either normalized scale such as 1-10, or its actual value, such as $500 for repair cost, etc.

Step #4: Since each allocation factor may be not equally important, we need to introduce the importance weight for each factor as shown in the 3rd column of Table 2. The higher the value the more important. For example, one can use 1-10 with 10 being the most important, and 1 the least important. For example, the team decides the failure severity should have the most impact for the failure rate allocation, then they may choose higher importance weight for the severity factor, such as 8-10. For another example, if the team decides the usage intensity has mild impact for the failure rate allocation, then they may choose a lower importance weight for the usage, such as 4-6, etc.

In general, for the sake of simplicity, the importance weight for each allocation factor can be assumed a global constant across different components or subsystems. But if needed and justified, they can be different across components and subsystems as well.

Table 2: Allocation Factors, Their Scoring, and Importance Weight for the Newly Proposed Importance-Weighted Geometric Mean FOO Method.

Allocation Factor	Rating Score*	Importance Weight
H1 (e.g., Complexity, Cx)	X_{H1} (1=least complex; 10=most complex)	W_{H1} (1=least important; 10=most important)
H2 (e.g., Usage, Us)	X_{H2} (1=least used; 10=most used)	W_{H2} (1=least important; 10=most important)
H3 (e.g., Stress, St)	X_{H3} (1=least stress; 10=highest stress)	W_{H3} (1=least important; 10=most important)
L1 (e.g., Failure Severity, Fs)	X_{L1} (1=least severe; 10=most severe)	W_{L1} (1=least important; 10=most important)
L2 (e.g., Design Maturity, Dm	X_{L2} (1=least mature; 10=most mature)	W_{L2} (1=least important; 10=most important)
L3 (e.g., Cost of Repair, Cr)	X_{L3} (1=least costly; 10=most costly)	W_{L3} (1=least important; 10=most important)

*Note that the rating score doesn't have to be always in normalized scale, such as 1-10, but can be actual value as well.

Step #5: Once we have the rating score and importance weight for each component or subsystem, we can calculate the combined score for each component or subsystem, i, using the following proposed Importance-Weighted Geometric Mean:

$$S_i = \left(\frac{X_{H1}^{W_{H1}} * X_{H2}^{W_{H2}} * X_{H3}^{W_{H3}}}{X_{L1}^{W_{L1}} * X_{L2}^{W_{L2}} * X_{L3}^{W_{L3}}} \right)_i^{\frac{1}{(W_{H1}+W_{H2}+W_{H3})+(W_{L1}+W_{L2}+W_{L3})}} \quad (4)$$

Step #6: Calculate the Total Score across all systems/sub-systems:

$$S = \sum_{j=1}^{m} S_j \quad (5)$$

Step #7: Calculate the Allocation Ratio/Proportion for each component or subsystem, $\boldsymbol{i}$:

$$\gamma_i = \frac{S_i}{S} = \frac{S_i}{\sum_{j=1}^{m} S_j} \quad (6)$$

Step #8: Calculate the allocated failure rate for each component or sub-system:

$$\lambda_i = \gamma_i * \lambda_{System} \quad (7)$$

4. Discussion on the Advantage of the Importance-Weighted Geometric Mean Method

Compared with the classical FOO method, the newly proposed Importance-Weighted Geometric Mean Method has the following advantages:

- Putting "H" category in the numerator of the combined score "$\boldsymbol{S_i}$" and "L" category in the denominator makes the scoring process much natural: high is high, and low is low. There is no need to twist the number to represent the language meaning, such as the "State-of-Arts" factor in the classical FOO algorithm where the highest score "10" represents the least developed state, while the lowest score "1" represents the most developed state. Another similar case is the failure detectability scoring in FMEA (failure modes and effects analysis) where high score stands for low detectability and low score stands for high detectability due to the multiplicative structure of risk priority number: RPN = Severity × Occurrence × Detectability.
- Introducing the importance weight for each allocation factor provides further distinction between factors and more refinement for factor scoring.
- The scoring doesn't have to be normalized, such as integer scales between 1 and 10, or 1 to 5, etc. The raw measurements for each factor can be used directly that would lead to the same results as using normalized scaling. For example, current failure rate, cost of failure repair, etc. can use their true values directly. This is so because of the unitless nature from multiplicative/ratio structure of the model that has a common power for each allocation factor in both numerator and denominator of the allocation proportion in Eq. (6). That is, multiplying a normalization scaler (constant) to an allocation factor score doesn't change the overall Allocation Ratio/Proportion.

Let $\vec{X} = (\vec{X}_H; \vec{X}_L) = (X_{H1}, X_{H2}, \ldots; X_{L1}, X_{L2}, \ldots)$ represents the vector of scoring for allocation factors.

Let $\vec{X'} = (\vec{X'}_H; \vec{X'}_L) = (h_1 * X_{H1}, h_2 * X_{H2}, \ldots; l_1 * X_{L1}, l_2 * X_{L2}, \ldots)$ represents the normalized vector of scoring for allocation factors where $h_1, h_2, \ldots$ represent the multipliers for "High" category factors, and $l_1, l_2, \ldots$ represent the multipliers for "Low" category factors.

Then the follow equivalence between their corresponding Allocation Ratios (Proportions) holds:

$$\gamma_i(\vec{X}_H; \vec{X}_L) = \frac{S_i(\vec{X}_H; \vec{X}_L)}{S(\vec{X}_H; \vec{X}_L)} = \frac{S_i(\vec{X'}_H; \vec{X'}_L)}{S(\vec{X'}_H; \vec{X'}_L)} = \gamma_i(\vec{X'}_H; \vec{X'}_L)$$

For a simple illustration, let's assume only one factor used the raw measurement, say X_{H2} while all other factors used normalized scoring. Let's see if normalize this factor by multiplying a constant, h_2, will change the overall allocation ratio.

$$S'_i = \left(\frac{X_{H1}^{W_{H1}} * (l_2 X_{H2})^{W_{H2}} * X_{H3}^{W_{H3}}}{X_{L1}^{W_{L1}} * X_{L2}^{W_{L2}} * X_{L3}^{W_{L3}}}\right)_i^{\frac{1}{(W_{H1}+W_{H2}+W_{H3})+(W_{L1}+W_{L2}+W_{L3})}}$$

$$S' = \sum_{j=1}^{m} S'_j = \sum_{j=1}^{m} \left(\frac{X_{H1}^{W_{H1}} * (l_2 X_{H2})^{W_{H2}} * X_{H3}^{W_{H3}}}{X_{L1}^{W_{L1}} * X_{L2}^{W_{L2}} * X_{L3}^{W_{L3}}}\right)_j^{\frac{1}{(W_{H1}+W_{H2}+W_{H3})+(W_{L1}+W_{L2}+W_{L3})}}$$

$$\gamma'_i = \frac{S'_i}{S'} = \frac{S'_i}{\sum_{j=1}^{m} S'_j} = \left[\left(\frac{X_{H1}^{W_{H1}} * (l_2 X_{H2})^{W_{H2}} * X_{H3}^{W_{H3}}}{X_{L1}^{W_{L1}} * X_{L2}^{W_{L2}} * X_{L3}^{W_{L3}}}\right)_i^{\frac{1}{(W_{H1}+W_{H2}+W_{H3})+(W_{L1}+W_{L2}+W_{L3})}}\right] / \left[\sum_{j=1}^{m} \left(\frac{X_{H1}^{W_{H1}} * (l_2 X_{H2})^{W_{H2}} * X_{H3}^{W_{H3}}}{X_{L1}^{W_{L1}} * X_{L2}^{W_{L2}} * X_{L3}^{W_{L3}}}\right)_j^{\frac{1}{(W_{H1}+W_{H2}+W_{H3})+(W_{L1}+W_{L2}+W_{L3})}}\right]$$

Dividing both the numerator and denominator by $(l_2)^{\frac{W_{H2}}{(W_{H1}+W_{H2}+W_{H3})+(W_{L1}+W_{L2}+W_{L3})}}$ yields

$$\gamma'_i = \left[\left(\frac{X_{H1}^{W_{H1}} * (X_{H2})^{W_{H2}} * X_{H3}^{W_{H3}}}{X_{L1}^{W_{L1}} * X_{L2}^{W_{L2}} * X_{L3}^{W_{L3}}}\right)_i^{\frac{1}{(W_{H1}+W_{H2}+W_{H3})+(W_{L1}+W_{L2}+W_{L3})}}\right] / \left[\sum_{j=1}^{m} \left(\frac{X_{H1}^{W_{H1}} * (X_{H2})^{W_{H2}} * X_{H3}^{W_{H3}}}{X_{L1}^{W_{L1}} * X_{L2}^{W_{L2}} * X_{L3}^{W_{L3}}}\right)_j^{\frac{1}{(W_{H1}+W_{H2}+W_{H3})+(W_{L1}+W_{L2}+W_{L3})}}\right]$$

$$= \frac{S_i}{\sum_{j=1}^{m} S_j} = \frac{S_i}{S} = \gamma_i$$

That is $\gamma'_i = \gamma_i$

Because of this property, mixed data entry formats can co-exist in the allocation process; i.e., some inputs are in normalized scaling while the others are in raw measurements format.

- Can leverage historical data including current reliability performance, in terms of failure rate, failure down time, etc.

5. Numerical Example

A newly designed electronic system is made of 11 subsystem modules labeled as M1 through M11, respectively. The system is a reliability-wise series system and is designed for 10-year non-stop operation with target failure rate of 5,000 FIT (failures per billion hours), or equivalently 5 failures per million hours. It is assumed that each module follows an Exponential life distribution.

The Reliability and Engineering Design teams have identified below 5 factors as most important to module failure rate allocation:

1. Module Failure Severity/Criticality
2. Module Complexity
3. Module Design Maturity
4. Module Usage Intensity
5. Module Operational Stress

They agreed on the importance weight for each allocation factor as shown in Table 3.

Table 3: Sample Importance Weight for Each Allocation Factor for the Numerical Example.

Allocation Factors	Failure Severity / Criticality	Complexity	Tech (Design) Maturity	Usage	Stress
Importance Level	Very High	High	High	Medium	Medium
Importance Weight	10	7	8	5	6

Upon agreeing on the importance weight for each allocation factor, they started assessing the scoring for each module and summarized their values in Table 4 below.

Table 4: Sample Scoring for Each Allocation Factor for the Numerical Example.

Modules	Failure Severity / Criticality	Complexity	Tech (Design) Maturity	Usage	Stress
M1	3	6	9	7	7
M2	7	10	3	8	10
M3	5	7	5	10	8
M4	10	8	6	9	6
M5	4	4	9	6	7
M6	6	5	9	5	7
M7	9	5	9	10	6
M8	6	2	10	9	2
M9	8	4	9	10	5
M10	2	7	8	5	2
M11	8	7	7	8	2

Obviously, the following three factors fall into "H" category (higher rank demands higher failure rate): Module Complexity, Module Usage Intensity, and Module Operational Stress. The other two factors fall into "L" category (higher rank demands lower failure rate): Module Failure Severity/Criticality and Module Design Maturity.

Applying Eqs. (4)-(7) yields the allocation results as listed in Table 5 below where the 2nd column is the combined scoring for each module, s_i, calculated by Eq. (4) and their total sum is calculated by Eq. (5), i.e., $S = \sum_{i=1}^{m} S_i$=10.81.

Table 5: Summary of Reliability Allocation Results for the Numerical Example.

Modules	Score, S_i	Allocated Failure Rate, FIT	MTTF, Hrs	10-Year Mission Reliability (assume 24x7 Operation)
M1	1.1613	537	1,861,524	95.40%
M2	1.3988	647	1,545,428	94.49%
M3	1.2713	588	1,700,471	94.98%
M4	0.9708	449	2,226,828	96.14%
M5	0.9698	449	2,229,010	96.15%
M6	0.8823	408	2,450,079	96.49%
M7	0.8460	391	2,555,303	96.63%
M8	0.6351	294	3,403,683	97.46%
M9	0.8120	376	2,662,403	96.76%
M10	1.0648	493	2,030,221	95.78%
M11	0.7966	369	2,713,596	96.82%
Total	10.81	5,000		

The 4th column is the mean time to failure (MTTF) for each module calculated by taking the reciprocal of the allocated failure rate. The 5th column is the 10-year mission reliability assuming 24x7 operation (or 87,600 hours of operation) under the Exponential life distribution assumption.

6. Further Extension of IWGM Method for Product Refresh or Enhancement

When reliability allocation is needed for a product that is not brand new, but a refined or evolved version of the previous model, then procedure introduced in Section 3 can be further extended to incorporate the reliability performance of previous model and changes in each allocation factor between two generations. Table 6 is an example of allocation scoring of such scenario by modifying the table in the Numerical Example where

- The failure rate performance of previous model is added as a new input factor for the allocation for the new model
- Failure Severity and Technology Maturity are scored using normalized scale 1-10
- The other three allocations factors, Complexity, Usage and Stress, are expressed in terms of their corresponding change ratio between new and old: either greater than 1 (increased) or less than 1 (decreased), depending on the actual situation.

Table 6: Sample Scoring incorporating both Reliability Performance of Previous Model and Changes in Certain Allocation Factors between Two Generations.

Modules	Failure Rate of Previous Model, FIT	Failure Severity / Criticality	Tech (Design) Maturity	Complexity Change Multiplier	Usage Change Multiplier	Stress Change Multiplier
M1	580	3	9	1.00	1.00	1.10
M2	620	7	3	0.70	1.40	1.00
M3	610	5	5	1.20	1.60	0.80
M4	470	10	6	0.80	1.00	1.30
M5	430	4	9	0.90	0.80	1.50
M6	401	6	9	1.00	0.90	1.00
M7	388	9	9	1.00	0.70	1.20
M8	301	6	10	1.00	1.10	1.00
M9	380	8	9	1.00	1.00	0.80
M10	420	2	8	0.90	1.00	0.90
M11	380	8	7	0.80	1.10	1.00

In this case, the following four factors fall into "H" category (higher rank demands higher failure rate): Failure Rate of Previous Model, Complexity Change Multiplier, Usage Change Multiplier, and Stress Change Multiplier. The other two factors fall into "L" category (higher rank demands lower failure rate): Failure Severity/Criticality and Design Maturity.

Applying Eqs. (4)-(7) yields the allocation results as listed in Table 7 below where the 2nd column is the combined scoring for each module, s_i, calculated by Eq. (4) and their total sum is calculated by Eq. (5), i.e., $S = \sum_{j=1}^{m} S_j$=17.95.

Table 7: Sample Allocation Results Summary for the New Generation Product.

Modules	Score, S_i	Allocated Failure Rate, FIT	MTTF, Hrs	10-Year Mission Reliability (assume 24x7 Operation)
M1	1.9166	534	1,872,946	95.43%
M2	1.8967	528	1,892,614	95.48%

M3	1.9932	555	1,800,968	95.25%
M4	1.4927	416	2,404,822	96.42%
M5	1.6938	472	2,119,372	95.95%
M6	1.4893	415	2,410,353	96.43%
M7	1.3471	375	2,664,675	96.77%
M8	1.4113	393	2,543,593	96.61%
M9	1.3574	378	2,644,565	96.74%
M10	1.9230	536	1,866,696	95.42%
M11	1.4274	398	2,514,810	96.58%
Total	17.95	5,000		

It may be seen that the reliability target for each module for the new generation, in terms of failure rate, MTTF, and mission reliability got re-allocated (adjusted) based on its performance in previous generation (indicator of underlying design and manufacturing capability), plus design and use condition change effects (design complexity change, usage change, and stress change), while still leveraging the consideration of failure severity and technology maturity.

7. Conclusion

Reliability allocation or apportionment is a very important step in product life cycle development. Over the years, there are many allocation methods and algorithms proposed and practiced in industry. The Feasibility of Objectives (FOO) Method is one of them and have been used widely. However, it has its certain limitations including assuming equal importance among all allocation factors which definitely do not reflect the true nature in real world applications. This paper presents a novel reliability allocation algorithm by introducing importance weight for each allocation factor and proposing an Importance-Weighted Geometric Mean approach to extend the traditional "Feasibility of Objectives" Method. The introduction of importance weight for each allocation factor provides further distinction between factors and more refinement for factor scoring. This extension makes the allocation method more flexible and general to accommodate a wide range of engineering factors in real world reliability allocation.

There are several advantages of the proposed method and its model structure including:

- Introduction of factor classification: "H" Category (higher rank demands Higher allocation metric, such as failure rate) and "L" Category (higher rank demands Lower allocation metric, such as failure rate).
- Putting "H" category factors in the numerator of the combined score "S_i" and "L" category factors in the denominator makes the scoring process much natural: high is high, and low is low. Note that this logic works assuming the allocation target metric falls into "H" category, such as failure rate, failure downtime, etc. However, if the allocation target metric falls into "L" category, such as MTTF, mission reliability, availability, etc., then we need to swap the order; i.e., put "L" category factors in the numerator of the combined score "S_i" and "H" category factors in the denominator.
- Due to the unique multiplicative/ratio structure of the model that has a common power for each allocation factor in both numerator and denominator of the allocation proportion in Eq. (6), mixed data entry formats can co-exist in the allocation process; i.e., some inputs are in normalized scaling, such as between 1 and 10, or 1 to 5, while the others are in raw measurements format. That is, multiplying a normalization scaler (constant) to an allocation factor score doesn't change the overall Allocation Ratio/Proportion.
- The proposed method can leverage historical data including current reliability performance, in terms of failure rate, failure down time, etc.
- The weighted geometric mean is particularly useful when dealing with rates of change, growth, or situations where a low value in one factor limits the overall result. This is especially important for reliability allocation of enhanced system design where the current reliability performance and changes in allocation factors are incorporated.

Since the reliability metric allocation for each sub-system or component is through multiplication of system target and allocation ratio or proportion as defined in Eq. (7), therefore their summation has to be equal to the system target: $\sum_{i=1}^{m} \gamma_i = 1$ and $\sum_{i=1}^{m} (\gamma_i \lambda_{System}) = \sum_{i=1}^{m} \lambda_i = \lambda_{System}$. Note that not all reliability metrics follow this summation relation between system and its subsystems or components, except failure downtime. Therefore, one can't apply this method directly to other reliability metric allocation, such as mission reliability, mean life, availability, etc. One needs to convert them into corresponding failure rate (or downtime) equivalence first. Then, allocate this converted failure rate (or downtime) target into subsystems or components, and calculate the corresponding mean life, reliability, and availability from allocated failure rate.

REFERENCES

1. D. Kececioglu, *Reliability Engineering Handbook,* 1st print by Prentice Hall in 1991, 2nd print by DEStech Publications, Inc in 2002.
2. D. J. Smith, *Reliability, Maintainability and Risk: Practical Methods for Engineers*, Elsevier, 2017.
3. C. E. Ebeling, *An Introduction to Reliability and Maintainability Engineering*, Waveland Press, 2010.
4. MIL-HDBK-338B, *Electronic Reliability Design Handbook.* U.S. Department of Defense, 1998.
5. B. S. Blanchard and W. J. Fabrycky, *Systems Engineering and Analysis*, (5th ed.), Pearson, 2011.
6. W. Kuo and M. J. Zuo, *Optimal Reliability Modeling: Principles and Applications*, Wiley, 2003.
7. B. S. Dhillon, *Maintainability, Maintenance, and Reliability for Engineers*, CRC Press, 2006.
8. M. Catelani, L. Ciani , G. Patrizi, and M. Venzi, "Reliability Allocation Procedures in Complex Redundant Systems," *IEEE Systems Journal*, Vol. 12, No. 2, June 2018.
9. H. Guo, M. Jiang, and W.Wang, "A method for reliability allocation with confidence level," in *Proc. Annu. Rel. Maintainability Symp.*, Colorado Springs, CO, USA, 2014, p. 1.
10. Mettas, "Reliability allocation and optimization for complex systems," *Proc. Annu. Rel. Maintainability Symp.*, Los Angeles, CA, USA, 2000, pp. 216–221.

A study on software reliability models considering the delayed S-shaped fault detection rates

Youn Su Kim[1], Kwang Yoon Song[2]*, In Hong Chang[3]*

[1]Institute of Well-Aging Medicare & CSU G-LAMP Project Group, Chosun University, Gwangju, 61452, Korea, imk92315@chosun.ac.kr

[2] Department of Computer Science and Statistics and institute of Well-Aging Medicare & CSU G-LAMP Project Group, Chosun University, Dong-gu, Gwangju, Korea, csssig@chosun.ac.kr

[3] Department of Computer Science and Statistics, Chosun University, Dong-gu, Gwangju, Korea, ihchang@chosun.ac.kr

* Corresponding author

Keywords: Software Reliability, NHPP software reliability model, finiteness of faults.

Abstract – Software reliability is very important because software is such a large part of our lives that software failures can cause major society and the economy. To improve software reliability, software reliability models have been developed in the past that include many assumptions such as independent and dependent failure, and operating environment uncertainty. In this study, we propose a new type of NHPP software reliability model that is not a differential equation with various assumptions in the past. It is a model that considers an initial explosion of failures followed by a slow development of a finite number of failures and defects until the maximum number of failures is reached. We demonstrated the superiority of the model by comparing it with eight traditional NHPP software reliability models using five criteria, and also checked the trend with the actual values and the estimated values of all the models, and found that the proposed model is superior.

1. Introduction

Our dependence on software has emphasized the importance of software reliability. The study of software reliability is necessary because software failures, both large and small, can have a significant impact on society and the economy. Software reliability research has been studied since 1972 by Jelinski and Moranda, and has continued to be studied, especially the NHPP software reliability model, which assumes that software failures follow a non-homogeneous Poisson Process (NHPP) [1, 2].

The traditional NHPP software reliability model was developed to model the diversity of forms in which software failures occur, and several assumptions were added to extend the software reliability model. First, several software reliability models that assume that software failures occur independently have been proposed, and software reliability models have been developed by various assumptions such as the dependent assumption of software failures that extend this assumption or operating environment uncertainty that may occur as the developed environment differs from the actual environment.

In this study, we propose a software reliability model through a new type of differential equation to derive a software reliability model. Instead of the structure of differential equations with various assumptions in the past, we propose a new NHPP software reliability model that considers the slow development of a finite number of faults through the transformation of differential equations. Section 2 introduces the new type of NHPP software reliability model, Section 3 presents data, criteria introduction and numerical example results, and Section 4 concludes.

2. Software reliability model

Software reliability is the field of testing whether software will not fail over a specified period of time. Software reliability models are used to estimate and predict software failures to determine reliability. The occurrence of software failures follows a non-homogeneous Poisson process (NHPP) in which the number of failures per unit time is a function rather than a constant value. Here, the mean number of failures per unit time is a function of the mean value from time 0 to time t, m(t). The traditional NHPP software reliability model developed in the past is proposed via the following differential equation [2]

$$\frac{dm(t)}{dt} = b(t)[a(t) - m(t)]$$

where $a(t)$ is the number of failures at time t, and $b(t)$ is the failure detection rate at time t.

The new type of software reliability model we propose in this work assumes a delayed S-shape, where when software fails, the probability of failure initially increases rapidly, followed by a finite number of failures once the maximum number of failures is reached [3].

$$\frac{dm(t)}{dt} = b(t)\left[1 - \frac{m(t)}{a(t)}\right]$$

Solving the corresponding differential equation with a(t) and b(t) as a and $\frac{b^2 t}{1+bt}$, leads to the following new type of NHPP software reliability model we propose.

$$m(t) = a\left(1 - e^{\frac{\ln(1+bt)-bt}{a}}\right)$$

We compare a total of eight existing NHPP software reliability models with the new type of NHPP software reliability model we propose. Table 1 contains the formulas for the eight models and the formulas for the new proposed model [2, 4-9].

Table 1. Software reliability model

No.	Model	Mean Value Function
1	GO	$a(1-e^{-bt})$
2	HDGO [4]	$\log\left[\frac{(e^{a}-c)}{(e^{ae^{-bt}}-c)}\right]$
3	DS [5]	$a(1-(1+bt)e^{-bt})$
4	IS [6]	$\frac{a(1-e^{-bt})}{1+\beta e^{-bt}}$
5	YE [7]	$a\left(1-e^{-\gamma\alpha(1-e^{-\beta t})}\right)$
6	YID1 [8]	$\frac{ab}{\alpha+b}(e^{\alpha t}-e^{-bt})$
7	YID2 [8]	$a(1-e^{-bt})\left(1-\frac{\alpha}{b}\right)+\alpha a t$
8	TP [9]	$\frac{a}{p-q}\left[1-\left(\frac{\beta}{\beta+(p-q)\ln\left(\frac{c+e^{bt}}{c+1}\right)}\right)^{\alpha}\right]$
9	NEW	$a\left(1-e^{\frac{\ln(1+bt)-bt}{a}}\right)$

3. Numerical Examples

3.1. Criteria

In this study, the dataset we utilize to judge the superiority of our proposed NHPP software reliability model is the failure data. We use five criteria measures to determine the goodness of the model. Mean Squared Error (MSE) and Mean Absolute Error (MAE) are based on the difference between the actual and estimated values, Predictive ratio risk (PRR) and Predictive Power (PP) are the difference between the actual and estimated values divided by the estimated and actual values, respectively, and R^2 is the coefficient of determination in the regression model. Among the five criteria, the closer R^2 is to 1, the better the result, and the closer to 0 for the other criteria [10].

3.2. Results

Table 1 shows the criteria results for comparison with the traditional NHPP software reliability model as a dataset to demonstrate the superiority of the new NHPP software reliability model proposed in this study. Among the five criteria, MSE, MAE, PRR, and PP showed the best results with 19.1675, 3.7329, 0.0974, and 0.1534, and R^2 also showed excellent results with 0.9937. Figures 1-3 is a comparison bar graph of each model for the five criteria. The proposed model shows better results than the traditional NHPP software reliability model.

Figure 4 shows the estimation results of the proposed model at each time point. The black dots are the actual values and the red solid line is the proposed NHPP software reliability model. The proposed model shows a similar trend to the true value compared to the other models.

Table 2. Result of criteria

Model	MSE	MAE	PRR	PP	R^2
GO	21.5128	3.9311	0.1465	0.279	0.9929
HDGO	22.7079	4.1495	0.1465	0.279	0.9929
DS	76.1734	7.7655	1.5617	0.4996	0.9748
IS	21.6236	3.944	0.1168	0.2009	0.9932
YE	24.1283	4.4036	0.1476	0.2821	0.9929
YID1	22.7283	4.1532	0.1468	0.2797	0.9929
YID2	22.7106	4.15	0.1465	0.2791	0.9929
TP	27.6009	5.0764	0.1142	0.1945	0.9933
NEW	**19.1675**	**3.7329**	**0.0974**	**0.1534**	**0.9937**

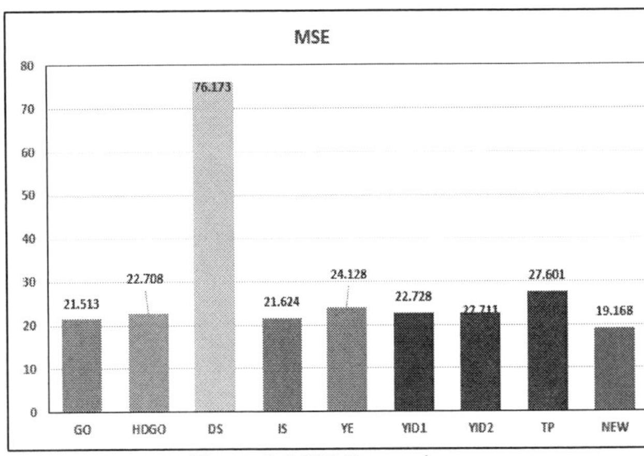

Figure 1. MSE Comparison

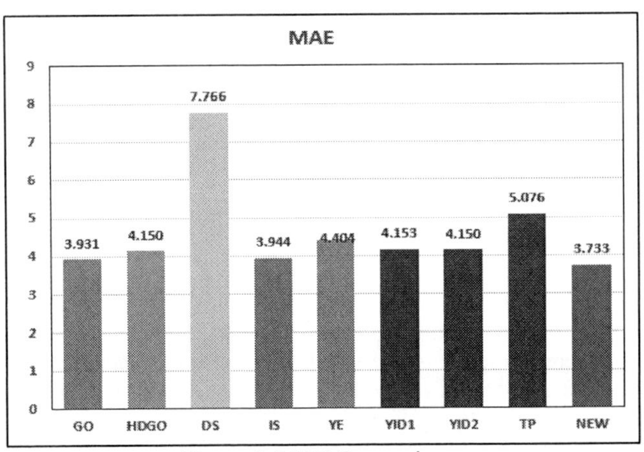

Figure 2. MAE Comparison

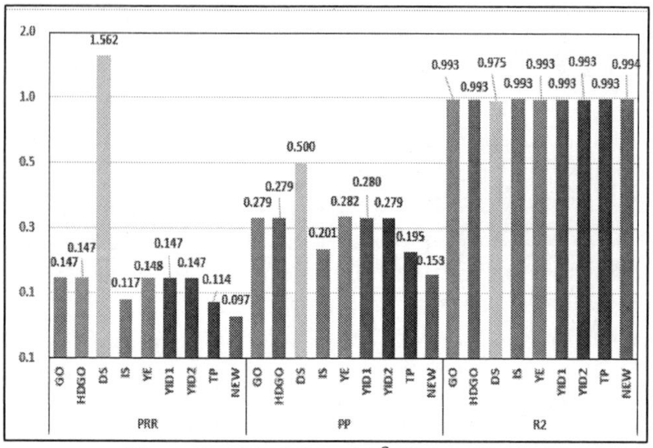

Figure 3. PRR, PP, and R^2 Comparison

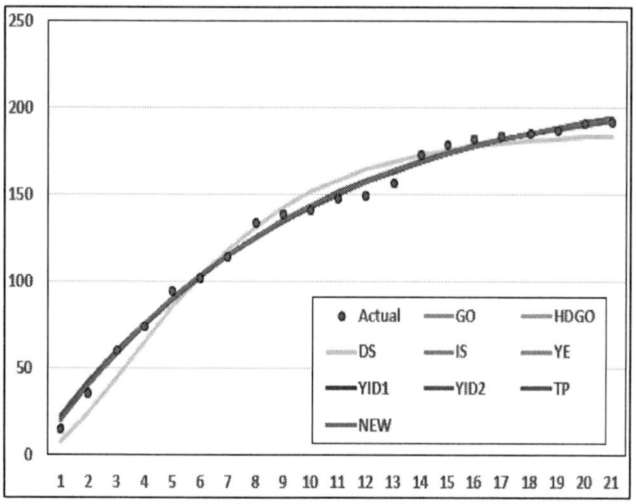

Figure 4. Actual values and estimated values

4. Conclusion

In the past, software reliability models have evolved from the independent occurrence of software failures to various assumptions such as dependent failure occurrence of software failures and operating environment uncertainty. In this study, we propose a new type of NHPP software reliability model that assumes a finite number of faults by extending the assumption in the other direction. As a result, we demonstrate the superiority of our proposed model by comparing it with eight traditional NHPP software reliability models with five criteria. We extend this work to develop NHPP software reliability models that assume finite faults with different functions.

Acknowledgement

This research was supported by Global-Learning & Academic research institution for Master's PhD students, and Postdocs (LAMP) Program of the National Research Foundation of Korea (NRF) grant funded by the Ministry of Education ((No. RS-2023-00285353) and, was supported by research fund from Chosun University, 2024.

References

[1] Jelinski, Z. ; Moranda, P. Software reliability research. In Statistical computer performance evaluation. Academic Press. 1972; 465-484.

[2] Goel, A.L.; Okumoto, K. Time-Dependent Error-Detection Rate Model for Software Reliability and Other Performance Measures. IEEE Trans. Reliab. 1979 ; R-28, 206–211.

[3] Song, K. Y.; Kim, Y. S.; Chang, I. H. Software reliability model for open-source software that considers the number of finite faults and dependent faults. Mathematical Biosciences and Engineering, 2023; 20, 11785-11804.

[4] Hossain, S.A.; Dahiya, R.C. Estimating the parameters of a non-homogeneous Poisson-process model for software reliability. IEEE Trans. Reliab. 1993 ; 42, 604–612.

[5] Yamada, S.; Ohba, M.; Osaki, S. S-shaped reliability growth modeling for software fault detection. IEEE Trans. Reliab. 1983; 32, 475–484.

[6] Osaki, S.; Hatoyama, Y. Inflexion S-Shaped Software Reliability Growth Models. In Stochastic Models in Reliability Theory; Springer: Berlin/Heidelberg, Germany, 1984; 144–162.

[7] Yamada, S.; Ohtera, H.; Narihisa, H. Software Reliability Growth Models with Testing-Effort. IEEE Trans. Reliab. 1986; 35, 19–23.

[8] Yamada, S.; Tokuno, K.; Osaki, S. Imperfect debugging models with fault introduction rate for software reliability assessment. Int. J. Syst. Sci. 1992; 23, 2241–2252.

[9] Teng, X.; Pham, H. A new methodology for predicting software reliability in the random field environments. IEEE Trans. Reliab. 2006; 55, 458–468.

[10] Pham, H. System Software Reliability; Springer: London, UK, 2006.

Interval Estimations of Software Functional Safety for E/E/PE Safety-Related Systems

Shinji INOUE†, Takaji FUJIWARA†† and Shigeru YAMADA†††

†Faculty of Informatics, Kansai University
2-1-1 Ryozenji-cho, Takatsuki-shi, Osaka 569-1095, Japan
E-mail: ino@kansai-u.ac.jp

††SRATECH Laboratory Inc.
1949-24, Yamakuni, Kato-shi, Hyogo 673-1421, Japan
E-mail: fujiwara.takaji@nifty.com

†††Graduate School of Engineering, Tottori University
4-101, Minami, Koyama-cho, Tottori-shi, Tottori 680-8552, Japan
E-mail: bex2yama@muse.ocn.ne.jp

Key Words: E/E/PE safety-related systems, Functional safety, Interval estimation, Target failure measures, Bootstrapping method.

Abstract

Among safety-related systems that are responsible for the functional safety of an overall system, the share of E/E/PE safety-related systems with embedded software is expanding. Under that situation, there is necessity to discuss the functional safety for the software installed into the E/E/PE safety-related system, not only for the hardware systems. We discuss quantitative software functional safety assessment methodologies for the software of the E/E/PE safety-related systems, which enable us to conduct simulation-based interval estimations of target failure measures even if the size of software failure data is small by applying a bootstrapping method. Numerical examples for our approaches to be proposed here are also shown to demonstrate our simulation-based interval estimation approaches.

1 Introduction

Recently, electorical / electronic / programmable electronic (E/E/PE) safety-related systems are widely applied in several industrial fields. Air-bag systems and pre-crash safety systems in automobiles can be shown as application examples for the E/E/PE safety-related systems. The principal role of the E/E/PE safety-related systems is maintaining the safety of overall systems from the functional aspects and these functional safety mechanism is mainly controlled by software embedded in the E/E/PE safety-related systems. Therefore, conducting functional safety assessment not only for the hardware but also the software of the E/E/PE safety-related systems is important issue to make the E/E/PE safety-related systems more reliable and safe.

In fact, IEC 61508 [1], the international basic standards for the functional safety of the E/E/PE safety-related systems, gives us quantitative functional safety assessment methodologies and the definition of the safety integrity level (SIL) for the hardware of the E/E/PE safety-related systems based on the notion of the random hardware failure mechanism. Table 1 shows the regulation defined by IEC 61508 for allocating the level of SIL. Those standards define the SIL for indicating the safety integrity of the E/E/PE safety-related systems and the target failure measures which are the average probability of failure on demand on the safety demand (PFD) and the average frequency of a dangerous failure of the safety function (PFH), for allocating the level of SIL. For the hardware of the E/E/PE safety-related systems, the standards give us quantitative estimation approaches for PFD and PFH. However, such quantitative estimation approaches have not been defined for the software of those systems in the standards. That is, it implies that the standards do not require conducting quantitative functional safety assessment for the software because software failures is treated as systematic failures.

Generally, software bugs that cause systematic software failures including dangerous software failures can be roughly classified into *Bohrbugs* and *Heisenbugs*. The Bohrbugs can be detected with near certainty under the right simple conditions. That is, it would be able to be considered that most of software bugs detected during the reviewing activities before the final testing phase are the Bohrbugs. On the other hand, the Heisenbugs are difficult to detect them in the reviewing because of the complex conditions with low repeatability required to manifest their existence as software failures. Furthermore, software failures caused by Heisenbugs occur apparently stochastically during the testing and operation phases. Under such situation, we can recognize the necessity of quantitative software

Table 1: Safety Integrity Level of Functional Safety [1].

SIL	Low Demand Mode	High Demand or Continuous Mode
4	$10^{-5} \leq \text{PFD} < 10^{-4}$	$10^{-9} \leq \text{PFH (1/hour)} < 10^{-8}$
3	$10^{-4} \leq \text{PFD} < 10^{-3}$	$10^{-8} \leq \text{PFH (1/hour)} < 10^{-7}$
2	$10^{-3} \leq \text{PFD} < 10^{-2}$	$10^{-7} \leq \text{PFH (1/hour)} < 10^{-6}$
1	$10^{-2} \leq \text{PFD} < 10^{-1}$	$10^{-6} \leq \text{PFH (1/hour)} < 10^{-5}$

functional safety assessment based on probability and statistical laws.

Recently, Inoue et al. [2] proposed mathematical fundamentals for conducting quantitative software functional safety assessment in the final testing phase of the E/E/PE safety-related software and for allocating SIL, applying the notion of software reliability modeling and assessment technologies. These approaches are based on the point estimation methods of PFD and PFH by following the probability and statistical laws. However, from the background above, it is easy to imagine a situation that bug detection data in the final test phase is extremely small. To handle this situation, we discuss internal estimation methods for the PFD and PFH based on the bootstrapping method that enables us to replicate observed small size data and to get distributions of the PFD and PFH.

2 Mathematical Approaches

2.1 Basic notions

First, we introduce the concepts underlying the mathematical models utilized for estimating these PFD and PFH [3] based on software reliability assessment technologies. The PFD can be essentially interpreted as the unavailability of the E/E/PE safety-related system at the time when the safety demand is received from the main systems with low frequency. If the time-duration to fix a bug is comparatively roughly short and constant against to the long operation or the proof-testing interval, then we could give the software PFD approximately as

$$\text{PFD} \approx 1 - \text{Software Reliability}. \tag{1}$$

Actually, a highly reliable system would be high availability if we consider the above situation. It should note that PFD is required to calculate time-averaged availability dividing by the proof test interval originally. However, Eq. (1) is not time averaged for the sake of simplicity for mathematical manipulation.

The PFH is defined as the time-averaged frequency of dangerous failure per hour for the E/E/PE safety-related systems. This can be considered as the dangerous failure intensity for the safety-related systems. Then, we consider the following equation for approximately estimating the PFH:

$$\text{PFH} \approx \frac{1}{\text{MTBF}}, \tag{2}$$

in which the mean time between software failures (abbreviated as MTBF) is one of the representative software reliability assessment measures. It is worth mentioning that the unit of PFH is 1/hour.

2.2 Mathematical approaches

Software reliability modeling technologies [4–6] can be utilized to obtain "Software Reliability"in Eq. (1) and "MTBF"in Eq. (2), respectively. Let us denote a counting process representing the number of software failure-occurrence by testing time t by $\{N(t), t \geq 0\}$. Supposing that process follows the non-homogeneous Poisson process (NHPP) [7,8]:

$$\Pr\{N(t) = n\} = \frac{\Lambda(t)^n}{n!} \exp[-\Lambda(t)] \quad (n = 0, 1, 2, \cdots), \tag{3}$$

the software reliability function that represents the failure-free probability on $(t, t+x]$ under that the testing has been conducted up to testing time t is derived as

$$R(x \mid t) = \exp[-\{\Lambda(t+x) - \Lambda(t)\}], \tag{4}$$

where $\Lambda(t)$ is the mean value function representing the expected number of software faults causing software failures observed up to time t. And the instantaneous MTBF that is the substitution of proper MTBF is given as

$$MTBF_I(t) = \frac{1}{\lambda(t)}, \tag{5}$$

where $\lambda(t)(= d\Lambda(t)/dt)$ is the intensity function representing the instantaneous number of software faults detected at time t. Furthermore, we introduce a dangerous software failure rate DFR ($0 < \text{DFR} < 1$) and an environment function $EF(x)$ to incorporate the fraction of software failures causing dangerous software failures and to enable us to transform the designed operation duration x into the testing time-duration. Then, we obtain the formulation of software PFD as

$$\begin{aligned} &PFD(x \mid t) \\ &= 1 - \exp\left[-\text{DFR}\{\Lambda(t + EF(x)) - \Lambda(t)\}\right] \\ &= 1 - \exp\left[-\text{DFR}\{\Lambda(t + \text{EC} \cdot x) - \Lambda(t)\}\right], \end{aligned} \tag{6}$$

and PFH as

$$PFH(t) = \frac{\text{DFR}}{EF^{-1}(MTBF_I(t))} = \frac{\text{DFR} \cdot \text{EC}}{MTBF_I(t)} \quad (7)$$

from Eqs. (1) and (2), respectively [2]. In the above equations, we assume $EF(x) = \text{EC} \cdot x$, in which the EC is the environment coefficient. And $EF^{-1}(\cdot)$ is the inverse function of the environment function that transform the MTBF in the testing into the one in the operation by using the environment function.

Suppose $\Lambda(t)$ follows well-known Goel-Okumoto model [4–6]. Then, it is well-known that the behavior of $\Lambda(t)$ is characterized by the following differential equation:

$$\frac{d\Lambda(t)}{dt} = \beta[\omega - \Lambda(t)], \quad (8)$$

where ω is the expected initial software fault content and β is the detection rate per software fault. Solving the differential equation above, we have $\Lambda(t) = \omega(1 - \exp[-\beta t])$. Furthermore $PFD(x \mid t)$ for the designed operation time duration x and $PFH(t)$ in Eqs. (6) and (7) can be obtained as

$$PFD(x \mid t) = 1 - \exp\left[-\text{DFR} \cdot \Lambda(\text{EC} \cdot x)e^{-\beta t}\right], \quad (9)$$

$$PFH(t) = \text{DFR} \cdot \text{EC} \cdot \omega\beta e^{-bt}, \quad (10)$$

respectively, .

3 Bootstrapping Approach

Generally, the probability distribution functions for $PFD(x \mid t)$ and $PFH(t)$ are needed to derive for conducting interval estimations of them. However, it is known that these probability distributions is hard to derive analytically even if we apply approximation approach assuming large number of sample, such as the asymptotic normality. Furthermore, it is also known that analytical approach to conduct interval estimation for that NHPP model is almost impossible [9].

To overcome the issues above, a simulation-based method [10] is discussed here. As one of the approaches, we apply a nonparametric bootstrap method. This method is known as a resampling technique for observed data to obtain a simulation-based distribution for an estimator. While it may be better to apply the parametric bootstrap method when assuming NHPP for software bug counting data, the nonparametric bootstrap method saves the effort of generating resampled data assuming that probability distribution.

Suppose software fault counting data (i, y_i) $(i = 0, 1, 2, \cdots, N;\ \ y_0 = 0)$ has been observed, where y_i represents the cumulative number of software faults detected up to the i-th testing period. Assuming the testing period is constant and same each other, we obtain the following regression equation from Eq. (8):

$$Y_i = C + Dy_i, \quad (11)$$

where

$$\begin{cases} Y_i = (y_{i+1} - y_{i-1})/2, \\ C = \omega\beta, \\ D = -\beta. \end{cases} \quad (12)$$

The estimations for C and D can be obtained by regression analysis and we denote them as $\widehat{C}$ and $\widehat{D}$). The, the parameters in Eq. (8) can be estimated as

$$\widehat{\omega} = -\widehat{C}/\widehat{D}, \quad (13)$$

$$\widehat{\beta} = -D, \quad (14)$$

respectively.

Based on the above preparation, the bootstrap samples and estimations for $PFD(x_c \mid t_c)$ and $PFH(t_c)$ at certain x_c and t_c can be obtained as the following procedure:

P1 Estimate C and D in Eq. (11) with observed data $(i, y_i)(i = 0, 1, 2, \cdots, N;\ \ y_0 = 0)$. Indicate $\widehat{C}$ and $\widehat{D}$ as $\widehat{C}_{(0)}$ and $\widehat{D}_{(0)}$, respectively.

P2 Calculate the residual errors $\widehat{r}_k$ at each observation points as $r_k = Y_k - (\widehat{C}_{(0)} + \widehat{D}_{(0)} y_k)(k = 1, 2, \cdots, N-1)$.

P3 Construct an empirical distribution function $\widehat{F}$ by putting mass $1/(N-2)$ at each ordered point $\{r_{[1]}, r_{[2]}, \cdots, r_{[N-1]}\}$.

P4 Set the total number of iteration B and denote the iteration count by b $(b = 1, 2, \cdots, B)$.

P5 Generate the bootstrap samples of the residual errors, $\boldsymbol{r}^*_{(b)} = \{r^*_{1(b)}, r^*_{2(b)}, \cdots, r^*_{N-1(b)}\}$ by sampling with replacement from $\widehat{F}$.

P6 Generate data pairs by using the above bootstrap sample $\boldsymbol{r}^*_{(b)}$, such as $\boldsymbol{d}^*_{(b)} = \{(y_1, E^*_{1(b)}), (y_2, E^*_{2(b)}), \cdots, (y_{N-1}, E^*_{N-1(b)})\}$, where

$$E^*_{k(b)} = \widehat{C}_{(0)} + \widehat{D}_{(0)} y_k + r^*_{k(b)}.$$

P7 Estimate $\widehat{C}^*_{(b)}$ and $\widehat{D}^*_{(b)}$ from the bootstrap sample $\boldsymbol{d}^*_{(b)}$.

P8 Calculate model parameters, $\widehat{\omega}^*_{(b)}$ and $\widehat{\beta}^*_{(b)}$, by the following equations:

$$\widehat{\omega}^*_{(b)} = -\frac{\widehat{C}^*_{(b)}}{\widehat{D}^*_{(b)}},$$

$$\widehat{\beta}^*_{(b)} = -\widehat{D}^*_{(b)}.$$

P9 Calculate $\widehat{PFD}(x_c \mid t_c)^*_{(b)}$ and $\widehat{PFH}(t_c)^*_{(b)}$ by following Eqs. (9) and (10), respectively.

P10 Set $b \leftarrow b + 1$ and go back to **P5** if $b \leq B$.

P11 We totally have B sets of estimations for $\widehat{\omega}^*$, $\widehat{\beta}^*$, $\widehat{PFD}^*(x_c \mid t_c)$, and $\widehat{PFH}^*(t_c)$ by each data pairs generated from bootstrap samples.

4 Numerical Examples

We show numerical examples for our nonparametric bootstrap interval estimation approach for the PFD and PFH. The following software fault counting data:

$(t_i, y_i)(i = 1, 2, \cdots, 21; t_{21} = 504(\text{hours}), y_{21} = 44)$ [11] is applied in this numerical examples, where y_i is the total number of software faults detected during $(0, t_i]$. Actually, this data set has not been collected from testing for E/E/PE safety-related software, but is just used for showing examples and results on our approach. Regarding the total number of iteration, we set $B = 2000$ because it is known that the number of iteration generally needs $B = 1000 \sim 2000$ for obtaining a bootstrap distribution of a parameter of interest.

4.1 Settings

Here we set DFR = 0.1 and EC = 0.1 for showing numerical examples, respectively, which means that 1 testing hour is equivalent to 10 operation hours under these settings. Following these settings, we now conduct interval estimations for $PFD(x_c \mid t_c)$ and $PFH(t_c)$, where we consider situation that the software testing has been conducted up to 95 days, i.e., $t_c = 2,280$ hours and the designed operation time duration is set as one year, i.e., $x_c = 8,760$ hours.

4.2 Bootstrapping

We first obtain $\widehat{C}_{(0)} = 0.19709$ and $\widehat{D}_{(0)} = -0.00373$ by the linear regression scheme from the actual data. Then, the residual errors for each observed point, $r_k(k = 1, 2, \cdots, 20)$, can be calculated. The 20 residual errors, $\boldsymbol{r}^*_{(1)} = \{r^*_{1(1)}, r^*_{2(1)}, \cdots, r^*_{20(1)}\}$, are generated by sampling with replacement from the ordered r_k. Then, the 1st bootstrap sample, $\boldsymbol{d}^*_{(1)} = \{(y_1, E^*_{1(1)}), (y_2, E^*_{2(1)}), \cdots, (y_{20}, E^*_{20(1)})\}$, is also generated as shown in **P6**.

From the 1st bootstrap sample, $\widehat{C}^*_{(1)}$ and $\widehat{D}^*_{(1)}$ can be estimated. Then, we obtain the 1st bootstrap estimation of ω and β, $\widehat{\omega}^*_{(1)}$ and $\widehat{\beta}^*_{(1)}$, respectively. Furthermore, $\widehat{PFD}^*(8,760 \mid 2,280)_{(1)}$ and $\widehat{PFH}^*(2,280)_{(1)}$ are also estimated as

$$\widehat{PFD}^*(8,760 \mid 2,280)_{(1)} = 1 - \exp\left[-0.1 \cdot \Lambda(0.1 \cdot 8,760) e^{-\widehat{\beta}^*_{(1)} 2,280}\right], \tag{15}$$

$$\widehat{PFH}^*(2,280)_{(1)} = 0.1 \cdot 0.1 \cdot \widehat{\omega}^*_{(1)} \widehat{\beta}^*_{(1)} e^{-\widehat{\beta}^*_{(1)} \cdot 2,280}, \tag{16}$$

from Eqs. (9) and (10), respectively.

Replicating the procedure above, we have 2000 bootstrap estimations for ω and β as $\widehat{\boldsymbol{\omega}}^* = \{\widehat{\omega}^*_{(1)}, \widehat{\omega}^*_{(2)}, \cdots, \widehat{\omega}^*_{(2000)}\}$ and $\widehat{\boldsymbol{\beta}}^* = \{\widehat{\beta}^*_{(1)}, \widehat{\beta}^*_{(2)}, \cdots, \widehat{\beta}^*_{(2000)}\}$. We also have 2000 bootstrap estimations for $\widehat{PFD}^*(8,760 \mid 2,280)$ and $\widehat{PFH}^*(2,280)$ as well.

4.3 Interval Estimation

Figs. 1 and 2 show bootstrap distributions for $\widehat{PFD}^*(8,760 \mid 2,280)$ and $\widehat{PFH}^*(2,280)$, respectively.

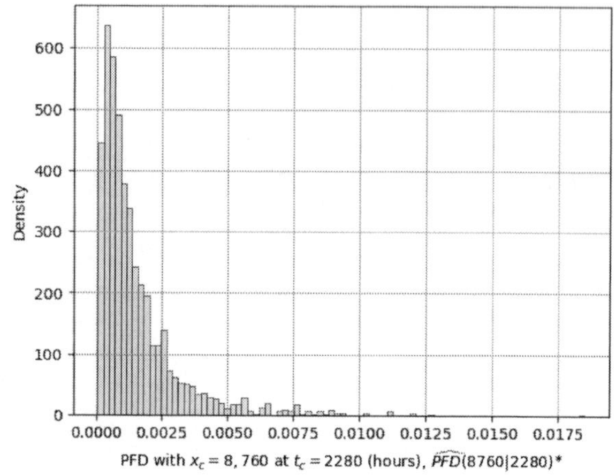

Fig. 1: Bootstrap distribution of $\widehat{PFD}^*(8,760 \mid 2,280)$.

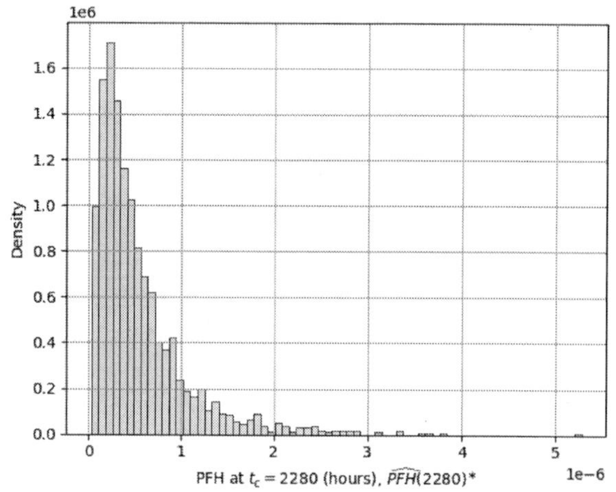

Fig. 2: Bootstrap distribution of $\widehat{PFH}^*(2,280)$.

From these bootstrap distributions, we can obtain bootstrap confidence intervals as the interval estimations for $\widehat{PFD}^*(8,760 \mid 2,280)$ and $\widehat{PFH}^*(2,280)$.

Let us θ be the parameter of interest, $\widehat{\theta}$ the statistic of θ, and $\widehat{\theta}^*$ the bootstrap estimator of θ. Bootstrap confidence intervals [12, 13] are established by approximately constructing the confidence intervals of θ from the bootstrap distribution of $\widehat{\theta}^*$. Generally, standard normal, basic, and percentile bootstrap confidence intervals are used to obtain the confidence intervals for the parameter of interest. However, the standard normal or basic bootstrap confidence intervals should not be used for the interval estimation of the target failure measures because there is no guarantee that the interval estimations of them within non-negative real values. Therefore, we use the percentile bootstrap confidence interval among them. This confidence interval is calculated from the empirical cumulative distribution function by the bootstrap iteration values: $\widehat{\theta}^*_{(1)}, \widehat{\theta}^*_{(2)}, \cdots, \widehat{\theta}^*_{(B)}$. Then, the $100(1-2\alpha)\%$ percentile bootstrap confidence interval is developed by

$$[\widehat{\theta}^*_{[B\alpha]}, \widehat{\theta}^*_{[B(1-\alpha)]}], \tag{17}$$

where $\widehat{\theta}^*_{[B\alpha]}$ represents the bootstrap estimation of $\widehat{\theta}^*$ at α quantile of the empirical cumulative distribution.

Following the percentile bootstrap confidence interval estimation method, the lower bound for the 95% percentile bootstrap confidence interval of $PFD(8,760 \mid 2,280)$ is obtained as

$$\widehat{PFD}^*(8,760 \mid 2,280)_{[0.025\times 2,000]} = 6.4511 \times 10^{-3} \tag{18}$$

The upper bound is estimated as

$$\widehat{PFD}^*(8,760 \mid 2,280)_{[0.975\times 2,000]} = 1.6709 \times 10^{-4} \tag{19}$$

From the bootstrap confidence intervals for $PFD(8,760 \mid 2,280)$, the SIL is allocated in levels ranging from SIL 2 to SIL 3 with the 95% confidence limit. By the way, if the mean of $\widehat{PFD}^*(8,760 \mid 2,280)$ is used as the results of point estimation, we obtain $\widehat{PFD}(8,760 \mid 2,280) \approx 1.5649 \times 10^{-3}$, which can be allocated to SIL 2. Furthermore, the lower and upper bounds for the 95% percentile bootstrap confidence interval of $PFH(2,280)$ are also obtained as The upper bound is estimated as

$$\widehat{PFH}^*(2,280)_{[0.025\times 2,000]} = 2.0739 \times 10^{-6},$$
$$\widehat{PFH}^*(2,280)_{[0.975\times 2,000]} = 7.6649 \times 10^{-8}, \tag{20}$$

respectively. That is, the SIL is allocated in levels ranging from SIL 1 to SIL 3 for the high demand or continuous mode. The mean of $\widehat{PFH}^*(2,280)$ is approximately 5.7598×10^{-7} which is corresponding to SIL 2. When bug data causing dangerous failures are scarce, as the dangerous software failure data collected from testing for the E/E/PE safety-related software, these interval estimations helps us to account for the uncertainty of the SIL allocation.

5 Conclusion

We have discussed interval estimations for target failure measures of the E/E/PE safety-related software based on the bootstrapping method. The interval estimation method generally needs to derive the probability distributions for parameters of interest, respectively. However, it is difficult to obtain the probability distributions of them especially for small number of data that cannot apply the asymptotic normality, and it is not always possible to conduct interval estimation analytically. Such cases must be often encountered in testing for the E/E/PE safety-related software. Our approach discussed here does not need to derive these distributions analytically and helps us because we obtain simulation-based distributions of them and to conduct interval estimations for each PFD and PFH. In our further studies, we need to revise our analytical formulation to estimate PFD in Eq. (6) to make it more close to the original definitions of PFD by considering a proof-testing interval and by deriving the time-averaged measure of the unavailability of the E/E/PE safety-related software. Furthermore, we need to apply other appropriate bootstrap confidence intervals to improve the accuracy of interval estimations of PFD and PFH.

References

[1] IEC 61508: Functional safety of electrical/electronic/programmable electronic safety-related systems, Edition 2.0, 2010.

[2] S. Inoue, T. Fujiwara and S. Yamada, "Mathematical approaches in functional safety assessment for E/E/PE safety-related software," *International Journal of Reliability, Quality and Safety Engineering*, Vol. 29, No. 1, pp. 2150043, 2022.

[3] T. Fujiwara, M. Kimura, Y. Satoh and S. Yamada, "A method of calculating safety integrity level for IEC 61508 conformity software," *Proceedings of the 17th IEEE Pacific Rim International Symposium on Dependable Computing*, pp. 296–301, 2011.

[4] H. Pham, *Software Reliability*, Springer-Verlag, Singapore, 2000.

[5] H. Pham, *System Software Reliability*, Springer-Verlag, London, 2006.

[6] S. Yamada, *Software Reliability Modeling — Fundamentals and Applications —* Springer, Tokyo, 2014.

[7] S. Osaki, *Applied Stochastic System Modeling.* Springer-Verlag, 1992.

[8] S.M. Ross, *Introduction to Probability Models* (10th Edition). Academic Press, 2009.

[9] T. Kaneishi and T. Dohi, "Parametric bootstrapping for assessing software reliability measures," *Proceedings of the 17th IEEE Pacific Rim International Symposium on Dependable Computing*, pp. 1–9, 2011.

[10] "Bootstrap methods: another look at the jackknife," *The Annals of Statistics*, Vol. 7, No. 1, pp. 1–26, 2022.

[11] S. Yamada, *Elements of Software Reliability: Modeling Approach.* (in Japanese), Kyoritsu-Shuppan, Tokyo, 2011.

[12] B. Efron, "Better bootstrap confidence intervals," *Journal of the American Statistical Association*, Vol. 82, No. 397, pp. 171–185, 1987.

[13] M. L. Rizzo, *Statistical Computing with R*, Chapman and Hall/CRC, Boca Raton, 2008.

A Determination System of Fault Correction Time for Software Development

Yuka MINAMINO, Masashi KUWANO, Mio HOSOE

Department of Social Systems and Civil Engineering,
Faculty of Engineering,
Tottori University,
4-101, Minami, Koyama-cho, Tottori-shi, Tottori 680-8552, Japan
E-mail: {minamino, kuwano, mhosoe}@tottori-u.ac.jp

Keywords: Random forest, AdaBoost, Software development management

Abstract

Software development managers estimate fault correction times and identify faults to be prioritized for correction before release. However, this time is influenced by factors such as fault characteristics, human involvement, and the testing environment, making accurate estimation difficult. To address this and enable AI (Artificial Intelligence)-driven decision support using small data, the current study develops a system that determines whether fault correction is completed within a defined time threshold. To this end, random forest and AdaBoost are trained on a small-scale fault dataset provided by LIMNO Co., Ltd. Two threshold-setting approaches are considered: one based on a decision tree analysis and the other on the distribution of correction times. The classification performance of the system was evaluated using confusion matrix, F1 score, and accuracy. By incorporating additional variables, the system achieves strong classification performance despite the limited dataset size, demonstrating the effectiveness of the proposed approach.

1. Introduction

In software development projects, products are typically developed through a process involving requirement definition, design, coding, and testing stages. Among these stages, final testing—which involves detecting and correcting faults to prevent post-deployment failures—is reported to account for 30% of the total development effort [2]. A software failure is defined as "the failure of software to operate as expected and to perform correctly" [8]. Such failures may occur, for example, when a malfunction interrupts processing or causes an output variable to take an incorrect value. The underlying cause of a software failure is known as a fault, defined as "a defect or error in the program that caused the software failure" [8].

Detected faults are managed using bug tickets, which record the importance of the fault and the environment in which it occurred. Once a ticket is created, it is assigned to a developer; the cause is investigated, the fault is corrected, the fix is verified, and the ticket is closed. In preparation for release, development managers must estimate the time required to correct each fault and prioritize the faults. Notably, fault correction time is directly related to the associated testing effort, typically measured in person–hours [11]. However, this time is influenced by several factors, including the fault's characteristics, differences in developer experience and skill, and testing environment such as the timing of detection and correction, as well as resource constraints. Consequently, accurately estimating fault correction time remains challenging.

Recent studies on fault correction time have primarily focused on open-source software (OSS) development [1,3,4,5,10]. OSS refers to software whose source code is freely available for public access, modification, reuse, and redistribution [12]. During OSS development, the bug tracking system (BTS) [7] remains publicly accessible, enabling developers and users to report failures. Given the frequency of version upgrades and long-term operation, large volumes of failure data accumulate in the BTS. Researchers leverage these data and apply machine learning techniques—such as random forest and logistic regression—to predict whether a fault will be corrected within a specified time threshold [1,5].

In OSS and general software development projects, decisions regarding version upgrade and release timings depend heavily on the accurate estimation of fault correction time. Unlike OSS development, fault data collection during general software development in private company projects is very limited. This is largely because private companies focus on minimizing failures during upstream processes, leading to fewer observable failures during testing. Additionally, time and budget limitations shorten the data collection period and limit the feasibility of extended data gathering. Consequently, data collected during general software development are often categorized as small data [6], characterized by a limited number of samples and data items. Companies that do not develop large-scale software, in particular, are unable to generate large failure datasets and therefore do not fully benefit from AI–driven decision-making automation or support. However, if methods for applying AI to small data can be developed, organizations could adopt AI without extensive data collection or infrastructure, enabling rapid, data-driven decision-making. Previous studies have been based on large-scale public data such as OSS, and the effectiveness of methods using AI to estimate fault correction time based on small-scale private data have not been verified.

In this study, we investigate the applicability of machine learning to small datasets collected from software development projects to support development management. Specifically, we develop a system that uses random forest and AdaBoost [9] to determine whether each fault in the electronic product data provided by LIMNO Co., Ltd. is corrected within a specified time threshold [9]. Unlike prior methods, the proposed approach aims to improve prediction accuracy by incorporating easily obtainable variables—such as the number of unresolved faults—from the collected fault data, thereby enabling the effective use of small datasets. A novel contribution of this study is the use of fault detection time series–based training and testing datasets, allowing the system to assess fault correction status even during ongoing project phases.

2. Summary of fault data

LIMNO Co., Ltd. records the status, importance, reporter, detection time, and resolution time for each fault/issue identified during software testing. Among these, status indicates how the fault was addressed and falls into one of four categories: "closed," "maintain present condition," "next time consideration," and "next model consideration." A status of "closed" means that the fault has been corrected. "Maintain present condition" indicates that the issue was not corrected because it is not a fault and does not substantially affect product usage. The "next time consideration" and "next model consideration" statuses indicate that the issue will not be addressed in the current product version but may be corrected in a future version. Each fault is also assigned an importance level— "high," "medium," or "low"—based on its symptoms and reproducibility. In the context of this study, fault detection time refers to the point at which a fault is logged, and fault correction time refers to the point at which it is resolved. The interval between these two timestamps serves as the basis for the analysis.

This study analyzed fault data collected between January 30 and July 1, 2019, during the quality verification of a software system embedded in a Linux-based display. A total of 354 faults were reported by 12 individuals, with 78.8% assigned a medium priority level. Table 1 provides an overview of the dataset.

Table 1. Data Overview

Data item	Summary
Total number of faults	354
Data collection period	2019/01/30～2019/07/01 (approximately 152 days)
Reporter	Reporter A to K, Client
Importance	"High," "Medium," "Low"
Status	"Closed," "Maintain present condition," "Next time consideration," "Next model consideration"
Fault detection time	Time when the fault was reported
Correction completion time	Time when the fault was corrected

3. System for fault correction time determination

3.1 Variables used in the determination system

We define a threshold to determine whether fault i is corrected within a specified timeframe after its detection. The variables used in the determination system are listed in Table 2. In addition to the variables "importance" and "reporter," which are available at the time of detection, new variables are introduced to represent the time segment of detection and the number of preceding faults.

Table 2. Variables used in this study

Variable	Summary
Importance	"High," "Medium," "Low"
Reporter	Reporter A to K, Client
Time segment	Morning, Afternoon
Day of week	Day on which the fault was detected (Monday to Saturday)
Faults detected in the last n days	Number of faults detected in the past n days from the detection of fault i ($n = 1, 3, 7, 10$)
Faults corrected on the detection date	Number of faults corrected on the day when fault i was detected
Uncorrected faults	Number of faults to be corrected at the time fault i was detected
Reporter-specific uncorrected faults	Cumulative number of uncorrected faults detected by each reporter
Reporter-specific faults in last 7 days	Cumulative number of faults detected by each reporter in the past 7 days

3.2 Random forest and AdaBoost

Ensemble learning involves training multiple weak classifiers and combining their outputs to produce the final prediction. A common ensemble learning approach is random forest, which uses decision trees as weak classifiers and bagging as the learning method [9]. Bagging involves generating multiple training datasets through bootstrap sampling of the training data. In random forest, the final output is determined by majority voting, where each weak classifier contributes one vote. Using multiple decision trees enhances classification accuracy and helps prevent overfitting. In this study, a random forest model was constructed using grid search for hyperparameter tuning.

AdaBoost [9], a boosting algorithm, trains weak classifiers sequentially, prioritizing learning from misclassified instances (Fig. 1). While random forest generates multiple training datasets from a single dataset through bootstrap sampling, AdaBoost uses a single training dataset and assigns weights to individual samples. This process enables sequential learning of weighted data. Variants of the AdaBoost algorithm include AdaBoost.M1 for binary classification and AdaBoost.M2 for multiclass classification. This study used AdaBoost.M1 with decision trees as weak classifiers to determine whether a fault is corrected within a defined threshold. The conceptual diagram of AdaBoost.M1 (hereafter referred to as AdaBoost) is presented in Fig. 1. Here, faults corrected within the threshold were labeled as one, while those not corrected within the threshold were labeled as zero. In the AdaBoost implementation, completed cases were assigned a label of 1 and incomplete cases a label of −1. The final output of AdaBoost was then transformed to one for complete and zero for incomplete cases.

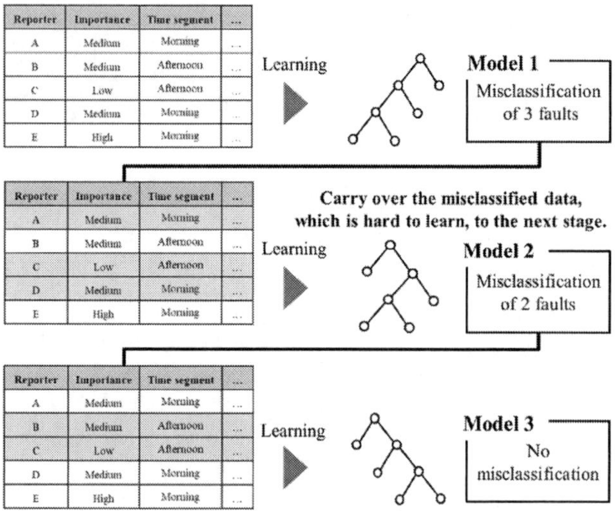

Fig. 1 Learning process of AdaBoost

3.3 Data splitting based on time series

In this study, we defined a start date as the reference point for evaluating whether a fault correction was completed within a given threshold. We arranged the faults in chronological order based on their detection time and split the dataset into 60% training data and 40% test data, using the start date as the dividing point. Faults with corrections completed by the start date were used as training data, while faults detected after the start date were used as test data. After data splitting, we removed training samples for which correction had begun but was not completed by the start date, as completion information for those samples was unavailable at that time. This time series–based data splitting resulted in a final dataset comprising 179 training and 121 test samples.

3.4 Threshold determination

We explored two approaches for determining the correction threshold: one based on a decision tree analysis and the other based on trends in the data distribution.

Specifically, we applied a decision tree to the training data to classify faults according to their correction time. Based on the number of samples, we set the threshold to approximately 9 days. In the training data, 98 samples were corrected within this threshold, while the correction time for 83 samples exceeded this threshold.

In the second approach, we examined the correction time distributions of the training and test datasets, as depicted in Fig. 2. These datasets exhibited similar patterns, particularly in the rise and fall of sample counts. Because the number of corrected faults declined around day 14, we set the threshold to 14 days. In the training data, 140 faults were corrected within 14 days, while 39 were not, indicating class imbalance. In classification tasks, training on imbalanced data can impair model performance. Therefore, class imbalance should be addressed to ensure reliable performance. In this study, we evaluated three approaches to handling class imbalance: no treatment, oversampling the minority class by generating new samples, and undersampling the majority class by reducing its sample size. We applied the synthetic minority oversampling technique (SMOTE) algorithm for oversampling and the k-means method for undersampling.

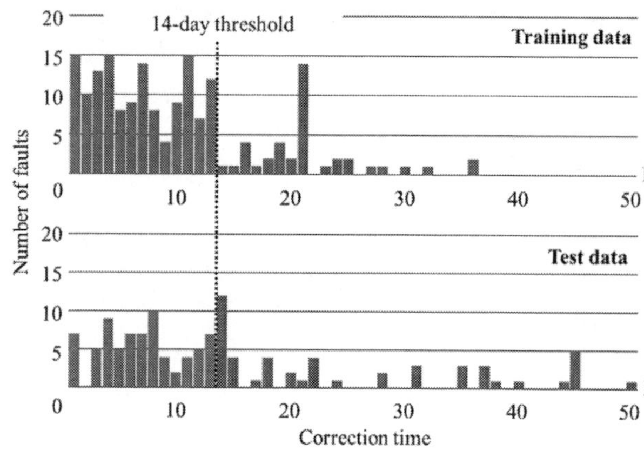

Fig. 2 Correction time distributions for the training and test datasets

4. Evaluation of models

In this study, we developed random forest and AdaBoost models to determine whether a fault correction was completed within 9 days or 14 days, using separate models for each threshold. Each of these four models was trained under three class imbalance conditions—no resampling, oversampling using SMOTE, and undersampling using the k-means method—resulting in a total of 12 models. To evaluate bias in the classification performance of each model, confusion matrices were used. Additionally, accuracy and F1 score were calculated to assess overall model performance.

Table 3 compares the model classification results for thresholds of 9 and 14 days. Among all models, the AdaBoost model with SMOTE-based oversampling achieved the highest classification accuracy. In contrast, models using the 9-day threshold showed lower classification accuracy compared to those using the 14-day threshold. Based on the F1 score and accuracy comparisons, we found that thresholds should be determined from the data distribution. Despite using a small dataset of approximately 350 faults and only four data items, this study achieved classification F1 score values comparable to or even exceeding those of previous studies using thousands to tens of thousands of OSS fault records.

To compare the classification accuracy of the models, we also constructed a logistic regression model, a conventional method commonly used for binary classification. With a 9-day threshold, the model achieved an F1 score of 0.24 and an accuracy of 0.41. In contrast, the 14-day threshold model yield an F1 score of 0.63, and an accuracy of 0.58. These results indicate that the AdaBoost model with a 14-day threshold performs better than

Table 3. Performance comparison

Threshold /Imbalance handling	9 days/ Undersampling				14 days/ Oversampling			
Model	Random forest		AdaBoost		Random forest		AdaBoost	
Actual	Incomplete	Complete	Incomplete	Complete	Incomplete	Complete	Incomplete	Complete
Incomplete	22 (0.18)	45 (0.37)	8 (0.07)	59 (0.49)	25 (0.21)	12 (0.10)	11 (0.09)	26 (0.21)
Complete	19 (0.16)	35 (0.29)	4 (0.03)	50 (0.41)	44 (0.36)	40 (0.33)	17 (0.14)	67 (0.55)
F1 Score	0.52		0.52		0.59		0.76	
Accuracy	0.47		0.48		0.54		0.64	

the logistic regression model.

For the model with a 9-day threshold, classification accuracy did not change between the no-treatment and undersampling conditions, as the class sizes were equal. In contrast, the 14-day model exhibited class imbalance. Undersampling reduced the majority class size to match the minority class size, removing approximately 100 samples. This resulted in insufficient training data and lower classification accuracy. However, oversampling increased the number of minority class samples, improving classification accuracy. Hence, the above comparison highlights the importance of carefully addressing class imbalance in small-scale datasets, ensuring that sufficient training data are preserved.

Furthermore, based on variable importance, the top 10 variables of the AdaBoost model with a 14-day threshold are shown in Table 4. Many of the top 10 variables relate to the number of unresolved faults at the time of detection and the number of faults detected a few days before the detection date. These results suggest that the newly added variables help improve the model's classification accuracy.

Table 4. Importance of variables

Rank	Variables	Importance
1	Reporter G	0.0537
2	Saturday	0.0535
3	Reporter D-specific faults in last 7 days	0.0515
4	Reporter B-specific faults in last 7 days	0.0461
5	Faults detected in the last 10 days	0.0427
6	Monday	0.0394
7	Reporter I-specific faults in last 7 days	0.0323
8	Reporter E-specific faults in last 7 days	0.0322
9	Uncorrected faults	0.0301
10	Faults detected in the last 1 day	0.0280

5. Conclusion

In this study, we trained two models—random forest and AdaBoost—on a small dataset to develop a system for estimating fault correction time, aiming to support software development management. The experiment involved approximately 350 samples provided by LIMNO Co., Ltd.

To apply machine learning to small data and improve model accuracy, this study introduces novelty in two main aspects: one is the addition of variables through easily implementable aggregation method, and the other is the construction of training and test datasets that consider the fault detection time. By not using the fault detection time as a variable and splitting the data considering the time series, the issue of extrapolation was avoided.

Two approaches were used to determine the correction time threshold: one based on a decision tree analysis and the other on the data's distribution. To address class imbalance, three strategies were evaluated: no resampling, SMOTE-based oversampling, and k means–based undersampling. The classification methods evaluated were random forest, AdaBoost, and logistic regression. Classification performance was assessed using confusion matrices, F1 score, and accuracy. The highest classification accuracy was achieved by setting a 14-day threshold (based on the data distribution), applying SMOTE-based oversampling, and using AdaBoost for classification. Additionally, AdaBoost outperformed logistic regression in classification accuracy. Overall, although machine learning techniques were applied to a small dataset of approximately 350 faults, reasonable classification accuracy could still be achieved. Thus, while existing machine learning–based development management approaches typically assume large-scale fault data, this study proposes a new method tailored to small datasets. However, because the training data is limited, there are still issues with the robustness and versatility of the model.

Future studies should apply fault data collected from other projects to identify variables that influence classification accuracy and to clarify guidelines for designing variables based on data aggregation. Additionally, further research is required to improve the accuracy and generalization performance of the developed system.

6. Acknowledgments

This work was supported by JSPS KAKENHI Grant Numbers. JP24K07948, JP23K26331. Our gratitude goes to LIMNO Co., Ltd. for providing the necessary data. We also would like to thank Mr. S. Ueda for the useful discussions.

7. References

[1] A. Ihara, R. Wakamoto, and K. Matsumoto, "A predicting method of issue-fixing time using development metrics in OSS projects," *Journal of Information Processing Society of Japan*, Vol. 59, No. 3, pp. 834–844, 2018.

[2] A. Kataoka, *White Paper on Software Development Data 2018–2019: Industry Edition – Information and Communications Sector*, Information-technology Promotion Agency, Japan (IPA), 2018.

[3] B.R.de O. Rodrigues, and F.S. Parreiras, "Predicting bug-fixing time with machine learning–a collaborative filtering approach," *Proceedings XV Computer on the Beach*, Balneário Camboriú, Brazil, July 2022, pp. 30–37.

[4] H. Masaki, O. Masao, A. Ihara, and K. Matsumoto, "Predicting the bug fixing time based on the bug assignment patterns in OSS development," *Journal of Information Processing Society of Japan*, Vol. 54, No. 2, pp. 933–944, 2013.

[5] H. Yoshiyuki, M. Ohira, and K. Toda, "Predicting bug-fix time using social relationships between assignors and assignees in OSS development," *Computer Software*, Vol. 32. No. 2, pp. 128–134, 2015.

[6] S. Akaho, "Machine learning for small data," *IEICE Fundamentals Review*, Vol. 16, No. 4, pp. 247–256, 2023.

[7] S. Miyamoto, Y. Tamura, and S. Yamada, "Reliability assessment tool based on deep learning and data preprocessing for OSS," *American Journal of Operations Research*, Vol. 12, pp. 111–125, 2022.

[8] S. Yamada, *Software Reliability Modeling—Fundamentals and Applications,* Springer-Verlag, Tokyo/Heidelberg, 2014.

[9] T. Hastie, R. Tibshirani, and J. Friedman, *The Elements of Statistical Learning*, Trans. by T. Kanamori, Kyoritsu Shuppan, Tokyo, Japan, 2014.

[10] Y. Kashiwa, M. Ohira, A. Hirohisa, and Y. Kamei, "A bug triaging method for reducing the time to fix bugs in large-scale open source software development," *Journal of Information Processing Society of Japan*, Vol. 56, No. 2, pp. 669–681, 2015.

[11] Y. Tamura, S. Miyamoto, L. Zhou, A. Anand, P.K. Kapur, and S. Yamada, "OSS reliability assessment method based on deep learning and independent Wiener data preprocessing," *International Journal of System Assurance Engineering and Management*, Vol. 15, No. 6, pp. 2668–2676, 2024.

[12] Y. Tamura and S. Yamada, *Applied OSS Reliability Assessment Modeling, AI and Tools—Mathematics and AI for OSS Reliability Assessment*, Springer, Cham, Switzerland, 2024.

FUSION: A Cloud-Based Framework for Integrated Software-Hardware Reliability Assessment Using Advanced Analytics and RBDs

Kazuhira Okumoto* and Hoang Pham**
* Sakura Software Solutions LLC, Naperville, IL, USA 60563.
** Department of Industrial and Systems Engineering, Rutgers University, Piscataway, NJ, USA 08854.

Keywords: Cloud-Based Digital Reliability Tools, Operational-Phase Analysis, Software-Hardware Integrated System Reliability, Reliability Block Diagrams

Abstract - As artificial intelligence, automation, and robotics become increasingly integral to modern systems, ensuring the reliability of both software and hardware components is paramount. Existing models primarily address software defects during development, leaving a critical gap in operational-phase reliability assessment. Similarly, while hardware reliability is well-studied, integrated models that encompass both software and hardware are limited. This paper introduces FUSION, a cloud-based tool designed to bridge this gap by aligning software failure rates with hardware reliability models, creating a unified framework for operational-phase reliability analysis. FUSION leverages advanced analytics and reliability block diagrams (RBDs) to provide comprehensive system evaluations. Key contributions include: (1) the development of an integrated software-hardware reliability model, (2) the implementation of automated reliability analysis algorithms, and (3) the creation of a digital tool for system-level reliability assessment. By integrating these elements, FUSION enhances reliability analysis, enabling practitioners to improve system resilience, user satisfaction, and operational efficiency

1. Introduction

In the era of rapid technological advancements, the integration of artificial intelligence (AI), automation, and robotics into modern systems has become increasingly prevalent. These technologies promise significant enhancements in efficiency, functionality, and user experience. However, they also introduce complex challenges, particularly in ensuring the reliability of both software and hardware components. Even minor defects can lead to substantial disruptions, underscoring the critical need for robust reliability assessment methodologies [11-12].

Current reliability models predominantly focus on software defects during the development phase, providing valuable insights into potential issues before deployment [4]. Despite their utility, a significant gap remains in assessing reliability during the operational phase, when software interacts with real-world conditions and user environments. This phase is crucial, as it is often when latent defects manifest, potentially leading to system failures [1]

On the hardware side, reliability assessment is well-established, with numerous models and methodologies developed to predict and mitigate failures [2]

However, the interaction between software and hardware components adds a layer of complexity that existing models do not fully address. Integrated reliability models that consider both software and hardware are limited, leaving practitioners without comprehensive tools to evaluate and enhance system resilience [3]

To bridge this gap, we introduce FUSION, a cloud-powered tool designed to integrate software and hardware reliability models for operational-phase analysis. FUSION aligns software failure rates with hardware reliability models, creating a unified framework that leverages advanced analytics and reliability block diagrams (RBDs) for comprehensive system evaluations. This tool not only facilitates accurate failure predictions but also provides actionable insights to improve system resilience, user satisfaction, and operational efficiency.

The key contributions of this paper are threefold: (1) the development of an integrated software-hardware reliability model, (2) the implementation of automated reliability analysis algorithms, and (3) the creation of a digital tool for system-level reliability assessment. By combining these elements, FUSION represents a significant advancement in reliability engineering, offering practitioners a powerful tool to anticipate and mitigate failures in integrated systems.

2. Literature Review

2.1 Software Reliability Models

Software reliability has been extensively studied, with numerous models developed to predict and mitigate software defects during the development phase [9-10]. Traditional models, such as the Jelinski-Moranda model and the Musa-Okumoto model, focus on defect prediction and reliability growth during software testing. These models have been instrumental in identifying potential issues before deployment, but they often fall short in addressing reliability during the operational phase, where software interacts with real-world conditions [5], [6].

Recent advancements have introduced more sophisticated approaches, such as Bayesian networks and machine learning-based models, which offer improved prediction accuracy by incorporating historical defect data and real-time monitoring. However, these models primarily concentrate on software reliability in isolation, without considering the interplay between software and hardware components [7], [8].

2.2 Hardware Reliability Models

Hardware reliability assessment is a well-established field, with models like the Weibull distribution and the Crow-AMSAA model being widely used to predict hardware failures. These models have been effective in various applications, from consumer electronics to aerospace systems, providing valuable insights into hardware performance and failure rates [15], [16].

In recent years, there has been a growing interest in reliability assessment methods for complex hardware systems, such as deep neural networks (DNNs) and their accelerators. These methods often employ fault injection, analytical, and hybrid approaches to evaluate the reliability of hardware components under different conditions. Despite their effectiveness, these models typically treat hardware reliability in isolation, without integrating software reliability considerations [17], [18].

2.3 Integrated Software-Hardware Reliability Models

The interaction between software and hardware components adds a layer of complexity that traditional models do not fully address. Some recent studies have attempted to bridge this gap by developing integrated reliability models. For instance, Zhu and Pham [13] proposed a novel system reliability model that incorporates hardware failures, software failures, and hardware-software interaction failures. This model provides a novel perspective by classifying interaction failures into software-induced hardware failures and hardware-induced software failures [13].

While these integrated models represent a significant advancement, they often rely on complex mathematical formulations and may not be easily applicable to real-world systems. Additionally, they may lack the scalability and flexibility required for modern, cloud-based environments [19], [20].

2.4 Novel Contributions of FUSION

FUSION addresses the limitations of existing models by providing a cloud-powered tool that integrates software and hardware reliability models for operational-phase analysis. Unlike traditional models that focus on either software or hardware reliability in isolation, FUSION offers a unified framework that aligns software failure rates with hardware reliability models. This approach leverages advanced analytics and reliability block diagrams (RBDs) to provide comprehensive system evaluations [21].

Key contributions of FUSION include:

1. **Integrated Software-Hardware Reliability Model**: FUSION develops a combined model that aligns software failure rates with hardware reliability behavior, creating a unified framework for operational-phase analysis.

2. **Automated Reliability Analysis Algorithms**: The tool implements algorithms for automated reliability analysis, enabling real-time predictions and assessments.

3. **Digital Tool for System-Level Assessments**: FUSION provides a user-friendly digital tool that facilitates the creation and evaluation of reliability block diagrams, offering actionable insights to improve system resilience and operational efficiency.

By integrating these elements, FUSION represents a significant advancement in reliability engineering, offering a practical and scalable solution for modern, integrated systems.

3. FUSION Overview

The methodology behind FUSION involves several key steps and algorithms to ensure accurate and comprehensive reliability assessments:

1. **Software Customer-Found Defect Prediction**:

    - **Operational Phase Segmentation**: The operational phase of software usage is divided into distinct periods: early customer testing, customer testing, post-deployment, and customer migration to the next release. Each period exhibits varying rates of defect identification.

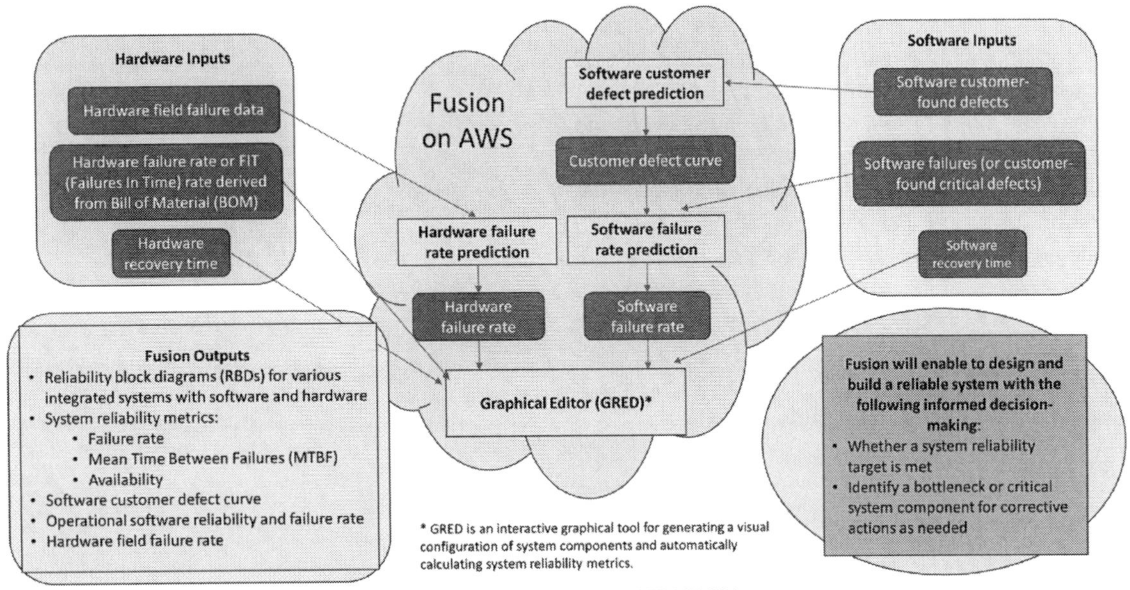

Fig. 1. An Overview of FUSION

- **Defect Trend Model**: A defect trend model spans the entire operational phase, represented as a sequence of empirically derived straight lines. An algorithm autonomously identifies the transitions (inflection points) between these lines, dynamically adapting to distinct patterns within the data.

2. **Software Failure Rate Prediction**:

- **Transformation of Defect Data**: The cumulative predicted defect curve is transformed into the cumulative failure curve using parameters α, β, and γ. These parameters represent horizontal shift, scaling factor, and vertical scaling factor, respectively.
- **Optimization Algorithm**: The algorithm optimizes the parameters to best fit the predicted failure curve to the actual one. The objective function is based on the absolute difference between predicted defects and actual failures over the last 10 weeks. The algorithm iterates over three levels to identify the global minimum sum of squared differences (SSQ).

3. **Intelligent Interactive Graphical Editor (iGRED) for RBDs**

- **RBD Construction**: iGRED allows users to construct detailed RBDs for software and hardware systems. Built-in real-time reliability metric calculations simplify assessments and accelerate system design.
- **Preconfigured Templates**: iGRED provides templates for single-unit, active-standby, and active-active systems. Users input failure rates and recovery times, and iGRED calculates and displays reliability metrics instantly.

4. **Reliability Metrics Calculation**

- **Key Metrics**: FUSION calculates key reliability metrics, including failure rate (λ), Mean Time to Failure (MTTF), Mean Time Between Failures (MTBF), Mean Time to Repair (MTTR), and availability (A). These metrics are computed for software, hardware, and the integrated system.
- **Formulas and Calculations**: The reliability metrics are derived using established formulas and methods, such as the exponential distribution for constant failure rates and the Markov chain method for complex configurations.

In the following subsections, we detail each of the above components.

3.1 Software Customer-Found Defect Prediction

The operational phase of software usage can be divided into distinct periods: early customer testing, customer testing, post-deployment, and customer migration to the next release. Each period exhibits varying rates of defect identification. To account for this variability, we developed a defect trend model that spans the entire operational phase, represented as a sequence of empirically derived straight lines. The primary technical challenge is creating an algorithm that autonomously identifies the transitions (inflection points) between these lines. This algorithm must dynamically adapt to the distinct patterns within the data and operate seamlessly in real-time as new defect data becomes available.

The segmented linear equation is expressed mathematically to capture the distinct defect trends in each period. The cumulative defects, *m*(*x*), found by time *x* during inflection points (*j* – 1) and *j* is described as:

$$m(x) = m(x_{j-1}) + \theta_j (x - x_{j-1}) \qquad \forall x_{(j-1)} \le x \le x_j \qquad (1)$$

Note that θ_j represents the slope of the curve during the period. Algorithm 1 shows the algorithm that we developed.

Algorithm 1 Finding inflection points and multiple curves

```
procedure LPM((x_i, y_i)  ∀0 ≤ i ≤ p)
    for i = x_s, i ≤ x_p, i++ do                    ▷ Start the loop at x_s, y_s to the end wee
        if i ≥ x_s + 3 then
            slope = (y_i − y_s)/(x_i − x_s)
            for j = x_s, j ≤ i, j++ do
                ŷ_j = slope × (x_j − x_s) + y_s       ▷ Calculate the predicted valu
                SSQ_j = (y_j − ŷ_j)^2                 ▷ This is a measure of goodness of fi
            end for
            SSQ_i = Σ_{j=x_s}^{i} SSQ_i/(i − x_s)     ▷ Goodness of fit for the week x_s to week
            if i ≥ x_s + 5 then ▷ Check if we have the last two weeks of SSQ value
                ΔSSQ_1 = (SSQ_{i−2} − SSQ_{i−1})/SSQ_{i−2}
                ΔSSQ_2 = (SSQ_{i−2} − SSQ_i)/SSQ_{i−2}
                if i ≥ x_s + 5 then
                    if (ΔSSQ_1 > 0.1) AND (ΔSSQ_2 > 0.1) then
                        IP = Week i − 2               ▷ IP is the Inflection Poin
                    else
                        x_s = x_{i−2}
                    end if
                end if
            end if
        end if
    end for
    return IP
end procedure
```

Algorithm 1. Algorithm for operational software defect prediction

3.2 Software Failure Rate Prediction

FUSION introduces groundbreaking methods for predicting software defects and failures, demonstrating that software defect and failure rates remain constant during the operational phase. This capability is significant as it aligns software reliability modeling with established hardware reliability models, offering a unified approach to system reliability. The analytics for predicting software defects are robust enough to extend to hardware field failure data, providing a versatile solution for reliability analysis across various system components.

An innovative algorithm has been developed to predict software failure rates during the operational phase. The required input data includes the defect-predicted curve (i.e., the output of the defect-predicted curve) and the software failure data (i.e., critical defects). The cumulative predicted defect curve (x, y) is transformed into the cumulative failure curve (u, v) using the parameters, α, β, and γ:

$$u = \alpha + \beta x \qquad (2)$$

$$v = \gamma y \qquad (3)$$

Parameters are interpreted as follows.

– α: Horizontal shift (right if positive, left if negative, no shift if zero).

– β: Scaling factor (delay if greater than 1, acceleration if less than 1, no change if 1).

– γ: Vertical scaling factor (doubles height if 2, reduces to 50% if 0.5, no change if 1).

Algorithm for Software Failure Prediction

The algorithm optimizes the parameters α, β, and γ to best fit the predicted failure curve to the actual one. The objective function is based on the absolute difference between predicted defects and actual failures over the last 10 (default) weeks. To calculate the objective function, follow these steps:

- Calculate transformed values (u, v) using the equations (2) and (3) for given values of α, β, and γ.
- The actual failure curve (xact, yact) remains on the original (x, y) scale. Calculate vact, for u = xact using interpolation:

$$v_{act} = v_1 + \frac{v_2 - v_1}{u_2 - u_1} \times (x_{act} - u_1) \qquad (4)$$

- Calculate the sum of the absolute differences (SSQ) between vact, and yact:

$$SSQ = \sum |v_{act} - y_{act}| \qquad (5)$$

The parameter ranges are:α = 5 to 0 with a decrement of 0.5, β = 0.7 to 1.1 with an increment of 0.05, and γ = 0.86 to 1.2 with an increment of 0.02.

Solving the non-linear optimization problem:

• The algorithm iterates over three levels:

– Level 1: Iterate over γ from 0.86 to 1.2 with an increment of 0.01.

– Level 2: For each value of γ, iterate over β from 0.7 to 1.1 with an increment of 0.01.

– Level 3: For each combination of γ and β, iterate over α from 5 to 0 with a decrement of 0.1

• Calculate SSQ for each combination and track the minimum SSQ value:

– For a fixed value of γ, iterate through α and β. Terminate Level 3 if the SSQ exceeds the previous value.

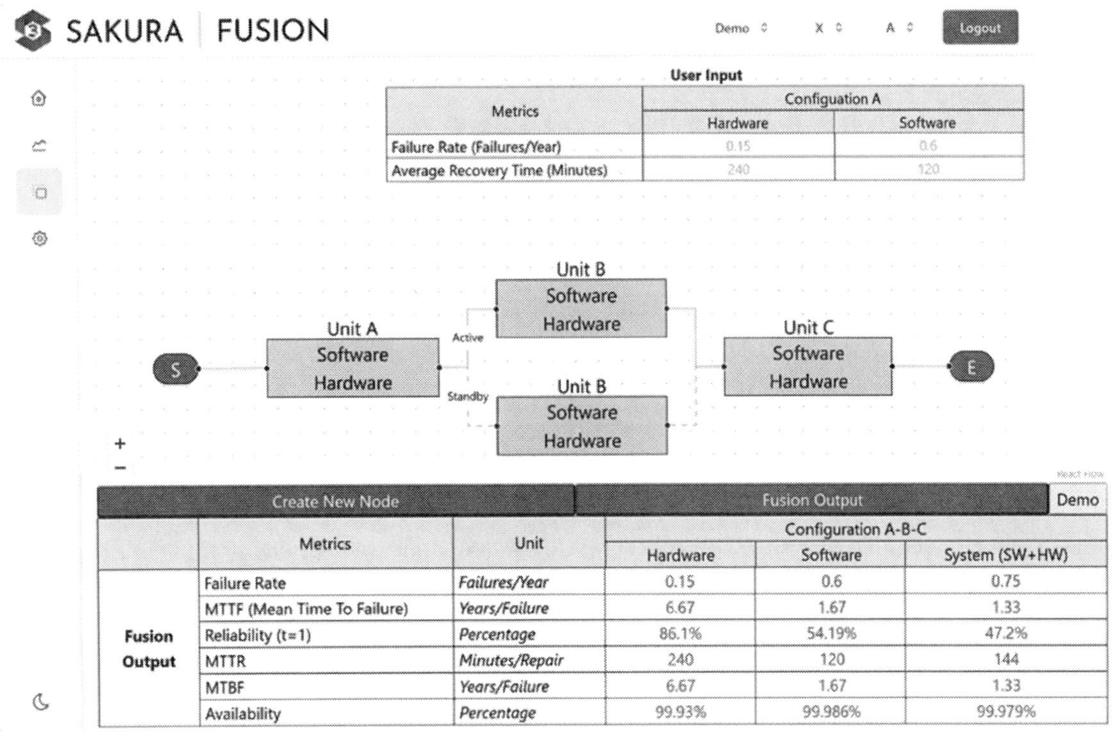

Fig. 2: A sample iGRED with the user input and the output

– Continue Level 2 until the minimum SSQ for the current γ is found.

– Repeat the process for γ until the global minimum SSQ is identified.

This algorithm provides a methodical approach to determining the best-fit parameters that minimize discrepancies between the predicted and actual software failure curves.

3.3 Intelligent Interactive Graphical Editor (iGRED) for Reliability Block Diagrams (RBDs)

iGRED, integrated into **FUSION**, allows users to construct detailed **reliability block diagrams (RBDs)** for software and hardware systems. Built-in real-time reliability metric calculations simplify assessments and accelerate system design. RBDs visually represent system configurations, enabling reliability analysis through **series and parallel equations**. iGRED also provides **preconfigured templates** for single-unit, active-standby, and active-active systems.

Users input **failure rates** and **recovery times**, and upon saving, iGRED instantly calculates and displays reliability metrics. Figure 2 shows a sample iGRED with the user input and the Fusion output.

3.3.1 Reliability Metrics

Reliability metrics evaluate system performance and operational efficiency. Key metrics include failure rate, Mean Time to Failure (MTTF), Mean Time Between Failures (MTBF), Mean Time to Repair (MTTR), and availability.

Failure Rate (λ): The failure rate measures how often a system or component fails over a specified time, expressed as failures per unit of time (e.g., per hour or year). It is crucial in reliability engineering to predict system reliability. A low failure rate indicates high reliability, while a high rate suggests frequent failures. Failure rates can be constant (common in electronics during the useful life period) or time-varying (changes over time, seen during early failures or wear-out phases).

Reliability Function (R(t)): The probability that a system operates without failure over time t. For a constant failure rate, it follows an exponential distribution.

MTTF (Mean Time to Failure): MTTF measures the average operational lifespan of non-repairable systems before failure. Higher MTTF indicates greater reliability. It applies to items like light bulbs or batteries.

	Hardware	Software	System
Failure Rate	λ_{hw}	λ_{sw}	$\lambda_{sys} = \lambda_{hw} + \lambda_{sw}$
MTTF	$\frac{2}{\lambda_{hw}}$	$\frac{2}{\lambda_{sw}}$	$\frac{2}{\lambda_{sys}}$
Reliability	$(1 + \lambda_{hw} t)e^{-\lambda_{hw} t}$	$(1 + \lambda_{sw} t)e^{-\lambda_{sw} t}$	$(1 + \lambda_{sys} t)e^{-\lambda_{sys} t}$
MTBF	$MTTF_{hw} + MTTR_{hw}$	$MTTF_{sw} + MTTR_{sw}$	$MTTF_{sys} + MTTR_{sys}$
MTTR	$\frac{1}{\mu_{hw}}$	$\frac{1}{\mu_{sw}}$	$\frac{1}{\mu_{sys}} = (\frac{\lambda_{hw}}{\mu_{hw}} + \frac{\lambda_{sw}}{\mu_{sw}})/\lambda_{sys}$
Availability	$\frac{MTTF_{hw}}{MTBF_{hw}}$	$\frac{MTTF_{sw}}{MTBF_{sw}}$	$\frac{MTTF_{sys}}{MTBF_{sys}}$

Fig. 3: Sample reliability metrics formulas for a two-unit active-active configuration

MTBF (Mean Time Between Failures): MTBF measures the average time between failures for repairable systems. It includes MTTF (Time before failure) and **MTTR (Time to Repair)**, which is the Time needed to restore functionality after failure. MTBF = MTTF + MTTR. Higher MTBF values indicate greater reliability, aiding maintenance planning and uptime estimation.

Availability (A): Availability reflects the proportion of operational time versus expected time. Calculated as **A = Uptime / (Uptime + Downtime)** or **A = MTTF / MTBF.** High availability (close to 1) indicates minimal downtime and is essential for critical industries like telecommunications, healthcare, and military applications. It supports **System Design (**ensuring systems meet operational requirements), **Maintenance Planning (**optimizing schedules to maximize uptime), and **SLAs (**defining reliability standards such as "99.9% uptime").

These metrics guide reliability engineering, enabling better design, maintenance, and operational strategies for minimizing failures and downtime.

3.3.2 Templates for Reliability Block Diagrams

Phase I iGRED development focuses on three primary configurations: A single-unit system with software and hardware, a two-unit active-standby system, and a two-unit active-active system. Phase II will address additional configurations.

FUSION calculates key reliability metrics, including **failure rate (**frequency of failures), **MTTF** (average operational lifespan before failure), **reliability** (percentage of systems expected to operate without failure over one year), **MTBF** (average time between successive failures, **MTTR** (average time required to restore functionality after a failure), and **availability** (proportion of operational time versus total expected time).

These metrics are computed for software, hardware, and the integrated system (HW + SW), providing a comprehensive overview of system reliability. Fig. 3 shows the reliability metrics formulas for a two-unit active-active template. Formulas for other templates have also been developed using the Markov chain method, although they are not shown here due to space limitations.

3.3.3 Combinations of the Basic Configurations / Templates

Each template requires specific starting and ending points to construct a network of templates. The network begins at the Start node and ends at the End node. Complex systems may combine series and parallel configurations. The reliability of such systems can be calculated by breaking them down into more straightforward series and parallel components and then combining their reliabilities using appropriate formulas. Sorting them topologically simplifies the metrics calculation. Fig. 2 shows an example with three configurations: two single-unit configurations and a two-unit active-active load-sharing configuration. These configurations are connected in series. Reliability metrics are already calculated for each template, allowing us to add them to determine the system failure rate. Figure 2 also shows the outputs for the sample configurations. FUSION will automatically calculate for any combinations of the templates.

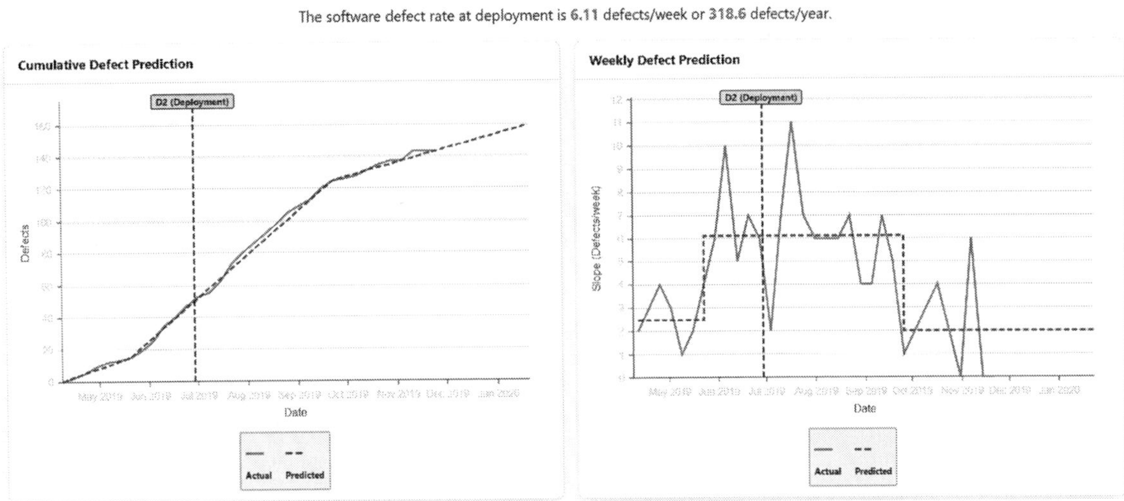

Fig. 4. A sample output of software defect prediction algorithm

3.4 System Design and Building

FUSION enables users to design and optimize reliable systems through advanced analytics and interactive modeling tools. Its software failure rate prediction component delivers accurate defect and failure forecasts, supporting proactive maintenance and system enhancements. With **iGRED's** intuitive interface and automated calculations, users can effortlessly create comprehensive **reliability block diagrams (RBDs)**, streamlining system evaluation and reliability improvement.

4. FUSION Implementation

FUSION is designed to streamline the entire workflow of reliability assessment, encompassing data extraction, pre-processing, core analytics, and post-processing. The system is built on the AWS platform, ensuring scalability and reliability. The architecture leverages several key components and technologies:

1. **Data Extraction and Pre-Processing**:
   - **APIs and Data Collection**: FUSION uses Flask APIs to collect data from various defect-tracking tools. This data is consolidated into two optimized databases: PostgreSQL for structured data and DynamoDB for unstructured data.
   - **Pre-Processing Steps**: Data undergoes rigorous pre-processing to ensure consistency and accuracy. This includes standardizing field and value mappings, categorizing field values, and detecting duplicates and cross-release defects. Data is aggregated into weekly or specified time frames to prepare inputs for the core analytics engine.
2. **Core Analytics Engine**:
   - **Predictive Modeling and Analytics**: Developed using the Python scientific stack, the core analytics engine performs advanced predictive modeling and reliability metrics calculation. It leverages libraries such as NumPy, SciPy, and scikit-learn for statistical analysis and machine learning.
   - **Reliability Block Diagrams (RBDs)**: The engine supports the creation and evaluation of RBDs, which visually represent system configurations and facilitate reliability analysis through series and parallel equations.
3. **User Interface**:
   - **Interactive and Intuitive Design**: The user interface is built with JavaScript ES6 and React, providing a responsive and intuitive experience. Users can design system reliability block diagrams, input failure rates and recovery times, and view real-time reliability metrics.
   - **Infrastructure Management**: Terraform AWS manages the system's infrastructure as code (IaC), ensuring efficient deployment and scalability.

5. Results and Discussion

Fig 4 illustrates these sequential lines, visually representing the algorithm's results. For enhanced clarity, the figure includes a weekly breakdown of the trend. The algorithm's

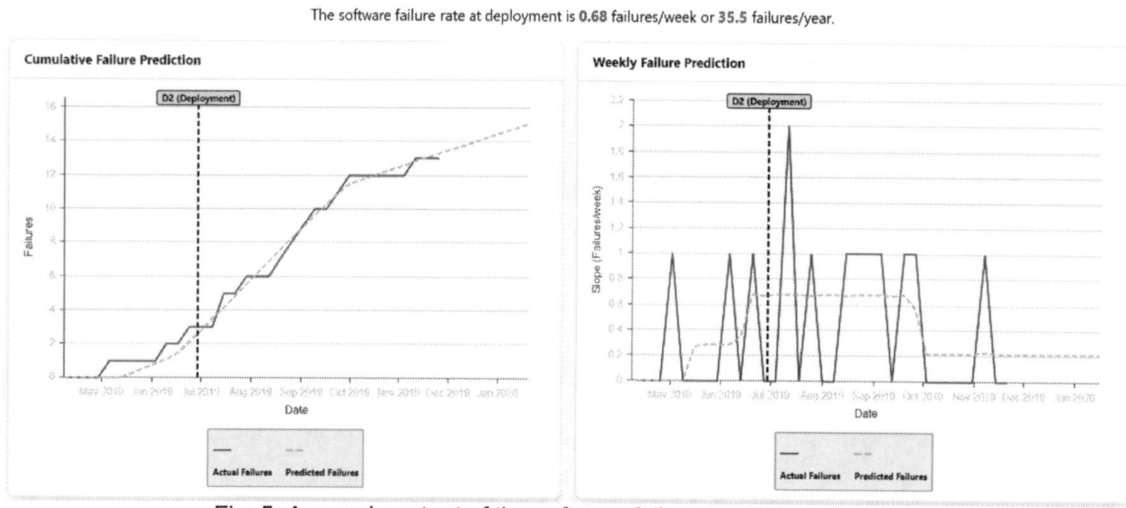

Fig. 5: A sample output of the software failure prediction algorithm.

utility extends beyond software defects, including hardware failure data. Additionally, we compare the observed hardware failure rates with those projected from the bill of materials (BOM) to deliver a comprehensive understanding of system reliability. This approach enables accurate modeling of defect trends and ensures timely and effective defect management throughout the software lifecycle. By integrating this capability, FUSION enhances reliability analysis for software and hardware components, providing actionable insights to improve system performance.

Fig 5 illustrates the predicted software failure curve alongside actual data, presented in cumulative and weekly views. These visualizations confirm that the software failure rate remains constant after deployment. This method has been applied to data from multiple projects, consistently validating these findings. A notable advantage of this approach is its effectiveness even when the number of failures is minimal, such as fewer than 10 occurrences. By integrating this method, FUSION enhances the accuracy and applicability of failure rate predictions, contributing to improved system reliability across diverse operational scenarios.

Figure 5: This figure showcases a sample configuration created using the Intelligent Interactive Graphical Editor (iGRED) integrated into FUSION. The figure includes a pop-up input table that appears when selecting a template, allowing users to input failure rates and recovery times. The RBD (Reliability Block Diagram) visually represents the system configuration, enabling reliability analysis through series and parallel equations. The figure demonstrates the use of preconfigured templates for single-unit, active-standby, and active-active systems. Once the RBD is completed, users can view real-time reliability metrics computed at the bottom of the page. These metrics include failure rate, Mean Time to Failure (MTTF), Mean Time Between Failures (MTBF), Mean Time to Repair (MTTR), and availability. iGRED simplifies the construction of detailed RBDs and accelerates system design by providing instant calculations and visual feedback, thereby enhancing the overall reliability assessment process.

6. Conclusion and Future Work

This paper introduced **FUSION**, a cloud-based tool that bridges a critical gap in operational-phase reliability modeling by aligning software and hardware reliability models. Our research shows that software failure rates during operation can be effectively modeled as segmented straight lines. With advanced analytics and a graphical editor, FUSION streamlines **reliability block diagram (RBD)** creation, accelerating reliability assessments and enabling targeted improvements. FUSION combines predictive analytics with an intuitive graphical interface, providing system reliability engineers with a powerful tool to anticipate and mitigate failures. This integrated approach enhances software and hardware reliability, ensuring overall system robustness.

By empowering practitioners to enhance system performance, FUSION significantly boosts reliability and customer satisfaction. This tool represents a significant advancement in reliability engineering, setting the stage for more resilient, integrated systems.

Acknowledgments

This research is supported by the National Science Foundation (NSF) Small Business Technology Transfer (STTR) program under Award Number 2348264. The author gratefully acknowledges Rashid Mijumbi, Joseph Good, Mike Okumoto, Andrew Raposo, Dylan Wong, and JiaXuan Mi for their valuable contributions to this paper.

References

[1] Ellison, Robert J. "Assuring software reliability." *Carnegie Mellon University, Tech. Rep.* (2014).

[2] Trivedi, Kishor. (2021). Reliability and Availability of Hardware-Software systems: Stochastic Reliability Models of Real Systems. 10.13140/RG.2.2.30286.48960.

[3] Sun, Bo, et al. "Physics-of-failure and computer-aided simulation fusion approach with a software system for electronics reliability analysis." *Eksploatacja i Niezawodność* 22.2 (2020). M. Dan, "The business model of 'Software-As-A-Service,'" in *Proc. 2007 IEEE Int. Conf. Services Comput.*, 2007, pp. 118-125.

[4] H. Pham, *Software Reliability*, Springer, Berlin, Heidelberg, 1999.

[5] P. D. T. O'Connor, "Software Reliability Engineering, John D. Musa, McGraw-Hill," *Quality and Reliability Engineering International*, vol. 16, no. 5, pp. 391-400, 2000.

[6] M. R. Lyu, *Handbook of Software Reliability Engineering*, McGraw-Hill, Inc., USA, 1996.

[7] D. D. Hanagal and N. N. Bhalerao, "Literature Survey in Software Reliability Growth Models," in *Software Reliability Growth Models*, Springer, Singapore, 2021, pp. 13-26.

[8] R. Mijumbi, K. Okumoto, and A. Asthana, "Software Reliability Assurance in Practice," in *Wiley Encyclopedia of Electrical and Electronics Engineering*, 2019.

[9] K. Okumoto, "Early Software Defect Prediction: Right-Shifting Software Effort Data into a Defect Curve," in *Proc. 2022 IEEE Int. Symp. Software Reliability Engineering Workshops (ISSREW)*, 2022, pp. 43-48.

[10] K. Okumoto, "Digital Engineering-driven Software Quality Assurance-as-a-Service," in *Proc. 28th ISSAT Int. Conf. Reliability and Quality in Design (RQD)*, 2023.

[11] X. Zhang and H. Pham, "Software field failure rate prediction before software deployment," *Journal of Systems and Software*, vol. 79, no. 3, pp. 43-56, 2006.

[12] K. Okumoto, "Experience Report: Practical Software Availability Prediction in Telecommunication Industry," in *Proc. Int. Symp. Software Reliability Engineering (ISSRE)*, 2016, pp. 19-25.

[13] M. Zhu and H. Pham, "A novel system reliability modeling of hardware, software, and interactions of hardware and software," *Mathematics*, vol. 7, no. 11, pp. 1049-1060, 2019.

[14] P. D. T. O'Connor and A. Kleyner, *Practical Reliability Engineering*, 5th ed., Wiley, 2011.

[15] U.S. Department of Defense, *Military Handbook MIL-HDBK-217E, Reliability Prediction of Electronic Equipment*, 1986.

[16] T. P. Ryan and W. Q. Meeker, "System Reliability Theory: Models, Statistical Methods, and Applications," *Journal of Quality Technology*, vol. 37, no. 1, pp. 5-10, 2005.

[17] W. Nelson, W. Q. Meeker, and L. A. Escobar, "Statistical Methods for Reliability Data," *Technometrics*, vol. 40, no. 3, pp. 293-297, 1998.

[18] A. Kleyner and V. Volovoi, "Application of Petri nets to reliability prediction of occupant safety systems with partial detection and repair," *Reliability Engineering and System Safety*, vol. 95, no. 6, pp. 123-130, 2010.

[19] A. Birolini, *Reliability Engineering: Theory and Practice*, 7th ed., Springer, 2014.

[20] Y. Jackson, P. Tabbagh, P. Gibson, and E. Seglie, "The new department of defense (DoD) guide for achieving and assessing RAM," in *Proc. Annual Reliability and Maintainability Symp.*, 2005, pp. 140-145.

[21] Relyence, "A Deep Dive into System Modeling Using Reliability Block Diagram (RBD) Analysis," Technical report, 2021.

Machine Learning-Based Spare Parts Demand Prediction under General Repair Turnaround Time Distributions

WANG Hongzhou, HART Brian

RTX, USA

Keywords: Spare Parts; Machine Learning; Queueing theory; M/M/c Queue, M/G/c Queue; Erlang C, Deep Learning

Abstract - Wang and Hart [1] introduced an Erlang C - based spare parts prediction model that addresses intermittent usage and prevents lost demand. It allows infinite spare parts requests, making it theoretically optimal. However, in practice, the repair turnaround time (RTAT) may not follow an Exponential distribution but a Lognormal distribution [5]. This paper will explore spares prediction when RTAT does not follow the exponential distribution which is assumed in the Erlang C queueing. Then this paper uses machine learning to refine the parameter of the spares prediction models, covering data preprocessing, feature engineering, train and test data preparation, variable importance, class balance, confounding, and the performance of various machine learning algorithms, including gradient boosting machine, distributed random forest, deep learning, and stacked ensemble. This paper has developed a machine learning algorithm with excellent performance. The length of this paper limits the discussions to prediction of repair outcomes only.

1. Introduction

Spare parts are essential across various industries. In the telecommunications industry, photonic service switch systems contain many FRUs (Field Replaceable Units) and FRU spares are used to ensure high operational availability, e.g., a typical requirement 0.99999. In aerospace and defense industry, airborne radar systems contain some WRAs (Weapon Replaceable Assemblies) and WRAs may contain SRUs (Shop Replaceable Units). WRA and/or SRU lay-in spares are widely used. Unlike photonic service switch systems which run continuously or are in uninterrupted 24/7 service, airborne radar systems operate intermittently or only for short periods during the day.

Figure 1 shows an airborne radar system spare parts replenishment process. If a WRA fails, a spare will be withdrawn from the base, and replace the failed one. The failed WRA will be sent to the base and then go to the depot for repair. Assume there are *n* aircraft's. The question is: How many WRA spares are required at the base and depot, respectively? How many SRU lay-in spares are required at the depot? Note that usually an aircraft does not fly continuously and may be airborne only for specific hours each month.. Therefore, aircraft flight hours h are not in calendar time. However, the repair turnaround time (RTAT) or spares replenishment time τ are in calendar time. So aircraft flight hours h and spares replenishment time τ are in different time scales. Their product τh represents total flight hours during the spares replenishment time. Assume that WRAs fail only during flight hours in this paper. Other parameters and acronyms are listed in the Notation and Acronyms sections.

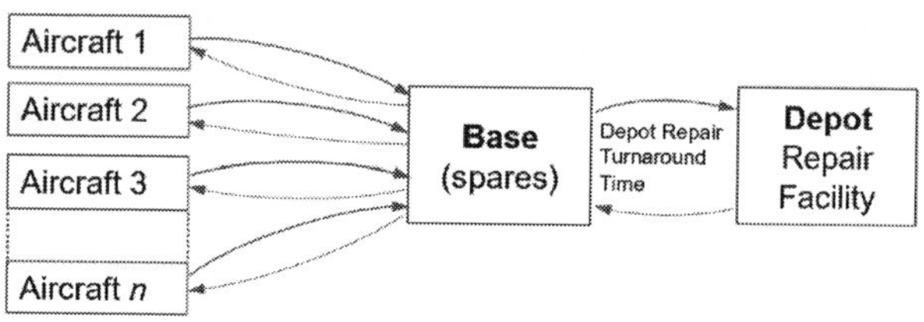

Figure 1. An airborne radar system spare parts replenishment process

Currently a Poisson process is often used to predict number of spare parts in aerospace & defense industry [1, 5]. Erlang B model is used in the telecommunications industry (24/7 service). However, they have a common drawback: if spares demand cannot be fulfilled it may be lost. Obviously, this is not practical. Wang and Hart [1, 5] introduced a new maintenance spare parts prediction model based on the Erlang C queuing and machine learning under general conditions including intermittent uses. This Erlang C model overcomes the drawback in the existing models and permits infinite spare parts requests and no spares demand is lost.

Acronyms

CNV	Cannot Verify
DRF	Distributed Random Forest
GBM	Gradient Boosting Machine
MFHBF	Mean Flight Hours Between Failures
MSE	Mean Squared Error
MTBF	Mean Time Between Failures
MTTR	Mean Time To Repair
NTF	No Trouble Found
RMSE	Root Mean Squared Error
RTAT	Repair Turnaround Time
WRA	Weapon Replaceable Assembly
XRT	Extremely Randomized Trees

Notation

- p stockout probability
- s number of spare parts
- N field population of parts, or number of fielded systems times part quantity per system
- τ repair turnaround time or spares replenishment time
- h monthly or daily operating or flight time (hours)
- π MFHBF or MTBF
- ν predicted failure rate $\nu = 1/\pi$
- m replacement factor, a multiplier of the predicted failure rate to account for CNVs or NTFs, induced damage, software failure, etc. $m\nu$ is the parts removal rate or field return rate.
- B number of parts to be replenished $B = N\tau hm\nu$
- A_q spares availability, $p + A_q = 1$
- A_o operational availability
- η MTTR
- c number of servers
- K Number of customers
- μ Exponential service time parameter
- λ Poisson process arrival rate
- R^2 R-Squared or the coefficient of determination

2. M/M/c Queue, M/G/c Queue and Spares Prediction

In queueing theory, the M/M/c queue represents a system where arrivals follow a Poisson process, service times are exponentially distributed, and there are c servers available [9. 10]. A M/M/c queue is a stochastic process whose state space is the set {0, 1, 2, 3, ...} where each state represents the total number of customers in the system, including those currently being served:

- Arrivals occur at rate λ according to a Poisson process and move the process from state *i* to *i*+1.
- Service times have an exponential distribution with parameter μ. If there are fewer than *c* jobs, some of the servers will be idle. If there are more than *c* jobs, the jobs queue in a buffer.
- The buffer is of infinite size (Erlang C), unlike Erlang B with 0 waiting positions (M/M/c/c).

Now imagine servers are spares and customers are failed or removed parts. Wang and Hart [1] obtained the spare parts stockout probability (i.e., queueing probability):

$$p = \frac{\frac{B^s}{s!}\frac{s}{s-B}}{\frac{B^s}{s!}\frac{s}{s-B} + \sum_{k=0}^{s-1}\frac{B^k}{k!}} \quad (1)$$

Wang and Hart compared the above Erlang C spares prediction model with Poisson Process and Erlang B models and conclude the Erlang C model has the most accurate prediction in theory [5]. The Erlang C model has been built into the Raytheon EAGLE software that is used by 100+ external customers. It has been used on many Raytheon products, resulting in millions of dollars savings.

Note that the above Erlang C spares prediction model (1) assume RTAT follows an exponential distribution. If they are not an exponential distribution [5] then this this is a M/G/c queue: where arrivals are Markovian and there are c servers with a general service time distribution and with no limit on the queue size. For a M/G/c queue, there is no closed-form expression for the queueing probability. Tijms *et al.* [2] believe it is not likely that computationally tractable methods can be developed to compute the exact numerical values of the steady-state probability in the M/G/*c* queue. Various approximations for the queueing probability have been developed. In fact, numerical experience shows that the Erlang C formula for a M/M/c queue is a good approximation for the M/G/c queue model [2, 3, 4, 9]. So Equation (1) is still a good approximation when RTAT follows a general distribution for some cases.

Tijms et al. [2] developed an approximate formula for the M/G/c queue. Using his results, we can approximate the stockout probability when RTAT is a general distribution:

$$p_{M/G/s}^{Appr1} \approx \beta p + 1 - \beta - \beta\left(\frac{\eta_1}{\eta_2} - 1\right)\frac{B^{s-1}}{(s-1)!}\Omega \quad (2)$$

where

$$\beta = \left\{1 + \frac{B^{s-1}B\Omega}{(c-1)!\,\eta_2(1-\frac{B}{s})E(\tau)}\left[\eta_1\left(\xi_2 - \frac{E(\tau)}{s}\right) - \eta_2\left(\xi_1 - \frac{E(\tau)}{s}\right)\right]\right\}^{-1}$$

$$\Omega = \left[\sum_{k=0}^{s-1}\frac{B^k}{k!} + \frac{B^s}{s!}\frac{s}{s-B}\right]^{-1}$$

$\eta_1, \eta_2, \xi_1, \xi_2$ are computed from the RTAT distribution [4].

Assume C_τ^2 the squared coefficient of variation of the RTAT distribution, defined as the ratio of variance in the RTAT and the mean RTAT squared: $C_\tau^2 = Var(\tau)/E^2[\tau]$. Based on the idea of the Pollaczek-Khinchine formula [4], the spare parts stockout probability for the M/G/s model can be approximated by

$$p_{M/G/s}^{Appr2} \approx p\frac{1 + C_\tau^2}{2} \quad (3)$$

In the above formula,

- If $C_\tau^2 = 1$, repair turnaround times follows an exponential distribution, and the formula reduces to the exact Erlang-C formula.
- If $C_\tau^2 > 1$, repair turnaround time times are more variable, increasing the stockout probability.
- If $C_\tau^2 < 1$, repair turnaround time times are more deterministic, leading to a lower stockout probability.
- If $C_\tau^2 = 0$, (M/D/c queue, service times (RTAT) is deterministic, or fixed, denoted "D"), reducing the stockout probability since less variability means less queueing.

The above equation (3) is only useful for quick engineering calculations for certain cases [9]. Another approximation is

$$p_{M/S/s}^{Appr3} \approx (1 - C_\tau^2)p_{M/D/s} + C_\tau^2 p \quad (4)$$

where $p_{M/D/c}$ and p are queueing probabilities for the M/D/s queue and the M/M/s queue respectively.

Wang and hart [5] have analyzed 5294 valid repair records of an airborne system with various WRAs and customers under intermittent use. The AIC (Akaike Information Criterion) values of the RTAT support that the RTAT fits the Lognormal distribution best, and does not fit the exponential distribution. Note also that sometimes the failure distribution may not be exponentially distributed.

The RTAT is an important parameter in spares prediction and may be impacted by many factors. Wang and Hart [5] developed machine learning algorithms with high accuracy to estimate RTAT. Another important parameter is the replacement factor *m*, which is determined from the repair outcome. Next we will explore machine learning algorithms to determine the replacement factor.

3. Machine Learning Algorithms

The replacement factor is a multiplier of the predicted failure rate to account for CNV (Cannot Verify) or NTF (No Trouble Found), induced damage, software failure, etc.. Generally, we classify repair outcomes into four categories: confirmed failures, CNV, induced hardware problem (damage, unusual aircraft environments induced, etc.), and software induced problem. The replacement factor will cover the last three types: CNVs, induced hardware problems, and software induced problems. There are many factors which may be correlated to the repair outcome: WRA, FSC (Federal Supply Classification), Service Contract, Customer, DODAAC (Department of Defense Activity Address Directory), RIC (Routing Identifier Codes), Repair Time, Repaired Part, Repair Location, and WRA Received Time. The FSC is used to categorize products. RIC serves multiple purposes in that they are source of supply codes, intersystem routing codes, intrasystem routing codes and consignor (shipper) codes. The DoDAAC uniquely identifies a unit, or organization.

In our machine learning models, the repair outcome will be the response variable while WRA, FSC, Contract, Customer, DODAAC, RIC, Repair Time, Repaired Part, Repair Location, and Received Time are independent variables or features. The receiving time will be separated into two variables: Receive Year and Receive Month. The Receive Year will be coded as a numerical variable to reflect its time series data nature and the Receive Month will be coded as a factor variable to capture possible seasonal effects. The Repair Time is coded as a numerical variable and others as factor variables. There are 5546 records or observations in our dataset after careful cleaning and removing outliers.

We will use the H2O package in R [11] since it contains some advanced machine learning algorithms such as GBM (Gradient Boosting Machine), Deep Learning (Fully-connected multi-layer artificial neural network), DRF (Distributed Random Forest), XRT (Extremely Randomized Trees), and Stacked Ensemble. The Stacked Ensemble model ensembles using subsets of the base models.

H2O's AutoML will automatically train and tune different models and construct a leaderboard of the best machine learning models. The results in Table 1 are generated by AutoML showing the best machine learning algorithms by Mean Per Class Error (MPCE) in ascending order, with the training and test data split at 70% :30%. MPCE in multi-class classification is the average of the errors of each class in a multi-class data set. This metric speaks toward misclassification of the data across the classes. Smaller MPCE values indicate better ML model performance. The Repair Outcome has four possible classes and therefore our model is a multi-class classification problem. The Logloss in Table 1 measures classification performance, specifically, uncertainty: it measures the uncertainty of the probabilities assigned to each class by the model. The lower the Logloss, the better the model's predictions are where 0 indicates perfect predictions.

The training and test data sets have 3883 and 1663 observations respectively. The Repaired Part feature is removed in this modeling considering this data is not readily available though machine learning model accuracy is improved with it included.

Table 1 Machine Learning Model Performance Metrics

Model	MPCE	Logloss	RMSE	MSE
1	0.4803	1.2853	0.5595	0.3131
2	0.4864	0.9641	0.5690	0.3238
3	0.4875	0.9429	0.5677	0.3223
4	0.4916	0.8946	0.5604	0.3141
5	0.4923	0.8884	0.5604	0.3141
6	0.4930	0.9279	0.5651	0.3194
7	0.4942	0.9448	0.5690	0.3238
8	0.4964	0.9282	0.5663	0.3207
9	0.5007	0.8924	0.5616	0.3154
10	0.5120	0.9229	0.5571	0.3104
11	0.5551	1.0766	0.5755	0.3313
12	0.6578	1.1325	0.6325	0.4000

The machine learning models in Table 1 are detailed below by model number [11]:

1 DRF_1_AutoML_1_20250330_122308
2 GBM_grid_1_AutoML_1_20250330_122308_model_1
3 GBM_4_AutoML_1_20250330_122308
4 GBM_1_AutoML_1_20250330_122308
5 StackedEnsemble_AllModels_1_AutoML_1_20250330_122308
6 GBM_2_AutoML_1_20250330_122308
7 GBM_3_AutoML_1_20250330_122308
8 GBM_5_AutoML_1_20250330_122308
9 StackedEnsemble_BestOfFamily_1_AutoML_1_20250330_122308
10 XRT_1_AutoML_1_20250330_122308
11 DeepLearning_grid_1_AutoML_1_20250330_122308_model_1
12 DeepLearning_1_AutoML_1_20250330_122308

In Table 1, MSE (Mean Squared Error) measures the average squared magnitude of the errors. RMSE measures the square root of the average squared magnitude of the errors.

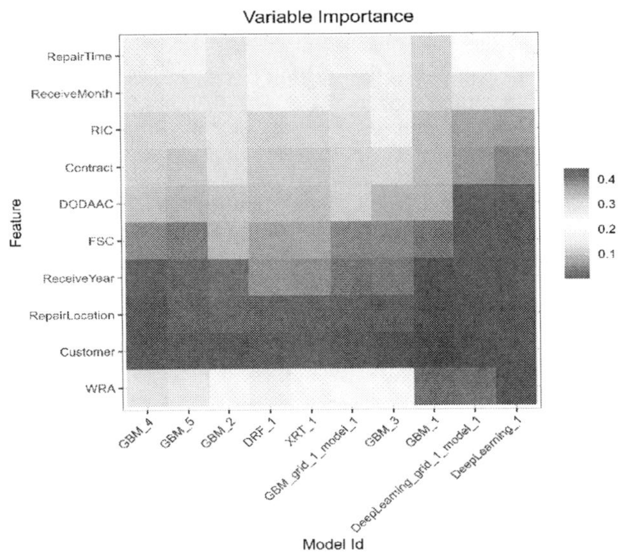

Figure 2. Variable Importance Heatmap

Figure 2 Variable Importance Heatmap shows the WRA and Repair Time have major impact on the Repair Outcome for most machine learning models. Note the color scale in Figure 2 ranges from blue (lowest importance) to red (highest importance). The Receive Year spans over a 20+ year period.

Table 1 shows that DRF and GBM algorithms perform best while Stacked Ensemble model are behind them. Next we will look into them further.

We have further tuned DRF and GBM models, and found the GBM model performs better with much improved model accuracy as shown in Table 2. This tuned GBM model has excellent performance: Logloss of 0.02703 and MPCE of 0.00503, much better than the leader in Table 1. Table 2 shows its R-Squared is excellent: 0.99333 on the training set.

The confusion matrix in Table 3 shows that the GBM performs excellently also since the Error is very small for all four levels. 1648 out of 1651 failures are predicted correctly by this GBM algorithm. Table 4 shows the Top-4 Hit Ratio which means that the correct class is within the top 4 predicted classes (based on probability scores). The model's prediction is considered correct if the actual class is among the 4 most probable classes predicted by the model.

Our trials show the training and test data 70% : 30% split tends to give the best fit. Generally, gradient boosting is one of the most effective techniques for building machine learning models [12] since it is based on the idea of improving the weak learners (learners with insufficient predictive power).

The Machine Learning Model Performance Metrics, shown in Table 1, indicate that base algorithms GBM, DRF, and Deep Learning are among the top performing models. Therefore, we built a stacked ensemble model using four base models: GBM, DRF, Deep Learning, and GLM. After tuning each of the four base models, our stacked ensemble model has good performance metrics but the tuned GBM algorithm performs best among all the models tested in this study so far.

Table 2 GBE Performance Metrics:

Logloss: (Extract with `h2o.logloss`)	0.02703
MPCE (Mean Per-Class Error)	0.00670
MSE: (Extract with `h2o.mse`)	0.00503
RMSE: (Extract with `h2o.rmse`)	0.07092
R^2: (Extract with `h2o.r2`)	0.99333

Table 3 Confusion Matrix from h2o.confusionMatrix GBM

	CNV	Failure	Induced	Software	Error	Rate
CNV	1200	8	1	1	0.0083	10/1,210
Failure	1	1648	1	1	0.0018	/1,651
Induced	1	2	787	0	0.0038	3 /790
Software	3	0	0	229	0.0129	3/232
Totals	1205	1658	789	231	0.0049	19/3,883

Table 4 GBM Top-4 Hit Ratios

k	Hit Ratio
1	0.995107
2	1.000000
3	1.000000
4	1.000000

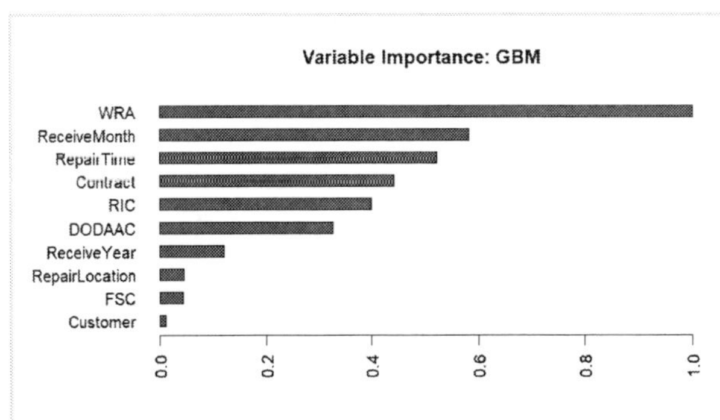

Figure 3. Feature Importance by GBM

Figure 3 shows for the GBM model the WRA has most impact on the Repair Outcome as expected. The Receive

Month has big impact also and this may reflect a seasonal effect. The Repair Time is also closely correlated to the Repair Outcome, as expected.

In this multi-class classification, class balance is critical for model performance. Our dataset is imbalanced (some classes appear much more frequently than others) and this problem has been treated by automatic balancing via oversampling/undersampling in our GBM algorithm.

The confounding issue is also addressed in our GBM model. A confounding variable is a variable that is correlated both with the dependent (target) variable and other independent variables (features), and can create misleading relationships between the features and the target. Confounders usually have a high correlation (>0.8) with other features and the target. We have found no strong confounders in our dataset based on the computed correlation matrix. However, since many values in our correlation matrix are missing, we removed the Repaired Part variable in our GBM model since we think it might be a confounding variable correlated with WRA, Repair Time, and Repair Location.

4. Concluding Remarks and Future Research

Wang and Hart [5] have compared three spares prediction models: Erlang C, Poisson, and Erlang B. The Erlang C model performs best in theory since it has infinite waiting positions and no spares demand will be lost. Wang and Hart tested the RTAT with 5294 observations, showing the RTAT fits the Lognormal distribution, and does not fit the Exponential distribution well. Section 2 has shown the stockout probability for Erlang C model in equation (1) is also a good approximation even for a general RTAT distribution. In this paper, we also introduced approximate spares prediction models when the RTAT is a general distribution, based on a M/G/c queue. Our future research will include spares prediction based on a G/G/c queue when both failure times and RTAT times are general distributions.

We have discussed spares model parameter estimation via machine learning. Section 3 has shown that machine learning results using our tuned GBE perform best for our data set. This GBE algorithm has excellent performance: Logloss of 0.02703, MPCE of 0.00503, and R-Squared of 0.99333. The WRA, Receive Month and Repair Time have most impact on the Repair Outcome.

We are currently developing an artificial intelligence/ machine learning system to predict spare parts automatically within the Raytheon EAGLE software system which contains all data on field failures, shipments, repairs, spares, etc. We have incorporated into the EAGLE software the best spares prediction model in theory: the Erlang C model. We are currently training and testing machine learning algorithms to estimate the spares prediction model parameters.

6. Acknowledgement

The authors thank our colleagues: Allison Duran for creating a raw data query, Sean Kenney for coding the Raytheon EAGLE online spares calculation tool, Isabelle Wang for coding the Microsoft Excel-based spares prediction tool, Zack Bellin, Gregory Wieber, Corina Serna, Aaron Feltman, and Jeff Guadagnin for their helpful discussions and support.

References

[1] Hongzhou Wang, Brian Hart, "An Optimal Maintenance Spare Parts Prediction Model and Its Complex Applications," *Proc. Ann. Reliability & Maintainability Symp.,* pp 1–7, Jan 2023

[2] H.C. Tijms, M.H. Van Hoorn, A. Federgruen. "Approximations for the Steady-State Probabilities in the M/G/c Queue". Advances in Applied Probability. 13 (1), pp 186–206, 1981.

[3] Per Hokstad. "Approximations for the M/G/m Queue". Operations Research, 26 (3), pp 510–523, 1978.

[4] B.N.W. Ma, J. W. Mark. "Approximation of the Mean Queue Length of an M/G/c Queueing System". Operations Research, 43 (1), pp 158–165, 1995.

[5] Hongzhou Wang, Brian Hart, "Queueing Theory-Based Spare Parts Prediction Through Machine Learning," Proc. Ann. Reliability & Maintainability Symp., pp 1–7, Jan 2023

[6] M. Ifraza, A. Aktepeb, S. Ersözb, T. Çetinyokusa, "Demand forecasting of spare parts with regression and machine learning methods: Application in a bus fleet," *Journal of Engineering Research*, vol. 11, pp 1–10, Mar 2023

[7] İ. Dursun, A. Akcay, G. Houtum, "How good must failure predictions be to make local spare parts stock superfluous?" *International Journal of Production Economics*, vol. 267, pp 1–13, Jan. 2024,

[8] Hongzhou Wang, Hoang Pham. "Reliability and Optimal Maintenance". London, Springer, 2006.

[9] H.C. Tijms. "A First Course in Stochastic Models". John Wiley & Son, 2003.

[10] Jyotiprasad Medhi. "Stochastic Models in Queueing Theory". Elsevier, 2003.

[11] M. Landry, A. Bartz. "Machine Learning with R and H2O", 7th ed., http://h2o.ai/resources, 2018.

[12] T. Hastie, R. Tibshirani, J.H. Friedman. "Boosting and Additive Trees," in *The Elements of Statistical Learning*, 2nd ed., New York, Springer, 2009, pp. 337–384, 2009.

Degradation Analysis of Multivariate Inverse Gaussian Process with Random Effects

Yi-Fu Wang and Tzu-Erh Huang
Department of Statistics, National Cheng Kung University, Tainan, Taiwan

Keywords: Degradation analysis, multivariate quality characteristics, inverse Gaussian process, random effect

Abstract - For high-reliability products, collecting sufficient failure data within a limited time is often challenging. To address this, degradation analysis is commonly employed to evaluate a product's quality characteristic to estimate the product lifetime. However, with the advancements in technologies, analyzing a single quality characteristic for degradation is no longer sufficient. This makes the analysis of multiple quality characteristics necessary. In this study, we propose a method that incorporates a common dependent framework with the inverse Gaussian process to address multivariate quality characteristics. By utilizing a conjugate conditional random effect within the inverse Gaussian process, we develop the Multivariate Inverse Gaussian Process with Random Effects (MIGP) model. This model effectively captures both the heterogeneity among samples and the correlations among quality characteristics. Finally, a case study was conducted to validate the proposed multivariate degradation model.

1. Introduction

To understand product lifetime information, manufacturers typically conduct reliability analysis. In the past, manufacturers often performed reliability analysis by conducting life tests, recording the failure time of products under normal usage to evaluate product lifetime. However, due to the high reliability of products, it is difficult to collect failure samples within a limited time. Therefore, if there exists the quality characteristics (QC) for product that is highly related to its lifetime, the product's lifetime information can be inferred by analyzing these QC. This method is known as degradation analysis.

However, with the increasing complexity of products and advancements in measurement technology, traditional single-QC degradation analysis can no longer meet manufacturers' needs. Nowadays, manufacturers face the challenge of monitoring and measuring multiple QCs. Therefore, multiple QCs degradation analysis will become more and more important. When conducting multiple QCs degradation analysis, the correlation between QCs should be considered. There are two main approaches in the literature to capture the correlation between QCs. One is to use the Copula functions, and the other is to consider the dependent random effects.

This study considers the degradation paths of multiple QCs following the inverse Gaussian process (IGP). Given that the common parameters of the IGP have random effects, we not only capture the heterogeneity of samples but also capture the correlation between multiple QCs. Consequently, we propose a multivariate inverse Gaussian process model with random effects (MIGP), which is based on the conjugate conditional random effects proposed by Peng [1]. In this work, both reliability predictions of marginal and system are provided, including the cumulative distribution function (CDF) of product lifetime, the quantile of lifetime, and the mean time to failure (MTTF). Finally, we validate the feasibility of our models through simulation study and two case studies.

2. Statistical models

Assuming there are Q quality characteristics. Let $X_q(t_j)$ be observed variable of q-th QC at t_j, $q = 1, 2, ..., Q$, $j = 1, 2, ..., m_q$, where m_q is the total measurements of q-th QC. Assume $\{\boldsymbol{X}(t)\}_{t\geq 0} = \{X_1(t), ..., X_Q(t)\}_{t\geq 0}$ being a MIGP$(\boldsymbol{\mu}, \boldsymbol{\tau}, \boldsymbol{\Lambda(t)}, \beta, \sigma^2)$ model with the following assumptions:

1. $\Pr(X_q(0) = 0) = 1$,
2. $Z_{q,j}|\delta, \lambda = (X_q(t_j) - X_q(t_{j-1}))|\delta, \lambda \sim IG\left(\frac{\mu_q \Delta\Lambda_q(t_j)}{\delta}, \lambda\tau_q(\Delta\Lambda_q(t_j))^2\right)$,
3. $\delta|\lambda \sim N\left(1, \frac{\sigma^2}{\lambda}\right), \lambda \sim \Gamma\left(\frac{1}{\beta}, \beta\right)$,
4. Degradation increment $Z_{q,j}(t)|\delta, \lambda$ is independent of each other, $\forall q, j$,

where $\Delta\Lambda_q(t_j) = \Lambda_q(t_j) - \Lambda_q(t_{j-1})$, and $\Lambda_q(t)$ is monotone increasing function of t with $\Lambda_q(0) = 0$. $IG(a, b)$ is the inverse Gaussian distribution, $N(1, \sigma^2/\lambda)$ is normal distribution with mean equal to 1 and variance equal to σ^2/λ. $\Gamma(\beta^{-1}, \beta)$ is gamma distribution with mean equal to 1 and variance equal to β. Let $\boldsymbol{\mu} = (\mu_1, ..., \mu_Q)$, $\boldsymbol{\tau} = (\tau_1, ..., \tau_Q)$, $\boldsymbol{\Lambda(t)} = (\Lambda_1(t), ..., \Lambda_Q(t))$, we then have $\boldsymbol{\theta}_1 = (\boldsymbol{\mu}, \boldsymbol{\tau}, \boldsymbol{\Lambda(t)}, \beta, \sigma^2)$ as the parameters of MIGP$(\boldsymbol{\mu}, \boldsymbol{\tau}, \boldsymbol{\Lambda(t)}, \beta, \sigma^2)$ model. Therefore, when $1/\beta \gg 0$ or $\sqrt{\beta/2} \gg \sigma$, we have $\Pr(\delta \leq 0) \to 0$. In addition, as $\beta \to 0$ and $\sigma^2 \to 0$, the dependent random effects between QCs will no longer exist, and the MIGP model will degenerate into Q independent IGP models.

In MIGP model, We define the lifetime of q-th QC by the first passage time of $X_q(t)$ crosses the threshold ω_q, that is

$$T_q = \inf\{t | X_q(t) \geq \omega_q\}.$$

By the definition, we can derive its cdf as

$$F_{T_q}(t|\boldsymbol{\theta}_1) = \frac{\Gamma(\frac{1}{\beta}+\frac{1}{2})}{\Gamma(\frac{1}{\beta})}\sqrt{\frac{\beta\tau_q\Lambda_q^2(t)}{2\pi}}\int_{\omega_q}^{\infty} x^{-\frac{3}{2}}\left(1+\frac{\tau_q\sigma^2 x}{\mu_q^2}\right)^{-\frac{1}{2}} \times \left(1+\frac{\beta}{2}\left(\frac{\tau_q\Lambda_q^2(t)}{x}+\frac{\frac{\tau_q x}{\mu_q^2}-2\frac{\tau_q\Lambda_q(t)}{\mu_q}-\sigma^2\left(\frac{\tau_q\Lambda_q(t)}{\mu_q}\right)^2}{1+\sigma^2\frac{\tau_q x}{\mu_q^2}}\right)\right)^{-(\frac{1}{\beta}+\frac{1}{2})} dx.$$

When a product has multiple QCs related to its lifetime, the product lifetime is defined based on the relationship with its QCs. There are two common definitions: one is the parallel system, where the product is considered to have failed when all QCs reach their failure thresholds. The other is the series system, where the product is considered to have failed when any one of the QCs reaches its failure threshold. Since the case studies follow the series system, we will use the series system as the rule for product lifetime in this research, that is

$$T = \inf\{t | X_1(t) \geq \omega_1 \text{ or ... or } X_Q(t) \geq \omega_Q\}.$$

Then we have the cdf of T as

$$F_T(t|\boldsymbol{\theta}_1) = 1-\frac{\Gamma\left(\frac{1}{\beta}+\frac{Q}{2}\right)}{\Gamma\left(\frac{1}{\beta}\right)}\left(\prod_{q=1}^{Q}\sqrt{\frac{\beta\tau_q\Lambda_q^2(t)}{2\pi}}\right)\int_0^{\omega_1}\cdots\int_0^{\omega_Q}\frac{\prod_{q=1}^{Q} x_q^{-\frac{3}{2}}}{\sqrt{1+\sigma^2\sum_{q=1}^{Q}\frac{\tau_q x_q}{\mu_q^2}}} \times \left(1+\frac{\beta}{2}\left(\sum_{q=1}^{Q}\frac{\tau_q\Lambda_q^2(t)}{x_q}+\frac{\sum_{q=1}^{Q}\frac{\tau_q x_q}{\mu_q^2}-2\sum_{q=1}^{Q}\frac{\tau_q\Lambda_q(t)}{\mu_q}-\sigma^2\left(\sum_{q=1}^{Q}\frac{\tau_q\Lambda_q(t)}{\mu_q}\right)^2}{1+\sigma^2\sum_{q=1}^{Q}\frac{\tau_q x_q}{\mu_q^2}}\right)\right)^{-(\frac{1}{\beta}+\frac{Q}{2})} \times dx_Q \ldots dx_1.$$

For the lifetime quantiles of the MIGP($\boldsymbol{\theta}_1$) model, assuming $\{\boldsymbol{X}(t)\}_{t\geq 0}$ follows the MIGP($\boldsymbol{\theta}_1$) model, the p-th quantile of q-th QC's lifetime is $t_{q,p}$, where $q = 1, 2, ..., Q$. Thus, under the failure threshold ω_q, $t_{q,p}$ satisfies $p = F_{T_q}(t_{q,p}|\boldsymbol{\theta}_1)$. However, since $F_{T_q}(t|\boldsymbol{\theta}_1)$ is too complex. We will directly compute $\hat{t}_{q,p} = F_{T_q}^{-1}(p|\hat{\boldsymbol{\theta}}_1)$ numerically to obtain the numerical solution $\hat{t}_{q,p}$. For the p-th quantile of product lifetime T under series system. t_p must satisfy $p = F_T(t_p|\boldsymbol{\theta}_1)$. Also, we will obtain $\hat{t}_p$ numerically by computing $\hat{t}_p = F_T^{-1}(p|\hat{\boldsymbol{\theta}}_1)$.

Then we consider the MTTF of q-th QC in MIGP($\boldsymbol{\theta}_1$) model. It is defined and derived as follows

$$\text{MTTF}_q = \int_0^{\infty}(1-F_{T_q}(t|\boldsymbol{\theta}_1))dt.$$

For MTTF of product under series system. It can be derived as follows

$$\text{MTTF} = \int_0^{\infty}(1-F_T(t|\boldsymbol{\theta}_1))dt.$$

For the derivation of the log-likelihood function of the MIGP($\boldsymbol{\theta}_1$) model, based on the definition of the MIGP($\boldsymbol{\theta}_1$) model, $\boldsymbol{\theta}_1 = (\boldsymbol{\mu}, \boldsymbol{\tau}, \boldsymbol{\Lambda}(\boldsymbol{t}), \beta, \sigma^2)$ is the vector of unknown parameters. Assume n observation samples, with $x_q(t_{i,j})$ being the j-th QC observation value of the q-th quality characteristic at time $t_{i,j}$ for the i-th sample, where $i = 1, 2, ..., n$, $q = 1, 2, ..., Q$, $j = 1, 2, ..., m_{i,q}$. This implies that different samples can have different observation times, but all Q QCs need to be observed simultaneously. Let $\boldsymbol{X} = \{x_q(t_{i,j})\}_{i=1}^{n}{}_{,q=1}^{Q}{}_{,j=1}^{mi,q}$. Assuming $\boldsymbol{X}$ follows the MIGP($\boldsymbol{\theta}_1$) model, the joint log-likelihood function of the parameters $\boldsymbol{\theta}_1$ given $\boldsymbol{X}$ is

$$\begin{aligned} l(\boldsymbol{\theta}_1|\boldsymbol{X}) &= \ln L(\boldsymbol{\theta}_1|\boldsymbol{X}) = \sum_{i=1}^{n}\ln L_i \\ &= \sum_{i=1}^{n}\ln\Gamma\left(\frac{1}{\beta}+\sum_{q=1}^{Q}\frac{m_{i,q}}{2}\right)-\sum_{i=1}^{n}\ln\Gamma\left(\frac{1}{\beta}\right)+\frac{1}{2}\sum_{i=1}^{n}\sum_{q=1}^{Q}\sum_{j=1}^{m_{i,q}}\ln\left(\frac{\beta\tau_q\Delta\Lambda_q^2(t_{i,j})}{2\pi z_{i,q,j}^3}\right) \\ &-\frac{1}{2}\sum_{i=1}^{n}\ln\left(1+\sigma^2\sum_{q=1}^{Q}\sum_{j=1}^{m_{i,q}}\frac{\tau_q z_{i,q,j}}{\mu_q^2}\right) \\ &-\sum_{i=1}^{n}(\frac{1}{\beta}+\sum_{q=1}^{Q}\frac{m_{i,q}}{2})\ln\left(1+\frac{\beta}{2}\left(\sum_{q=1}^{Q}\sum_{j=1}^{m_{i,q}}\frac{\tau_q\Delta\Lambda_q^2(t_{i,j})}{z_{i,q,j}}\right.\right. \\ &\left.\left.+\frac{\sum_{q=1}^{Q}\sum_{j=1}^{m_{i,q}}\frac{\tau_q z_{i,q,j}}{\mu_q^2}-2\sum_{q=1}^{Q}\sum_{j=1}^{m_{i,q}}\frac{\tau_q\Delta\Lambda_q(t_{i,j})}{\mu_q}-\sigma^2\left(\sum_{q=1}^{Q}\sum_{j=1}^{m_{i,q}}\frac{\tau_q\Delta\Lambda_q(t_{i,j})}{\mu_q}\right)^2}{1+\sigma^2\sum_{q=1}^{Q}\sum_{j=1}^{m_{i,q}}\frac{\tau_q z_{i,q,j}}{\mu_q^2}}\right)\right), \end{aligned}$$

where $z_{i,q,j} = x_q(t_{i,j}) - x_q(t_{i,j-1})$, $\Delta\Lambda_q(t_{i,j}) = \Lambda_q(t_{i,j}) - \Lambda_q(t_{i,j-1})$.

For the estimation of parameters $\boldsymbol{\theta}_1$ in the MIGP($\boldsymbol{\theta}_1$) model, this study intends to use maximum likelihood estimation (MLE) for point estimation of the parameters. That is, the MLEs $\hat{\boldsymbol{\theta}}_1$ should satisfy $\hat{\boldsymbol{\theta}}_1 = \arg\max_{\boldsymbol{\theta}_1} l(\boldsymbol{\theta}_1|\boldsymbol{X})$. However, due to the complexity of the likelihood functions, it is not possible to obtain the analytical solutions for $\hat{\boldsymbol{\theta}}_1$. Therefore, this study intends to use the optim function in R to solve for the numerical solutions. In addition, this study will use the bootstrap method to construct the $100(1-\alpha)\%$ confidence intervals (CI) for parameters, cdf, lifetime quantiles, and MTTF for the MIGP($\boldsymbol{\theta}_1$) model.

In this work, the goodness of fit (GOF) is to verify whether the data follow to the inverse Gaussian assumption. Based on Wang and Xu [2], when $X \sim IG(a, b)$, then $\xi(X) = b(X-a)^2/(a^2X) \sim \chi_1^2$, where χ_1^2 is a chi-square distribution with 1 degree of freedom. If the degradation path $X(t)$ follows IGP($\mu, \tau, \Lambda(t)$), given the increments $Z_{i,j} = X(t_{i,j}) - X(t_{i,j-1})$ which are mutually independent, then

$$\begin{aligned} \xi(Z_{i,j}) &= \frac{\tau(\Delta\Lambda(t_{i,j}))^2(Z_{i,j}-\mu\Delta\Lambda(t_{i,j}))^2}{(\mu\Delta\Lambda(t_{i,j}))^2 Z_{i,j}} \\ &= \frac{\tau(Z_{i,j}/\mu-\Delta\Lambda(t_{i,j}))^2}{Z_{i,j}}, \end{aligned}$$

where $\Delta\Lambda(t_{i,j}) = \Lambda(t_{i,j}) - \Lambda(t_{i,j-1})$, $i = 1, 2, ..., n$, $j = 1, 2, ..., m_i$. Therefore, we can deduce that $\xi(Z_{i,j})$ are independently and identically distributed as χ_1^2, $\forall i, j$. The Q-Q Plot of χ_1^2 is constructed to carry out the GOF of the MIGP($\boldsymbol{\theta}_1$) model.

3. Real case study

For the real case study, the data were come from the degradation data of heavy machine tools in Peng et al. [3]. This dataset includes observations of two QCs: positioning accuracy and output power. The degradation increments are all positive, and based on historical information and expert experience, the two QCs are correlated. The dataset comprises 3 observation samples $n = 3$

with observations of two QCs $Q = 2$. The predefined failure thresholds are $\omega_1 = 35$ and $\omega_2 = 120$. The lifetime of the heavy machine tool is considered as series system, meaning the machine is deemed to have failed when the positioning accuracy degrades beyond 35 or the output power degrades beyond 120. Figure 1 shows the corresponding degradation paths. Since there exists the correlation among the multiple QCs, we will use the proposed MIGP($\boldsymbol{\theta}_1$) model to carry out the multivariate degradation analysis.

From Figure 1, we find that the degradation data exhibits an exponential increasing trend. Therefore, we consider using the power-law function for $\Lambda(t)$, i.e., $\Lambda_q(t) = t^{\gamma_q}, q = 1, 2$. The unknown parameters of the MIGP($\boldsymbol{\theta}_1$) model are $\boldsymbol{\theta}_1 = (\mu_1, \mu_2, \tau_1, \tau_2, \gamma_1, \gamma_2, \beta, \sigma^2)$. The final prediction results of the MIGP($\boldsymbol{\theta}_1$) model indicate that the average lifetime of the heavy machine tool, considering the series system, is 33.9863.

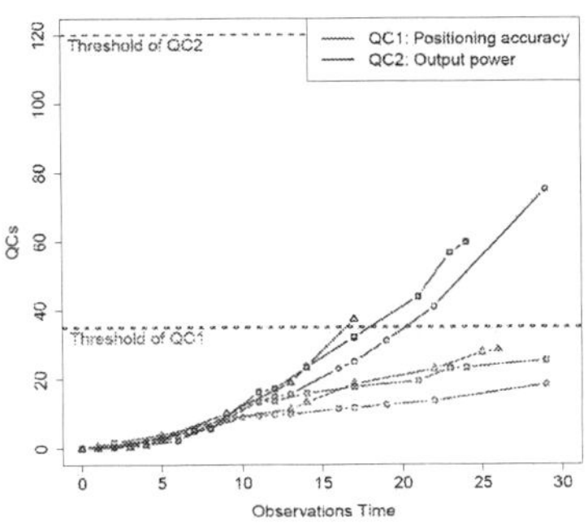

Figure 1: The degradation path of heavy machine tools data.

We fit the IGP model to the two QCs separately, and plot their χ_1^2 Q-Q plots in Figure 2. From Figure 2, we can see that the data points in both plots do not show significant deviations from the straight line, such that these GOFs perform well for this data.

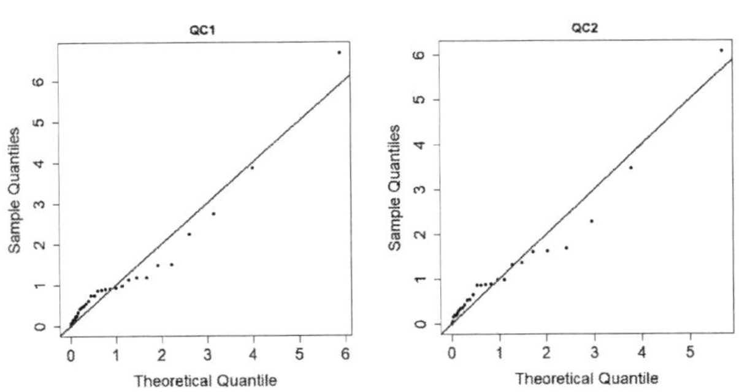

Figure 2: Q-Q Plots of heavy machine tools data.

Figure 3 shows the estimated of $F_T(t)$ for the lifetime T of the heavy machine tools data analyzed by the MIGP($\boldsymbol{\theta}_1$) model. It also includes the estimated curves of $F_{T_1}(t)$ and $F_{T_2}(t)$ for the lifetimes T_1 and T_2 of the two QCs, respectively. From Figure 3, we can see that under the series system lifetime definition, the product lifetime estimate will inevitably be lower than the individual lifetime estimates of each quality characteristic. That is, the black curve will be to the left of the red and blue curves in the graph.

The pseudo-failure time (PFT) for the data is used. We also plot $F^*(t_i)$ (green dots) in Figure 3, and observe that $F^*(t_i)$ closely matches the estimated $F_T(t)$ from the MIGP($\boldsymbol{\theta}_1$) model and falls within its 95% CI (gray dashed lines), indicating good predictive performance of the MIGP($\boldsymbol{\theta}_1$) model for this data.

Additionally, we calculate the estimated CDF of the lifetime under a traditional IGP model (which does not consider correlation) for the series system (purple line), and find that the results deviate more from $F^*(t_i)$, indicating that it is indeed necessary to use the MIGP($\boldsymbol{\theta}_1$) model, which incorporates correlation, for reliability analysis of this heavy machine tools data from Peng et al. [3].

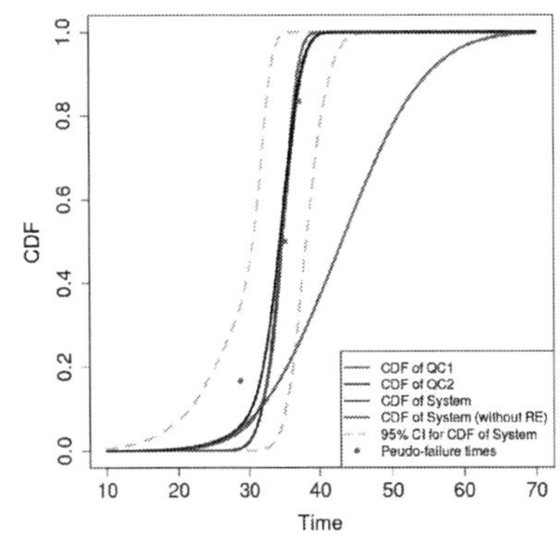

Figure 3: The cdf and $F^*(t_i)$ of heavy machine tools data.

4. Conclusion

Degradation analysis is used to infer the reliability of products. However, traditional degradation analysis cannot be applied when products have multiple QCs. Therefore, this study considers the correlations between QCs and proposes the MIGP model, which can analyze degradation data with multiple QCs and provide the comprehensive statistical and reliability inferences.

In the simulation study, we found that the MIGP model, with a sufficient sample size, ensures more accurate parameter estimation. In the case study, we performed a complete reliability analysis on the bivariate degradation data of heavy machine tools using the MIGP model, obtaining lifetime inferences for the product under a series system. In addition, the model proposed in this study still has some flaws that deserve improvement. For example, when there are too many QCs, it will be difficult to estimate the model and obtain reliability information. When sample heterogeneity does not exist, it becomes difficult to estimate dependent random effects.

References

[1] Peng, C.Y. "Inverse Gaussian processes with random effects and explanatory variables for degradation data"; *Technometrics*, 57, 100–111, 2015.

[2] Wang, X. and Xu, D. "An inverse Gaussian process model for degradation data"; *Technometrics*, 52, 188–197, 2010.

[3] Peng, W., Li, Y.F., Yang, Y.J., Zhu, S.P., and Huang, H.Z. "Bivariate analysis of incomplete degradation observations based on inverse Gaussian processes and copulas"; *IEEE Transactions on Reliability*, 65, 624–639, 2016.

AI-Driven Predictive Maintenance: Bayesian Reliability Assessment and XGBoost for Smart Industrial Systems

Kuo-Yi Lin[1,*], Yu-He Hong[1], Meng-Hua Li[2,3], Ming-Lang Tseng[4]

[1]Department of Industrial Engineering and Management, National Kaohsiung University of Science and Technology, No. 415, Jiangong Road, Sanmin District, Kaohsiung City, Taiwan, kylin@nkust.edu.tw

[2] Department of Industrial Management, National Formosa University, Taiwan

[3] Smart Machinery and Intelligent Manufacturing Research Center, National Formosa University, Taiwan

[4] Institute of innovation of circular economy, Asia University, Taiwan

Keywords: Predictive Maintenance (PdM), Remaining Useful Life (RUL), XGBoost, SHAP, Bayesian Reliability, Industry 4.0, Industry, Innovation and Infrastructure

Abstract

Predictive Maintenance (PdM) enhances industrial reliability by mitigating unexpected failures and optimizing resources. This study proposes a PdM framework that combines XGBoost-based failure time prediction with Bayesian reliability analysis, allowing dynamic updates of failure probabilities using real-time sensor data. The integration improves Remaining Useful Life (RUL) estimation, risk assessment, and decision support. Evaluated on the PHM08 dataset, the proposed model outperforms Random Forest and LSTM in predictive accuracy, uncertainty quantification, and interpretability. SHAP analysis reveals key factors influencing equipment degradation, increasing model transparency and stakeholder trust.

Aligned with Sustainable Development Goal 9 (Industry, Innovation and Infrastructure), this approach supports smart manufacturing by enabling reliable, explainable, and adaptive maintenance strategies. It fosters resilient industrial systems through reduced downtime, better maintenance planning, and efficient decision-making. The results highlight the model's scalability and practical value in advancing intelligent, sustainable industrial operations.

1. Introduction

In the era of Industry 4.0, predictive maintenance (PdM) plays a critical role in intelligent manufacturing by enabling early fault detection, minimizing downtime, and extending equipment lifespan through real-time monitoring and machine learning [1]. PdM is applied across sectors such as aerospace, energy, and manufacturing to optimize resources and support data-driven decision-making. As systems grow more interconnected and complex, explainable AI (XAI) techniques like SHAP have become essential for enhancing model transparency and building stakeholder trust [2], [3]. Frameworks such as UNISONE integrate circular supply chain (CSC) strategies with Industry 4.0 technologies to support adaptive and sustainable maintenance planning [4], [5]. Applications including spare parts optimization [6], gas turbine diagnostics [7], and battery degradation forecasting using CNN-XGBoost models [8] highlight the growing importance of interpretable machine learning models. Among them, XGBoost stands out for its robustness and flexibility across industrial domains [9].

Despite progress, PdM implementation still faces challenges. Many advanced machine learning models, including deep neural networks and ensemble methods, lack interpretability, which limits stakeholder confidence and complicates regulatory compliance [10]. Even newer techniques—like temporal convolutional networks (TCNs) for aero-engine RUL prediction—often fall short in uncertainty quantification and explainability [11]. These limitations underscore the need for PdM frameworks that combine predictive accuracy, transparency, and risk-aware reasoning.

This study proposes a unified PdM framework that integrates XGBoost, SHAP, and Bayesian reliability analysis. The approach aims to enhance accuracy, provide interpretable outputs, and embed probabilistic logic for adaptive, risk-informed maintenance decisions. In alignment with the United Nations Sustainable Development Goal 9 (Industry, Innovation and Infrastructure), the framework contributes to building resilient, intelligent industrial systems by advancing data-driven reliability assessment and sustainable innovation. Expected outcomes include more accurate and explainable RUL predictions, improved stakeholder confidence, reduced risk, and enhanced resource efficiency—supporting both industrial competitiveness and sustainable development.

The remainder of this paper is structured as follows. Chapter 2 reviews the literature on PdM, explainable AI, and Bayesian analysis. Chapter 3 details the methodology. Chapter 4 describes the experimental setup. Chapter 5 presents the results and discussion. Chapter 6 concludes with key findings and future directions.

2. Literature Review

2.1 Predictive Maintenance (PdM) and Reliability Analysis

Predictive maintenance (PdM) is central to Industry 4.0, enhancing real-time monitoring to reduce equipment failures. Traditionally relying on condition-based monitoring and heuristic thresholds, PdM has advanced with machine learning techniques, notably XGBoost, which offers high accuracy and robust generalization across industries [12]. When paired with optimized preprocessing and feature selection, these models excel in applications like battery and gas turbine monitoring [7]. However, challenges like missing data, uncertainty, and lack of transparency persist. To address these, solutions such as SHAP for interpretability and robust imputation methods have been introduced [13]. These innovations suggest PdM must go beyond accuracy, incorporating explainability, risk-awareness, and resilience to support sustainable decision-making.

As PdM evolves, analytical methods have shifted from traditional machine learning to more complex models, including quantum machine learning and deep neural networks. Models like LSTM and TCN effectively capture spatiotemporal patterns in large datasets, improving Remaining Useful Life (RUL) predictions in bearings and fuel cells. However, these models are often criticized for their opacity, especially in high-stakes environments where interpretability is crucial. To address this, SHAP-based methods help interpret feature contributions and improve transparency, while combining deep learning with interpretable feature extraction enhances both performance and transparency. These developments highlight the growing need for interpretable, risk-aware PdM systems for real-time decision support in industrial settings.

In summary, PdM research increasingly blends advanced analytics, interpretability, and uncertainty-aware modeling. Hybrid frameworks combining deep learning, Bayesian reasoning, and explainable AI are emerging to support adaptive, transparent decision-making [2]. These frameworks align with Industry 4.0 and 5.0 goals, where real-time insights, trust, and sustainability are essential. As PdM systems integrate into complex environments, incorporating interpretable, risk-aware intelligence will be key to ensuring resilience, operational excellence, and regulatory compliance.

2.2 Challenges in Predictive Maintenance

Despite significant advancements, PdM faces challenges hindering broader adoption. One major issue is the "black-box" nature of machine learning models, which often lack interpretability, reducing stakeholder trust and complicating regulatory compliance [2]. The increasing diversity of model architectures also complicates model selection. Without systematic evaluation frameworks, high-performing models like XGBoost and deep learning variants are often deployed suboptimally. This is especially problematic in high-risk sectors, where understanding the rationale behind predictive decisions is critical for compliance and risk mitigation. Moreover, conventional PdM models often fail to quantify uncertainty, leading to inaccurate risk assessments and suboptimal decision-making.

Recent research has focused on integrating interpretability, uncertainty quantification, and predictive accuracy in PdM models. Explainable AI methods like SHAP clarify feature contributions and model behaviors, improving decision-making [10],[2]. SHAP has proven effective in visualizing feature importance and aligning predictive performance with reliability metrics. Studies show that SHAP values can assess the quality of prognostic models and provide actionable insights. SHAP has also been validated in safety-critical domains like seismic risk assessment, where explainable XGBoost models assess structural vulnerabilities under uncertainty [3]. Bayesian methods offer robust frameworks for uncertainty quantification, dynamically updating models to reflect changing conditions, improving reliability and stakeholder confidence. Hybrid approaches combining Bayesian networks with machine learning algorithms offer resilient predictive solutions.

This study addresses these challenges by developing an integrated PdM framework. The framework uses XGBoost to ensure predictive accuracy, SHAP for interpretability, and Bayesian methods for uncertainty quantification. Extensive empirical validation with the PHM08 dataset demonstrates the framework's practical feasibility, offering organizations tools to optimize maintenance strategies, manage risks, and comply with safety regulations, ultimately increasing stakeholder confidence in predictive decision-making [14].

2.3 UNISONE Framework

The UNISONE framework integrates Circular Supply Chain (CSC) concepts, Knowledge Discovery in Databases (KDD), and Industry 4.0 technologies to create a robust decision-making system. Proposed by Lin [4], UNISONE emphasizes a cyclic decision-making process designed to enhance industrial system reliability and sustainability. The framework incorporates generative AI to support dynamic decision-making and uses sparse autoencoders to handle complex, noisy industrial data. Additionally, SHAP is integrated to ensure interpretability and enhance communication of model insights, promoting stakeholder confidence. UNISONE's decision cycle consists of seven phases: problem identification, data collection, feature extraction, predictive modeling, interpretability analysis, uncertainty quantification, and continuous knowledge integration. Real-time monitoring and adaptive learning mechanisms allow for continuous updates to predictive models and maintenance strategies, improving proactive maintenance capabilities.

UNISONE has gained attention for its ability to address data-driven challenges in manufacturing environments. Studies show that integrating generative AI methods within UNISONE enhances decision-making in dynamic settings. Sparse autoencoders effectively manage data complexity and improve predictive performance. SHAP analysis enhances UNISONE's ability to provide interpretable insights, ensuring stakeholders can trust and utilize predictive outputs effectively. Empirical validations show that UNISONE's structured decision-making improves operational efficiency and reduces uncertainty, positively impacting maintenance strategies and sustainability.

The strength of UNISONE lies in its flexibility to incorporate advanced analytics and hybrid intelligence for adaptive decision-making. Integrating models like XGBoost and Bayesian inference provides high predictive accuracy and probabilistic reasoning, essential for safety-critical environments. Real-time feedback loops enable rapid responses to changing operational conditions, while combining ultrasonic sensing with AI-based prediction models, such as Bayesian optimization applied to XGBoost, has proven effective in predicting structural defects in complex systems like concrete-filled steel tubes. UNISONE's alignment with Industry 4.0 principles ensures that data complexity, real-time responsiveness, uncertainty handling, and transparency come together in a unified system for sustainable maintenance strategies.

3. Methodology

This study adopts the UNISONE framework to address the complex demands of predictive maintenance (PdM) in Industry 4.0. Unlike traditional linear approaches, UNISONE uses a cyclic, adaptive decision-making model that integrates sensor data processing, machine learning, interpretability analysis, and Bayesian uncertainty quantification. This methodology is a reflective process, focusing on understanding industrial problems, identifying opportunities, modeling predictions, and evaluating decisions. The following subsections describe how this framework is applied in this study, using the PHM08 dataset and a hybrid XGBoost–Bayesian–SHAP architecture.

3.1 Understand and Define the Problem

A key challenge in PdM is defining the real-world problems it aims to solve. Many existing models focus solely on algorithmic performance without considering the industrial context. In this study, the problem is framed not just as forecasting but as improving decision-making in maintenance scheduling, resource allocation, and risk management. Systems like aviation engines face high costs from false predictions, and a model that merely predicts failure time is insufficient unless it can be trusted, interpreted, and acted upon. This phase explores the importance of interpretability and adaptability in predictive decision-making to ensure safety and reliability in industry.

3.2 Identify the Niche of PdM in Circular Supply Chains under Industry 4.0

While PdM is a strategic goal in Industry 4.0, its implementation often lacks contextual alignment. This study positions PdM at the intersection of circular supply chains (CSC) and PdM strategies. The goal is to provide interpretable, risk-aware, and data-driven maintenance recommendations that align with broader goals such as minimizing waste, extending asset lifespan, and enhancing system resilience. Most PdM systems optimize for short-term performance, but integrating PdM with CSC addresses long-term value, making PdM a strategic enabler for sustainable industry.

3.3 Structure the Objective Hierarchy and Influence Relationship

A coherent structure linking predictive targets with operational variables is essential for a meaningful PdM model. The PHM08 dataset, which includes 24 sensor features across 54,727 records, is used to capture meaningful degradation trends. The dataset's feature dimensionality is manageable for XGBoost, and operational variables like temperature, pressure, and vibration are analyzed to understand the influence on engine wear. The model construction is guided by this relationship, ensuring the model reflects the causal paths leading to failure, which supports interpretable and reliable predictions.

Table 1. Basic statistical information table

Dataset	Samples	Features
Training Set	20631	24
Testing Set	13096	24
Final Test Set	10000	24

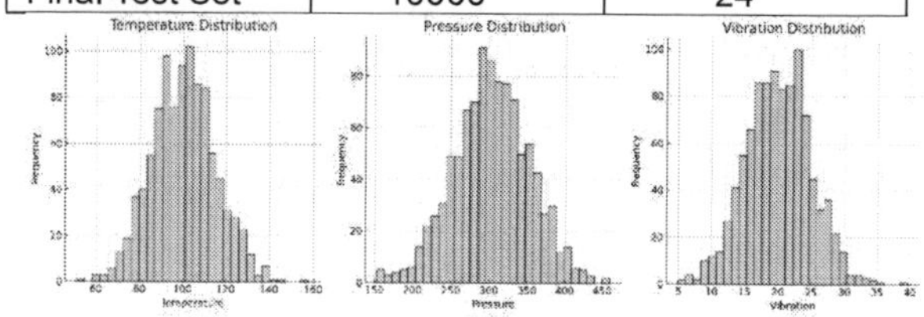

Fig.1. Feature Distribution Histograms

3.4 Sense and Describe Expected Outcomes

This methodology focuses on providing not just RUL predictions, but also interpretable, uncertainty-aware insights to guide real-world decision-making. XGBoost is used for its speed, accuracy, and robustness to missing values, while SHAP allows for feature contribution analysis, ensuring transparency. The model's output is reframed as a probabilistic assessment of degradation risk rather than a deterministic failure timeline. This allows maintenance decisions to account for variability and confidence levels, ensuring that the predictions are trusted and aligned with operational needs.

3.5 Overall Judgments and Value Assessments

A central challenge in AI-driven PdM is aligning model outputs with human judgment, especially in contexts where decisions impact safety, cost, and reliability. SHAP provides localized interpretability, helping operators assess predictions against domain knowledge. Bayesian reliability analysis translates predictions into dynamic risk profiles, reflecting new data over time. These methods support nuanced decision-making, allowing stakeholders to balance trade-offs, such as the cost of downtime versus premature replacement. The model enhances human judgment by providing a structured, explainable basis for evaluating maintenance options.

3.6 Trade-off and Decision

In real-world industrial settings, maintenance planning involves trade-offs between preventive and reactive actions, short-term costs, and long-term system health. This study addresses these tensions by embedding Bayesian updating in the XGBoost–SHAP framework, enabling the model to adapt to new data and priorities in real time. The model generates probabilistic degradation trajectories, supporting scenario-based decision-making. These decisions are informed by contextual factors such as component reuse and sustainability, transforming PdM from a static forecasting tool into an interactive decision support system that reflects the complexity of modern industrial operations.

3.7 Evaluate the Decisions and Consolidate the Knowledge

The final phase of the methodology ensures the system evolves with its predictions. After maintenance decisions are made, their outcomes are used to update both the predictive model and Bayesian priors, creating a feedback loop that enhances long-term reliability. SHAP-based explanations are archived to monitor model drift and stability, consolidating predictive insights and operational feedback. This self-adaptive cycle enables the PdM system to continuously improve, embodying the resilience and adaptability required for Industry 4.0 environments.

4. Experimental Results & Analysis

This chapter evaluates the proposed predictive maintenance framework that integrates XGBoost, SHAP, and Bayesian reliability analysis using the PHM08 dataset. The goal is to assess the model's effectiveness in predicting Remaining Useful Life (RUL), while also supporting interpretable and risk-aware decision-making. Experiments were conducted across training, testing, and final validation sets, comparing the model's performance against LSTM and Random Forest baselines. Results focus on prediction accuracy, SHAP-based feature interpretability, and Bayesian uncertainty quantification, demonstrating that the proposed approach provides reliable, explainable, and adaptable outputs suitable for Industry 4.0 applications.

4.1 Data Context and Problem Framing

To predict RUL for aircraft engines, the PHM08 Challenge dataset is used, which includes sensor readings like temperature, pressure, and vibration, along with engine operational data. The problem is framed as estimating RUL, defined as the difference between the maximum cycle and the current cycle. This context highlights the high-stakes nature of PdM in aviation, where accurate predictions impact system availability, safety, and cost-efficiency. The study aims to produce models that not only perform well but also provide interpretable, reliable outputs to guide real-time maintenance decisions under uncertainty.

4.2 Application Scope and Industrial Relevance

While focused on aviation, the proposed framework addresses broader industrial needs. PdM is crucial in sectors such as manufacturing, energy, and transportation, where equipment failure incurs high costs. This flexible approach, compatible with real-time data inputs and scalable to edge computing, positions PdM as a strategic function within Industry 4.0 ecosystems. The methodology's cross-domain adaptability allows models trained on engine degradation data to inform similar applications in other sensor-driven systems, contributing to the shift from reactive to proactive maintenance.

4.3 Feature Construction and Relevance Mapping

To capture degradation behavior, time-series feature engineering is applied to the raw sensor data. Statistical indicators such as mean and standard deviation are extracted over sliding windows to detect patterns indicative of wear and failure. Dimensionality reduction techniques, like correlation filtering and PCA, are used to remove redundancy and noise while preserving important variables. These features reflect physical degradation processes and provide a transparent structure linking sensor data to RUL predictions.

4.4 Model Construction and Predictive Performance

This study evaluates three models: XGBoost, Random Forest, and LSTM. XGBoost consistently outperforms the alternatives across metrics like RMSE, F1-Score, and Recall, with significantly shorter training times than LSTM. While LSTM captures temporal dependencies, its high computational cost limits its practicality. These results validate the use of structured, tree-based models like XGBoost in PdM applications where performance and interpretability are crucial.

4.5 Interpretability and Reliability Insights

Model transparency is vital for trust in PdM systems. SHAP is used to quantify the influence of individual features on RUL predictions. Summary plots show that pressure, temperature, and vibration are dominant features across test scenarios. SHAP value distributions remain stable, with less than ±5% variation, confirming the robustness and explainability of XGBoost. This transparency bridges the gap between algorithmic predictions and human reasoning, enabling maintenance teams to understand both the "what" and the "why" of model outputs.

4.6 Uncertainty, Risk Assessment, and Evaluation

Uncertainty is a key consideration in high-risk domains like aviation. Bayesian reliability analysis is incorporated to model RUL prediction variability under different sensor conditions. Monte Carlo simulations with Gaussian noise injection achieve a Prediction Interval Coverage Probability (PICP) of 93.5%, indicating well-calibrated predictive intervals. These probabilistic insights support risk-aware maintenance planning, enabling decisions based not only on expected RUL but also on confidence bounds around failure risk.

4.7 Generalization Testing and Method Refinement

To test the framework's applicability, the XGBoost model is evaluated on alternative datasets such as C-MAPSS and on unseen operational conditions. Despite distribution shifts, RMSE increases by only 8.2%, with prediction accuracy remaining above 85%. Feature importance patterns identified by SHAP are consistent across datasets, demonstrating the model's stability. These results suggest that the framework can adapt to different engine types and usage scenarios. Future refinements include integrating time-series models like LSTM and Transformer, applying AutoML for feature selection, and deploying models for real-time inference at the edge. These enhancements will ensure the framework remains adaptive, interpretable, and scalable for PdM across industrial domains.

5. Discussion & Practical Implications

This study highlights the value of machine learning in predictive maintenance, especially through integrating XGBoost, Random Forest, and LSTM within the UNISONE framework. XGBoost proved to be the most effective, offering a strong balance of accuracy, efficiency, and interpretability. SHAP analysis enhanced the framework by identifying key predictors like pressure, temperature, and vibration, clarifying their impact on model outputs. Bayesian reliability analysis was used to quantify prediction uncertainty, providing probabilistic insight into failure likelihood and remaining useful life, which aids in proactive, data-driven decision-making. Practically, the framework supports optimized scheduling, reduced downtime, and lower operational costs, directly benefiting aviation safety and reliability. Additionally, the approach is applicable to other industries, such as manufacturing, energy, and transportation. By aligning with Industry 4.0 objectives and supporting real-time analytics through Edge AI and cloud computing, the method contributes to scalable, uncertainty-aware maintenance systems.

6. Conclusion

This study demonstrates the effectiveness of machine learning, particularly XGBoost, in predictive maintenance, delivering accurate, efficient, and interpretable RUL predictions within the UNISONE framework. The integration of SHAP and Bayesian reliability analysis enhances transparency and uncertainty awareness, enabling proactive decision-making. The framework optimizes maintenance scheduling in aviation and shows strong potential for cross-industry applications aligned with Industry 4.0.

Future research will focus on hybrid architectures combining XGBoost with deep learning models like LSTM or Transformers to capture both structural and temporal patterns. Advancements toward real-time PdM through Edge AI and cloud-based deployment will be key for low-latency, decentralized decision-making. Automated model optimization, advanced feature engineering, and synthetic data augmentation (e.g., via GANs) will further improve scalability. Expanding interpretability tools beyond SHAP and validating the framework across sectors like manufacturing, energy, and healthcare will ensure broader applicability. Integration with emerging technologies, such as Digital Twins, IIoT, and Blockchain, will foster secure, explainable, and intelligent maintenance ecosystems, paving the way toward Industry 5.0.

Acknowledgements

This research was funded by the Ministry of Science and Technology of Taiwan (MOST 113-2622- E-992-024-, 114-2622-8-150 -001 -TE3) and NKUST Industry-Academic Cooperation Project (20241129170433, 20241209141747, 20250420145108).

References

[1]. S.S. Shah, T. Daoliang, S.C. Kumar, "RUL forecasting for wind turbine predictive maintenance based on deep learning"; *Heliyon* (Cell Press), Vol. 10, e39268, pp. 1–12, January 2024.

[2]. M.L. Ndao, G. Youness, N. Niang, G. Saporta, "Improving predictive maintenance: Evaluating the impact of preprocessing and model complexity on the effectiveness of eXplainable Artificial Intelligence methods"; *Engineering Applications of Artificial Intelligence* (Elsevier), Vol. 144, 110144, pp. 1–15, January 2025.

[3]. M.M. Gharagoz, M. Noureldin, J. Kim, "Explainable machine learning (XML) framework for seismic assessment of structures using Extreme Gradient Boosting (XGBoost)"; *Engineering Structures* (Elsevier), Vol. 327, 119621, pp. 1–15, February 2025.

[4]. K.-Y. Lin, "Circular supply chain for smart production in Industry 4.0"; *Computers & Industrial Engineering* (Elsevier), Vol. 198, 110682, pp. 1–10, March 2024.

[5]. Q. Su, L. Chen, L. Qian, "Optimization of big data analysis resources supported by XGBoost algorithm: Comprehensive analysis of Industry 5.0 and ESG performance"; *Measurement: Sensors* (Elsevier), Vol. 36, 101310, pp. 1–12, January 2024.

[6]. U. Dereci, G. Tuzkaya, "An explainable artificial intelligence model for predictive maintenance and spare parts optimization"; *Supply Chain Analytics* (Elsevier), Vol. 8, 100078, pp. 1–10, February 2024.

[7]. N.B. Shaik, K. Jongkittinarukorn, K. Bingi, "XGBoost based enhanced predictive model for handling missing input parameters: A case study on gas turbine"; Case Studies in Chemical and Environmental Engineering (Elsevier), Vol. 10, 100775, pp. 1–12, February 2024.

[8]. V. Safavi, A.M. Vaniar, N. Bazmohammadi, J.C. Vasquez, O. Keysan, J.M. Guerrero, "Early prediction of battery remaining useful life using CNN-XGBoost model and Coati optimization algorithm"; *Journal of Energy Storage* (Elsevier), Vol. 98, 113176, pp. 1–13, January 2024.

[9]. S. Hakkal, A.A. Lahcen, "XGBoost to enhance learner performance prediction"; *Computers and Education: Artificial Intelligence* (Elsevier), Vol. 7, 100254, pp. 1–10, January 2024.

[10]. M. Alizamir, M. Wang, R.M.A. Ikram, A. Gholampour, K.O. Ahmed, S. Heddam, S. Kim, "An interpretable XGBoost-SHAP machine learning model for reliable prediction of mechanical properties in waste foundry sand-based eco-friendly concrete"; *Results in Engineering* (Elsevier), Vol. 25, 104307, pp. 1–15, March 2025.

[11]. W. Zha, Y. Ye, "An aero-engine remaining useful life prediction model based on feature selection and the improved TCN"; *Franklin Open* (Elsevier), Vol. 6, 100083, pp. 1–14, January 2024.

[12]. S. Jafari, J.H. Yang, Y.C. Byun, "Optimized XGBoost modeling for accurate battery capacity degradation prediction"; *Results in Engineering* (Elsevier), Vol. 24, 102786, pp. 1–11, February 2024.

[13]. A. Homafar, H. Nasiri, S.C. Chelgani, "Modeling coking coal indexes by SHAP-XGBoost: Explainable artificial intelligence method"; *Fuel Communications* (Elsevier), Vol. 13, 100078, pp. 1–10, September 2022.

[14]. J. Alam, H. Zhang, L.A.C. Neves, D. Dias-da-Costa, "Sequential Bayesian updating for time-variant reliability analysis of ageing structures"; *Mechanical Systems and Signal Processing* (Elsevier), Vol. 204, 110774, pp. 1–14, December 2023.

Resilience Comparison of CNN-enabled Systems under Adversarial Attacks on Different Computing Environments

Karen Da Mata[1], Priscila Silva[1], Fatemeh Salboukh[2], and Lance Fiondella[1]
[1] Electrical and Computer Engineering, University of Massachusetts Dartmouth, MA, USA
[2] Engineering and Applied Science, University of Massachusetts Dartmouth, MA, USA
Email: {psilva4, fsalboukh, lfiondella}@umassd.edu, karenadamata@gmail.com

***Abstract*—Convolutional Neural Networks (CNN) are widely used in applications such as image classification and autonomous systems but are vulnerable to adversarial attacks, requiring adaptation to dynamic and hostile conditions while maintaining high performance. Previous studies have considered the impact of different Python frameworks and hyperparameters on CNN model performance. However, fewer studies have considered the role of computing environments in resilience under attack scenarios. This study compares a CNN resilience model in adversarial situations in three different computing environments, including MacOS, Linux, and Windows, which are composed of diverse hardware elements. An image classification model is subjected to two generative adversarial attacks and iteratively retrained to improve system performance whenever it falls below a pre-specified threshold. Data related to performance is collected from each computer and then employed to compute several resilience metrics that quantify the computer's ability to preserve the CNN model's performance. The results indicate that the Linux machine outperformed the other two platforms, preserving performance by 2.7% more and reducing performance loss by 16.16%. Thus, the Linux system was more suitable for running the CNN-enabled application under adversarial conditions, enabling greater resilience.**

***Index Terms*—Resilience engineering, Machine learning resilience, Convolutional neural network, Adversarial attacks, AI test and evaluation**

I. Introduction

Convolutional Neural Networks (CNNs) [1] have proven effective in many applications, including image classification [2] and autonomous systems [3]. These models operate in dynamically changing and hostile environments, requiring constant adaptation while maintaining high performance. Many studies have analyzed the impact of different Python frameworks [4] and hyperparameters [5] on CNN performance. However, they did not consider the influence of computing devices under attack scenarios on system performance and resilience.

Previous studies have examined several factors affecting CNN performance. Li et al. [6] and Kim et al. [4] studied the impact of frameworks on GPU-based CNN models concerning execution time and memory utilization. Nasser et al. [5] compared three CNN architectures and optimization algorithms according to accuracy, specificity, sensitivity, positive predictive value, false omission rate, negative predictive value, and F1 score, while Baye et al. [7] analyzed the effects of learning rates, batch sizes, training epochs, and class balances on OpenSetRecognition algorithms. Zhang et al. [8] compared adversarial detection models exposed to different attacks using the area under the ROC curve as a performance indicator. However, they did not consider how the computing devices running these models impact resilience. Faddi et al. [9] applied reliability and resilience models to track and predict ML system performance under adversarial scenarios using a CNN model, comparing attack ranges. However, their focus was on predictive modeling, not the role of computing environments in resilience. Resilience metrics [10] offer potential methods to quantify resilience and compare computing environments to identify the most suitable environment for a given application.

Previous research on resilience metrics includes Bruneau and Reinhorn [11], who defined performance preserved by measuring the area under the curve, and Yang and Frongopol [12], who quantified performance lost as the area above the curve. Zhou et al. [13] defined resilience as the ratio of performance loss to target performance during disruption and recovery. Reed et al. [14] proposed average preserved performance as a metric, while Cimerallo [15] suggested a user-specified weighting method to emphasize pre- and post-critical performance. These metrics quantify CNN-enabled system resilience, enabling retrospective analyses to compare designs and inform future decisions.

This paper performs a comparative resilience analysis of a CNN model under adversarial scenarios across three computing environments to determine which is most resilient for hosting an application. Specifically, it: i) Implements a CNN-enabled system under adversarial attacks in three computing environments. ii) Quantifies resilience using interval- and point-based resilience metrics [16]. iii) Provides applications and interpretations of these metrics to assess resilience and compare adaptability to adversarial attacks.

An image classification CNN [1] is deployed on three computers and subjected to the Fast Gradient Sign Method (FGSM) [17] and Projected Gradient Descent (PGD) [18] attacks. Adaptive Adversarial Training (AAT) [19] is performed to enhance performance and produce resilience trends. The environments include MacOS, Linux, and Windows, with varying CPU and GPU specifications. The CNN is trained on a dataset and tested on real and adversarial images. If the F1 score falls below a threshold, AAT is applied to improve robustness. Metrics such as the F1 score, CPU usage, and memory utilization are collected from each computer to quantify resilience. The results indicate the Linux system exhibited a 2.7% increase in preserved performance and a 16.16% decrease in performance loss, suggesting it is the most resilient for hosting CNN-enabled applications.

The remainder of this paper is structured as follows: Section II discusses ML techniques for attacking and defending CNN-enabled systems. Section III presents resilience engineering concepts and metrics. Section IV describes the experiment and discusses findings. Section V presents conclusions and outlines future research.

II. Machine Learning Techniques

This section provides an overview of three ML techniques to degrade and enhance performance of a CNN model. Section II-A introduces CNN for image classification applications. Section II-B summarizes two attacks a CNN model may face, while Section II-C describes a defensive measure to enhance system resilience.

A. Convolutional Neural Networks

Convolutional Neural Networks (CNNs) [1] are widely used in image classification and object recognition, enabling applications like self-driving cars [3] and face recognition [20]. Their strength lies in identifying patterns and features, but they are vulnerable to adversarial attacks, where small perturbations in images cause misclassification, significantly impacting performance. Some attacks exploit CNN structures to generate deceptive images, necessitating an understanding of their architecture before discussing attack strategies and defenses.

A CNN architecture [21] consists of input, convolutional, pooling, and fully connected layers that process images by reducing dimensionality and extracting features to classify them. The model is trained using labeled images, with an optimization algorithm adjusting weights and biases to minimize loss. Once trained, it can predict image classes based on new inputs. The next subsection discusses adversarial techniques that maximize loss by manipulating input images.

B. Generative Adversarial Attacks (GAA)

In image classification, generative adversarial attacks create realistic-looking images to deceive the target model into making incorrect predictions. Common generative models used for these attacks include the Fast Gradient Sign Method (FGSM) [17] and Projected Gradient Descent (PGD) [18].

Fast Gradient Sign Method (FGSM) is a white-box attack [22] where the attacker has full access to the model architecture and parameters. This attack generates adversarial examples by computing the sign of the gradient of the loss function with respect to the input image and perturbing the image in the direction that maximizes classification error. FGSM is faster than other gradient-based methods, making it an efficient adversarial attack. The following equation summarizes the FGSM method.

$$x_{adv} = x + \varepsilon \times \text{sign}(\nabla_x \mathcal{L}(\theta, x, y)) \quad (1)$$

where x_{adv} is the generated image, x the original input image, $\varepsilon > 0$ an arbitrarily small positive number that controls the intensity of the noise added to the image, sign is the signum function, $\mathcal{L}$ the cross-entropy loss, θ the model parameters, and y the original input label.

Projected Gradient Descent (PGD) uses the magnitude of the gradient, taking multiple steps towards the direction of the gradient of the classification model output with respect to the input image. At each step, the input is projected back onto the space of valid inputs, ensuring that the adversarial examples generated are similar to the original image and in the same space. The PGD iterative procedure is

$$x_{adv_{t+1}} = \prod_{\Delta}(x_{adv} + \alpha \times \text{sign}(\nabla_x \mathcal{L}(\theta, x, y))) \quad (2)$$

where $x_{adv_{t+1}}$ is the projection-generated image at time $(t+1)$, $\prod$ the projection operator, Δ the set of perturbations, and α the gradient step size.

C. Defensive Measures

Adaptive Adversarial training (AAT) [19] is a defensive technique that combines adversarial and online training to improve the stability of neural network models against input perturbations, where adversarial examples are included in the model training as they become available.

AAT is an optimization procedure where online training considers a newly available adversarially perturbed dataset.

$$\min_{\theta}[\max_{\delta \in \Delta}[\mathcal{L}(x + \delta, y, \theta)]] \quad (3)$$

where $\delta \in \Delta$ is a set of perturbations. In this min-max problem, the inner maximization represents the adversary attempting to maximize the loss of a classification model in which the parameters θ are known. The subsequent minimization trains the classifier on adversarial attacks to ensure that the model cannot be tricked by that type of attack.

III. Resilience Engineering

Resilience engineering [23] studies a system's ability to sustain performance and recover from disruptive events. This section covers two key components: (i) the resilience curve and its four stages and (ii) common resilience metrics for assessing system performance, such as CNN-enabled systems under adversarial attacks. Although system performance is domain-dependent, it pertains to task accomplishment, which fluctuates due to disruptive events and restorative activities, also known as covariates, giving rise to the resilience curve.

A. Resilience Curve

Figure 1 illustrates the four stages of a canonical resilience curve, as described by The National Academy of Sciences [24]: (i) prepare, (ii) absorb, (iii) recover, and (iv) adapt. In the prepare stage, system performance $P(t)$ remains nominal (dotted horizontal line) until time t_h when a disruption occurs. The absorb stage follows, where performance declines until reaching a minimum at time t_d before improving in the recovery stage. Resilient systems recover smoothly to a new steady performance at time t_r and enter the adapt stage. Some systems recover beyond nominal performance (dashed line), while others, such as power generation systems, may only return to nominal (solid) or degraded (dash-dotted) performance due to equipment damage. In many real cases, resilience is insufficient for an immediate performance recovery, leading to multiple declines (dotted) at time t_ℓ.

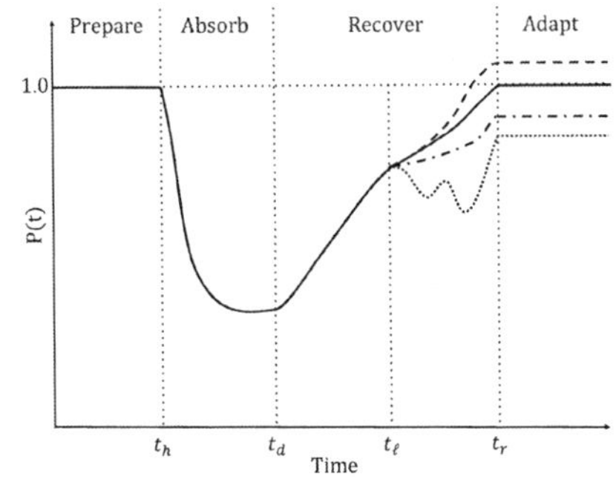

Figure 1: Canonical resilience curve.

B. Resilience Metrics

This subsection introduces four commonly used resilience metrics, evaluating a system's ability to maintain functionality and recover performance after a disruption, aiding comparisons and restorative decisions.

Performance Preserved (PP) [11]

$$PP = \int_{t_h}^{t_r} P(t)dt \tag{4}$$

measures the portion of system performance maintained between a disruption (t_h) and recovery time (t_r).

Performance Lost (PL) [12]

$$PL = P(t_h)(t_r - t_h) - \int_{t_h}^{t_r} P(t)dt \tag{5}$$

computes the portion of system performance lost during a disruption.

Instantaneous Resilience (IR) [16]

$$IR(t_r) = \frac{P(t_r) - P(t_d)}{P(t_h) - P(t_d)} \tag{6}$$

quantifies the ratio of the recovered and degraded performance at time t_r.

Normalized Instantaneous Resilience (NIR) [25]

$$NIR(t_d) = \frac{Max\{P(t_h) - P(t_d)\} - (P(t_h) - P(t_d))}{Max\{P(t_h) - P(t_d)\}} \tag{7}$$

quantifies the normalized impact of the hazardous consequences absorbed by the system, where $Max\{P(t_h) - P(t_d)\}$ is the worst degradation scenario.

Higher values for PP and IR indicate better performance retention and faster recovery, while lower PL values indicate minimal performance loss. For NIR, values closer to one suggest a smaller drop than the worst-case scenario, whereas values near zero indicate severe performance degradation.

IV. Illustrations

This section presents the experimental setup and comparative analysis of CNN resilience across different computing environments under adversarial conditions.

A. Experiment

This experiment compares the resilience of different devices operating a CNN-enabled system in adversarial scenarios using the techniques in Section II and resilience methodology in Section III. It helps identify the most suitable device for maintaining CNN functionality under adversarial attacks and recovering performance after disruptions.

Figure 2 provides an overview of the experimental setup. Three devices, described in Subsection IV-A1, operate the same CNN-enabled image classification system under adversarial conditions, as detailed in Subsection IV-A2. The CNN is trained and tested on real and adversarial images across multiple iterations, with performance and resource utilization data collected from each device. These data are then used to compute resilience metrics, followed by the comparative analysis in Section IV-B.

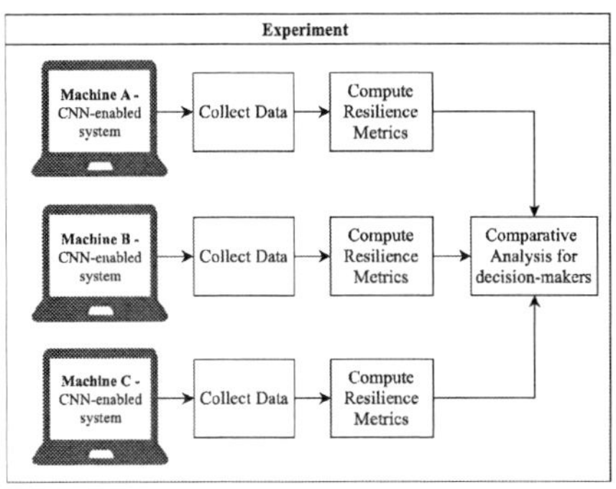

Figure 2: The overview of the experimental setup.

1) Setup: The approach is generalizable to other devices. Three machines were selected based on availability and common usage. Their specifications, including operating system, CPU/GPU cores, and hardware type, are shown in Table I. The same Python library, TensorFlow [26], [27], was used to ensure device-focused comparisons.

Table I: The specifications of each machine in the experimental setup.

Specification \ Machine	A	B	C
Test unit	Apple M2 Max	Unity Cluster (gypsum-gpu024)	Dell Precision 5570
Processor	arm64-arm-64bit	159-generic-x86_64-with-glibc2.29	12th Gen Intel® Core™ i9
OS	MacOS Sonoma	Linux	Windows 10 Enterprise
OS version	14.0	5.4.0	10.0.19045
CPU number of cores	12	12	20
Number of GPU Devices	1	2	1
GPU	Apple M2 Max	NVIDIA Tesla M40 24GB	NVIDIA RTX A2000 8GB
GPU number of cores	30	3072 (workstation card)	3328 (workstation card)
Memory (GB)	32	32	32
Memory Type	LPDDR5	DDR5	DDR5
Python Library	TensorFlow	TensorFlow	TensorFlow

2) Data Collection: The experiment used the CIFAR-10 dataset [28], containing $60,000$ 32x32 images across ten classes, with $6,000$ images per class. Figure 3 illustrates the CNN architecture model (Model$_X$) where layer sizes follow Section II-A.

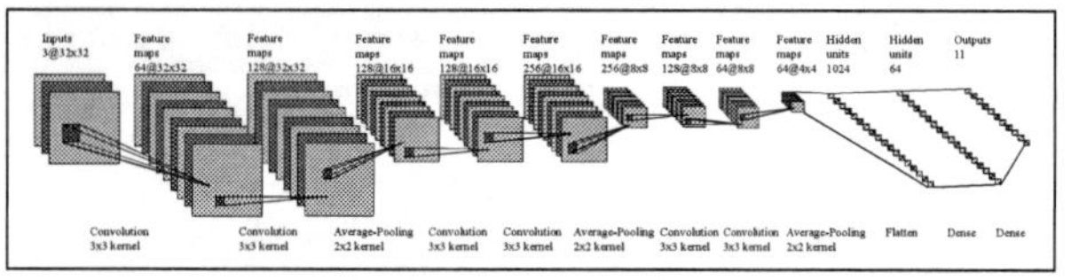

Figure 3: Architecture of the convolutional neural network.

Figure 4 outlines the steps taken for data collection on each machine.

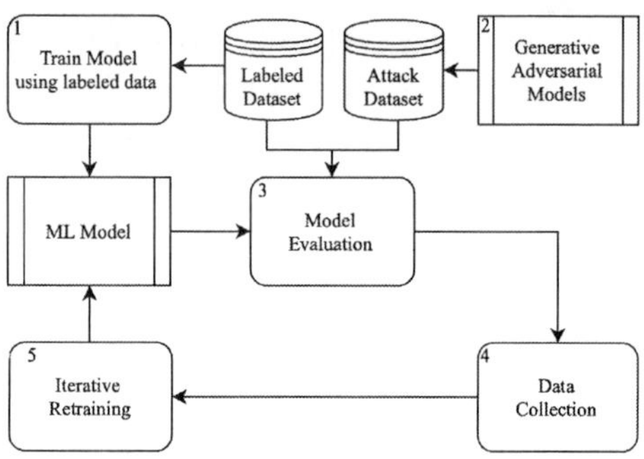

Figure 4: Framework for the CNN-enabled system in each device.

The CIFAR-10 dataset was split into training ($40,000$ images), validation ($10,000$), and testing ($10,000$), with mutually exclusive classes. The first $50,000$ labeled images were used to train and validate $Model_X$ until it reached 70% accuracy, ensuring a baseline for improvement. The following steps were then repeated 40 times: (1) 5,000 adversarial images were generated using FGSM and PGD on the remaining $10,000$ images, with a random ε value sampled from a uniform distribution ($0 \leq \varepsilon_l, \varepsilon_u \leq 1$) to simulate varying attack intensities. These were combined with 5,000 real images to create a 10,000-image poisoned dataset, which was split into ten batches for faster processing. (2) $Model_X$ was evaluated on each batch, and performance metrics were recorded. (3) If the F1 Score fell below a 0.9 threshold, iterative retraining was performed using the poisoned dataset. (4) System performance and resource usage data were collected (Table II).

The F1 Score was chosen as the primary performance metric due to its balanced evaluation of classification accuracy and precision. Since the data was split into batches, at the end of the experiment, 402 data points were collected for each factor described in Table II for each machine. The resilience metrics described in Section III-B treats the F1 Score as the performance indicator of the CNN-enabled system.

Table II: Factor collected during the experiment in each device.

Related to	Name	Description
Performance	Duration	Duration of each iteration in seconds
	F1 Score	F1 Score of Model$_X$ on a batch of the poisoned data set
	Training frequency	Whether iterative retraining was required or not
Resources	CPU utilization	CPU utilization in percentage
	Memory utilization	Physical memory utilization in percentage
	Swap utilization	Swap memory utilization in percentage

B. Analysis

This section discusses the findings of the comparative analysis of the resilience of three devices operating a CNN-enabled system under adversarial attacks. Data on CNN performance and resource utilization were collected following Section IV-A2, and resilience metrics from Section III-B were computed using the F1 Score as the performance indicator.

In order to determine if there is a statistically significant difference in the performance of the CNN-enabled systems, a hypothesis test [29] was conducted, where the null hypothesis states that there is no difference in performance among the computers, while the alternative hypothesis suggests that at least one computer performs differently. Thus, Figure 5 shows the normal probability plot and histogram with the best-fitting normal plot based on the mean and standard deviation of the F1 Score of each machine.

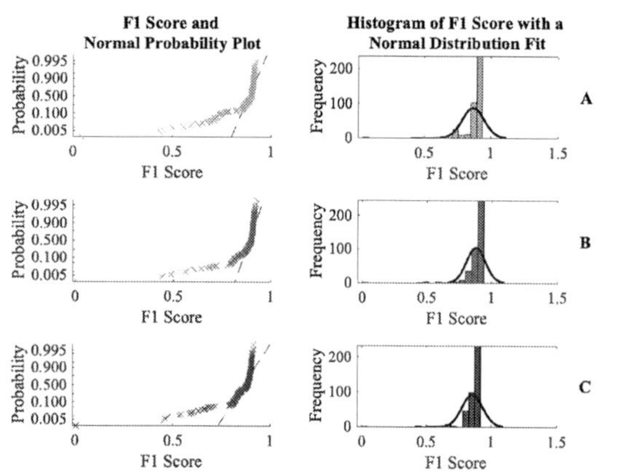

Figure 5: Normal probability plot and histogram with the best fitting normal plot for the F1 Score of each machine.

The left plots in Figure 5 show deviations from the best-fit line, suggesting the F1 Score data are not normally distributed. The right-side histograms further confirm this, as the bars do not follow a bell-shaped curve. Given the non-normality, the Friedman test [30], suitable for repeated measures without normal distribution, was applied. A p-value smaller than 0.0001 rejected the null hypothesis at the 5% significance level, indicating a statistically significant performance difference among the computers.

Figure 6 shows the F1 Scores of the CNN-enabled system under adversarial attacks throughout the experiment, including the performance threshold in red. All machines exhibited similar F1 score trends. Sharp drops within the first 100 iterations likely resulted from adversarial attacks. As adaptive adversarial training progressed, the model adapted, resulting in a recovery of performance with fewer sharp drops. However, adaptation varied. Machines A (MacOS) and C (Windows) had multiple degradations, while Machine B (Linux) remained near the performance threshold. This suggests Machines A and C struggled more in learning from attacks and maintaining performance, while Machine B adapted better. Figure 7 shows the duration of each experimental iteration in seconds and the frequency of adaptive adversarial training sessions, indicating how often the F1 Score dropped below 0.9.

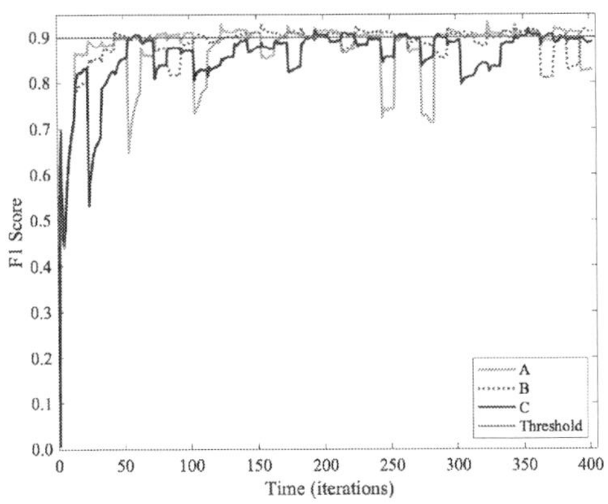

Figure 6: F1 Scores of the CNN-enabled system on each machine during the experiment and the F1 Score threshold.

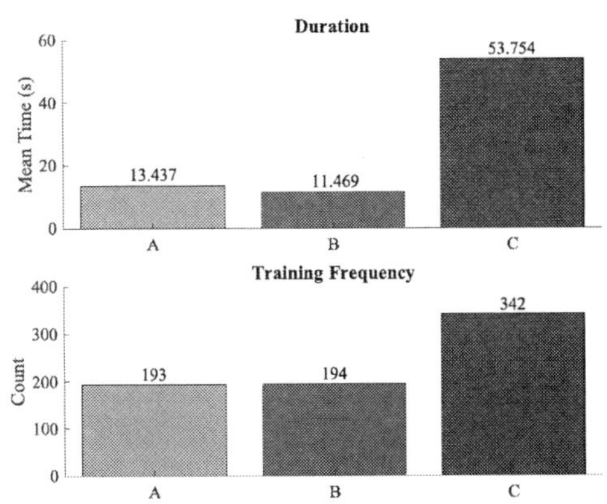

Figure 7: Mean duration of each iteration, measured in seconds, and the frequency of iterative retraining occurrences in each machine.

On average, Machine A required 13.44 seconds per iteration, while Machine B completed iterations 2 seconds faster. Machine C required $\frac{53.75}{\frac{13.44+11.47}{2}} = 4.31$ times more than the other machines. Regarding training frequency, Machines A and B had similar results, whereas Machine C required retraining $\frac{342}{\frac{193+194}{2}} = 1.76$ times more. These findings suggest Machine C was less resilient, needing nearly twice as much retraining.

Table III presents the resilience metrics computed from CNN performance data, with the best values in bold. Interval-based metrics, including performance preserved (PP) and performance lost (PL), were computed by discretizing Equations (4) and (5). Point-based metrics, instantaneous resilience (IR) (Equation (6)) and normalized instantaneous resilience (NIR) (Equation (7)), were computed considering the last drop occurrence and the worst degradation scenario, where $(MaxP(t_h = 1) - P(t_d = 0) = 1)$ represents the highest possible drop in F1 Score from 1 to 0.

Table III: Resilience metrics applied to the CNN performance data of each machine with the best values in bold.

Metrics \ Machine	A	B	C
PP	349.7357	**353.6743**	344.3548
PL	52.2643	**48.3257**	57.6453
IR	0.0226	**0.1410**	0.0454
$IR_{average}$	2.2663	**3.2901**	2.5249
NIR	0.8926	**0.9815**	0.9704
$NIR_{average}$	0.9553	**0.9637**	0.9564

Table III shows that Machine B outperformed the others in all metrics, improving PP by $\frac{353.67-344.35}{344.35} \times 100\% = 2.7\%$ and achieving a $\frac{57.64-48.32}{57.64} \times 100\% = 16.16\%$ lower PL than the worst-performing machine. These results indicate superior resilience in preserving performance under adversarial conditions. Machine A performed second-best in PP and PL, while Machine C ranked second in point-based metrics. This suggests Machine A maintained resilience over time, whereas Machine C performed better in specific instances. Overall, Machine B demonstrated the highest resilience and may be the best choice for operating the CNN-enabled system.

Figure 8 shows the scatter plot of the F1 Score and the percentage of CPU, Memory, and Swap Memory utilized by each machine during the experiment.

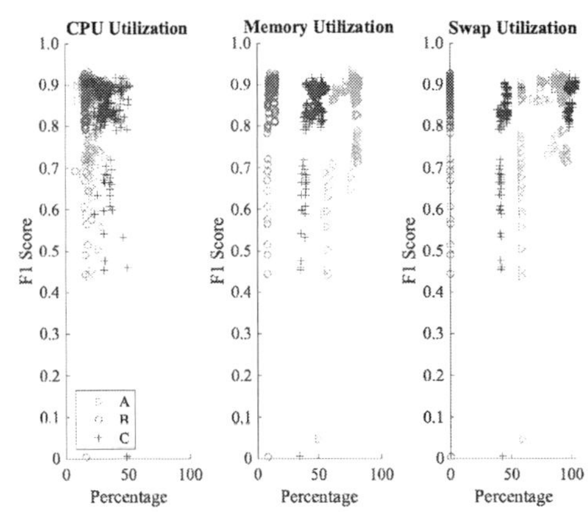

Figure 8: Scatter plot of the F1 Score and the percentage of resources utilized by each machine.

Machine C's CPU usage was around 50%, while Machines A and B remained around 30%, maintaining F1 Scores between 0.8 and 0.9. Machine A used approximately 80% of its memory, while Machine C ranged between 40% and 60%. Both Machines A and C had swap memory utilization around 100% at times, whereas Machine B had minimal to zero usage. Although no strong correlation between resource usage and CNN performance is evident, Machine B consumed fewer resources while achieving the best resilience metrics (Table III), further supporting it as the optimal choice for CNN-enabled system deployment.

V. Conclusion

This paper compared the resilience of a CNN model under adversarial conditions across three computing environments to determine which environment is most suitable for hosting the application. A convolutional neural network with adaptive adversarial training was subjected to fast gradient sign method and projected gradient descent attacks and tested on three computers with different operating systems such as MacOS, Linux, and Windows, as well as varying CPU/GPU configurations. Performance data was collected from each machine and analyzed using resilience metrics. Results indicate that the Linux machine significantly outperformed the other two, increasing performance preservation by 2.7% and reducing performance loss by 16.16%. These findings suggest that Linux provided a more resilient environment for CNN-enabled applications, maintaining higher performance under adversarial attacks.

Further research could explore a wider range of adversarial attacks and datasets to enhance generalizability. Additionally, predictive resilience models incorporating hardware and attack-specific factors could offer a more dynamic assessment of CNN system robustness.

Acknowledgment

This research was supported by the Homeland Security Community of Best Practices (HS CoBP) through the U.S. Department of the Air Force under contract FA8075-18-D-0002/FA8075-21-F-0074. Any opinions, findings, and conclusions or recommendations expressed in this material are those of the authors and do not necessarily reflect the views of the U.S. Department of Homeland Security or the U.S. Department of the Air Force.

References

[1] C. Szegedy, W. Zaremba, I. Sutskever, J. Bruna, D. Erhan, I. Goodfellow, and R. Fergus, "Intriguing properties of neural networks," *arXiv preprint arXiv:1312.6199*, 2013.

[2] G. Apruzzese, M. Colajanni, L. Ferretti, and M. Marchetti, "Addressing adversarial attacks against security systems based on machine learning," in *International Conference on Cyber Conflict (CyCon)*, vol. 900, 2019, pp. 1–18.

[3] A. Gupta, A. Anpalagan, L. Guan, and A. Khwaja, "Deep learning for object detection and scene perception in self-driving cars: Survey, challenges, and open issues," *Array*, vol. 10, p. 100057, 2021.

[4] H. Kim, H. Nam, W. Jung, and J. Lee, "Performance analysis of cnn frameworks for gpus," in *IEEE International Symposium on Performance Analysis of Systems and Software*, 2017, pp. 55–64.

[5] I. Naseer, S. Akram, T. Masood, A. Jaffar, M. Khan, and A. Mosavi, "Performance analysis of state-of-the-art cnn architectures for LUNA16," *Sensors*, vol. 22, no. 12, 2022.

[6] X. Li, G. Zhang, H. Huang, Z. Wang, and W. Zheng, "Performance analysis of gpu-based convolutional neural networks," in *International Conference on Parallel Processing*, 2016, pp. 67–76.

[7] G. Baye, P. Silva, A. Broggi, L. Fiondella, N. Bastian, and G. Kul, "Performance analysis of deep-learning based open set recognition algorithms for network intrusion detection systems," in *IEEE/IFIP NOMS Network Operations and Management Symposium*, 2023, pp. 1–6.

[8] S. Zhang, S. Chen, X. Liu, C. Hua, W. Wang, K. Chen, J. Zhang, and J. Wang, "Detecting adversarial samples for deep learning models: A comparative study," *IEEE Transactions on Network Science and Engineering*, vol. 9, no. 1, pp. 231–244, 2022.

[9] Z. Faddi, K. da Mata, P. Silva, V. Nagaraju, S. Ghosh, G. Kul, and L. Fiondella, "Quantitative assessment of machine learning reliability and resilience," *Risk Analysis*, 2024.

[10] S. Hosseini, K. Barker, and J. Ramirez-Marquez, "A review of definitions and measures of system resilience," *Reliability Engineering & System Safety*, vol. 145, pp. 47–61, 2016.

[11] M. Bruneau and A. Reinhorn, "Exploring the concept of seismic resilience for acute care facilities," *Earthquake Spectra*, vol. 23, no. 1, pp. 41–62, 2007.

[12] D. Yang and D. Frangopol, "Life-cycle management of deteriorating civil infrastructure considering resilience to lifetime hazards: A general approach based on renewal-reward processes," *Reliability Engineering & System Safety*, vol. 183, pp. 197–212, 2019.

[13] Y. Zhou, J. Wang, and H. Yang, "Resilience of transportation systems: Concepts and comprehensive review," *IEEE Transactions on Intelligent Transportation Systems*, vol. 20, no. 12, pp. 4262–4276, 2019.

[14] D. Reed, K. Kapur, and R. D. Christie, "Methodology for assessing the resilience of networked infrastructure," *Systems Journal*, vol. 3, no. 2, pp. 174–180, 2009.

[15] G. Cimellaro, A. Reinhorn, and M. Bruneau, "Seismic resilience of a hospital system," *Structure and Infrastructure Engineering*, vol. 6, no. 1-2, pp. 127–144, 2010.

[16] Y. Cheng, E. Elsayed, and Z. Huang, "Systems resilience assessments: a review, framework and metrics," *International Journal of Production Research*, vol. 60, no. 2, pp. 595–622, 2022.

[17] I. Goodfellow, J. Shlens, and C. Szegedy, "Explaining and harnessing adversarial examples," *arXiv preprint arXiv:1412.6572*, 2014.

[18] A. Madry, A. Makelov, L. Schmidt, D. Tsipras, and A. Vladu, "Towards deep learning models resistant to adversarial attacks," *arXiv preprint arXiv:1706.06083*, 2017.

[19] Y. Balaji, T. Goldstein, and J. Hoffman, "Instance adaptive adversarial training: Improved accuracy tradeoffs in neural nets," *arXiv preprint arXiv:1910.08051*, 2019.

[20] S. Lawrence, C. Giles, A. Tsoi, and A. Back, "Face recognition: A convolutional neural-network approach," *IEEE Transactions on Neural Networks*, vol. 8, no. 1, pp. 98–113, 1997.

[21] K. O'Shea and R. Nash, "An introduction to convolutional neural networks," *arXiv preprint arXiv:1511.08458*, 2015.

[22] N. Papernot, P. McDaniel, S. Jha, M. Fredrikson, Z. Celik, and A. Swami, "The limitations of deep learning in adversarial settings," in *IEEE European Symposium on Security and Privacy*, 2016, pp. 372–387.

[23] E. Hollnagel, D. Woods, and N. Leveson, *Resilience Engineering: Concepts and Precepts*. Ashgate Publishing, Ltd., 2006.

[24] T. Academies, Committee on Increasing National Resilience to Hazards and Disasters, and Committee on Science, Engineering, and Public Policy, *Disaster Resilience: A National Imperative*. Washington, DC: The National Academies Press, 2012.

[25] A. Rose, "Economic resilience to natural and man-made disasters: Multidisciplinary origins and contextual dimensions," *Environmental Hazards*, vol. 7, no. 4, pp. 383–398, 2007.

[26] M. Abadi, P. Barham, J. Chen, Z. Chen, A. Davis, J. Dean, M. Devin, S. Ghemawat, G. Irving, M. Isard, M. Kudlur, J. Levenberg, R. Monga, S. Moore, D. G. Murray, B. Steiner, P. Tucker, V. Vasudevan, P. Warden, M. Wicke, Y. Yu, and X. Zheng, "TensorFlow: A system for Large-Scale machine learning," in *USENIX Symposium on Operating Systems Design and Implementation*. Savannah, GA: USENIX Association, Nov. 2016, pp. 265–283.

[27] M. Abadi, A. Agarwal, P. Barham, E. Brevdo, Z. Chen, C. Citro, G. Corrado, A. Davis, J. Dean, M. Devin *et al.*, "Tensorflow: Large-scale machine learning on heterogeneous distributed systems," *arXiv preprint arXiv:1603.04467*, 2016.

[28] A. Krizhevsky and G. Hinton, "Learning multiple layers of features from tiny images," University of Toronto, Toronto, Ontario, Tech. Rep., 2009.

[29] W. Newey and D. McFadden, "Large sample estimation and hypothesis testing," *Handbook of Econometrics*, vol. 4, pp. 2111–2245, 1994.

[30] T. Cleophas and A. Zwinderman, *Non-parametric Tests for Three or More Samples (Friedman and Kruskal-Wallis)*. Cham: Springer International Publishing, 2016, pp. 193–197.

Reliability Modelling of Data Transmission Model with CSMA/CA in Wireless Environments

MITSUTAKA KIMURA
Faculty of Business Administration,
Aichi University
4-60-6 Hiraike-cho, Nakamura-ku,
Nagoya, Aichi, 453-8777, Japan.

MITSUHIRO IMAIZUMI
Affiliated Research Center,
Aichi Gakusen University
28 Kamikawanari, Hegoshi-cho,
Okazaki, Aichi, 444-8520, Japan.

TOSHIO NAKAGAWA
Department of Business Administration, Aichi Institute of Technology
1247 Yachigusa, Yakusa-cho, Toyota, Aichi, 470-0392, Japan

Key Words: Wireless Channel, Avoid Collisions, CSMA/CA, Window Flow Control, Reliability.

Abstract

In wireless communication networks, where multiple devices must share a common communication channel, it is essential to prevent data collisions that may occur when two or more devices attempt to transmit simultaneously. Such collisions can lead to transmission failures, retransmissions, and overall degradation of network performance. To address this issue, media access control (MAC) mechanisms have been developed, which regulate access to the communication channel. One common approach is to allow each device to monitor the status of the channel and determine whether it is idle before initiating transmission, thereby reducing the likelihood of collision.

In this study, we examine a stochastic model of a wireless communication system that employs Carrier Sense Multiple Access with Collision Avoidance (CSMA/CA)—a widely adopted MAC protocol used in IEEE 802.11 wireless networks. In this model, each terminal senses the channel's availability and, in order to avoid potential collisions, introduces a random backoff time before transmission. The decision to transmit is made probabilistically, based on the sensed state of the channel and predefined transmission rules. We analytically derive the mean time until packet transmissions succeed and discuss an optimal transmission strategy analytically.

1. Introduction

In wireless communication networks where multiple terminals share common network resources, it is crucial to avoid collisions that occur when multiple devices transmit data simultaneously [1]. The mechanisms used to prevent such collisions, as well as to handle them when they occur, are referred to as media access control (MAC) [1]. While various MAC protocols exist for wireless LANs, this study focuses on the widely adopted IEEE 802.11 standard. Specifically, we consider an IEEE 802.11-based wireless LAN composed of a single access point and one or more wireless terminals.

One of the most effective and simple approaches to avoiding contention among wireless terminals is to confirm the availability of wireless channel before transmitting a frame. This process is known as carrier sensing, and MAC protocols that adopt this mechanism are categorized under Carrier Sense Multiple Access (CSMA) [1]. CSMA significantly reduces the likelihood of collisions. However, because the sensing information is received at the terminal with some delay, other terminals may begin transmission during this delay, resulting in a frame collision and subsequent transmission failure. To address this issue, the IEEE 802.11 standard employs Carrier Sense Multiple Access with Collision Avoidance (CSMA/CA), which reduces simultaneous transmissions by introducing a random backoff period after sensing an idle channel before transmission begins [1]. Nevertheless, this random waiting period can decrease communication efficiency, prompting research aimed at improving the performance of CSMA/CA [2].

In this study, we construct a reliability model to mathematically examine the impact of the backoff period. We have already considered previous work on congestion-aware communication models. For example, models using Explicit Congestion Notification (ECN) adjust the packet transmission interval based on explicit feedback about network congestion at the time of connection establishment [3]. Inspired by such approaches, we develop a communication model that uses CSMA/CA to transmit frames (i.e., packets).

Specifically, we consider a wireless communication system between a client and a WWW server. Upon receiving a data request from the client, the server transmits multiple packets corresponding to the TCP window size, using a TCP-based communication method[4],

[5]. The client performs acknowledgment while also checking the channel status; if the channel is idle, it waits for a certain period with some probability before sending data. We analytically derive the mean time until packet transmissions succeed and then discuss the optimal transmission policy that maximizes throughput analytically.

2. Model and Analysis

We consider a communication system which consists of a web server and a client. In network systems, congestion is assumed to occur randomly during which no wireless channel is available. This congestion persists for a certain period and is resolved afterward, allowing the wireless channel to become available again. When the client sends a data request to the server, the server performs a connection establishment procedure with the client. Upon receiving a response from the server, the client confirms the availability of wireless channel. If a channel is available, the client waits for a predetermined period before initiating data transmission. After waiting, the server transmits data packets $n (n = 1, 2, \cdots)$ corresponding to a specified window size to a client.

We formulate the following stochastic model:

(1) Congestion occurs in the network according to an exponential distribution $(1 - e^{-\lambda t})(0 < \lambda < \infty)$ during which no wireless channels are available and continues according to an exponential distribution $(1 - e^{-\beta t})(0 < \beta < \infty)$ and is resolved afterward, allowing wireless channels to become available again. We define the following states of a network system:

State 0: No congestion occurs and the wireless channel is available.

State 1: Congestion occurs and no wireless channel is available.

The network system states defined above form a two-state Markov process [6]. Thus, we have the following probabilities under the initial condition that $P_{00}(0) = P_{11}(0) = 1, P_{01}(0) = P_{10}(0) = 0$:

$$\begin{aligned} P_{00}(t) &\equiv \frac{\beta}{\lambda+\beta} + \frac{\lambda}{\lambda+\beta} e^{-(\lambda+\beta)t}, \\ P_{11}(t) &\equiv \frac{\lambda}{\lambda+\beta} + \frac{\beta}{\lambda+\beta} e^{-(\lambda+\beta)t}, \\ P_{01}(t) &= 1 - P_{00}(t), \\ P_{10}(t) &= 1 - P_{11}(t), \end{aligned}$$

where $P_{ij}(t)$ are probabilities that the network system is in State $i (i = 0, 1)$ at time 0 and State $j (j = 0, 1)$ at time $t (> 0)$.

(2) When a client requests data packets, the server confirms the availability of wireless channel. Let $A(t)$ denote a general distribution describing the time required for the occurrence of data request with mean a and $A_1(t) \equiv 1 - e^{-a_1 t}$ denote an exponential distribution describing the time required for confirmation of the availability of wireless channel with mean $1/a_1$.

(i) If availability can be confirmed, a random waiting time is introduced in order to avoid collisions due to simultaneous communications with other clients. It is assumed that a client waits for a fixed period of time with probability $q (0 < q < 1)$, and the distribution of this waiting time is denoted by $W(t) \equiv 1 - e^{-wt}$ with a mean of $1/w$.

(a) If a collision due to simultaneous communications occurs, the transmission is interrupted, the transmission channel is monitored, and a retransmission is attempted. The distribution of the time elapsed until the retransmission is denoted by $G(t)$, with an expected value of μ, where $G(t) \equiv 0$ for $t < \mu$ and 1 for $t \geq \mu$.

(b) If no collision due to simultaneous communications occurs, the process to establish a connection with the server is initiated. Let $A_2(t) \equiv 1 - e^{-a_2 t}$ denote an exponential distribution describing the time required for connection establishment with mean $1/a_2$.

(ii) If availability cannot be confirmed, the checking process is repeated until availability is successfully confirmed.

(3) After the connection establishment can be executed, n data packets corresponding to a window size are transmitted by the server successively. The transmission interval of each packet needs the time according to a general distribution $B(t)$ with mean b.

(i) If the data packet transmission successes, a client returns Acknowledgement (ACK) according to a general distribution $D(t)$ with mean d.

(ii) If the data packet transmission fails, a client returns Negative Acknowledgement (NAK) according to a general distribution $D(t)$ with mean d and requests loss packet. The probability that each packet is lost at data transmission is p $(0 < p < 1)$.

(4) If the retransmission has been failed at $k (k = 1, 2, \cdots)$ times, the connection is made newly after constant time $G(t)$.

(5) If the server has received ACK of all packets n, the transmission succeeds.

Under the above assumptions, we define the following states of the system:

State 2: Data packets are requested from a client.

State 3: Availability of wireless channel is confirmed.

State 4: If availability cannot be confirmed, the checking process is repeated.

State 5: If availability can be confirmed, connection establishment between a client.

State 6: n packets are transmitted from a server to a client.

State F: When a retransmit at k times fails, the connection is made newly.

State S: Transmission of all n packets succeeds.

The system states defined above form a Markov renewal process [7], [8], where S is an absorbing state. A transition diagram between system states is shown in Figure 1.

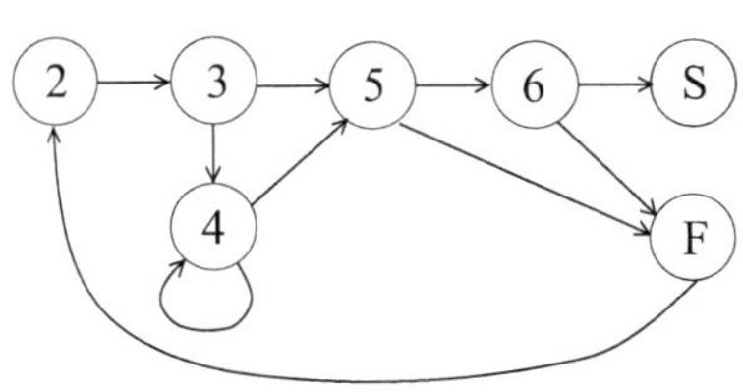

Figure 1: Transition diagram between system states .

In case of $k = 2$, transition probabilities $Q_{i,j}(t)$ from State $i (i = 3, 4, 5, 6)$ to State $j (j = 4, 5, 6, F, S)$ are :

$$Q_{3,5}(t) = \int_0^t P_{00}(x) dA_1(x), \tag{1}$$

$$Q_{3,4}(t) = \int_0^t P_{01}(x) dA_1(x), \tag{2}$$

$$Q_{4,4}(t) = \int_0^t P_{11}(x) dA_1(x), \tag{3}$$

$$Q_{4,5}(t) = \int_0^t P_{10}(x) dA_1(x), \tag{4}$$

$$\begin{aligned} Q_{5,6}(t) &= \\ & q\left\{ \left[\int_0^t P_{00}(x) dW(x)\right] * \left[\int_0^t P_{00}(x) dA_2(x)\right] \right. \\ & \left. + \left[\int_0^t P_{01}(x) dW(x)\right] * \left[\int_0^t P_{10}(x) dA_2(x)\right] \right\} \\ & + (1-q)\left[\int_0^t P_{00}(x) dA_2(x)\right], \end{aligned} \tag{5}$$

$$\begin{aligned} Q_{5,F}(t) &= \\ & q\left\{ \left[\int_0^t P_{00}(x) dW(x)\right] * \left[\int_0^t P_{01}(x) dA_2(x)\right] \right. \\ & \left. + \left[\int_0^t P_{01}(x) dW(x)\right] * \left[\int_0^t P_{11}(x) dA_2(x)\right] \right\} \\ & + (1-q)\left[\int_0^t P_{01}(x) dA_2(x)\right], \end{aligned} \tag{6}$$

$$\begin{aligned} Q_{6,S}(t) &\equiv (1-p)^n B^{(n)}(t) * D(t) \\ & + \sum_{m_1=1}^{n} \binom{n}{m_1} p^{m_1} (1-p)^{n-m_1} B^{(n)}(t) * D(t) \\ & * (1-p)^{m_1} B^{(m_1)}(t) * D(t), \end{aligned} \tag{7}$$

$$\begin{aligned} Q_{6,F}(t) &\equiv \\ & \sum_{m_1=1}^{n} \binom{n}{m_1} p^{m_1} (1-p)^{n-m_1} B^{(n)}(t) * D(t) \\ & * [1 - (1-p)^{m_1}] B^{(m_1)}(t) * D(t). \end{aligned} \tag{8}$$

$\Phi^{(i)}(t)$ is the i-fold convolution of $\Phi(t)$, $\Phi^{(0)}(t) \equiv 1$, and the asterisk mark denotes the Stieltjes convolution.

Laplace-Stieltjes (LS) transforms $q_{i,j}(s)$ of transition probabilities $Q_{i,j}(t)$ are :

$$\begin{aligned} & q_{3,5}(s) = a_1 \widetilde{P}_{0,0}(s + a_1), \quad q_{3,4}(s) = a_1 \widetilde{P}_{0,1}(s + a_1), \\ & q_{4,4}(s) = a_1 \widetilde{P}_{1,1}(s + a_1), \quad q_{4,5}(s) = a_1 \widetilde{P}_{1,0}(s + a_1), \\ & q_{5,6}(s) = q a_2 w \left[\widetilde{P}_{0,0}(s + w) \widetilde{P}_{0,0}(s + a_2) \right. \\ & \left. + \widetilde{P}_{0,1}(s + w) \widetilde{P}_{1,0}(s + a_2) \right] + (1-q) w \widetilde{P}_{0,0}(s + w), \\ & q_{5,F}(s) = q a_2 w \left[\widetilde{P}_{0,0}(s + w) \widetilde{P}_{0,1}(s + a_2) \right. \\ & \left. + \widetilde{P}_{0,1}(s + w) \widetilde{P}_{1,1}(s + a_2) \right] + (1-q) w \widetilde{P}_{0,1}(s + w), \end{aligned}$$

$$\begin{aligned} q_{6,S}(s) &= [(1-p) b(s)]^n d(s) \\ & \times [1 + d(s)\{[1 + p b(s)]^n - 1\}], \\ q_{6,F}(s) &= [(1-p) b(s)]^n [d(s)]^2 \\ & \times \left\{ \left[1 + \frac{p b(s)}{1-p}\right]^n - [1 + p b(s)]^n \right\}, \end{aligned}$$

where $\phi(s) \equiv \int_0^\infty e^{-st} d\Phi(t)$,

$$\begin{aligned} & \widetilde{P}_{ij}(s) \equiv \int_0^\infty e^{-st} P_{i,j}(t) dt, (i, j = 0, 1), \\ & q_{3,4}(0) + q_{3,5}(0) = 1, \\ & q_{4,4}(0) + q_{4,5}(0) = 1, \\ & q_{5,6}(0) + q_{5,F}(0) = 1, \\ & q_{6,S}(0) + q_{6,F}(0) = 1. \end{aligned}$$

We derive the mean time $\ell_{2,S}$ until transmission of n packets succeeds. Let LS transform $h_{2,S}(s)$ be the first-passage time distribution $H_{2,S}(t)$ from State 2 to State S. Then, we have

$$h_{2,S}(s) = \frac{\left[q_{2,3}(s)q_{3,5}(s) + \frac{q_{2,3}(s)q_{3,4}(s)q_{4,5}(s)}{1-q_{4,4}(s)}\right] \times q_{5,6}(s)q_{6,S}(s)}{1 - \left[q_{2,3}(s)q_{3,5}(s) + \frac{q_{2,3}(s)q_{3,4}(s)q_{4,5}(s)}{1-q_{4,4}(s)}\right] \times [q_{5,F}(s) + q_{5,6}(s)q_{6,F}(s)]\, g(s)}. \tag{9}$$

Hence, the mean time $\ell_{2,S}(n)$ is given by

$$\ell_{2,S}(n) \equiv \int_0^\infty t dH_{2,S}(t) = \lim_{s\to 0} -\frac{dh_{2,S}(s)}{ds}$$
$$= \frac{a + \frac{1}{w} + \frac{\lambda+\beta}{a_1\beta} + \frac{q}{a_2} + X\{nb(1+p) + d[2-(1-p)^n]\} + \mu}{X(1-p^2)^n} - \mu, \tag{10}$$

where

$$X \equiv \frac{(w+\beta)(a_2+\beta) + \lambda[\beta + (1-q)w]}{(a_2+\lambda+\beta)(w+\lambda+\beta)}.$$

3. Optimal Policy

We discuss an optimal policy which maximizes the transmission of all packets per unit of time until it succeeds. Then, we define throughput $E(n)$, which represents the rate of n packets to their mean transmission times,

$$E(n) \equiv \frac{n}{\ell_{2,S}(n)}. \tag{11}$$

We seek an optimal window size n^* to maximize $E(n)$. When $k = 2$, the mean times are given by

$$\ell_{2,S}(n) = Z(n) - \mu,$$

where

$$Z(n) \equiv \frac{a + \frac{1}{w} + \frac{\lambda+\beta}{a_1\beta} + \frac{q}{a_2} + X\{nb(1+p) + d[2-(1-p)^n]\} + \mu}{X(1-p^2)^n}.$$

We discuss optimal n^* to maximize $E(n)$. The mean time $\ell_{2,S}(n)$ increases strictly with n from $\ell_{2,S}(1)$ to ∞. Then, because

$$\lim_{n\to\infty} \frac{\ell_{2,S}(n)}{n} = \infty,$$

a finite n^* exists.

We put formally that $A(n) \equiv 1/E(n)$ and seek n^* to minimize $A(n)$. From the inequality $A(n+1) - A(n) \geq 0$,

$$nZ(n+1) - (n+1)Z(n) + \mu \geq 0. \tag{12}$$

Denoting the left side of (12) by $L(n)$, we have

$$L(n+1) - L(n) = (n+1)\{[Z(n+2) - Z(n+1)] - [Z(n+1) - Z(n)]\}.$$

Hence, when $Z(n)$ is a convex function, $L(n)$ is strictly increasing in n from $L(1)$ to ∞.

Therefore, we have the following optimal policy:

(i) If $L(1) < 0$ then there exists a finite and unique $n^*(> 1)$ which satisfies (12).

(ii) If $L(1) \geq 0$ then $n^* = 1$.

4. Numerical Examples

We compute numerically the optimal window size n^*. Suppose that the mean time b until transmitting one packet is a unit time. It is assumed that the mean time for occurrence of congestion during which no wireless channels are available is $(1/\lambda)/b = 10, 30$, the mean time that congestion is resolved afterward, allowing wireless channels to become available again is $(1/\beta)/b = 10$, the mean time required for data packets is $a/b = 10$, the mean time required for confirmation of the availability of wireless channel is $(1/a_1)/b = 5$, the probability that the client waits for a fixed period of time randomly is $q = 0.1, 0.5$, the mean time of this waiting time is $(1/w)/b = 10, 50$, the mean time required for connection establishment is $(1/a_2)/b = 5$, the mean time for the server to transmit all packets to receive ACK or NAK is $d/b = 2$, the mean time for the server to interrupt n retransmission to restart again is $\mu/b = 30$ and the probability that loss packets occur is $p = 0.05, 0.1$.

Table 1 presents the optimal window size n^* to maximize the throughput, the mean time $\ell_{2,S}(n^*)$ and the throughput $E(n^*)$ when $k = 2$. For example, when $(1/\lambda)/b = 10, (1/\beta)/b = 10, a/b = 10, (1/a_1)/b = 5, (1/a_2)/b = 5, d/b = 2, q = 0.1, p = 0.05, (1/w)/b = 10$, the optimal number of packets is $n^* = 136$, the mean time is $\ell_{2,S}(n^*) = 305.5$ and the throughput is $E(n^*) = 0.4452$. This indicates that n^* decrease with p and $(1/\lambda)/b$ and increase with $(1/w)/b$ and q. But $E(n^*)$ increase with $(1/\lambda)/b$ and decrease with $(1/w)/b$ and q conversely.

5. Conclusions

We have considered a stochastic model that applies CSMA/CA (Carrier Sense Multiple Access with Collision Avoidance). That is, in order to avoid collisions, a client wait with a probability such that each terminal senses the availability of the wireless channel prior to frame transmission. After waiting, the server transmits data packets $n(n = 1, 2, \cdots)$ corresponding to a

Table 1: Optimal window size n^* to maximize $E(n)$ when $k = 2, (1/\beta)/b = 10, a/b = 10, (1/a_1)/b = 5, (1/a_2)/b = 5, d/b = 2$.

q	p	$(1/\lambda)/b$	$(1/w)/b$	n^*	$\ell_{2S}(n^*)$	$E(n^*)$
0.1	0.05	10	10	136	305.5	0.4452
			50	184	575.8	0.3195
		30	10	116	227.8	0.5092
			50	156	401.7	0.3883
	0.1	10	10	53	232.7	0.2278
			50	67	485.2	0.1381
		30	10	47	166.8	0.2816
			50	60	325.2	0.1844
0.5	0.05	10	10	142	331.1	0.4288
			50	186	593.2	0.3136
		30	10	119	239.1	0.4978
			50	158	412.1	0.3834
	0.1	10	10	55	255.9	0.2149
			50	68	506.2	0.1343
		30	10	48	176.7	0.2717
			50	60	331.5	0.1810

specified window size to a client. We have derived the mean time until packet transmissions succeed, and discussed an optimal policy to maximize the amount of packets per unit of time until the transmission succeeds. From numerical examples, we have shown that the optimal window size decrease with the probability that loss packets occur and the time for occurrence of congestion during which no wireless channels, and increase with the probability that the client waits for a fixed period of time and waiting time. But the optimal throughput decrease with the probability that the client waits for a fixed period of time and waiting time conversely.

Acknowledgments

This research received funding from the Joint Research Project of the Institute of Managerial Research, Aichi University.

References

[1] S. Shioda, "Queueing Models for the Analysis of Wireless LANs with Consideration on Conflicts between Terminals", *The Institute of Electronics, Information and Communication Engineers*, Vol.100, No. 4, pp. 259-265, 2017.

[2] R. Umezawa and T. Yoshihiro, "A Study on Improving the Efficiency of CSMA/CA by Detecting Control Frames Using RSSI", *IPSJ Technical Report*, Vol.2019-MBL-93, No.1 / Vol.2019-ITS-79, No.1, pp. 1-4, 2019.

[3] M. Kimura, M. Imaizumi and T. Nakagawa, "Optimal Policy of Window Flow Control Based on Packet Transmission Interval with Explicit Congestion Notification", *International Journal of Reliability, Quality and Safety Engineering*, Vol.26, No. 5, pp.1950024-1 - 1950024-14, (14pages), DOI:10.1142/S0218539319500244, May, 2019.

[4] W. R. Stevens,"TCP/IP illustrated, volume 1:The protocols," Addison-Wesley, Reading, Massachusetts, 1994.

[5] Mathis M., Mahdavi J., Floyd S., Romanow A., TCP Selective Acknowledgements Options, RFC2018, October 1996.

[6] S. Osaki, *Applied Stochastic System Modeling*, Springer-Verlag, Berlin, (1992).

[7] K. Yasui, T. Nakagawa and H. Sandoh, Reliability models in data communication systems, *Stochastic Models in Reliability and Maintenance* (edited by S.Osaki), pp.281-301, Springer-Verlag, Berlin(2002).

[8] T. Nakagawa, *Stochastic Processes with Applications to Reliability Theory*, Springer, London, 2011.

Reliability Analysis of a System Considering Loss Costs for Different Types of Server Attacks

Mitsuhiro Imaizumi[1], Mitsutaka Kimura[2]

[1] Aichi Gakusen University, Faculty of Home Economics, 28 Kamikawanari, Hegoshi-cho, Okazaki 444-8520, Japan.

[2] Aichi University, Faculty of Business Administration, 4-60-6 Hiraike-cho, Nakamura-ku, Nagoya, 453-8777, Japan.

Key Words: Security, WAF, IDS, Defense-in-depth, Expected Cost

Abstract-

In recent years, cyber attacks against server systems have become increasingly diverse and sophisticated. It is difficult to prevent these attacks with a single measure alone, and it is effective to combine multiple security measures. In redundant defense, attacks are monitored using tools such as Firewalls and IDS. Since servers are typically exposed to various types of attacks,it is more realistic to model these attacks using multiple probability distributions. This paper formulates three stochastic models for a server system with multiple security tools to monitor multiple types of attacks which are represented by multiple probability distributions. In this model, we consider loss costs that depend on the type of attack. The total expected costs until cyber attacks are detected are derived and optimal policies which minimize them are discussed.

1 Introduction

In recent years, cyber attacks against server systems have become increasingly diverse and sophisticated, with a tendency to combine various attack methods. Once a server is attacked, it may suffer serious damage, such as loss of trust due to information leakage, financial loss due to service disruption, and destruction of data. It is difficult to prevent these attacks with a single measure alone, and it is effective to combine multiple security measures. Defense-in-depth is a security strategy in which multiple security measures are implemented across different layers. It involves the deployment of controls at three key levels: measures to prevent intrusion from the outside, measures to contain the spread of infection within the system, and measures to prevent data leakage to the outside. In addition, redundant defense is an effective approach to enhancing protection at critical points by deploying multiple security measures at the same layer.

In redundant defense, attacks are monitored by security tools such as Firewalls and IDS (Intrusion Detection System)[1, 2, 3]. Firewalls include static packet filtering firewalls, which detect attacks based on packet header information such as source address and port number, and stateful packet inspection firewalls, which monitor session states and communication context to detect attacks. On the other hand, IDS has been widely used to detect anomalous communications or signs of attacks that cannot be identified by the aforementioned firewalls. It can detect attacks that target OS vulnerabilities including buffer overflow. Furthermore, WAF (Web application Firewall)[4] has been used specifically to detect attacks targeting web applications. It monitors the HTTP traffic between a web application and the Internet. It is particularly effective against application-layer attacks such as SQL injection.

We have proposed some stochastic models of a system subject to cyber attacks by using the maintenance theory [5, 6, 7, 8]. In [9], we have proposed a random inspection policy for a system with cyber attack. In [10], we have proposed a model with a non-linear parameter, assuming that the loss cost between attack occurrence and its detection increases non-linearly with T. In [11], we have proposed a model that takes false detection of attacks into account. In these models, it was assumed that the time until an attack occurs is represented by a single probability distribution. Since servers are typically exposed to various types of attacks, including DoS (Denial of Service), buffer overflows, and SQL injection, it is more realistic to model these attacks using multiple probability distributions. In [12], we have proposed a model in which various types of attacks on a server system are represented by multiple probability distributions. In that model, the loss cost was assumed to be the same regardless of the type of attack.

This paper formulates three stochastic models for a server system which has the function of IDS and WAF. Attacks due to unauthorized access are detected by IDS, and attacks due to web application vulnerabilities are detected by WAF. In this paper, we extend the model presented in [12], and formulate new models under the assumption that loss costs are incurred depending on the type of attack. The expected costs until attacks are detected are derived and optimal policies which minimize them are discussed. Finally, numerical examples are given.

2 Model 1

We pay attention to only a server connected with the Internet. The server has the function of IDS and WAF. In this model, we consider two types of attacks: one due to unauthorized access (Attack 1), and the other due to web application vulnerabilities (Attack 2). Since these attacks typically follow different probability distributions, we distinguish between Attack 1 and Attack 2.

(1) After the server begins to operate, Attack 1 occurs according to a general distribution $F(t)$ with finite mean $1/\lambda$, and Attacks 2 occurs according to a general distribution $G(t)$ with finite mean $1/\mu$. Attack 1 and Attack 2 occur independently.

(2) Cyber attacks are checked by IDS and WAF at periodic times $kT(k = 1, 2, \cdots)$. T represents the checking interval.

(3) Attack 1 is detected with probability 1 by the IDS. Similarly, Attack 2 is detected with probability 1 by WAF.

Let c_1 be the cost of one check, and c_2 be the cost per unit of time elapsed time between Attack 1 and its detection, and c_3 be the cost per unit of time elapsed time between Attack 2 and its detection. In Model 1, it is assumed that the loss cost incurred depends on the type of the first attack that occurs. Then, the expected cost $C_1(T)$ until cyber attacks are detected is

$$\begin{aligned} &C_1(T) \\ &= \sum_{k=0}^{\infty} \int_{kT}^{(k+1)T} \{(k+1)c_1 + c_2[(k+1)T - t]\}\overline{G}(t)dF(t) \\ &+ \sum_{k=0}^{\infty} \int_{kT}^{(k+1)T} \{(k+1)c_1 + c_3[(k+1)T - t]\}\overline{F}(t)dG(t). \end{aligned} \quad (1)$$

In particular, when $F(t) = 1 - e^{-\lambda t}$ and $G(t) = 1 - e^{-\mu t}$, the expected cost $C_1(T)$ becomes

$$\begin{aligned} C_1(T) &= \frac{c_1 + \left(c_2\frac{\lambda}{\lambda+\mu} + c_3\frac{\mu}{\lambda+\mu}\right)T}{1 - e^{-(\lambda+\mu)T}} \\ &\quad - \left(c_2\frac{\lambda}{\lambda+\mu} + c_3\frac{\mu}{\lambda+\mu}\right)\frac{1}{\lambda+\mu}. \end{aligned} \quad (2)$$

We seek an optimal time T_1^* which minimizes $C_1(T)$. Differentiating $C_1(T)$ with respect to T and setting it equal to zero,

$$e^{(\lambda+\mu)T} - 1 - (\lambda+\mu)T = \frac{c_1(\lambda+\mu)^2}{c_2\lambda + c_3\mu}, \quad (3)$$

whose left-hand side increases strictly with T from 0 to ∞. Thus, there exists a finite $T_1^*(0 < T_1^* < \infty)$ which satisfies (3).

3 Model 2

The loss cost increases non-linearly after a cyber attack, as the damage often escalates over time. For example, the longer it takes to detect and respond to an attack, the more data may be stolen, corrupted, or leaked. We modify Model 1 considering non-linear parameter: Let c_1 be the cost of one check, and the cost between Attack 1 and its detection increases with T non-linearly, i.e., $c_2 e^{\alpha[(k+1)T-t]}$, and the cost between Attack 2 and its detection increases with T non-linearly, i.e., $c_3 e^{\alpha[(k+1)T-t]}$. Then, the expected cost $C_2(T)$ until cyber attacks are detected is

$$\begin{aligned}
&C_2(T)\\
&=\sum_{k=0}^{\infty}\int_{kT}^{(k+1)T}\{(k+1)c_1+c_2e^{\alpha[(k+1)T-t]}\}\overline{G}(t)dF(t)\\
&+\sum_{k=0}^{\infty}\int_{kT}^{(k+1)T}\{(k+1)c_1+c_3e^{\alpha[(k+1)T-t]}\}\overline{F}(t)dG(t).
\end{aligned} \tag{4}$$

In particular, when $F(t)=1-e^{-\lambda t}$ and $G(t)=1-e^{-\mu t}$, the expect cost in (4) becomes

$$\begin{aligned}
C_2(T) &= \frac{c_1}{1-e^{-(\lambda+\mu)T}}\\
&+\frac{c_2\lambda+c_3\mu}{\lambda+\mu+\alpha}\frac{e^{\alpha T}-e^{-(\lambda+\mu)T}}{1-e^{-(\lambda+\mu)T}}.
\end{aligned} \tag{5}$$

We seek an optimal time T_2^* which minimizes $C_2(T)$. Differentiating $C_2(T)$ with respect to T and setting it equal to zero, we have

$$\begin{aligned}
&e^{\alpha T}\left[\frac{\alpha}{\lambda+\mu+\alpha}e^{(\lambda+\mu)T}-1\right]+\frac{\lambda+\mu}{\lambda+\mu+\alpha}\\
&=\frac{c_1(\lambda+\mu)}{c_2\lambda+c_3\mu},
\end{aligned} \tag{6}$$

whose left-hand side increases strictly with T from 0 to ∞. Thus, there exists a finite $T_2^*(0<T_2^*<\infty)$ which satisfies (6).

4 Model 3

We modify Model 1 to take into account not only the loss cost incurred by the first attack but also that incurred by the second attack, in order to better reflect the loss costs associated with each type of attack.

The probability that Attack 1 occurs during the interval from kT to $(k+1)T$ $(k=0,1,2,\cdots)$, and then Attack 2 occurs before $(k+1)T$ is

$$\sum_{k=0}^{\infty}\int_{kT}^{(k+1)T}\int_{t}^{(k+1)T}dG(x)dF(t).$$

The probability that Attack 1 occurs during the interval from kT to $(k+1)T$ $(k=0,1,2,\cdots)$, and then Attack 2 dose not occur before $(k+1)T$ is

$$\sum_{k=0}^{\infty}\int_{kT}^{(k+1)T}\overline{G}[(k+1)T]dF(t).$$

The probability that Attack 2 occurs during the interval from kT to $(k+1)T$ $(k=0,1,2,\cdots)$, and then Attack 1 occurs before $(k+1)T$ is

$$\sum_{k=0}^{\infty}\int_{kT}^{(k+1)T}\int_{t}^{(k+1)T}dF(x)dG(t).$$

The probability that Attack 2 occurs during the interval from kT to $(k+1)T$ $(k=0,1,2,\cdots)$, and then Attack 1 does not occur before $(k+1)T$ is

$$\sum_{k=0}^{\infty}\int_{kT}^{(k+1)T}\overline{F}[(k+1)T]dG(t).$$

Let c_1 be the cost of one check, and c_2 be the cost per unit of time elapsed time between Attack 1 and its detection, and c_3 be the cost per unit of time elapsed time between Attack 2 and its detection. Then, the expected cost $C_3(T)$ until cyber attacks are detected is

$$\begin{aligned}
&C_3(T)\\
&=\sum_{k=0}^{\infty}\int_{kT}^{(k+1)T}\int_{t}^{(k+1)T}\{(k+1)c_1+c_2[(k+1)T-t]\\
&+c_3[(k+1)T-x]\}dG(x)dF(t)\\
&+\sum_{k=0}^{\infty}\int_{kT}^{(k+1)T}\{(k+1)c_1\\
&+c_2[(k+1)T-t]\}\overline{G}[(k+1)T]dF(t)\\
&+\sum_{k=0}^{\infty}\int_{kT}^{(k+1)T}\int_{t}^{(k+1)T}\{(k+1)c_1\\
&+c_3[(k+1)T-t]\\
&+c_2[(k+1)T-x]\}dF(x)dG(t)\\
&+\sum_{k=0}^{\infty}\int_{kT}^{(k+1)T}\{(k+1)c_1\\
&+c_3[(k+1)T-t]\}\overline{F}[(k+1)T]dG(t).
\end{aligned} \tag{7}$$

In particular, when $F(t)=1-e^{-\lambda t}$ and $G(t)=1-e^{-\mu t}$, the expect cost in (7) becomes

$$\begin{aligned}
C_3(T) &= \frac{c_1+(c_2+c_3)T}{1-e^{-(\lambda+\mu)T}}\\
&-\frac{\left[\frac{c_2}{\lambda}(1-e^{-\lambda T})+\frac{c_3}{\mu}(1-e^{-\mu T})\right]}{1-e^{-(\lambda+\mu)T}}.
\end{aligned} \tag{8}$$

We seek an optimal time T_3^* which minimizes $C_3(T)$. Differentiating $C_3(T)$ with respect to T and setting it equal to zero,

$$\frac{[c_2(1-e^{-\lambda T})+c_3(1-e^{-\mu T})]\,[e^{(\lambda+\mu)T}-1]}{(c_2+c_3)(\lambda+\mu)} + \frac{c_2}{c_2+c_3}\frac{1-e^{-\lambda T}}{\lambda} + \frac{c_3}{c_2+c_3}\frac{1-e^{-\mu T}}{\mu} - T = \frac{c_1}{c_2+c_3}. \tag{9}$$

Denoting the left-hand side of (9) by $L_3(T)$,

$$L_3(0) = 0, \quad L_3(\infty)=\infty,$$

$$L_3'(T) = \left(1-\frac{c_2}{c_2+c_3}\frac{\mu}{\lambda+\mu}e^{-\lambda T} - \frac{c_3}{c_2+c_3}\frac{\lambda}{\lambda+\mu}e^{-\mu T}\right)[e^{(\lambda+\mu)T}-1] > 0.$$

$L_3(T)$ is strictly increasing in T from 0 to ∞. Thus, there exists a finite optimal $T_3^*(0 < T_3^* < \infty)$ which satisfies (9).

5 Numerical examples

We give optimal T_1^*, T_2^* and T_3^* numerically which minimize the expected costs $C_1(T)$, $C_2(T)$ and $C_3(T)$. It is assumed that the mean time to Attack 1 is $1/\lambda = 20 \sim 80$, the mean time to Attack 2 is $1/\mu = 100$, the cost of the periodic check is $c_1 = 10 \sim 50$, the cost per unit of time for the time elapsed between Attack 1 and its detection is $c_2 = 1$ and the cost per unit of time for the time elapsed between Attack 2 and its detection is $c_3 = 1 \sim 3$. In general, attacks on the network layer occur more frequently than those on the application layer. Attack 1, for example, can be executed using automated tools. Therefore, we assume that $1/\lambda$ is smaller than $1/\mu$.

Table 1 presents the optimal T_1^* which minimizes the expected cost $C_1(T)$. For example, when $1/\lambda = 60$, $c_1 = 30$ and $c_3 = 2$, the optimal $T_1^* = 34$. This indicates that T_1^* decreases with c_3, however, increases with $1/\lambda$ and c_1. When $1/\lambda$ is small, T_1^* is small. In this case, we should perform the check at short intervals.

Table 2 presents the optimal T_2^* which minimizes the expected cost $C_2(T)$ when $c_1 = 10$. This indicates that T_2^* decreases with c_3 and α, however, increases with $1/\lambda$. When α is large, T_2^* is small.

Table 3 presents the optimal T_3^* which minimizes the expected cost $C_3(T)$. This indicates that T_3^* decreases with c_3, however, increases with $1/\lambda$ and c_1. T_3^* is smaller than T_1^*. In Model 3, we take into account the loss costs of two types of attacks. therefore, the loss costs until attack are detected becomes larger than that of Model 1. Thus, it is better to perform checks at short intervals as early as possible in Model 3.

Table 1: Optimal T_1^* to minimize $C_1(T)$ when $c_2 = 1$ and $1/\mu = 100$.

c_3	$1/\lambda$	c_1				
		10	20	30	40	50
1	20	15	21	24	27	29
	40	21	28	33	37	41
	60	24	33	39	44	48
	80	27	36	43	49	53
2	20	14	19	23	25	28
	40	19	25	30	34	37
	60	21	29	34	39	42
	80	23	31	37	42	46
3	20	14	18	22	24	26
	40	17	23	28	31	34
	60	19	26	31	35	38
	80	20	28	33	37	41

Table 2: Optimal T_2^* to minimize $C_2(T)$ when $c_1 = 10$ and $c_2 = 1$.

c_3	$1/\lambda$	α				
		0.01	0.02	0.03	0.04	0.05
1	20	62	48	40	35	31
	40	65	65	53	45	39
	60	103	75	60	50	44
	80	114	81	64	54	46
2	20	60	47	39	34	30
	40	83	61	50	42	37
	60	96	69	55	46	40
	80	104	74	58	49	42

6 Conclusions

We have investigated stochastic models for a server system with multiple security tools to check and monitor multi types of attacks. We have assumed that cyber attacks due to unauthorized access are detected by IDS, and cyber attacks due to web application vulnerabilities are detected by WAF. We have derived the expected costs by considering loss costs for different

Table 3: Optimal T_3^* to minimize $C_3(T)$ when $c_2 = 1$ and $1/\mu$=100.

c_3	$1/\lambda$	c_1				
		10	20	30	40	50
	20	15	19	22	25	27
1	40	20	26	30	34	37
	60	23	30	36	40	43
	80	25	33	39	44	48
	20	13	18	21	23	25
2	40	17	23	27	30	33
	60	20	26	31	35	38
	80	21	29	34	38	41
	20	13	17	19	22	23
3	40	16	21	25	28	30
	60	18	24	28	32	34
	80	19	25	30	34	37

types of attacks. Further, we have discussed the optimal policies which minimize them.

From the numerical examples, we have shown the optimal checking time to minimize the expected cost. In numerical examples, we have shown that optimal checking time increases with the mean time to cyber attack occurrence and the cost of the periodic check, however, it decreases with the cost per unit of time for the time elapsed between attack occurrence and its detection.

It would be very important to evaluate and improve the reliability of a server system with multiple types of attacks. It is essential to assess and improve the reliability of server systems exposed to various types of attacks. The results derived in this paper would be applied in practical fields by making some suitable modification and extensions. Further studies for such subject would be expected.

ACKNOWLEDGMENT

This research received funding from the Joint Research Project of the Institute of Managerial Research, Aichi University.

References

[1] Information Security Handbook, Ohmsha, pp.354 2004.

[2] K. Ohta and G. Mansfield, "Illegal Access Detection on the Internet -Present status and future directions-", *Trans. IEICE of Japan*, Vol.J83-B, No.9, pp.1209-1216, 2000.

[3] T. Miyamoto, A. Kojima, M. Izumi and K. Fukunaga, "Network Traffic Anomaly Detection Using SVM", *Trans. IEICE of Japan*, Vol.J87-B, No.4, pp.593-598, 2004.

[4] Information technology Promotion Agency, Japan, "How to Secure Your Website 5th Edition", https://www.ipa.go.jp/ security/vuln/ websecurity/ug65p900000196e2-att/ 000017318.pdf, 2011.

[5] R. E. Balow and F. Proschan, Mathematical theory of reliability, JohnWiley & Sons, New York, 1965.

[6] T. Nakagawa, Maintenance Theory of Reliability, Springer, London, 2005.

[7] T. Nakagawa, Random Maintenance Policies, Springer, London, 2014.

[8] K. Ito and T. Nakagawa, Optimal Inspection models with Their Applications, Springer-Verlag, London, 2023.

[9] M. Imaizumi and M. Kimura, "Probabilistic Analysis of a System with Illegal Access", Proceedings of the 2011 International Conference on Advanced Software Engineering and Its Applications, pp.370-375, 2011.

[10] M. Imaizumi and M. Kimura, "Optimal Monitoring Policy for a System with Network", Advanced reliability and maintenance modeling VI, pp.168-175, 2014.

[11] M. Imaizumi and M. Kimura, "Reliability Evaluation of a Server System Considering Signature Update", International Journal of Reliability, Quality and Safety Engineering, Vol.28, No.1, pp.1-15(2150003).

[12] M. Imaizumi and M. Kimura, "Optimal Monitoring Policy for a Server System with Multiple Types of Attacks", Proceedings of 29th ISSAT International Conference on Reliability and Quality in Design, pp.69-73, 2024.

Investigation of Residual Stress and Fatigue Reliability Enhancement in Polyimide-Coated Lead Conductor Wires

Haitao Zhang, Bernard Li, Mingxiao Jiang

Medtronic, Plc., 7000 Central Ave NE, Minneapolis, MN 55432, USA

Keywords: Implantable Medical Devices, Fatigue Reliability, Thermal Residual Stress, P-S-N (probabilistic stress-life), Accelerated Life Testing (ALT)

Abstract - In the field of Implantable Electric Stimulation, PTFE and ETFE coatings have conventionally been employed as insulation materials for metal wires used in lead conductor coils. Recently, due to its superior insulation performance, polyimide coating starts to find wide application as insulation materials for lead conductors. It was observed that coated wire has a higher fatigue performance than bare wire. It is expected that residual stress may be present following the coating process. This study aims to develop an exact analytical thermal elastic solution to assess the residual stress of the metal wire due to the polyimide coating. The analytical result indicates that a compression residual stress is on the wire which may enhance the fatigue life of the wire.

1. Introduction

Implantable Electric Stimulation has found wide application of therapies, such as Spinal cord stimulation, Deep brain stimulation (DBS) device, Sacral nerve stimulation (SNS), pacemakers and defibrillators. Implantable Electric Stimulation is commonly composed of two primary parts: an implantable electric stimulator and leads. Implantable electric stimulator generates electric pulse/signal and the electric pulse/signal is sent to the physiological target through a lead.

Leads are integral components of implantable electric stimulation systems, serving as the conduit for electrical pulses from the stimulator to the target physiological site. A typical lead consists of a conductor, insulation, and electrodes. The conductor, often made from biocompatible metals like Pt-20Ir, MP35. The electrodes interface directly with the physiological target, delivering electrical impulses required for therapeutic effects. The conductor is often designed in either a coil or cable configuration to provide flexibility and fatigue resistance, accommodating the dynamic movements of the body. In coil-shaped conductors, the filars—thin wires that form the coil—are individually coated with an insulating polymer, such as ETFE (ethylene tetrafluoroethylene) or PTFE (polytetrafluoroethylene), to prevent electrical shorting between filars and enhance durability.

Lead fatigue performance is critical in ensuring the long-term reliability and safety of implantable electric stimulation devices. Leads are subjected to continuous mechanical stresses from bodily movements, including bending, stretching, and twisting. Poor fatigue performance can lead to conductor failure, such as fractures or insulation breaches, which may compromise the delivery of electrical signals to the target site. Such failures can result in reduced therapeutic efficacy, device malfunction, or the need for surgical intervention to replace the leads. Enhancing the fatigue performance of lead conductors not only improves the durability of the device but also reduces patient risks, extends the lifespan of the implant, and minimizes healthcare costs associated with device failure or replacement.

Traditionally, PTFE and ETFE coatings have been widely applied as lead conductor insulation materials. Spin fatigue testing has not shown noticeable differences in fatigue performance between bare wires and those with these coatings. Recently, polyimide has been introduced as a coating material for lead conductors. Spin fatigue testing indicates that polyimide coated metal conductor wires exhibit significant improvement in fatigue life compared to bare metal wires.

In this paper, an analytical mechanics model was developed based on elasticity theory to analyze the residual stress on the coated metal wire due to coating process. The effect of residual stress on the fatigue life of the wires was discussed. Additionally, a reliability modelling is constructed to understand the difference of coated vs. non-coated configuration in terms of fatigue reliability.

2. Fatigue Testing and P-S-N (probabilistic stress-life) Curve

Bare cold drawn Pt-20Ir (Pt based alloy with 80% Pt and 20% Ir) wire and PI coated device cold drawn Pt-20Ir wire were studied. The bare wire diameter is 0.102 mm and PFTE coating thickness is 0.025mm. The wires were fatigue tested in a rotary beam tester (Positool Technologies, model 100, Brunswick OH) [1] with a testing frequency of 60Hz.

Given the material level testing data, P-S-N curves for material can be constructed using ALT modeling. In practice, the P-S-N curves are only of point estimates based on available testing results. Due to limit testing samples, reliability model should be constructed to further obtain results under various confidence levels (CL), since the reliability requirement is that the product has to meet Bx life at certain CL, where Bx indicates the lifetime that x% product fail.

P-S-N curves for material can be constructed using ALT modeling as the followings, based on the Log-location-scale regression model approach [2], the probability of failure time of such a structure, T, can be described by

$$\Pr(T \leq t) = F(t, S) = \Phi\left[\frac{t' - \mu_{t'}(S)}{\sigma}\right] \quad (1)$$

where $t' = \ln(t)$, in which t is the testing duration in cycle, S is the stress/strain level used in the testing.

The log-location parameter under stress level S, is a function of stresses:

$$\mu_{t'}(S) = \beta_0 + \beta_1 \ln(S) \quad (2)$$

Where β_0, β_1 are unknown parameters to be determined through life testing data and physics-of-failure models. So, in total, three parameters β_0, β_1 and σ need to be determined from testing data. The scale parameter σ does not depend on the stress levels.

Some distributions for log-location-scale model are Lognormal distribution, Loglogistic distribution, and Weibull distribution. In this paper, the Weibull distribution is used:

$$\Phi(u) = \Phi_{sev}(u) = 1 - \exp[-\exp(u)] \quad (3)$$

with $\sigma = \frac{1}{\beta}$ and $\mu = \ln(\eta)$. β and η are the shape and scale parameters of Weibull distribution.

After point estimates of parameters ($\hat{\beta}_0, \hat{\beta}_1, \hat{\sigma}$) are obtained, the relationship between Bx life and stress levels can be obtained as:

$$x\% = \Phi\left[\frac{\ln(\hat{B}x) - \hat{\beta}_0 - \hat{\beta}_1 \ln(S_i)}{\hat{\sigma}}\right] \quad (4)$$

Such a method was used in an early study by the authors for un-coated Pt-20Ir fatigue reliability [3].

3. Coating Process and Coating Induced Residual Stress

During coating process, Pt-20Ir wire goes from room temperature 25°C through a 400°C furnace to be coated with liquid polyimide for about 2-4 minutes, then comes out from the furnace to room temperature and get a coating about 0.0005 inch (0.0127 mm). Figure 1 shows the thermal expansion of the wire and coating during coating process.

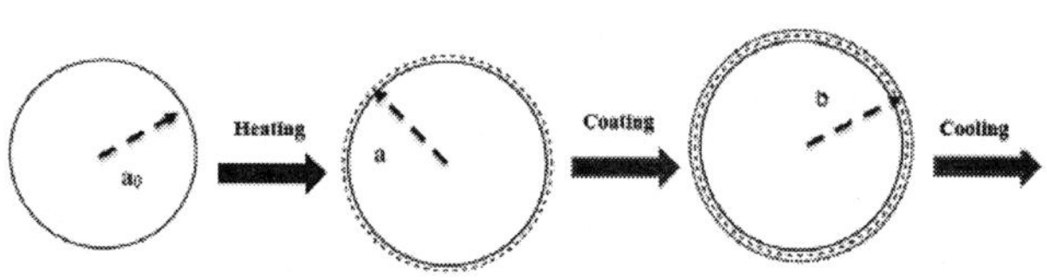

Figure 1 – Schematic description of coating process

The coating process can be divided into two mechanics problem as shown in Figures 2 (a), for bare wire thermal expansion, and 2(b) for coating process and cooling.

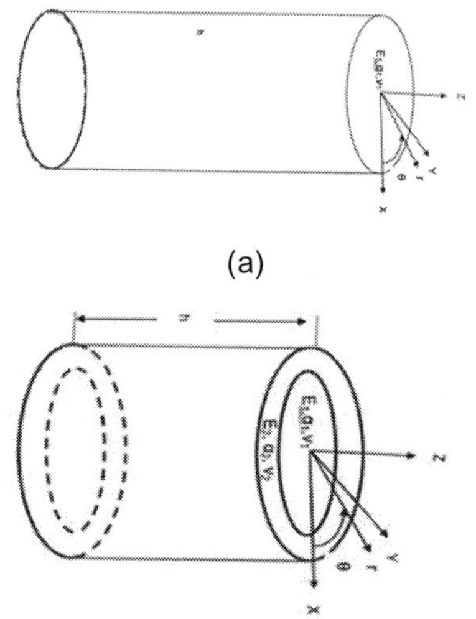

(a)

(b)

Figure 2 – Schematic description of mechanics problem

The equilibrium equations in each material is

$$\frac{d\sigma_{\gamma i}}{d\gamma} + \frac{1}{\gamma}(\sigma_{\gamma i} - \sigma_{\theta i}) = 0 \quad (5)$$

where i denotes the material, σ_{ri} is radial stress, $\sigma_{\theta i}$ is tangential stress, and σ_{zi} is axial stress (longitudinal stress).

The strain-displacement relations are:

$$\varepsilon_{\gamma i} = \frac{du_i}{d\gamma} \text{ and } \varepsilon_{\theta i} = \frac{u_i}{\gamma} \quad (6)$$

Since the wire is very long during coating process, the problem can be simplified as a plan strain problem, where $\varepsilon_{zi} = 0$. The stress-strain relations for isotropic linear elastic material from temperature change T can be written as

$$\varepsilon_{ri} = \frac{1}{E_i}[\sigma_{ri} - v_i(\sigma_{\theta i} + \sigma_{zi})] + \alpha_i T \quad (7a)$$

$$\varepsilon_{\theta i} = \frac{1}{E_i}[\sigma_{\theta i} - v_i(\sigma_{ri} + \sigma_{zi})] + \alpha_i T \quad (7b)$$

$$\varepsilon_{zi} = \frac{1}{E_i}[\sigma_{zi} - v(\sigma_{\theta i} + \sigma_{ri})] + \alpha_i T \quad (7c)$$

where E_i, v_i, and α_i are Young's modulus, Poisson's ratio and linear thermal expansion coefficient in material i, respectively; T is the temperature difference between the room temperature and the coating temperature. During the heating process, the wire is heated to a temperature from room temperature 25°C to 400 °C. The wire diameter is a_0 before expansion and a after the thermal expansion. The boundary conditions are:

$$u_1(r=0)=0 \quad (8a)$$
$$\sigma_{r1}(r=a_0)=0 \quad (8b)$$

During the coating and cooling down process, the wire with coating is cooling down from 400 °C to room temperature 25°C, The boundary conditions are:

$$u_1(r=0)=0 \quad (9a)$$
$$u_{r1}(r=a)=u_{r2}(r=a) \quad (9b)$$
$$\sigma_{r1}(r=a)=\sigma_{r2}(r=a) \quad (9c)$$
$$\sigma_{r2}(r=b)=0 \quad (9d)$$

After solving the partial differential equation (PDE), using superposition principle, the residual stress in longitudinal direction is:

$$\sigma_z=\sigma_{z1}+\sigma_{z2}=-E_1\alpha_1 T+\frac{E_1}{1-v_1}\left(2v_1\frac{E_{c1}\frac{\alpha_1 T}{2}a^2+E_{c2}\frac{1}{2}\left(\frac{1+v_2}{1+v_1}\right)\alpha_2 T(b^2-a^2)}{E_{c1}a^2+E_{c2}(b^2-a^2)}-\alpha_1 T\right) \quad (10)$$

where

$$E_{c_1}=E_1+\frac{E_1(1+v_2)-E_2(1+v_1)}{2(1-v_2^2)}\left(\frac{b^2}{a^2}-1\right)$$

and

$$E_{c_2}=E_2\left(\frac{1-v_1^2}{1-v_2^2}\right)$$

Table 1: Material Properties of polyimide and Pt-20Ir

	E(Gpa)	Poisson's ratio	Linear CTE um/m/°C
polyimide	3.7	0.34	21.6
Pt-20Ir[4]	230	0.368	9.50

4. Results

Figure3 and Figure 4 show the p-s-n curves for bare Pt-20Ir and coated Pt-20Ir metal wires, respectively.

The two ALT regression model for bare and coated wires are obtained (JMP 17) as the followings:

$\mu_{t'}(S;bare)=-9.832-19.364\cdot\ln(S)$, for bare wire

$\mu_{t'}(S;coated)=-5.754-19.082\cdot\ln(S)$, for coated wire

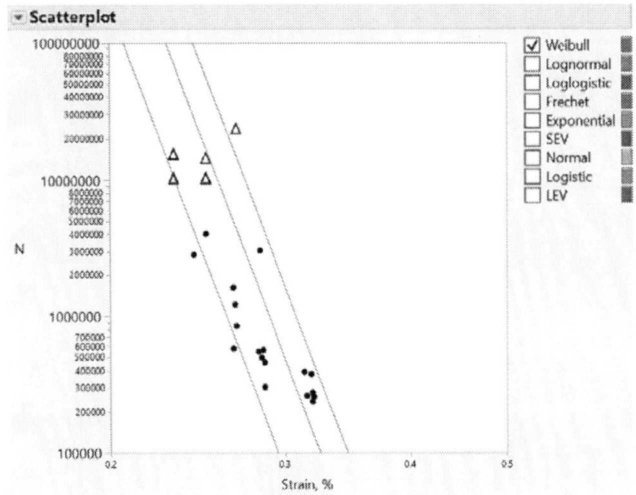

Figure 3: Bare wire raw data and P-S-N curves (B10, B50 and B90 life). Strain is strain amplitude.

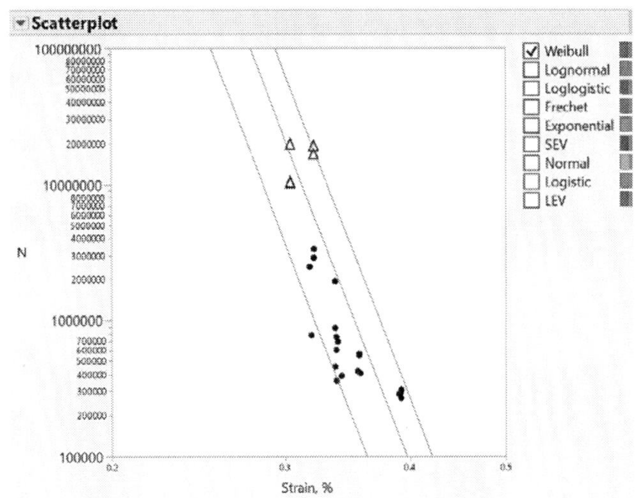

Figure 4: Coated wire raw data and P-S-N curves (B10, B50 and B90 life). Strain is strain amplitude.

The ratio of Weibull characteristic life, indicating fatigue life improvement from bare to coated wire, is defined as:

$$r(S)=\frac{\eta(S;coated)}{\eta(S;bare)} \quad (11)$$

Figure 5 shows that r is a linear function of strain. It can be seen that the coated wire has dramatic (over 40 times) life improvement over bare wire. As the strain increases, the improvement becomes more pronounced. This may be because, at higher strain levels, the compressive residual stress more effectively inhibits the initiation of small fatigue cracks on the outer surface of the metal wire.

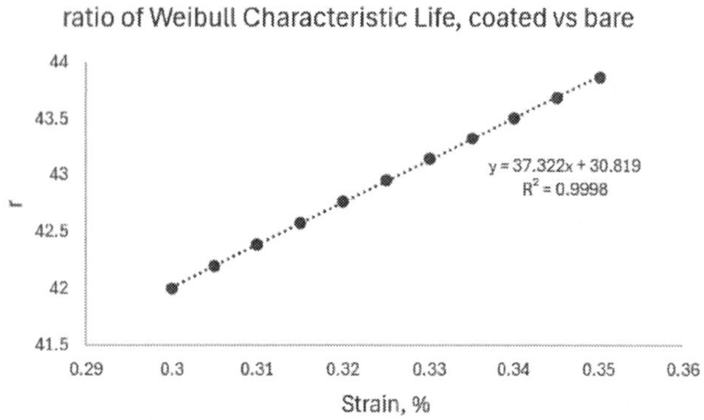

Figure 5: Ratio of Weibull characteristic life as a function of strain

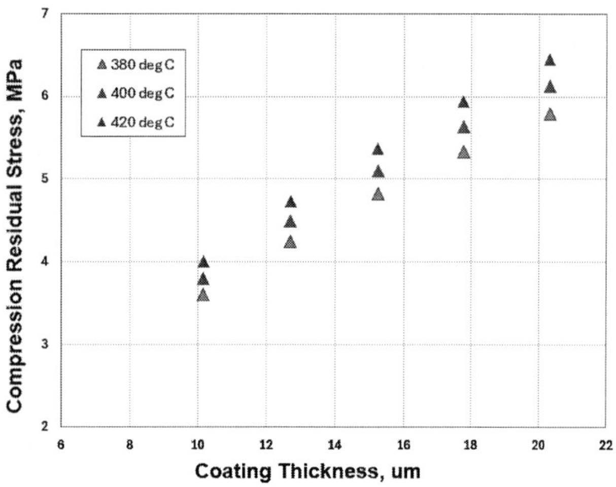

Figure 6 – Compression thermal residual stress as a function of coating thickness and coating temperature (°C)

Figure 6 shows the compression residual stress as a function of coating thickness and coating temperature. The plot shows that an increase in coating thickness results in a corresponding increase in compressive residual stress. Similarly, the coating temperature also affects the compressive residual stress in the same way. This compressive residual stress plays a role in enhancing the fatigue life of the wire.

5. Conclusions

P-S-N curves for coated and uncoated Pt-20Ir wires were obtained with spin fatigue testing. The P-S-N curves show polyimide coated wire has over 40 times improvement in fatigue life compared to bare metal wires. Analytical equation for thermal residual stress due to coating process were derived with elasticity theory. The results show the compression residual stress were induced by the coating process and this increases the wire fatigue durability. It is shown that as coating thickness and temperature increase, so is the compression residual stress, which enhances wire fatigue life and reliability.

6. References

[1] Fatigue Tester Model #100 Manual, Valley Instruments, Brunswick, OH.

[2] Meeker, W. Q., and L. A. Escobar, Statistical Models for Reliability Data. John Wiley & Sons), 1998.

[3] H. Zhang and M. Jiang, An Integrated Approach for Implantable Medical Devices Fatigue Reliability Test, IEEE, PROCEEDINGS Annual Reliability and Maintainability Symposium, 2017

[4] Haitao Zhang & Bernard Li, "Fatigue Behavior of Pt-20%Ir Coils Used as Implanted Electrodes in Medical Devices." Proceedings of the ASME 2013 International Mechanical Engineering Congress and Exposition. Volume 9: Mechanics of Solids, Structures and Fluids. San Diego, California, USA. November 15–21, 2013. V009T10A014. ASME. https://doi.org/10.1115/IMECE2013-63779

Extended Maintenance Policies with Working and Stopping Periods

Satoshi MIZUTANI Toshio NAKAGAWA

Department of Business Administration, Aichi Institute of Technology,
1247 Yachigusa, Yakusa-cho, Toyota 470-0392, Japan,

Keywords: Replacement policy, Operating period, Expected benefit, Standard operating time

Abstract - We treat optimal maintenance policy with the operation and stopping period. We suppose that the system consists of one unit. The operating period is given as random variable. When the unit has failed in the operating period, the failed unit is repaired in the stopping period. We suppose that the unit might has only one failure, and there is no fatal failure which is should be repaired immediately. The system operates again when the unit has no failure or its failure is repaired. When the repairment has not done by the planned cycle time, loss cost per unit of time is incurred from the time to the repair completion. We consider following two models for the system: (1) Maximizing benefits model: a constant income is generated when an operation has completed. (2) Low bound operating period model: This is a special case of (1), the distribution of operating period has location parameter. We consider the benefit as a difference of the income and the loss cost and derive the expected benefit per unit of time for these models. Further, we discuss analytically the optimal planned cycle time which maximizes the expected benefit per unit of time.

1 Introduction

Many systems which provide several services in its operating time repeat to operate again and again. If its operation has not completed by the planned time, then it might give large influence to the subsequent operation. On the other hand, it would be no problem when the service has complete by the planned time, even if the operating time is vary. Of course, reducing the variance should be an object to improve the system. For example, when the unit has failed, it would be necessary to repair it, and so the operation might has not completed by the planned time. Thus, slack time is necessary to increase the completion rate of the operation. On the other hand, the efficiency of the operation would decrease when the slack time is large. Therefore, we should consider trade-off of the slack time. We consider a system with operating period and its failure is repaired in the stopping period. For example, the system such as airplane, space satellite, unmanned vehicle, or service system with severe mission would be difficult to repair its failure at the operating time. The maintenance would be done after the operation.

There have been many researches of maintenance policies in theory [1–3]; In general, it is difficult to do some maintenance during the interval when the unit is operating, and it would be better to do maintenance when the operation completes. The maintenance model that maintaining a unit after it completes some works of which the times are random [4]. Replacement times between two successive failed units were studied for a system which replaced only at random times [5]. System with random and age replacement were discussed in which operating unit repeats some works over again [6]. The maintenance model with age and number of jobs completed has been considered [7]. First and last policies for replacement and inspections when the policies are triggered by two factors. [8, 9]. Replacement first and last polices with the termination time of the project [10]. Replacement first and last model with two kinds of failures were were discussed [11]. Replacement policies with delay time due to inspection test were studied [12]. Further, maintenance policies with shortage time and excess time were discussed [4]. Comparing these model and selecting suitable one, that is, Which-is-better problem, are very important because so many models are proposed [13–16]. Most maintenance policy planned to minimizes the expected cost rate. The reason be that most companies have responsibility to minimize the impact of its failure and the loss cost. On the other hand, it is discussed that maximizing the benefit is very important to intensify the incentive to maintain the system [17]. In fact, there are some studies to maximize the benefit [18–21].

We considered some maintenance policies with operating period and resting period [22]. In these models, if some faults in a unit are detected, then the unit is repaired in the resting period. It is no problem when the maintenance completes by the next operation. But if the maintenance does not completes by the next operation, large loss cost per unit of time is incurred from the last time of the resting period and the repair completion. Further, loss cost per unit of time is incurred during the resting period to discuss the optimal resting period interval. We obtained the expected cost rate for theses models and discussed analytically optimal resting periods which minimize the expected cost rates.

We treat optimal maintenance policy with the operation and stopping period. They are extended models for previous ones [22]. We suppose that the system consists of one unit.

The operating period is a random variable and has a general time distribution. When the unit has failed in the operating period, the failed unit is repaired in the stopping period. We suppose that the unit might has only one failure, and there is no fatal failure which is should be repaired immediately. The system operates again when the unit has no failure or its failure is repaired. When the repairment has not done by given *planned cycle time*, loss cost per unit of time is incurred from the time to the completion time of repair.

We consider the following two models for the system: (1) Maximizing benefits model: a constant income is generated when an operation has completed. (2) Low bound operating period model: This is a special case of (1), the distribution of operating period has location parameter. We consider the benefit as a difference of the income and the loss cost and derive the expected benefit per unit of time for these models. Further, we discuss analytically the optimal planned cycle time which maximize the expected benefit per unit of time.

Section 2 shows the assumptions for these models. Section 3 discusses (1) Maximizing benefits model. We derive the expected benefit per unit of time and discusses analytically optimal planned cycle time which maximizes the expected benefit. Section 4 discusses (2) Low bound operating period model, and discusses analytically optimal planned cycle time which maximizes the expected benefit.

2 Assumptions

We make the following assumptions for the models:

(i) The system consists of one unit, and starts its operation at time 0. When the unit has not failed or the failed unit is repaired, it is nothing to do in the stopping period, and it operates again at planned cycle time T (> 0). When the unit has failed, it is repaired in the stopping period. If the failed unit is repaired before time T, the system operates again at time T. We refer to an interval from starting an operation to the next operation as one cycle. When a new cycle starts again, the system becomes as good as new, and only one failure might occur in the cycle.

(ii) Let X be a random variable that denotes the failure time of the unit with a general distribution $F(t) \equiv \Pr\{X \leq t\}$, finite mean $\mu \equiv \int_0^\infty \overline{F}(t)\mathrm{d}t$, and a density function $f(t) \equiv \mathrm{d}F(t)/\mathrm{d}t$, where $\Phi(t) \equiv 1 - \Phi(t)$ for any function $\Phi(t)$. The failure rate $h(t) \equiv f(t)/\overline{F}(t)$ has IFR (Increasing Failure Rate).

(iii) Let Y be a random variable that denotes the repair time of the failed unit with a general distribution $G(t) \equiv \Pr\{Y \leq t\}$, finite mean $\gamma \equiv \int_0^\infty \overline{G}(t)\mathrm{d}t$, and a density function $g(t) \equiv \mathrm{d}G(t)/\mathrm{d}t$.

(iv) Let U be a random variable that denotes the operation time of the unit with a general distribution $W(t) \equiv \Pr\{U \leq t\}$, finite mean $\beta \equiv \int_0^\infty \overline{W}(t)\mathrm{d}t$, and a density function $w(t) \equiv \mathrm{d}W(t)/\mathrm{d}t$.

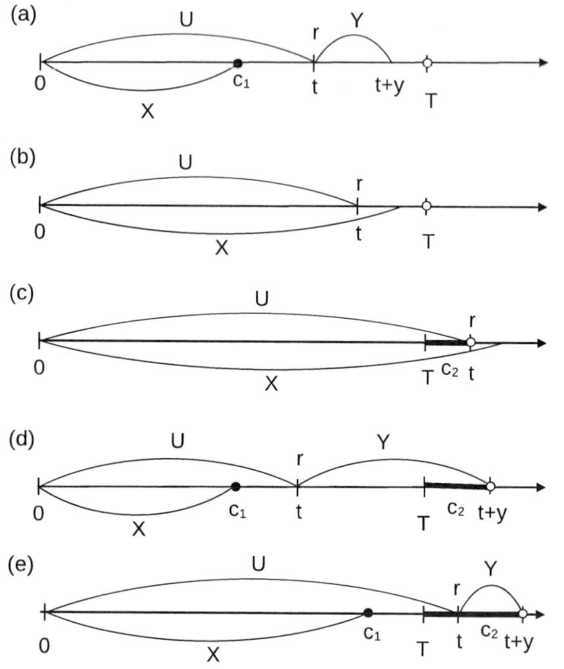

Figure 1: Process of operating and stopping periods.

(v) Let c_1 be the failure cost, and c_2 be the loss cost per unit of time from T to the repair completion. Let r (> 0) be the income generated at the completion of system operation.

3 Maximizing Benefits Model

We consider the following model maximizing the expected benefits per unit of time in Fig. 1.

(a) The probability that the unit has failed in operating period and the failure is repaired before time T is

$$\int_0^T \left[\int_0^{T-t} \mathrm{d}G(y)\mathrm{d}y\right] F(t)\mathrm{d}W(t) = \int_0^T G(T-t)F(t)\mathrm{d}W(t). \tag{1}$$

(b) The probability that the the operating period is completed before time T and unit failure is

$$\int_0^T \overline{F}(t)\mathrm{d}W(t). \tag{2}$$

(c) The probability that the operation is completed after time T before unit failure is

$$\int_T^\infty \overline{F}(t)\mathrm{d}W(t). \tag{3}$$

(d) The probability that the operation is completed before time T and after unit failure, and its is repaired after time T is

$$\int_0^T \left[\int_{T-t}^\infty \mathrm{d}G(y)\right] F(t)\mathrm{d}W(t) = \int_0^T \overline{G}(T-t)F(t)\mathrm{d}W(t). \tag{4}$$

(e) The probability that the operation is completed after time T and unit failure is

$$\int_T^\infty \left[\int_0^\infty \mathrm{d}G(y)\right] F(t)\mathrm{d}W(t) = \int_T^\infty F(t)\mathrm{d}W(t). \tag{5}$$

Clearly, (1) + (2) + (3) + (4) + (5) = 1.

Furthermore, the probability that the unit has no failure before the completion of operation is

$$\int_0^\infty F(t)\mathrm{d}W(t). \tag{6}$$

Then, the mean time from time T to the completion of repir is

$$\begin{aligned}&\int_T^\infty \overline{W}(t)\mathrm{d}t + \gamma\int_T^\infty F(t)\mathrm{d}W(t) \\ &+ \int_0^T \left[\int_{T-t}^\infty \overline{G}(y)\mathrm{d}y\right] F(t)\mathrm{d}W(t) \\ &= \int_T^\infty \overline{W}(t)\mathrm{d}t + \gamma\int_0^\infty F(t)\mathrm{d}W(t) \\ &- \int_0^T \left[\int_0^{T-t} \overline{G}(y)\mathrm{d}y\right] F(t)\mathrm{d}W(t).\end{aligned} \tag{7}$$

Thus, the expected benefit of one cycle is,

$$\begin{aligned}&\text{benefit} = \text{income} - \text{maintenance cost} \\ &= r - \left[c_1 + c_2\gamma\int_0^\infty F(t)\mathrm{d}W(t)\right] \\ &+ c_2\left\{\int_0^T \left[\int_0^{T-t} \overline{G}(y)\mathrm{d}y\right] F(t)\mathrm{d}W(t) - \int_T^\infty \overline{W}(t)\mathrm{d}t\right\},\end{aligned} \tag{8}$$

and the mean time of one cycle is

$$\begin{aligned}&T + \int_T^\infty \overline{W}(t)\mathrm{d}t + \gamma\int_T^\infty F(t)\mathrm{d}W(t) \\ &+ \int_0^T \left[\int_{T-t}^\infty \overline{G}(y)\mathrm{d}y\right] F(t)\mathrm{d}W(t) \\ &= T + \int_T^\infty \overline{W}(t)\mathrm{d}t + \gamma\int_0^\infty F(t)\mathrm{d}W(t) \\ &- \int_0^T \left[\int_0^{T-t} \overline{G}(y)\mathrm{d}y\right] F(t)\mathrm{d}W(t).\end{aligned} \tag{9}$$

Therefore, the expected benefit rate is

$$\begin{aligned}B(T) &= \frac{\begin{matrix} r - [c_1 + c_2\gamma]\int_0^\infty F(t)\mathrm{d}W(t) \\ -c_2\left\{\int_T^\infty \overline{W}(t)\mathrm{d}t - \int_0^T \left[\int_0^{T-t}\overline{G}(y)\mathrm{d}y\right] F(t)\mathrm{d}W(t)\right\}\end{matrix}}{\begin{matrix} T + \int_T^\infty \overline{W}(t)\mathrm{d}t + \gamma\int_0^\infty F(t)\mathrm{d}W(t) \\ - \int_0^T \left[\int_0^{T-t}\overline{G}(y)\mathrm{d}y\right] F(t)\mathrm{d}W(t)\end{matrix}} \\ &= \frac{r - c_1\int_0^\infty F(t)\mathrm{d}W(t) + c_2 T}{\begin{matrix} T + \int_T^\infty \overline{W}(t)\mathrm{d}t + \gamma\int_0^\infty F(t)\mathrm{d}W(t) \\ - \int_0^T \left[\int_0^{T-t}\overline{G}(y)\mathrm{d}y\right] F(t)\mathrm{d}W(t)\end{matrix}} - c_2.\end{aligned} \tag{10}$$

We obtain optimal T^* which maximize $B(T)$. Differentiating $B(T)$ with T and set it equal to 0,

$$\frac{\begin{matrix} T + \int_T^\infty \overline{W}(t)\mathrm{d}t + \gamma\int_0^\infty F(t)\mathrm{d}W(t) \\ - \int_0^T \left[\int_0^{T-t}\overline{G}(y)\mathrm{d}y\right] F(t)\mathrm{d}W(t)\end{matrix}}{\int_0^T [1 - \overline{G}(T-t)F(t)]\mathrm{d}W(t)} - T = \frac{r - c_1\int_0^\infty F(t)\mathrm{d}W(t)}{c_2}. \tag{11}$$

Letting $L(T)$ be the left-hand side of (11), we have

$$L(0) \equiv \lim_{T\to 0} L(T) = \infty, \qquad L(\infty) \equiv \lim_{T\to\infty} L(T) = 0.$$

Furthermore, we have $L'(T) < 0$ from Appendix. Thus, if $r > c_1\int_0^\infty F(t)\mathrm{d}W(t) > 0$, then there exists optimal T^* $(0 < T^* < \infty)$ which satisfies (11). If $r \le c_1\int_0^\infty F(t)\mathrm{d}W(t)$, then $T^* = \infty$.

4 Low bound operating period model

If the operating period has an exponential distribution, then there are possibility that its operation is completed immediately after the starting time. However, it is not proper for some systems such as airplane, because a certain amount of time is necessary to move from a airport to another one. So, we consider that the operation is not completed immediately after its starting time, and at least, itis completed after a constant time η (> 0).

For the purpose, we consider a distribution $K(s)$ with finite mean θ, and completion time of the operating period is given as $\eta + s$. This means that the time distribution of the operating period $W(t)$ has a location parameter, that is,

$$W(t) = \begin{cases} K(t-\eta) & (t \ge \eta) \\ 0 & (0 \le t < \eta). \end{cases}$$

We consider a modified model with $K(s)$, because it is useful to compute it numerically.

Similarly with Section 3,

(a) The probability that the unit has failed in operating period and the failure is repaired before time T is

$$\begin{aligned}&\int_0^{T-\eta}\left[\int_0^{T-\eta-s}\mathrm{d}G(y)\right] F(s+\eta)\mathrm{d}K(s) \\ &= \int_0^{T-\eta} G(T-\eta-s)F(t+\eta)\mathrm{d}K(s).\end{aligned} \tag{12}$$

(b) The probability that the the operating period is completed before time T and unit failure is

$$\int_0^{T-\eta} \overline{F}(t+\eta)\mathrm{d}K(s). \tag{13}$$

(c) The probability that the operation is completed after time T before unit failure is

$$\int_{T-\eta}^\infty \overline{F}(s+\eta)\mathrm{d}K(s). \tag{14}$$

(d) The probability that the operation is completed before time T and after unit failure, and its is repaired after time T is

$$\int_0^{T-\eta}\left[\int_{T-\eta-s}^{\infty}\mathrm{d}G(y)\right]F(s+\eta)\mathrm{d}K(s)$$
$$=\int_0^{T-\eta}\overline{G}(T-\eta-s)F(s+\eta)\mathrm{d}K(s). \quad (15)$$

(e) The probability that the operation is completed after time T and unit failure is

$$\int_{T-\eta}^{\infty}\left[\int_0^{\infty}\mathrm{d}G(y)\right]F(s+\eta)\mathrm{d}K(t)$$
$$=\int_{T-\eta}^{\infty}F(s+\eta)\mathrm{d}K(s). \quad (16)$$

Clearly, (12) + +(13) + (14) + (15) + (16) = 1.

Furthermore, the probability that the unit has no failure before the completion of operation is

$$\int_0^{\infty}F(s+\eta)\mathrm{d}K(s). \quad (17)$$

Then, the mean time from time T to the completion of repir is

$$\int_{T-\eta}^{\infty}\overline{K}(s)\mathrm{d}s+\gamma\int_{T-\eta}^{\infty}F(s+\eta)\mathrm{d}K(s)$$
$$+\int_0^{T-\eta}\left[\int_{T-\eta-s}^{\infty}\overline{G}(y)\mathrm{d}y\right]F(s+\eta)\mathrm{d}K(s)$$
$$=\int_{T-\eta}^{\infty}\overline{K}(s)\mathrm{d}s+\gamma\int_0^{\infty}F(s+\eta)\mathrm{d}K(s)$$
$$-\int_0^{T-\eta}\left[\int_0^{T-\eta-s}\overline{G}(y)\mathrm{d}y\right]F(s+\eta)\mathrm{d}K(s). \quad (18)$$

and the expected time of one cycle is

$$T+\int_{T-\eta}^{\infty}\overline{K}(s)\mathrm{d}s+\gamma\int_0^{\infty}F(s+\eta)\mathrm{d}K(s)$$
$$-\int_0^{T-\eta}\left[\int_0^{T-\eta-s}\overline{G}(y)\mathrm{d}y\right]F(s+\eta)\mathrm{d}K(s). \quad (19)$$

Therefore, the expected benefit per unit of time is

$$B_\eta(T)=\frac{r-[c_1+c_2\gamma]\int_0^{\infty}F(s+\eta)\mathrm{d}K(t)-c_2\left\{\int_T^{\infty}\overline{W}(t)\mathrm{d}t-\int_0^{T-\eta}\left[\int_0^{T-\eta-s}\overline{G}(y)\mathrm{d}y\right]F(s+\eta)\mathrm{d}K(s)\right\}}{T+\int_{T-\eta}^{\infty}\overline{K}(s)\mathrm{d}s+\gamma\int_0^{\infty}F(s+\eta)\mathrm{d}K(t)-\int_0^{T-\eta}\left[\int_0^{T-\eta-s}\overline{G}(y)\mathrm{d}y\right]F(s+\eta)\mathrm{d}W(s)}$$
$$=\frac{r-c_1\int_0^{\infty}F(s+\eta)\mathrm{d}K(s)+c_2T}{T+\int_{T-\eta}^{\infty}\overline{K}(s)\mathrm{d}s+\gamma\int_0^{\infty}F(s+\eta)\mathrm{d}K(t)-\int_0^{T-\eta}\left[\int_0^{T-\eta-s}\overline{G}(y)\mathrm{d}y\right]F(s+\eta)\mathrm{d}W(s)}-c_2. \quad (20)$$

We obtain optimal T^* which maximize $B_\eta(T)$. Differentiating $B_\eta(T)$ with T and set it equal to 0, we have

$$\frac{T+\int_{T-\eta}^{\infty}\overline{K}(s)\mathrm{d}s+\gamma\int_0^{\infty}F(s+\eta)\mathrm{d}K(s)-\int_0^{T-\eta}\left[\int_0^{T-\eta-s}\overline{G}(y)\mathrm{d}y\right]F(s+\eta)\mathrm{d}K(s)}{\int_0^{T-\eta}[1-\overline{G}(T-\eta-s)F(s+\eta)]\mathrm{d}K(s)}-T$$
$$=\frac{r-c_1\int_0^{\infty}F(s+\eta)\mathrm{d}K(s)}{c_2}. \quad (21)$$

Let $L_\eta(T)$ be the left hand of (21). Then, we have

$$L_\eta(0)\equiv\lim_{T\to 0}L_\eta(T)=\infty,\quad L_\eta(\infty)\equiv\lim_{T\to\infty}L_\eta(T)=0.$$

Further, we have $L'_\eta(T)<0$. Thus, if $[r-c_1\int_0^{\infty}F(s+\eta)\mathrm{d}K(s)]/c_2>0$, that is $r>c_1\int_0^{\infty}F(s+\eta)\mathrm{d}K(s)>0$, then there is optimal T^* $(0<T^*<\infty)$ which satisfies (21). If $r\le c_1\int_0^{\infty}F(s+\eta)\mathrm{d}K(s)>0$ then $T^*=\infty$.

5 Conclusions

We considered some models with operating and stopping period, and discussed analytically the optimal planned cycle time. (1) Maximizing benefits model and (2) Low bound operating period model which is a special case were proposed. For the future works, we should give numerical examples and compare them with previous models.

Appendix: Proof of $L'(T)<0$

Letting $L_1(t)$ be the numerator of the first term of $L(T)$,

$$L_1(T)\equiv T+\int_T^{\infty}\overline{W}(t)\mathrm{d}t+\gamma\int_0^{\infty}F(t)\mathrm{d}W(t)$$
$$-\int_0^{T}\left[\int_0^{T-t}\overline{G}(y)\mathrm{d}y\right]F(t)\mathrm{d}W(t)$$
$$=T+\int_T^{\infty}\overline{W}(t)\mathrm{d}t+\gamma\int_T^{\infty}F(t)\mathrm{d}W(t)$$
$$+\int_0^{T}\left[\int_{T-t}^{\infty}\overline{G}(y)\mathrm{d}y\right]F(t)\mathrm{d}W(t)>0. \quad (22)$$

Then, $L'_1(T)$ is equal to the denominator of the first term of $L(T)$, i.e.,

$$L'_1(T)=\int_0^{T}[1-\overline{G}(T-t)F(t)]\mathrm{d}W(t). \quad (23)$$

Thus,

$$L''_1(T)=\overline{F}(T)w(T)+\int_0^{T}g(T-t)F(t)\mathrm{d}W(t)>0. \quad (24)$$

Because

$$L(T)=\frac{L_1(T)}{L'_1(T)}-T,$$

differentiating $L(T)$ with T,

$$L'(T)=\frac{[L_1(T)-TL'_1(T)]'L'_1(T)-[L_1(T)-TL'_1(T)]L''(T)}{[L'_1(T)]^2}$$
$$=-\frac{L_1(T)L''_1(T)}{[L_1(T)]^2}<0. \quad (25)$$

Acknowledgment

This work is supported by JSPS KAKENHI Grant Number 24K07937.

References

[1] R.E. Barlow and F. Proschan, Mathematical Theory of Reliability, John Wiley & Sons, New York, 1965.

[2] S. Osaki, Applied Stochastic System Modeling, Springer Verlag, Berlin, 1992.

[3] T. Nakagawa. Maintenance Theory of Reliability. Springer, London, 2005.

[4] T. Nakagawa. Random Maintenance Policies. Springer, London, 2014.

[5] W. Stadje. Renewal analysis of a replacement process. Operational Research Letter, 31, 2013, 1-6.

[6] M. Chen, S. Mizutani and T. Nakagawa, "Random and age replacement policies", International Journal of Reliability, Quality and Safety Engineering, 17, 27-39, 2010.

[7] M. Chen, S. Nakamura, and T. Nakagawa, "Replacement and preventive maintenance models with random working times", IEICE Transactions on Fundamentals of Electronics, Communications and Computer Sciences, E93-A(2), 500-507, 2010.

[8] X. Zhao and T. Nakagawa, "Optimization problems of replacement first or last in reliability theory". European Journal of Operational Research, 223, 2012, 141-149.

[9] X. Zhao and T. Nakagawa, "Optimal periodic and random inspection with first, last, and overtime policies". International Journal of Systems Science, DOI: 10.1080/00207721.2013.827263, 2013.

[10] M. Hamidi, F. Szidarovszky, M. Szidarovszky, New one cycle criteria for optimizing preventive replacement policies. Reliability Engineering and System Safety, 154, 2016, 42-48.

[11] S. Sheu, H. Tsai, U. Sheu and G. Zhang, Optimal replacement policies for a system based on a one-cycle criterion. Reliability Engineering and System Safety, 191, 2019, 106527.

[12] M. Berrade, P. Scarf and C. Cavalcante, A study of postponed replacement in a delay time model. Reliability Engineering and System Safety, 168, 2017, 70-79.

[13] X. Zhao and T. Nakagawa, "Comparisons of periodic and random replacement policies", in Applied Reliability Engineering and Risk Analysis: Probabilistic Models and Statistical Inference, (Eds) by Ilia B. Frenkel, A. Karagrigoriou, A. Lisnianski and A. Kleyner, John Wiley & Sons, 2014.

[14] X. Zhao, S. Mizutani and T. Nakagawa, "Which is better for replacement policies with continuous or discrete scheduled times?", European Journal of Operational Research, 242, 477-486, 2015.

[15] X. Zhao, C. Qian and T. Nakagawa, "Comparisons of replacement policies with periodic times and repair numbers", Reliability Engineering and System Safety, 168, 161-170, 2017.

[16] S. Mizutani, X. Zhao and T. Nakagawa, "Which replacement is better at working cycles or numbers of failures", IEICE Transaction, Fundamentals, E103-A(2), 523-532, 2020.

[17] R. Gulati, Maintenance and Reliability Best Practices Third Edition, Industrial Press. Inc. 2021.

[18] T. Nakagawa, "Optimum preventive maintenance and repair limit policies maximizing the expected earning rate", RAIRO-Operations Research, 11, 1, 1977.

[19] T. Dohi, T. Aoki, N. Kaio and S. Osaki, "Nonparametric Preventive Maintenance Policy Under Earning Rate Criterion", IFAC Proceedings Volumes, 30, 18, 1165-1170, 1997.

[20] H. B. Fakher, M. Nourelfath and M. Gendreau, "Integrating production, maintenance and quality: A multi-period multi-product profit-maximization model" Reliability Engineering and System Safety 170, 2018, 191-201, 2018.

[21] R. Ghandali, M. H. Abooei and M. S. Fallah Nezhad, "A POMDP Framework to Find Optimal Inspection and Maintenance Policies via Availability and Profit Maximization for Manufacturing Systems", International Journal of Engineering, 31, 12, 2077-2084, 2018.

[22] S. Mizutani and T. Nakagawa, "Optimal Maintenance Policy for Delays in the Next Operation" Proceedings of 29th ISSAT International Conference on Reliability & Quality in Design, 2024.

An enhanced cumulative quantity control chart based on asymmetric runs rules

Chen Pei-Wen

Department of Industrial Engineering and Management, Yuan Ze University,
No. 135, Yuan-Tung Road, Chung-Li District, Taoyuan City 32003, Taiwan, ieiris@saturn.yzu.edu.tw

Keywords: CQC chart, runs rules, high-yield, Markov chain

Abstract - The cumulative quantity control (CQC) chart is a statistical process control tool designed for monitoring high-quality processes, particularly those with very low defect rates. Unlike traditional control charts that track defect counts or proportions over fixed sample sizes, the CQC chart accumulates production quantities until a defective item is observed. This approach allows for more efficient monitoring in processes where defect rates are rare. Its applications extend beyond manufacturing, such as microchip production, circuit board assembly, and other precision manufacturing processes with extremely low defect rates. In non-manufacturing sectors, it tracks the occurrence of errors in transaction processing or monitors defective drug batches. Improving the sensitivity of control charts remains a key focus in statistical process control research. Most existing studies concentrate rely on symmetric runs rules which apply identical decision criteria to both sides of the control limits. However, symmetric rules do not offer balanced detection performance for the CQC chart due to the asymmetric nature of the statistics. This imbalance can result in improved detection on one side while severely limiting the effectiveness on the other. In this study, a one-sided m-of-k rule is applied to establish the lower control limit of the CQC chart, while retaining the original upper control limit. A Markov chain model is developed to assess the effectiveness of control charts incorporating various runs rules. The results demonstrate that the one-sided m-of-k rule scheme not only overcomes the limitations of current methods for monitoring high-yield production, but also enhances sensitivity in detecting increases in the defect rate.

1. Introduction

The cumulative quantity control (CQC) chart, a Shewhart-type time-between-events (TBE) control chart, bases its decision-making on the most recent charting statistic, similar to traditional Shewhart charts. While effective for detecting large process shifts, its sensitivity to small shifts can be limited. To address this, several runs rules are incorporated into the CQC chart to enhance its ability to detect small process changes. The performance of these enhanced CQC schemes is evaluated using a Markov chain approach. Designed for high-yield processes where non-conforming items are rare, the CQC chart monitors the time between successive events rather than their count or proportion, offering an efficient alternative for monitoring quality and reliability in various fields.

Runs rules are known for the enhancement of control charts in detecting small process changes. A widely recognized approach involves incorporating supplementary rules [1-8]. Klein [9] proposed the m of k rules to improve the performance of $\bar{X}$ chart by incorporating earlier information. Building on this idea, Khoo [10] introduced additional rules for interpreting the p chart, resulting in enhanced detection performance with the inclusion of runs rules. Khoo and Ariffin [11] introduced the improved m of k rule (hereafter referred to as I-m/k), which combines the m of k rule with the single-point determination concept from traditional Shewhart control charts. Compared to the earlier runs rules proposed by Klein [9], I-m/k significantly improves the detection of larger process shifts. Antzoulakos and Rakitzis [12] combined the Western Electric rules with I-m/k and proposed the revised m of k rules. Their study demonstrated that these revised rules provide superior detection performance for $\bar{X}$ charts compared to the I-m/k rules. Jalilibal et al. [8] reviewed over a hundred related researched on runs rules and found that approximately 91% of the research still focuses on traditional control charts. There is still very little research on the application of runs rules to dependent high-yield processes.

Most existing studies focus on symmetric runs rules, which apply identical decision criteria to both the upper and lower control limits. However, these symmetric rules fail to provide balanced detection performance for the CQC chart due to the inherent asymmetry of its charting statistics. To address this limitation, this study proposes one-sided m of k rules and I-m/k rules specifically tailored for monitoring high-yield production processes. A Markov chain model is developed to evaluate the effectiveness of control charts incorporating these alternative runs rules.

2. Description of the CQC chart

The CQC chart, proposed by Chan et al. [13], is designed as an alternative to the Shewhart c chart and u chart. The basic idea is that instead of concentrating on the number of defects or nonconformities, the number of units required to observe exactly one defect is counted. Suppose that defects in a process occur according to a Poisson process with mean rate of occurrence equal to λ_0 defects per unit quantity of product. Then the number of units X required to observe one defect (which is not necessarily an integer) is an exponential random variable. Instead of using traditional control limits, some researchers [13-15] suggested the use of probability limits. Assume the type I error is α,These limits are established based on equal tail probabilities of false alarms and are presented in Equations (1) and (2).

$$\mathrm{UCL} = -\ln\,(\alpha/2)/\lambda_0 \tag{1}$$

$$\mathrm{LCL} = -\ln\,(1-\alpha/2)/\lambda_0 \tag{2}$$

The process is considered to be out-of-control if there is one point falls outside the control limits. If a plotted point of the CQC chart is above the upper control limit, the process is likely to have improved. In other words, a point below the lower control limit is an indication of process deterioration.

3. Designs of runs rules scheme

Runs rules are widely recognized for improving the sensitivity of control charts in detecting small process shifts. In this study, we introduce several runs rule schemes to the CQC chart, which can be categorized into two types: symmetric and asymmetric runs rules. The symmetric runs rules include the m of k rules (Klein [9]) and I-m/k rules (Khoo and Ariffin [11]). The asymmetric runs rules, also referred to as one-sided runs rules, developed in this study are combinations of the m of k rules and I-m/k rules applied to both sides of the CQC chart.

Figure 1 illustrates a control chart where the area between the upper and lower control limits is divided into six distinct regions. This zoning framework is used to define various runs rule schemes by tracking the frequency and pattern of plotted points in specific regions. Two sets of control limits, outer (UOCL/LOCL) and inner (UICL/LICL), are introduced based on the I-m/k rules while the m of k rules use only the outer control limits. Let {Upper, Lower} denote the runs rules applied to the respective sides of the control chart. All out-of-control conditions are summarized in Table 1.

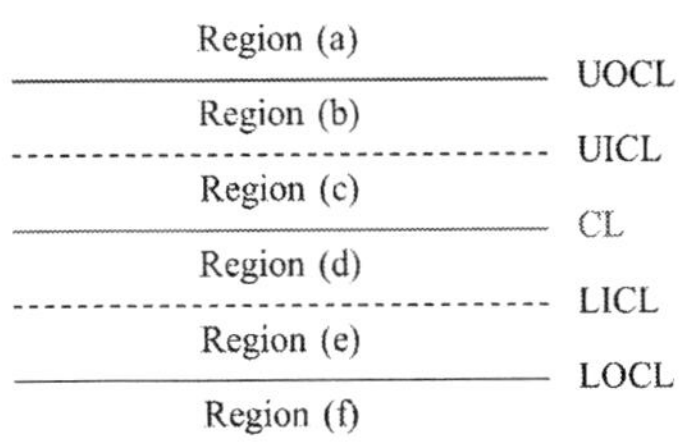

Figure 1. The zoning framework of a control chart

Table 1. All the out-of-control conditions of various schemes

Schemes	{Upper, Lower}	OOC conditions
None	$\{1/1, 1/1\}$	$\{a\,;f\}$
2 of 2	$\{2/2, 2/2\}$	$\{aa\,;ff\}$
2 of 3	$\{2/3, 2/3\}$	$\{aa\,;ff\}$ $\{a(b+c+d+e)a\}$ $\{f(e+d+c+b)f\}$
I-2 of 2	$\{\text{I-}2/2, \text{I-}2/2\}$	$\{a\,;f\}$ $\{bb\,;ee\}$
I-2 of 3	$\{\text{I-}2/3, \text{I-}2/3\}$	$\{a\,;f\}$ $\{bb\,;ee\}$ $\{b(c+d)b\,;e(d+c)e\}$
One-sided 2 of 2	$\{1/1, 2/2\}$	$\{a\,;ff\}$
One-sided 2 of 3	$\{1/1, 2/3\}$	$\{a\,;ff;f(e+d+c+b)f\}$
One-sided I-2 of 2	$\{1/1, \text{I-}2/2\}$	$\{a\,;f;ee\}$
One-sided I-2 of 3	$\{1/1, \text{I-}2/3\}$	$\{a\,;f;ee;e(d+c+b)e\}$

A Markov chain approach is utilized to determine suitable inner and outer control limits in a way that guarantees the in-control average run length (ARL). The following steps detailing how to acquire the control limits for the CQC chart incorporating the one-sided 2 of 3 rules and one-sided I-2 of 3 rules schemes are outlined below.

- Determine an acceptable occurrence rate λ_0 and a required in-control ARL (i.e. $1/\alpha$).
- Define the transient and absorbing states of Markov chain for each runs rule scheme and construct the one-step transition probability matrix $\mathbf{P}$. The transition probability of the CQC chart is derived from the exponential distribution.
- Given the probability in Region (f), denoted as p_a, the probability in Region (e), denoted as p_b, is then calculated to achieve the desired in-control ARL, based on the condition that the probability in Region (a) equals $\alpha/2$.
- For the one-sided 2 of 3 rules, the lower outer control limits can be calculated using Equations (3) while the upper outer control limit (UOCL) is determined using Equation (1).

$$\text{LOCL} = -\ln\left(1 - p_a - p_b\right)/\lambda_0 \quad (3)$$

- For the one-sided I-2 of 3 rules, the lower outer and inner control limits can be calculated using Equations (4) and (5), respectively, while the upper outer control limit (UOCL) is determined using Equation (1).

$$\text{LOCL} = -\ln\left(1 - p_a\right)/\lambda_0 \quad (4)$$

$$\text{LICL} = -\ln\left(1 - p_a - p_b\right)/\lambda_0 \quad (5)$$

Let X_t represent the statistic at time point t and Table 2 displays the states of the Markov chain model for the CQC chart using the one-sided 2 of 3 rules and one-sided I-2 of 3 rules, respectively.

Table 2. The states of the Markov chain model

The one-sided 2 of 3 rules
State $\{0\}$: X_t falls in Region (b), (c), (d) or (e) State $\{1\}$: X_t falls in Region (f) State $\{2\}$: X_t falls in Region (d) or (e) and X_{t-1} falls in Region (f) State $\{3\}$: Absorbing state
The one-sided I-2 of 3 rules
State $\{0\}$: X_t falls in Region (b) or (c) or (d) State $\{1\}$: X_t falls in Region (e) State $\{2\}$: X_t falls in Region (d) and X_{t-1} falls in Region (e) State $\{3\}$: Absorbing state

Let p_C denote the probability of points fall within UOCL and LOCL, i.e. Region (b), (c), (d) and (e), and let p_L denote the probability of points fall within Region (f). The one-step transition probability matrix of the Markov chain for the one-sided 2 of 3 rules can be expressed as Equations (6).

$$\mathbf{P} = \begin{bmatrix} p_C & p_L & 0 & 1-p_C-p_L \\ 0 & 0 & p_C & 1-p_C \\ p_C & 0 & 0 & 1-p_C \\ 0 & 0 & 0 & 1 \end{bmatrix} \quad (6)$$

The in-control ARL, denoted as ARL_{in}, is given by the expected value of the first passage time from the starting state 0 to the absorbing state 3 and can be derived as Equations (7).

$$\text{ARL}_{in} = M_{03} = \frac{1+p_L+p_L p_C}{1-p_C-p_L p_C^2} \quad (7)$$

The out-of-control ARL can be obtained from the first element of vector **ARL** which is shown in Equations (8).

$$\mathbf{ARL} = (\mathbf{I} - \mathbf{R})^{-1}\mathbf{1} \quad (8)$$

where **R** is a submatrix obtained from the transition probability matrix **P** by deleting its last row and column and **1** is a column vector of 1's [16].

Similar to the one-sided 2 of 3 rules, let p_C denote the probability of points fall within UOCL and LICL, i.e. Region (b), (c) and (d), and let p_L denote the probability of points fall within Region (e). The one-step transition probability matrix of the Markov chain for the one-sided I-2 of 3 rules is likewise provided in Equation (6). Following the same approach, the performance of the one-sided I-2 of 3 rules can also be evaluated using Equation (8).

4. Performance Evaluation

This section presents the ARLs of the CQC chart under various runs rules schemes. In this study, the ARL of the basic CQC chart serves as the baseline for comparison. Assuming an acceptable occurrence rate equal to λ_0 and a significance level is α, the target in-control ARL is approximately 370. Let ρ represent the ratio of the actual occurrence rate λ_1 to the acceptable occurrence rate λ_0. A value of $\rho > 1$ indicates process deterioration ($\lambda_1 > \lambda_0$), while $\rho < 1$ signifies process improvement ($\lambda_1 < \lambda_0$).

Tables 3 and 4 show the performance of symmetric and asymmetric runs rules schemes, respectively. The symmetric runs rules include the m of k rules and I-m/k rules, which apply rules to both sides of the control limits. In contrast, the asymmetric schemes developed in this study apply rules only to the lower control limit and are referred to as one-sided runs rules schemes.

Table 3. Performance of symmetric runs rules schemes

ρ	CQC-1	2 of 2	2 of 3	I-2 of 2	I-2 of 3
0.01	1.07	2.10	2.07	1.10	1.10
0.02	1.14	2.21	2.16	1.21	1.21
0.03	1.22	2.32	2.24	1.32	1.32
0.04	1.30	2.44	2.33	1.43	1.43
0.05	1.39	2.57	2.43	1.55	1.54
0.06	1.49	2.70	2.53	1.67	1.66
0.07	1.59	2.84	2.64	1.79	1.78
0.08	1.70	2.99	2.76	1.93	1.91
0.09	1.81	3.15	2.89	2.07	2.04
0.1	1.94	3.32	3.02	2.21	2.18
0.2	3.75	5.65	4.87	4.24	3.97
0.3	7.24	9.84	8.22	7.97	7.13
0.4	13.95	17.50	14.44	15.00	13.01
0.5	26.73	31.52	26.15	28.27	24.23
0.6	50.54	57.02	48.29	53.01	45.77
0.7	93.06	101.81	89.29	97.34	86.21
0.8	162.83	174.13	159.85	170.09	156.69
0.9	261.16	272.23	262.35	269.99	260.15
1	**370.37**	**370.00**	**370.37**	**370.27**	**370.00**
2	370.37	198.72	201.89	200.89	203.68
3	247.25	94.70	97.44	96.01	98.58
4	185.56	56.96	59.26	57.81	60.02
5	148.55	38.90	40.86	39.50	41.40
6	123.87	28.76	30.47	29.21	30.87
7	106.25	22.46	23.97	22.81	24.28
8	93.03	18.25	19.59	18.53	19.85
9	82.75	15.27	16.49	15.50	16.70
10	74.53	13.09	14.20	13.28	14.38

According to the data shown in Table 3, it can be observed that the 2 of 2 rule outperforms the I-2 of 2 rule for values of $\rho > 1$. However, the I-2 of 2 rule shows marginal improvement for ρ values less than 1. The results indicate that incorporating outer control limits improves the ability to detect a decrease in the occurrence rate but performs less effectively in identifying an increase in defect occurrences. Similarly, the same approach is applied to the 2 of 3 and the I-2 of 3 rules, as also illustrated in Table 3.

Table 4. Performance of asymmetric runs rules schemes

ρ	CQC-1	One-sided 2 of 2	One-sided 2 of 3	One-sided I-2 of 2	One-sided I-2 of 3
0.01	1.07	1.07	1.07	1.11	1.11
0.02	1.14	1.14	1.14	1.23	1.23
0.03	1.22	1.22	1.22	1.36	1.36
0.04	1.30	1.30	1.30	1.51	1.51
0.05	1.39	1.39	1.39	1.68	1.68
0.06	1.49	1.49	1.49	1.86	1.86
0.07	1.59	1.59	1.59	2.07	2.07
0.08	1.70	1.70	1.70	2.29	2.29
0.09	1.81	1.81	1.81	2.54	2.54
0.1	1.94	1.94	1.94	2.82	2.82
0.2	3.75	3.75	3.75	7.94	7.94
0.3	7.24	7.25	7.25	22.26	22.26
0.4	13.95	14.01	14.01	61.33	61.32
0.5	26.73	26.96	26.96	157.93	157.79
0.6	50.54	51.34	51.34	332.97	332.14
0.7	93.06	95.44	95.43	484.70	482.89
0.8	162.83	168.35	168.32	500.01	498.43
0.9	261.16	268.98	268.90	439.26	438.63
1	**370.37**	**370.00**	**370.00**	**370.17**	**370.41**
2	370.37	198.54	201.41	104.02	106.14
3	247.25	94.61	97.23	50.92	52.80
4	185.56	56.91	59.14	31.39	32.97
5	148.55	38.86	40.78	21.93	23.28
6	123.87	28.74	30.41	16.56	17.74
7	106.25	22.44	23.92	13.19	14.23
8	93.03	18.23	19.56	10.91	11.84
9	82.75	15.26	16.46	9.29	10.14
10	74.53	13.08	14.17	8.10	8.87

As indicated by the findings in Table 3, the application of rules in the CQC control chart enhances detection performance only when the process defect rate increases ($\rho > 1$). Conversely, when the defect rate decreases, incorporating additional rules leads to delayed signaling, suggesting an inability to promptly detect process degradation. The improved I-m/k rules incorporate single-point criteria into the m of k rules, which helps reduce the ARL when the process shift is large, thereby enhancing the detection capability for substantial shifts.

In the asymmetric runs rules scheme proposed in this study, runs rules are applied exclusively to the lower side of the CQC chart, while the upper side retains the original control limit of the basic CQC chart. This design reflects a targeted monitoring strategy focused on detecting increases in the process defect rate. As evidenced by the results in Table 4, all the one-sided runs rules effectively achieve the intended objective. When $\rho > 1$, the ARLs of control charts with one-sided runs rules are consistently shorter than those of the basic CQC chart. However, when $\rho < 1$, the schemes demonstrate limited effectiveness in detecting small process shifts, although it maintains comparable performance in the presence of large shifts.

To enable clearer comparisons, this study employs the Relative Detection Efficiency Index (RDEI) to evaluate the performance of various runs rules schemes relative to the basic CQC chart. The RDEI is defined in Equation (9). In this study, the in-control ARL is held constant and the out-of-control ARL is compared across various conditions. A smaller RDEI indicates that the runs rules scheme achieves higher detection efficiency compared to the basic CQC chart, meaning it can identify process shifts more quickly or accurately. An RDEI value of 1 indicates that the runs rules scheme and the basic CQC chart exhibit equivalent detection efficiency, suggesting no relative advantage in identifying process shifts.

$$\mathrm{RDEI} = \frac{\mathrm{ARL}_{Runs\ Rules}}{\mathrm{ARL}_{CQC}} \tag{9}$$

Figures 1 through 4 respectively present the performance of the m/k, I-m/k, one-sided m/k, and one-sided I-m/k runs rules schemes. The x-axis represents the value of ρ, while the y-axis displays the RDEI value, both on a logarithmic scale for illustration purposes. When $\rho = 1$, all RDEI values converge to approximately 1, since the in-control ARL is fixed in our comparative analysis.

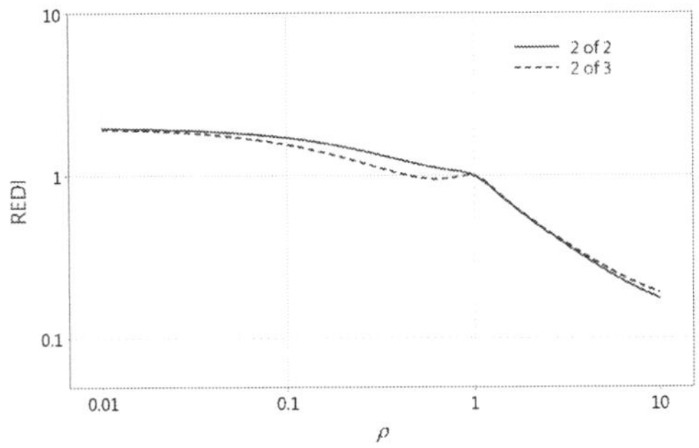

Figure 1. Performance of m/k runs rules

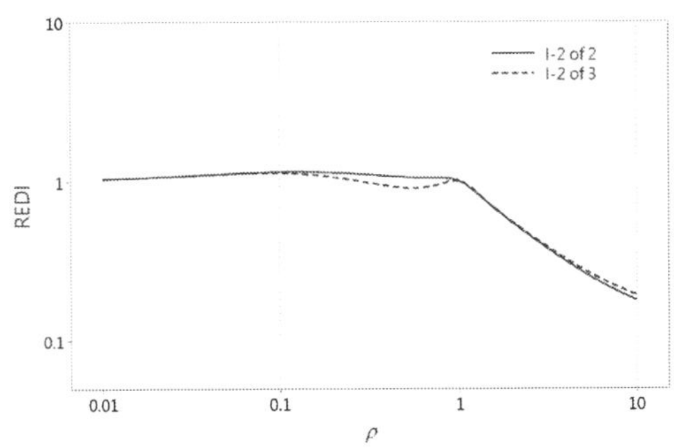

Figure 2. Performance of I-m/k runs rules

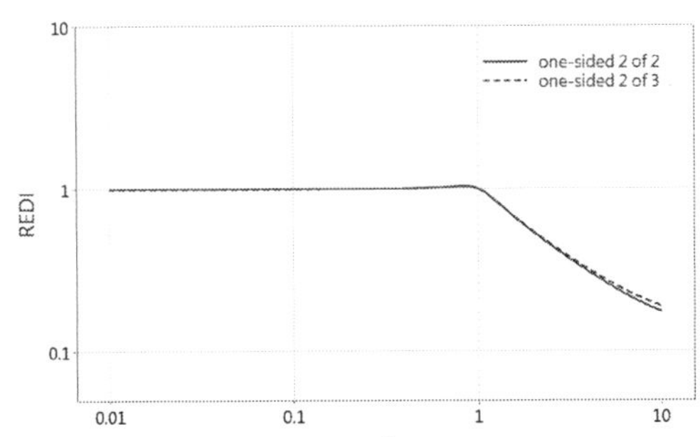

Figure 3. Performance of one-sided m/k runs rules

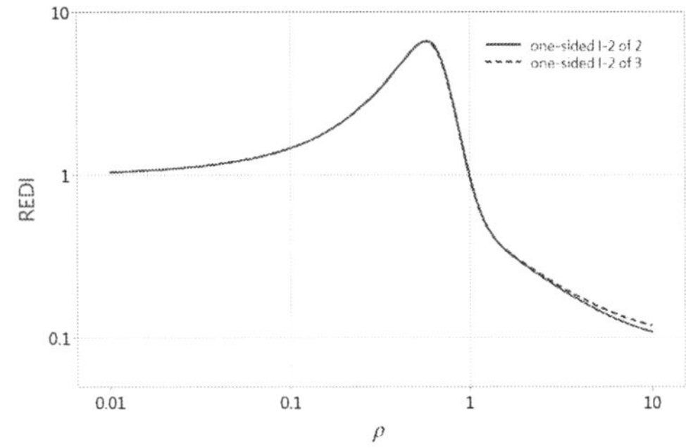

Figure 4. Performance of one-sided I-m/k runs rules

As illustrated in Figures 1 and 2, it is observed that the 2 of 3 rule slightly outperforms the 2-of-2 rule when $\rho < 1$, and maintains comparable performance when $\rho > 1$. A similar pattern is observed in the I-m/k rules: the I-2 of 3 rule demonstrates slightly better performance in detecting decreases in λ_0, while maintaining similar effectiveness in detecting increases in λ_0, compared to the I-2 of 2 rule. A comparison between Figures 1 and 2 reveals that, when $\rho < 1$, the I-m/k rules exhibit smaller RDEI values (closer to 1) than the m/k rules, indicating enhanced sensitivity in detecting decreases in λ_0. When $\rho > 1$, the I-m/k rules maintain comparable detection efficiency.

Based on the above findings, it can be concluded that, for the CQC chart, incorporating additional runs rules does not necessarily enhance detection performance in both directions. Figures 3 and 4 display the performance curves of the one-sided rule-based control charts proposed in this study. Applying the runs rule solely to the lower side of the CQC chart not only effectively reduces the detection time for downward process shifts, but also preserves the original upper control limit on the chart, thereby maintaining the same performance as the basic CQC chart in detecting upward shifts. As shown in Figure 4, the one-sided I-m/k runs rules demonstrate enhanced detection efficiency for large upward process shifts. Nevertheless, they exhibit diminished sensitivity in detecting small downward shifts, particularly during the early phase of shifting. Overall, this study recommends the one-sided m/k rule as the most effective approach, as it demonstrates generally superior detection performance compared to the basic CQC chart. In some situations where process monitoring primarily focuses on detecting process deterioration (i.e., an increase in process defects λ_0), and shifts in the opposite direction can be reasonably disregarded, the one-sided I-m/k runs rules may be considered as a suitable alternative.

5. Conclusion

This study extends the application of the CQC chart by addressing its limitations under symmetric runs rules, which are often inadequate due to the asymmetric nature of its underlying statistic. To improve detection performance, especially in high-quality processes, the one-sided m/k and the one-sided I-m/k runs rules, were proposed—applying the runs rules only to the lower control limit while retaining the original upper limit. Through a Markov chain modeling approach, the proposed method was shown to significantly enhance sensitivity to increases in defect rates without compromising performance in the opposite direction.

These findings suggest that the one-sided m/k runs rules offer a more effective and balanced monitoring strategy, particularly in contexts where detecting process deterioration—namely, an increase in the process defect rate— is the primary concern, and shifts in the opposite direction can be reasonably disregarded. In scenarios where the primary objective of process monitoring is to detect deterioration—specifically, an increase in the process defect rate, and shifts in the opposite direction are negligible or of limited concern, the one-sided I-m/k runs rules present a viable and effective alternative to traditional symmetric schemes.

6. References

[1] Western Electric Company. Statistical Quality Control Handbook. Indianapolis, Indiana: Western Electric Co. Inc.;1956.

[2] Nelson LS. The Shewhart control chart – tests for special causes. Journal of Quality Technology. 1984; 16(4): 255-256.

[3] Champ CW, Woodall WH. Exact results for Shewhart control charts with supplementary runs rules. Technometrics. 1987; 29:393-399.

[4] Shmueli G, Cohen A. Run-length distribution for control charts with runs and scans rules. Communications in Statistics-Theory and Methods. 2003; 32(2):475-495.

[5] Chen PW, Cheng CS. An ARL-unbiased approach to setting control limits of CCC-r chart for high-yield processes. Journal of Quality.2010;17(6):435-452.

[6] Riaz M, Mehmood R, Does R. J. M. M. On the performance of different control charting rules. Quality Reliability Engineering International. 2011; 27(8):1059-1067.

[7] Rakitzis AC. On the performance of modified runs rules charts with estimated parameters. Communications in Statistics-Simulation and Computation. 2017; 46(2): 1360-1380.

[8] Jalilibal Z, Karavigh, MHA, Amiri, A, et al. Run rules schemes for statistical process monitoring: a literature review. Quality Technology and Quantitative Management, 2022; 21-52.

[9] Klein M. Two alternatives to the Shewhart $\bar{X}$ control chart. Journal of Quality Technology. 2000; 32(4):427-431.

[10] Khoo MBC. Increasing the sensitivity of control chart for fraction nonconforming. Quality Engineering. 2003; 16(2):307-319.

[11] Khoo MBC, Ariffin KNB. Two improved runs rules for the Shewhart $\bar{X}$ control chart. Quality Engineering. 2006; 18(2):173-178.

[12] Antzoulakos DL, Rakitzis CA. The revised m-of-k runs rule. Quality Engineering. 2008; 20(1):175-81.

[13] Chan LY, Xie M, Goh TN. Cumulative quantity control charts for monitoring production processes. International Journal of Production Research. 2000; 38(2): 397-408.

[14] Xie M, Goh TN. The use of probability limits for process control based on geometric distribution. International Journal of Quality and Reliability Management. 1997; 14(1):64-73.

[15] Zhang CW, Xie M, Liu JY and Goh TN. A control chart for the Gamma distribution as a model of time between events. International Journal of Production Research. 2007; 45(23): 5649-5666.

[16] Brook D and Evans DA. An approach to the probability distribution of run length. Biometrika. 1972; 59(3): 539-549.

Performance evaluation and improvement decision-making rules for e-learning system

CHEN Yen-Po [1], CHEN Yu-Ling [2], YU Chun-Hung [3,4*], YU Chun-Min [2]

[1] Department of English, National Chengchi University, Taipei 116011, Taiwan; y92200b@gmail.com
[2] Department of Industrial Engineering and Management National Chin-Yi University of Technology Taichung 411030, Taiwan; erin1611809@gmail.com (CHEN Y. L.); Yu2013000@gmail.com (YU C. M.)
[3] Language Center, National Chin-Yi University of Technology, Taichung 411030, Taiwan; sylvia@ncut.edu.tw
[4] Language Teaching Center, National Chi Nan University, Nantou County 545301, Taiwan
* Corresponding author. Address: No.57, Sec. 2, Zhongshan Rd., Taiping Dist., Taichung 411030, Taiwan (R.O.C.); Tel: +886 4 23924505; Fax: +886 4 23934620; E-mail addresses: sylvia@ncut.edu.tw

Keywords: E-learning system, IoT, Satisfaction index, Influence index, Performance evaluation matrix.

Abstract – With the maturity of the Internet of Things (IoT), and especially after the COVID-19 pandemic, online courses at all levels of education have become mainstream, often replacing in-person instruction. Improving the operational performance of e-learning systems can enhance learner satisfaction, attract more geographically dispersed learners, create more business and increase economic activity. Additionally, since learners can study from home, this reduces traffic impact and lowers carbon emissions, thereby alleviating environmental pollution. A solid evaluation and improvement decision model for e-learning systems helps system administrators understand user satisfaction across various service components. Therefore, this paper designed a questionnaire to investigate user satisfaction. A performance evaluation matrix was constructed using the satisfaction index of each service item as the horizontal axis and the influence index of the correlation between each service item and overall satisfaction as the vertical axis. Using statistical testing principles, we also propose an improvement decision model to identify critical-to-quality (CTQ) items. Under limited resources, this model can assist administrators in prioritizing which service items to improve to enhance overall learner satisfaction.

1. Introduction

During the COVID-19 pandemic, online courses became mainstream, often replacing physical classes [1]. As the quality and environment of the Internet of Things (IoT) more common and mature, enabling online courses to proceed smoothly. Online learning systems or e-learning systems allow learners to decide freely when and where to learn, so that teaching and learning are no longer restricted by physical constraints, which can improve participation [2]. After the COVID-19 epidemic, e-learning system has become the new mainstream learning modes in recent years [3]. It is important to continue to improve the performance of e-learning to increase learners' satisfaction and attract more learners from all over the world, thereby creating more business and increasing economic activity [4]. In addition, since customers can study at home, they can reduce the impact of traffic on the environment, which is mostly caused by carbon emissions from vehicles. [5].

The e-learning system can be regarded as a service operation system. Establishing a robust system evaluation and analysis model will help system managers determine user satisfaction with various service elements and enable designers to make improvements [6]. The performance evaluation matrix (PEM) is a convenient and effective tool for evaluating the performance of service operation systems [7]. The current paper designed questionnaire items for all service items provided by the e-learning system. For the sake of generality, it is assumed that there are q questionnaire items in total. We then investigate the satisfaction of students with these q questionnaire items and their overall satisfaction.

Drawing on the work of Liu et al. [8], we let random variable X_h represent the satisfaction of the hth questionnaire item. Then, X_h is distributed as $Beta(a_h, b_h)$, where a_h and b_h are two parameters of this satisfaction distribution. These two indices can be defined as follows:

$$\text{Satisfaction index: } \theta_h = \frac{a_h}{a_h + b_h} \quad (1)$$

where $h = 1, 2, \ldots, q, q+1$ and X_{q+1} represents the learner's overall satisfaction with the e-learning system. As noted by Yu et al. [2], the value of index θ_h is between 0 and 1. In addition, according to Chen and Yu [7], the influence index is based on the correlation between the satisfaction of each service item and the overall satisfaction as follows:

$$\text{Influence index: } \rho_h = \frac{COV(X_h, X_{q+1})}{\sigma_h \sigma_{q+1}} \quad h = 1, 2, \ldots, q \quad (2)$$

where σ_h is the standard deviation of random variable X_h, $h = 1, 2, \ldots, q, q+1$ and $COV(X_h, X_{q+1})$ is covariance of X_h and X_{q+1}. As noted by Wang et. al. [9], although in theory $-1 \le \rho_h \le 1$, in practice $0 \le \rho_h \le 1$. Drawing on the work of Yu et al. [2], we use influence index ρ_h as the vertical coordinate and satisfaction index θ_h as the horizontal coordinate to construct the service performance evaluation matrix of the e-learning system. Since both the satisfaction index and the influence index are unknown parameters, they must be estimated using sample data gathered from interviewed learners [10]. This paper first divides the performance evaluation matrix of the e-learning system into four evaluation quadrants based on the average of all estimated observations for the satisfaction and influence indices. Next, this study uses the average of all satisfaction index observations as the calibration standard, and derives the upper confidence limit of all satisfaction indices. When the observed value of the upper confidence limit of the h-th satisfaction index is less than the calibration standard, the satisfaction of the h-th questionnaire item must increase. Finally, the h-th influence indicator is used to perform statistical verification on each questionnaire item based on the upper confidence interval of the h-th influence indicator. When the upper confidence limit of the influence indicator is greater than or equal to the verification standard, the questionnaire item has a higher improvement priority. When the upper confidence limit of the influence indicator is equal to the verification standard, the improvement priority of the questionnaire item is higher. When the upper confidence limit of the influence indicator is less than the verification standard, the improvement priority of the questionnaire item is lower.

The remainder of this paper is organized as follows. In Section 2, we derive the $1-\alpha$ upper confidence limits for the satisfaction index and the influence index. Then, the upper confidence limits of these two indices are used to form evaluation coordinate points of questionnaire item. In Section 3, we use the satisfaction indices as the horizontal axis and the influence indices as the vertical axis to construct the performance evaluation matrix of the e-learning system. Based on the concept of continuous quality improvement from total quality management, the performance evaluation matrix is divided into four evaluation blocks to establish evaluation criteria. Section 4 presents a practical example to illustrate the applicability of the proposed model. Section 5 presents the conclusion.

2. Upper confidence limits and evaluation coordinate points

In this section, we derive the $1-\alpha$ upper confidence limits for the satisfaction index and the influence index. Then, the upper confidence limits of these two indices are used to form evaluation coordinate points of questionnaire item.

As mentioned above, since the satisfaction index and the influence index are unknown parameters; thus, they must be estimated using sample data collected from interviewed learners. Assuming that there are n learners to be interviewed, we let random variable $X_{h,j}$ represent the satisfaction of the respondent to the hth question, and the group observation value of random variable $X_{h,j}$ is $x_{h,j}$. Then, the observation values of the hth question are as follows:

$$\left(X_{h,1},\cdots,X_{h,j},\cdots,X_{h,n}\right)=\left(x_{h,1},\cdots,x_{h,j},\cdots,x_{h,n}\right) \quad (3)$$

The sample mean and sample standard deviation for h^{th} question can be show respectively, as follows:

$$\bar{X}_h=\frac{1}{n}\times\sum_{j=1}^{n}X_{h,j} \text{ and } S_h=\sqrt{\frac{1}{n-1}\times\sum_{j=1}^{n}\left(X_{h,j}-\bar{X}_h\right)^2} \quad (4)$$

The observation values of $\bar{X}_h$ and S_h are as follows:

$$\bar{x}_h=\frac{1}{n}\times\sum_{j=1}^{n}x_{h,j} \text{ and } s_h=\sqrt{\frac{1}{n-1}\times\sum_{j=1}^{n}\left(x_{h,j}-\bar{x}_h\right)^2} \quad (5)$$

Then, the estimator of the satisfaction index and its observation values for the hth question are as follows:

$$\hat{\theta}_h=\bar{X}_h=\frac{1}{n}\sum_{j=1}^{n}X_{h,j} \text{ and } \hat{\theta}_{h0}=\bar{x}_h=\frac{1}{n}\sum_{j=1}^{n}x_{h,j} \quad (6)$$

We define random variable Z_h as follows:

$$Z_h=\frac{\hat{\theta}_h-\theta_h}{S_h/\sqrt{n}} \quad (7)$$

According to the *Central Limits Theorem* (*CLT*), random variable Z_h approximates standard normal distribution when sample size n is large enough [11]. Thus,

$$1-\alpha=p\left(Z_h\geq -z_\alpha\right)=p\left(\frac{\hat{\theta}_h-\theta_h}{S_h/\sqrt{n}}\geq -z_\alpha\right)=p\left(\theta_h\leq U\theta_h\right) \quad (8)$$

where $U\theta_h$ is the $1-\alpha$ upper confidence limit of satisfaction index θ_h as follows:

$$U\theta_h=\hat{\theta}_h+z_\alpha\frac{S_h}{\sqrt{n}} \quad (9)$$

The observation values of $1-\alpha$ upper confidence limit $U\theta_h$ are

$$U\theta_{h0}=\hat{\theta}_{h0}+z_\alpha\frac{s_h}{\sqrt{n}} \quad (10)$$

According to Eq. (2), estimator of influence index ρ_h can be written as follows:

$$\hat{\rho}_h=\frac{\sum_{j=1}^{n}X_{h,j}X_{q+1,j}-n\bar{X}_h\bar{X}_{q+1}}{(n-1)S_hS_{q+1}} \quad (11)$$

The observation values of $\hat{\rho}_h$ are then

$$\hat{\rho}_{h0}=\frac{\sum_{j=1}^{n}x_{h,j}x_{q+1,j}-n\bar{x}_h\bar{x}_{q+1}}{(n-1)s_hs_{q+1}} \quad (12)$$

Drawing on the work of Chen and Yu [7], this paper uses Fisher transformation to derive the upper confidence limit of the influence indicator and conducts statistical testing based on this limit. We set the following random variable:

$$W_h=F(\hat{\rho}_h)=\frac{1}{2}\ln\frac{1+\hat{\rho}_h}{1-\hat{\rho}_h}=\tan^{-1}(\hat{\rho}_h) \quad (13)$$

As noted by Chen and Yu [7], random variable W_h approximates the normal distribution with mean $\tan^{-1}(\rho_h)$ and variance $(n-3)^{-1}$ when sample size n is large enough, denoted by $W_h\sim N\left(\tan^{-1}(\rho_h),\frac{1}{n-3}\right)$. If we let

$$Z_h=\frac{W_h-\tan^{-1}(\rho_h)}{1/\sqrt{n-3}}=\sqrt{n-3}\left(\tan^{-1}(\hat{\rho}_h)-\tan^{-1}(\rho_h)\right) \quad (14)$$

then random variable Z_h approximates standard normal distribution. We then derive the upper confidence limit of influence index ρ_h as follows:

$$1-\alpha = P\{Z_h \geq -z_{\alpha/2}\}$$

$$= P\left\{\sqrt{n-3}\left(\tan^{-1}(\hat{\rho}_h)-\tan^{-1}(\rho_h)\right) \geq -z_{\alpha/2}\right\}$$

$$= P\left\{\tan^{-1}(\rho_h) \leq \tan^{-1}(\hat{\rho}_h)+\frac{z_\alpha}{\sqrt{n-3}}\right\}$$

$$= P\left\{\rho_h \leq \tan\left(\tan^{-1}(\hat{\rho}_h)+\frac{z_\alpha}{\sqrt{n-3}}\right)\right\} \tag{15}$$

where z_α is the upper α quintile of standard normal distribution. Obviously, the $1-\alpha$ upper confidence limit of ρ_h is

$$U\rho_h = \tan\left(\tan^{-1}(\hat{\rho}_h)+\frac{z_\alpha}{\sqrt{n-3}}\right) \tag{16}$$

The observation values of $U\rho_h$ are then

$$U\rho_{h0} = \tan\left(\tan^{-1}(\hat{\rho}_{h0})+\frac{z_\alpha}{\sqrt{n-3}}\right) \tag{17}$$

As noted above, the upper confidence limits of these two indices can be used to form evaluation coordinate points of questionnaire item *h* as follows:

$$(x_h, y_h) = (U\theta_{h0}, U\rho_{h0}) = \left(\hat{\theta}_{h0}+z_\alpha\frac{s_h}{\sqrt{n}}, \tan\left(\tan^{-1}(\hat{\rho}_{h0})+\frac{z_\alpha}{\sqrt{n-3}}\right)\right) \tag{18}$$

3. Performance evaluation matrix of the e-learning system and its evaluation rules

As noted above, the performance evaluation matrix is a good tool for evaluating the performance of service operation systems [7]. Therefore, we use the satisfaction index as the horizontal axis and the influence index as the vertical axis to construct the performance evaluation matrix of the e-learning system. Based on the concept of continuous quality improvement from total quality management, the performance evaluation matrix is divided into four evaluation blocks using the average of the estimated observation values of the satisfaction index (θ_0) and the average of the estimated observation values of the influence index (ρ_0).

The average of all estimated observations for the satisfaction index (θ_0) is defined as follows:

$$\theta_0 = \frac{1}{q}\sum_{h=1}^{q}\hat{\theta}_{h0} \tag{19}$$

Similarly, the average of all estimated observations for the influence index (ρ_0) is defined as follows:

$$\rho_0 = \frac{1}{q}\sum_{h=1}^{q}\hat{\rho}_{h0} \tag{20}$$

Thus, the four evaluation quadrants can be represented as follows:

Quadrant 1: $Q_1 = \{(x_h, y_h) \mid \theta_0 \leq x_h \leq 1, \rho_0 \leq y_h \leq 1\}$,

Quadrant 2: $Q_2 = \{(x_h, y_h) \mid 0 \leq x_h \leq \theta_0, \rho_0 \leq y_h \leq 1\}$,

Quadrant 2: $Q_3 = \{(x_h, y_h) \mid 0 \leq x_h \leq \theta_0, 0 \leq y_h < \rho_0\}$,

Quadrant 4: $Q_4 = \{(x_h, y_h) \mid \theta_0 \leq x_h \leq 1, 0 \leq y_h < \rho_0\}$.

Drawing on the work of Chen et al. [6] and the concept of continuous improvement, we use the average of all estimated observations of satisfaction index θ_0 as the statistical standard. Thus, we define the following:

null hypothesis H_0: $\theta_h \geq \theta_0$,

alternative hypothesis H_1: $\theta_h < \theta_0$.

We use $U\theta_{h0}$ to perform statistical testing. The test rules for the satisfaction index are as follows:

1. When the upper confidence limit of the satisfaction index is $U\theta_{h0} \geq \theta_0$, it can be inferred that $\theta_h \geq \theta_0$, indicating that no improvement is needed.
2. When the upper confidence limit of the satisfaction index is $U\theta_{h0} < \theta_0$, it can be inferred that $\theta_h < \theta_0$, indicating that the j-th questionnaire item is in need of improvement.

Yu et al. [2] pointed out that when resources are limited, the priority of each service item can be determined through statistical testing of impact indicators. As with the satisfaction index, we use the average of all estimated observations of influence index ρ_0 as the statistical standard. Thus, we define the following:

null hypothesis H_0': $\rho_h \geq \rho_0$,

alternative hypothesis H_1': $\rho_h < \rho_0$.

Observation values $U\rho_{h0}$ are applied for statistical testing according to the following rules:

3. When observation value $U\rho_{h0}$ is bigger than or equal to ρ_0 ($U\rho_{h0} \geq \rho_0$), it can be inferred that ($\rho_h \geq \rho_0$), indicating that the h-th question has a higher influence and therefore should be prioritized for improvement.
4. When observation value $U\rho_{h0}$ is smaller than ρ_0 ($U\rho_{h0} < \rho_0$), it can be inferred that ($\rho_h < \rho_0$), indicating that the h-th question has a lower influence and therefore does not need to be prioritized for improvement

Next, we analyze the location of evaluation coordinate points (x_h, y_h) in the four evaluation quadrants to establish decision rules for improving the e-learning system, as follows:

1. When evaluation coordinate point (x_h, y_h) falls into quadrant 1, it means that upper confidence limit $U\theta_{h0}$ is greater than or equal to θ_0 ($U\theta_{h0} \geq \theta_0$). We thus do not reject null hypothesis H_0 and conclude that $\theta_h \geq \theta_0$. Item *h* can be maintained without any need for improvement.
2. When evaluation coordinate point (x_h, y_h) falls into quadrant 4, it means that upper confidence limit $U\theta_{h0}$ is greater than or equal to θ_0 ($U\theta_{h0} \geq \theta_0$).We thus do not reject null hypothesis H_0 and conclude that $\theta_h \geq \theta_0$. Item *h* can be maintained without any need for improvement.

3. When evaluation coordinate point (x_h, y_h) falls into quadrant 2, it means that upper confidence limit $U\theta_{h0}$ is less than θ_0 ($U\theta_{h0} < \theta_0$). We thus reject the null hypothesis and conclude that $\theta_h < \theta_0$, so item h must be improved. In addition, it means that upper confidence limit $U\rho_{h0}$ is greater than or equal to ρ_0 ($U\rho_{h0} \geq \rho_0$). The priority of improving item h is thus high.
4. When evaluation coordinate point (x_h, y_h) falls into quadrant 3, it means that upper confidence limit $U\theta_{h0}$ is less than θ_0 ($U\theta_{h0} < \theta_0$). We thus reject the null hypothesis and conclude that $\theta_h < \theta_0$, so item h must be improved. In addition, it means that upper confidence limit $U\rho_{h0}$ is less than ρ_0 ($U\rho_{h0} < \rho_0$). The priority of improving item h is low.

4. Conclusion

After the COVID-19 pandemic, e-learning systems have become a mainstream learning model, as learners can access education from home without travel. Improving the performance of an e-learning system enhances user satisfaction, attracting more learners from various locations, thus creating greater business value and increasing economic benefits. This study establishes a performance evaluation matrix to develop a decision-making model for assessing and improving e-learning systems. It helps system administrators understand learner satisfaction with different service items and identify items that need improvement to enhance overall user satisfaction. To maintain general applicability, the study assumes there are q questionnaire items. With customer satisfaction following a Beta distribution, the research defines a satisfaction index. Additionally, an influence index is created based on the correlation between individual and overall satisfaction. This approach reduces response volume by 50%, increasing response willingness and accuracy. As the indices have unknown parameters, the study derives upper confidence limits for all indices and uses these observations for statistical tests, minimizing misjudgment risks caused by sampling errors. Using the average satisfaction index values as evaluation criteria, the performance evaluation matrix is divided into four quadrants. The upper confidence limits of two indices serve as evaluation coordinates, determining quadrant positioning. Based on statistical test rules, this research develops a performance evaluation and improvement decision-making model for e-learning systems. This assists administrators in identifying service items that require enhancement and prioritizing improvements when resources are limited.

5. References

[1] T. H. Le Vo. "Online simulated workplace tasks to enhance business english learning", Journal of Asian Business and Economic Studies, Vol. 29, No. 3, 205-221, 2022.

[2] C. M. Yu, H. T. Chang, and K. S. Chen. "Developing a performance evaluation matrix to enhance the learner satisfaction of an e-learning system", Total Quality Management and Business Excellence, Vol. 29, No. 7-8, 272-745, 2018.

[3] Y. T. Wang, and K. Y. Lin. "Virtual reality-based online learning system adoption: a research framework and empirical study", Online Information Review, Vol. 48, No. 6, 1233-1251, 2024.

[4] C. M. Chen, L. Ming-Chaun, and C. P. Kuo. "A game-based learning system based on octalysis gamification framework to promote employees' Japanese learning", Computers and Education, Vol. 205, 104899, 2023.

[5] S. Zuo, Y. Zhao, L. Zheng, Z. Zhao, S. Fan, and J. Wang. "Assessing the influence of the digital economy on carbon emissions: Evidence at the global level", Science of the Total Environment, Vol. 946, 174242, 2024.

[6] K. S. Chen, H. T. Chang, and C. M. Yu. "Development and application of performance improvement verification model: A case study of an e-learning system", Total Quality Management and Business Excellence, Vol. 30, No. 7-8, 936-952, 2019.

[7] K. S. Chen, and C. M. Yu. "Fuzzy test model for performance evaluation matrix of service operating systems", Computers and Industrial Engineering, Vol. 140, 106240, 2020.

[8] C. C. Liu, C. H. Yu, and K. S. Chen. "Using Statistical Test Method to Establish a Decision Model of Performance Evaluation Matrix", Applied Sciences, Vol. 13, No. 8, 5139, 2023.

[9] K. J. Wang, T. C. Chang, and K. S. Chen. "Determining critical service quality from the view of performance influence", Total Quality Management and Business Excellence, Vol. 26, No. 3-4, 368-384, 2015.

[10] K. S. Chen. "Fuzzy testing of operating performance index based on confidence intervals", Annals of Operations Research, Vol. 311, No. 1, 19-33, 2022.

[11] R. V. Hogg, and E. A. Tanis. "Probability and statistical inference", 6th ed., Prentice-Hall, New Jersey, 2001.

Application of SPC and AHP in Quality Control: Case of Electronic Components at a Manufacturing Company

KHAC-HIEU Nguyen[1], ANH-VAN Nguyen[2], MY-HANH Nguyen[3]

[1]Faculty of Economics, Ho Chi Minh City University of Technology and Education, Vietnam, Email: hieunk@hcmute.edu.vn
[2]Faculty of Economics, Ho Chi Minh City University of Technology and Education, Vietnam, Email: anhvan@hcmute.edu.vn
[3]Department of Industrial Engineering and Management, Yuan Ze University, Taiwan, Email: ntmhanh@saturn.yzu.edu.tw (Corresponding author)

Keywords: SPC, AHP, quality control, defect analysis, manufacturing, Industry 4.0

Abstract - Quality control is essential in electronic component manufacturing, where defect prevention directly impacts production efficiency. People widely use Statistical Process Control (SPC) to monitor and improve quality, but it fails to prioritize the most critical defect causes. This study integrated SPC with the Analytic Hierarchy Process (AHP) to improve defect identification and root cause analysis. The authors conducted a case study in an electronic components manufacturing company, concentrating on the welding process. The Pareto chart identified damaged cores as the most frequent defect. We analyzed potential causes using the 4M method and applied AHP to rank them based on expert evaluations. The results indicated inappropriate installation and excessive force testing parameters were the primary contributors. The study implemented a corrective solution by adjusting the settings of the force testing machine, which reduced the applied force while maintaining the quality of the product. Post-adjustment data confirmed the effectiveness of this approach. This study demonstrates that combining SPC and AHP enhances quality control decision-making, supporting continuous improvement in Industry 4.0 manufacturing.

1. Introduction

In today's highly competitive manufacturing environment, ensuring consistent product quality is essential for enterprises to maintain their market position and meet international standards. Statistical Process Control (SPC) has been widely adopted as an effective tool to monitor and improve production quality by detecting variations and reducing defects in manufacturing processes [1]. By systematically analyzing production data, SPC enables companies to maintain process stability and enhance product reliability [1]. Even though SPC works, it might not always give clear information about the most important reasons for defects, which is a big problem in manufacturing environments that are very complicated [1, 2].

The electronics manufacturing industry plays a pivotal role in Vietnam's economy, significantly contributing to employment, exports, and economic growth. According to the Vietnam Economic Annual Report 2021, the export value of electronic components experienced an average annual growth rate of 28.6% between 2011 and 2020 [3]. With increasing global competition and stringent customer requirements, manufacturers must continuously improve their quality control strategies to minimize defects and production inefficiencies. One of the most common challenges in electronics manufacturing is defect prevention during critical processes such as welding, where precision and consistency are crucial [4].

Although SPC methods effectively identify defect trends, they do not inherently prioritize the most critical defect causes. To address this limitation, this study integrates the Analytic Hierarchy Process (AHP) with SPC to enhance root cause analysis and decision-making. AHP is a multi-criteria decision-making approach that allows manufacturers to rank defect causes based on their severity and impact on quality [5] [6]. Applying AHP, this research systematically evaluates the most significant factors contributing to defects and proposes targeted solutions to mitigate quality issues effectively. New studies show that AHP is very important in modern quality management systems. They show how it helps make decisions in Total Quality Management (TQM) 4.0 and Industry 4.0 settings [6].

Furthermore, as manufacturing industries transition toward Industry 4.0, enterprises are under increasing pressure to ensure sustainable quality management practices that align with digital transformation strategies. Integrating SPC and AHP not only enhances defect detection and prevention but also contributes to long-term sustainable excellence in production. The shift to Quality 4.0, which incorporates data-driven decision-making, intelligent process monitoring, and real-time analytics, underscores the need for adaptive quality control methodologies [7].

This study focuses on analyzing defects in the welding process at an electronic components manufacturing company. To improve defect detection and corrective actions, this research combines SPC for defect identification and AHP for root cause prioritization, providing a more structured approach to quality control enhancement. By implementing this integrated approach, the study aims to: (1) Identify major defects in the welding process using SPC techniques; (2) Determine key influencing factors using the 4M method (Man, Machine, Method, Material); (3) Prioritize the most critical causes using AHP analysis; (4) Propose practical solutions to mitigate defects and improve production efficiency.

This research's findings provide theoretical contributions to quality management literature and practical insights for manufacturing enterprises seeking to optimize their quality control systems. Ultimately, integrating SPC and AHP presents a more data-driven, systematic approach to enhancing product quality, reducing defects, and supporting continuous improvement in the electronics manufacturing industry.

2. Methodology

This study follows a structured four-step approach to identify, analyze, prioritize, and propose solutions to address the root causes of defects in the production process. The methodology consists of the following steps:

In the first step, the Pareto chart was utilized to determine the most frequently occurring defect in Production Line 2. The Pareto principle (80/20 rule) suggests that a small number of causes contribute to most defects. To apply this principle, production defect data were collected, categorized, and analyzed to visualize their frequency distribution. The results highlighted the most significant defect, which required further investigation. This step allowed the study to focus on the most critical quality issue in production, ensuring that resources and efforts were directed toward its resolution.

In the second step, the 4M method (Man, Machine, Method, and Material) was employed to identify potential causes of the defect systematically. This method categorizes defect causes into four key areas: Man (human factors related to worker skills, experience, and handling), Machine (issues related to equipment performance, maintenance, and calibration), method (process-related inefficiencies, procedural deviations, and quality control measures), and Material (raw material quality, consistency, and supplier-related issues). To gain a comprehensive understanding of these factors, structured interviews were conducted with 18 industry experts, including one manager from the welding process, five workers from the Quality Control (QC) department, four workers from the Production department, four workers from the Incoming Quality Control (IQC) department, and four workers directly involved in production. The experts provided insights into the key factors influencing defect occurrence, which were then analyzed to identify the most critical causes under each 4M category.

In the third step, the Analytic Hierarchy Process (AHP) was applied to prioritize the identified causes based on their impact. A structured AHP questionnaire was developed, listing the causes categorized under the 4M framework, and distributed to 10 experts, including one manager responsible for the welding process, five workers from the QC department, and four workers from the production department.

In this survey, the authors determined the relative importance of each factor and indicator level through pairwise comparative judgments. According to Deng et al. [1], panelists were required to simultaneously compare two factors or indicators. The respondents expressed their preference between every two factors and translated these preferences into numerical ratings of 1-3-5-7-9, where 1 indicated equal importance, and 9 represented the highest level of importance. Intermediate values (2-4-6-8) were used to indicate varying degrees of importance. If factor A was considered more important than factor B, a value between 2 and 9 was assigned in favor of A; otherwise, the value was assigned to B. If both factors were equally important, a score of 1 was selected. Several important indices are calculated using the AHP method. These include the Pairwise Comparison Matrix, which shows how experts feel about each factor by comparing it to others; the Normalized Matrix, which makes the pairwise comparison matrix more consistent so experts can make fair decisions; and the Priority Weights (Eigenvalues), which show how much each factor is worth.

The collected data were then assessed for consistency and reliability using the Consistency Index (CI). According to Saaty [2], the Consistency Ratio (CR) was calculated as CR (consistency ratio) = CI/RI (random index), where RI represents the Random Consistency Index. The Consistency Index (CI) was computed using $CI=(\lambda max-n)/(n-1)$, where λmax is the largest eigenvalue of the pairwise comparison matrix, and n is the number of factors being compared. A CR value below 0.10 indicates acceptable consistency, meaning the evaluations provided by respondents are reliable. If CR > 0.10, the judgments are inconsistent and require reassessment.

In the final step, after identifying the most significant root cause, a corrective solution was proposed to minimize its impact.

3. Results

The company conducting the research specializes in the production of electronic components. The organization has its quality assurance system, which is ISO 9001 certified. The company's main products are RF component assembly, filters, VCOs, robust lead circulators, air coils, ferrite, PCB assembly, and mini inductors. In this study, we concentrate on the welding process of the Air Coil Product.

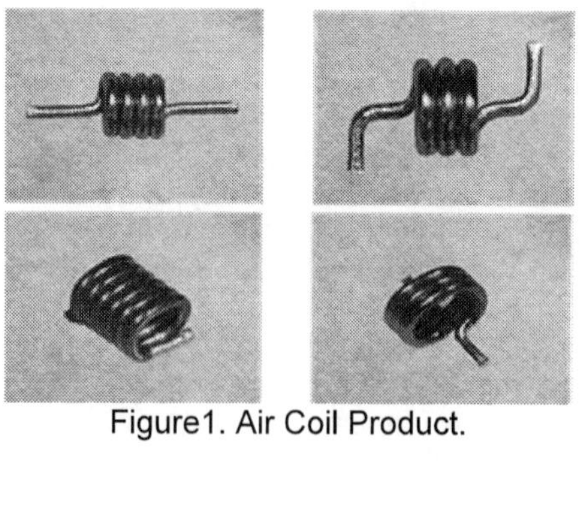

Figure1. Air Coil Product.

3.1 Applying Pareto to find the main defects

In the welding process, the product acceptance standards are clearly defined as follows. The wire must be correctly positioned without defects. Minor lead loss on pins is acceptable for wire quality if the missing area is less than 5% of the pin's surface. Melted lead on pins is acceptable only if the blackened area remains above the elbow of the pin and does not reach the bottom contact area. Pins may have slight scratches, provided they do not significantly affect their function or appearance. Pins must not be visibly deformed or broken.

The product background may have minor scratches if they do not damage the gold-plated surface. The cores must not be chipped; minor surface imperfections such as small, faint white spots are acceptable as long as they do not result in peeling of the core material. Additionally, wires should be secured appropriately without significant gaps or damages. Any lead loss must not exceed the specified tolerance (less than 5%). All cores must be free from major chips or significant surface damage, although minor white spots from previous usage that do not affect the core integrity or surface are permissible.

Table 1 summarizes the data on defects in the welding process over two months, from May to June 2024.

Table 1. Defects in the welding process from May to June 2024

No	Defects	Q'ty	Cumulative
1	Damaged core	206	34.33%
2	Side turn	108	52.33%
3	Damaged substrate	78	65.33%
4	Bad epoxy	72	77.33%
5	Missing wire	46	85.00%
6	Overlapped wire	41	91.83%
7	Wrong wound wire	29	96.67%
8	Excess round	15	99.17%
9	Wrong taped wire	4	99.83%
10	Paste backwards	1	100.00%
Total		600	100.00%

Based on the Pareto chart, we identify and analyze the most significant types of defects during production. Applying the Pareto principle (80/20 rule), we observe that two primary defects—"Damaged core" and "Side turn"—together account for 52.33% of the total defects in the manufacturing process for product code MABA-011085 on line 2. Specifically, the "Damaged core" error alone contributes 34.33%, while the "Side turn" error represents 18% of defects. These issues significantly impact product quality and production efficiency due to their high occurrence rates. Consequently, the involved production departments prioritize addressing these defects. This study aims to deeply analyze these specific defects, employing appropriate quality control tools to investigate their root causes comprehensively, thus proposing practical solutions to mitigate and prevent such problems from recurring in the production line.

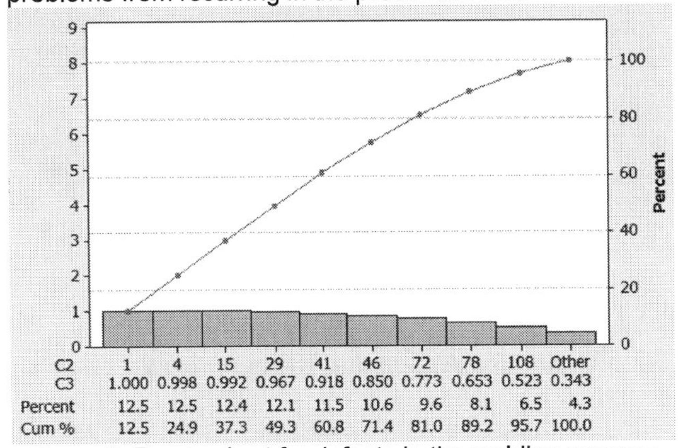

Figure 2. Pareto chart for defects in the welding process

3.2 Applying the 4M method to find the root causes of the main defects

Pareto analysis revealed that "damaged core" was the defect that occurred most frequently. Given its high occurrence rate, the authors focused on identifying the root causes of this defect and proposing practical corrective actions to improve production quality. To determine the key factors contributing to the "damaged core" defect, the authors employed the 4M method. A survey was conducted involving industrial experts, including one manager responsible for supervising employees in the welding process, five workers from the Quality Control (QC) department, four workers from the production department, four workers from the Incoming Quality Control (IQC) department, and four workers directly engaged in the production process.

Based on the collected data, the study identified four major categories of influencing factors: human factors, machinery and equipment, methodological factors, and material factors. These factors were then further analyzed to determine their specific impact on the defect. The specific results are presented in Table 2.

Table 2. Influencing factors of "damaged core" defect

No	Factors	Factors explanation
1	Setting	Inappropriate installation parameters and force testing parameters (force too strong) lead to core breakage.
2	Procedure	Workers have not been fully provided with quality procedures for new product codes.
3	Work instruction s	After a long time, the welding tip will wear out, leaving white spots on the core and possibly breaking it. However, employees lack instructions on recycling the soldering tip and continue using the old one.
4	Worker	Workers adjusted the strings vigorously during the winding process, causing white spot errors.
5	Supplier	Broken cores/tank cores due to input materials not being well controlled.
6	Goods-making	The core has acceptable light white spots, but after the process of making the goods and going

	process	through many stages, the core is affected, leading to severe white spots.
7	Material	The core has a poor coating, so when the wire is wound, friction causes the coating to peel off, leading to severe white spots.
8	Delivery	The delivered goods had light white spots, and when it came to the welding stage, after cutting and adjusting the wires, the strong impact caused the core to have heavy white spots.
9	Inspection	During the inspection, the winding wire overflowed the core surface, so the winding loop had to be adjusted, causing the core to have white spots

3.3 Applying the AHP method to prioritize the factors

We designed an AHP questionnaire outlining the factors influencing the "damaged core" defect. Ten experts evaluate the questionnaire. The respondents included one manager responsible for supervising employees in the welding process, five workers from the Quality Control (QC) department, and four workers from the production department. Each expert was asked to assess the relative importance of these factors in contributing to the defect.

The authors calculated the Pairwise Comparison Matrix, Normalized Matrix, and Priority Weights based on the responses from 10 experts. The individual results were then averaged to obtain the final values. The specific results are presented in Table 3.

Table 3. Ranking of influenced factors of "damaged core" defect

Ranking	Factors	Criteria weights
1	Setting	0.23
2	Worker	0.17
3	Work instructions	0.16
4	Procedure	0.13
5	Supplier	0.08
6	Material	0.075
7	Inspection	0.07
8	Delivery	0.06
9	Goods-making process	0.04

The authors calculated the maximum eigenvalue (λmax) as 9.93, obtained as the arithmetic mean of the Consistency Vector column. Based on this value, the Consistency Index (CI) was computed using the formula:

$CI = (9.93 - 9) / (9 - 1) = 0.12$

The Consistency Ratio (CR) was then determined using the formula:

$CR = CI / RI$

Where RI (Random Consistency Index) is derived from the standard RI table based on the number of criteria. In this case, with nine criteria, the corresponding RI value is 1.45. Thus,

$CR = 0.12 / 1.45 = 0.083$

The results are considered consistent and reliable since the CR value is less than 0.10 (8.3%). This evidence confirms that the ranking outcome is valid. Based on the findings, the most critical root cause of the "damaged core" defect is identified as: *"Inappropriate installation parameters and force testing parameters (force too strong) lead to core breakage."*

This result highlights the importance of optimizing machine settings and force testing parameters to reduce the occurrence of defects in production

3.4 Proposing solution

After identifying the most significant root cause, a corrective solution was proposed to minimize its impact. Based on the AHP analysis, the study focused on optimizing machine settings and force-testing parameters to reduce the likelihood of core breakage.

The proposed solution involved adjusting the settings of the force testing machine to lower the applied force while ensuring product quality. Specifically, the 5000g force testing machine was recalibrated, reducing the testing force from 420g to 405g. We identified excessive pressure on the core as the primary factor contributing to core damage and adjusted to decrease it. The specific configuration parameters are presented in Table 4.

Table 4: Setting parameters

<table>
<tr><th rowspan="3">Testing</th><th colspan="5">Setting parameters</th><th colspan="3">Parameters during force testing</th><th rowspan="3">Force testing machine 5000g</th></tr>
<tr><th rowspan="2">Force (kg)</th><th rowspan="2">Time (ms)</th><th rowspan="2">Setting current (A)</th><th rowspan="2">Lower limit current (A)</th><th rowspan="2">Upper limit current (A)</th><th colspan="2">Single wire</th><th rowspan="2">Double wire</th></tr>
<tr><th>Pin 1 and 3</th><th>Pin 4 and 6</th></tr>
<tr><td>Before</td><td>1.2</td><td>9</td><td>204</td><td>189</td><td>219</td><td>290
221
152</td><td>353
282
211</td><td>626
420
214</td><td>420</td></tr>
<tr><td>After</td><td>1.2</td><td>9</td><td>204</td><td>189</td><td>219</td><td>266
200
150</td><td>350
250
190</td><td>610
405
200</td><td>405</td></tr>
</table>

To validate the effectiveness of this solution, post-adjustment data were collected and compared with pre-adjustment values. The results showed a slight reduction in force values applied during testing, which is expected to mitigate core breakage without compromising product quality. Further monitoring and quality assessments will be conducted to ensure the long-term effectiveness of this adjustment.

4. Conclusion

This study successfully combined statistical process control (SPC) and the analytical hierarchy process (AHP) to improve quality control in a company that makes electronic parts. With the help of SPC, the most common problems in the welding process were found. Then, AHP made it possible to organize the root causes to ensure the most important ones got fixed first.

The results confirmed that inappropriate installation and excessive force testing parameters were the primary contributors to the damaged core defect. Implementing an optimized setting for the force testing machine reduced the applied force, minimizing core breakage without compromising product quality. This adjustment demonstrates the effectiveness of a data-driven, structured approach in addressing quality issues and improving manufacturing efficiency.

In addition to this case study, the results show how important it is to use both SPC and multi-criteria decision-making tools such as AHP to prevent defects better and promote continuous improvement in production settings. Other manufacturing processes can further apply this methodology, thereby contributing to sustainable quality management within the context of Industry 4.0. In the future, researchers might look into combining machine learning and real-time analytics with SPC and AHP to improve defect prediction and process optimization.

5. References

[1] D. C. Montgomery. "Introduction to Statistical Quality Control", 8th ed. New York: Wiley, 2020.

[2] J. Oakland and J. S. Oakland, "Statistical Process Control". London, UK: Routledge, 2007.

[3] Vietnam Institute for Economic and Policy Research (VEPR). "Vietnam Economic Annual Report 2021", Vietnam National University Press, 2021.

[4] L. A. M. Huertas-Quintero, P. P. Conway, D. M. Segura-Velandia, and A. A. West. "Root cause analysis support for quality improvement in electronics manufacturing"; Assembly Automation, vol. 31, no. 1, pp. 38–46, 2011.

[5] T. L. Saaty. "The Analytic Hierarchy Process: Planning, Priority Setting, Resource Allocation". New York: McGraw-Hill, 1990.

[6] T. A. V. Nguyen, D. Tucek, and N. T. Pham. "Indicators for TQM 4.0 model: Delphi method and analytic hierarchy process (AHP) analysis"; Total Quality Management & Business Excellence, vol. 34, no. 1–2, pp. 220–234, 2023.

[7] T. A. V. Nguyen, D. Tucek, N. T. Pham, and K. H. Nguyen. "Quality 4.0 practices toward sustainable excellence in the manufacturing sector"; Total Quality Management & Business Excellence, vol. 35, no. 13-14, pp. 1593-1610, 2024.

IC packaging process quality evaluation for smart manufacturing environments

CHEN Kuen-Suan [1, 2, 3], YU Chun-Min [1,*]

[1] Department of Industrial Engineering and Management, National Chin-Yi University of Technology, Taichung 411030, Taiwan, R.O.C. kuensuan.chen@gmail.com
[2] Department of Business Administration, Chaoyang University of Technology, Taichung 413310, Taiwan, R.O.C.
[3] Department of Business Administration, Asia University, Taichung 413305, Taiwan, R.O.C.
* Corresponding author. Address: No.57, Sec. 2, Zhongshan Rd., Taiping Dist., Taichung 411030, Taiwan (R.O.C.); Tel: +886 4 23924505; Fax: +886 4 23934620; E-mail addresses: yu2013000@gmail.com

Keywords: process capability index; product yield; operating performance of IC component; confidence interval; Poisson distribution.

Abstract – The output of Taiwan's wafer foundry and IC packaging and testing industries ranks first in the world. Its electronic industry boasts a high cluster density, securing its key position in the global market. Increasing the process quality and yield of IC packaging can reduce the scrap rates of IC components and the replacement rates of failed components. Many studies have indicated that wire bonding is a crucial process in the IC packaging industry chain, which follows a professional division of labor model. According to Taguchi loss functions, inadequate process capabilities in gold wire bonding will affect the operating performance of IC components and cause them to malfunction within a short period of time. IC components are widely used in products in network communications, consumer electronics, automobiles, industry, aerospace, and national defense. If any of the IC components in these products malfunction, they will cease to operate normally and require repairs, causing economic losses and increases in carbon emissions. Firms require swift responses, which means that decisions must be made with small sample sizes. We therefore propose a fuzzy evaluation model for the operating performance of IC components based on the process capability of gold wire bonding. We first create an IC component operating performance index. This is achieved by combining all of the process capability indices (PCIs) used to evaluate gold wire bonding and utilizing both the inequality between the PCIs and product yield and the principle in which the number of failures follows a Poisson distribution. By deriving the confidence intervals of the PCIs, we next obtain the confidence interval of this index and use this as the basis of our fuzzy evaluation model. The proposed model aids firms in the electronics industry in the assessment and improvement of process quality.

1. Introduction

Taiwan's wafer foundry and IC packaging and testing industries respectively take up 70% and 50% of the global market, thereby ranking first in the world [1][2]. The high density of Taiwan's electronics industry cluster and complete industry chain for information and communication technology (ICT) secures this position [3]. For example, Mediatek's IC design and TSMC's wafer foundries and semiconductor packaging and testing have formed an electronics industry chain with vertically-integrated services in Taiwan [1]. Increasing the process quality and yield of IC packaging can reduce scrap rates, lengthen component service life, and decrease replacement rates [4].

Wire bonding, a crucial process in IC packaging, involves welding gold wire onto chips and the inner pins of lead frames to serve as an important medium for electrical connection and signal transmission between the internal and external components [5]. Wire pull and ball shear are two important characteristics of the process quality of wire bonding [6]. Poor process quality can cause defective bonding between the gold wire and the chip or lead frame; the gold wire may therefore break and cause electronic products to malfunction [7].

IC components are widely used in products made for information and network communications, consumer electronics, automobiles, aerospace, and national defense. To ensure the quality and reliability of these products, enhancing the process capabilities of IC component products is critical. If any of the IC components in these products malfunction, they will cease to operate normally and require repairs, causing economic losses and increases in carbon emissions. Chen et al. [5] specified that the gold wires in IC components have two larger-the-better quality characteristics: 1. wire pull and 2. ball shear. Without loss of generality, suppose an IC component has k wires. Let random variable $X_{i,j}$ represent the i-th quality characteristic of the j-th wire and follow a normal distribution with mean $\mu_{i,j}$ and variance $\sigma_{i,j}^2$. Let random variable $Y_{i,j}$ follow a normal distribution with mean $\delta_{i,j}$ and variance $\gamma_{i,j}^2$, where

$$Y_{i,j} = \frac{X_{i,j} - T_{i,j}}{d_{i,j}} = \frac{X_{i,j} - 2LSL_{i,j}}{T_{i,j} - LSL_{i,j}} = \frac{X_{i,j}}{LSL_{i,j}} - 2 \quad (1)$$

Where $LSL_{1,j}$ and $LSL_{2,j}$ represent the lower specification limits of the j-th wire for wire pull and ball shear, respectively. Thus, random variable $Y_{i,j} \sim N(\delta_{i,j}, \gamma_{i,j}^2)$, where $i = 1, 2$ and $j = 1, 2, ..., k$. The process capability indices (PCIs) used to assess these $2k$ larger-the-better quality characteristics can therefore be written as follows:

$$C_{PL(i,j)} = \frac{1+\delta_{i,j}}{3\gamma_{i,j}} \quad (2)$$

Similar to Chang and Chen [7], this paper integrates the evaluation indices of the two quality characteristics (i = 1 and i = 2) of the j-th bonding wire into the process capability index of the j-th bonding wire as follows:

$$C_{PLj} = \frac{1}{3}\Phi^{-1}\left\{1 - \sum_{i=1}^{2}\left[1 - \Phi\left(3C_{PL(i,j)}\right)\right]\right\} \quad (3)$$

Let event $E_{i,j} = \{Y_{i,j} \geq -1\}$ and its complement $E_{i,j}^c = \{Y_{i,j} < -1\}$, where $i = 1, 2$ and $j = 1, 2, ..., k$. Then the defective rate p and defective rate q of the j-th welding wire are as follows:

$$p_{i,j} = p(E_{i,j}) = \Phi\left(3Q_{PL(i,j)}\right)$$
$$q_{i,j} = p(E_{i,j}^c) = 1 - \Phi\left(3Q_{PL(i,j)}\right) \quad (4)$$

Next, let event $E_j = E_{1,j} \cap E_{2,j}$. According to the De Morgan theorem and Boole's inequality, the yield of the j-th wire is

$$p_j = p(E_j) = p(E_{1,j} \cap E_{2,j}) \geq 1 - \sum_{i=1}^{2} p(E_{i,j}^c) = 1 - \sum_{i=1}^{2}\left[1 - \Phi\left(3C_{PL(i,j)}\right)\right] = \Phi\left(3C_{PLj}\right) \quad (5)$$

Clearly, the relationship between PCI C_{PLj} and the yield of the j-th wire must be an inequality. Following this concept, we combined the PCIs of the k wires and defined the PCI of an IC component as follows:

$$C_{PL} = \frac{1}{3}\Phi^{-1}\left\{1 - \sum_{j=1}^{k}\left[1 - \Phi\left(3C_{PLj}\right)\right]\right\} \quad (6)$$

Equivalently,

$$C_{PL} = \frac{1}{3}\Phi^{-1}\left\{1 - \sum_{j=1}^{k}\left[1 - \left\{1 - \sum_{i=1}^{2}\left[1 - \Phi\left(3C_{PL(i,j)}\right)\right]\right\}\right]\right\} \quad (7)$$

Let event $E = \bigcap_{j=1}^{k} E_j$ represent the event that the IC component is a good product. According to the De Morgan theorem and Boole's inequality, the yield rate of the IC component is as follows

$$p = p(E) = p\left(\bigcap_{j=1}^{k} E_j\right) \geq 1 - \sum_{j=1}^{k} p(E_j^c) = 1 - \sum_{j=1}^{k}\left[1 - \Phi\left(3C_{PLj}\right)\right] = \Phi\left(3C_{PL}\right) \quad (8)$$

Obviously, the relationship between PCI C_{PL} and the yield rate must be an inequality. When the value of the IC component's PCI C_{PL} is larger, product yield p is also higher. Assume that among the products sold by an IC component manufacturer, the number of IC components that fail due to insufficient wire bonding process capability per unit of time is N and the average number is λ, where $\lambda = N \times (1-p)$. Because $(1-p) \leq \left(1 - \Phi\left(3C_{PL}\right)\right)$, then $\lambda < N \times \left(1 - \Phi\left(3C_{PL}\right)\right)$. Obviously, when the value of the process capability index is larger, the average number of failures λ is smaller. According to Eq. (8), the process capability of the IC component is composed of the process capability of each bonding wire. If the process capability of one of the bonding wires is insufficient, then the IC component may fail during the product warranty period. Therefore, this study uses PCIs to evaluate these 2k quality characteristics for our fuzzy evaluation and improvement model

The remainder of this paper is organized as follows. In Section 2, we propose an operating performance index for IC components and derive the 100($1-\alpha$)% confidence interval for this index. In Section 3, a fuzzy evaluation model is developed based on this confidence interval. Finally, Section 4 provides our conclusions.

2. Operating performance index for IC components

As noted above, random variable $N(x)$ follows a Poisson distribution with mean λx:

$$p\left(N(x) = n \mid \lambda x\right) = \frac{e^{-\lambda t}(\lambda x)^n}{n!}, \quad n = 0, 1, 2, \ldots \quad (9)$$

Furthermore, total loss TL caused by the functional failure of these IC components can be expressed as follows:

$$TL = \sum_{h=1}^{N} L_h \quad (10)$$

According to Eq. (9), the expected value of TL is

$$\mu_{TL} = E[TL] = E[N] \times E[L_h] = \lambda \times \mu \quad (11)$$

According to Chen et al. [8], losses are an inevitable result of IC component malfunction; total expected loss μ_{TL} can only be effectively reduced by decreasing λ, which is the mean number of failures in a unit of IC components within a unit of time. From a management perspective, manufacturers can set the upper limit requirement for the number of IC component malfunctions per unit time as N_0; that is, $N < N_0$ [9]. Let $N_0 = N(1-p_0)$, where p_0 is the required level of product yield. Thus, the manager's requirement can be rewritten as $p \geq p_0$. Based on this concept and Eq. (7), we define an operating performance index for IC components as follows:

$$\theta_{IC} = \frac{p}{p_0} = \frac{\Phi\left(3C_{PL}\right)}{p_0} = \frac{1}{p_0}\left\{1 - \sum_{j=1}^{k}\left[1 - \left\{1 - \sum_{i=1}^{2}\left[1 - \Phi\left(3C_{PL(i,j)}\right)\right]\right\}\right]\right\} \quad (12)$$

According to Eqs. (2), (3), and (6), we first deduce the 100($1-\alpha$)% confidence interval of indices C_{PLj}, then that of index C_{PL}, and finally, the 100($1-\alpha$)% confidence interval of index θ_{IC}.

As stated above, random variable $Y_{i,j} \sim N(\delta_{i,j}, \gamma_{i,j}^2)$. Let $Y_{i,j,1}, ..., Y_{i,j,l}, ..., Y_{i,j,n}$ be a set of random samples. Thus, the mean and standard deviation of the samples are as follows:

$$\delta_{i,j}^* = \frac{1}{n}\sum_{l=1}^{n} Y_{i,j,l} \text{ and } \gamma_{i,j}^* = \frac{1}{n}\sum_{l=1}^{n}\left(Y_{i,j,l} - \delta_{i,j}^*\right)^2 \quad (13)$$

Thus, operating performance index $C_{PL(i,j)}$ of the two larger-the-better quality characteristics of the j-th wire is estimated to be

$$C^*_{PL(i,j)} = \frac{1+\delta^*_{i,j}}{3\gamma^*_{i,j}} \quad (14)$$

Under the assumption of normality, we let

$$T_n = \frac{\sqrt{n}\left(\delta^*_{i,j} - \delta_{i,j}\right)}{\gamma^*_{i,j}} \quad (15)$$

and

$$K_n = \frac{n\gamma^{*2}_{i,j}}{\gamma^2_{i,j}} \quad (16)$$

Thus, T_n follows a t distribution with $n-1$ degrees of freedom, noted as $T_n \sim t_{n-1}$. Furthermore, K_n follows a chi-square distribution with $n-1$ degrees of freedom, noted as $K_n \sim \chi^2_{n-1}$. Next, events $E_1 = \{T_n \ge -t_{\alpha/2;n-1}\}$ and $E_2 = \{K_n \le \chi^2_{\alpha/2;n-1}\}$ are defined, where $t_{\alpha/2;n-1}$ is the $1-\alpha/2$ upper quantile of t_{n-1}, and $\chi^2_{\alpha/2;n-1}$ is the $1-\alpha/2$ lower quantile of χ^2_{n-1}. Based on the De Morgan theorem and Boole's inequality [10].

$$p(E_1 \cap E_2) = p\left(T_n \ge -t_{\alpha/2;n-1}, K_n \le \chi^2_{\alpha/2;n-1}\right) \ge 1 - \sum_{i=1}^{2} p\left(E_i^c\right) = 1-\alpha \quad (17)$$

$$\Rightarrow p\left(\delta_{i,j} \le \delta^*_{i,j} + t_{\alpha/2;n-1}\frac{\gamma^*_{i,j}}{\sqrt{n}}, \gamma_{i,j} \ge \gamma^*_{i,j}\sqrt{\frac{n}{\chi^2_{1-\alpha/2;n-1}}}\right) \ge 1-\alpha \quad (18)$$

According to Eq. (17), $p\left(C_{PL(i,j)} \le UC_{PL(i,j)}\right) \ge 1-\alpha$, where $UC_{PL(i,j)}$ is the $1-\alpha$ upper confidence limit of index $C_{PL(i,j)}$, as follows:

$$UC_{PL(i,j)} = \left(C^*_{PL(i,j)} + \frac{t_{\alpha/2;n-1}}{\sqrt{n}}\right)\sqrt{\frac{n}{\chi^2_{1-\alpha/2;n-1}}} \quad (19)$$

According to Eqs. (5) and (18), the $1-\alpha$ upper confidence limit of operating performance index C_{PLj} for the j-th wire is as follows:

$$UC_{PLj} = \frac{1}{3}\Phi^{-1}\left\{1 - \sum_{i=1}^{2}\left[1 - \Phi\left(3\left(C^*_{PL(i,j)} + \frac{t_{\alpha/2;n-1}}{\sqrt{n}}\right)\sqrt{\frac{n}{\chi^2_{1-\alpha/2;n-1}}}\right)\right]\right\} \quad (20)$$

Next, according to Eqs. (8) and (19), the $1-\alpha$ upper confidence limit of evaluation index C_{PL} for the j-th wire is as follows:

$$UC_{PL} = \frac{1}{3}\Phi^{-1}\left\{1 - \sum_{j=1}^{k}\left[1 - \Phi\left(3UC_{PLj}\right)\right]\right\} \quad (21)$$

Equivalently,

$$UC_{PL} = \frac{1}{3}\Phi^{-1}\left\{1 - \sum_{j=1}^{k}\left[1 - \left\{1 - \sum_{i=1}^{2}\left[1 - \Phi\left(3\left(C^*_{PL(i,j)} + \frac{t_{\alpha/2;n-1}}{\sqrt{n}}\right)\sqrt{\frac{n}{\chi^2_{1-\alpha/2;n-1}}}\right)\right]\right\}\right]\right\} \quad (22)$$

Therefore,

$$U\theta_{IC} = \frac{1}{p_0}\left(1 - \sum_{j=1}^{k}\left[1 - \left\{1 - \sum_{i=1}^{2}\left[1 - \Phi\left(3\left(C^*_{PL(i,j)} + \frac{t_{\alpha/2;n-1}}{\sqrt{n}}\right)\sqrt{\frac{n}{\chi^2_{1-\alpha/2;n-1}}}\right)\right]\right\}\right]\right) \quad (23)$$

The proposed fuzzy evaluation model is based on the upper confidence limit of operating performance index $U\theta_{IC}$.

3. Fuzzy evaluation model of IC component performance

Suppose the operating performance index θ_{IC} is required to reach threshold C. Then, the required level of product yield is $p_0 = \Phi(3C)$. Thus,

$$\theta_{IC} = \frac{\Phi(3C_{PL})}{\Phi(3C)}, \quad (24)$$

Equivalently,

$$\theta_{IC} = \frac{1}{\Phi(3C)}\left\{1 - \sum_{j=1}^{k}\left[1 - \left\{1 - \sum_{i=1}^{2}\left[1 - \Phi\left(3C_{PL(i,j)}\right)\right]\right\}\right]\right\} \quad (25)$$

Null hypothesis H_0 and alternative hypothesis H_1 can then be expressed as follows:

$H_0: \theta_{IC} \ge 1$;

$H_1: \theta_{IC} < 1$.

Obviously, when the value of operating performance index θ_{IC} is bigger than or equal to 1 ($\theta_{IC} \ge 1$), the value of process capability index C_{PL} is bigger than or equal to C ($C_{PL} \ge C$).

The fuzzy evaluation model for operating performance index is based on Eq. (23) and statistical testing rules. According to Chen and Yu (2021), α-cuts of the semi-triangular fuzzy number $\tilde{\theta}_{IC}$ can be defined as follows:

$$\tilde{\theta}_{IC}[\alpha] = \begin{cases} \left[\theta_{IC}(1), \theta_{IC}(\alpha)\right], & for\ 0.01 \le \alpha \le 1 \\ \left[\theta_{IC}(1), \theta_{IC}(0.01)\right], & for\ 0 \le \alpha \le 0.01 \end{cases} \quad (26)$$

where

$[LS_{PK}, US_{PK}]$ is the $1-\alpha$ confidence interval of index S_{PK}. Based on the definition of product failure evaluation index Q_λ, the upper and lower limits of the $1-\alpha$ confidence interval can be expressed as follows:

$$\theta_{IC}(1) = \frac{1}{\Phi(3C)}\left(1 - \sum_{j=1}^{k}\left[1 - \left\{1 - \sum_{i=1}^{2}\left[1 - \Phi\left(3\left(C^*_{PL(i,j)}\right)\sqrt{\frac{n}{\chi^2_{0.5;n-1}}}\right)\right]\right\}\right]\right) \quad (27)$$

$$\theta_{IC}(\alpha) = \frac{1}{\Phi(3C)}\left(1 - \sum_{j=1}^{k}\left[1 - \left\{1 - \sum_{i=1}^{2}\left[1 - \Phi\left(3\left(C^*_{PL(i,j)} + \frac{t_{\alpha/2;n-1}}{\sqrt{n}}\right)\sqrt{\frac{n}{\chi^2_{1-\alpha/2;n-1}}}\right)\right]\right\}\right]\right) \quad (28)$$

As noted above, the semi-triangular fuzzy number $\tilde{\theta}_{IC} = \Delta(\theta_M, \theta_R)$, where $\theta_M = \theta_{IC}(1)$ and

$$\theta_R = \frac{1}{\Phi(3C)}\left(1 - \sum_{j=1}^{k}\left[1 - \left\{1 - \sum_{i=1}^{2}\left[1 - \Phi\left(3\left(C^*_{PL(i,j)} + \frac{t_{0.005;n-1}}{\sqrt{n}}\right)\sqrt{\frac{n}{\chi^2_{0.995;n-1}}}\right)\right]\right\}\right]\right) \quad (29)$$

Thus, the fuzzy membership function can be expressed as follows:

$$\eta(x)=\begin{cases}0 & if\ x<\theta_M\\ 1 & if\ x=\theta_M\\ \alpha & if\ \theta_M<x\le\theta_R\\ 0 & if\ x>\theta_R\end{cases} \tag{30}$$

where the value of α is determined by

$$x=\frac{1}{\Phi(3C)}\left(1-\sum_{j=1}^{k}\left[1-\left\{1-\sum_{i=1}^{2}\left[1-\Phi\left(3\left(C^{*}_{PL(i,j)}+\frac{t_{\alpha/2;n-1}}{\sqrt{n}}\right)\sqrt{\frac{n}{\chi^2_{1-\alpha/2;n-1}}}\right)\right]\right\}\right]\right) \tag{31}$$

Based on Eq. (30), we can construct a graph of membership functions of $\eta(x)$ with vertical line $x=1$. This is presented in Figure 1.

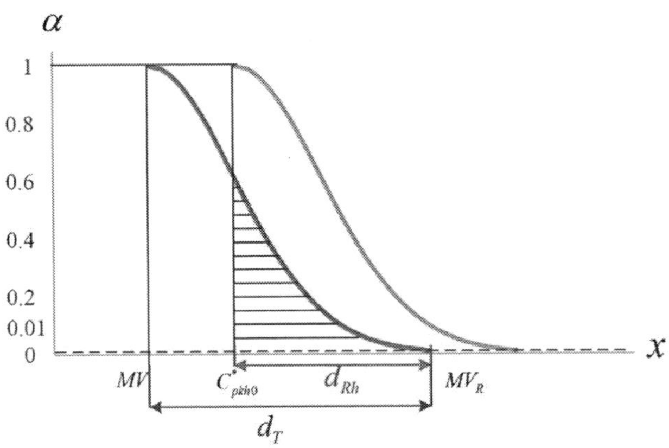

Figure 1. Graph of membership functions of $\eta(x)$ with vertical line $x=1$

Drawing on the work of Chen and Yu [11], we let set A_T be the area between the fuzzy membership function $\eta(x)$ and the x-axis as follows:

$$A_T=\{(x,\alpha)|\theta_M\le x<\theta_{IC}(\alpha),0\le\alpha\le1\} \tag{32}$$

Similarly, we let set A_R be the area between the vertical line $x=1$, the fuzzy membership function $\eta(x)$, and the x-axis as follows:

$$A_R=\{(x,\alpha)|1\le x<\theta_{IC}(\alpha),0\le\alpha\le a\} \tag{33}$$

where $\alpha=1$ such that $\theta_{IC}(a)=1$. According to Eq. (28), we define $d_T=\theta_R-\theta_M$ as follows:

$$d_T=\frac{2}{\Phi(3C)}\left(1-\sum_{j=1}^{k}\left[1-\left\{1-\sum_{i=1}^{2}\left[1-\Phi\left(3\left(C^{*}_{PL(i,j)}+\frac{t_{0.005;n-1}}{\sqrt{n}}\right)\sqrt{\frac{n}{\chi^2_{0.995;n-1}}}\right)\right]\right\}\right]\right)$$
$$-\frac{2}{\Phi(3C)}\left(1-\sum_{j=1}^{k}\left[1-\left\{1-\sum_{i=1}^{2}\left[1-\Phi\left(3\left(C^{*}_{PL(i,j)}\right)\sqrt{\frac{n}{\chi^2_{0.5;n-1}}}\right)\right]\right\}\right]\right) \tag{34}$$

Similarly, we let $d_T=\theta_R-\theta_M$ as follows:

$$d_R=\frac{1}{\Phi(3C)}\left(1-\sum_{j=1}^{k}\left[1-\left\{1-\sum_{i=1}^{2}\left[1-\Phi\left(3\left(C^{*}_{PL(i,j)}+\frac{t_{0.005;n-1}}{\sqrt{n}}\right)\sqrt{\frac{n}{\chi^2_{0.995;n-1}}}\right)\right]\right\}\right]\right)-1 \tag{35}$$

Process engineers can determine the value of ϕ based on historical production data to establish the following fuzzy evaluation rules based on d_R/d_T and ϕ [12]:

(1). If $d_R/d_T\le\phi$, then reject H_0 and conclude that $\theta_{IC}<1$. That is, the operating performance is poor and requires improvement.

(2). If $\phi<d_R/d_T\le0.5$, then do not reject H_0 and conclude that $\theta_{IC}\ge1$. That is, that is the operating performance is good.

As these rules are based on accumulated data, they are applicable to small sample sizes with greater errors [13]. However, because the rules are based on d_R/d_T, engineers may have difficulty to comprehend and then implement it in practice. We therefore designed fuzzy evaluation value EV to simplify the testing rules as follows:

(1). If $EV\ge1$, then reject H_0 and conclude that $\theta_{IC}<1$. That is, the operating performance is poor and requires improvement.

(2). If $EV<1$, then do not reject H_0 and conclude that $\theta_{IC}\ge1$. That is, the operating performance is good.

The value of EV can be obtained as follows:

$$\frac{\theta_R-EV}{2(\theta_R-\theta_M)}=\phi \tag{36}$$

Thus,

$$EV=(1-2\phi)\theta_R+2\phi\theta_M \tag{37}$$

Equivalently,

$$EV=\frac{1-2\phi}{\Phi(3C)}\left(1-\sum_{j=1}^{k}\left[1-\left\{1-\sum_{i=1}^{2}\left[1-\Phi\left(3\left(C^{*}_{PL(i,j)}+\frac{t_{0.005;n-1}}{\sqrt{n}}\right)\sqrt{\frac{n}{\chi^2_{0.995;n-1}}}\right)\right]\right\}\right]\right)$$
$$+\frac{2\phi}{\Phi(3C)}\left(1-\sum_{j=1}^{k}\left[1-\left\{1-\sum_{i=1}^{2}\left[1-\Phi\left(3\left(C^{*}_{PL(i,j)}\right)\sqrt{\frac{n}{\chi^2_{0.5;n-1}}}\right)\right]\right\}\right]\right) \tag{38}$$

4. Conclusion

In smart manufacturing environments, increasing the process quality and yield of IC packaging can reduce the replacement rates of components due to malfunctioning. A crucial process in IC packaging, wire bonding, involves welding gold wire onto chips and the inner pins of lead frames to serve as an important medium for electrical connection and signal transmission between the internal and external components of IC devices. Poor process quality in wire pull and ball shear can cause defective bonding between the gold wire and the chip or lead frame; the gold wire may therefore break and cause electronic products to malfunction [7]. IC components are widely used in products in the fields of information and network communications, consumer electronics, automobiles, aerospace, and national defense. If any of the IC components in these products malfunction, they will cease to operate normally and require repairs, causing economic losses and increases in carbon emissions.

We hypothesized that an IC component has k wires and that each wire has the following two larger-the-better quality characteristics: wire pull and ball shear. We first combined the evaluation indices of these two quality characteristics to construct evaluation index C_{PLj} for wires and then combined the evaluation indices for k wires to establish the operating performance evaluation index C_{PL} for IC components. The relationship between process capability index C_{PL} and the yield rate must be an inequality. When the value of the IC component's process capability index C_{PL} is larger, the product yield p is also higher.

If the process capability of one of the bonding wires is insufficient, then the IC component may fail during the product warranty period. Therefore, this paper proposes a fuzzy evaluation and improvement model for IC component wire bonding. We first propose an operating performance index θ_{IC} based on process capability index C_{PL}. We then derive the $100(1-\alpha)\%$ confidence interval of process capability index C_{PL} and derive that of index θ_{IC} based on the confidence interval of process capability index C_{PL}. Finally, we present the proposed fuzzy evaluation model of index θ_{IC} based on this confidence interval.

5. References

[1] K. S. Chen, C. M. Yu and M. L. Huang. "Fuzzy selection model for quality-based IC packaging process outsourcers", IEEE Transactions on Semiconductor Manufacturing, Vol. 35, No.1, 102–109, 2022a.

[2] K. S. Chen, M. C. Huang, C. M. Yu and H. Y. Chen. "Quality-based supplier selection model for products with multi-quality characteristics", Sustainability, Vol. 14, No. 14, 8532, 2022b.

[3] A. Amindoust, S. Ahmed, A. Saghafinia and A. Bahreininejad. "Sustainable supplier selection: A ranking model based on fuzzy inference system", Applied Soft Computing Journal, Vol. 12, No.6, 1668–1677,2020.

[4] K. S. Chen, K. C. Chiou and C. M. Yu. "Lifetime performance index of electronic products", Microelectronics Reliability, Vol. 113, 113941, 2020.

[5] K. S. Chen, C. M. Yu and M. L. Huang "Fuzzy selection model for quality-based IC packaging process outsourcers", IEEE Transactions on Semiconductor Manufacturing, Vol. 35, No. 1, 102–109, 2022c.

[6] S. Roy, A. K. Das and R. Banerjee. "Grey-Fuzzy Taguchi Approach for Multi-objective Optimization of Performance and Emission Parameters of a Single Cylinder CRDI Engine Coupled with EGR", International Journal of Automotive Technology, Vol. 17, No. 1, 1–12, 2016.

[7] T. C. Chang and K. S. Chen. "Testing process quality of wire bonding with multiple gold wires from viewpoint of producers", International Journal of Production Research, Vol. 57, No. 17, 5400–5413, 2019.

[8] T. Chen, C. M. Yang, K. S. Chen and T. H. Hsu. "Fuzzy evaluation model of bank APP performance based on circular economy thinking", Mathematics, Vol. 9, No. 21, 2761, 2021.

[9] A. Aghsami, Y. Samimi and A. Aghaei. "A novel markovian queueing-inventory model with imperfect production and inspection processes: A hospital case study", Computers and Industrial Engineering, Vol. 162, 107772, 2021.

[10] K. S. Chen and C. M. Yu. "Dual dimensional fuzzy testing based on the upper confidence limits for supplier selection", Journal of Intelligent & Fuzzy Systems, Vol. 40, No. 6, 11145–11158, 2021.

[11] K. S. Chen and C. M. Yu. "Lifetime performance evaluation and analysis model of passive component capacitor products", Annals of Operations Research, Vol. 311, No. 1, 51–64, 2022.

[12] H. Y. Chen and K. P. Lin. "Fuzzy supplier selection model based on lifetime performance index", Expert Systems with applications, Vol. 208, 118135, 2022.

[13] C. M. Yu, W. J. Luo, T. H. Hsu and K. K. Lai. "Two-Tailed Fuzzy Hypothesis Testing for Unilateral Specification Process Quality Index", Mathematics, Vol. 8, No. 2129, 1–18, 2020.

Self-Training for Accuracy Improvement in Wafer Map Defect Pattern Classification Using AI

KUROKAWA Masaru[1], NAGAMURA Yoshikazu[1], ARAI Masayuki[2], FUKUMOTO Satoshi[1]

[1]Tokyo Metropolitan University, Japan
[2]Nihon University, Japan

Keywords: wafer map, defect pattern classification systematic defect, self-training, adjusted confidence score, ResNet

Abstract - Classification of wafer map defect patterns is important to monitor occurrence and further to assist root cause analysis of manufacturing-process-induced systematic defects. Recently, AI-based methods have attracted particular attention, but they require a large amount of labeled data for highly accurate learning. In this study, we propose a self-training-based labeling method to increase the number of training data by labeling unlabeled data. In the proposed method, a small amount of labeled data is first used to train the AI. The trained AI then makes predictions on unlabeled data. We adjust confidence score of prediction for the data that is likely to be misrecognized, and then label a part of unlabeled data based on the score. We report the results of a simulated application of the proposed method to labeled data and show that the labeling accuracy was 96.7%.

1. Introduction

With advances in semiconductor manufacturing technology such as shrinking technology node and higher integration, subtle and complicated defects have more impacts on yield and reliability of the LSI devices. It is difficult to predict the occurrence of systematic defects, and if occur they strongly impact to yield and reliability. Thus, for yield ramp-up it is important to quickly detect the occurrence of systematic defects and analyze the root cause of the defects.

Wafer map, which plots the locations of defective dies on a wafer image, is an effective tool to monitor the occurrence of systematic defects and further to classify them. With the advancement of computing capability, deep-learning-based approaches have been focused. Nakazawa et al. introduced convolutional neural network [1] (CNN)-based classifier, and reported the proposed scheme showed 97.8% accuracy for simulated set of wafer maps consisting of 22 categories [2].

Training CNNs for wafer map classification requires a large amount of wafer map images which are labeled by their defect pattern categories. However, the amount of wafer maps obtained during the manufacturing process is enormous, and it is difficult to manually label all wafer maps. In addition, the frequency of defects that occur during manufacturing differs depending on the defect categories, resulting in a bias in the defect patterns that can be collected and then degradation of classification accuracy. For example, a real wafer map dataset WM-811K [3] consists of about 811 thousand images, but among them only about 172 thousand images are labeled, and the smallest defect category has just 149 images. In Ref. [4], Huang et al. introduced semi-supervised learning [5] to add labels to unlabeled wafer maps. By optimizing the loss function used during training, they eliminated the bias between defect categories. However, their scheme labels all of unlabeled images at the same time, then it has still the problem of uncertainties on labeling and classification accuracy.

In this study we propose a labeling scheme for unlabeled wafer map images by self-training strategy, aiming at high accuracy labeling as well as reduction of the bias of defect categories. The self-training strategy takes an incremental approach: first, we train a CNN model by a small number of labeled images, and then, we repeat labeling and training phases. In every labeling phase only a part of the images which shows high confidence for the prediction results is labeled. Labeled images are then added to the training dataset in the next training phases. To determine if the predicted label is assigned or not, we calculate adjusted confidence score, based on the original confidence level and the training accuracy, which is given as the form of a confusion matrix. From experimental results using labeled data in WM-811K, we show our proposed scheme has high labeling accuracy of 96.7%.

2. Preliminaries

2.1. WM-811K

WM-811K is a wafer map dataset published by MIR (Multimedia Information Retrieval) Laboratory [3], which is collected as 46,393 real fabricated lots of wafers and test results for every die on them. The dataset consists of 811,457 wafer map images.

Figure 1 shows examples of wafer map images in each category. White dots indicate faulty dies in a fabricated wafer. Table 1 shows the breakdown of the number of images. 172,950 images are manually labeled as any of 9 defect pattern categories of Center, Donut, Edge-Loc, Edge-Ring, Loc, Near-full, Random, Scratch, or None, while the other 638,507 images are left

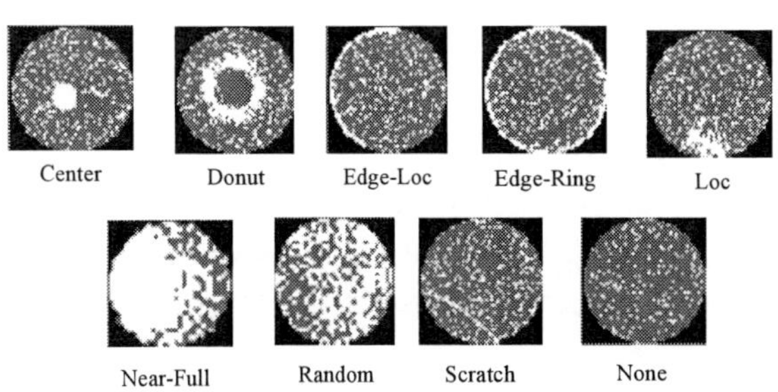

Figure 1. Examples of wafer maps in WM-811K.

Table 1. Breakdown of categories in WM-811K dataset

defect category	# of data
Center	4,294
Donut	555
Edge-Loc	5,189
Edge-Ring	9,680
Loc	3,593
Near-full	149
Random	866
Scratch	1,193
None	147,431
Unlabeled data	638,507
Total	811,457

unlabeled. Images in None category show only random (that is, non-systematic) defects, and the other 8 categories including Random show characteristics of systematic defects corresponding to the category name, in addition to random defects. Vast majority of labeled data are in None category, and we have only 25,519 images for systematic defects. The table also shows unavoidable bias between categories.

2.2. ResNet

In our experiments we apply a variation of CNN called ResNet (Residual Network) [6]. In deep convolutional neural networks, it is in general expected that the more layers in the training model, the more diverse features can be learned. However, the deeper the layers, the less the gradient becomes as the learning progresses, and this leads to the problem of suboptimal learning results. ResNet skips the convolutional layer by shortcut connections, and calculates an output of a residual block by adding the original input and the output of the convolutional layer. It can manage the problem of vanishing gradients by allowing error back propagation using residuals more easily than back propagation in stacked layers in sequence.

ResNet is classified according to the number of convolutional layers it consists of. The model with the fewest number of layers is ResNet-18, which consists of 18 convolutional layers, 8 residual connections and residual blocks.

3. Self-Training-based Wafer Map Labeling

We propose a labeling method for unlabeled wafer map images based on self-training strategy. Self-training, or also called bootstrap, is a category of semi-supervised learning, which uses training dataset consisting of both labeled and unlabeled data. With self-training approach, the classifier is first trained by only labeled data. Then the trained model is applied over unlabeled data to predict their categories. The training dataset is then expanded by newly-labeled data to improve prediction accuracy, and the phases of training and prediction are repeated.

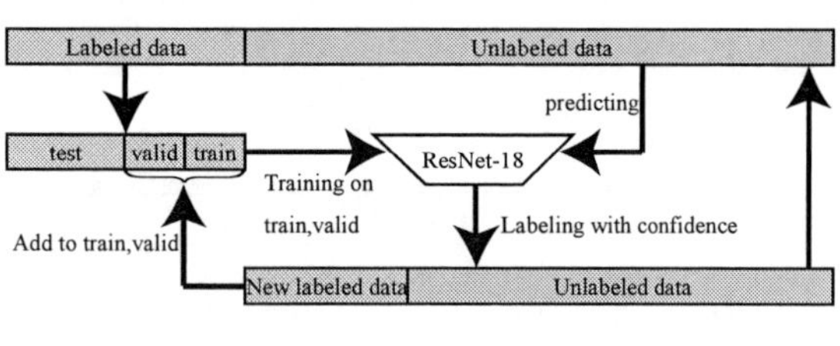

Figure 2. Overview of the prosed self-training-based wafer map defect pattern labeling.

Figure 2 shows an overview of the flow of training and labeling in our proposed scheme. First, the initial set of labeled data is divided into 3 classes of training, validation, and test datasets, and ResNet is trained by using training and validation datasets. After completion of the first training phase, the trained ResNet-18 is applied to all unlabeled data to predict their defect categories. The prediction results are output along with their confidence level, and only for the data which show higher confidence than a given threshold value the predicted labels are assigned. The newly labeled data is then added to either training or validation dataset, and training of ResNet is performed again. The training and prediction phases are repeated until no unlabeled data exists. A prediction phase, if there are still unlabeled data but no new labels are assigned, the threshold value is reduced to the highest confidence level. When all data is labeled, ResNet is again trained, and then prediction for test data is performed to evaluate final accuracy.

Targeting WM-811K, ResNet is built as a 9-class, single-label classifier, and thus the output layer consists of 9 neurons, each of which corresponds to a label of defect pattern category. For an input image under prediction, the confidence level is calculated for each label as output value of activation function for corresponding output neuron, and the predicted label for the image is indicated as the one with highest confidence level. For an activation function, sigmoid or softmax is typically applied. Softmax normalizes the output values so that summation of all neurons' output becomes 1.

4. Experiments on Wafer Map Labeling based on Naïve Confidence Level

First, we evaluated the proposed scheme, when the confidence level mentioned above is applied as it is at determining label assignment.

To evaluate accuracy of labeling, we only used labeled data in WM-811K. Table 2 summarizes the breakdown of the initial dataset. We used all of labeled wafer maps, except for None (we just utilized 14,000 among 147,431 images). Training and validation datasets consist of 900 and 300 images, respectively, where the numbers of images for the categories are set so that the

Table 2. Breakdown of initial dataset for labeling experiment.

Label	train	validation	test	unlabeld	total
Center	97	33	288	3,876	4,294
Donut	13	4	37	501	555
Edge-Loc	118	40	349	4,682	5,189
Edge-Ring	221	73	650	8,736	9,680
Loc	82	27	241	3,243	3,593
Near-full	4	1	10	134	149
Random	19	7	58	782	866
Scratch	27	9	80	1,077	1,193
none	319	106	940	12,635	14,000
total	900	300	2,653	35,666	39,519

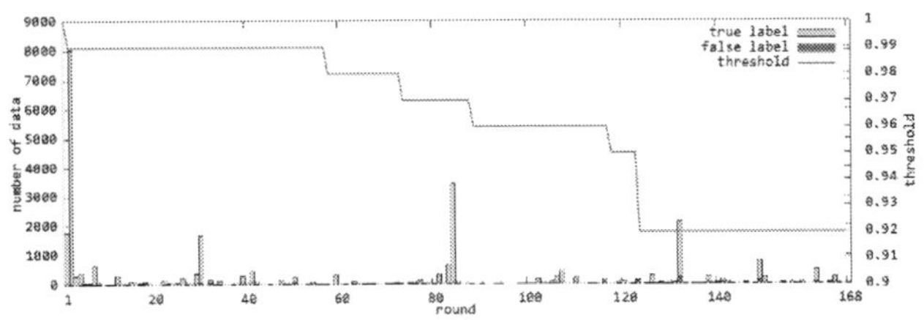

Figure 3. Results of labeling experiments: threshold, correct and false labeling at each round

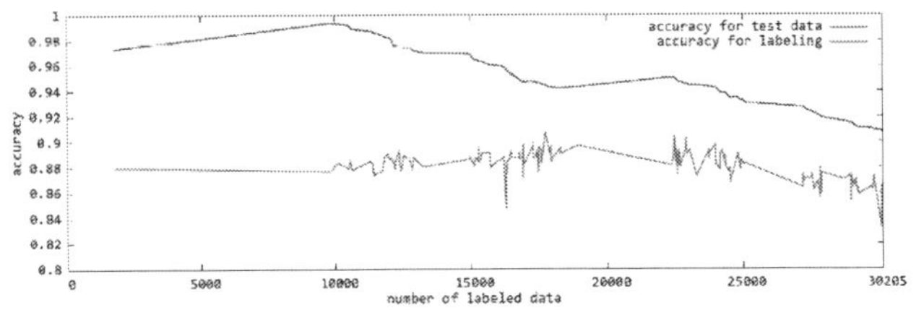

Figure 4. Results of labeling experiments: labeling accuracy and classification accuracy on test data.

ratio of original category size is maintained. 35,666 images were treated as unlabeled, and our algorithm tried to label them. Accuracy of labeling was calculated based on the assigned and the original (correct) labels.

We applied ResNet-18, where LDAM Loss [7] was applied as loss function. For activation function we firstly used softmax. Threshold value for labeling is initially set to 1.0. In the end of a round of training and prediction, if there are no new label assignments, the threshold value is reduced by 0.01 and label assignment is performed again. Newly labeled data is added into training or validation dataset, so that the ratio of their sizes is kept 3:1.

Figure 3 shows the results of labeling. Threshold value, the number of correctly assigned labels, and the number of falsely assigned labels are plotted at each round. Starting from 1.0, the threshold value finally falls into 0.92. We observe several false labeling between rounds 30 to 40, despite the threshold is still 0.99 in this range. That is, high confidence level does not always guarantee high accuracy of labeling. We also see rapid reduction of threshold around round 120, and after that we see frequent false labeling. Thus, we think low confidence such as < 0.95 is unreliable for label assignments.

Figure 4 shows the results of experiments, where accuracy of labeling as well as classification accuracy for test data is plotted. Please note that evaluation of classification accuracy for test data was performed at the end of every round, but the x-axis is not the round number but the number of labeled data, then the intervals between sample points are not even. We expected that labeling and/or classification accuracy would go up as the number of labeled data increases, but the figure shows complicated behavior. When the number of labeled data ranges from 10,000 to 18,000, labeling accuracy proportionally decreases while classification accuracy gently increases. This might be due to increased training data with relatively high labeling accuracy. On the other hand, with more than 22,000 images both labeling and classification accuracy decrease. That is, wrong labeling is rather harmful for high classification accuracy.

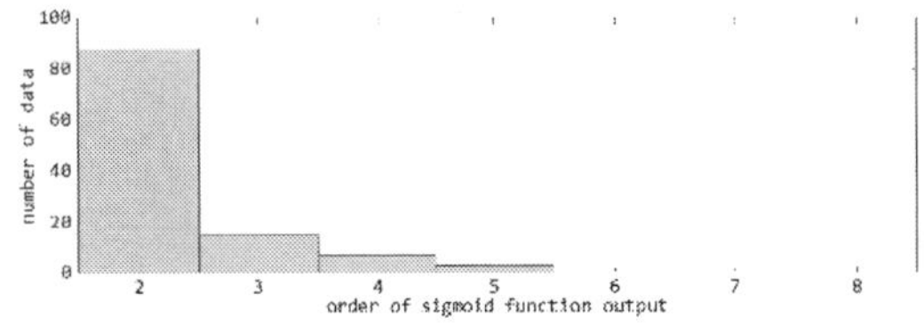

Figure 5. Results of labeling experiments: labeling accuracy and classification accuracy on test data.

Table 3. Classification accuracy at the best case of labeling.

Activation function	classification accuracy
softmax	0.9582
sigmoid	0.9574

While omitting the detail in this paper due to the page limit, we also performed the same experiments by using sigmoid as activation function to calculate confidence level. The results were almost the same or rather worse than the case of softmax.

Then we investigated the causes of false labeling. Figure 5 shows frequency of ranks of correct label for falsely predicted data: the data was taken by the experiments for sigmoid, but the order of ranking is identical to softmax. When a false label is assigned to an image, in most cases the correct label shows the second-highest confidence level. Furthermore, mispredictions do not occur equally for all pairs of labels: specific pairs show higher misprediction probabilities than the others. Therefore, by considering not only the highest but also the second and the following confidence levels, labeling accuracy would be improved.

We also investigated the upper limit of classification accuracy in the best case of labeling. We used all data in Table 2, that is 39,519 images to train ResNet with their correct labels, and then performed predictions over all images. The result shown in Table 3 indicates that even if labeling is perfectly performed, there are still about 4.2% of misclassified wafer maps. That is, the WM-811K dataset would have several wafer maps difficult to classify, or, some wafer maps may be manually misclassified.

5. Adjusted Confidence Score for label assignments

Based on the observations in the previous section, we introduce adjusted confidence score used to determine whether the predicted label is assigned or not. Considering confidence levels other than the highest and the results of misprediction in test dataset, we reduce the confidence level for the data which is likely to be mispredicted.

We take two-step approach to calculate the adjusted confidence score. At the first step the confidence score for a label having highest confidence level is calculated based on the values of confidence levels for all labels. Then, the confidence score at the first step is further adjusted in the second step, considering the probability of misprediction derived from prediction results for the test dataset.

In the experiments shown in the previous section, softmax showed better accuracy than sigmoid, in terms of both labeling and classification. However, softmax normalizes confidence levels, boosting the highest value while reducing the others, and thus uncertainty on the first and the second ranks tends to be sometimes concealed. Therefore, to calculate the adjusted confidence score, we apply sigmoid as activation function of the output neurons of ResNet and use the value of sigmoid output as the original confidence level for each label.

Let $\mathbb{L} = \{Center, Donut, \ldots, None\}$ denote the set of labels, $l* \in \mathbb{L}$ denote the label having the highest confidence level, and s_l denote the confidence level for a label $l \in \mathbb{L}$. Then, the confidence score for $l*$ at the first step, r_1, is calculated as

$$r_1 = s_{l*} \times \prod_{l \in \mathbb{L}, l \neq l*} (1 - s_l).$$

As the confidence levels for the second and the following ranks become larger, confidence score r_1 becomes smaller. Then, depending on the value of threshold, uncertain labels tend to be postponed for assignment.

As shown in Fig. 5, when a misprediction occurs the true label is likely to have the second-highest confidence level. In addition, as mentioned earlier specific pairs of labels have higher probability of misprediction than the others. Then, in the second step, we search the prediction results for the test dataset, and reduce the value of confidence score calculated in the first step if the pair of the first and second labels is suspicious.

In the end of training at every round we perform prediction for the test dataset, and obtain the result in the form of a confusion matrix. Let $c_{l_{true} l_{pred}}$ $(l_{true}, l_{pred} \in \mathbb{L})$ denote an element of the confusion matrix, that is, the number of data which is predicted as l_{pred} and is actually l_{true}. Then, for an unlabeled input image under prediction, let $[l_1, l_2, \ldots, l_9]$ $(l_1, \ldots l_9 \in \mathbb{L})$ denote the list of labels which are arranged in the descending order of original confidence level. The adjusted confidence score at the second step, r_2, is calculated as shown in Table 4. If the probability that the label having second-highest confidence level is actually the true label is not zero, the value calculated at the first step is reduced to half. The conditions in the table are checked from top to bottom, and only the first condition matched is applied.

Figure 6 shows an example of calculation of adjusted confidence score at the second step. The top is a confusion matrix for the test dataset at a round, and in the middle the output of sigmoid for all labels for an input image is shown. The label with highest confidence level is Center, and None and Edge-Loc follow as 2nd and 3rd, respectively. The confidence score at the first step, r_1, is already calculated based on Center's confidence level 0.9707 and other values. Looking at the confusion matrix, there are no cases that the second label of None is mispredicted as Center, but Edge-Loc might be mispredicted as Center. Then the second condition in Table 4 matches and r_1 is reduced to 75%.

6. Evaluation of Self-Training-based Wafer Map Labeling with Adjusted Confidence Score

We evaluated the effectiveness of the proposed self-training-based wafer map labeling combined with adjusted confidence score.

As shown in Table 3, WM-811K contains several difficult-to-classify wafer maps. Then we removed such wafer maps from our dataset, in order to evaluate the best performance of the proposed scheme. Table 5 shows a new initial dataset. While omitting the details of procedure, we removed 2,614 images from the original dataset shown in Table 2.

Figures 7 and 8 show experimental results of labeling based on adjusted confidence score. Since the adjusted confidence score is slightly reduced from the original confidence level output by sigmoid, the threshold value steadily falls as the round progresses, and finally goes below 0.2. In addition, due to lower score, the number of labels assigned at one round is reduced in comparison to the case with original confidence level, resulting in larger number of rounds until terminating. However, as shown in Fig. 8, labeling accuracy is maintained at a high level throughout all rounds. First 10,000 labels showed more than 99.5% labeling accuracy, and final labeling accuracy, that is, average for all labels, was 96.7%. Then, due to such high labeling accuracy, classification accuracy for test dataset also gently goes up as the number of labeled data increases.

Table 4. Calculation of adjusted confidence score

Conditional expression	Correction formula
$c_{l_2 l_1} > 0$	$r_2 = r_1 \times 0.5$
$c_{l_3 l_1} > 0$	$r_2 = r_1 \times 0.75$
$c_{l_4 l_1} > 0$	$r_2 = r_1 \times 0.875$
$c_{l_5 l_1} > 0$	$r_2 = r_1 \times 9375$

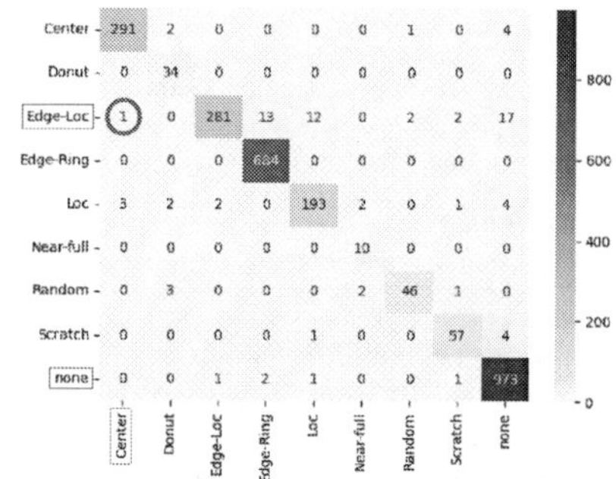

Center	none	Edge-Loc	Loc	Donut	Edge-Ring	Scratch	Nearfull	Random
0.9707	0.0356	0.0252	0.0094	0.0057	0.0018	0.0004	0.0002	0.0001

$C_{ture\_label\ pred\_label} = C_{none\ Center} = 0$

$C_{ture\_label\ pred\_label} = C_{Edge\text{-}Loc\ Center} = 1 > 0 \longrightarrow r_2 = r_1 \times 0.75$

Figure 6. Example of adjusted confidence score calculation

Table 5. New initial dataset for labeling experiment, where difficult-to-classify wafer maps are removed

Label	train	validation	test	unlabeld	total
Center	101	34	298	3,717	4,150
Donut	12	4	34	429	479
Edge-Loc	112	37	328	4,093	4,570
Edge-Ring	232	77	684	8,513	9,506
Loc	70	23	207	2,573	2,873
Near-full	3	1	10	123	137
Random	18	6	52	647	723
Scratch	21	7	62	776	866
none	331	111	978	12,181	13,601
total	900	300	2,653	33,052	36,905

Table 6 shows accuracy of labeling, for each defect category. While top 5 categories show more than 98% of accuracy, Edge-Loc shows lowest value of 85%, despite the numbers of labeled and unlabeled data in the initial dataset is not so small. This may be due to similarity of the characteristics of Edge-Ring and Loc.

Let us finally discuss the combinational effect of self-training and adjusted confidence score. Figure 9 shows the results

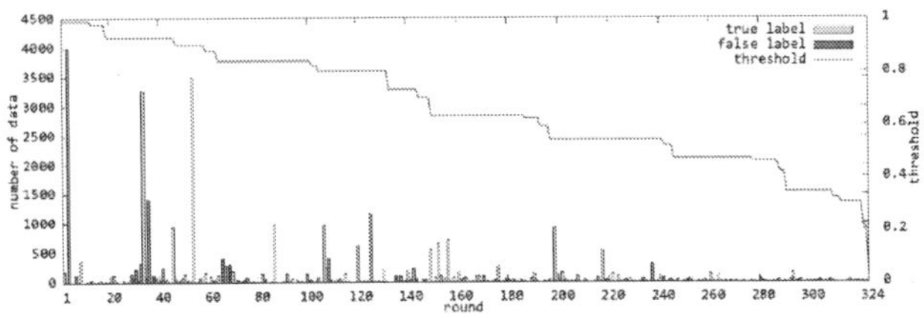

Figure 7. Results of labeling experiments using adjusted confidence score: threshold, correct and false labeling at each round

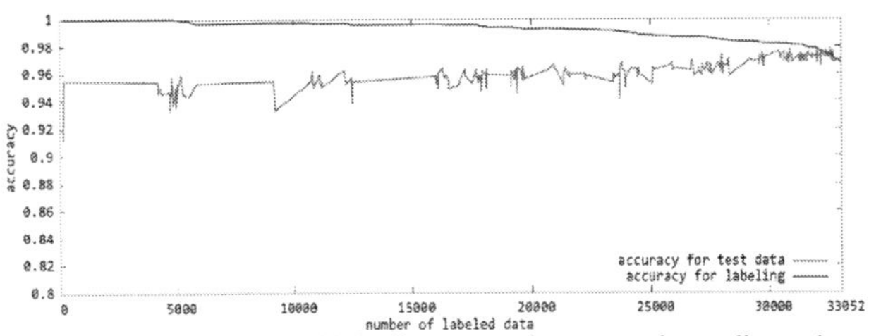

Figure 8. Results of labeling experiments using adjusted confidence score: labeling accuracy and classification accuracy on test data

Table 6. Labeling accuracy for each defect category

Label name	Labeling accuracy
Center	0.9814
Donut	0.9860
Edge-Loc	0.8517
Edge-Ring	0.9986
Loc	0.9223
Near-full	1.0000
Random	0.9119
Scratch	0.9704
none	0.9914
total	0.9674

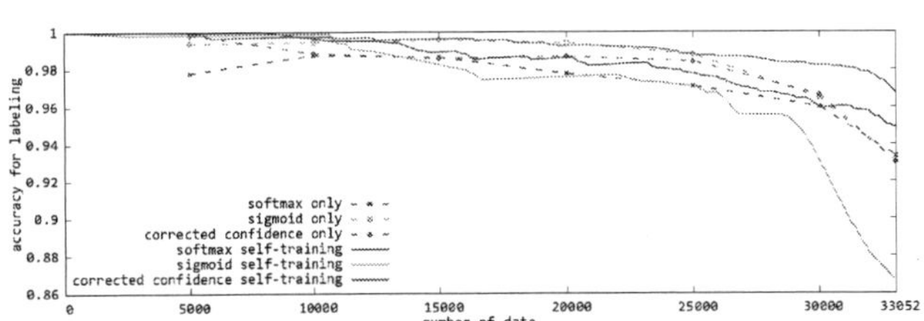

Figure 9. Evaluation of labeling accuracy: with and without self-training, and with and without adjusted confidence score

of labeling accuracy, where self-training and adjusted confidence score (corrected confidence in the figure) are independently applied. Without self-training, all predicted labels are assigned at the first round. Adjusted confidence score just reduces the value of top-ranked confidence level, so without self-training we see about 5% of prediction error for the last 10,000 images. As mentioned in Sec. 4 naïve confidence level does not work well with self-training: for sigmoid, accuracy goes much worse than single-round labeling. By combining these two schemes we can see high labeling accuracy, especially on the latest 8,000 images.

7. Conclusion

In this study we proposed a self-training-based labeling method for systematic wafer map images. In the proposed method, a small amount of labeled data is first used to train ResNet. Then, using output of confidence score and prediction results for test dataset we calculate adjusted confidence score, and assign predicted label only to the unlabeled image with high score, in order to reduce the opportunity of assignment under misprediction. Newly-labeled data is used to expand the training dataset in the next round. Experimental results indicated that the proposed method shows 96.7% labeling accuracy, and these newly-labeled images contributed to increasing classification accuracy.

Using the proposed method, we have already labeled 638,507 unlabeled images in the original WM-811K dataset. Now we are investigating several schemes to further gain classification accuracy using large dataset.

References

[1] A. Krizhevsky, I. Sutskever and G. E. Hinton, "ImageNet Classification with Deep Convolutional Neural Networks", Proc. NIPS'12, pp. 1097-1105, Dec. 2012.

[2] T. Nakazawa and D. V. Kulkarni, "Wafer Map Defect Pattern Classification and Image Retrieval Using Convolutional Neural Network," IEEE Trans. Semicond. Manuf., Vol. 31, No. 2, pp. 309-314, Mar. 2018.

[3] M.-J. Wu, J.-S. R. Jang and J.-L. Chen, "Wafer Map Failure Pattern Recognition and Similarity Ranking for Large-Scale Data Sets," IEEE Trans. Semicond. Manuf., Vol. 28, No. 1, pp. 1-12, Feb. 2015, Available: http://mirlab.org/dataSet/public/

[4] J. Huang, K.-Y. Lin and J. Xu, "Imbalanced Wafer Map Dataset Classification with Semi-Supervised Learning Method and Optimized Loss Function," Proc. CASE, pp. 1815-1819, Aug. 2022.

[5] O. Chapelle, B. Schölkopf, A. Zien, Semi-Supervised Learning, MIT press Cambridge, Sep. 2006.

[6] K. He, X. Zhang, S. Ren and J. Sun, "Deep Residual Learning for Image Recognition," Proc. CVPR, pp. 770-778, Jun. 2016.

[7] K. Cao, C. Wei, A. Gaidon, N. Arechiga and T. Ma, "Learning Imbalanced Datasets with Label-distribution-aware Margin Loss," Proc. NIPS'19, pp. 1565-1576, Dec. 2019.

An Evaluation of Forecasting Precision with Forecasting Method Concerning Water Demand for A Prefecture

MARUYAMA Yukio[1], SHIRAI Yutaka[2], KIHARA Kazuo[3]

[1]Department of Digital Transformation/Chiba Institute of Technology, Japan
[2]Department of Business System Design and Management/Chiba Institute of Technology, Japan
[3]Real Futures Co., Ltd., Japan

Keywords: Water demand, statistical model, multiple regression analysis, forecasting precision, estimation of parameters.

Abstract - Forecasting the water demands is very important for pure-water reservoirs. Because the amount of water supply to the water supply stations cannot be changed frequently according to the variation of water demands. In our studies, we proposed three kinds of forecasting method and one kind of correcting method for water demand using data of five prefectures or town in Japan. The points of these forecasting methods are following three matters. 1) Based on a multiple regression analysis. 2) Using multiple year's data of the value of water supply per day. 3) Correcting the obtained multivariate regression formula by single regression analysis. In previous study, it was confirmed that our proposed forecasting method can be applied to forecasting the duration of COVID-19. The purpose of this paper is to examine parameter combinations that improve the forecasting precision in our proposed forecasting method. As the result of this examination, different parameter combination is obtained than previous studies. We hope that the result of this examination can be applied as one of the parameter selection methods in other forecasting methods using deep learning.

1. Introduction

The amount of water supply to the water supply stations cannot be changed frequently according to the variation of water demands, because management of water resources, e.g., river water, has various restrictions (e.g. the amount of extracted water from a river around unit time, etc.). Therefore, forecasting the water demand is very important for pure-water reservoirs. The goal of this study is to propose forecasting method of water demands applying all over the country in Japan. In our studies, we proposed three kinds of forecasting method and one kind of correcting method for water demand using data of five prefectures or town in Japan. The points of these forecasting methods are following three matters.

- Based on a multiple regression analysis
- Using multiple year's data of the value of water supply per day
- Correcting the obtained multivariate regression formula by single regression analysis

In our studies, forecasting precision of our proposed method was leaded approximately 2%. In addition, it was confirmed that our proposed forecasting method can be applied to forecasting the duration of COVID-19 using data of amount of daily water supply of A prefecture in previous study [1]. In this confirmation, parameter combinations of forecasting method were set at that improve the forecasting precision in our original proposed forecasting method [2]. However, there is different between currently used forecasting method in this confirmation and our original proposed forecasting method. The purpose of this paper is to examine parameter combinations that improve the forecasting precision with daily water supply in currently used forecasting method. These parameter combinations are described in section 3.

2. Characteristics of water supply of A prefecture

In this section, characteristics of daily water supply of A prefecture are described. A transition of the amount of daily water supply of A prefecture in 2020 FY is shown in Figure 1. As shown in Figure 1, characteristic of transition of the amount of daily water supply is that the amount of daily water supply in the summer period tends to increase than that in the other seasons period. The average amount of daily water supply of each the day of the week in 2020 FY is shown in Figure 2. In addition, differences of the average amount of daily water supply among day of the week in 2020 FY by t-test are shown in Table 1. As shown in Figure 2 and Table 1, the average amount of daily water supply of Friday and Saturday tend to decrease than that of other day of the week. Here, 2020 FY was during COVID-19. There is difference between transition of the amount of daily water supply in 2019 FY (before COVID-19) and that

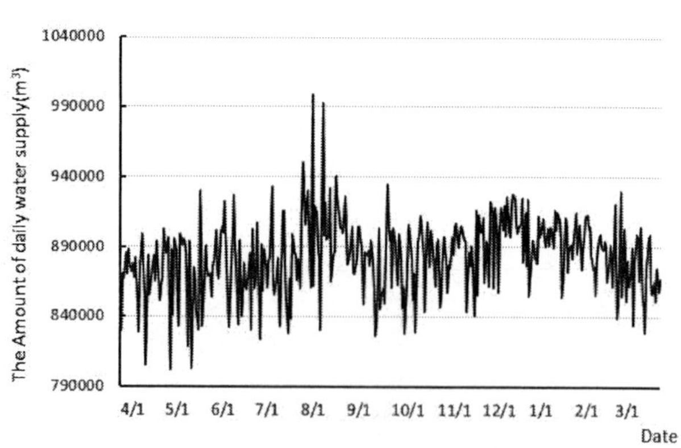

Figure 1. The transition of daily water supply in 2020 FY

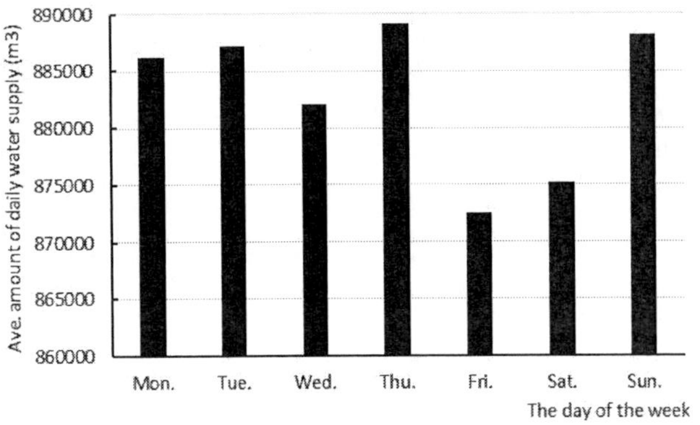

Figure2. The average amount of daily water supply of each the day of the week in 2020 FY

Table 1. Differences of the averaged amount of daily water supply among day of the week in 2020 FY by t-test

	Mon.	Tue.	Wed.	Thu.	Fri.	Sat.	Sun.
Mon.					**		
Tue.					**	*	
Wed.					*		
Thu.					**	*	
Fri.							**
Sat.							*
Sun.							

*: 5% significance, **: 1% significance

in 2020 FY. However, the amount of daily water supply in the summer period of 2019 FY tends to increase than that in the other seasons period. There is also difference between the average amount of daily water supply among day of the week in 2020 FY and that in 2019 FY. In 2019 FY, the average amount of daily water supply of Wednesday and Friday tend to decrease than that of other day of the week. In addition, that of Sunday tends to increase than that of other day of the week. Although there are differences of characteristics of the amount of daily water supply between in 2019 FY and in 2020 FY, it was confirmed that our proposed forecasting method can be applied to forecasting the duration of COVID-19 (2020 FY) using data of amount of daily water supply of A prefecture in previous study.

3. Concept of forecasting method

In this section, concept of forecasting method is described. Figure 3 shows the concept of forecasting method. In this figure, the horizontal axis represents "date" and the vertical axis represents "year". D_M in Y year is assumed as the forecasting day. The procedures of this forecasting method are as follows:

Step 1: Collecting weather information data that correlate with the amount of daily water supply and analyzing by correlation analysis for the regression period (from $D_M - t$ to $D_M + t$) until $Y - 1$ year (see Figure 3).

Step 2: Constructing the multiple regression formula for each year using the collected data in Step 1, which is

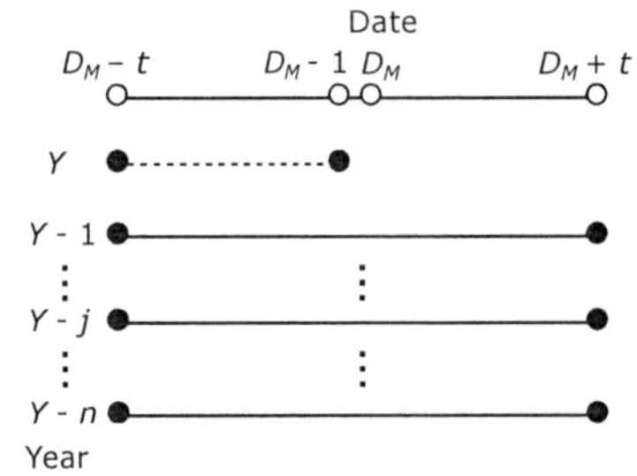

Figure 3. Concept of forecasting method

expressed in equation (1).

$$\hat{Z}^{(Y-n)} = \sum_{i=0}^{m}\sum_{j=1}^{n} \hat{a}_i^{(Y-j)} x_i, (x_0 \equiv 1) \quad (1)$$

The notations are defined as follows:

- Y : A variable representing the year in the western calendar.
- M : A variable representing the month (M = 1, ..., 12).
- D : A variable representing a specific day of the year (D = 1, ⋯, 366). A value of D = 1 corresponds to January 1, and D = 366 corresponds to December 31. February 29 is assumed to exist even in non-leap years, and is treated as a missing day in the actual data.
- D_M : The first day of the year and month of the forecasting date.
- t : A variable representing the period of using data to make the forecasting formula. Here, this variable is called "regression period."
- x : Explanatory variables (i = 0, 1, ..., m).
- $\hat{a}_i^{(Y-j)}$: Estimator of the partial regression coefficients for $Y - j$ year (i = 0, 1, ..., m; j = 1, ..., n)
- m : Number of explanatory variables.
- n : Number of past years.

Thus, n of multiple regression formulas are obtained by the multiple regression analysis.

Step 3: Calculating the temporary forecasting values of daily water supply from $D_M - t$ in Y year to $D_M - 1$ in Y year (period of dotted line in Figure 3) using obtained n from multiple regression formulas.

Step 4: Correcting each obtained multiple regression formula by three correction methods using the correlation between the actual amounts of daily water supply and the calculated temporary forecasting values of daily water supply in Step 3. Figure 4 shows the concept of correction method. In each figure, the horizontal axis represents the temporary forecasting values, while the vertical axis represents the actual amounts of daily water supply. The relationship of these values is also examined, where the obtained temporary forecasting values should ideally represent the actual amounts of daily water supply ($y = x$). As shown in this figure, however, the obtained temporary forecasting values deviate from the actual amounts of daily water supply. One of the reasons may be annual economic

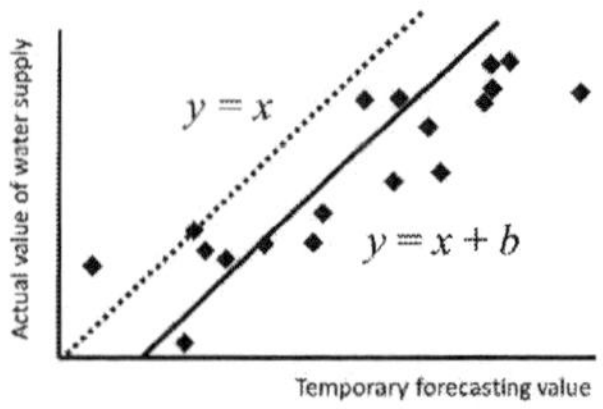

(a) Increment Type

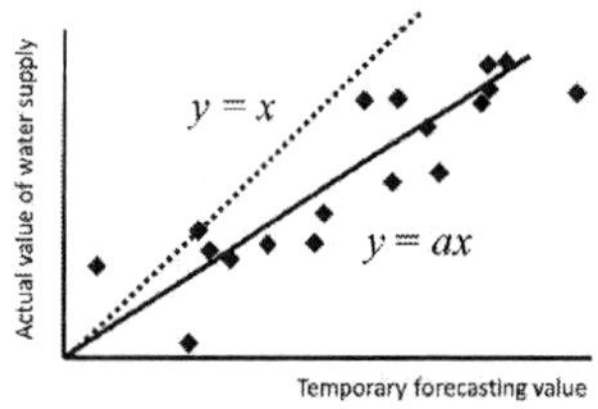

(b) Proportional Type

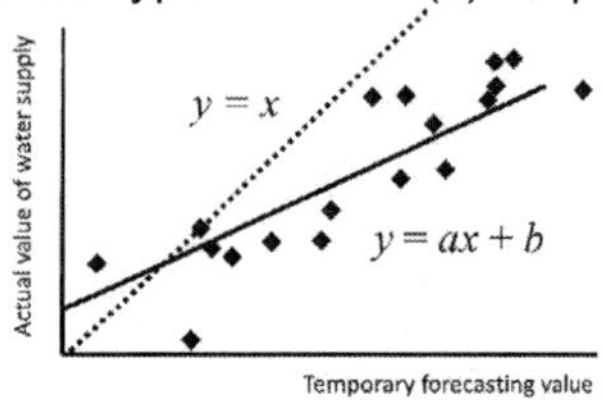

(c) Regression Type

Figure 4. Concept of correction method

fluctuations. Then, it assumes that a linear relationship is established between the temporary forecasting values and actual amounts of daily water supply. In order to minimize this deviation, the obtained temporary forecasting values are corrected by assuming three kinds of linear relationships. In this study, these correction methods are called “increment type” (Figure 4(a)), “proportional type” (Figure 4(b)), and “regression type” (Figure 4(c)), respectively.

In “increment type,” it is assumed that an annual fluctuation ensures a constant increase (decrease) compared to past years (it is assumed $y = x + b$). The obtained multiple regression formula is corrected by applying the obtained estimator of increased amount ($\hat{\delta}_1$) by single regression analysis. In “proportional type,” it is assumed that an annual fluctuation ensures a constant ratio to past years (it is assumed $y = ax$). The obtained multiple regression analysis is corrected by applying the obtained estimator of ratio ($\hat{\beta}_1$) by single regression analysis. In “regression type,” an annual fluctuation ensures a constant increase and ratio to past years (it is assumed $y = ax + b$). The obtained multiple regression formula is corrected by applying the obtained estimators of the increased (decrease) amount and ratio ($\hat{\delta}_2$, $\hat{\beta}_2$) by single regression analysis. Thus, n values of the corrected multiple regression formula are obtained.

Step 5: Averaging the corrected n of multiple regression formula. Moreover, this averaged formula is the forecasting formula ($\widehat{W}_1$: increment type, $\widehat{W}_2$: proportional type, $\widehat{W}_3$: regression type). The forecasting formulas of each correction method are expressed in equations (2) to (4), respectively.

$$\widehat{W}_1 = \frac{1}{n}\sum_{j=1}^{n}\left(\hat{z}^{(Y-j)} + \hat{\delta}_1^{(Y-j)}\right) \quad (2)$$

$$\widehat{W}_2 = \frac{1}{n}\sum_{j=1}^{n}\hat{\beta}_1^{(Y-j)}\hat{z}^{(Y-j)} \quad (3)$$

$$\widehat{W}_3 = \frac{1}{n}\sum_{j=1}^{n}\left(\hat{\beta}_2^{(Y-j)}\hat{z}^{(Y-j)} + \hat{\delta}_2^{(Y-j)}\right) \quad (4)$$

Actually, one correction method is selected from three kinds of correction methods. The forecasting value of daily water supply is calculated by substituting weather information, etc. of the forecasting day in the forecasting formula.

4. Examination of forecasting precision

In this section, parameter combinations that improve the forecasting precision in currently used forecasting method are examined.

4.1. Outline of our original forecasting method

In our original forecasting method, values of daily water supply for weekdays and holidays were forecasted, respectively. This reason is because there was a large difference in the amount of daily water supply between weekdays and holidays using data of the amount of daily water supply of Kanagawa Prefecture and Tokyo Metropolitan. Here, weekdays refer to Monday through Friday, and holidays refer to Saturday, Sunday, and national holidays. Our original forecasting method for weekdays is based on the concept of forecasting method presented in Chapter 3. In this paper, outline of our original forecasting method for holidays is omitted. In the result of forecasting precision examination using our original forecasting method, it was found that the combination which past year set at 4 years ($n = 4$ in Figure 3) and regression period set at 84 days ($t = 42$ in Figure 3) had higher forecasting precision.

4.2. Outline of currently used forecasting method

In currently used forecasting method, forecasting method for weekdays and holidays is same one. The currently used forecasting method based on the concept forecasting method represented in Chapter 3. In addition, it was confirmed that currently used forecasting method can be applied to forecasting the duration of COVID-19 using data of amount of daily water supply of A prefecture in previous study. From next section, parameter combinations that improve the forecasting precision in currently used forecasting method are examined.

4.3. Data and setting parameters

Data on the amount of daily water supply for six years (April 1, 2015 to March 31, 2021) are obtained from A Prefecture Public Enterprises Bureau. In addition, the data on weather information for the aforementioned period are downloaded from the Japan Meteorological Agency’s website [3].

The regression period is set at 56 days, 70days, 84 days and 98 days (t = 28, 35, 42, 49 in Figure 3), while the past year is set at 1, 2, 3, 4 and 5 years (n = 1, 2, 3, 4, 5 in Figure 3).

4.4. Evaluation method

In the present study, the evaluation method is expressed in equation (5).

$$q = \frac{|(Forecasting\ value) - (Actual\ amount)|}{(Actual\ amount)} \times 100 \quad (5)$$

In equation (5), forecasting precision (q) is evaluated using the absolute value of relative error ratio of the forecasted value of daily water supply to its actual value. Here, the evaluation period is set from June 1, 2020 to March 31, 2021 (for 8 months).

4.5. Explanatory variables

The explanatory variables of multiple regression analysis are set into two categories: weather information and days of the week. Weather information include maximum daily temperature, maximum daily temperature squared, temperature difference between today and yesterday, rainy in the morning, rainy in the afternoon, cloudy in the morning, cloudy in the afternoon, cloudy after sunny in the morning, cloudy after sunny in the afternoon, sunny after cloudy in the morning, and sunny after cloudy in the afternoon (11 factors). Days of the week include Friday and Saturday (2 factors). Thus, a total of 13 factors are set as explanatory variables.

4.6. Forecasting result and precision

In this section, one of forecasting result and precision in evaluation period are presented. The part of forecasting results of daily water supply (regression period set at 56 days (t = 28 in Figure 3) and past year is set at 1 years (n = 1 in Figure 3)) is shown in Table 2. In Table 2, The values of "No correction" are forecasted without applying a correction method. The part of forecasting precision results of daily water supply (regression period set at 56 days (t = 28 in Figure 3) and past year is set at 1 years (n = 1 in Figure 3)) is shown in Table 3. In Table 3, the absolute values of relative error ratio drawn background color (orange) represent highest forecasting precision on each day. In addition, the absolute values of average relative error ratio drawn background color (blue) represent highest forecasting precision during all evaluation period. As shown in Table 3, it is found that there is difference of forecasting precision on each day among correction methods.

4.7. Comparing forecasting precision

In this section, forecasting precision of all combination of regression period and past year is compared. The

Table 2. The part of the forecasting results of daily water supply (t = 28, n = 1) (Units: m^3)

Date	Actual	No correction	Increment	Proportional	Regression
2020/6/1	854378	849591.3704	854884.2323	854844.5531	853055.2507
2020/6/2	875481	874944.5082	880237.3701	880354.4541	881309.5524
2020/6/3	879696	881987.865	887280.7269	887441.3613	889158.8817
2020/6/4	901481	884363.2618	889656.1238	889831.4456	891806.0956
2020/6/5	872257	873680.7688	878973.6308	879082.9008	879901.2031
⋮					
2021/1/28	889391	845661.7326	867586.5133	866719.0555	862856.1145
2021/1/29	891618	873204.6979	895129.4787	894947.8519	894055.8137
2021/1/30	881360	871099.8043	893024.5851	892790.5456	891671.4645
2021/1/31	896660	899648.3291	921573.1098	922049.9403	924010.2258

Table 3. The part of the forecasting precision results of daily water supply (t = 28, n = 1) (Units: %)

Date	No correction	Increment	Proportional	Regression
2020/6/1	0.5602	0.0593	0.0546	0.1548
2020/6/2	0.0613	0.5433	0.5567	0.6658
2020/6/3	0.2605	0.8622	0.8805	1.0757
2020/6/4	1.8988	1.3117	1.2923	1.0732
2020/6/5	0.1632	0.7700	0.7826	0.8764
⋮				
2021/1/28	4.9168	2.4516	2.5492	2.9835
2021/1/29	2.0652	0.3938	0.3735	0.2734
2021/1/30	1.1641	1.3235	1.2969	1.1699
2021/1/31	0.3333	2.7784	2.8316	3.0502
Average	2.3599	1.8072	1.8171	2.1568

forecasting precision results of combination of all parameters during all evaluation period is shown in Table 4. In Table 4, the absolute value of average relative error ratio drawn background color (blue, q = 1.6462; t = 42; n = 4; correction method is proportional) represents highest forecasting precision in the result of previous study. The absolute value of average relative error ratio drawn background color (pink, q = 1.6007; t = 28; n = 4; correction method is proportional) represents highest forecasting precision in the result of this examination. As shown in Table 4, other parameter combinations (background color is green) also obtained higher forecasting precision than the result of the previous study. Furthermore, for these parameter combinations of higher forecasting precision than the result of the previous study, the differences of forecasting value of daily water supply between in this

Table 4. The forecasting precision results of combination of all parameters during all evaluation period (Units: %)

Nunber of regression period (t: days)		Correction method	Number of past year (n: year) 1	2	3	4	5
	± 28	No correction	2.3599	1.8918	1.8941	1.8569	1.9144
		Increment	1.8072	1.6644	1.6377	1.6025	1.6608
		Proportional	1.8171	1.6646	1.6362	1.6007	1.6608
		Regression	2.1568	1.9246	1.8752	1.8114	1.8625
	± 35	No correction	2.3842	1.8847	1.8809	1.8455	1.8977
		Increment	1.8346	1.6923	1.6696	1.6345	1.6738
		Proportional	1.8415	1.6918	1.6689	1.6334	1.6728
		Regression	1.8869	1.8087	1.7637	1.7292	1.7351
	± 42	No correction	2.4389	1.9069	1.8931	1.8498	1.9039
		Increment	1.8755	1.6964	1.6834	1.6491	1.6845
		Proportional	1.8798	1.6978	1.6813	1.6462	1.6821
		Regression	1.8771	1.7401	1.7247	1.6980	1.7112
	± 49	No correction	2.4181	1.9046	1.8865	1.8331	1.8865
		Increment	1.8108	1.6674	1.6726	1.6225	1.6644
		Proportional	1.8121	1.6679	1.6713	1.6204	1.6630
		Regression	1.8032	1.6853	1.6803	1.6337	1.6499

examination and in the previous study are tested by using t-test. This result of t-test is shown in Table 5. As shown in Table 5, a statistical significance is observed forecasting value of daily water supply between in this examination of parameter combination (except for No. 4 in Table 5) and in the result of previous study. However, a statistical significance is not observed relative error ratio (q) between in this examination of all parameter combination and in the result of previous study.

In addition, the forecasting precision results of combination of all parameters in July 2020 is shown in Table 6. In Table 6, the absolute value of average relative error ratio drawn background color (blue, q = 2.0405; t = 42; n = 4; correction method is regression) represents highest forecasting precision in the result of previous study. The absolute value of average relative error ratio drawn background color (pink, q = 1.8551; t = 28; n = 4; correction method is regression) represents highest forecasting

Table 5. The result of t-test

No.	q	t	n	Correction	Decision
1	1.6007	28	4	Proportional	*
2	1.6025	28	4	Increment	*
3	1.6204	49	4	Proportional	△
4	1.6225	49	4	Increment	
5	1.6337	49	4	Regression	**
6	1.6362	28	3	Proportional	*
7	1.6377	28	3	Increment	*

△: 10% significance, *: 5% significance, **: 1% significance

Table 6. The forecasting precision results of all combination of parameters in July 2020 (Units: %)

		Correction method	Number of past year (n: year)				
			1	2	3	4	5
Nunber of regression period (t: days)	± 28	No correction	2.2330	2.2441	2.3829	2.1436	2.1375
		Increment	2.1456	2.2107	2.0049	1.8840	1.9385
		Proportional	2.1505	2.2043	1.9998	1.8789	1.9333
		Regression	2.0387	2.0740	1.9503	1.8551	1.9048
	± 35	No correction	2.6747	2.4353	2.4906	2.2989	2.2862
		Increment	2.4770	2.4231	2.2808	2.1264	2.1376
		Proportional	2.4896	2.4191	2.2783	2.1239	2.1353
		Regression	2.1637	2.1874	2.1304	2.0447	2.0651
	± 42	No correction	2.5111	2.3065	2.3635	2.2006	2.1979
		Increment	2.2955	2.3228	2.2400	2.1534	2.1755
		Proportional	2.3082	2.3218	2.2318	2.1415	2.1648
		Regression	2.0797	2.1142	2.1050	2.0405	2.0471
	± 49	No correction	2.5503	2.2652	2.2721	2.0892	2.1089
		Increment	2.2927	2.2793	2.1763	2.0520	2.0995
		Proportional	2.3021	2.2796	2.1723	2.0464	2.0924
		Regression	2.0968	2.1120	2.0818	1.9922	2.0011

precision in the result of this examination. As shown in Table 6, other parameter combinations (background color is green) also obtained higher forecasting precision than the result of the previous study.

4.8. Evaluation of this examination

In this section, this examination is evaluated. In our previous studies, parameter settings (t and n) were decided when our original forecasting method was proposed. These parameter settings have been used for convenience in our previous studies. From the result of this examination (Table 4, Table 5 and Table 6), following three matters are considered.

- Setting number of past year (n) to 4 tends to improve forecasting precision
- Setting number of regression period (t) to 49 or 28 tends to improve forecasting precision
- There is no tendency in the correction method that improve forecasting precision

5. Conclusion

The purpose of this paper is to examine parameter combinations that improve the forecasting precision with daily water supply in currently used forecasting method. As the results of this examination, there is difference of parameter combination that improve forecasting precision between in currently used forecasting method and in our original forecasting method.

In future tasks, it is considered that forecasting precision of currently forecasting method is examined using different parameter combination setting than this examination. We hope that the result of this examination can be applied as one of the parameter selection methods in other forecasting methods using deep learning.

6. Acknowledgement

We wish to thank A Prefecture Public Enterprises Bureau for offering the data of amount of daily water supply.

7. References

[1] Y. Maruyama, Y. Shirai. "A study of Statistical Forecasting Method Concerning Water Demand of A Prefecture"; Proceedings of The 22nd Asia Pacific Industrial Engineering And Management Systems (Nov 2022).

[2] Y. Maruyama, K. Matsumoto, H. Yamamoto, T. Nakazawa, M. Tanabe. "Forecasting demand for water supply in the service area of the Kanagawa prefectural water works"; Journal of Japan Industrial Management Association, Vol.55, No.5, 283—292, (Dec 2004). (In Japanese)

[3] Japan Meteorological Agency. "Japan Meteorological Agency Home Page"; http://www.jma.go.jp/jma/index.html (Apr 2022).

Reliability Evaluation of a Standby Redundant System with Two Types of Components and Secondary Repair

Chia-Huang WU[1], Yin-Ying DAI[2], Dong-Yuh YANG[3]

[1]Department of Industrial Engineering and Management, National Yang Ming Chiao Tung University, Hsinchu, Taiwan
jacalwu@nycu.edu.tw
[2]Department of Industrial Engineering and Management, National Yang Ming Chiao Tung University, Hsinchu, Taiwan
yy.mg12@nycu.edu.tw
[3]Institute of Information and Decision Sciences, National Taipei University of Business, Taipei, Taiwan
yangdy@ntub.edu.tw

Keywords: MTTF, reliability, secondary repair, sensitivity analysis.

Abstract - This research investigates a standby redundant system composed of two distinct types of operating components and two distinct types of standby components. All components are subject to failure, and a repairman is responsible for restoring failed components. While failed components receive basic repair, some may require advanced repair depending on the severity of the damage, safety requirements, or performance considerations. The repair times for the two types of failed components under basic and advanced repair services follow different exponential distributions. Using the Laplace transform and matrix-analytical methods, we derive the reliability function and mean time to failure (*MTTF*) under consideration. Finally, we perform a sensitivity analysis of system reliability and *MTTF* through comprehensive numerical computations to identify critical parameters that have significant impacts.

1. Introduction

Redundant systems have been widely applied across a broad range of application areas, such as aerospace systems, communication networks, intelligent manufacturing, and energy systems. Due to their essential role in ensuring high system reliability and availability, these systems have attracted considerable research attention in the past. Integrating redundancy techniques and maintenance strategies involving component repair can significantly enhance the performance of repairable systems [1]. In the reliability literature, extensive studies have focused on three main types of standby components: cold, warm, and hot standby. A standby component is called a cold standby if it has a failure rate of zero. In contrast, a warm standby component has a non-zero failure rate lower than that of an operating component. On the other hand, a hot standby component experiences the same failure rate as an operating component. Interested readers may refer to [2-5].

In repairable systems with a two-phase repair service, all failed components initially undergo the essential repair phase, including preliminary fault diagnosis, visual inspection, or replacing worn internal parts. If the issue cannot be resolved during this phase, the component may proceed to the advanced repair phase for further repair and testing. Wang *et al.* [6] conducted a cost optimization analysis of a multi-server machine repair system with second optional repair. El-Said and El-Sherbeny [7] addressed the cost-benefit analysis of a two-unit cold standby system, in which the repair process is divided into two stages. The time elapsed between these two stages is referred to as the waiting time, which was also discussed in the study. Jain and Chauhan [8] studied a machine repair problem involving an unreliable repairman, a second optional repair, and mixed spares. In their model, the repairman may take a vacation when the system becomes empty, and the repair service resumes when at least N ($N \geq 1$) failed machines have accumulated. Gupta and Agarwal [9] analyzed the machine repairable system with warm spares and two repairmen under N-policy vacation, where one repairman is always available; the other performs the essential repair to all failed units and then may provide a second optional repair to some failed units as needed. Recently, Wang *et al.* [10] used the Markov process, matrix analysis and the technique of solving differential equations to develop reliability indices of the linear consecutive k/n: F retrial system with two-phase repair and Bernoulli vacation. Furthermore, the authors also conducted a numerical comparison of the cost-benefit ratio among system models with and without retrial and/or vacation mechanisms. Gao [11] focused on the availability and reliability characteristics of a repairable retrial system with warm standbys and second optional repair service. In the past, many researchers have studied repairable systems with two different types of components (see, e.g., [12-15]). However, most of these studies assume that the repairman performs only a single-phase repair for failed components. To the best of our knowledge, no prior work has investigated a repairable system with two types of components, in which the repairman is capable of providing a two-phase repair service. It motivates us to propose a novel redundant system that incorporates two types of operating and standby components and a second optional repair service.

The rest of this paper is organized as follows. Section 2 presents the reliability model of the redundant system under consideration and outlines the model assumptions. Section 3 formulates the system's differential-difference equations and derives the transient probabilities of the system. Section 4 conducts the reliability characteristics and provides numerical experiments to illustrate their behavior. Finally, Section 5 concludes the paper and suggests directions for future research.

2. Model assumptions

In this section, we outline the assumptions of the redundant system with two types of components and a second optional repair service as follows:

- The system consists of M_1 type I operating components, S_1 type I standby components, M_2 type II operating components, S_2 type II standby components, and a repairman.
- The system operates only when at least one component of type I and one of type II are operational simultaneously.
- The failures of type I and type II operating components follow a Poisson process with parameters λ and Λ, respectively.
- The failure intervals of type I and type II standby components follow exponential distributions with parameters δ_1 and δ_2, respectively, where $\lambda>\delta_1>0$ and $\Lambda>\delta_2>0$.
- The repairman is responsible for repairing failed components. Once a failed component is completely repaired, if there are failed components of the same type waiting for repair, priority is given to repairing components of the same type. Otherwise, the repairman proceeds to repair failed components of another type.
- All failed components undergo the first-stage basic repair, but only some severely damaged components require further second-stage advanced repair. The probabilities that type I and type II failed components will undergo further advanced repair are θ_1 and θ_2, respectively.
- For type I and type II failed components, the first-stage repair time follows an exponential distribution with parameters μ_1^1 and μ_1^2, respectively. If advanced repair is needed, the second-stage repair time follows an exponential distribution with μ_2^1 and μ_2^2, respectively.
- Various stochastic processes involved in the system are independent of each other.

3. Computation of transient probabilities

Let $I(t)$ and $J(t)$ denote the number of type I and type II failed components in the system at time t, respectively. $K(t)$ represents the state of the repairman at time t, where $K(t)=-1,-2,0,1,2$ indicate the repairman provides basic repairs to type I components, the repairman provides advanced repairs to type I components, the repairman is idle, the repairman provides basic repairs to type II components, the repairman provides advanced repairs to type II components, respectively. $F(t)$ represents the state in which the system failed at time t. Thus, the stochastic process $\{(K(t),I(t),J(t))\cup F(t),\ t\geq 0\}$ forms a continuous-time Markov chain with the state space $\Omega=\{(k,\ i,\ j):\ k=-1,-2;\ 1\leq i\leq L_1-1;\ 0\leq j\leq L_2-1\}\cup\{(k,\ i,\ j):\ k=1,2;\ 0\leq i\leq L_1-1;\ 1\leq j\leq L_2-1\}\cup\{(0,0,0),\ F_1,\ F_2\}$, where $L_1=M_1+S_1$ and $L_2=M_2+S_2$. We define $P_{i,j}^k(t)=\Pr\{K(t)=k,\ I(t)=i,\ J(t)=j\}$, $(k,\ i,\ j)\in\Omega$ and $F_i(t)=P(F(t)=F_i)$, $i=1,2$ be the transient probabilities. Figure 1 illustrates the system state-transition-rate diagram based on the assumptions outlined in Section 2.

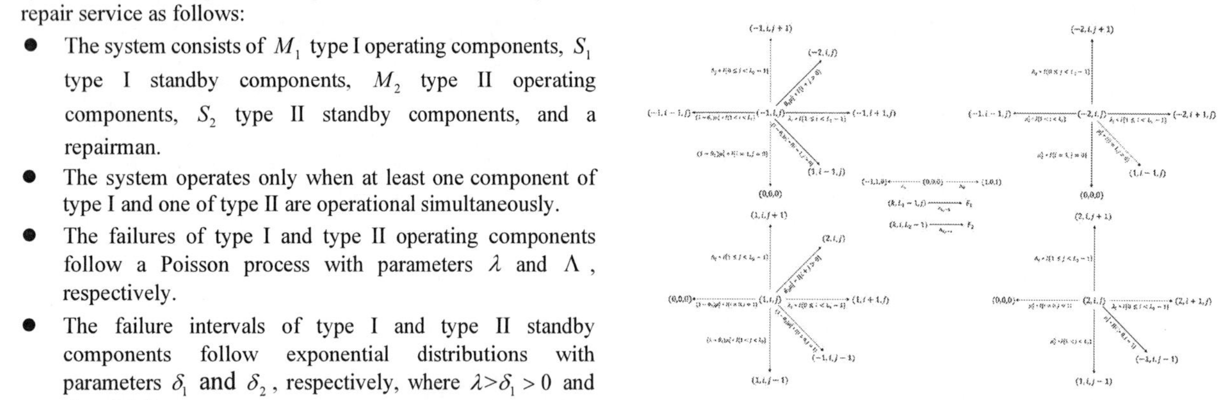

Figure 1. State transition diagram of the system.

Referring to Figure 1, the differential-difference equations governing the system are given as follows:

$$\frac{dP_{0,0}^0(t)}{dt}=-(\lambda_0+\Lambda_0)P_{0,0}^0(t)+(1-\theta_1)\mu_1^1P_{1,0}^{-1}(t)+\mu_2^1P_{1,0}^{-2}(t)+(1-\theta_2)\mu_1^2P_{0,1}^1(t)+\mu_2^2P_{0,1}^2(t), \tag{1}$$

$$\frac{dP_{1,0}^{-1}(t)}{dt}=-(\lambda_1+\Lambda_0+(1-\theta_1)\mu_1^1+\theta_1\mu_1^1)P_{1,0}^{-1}(t)+\lambda_0P_{0,0}^0(t)+(1-\theta_1)\mu_1^1P_{2,0}^{-1}(t)+\mu_2^1P_{2,0}^{-2}(t)+(1-\theta_2)\mu_1^2P_{1,1}^1(t)+\mu_2^2P_{1,1}^2(t), \tag{2}$$

$$\frac{dP_{i,0}^{-1}(t)}{dt}=-(\lambda_i+\Lambda_0+(1-\theta_1)\mu_1^1+\theta_1\mu_1^1)P_{i,0}^{-1}(t)+\lambda_{i-1}P_{i-1,0}^{-1}(t)+(1-\theta_1)\mu_1^1P_{i+1,0}^{-1}(t)+\mu_2^1P_{i+1,0}^{-2}(t)+(1-\theta_2)\mu_1^2P_{i,1}^1(t)+\mu_2^2P_{i,1}^2(t),\ i=2,3,\ldots,L_1-2, \tag{3}$$

$$\frac{dP_{L_1-1,0}^{-1}(t)}{dt}=-(\lambda_{L_1-1}+\Lambda_0+(1-\theta_1)\mu_1^1+\theta_1\mu_1^1)P_{L_1-1,0}^{-1}(t)+\lambda_{L_1-2}P_{L_1-2,0}^{-1}(t)+(1-\theta_2)\mu_1^2P_{L_1-1,1}^1(t)+\mu_2^2P_{L_1-1,1}^2(t), \tag{4}$$

$$\frac{dP_{1,j}^{-1}(t)}{dt}=-(\lambda_1+\Lambda_j+(1-\theta_1)\mu_1^1+\theta_1\mu_1^1)P_{1,j}^{-1}(t)+\Lambda_{j-1}P_{1,j-1}^{-1}(t)+(1-\theta_1)\mu_1^1P_{2,j}^{-1}(t)+\mu_2^1P_{2,j}^{-2}(t),\ j=1,2,\ldots,L_2-1, \tag{5}$$

$$\frac{dP_{i,j}^{-1}(t)}{dt}=-(\lambda_i+\Lambda_j+(1-\theta_1)\mu_1^1+\theta_1\mu_1^1)P_{i,j}^{-1}(t)+\lambda_{i-1}P_{i-1,j}^{-1}(t)+\Lambda_{j-1}P_{i,j-1}^{-1}(t)+(1-\theta_1)\mu_1^1P_{i+1,j}^{-1}(t)+\mu_2^1P_{i+1,j}^{-2}(t),$$
$$i=2,3,\ldots,L_1-2,\ j=1,2,\ldots,L_2-1, \tag{6}$$

$$\frac{dP^{-1}_{L_1-1,j}(t)}{dt}=-(\lambda_{L_1-1}+\Lambda_j+(1-\theta_1)\mu_1^1+\theta_1\mu_1^1)P^{-1}_{L_1-1,j}(t)+\lambda_{L_1-2}P^{-1}_{L_1-2,j}(t)+\Lambda_{j-1}P^{-1}_{i,j-1}(t),\quad j=1,2,\ldots,L_2-1, \tag{7}$$

$$\frac{dP^{-2}_{1,0}(t)}{dt}=-(\lambda_1+\Lambda_0+\mu_2^1)P^{-2}_{1,0}(t)+\theta_1\mu_1^1P^{-1}_{1,0}(t), \tag{8}$$

$$\frac{dP^{-2}_{i,0}(t)}{dt}=-(\lambda_i+\Lambda_0+\mu_2^1)P^{-2}_{i,0}(t)+\lambda_{i-1}P^{-2}_{i-1,0}(t)+\theta_1\mu_1^1P^{-1}_{i,0}(t),\ i=2,3,\ldots,L_1-1, \tag{9}$$

$$\frac{dP^{-2}_{1,j}(t)}{dt}=-(\lambda_1+\Lambda_j+\mu_2^1)P^{-2}_{1,j}(t)+\Lambda_{j-1}P^{-2}_{1,j-1}(t)+\theta_1\mu_1^1P^{-1}_{1,j}(t),\ j=1,2,\ldots,L_2-1, \tag{10}$$

$$\frac{dP^{-2}_{i,j}(t)}{dt}=-(\lambda_i+\Lambda_j+\mu_2^1)P^{-2}_{i,j}(t)+\lambda_{i-1}P^{-2}_{i-1,j}(t)+\Lambda_{j-1}P^{-2}_{i,j-1}(t)+\theta_1\mu_1^1P^{-1}_{i,j}(t),\quad i=2,3,\ldots,L_1-1,\ j=1,2,\ldots,L_2-1, \tag{11}$$

$$\frac{dP^{1}_{0,1}(t)}{dt}=-(\lambda_0+\Lambda_1+(1-\theta_2)\mu_1^2+\theta_2\mu_1^2)P^{1}_{0,1}(t)+\Lambda_0P^0_{0,0}(t)+(1-\theta_2)\mu_1^2P^1_{0,2}(t)+\mu_2^2P^2_{0,2}(t)+(1-\theta_1)\mu_1^1P^{-1}_{1,1}(t)+\mu_2^1P^{-2}_{1,1}(t), \tag{12}$$

$$\frac{dP^{1}_{i,1}(t)}{dt}=-(\lambda_i+\Lambda_1+(1-\theta_2)\mu_1^2+\theta_2\mu_1^2)P^{1}_{i,1}(t)+\lambda_{i-1}P^1_{i-1,1}(t)+(1-\theta_2)\mu_1^2P^1_{i,2}(t)+\mu_2^2P^2_{i,2}(t),\quad i=1,2,\ldots,L_1-1, \tag{13}$$

$$\frac{dP^{1}_{0,j}(t)}{dt}=-(\lambda_0+\Lambda_j+(1-\theta_2)\mu_1^2+\theta_2\mu_1^2)P^{1}_{0,j}(t)+\Lambda_{j-1}P^1_{0,j-1}(t)+(1-\theta_2)\mu_1^2P^1_{0,j+1}(t)+\mu_2^2P^2_{0,j+1}(t)+(1-\theta_1)\mu_1^1P^{-1}_{1,j}(t)+\mu_2^1P^{-2}_{1,j}(t),\ j=2,3,\ldots,L_2-2, \tag{14}$$

$$\frac{dP^{1}_{i,j}(t)}{dt}=-(\lambda_i+\Lambda_j+(1-\theta_2)\mu_1^2+\theta_2\mu_1^2)P^{1}_{i,j}(t)+\lambda_{i-1}P^1_{i-1,j}(t)+\Lambda_{j-1}P^1_{i,j-1}(t)+(1-\theta_2)\mu_1^2P^1_{i,j+1}(t)+\mu_2^2P^2_{i,j+1}(t),\quad i=1,2,\ldots,L_1-1,\ j=2,3,\ldots,L_2-2, \tag{15}$$

$$\frac{dP^{1}_{0,L_2-1}(t)}{dt}=-(\lambda_0+\Lambda_{L_2-1}+(1-\theta_2)\mu_1^2+\theta_2\mu_1^2)P^{1}_{0,L_2-1}(t)+\Lambda_{L_2-2}P^1_{0,L_2-2}(t)+(1-\theta_1)\mu_1^1P^{-1}_{1,L_2-1}(t)+\mu_2^1P^{-2}_{1,L_2-1}(t), \tag{16}$$

$$\frac{dP^{1}_{i,L_2-1}(t)}{dt}=-(\lambda_i+\Lambda_{L_2-1}+(1-\theta_2)\mu_1^2+\theta_2\mu_1^2)P^{1}_{i,L_2-1}(t)+\lambda_{i-1}P^1_{i-1,L_2-1}(t)+\Lambda_{L_2-2}P^1_{i,L_2-2}(t),\quad i=1,2,\ldots,L_1-1, \tag{17}$$

$$\frac{dP^{2}_{0,1}(t)}{dt}=-(\lambda_0+\Lambda_1+\mu_2^2)P^{2}_{0,1}(t)+\theta_2\mu_1^2P^1_{0,1}(t), \tag{18}$$

$$\frac{dP^{2}_{i,1}(t)}{dt}=-(\lambda_i+\Lambda_1+\mu_2^2)P^{2}_{i,1}(t)+\lambda_{i-1}P^2_{i-1,1}(t)+\theta_2\mu_1^2P^1_{i,1}(t),\ i=1,2,\ldots,L_1-1, \tag{19}$$

$$\frac{dP^{2}_{0,j}(t)}{dt}=-(\lambda_0+\Lambda_j+\mu_2^2)P^{2}_{0,j}(t)+\Lambda_{j-1}P^2_{0,j-1}(t)+\theta_2\mu_1^2P^1_{0,j}(t),\ j=2,3,\ldots,L_2-2, \tag{20}$$

$$\frac{dP^{2}_{i,j}(t)}{dt}=-(\lambda_i+\Lambda_j+\mu_2^2)P^{2}_{i,j}(t)+\lambda_{i-1}P^2_{i-1,j}(t)+\Lambda_{j-1}P^2_{i,j-1}(t)+\theta_2\mu_1^2P^1_{i,j}(t),\quad i=1,2,\ldots,L_1-1,\ j=2,3,\ldots,L_2-2, \tag{21}$$

$$\frac{dF_1(t)}{dt}=\lambda_{L_1-1}\Big(\sum_{j=0}^{L_2-1}P^{-1}_{L_1-1,j}(t)+\sum_{j=0}^{L_2-1}P^{-2}_{L_1-1,j}(t)+\sum_{j=1}^{L_2-1}P^{1}_{L_1-1,j}(t)+\sum_{j=1}^{L_2-1}P^{2}_{L_1-1,j}(t)\Big), \tag{22}$$

$$\frac{dF_2(t)}{dt}=\Lambda_{L_2-1}\Big(\sum_{i=1}^{L_1-1}P^{1}_{i,L_2-1}(t)+\sum_{i=1}^{L_1-1}P^{2}_{i,L_2-1}(t)+\sum_{i=0}^{L_1-1}P^{1}_{i,L_2-1}(t)+\sum_{i=0}^{L_1-1}P^{2}_{i,L_2-1}(t)\Big), \tag{23}$$

where

$$\lambda_i=\begin{cases}M_1\lambda+(S_1-i)\delta_1, & i=0,1,2,\cdots,S_1,\\ (M_1+S_1-i)\lambda, & i=S_1+1,S_1+2,\cdots,L_1-1,\\ 0, & \text{otherwise},\end{cases}$$

and

$$\Lambda_j=\begin{cases}M_2\Lambda+(S_2-j)\delta_2, & j=0,1,2,\cdots,S_2,\\ (M_2+S_2-j)\Lambda, & j=S_2+1,S_2+2,\cdots,L_2-1,\\ 0, & \text{otherwise}.\end{cases}$$

Equations (1)–(23) are reformulated in matrix form for computational convenience, as shown below:

$$\frac{d}{dt}\mathbf{P}(t)=\mathbf{P}(t)\mathbf{Q} \tag{24}$$

with the initial condition $\mathbf{P}(0)=[1,0,0,\ldots,0]$, where $\mathbf{P}(t)=[P^0_{0,0}(t),\ \mathbf{P}^{-1}(t),\ \mathbf{P}^{-2}(t),\ \mathbf{P}^{1}(t),\ \mathbf{P}^{2}(t),\ F_1(t),\ F_2(t)]$ with $\mathbf{P}^k(t)=[P^k_{1,0}(t),\cdots,P^k_{L_1-1,0}(t),P^k_{1,1}(t),\cdots,P^k_{L_1-1,1}(t),\cdots,P^k_{1,L_2-1}(t),\cdots,P^k_{L_1-1,L_2-1}(t)]$, $k=-1,-2$, and $\mathbf{P}^k(t)=[P^k_{0,1}(t),\cdots,P^k_{L_1-1,1}(t),P^k_{0,2}(t),\cdots,P^k_{L_1-1,2}(t),\cdots,P^k_{0,L_2-1}(t),\cdots,P^k_{L_1-1,L_2-1}(t)]$, $k=1,2$. The matrix $\mathbf{Q}$ is a square matrix of order $2[(L_1-1)\bullet L_2+L_1\bullet(L_2-1)]+3$.

Then, using the Laplace transform method, we can get the following:

$$\tilde{\mathbf{Q}}_s\tilde{\mathbf{P}}(s)=\tilde{\mathbf{P}}(0), \tag{25}$$

where $\tilde{\mathbf{Q}}_s=s\mathbf{I}-\mathbf{Q}^T$, $\tilde{\mathbf{P}}(s)=[\tilde{\mathbf{P}}^{-2}(s),\ \tilde{\mathbf{P}}^{-1}(s),\ \tilde{P}^0_{0,0}(s),\ \tilde{\mathbf{P}}^{1}(s),\ \tilde{\mathbf{P}}^{2}(s),\ \tilde{F}_1(s),\ \tilde{F}_2(s)]^T$, $\tilde{\mathbf{P}}^k(s)=[\tilde{P}^k_{1,0}(s),\cdots,\tilde{P}^k_{L_1-1,0}(s),\tilde{P}^k_{1,1}(s),\cdots,$

$\tilde{P}^k_{L_1-1,1}(s),\cdots,\tilde{P}^k_{1,L_2-1}(s),\cdots,\tilde{P}^k_{L_1-1,L_2-1}(s)]$, $k=-1,-2$, $\tilde{\mathbf{P}}^k(s)=[\tilde{P}^k_{0,1}(s),\cdots,\tilde{P}^k_{L_1-1,1}(s),\tilde{P}^k_{0,2}(s),\cdots,\tilde{P}^k_{L_1-1,2}(s),\cdots,\tilde{P}^k_{0,L_2-1}(s),\cdots,\tilde{P}^k_{L_1-1,L_2-1}(s)]$, $k=1,2$, $\tilde{\mathbf{P}}(0)=[1,0,0,...,0]$, and $\tilde{P}^k_{i,j}(s)=\int_0^\infty e^{-st}P^k_{i,j}(t)dt$, $(k,\ i,\ j)\in\Omega$. $\tilde{F}_1(s)$ and $\tilde{F}_2(s)$ are the Laplace transform of $F_1(t)$ and $F_2(t)$, respectively. $\mathbf{I}$ is the identity matrix with an appropriate order.

We determine the transient probabilities $P^k_{i,j}(t)$, $(k,i,j)\in\Omega$, by solving Equation (25) and applying the inverse Laplace transform. As analytical solutions are not available, we resort to numerical computation using R software.

4. Reliability Characteristics

Let Y denote the random variable corresponding to the time until the first failure of the system. Then, the reliability function at time t is given by

$$R_Y(t)=\Pr(Y>t)=1-F_1(t)-F_2(t). \tag{26}$$

The mean time to failure (*MTTF*) of the system is the expected time until the system experiences the first failure. Thus, the *MTTF* can be expressed as follows:

$$\begin{aligned} MTTF &= E[Y]=\int_0^\infty R_Y(t)dt=\lim_{s\to 0}\int_0^\infty e^{-st}R_Y(t)dt \\ &=\lim_{s\to 0}\left[\frac{1}{s}-\tilde{F}_1(s)-\tilde{F}_2(s)\right]. \end{aligned} \tag{27}$$

4.1. Numerical examples

The default parameters are set as follows: M_1=3 , M_2=2 , S_1=2 , S_2=1 , λ=2.0 , Λ=1.5 , δ_1=0.4 , δ_2=0.36 , μ_1^1=20 , μ_2^1=16, μ_1^2=14 , μ_2^2=12 , θ_1=0.3 , and θ_2=0.4 . We perform a sensitivity analysis to evaluate the effects of parameter variations on $R_Y(t)$ and *MTTF*. Tables 1-10 show the effect of various system parameters on $R_Y(t)$ and *MTTF*.

Table 1. Impacts of λ and Λ on $R_Y(t)$.

$(\lambda,\ \Lambda)$	t=0.1	t=0.3	t=0.5	t=0.7	t=0.9
(1.0, 2.0)	0.997	0.968	0.927	0.883	0.841
(1.5, 1.0)	1.000	0.994	0.983	0.971	0.957
(1.5, 2.0)	0.997	0.966	0.920	0.870	0.820
(1.5, 3.0)	0.991	0.914	0.813	0.715	0.626
(2.0, 2.0)	0.997	0.963	0.910	0.849	0.789

Table 2. Impacts of δ_1 and δ_2 on $R_Y(t)$.

$(\delta_1,\ \delta_2)$	t=0.1	t=0.3	t=0.5	t=0.7	t=0.9
(0.2, 0.2)	0.999	0.982	0.953	0.918	0.881
(0.4, 0.2)	0.999	0.982	0.952	0.916	0.878
(0.4, 0.36)	0.999	0.981	0.950	0.913	0.874
(0.4, 0.56)	0.998	0.980	0.948	0.910	0.870
(0.6, 0.2)	0.999	0.981	0.951	0.914	0.875

Table 3. Impacts of μ_1^1 and μ_1^2 on $R_Y(t)$.

$(\mu_1^1,\ \mu_1^2)$	t=0.1	t=0.3	t=0.5	t=0.7	t=0.9
(16, 16)	0.999	0.981	0.948	0.908	0.865
(20, 12)	0.998	0.980	0.946	0.906	0.864
(20, 14)	0.999	0.981	0.950	0.913	0.874
(20, 16)	0.999	0.982	0.953	0.919	0.883
(22, 16)	0.999	0.982	0.955	0.922	0.888

Table 4. Impacts of μ_2^1 and μ_2^2 on $R_Y(t)$.

$(\mu_2^1,\ \mu_2^2)$	t=0.1	t=0.3	t=0.5	t=0.7	t=0.9
(14, 12)	0.998	0.981	0.949	0.910	0.870
(16, 10)	0.998	0.980	0.948	0.909	0.868
(16, 12)	0.999	0.981	0.950	0.913	0.874
(16, 14)	0.999	0.981	0.952	0.916	0.879
(18, 12)	0.999	0.981	0.951	0.915	0.878

Table 5. Impacts of θ_1 and θ_2 on $R_Y(t)$.

$(\theta_1,\ \theta_2)$	t=0.1	t=0.3	t=0.5	t=0.7	t=0.9
(0.1, 0.4)	0.999	0.982	0.954	0.923	0.890
(0.3, 0.2)	0.999	0.983	0.956	0.923	0.889
(0.3, 0.4)	0.999	0.981	0.950	0.913	0.874
(0.3, 0.6)	0.998	0.979	0.944	0.903	0.860
(0.5, 0.4)	0.998	0.980	0.946	0.903	0.859

Table 6. Impacts of λ and Λ on *MTTF*.

λ	Λ = 1.0	Λ = 1.5	Λ = 2.0	Λ = 2.5	Λ = 3.0
1.0	19.443	7.745	4.160	2.638	1.856
1.5	13.783	6.152	3.504	2.307	1.665
2.0	9.135	4.694	2.879	1.984	1.477
2.5	6.058	3.551	2.348	1.696	1.304
3.0	4.170	2.724	1.926	1.454	1.152

Table 7. Impacts of δ_1 and δ_2 on *MTTF*.

δ_1	δ_2 = 0.2	δ_2 = 0.4	δ_2 = 0.6	δ_2 = 0.8	δ_2 = 1.0
0.2	4.953	4.788	4.641	4.508	4.388
0.4	4.822	4.664	4.522	4.394	4.278
0.6	4.701	4.549	4.412	4.288	4.177
0.8	4.589	4.442	4.309	4.190	4.083
1	4.485	4.342	4.214	4.099	3.995

Table 8. Impacts of μ_1^1 and μ_1^2 on *MTTF*.

μ_1^1	μ_1^2 = 12	μ_1^2 = 14	μ_1^2 = 16	μ_1^2 = 18	μ_1^2 = 20
12	2.890	3.047	3.175	3.279	3.366
14	3.288	3.509	3.692	3.844	3.970
16	3.655	3.944	4.187	4.390	4.562
18	3.984	4.341	4.644	4.901	5.121
20	4.272	4.694	5.056	5.367	5.634

Table 9. Impacts of μ_2^1 and μ_2^2 on *MTTF*.

μ_2^1	μ_2^2 = 10	μ_2^2 = 12	μ_2^2 = 14	μ_2^2 = 16	μ_2^2 = 18
10	3.711	3.892	4.030	4.139	4.225
12	4.001	4.220	4.388	4.521	4.627
14	4.232	4.483	4.677	4.831	4.955
16	4.416	4.694	4.911	5.083	5.222
18	4.564	4.865	5.101	5.289	5.441

Table 10. Impacts of θ_1 and θ_2 on *MTTF*.

θ_1	$\theta_2 = 0.2$	$\theta_2 = 0.3$	$\theta_2 = 0.4$	$\theta_2 = 0.5$	$\theta_2 = 0.6$
0.2	5.978	5.517	5.126	4.788	4.494
0.3	5.392	5.017	4.694	4.412	4.164
0.4	4.889	4.583	4.315	4.079	3.869
0.5	4.457	4.204	3.981	3.783	3.605
0.6	4.082	3.873	3.687	3.519	3.368

We present the effect of various system parameters on the $R_Y(t)$ for different values of t in Tables 1-5. One can easily see that the system reliability decreases as t increases. Table 1 indicates that $R_Y(t)$ declines as λ or Λ increases, while Table 2 shows a similar trend with increasing δ_1 or δ_2. Tables 3 and 4 reveal that higher μ_1^1, μ_1^2, μ_2^1, or μ_2^2 enhance $R_Y(t)$, whereas Table 5 demonstrates that increasing θ_1 or θ_2 reduces $R_Y(t)$. The numerical results of *MTTF* are summarized in Tables 6-10. From Table 6, it shows that increasing λ decreases *MTTF* across all Λ. Table 7 reveals that increasing δ_1 or δ_2 lowers *MTTF*. Tables 8 and 9 indicate that higher μ_1^1, μ_1^2, μ_2^1, or μ_2^2 increase *MTTF*, highlighting the benefits of faster repair rates. Table 10 shows that increasing θ_1 or θ_2 reduces *MTTF*. Based on the numerical results, system managers or decision-makers can enhance system reliability and extend *MTTF* by adjusting key system parameters.

5. Conclusion

This paper conducted a reliability analysis of a standby redundant system with two types of components and a second optional repair service. We utilized the matrix analytical method and Laplace transforms to obtain the transient probabilities. Two reliability characteristics, namely the reliability function and *MTTF*, were developed. We provided numerical experiments to demonstrate how variations in system parameters influence the reliability function and *MTTF*. Our numerical results offer valuable insights for improving system performances and have important managerial implications for decision-makers. In the future, an interesting research topic could be to explore the Markov model of the proposed standby redundant systems for steady-state availability analysis.

6. Acknowledgement

This work was partially supported by National Science and Technology Council, Taiwan, under Grant NSTC 112-2221-E-A49-124-MY3 and Grant NSTC 112-2221-E-141-009-MY2.

7. References

[1] S. Gao, "Reliability analysis and optimization for a redundant system with dependent failures and variable repair rates," *Math. Comput. Simul.*, vol. 208, pp. 637–659, 2023.

[2] R. Subramanian and V. Anantharaman, "Reliability analysis of a complex standby redundant systems," *Reliab. Eng. Syst. Saf.*, vol. 48, pp. 57–70, 1995.

[3] M. Jain, "Reliability prediction of repairable redundant system with imperfect switching and repair," *Arab. J. Sci. Eng.*, vol. 41, pp. 3717–3725, 2016.

[4] A. Azaron, H. Katagiri, K. Kato, and Sakawa, M. "Reliability evaluation of multi-component cold-standby redundant systems ", *Appl. Math. Comput.*, vol. 173, pp. 137-149, 2006.

[5] M. Oszczypała, J. Ziółkowski, and J. Małachowski, "Redundancy allocation problem in repairable *k*-out-of-*n* systems with cold, warm, and hot standby: A genetic algorithm for availability optimization," *Appl. Soft Comput.*, vol. 165, p. 112041, 2024.

[6] K.-H. Wang, C.-W. Liao, and T.-C. Yen, "Cost analysis of the M/M/R machine repair problem with second optional repair: Newton-quasi method," *J. Ind. Manag. Optim.*, vol. 6, pp. 197–207, 2009.

[7] K. M. El-Said and M. S. El-Sherbeny, "Stochastic analysis of a two-unit cold standby system with two-stage repair and waiting time," *Sankhya B*, vol. 72, pp. 1–10, 2010.

[8] M. Jain and D. Chauhan, "Unreliable server machine repair problem with second optional service, mixed spares and multi-phase repair," *Int. J. Eng. Math. Comput. Sci.*, vol. 3, pp. 1–9, 2014.

[9] R. Gupta and D. Agarwal, "Cost analysis of N-policy vacation machine repair problem with optional repair," *Int. J. Math. Oper. Res.*, vol. 19, pp. 354–374, 2021.

[10] Y. Wang, L. Hu, B. Zhao, and R. Tian, "Stochastic modeling and cost-benefit evaluation of consecutive *k*/*n*: F repairable retrial systems with two-phase repair and vacation," *Comput. Ind. Eng.*, vol. 175, p. 108851, 2023.

[11] S. Gao, "Availability and reliability analysis of a retrial system with warm standbys and second optional repair service," *Commun. Stat. Theory Methods*, vol. 52, pp. 1039–1057, 2023.

[12] S. Eryilmaz, "The number of failed components in a *k*-out-of-*n* system consisting of multiple types of components," *Reliab. Eng. Syst. Saf.*, vol. 175, pp. 246–250, 2018.

[13] S. Eryilmaz and K. Sarikaya, "Modeling and analysis of weighted-*k*-out-of-*n*: G system consisting of two different types of components," *Proc. Inst. Mech. Eng. O: J. Risk Reliab.*, vol. 228, pp. 265–271, 2014.

[14] C. Franko, G. Y. Tütüncü, and S. Eryilmaz, "Reliability of weighted *k*-out-of-*n*: G systems consisting of two types of components and a cold standby component," *Commun. Stat. Simul. Comput.*, vol. 46, pp. 4067–4081, 2017.

[15] G. Wang, L. Hu, T. Zhang, and Y. Wang, "Reliability modeling for a repairable (k_1, k_2)-out-of-*n*: G system with phase-type vacation time," *Appl. Math. Model.*, vol. 91, pp. 311–321, 2021.

Which is Better Problem in Backward Model

Toshio NAKAGAWA†, Xufeng ZHAO‡, Satoshi MIZUTANI†

†Department of Business Administration, Aichi Institute of Technology, Toyota, Japan
‡College of Economics and Management
Nanjing University of Aeronautics and Astronautics, Nanjing, China

Keywords: Maintenance Policy, Checking times, Backward model, Reversed failure rate.

Abstract - We consider some maintenance policies in backward model with the reversed failure rate. When the unit has failed, we consider two models: we trace back from time 0 to detect the failure time, and from time S to detect the failure time. We discusses optimal checking times for the models using finite interval model, and show the numerical examples when the failure distribution is Weibull.

1 Introduction

There are some cases that investigating the failure time is important when the failure has detected. If we can estimate the time previously before operating the system, it would be useful to estimate the failure cost and plan the optimal maintenance schedule. The maintenance models in backward models are planned using the reversed failure rate [1,2]. Further, it is important to compare the maintenance models to select optimal one [3,4]. We compare, in this paper, some maintenance policies in backward model extending finite interval models [5,6]. That it, we consider the time that a failure for a unit is detected like a finite interval. Section 2 shows some backward models.

2 Backward Model

Suppose that when a failure for a unit is detected at time S $(0 < S < \infty)$ and its failure time is unknown, we often investigate the past time at failure [1,2]. For this purpose, we consider two cases in Fig 1. One is that the operational behaviors of the unit are on record, and its failure time is traced back from time 0 and is detected at time t. The other is that the failure time is traced back time S and its detected at time $S-t$ $(0 < t < S)$.

We propose the following which is Better (WIB) problem [3,4], of the backward model:

(1) We trace back from time 0 to detect the failure time.

(2) We trace back from time S to detect the failure time.

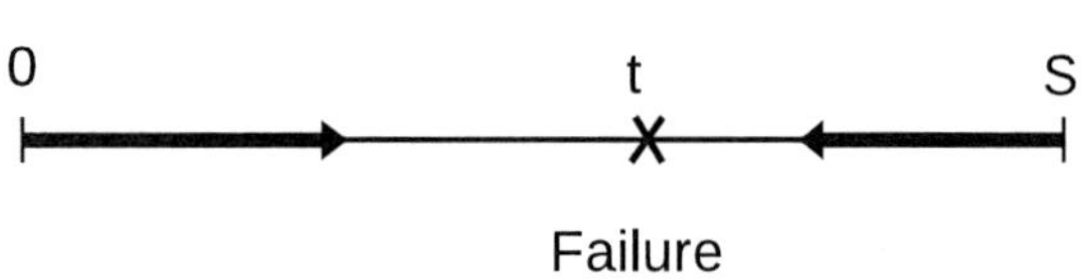

Figure 1: Two backward policies.

It is assumed that unit has a failure distribution $F(t)$ with finite mean $\mu \equiv \int_0^\infty \overline{F}(t)\mathrm{d}t$, a density function $f(t) \equiv \mathrm{d}F(t)\mathrm{d}t$, and a reversed failure rate $r(t) \equiv f(t)/F(t)$, where $\overline{\Phi}(t) \equiv 1-\Phi(t)$ for a general function $\Phi(t)$. Then, when $r(t)$ decreases with t, we easily have [1,2], for $0 < t < \infty$,

$$\frac{\overline{F}(t)}{\int_t^\infty F(u)\,\mathrm{d}u} \le r(t) \le \frac{F(t)}{\int_0^t F(u)\,\mathrm{d}u}, \tag{1}$$

all of which decrease with t.

The mean time from 0 to detect the failure time in case **(1)** is

$$Q_1(S) = \frac{1}{F(S)}\int_0^S t\,\mathrm{d}F(t) = \frac{1}{F(S)}\int_0^S [F(S)-F(t)]\mathrm{d}t, \tag{2}$$

and the mean time from S to detect the failure time is case **(2)** is

$$Q_2(S) = \frac{1}{F(S)}\int_0^S (S-t)\,\mathrm{d}F(t) = \frac{1}{F(S)}\int_0^S F(S)\,\mathrm{d}t, \tag{3}$$

where $Q_1(S)+Q_2(S)=S$. Clearly,

$$\lim_{S\to 0} Q_1(S) = 0, \qquad \lim_{S\to\infty} Q_1(S) = \mu,$$

$$\lim_{S\to 0} Q_2(S) = \frac{1}{r(0)}, \qquad \lim_{S\to\infty} Q_2(S) = \infty.$$

Thus, it is easily proved that $Q_1(S)$ increases with S from to μ and $Q_2(S)$ increases with S from $1/r(0)$ to ∞.

We consider the problems *which is smaller, $Q_1(S)$ and $Q_2(S)$*: Forming $Q_2(S)$ - $Q_1(S)$,

$$L_1(S) \equiv 2\int_0^S F(t)\mathrm{d}t - SF(S).$$

Noting that

$$L_1(0)=0, \quad L_1'(S) = F(S) - Sf(S) = SF(S)\left[\frac{1}{S} - r(S)\right].$$

Thus, if $r(S) \le 1/S$, then we should trace back from time 0, and if $r(S) > 1/S$, then we should trace back from time S.

In particular, when $F(t)$ is symmetric for $0 \le t \le S$ such as uniform and triangular distributions with mean $S/2$, i.e.,

$$f(t) = f(S-t), \qquad Q_1(S) = Q_2(S).$$

Table 1: Value of $\widetilde{x}$.

m	1.0	1.5	2.0	2.5	3.0	3.5
$\widetilde{x}$	0	0.835	1.121	1.212	1.239	1.242

Example. 1. When $F(t) = 1 - e^{-\lambda t}$,

$$Q_1(S) = \frac{1}{\lambda}\frac{1-(1+\lambda S)e^{-\lambda S}}{1-e^{-\lambda S}} < \frac{S}{2}, \tag{4}$$

which increases strictly with S from 0 to $1/\lambda$, and

$$Q_2(S) = \frac{1}{\lambda}\frac{\lambda S - (1-e^{-\lambda S})}{1-e^{-\lambda S}} > \frac{S}{2}, \tag{5}$$

which increases strictly with S from 0 to ∞, which follows that $Q_2(S) > Q_1(S)$. Furthermore, noting that

$$F\left(\frac{S}{2}\right) - \left[F(S) - F\left(\frac{S}{2}\right)\right] = 1 - e^{-\lambda S/2} - (e^{-\lambda S/2} - e^{-\lambda S}) > 0,$$

$$\frac{1}{S} - r(S) = \frac{1}{S} - \frac{\lambda e^{-\lambda S}}{1-e^{-\lambda S}} = \frac{1}{S} - \frac{\lambda}{e^{\lambda S}-1} > 0,$$

we also have $Q_2(S) > Q_1(S)$. ■

Example. 2. When $F(t) = 1 - e^{-(\lambda t)^m}$ $(m \geq 1)$,

$$r(S) = \frac{m\lambda(\lambda S)^{m-1}e^{-(\lambda t)^m}}{1-e^{-(\lambda S)^m}} - \frac{1}{S} = \frac{m\lambda(\lambda S)^{m-1}}{e^{(\lambda S)^m}-1} - \frac{1}{S}. \tag{6}$$

If $r(S) < 1/S$, i.e.,

$$e^{(\lambda S)^m} > 1 + m(\lambda S)^m,$$

then we should trace back from time 0. Let $\widetilde{x}$ be a solution of the equation:

$$L_2(x) \equiv e^{x^m} - 1 - mx^m = 0.$$

Table 1 presents values of $\widetilde{x}$ for $m = 1.0$, 1.5, 2.0, 2.5, 3.0, 3.5.

(i) If $x \geq \widetilde{x}$, i.e., $\lambda S \geq \widetilde{x}$, then we should trace back from time 0.

(ii) If $x < \widetilde{x}$, i.e., $\lambda S < \widetilde{x}$, then we should trace back from time S.

■

3 Optimal Checking Times

Suppose that the unit has failed and its failure is detected at time S $(0 < S < \infty)$. To search for the failure time, checking times T_k $(k = 1, 2, \ldots, N)$ are placed at successive times from 0 in case (**1**), when $T_N \equiv S$ $(N = 1, 2, \ldots)$ in Fig. 2.

It is assumed that c_1 is checking cost and c_2 is tracing cost per unit of time from failure time t to checking time

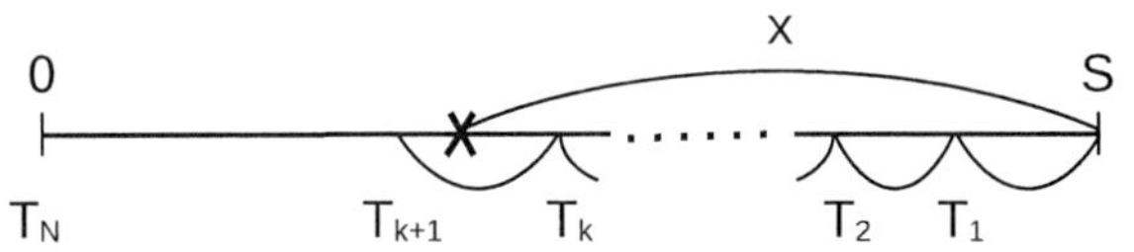

Figure 2: Checking times T_k $(k = 1, 2, \ldots, N)$ from time 0.

T_{k+1}. Then, the total cost until the detection of failure time is, for $\boldsymbol{T} \equiv \{T_0, T_1, T_2, \ldots, T_N\}$ where $T_0 \equiv 0$ and $T_N \equiv S$,

$$\begin{aligned} C_1(\boldsymbol{T}|N) &= \frac{1}{F(S)}\sum_{k=0}^{N-1}\int_{T_k}^{T_{k+1}}[c_1(k+1) + c_2(T_{k+1} - t)]dF(t) \\ &= \frac{1}{F(S)}\left(\sum_{k=0}^{N-1}\{[c_1 + c_2(T_{k+1} - T_k)][F(S) - F(T_k)]\}\right. \\ &\quad \left. - c_2\int_0^S [F(S) - F(t)]dt\right) \quad (N = 1, 2, \ldots). \end{aligned} \tag{7}$$

Clearly,

$$C_1(\boldsymbol{T}|1) = \frac{1}{F(S)}\left[c_1 + c_2\int_0^S F(t)dt\right]. \tag{8}$$

We find optimal T_k^* $(k = 1, 2, \ldots, N)$ to minimize $C_1(\boldsymbol{T}|N)$. Differentiating $C_1(\boldsymbol{T}|N)$ in (7) with respect to T_k and setting it equal to zero,

$$T_{k+1} - T_k = \frac{F(T_k) - F(T_{k-1})}{f(T_k)} - \frac{c_1}{c_2}, \tag{9}$$

i.e.,

$$T_2 - T_1 = \frac{F(T_1)}{f(T_1)} - \frac{c_1}{c_2},$$

$$T_{k+1} - T_k = \frac{F(T_k) - F(T_{k-1})}{f(T_k)} - \frac{c_1}{c_2} \quad (k = 2, 3, \ldots, N-2),$$

$$S - T_{N-1} = \frac{F(T_{N-1}) - F(T_{N-2})}{f(T_{N-1})} - \frac{c_1}{c_2}.$$

In particular, when $F(t) = 1 - e^{-\lambda t}$,

$$T_{k+1} - T_k = \frac{e^{-\lambda T_{k-1}} - e^{-\lambda T_k}}{\lambda e^{-\lambda T_k}} - \frac{c_1}{c_2}.$$

Let T_1 be a solution of the equation

$$T_1 = \frac{1}{\lambda}(e^{\lambda T_1} - 1) - \frac{c_1}{c_2}. \tag{10}$$

Then, from the equation

$$T_2 - T_1 = \frac{1-e^{-\lambda T_1}}{\lambda e^{-\lambda T_1}} - \frac{c_1}{c_2} = \frac{1}{\lambda}(e^{\lambda T_1} - 1),$$

we easily have $T_2 = 2T_1$. Using a mathematical induction, $T_k = kT_1^*$, i.e., the unit would be replaced at about periodic times kT_1^* $(k = 1, 2, \ldots, N)$ when $NT_1^* = S$.

Next, checking times T_k $(k = 1, 2, \dots, N)$ are replaced at successive times from S in case (**2**), where $T_N \equiv S$ $(N = 1, 2, \dots)$.

The total cost until the detection of failure time is

$$\begin{aligned} C_2(\boldsymbol{T}|N) &= \frac{1}{F(S)} \sum_{k=0}^{N-1} \int_{T_k}^{T_{k+1}} [c_1(k+1) \\ &\quad + c_2(T_{k+1} - x)]\mathrm{d}[F(S) - F(S-x)] \\ &= \frac{1}{F(S)} \left(\sum_{k=0}^{N-1} \{[c_1 + c_2(T_{k+1} - T_k)]F(S - T_k)\} \right. \\ &\quad \left. - c_2 \int_0^S F(x)\mathrm{d}x \right) \qquad (N = 1, 2, \dots). \end{aligned} \tag{11}$$

Clearly,

$$C_2(\boldsymbol{T}|1) = \frac{1}{F(S)} \left\{ c_1 + c_2 \int_0^S [F(S) - F(x)]\mathrm{d}x \right\}. \tag{12}$$

We find optimal T_k^* $(k = 1, 2, \dots, N)$ to minimize $C_2(\boldsymbol{T}|N)$. Differentiating $C_2(\boldsymbol{T}|N)$ in (11) with respect to T_k and setting it equal to zero,

$$T_{k+1} - T_k = \frac{F(S - T_{k-1}) - F(S - T_k)}{f(S - T_k)} - \frac{c_1}{c_2},$$

i.e.,

$$\begin{aligned} T_2 - T_1 &= \frac{F(S) - F(S - T_1)}{f(S - T_1)} - \frac{c_1}{c_2}, \\ T_{k+1} - T_k &= \frac{F(S - T_{k-1}) - F(S - T_k)}{f(S - T_k)} - \frac{c_1}{c_2} \\ &\qquad (k = 2, 3, \dots, N-2), \\ S - T_{N-1} &= \frac{F(S - T_{k-2}) - F(S - T_{k-1})}{f(S - T_{N-1})} - \frac{c_1}{c_2}. \end{aligned}$$

In particular, when $F(t) = 1 - \mathrm{e}^{-\lambda t}$,

$$\begin{aligned} T_{k+1} - T_k &= \frac{\mathrm{e}^{-\lambda(S-T_k)} - \mathrm{e}^{-\lambda(S-T_{k-1})}}{\lambda \mathrm{e}^{-\lambda(S-T_k)}} - \frac{c_1}{c_2}, \\ &= \frac{\mathrm{e}^{\lambda T_k} - \mathrm{e}^{\lambda T_{k-1}}}{\lambda \mathrm{e}^{\lambda T_k}} - \frac{c_1}{c_2}. \end{aligned} \tag{13}$$

Then, from the equation

$$T_1 = \frac{\mathrm{e}^{\lambda T_1} - 1}{\lambda \mathrm{e}^{\lambda T_1}} - \frac{c_1}{c_2} = \frac{1}{\lambda}(1 - \mathrm{e}^{-\lambda T_1}) - \frac{c_1}{c_2}. \tag{14}$$

Then, from the equation

$$T_2 - T_1 = \frac{1}{\lambda}(1 - \mathrm{e}^{-\lambda T_1}) - \frac{c_1}{c_2},$$

we easily have $T_2 = 2T_1$. Using a mathematical induction, $T_k = kT_2^*$, i.e., the unit should be checked at about periodic times kT_2^* $(k = 1, 2, \dots)$ in case (ii).

Noting that $\mathrm{e}^{\lambda T} - 1 > 1 - \mathrm{e}^{-\lambda T}$, we have $T_1^* > T_2^*$.

Table 2: Optimal cost $C(\boldsymbol{T}^*|N))/c_2$.

c_1/c_2	5	7	10
N^*	6	5	4
$C(\boldsymbol{T}^*\|N))/c_2$	23.646	28.550	35.000

Table 3: Optimal $\boldsymbol{T}$ for $C_1(\boldsymbol{T}|N)/c_2$ when $m = 1.0$, $S = 100$, $\lambda = 0.01$, $c_1/c_2 = 5$.

T_k	1	2	3	4	5	6
T_1	100.0	46.2	32.4	26.9	24.5	23.5
T_2		100.0	65.6	52.7	47.2	45.0
T_3			100.0	77.2	67.7	63.9
T_4				100.0	85.5	79.8
T_5					100.0	92.0
T_6						100.0
$\frac{C_1(\boldsymbol{T}\|N)}{c_2}$	463.2	307.8	263.6	244.3	234.9	230.5

Example. 3. When the failure time has a uniform distribution in $[0, t]$, i.e., $F(t) = t/S$ for $0 \le t \le S$ and 1 for $t > S$. Then, both $C_1(\boldsymbol{T}|N)$ and $C_2(\boldsymbol{T}|N)$ are the same as

$$C(\boldsymbol{T}|N) = \frac{1}{S} \sum_{k=0}^{N-1} \int_{T_k}^{T_{k+1}} [(k+1)c_1 + c_2(T_{k+1} - t)]\mathrm{d}t.$$

Differentiating $C(\boldsymbol{T}|N)$ with respect to T_k and setting it equal to zero,

$$T_{k+1} - T_k = T_k - T_{k-1} - \frac{c_1}{c_2}.$$

Solving for T_k,

$$T_k = kT_1 - \frac{k(k-1)}{2} \frac{c_1}{c_2}.$$

Setting for T_k,

$$T_k = \frac{kS}{N} + k(N-k)\frac{c_1}{2c_2} \qquad (k = 0, 1, \dots, N).$$

When $k = N - 1$,

$$\frac{N(N-1)}{2} < \frac{c_2 S}{c_1}, \qquad i.e., \qquad \frac{N(N+1)}{2} \ge \frac{c_2 S}{c_1}.$$

We compute N^* and the cost in Table 3 when $c_1/c_2 = 5, 7, 10$. ■

Example. 4. When $F(t) = 1 - \mathrm{e}^{-(\lambda t)^m}$ $(m \ge 1)$, compute $C_1(\boldsymbol{T}|N)$ and $C_2(\boldsymbol{T}|N)$ for $N = 1, 2, \dots$ when $S = 100, 150, 200$, $1/\lambda = 0.01$ in Table 3∼16. ■

4 Conclusions

We considered some maintenance policies in backward models, and showed the numerical examples. We could not compute optimal checking times when N is greater than 6, and not obtain the optimal N^* which minizes the expected costs. To compute these values, it might be necessary to check the model and numerical algorithms.

Table 4: Optimal $\boldsymbol{T}$ for $C_1(\boldsymbol{T}|N)/c_2$ when $m = 1.2$, $S = 100$, $\lambda = 0.01$, $c_1/c_2 = 5$.

T_k	1	2	3	4	5	6
T_1	100.0	51.2	37.6	32.1	29.7	28.8
T_2		100.0	69.3	57.5	52.5	50.6
T_3			100.0	80.1	71.9	68.8
T_4				100.0	87.8	83.4
T_5					100.0	93.9
T_6						100.0
$\frac{C_1(\boldsymbol{T}\|N)}{c_2}$	58.40	32.68	26.15	23.90	23.15	22.98

Table 5: Optimal $\boldsymbol{T}$ for $C_1(\boldsymbol{T}|N)/c_2$ when $m = 1.5$, $S = 100$, $\lambda = 0.01$, $c_1/c_2 = 5$.

T_k	1	2	3	4	5	6
T_1	100.0	57.2	44.4	39.0	36.8	36.1
T_2		100.0	73.8	63.5	59.2	57.9
T_3			100.0	83.5	77.0	75.0
T_4				100.0	90.6	87.8
T_5					100.0	96.2
T_6						100.0
$\frac{C_1(\boldsymbol{T}\|N)}{c_2}$	452.49	335.83	299.87	284.06	276.79	274.27

References

[1] Nakagawa, T., Mizutani, S. and Sugiura, T. (2005) Note on the backward time of reliability models, Eleventh ISSAT International Conference on Reliability and Quality in Design, pp. 219-222.

[2] Nakagawa, T. and Mizutani, S. (2008) Optimum Problems in Backward Times of Reliability Models, IIE Transactions, 41, 1, pp. 65-71.

[3] Zhao, X., Mizutani, S and Nakagawa, T (2015) Which is better for replacement policies with continuous or discrete scheduled time. European Journal of Operational Research, 242: pp. 477-486.

Table 6: Optimal $\boldsymbol{T}$ for $C_1(\boldsymbol{T}|N)/c_2$ when $m = 1.2$, $S = 100$, $\lambda = 0.01$, $c_1/c_2 = 3$.

T_k	1	2	3	4	5	6
T_1	100.0	50.8	36.7	30.7	27.9	26.6
T_2		100.0	68.4	55.7	49.8	47.1
T_3			100.0	78.7	69.1	64.8
T_4				100.0	85.9	79.6
T_5					100.0	91.5
T_6						100.0
$\frac{C_1(\boldsymbol{T}\|N)}{c_2}$	57.40	31.25	24.31	21.72	20.71	20.37

Table 7: Optimal $\boldsymbol{T}$ for $C_1(\boldsymbol{T}|N)/c_2$ when $m = 1.2$, $S = 100$, $\lambda = 0.01$, $c_1/c_2 = 6$.

T_k	1	2	3	4	5	6
T_1	100.0	51.6	38.5	33.4	31.4	30.9
T_2		100.0	70.2	59.3	55.1	54.0
T_3			100.0	81.5	74.6	72.8
T_4				100.0	89.8	87.1
T_5					100.0	96.3
T_6						100.0
$\frac{C_1(\boldsymbol{T}\|N)}{c_2}$	59.40	34.10	27.96	26.03	25.51	25.45

Table 8: Optimal $\boldsymbol{T}$ for $C_1(\boldsymbol{T}|N)/c_2$ when $m = 1.2$, $S = 150$, $\lambda = 0.01$, $c_1/c_2 = 5$.

T_k	1	2	3	4	5	6
T_1	150.0	71.0	49.8	40.7	36.3	34.0
T_2		150.0	96.7	76.2	66.4	61.5
T_3			150.0	112.0	95.0	86.7
T_4				150.0	122.8	110.0
T_5					150.0	131.2
T_6						150.0
$\frac{C_1(\boldsymbol{T}\|N)}{c_2}$	92.17	46.49	34.66	30.03	28.01	27.15

[4] Mizutani, S, Zhao, X. and Nakagawa, T. (2023) Which-Is-Better (WIB): Problems in reliability theory. Springer, London.

[5] Nakagawa, T. and Mizutani, S. (2009) A summary of maintenance policies for a finite interval. Reliability Engineering & System Safety, 94, 1, pp. 89-96.

[6] Nakagawa, T. (2008) Advanced Reliability Models and Maintenance Policies, Springer, London.

Table 9: Optimal $\boldsymbol{T}$ for $C_1(\boldsymbol{T}|N)/c_2$ when $m = 1.2$, $S = 200$, $\lambda = 0.01$, $c_1/c_2 = 5$.

T_k	1	2	3	4	5	6
T_1	200.0	88.3	59.8	47.7	41.4	38.0
T_2		200.0	121.0	91.8	77.7	70.2
T_3			200.0	140.6	114.7	101.4
T_4				200.0	154.6	132.9
T_5					200.0	165.4
T_6						200.0
$\frac{C_1(\boldsymbol{T}\|N)}{c_2}$	130.46	60.55	42.95	35.79	32.38	30.68

Table 10: Optimal $\boldsymbol{T}$ for $C_2(\boldsymbol{T}|N)/c_2$ when $m = 1.0$, $S = 100$, $\lambda = 0.01$, $c_1/c_2 = 5$.

T_k	1	2	3	4	5	6
T_1	100.0	59.9	45.9	40.0	37.7	37.5
T_2		100.0	77.7	68.0	64.1	63.7
T_3			100.0	87.4	82.3	81.8
T_4				100.0	94.0	93.4
T_5					100.0	99.3
T_6						100.0
$\frac{C_2(\boldsymbol{T}\|N)}{c_2}$	46.80	51.69	56.64	61.61	66.59	71.57

Table 11: Optimal $\boldsymbol{T}$ for $C_2(\boldsymbol{T}|N)/c_2$ when $m = 1.2$, $S = 100$, $\lambda = 0.01$, $c_1/c_2 = 5$.

T_k	1	2	3	4	5	6
T_1	100.0	57.9	43.6	37.5	34.9	34.1
T_2		100.0	75.2	64.6	60.1	58.6
T_3			100.0	84.7	78.3	76.3
T_4				100.0	91.3	88.7
T_5					100.0	96.4
T_6						100.0
$\frac{C_2(\boldsymbol{T}\|N)}{c_2}$	51.60	56.46	61.41	66.38	71.36	76.33

Table 12: Optimal $\boldsymbol{T}$ for $C_2(\boldsymbol{T}|N)/c_2$ when $m = 1.5$, $S = 100$, $\lambda = 0.01$, $c_1/c_2 = 5$.

T_k	1	2	3	4	5	6
T_1	100.0	55.0	40.6	34.5	31.7	30.7
T_2		100.0	71.8	60.3	55.3	53.3
T_3			100.0	81.2	73.4	70.4
T_4				100.0	87.8	83.4
T_5					100.0	93.0
T_6						100.0
$\frac{C_2(\boldsymbol{T}\|N)}{c_2}$	57.51	62.36	67.31	72.27	77.24	82.21

Table 13: Optimal $\boldsymbol{T}$ for $C_2(\boldsymbol{T}|N)/c_2$ when $m = 1.2$, $S = 100$, $\lambda = 0.01$, $c_1/c_2 = 4$.

T_k	1	2	3	4	5	6
T_1	100.0	57.3	42.4	35.8	32.6	31.2
T_2		100.0	74.2	62.5	56.9	54.5
T_3			100.0	83.3	75.4	72.0
T_4				100.0	89.4	85.0
T_5					100.0	94.1
T_6						100.0
$\frac{C_2(\boldsymbol{T}\|N)}{c_2}$	50.60	54.47	58.42	62.39	66.37	70.35

Table 14: Optimal $\boldsymbol{T}$ for $C_2(\boldsymbol{T}|N)/c_2$ when $m = 1.2$, $S = 100$, $\lambda = 0.01$, $c_1/c_2 = 6$.

T_k	1	2	3	4	5	6
T_1	100.0	58.4	44.8	39.3	37.3	36.9
T_2		100.0	76.2	66.7	63.2	62.6
T_3			100.0	86.2	81.2	80.4
T_4				100.0	93.2	92.0
T_5					100.0	98.4
T_6						100.0
$\frac{C_2(\boldsymbol{T}\|N)}{c_2}$	52.60	58.46	64.41	70.37	76.34	82.32

Table 15: Optimal $\boldsymbol{T}$ for $C_2(\boldsymbol{T}|N)/c_2$ when $m = 1.2$, $S = 150$, $\lambda = 0.01$, $c_1/c_2 = 5$.

T_k	1	2	3	4	5	6
T_1	150.0	92.5	70.1	59.2	53.8	51.2
T_2		150.0	115.4	98.5	89.9	85.8
T_3			150.0	127.4	116.0	110.6
T_4				150.0	135.4	128.7
T_5					150.0	141.5
T_6						150.0
$\frac{C_2(\boldsymbol{T}\|N)}{c_2}$	67.83	72.71	77.67	82.64	87.62	92.61

Table 16: Optimal $\boldsymbol{T}$ for $C_2(\boldsymbol{T}|N)/c_2$ when $m = 1.2$, $S = 200$, $\lambda = 0.01$, $c_1/c_2 = 5$.

T_k	1	2	3	4	5	6
T_1	200.0	132.0	102.2	86.6	78.0	73.4
T_2		200.0	158.7	136.8	124.5	117.8
T_3			200.0	172.3	157.0	148.7
T_4				200.0	181.2	171.3
T_5					200.0	187.9
T_6						200.0
$\frac{C_2(\boldsymbol{T}\|N)}{c_2}$	79.54	84.46	89.42	94.40	99.39	104.38

Smart Manufacturing Acceptance Rate Prediction Model: A Deep Learning Approach

Chiao-Tzu HUANG [1], Yi Peng LIAO [2], Cheng-Kai HUNG[2]

[1] National Chin-Yi University of Technology, Industrial Engineering & Management, Taiwan, huang501@mail.ncut.edu.tw
[2] Universal AI Technology Co., Ltd., Taiwan

Keywords: Smart Acceptance Prediction, Quality Control, Transfer Learning, Model Adaptation

Abstract -This paper presents a novel Smart Acceptance Prediction Model that transforms In-Process Quality Control (IPQC) by predicting customer acceptance rates at early production stages. By implementing deep learning techniques—specifically a Deep GAN LRCN-GPR architecture with Model Adaptation (Transfer Learning with Domain Adaptation) framework—our model identifies potential defects at upstream workstations, preventing defective products from flowing into downstream processes. This enables intelligent production line segregation, where only output from problematic workstations undergoes 100% inspection while maintaining high precision in quality prediction. The proposed model demonstrates remarkable performance with up to 95% prediction accuracy across diverse production scenarios. The implementation of this Smart Acceptance Prediction Model delivers a crucial benefit by significantly reducing the burden of 100% inspection on production lines. By achieving consistently high prediction accuracy, the model enables manufacturers to confidently transition from comprehensive inspection of all products to a more efficient sampling inspection methodology. This shift not only alleviates production bottlenecks and resource constraints but also maintains rigorous quality standards while improving overall production throughput and operational efficiency. The model thus provides a data-driven foundation for optimizing inspection protocols without compromising product quality or customer satisfaction

1. Introduction

Modern manufacturing enterprises face increasing pressure to deliver defect-free products while optimizing production efficiency. Traditional quality control approaches often rely on costly and time-consuming 100% inspection procedures or statistical sampling methods that may miss critical defects. These conventional approaches create production bottlenecks and increase manufacturing costs while still failing to guarantee optimal product quality.

The emergence of smart manufacturing and Industry 4.0 technologies presents new opportunities to transform quality control processes through advanced data analytics and machine learning techniques. This paper introduces a novel Smart Acceptance Prediction Model that leverages deep learning algorithms to predict product acceptance rates at early production stages, enabling manufacturers to make informed decisions about inspection strategies and resource allocation.

Our approach combines Generative Adversarial Networks (GANs) with Long-term Recurrent Convolutional Networks (LRCNs) and Gaussian Process Regression (GPR) to create a robust prediction framework that achieves high accuracy with minimal training data. The model enables manufacturers to implement selective inspection protocols, where only products from potentially problematic workstations undergo comprehensive inspection, significantly reducing inspection costs while maintaining quality standards.

2. Related Work

2.1. Deep Learning in Manufacturing Quality Control

Deep learning techniques have demonstrated significant potential for improving manufacturing quality control processes. Wang et al. [1] proposed a convolutional neural network (CNN) for defect detection in semiconductor manufacturing, achieving 92% accuracy in identifying defective wafers. Similarly, Zhang and Tao [2] developed a deep learning framework for fault diagnosis in complex manufacturing systems that outperformed traditional machine learning approaches.

2.2. Generative Adversarial Networks in Manufacturing

Generative Adversarial Networks (GANs) have emerged as powerful tools for manufacturing applications due to their ability to generate synthetic data and learn complex data distributions. Lee et al. [3] utilized GANs for anomaly detection in manufacturing processes, demonstrating their effectiveness in identifying rare defects with limited training examples. Wang et al. [4] applied GANs for generating synthetic defect images to augment training datasets for inspection systems.

2.3. Transfer Learning and Domain Adaptation

Transfer learning approaches enable knowledge transfer between related domains, addressing challenges associated with limited training data in manufacturing environments. Kang et al. [5] demonstrated that transfer learning could significantly improve defect detection accuracy when applied to new product variants with minimal retraining. Domain adaptation techniques further enhance this capability by adapting models to changing production conditions, as shown by Chen and Feng [6] in their work on cross-production line quality prediction.

3. Methodology

3.1. System Architecture

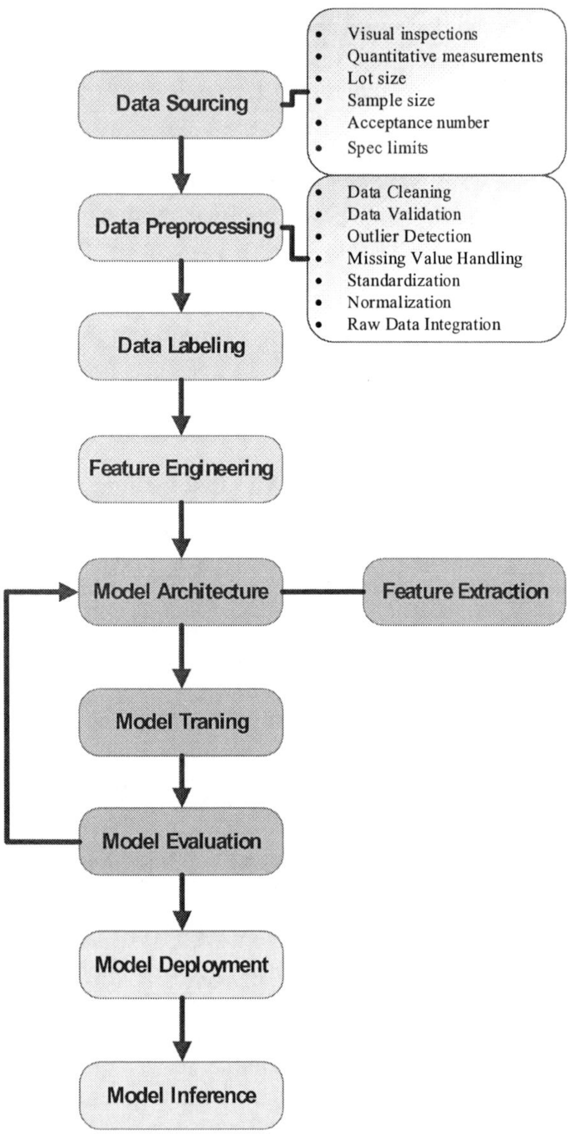

Figure 1. AI Modeling Workflow

The proposed Smart Acceptance Prediction Model consists of three main components: Input, Process, and Output modules, as illustrated in Figure 1. This architecture creates an end-to-end system that integrates with existing manufacturing execution systems while providing advanced prediction capabilities.

3.1.1 Input Module

The input module establishes quality measurement units (N-type product parameters and N-type quality measurement units), lot size, sample size and acceptance number. It collects inspection values including visual inspections (such as appearance defects) and quantitative measurements (such as dimensions) at production stations. The system interfaces with manufacturing execution systems to obtain real-time measurement data through digital measurement instruments.

3.1.2 Process Module

The core process module implements our GAN-LRCN hybrid model architecture. This module processes measurement data through feature transformation and standardization before feeding it into the deep learning model. The architecture integrates generative adversarial networks with long-term recurrent convolutional networks, enabling robust pattern recognition with temporal dependencies. One key advantage of our approach is the ability to achieve high accuracy with minimal training data. The LRCN model structure requires as few as 30 samples to effectively adapt to different acceptance standards across manufacturing scenarios.

3.1.3 Output Module

The output module delivers prediction results for:
- In-factory self-inspection: Predicting post-processing rejection rates
- Outbound inspection: Predicting customer acceptance rates

3.2. Deep Learning Model Architecture

Our model employs a hybrid architecture combining DEEP GAN, LRCN, GPR, Model Adaptation and Transfer Learning techniques, as shown in Figure 2. This innovative integration creates a powerful predictive framework capable of learning from limited data while maintaining high generalization capability.

3.2.1 GAN-LRCN Architecture

The GAN component consists of a generator and discriminator network working in adversarial fashion. The generator creates synthetic quality measurement data that mimics real production patterns, while the discriminator learns to distinguish between real and synthetic data. This adversarial training process enhances the model's ability to recognize subtle quality patterns with limited training examples.

The LRCN component combines convolutional neural networks with long short-term memory (LSTM) networks to capture both spatial and temporal dependencies in production data. This temporal modeling capability is particularly valuable for predicting quality outcomes that depend on process sequences and time-series measurement data.

3.2.2 Gaussian Process Regression

We integrate Gaussian Process Regression (GPR) to provide uncertainty quantification for our predictions, enabling risk-aware decision-making. The GPR component models the relationship between input quality measurements and final acceptance rates while providing confidence intervals for predictions.

3.2.3 Transfer Learning and Domain Adaptation

To address the challenge of limited training data in manufacturing environments, we implement transfer learning with domain adaptation. This approach allows knowledge transfer from base models trained on larger datasets to specific product lines with minimal retraining. The domain adaptation technique adjusts for differences between source and target domains, enabling high prediction accuracy even when production conditions change.

3.3. Training Process

The training process follows a three-stage approach:

Stage1. Pre-training of base models using historical data from similar production processes

Stage 2. Fine-tuning with product-specific data using transfer learning

Stage 3. Online adaptation during production to maintain prediction accuracy despite process drift

This efficiency enables rapid deployment across different product lines and manufacturing scenarios.

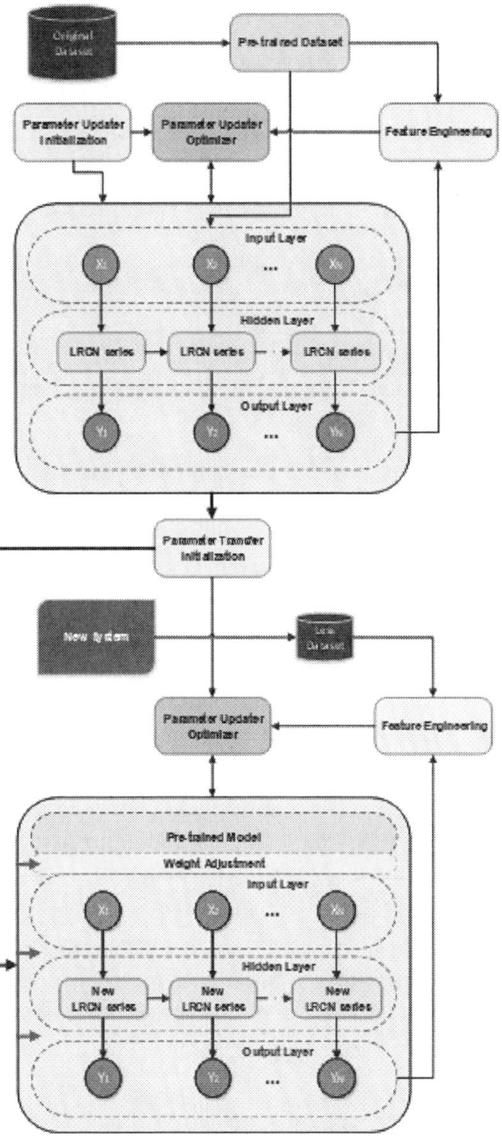

Figure 2. Model Architecture

4. Conclusion

This paper presents a Smart Manufacturing Acceptance Rate Prediction Model that transforms quality control processes through deep learning techniques. By combining GANs, LRCNs, and GPR with transfer learning and domain adaptation, our approach achieves high prediction accuracy with minimal training data, enabling selective inspection protocols that significantly reduce quality control costs while maintaining product quality standards.

The proposed model offers several key contributions to smart manufacturing:

1. A novel hybrid architecture that integrates generative adversarial networks with recurrent convolutional networks for robust quality prediction
2. A transfer learning approach that enables rapid deployment across different product lines with minimal retraining
3. An uncertainty quantification framework that supports risk-aware decision-making in quality control

5. Acknowledgement

This research was supported by the National Chin-Yi University of Technology, Industrial Engineering & Management, Taiwan. The authors would like to thank the participating manufacturing companies for providing data and implementation support.

6. References

[1] Wang, J., Ma, Y., Zhang, L., Gao, R.X. and Wu, D. "Deep learning for smart manufacturing: Methods and applications"; Journal of Manufacturing Systems, Vol. 48, pp. 144-156, 2018.

[2] Zhang, C. and Tao, F. "Manufacturing big data-driven intelligent diagnosis: A transfer learning framework for fault diagnosis with limited labeled data"; Computers in Industry, Vol. 123, 103318, 2020.

[3] Lee, K.B., Cheon, S. and Kim, C.O. "A convolutional neural network for fault classification and diagnosis in semiconductor manufacturing processes"; IEEE Transactions on Semiconductor Manufacturing, Vol. 30, Issue 2, pp. 135-142, 2017.

[4] Wang, T., Chen, Y., Qiao, M. and Snoussi, H. "A fast and robust convolutional neural network-based defect detection model in product quality control"; International Journal of Advanced Manufacturing Technology, Vol. 94, pp. 3465-3471, 2018.

[5] Kang, S., Joo, S. and Choi, Y. "Generative adversarial networks with long short-term memory for time series anomaly detection in industrial processes"; Expert Systems with Applications, Vol. 168, 114240, 2021.

[6] Chen, B. and Feng, Q. "Domain adaptation transfer learning for fault diagnosis of rolling bearings"; IEEE Access, Vol. 9, pp. 82470-82480, 2021.

[7] Liu, Y., Zhao, T. and Wang, W. "Learning deep features using generative adversarial networks with application to semiconductor wafer defect detection"; IEEE Transactions on Semiconductor Manufacturing, Vol. 33, Issue 3, pp. 404-414, 2020.

[8] Pan, S.J. and Yang, Q. "A survey on transfer learning"; IEEE Transactions on Knowledge and Data Engineering, Vol. 22, Issue 10, pp. 1345-1359, 2010.

Using A2C for Hyperparameter Optimization of Deep Learning Models

LIN, Shun-Chang, LIN, Gi-Wei, TIEN, Fang-Chih.[1]

[1] National Taipei University of Technology, ROC
Department of Industrial Engineering and Management, 1, Section 3, Chung-Hsiao E. Rd. Taipei, ROC,
fctien@ntut.edu.tw

Keywords: Reinforcement Learning, Deep Learning, Hyperparameter optimization

Abstract - Deep learning has made remarkable advancements in machine learning, demonstrating exceptional performance in defect detection, object recognition, and image processing. AI models are widely adopted in industry due to their adaptability, efficiency, and accuracy. Reinforcement Learning (RL), a critical branch of machine learning, empowers algorithms to make optimal decisions through continuous interaction with the environment. This paper presents **A2C-HOD** (Advantage Actor-Critic-based Hyperparameter Optimization for Deep Neural Networks), an innovative method that applies the A2C reinforcement learning framework to hyperparameter optimization. We integrated A2C-HOD into the training pipeline of the YOLO model and evaluated its effectiveness on both standard and custom-built datasets. Experimental results demonstrate that A2C-HOD significantly enhances model performance and stability by efficiently identifying optimal hyperparameter configurations.

1. Introduction

In recent years, deep learning has made significant advances in the field of machine learning and has demonstrated outstanding performance in areas such as defect detection, object recognition, and image processing. Models such as CNN, YOLO, GAN, Transformer, and LSTM are widely applied in the industry due to their high efficiency and accuracy. However, the performance of these models is highly dependent on the configuration of hyperparameters, especially when training data is limited. Under such conditions, proper hyperparameter tuning becomes critically important.

Reinforcement Learning (RL) is a crucial subfield of machine learning that enables agents to learn optimal policies through trial-and-error interactions with an environment, with the aim of maximizing cumulative rewards [3][12][16]. It involves learning from sequences of states, actions, and rewards, which is particularly advantageous for tasks like hyperparameter optimization where the effects of parameter adjustments unfold over time. RL algorithms can be broadly categorized into on-policy and off-policy methods. On-policy methods, such as SARSA [13], learn from actions taken according to the current policy, while off-policy methods like Deep Q-Networks (DQN) [8] learn from actions that may be taken by a different policy. Given the rapidly changing nature of hyperparameter environments, this study adopts the on-policy Advantage Actor-Critic (A2C) algorithm [7], known for its improved convergence speed and policy consistency.

The A2C algorithm is part of the Actor-Critic family and integrates both value-based and policy-based approaches. The Actor selects actions based on the policy, and the Critic evaluates those actions by estimating value functions. The use of an advantage function allows the agent to assess how much better an action is compared to the average, enhancing learning stability [7]. In the context of action space design, hyperparameter optimization poses a unique challenge as it often involves both discrete and continuous variables. Traditional methods such as DQN [8] handle discrete actions well, while continuous approaches like Proximal Policy Optimization (PPO) use parameter distributions like Beta [9] to address continuous spaces. For mixed action spaces, methods such as PA-DDPG [2], hybrid action strategies [6], and discretization techniques [4] have been proposed. To ensure robust exploration and avoid convergence to suboptimal configurations, several noise-based exploration strategies have been proposed, including Gaussian (Normal) noise, Ornstein-Uhlenbeck (OU) noise [19], and Parameter Noise [10]. Selecting an appropriate exploration technique is essential for effective learning and efficient search in high-dimensional parameter spaces. Traditional hyperparameter optimization methods include grid search [5], random search, and Bayesian optimization [15], each with their strengths and limitations. While exhaustive, grid search is computationally expensive. Bayesian optimization provides a probabilistic approach to model performance estimation but may not scale well with high-dimensional spaces. Heuristic algorithms such as genetic algorithms and particle swarm optimization [18] are more adaptable but demand significant resources. In contrast, reinforcement learning has recently emerged as a compelling alternative for hyperparameter tuning. Applications include CNN tuning [17], reward-driven architecture adjustments [14], and the Google AutoML-Zero project [11], which combines evolutionary strategies and RL to design entire learning pipelines. Furthermore, Neural Architecture Search (NAS) [21] and its variants [20] have demonstrated the feasibility of using RL to automate the design of deep learning architectures.

This study proposes a hyperparameter optimization method based on the Advantage Actor-Critic (A2C) algorithm to enhance the performance of deep learning models across various architectures and datasets.

2. Proposed Method

This study proposes a novel hyperparameter optimization method called A2C-HOD (Advantage Actor-Critic for Hyperparameter Optimization in Deep learning), which applies the reinforcement learning framework to systematically adjust and improve hyperparameter configurations during model training as shown in Figure 1. The proposed method consists of three core components: Agent, Environment, and Action Space Design.

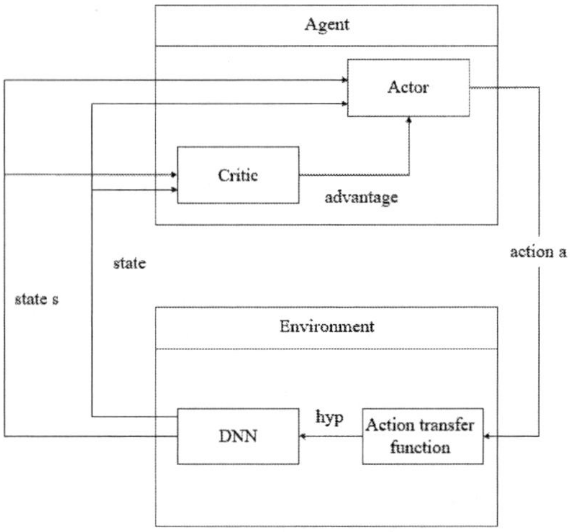

Figure 1. Proposed Structure

2.1 Agent

The agent serves as the decision-making entity responsible for selecting hyperparameters based on the current environment state. Its architecture is inspired by the Parameterized Action Deep Deterministic Policy Gradient (PA-DDPG) network proposed by Hausknecht et al. [2] as show in Figure 2. In this framework, the state input is fed into the Actor network, which outputs a set of actions (hyperparameter suggestions). These actions, combined with the state, are then evaluated by the Critic network to estimate the value (V). This configuration enables effective handling of hybrid action spaces and facilitates robust policy learning.

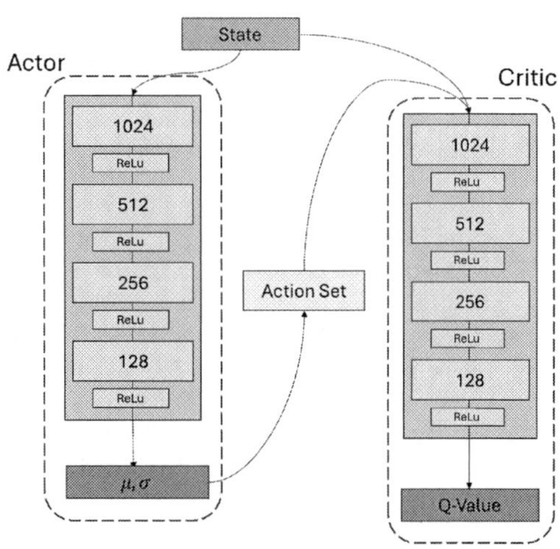

Figure 2. PA-DDPG network architecture [2]

2.2 Environment

The environment simulates the training process of the deep learning model and provides feedback to the agent. It includes a reward mechanism, state representation, and allowable actions. The state space represents the current training configuration, such as architecture features and performance outcomes. Actions correspond to potential changes in hyperparameters. Rewards are determined by comparing the performance of the model under the new hyperparameter configuration against a baseline. This setup allows the agent to iteratively learn the effects of hyperparameter changes and converge towards an optimal policy. The reward function is designed to guide the learning process while maintaining numerical stability by bounding reward values between -100 and 100.

2.3 Action Space and Exploration

The action space is structured using mixed discrete and continuous domains as shown in Figure 3. Discrete hyperparameters such as batch size and kernel size are modeled with arithmetic or geometric progressions, while continuous parameters like learning rate and momentum are treated as normalized values within a defined range. The Actor network outputs normalized values which are then transformed (de-normalized) into actual hyperparameter values for training. To enhance exploration and avoid local minima, the agent employs different exploration strategies including Gaussian (Normal) noise, Ornstein-Uhlenbeck (OU) noise [19], and Parameter Noise [10]. The choice of noise directly influences the spread of action exploration and ultimately the learning stability.

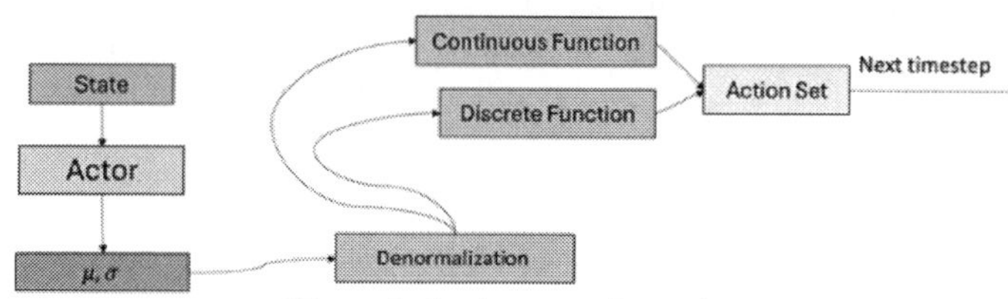

Figure 3. Action transformation

We design three different types of ranges, including an arithmetic sequence for the discrete action space, a geometric sequence for the discrete action space, and a continuous action space. The specific methods for setting these ranges are described as Equation (1).

$$Domain = \begin{cases} Arithmetic\ Discrete\ Action\ Space, ex: [2^{log(L)}, 2^{log(U)}], if\ s = 0, \\ Geometric\ Discrete\ Action\ Space, ex: [L, L + s, L + s * 2, \ldots, Upper], if\ s > 0, \\ Continuous\ Action\ Space, ex: [L, U], if\ s < 0. \end{cases}$$

(1)

where s is the state, and the domain is determined based on the different ranges of states

2.4 Rewards

The design of the reward function has a decisive impact on the overall effectiveness of model training. According to existing theories [16], a well-designed reward function can effectively guide the learning process by focusing on enhancing specific variables such as accuracy or precision. This study adopts a simple yet effective reward function that compares model performance against a predefined baseline and provides either positive or negative feedback based on the comparison result.

The reward functions designed for different deep learning models are shown in Table 1. These reward mechanisms were tailored to the characteristics and training objectives of each model, ensuring consistency between the reward function and the model's learning goals. The range of rewards was constrained between -100 and 100 to promote convergence. The baseline values were determined by considering the average performance and expected outcomes during training, further ensuring model convergence

Table 1. Reward for different models

Model	Reward Function
LeNet	$Reward = (acc - 0.8) * 100$
VGG16	$Reward = (acc - 0.5) * 100$
Yolov7	$Reward = (map - 0.5) * 10 + (map_{95} - 0.1) * 10$

2.5 State

Adapting the work of Talaat et al. [17], this study defines the environmental state as the current set of hyperparameters, which describe the model's configuration at a specific training stage. To make these hyperparameters more suitable for the learning process of reinforcement learning algorithms, they are normalized. This state design enables the reinforcement learning algorithm to learn how to adjust according to changes in hyperparameters, thereby maximizing rewards and identifying more optimal parameter configurations.

3. Implementation

The experiment was structured to validate the effectiveness and generalizability of the proposed method. Initial experiments were conducted using LeNet and VGG16, which are relatively simple network architectures. The proposed method was later applied to YOLOv7[1], for which the related information of UAV dataset used is shown in Table 2. Each model was trained using different setups of hyperparameters reflecting various domain types (discrete/continuous), steps, and parameter ranges. For LeNet and VGG16, structural parameters such as the number of output layers, kernel size, and the fully connected output size were included in the optimization. Due to YOLOv7's structural complexity, only the parameters relevant to the evolution process were optimized, including learning rate, momentum, and data augmentation settings. Reward functions were designed per model to guide the learning process. These functions compare the model's performance using current hyperparameters against a baseline and produce feedback in a range between -100 to 100 to ensure stability during learning. The state representation included the normalized values of the current hyperparameter set. These representations allowed the reinforcement learning agent to evaluate and adjust the settings dynamically, enhancing generalization capabilities and convergence speed.

Table 2. Dataset and related information for training Yolov7

Model	Datasets
Yolov7	UAV Dataset
LeNet	MNIST
VGG16	CIFAR 100

3.1 Experimental Design

Two key evaluation strategies were implemented: (1) performance before and after hyperparameter optimization under reduced training data conditions, and (2) performance differences between original and optimized settings using the full dataset. After each optimization cycle, the resulting parameters were validated using 30 epochs of training with 10 iterations per epoch.

Baseline configurations were randomly selected within the parameter constraints. Performance indicators such as accuracy (for LeNet and VGG16) and mAP (for YOLOv7) were used for evaluation

3.2 LeNet-MNIST Results

The LeNet model was evaluated on the MNIST dataset, and the comparative results are shown in Figure 4(a) and (b). After hyperparameter optimization, the model achieved an accuracy of 0.99, compared to 0.965 with the original configuration. Testing on randomly segmented data yielded 0.99 accuracy with optimized parameters versus 0.93 with the original setup. This demonstrates that the A2C-HOD method significantly improves classification performance as shown in Figure.

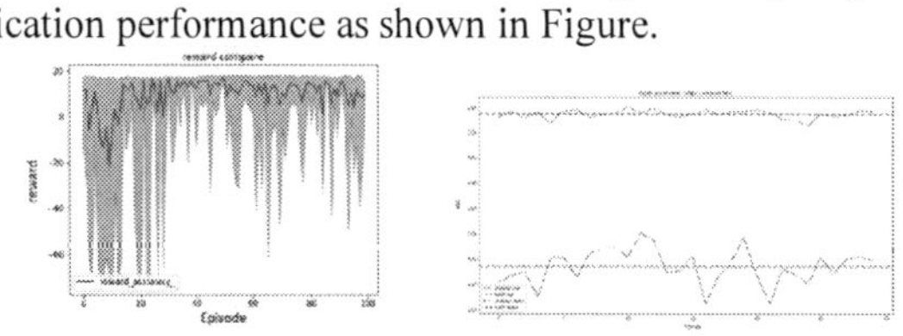

(a) Rewards (b) Accuracy

Figure 4. Comparative Results of LeNet-MNIST

3.3 VGG16-CIFAR100 Results

On the CIFAR100 dataset, the proposed method also achieved significant results. After hyperparameter optimization, the accuracy improved from 0.35 to 0.46, as shown in Figures 5 (a) and (b)

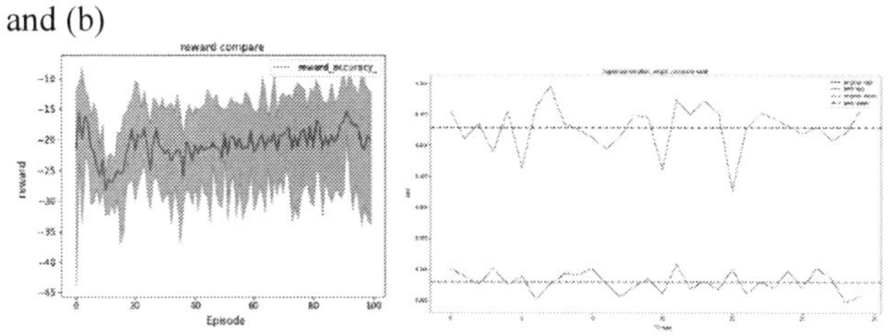

(a) Reward (b) Accuracy

Figure 5. The comparison of optimization process of CIFAR100

3.4 YOLOv7 UAV Dataset Results

The YOLOv7 model was tested using a custom drone image dataset. The optimized hyperparameters enabled the model to reach an mAP95 of 0.65, showing a marked improvement over unstable performance with original settings as shown in Figure 6. Even after augmenting the dataset with additional UAV images, the optimized parameters maintained stable convergence with an mAP95 of approximately 0.50.

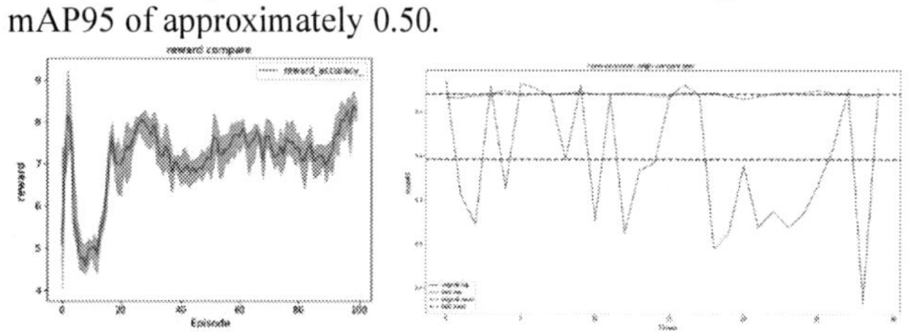

(a) Reward (b) Accuracy

Figure 6. The comparison of optimization process of Yolov7

The results confirm that the optimized parameters are generalizable across changes in training data, proving the robustness of the A2C-HOD approach.

4. Conclusion

This study addresses the challenge of suboptimal long-range UAV detection by proposing a novel hyperparameter optimization framework based on the Advantage Actor-Critic (A2C) algorithm. By incorporating a DDPG-inspired network design and carefully structured action space transformations, the proposed A2C-HOD method enables reinforcement learning agents to adaptively tune hyperparameters with greater stability and learning efficiency. Experimental results across multiple deep learning models confirm the effectiveness of this approach. LeNet achieved an accuracy of 0.99 on the MNIST dataset; VGG16 saw accuracy improvements from 0.35 to 0.46 on CIFAR100; and YOLOv7 maintained a stable mAP@0.95 around 0.65 after optimization. Notably, even with an expanded UAV dataset, the optimized configuration demonstrated strong generalization and robustness.

This study shows the potential of reinforcement learning for dynamic hyperparameter optimization, especially in scenarios where traditional methods struggle with scalability and adaptation. However, the method's performance on more complex and noisy datasets remains an open challenge. Future work will explore integrating other policy optimization techniques, such as PPO or SAC, and extending the approach to transformer-based models and real-time learning environments. Additionally, incorporating automated reward shaping and multi-agent collaboration could further enhance adaptability and convergence speed.

Acknowledgement

This research was supported by the National Science and Technology Council of Taiwan under project number MOST 113-2221-E-027-110.

References

[1] C.-Y. Wang, A. Bochkovskiy, and H.-Y. M. Liao, "Yolov7: Trainable bag-of-freebies sets new state-of-the-art for real-time object detectors," IEEE/CVF Conference on Computer Vision and Pattern Recognition (CVPR), 2023.

[2] Hausknecht, Matthew J. and Peter Stone. "Deep Reinforcement Learning in Parameterized Action Space." CoRR abs/1511.04143 (2015)

[3] Kaelbling, Leslie Pack et al. "Reinforcement Learning: A Survey." J. Artif. Intell. Res. 4, 1996: 237-285.

[4] Kanervisto, Anssi et al. "Action Space Shaping in Deep Reinforcement Learning." 2020 IEEE Conference on Games (CoG) (2020): 479-486.

[5] Liashchynskyi, Petro B. and Pavlo Liashchynskyi. "Grid Search, Random Search, Genetic Algorithm: A Big Comparison for NAS." ArXiv abs/1912.06059 (2019)

[6] Masson, W. et al. "Reinforcement Learning with Parameterized Actions." AAAI Conference on Artificial Intelligence (2015).

[7] Mnih, Volodymyr et al. "Asynchronous Methods for Deep Reinforcement Learning." International Conference on Machine Learning (2016).

[8] Mnih, Volodymyr et al. "Playing Atari with Deep Reinforcement Learning." ArXiv abs/1312.5602, 2013

[9] Petrazzini, Irving G. B. and Eric A. Antonelo. "Proximal Policy Optimization with Continuous Bounded Action Space via the Beta Distribution." 2021 IEEE Symposium Series on Computational Intelligence (SSCI) (2021): 1-8.

[10] Plappert, Matthias et al. "Parameter Space Noise for Exploration." ArXiv abs/1706.01905 (2017)

[11] Real, Esteban et al. "AutoML-Zero: Evolving Machine Learning Algorithms From Scratch." International Conference on Machine Learning (2020).

[12] Richard S. Sutton and Andrew G. Barto. 2018. Reinforcement Learning: An Introduction. A Bradford Book, Cambridge, MA, USA.

[13] Rummery, Gavin Adrian and Mahesan Niranjan. "On-line Q-learning using connectionist systems.", 1994.

[14] S. Dubbioso et al., "A deep reinforcement learning approach for vertical stabilization of Tokamak Plasmas," Fusion Engineering and Design, vol. 194, p. 113725, 2023.

[15] Snoek, Jasper et al. "Practical Bayesian Optimization of Machine Learning Algorithms." Neural Information Processing Systems (2012).

[16] Sowerby, Henry et al. "Designing Rewards for Fast Learning." ArXiv abs/2205.15400, 2022.

[17] Talaat, F.M., Gamel, S.A. RL based hyper-parameters optimization algorithm (ROA) for convolutional neural network. J Ambient Intell Human Comput 14, 13349–13359, 2023.

[18] Tani, Laurits et al. "Evolutionary algorithms for hyperparameter optimization in machine learning for application in high energy physics." The European Physical Journal C 81, 2020.

[19] Uhlenbeck, George E and Ornstein, Leonard S. "On the theory of the brownian motion." Physical review, 36(5):823, 1930.

[20] White, Colin et al. "Neural Architecture Search: Insights from 1000 Papers." ArXiv abs/2301.08727 (2023)

[21] Zoph, Barret and Quoc V. Le. "Neural Architecture Search with Reinforcement Learning." ArXiv abs/1611.01578 (2016)

Analyzing arXiv Publication Trends of Generative AI After DeepSeek Release

Kai-Yuan Hsiao[1], Wei-Shan Chang[3], Mingchih Chen[1,2], Ben-Chang Shia[1,2]

[1] Artificial Intelligence Development Center, Fu Jen Catholic University, No. 510, Zhongzheng Rd., Xin-Zhuang Dist., New Taipei City 242062, Taiwan

[2] Graduate Institute of Business Administration, College of Management, Fu Jen Catholic University, No. 510, Zhongzheng Rd., Xinzhuang Dist., New Taipei City 242062, Taiwan

[3] Institute of Statistical Science, Academia Sinica

Keywords: Generative AI, large language model, Natural Language Processing, Text mining

Abstract

This study investigates publication trends in generative artificial intelligence by analyzing preprints submitted to arXiv between November 2022 and March 2025, a period marked by the rapid development of large language models (LLMs) and the release of the DeepSeek model series. Using Latent Dirichlet Allocation (LDA) for topic modeling, we extracted key thematic patterns from over 60,000 articles classified under machine learning and AI. The results reveal three dominant research directions: foundational machine learning methods and training strategies, reasoning capabilities and task-oriented applications of LLMs, and the emergence of multimodal systems that integrate vision and language. The release of DeepSeek, which emphasizes computational efficiency and open accessibility, coincides with increased academic interest in scalable architectures and human-centric AI. These findings highlight the evolving priorities in generative AI research and suggest that future developments will continue to focus on efficiency, reasoning, and multimodal integration.

1. Introduction

Natural Language Processing (NLP) has made significant progress in recent years, largely driven by advancements in machine learning and the widespread use of transformer-based models. New developments now quickly spread across the research community, thanks mainly to preprint platforms like arXiv, which allow researchers to share findings almost instantly. arXiv has become an essential resource for AI research, hosting over 2.6 million papers and receiving approximately 20,000 new submissions monthly [1]. Notably, many groundbreaking NLP discoveries first appear on arXiv. For example, the influential "Transformer" architecture paper, which initiated significant advances in artificial intelligence, was first published there [2]. This open-access approach enables NLP advancements to be rapidly shared, discussed, and reviewed by researchers worldwide.

In late 2022, ChatGPT, a conversational system based on Large Language Model (LLM) technology, quickly gained massive popularity, reaching 100 million users within just two months and firmly establishing AI-generated text in mainstream culture. GPT-4, released by OpenAI in 2023, further expanded these capabilities with enhanced reasoning, a larger context window, and the ability to perform complex tasks like writing code and even passing exams.

Meanwhile, the generative AI landscape diversified as other organizations introduced their own models, such as Google's Bard, Meta's LLaMA, and Anthropic's Claude. Most recently, the DeepSeek model series, introduced by a new AI startup in early 2025, has quickly attracted significant attention as a potential breakthrough in the LLM space. DeepSeek differs from GPT-based models by emphasizing efficiency and open accessibility. Its architecture incorporates a Mixture-of-Experts mechanism and other optimizations that significantly reduce computational requirements, delivering performance similar to GPT-4 at less computational cost on certain benchmarks [3]. The DeepSeek product line also includes multimodal models, which can process both text and images. These characteristics have made DeepSeek an appealing alternative to the dominant GPT approach, explaining the extensive interest it has generated.

Overall, generative AI research has undergone rapid growth and profound transformation. These trends highlight the importance of understanding how the field's focus is evolving. In this study, we utilize text mining methods to examine publication patterns and thematic shifts within AI literature, applying quantitative analysis and topic modeling to explore differences in generative AI research across various time points.

2. Method

2.1. Data Sources

The present study utilized data sourced from arXiv, a widely recognized open-access repository that was established in 1991[4]. arXiv hosts a large and continually growing collection of preprints in disciplines such as physics, mathematics, computer science, and quantitative biology, with more than two million submissions as of 2025. This repository serves as a critical platform for the dissemination of early-stage research outputs prior to formal peer review, thereby supporting rapid communication and open access to scientific findings. All submissions to arXiv are subject to a moderation process that ensures submissions meet minimal standards of academic relevance, are appropriately classified, and do not contain non-scientific or offensive content. Moderation does not constitute peer review but serves to maintain the scholarly scope and integrity of the repository [5]. The metadata associated with each preprint, including title, authorship, subject classification, and submission history, is publicly accessible and consistently formatted, making arXiv a valuable resource for large-scale bibliometric and text-based analyses. Since arXiv does not contain personal or patient-level information, issues related to data confidentiality and ethical review were not applicable in this study.

2.2. Statistical Analysis

Topic modeling is a statistical method used in natural language processing to uncover hidden thematic structures within a large corpus of text. It enables the identification and clustering of semantically related words, which are interpreted as "topics." One of the most widely used algorithms for topic modeling is Latent Dirichlet Allocation (LDA). LDA is a generative probabilistic model that assumes documents are mixtures of topics and that each topic is characterized by a distribution over words [6-8]. The model works by inferring the latent topic structure through a process of iterative estimation, typically using variational inference or Gibbs sampling. LDA allows researchers to capture the abstract themes in text data without requiring labeled training sets, making it particularly useful for exploratory data analysis in fields such as digital humanities, marketing, and biomedical informatics.

3. Results

3.1. Dataset

This study collected articles published on arXiv between November 2022 and March 2025, classified under "machine learning," "deep learning," and "AI." A total of 60,482 entries were gathered, including the title, authors, abstract, publication date, and category of each article.

Table1. Descriptive statistics of datasets.

Dataset	#document	Vocab Size	Avg Words
arXiv	60,482	80,077	121

3.2. Topic Modeling Results and Semantic Labeling

This study applied LDA to explore the latent topics within the texts after cleaning the textual data. Through this approach, it aimed to observe the research trends and directions in the field of computer science amid the rapid advancement of generative AI. Table 2 presents the patterns of three topics, each represented by ten keywords. The publication trends of the articles appear to converge into three main areas: (1) general machine learning methodologies and training strategies, (2) reasoning mechanisms and task-oriented applications of large language models, and (3) multimodal models with images, vision, and agents.

Topic 1 is centered on foundational elements of machine learning, highlighting core concepts such as models, learning algorithms, methods, and training processes. The frequent appearance of terms like "performance," "time," and "network" suggests an emphasis on optimizing model efficiency, evaluation, and implementation strategies. This theme likely captures general research addressing algorithm design, empirical evaluations, and scalable learning techniques across a wide range of machine learning applications [9].

Topic 2 shows research efforts centered on large language models (LLMs) with a particular focus on their reasoning capabilities. The prevalence of terms such as "llm," "language," "reasoning," and "system" indicates a concentration on the development and evaluation of LLMs designed for complex cognitive tasks that go beyond pattern recognition, including logical inference, multi-step reasoning, and decision-making. Moreover, the presence of keywords like "task," "AI," and "performance" underscores the drive to benchmark and extend the generalization abilities of such models across diverse downstream applications. This research trajectory reflects the growing ambition to align LLMs more closely with attributes of artificial general intelligence.

The last topic is characterized by an intersection of visual and linguistic data, with keywords such as "image," "text," "video," and "agent" pointing to research in multimodal learning [10]. The inclusion of "human" and "task" suggests that many studies under this theme may focus on human-centered applications, such as embodied agents or interactive systems that integrate visual perception and natural language understanding.

Table2. Top-3 topics.

Topic	Top 10 Keywords and Their Weights in Terms of Topic Relevance
Topic 1	0.014*"model" + 0.011*"learning" + 0.009*"method" + 0.007*"data" + 0.007*"network" + 0.007*"based" + 0.006*"approach" + 0.006*"performance" + 0.006*"time" + 0.005*"training"
Topic 2	0.024*"model" + 0.019*"llm" + 0.011*"language" + 0.008*"data" + 0.008*"task" + 0.007*"ai" + 0.007*"large" + 0.006*"performance" + 0.005*"reasoning" + 0.005*"system"
Topic 3	0.015*"model" + 0.011*"image" + 0.008*"method" + 0.007*"task" + 0.006*"based" + 0.006*"data" + 0.006*"agent" + 0.005*"text" + 0.005*"human" + 0.005*"video"

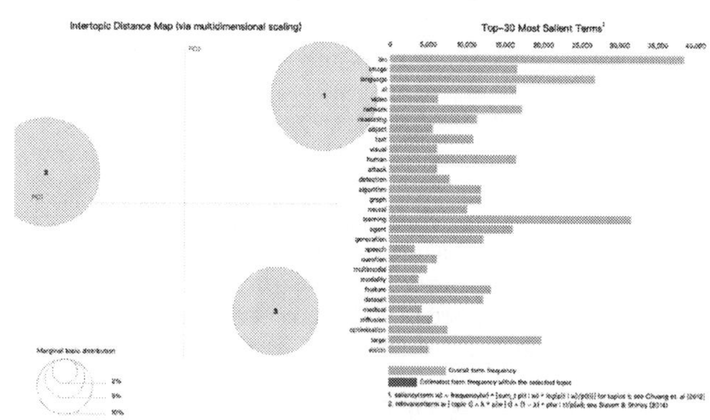

Fig1. 10 topics with all articles

4. Conclusion

This study analyzed arXiv publication trends related to generative AI from November 2022 to March 2025, with a particular focus on the post-release period of the DeepSeek model series. By applying Latent Dirichlet Allocation for topic modeling, we identified three dominant research themes: foundational machine learning methodologies, reasoning capabilities of large language models, and multimodal systems integrating vision and language. These findings illustrate a clear thematic diversification within generative AI research, reflecting both ongoing optimization efforts and the pursuit of more cognitively capable and context-aware systems. The emergence of DeepSeek and similar innovations appears to have accelerated interest in efficient architectures and multimodal integration, signaling a broader shift toward scalable and human-centric AI applications. Future work should continue to monitor how evolving model architectures and capabilities influence the direction of AI research across both technical and applied domains.

Reference

[1] arXiv. arXiv monthly submission statistics. https://arxiv.org/stats/monthly_submissions.

[2] Vaswani, A., Shazeer, N., Parmar, N., Uszkoreit, J., Jones, L., Gomez, A. N., ... & Polosukhin, I. (2017). Attention is all you need. Advances in neural information processing systems, 30.

[3] Liu, A., Feng, B., Xue, B., Wang, B., Wu, B., Lu, C., ... & Piao, Y. (2024). Deepseek-v3 technical report. arXiv preprint arXiv:2412.19437.

[4] Ginsparg, P. (2011). ArXiv at 20. Nature, 476(7359), 145-147.

[5] arXiv. Moderation process. https://arxiv.org/help/moderation

[6] Blei, D. M., Ng, A. Y., & Jordan, M. I. (2003). Latent dirichlet allocation. Journal of machine Learning research, 3(Jan), 993-1022.

[7] Heinrich, G. (2005). Parameter estimation for text analysis (pp. 1-32). Darmstadt, Germany: Technical report.

[8] Griffiths, T. L., & Steyvers, M. (2004). Finding scientific topics. Proceedings of the National academy of Sciences, 101(suppl_1), 5228-5235.

[9] Bommasani, R., Hudson, D. A., Adeli, E., Altman, R., Arora, S., von Arx, S., ... & Liang, P. (2021). On the opportunities and risks of foundation models. arXiv preprint arXiv:2108.07258.

[10] Alayrac, J. B., Donahue, J., Luc, P., Miech, A., Barr, I., Hasson, Y., ... & Simonyan, K. (2022). Flamingo: a visual language model for few-shot learning. Advances in neural information processing systems, 35, 23716-23736.

Fault Tree Analysis Model for Remanufactured Machine Tools by Using Generative AI and Analytic Hierarchy Process

Kuo-Ping Lin[1], Yueh-Ju Kuo[2], Ting-Yu Lin[3], I-Jan Wang[4]

[1] Department of Industrial Engineering and Enterprise Information Tunghai University, Taichung City, Taiwan, Email: kplin@thu.edu.tw
[2]Department of Industrial Engineering and Enterprise Information Tunghai University, Taichung City, Taiwan, Email: G12330013@thu.edu.tw
[3] Department of Industrial Engineering and Enterprise Information Tunghai University, Taichung City, Taiwan, Email: tylin0114@thu.edu.tw
[4] Department of Industrial Engineering and Enterprise Information Tunghai University, Taichung City, Taiwan, Email: ijwang@thu.edu.tw

Keywords: Remanufactured machine tools; Fault tree analysis; Large language models

Abstract - This study develops a systematic framework for reliability allocation in remanufactured machine tools by using Fault Tree Analysis (FTA), Analytic Hierarchy Process (AHP), and the application of large language models (LLMs) to optimize reliability distribution across subsystems. The framework leverages Artificial Intelligence-Generated Content (AIGC) models to refine allocation strategies based on expert inputs and predefined criteria, enhancing predictive accuracy. A case study on an NC gear hobbing machine demonstrates the proposed method's effectiveness. The LLM-generated reliability values exhibit comparable accuracy to those obtained from expert surveys, while significantly reducing the time and resources required for data collection and processing. This approach not only streamlines the reliability allocation process but also mitigates potential biases inherent in expert assessments, providing a scalable, consistent, and cost-effective alternative for reliability analysis in remanufactured systems.

1. Introduction

Remanufacturing of machine tools has become a critical component of the remanufacturing industries in developed countries such as those in Europe, the United States, and Japan. In Europe, the remanufacturing industry accounts for approximately 2% of total manufacturing, with an annual turnover of around €30 billion [1]. Compared to newly manufactured machine tools, remanufactured machine tools typically have shorter service lives due to the wear and aging of foundational components, which have often been used for many years. Even after undergoing the remanufacturing process, it is difficult for these tools to return to a condition equivalent to new machines. Moreover, remanufactured machine tools are often perceived as second-hand products, which reduces their value and appeal in the market.

Thus, ensuring high reliability while meeting target reliability goals has become a crucial issue for remanufactured machine tools. Maintaining high reliability not only ensures product quality but also reduces maintenance costs and promotes environmental benefits. Achieving reliability targets involves allocating reliability goals to individual components and optimizing the integration of reused and new parts. This approach ensures that the overall system meets reliability requirements while highlighting the criticality of each component within the remanufactured tool. A rational reliability allocation strategy helps ensure that the assembled remanufactured machine tool meets system-level reliability requirements. To this end, it is necessary to incorporate the constraints and impacts of the remanufacturing process into the reliability allocation framework, thereby enhancing the effectiveness and feasibility of reliability improvement for remanufactured machine tools [2]. The literature indicates that the failure mechanisms of remanufactured machine tools are complex, difficult to predict, and often based on limited data samples. Accurately predicting their reliability enables proactive intervention before failures occur, thus avoiding additional repair costs and potential production downtime [2]. Machine learning (ML) techniques have recently been widely adopted by researchers as predictive models, with their effectiveness and accuracy validated across various domains. For example, Li et al. [3] noted that frequent failures of CNC machine tools during actual production have adverse effects on sustainable manufacturing and directly impact a company's economic performance.

Therefore, reliability prediction of CNC remanufactured machine tools has emerged as a key challenge in the machine tool industry. Although the reliability of remanufactured tools is vital, acquiring sufficient data for reliability prediction remains difficult. Traditional data collection methods are often time-consuming and costly. With the rapid advancement of generative artificial intelligence (AI), tools such as ChatGPT-4 offer a novel approach to generating synthetic reliability data for remanufactured machine tools. This not only improves data completeness but also significantly accelerates the data acquisition process.

Therefore, this study attempts that (1) This study utilizes generative artificial intelligence (AI) to synthesize reliability data, which is then integrated with machine learning models to predict reliability allocation at the component and subsystem levels of remanufactured machine tools. (2) Large language models (LLMs) are employed to generate textual outputs that serve as substitutes for expert evaluations in calculating post-allocation reliability values. (3) Taking a CNC machine tool (gear hobbing machine) as a case study, the proposed prediction model and LLM-generated reliability values are compared with those derived from traditional allocation methods proposed by previous scholars to examine their differences. (4) An integrated model is developed to combine the prediction results with reliability values obtained through the fuzzy comprehensive evaluation method, thereby enhancing the alignment of the predicted reliability with actual post-allocation reliability observed in practical cases. This paper is organized as follows. The following section (section 2) introduces the Generative AI and Analytic Hierarchy Process. Section 3 presents the remanufactured machine numerical example. Section 4 gives concludes.

2. Generative AI and Analytic Hierarchy Process

The structure of remanufactured machine tools is intricate and consists of numerous interconnected parts, making direct allocation of system reliability to individual components challenging. Therefore, the system is systematically divided into subsystems and individual parts for effective reliability allocation. The following steps and Fig. 1 describe the reliability allocation process:

Step 1. Data Collection

Collect essential data on reliability-related performance, system configuration, and past operational data of machine tools.

Step 2. Construction of the Reliability Model Using Fault Tree Analysis (FTA)

The reliability model is constructed using Fault Tree Analysis (FTA), which visually represents the hierarchical structure and functional interdependence of the subsystems and parts. This step ensures that failure propagation paths are well-understood, providing a foundation for analysis and allocation.

Step 3. Determining the Reliability Target for the Remanufactured Machine Tool

Based on the reliability model, the reliability target of the entire remanufactured system is determined. The target is defined by Mean Time Between Failures (MTBF), adjusted according to customer requirements and the remanufacturing processing capacity.

Any conversion of reliability indicators occurs during this step.

Step 4. Reliability Allocation from System to Subsystems

The system-level reliability target is initially distributed to individual subsystems using historical data. The neural network takes inputs such as system reliability, probability importance of subsystems, and their complexity, and outputs the reliability allocation for each subsystem. This allocation is verified to ensure it meets the overall system reliability target. If verification fails, reallocation is performed.

Step 5. AIGC-Based Reliability Allocation Approaches

This stage involves Artificial Intelligence-Generated Content (AIGC) models assisting in refining reliability allocation. There are two main AIGC allocation mechanisms: AIGC Based on Criteria: Allocation is optimized using predefined criteria and manufacturing coefficients.

AIGC Based on Experts: Inputs from reliability experts are incorporated into the allocation process to balance and validate the distribution. Various AI models like Google's Gemma (2B, 7B), Microsoft's Phi-3-mini (3.8B), and Meta's Llama (38B) are employed to enhance decision-making during allocation.

Step 6. Reliability Allocation from Subsystems to Parts

At this stage, a remanufacturing coefficient is introduced, accounting for factors like wear, rework, and the condition of the components. Reliability targets are allocated from subsystem level to part level, ensuring that each part's reliability contribution aligns with its subsystem's target. If allocation results fail to meet subsystem reliability targets, reallocation is conducted until the requirements are satisfied.

Step 7. Final Reliability Allocation Verification

After successful allocation from subsystems to parts, the final reliability allocation results are evaluated to ensure they align with the system-level target. If confirmed, the process concludes, and the optimized reliability distribution can be implemented during remanufacturing.

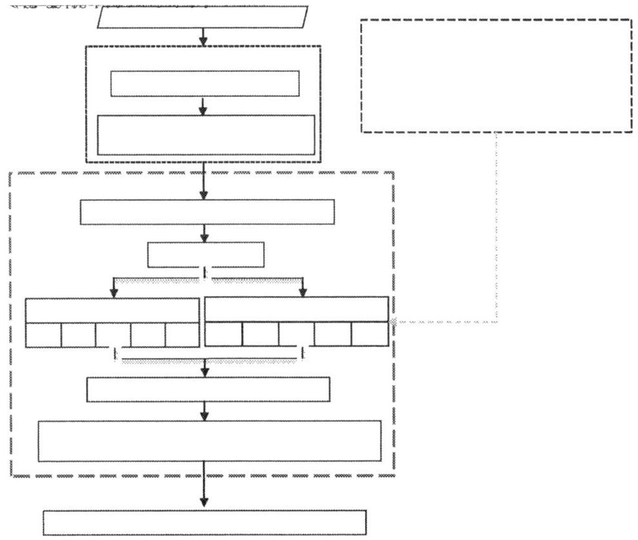

Fig. 1 The flowchart of the proposed reliability allocation.

3. Case: Remanufactured machine

A remanufactured machine tool can be viewed as a complex system consisting of various subsystems, including the spindle system, feed system, and numerical control system [4]. Each of these subsystems is further composed of individual components. In the context of reliability allocation for remanufactured machine tools, the entire system is considered, with the failure of the machine tool serving as the top event in the fault tree analysis. Since different types of machine tools comprise unique subsystems, a failure in any of these subsystems can result in the failure of the overall machine tool system. In this study, the weight factors for each criterion in this system are established using the Analytic Hierarchy Process (AHP), and Table2 shows AHP weight of Knife rest by LLMs. The standard weights of Aspect 1,2,3,4, and 5 using LLMs are 0.1892, 0.2102, 0.2027, 0.2094, and 0.1885, respectively. Table3 shows the reliability allocation of subsystems based on LLMs (Achieve reliability<0.05 and 0.1). The results demonstrate that the reliability allocation for each subsystem is consistently optimized, with slight variations across different reliability thresholds. Specifically, the Knife rest subsystem exhibits a reliability allocation of 0.8819, increasing to 0.890 and 0.899 as the target reliability thresholds are adjusted to below 0.05 and 0.1, respectively. Similarly, the Table components subsystem shows a reliability allocation of 0.8853, which progressively rises to 0.894 and 0.903 under the same conditions. The Bed subsystem maintains the highest reliability allocation among all subsystems, ranging from 0.915 to 0.927. In contrast, the Big column subsystem presents the lowest allocation values, ranging from 0.8429 to 0.868, indicating a potential area for further reliability improvement. The NC system subsystem shows a moderately stable reliability allocation, increasing from 0.8916 to 0.908. These findings suggest that while LLM-based reliability allocation is effective in maintaining subsystem reliability, specific components, such as the Big column, may require additional focus to achieve higher reliability targets.)

Table 1. Components and subsystems requiring reliability allocation in the NC gear hobbing machine

Subsystems	Parts
Knife rest	Spindle, bevel gear 1, bearing bush
Table components	Workbench, table housing, indexing turbine, indexing worm
Bed	None
Big column	Bevel gear 2, bearing, screw rod, turbine, worm
Small column	Transmission gear, center
NC system	Man-machine dialogue interface, feed shaft control interface, spindle control interface, auxiliary control interface

Table 2. AHP weight of Knife rest by LLMs

	Aspect 1	Aspect 2	Aspect 3	Aspect 4	Aspect 5
Aspect 1	1	1.04	0.94	0.97	1.04
Aspect 2	0.96	1	0.91	0.94	1.01
Aspect 3	1.06	1.11	1	1.03	1.11
Aspect 4	1.03	1.07	0.97	1	1.08
Aspect 5	0.96	1.01	0.91	0.94	1

Table3. The reliability allocation of subsystems based on LLMs.

Subsystems	reliability allocation	Achieve reliability<0.05	Achieve reliability<0.1
Knife rest	0.8819	0.890	0.899
Table components	0.8853	0.894	0.903
Bed	0.915	0.921	0.927
Big column	0.8429	0.855	0.868
Small column	0.9101	0.917	0.923
NC system	0.8916	0.900	0.908

4. Conclusion

This study presents a systematic framework for reliability allocation in remanufactured machine tools, addressing the inherent complexity of machine tool structures composed of multiple interconnected subsystems and parts. By employing a structured reliability allocation process involving data collection, fault tree analysis (FTA), and the application of large language models (LLMs), the proposed approach effectively distributes reliability targets from the system level down to individual subsystems and parts. The incorporation of AIGC-based reliability allocation mechanisms further refines the allocation by considering expert inputs and predefined manufacturing criteria, enhancing overall reliability prediction accuracy. The case study on NC gear hobbing machines illustrates that while the overall reliability allocation is optimized, specific subsystems, such as the Big column, exhibit relatively lower reliability values, suggesting the need for targeted interventions to mitigate potential reliability deficiencies. Additionally, the results demonstrate the capability of LLMs to facilitate adaptive reliability allocation, providing a robust framework for addressing variability in component wear and rework during the remanufacturing process. Future research should focus on refining the AIGC-based reliability allocation mechanisms by integrating advanced machine learning algorithms to improve predictive accuracy and adaptability in dynamic remanufacturing environments. Additionally, the development of a multi-objective optimization framework that simultaneously considers cost, time, and reliability allocation could further enhance the proposed model's applicability in industrial settings. Further validation through extensive testing on diverse remanufactured machine tools with varying subsystem configurations would provide a comprehensive evaluation of the model's effectiveness. Moreover, the integration of real-time sensor data and digital twin technology could offer deeper insights into component degradation patterns, enabling proactive reliability allocation and predictive maintenance strategies. Finally, exploring the use of ensemble learning techniques to incorporate multiple AI models, such as LLMs, reinforcement learning, and Bayesian networks, could further bolster the robustness and accuracy of the reliability allocation process.

5. Acknowledgement

This research was funded by the National Science and Technology Council of the Republic of China, Taiwan, grant number NSTC-113-2221-E-029-022-MY3,

6. References

[1] Parker, D., Riley, K., Robinson, S., Symington, H., Tewson, J., Jansson, K., Ramkumar, S., Peck, D. "Remanufacturing market study". European Remanufacturing Network (ERN), http://www.remanufacturing.eu/assets/pdfs/remanufacturing-market-study.pdf. (2015).

[2] Du, Y., He, G., Li, B., Zhou, Z., Wu, G. (2022). "In-service machine tool remanufacturing: A sustainable resource-saving and high-valued recovery approach. Environment"; Development and Sustainability, Vol. 24, 1335-1358, 2022.

[3] Li, Y., Zhang, G., Wang, Y., Zhang, X., Ran, Y. "Research on reliability allocation technology for NC machine tool meta-action. "; Quality and Reliability Engineering International, Vol. 35, Issue No. 6, 2016–2044, 2019.

[4] Du, Y., Wu, G., Tang, Y., Liu, S., "A two-stage reliability allocation method for remanufactured machine tools integrating neural networks and remanufacturing coefficient"; Computers & Industrial Engineering, Vol. 163, 107834, 2022.

Enhancing E-Commerce Service Quality: Strategic Insights and Evaluation

Tsai Chih-Ming[1], Yu Chun-Hung[2,*], Yu Chun-Min[1], Chu Chih-Han[1]

[1] Dept. of Industrial Engineering and Management / National Chin-Yi University of Technology, Taiwan.
[2,*] Language Teaching Center / National Chi Nan University, Taiwan. Email: chyu@ncnu.edu.tw (corresponding author)

Keywords: Electronic Service Quality (E-S-QUAL), Electronic Recovery Service Quality (E-RecS-QUAL), Refined Kano Model, Importance-Performance Analysis (IPA), Customer Satisfaction

Abstract - With the rapid advancement and continuous innovation of internet technology, the development of online platforms has become the business model that dominates consumer shopping behavior for e-commerce businesses. In such a fiercely competitive environment, enhancing service quality of e-commerce platforms has become an important topic that drives customer satisfaction and e-commerce businesses profits. By employing both electronic service quality (E-S-QUAL) and electronic recovery service quality (E-RecS-QUAL), the research framework of establishing e-commerce service quality was identified. Based on the results of 30 service quality attributes obtained from 136 Taiwanese respondents, the responsiveness construct falls into the "Concentrate here" field of Importance-Performance Analysis (IPA). Two questionnaire items of "The platform provides good product guarantees" and "When a problem occurs in my transaction, the platform guides me on how to resolve it" in the responsiveness construct, classified into the high value-added of refined Kano model, are also the essential service quality attributes in enhancing customer satisfaction. Finally, we provide the strategic insights and valuable guidance for e-commerce businesses in developing strategies to enhance service quality on their platforms.

1. Introduction

With the rapid technological advancements and the advent of the digital age, consumers' shopping habits have shifted from physical stores to online e-commerce platforms. This paradigm shift has catalyzed the emergence of e-commerce as a dominant business model. In such a highly competitive environment, our study addresses the critical challenge of measuring and enhancing service quality in e-commerce platforms to optimize corporate performance and profitability. This study is based on the refined Kano model, which has been widely used in recent years to explore service quality. Our methodology also integrates Importance-Performance Analysis (IPA) complemented by the importance analysis that is not considered in the refined Kano model. This comprehensive approach aims to evaluate the correlation between the perceived importance and satisfaction levels of various service quality attributes by analyzing consumers' needs and conducting surveys to explore the essential service quality attributes of e-commerce platforms. It then provides data-driven strategic insights for e-commerce platform management to continuously strengthen or maintain service quality with existing advantages, while suggesting appropriate adjustments for over-serviced quality attributes. The anticipated outcomes of this study is to continuously optimize service quality and processes, achieving sustainable development in the e-commerce operation.

2. Literature review

2.1. E-commerce and service quality

E-commerce platforms are transaction platforms based on multimedia content and the internet infrastructure. Their purpose is to facilitate the exchange of goods and services in virtual environments, offering a streamlined interface for commercial interactions of buyers and sellers, which vary significantly from face-to-face sales model in physical retail establishments [1].

With the popularization of e-commerce services, the conceptualization of service quality has developed and expanded from physical stores to the digital realm. Therefore, Parasuraman et al. [2] proposed two distinct dimensions: the Electronic Service Quality Scale (E-S-QUAL) and the Electronic Recovery Service Quality Scale (E-RecS-QUAL). Through the related research [2], more scholars have been able to conduct efficacious research on online service quality analysis. For instance, convenience, price, network assurance, network security and privacy, website design, customization and personalization, reliability, flexibility, etc. have been widely included in the e-commerce service quality attributes [3]. Huang [4] stated that both electronic service quality and electronic recovery service quality exert a positive influence on customer loyalty. E-commerce platform brand, encryption mechanism, and payment method will also influence the consumers' willingness to use e-commerce platforms [1].

2.2. Kano model and refined Kano model

The Kano model [5], a widely used research method since 1984, has proven its reliability and inspired a number of scholars to further extend it. In 2005, Yang [6] proposed an expanded version called the refined Kano model, which elaborates on the original four quality attributes.

1. Highly attractive quality attributes: these attributes are the most appealing ones to customers and therefore are the best tools for businesses.
2. Less attractive quality attributes: these attributes have a limited influence on customers and can be omitted based on cost considerations.

3. High value-added quality attributes: these attributes contribute significantly to customer satisfaction and should be provided on a best-effort basis.
4. Low value-added quality attributes: these attributes contribute marginally to customer satisfaction but still shouldn't be ignored.
5. Critical quality attributes: these attributes are crucial to customer satisfaction and it's essential for business to meet customers' demand fully.
6. Necessary quality attributes: these attributes are indispensable on a desired level in order to avoid customer dissatisfaction.
7. Potential quality attributes: these attributes may be potential attractions and should be considered as effective tools in the future.
8. Care-free quality attributes: these attributes are the least priority ones that customer don't care about and therefore business need not provide to save costs.

2.3. Importance-Performance Analysis (IPA)

In the study of satisfaction, the IPA method is often used to better understand customers' subjective feelings about products or services provided by businesses. The method proposed by Martilla and James [7] developed a two-dimensional matrix analysis diagram based on customer satisfaction and the importance of each issue, divided into four quadrants which are listed as follows:

1. Concentrate here: The quadrant indicates low satisfaction, high importance and requires strengthening improvement.
2. Keep up the good work: The quadrant indicates high satisfaction, high importance and requires maintaining.
3. Low priority: The quadrant indicates low satisfaction, low importance and requires minor improvements
4. Possible overkill: The quadrant indicates high satisfaction, low importance – and is considered oversupplied.

IPA was initially used in marketing field to evaluate consumer satisfaction and expectations. With the development of recent research, this analytical method has been widely adopted as an analytical tool in various fields such as education, management, and tourism. A number of studies [3, 8] have shown that IPA can not only identify problems effectively but also provide valuable analysis for resource allocation efficiently.

By integrating various analytical tools, the refined Kano model can make up for the deficiency of IPA analysis that only considers a single dimension, and IPA analysis can also make up for the lack of consideration of the refined Kano model in terms of consumers' actual usage experience and degree of importance [3]. Furthermore, the refined Kano model also provides different considerations from the traditional Kano model in terms of customer importance [6]. Such combinations are expected to help businesses effectively identify the key factors to improve user satisfaction when evaluating resource allocation strategies [4, 8].

3. Methodology

3.1. Research framework

This study is based on two different constructs: E-S-QUAL and E-RecS-QUAL as the basis for studying e-service quality [2], as shown in Figure 1. The questionnaire was designed based on different seven aspects such as efficiency, fulfillment, system reliability, privacy, responsiveness, compensation, and contact. After the collected questionnaires were sorted, the research conclusions were proposed through the analysis of the refined Kano model and IPA.

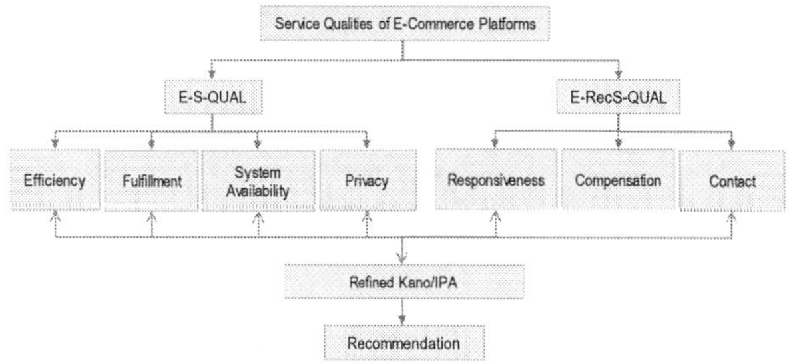

Figure 1. Research framework

3.2. Questionnaire design

The questionnaire used is divided into two parts. The first part is the basic information of the respondents, including gender, age, income, education level, relevant experience in using e-commerce online shopping services, etc. Respondents are requested to fill in the answers based on their actual situation. The second part collects the respondents' experience and opinions based on the items established within the E-S-QUAL and E-RecS-QUAL framework as shown in Table 1.

Table 1. Questionnaire items for E-S-QUAL and E-RecS-QUAL

Construct	Definition	Items [Reference]
A. efficiency	The degree to which the website provides speed and ease of use.	5 [4]
B. fulfillment	The extent to which the website delivers on its promises regarding products or services.	5 [4]
C. system reliability	The stability and smoothness of the website's system and	4 [4]

Construct	Definition	Items [Reference]
	technical performance.	
D. privacy	The extent to which the website provides security and protection for customer information.	4 [4]
E. responsiveness	The degree to which the website can effectively handle customer issues.	4 [4]
F. compensation	The extent to which the website offers compensation for customer issues.	4 [9]
G. contact	The extent to which the website provides customer service through communications or online contact.	4 [9]

3.3. Data Analysis

After classifying service quality attributes from refine Kano model, we can find out highly attractive attributes, high value-added attributes, critical attributes, and potential attributes that need attention. Through the calculation of the satisfaction index (CS value and –CS value), we can identify the key service quality attributes that have higher CS value (closer to 1) along with lower -CS value (closer to -1) as the important factors affecting customer satisfaction [10]. Furthermore, IPA can also be used to identify the service quality attributes falling into the field of concentrate here by analyzing satisfaction and importance, thereby improving customer satisfaction [8].

4. Results

This study aims to explore the service quality of online shopping platforms. We used Facebook and Line to distribute the questionnaire. The questionnaires were distributed to respondents who had used online shopping platforms for consumption. The survey was conducted from October to December 2024, and a total of 167 questionnaires were distributed, of which 136 were valid and 31 were invalid. The valid response rate was 81.44%.

This study used SPSS 23.0 as the analysis software. The Cronbach's alpha of the seven constructs, including efficiency, fulfillment, system reliability, privacy, responsiveness, compensation, and connection, were all greater than 0.7, indicating that the results have high reliability. In addition, the factor loadings of each item were greater than 0.5; the composite reliability and KMO value of each construct were also greater than 0.7; all values of Average Variance Extracted (AVE) were greater than 0.5, indicating that the results meet the validity requirements.

The classifications of service quality attributes obtained by Kano model and refined Kano model are shown in Table 2. After calculating the customer satisfaction indexes: CS value = (A+O)/(A+O+M+I) and -CS value = (-1) (O+M)/(A+O+M+I), the benefits improvement area can be figured out with higher CS value and lower -CS value [10]. The results are shown in Figure 2. Moreover, IPA were conducted based on the respondents' answers we collected. With satisfaction and importance set as the X-axis and Y-axis respectively, the average value of satisfaction and importance are the origin of the quadrant coordinates. As shown in Figure 3, the responsiveness construct is rated 4.382 in terms of importance, which is higher than the total average of all constructs, while the satisfaction construct is rated 3.851, which is lower than the total average of all constructs. Therefore, it is concluded that the responsiveness is considered a key construct that needs to be highly improved.

Table 2. Service quality attribute classification

Item	Kano class-ification	Import-ance (average)	Refined Kano class-ification	Item	Kano class-ification	Import-ance (average)	Refined Kano class-ification
A01	O	4.29412	HV	F01	O	4.28677	HV
A02	O	4.18382	LV	F02	O	4.08088	LV
A03	O	4.22794	LV	F03	O	4.16912	LV
A04	O	4.19853	LV	F04	O	4.09559	LV
A05	O	4.27206	HV	G01	O	4.12500	LV
B01	I	3.94853	CF	G02	O	4.03677	LV
B02	O	4.38235	HV	G03	I	3.71324	CF
B03	O	4.26471	LV	G04	O	4.13235	LV
B04	O	4.17647	LV				
C01	M	4.37500	C	Kano Model classification A：Attractive； O：One-Dimensional； M：Must-be； I：Indifferent。			
C02	I	4.07353	CF				
C03	O	4.22794	LV				
C04	O	4.21324	LV				
C05	O	4.48529	HV	Refined Kano Model classification HA：Highly attractive； LA：Less attractive； HV：High value-added； LV：Low value-added； C：Critical； N：Necessary； P：Potential； CF：Care-free			
D01	O	4.49265	HV				
D02	O	4.65441	HV				
D03	O	4.74265	HV				
D04	O	4.57353	HV				
E01	O	4.38235	HV				
E02	O	4.31618	HV				
E03	O	4.49265	HV				
E04	O	4.33824	HV				

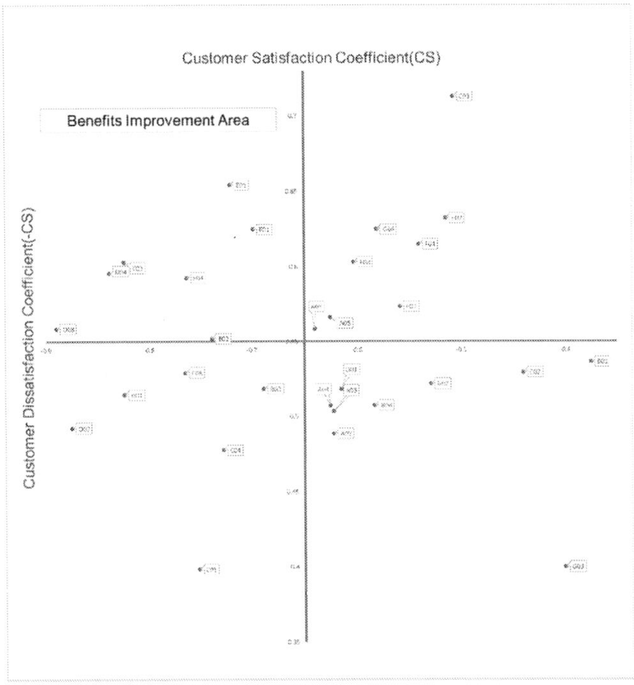

Figure 2. CS/ -CS Results

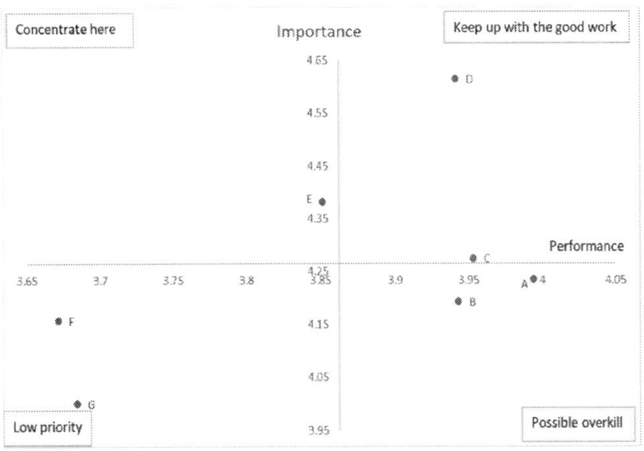

Figure 3. IPA Results

5. Conclusion: Discussion and Implications

The purpose of this study is to integrate Kano model, refined Kano model, and IPA to investigate the correlation between various service quality attributes based on customer satisfaction and importance. The results can also provide an evaluation mechanism for manages to develop relevant strategies when operating online shopping platforms.

In the context of service quality management, the integrations among Kano model, refined Kano model, and IPA have been widely adopted in numerous studies [3, 4, 8, 10]. By synthesizing these analytical frameworks shown in Table 3, two items of "(E03) The platform provides good product guarantees" and "(E04) When a problem occurs in my transaction, the platform guides me on how to resolve it" in the responsiveness construct both fall into the high value-added (refined Kano), Concentrate here (IPA), and Benefits Improvement Area (CS/ -CS results). Based on the comprehensive analysis, it is concluded that the items E03 and E04 within responsiveness are the key factors that should be improved first. Such results also show that online shopping platforms can effectively improve customer satisfaction by optimizing the transaction processes such as product guarantees and exception troubleshooting.

Table 3. Service quality attribute classification

IPA	Construct	Questionnaire item	Refined KANO	CS/-CS results
Concentrate here	Responsiveness	E03	high value-added	Benefits Improvement Area
		E04		

While doing online shopping, consumers cannot touch the products physically, so product guarantee becomes a significant reference to make purchasing decisions. To optimize this service, the following measures are suggested to be taken. First, simplify the guarantee terms. Using plain and clear language helps consumers to understand the content quickly. Second, extend product protection for specific products especially for frequently purchased items. Tailor more attractive guarantee plans (e.g., extended warranties, free repairs, replacement services) to better meet the demand of different age group in order to enhance product competitiveness and consumer loyalty. Lastly, utilize customer testimonials to build trust and to reassure potential clients. By implementing these strategic enhancements, purchase concerns can be reduced, thereby the overall shopping experience can be improved.

In terms of handling transaction anomalies, the platform should proactively notify users of processing steps to enhance user experience. It can provide humanized operating instructions through AI guidance to rest assured that users of different age groups understand the process in time without worrying about searching for information themselves or making operating errors. Meanwhile, instant updates should be provided to ensure users clearly grasp the progress. Additionally, dedicated customer service that provides prompt assistance at critical moments ensures users feel valued. A user feedback mechanism can also be set up to understand different consumers' voices and prioritize the handling process based on their needs. This set of strategies seeks to reassure consumers, expedite issue resolution, minimize delays, and help retain customer loyalty even when clients are in negative emotions or frustrating circumstances.

For future research, as society transitions into a post-pandemic era and embraces the transformative potential of AI, further exploration into optimizing e-commerce platform service quality should be conducted. By developing innovative and user-centric e-commerce service offerings, businesses can not only consolidate the trust relationship between the platform and customers but also drive long-term growth, ultimately achieving sustainable development in e-commerce.

6. References

[1] Pan, Yi-Xuan. “The Impact of E-commerce Platform Brand, Consumption Amount, Encryption Mechanism, and Payment Method on Consumers’ Willingness to Use E-commerce Platforms“ [Unpublished master’s thesis]. Pingtung University, (2024).

[2] Parasuraman, A., Zeithaml, V. A., and Malhotra, A.. “E-S-QUAL a Multiple-item Scale for Assessing Electronic Service Quality”. Journal of Service Research, 7(3), 213—233, (2005).

[3] Yang, Shu-Fen. “Using Kano Model and IPA Analysis Discussion on The Service Qualities of Coffee Bean E-commerce” [Unpublished master’s thesis]. Chien Hsin University of Science and Technology, (2024).

[4] Huang, Shu-Mei. “Investigating the Influences of E-service Quality and E-recovery Service Quality on Customer Loyalty: A Gender Difference Approach” [Unpublished master’s thesis]. Hsing Wu University, (2023).

[5] Kano, N., Seraku, N., Takahashi, F., Tsuji, S. “Attractive Quality and Must-be quality“. The Journal of the Japanese Society for Quality Control, 39—48, (1984).

[6] Yang, C.C.. “The Refined Kano’s Model and Its Application“. Total Quality Management, 16, 1127—1137, (2005).

[7] Martilla, J. A., & James, J. C. “Importance-Performance Analysis“. Journal of Marketing, 41(1), 77—79, (1977).

[8] Yeh, Tsu-Ming, Hung, Hsiang-Yung, Chiang, Ka-Him, Chen, Lung-Hung, Wang, Hao-Ping. “The Application of Refined Kano Model and IPA to Explore the Domestic Airlines' Outlying Island Routes Service Quality“. Journal of Quality, 27(6), 347—365, (2020).

[9] Lin, Yu-Chen. “The Perception Research in National Pingtung University Students in E-commerce Trading Platform Service Quality - A Case on Shopping Site“ [Unpublished master’s thesis]. Pingtung University, (2015).

[10] Meng, Chen-Yu. “The Application of Kano Model to Investigate the Business Strategy of Airlines“ [Unpublished master’s thesis]. Feng Chia University, (2023).

The Impact of Chinese Herbal Medicine on Survival in Lung Cancer Patients Receiving Targeted Therapy

Wei-Shan Chang[1], Kai-Yuan Hsiao[1], Shi-Chen Ou[3,4], Hao-Ren Yao[5], Der-Chen Chang[6], Ben-Chang Shia[1,2], Mingchih Chen[1,2], Meng-Che Hsieh[7,8]

[1] Artificial Intelligence Development Center, Fu Jen Catholic University, No. 510, Zhongzheng Rd., Xin-Zhuang Dist., New Taipei City 242062, Taiwan

[2] Graduate Institute of Business Administration, College of Management, Fu Jen Catholic University, No. 510, Zhongzheng Rd., Xinzhuang Dist., New Taipei City 242062, Taiwan

[3]Department of Chinese Medicine, China Medical University Hospital, Taichung city 40402, Taiwan.

[4]School of Post Baccalaureate Chinese Medicine, China Medical University, Taichung city, Taiwan.

[5]National Institute of Health, Bethesda, MD 20892, USA.

[6]Department of Mathematics and Statistics, Georgetown University, Washington DC 20057, USA.

[7]College of Medicine, I-Shou University, Kaohsiung city 84001, Taiwan

[8]Department of Hematology-Oncology, E-Da Cancer Hospital, Kaohsiung city 82445, Taiwan

Keywords: Machine learning, Associate analysis, Chinese herbal medicine, Lung cancer

Abstract

There is limited large-scale cohort evidence regarding the benefits of CHM on lung cancer survival, particularly in patients receiving targeted therapies. This nationwide population-based study aimed to investigate the prognostic impact of CHM on survival outcomes in lung cancer patients undergoing standard treatments, including targeted therapies.

Lung cancer patients diagnosed between 2015 and 2020 were identified, and those receiving targeted therapies were further analyzed. Patients were categorized into CHM and non-CHM groups based on medical records.

A total of 9,343 patients were included in the final analysis, with 1,583 patients in CHM group.

Data mining techniques revealed prevalent CHM utilization patterns, with Hedyotis diffusa Willd, Scutellaria barbata, and Astragalus membranaceus as the most frequently prescribed herbs. Network analysis further elucidated common herbal combinations. This study provides robust real-world evidence supporting the adjunctive role of CHM in enhancing survival outcomes for lung cancer patients receiving targeted therapy, emphasizing the importance of integrated care in clinical oncology.

1. Introduction

Lung cancer remains a predominant cause of cancer-associated mortality globally, with Taiwan reflecting similar epidemiological trends[1]. Over the past decade, significant advancements in therapeutic approaches, particularly the advent of targeted therapies, have markedly enhanced clinical outcomes for patients diagnosed with advanced-stage lung cancer. Notably, epidermal growth factor receptor (EGFR) tyrosine kinase inhibitors, including gefitinib, erlotinib, and afatinib, have emerged as integral components of the therapeutic landscape in Taiwan. The incorporation of these targeted agents into clinical practice has substantially improved survival rates among eligible patient cohorts. Nonetheless, despite these therapeutic advancements, the long-term prognosis for a substantial proportion of patients continues to be suboptimal. Consequently, there is ongoing clinical and research interest in exploring adjunctive supportive treatments aimed at further enhancing patient outcomes.

Chinese herbal medicine (CHM) is a widely used complementary therapy among cancer patients in Taiwan[2]. As an integral part of the Taiwanese healthcare system, CHM is often employed alongside conventional treatments to manage symptoms and enhance well-being. Real-world health records indicate that a substantial proportion of lung cancer patients receiving targeted therapy also utilize CHM as part of their care. This prevalent concurrent use of CHM raises important questions about its potential impact on patient outcomes, including survival. However, evaluating the effectiveness of CHM through traditional clinical research methods is challenging. Herbal treatments are highly individualized and used in diverse combinations, and patients who choose CHM may differ in baseline characteristics that make it difficult to isolate the effects of CHM with standard prospective studies.

In this study, data mining provides a powerful approach to analyze large-scale health databases for insights into CHM usage and outcomes. Taiwan's National Health Insurance Research Database (NHIRD) and Taiwan Cancer Registry (TCR) offer an unprecedented opportunity to study these issues. These databases comprehensively capture healthcare utilization and cancer diagnoses nationwide, covering virtually the entire Taiwanese population and nearly all cancer cases. By applying data mining techniques to these robust data sources, it is possible to identify patterns of CHM use and evaluate associations with survival in a real-world setting[3-4]. The objective of the present study is to investigate the patterns of CHM utilization and its association with survival outcomes among lung cancer patients undergoing targeted therapy in Taiwan. This study leverages nationwide healthcare and cancer registry data to elucidate real-world CHM usage patterns with data mining and the potential influence on real world Chinese herbal Medicine database in the era of data science.

2. Method

2.1. Data Sources

The present study leveraged data from the National Health Insurance Research Database (NHIRD), which encompasses over 99% of the Taiwanese population, providing a robust and comprehensive dataset[5]. Additionally, data were integrated from the Taiwan Cancer Registry (TCR), a well-established database with an extensive coverage rate exceeding 98% of all cancer cases in Taiwan. Cancer diagnoses recorded in the TCR are rigorously validated through histological or cytological examinations, ensuring data reliability. This retrospective, nationwide, population-based study synthesizes detailed information from both the NHIRD and TCR, including cancer diagnosis, staging, and treatment modalities. All diagnoses in the NHIRD and TCR adhere to the International Classification of Diseases, Ninth Revision, Clinical Modification (ICD-9-CM), and Tenth Revision (ICD-10-CM). To safeguard patient confidentiality, all personal identifiers are encrypted prior to database release. The study protocol was reviewed and approved by the Institutional Review Board of Fu Jen Catholic University (IRB No. C110199), with a waiver granted for the requirement of individual written informed consent.

2.2. Study Populations

In this population-based retrospective study, patients diagnosed with lung cancer, as identified by the International Classification of Diseases for Oncology, Third Edition (ICD-O-3) codes C33 and C34, between 2013 and 2015 were retrieved from the Taiwan Cancer Registry (TCR). The index date was defined as the date of the first recorded lung cancer diagnosis for each patient. The observation period extended from the index date until either the date of death or the last available follow-up date in the National Health Insurance Research Database (NHIRD), which was December 31, 2021.

To explore the utilization of complementary therapies, patients who received Chinese herbal medicine (CHM) treatments excluding acupuncture and traumatology therapies and after the index date and continued CHM use for more than 14 consecutive days were categorized as CHM users[6]. Conversely, patients without any CHM treatment records were classified as non-CHM users. Figure 1 provides a detailed flow diagram outlining the enrollment and categorization processes employed in the study.

2.3. Statistical Analysis

Between-group differences for continuous variables were analyzed using the Student's t-test, while categorical variables were compared using the Chi-square test. All statistical analyses were conducted using SAS software (version 9.4; SAS Institute Inc., Cary, NC, USA) and R software (version 4.4.1). Statistical significance was determined by a two-sided P-value threshold of less than 0.05.

Association analysis was performed to explore common patterns of traditional Chinese medicine usage. This method aims to identify frequent co-prescriptions or combinations of herbal medicines based on large-scale prescription records. Association rules were evaluated using three key metrics: support, confidence, and lift.

$$\text{Support}(A\rightarrow B) = \frac{\textit{Number of prescriptions containing both A and B}}{\textit{Total number of prescriptions}} \quad (1)$$

$$\text{Confidence}(A\rightarrow B) = \frac{\textit{Number of prescriptions containing both A and B}}{\textit{Number of prescriptions containing A}} \quad (2)$$

$$\text{Lift}(A\rightarrow B) = \frac{\text{Confidence(A"B)}}{\text{Support(A"B)}} \quad (3)$$

A lift value greater than 1 suggests a positive association, implying that herbs A and B are more likely to be prescribed together than by chance alone.

3. Results

3.1. Demographic statistics

Using data from the National Health Insurance Research Database (NHIRD) and the Taiwan Cancer Registry (TCR), we identified patients diagnosed with lung cancer between 2015 and 2020 (Figure 1). Among 47,751 eligible lung cancer patients, 9,343 individuals were identified as having received at least one of the targeted therapies Gefitinib, Erlotinib, or Afatinib. Of these, 1,583 patients underwent concurrent Chinese herbal medicine (CHM) treatment, while 7,760 did not utilize CHM.

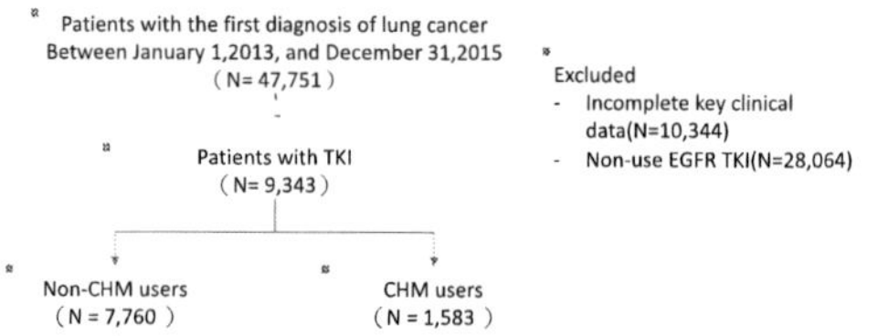

Fig1. Flow chart of patients' collection

Table 1 summarizes the demographic and clinical characteristics of patients in the CHM and non-CHM groups. Key findings revealed a higher proportion of female patients in the CHM group, whereas the mean age of patients in the non-CHM group was marginally higher than that in the CHM group. Furthermore, patients in the CHM group exhibited a greater frequency of outpatient and inpatient treatments compared with their counterparts in the non-CHM group. According to chi-square test results, there was a statistically significant difference in the 5-year mortality between the CHM and non-CHM groups.

Table1. Baseline Characteristics of the Patients.

	level	CHM Users	Non-CHM Users	p
N		1583	7760	
Gender	Male	579 (36.6)	3436 (44.3)	<0.001
	Female	1004 (63.4)	4324 (55.7)	
Age(mean(SD))		60.00 (10.70)	65.95 (12.13)	<0.001
Age Group	<60	779 (49.2)	2393 (30.8)	<0.001
	>=60	804 (50.8)	5367 (69.2)	
Pathologic stage	Other	819 (51.7)	4565 (58.8)	<0.001
	I-II	200 (12.6)	593 (7.6)	
	III-IV	564 (35.6)	2602 (33.5)	

	level	CHM Users	Non-CHM Users	p
CCI SCORE (mean (SD))		1.20 (1.93)	1.20 (2.09)	0.962
Outpatient visit frequency (mean (SD))		136.16 (101.48)	103.61 (90.46)	<0.001
Inpatient visit frequency (mean (SD))		8.01 (10.06)	5.74 (7.49)	<0.001
Overall mortality within 5 years	No	529 (33.4)	1984 (25.6)	<0.001
	Yes	1054 (66.6)	5776 (74.4)	

3.2. Drug Network

The top three single herbs prescribed for the treatment of lung cancer patients in CHM services were hedyotis diffusa willd, scutellaria barbata, and astragalus membranaceus. Figure 2 shows the ten most commonly used single-herb traditional Chinese medicines (CHMs) among lung cancer patients, while Figure 3 displays the ten most commonly used single-herb CHMs and their highly associated co-prescribed herbs. Both figures are presented as network graphs. In Figure 2, the size of each node represents the frequency with which the corresponding herb appears in prescriptions, with larger nodes indicating higher frequencies. The connecting lines between nodes represent the number of times two herbs co-occurred within prescriptions, with thicker lines denoting stronger associations[7]. In Figure 3, the size of each node corresponds to the support value, indicating the frequency of herb occurrence within the database, whereas the thickness of the connecting lines reflects the lift value, representing the strength of association between paired herbs[8].

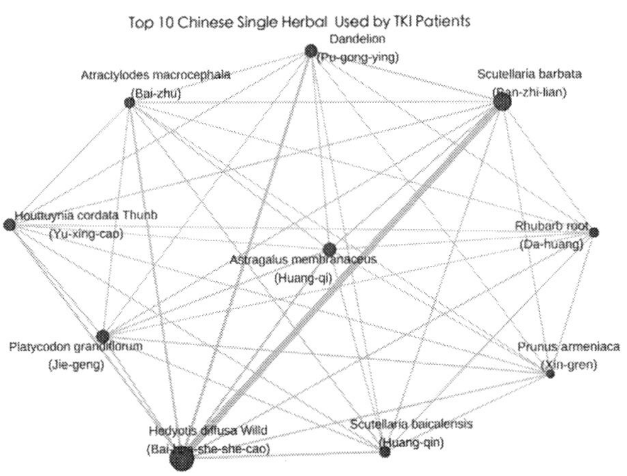

Fig2. Top 10 Chinese single herbal used by TKI patients

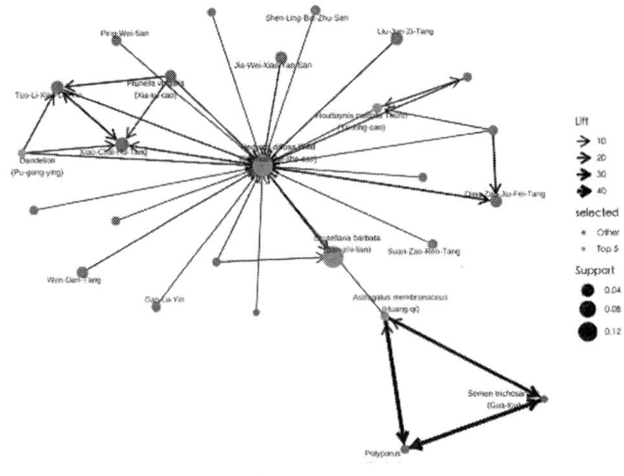

Fig3. Network analyses of the most frequent 5 herbs and formulas combination for patients with TKI patients.

4. Conclusion

Our study included the largest cohort and provided real-world evidence for physicians treating patients with lung cancer. Our results demonstrated that lung cancer patients receiving both standard care and concomitant CHM therapy had longer survival compared to those treated with standard care alone in Taiwan. Furthermore, our research revealed the patterns of CHM usage among lung cancer patients receiving tyrosine kinase inhibitor (TKI) therapy, and explored the combinations of different CHMs based on data mining from a real-world health database.

Reference

[1] Chang, Y. J., Huang, J. Y., Lin, C. H., & Wang, B. Y. (2021). Survival and treatment of lung cancer in Taiwan between 2010 and 2016. Journal of Clinical Medicine, 10(20), 4675.

[2] F A (2021) Discovering the Use of Complementary and Alternative Medicine in Oncology Patients: A Systematic Literature Review. Evid Based Complement Alternat Med 2021, 6619243.

[3] Huang, K. C., Su, Y. C., Sun, M. F., & Huang, S. T. (2018). Chinese herbal medicine improves the long-term survival rate of patients with chronic kidney disease in Taiwan: a nationwide retrospective population-based cohort study. Frontiers in Pharmacology, 9, 1117.

[4] Wang, J., Li, R., Chang, W. S., Hsiao, K. Y., Shia, B. C., & Ma, S. (2025). Heterogeneous network analysis of disease clinical treatment measures via mining electronic medical record data. The Annals of Applied Statistics, 19(1), 637-654.

[5] Chiang CJ, Wang YW, Lee WC. Taiwan's nationwide cancer registry system of 40 years: past, present, and future. J Formos Med Assoc. 2019;118(5):856-858.

[6] Chen, P. E., Hung, H. H., Huang, W. T., Yeh, C. H., Kao, Y. W., Shia, B. C., & Huang, S. T. (2023). Chinese Herbal Medicine Improved Survival in Stage IV Breast Cancer

Patients: Data Mining of the Incorporated Taiwan Cancer Registry Database and Hospital Database. Integrative Cancer Therapies, 22, 15347354231178898.

[7] Chang, C. C., Bi, K. W., Lin, H. J., Su, Y. C., Wang, W. L., Lin, C. Y., ... & Huang, S. T. (2019). Conventional Western treatment associated with Chinese herbal medicine ameliorates the incidence of head and neck cancer among patients with esophageal cancer. Integrative cancer therapies, 18, 1534735419834353.

[8] Guo, J. C. L., Pan, H. C., Yeh, B. Y., Lu, Y. C., Chen, J. L., Yang, C. W., ... & Chen, H. Y. (2021). Associations between using Chinese herbal medicine and long-term outcome among pre-dialysis diabetic nephropathy patients: a retrospective population-based cohort study. Frontiers in Pharmacology, 12, 616522.

Integrating Delphi method into design of experiments for improving quality control: a case study of mechanical company

ANH-VAN Nguyen[1], KHAC-HIEU Nguyen[2], MY-HANH Nguyen[3]

[1]Faculty of Economics, Ho Chi Minh City University of Technology and Education, Vietnam, Email: anhvan@hcmute.edu.vn
[2]Faculty of Economics, Ho Chi Minh City University of Technology and Education, Vietnam, Email: hieunk@hcmute.edu.vn
[3]Department of Industrial Engineering and Management, Yuan Ze University, Taiwan, Email: ntmhanh@saturn.yzu.edu.tw (Corresponding author)

Keywords: Forging process, Design of Experiments (DOE), ANOVA, optimization, quality improvement, Delphi method.

Abstract - The forging industry plays a crucial role in various manufacturing sectors, where process optimization is essential for improving product quality and efficiency. This study applies the Design of Experiments (DOE) method to optimize the Ratchet forging process, addressing the limitations of the traditional One Variable at a Time (OVAT) approach. Using the Delphi method, key influencing factors were identified, including billet heating temperature, heating time, and forging force. A randomized experimental design with 32 trials was conducted using Minitab (Version 20), followed by statistical analysis through ANOVA. The optimal process parameters were determined as a billet heating temperature of 1131.92°C, a heating time of 112.015 seconds, an upsetting force of 441.45 kN, a rough and finish forging force of 1226.25 kN, and a flash trimming force of 441.4 kN. Validation tests showed that these conditions consistently got a 30/30 quality score for the product while cutting processing time by 20%, costs by 22.22%, and the number of trials by 38.82%. The quality also got better by 6.67%. Based on these results, DOE is a very useful tool for optimization, providing better quality and efficiency gains than traditional trial-and-error methods.

1. Introduction

The forging industry is a vital component of modern manufacturing, playing a crucial role in sectors such as automotive, aerospace, transportation, agriculture, and defense. According to the Forging Industry Association (FIA), forged components are extensively used in essential machinery, with an average car containing over 250 forged parts, an aircraft incorporating more than 450 forged structural components, and a heavy battle tank requiring over 550 forged parts [1]. The global forging market has experienced steady growth, rising from $84.1 billion in 2021 to $89.43 billion in 2022. It is projected to reach $137.52 billion by 2030, with an annual growth rate of 6.34%. However, despite this expansion, the industry faces challenges such as the impact of the COVID-19 pandemic, rising global inflation, geopolitical conflicts, and supply chain disruptions [2]. These factors emphasize the need for process optimization to improve efficiency, reduce costs, and maintain high product quality.

With the emergence of Industry 4.0, manufacturers are increasingly adopting smart technologies, automation, and data-driven decision-making to enhance production efficiency and quality. The Total Quality Management 4.0 (TQM 4.0) framework highlights the importance of integrating advanced analytical tools and systematic optimization methods to improve manufacturing performance [3]. Traditional optimization approaches, such as the One Variable at a Time (OVAT) method, remain widely used in forging. However, OVAT has significant limitations, including high resource consumption, an inability to assess interactions between factors, and reliance on trial-and-error experimentation. To address these challenges, this study applies the Design of Experiments (DOE) methodology, which is a structured and efficient method for process optimization [4]. To ensure the effective application of DOE, the Delphi method was employed to identify and refine the key influencing factors in the forging process. The Delphi method is widely recognized for its reliability in expert-driven decision-making [6].

The following sections detail the methodology, experimental design, results, and analysis of DOE in the forging process.

2. Methodology

This study employs the Design of Experiments (DOE) approach to optimize the forging process for Ratchet products. The methodology consists of the following steps:

Step 1: Defining research objectives

This study aims to optimize the forging process by improving product quality, production efficiency, and resource utilization.

Step 2: Identifying factors

The Delphi method was used to consult 10 industry experts, identifying key factors influencing the forging process and determining their levels of impact.

Step 3: Experimental design

A randomized experimental plan was developed using Minitab, incorporating five independent variables and 32 trials to ensure robust statistical analysis.

Step 4: Experimental execution

The experiments were conducted under controlled conditions, ensuring precise parameter settings while

Quality Control (QC) monitoring minimized environmental variations.

Step 5: Data analysis

Statistical methods, including Analysis of Variance (ANOVA), were applied to evaluate factor significance and interactions affecting the forging process.

Step 6: Determination of optimal values

Based on the analysis, optimal forging parameters were identified to achieve the study's objectives.

Step 7: Validation and verification

Additional trials were conducted under optimized conditions to validate effectiveness and ensure process stability.

Step 8: Reporting and conclusion

The results were compiled into a research report assessing the impact of DOE on quality improvement, production efficiency, and waste reduction.

3. Results

3.1. Project scope and objectives

This project focuses on optimizing the forging process for Ratchet production using an assembly line system. The key objectives include enhancing product quality, improving production efficiency, and reducing material waste and processing time. The project is structured into three main phases: Definition, Implementation, and Summary and reporting, with a 10-member team executing tasks within a 15-day timeline.

3.2. Implementation and technical requirements

The project aims to increase forging efficiency by 20%, reduce material waste by 30%, and enhance product quality by 5%. The main material used is Chrome Vanadium Steel (Cr-V, AISI 6150). It is known for being strong, resistant to wear, and able to be heated and shaped at temperatures between 850°C and 1175°C. The billet dimensions are 30.8 cm (±0.5 mm) in length and 2 cm (±0.1 mm) in diameter. At the same time, the final product must meet strict dimensional accuracy, surface smoothness, and durability requirements to ensure optimal performance and longevity.

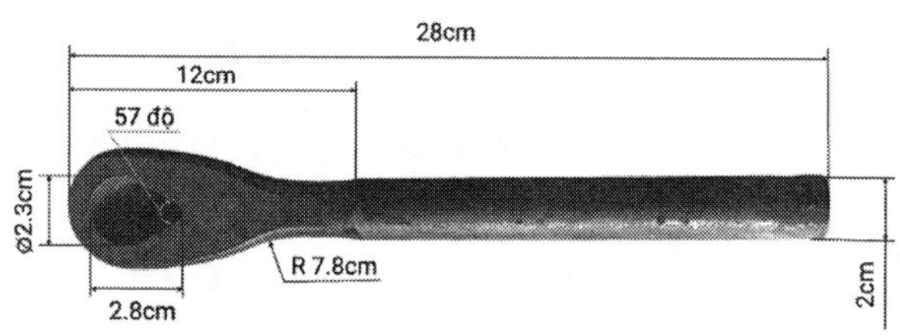

Figure 1. Technical specifications requirements

3.3. Apply Delphi method to identify factors influencing the forging process

To accurately determine the key factors influencing the forging process, 10 experienced engineers from a mechanical company were interviewed. These experts provided insights into the critical variables affecting the forging process and their respective levels of influence.

The authors calculate the Mean and CVR (Content Validity Ratio) to analyze expert opinions.

Mean = $(X_1 + X_2 + ... + Xn)/n$; where $X_1, X_2, ..., Xn$ represent individual values provided by experts, and n is the sample size (10 experts).

CVR = (Ne - N/2)/(N/2), where Ne is the number of experts considering the essential factor, and N is the total number of experts. Table 1 shows the results of the Delphi method.

Table 1. The results of the Delphi method.

No.	Product Complexity	Billet Heating Temperature	Billet Heating Time	Billet Shape	Forging Speed	Forging Force
1	2	5	4	2	4	5
2	3	5	5	4	3	5
3	4	5	5	3	4	5
4	4	5	5	2	5	5
5	3	5	5	3	4	5
6	3	5	5	3	3	5
7	3	5	4	4	3	5
8	4	5	4	3	4	5
9	3	5	5	3	4	5
10	4	5	4	2	2	5
Mean	**3.3**	**5**	**4.6**	**2.9**	**3.6**	**5**
Ne	**4**	**10**	**10**	**2**	**6**	**10**
CVR	**-0.2**	**1**	**1**	**-0.6**	**0.2**	**1**

Following the survey, the Ratchet forging process was determined to have moderate difficulty. Among the influencing factors, billet heating temperature and forging force were identified as the most significant, both with an average coefficient of 5 and a CVR of 1. Billet heating time also showed a strong influence, with an average coefficient of 4.6 and a CVR of 1. Meanwhile, forging speed had a moderate impact (average coefficient of 3.6, CVR of 0.2), whereas billet shape had the least influence (average coefficient of 2.9, CVR of -0.6).

Because the Content Validity Ratio (CVR) was at least 0.62, the temperature, time, and force used to forge the billet were kept as important factors for further improvement. On the other hand, the billet shape was thrown out because it had a low average coefficient (2.9 to 3.5), and the forging speed was thrown out because its CVR (0.2) did not meet the selection criteria. These findings will guide the subsequent experimental design to improve the forging process's efficiency, precision, and quality.

3.4. Experimental design

The experimental plan was developed based on the survey results, focusing on three key factors: billet heating temperature, billet heating time, and forging force. The Ratchet forging process consists of three stamping stages: upsetting, rough and finish forging, and flash trimming. Consequently, the forging force is divided into three components: upsetting force, rough and finish forging force, and flash trimming force. The specific levels for each factor are detailed in Table 2.

Table 2. Experimental Factors and Their Levels

Symbol	Factor	Low Level	High Level
A	Billet heating temperature	850°C	1175°C
B	Billet heating time	60 s	120 s
C	Upsetting force	294.3 kN	588.6 kN
D	Rough & finish forging force	981 kN	1471.5 kN
E	Flash trimming force	294.3 kN	588.6 kN

We used Minitab (Version 20) to design the experiment, randomly generating a test plan based on these factors and levels. The experiment includes five variables and 32 trials, ensuring accuracy by randomizing the trial order, as detailed in Table 3.

Due to potential variations in machine settings and environmental conditions, experimental results will be considered acceptable within the following tolerance ranges:

- Billet heating temperature: ± 3°C
- Billet heating time: ± 0.5 s
- Forging force (upsetting, rough & finish forging, flash trimming): ± 5 kN

Table 3: Experimental plan

No	A	B	C	D	E
31	1012.5	120	441.45	1226.25	441.4
18	1337.5	120	441.45	1226.25	441.4
24	1012.5	120	441.45	1716.75	441.4
1	850.0	60	294.30	981.00	588.5
10	1175.0	60	294.30	1471.50	588.5
4	1175.0	180	294.30	981.00	588.5
15	850.0	180	588.60	1471.50	294.3
11	850.0	180	294.30	1471.50	588.5
8	1175.0	180	588.60	981.00	294.3
29	1012.5	120	441.45	1226.25	441.4
26	1012.5	120	441.45	1226.25	735.6
20	1012.5	240	441.45	1226.25	441.4
21	1012.5	120	147.15	1226.25	441.4
16	1175.0	180	588.60	1471.50	588.5
2	1175.0	60	294.30	981.00	294.3
12	1175.0	180	294.30	1471.50	294.3
19	1012.5	60	441.45	1226.25	441.4
27	1012.5	120	441.45	1226.25	441.4
13	850.0	60	588.60	1471.50	588.5
5	850.0	60	588.60	981.00	294.3
3	850.0	180	294.30	981.00	294.3
28	1012.5	120	441.45	1226.25	441.4
14	1175.0	60	588.60	1471.50	294.3
23	1012.5	120	441.45	735.75	441.4
9	850.0	60	294.30	1471.50	294.3
7	850.0	180	588.60	981.00	588.5
25	1012.5	120	441.45	1226.25	147.2
30	1012.5	120	441.45	1226.25	441.4
6	1175.0	60	588.60	981.00	588.5
22	1012.5	120	735.75	1226.25	441.4
32	1012.5	120	441.45	1226.25	441.4
17	687.5	120	441.45	1226.25	441.4

3.5 Experiment execution and data collection and analysis

The operators set up the machines according to the predefined experimental sequence. The authors recorded data on the product evaluation forms. The collected data were analyzed using Minitab (Version 20) to design and optimize the experiment.

We made a regression equation to show how the chosen factors—billet heating temperature (A), billet heating time (B), upsetting force (C), rough and finish forging force (D), and flash trimming force (E)—affect the response variable (quality score). The obtained regression equation is as follows:

$$\text{Quality score} = -100.40 + 0.15309A + 0.1941B + 0.02257C + 0.02214D + 0.05858E - 0.000066A*A - 0.000863B*B - 0.000028C*C - 0.000008D*D - 0.000034E*E - 0.000013A*B + 0.000005A*C + 0.000000A*D - 0.000010A*E + 0.000071B*C - 0.000000B*D + 0.000000B*E + 0.000000C*D - 0.000023C*E - 0.000003\,D*E$$

Based on regression analysis, the findings confirm that billet heating temperature (A), billet heating time (B), and flash trimming force (E) play the most significant roles in optimizing the Ratchet forging process. The quality of the final product is also affected by how different factors interact with each other. This result shows that multifactorial optimization is more important than single-variable adjustments.

We used Analysis of Variance (ANOVA) to check the regression model's statistical significance. We looked at how linear terms, quadratic terms, and two-way interactions affected the forging process. Table 4 presents the ANOVA results.

Table 4. ANOVA Results

Source	DF	Sum of Squares	Mean Square	F-Value	P-Value
Model	20	470.044	23.502	311.12	0.000
Linear Terms	5	169.419	33.884	448.55	0.000
A (Billet Heating Temperature)	1	160.167	160.167	2120.28	0.000
B (Billet Heating Time)	1	1.919	1.919	25.40	0.000
C (Upsetting Force)	1	0.667	0.667	8.83	0.013
D (Rough & Finish Forging	1	0.667	0.667	8.83	0.013

Force)					
E (Flash Trimming Force)	1	6.000	6.000	79.43	0.000
Quadratic Terms	5	285.472	57.094	755.81	0.000
A^2	1	89.134	89.134	1179.95	0.000
B^2	1	166.542	166.542	2204.67	0.000
C^2	1	11.109	11.109	147.06	0.000
D^2	1	7.046	7.046	93.27	0.000
E^2	1	16.094	16.094	213.05	0.000
Two-Way Interactions	10	12.000	1.200	15.89	0.000
A × B	1	0.250	0.250	3.31	0.096
A × C	1	0.250	0.250	3.31	0.096
A × D	1	0.000	0.000	0.00	1.000
A × E	1	1.000	1.000	13.24	0.004
B × C	1	6.250	6.250	82.74	0.000
B × D	1	0.000	0.000	0.00	1.000
B × E	1	0.000	0.000	0.00	1.000
C × D	1	0.000	0.000	0.00	1.000
C × E	1	4.000	4.000	52.95	0.000
D × E	1	0.250	0.250	3.31	0.096

The overall model is highly significant (P-value = 0.000), confirming that the regression model effectively explains the variation in the forging process. All linear terms (A, B, C, D, E) and quadratic terms (A^2, B^2, C^2, D^2, E^2) have very low P-values (0.000 or close to 0), indicating their strong influence on the process. Billet heating temperature (A), billet heating time (B), and flash trimming force (E) show the highest significance in both linear and quadratic terms. Three interaction terms (A × E, B × C, and C × E) have P-values below 0.05, indicating notable effects on the forging process. Other interaction terms, including A × B, A × C, and D × E, have P-values greater than 0.05, suggesting they are statistically insignificant.

These findings indicate that billet heating temperature, billet heating time, and flash trimming force are the most critical factors, and their quadratic effects significantly impact the process. Some two-way interactions (A×E, B×C, and C×E) also make a difference, which shows that multifactorial optimization is more important than single-variable adjustments.

3.6 Determination of optimal values

The main factors and how they interact with each other that affect the forging process were found using statistical analysis and ANOVA. We established the optimal conditions to enhance product quality, improve efficiency, reduce waste, and ensure process stability and reproducibility.

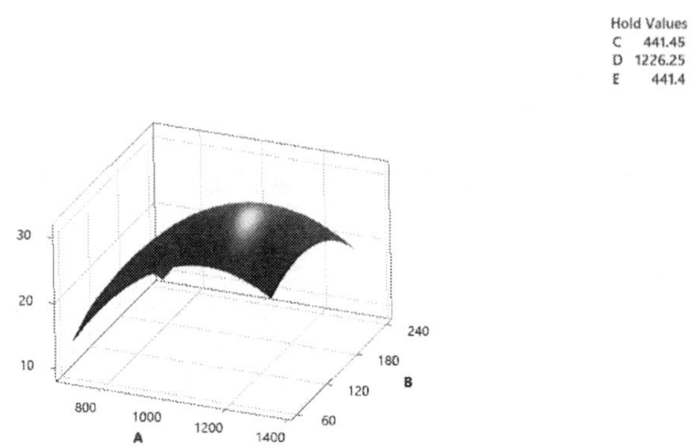

Figure 2. Surface Plot of Quality Score, Billet Heating Temperature (A), and Heating Time (B)

To see the relationship between the response variable (quality score), the heating temperature (A), and the heating time (B), we set the other factors (C, D, and E) to constant values (C = 441.45 kN, D = 1226.25 kN, and E = 441.4 kN). This result is shown in Figure 2. The plot highlights an optimal range where both A and B maximize the response while extreme values reduce effectiveness. This insight helps refine forging parameters for improved efficiency and product quality.

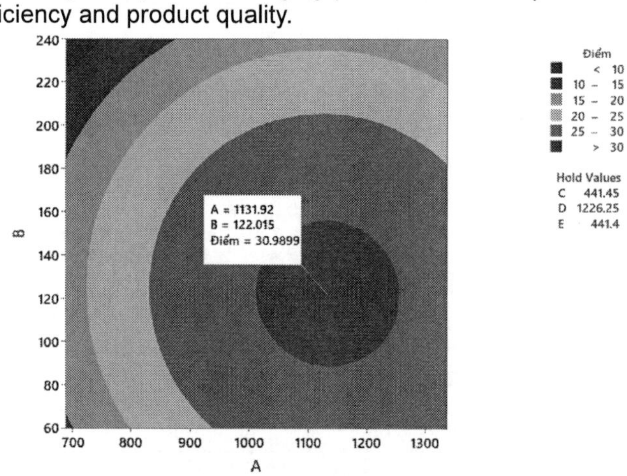

Figure 3. Contour Plot of Quality Score, Billet Heating Temperature (A), and Heating Time (B)

The contour plot in Figure 3 shows the relationship between the response variable, the temperature at which the billet is heated (A), and the time it takes to heat up (B), with all other factors staying the same (C = 441.45 kN, D = 1226.25 kN, E = 441.4 kN). At A = 1131.92°C and B = 122.015 s, we achieve the highest response value (30.99) in the darkest region, representing the optimal range.

Table 5. Optimal Conditions for Forging Parameters

8	Factor	Optimal Values
1	Billet Heating Temperature (A)	1131.92°C
2	Billet Heating Time (B)	122.015 s
3	Upsetting Force (C)	441.45 kN

4	Rough & Finish Forging Force (D)	1226.25 kN
5	Flash Trimming Force (E)	441.4 kN

3.7 Validation and Verification

To confirm the effectiveness of the optimal conditions, as shown in Table 5, 20 experimental trials were conducted. The objective was to assess whether the identified parameters consistently produced high-quality products and maintained stability across multiple trials. Experimental results are shown in Table 6.

Table 6: Validation Results with Optimal Conditions

No	A	B	C	D	E	Score
1	1131.92	112.015	441.45	1226.25	441.4	30
2	1131.92	112.015	441.45	1226.25	441.4	30
3	1131.92	112.015	441.45	1226.25	441.4	30
4	1131.92	112.015	441.45	1226.25	441.4	30
5	1131.92	112.015	441.45	1226.25	441.4	30
6	1131.92	112.015	441.45	1226.25	441.4	30
7	1131.92	112.015	441.45	1226.25	441.4	30
8	1131.92	112.015	441.45	1226.25	441.4	30
9	1131.92	112.015	441.45	1226.25	441.4	30
10	1131.92	112.015	441.45	1226.25	441.4	30
11	1131.92	112.015	441.45	1226.25	441.4	30
12	1131.92	112.015	441.45	1226.25	441.4	30
13	1131.92	112.015	441.45	1226.25	441.4	30
14	1131.92	112.015	441.45	1226.25	441.4	30
15	1131.92	112.015	441.45	1226.25	441.4	30
16	1131.92	112.015	441.45	1226.25	441.4	30
17	1131.92	112.015	441.45	1226.25	441.4	30
18	1131.92	112.015	441.45	1226.25	441.4	30
19	1131.92	112.015	441.45	1226.25	441.4	30
20	1131.92	112.015	441.45	1226.25	441.4	30

The results confirm that under optimal conditions, the product quality remained consistent (Score = 30) across all 20 trials. No negative variations were observed, indicating process stability and repeatability.

Thus, the optimal forging parameters for Ratchet production are:

- Billet Heating Temperature: 1131.92°C
- Billet Heating Time: 112.015 s
- Upsetting Force: 441.45 kN
- Rough & Finish Forging Force: 1226.25 kN
- Flash Trimming Force: 441.4 kN

These conditions ensure high product quality, efficiency, and process reliability.

4. Conclusion

This study successfully applied the Design of Experiments (DOE) method to optimize the Ratchet forging process, identifying billet heating temperature, heating time, and forging force as the most critical factors. Through statistical analysis and ANOVA, the optimal process parameters were determined as a billet heating temperature of 1131.92°C, a heating time of 112.015 seconds, an upsetting force of 441.45 kN, a rough and finish forging force of 1226.25 kN, and a flash trimming force of 441.4 kN. Validation experiments confirmed that these optimal conditions consistently produced high-quality products (30/30 score) while maintaining process stability and repeatability. The findings demonstrate that DOE is a powerful tool for process optimization, offering significant advantages over traditional trial-and-error methods.

Table 7: Comparison before and after applying DOE

Factor	OVAT Method	DOE Method	Improvement (%)
Implementation Time	15 days	12 days	20% reduction
Implementation Cost	~2,300 USD	~1,800 USD	22.22% cost saving
Number of Trials	85 trials	52 trials	38.82% fewer trials
Average Product Quality Score (20 samples)	28/30	30/30	6.67% improvement
Workforce Required	15 people	11 people	26.67% reduction

Before applying DOE, the optimization process required significant time, effort, and material consumption, relying heavily on product complexity, billet properties, and worker experience. The traditional OVAT method took 15 days, required 15 workers, and involved 85 trials, resulting in an average product quality score of 28/30 at approximately $2,300. However, the process became significantly more efficient and cost-effective after implementing DOE. The execution time was reduced to 12 days (-20%), workforce requirements dropped to 11 workers (-26.67%), and the number of trials decreased to 52 (-38.82%), leading to a 6.67% improvement in product quality while cutting costs by 22.22% (down to ~$1,800). These results confirm that DOE not only optimizes production efficiency but also enhances quality and reduces resource consumption, making it a highly effective approach for manufacturing improvement.

5. References

[1] Forging Industry Association (FIA), "Common Applications of Forgings", 2017. [Online]. Available at: https://www.forging.org/fia/content/about/design-engineering-center-content/Common_Applications_of_Forgings.aspx

[2] World Bank, "Global Economic Prospects Report 2023". Washington, DC, 2023.

[3] T. A. Van Nguyen, K. H. Nguyen, and D. Tucek, "Total quality management 4.0 framework: present and future"; Total Quality Management, vol. 16, no. 3, pp. 311–322, 2023.

[4] Jiju Antony, "Design of Experiments for Engineers and Scientists", 2nd ed. Amsterdam: Elsevier, 2020.

[5] T. A. V. Nguyen, D. Tucek, and N. T. Pham, "Indicators for TQM 4.0 model: Delphi method and analytic hierarchy process (AHP) analysis"; Total Quality Management & Business Excellence, vol. 34, no. 1–2, pp. 220–234, 2023.

A Smartphone Quality Evaluation Model Based on Quality Loss Function and Gamma Distribution

Kuen-Suan CHEN, Tsun-Hung HUANG* and Yen-Chun HUANG

Department of Industrial Engineering and Management, National Chin-Yi University of Technology, Taiwan
*toby@ncut.edu.tw

Keywords: Smartphone, information product, quality loss function, gamma distribution

Abstract

The smartphone penetration rate in advanced countries has reached nearly 80%, with some nations approaching 90%, making smartphones the most widely used information product ever invented. The smartphone industry has thus become a key driver of global economic development. People use smartphones for communication, information acquisition, work, learning, social interaction, health monitoring, and even investment activities. Losing access to a smartphone can cause severe disruptions to daily life, making smartphone quality a critical factor in user experience and, consequently, in market competitiveness for manufacturers.

To assess smartphone quality, manufacturers can rely on historical repair and complaint records to evaluate product performance over its lifecycle. However, accumulating such long-term data takes considerable time, making this approach too slow to provide timely feedback for improvement during the limited product lifecycle. To enable rapid smartphone quality evaluation, this study applies the concept of the quality loss function alongside probabilistic models based on the gamma distributions. We propose an indicator derived from the time intervals between repair events to quickly assess smartphone quality, determine whether the quality falls below expectations, and provide timely recommendations for improvement to prevent quality degradation.

1. Introduction

The importance of smartphones in people's lives cannot be overstated. Beyond being communication tools, smartphones serve as channels for information, platforms for financial transactions, tools for learning and teaching, devices for health monitoring, and the primary means for social interaction for many.

Therefore, smartphone malfunctions can be catastrophic, causing major disruptions to both personal life and work. In modern society, a smartphone breakdown can result in communication failures, economic losses, limited educational access, exacerbated health and psychological issues, and social isolation. Given the widespread use and even addictive reliance on smartphones, these impacts cannot be ignored. Smartphone quality has thus escalated beyond mere manufacturer reputation and profits, becoming an issue of broader social and economic significance.

As a result, manufacturers face a heightened responsibility for product quality, requiring more timely and sensitive evaluation and monitoring systems. Such systems should continuously track whether each smartphone model maintains acceptable quality levels and detect any unexpected drops in quality early in the product lifecycle, providing a basis for improvement.

A smartphone comprises major components such as the screen, battery, motherboard, processor, communication modules, sensors, memory, camera, antenna, speaker, casing, and charging/data transfer hardware, all assembled with precision. Smartphone malfunctions can stem from individual component failures, assembly issues, or software problems. Common failures include overheating, rapid battery drain, connectivity issues, screen malfunctions, freezing or crashing, charging problems, hardware damage, and water damage.

Some failures are user-induced—such as water exposure, screen cracks from drops, or hardware damage from improper cable insertion—and these should reasonably be borne by the user. Other failures, especially non-user-induced failures occurring early in the product's life, are attributable to manufacturing or assembly quality and fall under warranty obligations. While the visible, calculable costs of warranty repairs are relatively limited, the larger impact lies in consumer losses, both tangible and intangible, and the erosion of trust in the product and brand, which can lead to negative reviews and declining sales.

Therefore, smartphone manufacturers require real-time, accurate quality monitoring. This study develops a smartphone quality assessment model based on the quality loss function and the gamma distribution, aiming to detect changes in product quality promptly.

2. Literature Review

According to quality loss function concept described in Chen et al. [4], the total loss cost TL increases with the number of failures N over a certain period.

$$TL = \sum_{j=1}^{N} Loss(j) \tag{1}$$

Where $Loss(j)$ represents the cost caused by the jth failure. The study in Chen and Yang [1] shows that the number of failures N over a certain period of time follows a Poisson distribution with mean λ ($N \sim Poisson(\lambda)$), and λ is the average number of failures in that period of time. The probability density function of failures number N is as follows:

$$f_N(n) = \frac{e^{-\lambda}\lambda^n}{n!}, n = 0,1,2,3... \tag{2}$$

The expected value of total loss TL is

$$E[TL] = \lambda \times \mu_{Loss} \tag{3}$$

Where λ denote the mean of failure times and μ_{Loss} is the average loss per failure. To control repair costs within the smartphone's lifecycle, manufacturers can set an acceptable total loss threshold.

Due to the high penetration rate of smartphones, a best-selling brand of smartphone will be sold all over the world. There may be demand for this smartphone in various countries, cities, towns and even villages. However, due to the rapid update speed of smartphone functions and models, the product life cycle is very short. Therefore, local telecom operators and smartphone dealers do not prepare a large number of various smartphone stocks. In case of poor sales, the smartphone may not be sold and become a stock loss. Therefore, smartphone stocks are usually concentrated in regional delivery centers. When consumers purchase, the smartphones are delivered to various demand locations through a highly efficient logistics system. On the contrary, smartphone repairs are not available in every region. When a customer's smartphone fails or is damaged, the smartphone will be concentrated in the regional repair center for inspection and repair quotation in a reverse logistics manner. If it is within the warranty period, it will be updated or repaired free of charge. If it is out of warranty or without warranty, the repair and subsequent charges will be made only after the customer confirms that he wants to repair it.

When a customer sends a faulty smartphone for repair, unless it is a more special fault condition, the telecom operator or smartphone dealer can determine the type of fault based on the customer's description and smartphone inspection, and record the time of the fault. The time and type of the smartphone failure can be collected before the reverse logistics. The smartphone manufacturer can use the information system to timely integrate the fault information collected from various countries, cities, sales points, and repair points. We can conduct timely statistical analysis based on this information and evaluate whether the quality of the smartphone is still within an acceptable range before the repair is carried out.

3. Smartphone Operation Performance Index

As mentioned above, the number of smartphone failures N in a certain period obeys the Poisson distribution with an average number λ. From a management perspective, managers can set a quality cost amount TL_{Most} as the upper limit of the total maintenance cost that can be tolerated within a certain period of time, and convert it into the upper limit of the number $N_0 = TL_{Most}/\mu_{Loss}$ of failures that occur within a certain period of time; by recording the number of failures that occur within a certain period of time, it is possible to determine whether the quality of the smartphone is lower than expected. On the other hand, the longer the failure interval, the fewer failures occur in a certain period; in comparison, we can know that evaluating the quality of smartphones by the interval between smartphone failures is more efficient than recording the number of failures N in a certain period.

Let the random variable X represent the time interval between smartphone failures, then X obeys an exponential distribution with an average number $\tau = 1/\lambda$, denoted by $X \sim Exp(\tau)$. Obviously, the larger τ is, the smaller N is, which means the better the quality of the smartphone is. According to the application of six-sigma process quality index [2, 3], the smartphone operation performance index is defined as follows:

$$\xi_p = \frac{\mu - A_T}{\sigma} \tag{4}$$

And since the mean and standard deviation of an exponential distribution are all equal to the average time interval τ, we have the equation as follows:

$$\xi_p = \frac{\tau - A_T}{\tau} = 1 - \frac{A_T}{\tau} \tag{5}$$

Where $A_T = 1/N_0 = 1/(TL_{Most}/\mu_{Loss}) = \mu_{Loss}/TL_{Most}$, represents the shortest acceptable time interval of smartphone failure.

The larger the smartphone performance quality index ξ_p is, the better the quality of the smartphone is. Conversely, the smaller ξ_p is, the higher the failure rate of the smartphone is and the worse the quality is.

The relationship between the failure interval τ and acceptable time interval A_T and smartphone operation index ξ_p is as follows:

$If\ \tau > A_T \Rightarrow 1 - \frac{A_T}{\tau} > 0 \Rightarrow \xi_p > 0$, ξ_p is greater than zero, it means that the quality of the smartphone is better than the acceptable level.

$If\ \tau = A_T \Rightarrow 1 - \frac{A_T}{\tau} = 0 \Rightarrow \xi_p = 0$, ξ_p is equal to zero, it means that the quality of the smartphone is equal to the acceptable level.

$If\ \tau < A_T \Rightarrow 1 - \frac{A_T}{\tau} < 0 \Rightarrow \xi_p < 0$, ξ_p is less than zero, it means that the quality of the smartphone is worse than the acceptable level.

In addition, the indicator ξ_p has a one-to-one mathematical relationship with the standard ratio of the smartphone operation performance p_r, as follows:

$$p_r = p(X_j > A_T) = \int_{A_T}^{\infty} \frac{1}{\tau} e^{-\frac{1}{\tau}t} dt = e^{-\frac{A_T}{\tau}} = e^{\xi_P - 1} \tag{6}$$

Which means the ratio of the smartphone failure time interval greater than the minimum acceptable time interval.

Based on Equations (6), partial differentiation for the standard ratio of smartphone operation performance p_r divided by ξ_p is expressed as follows:

$$p_r' = \frac{dp_r}{d\xi_r} = e^{\xi_P - 1} \tag{7}$$

Obviously, the value of p_r is positive ($p_r' > 0$). Thus, the standard ratio of smartphone operation performance p_r is an increasing function of ξ_p. As shown in Figure 1, the curve of p_r versus ξ_p is absolutely increasing.

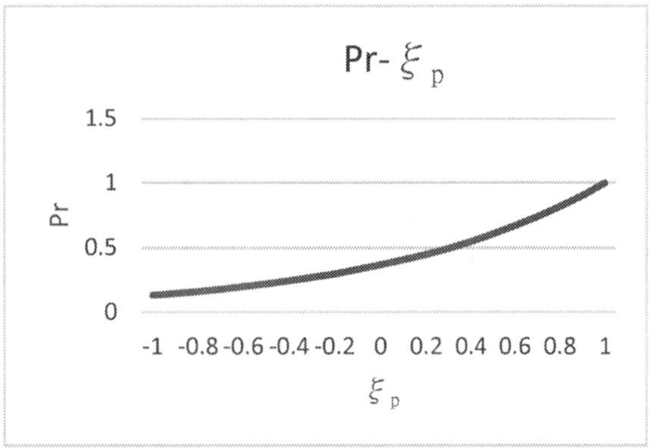

Figure 1. Curve of standard ratio to the smartphone operation performance index

4. Smartphone quality evaluation and decision-making model

As mentioned above, the greater ξ_P is, the better the smartphones are. If v is the manager's minimum requirement for the smartphone performance index ξ_P, we can test the index by setting the null hypothesis and alternative hypothesis as follows:

$$H_0 : \xi_P \ge v$$
$$H_1 : \xi_P < v \qquad (8)$$

The rules for statistical testing are as follows:

$$\phi(Z) = \begin{cases} 1, & \text{if } \hat{\xi}_P \le C_0 \\ 0, & \text{otherwise} \end{cases} \qquad (9)$$

Where $\hat{\xi}_P$ is the uniformly minimum variance unbiased estimator of ξ_P can be show as following:

$$\hat{\xi}_P = 1 - \frac{A_T}{\sum_{j=1}^{n} X_j \big/ (n-1)} = 1 - \frac{(n-1)A_T}{V(Z)} \qquad (10)$$

Based on equation (5), we can derive another representation for A_T:

$$\xi_P = 1 - \frac{A_T}{\tau} \Rightarrow \frac{A_T}{\tau} = 1 - \xi_P \Rightarrow A_T = \tau(1 - \xi_P) \qquad (11)$$

$$\hat{\xi}_P = 1 - \frac{A_T}{\sum_{j=1}^{n} X_j \big/ (n-1)} = 1 - \frac{(n-1)A_T}{V(Z)}$$

$$\Rightarrow \frac{(n-1)A_T}{V(Z)} = 1 - \hat{\xi}_P$$

$$\Rightarrow V(Z) = \frac{(n-1)A_T}{1-\hat{\xi}_P} = \frac{(n-1)\tau(1-\xi_P)}{1-\hat{\xi}_P} \qquad (12)$$

Where $Z = (X_1, \dots, X_n)'$, $X_1, \dots, X_n$ be an independent identity distribution $(i.i.d.)$ random variables with $Exp(\tau)$ and $V(Z) = \sum_{j=1}^{n} X_j$. Then the random variable $V(Z)$ is distributed as $G(n,\tau)$. Furthermore, with the significance level α, let

$$W = \frac{V(Z)}{\tau} = \frac{(n-1)(1-\xi_P)}{1-\hat{\xi}_P} \qquad (13)$$

Then W is distributed as $G(n,1)$ and the critical value C_0 can be determined by

$$E_v[\phi(Z)] = p\{\hat{\xi}_P \le C_0 | \xi_P \ge v\} = \alpha$$

$$p\left\{ W \le \frac{n-1}{1-C_0}(1-v) \right\} = \alpha \qquad (14)$$

Hence, we have

$$\frac{n-1}{1-C_0}(1-v) = G_\alpha(n,1)$$

$$C_0 = 1 - \frac{(n-1)(1-v)}{G_\alpha(n,1)} \qquad (15)$$

Based on the above inferences, we can summarize the statistical decision-making rules as follows:

1. If $\hat{\xi}_P < C_0$, H_0 is rejected, and the conclusion is $\xi_P < v$, indicating that the quality of the smartphone is below the standard and needs to be improved

2. If $\hat{\xi}_P \ge C_0$, H_0 is not rejected, and the conclusion is $\xi_P \ge v$, indicating that the quality of the smartphone meets the standard and can be maintained

5. Conclusion

The method proposed in this study, which uses the failure interval time to detect whether the quality of smartphones is maintained at a reasonable level, can calculate or recalculate whether the quality of the smartphone is qualified when any failure occurs. There is no need to calculate the cumulative number of failures over a period of time to judge the quality of the smartphone. This method is faster and more agile than traditional methods. The quality of smartphones can be evaluated based on maintenance and customer complaint records. This method is quite applicable to many household and personal information products.

6. References

[1] Chen, K.S.; Yang, C.M. Developing a performance index with a Poisson process and an exponential distribution for operations management and continuous improvement. J. Comput. Appl. Math. **2018**, 343, 737–747.

[2] Chen, K.S.; Wang, C.H.; Tan, K.H.; Chiu, S.F. Developing one-sided specification Six-Sigma fuzzy quality index and testing model to measure the process performance of fuzzy information. Int. J. Prod. Econ. **2019**, 208, 560–565.

[3] Chen, K.S.; Wang, C.H.; Tan, K.H. Developing a fuzzy green supplier selection model using Six Sigma quality indices. Int. J. Prod. Econ. **2019**, 212, 1–7.

[4] Chen, K.S.; Wu, C.F.; Tsaur, R.C.; Huang, T.H. Fuzzy Evaluation and Improvement Decision-Making Model for Machining Operation Performance. Applied Sciences. 2023, 13, 1430.

A Study on the Development of Route Recommendation Based on Trajectory Clustering for Autonomous Ship

CHOI Jungyeon[1,2], HWANG Taewoong[3], HWANG Hyoseon[4], YOUN Ik-Hyun[3,*]

[1]Department of Computer Science and Statistics,
[2]Institute of Well-Aging Medicare & CSU G-LAMP Project Group, Chosun University, Gwangju, jchoi@chosun.ac.kr,
[3]Division of Navigation & Information Systems, Mokpo National Maritime University, Mokpo, Republic of Korea,
*iyoun@mmu.ac.kr
[4]Department of Maritime Transportation System, Mokpo National Maritime University, Mokpo, Republic of Korea

Keywords: Autonomous ship, Trajectory clustering, K-means, DBSCAN, MASS

Abstract - The development of autonomous ships promises to revolutionize maritime transportation by enhancing efficiency, safety, and reducing human error. A crucial aspect of autonomous navigation is the ability to recommend optimal routes that minimize fuel consumption, reduce travel time, and avoid hazards. This study explores a route recommendation system for autonomous ships based on trajectory clustering. Using K-means and DBSCAN clustering algorithms, distinct ship trajectory patterns were identified to improve route accuracy. DBSCAN effectively handled noisy, complex data and detected arbitrarily shaped clusters, while K-means excelled with well-defined, regular trajectories. Additionally, an automated altering point detection system was incorporated to adapt to changes in ship movement and adjust routes. This study highlights the potential of data-driven techniques to enhance the safety and efficiency of autonomous ship navigation. Future work should focus on improving data handling, especially for noisy or incomplete data, and incorporating real-time environmental inputs to further optimize route planning.

1. Introduction

As the maritime industry explores the potential of autonomous ships, also known as maritime autonomous surface ships (MASS), the need for efficient, safe, and intelligent navigation systems becomes more apparent. Autonomous ships have the potential to revolutionize the maritime industry by reducing human error, improving operational efficiency, and enhancing safety [1]. One of the key challenges in autonomous navigation is determining optimal routes that balance factors such as fuel efficiency, time, safety, and traffic avoidance [2].

Route recommendation systems play a crucial role in this process by suggesting the most efficient and safest paths for autonomous ships to follow. Traditionally, route planning in maritime navigation has relied on predefined paths or human decision-making, which may not always be flexible enough to handle real-time dynamic conditions, such as sudden changes in weather or vessel congestion [1,3]. To address these limitations, intelligent route recommendation systems leveraging historical data and advanced machine learning techniques, such as trajectory clustering, have gained significant attention.

Trajectory clustering is a promising approach for identifying patterns in ship movements by analyzing historical trajectory data. By clustering similar trajectories, it is possible to recommend routes based on past patterns and adapt to real-time conditions [4,5]. This study focuses on developing an autonomous route recommendation system based on trajectory clustering techniques, specifically using K-means clustering and density-based spatial clustering of applications with noise (DBSCAN) algorithms. Additionally, an automated detection of altering points (i.e., significant changes in a ship's trajectory) is incorporated to improve the accuracy and adaptability of the system.

The goal of this study is to explore how clustering algorithms can be applied to historical maritime data to recommend efficient and safe routes for autonomous ships, while accounting for real-time navigational challenges. By integrating both K-means clustering and DBSCAN, the system aims to provide more adaptive and resilient route recommendations.

2. Methods

2.1. Data collection

The first step in developing the system was to gather trajectory data from ships operating in different regions. The dataset was primarily collected from Automatic Identification System (AIS) data, which is used to track the movements of ships. This data includes information on the ship's position (latitude and longitude), speed, heading, and timestamp. For the purposes of this study, data from vessels operating in both commercial shipping routes and areas with high traffic density were considered. The dataset was cleaned and filtered to remove outliers and incomplete entries to ensure its reliability.

2.2. Data preprocessing

Data preprocessing is crucial for transforming raw trajectory data into a format suitable for clustering algorithms. The preprocessing steps involved:

o ***Data Cleaning***: Outliers, erroneous entries, and missing data were removed to improve the overall quality of the dataset.

o ***Trajectory Segmentation***: Raw trajectory data was divided into smaller segments based on certain criteria such as distance or time intervals. This step helps break down the trajectory into more manageable portions, making clustering more effective [6,7].

o ***Normalization***: The data was standardized to ensure uniformity in scale, which prevents certain variables (e.g., speed or heading) from disproportionately influencing the clustering process.

Figure 1a represents a sample of the processed ship trajectories after performing data cleaning, trajectory segmentation, and normalization.

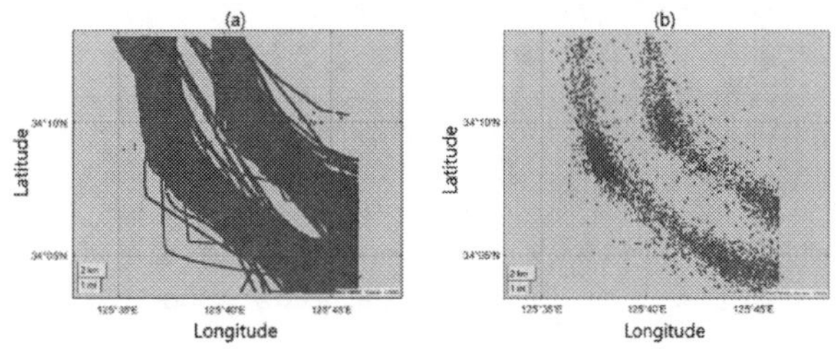

Figure 1. A sample of plots for: (a) data preprocessed trajectories and (b) detected altering points

2.3. Automated detection of altering points

A crucial component of the route recommendation system is the ability to detect significant alterations in a ship's trajectory—referred to as altering points. These points are instances where the ship's trajectory deviates significantly from its expected path, such as course changes due to navigation obstacles or sudden changes in environmental conditions.

The automated detection of altering points was implemented by analyzing the velocity and heading changes between consecutive trajectory points []. If the change in heading or velocity exceeded a predefined threshold, it was classified as an altering point. The detection of altering points helps identify critical moments in a ship's trajectory where dynamic changes might affect route planning. Figure 1b shows the detected altering points from the ship's trajectories.

By incorporating altering points, the system can adapt in real time and recommend safer and more efficient routes. For instance, if an altering point is detected due to a sudden course change (e.g., to avoid a collision or unfavorable weather conditions), the system can immediately adjust the recommended route to avoid potential hazards or inefficient paths.

2.4. Clustering algorithms

Two clustering algorithms were applied to the preprocessed trajectory data: K-means clustering and DBSCAN. K-means is a popular algorithm for dividing data into K clusters based on the Euclidean distance between points [8]. This method is highly effective for finding common patterns in well-defined trajectories, particularly when the clusters are roughly spherical. However, K-means requires the number of clusters (K) to be predefined, which may be a limitation in dynamic environments like maritime navigation. Unlike K-means, DBSCAN does not require the number of clusters to be predefined and can detect clusters of arbitrary shapes. DBSCAN works well in the maritime context, where ship trajectories can vary significantly and may not follow a linear or predictable pattern [9]. DBSCAN can also identify noise points—those data points that do not belong to any cluster—making it suitable for maritime data, where outliers are common.

Both algorithms were evaluated based on their ability to capture meaningful patterns in the trajectory data, the quality of the clusters, and the computational efficiency. Figure 2 shows the result of DBSCAN and K-means clustering.

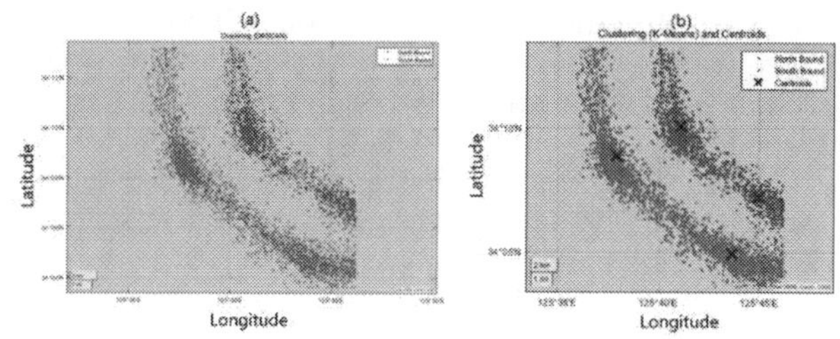

Figure 2. The results of DBSCAN and K-means clustering

3. Results

The clustering process using K-means and DBSCAN generated distinct clusters of ship trajectories, each representing common travel patterns. DBSCAN performed well in detecting arbitrarily shaped clusters and noise points, while K-means was effective in identifying well-defined, regular trajectories. The integration of altering point detection further enhanced the system's ability to adapt to unexpected changes in ship movement. The system was able to detect moments of trajectory alteration and adjust

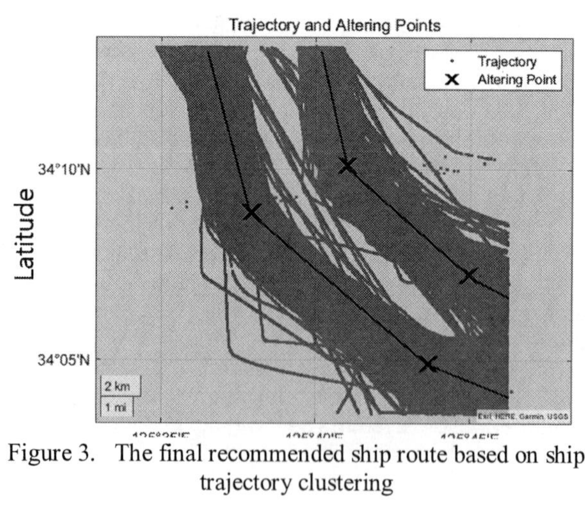

Figure 3. The final recommended ship route based on ship trajectory clustering

the recommended route accordingly. The final recommended route was determined as shown in Figure 3.

4. Discussion

This study demonstrates that combining K-means clustering, DBSCAN, and automated detection of altering points can significantly enhance the route recommendation process for autonomous ships. DBSCAN's ability to handle complex and noisy data makes it well-suited for maritime environments, while K-means provides useful insights when the trajectory patterns are well-defined.

The addition of altering point detection is a major contribution to the adaptability and robustness of the system. By detecting critical changes in a ship's trajectory, the system can adjust recommendations to ensure that the ship avoids potential hazards or inefficient routes. This feature is essential for autonomous navigation, where dynamic and real-time decision-making is critical for safety and efficiency [10,11].

However, a limitation of the system is the inability to make real-time adjustments to route recommendations. While the system performs well in recommending safe and efficient routes based on historical data, challenges remain in dealing with incomplete or noisy data, and more improvements are needed for handling real-time environmental changes and other dynamic factors such as weather or vessel traffic.

5. Conclusion

This study highlights the effectiveness of combining K-means clustering, DBSCAN, and altering point detection for route recommendation in autonomous ships. The clustering techniques successfully identified common travel patterns and enabled the system to recommend highly accurate routes based on historical trajectory data. DBSCAN's ability to handle complex and noisy maritime data, along with K-means' capacity for identifying well-defined trajectory patterns, contributed to the robustness and adaptability of the system.

The integration of altering point detection proved to be a key feature, allowing the system to recognize critical changes in ship movement and adjust the recommended routes accordingly. However, a significant limitation remains in the system's inability to make real-time route adjustments based on dynamic environmental factors such as weather or vessel traffic.

Future work should focus on enhancing the system's ability to handle incomplete or noisy data, as well as incorporating real-time environmental data to further improve route recommendations and ensure even safer and more efficient autonomous navigation. Despite these challenges, the findings of this study demonstrate the potential of data-driven techniques for improving route planning in autonomous maritime operations.

6. Acknowledgement

This research was supported by Global-Learning & Academic research institution for Master's·PhD students, and Postdocs(LAMP) Program of the National Research Foundation of Korea(NRF) grant funded by the Ministry of Education(No. RS-2023-00285353).

7. References

[1] ZHAO, Liang, et al. “Intelligent shipping: integrating autonomous maneuvering and maritime knowledge in the Singapore-Rotterdam Corridor”, *Communications Engineering*, 4(1), 2025.

[2] Hosseinian, S. M., & Mirzahossein, H. “Efficiency and safety of traffic networks under the effect of autonomous vehicles”, *Iranian Journal of Science and Technology, Transactions of Civil Engineering*, 48(4), 1861-1885, 2024.

[3] Öztürk, Ü., Akdağ, M., & Ayabakan, T. “A review of path planning algorithms in maritime autonomous surface ships: Navigation safety perspective”, *Ocean engineering*, *251*, 2022.

[4] Zhang, C., Liu, S., Guo, M., & Liu, Y. “A novel ship trajectory clustering analysis and anomaly detection method based on AIS data”, *Ocean Engineering*, *288*, 2023.

[5] Zhuang, C., & Chen, C. “Research on autonomous route generation method based on AIS ship trajectory big data and improved LSTM algorithm”, *Frontiers in neurorobotics*, 16, 2022.

[6] Yan, Z., Yang, G., He, R., Yang, H., Ci, H., & Wang, R. “Ship trajectory clustering based on trajectory resampling and enhanced birch algorithm”, *Journal of Marine Science and Engineering*, *11*(2), 407, 2023.

[7] Sheng, P., & Yin, J. “Extracting shipping route patterns by trajectory clustering model based on automatic identification system data”, *Sustainability*, *10*(7), 2018.

[8] Park, J., & Choi, M. “A K-means clustering algorithm to determine representative operational profiles of a ship using AIS data”, *Journal of Marine Science and Engineering*, *10*(9), 2022.

[9] Wang, L., Chen, P., Chen, L., & Mou, J. “Ship AIS trajectory clustering: An HDBSCAN-based approach”, *Journal of Marine Science and Engineering*, *9*(6), 2021.

[10] Wu, G., Guo, L., Shi, D., Han, B., & Yang, F. “Hybrid Probabilistic Road Map Path Planning for Maritime Autonomous Surface Ships Based on Historical AIS Information and Improved DP Compression”, *Journal of Marine Science and Engineering*, *13*(1), 2025.

[11] Liu, Z., Yang, H., Xiong, C., Xu, F., Gan, L., Yan, T., & Shu, Y. “Research on the optimization of ship trajectory clustering based on the OD–Hausdorff distance”, *Journal of Marine Science and Engineering*, *12*(8), 2024.

Examining Future Trends in Population Changes in Tourist Destinations

Masahide Yamamoto

Faculty of Foreign Studies, Nagoya Gakuin University, Japan, myama@ngu.ac.jp

Keywords: Tourism, Statistical Population Data, Noto region, Keyword search volume, Correlation analysis, Regression analysis

Abstract - This study uses statistical population data created by the operational data of mobile phone networks to identify the number of visitors in different periods at specific tourist destinations. The service makes it possible to estimate the population structure of a region by gender, age, and residential area. In addition, it attempts to demonstrate an alternative method to infer the number of visitors in specific areas more accurately. The various interests of tourists influence their keyword search before or during travel and ultimately emerge as some kind of trend in a specific keyword's search volume. By connecting the data and keyword search volume, linear equations could be derived. These findings could lead to a model to forecast tourism demand in a destination.

1. Introduction

Japan's tourism industry has been strategically navigating the challenging recovery from the COVID-19 pandemic. According to Japan Tourism Agency's Travel and Tourism Trends Survey, travel spending in 2023, including both domestic and international visitors to Japan, is expected to reach 28.1 trillion yen—a figure that marginally surpasses the pre-pandemic spending of 27.9 trillion yen in 2019. However, many regions continue to confront substantial challenges, including sudden drop in tourism demand due to natural disasters such as typhoons, heavy rain, and earthquakes. Consequently, tourism demand remains inherently volatile and unpredictable.

Basically, it is important to verify the number of visitors to effectively market a tourist destination regardless of events being held there. Although measuring the exact number of visitors to open tourist areas has been quite difficult so far, it has now become possible to estimate the number by obtaining some population data.

This study used statistical population data created by operational data from mobile phone networks to count the number of visitors at specific tourist destinations. This study also attempts to demonstrate an alternative method to more accurately infer the number of visitors in specific areas.

2. Related Studies

Previous tourism marketing research has primarily focused on the ways service promises are made and kept, mostly generating frameworks to improve managerial decisions or providing insights on associations between constructs (Dolnicar and Ring, 2014, p. 31). Big data have become important in many research areas, such as data mining, machine learning, computational intelligence, information fusion, the semantic Web, and social networks (Bello-Orgaz et al., 2016, p. 46). To date, several attempts have been made to use large-scale data or mobile phone location data in tourism marketing studies.

Most studies dealing with big data in tourism were published after 2010. Fuchs et al. (2014, pp. 198-208) presented a knowledge infrastructure that has recently been implemented at the leading Swedish mountain tourism destination, Åre. Using a Business Intelligence approach, the Destination Management Information System Åre (DMIS-Åre) drives knowledge creation and application as a precondition of organizational learning at tourism destinations. Xiang et al. (2015) tried to apply big data to tourism marketing. The study aimed to explore and demonstrate the utility of big data analytics to better understand important hospitality issues, namely, the relationship between hotel guest experience and satisfaction. Specifically, the investigators applied a text analytical approach to a large number of consumer reviews extracted from Expedia.com to deconstruct hotel guest experiences and examine the association with satisfaction ratings (pp. 120-129). These studies are similar to this study in that they attempted to utilize big data in tourism. However, the research methods and objectives of these studies are different from that of the present study.

Studies on using mobile phone location data for tourism surveys can be traced back to 2008. Ahas et al. (2008, pp. 469-485) introduced the applicability of passive mobile positioning data for studying tourism. They used a database of roaming location (foreign phones) and call activities in network cells: the location, time, random identification, and country of origin of each called phone. Using examples from Estonia, their study described the peculiarities of the data, data gathering, sampling, the handling of the spatial database, and some analytical methods to demonstrate that mobile positioning data have valuable applications for geographic studies. Japan Tourism Agency conducted a similar study using international roaming service in December 2014 (Japan Tourism Agency, 2014).

Since the work of Ahas et al. (2008), several studies employing location data have emerged. Liu et al. (2013, pp. 3299-3311) investigated the extent to which behavioral routines could reveal the activities being performed at mobile phone call locations captured when users initiate or receive voice calls or messages. Using data collected from the natural mobile phone communication patterns of 80 users over more than a year, they assessed the approach via a set of extensive experiments. Based on the ensemble of models, they achieved prediction accuracy of 69.7%. The experiment results demonstrated the potential to annotate mobile phone locations based on the integration of data mining techniques with the characteristics of underlying activity-travel behavior.

3. Method

The survey areas are presented in Figure 1. There are two reasons why the area around two hot springs was chosen. First, both hot springs are close to Kanazawa City and thus compete with each other. Second, they are also popular enough to obtain sufficient search volume of keywords related to the areas. Kenrokuen Park, one of the most famous gardens in Japan, is located in Kanazawa City as well and was added to the survey area to see the difference of trends in population change from those at the hot springs.

This research also uses Google Trends, which is a website provided by Google which indicates the search volume of specific keywords in Google Search over time and analyzes the popularity of top search queries across various regions and languages. The trends in the keyword search volume are expected to suggest tourists' behaviors and routes. Their various interests might influence their keyword search before or during the travel and ultimately emerge as some kind of trend in a specific keyword's search volume.

Fig. 1. Survey areas

Table 1. The cross-correlation coefficients between the transition of the population at Kenrokuen and the keyword search volume (N=55)

		Kenrokuen	Kanazawa Tourism	Kanazawa Station	Higashi chayagai	21st CMCA	Omicho Market
The same week	correlation coefficient	.265	-.023	.168	.143	**.403****	.039
	significance probability	.051	.868	.221	.297	.002	.780
1 week later	correlation coefficient	**.366****	-.129	.230	.185	.312*	.239
	significance probability	.006	.346	.091	.180	.020	.079
2 weeks later	correlation coefficient	.236	-.249	-.005	-.081	.197	.007
	significance probability	.082	.067	.974	.565	.150	.959
1 week before	correlation coefficient	**.354****	.208	**.460****	.314*	**.474****	.188
	significance probability	.008	.128	.000	.020	.000	.169
2 weeks before	correlation coefficient	.225	.249	**.552****	**.358****	**.506****	**.346****
	significance probability	.099	.067	.000	.007	.000	.010
3 weeks before	correlation coefficient	.183	**.432****	**.495****	.266*	**.465****	.254
	significance probability	.182	.001	.000	.050	.000	.062
4 weeks before	correlation coefficient	-.040	**.355****	.318*	.177	**.375****	-.008
	significance probability	.774	.008	.018	.196	.005	.953
5 weeks before	correlation coefficient	-.163	**.401****	.261	.134	.250	-.071
	significance probability	.234	.002	.054	.329	.066	.605
6 weeks before	correlation coefficient	-.081	.272*	.281*	.148	**.451****	.045
	significance probability	.556	.044	.038	.282	.001	.746

*. The correlation coefficient is significant at the 5% level. **. The correlation coefficient is significant at the 1% level.
Note: The table only includes part of the results.

4. Results

Here onwards, the paper presents an analysis by connecting the statistical population data and the keyword search volume. Then, this survey obtained search volume data for 42 keywords through Google Trends, provided by Google Inc., and attempted correlation analysis between the statistical population data and the tourism related keywords' (e.g., name of tourism site) search volume data.

It figured out that travelers do not necessarily search keywords of what they are currently enjoying but normally of what they are going to visit later.

Then, what kind of process should be done when faced with the case of the Kenrokuen? This study also attempted cross correlation analyses among them. With regard to the word Kenrokuen, its correlation coefficient rises when it comes to one week later or before (Table 1).

Table 2. The summary of the model (Kenrokuen)

Model	R	R^2	Adjusted R^2	Standard error of estimated value
Kenrokuen	.884^{a}	.782	.664	720.10244

Table 3. The analysis of the variance (Kenrokuen)

Model	Sum of squares	Degree of freedom	Average square	F value	Significance probability

Kenrokuen	Regression	65161023.47	19	3429527.551	6.614	.000[b]
	Residual error	18149163.51	35	518547.529		
	Total	83310186.98	54			

Table 4. The factors of the model (Kenrokuen)

Model		Non-standardization factor		Standardization factor	t value	Significance probability
		B	Standard error	β		
Kenrokuen	(constant)	9720.875	1740.55		5.585	0
	Kenrokuen (+1)	8.908	9.094	0.1	0.98	0.334
	Kanazawa Tourism (-3)	9.094	15.01	0.096	0.606	0.549
	Kanazawa Station (-2)	27.271	25.828	0.193	1.056	0.298
	Higashichayagai (-2)	-2.773	11.5	-0.032	-0.241	0.811
	21st CMCA (-2)	-2.35	12.498	-0.029	-0.188	0.852
	Omicho (-2)	0.731	12.365	0.009	0.059	0.953
	Kazuemachi (+2)	-15.87	5.335	-0.275	-2.974	0.005
	Yuwaku (-6)	16.655	7.329	0.238	2.273	0.029
	ToshiieMaeda (-6)	14.418	8.88	0.178	1.624	0.113
	Wakura (-3)	-2.986	11.76	-0.03	-0.254	0.801
	Wajima Market (-1)	11.086	9.627	0.14	1.152	0.257
	Notojima (-6)	-16.375	12.104	-0.227	-1.353	0.185
	Chirihama (-3)	-13.94	11.129	-0.239	-1.253	0.219
	Suzu (-6)	21.253	11.699	0.259	1.817	0.078
	Komatsu Airport (-3)	-8.343	13.956	-0.078	-0.598	0.554
	Fukui Station (-1)	20.786	11.77	0.187	1.766	0.086
	Tojinbo (-3)	17.45	14.145	0.192	1.234	0.226
	Toyama Station (-6)	14.146	15.776	0.118	0.897	0.376
	Unazuki (-3)	22.361	9.794	0.289	2.283	0.029

Note: A dependent variable is population at Kenrokuen Park. "+1" means "1 week later," while "-1" stands for "1 week before."

Table 5. The cross-correlation coefficients between the transition of the population at Kenrokuen and search volume in each period for the keyword Kenrokuen (N=55)

		The same time	1 week before	1 week later	Average (previous 2weeks)	Average (successive 2weeks)	Average (3weeks)
Kenrokuen (population)	correlation coefficient	.265	.354**	.366**	.356**	.361**	.426**
	significance probability	.051	.008	.006	.008	.007	.001

**. The correlation coefficient is significant at the 1% level.

As for other keywords, Kanazawa Tourism showed higher correlation three to five weeks before, and Kanazawa Station from one week to three weeks before as well. In this way, people search each keyword at different times. Similar findings which include negative correlations, were observed for Wakura and Yamanaka Hot Springs. However, the tendency of the correlations to become more apparent in different periods is not as distinctive as in the case of Kenrokuen.

Using the above data, the linear equation for Kenrokuen Park can be obtained. However, fewer correlation coefficients are significant at the 1% level for Kenrokuen.

Next, this study incorporates the concept of time lag, as shown in Table 1. The value of R2 is 0.782 and the adjusted R2 is 0.664 (see Tables 2, 3, and 4). Table 13 contains several keywords indicating low correlations with the population of Kenrokuen at the same time, such as "Kanazawa tourism" and "Unazuki." Those keywords showed higher correlations with the population when a different time was selected. The linear equations for Wakura and Yamanaka Hot Springs can be modified by also incorporating such keywords (see Tables 6, 7, and 8).

Table 6. The summary of the model (Wakura and Yamanaka Hot Springs)

Model	R	R^2	Adjusted R^2	Standard error of estimated value
Wakura	.819[a]	.671	.533	95.23022
Yamanaka	.765[a]	.586	.395	79.88023

Note: "a" is predicted value (constant).

5. Conclusion

This study demonstrated an analysis by connecting the statistical population data and keyword search volume.

The various interests of the tourists influence their keyword search before or during travel and ultimately emerge as some kind of trend in a specific keyword's search volume. This study also attempted cross correlation analyses among them. As a result, a linear equation could be derived. These findings could lead to a model to forecast tourism demand in a destination.

Table 7. The analysis of the variance (Wakura and Yamanaka Hot Springs)

Model		Sum of squares	Degree of freedom	Average square	F value	Significance probability
Wakura	Regression	704171.774	16	44010.736	4.853	.000[b]
	Residual error	344614.226	38	9068.795		
	Total	1048786.000	54			
Yamanaka	Regression	333845.316	17	19637.960	3.078	.002[b]
	Residual error	236091.521	37	6380.852		
	Total	569936.836	54			

Note: "b" is predicted value (constant).

Table 8. The factors of the model (Wakura Hot Springs)

Model		Non-standardization factor		Standardization factor	t value	Significance probability
		B	Standard error	β		
Wakura	(constant)	1164.225	297.384		3.915	.000
	PopulationYamanaka	.236	.184	.174	1.284	.207
	Kenrokuen	-.537	1.365	-.054	-.393	.696
	KanazawaStation	.029	3.154	.002	.009	.993
	Higashichayagai	1.921	1.504	.198	1.277	.209
	Korinbo	1.460	1.466	.124	.996	.326
	Omicho	1.060	1.969	.110	.538	.593
	WakuraStation	.551	.874	.074	.630	.532
	Yamanaka	-.202	1.580	-.019	-.128	.899
	Yamashiro	1.592	1.613	.127	.987	.330
	Kaga	-2.005	1.049	-.232	-1.910	.064
	KagaStation	-.559	1.455	-.049	-.384	.703
	Awazu	.945	.909	.123	1.039	.306
	Gokayama	-.149	1.382	-.017	-.108	.915
	Shirakawago	.124	1.444	.014	.086	.932
	Eiheiji	2.636	1.776	.211	1.484	.146
	Tateyama	-1.322	.819	-.227	-1.615	.115

Note: A dependent variable is the population at Wakura Hot Springs.

Table 9. The factors of the model (Yamanaka Hot Springs)

Model		Non-standardization factor		Standardization factor	t value	Significance probability
		B	Standard error	β		
Yamanaka	(constant)	624.041	242.581		2.573	.014
	PopulationWakura	.239	.127	.325	1.885	.067
	Kenrokuen	-.107	1.284	-.015	-.083	.934
	KanazawaTourism	1.229	1.876	.151	.655	.516
	KanazawaStation	-.610	3.006	-.050	-.203	.840
	Higashichayagai	.357	1.384	.050	.258	.798
	Korinbo	-1.035	1.293	-.119	-.800	.429
	Omicho	.999	1.717	.141	.582	.564
	Itaru	.590	.830	.095	.711	.482
	Yamanaka	.009	1.211	.001	.007	.994

Katayamazu	-.147	1.252	-.019	-.118	.907
KagaStation	.691	1.240	.083	.557	.581
Awazu	-.925	.818	-.163	-1.130	.266
HokurikuShinkansen	1.858	1.104	.241	1.683	.101
Gokayama	.818	.998	.130	.819	.418
FukuiStation	-.561	1.702	-.061	-.330	.744
Eiheiji	3.258	1.547	.355	2.107	.042
Awara	-.099	1.427	-.012	-.069	.945

Note: A dependent variable is the population at Yamanaka Hot Springs.

The linear equations illustrated above can be made more accurate by incorporating the average. For example, that of Kenrokuen used the keyword search volume in one week after the transition of the population regarding the word "Kenrokuen" and the correlation coefficient was 0.366 (Table 5). Taking the average volume of the three weeks (previous, present, and successive), the correlation coefficient would be slightly higher (0.426).

Of course, these equations still have room to be made more reliable by adopting several other factors such as the population of the same week in the previous year. Further search for better factors would be a future challenge of this study as well as attempting the same approach in different areas. In addition, building linear equations by tourists' characteristic such as gender, age, and residence should also be considered since the Mobile Kukan Toukei can examine them.

6. References

[1] Ayanso, A., and Karimi, A. (2015). The moderating effects of keyword competition on the determinants of ad position in sponsored search advertising, Decision Support Systems, Vol. 70, 42-59.

[2] Ahas, R., Aasa, A., Roose, A., Mark, Ü., and Silm, S. (2008). Evaluating passive mobile positioning data for tourism surveys: An Estonian case study. Tourism Management, Vol. 29, No. 3, 469-485.

[3] Gao, H., and Liu, F. (2013). Estimating freeway traffic measures from mobile phone location data. European Journal of Operational Research, Vol. 229, No. 1, 252-260.

[4] Japan Tourism Agency. (2014). Keitaidenwa kara erareru ichijouhou tou wo katuyousita hounichi gaikokujin doutaichousa houkokusho [Foreign visitors' dynamics research report utilizing mobile phone location information]. Retrieved September 28, 2018, from http://www.mlit.go.jp/common/001080545.pdf

[5] Liu, F., Janssens, D., Wets, G., and Cools, M. (2013). Annotating mobile phone location data with activity purposes using machine learning algorithms. Expert Systems with Applications, Vol. 40, No. 8, 3299-3311.

[6] Okinawa Prefecture Culture, Sports, and Tourism Department. (2013). Senryakuteki repeater souzou jigyou houkokusho [Report on strategic creation of repeaters]. Retrieved October 5, 2019, from http://

[7] www.pref.okinawa.jp/site/bunka-sports/kankoseisaku/kikaku/report/houkokusixyo/documents/07dairokusiyou.pdf

[8] Pan, B., and Li, X. R. (2011). The Long Tail of Destination Image and Online Marketing, Annals of Tourism Research, Vol. 38 (1) , 132-152.

[9] Pan, B., Litvin, S. W., and O'Donnell, T. E. (2007). Understanding accommodation search query formulation: The first step in putting 'heads in beds', Journal of Vacation Marketing, Vol. 13, 371–381.

[10] Sheldon, P, J. (1997). Tourism Information Technology. CABI Publishing, 1-3.

[11] Steenbruggen, J., Tranos, E., and Nijkamp, P. (2015). Data from mobile phone operators: A tool for smarter cities? Telecommunications Policy, Vol. 39, No. 3-4, 335-346.

[12] Xiang, Z., and Gretzel, U. (2010). Role of Social Media in Online Travel Information Search Original, Tourism Management, Vol. 31 (2) , 179-188.

[13] Xiang, Z., and Pan, B. (2011). Travel Queries on Cities in the United States: Implications for Search Engine Marketing for Tourist Destinations, Tourism Management, Vol. 32 (1): 88-97.

[14] Yamamoto, M. (2019). Furthering Big Data Utilization in Tourism. In F. García Márquez, & B. Lev (Eds.) Data Science and Digital Business. Springer, pp-157-171.

Golf Chipping Analysis Using a Feed-Forward Neural Network

CHOI Jungyeon[1,2], NG Hui Ru[3,*], YOUN Jong-Hoon[3]

[1]Department of Computer Science and Statistics,
[2]Institute of Well-Aging Medicare & CSU G-LAMP Project Group, Chosun University, Gwangju, Republic of Korea,
jchoi@chosun.ac.kr,
[3]Department of Computer Science, University of Nebraska at Omaha, Omaha, NE, USA, *hng88.ru@gmail.com,
jyoun@unomaha.edu

Keywords: Wearable Sensor, Machine Learning, Deep Learning, Golf Chip Shot, Feed-Forward Neural Network

Abstract - Wearable technology has become increasingly prominent in sports analytics, enabling cost-effective and portable approaches to performance assessment. This study investigated the feasibility of using a single accelerometer sensor attached to a pitching wedge to classify golf chip shots as Good or Bad from a 25-yard distance. Eight participants, each with a unique handicap, performed 20 shots; a total of 160 shots were recorded. Linear acceleration data were collected at 100 Hz, clipped for each swing, and used to extract 16 features indicative of backswing, strike, and follow-through phases. Four machine learning algorithms (Random Forest, Logistic Regression, Decision Tree, and K-Nearest Neighbors) and a feed-forward neural network (FFNN) were trained and optimized with Python's scikit-learn and Tensorflow, respectively. The FFNN, along with the best-performing traditional models, demonstrated relatively high classification accuracy. These findings underscore the potential for a compact, single-sensor system to provide effective shot evaluation. Future work will include larger and more diverse participant groups in real golfing conditions, aiming to improve model generalizability and facilitate real-time feedback for golf chipping.

1. Introduction

Wearable technology has undergone rapid expansion, and its application in the analysis of athletic movements is increasingly prevalent. By employing wearable sensors, it becomes possible to detect sport-specific motions in both individual and team settings. Integrating these sensors into sports analytics can help streamline coaching and feedback [1]. The primary advantages of wearable sensors in performance analysis lie in their affordability and compact design, allowing them to be positioned in multiple locations.

Golf provides an illustrative example of a sport that demands proficiency in a variety of skills, including driving, chipping, and putting. The traditional systems used to evaluate golf swings have been costly and cumbersome, often involving numerous sensors affixed to different parts of the body in combination with multiple cameras, such as the Golf 3DMA system. Recent investigations, however, have concentrated on using sensors attached to the club or the golfer to more precisely evaluate golf swings. For instance, Huang et al. [2] positioned a sensor on a club to study its trajectory and velocity near the point of impact, concluding that Euler angles could gauge the swing's consistency and stability. Similarly, Ghasemzadeh et al. [3] utilized sensors across the golfer's body and on the club to determine swing quality based on wrist rotation angles. Grober [4] further investigated club and hand acceleration to interpret the tempo, rhythm, timing, and torques constituting a complete golf swing.

Moreover, multiple studies have sought to identify the most effective way to differentiate between various skill levels in golf. Mitsui et al. [5] reported that beginner and experienced golfers exhibit distinct Y-axis acceleration patterns in the left wrist. In parallel, Lai et al. [6] evaluated how novice and advanced swings vary by using sensors on the lead hand, swing lead arm, pelvis, and upper trunk. Their findings showed that the skilled group displayed lower standard deviation in measurements than the beginner group, a reasonable outcome given that skilled golfers generally exhibit more consistency across multiple attempts [6].

This paper examines the unique features of both good and bad chip shots, aiming to optimize coaching and feedback for golfers. Specifically, we propose an analysis model for good and bad chip shots by attaching an accelerometer sensor to the club. To distinguish the characteristics of good and bad performances, we use machine learning and deep learning techniques to analyze acceleration and deceleration profiles. The implementation of wearable sensors that are both cost-effective and portable in the assessment of golf swings holds considerable promise for assisting golfers in refining and enhancing their technique.

2. Methods

2.1. Data collection

Eight participants—two women and six men—took part in this study. Their ages ranged from 42 to 57 years, with golf handicaps of 4 to 22. A Mbient sensor (MetaMotionR, Mbient Lab, San Francisco, CA, USA) was positioned on the pitching wedge's shaft just above the club head, and the accelerometer data were collected at 100 Hz.

A distance of 25 yards was measured such that the golf ball was placed exactly 25 yards from the target. Around the target, a circle with a 10-foot radius marked the designated "good-shot" zone. Each participant performed

20 shots from this 25-yard distance. Figure 1 illustrates both the sensor's placement on the club head and the overall testing arrangement. Shot outcomes were categorized as follows: G (good) if the golf ball landed on or in the designated target area, and B (bad) if the ball landed outside that area.

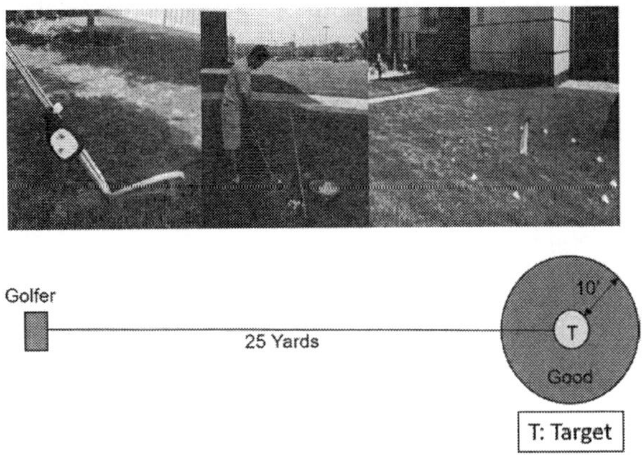

Figure 1. Sensor placement and experimental setup

2.2. Data pre-processing and feature selection

The Mbient sensor collected linear acceleration data for each shot, providing x, y, and z-axis measurements for every chip. The x-axis captures the vertical movement of the pitching wedge—essentially the action of lifting the club off the ground. The y-axis registers horizontal movement, encompassing any wobble during the swing, while the z-axis corresponds to backward and forward motion. For data analysis, the raw acceleration data were clipped from the start to the end of the golf swing, enabling a focused examination of acceleration and deceleration characteristics in each phase.

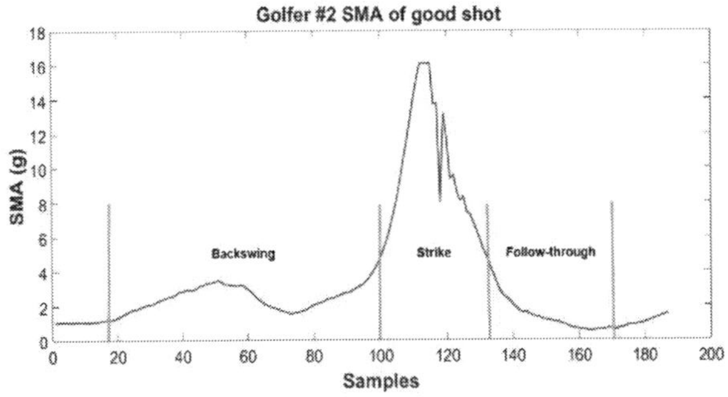

Figure 2. A sample of swing phases for a good shot

As shown in Figure 2, each swing comprised the backswing, strike, and follow-through phases, with a pronounced spike indicating the moment the ball was struck. The clipped acceleration data were subsequently used to calculate the signal magnitude area (SMA) [7], thereby distinguishing the backswing, strike, and follow-through phases. All 20 shots from the 25-yard distance were labeled as G (Good) or B (Bad) to facilitate machine learning-based analyses of swing patterns, yielding a dataset of 100 Good shots and 60 Bad shots. From the raw ball-strike signals, 16 features were extracted for each clipped portion as shown in Table 1. These features were normalized to a zero mean and scaled to unit variance.

Prior to training the machine learning models, we applied L1-regularized logistic regression to select a subset of relevant features for the 25-yard datasets separately. This method was chosen because it is known to be able to simplify models and improve prediction metrics. L1 regularization, uses a penalty term to penalize the absolute sum of the coefficients to produce sparse models. It addresses highly correlated features by keeping the coefficient of one feature and shrinking the rest to zero [8]. For our feed-forward neural network (FFNN) model, instead of conducting a separate feature selection procedure, we used L1 regularization within the FFNN training process to achieve a similar effect. L1 regularization encourages sparsity in the weights, which effectively excludes non-informative features. Thus, we trained the network on the entire feature set without an explicit feature selection stage.

Table 1. Description of Features

Feature	Description
L_mean	Mean value of lateral accelerations at ball strike
V_mean	Mean value of vertical accelerations at ball strike
A_mean	Mean value of anterior accelerations at ball strike
L_std	Standard deviation of lateral accelerations at ball strike
V_std	Standard deviation of vertical accelerations at ball strike
A_std	Standard deviation of anterior accelerations at ball strike
Mean_angle_VA	Mean angle between vertical and anterior directions
Mean_angle_VL	Mean angle between vertical and lateral directions
Mean_angle_AL	Mean angle between anterior and lateral directions
L_max	Maximum value of lateral accelerations at ball strike
V_max	Maximum value of vertical accelerations at ball strike
A_max	Maximum value of anterior accelerations at ball strike
L_mode	Most frequent value of lateral accelerations at ball strike
V_mode	Most frequent value of vertical accelerations at ball strike
A_mode	Most frequent value of anterior accelerations at ball strike
SMA	Signal vector magnitude area

2.3. Golf Chipping Analysis Models

In this study, four conventional machine learning algorithms and a feed-forward neural network (FFNN) were assessed for their performance in classifying chip shots as Good or Bad. The machine learning algorithms evaluated included Random Forest (RF), Logistic Regression (LR), Decision Tree (DT), and K-Nearest Neighbors (KNN), all of which are well-established for supervised binary classification. Each model was implemented in Python's scikit-learn module [9], and its parameters were optimized before evaluation.

The FFNN was constructed and evaluated using the Tensorflow module [13]. We employed a FFNN with two hidden layers to classify golf chip shots. The network accepts a 16-dimensional input vector, which is the number of extracted features. Each hidden layer consists of 16 units with a rectified linear unit (ReLU) activation function and an L1 penalty term $\lambda = 0.01$. The final output layer is a single neuron with a sigmoid activation, yielding a predicted probability of the input belonging to the "good" class. The network is trained using the Adam opshown in Table 1timizer, a binary cross-entropy loss function and a batch size of 8 to ensure stable convergence. We employed an early stopping strategy to prevent overfitting and reduce computational overhead. Specifically, we monitor the validation loss at each epoch and halt training if no improvement is observed for 10 consecutive epochs. This ensures that we capture the best-performing model based on validation metrics once the model has converged. This configuration effectively captures key patterns in the data while minimizing overfitting, making it well-suited for the relatively small (16-feature) input space in this application.

Given the slight class imbalance, the machine learners and neural network were evaluated using AUC metric, which is the area under the receiver operating characteristics (ROC) curve, as it remains robust to skewed data [11]. The AUC is a useful measure for binary classifier performance that summarizes the ROC curve into a single value between 0 and 1 where 1 is the perfect score.

We used a stratified 5-fold cross-validation (CV) to evaluate the performance of each model [12]. Stratified CV ensures that class distribution in each fold matches the original distribution of the datasets. The CV process was repeated 5 times to reduce bias attributed to random selection. The validation performance metrics were averaged to obtain the final results for comparison.

3. Results

The L1-regularized logistic regression method identified a subset of 12 features for the 25-yard dataset. Across all classifiers, using only these 12 features produced results comparable to those obtained from the complete feature set. The selected features used to train the classifiers are: *L_mean, V_mean, A_mean, L_std, Mean_angle_VA, Mean_angle_VL, Mean_angle_AL, V_max, L_mode, V_mode, A_mode and SMA.*

Table 2. The average AUCs for each model

Model	AUC
RF	0.81
LR	0.82
DT	0.80
KNN	0.78
FFNN	0.85

Table 2 reports the classification results for each model trained with optimized parameters. All classifiers—except for KNN—exceeded an AUC of 80%, with the FFNN achieving the highest score at 85%. For completeness, Figure 3 presents the validation ROC curve from a single iteration of the repeated 5-fold CV for FFNN training with performance closest to the highest average AUC, achieving an area under the curve of 86%.

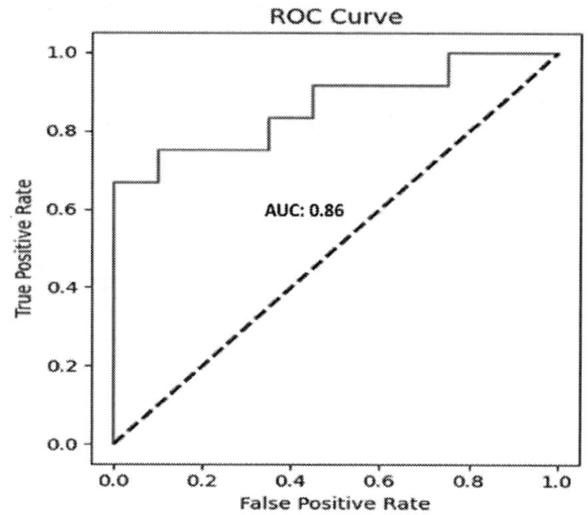

Figure 3. The ROC curve of one of the repeated 5-fold cross-validation iterations

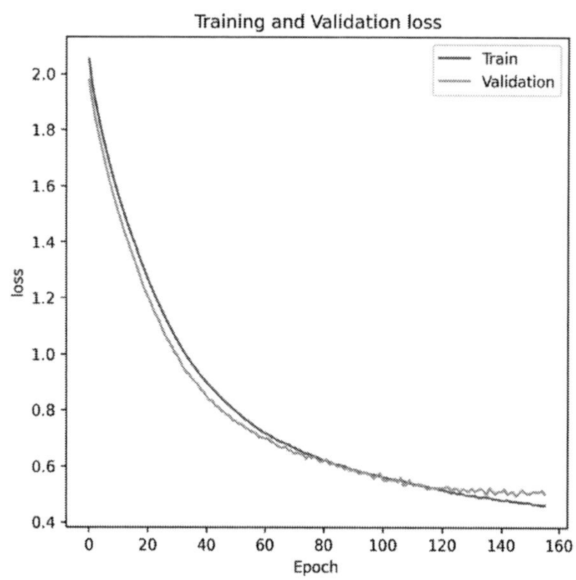

Figure 4. Training progress of one of the repeated 5-fold cross-validation iterations

Figures 4 and 5 illustrate the training progress of one of the repeated 5-fold cross-validation iterations. Throughout training, the validation loss decreased gradually, while the validation AUC stabilized—an indication that the model had converged. With the early-stopping mechanism, the training was halted at epoch 156 when the validation loss failed to improve after 10 consecutive epochs, thus mitigating overfitting. The small gaps observed between the training and validation curves across both figures suggest the L1 regularization effectively prevented overfitting.

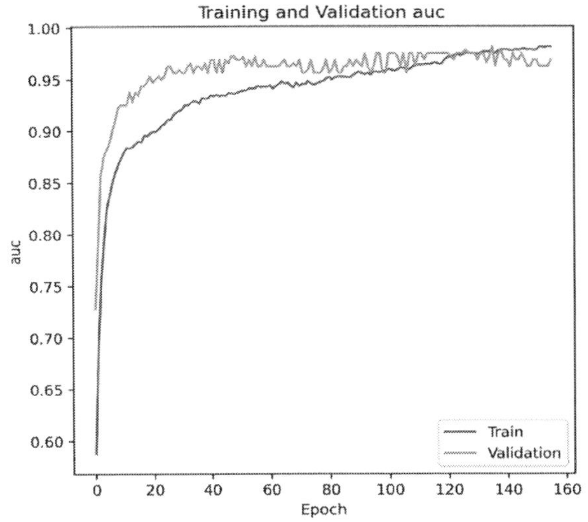

Figure 5. Training and validation AUC at each epoch for one of the repeated 5-fold cross-validation iterations

4. Discussion and Conclusions

In this study, we introduced and validated a FFNN for analyzing golf chipping shots using a single sensor affixed to the clubhead, benchmarking its performance against conventional machine learning methods. The results indicated relatively high accuracy in classifying chip shots as Good or Bad at 25-yard distances, thereby demonstrating the feasibility and utility of machine learning approaches applied to accelerometer data. Following proper training, this system could offer golfers real-time feedback for each shot without requiring a specialized chipping training setup. Moreover, the set of features identified here may also apply to other golf swing analysis systems.

Despite these findings, the study has certain limitations. First, the participant group was restricted to eight individuals. Second, data collection took place in a controlled environment, which may not accurately mirror real-world golfing conditions. Consequently, future work will involve recruiting a larger and more diverse group of participants and assessing performance in genuine golfing scenarios to enhance the model's generalizability. Such advances could ultimately support the development of an automatic, real-time feedback system for golf chipping.

5. Acknowledgement

This research was partially funded by the NSF under grant number CNS-1711386, and also supported by Global-Learning & Academic research institution for Master's·PhD students, and Postdocs(LAMP) Program of the National Research Foundation of Korea(NRF) grant funded by the Ministry of Education(No. RS-2023-00285353).

6. References

[1] R. Chambers et al., "The Use of Wearable Microsensors to Quantify Sport-Specific Movements," Sports Medicine, vol. 45, no. 7, pp. 1065–1081, 2015.

[2] Y. C. Huang et al., "Calculate golf swing trajectories from IMU sensing data," Proc. of the International Conference on Parallel Processing Workshops, pp. 505–513, 2012.

[3] H. Ghasemzadeh et al., "Sport training using body sensor networks: a statistical approach to measure wrist rotation for golf swing," Proc. of the Fourth International Conference on Body Area Networks, pp. 1-8, 2009.

[4] R. D. Grober, "An Accelerometer Based Instrumentation of the Golf Club: Measurement and Signal Analysis," arXiv preprint, 2010.

[5] T. Mitsui, S. Tang, and S. Obana, "Support system for improving golf swing by using wearable sensors," 2015 8th International Conference on Mobile Computing and Ubiquitous Networking, ICMU 2015, pp. 100–101, 2015.

[6] D. T. H. Lai et al., "On the difference in swing arm kinematics between low handicap golfers and non-golfers using wireless inertial sensors," Procedia Engineering, vol. 13, pp. 219–225, 2011.

[7] M. T. Redfield et al., "Classifying Prosthetic Use via accelerometry in persons with trans-tibial amputations," Journal of rehabilitation research and development, vol. 50, no. 9, 2013.

[8] A. Y. Ng, "Feature selection, L1 vs. L2 regularization, and rotational invariance," in Proceedings of the Twenty-first International Conference on Machine Learning (ICML, p. 78), 2004.

[9] F. Pedregosa et al., "Scikit-learn: Machine learning in Python," Journal of machine Learning research, pp. 2825-2830, 2011.

[10] N. V. Chawla et al., "SMOTE: synthetic minority over-sampling technique," Journal of artificial intelligence research, vol. 16, pp. 321-357, 2002.

[11] L. A. Jeni et al., "Facing imbalanced data--recommendations for the use of performance metrics," In 2013 Humaine association conference on affective computing and intelligent interaction, pp. 245-251, 2013.

[12] H. He, and Y. Ma, "Imbalanced learning: foundations, algorithms, and applications," Wiley-IEEE Press, 2013.

[13] M. Abadi, A. Agarwal, P. Barham, E. Brevdo, Z. Chen, C. Citro, G. Corrado, A. Davis, J. Dean, M. Devin, et al., "TensorFlow: Large-Scale Machine Learning on Heterogeneous Systems," arXiv:1603.04467, 2015.

Improving Methodology for Calculating Automotive Industry Localization Rates

ZAYTSEV, Dmitry,[1] KUSKOVA, Valentina V.[2]

[1] Lucy Family Institute for Data & Society, University of Notre Dame, Notre Dame, IN, USA, dzaytsev@nd.edu
[2] Lucy Family Institute for Data & Society, University of Notre Dame, Notre Dame, IN, USA, vkuskova@nd.edu

Keywords: Localization, automotive industry, inter-industry balances method

Abstract - The automotive industry, due to the volume and complexity of its products, has a serious impact on the most diverse areas of the country's economy, being tightly integrated with most industrial sectors. One of the key factors in evaluating the industry's impact is the localization rate of production of finished goods and their components. The goal of this paper is to evaluate the methodology of calculating the localization rate of an automotive industry, using the country of Russia as an example, demonstrate the calculation of the localization rate of the automotive industry as a whole and its passenger car segment; and demonstrate the new approach for calculating the localization rate of key industries for the passenger car segment of the automotive industry based on the method of interindustry balances.

1. Introduction

Global motor-vehicle production epitomizes the tensions and opportunities that arise when manufacturing is embedded in extended, trans-national supply networks [1]. On the one hand, highly distributed sourcing enables firms to reap economies of specialization and scale; on the other, it complicates the task of determining how much value is genuinely created within a given jurisdiction. The answer matters for a broad array of stakeholders: governments use localization metrics to calibrate industrial-policy incentives and to evaluate compliance with trade agreements; assemblers and tier-one suppliers rely on them to benchmark procurement strategies; and scholars treat them as indicators of technological upgrading and developmental spill-overs [2]. Yet despite this practical salience, the literature offers no single, universally accepted technique for measuring domestic content [3]. Instead, a spectrum of methodological traditions – ranging from simple bill-of-materials audits to sophisticated multi-regional input–output decompositions – has emerged, each grounded in a distinct view of how and where economic value is generated.

The present review interrogates that spectrum with specific reference to the automotive sector, synthesizing contributions from trade economics, industrial engineering and policy analysis. By reconstructing the intellectual genealogy, data requirements, and inferential limits of four dominant approaches – cost-share accounting, investment–turnover ratios, technology-stage scorecards, and input–output modelling – it seeks to clarify the comparative advantages of each and to illuminate why recent empirical work increasingly triangulates among them. The goal is not merely taxonomic; it is to furnish researchers and policymakers with a coherent analytical framework capable of guiding the selection – or combination – of measurement strategies best suited to the question at hand.

Currently, there is no unified methodology for calculating the rate of localization of an industry. The term "localization rate" is interpreted in different ways, depending on the application and availability of data. There are several approaches to defining and calculating localization rate [4].

- Balance method. Calculations are made based on the ratio of local investment (capital expenditures) to the annual turnover (revenue) of organizations averaged over several periods.

- Product method. The localization level is calculated on the basis of the percentage of the cost of the locally-produced components in the cost of the finished product.

- Technological method. The expert community of the industry, based on objective criteria which are established by the experts themselves, determines the percentage of the various products in the value chain, where the final product as a whole can be considered localized in the territory of the country. However, this method is quite complicated to calculate, and its results are not always clear to stakeholders outside the industry expert community [4]. The difficulty lies in the fact that information about the production of individual components is not always available; the contracts that manufacturers engage in with their suppliers are trade secrets, etc. If the calculations use the method of assessment (by the volume of imported components in the total volume of used components) rather than the cost method of assessment, such information is often not available outside of individual enterprises.

There are other methods for calculating localization rates, which are used less frequently. What we propose is a method based on the system of inter-industry balances, supplemented by calculations based on the product method.

To demonstrate our proposed approach, we have chosen an automotive industry, which offers a particularly revealing context for calculating localization rate because of its extensive integration across multiple industrial sectors, the complexity of its supply chain, and the sheer volume of its products. Automobiles rely on an intricate network of components produced by a variety of manufacturers, which means that understanding the degree to which those components are sourced domestically has broad implications for evaluating the overall health and self-sufficiency of the national economy. Furthermore, the automotive sector is an ideal laboratory for refining these localization rate calculations because its domestic impact stretches beyond the immediate manufacture of vehicles.

It draws on raw materials such as steel, textiles, and rubber, as well as services like warehousing, transportation, and various business operations. As a result, calculating the localization rate for automotive production can reveal how deep domestic supply chains run across multiple sectors of the economy. This makes the automotive industry's localization rate numbers highly significant when policymakers want to gauge how effectively local production capabilities are being developed and how much foreign dependence remains. Finally, automotive industry is considered one of the most standardized industries in terms of localization rate requirements [5].

The empirical measurement of domestic value creation in the automotive sector has evolved along four principal methodological lines, each resting on distinct theoretical premises and data sources. Early work conceptualized localization as a simple cost share derived from the manufacturer's bill of materials. Under the American Automobile Labelling Act (AALA) a vehicle's window sticker must display the percentage of U.S.–Canadian parts content; the proportion is obtained by dividing the customs value of imported components by the ex-works price of the vehicle and subtracting that ratio from one [6]. A closely related framework is embedded in international trade agreements. Annex 4-B of the United States-Mexico-Canada Agreement (USMCA) stipulates a regional-value-content threshold of 62.5 percent for passenger cars when calculated by the net-cost formula, or 72.5 percent when the transaction-value option is elected [7]. These cost-share approaches are tractable because they rely on data that are already collected for tariff assessment, yet they systematically overstate domestic value when first-tier suppliers themselves source intermediate inputs from abroad.

Recognizing that physical purchases capture only one dimension of embedded knowledge and capital, a second body of literature turns to investment–turnover ratios as an indicator of "stickiness" of production. One study [4] proposes an import-substitution efficiency index that juxtaposes cumulative domestic capital expenditure and R&D outlays with annual revenue to infer localization trajectories across Russian manufacturing branches [4]. Multinational consulting firms have adapted similar metrics when counselling governments on whether joint ventures are meeting indigenization milestones. While the measure is appealing for policy because plant and tooling investments are durable, its timing sensitivity can confound inference: a surge of capital spending in one year depresses the indicator even if domestic sourcing remains stable.

A third stream emphasizes the technological locus of value added. Since 2019 the Russian Ministry of Industry and Trade has employed a point-based checklist that assigns up to 2,000 points to domestically executed operations ranging from metal stamping to ECU programming; eligibility for preferential procurement and credit hinges on surpassing the threshold [8]. Comparable scorecards have been piloted in Brazil and India. The expert calibration of such systems allows regulators to privilege future-oriented capabilities – battery-pack assembly or ADAS software – yet their composite weighting is often opaque and their validity difficult to replicate outside the juristic context in which they were devised.

Taken together, the literature demonstrates that no single metric can exhaustively capture the multifaceted nature of localization, especially in automotive industry. Cost-share measures are transparent but myopic, investment ratios illuminate enduring productive capacity but are temporally volatile, scorecards reward strategic technologies yet rest on contested weighting schemes, and IO models achieve completeness at the cost of real-time relevance. Contemporary scholarship is therefore converging on integrative frameworks that layer these instruments, thereby producing a more nuanced and policy-usable cartography of where, and in which industries, the value of an automobile is truly generated.

2. Product method of localization evaluation

The product method is widely used in the automotive industry and is simple enough to calculate [9]. The average annual level of localization rate of production of assemblies and units, for example, is calculated by the formula:

where V is the customs value of all car components and their parts imported by the company into a country to produce assemblies and units, and P is the total value of all assemblies and units produced in the country. Calculation is carried out according to the funds spent, i.e. in monetary terms, rather than in physical terms. The localization level is calculated by calculating the share of costs for components, materials and services of local origin in the total production costs.

At the same time there are certain discrepancies in how component P is calculated. Under the "total cost" of products manufactured on the territory of a given country there are the following understandings of cost categories [10]:

- All costs of producing a particular component. This includes all material costs, as well as labor costs, mandatory insurance premiums and fees. This is the most common cost for localization rate calculation in the automotive industry.
- Material costs, which include the cost of purchasing raw materials and supplies, as well as transportation and storage costs, the purchase of fuel, third-party services, repair and maintenance costs for production sites and residential facilities, and many other similar costs.
- Expenses for purchasing raw materials, materials, purchased semi-finished products and components for production and sale of products (goods, works, services), but not including other material costs.

3. Calculation of localization based on the "Input-Output" (Inter-industry balance) system

The product method of calculating localization is quite simple in its underlying principles and intuitive, but it seriously complicates localization schemes within the industry. This happens for several reasons. First, it does not consider the objective level of localization, i.e. whether the materials used were produced in the country. For example, if an automobile manufacturer purchases components from a supplier within the country, then this purchase is considered local in official reporting and is not included in import costs. If, however, the component was imported by the supplier, then it was accounted for as imported at the supplier level, but not at the level of the automaker. And the problem is that such a notion of "localization rate" of procurement does not accurately reflect the actual level of localization rate of production and procurement from local manufacturers.

Secondly, only the total figure of imported components in all production is known, without dividing it into costs for individual industries. Therefore, it is impossible to isolate the localization of individual industries from the total figure of localization, which can be very different. For example, according to automotive industry companies, several industries are currently 100% localized in their home country, such as warehousing and auxiliary transportation activities, some business services (rental of premises, administrative services, etc.), electricity and water supply, and others. At the same time, there are several industries where localization remains at a minimal level. As a result, the average localization rate of the entire automotive industry, calculated using the product method, does not provide an understanding of the localization of purchases in individual key industries. To calculate this indicator at the level of individual industries in which the automotive industry makes purchases, we propose to use the Input-Output tables, a method developed by W. Leontief, for which he was awarded the Nobel Prize in Economics in 1973) [11].

Input-output tables [12], or inter-industry balance sheets, contain information on all the products produced in the economy as well as the elements of value added - labor compensation and profits. These tables also contain information about the sources of final demand, such as household consumption, gross savings, exports, and government consumption. In addition, the tables contain information on imports (with negative values). The process of calculating the balance between industries is structured as follows: from each industry, the costs necessary to produce secondary products (in this case, the costs of the auto industry to produce various components from different components) are removed, which are redirected to those activities where these products are primary (for example, the value of purchased steel is transferred to the steel industry, the value of purchased leather to the textile industry, etc.). The same calculations are made for all suppliers to the automobile industry, for which imports are also removed from their activity costs. Separately for each industry, imports of primary products produced outside the country are subtracted. As a result, imports are completely removed from all stages of production in the country's economy, leaving only local production and local purchases.

Input-output tables are used for a variety of purposes, including balancing national accounts, forecasting economic development, and calculating imports [12] (and thus the level of localization rate). Based on information about the products purchased by an industry and imports by the same industry, the localization percentage of each individual industry is calculated. As a result, this approach solves the problem that arises when only the product method of measuring localization is used; this methodology makes it possible to estimate what percentage of the components used in production were produced in the local economy.

4. Data sources

For an illustrative example, we have used the country of the Russian Federation prior to 2022 – the start of Putin's war and withdrawal of many international companies from the country. The Russian Federation in the period prior to 2022 provides a particularly instructive case for calculating localization rates due to its sizable and diverse industrial landscape, significant government focus on developing domestic manufacturing, and the availability of detailed economic data. Russia's automotive industry, for instance, requires massive volumes of parts and services, which means there is a complex network of suppliers operating at different tiers of production. This level of industrial activity creates ample opportunities to track and measure the proportion of domestically sourced components and thereby derive meaningful localization rates.

Prior to 2022, the Russian government had placed a strong emphasis on policies aimed at boosting local content, not only to stimulate its own industries but also to reduce reliance on imports. This was reflected in specific regulations, incentive programs, and data monitoring initiatives, all of which encouraged manufacturers to produce domestically as much as possible. As a result, the data emerging from these efforts - both from state statistical agencies such as Rosstat and from private firms - tended to be relatively comprehensive, allowing analysts to compare different calculation methods (like product-based approaches and input-output balances) and to verify results through triangulation. Another factor that makes Russia useful as an example is the diversity of sectors and materials required for large-scale manufacturing, particularly in industries like automotive. Steel, textiles, plastics, and various services feed into vehicle production, and these inputs may originate both within and outside the country. This variety allows for clear illustrations of how localization calculations must account for secondary and tertiary suppliers, each of which may be importing some of its raw materials. Consequently, examining localization in Russia offers insights into globalized supply chains and highlights where certain segments of production are more readily substitutable by domestic equivalents than others.

The calculations use data from Rosstat and Euromonitor, as well as data from industry companies. Information on imported raw materials and supplies and detailed information on all expenditure categories for the automotive industry as a whole, as well as for its participants - the passenger car segment, the truck segment and the production of components and spare parts - are used. These expenses include expenses for imported raw materials, supplies, and purchased products, which are listed in the official reports as expenses for the purchase of raw materials, supplies, and components. Separately, there are all material costs, which include raw materials and components, as well as all costs of production activities, which include material costs.

For the localization calculations in this study, the source of the input-output tables was the Economic Cooperation Organization (OECD) database [13]. This database was preferred because the Input-Output tables are calculated for each individual year. For comparison, Rosstat releases these tables once every five years (for the period of this study it was 2011 and 2016) [14]. From the OECD database, we obtained tables of GDP and imports, Leontiev multiplier tables with and without imports, as well as a table of the percentage of imports in exports to correctly calculate the residual amount of import purchases to produce goods for domestic use. Euromonitor data for 2010-2019 were used to calculate purchases by industry. Procurement data was broken down into 133 sectors of the economy, which, for comparison with the Input-Output tables, were aggregated into 37 major industries according to OKVED-2.

5. Results

To calculate the localization of automotive industry purchases in related industries, the volume of domestic production ("domestic") was subtracted from the industry's total impact on related industries ("total"). The resulting figures were then multiplied by the import adjustment in exported products. When exporting manufactured products that contain imported components, the amounts of imports must be factored into the exports to obtain the final localization factor in each individual industry. This was done in order to estimate the real volumes of exports produced by Russian manufacturers. Otherwise, if the amounts of imports are accounted for as produced in the Russian Federation, there will be an overestimation of exports of local production and an underestimation of it for the goods that remain in the Russian economy. All calculations were made for each year for the period 2010-2019. This made it possible to consider the dynamics of the level of localization of all major industries with which the automotive industry interacts.

Product method of calculation of the localization rate was done by dividing the costs of imported components separately by each of these cost levels to account for different understandings of the term "localization. Data from individual companies that provided detailed information on purchases were used to refine the resulting calculations. It is known that some companies purchase far more locally produced components than others. The availability of this information may allow us to make the calculations more accurate, since inter-industry balance sheets allow for a fairly high level of rounding error at the level of entire industries.

To verify the calculations made, we triangulated [15] the calculations made on Euromonitor data with the data on imports provided by Rosstat, based on the product method. The automotive industry purchases in each industry obtained from the Euromonitor database were multiplied by the localization coefficients for that industry and added together to obtain the total amount of local purchases. This total was compared with Rosstat data for each year for the period 2010-2019 and separately for each automotive industry segment. The results of calculations for the passenger car industry segment are shown in Table 1. Note that the average value of the "mean absolute percentage error" ("MAPE") is 2.7% and is within the tolerance range.

Table 1. Comparison of calculations of local purchases of the passenger car segment of the automotive industry using the "Input-Output" tables, Euromonitor and Rosstat data in 2010-2019, billion rubles.

	2010	2011	2012	2013	2014	2015	2016	2017	2018	2019
Suggested method expenses, bln rubles[1]	275	365	411	432	496	430	556	650	799	845
Product-based exneses, bln rubles	279	351	401	422	482	442	563	633	833	873
Absolute deviation, %	*1.6*	*4.0*	*2.4*	*2.3*	*2.9*	*2.6*	*1.3*	*2.5*	*4.3*	*3.2*

Notes: Source: Rosstat, Euromonitor, authors' calculations

[1] Calculation of expenses according to the "Input-Output" tables and Euromonitor data

[2] Expenses according to Rosstat, product method of calculation

The data presented in Table 1 show that the absolute deviation in any one year does not exceed 5%. If we consider the average statistical deviation (without conversion to absolute values), it is equal to 0.9%. Therefore, deviations can be called arbitrary - they are not systematic and rather reflect differences in rate fluctuations, rounding calculations, etc. Therefore, both sources of information were deemed acceptable to be used in various methods of calculation.

Both methods – product and input-output – were used to calculate the localization rates. In addition, localization was calculated for related industries. Selected results are presented in Table 2, including localization of the passenger car (PC) segment and several supporting industries.

Table 2. Localization rates of Passenger Car Segment of Russian Automotive Industry using two different methods, and Localization rates of several supporting industries using IO method, 2010-2019, percentage.

	2010	2011	2012	2013	2014	2015	2016	2017	2018	2019
Localization of Passenger Car Segment, Two Different Methods										
Product method	61.3	46.8	41.1	40.2	45.4	50.8	59.4	57.4	57.9	57.7
IO method	37.2	29.8	25.7	27.8	32.3	36.6	41.7	43.7	44.5	45.3
Localization of Supporting Industries, IO Balance Method										
Rare minerals	30.6	30.3	23.4	25.9	30.7	36.2	33.5	42.8	39.6	46.8
Textiles	20.0	26.0	26.0	22.3	32.1	25.3	37.4	30.8	39.0	29.7
Lumber	33.3	34.7	24.4	26.8	30.0	38.0	44.5	48.4	47.1	46.5
Oil products	50.0	31.2	21.7	33.5	30.0	38.0	41.7	47.3	43.9	44.2
Metals	39.0	26.0	27.9	25.1	28.1	33.8	38.1	42.4	41.9	40.0
Metal[1] products	37.5	31.2	26.0	27.9	34.6	38.0	44.4	46.3	44.5	44.2
Electro-nics	28.6	26.0	16.3	22.3	25.0	27.6	32.0	35.2	34.0	33.2
Electr. Equipm.	41.7	32.1	26.0	29.8	33.3	36.2	45.2	41.5	42.6	39.4
Ware-housing	43.8	33.9	31.1	30.9	36.1	42.8	50.3	52.2	51.6	50.5

Notes: Source: Rosstat, Euromonitor, authors' calculations

[1] Metal products except motor vehicles and equipment

Comparison of the localization level calculated by the product method and the method of inter-industry balances shows to what extent the product method of calculation underestimates the level of imports in the industry. Thus, in terms of material costs, the localization of the passenger car segment by the product method was 57.7% in 2019. However, in the detailed breakdown by industry calculated for the passenger car segment by the inter-industry balance method, none of the industries, except for warehousing (50.5%), is even close to this level of localization. In all industries, the level of localization calculated by the method of inter-industry balances is lower, more often significantly.

The source of discrepancies is intuitively clear. The product method calculates the localization level based on the territory of material costs. If the components were purchased in Russia, the product method calculates the purchase as localized. However, this may not be the case if the seller of the product is not a manufacturer in Russia, but an intermediary importer. There are no such discrepancies when calculated by the method of inter-industry balances. If the goods were imported into Russia, the amount of costs is attributed to imports within the relevant industry, and when the automotive industry calculates with this industry, the supplier's share of imports is taken into account. As a result, the localization level is calculated more accurately. Therefore, the localization level of passenger car production did not decrease, as shown by the product method (from 61.3 in 2010 to 57.7 in 2019 for all production), but increased, compared to 2010, in all but oil (coke and petroleum) products. Most importantly, it shows an increase for the automotive industry.

In 2012-2013, there was indeed a decrease in the rate of localization for almost all industries, caused by the expansion of production sites and a corresponding increase in imports required to sustain this expansion. But the increase in the level of localization rates started in 2013-2014, and localization rate continued to grow.

6. Conclusion

The findings presented here highlight the importance of adopting multiple methodologies for accurately assessing localization in the automotive sector. Although the product method remains a more straightforward and intuitive tool - widely applied to evaluate localization levels for parts, components, and overall production - it has notable drawbacks that limit its ability to capture the full extent of domestic value addition. By incorporating an approach based on inter-industry balances, which considers imports across all relevant sectors and stages of the value chain, the study addresses these shortcomings and offers a more precise perspective. This refinement reveals that the initial product-method calculation, which suggested a 57.7% localization rate in the passenger car segment for 2019, is likely inflated; a more accurate weighted average of approximately 45.3% emerges once the inter-industry balance method is employed. In examining trends, it is evident that despite a brief decline from 2010 to 2012, localization in the passenger segment has grown considerably throughout the study period, with almost every linked industry showing signs of increased domestic integration.

Nevertheless, the potential for further growth in localization rates varies markedly across different economic sectors. In industries such as metal production, oil, and lumber production, limited annual production capacity may constrain immediate gains, underscoring the need for expanded capacity to foster deeper localization. By contrast, sectors like information technology, electrical equipment production, telecommunications, and textile manufacturing can enhance localization more readily, given their existing capabilities. Strengthening localization in these latter industries has the added benefit of amplifying secondary effects on value added across the economy. Taken together, these observations highlight the necessity of a nuanced, multi-method strategy that accounts for capacity constraints, sectoral differences, and complex supply chains when formulating policies and practices to advance localization in the automotive industry. The proposed method of inter-industry balances provides exactly the approach needed to account for such complexities.

7. References

[1] Hertenstein, P., 2019. Multinationals, global value chains and governance: the mechanics of power in inter-firm relations. Routledge.

[2] Flaig, D. and Stone, S.F., Localization measures: A global perspective. In Local Content Requirements (pp. 14-47). Routledge.

[3] Veloso, F.M., 2006. Understanding local content decisions: Economic analysis and an application to the automotive industry. Journal of Regional Science, 46(4), pp.747-772.

[4] Losev, A.A., Soloviev, V.I. and Sunchalin, A.M., 2017. Import substitution efficiency indicators. Russian Foreign Economic Journal, (4), pp.55-70.

[5] https://www2.deloitte.com/content/dam/Deloitte/ru/Documents/manufacturing/russian/automotive-news-october-2018-ru.pdf

[6] Klier, T.H. and Rubenstein, J.M., 2007. Whose part is it? Measuring domestic content of vehicles. Chicago Fed Letter, 243.

[7] https://ustr.gov/sites/default/files/files/agreements/FTA/USMCA/Text/04-Rules-of-Origin.pdf?utm_source=chatgpt.com

[8] Kandrashina, E.A., Ashmarina, S.I., Aleshkova, D.V. and Vorotnikova, M.V., 2020. The level of production localization of automotive industry enterprises in Russia. In SHS Web of Conferences (Vol. 73, p. 01011). EDP Sciences.

[9] Lashgari, S., Abedi, S. and Iranban, S., 2021. Dynamic System Analysis of R&D Based on Localization Capabilities in the Commercial Auto Industry. Journal of System Management, 7(1), pp.101-120.

[10] Yamashina, H. and Kubo, T., 2002. Manufacturing cost deployment. International Journal of Production Research, 40(16), pp.4077-4091.

[11] Leontief, W. ed., 1986. Input-output economics. Oxford University Press.

[12] Almon, C., 2018. Why are input-output tables important?. Studies on Russian Economic Development, 29, pp.584-587.

[13] http://www.oecd.org/sti/ind/input-outputtables.htm

[14] https://rosstat.gov.ru/central-news/document/75139

[15] Denzin, N., 2010. The fundamentals. An Introduction to Triangulation, D. Rugg, editor. UNAIDS Monitoring and Evaluation Fundamentals, Geneva, Switzerland, 12.

[16] Gravino, D., 2012. Economic and policy implications of industry interdependence: An Input-output approach. International Journal of Economics and Finance, 4(6), pp.22-31.

Ensemble SHAP-Based Feature Selection for Credit Card Fraud Detection

Huanjing Wang
Western Kentucky University
huanjing.wang@wku.edu

Qianxin Liang
Florida Atlantic University
qliang1@fau.edu

Taghi M. Khoshgoftaar
Florida Atlantic University
khoshgof@fau.edu

***Abstract*—Feature selection plays a critical role in enhancing the performance and interpretability of machine learning models, particularly in high-dimensional datasets. In this study, we introduce an ensemble SHAP-based feature selection approach that integrates SHAP value rankings produced by three distinct base learners: Decision Tree, Random Forest, and XGBoost. The ensemble method combines individual SHAP value rankings using a median approach, resulting in a more stable and reliable feature selection strategy. We evaluate the effectiveness of the proposed approach by training Random Forest classifier on various subsets of top-ranked features, as well as on the full feature set. Model performance is assessed using the Area Under the Precision-Recall Curve (AUPRC). The experiments in this study employ the Kaggle Credit Card Fraud Detection Dataset. The results demonstrate that using the top 15 features, selected by the ensemble method, achieves performance nearly equivalent to that of the full feature set, significantly reducing dimensionality with minimal loss in predictive accuracy. These findings suggest that the ensemble SHAP-based feature selection technique effectively balances model accuracy and feature efficiency. This method holds promise for applications requiring interpretable and computationally efficient models.**

Keywords: Ensemble, SHAP, Feature Selection, Credit Card Fraud Detection, Machine Learning

I. Introduction

In recent years, the rise of high-dimensional data across various domains has highlighted the need for effective feature selection methods in machine learning, especially in credit card fraud detection systems. Reducing dimensionality not only improves computational efficiency but also enhances model interpretability and generalization. However, identifying the most relevant features without sacrificing predictive performance remains a key challenge [6].

Among many feature selection techniques, SHAP (SHapley Additive exPlanations) [12] has gained considerable attention due to its strong theoretical foundation in cooperative game theory and its ability to provide consistent, model-agnostic explanations for feature contributions. Despite its usefulness in interpretability, SHAP-based feature selection often depends on the choice of the underlying learning model, which can introduce variability and bias in the ranking of feature importance through SHAP values.

To overcome this limitation, we introduce an ensemble SHAP-based feature selection method that combines feature importance rankings (SHAP values) derived from multiple base models, namely Decision Tree, Random Forest, and XGBoost. By aggregating these diverse perspectives, our ensemble method aims to produce a more robust and reliable ranking of features for downstream classification tasks.

We utilize the Kaggle Credit Card Fraud Detection Dataset [8], which contains real credit card transaction data, with features anonymized by the original dataset creators. To the best of our knowledge, this dataset is the only publicly available large data for credit card fraud analysis, with 284,807 transactions and 30 independent features; only 492 (0.172%) records are labeled fraudulent. In this study, we evaluate the effectiveness of the ensemble feature selection method by training a Random Forest classifier on feature subsets of various sizes derived from the ensemble ranking. The classifiers are evaluated using the Area Under the Precision Recall Curve (AUPRC) metric [5], [10], and we additionally perform a statistical test with a significance level of $\alpha = 1\%$ to assess the statistical significance of our results.

To the best of our knowledge, this study is the first comprehensive empirical investigation comparing the performance of ensemble of SHAP-based feature selection in the context of fraud detection and potentially other application domains in machine learning.

The remainder of the paper is organized as follows. Section II provides an overview of related work, while Section III presents detailed information about SHAP-based feature selection, ensemble method, and classifiers. Section IV describes the dataset, performance metric, cross-validation, and experimental setup. Section V presents and discusses our results. Finally, Section VI concludes the paper and outlines directions for future work.

II. Related Work

Feature selection is a fundamental step in machine learning and data mining, particularly when dealing with high-dimensional datasets [20]. It can help improve model performance, reduce overfitting, and enhance interpretability by identifying the most informative features. Recently, explainable machine learning has introduced new perspectives on feature selection through model-agnostic explanation techniques. SHAP (SHapley Additive exPlanations) has emerged as a powerful tool for interpreting model predictions.

After performing an extensive literature review on existing research utilizing SHAP values for feature selection, we observed that relatively few studies have applied SHAP-based methods across different domains. Our work offers a novel contribution to the field of credit card fraud detection by examining the performance of models trained on datasets with features selected through an ensemble SHAP-based feature selection—an angle that has received limited attention in current literature.

In their study, Liu et al. [11] utilized SHAP for, feature selection on the UCI Parkinson's disease medical dataset [17]. They combined SHAP values with four classifiers: Deep Forest (gcForest), Extreme Gradient Boosting (XGBoost), Light Gradient Boosting machine (LightGBM), and Random Forest (RF). Each classifier was used to calculate the SHAP values of individual features. To assess the effectiveness of SHAP feature selection, they compared it with three filter-based feature selection methods: F1-score, Analysis of Variance (Anova-F), and Mutual Information. The experiments were conducted with a training and testing ratio of 70:30, feature selection was applied to the training dataset. The results showed that the gcForest model based on SHAP-value feature selection achieved an impressive classification accuracy of 91.78% and an F1-score of 0.945, with 150 features selected. This performance surpassed the outcomes of other feature selection methods considered in their study. While the authors conducted SHAP-value-based feature selection exclusively on the training dataset, our study took a different approach. We applied the SHAP method to the entire dataset, and then performed cross-validation after the feature selection process.

Marcilio and Eler [13] employed the SHAP method as a feature selection technique and compared it against three widely used feature selection methods: Mutual Information, Recursive Feature Elimination, and ANOVA. The SHAP process involved utilizing XGBoost as the underlying model. They conducted experiments on five UCI datasets using the XGBoost classifier and three other UCI datasets using the XGBoost regressor. The results of their study revealed that SHAP outperformed the three commonly used methods in terms of the Area Under the Receiver Operating Characteristic Curve (AUC) metric. It is worth noting that the datasets used in Marcilio and Eler's experiments were significantly smaller in size compared to the Kaggle Credit Card Fraud Detection Dataset.

Waspada et al. [21] use the RF classifier to calculate the importance score of each feature. Features with a low importance score will be discarded. The paper lists the importance score of all features. The authors analyze several factors (dataset split ratio, the selection of top k features, the amount of fraud data on training data, and the setting of hyper-parameter values) that influence the performance of the Isolation Forest (IF) model to detect fraud on credit card transactions. Isolation Forest is a popular unsupervised outlier detection method. Their findings indicate that the best results can be obtained by setting training-testing ratio of 60:40, using the top five features ($V_{14}, V_4, V_{17}, V_{12}, V_{11}$), using only 60% of fraud data, and setting hyper-parameters with the number of trees 100, 128 sample maximum, and 0.001 contamination. The model shows impressive results obtaining precision of 80.7143%, recall of 76.3514%, F1-score of 78.4722%, AUC of 0.97371, and AUPRC of 0.759228. Waspada et al. utilized only a single importance-based feature selection method and did not incorporate any ensemble method, which we have implemented in our study.

In another study, Hancock et al. [6] proposed a flexible feature selection method that can be applied across different data labeling contexts, including no label. The approach enables the identification and ranking of feature importance independent of label availability, supporting both efficient data reduction and enhanced model interpretability.

The effectiveness of SHAP for feature selection can differ based on the choice of base model. Prior studies, including those by Lundberg et al. [12] and Wang et al. [20], have shown that different models may produce varying SHAP values for the same dataset, leading to inconsistent feature rankings. To address this challenge, we evaluate an ensemble SHAP-based feature selection strategy across different feature subset sizes, employing Random Forest as the classification model. By aggregating SHAP value rankings from multiple base learners, our approach aims to achieve a more consistent and reliable selection process, preserving high classification accuracy while effectively reducing feature dimensionality.

III. Methodology

A. SHAP-based feature selection

Shapley Additive exPlanations (SHAP), introduced by Lundberg and Lee [12], has gained significant popularity as a tool for interpreting the predictions of machine learning models. Rooted in Game Theory [18], SHAP provides a way to understand the contribution of each individual feature to a model's output. As an additive feature attribution method, SHAP is model-agnostic, meaning it can be applied to a wide variety of machine learning and deep learning models. By assigning importance scores to input features, SHAP helps to demystify how models make decisions.

In feature-selection tasks, SHAP-based methods typically follow this procedure: the dataset is split into training and test sets in an 80:20 ratio, after which a classification model (base learner) is trained. SHAP values are then computed by comparing the model's predictions with and without each feature, for every data instance. The per-instance SHAP values are averaged (often as mean absolute values) to yield one score per feature, representing its typical influence on the model. Finally, features are ranked in descending order of these mean absolute SHAP values, and the top–k most influential features are selected.

B. Ensemble feature selection

This study aims to improve the stability and reliability of selected features by employing ensemble methods that combine multiple feature rankings. The process of generating a single, unified feature ranking from multiple individual lists involves two key stages. First, diverse ranking lists are produced by applying SHAP-based feature selection using different base learners. These distinct rankings capture varied perspectives on feature importance, contributing to diversity in the ensemble.

In the second stage, the individual rankings are aggregated through a rank-ordering process. In this study, we adopt the median as the aggregation method. Specifically, each feature is assigned a final ranking score based on the median of its positions across all generated ranking lists. Once the aggregated rankings are determined, the top k features are selected for further use.

C. Classification models

In this study, credit card fraud detection models were developed using three classification algorithms: Decision Tree (DT) [1], Random Forest (RF) [14], and XGBoost [2]. All three classifiers served as base learners in the SHAP analysis, while Random Forest was selected for model evaluation. These algorithms are widely used in classification tasks due to their effectiveness and interpretability [9].

DT, RF, and XGBoost are all tree-based classifiers [9]. A Decision Tree constructs a hierarchical structure by recursively splitting the data based on the most informative features, forming a sequence of decision rules that lead to an outcome. Random Forest and XGBoost extend this concept through ensemble learning [9]. Random Forest builds multiple decision trees in parallel using the bagging technique, combining their outputs to improve predictive performance and reduce overfitting [4]. XGBoost, on the other hand, is a more sophisticated implementation of the Gradient Boosted Decision Trees (GBDT) framework, originally introduced by Friedman in 2001 [3], which builds trees sequentially to correct errors from previous iterations.

The hyperparameter settings for all models were left at their default values, except for the "tree_method" setting for XGBoost, which was set to "gpu_hist" in order to run experiments on Graphics Processing Units (GPUs).

IV. Experimental Design

A. Dataset Description

This study employed the Credit Card Fraud Detection Dataset [8], available for download on the Kaggle platform. The dataset contains anonymized credit card transactions made by European cardholders over a two-day period in September 2013. Out of 284,807 total transactions, only 492 are labeled as fraudulent, resulting in a highly imbalanced dataset with just 0.172% of transactions classified as fraud, and the remainder as legitimate.

The dataset includes 30 numerical input features. Among these, features V_1 through V_{28} are anonymized and transformed using Principal Component Analysis (PCA) to ensure confidentiality. The remaining two features, "Time" and "Amount," were not transformed. "Time" indicates the number of seconds elapsed since the first recorded transaction, while "Amount" represents the monetary value of the transaction. For this analysis, the "Amount" feature was normalized to improve comparability, whereas the "Time" feature was excluded to avoid introducing bias, as its uniqueness may lead the model to memorize specific transactions.

The target variable, labeled as "Class," indicates the transaction's legitimacy—where a value of 1 denotes a fraudulent transaction and 0 indicates a normal one.

B. Performance Metric

To evaluate the effectiveness of the proposed feature selection methods, classification models were built using the reduced datasets. These models were assessed using the Area Under the Precision-Recall Curve (AUPRC) as the primary performance metric.

In binary classification tasks, such as identifying fraudulent (positive) versus legitimate (negative) transactions, four possible prediction outcomes can occur: true positives (correctly identified fraudulent instances), false positives (legitimate instances incorrectly classified as fraudulent), true negatives (correctly identified legitimate instances) and false negatives (fraudulent instances missed by the model).

The AUPRC quantifies the area under the Precision-Recall curve, which illustrates the trade-off between precision and recall across various classification thresholds. Precision is defined as:

$$\frac{true\ positives}{true\ positives + false\ positives} \tag{1}$$

while recall (also known as the true positive rate) is given by:

$$\frac{true\ positives}{true\ positives + false\ negatives} \tag{2}$$

To compute AUPRC, the precision is plotted against the recall at multiple threshold levels and the area under this curve is calculated. Higher AUPRC values indicate better model performance. The AUPRC score ranges from 0 to 1, with 1 representing perfect precision and recall. Importantly, AUPRC provides a more sensitive evaluation of false positives, making it particularly well-suited for imbalanced classification problems like fraud detection [7].

C. Cross-Validation

Cross-validation is a method that intelligently involves the reuse of data from a single dataset. The process involves dividing the dataset into a predetermined number of subsets or folds in a relatively balanced manner. In this study, we utilized five-fold cross-validation, where one fold served as the test data, while the remaining four folds were designated as the training data. To minimize any potential bias arising from a fortuitous or unfavorable split, we conducted ten independent runs of the five-fold cross-validation. It is important to note that the feature selection procedures were performed on the original dataset.

D. Experimental Setup

In our experiments, we explored an ensemble SHAP-based feature selection technique. To evaluate its effectiveness, we built classification models using subsets of features selected by this ensemble method. All classification models were

TABLE I: Ensemble SHAP-based feature selection ordered from top to bottom

Ranking	Feature
1	V_{14}
2	V_{17}
3	V_{12}
4	V_4
5	V_1
6	V_8
7	V_{11}
8	V_{10}
9	V_{19}
10	V_7
11	V_{16}
12	V_{20}
13	V_3
14	V_{21}
15	V_{26}

developed using the Random Forest classifier. For comparison, we also reported results from models trained on the full feature set.

Initially, we ranked the features using SHAP-based methods applied to three different base learners: Decision Trees (DT), Random Forest (RF), and XGBoost. This resulted in three separate feature ranking lists. We then combined these rankings into a single ensemble ranking. From this ensemble list, we selected the top 3, 5, 7, 10, and 15 features for further analysis. Using these selected subsets, as well as the full set of features, we trained Random Forest classifiers and evaluated their performance using the Area Under the Precision-Recall Curve (AUPRC).

The experiments were conducted on a distributed computing platform with nodes equipped with 16-core Intel Xeon CPUs, 256 GB of RAM per CPU, and Nvidia V100 GPUs. All training and evaluation procedures were implemented in Python. The Python data science stack [15] was employed for experiment implementations. SHAP is publicly available as an open source library for the Python programming language [16]. In addition to the SHAP values for feature importance, this library also supplies several tools for visualizing SHAP feature importance values.

V. Results and Analysis

As previously discussed, we employed SHAP-based feature selection methods in conjunction with three base learners. We present the aggregated feature ranking derived from the ensemble of the three individual rankings, with a focus on a maximum of 15 features. Table I shows the resulting rankings, where rank 1 indicates the highest ensemble SHAP value. Notably, features V_{14}, V_{17}, and V_{12} emerged as the top three most influential features.

The classification performance results of the Random Forest models, measured by AUPRC, are presented in Table II. Each row in the table represents the number of features used. These values represent the average results across ten runs of five-fold cross-validation. For instance, the value 0.8092 on the top row indicates the performance of the Random Forest classifier on a training dataset with a feature subset size of 3. It can be observed from the table that the AUPRC score improves as the feature subset size increases. This indicates that incorporating more features tends to enhance the model's predictive performance, at least up to the full feature set (29 features). While using all 29 features gives the highest AUPRC (0.8496), using just 15 features results in a very close score (0.8464), which is only 0.0032 lower. This suggests that the top 15 features capture most of the predictive power, offering a good balance between performance and feature efficiency, which we validated using ANOVA and Tukey's HSD tests.

TABLE II: Classification Results: AUPRC

Feature Subset Size	RF
3	0.8092
5	0.8370
7	0.8377
10	0.8396
15	0.8464
29 (All)	0.8496

We performed a one-way ANOVA test to statistically examine the effects of feature subset size on the performance of the classification models in terms of AUPRC. Factor Size represents the six feature subset sizes. A significance level of $\alpha = 1\%$ was used for the statistical test. The ANOVA results are presented in Table III. The test results indicate that the performance values were not the same for all groups in the main factor in terms of the AUPRC metric since the p-values were less than the specified cutoff 0.01. Therefore, the factor size have a statistically significant effect on AUPRC scores.

TABLE III: One-way ANOVA in terms of AUPRC

	Df	Sum Sq	Mean Sq	F value	Pr(>F)
Size	5	0.010253	0.0020506	242.9	less than $2e^{-16}$
Residuals	54	0.0000456	0.0000084		

TABLE IV: Tukey's HSD Results in terms of AUPRC

Group a consists of: 15, 29
Group b consists of: 5, 7, 10
Group c consists of: 3

The ANOVA test results reveal that the factor Size had a significant impact on AUPRC scores. As a result, we conducted multiple comparison test using Tukey's Honestly Significant Difference (HSD) tests [19] to rank the feature subset size based on their impact on AUPRC scores. The performance was ranked alphabetically, with group 'a' having the highest AUPRC scores. Table IV presents the results of the HSD test conducted to compare AUPRC performance across different feature subset sizes. The feature subset sizes were grouped based on statistical similarity in their classification performance. A summary of the findings from Tables II and IV highlights the following:

- **Group a (15, 29):** This group achieved the highest AUPRC scores and is statistically significantly better than the other groups. Feature sets of size 15 and 29 yielded the most accurate models, suggesting that the top 15 features capture most of the predictive power in the data, with little gain from using all 29 features.
- **Group b (5, 7, 10):** These feature sizes performed moderately well and are not statistically different from each other. However, their performance was significantly lower than that of group a, indicating that while smaller subsets still offer decent predictive capability, they do not match the effectiveness of the top 15 or all features.
- **Group c (3):** This group represents the lowest AUPRC performance and is statistically significantly worse than both group a and group b. Using only three features resulted in a substantial drop in classification performance, highlighting the limitation of overly aggressive feature selection.

In summary, the HSD test supports the observation that increasing the number of selected features generally improves model performance. A feature size of 15 offers a strong balance between dimensionality reduction and predictive accuracy, performing nearly as well as using the full feature set.

VI. Conclusion

In this study, we propose an ensemble approach to SHAP-based feature selection by integrating SHAP-value based feature rankings from multiple base learners, including Decision Tree, Random Forest, and XGBoost. The ensemble method effectively aggregate these rankings to identify the most informative features for classification tasks.

To evaluate the impact of feature selection, we construct Random Forest classifiers using subsets of features selected from the ensemble rankings, as well as the full feature set. Our experimental results, assessed using AUPRC, demonstrate that models trained on a reduced set of top-ranked features achieve performance comparable to those using all features. Notably, the subset of the top 15 features result in an AUPRC score that is not statistically different from the full feature set, suggesting that a subset of features can maintain high predictive power while improving model interpretability and efficiency.

Overall, our findings indicate that the ensemble SHAP-based feature selection technique is a robust and effective strategy for dimensionality reduction, enabling the construction of efficient and accurate classification models. Future work may explore extending this approach to other model architectures and datasets, as well as investigating its applicability in real-world decision-support systems.

References

[1] L. Breiman, "Classification and regression trees," *Routledge*, 2017.

[2] T. Chen and C. Guestrin, "Xgboost: A scalable tree boosting system," *Proceedings of the 22nd ACM SIGKDD International Conference on Knowledge Discovery and Data Mining - KDD '16*, 2016.

[3] J. H. Friedman, "Greedy function approximation: a gradient boosting machine," *Annals of statistics*, pp. 1189–1232, 2001.

[4] S. González, S. García, J. D. Ser, L. Rokach, and F. Herrera, "A practical tutorial on bagging and boosting based ensembles for machine learning: Algorithms, software tools, performance study, practical perspectives and opportunities," *Information Fusion*, vol. 64, pp. 205–237, December 2020.

[5] J. T. Hancock, T. M. Khoshgoftaar, and J. M. Johnson, "Evaluating classifier performance with highly imbalanced big data," *Journal of Big Data*, vol. 10, no. 42, April 2023.

[6] J. T. Hancock, T. M. Khoshgoftaar, and . Q. Liang, "A problem-agnostic approach to feature selection and analysis using shap," *Journal of Big Data*, vol. 12, no. 12, January 2025.

[7] J. T. Hancock, T. M. Khoshgoftaar, and J. M. Johnson, "A comparative approach to threshold optimization for classifying imbalanced data," in *The International Conference on Collaboration and Internet Computing (CIC)*. IEEE, 2022.

[8] Kaggle, "Credit card fraud detection," *https://www.kaggle.com/mlg-ulb/creditcardfraud*, 2018.

[9] J. S. Kushwah, A. Kumar, S. Patel, R. Soni, A. Gawande, and S. Gupta, "Comparative study of regressor and classifier with decision tree using modern tools," *Materials Today: Proceedings*, vol. 56, no. 6, pp. 3571–2576, 2022.

[10] J. L. Leevy, T. M. Khoshgoftaar, and J. T. Hancock, "Evaluating performance metrics for credit card fraud classification," in *2022 IEEE 34th International Conference on Tools with Artificial Intelligence (ICTAI)*, 2022, pp. 1336–1341.

[11] Y. Liu, Z. Liu, X. Luo, and H. Zhao, "Diagnosis of parkinson's disease based on shap value feature selection," *Biocybernetics and Biomedical Engineering*, vol. 42, no. 3, pp. 856–869, July-September 2022.

[12] S. M. Lundberg and S.-I. Lee, "A unified approach to interpreting model predictions," *Advances in neural information processing systems*, vol. 30, 2017.

[13] W. E. Marcilio and D. M. Eler, "From explanations to feature selection: assessing shap values as feature selection mechanism," in *2020 33rd SIBGRAPI Conference on Graphics, Patterns and Images (SIBGRAPI)*, Los Alamitos, CA, USA, nov 2020, pp. 340–347.

[14] A. Muaz, M. Jayabalan, and V. Thiruchelvam, "A comparison of data sampling techniques for credit card fraud detection," *International Journal of Advanced Computer Science and Applications (IJACSA)*, vol. 11, no. 6, pp. 477–485, 2020.

[15] T. Oliphant, "Python for scientific computing," *Computing in Science & Engineering*, vol. 9, no. 3, pp. 10–20, 2007.

[16] S. Lundberg and others, "shap," https://github.com/slundberg/shap/tree/v0.41.0, accessed: 2023-07-09.

[17] C. O. Sakar, G. Serbes, A. Gunduz, H. Tunc, H. Nizam, B. Sakar, M. Tütüncu, T. Aydin, M. Isenkul, and H. Apaydin, "A comparative analysis of speech signal processing algorithms for parkinson's disease classification and the use of the tunable q-factor wavelet transform," *Applied Soft Computing*, vol. 74, pp. 255–263, January 2019.

[18] L. Shapley, "A value for n-person games," *Contributions to the Theory of Games*, pp. 307–317, 1953.

[19] J. W. Tukey, "Comparing individual means in the analysis of variance," *Biometrics*, pp. 99–114, 1949.

[20] H. Wang, Q. Liang, J. T. Hancock, and T. M. Khoshgoftaar, "Feature selection strategies: A comparative analysis of shap-value and importance-based methods," *Journal of Big Data*, vol. 11, no. 44, March 2024.

[21] I. Waspada, N. Bahtiar, P. W. Wirawan, and B. D. A. Awa, "Performance analysis of isolation forest algorithm in fraud detection of credit card transactions," *Khazanah Informatika Jurnal*, October 2022.

An Evaluation of CNN and Vision Transformer Models for Mars Surface Image Classification

Kehan Gao and Sarah Tasneem
Eastern Connecticut State University
Willimantic, Connecticut 06226
gaok@easternct.edu, tasneems@easternct.edu

Taghi M. Khoshgoftaar
Florida Atlantic University
Boca Raton, Florida 33431
khoshgof@fau.edu

Abstract—**This paper examines the effectiveness of three Convolutional Neural Network (CNN) architectures (InceptionNet, DenseNet, and EfficientNet) and a Vision Transformer (ViT) model in classifying Mars surface images, with a particular focus on their performance under varying degrees of class imbalance. Using NASA's HiRISE imagery, we evaluate model robustness under two scenarios: one with severe imbalance across six terrain categories and another with moderate imbalance across four. While CNNs capture spatial hierarchies, ViTs treat images as sequences of patches and leverage self-attention, offering a contrasting approach to handling imbalanced planetary datasets. Experimental results demonstrate that all models perform well under moderate imbalance. However, a clear decline in classification performance is observed as imbalance becomes more severe. Among the models, the ViT consistently demonstrates greater robustness compared to the CNN architectures, achieving higher F1-scores and accuracy, particularly in the severely imbalanced setting. These findings highlight the potential of transformer-based models in addressing challenges posed by imbalanced datasets in image classification tasks.**

Index Terms—**Convolutional Neural Networks (CNNs), InceptionNet, DenseNet, EfficientNet, Vision Transformer (ViT), Image Classification, Class Imbalance**

I. Introduction

Deep learning has significantly enhanced image classification capabilities, particularly through the use of Convolutional Neural Networks (CNNs) and, more recently, Vision Transformer (ViT) models. CNNs have long been the standard architecture for image-related tasks due to their ability to effectively capture spatial hierarchies in images. In contrast, ViTs, adapted from the success of transformers in natural language processing, offer a new approach by treating images as sequences of patches and leveraging self-attention mechanisms [1]. While both CNNs and ViTs have demonstrated remarkable success across a variety of domains, an ongoing challenge remains: the impact of class imbalance on model performance.

Class imbalance, referring to situations in which some categories are significantly overrepresented compared to others, can adversely affect the training of machine learning models by biasing predictions toward the dominant classes. This challenge is especially critical in specialized domains like planetary science, where data collection is limited and naturally imbalanced. Our previous research applied two basic CNNs, AlexNet and ResNet, to NASA's HiRISE landmark dataset and found that ResNet outperformed AlexNet as class imbalance increased in Mars surface images [2]. We now aim to build on this foundation by evaluating three more advanced CNN models, InceptionNet [3], DenseNet [4], and EfficientNet [5], along with a ViT model [6]. Our goal is to gain deeper insights into the robustness of these models, particularly when faced with varying degrees of class imbalance.

The Mars image datasets used in this study consist of cropped landmark images representing different surface features. Two classification scenarios are examined: one using the full six-category dataset with severe imbalance, and the other using a subset of this data without the two largest categories, providing only moderate imbalance. Performance is measured using standard metrics, such as precision, recall, F1-score, and accuracy, with a focus on evaluating how each model handles the distribution disparities across categories. Through systematic experimentation and analysis, we seek to answer two key questions: How do CNN and ViT models perform under varying degrees of class imbalance? And which architecture demonstrates greater robustness to imbalanced datasets? While we hypothesize that more balanced data should support better classification performance, it is important to note that the more balanced dataset in this study is also smaller. This introduces a tradeoff: although balancing class distributions can reduce prediction bias, reduced data volume may limit the model's ability to learn generalizable patterns. We account for this in our analysis and interpretation of the results. The insights from this study are valuable not only for developing more effective classification models for Mars imagery but also for addressing similar issues in other real-world classification tasks.

Our experimental results show that while all models perform well under moderate imbalance, classification performance declines as the imbalance becomes more severe. Among the evaluated models, the ViT demonstrates superior robustness, achieving higher F1-scores and accuracy compared to the CNN architectures, especially in the severely imbalanced setting.

The rest of the paper is organized as follows: Section II discusses the methods used, including three CNNs and a ViT. A case study is presented in Section III, where a NASA Mars image dataset is introduced and two scenarios with various class distributions are created. Their classification results, along with corresponding assessments, are presented. Finally, the conclusions and future work are summarized in Section IV.

II. METHODOLOGY

Convolutional Neural Networks (CNNs) [7] process images using convolutional, pooling, and fully connected layers to extract hierarchical features and perform classification. In contrast, Vision Transformers (ViTs) treat images as sequences of patches and use self-attention to model global relationships. The following subsections provide detailed descriptions of each model architecture.

A. InceptionNet

InceptionNet [3] introduces 1×1 convolutions to reduce dimensionality, lowering computation cost and parameter counts while preserving important features. Its core component, the Inception module, applies multiple filter sizes (1×1, 3×3, and 5×5) and max pooling in parallel to capture multi-scale features. The outputs are concatenated, enabling the network to learn which feature resolutions are most relevant to a task. This design increases depth and efficiency while balancing complexity and accuracy.

This study uses Inception-v3 [8], an improved version featuring aggressive factorization. Larger convolutions such as 5×5 are decomposed into asymmetric convolutions (e.g., 1×5 followed by 5×1), reducing parameters while maintaining performance. Inception-v3 also incorporates label smoothing to mitigate overfitting by assigning small probabilities to incorrect labels, and uses an auxiliary classifier at intermediate layers to address vanishing gradients, though this component is discarded during testing.

Instead of conventional fully connected layers, Inception-v3 adopts global average pooling to compress feature maps, resulting in a more compact model. A final softmax layer produces classification outputs. Pre-trained Inception-v3 models are widely used in transfer learning for tasks such as fine-grained image classification, medical imaging analysis, and facial recognition.

B. DenseNet

DenseNet, proposed by Huang et al. [4], introduces dense connectivity, where each layer receives input from all preceding layers by concatenating their feature maps. Formally, the output of the l-th layer is: $output_l = concat(x_1, x_2, ..., x_l)$, where x_l is the output of layer l.

Dense connections are grouped into dense blocks, which maintain constant feature map dimensions to enable concatenation. Between dense blocks, transition layers perform downsampling using 1×1 convolutions and 2×2 average pooling. After the final blocks, global average pooling reduces feature maps to a single vector, followed by a softmax layer for classification.

This architecture promotes feature reuse and mitigates overfitting, especially with limited data, while using fewer parameters. Dense connectivity improves gradient flow, addressing the vanishing gradient problem and facilitating deeper architectures. Among the variants, DenseNet-121 offers an effective balance between computational efficiency and representational capacity, with significantly fewer parameters than deeper variants like DenseNet-201, while still achieving high accuracy. This makes it a practical and suitable choice for this study.

C. EfficientNet

EfficientNet [5] introduces a compound scaling method that uniformly scales a model's depth, width, and resolution using a set of predefined coefficients. In contrast to conventional scaling, which modifies one dimension at a time, EfficientNet's balanced approach yields more efficient and higher-performing models.

The baseline EfficientNet-B0 model scales dimensions based on the formula: $d = \alpha^{\lambda}$, where α is a compound coefficient and λ is an empirically tuned exponent. This approach achieves high accuracy with fewer parameters and less computational cost.

EfficientNet is widely adopted in transfer learning for image classification, object detection, and segmentation. Its compact structure design also makes it suitable for mobile and embedded systems. The family includes models from EfficientNet-B0 to B7, with B0 optimized for speed and resource efficiency, and B7 optimized for maximum classification performance, achieving 84.3% top-1 accuracy on ImageNet with less than half the parameters of models like ResNet-152 or Inception-V4. In this study, EfficientNet-B7 was selected due to its superior accuracy and ability to handle fine-grained, imbalanced classifications, while remaining relatively efficient in parameter usage.

In addition, EfficientNet replaces traditional ReLU activation with Swish, which provides smoother gradients and improves performance in deeper networks.

D. Vision Transformer (ViT) and ViT/B-32

The Vision Transformer (ViT) [6] adapts transformer architecture, originally developed for natural language processing (NLP), to visual tasks. Rather than relying on convolutional layers, ViT divides images into fixed-size non-overlapping patches, treats each as a token, and processes them using self-attention mechanisms.

Each patch (e.g., 16×16 or 32×32 pixels) is flattened into a vector and linearly embedded. Position encodings are added to retain spatial relationships. These patch embeddings form a sequence input to a transformer model, where self-attention enables the capture of both local and global dependencies across the image.

ViT/B-32 is a specific configuration of the Vision Transformer. The "B" refers to the base model size (12 transformer blocks, 768 hidden dimensions, 12 attention heads), while "32" indicates that the image is split into 32x32 patches. This configuration offers a balance between computational efficiency and performance, making it suitable for tasks involving high-resolution images or constrained compute budgets.

ViT models have demonstrated competitive or superior performance compared to state-of-the-art CNNs like ResNet and EfficientNet, especially when trained on large-scale datasets such as ImageNet-21k or JFT-300M. Their scalability and

TABLE I
MODEL COMPLEXITY AND FEATURES COMPARISON (PRETRAINED ON IMAGENET)

Model	Parameters (notop)	Key Features
InceptionNet-v3	21.8 million	Inception blocks, auxiliary classifiers, optimized for speed and accuracy
DenseNet-121	7 million	Dense connections, fewer parameters, efficient use of features
EfficientNet-B7	63.8 million	Compound scaling, optimized for accuracy while keeping efficiency
ViT/B-32	85 million	Transformer-based architecture, attention mechanism, excels at capturing long-range dependencies

ability to learn global context from the start make them particularly effective in transfer learning, especially for downstream tasks like medical image analysis, satellite imagery classification, and fine-grained object recognition.

Table I summarizes the model complexity and architectural highlights of the four models, with parameter counts based on pretrained weights from ImageNet.

III. CASE STUDY

In this study, we applied three CNN models, InceptionNet, DenseNet, and EfficientNet, and the Vision Transformer (ViT/B-32) to the NASA Mars surface image dataset. We explored two scenarios based on different levels of class distribution (balance). Detailed information on these scenarios is provided in the subsequent sections.

A. NASA Mars Image Datasets

This study uses image data from the HiRISE (High-Resolution Imaging Science Experiment) camera aboard the Mars Reconnaissance Orbiter [9]. HiRISE captures long image strips at 30 cm/pixel resolution. Rather than labeling entire strips, the dataset focuses on "landmarks" identified using dynamic landmarking. Square crops with a 30-pixel margin are extracted around each landmark for classification. From 168 map-projected HiRISE images, 3,820 grayscale landmark images were created, each resized to 227×227 pixels. Labels include craters, bright dunes, dark dunes, dark slope streaks, and an "other" class. To handle false detections caused by triangular black image borders, an "edge" class was added. The labeled dataset is available at [10], and Figure 1 shows a sample from each category. More details can be found in [9].

TABLE II
HIRISE DATASET WITH 6 CATEGORIES

Class ID	Class name	Count	Percent
0	Other	2018	53%
1	Crater	369	10%
2	Dark dune	408	11%
3	Streak	37	1%
4	Bright dune	156	4%
6	Edge	832	22%
Total		3820	100%

B. Two Scenarios Setup

It is well known that the classification performance of machine learning algorithms often deteriorates when there is significant class imbalance in a training dataset [11]. This study aims to compare three types of CNNs and a vision transformer (ViT/B-32) across two different class imbalance scenarios in the classification of Martian image data. One scenario used the full dataset of 3,820 images. The other excluded the two largest classes ('Edge' and 'Other'), reducing the dataset to 970 images. This second scenario reduced class imbalance but introduced the challenge of having less training data, which could limit the model's ability to learn generalizable patterns. Both scenarios employed five-fold cross-validation to maximize data use. Although Scenario 2 had fewer training samples per fold, we hypothesize that the improved class balance may offset the reduced data volume, potentially leading to better overall classification performance.

TABLE III
HIRISE DATASET WITH 4 CATEGORIES

Class ID	Class name	Count	Percent
1	Crater	369	38%
2	Dark dune	408	42%
3	Streak	37	4%
4	Bright dune	156	16%
Total		970	100%

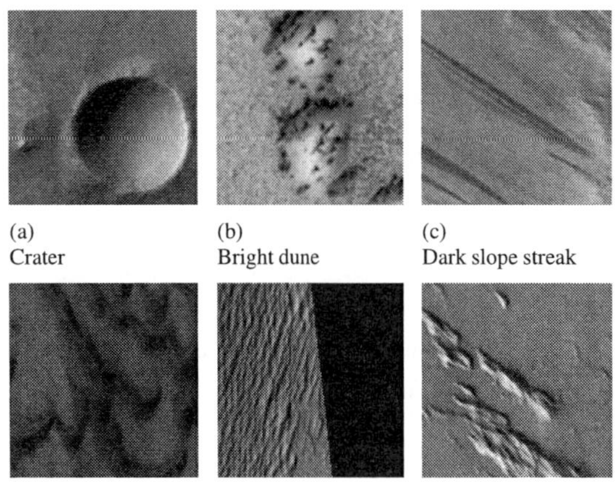

(a) Crater (b) Bright dune (c) Dark slope streak
(d) Dark dune (e) Edge (f) Other

Fig. 1. HiRISE image classes

The two datasets, along with their categories and class distributions, are shown in Tables II and III. Scenario 1 included six classes, with 'Other' comprising 53% of the dataset and 'Streak' only 1%, resulting in severe imbalance. 'Other' was 53 times larger than 'Streak.' Scenario 2 removed the two largest classes, leaving four classes. In this scenario, 'Dark dune' became the largest at 42%, while 'Streak' remained the smallest at 4%, yielding an 11-fold difference. Compared to the full dataset, Scenario 2 presented a more moderately imbalanced distribution.

TABLE IV
CLASSIFICATION PERFORMANCE FOR HIRISE SCENARIO 1

InceptionNet

Class	Precision	Recall	F1-score	Support
Bright dune	0.877	0.865	0.871	156
Crater	0.841	0.762	0.799	369
Dark dune	0.915	0.953	0.934	408
Edge	0.856	0.964	0.907	832
Other	0.942	0.904	0.923	2018
Streak	0.735	0.676	0.704	37
Overall	0.906	0.905	0.904	3820

DenseNet

Class	Precision	Recall	F1-score	Support
Bright dune	0.883	0.872	0.877	156
Crater	0.823	0.783	0.803	369
Dark dune	0.963	0.946	0.954	408
Edge	0.872	0.942	0.906	832
Other	0.932	0.919	0.925	2018
Streak	1.000	0.676	0.806	37
Overall	0.910	0.909	0.909	3820

EfficientNet

Class	Precision	Recall	F1-score	Support
Bright dune	0.820	0.904	0.860	156
Crater	0.853	0.878	0.865	369
Dark dune	0.962	0.936	0.949	408
Edge	0.866	0.959	0.910	832
Other	0.963	0.904	0.932	2018
Streak	0.630	0.919	0.747	37
Overall	0.922	0.917	0.918	3820

ViT

Class	Precision	Recall	F1-score	Support
Bright dune	0.937	0.853	0.893	156
Crater	0.914	0.864	0.889	369
Dark dune	0.939	0.983	0.960	408
Edge	0.892	0.948	0.919	832
Other	0.949	0.940	0.945	2018
Streak	1.000	0.514	0.679	37
Overall	**0.932**	**0.931**	**0.931**	3820

C. Results and Analysis

We applied the InceptionNet, DenseNet, EfficientNet, and ViT models to the two datasets, and the results are shown in Tables IV to V. These results are based on five-fold cross-validation used during the training process. Each table presents the performance of the four models, including precision, recall, and F1-score metrics for each category in the datasets. The tables also report support, which refers to the number of actual instances of each class in the dataset.

For the complete dataset (Scenario 1), ViT/B-32 demonstrated the best overall performance, with precision, recall, and F1-score of 0.932, 0.931, and 0.931, respectively, followed by EfficientNet and DenseNet. InceptionNet showed the weakest performance among the four techniques. This can also be observed in Figure 2(a), where F1-score and accuracy are displayed for the four techniques. Figure 2(b) presents the average F1-score of the four techniques across the six categories. Among these, the smallest class, 'Streak' (support = 37), had the lowest F1-score of 0.734. In contrast, 'Dark dune' achieved the highest F1-score of 0.949, despite representing only 11% of the dataset. The largest class, 'Other' (support = 2018), also performed well with an F1-score of 0.931, though it was not the highest. These results demonstrate that high performance is not strictly correlated with class size, as minority classes like 'Dark dune' can still achieve superior accuracy.

For the four-category dataset (Scenario 2), all models demonstrated excellent performance, with overall precision, recall, and F1-scores above 0.95 (see Table V). InceptionNet and DenseNet achieved the best balance of precision and recall for 'Streak,' the class with the smallest support. Figure 3(a) presents the overall F1-score and accuracy for the four techniques. Class-level performance, shown in Figure 3(b), reveals that 'Crater' and 'Dark dune,' the two largest remaining classes, were classified most accurately across all models, with F1-scores exceeding 0.96. In contrast, 'Streak' remained the most difficult class to detect. These results demonstrate the robustness of the models in moderately imbalanced settings, while also underlining the persistent difficulty in accurately detecting underrepresented classes.

Furthermore, when comparing the two scenarios with different degrees of class imbalance, all classification models performed significantly better in Scenario 2 (moderate imbalance) than in Scenario 1 (severe imbalance), indicating that the severe imbalance in Scenario 1 had a significant negative impact on all model performance. Notably, ViT showed the lowest drop in performance between the scenarios, suggesting greater robustness to class imbalance compared to the other models.

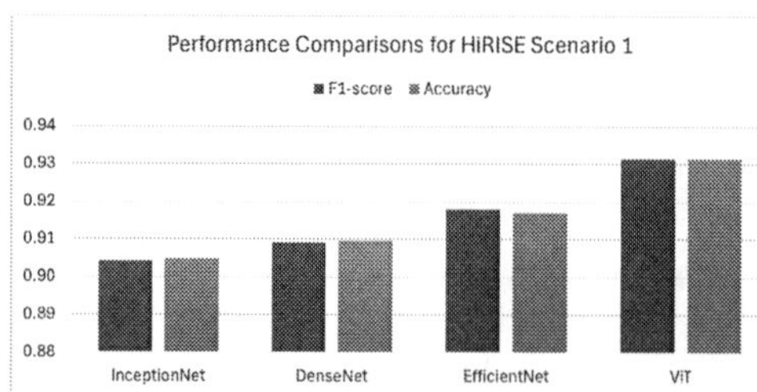

(a) F1-score and accuracy

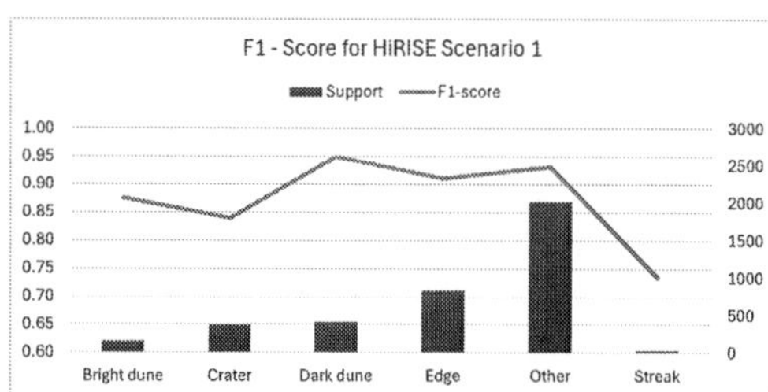

(b) F1-score across six categories

Fig. 2. Performance comparisons for HiRISE Scenario 1

IV. CONCLUSION

In this paper, we examined the efficacy of three CNN architectures, InceptionNet, DenseNet and EfficientNet, as well as a Vision Transformer (ViT/B-32) in the context of varying degrees of class imbalance. Our investigation included a case study conducted on a NASA Mars surface image

TABLE V
CLASSIFICATION PERFORMANCE FOR HIRISE SCENARIO 2

InceptionNet

Class	Precision	Recall	F1-score	Support
Bright dune	0.933	0.891	0.911	156
Crater	0.976	0.989	0.983	369
Dark dune	0.952	0.971	0.961	408
Streak	1.000	0.838	0.912	37
Overall	0.960	0.960	0.959	970

DenseNet

Class	Precision	Recall	F1-score	Support
Bright dune	0.933	0.897	0.915	156
Crater	0.968	0.989	0.979	369
Dark dune	0.964	0.971	0.967	408
Streak	0.969	0.838	0.899	37
Overall	0.961	**0.961**	**0.960**	970

EfficientNet

Class	Precision	Recall	F1-score	Support
Bright dune	0.909	0.955	0.931	156
Crater	0.994	0.962	0.978	369
Dark dune	0.987	0.949	0.968	408
Streak	0.632	0.973	0.766	37
Overall	**0.964**	0.956	0.958	970

ViT

Class	Precision	Recall	F1-score	Support
Bright dune	0.972	0.885	0.926	156
Crater	0.958	0.997	0.977	369
Dark dune	0.950	0.985	0.968	408
Streak	1.000	0.568	0.724	37
Overall	0.959	0.958	0.955	970

dataset, from which we extracted two sets: a four-category dataset with moderate imbalance and a six-category complete dataset with severe imbalance.

The results demonstrated that all models performed well under moderate class imbalance, indicating their suitability for this type of classification task. However, as class imbalance became more severe, performance declined across all models. It is worth noting that the ViT model outperformed the CNNs under severe data imbalance and performed comparably under moderate imbalance, resulting in a notably smaller performance drop between the two scenarios. This suggests that Vision Transformers may offer greater robustness to class imbalance in planetary or terrestrial surface imagery applications.

Future work could involve investigating additional variants of Vision Transformers (ViT), such as DeiT [12] and Swin Transformer [13], and applying them to a broader range of image classification tasks, including satellite imagery, medical imaging, and natural scene recognition. This would help evaluate their generalizability and performance across different domains.

ACKNOWLEDGEMENTS

We thank Dylan Chamberlin and Gabriel Arevalo for their contributions to part of the experiments. We also thank Preston Billion-Polak for his constructive suggestions. This study is partially supported by NASA Connecticut Space Grant Consortium.

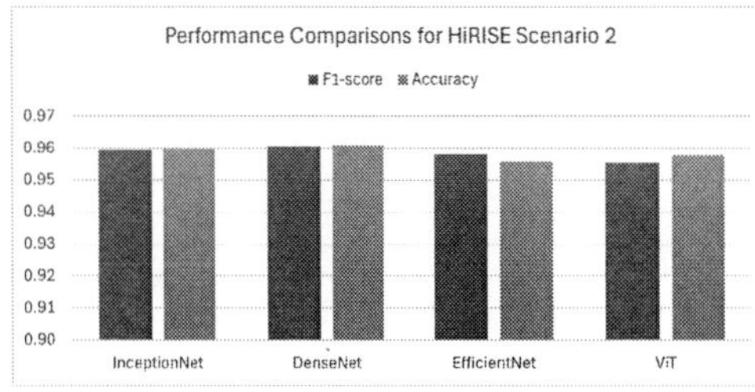

(a) F1-score and accuracy

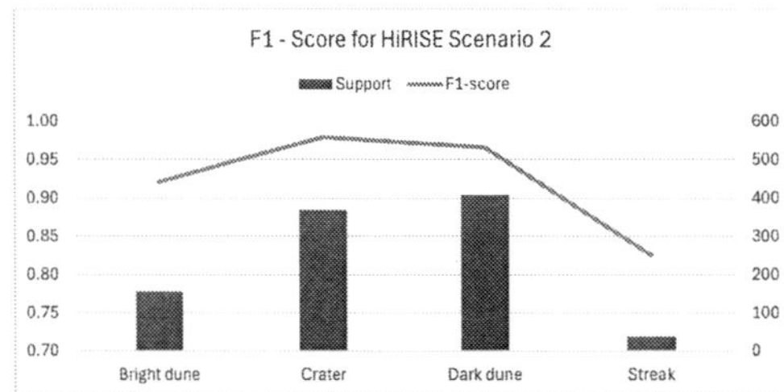

(b) F1-score across four categories

Fig. 3. Performance comparisons for HiRISE Scenario 2

REFERENCES

[1] A. Vaswani *et al.*, "Attention is all you need." [Online]. Available: https://arxiv.org/abs/1706.03762

[2] K. Gao, S. Tasneem, and T. M. Khoshgoftaar, "Exploring Convolutional Neural Networks for NASA Mars Image Data," in *Proceedings of the 29th ISSAT International Conference on Reliability and Quality in Design*, Miami, FL, August 8-10 2024, pp. 159–163.

[3] C. Szegedy *et al.*, "Going deeper with convolutions," 2014. [Online]. Available: https://arxiv.org/abs/1409.4842

[4] G. Huang, Z. Liu, L. van der Maaten, and K. Q. Weinberger, "Densely connected convolutional networks," 2018. [Online]. Available: https://arxiv.org/abs/1608.06993

[5] M. Tan and Q. V. Le, "Efficientnet: Rethinking model scaling for convolutional neural networks," 2020. [Online]. Available: https://arxiv.org/abs/1905.11946

[6] A. Dosovitskiy *et al.*, "An image is worth 16x16 words: Transformers for image recognition at scale," 2021. [Online]. Available: https://arxiv.org/abs/2010.11929

[7] L. Alzubaidi, J. Zhang, and A. Humaidi, "Review of deep learning: concepts, CNN architectures, challenges, applications, future directions," *Journal of Big Data*, vol. 8, no. 53, March 2021.

[8] C. Szegedy, V. Vanhoucke, S. Ioffe, J. Shlens, and Z. Wojna, "Rethinking the inception architecture for computer vision," in *Proceedings of the IEEE Conference on Computer Vision and Pattern Recognition (CVPR)*, 2016, pp. 2818–2826.

[9] K. L.Wagstaff, Y. Lu, A. Stanboli, K. Grimes, T. Gowda, and J. Padams, "Deep Mars: CNN Classification of Mars Imagery for the PDS Imaging Atlas," in *The Thirtieth AAAI Conference on Innovative Applications of Artificial Intelligence (IAAI-18)*, April 2018, pp. 7867–7872.

[10] Y. Lu and K. Wagstaff, "Mars orbital image (hirise) labeled data set," Zenodo, November 13 2017. [Online]. Available: http://doi.org/10.5281/zenodo.1048301

[11] K. Ghosh, C. Bellinger, and R. Corizzo, "The class imbalance problem in deep learning," *Machine Learning*, Dec 2022.

[12] H. Touvron *et al.*, "Training data-efficient image transformers & distillation through attention," 2021. [Online]. Available: https://arxiv.org/abs/2012.12877

[13] Z. Liu *et al.*, "Swin transformer: Hierarchical vision transformer using shifted windows," 2021. [Online]. Available: https://arxiv.org/abs/2103.14030

Integrating Socioeconomic Determinants with Medical Risk Factors for Diabetes

McCORMACK James and SELIYA, Naeem

Department of Computer Science
University of Wisconsin – Eau Claire, USA

Keywords: Diabetes, Socioeconomic Attributes, Medical Risk Factors, Machine Learning, Feature Importance.

Abstract – Diabetes mellitus is a metabolic disease of inadequate control of elevated blood glucose levels. Among the subtypes, Type 2 has a higher prevalence in our population. The likelihood of a Type 2 diagnosis is affected by medical risk factors such as age, body mass index, hyperglycemia, and heart health. The variation of people with diabetes is significant across many levels of social, economic, geographic, cultural, and other non-medical aspects. In the literature, medical risk factors are the predominant features in machine learning based studies of diabetes. However, in comparison, we observe a significant gap in examining non-medical data as potential, important predictive attributes. In this work, an objective is to study the effects of incorporating social and economic determinants with medical risk factors, to form the features in a dataset for developing learners for a binary (yes/no) prediction of diabetes. The case study data, part of a large health-related survey, includes social and economic determinants as well as medical risk factors as features. A total of six machine learners were developed with the integrated dataset. A feature-importance study with SHapley Additive exPlanations provided insight into the social and economic determinants as features. The main observations include: most learners yielded an F-1 of 82%, AUC of 80%, and AUPRC of 81%. The feature-importance study indicated Blood Pressure, Cholesterol, and BMI as important medical risk factors, as well as various social and economic determinants were among the top 10 features. The relative importance of the latter features lends to including them in predictive diabetes analysis.

1. Introduction

Diabetes mellitus is a prevalent disease and a significant public health concern. Its widespread occurrence places a substantial burden on patients and healthcare systems, underscoring the need for early detection and prevention efforts[1][2]. While traditional approaches have relied on statistical analysis, advancements in computational technologies have introduced new tools for disease prediction.

Machine learning algorithms, capable of analyzing extensive and complex datasets, can identify patterns connecting patient attributes to chronic diseases. In predicting conditions like diabetes, these models utilize vast amounts of patient data available in modern healthcare research. Emerging artificial intelligence techniques may have the potential to improve prediction accuracy and facilitate earlier detection [3] through their more holistic approach to data analysis.

Although machine learning is already employed in diabetes predictive modeling, existing studies emphasize biological attributes [4][5]. While these methods have demonstrated some success, incorporating social determinants of health may enhance predictive accuracy further. Broadening the scope of risk factors could enable machine learning models to provide a more comprehensive assessment of diabetes risk, uncovering trends that are only apparent through a social determinant perspective.

To address this gap, our study analyzes data obtained from a large health-related survey of medical, social, economic, and other factors of the survey respondents. Using different machine learners (six), including XGBoost, Logistic Regression, Random Forest, AdaBoost, Naïve Bayes, and LightGBM we predict status of diabetes (yes/no). By evaluating multiple models, we aim to assess their performance based on a case study dataset with features consisting of medical risk factors as well as social and economic attributes. In addition, we examine feature importance to gain meaningful insight into the effects of integrating social and economic attributes with medical risk factors.

By integrating the two groups as a collective set of features used for machine learning based analysis of diabetes occurrence, this study seeks to contribute to an improved understanding of diabetes from a non-medical perspective. Studying the effects of incorporating social and economic attributes with medical risk factors predictive assessment of diabetes may reveal essential insights into diabetes risk characteristics and its prevalence.

The remainder of the paper is structured as follows: Section II reviews related studies; Section III outlines empirical methods, including dataset details and data preprocessing; Section IV describes the machine learning algorithms utilized; Section V presents results, along with tables and analysis; Section VI concludes the study.

2. Related Works

This section reviews key studies that have contributed to the integration of social variables in diabetes prediction models, covering their methodologies and findings.

Horestani and Owrang [6] trained Logistic Regression and Random Forest models using 33 selected features from the 2015 BRFSS study to analyze the relationship between diabetes and various health factors, including income. Their findings identified blood pressure, cholesterol, BMI, and income as key risk factors, with lower income levels correlating with a higher risk of diabetes. However, they concluded that medical indicators exhibited a stronger predictive relationship with diabetes than income.

Tanner et al. [7] employed gradient boosting models to assess the impact of social determinants on diabetes diagnosis in New York City. They trained XGBoost models using two datasets, one with 16 selected variables and another with 81, with both datasets exclusively having social determinants. Feature importance analysis with the SHapley Additive exPlanations (SHAP) algorithm revealed low education and poverty were the most influential predictors.

Islam et al. [8] examined Type 2 diabetes risk factors with the Logistic Regression, Naïve Bayes, J48, Multilayer Perceptron, and Random Forest machine learners with two datasets obtained from the National Health and Nutrition Examination Survey (2009–2010 and 2011–2012), with each containing 14 features. Their analysis identified age, marital status, smoking, and BMI as key risk factors across both datasets.

Arockiasamy [9] present a healthcare analytics framework for early diabetes prediction, which integrated social determinants for predictive analysis. The two machine learners, LightGBM and Optimized XGBoost, were utilized for a case study across multiple datasets, including County Health Rankings, BRFSS Surveys, and USDA Food Access Research Atlas. Their findings indicated the effectiveness of social risk factors in population-level diabetes prediction.

While prior studies have explored the integration of medical risk factors and social determinants in diabetes prediction, they often exhibit a strong imbalance between the respective numbers of medical risk factors and social determinants. To provide an example of such imbalance: Horestani and Owrang [6] included numerous medical factors but only one social determinant, whereas Tanner et al. [7] exclusively focus on social determinants and no medical factors. These studies provide good insights, however, underscore a justifiable necessity for improved feature selection as well as comprehensive feature importance analysis.

Building upon these works, this case study involves a dataset that provides a more balanced representation of medical factors and social determinants. In addition, we investigated SHAP and its feature importance ranking capability for a deeper analysis of the influence of various risk factors for diabetes.

3. Methodology

3.1 Data Source and Preprocessing

The dataset of this study is obtained from a large nationally representative health-related survey [10] performed in 2021.

To prepare the dataset for prediction for diabetes prediction, several preprocessing steps were applied. First, columns recorded only in specific states or regions were removed to ensure uniformity across all records. Next, features with more than 50% missing or unanswered responses were excluded to minimize incomplete data.

Subsequently, an expert-based targeted feature selection was performed on medical factors and socioeconomic determinants that were relevant to diabetes risk. The medical factors such as blood glucose levels, blood pressure, cholesterol, and body mass index were included due to their established correlation with the risk of diabetes. In addition, socioeconomic attributes such as education level, income, healthcare access, and lifestyle behaviors were selected for their broader health risk influences.

In addition, data records containing any remaining missing values were removed, resulting in a complete and clean dataset with 223,022 records and 29 features.

3.2 Data Splitting and Class Imbalance

The dataset was split into 80% training and 20% testing. The training set was used for further preprocessing, including oversampling techniques, while the test set was reserved for final performance assessment.

A substantial class imbalance was observed with an 85:15 class imbalance ratio of the non-diabetes and diabetes categories. To address the class imbalance, SMOTE (Synthetic Minority Oversampling Technique) was applied [11]. The oversampling algorithm generates synthetic data points for the minority class, improving model training through increased representation of minority (diabetes) class.

While SMOTE has been shown to enhance model performance in diabetes prediction, its impact can vary. Some studies report improved classification accuracy [12], while others highlight multifaceted [13] or even negative effects [14]. To account for this variability, SMOTE was applied with three class imbalance ratios: baseline (85:15), 50% oversampling, and 100% oversampling. These levels of class ratios allow for a more consistent comparative analysis and effects of class imbalance on performance of machine learners (classifiers) and the trade-offs associated with oversampling for substantial class imbalance. Subsequently, a five-fold cross-validation model training was implemented with training dataset [15]

3.3 Model Evaluation and Feature Analysis

We use multiple performance metrics [16] to assess the machine learners' ability to distinguish between diabetes and non-diabetes cases. Models are evaluated by the following performance measures: accuracy (Acc), F1-score (F1), area under the receiver operating characteristic curve (AUROC), precision (Prec), and recall (Rec). These metrics represent different performance characteristics for broader assessment of the machine learners.

Beyond performance evaluation, this study incorporates SHapley Additive exPlanations (SHAP) and its built-in feature importance ranking from top-performing models to analyze the influence of individual features on model decision-making [17]. The objective of this analysis is to directly compare the predictive strength of biomedical attributes and social determinants of health in diabetes prediction. By quantifying feature importance, this study provides a structured comparison of risk factors, offering insights into their relative contributions to diabetes classification.

The following 29 features are represented in our case study: Diabetes Status, Body Mass Index, Blood Pressure, Cholesterol, Smoking History, Alcohol Consumption, Stroke History, Asthma, Heart Disease, Skin Cancer, Other Cancers, Heart Attack History, C.O.P.D., Kidney Disease, State of Residence, Source of Health Insurance, Primary Healthcare Provider, Affording Doctor Visit, Marital Status, Education Level, Own or Rent Home, Served in U.S. Armed Forces, Employment Status, Annual Income, Time Since Last Checkup.

4. Machine Learning Algorithms

XGBoost [18] is an optimized, distributed gradient boosting framework designed for efficiency and scalability. It employs an ensemble approach, combining multiple weak learners to enhance predictive accuracy. By iteratively refining its trees, XGBoost minimizes errors and improves model performance.

Random Forest [19] is an ensemble learning method that constructs multiple decision trees during training and determines the final classification based on the majority decision. It creates randomness by selecting subsets of features at each split, reducing overfitting and enhancing generalization.

Naïve Bayes [20] is a probabilistic classifier based on Bayes' Theorem, assuming strong independence among features. Despite its simplicity, it performs well in scenarios where features exhibit conditional independence or functional dependencies, making it effective for text and medical diagnosis classification problems.

Logistic Regression [21] is a statistical model used for binary classification that models the relationship between input features and output probabilities with a logarithmic function. It is widely applied in healthcare, finance, and economics due to its interpretability and efficiency in handling linear relationships.

AdaBoost (Adaptive Boosting) [22] is an ensemble boosting algorithm that iteratively trains weak classifiers on weighted versions of the dataset. By adjusting weights to emphasize misclassified instances, AdaBoost continually improves model accuracy, making it effective for complex classification tasks.

LightGBM (Light Gradient Boosting Machine) [23] is a gradient boosting framework optimized for speed and efficiency on large datasets. Unlike XGBoost and AdaBoost, LightGBM employs a leaf-wise tree growth strategy, splitting the leaf that minimizes loss the most, resulting in deeper trees and potentially higher accuracy. Additionally, it utilizes Exclusive Feature Bundling (EFB) to efficiently handle sparse data.

5. Empirical Case Study Results

Table 1. XGBoost Performance

CV	Acc	F1	AUROC	Prec	Rec
0.8553	0.8555	0.8231	0.8101	0.8242	0.8555
0.8576	0.8559	0.8233	0.8105	0.8248	0.8559
0.8623	0.8562	0.8237	0.8115	0.8253	0.8562

Tables Note: The rows are SMOTE at baseline, 50%, and 100%.

Table 2. Random Forest Performance

CV	Acc	F1	AUROC	Prec	Rec
0.8553	0.8536	0.8173	0.7994	0.8200	0.8536
0.8558	0.8552	0.8200	0.7979	0.8228	0.8552
0.8617	0.8556	0.8208	0.7999	0.8229	0.8556

Table 3. Naïve Bayes Performance

CV	Acc	F1	AUROC	Prec	Rec
0.7895	0.7900	0.7996	0.7648	0.8116	0.7900
0.7735	0.7875	0.7985	0.7673	0.8125	0.7875
0.7558	0.7852	0.7982	0.7691	0.8159	0.7852

Table 4. Logistic Regression Performance

CV	Acc	F1	AUROC	Prec	Rec
0.8531	0.8532	0.8081	0.7900	0.8168	0.8532
0.8242	0.8514	0.818	0.7849	0.8159	0.8514
0.7890	0.8463	0.8254	0.7847	0.8177	0.8463

Table 5. AdaBoost Performance

CV	Acc	F1	AUROC	Prec	Rec
0.8567	0.8568	0.8250	0.8095	0.8266	0.8567
0.8455	0.8551	0.8281	0.8052	0.8256	0.8551
0.8530	0.8527	0.8299	0.8030	0.8247	0.8527

Table 6. LightGBM Performance

CV	Acc	F1	AUROC	Prec	Rec
0.8553	0.8536	0.8173	0.7994	0.8200	0.8536
0.8558	0.8552	0.8200	0.7979	0.8228	0.8552
0.8617	0.8556	0.8208	0.7999	0.8229	0.8556

Table 7. XGBoost Feature Importance Ranking

Feature	Imp.	Feature	Imp.
Blood Pressure	0.5557	Blood Pressure	0.4180
BMI	0.4383	Cholesterol	0.0952
Cholesterol	0.3346	Kidney Disease	0.0642
Alcohol Consumption	0.3284	Time Since Last Checkup	0.0494
Time Since Last Checkup	0.2628	Employment Status	0.0374
Employment Status	0.2889	Heart Disease	0.0356
Sex	0.1858	Alcohol Consumption	0.0328
Race	0.1140	Heart Attack	0.0264
Income	0.1111	BMI	0.0255
Personal Provider	0.1873	Sex	0.0244
Source of Health Insurance	0.0957	Race	0.0200
Kidney Disease	0.0745	Personal Provider	0.0160
State of Residence	0.0715	Stroke	0.0143
Education Level	0.0700	Income	0.0129
Heart Attack	0.0483	Health Insurance Source	0.0123

Note: In Tables 7, 8, and 9, the two left columns represent feature importance values obtained with SHAP, while the two right columns represent the feature ranking obtained by the built-in functions.

Table 8. LightGBM Feature Importance Ranking

Feature	Imp.	Feature	Imp.
Blood Pressure	0.5502	Blood Pressure	0.3600
BMI	0.4054	BMI	0.1507
Cholesterol	0.3437	Alcohol Consumption	0.1112
Alcohol Consumption	0.3306	Employment Status	0.0578
Time Since Last Checkup	0.2917	Time Since Last Checkup	0.0502
Employment Status	0.1915	Kidney Disease	0.0338
Sex	0.1715	Income	0.0230
Income	0.1031	Race	0.0217
Race	0.0979	Sex	0.0167
Personal Provider	0.0876	Heart Attack	0.0162
Source of Health Insurance	0.0804	Heart Disease	0.0141
Kidney Disease	0.0608	Source of Health Insurance	0.0137
Education Level	0.0562	Personal Provider	0.0102
Heart Atack	0.0412	State of Residence	0.0129
Heart Disease	0.0376	Education Level	0.0060

Table 1. Random Forest Feature Importance Ranking

Feature	Imp.	Feature	Imp.
Blood Pressure	0.0539	Blood Pressure	0.2057
BMI	0.0373	BMI	0.1732
Cholesterol	0.0350	Cholesterol	0.1012
Alcohol Consumption	0.0256	Alcohol Consumption	0.0900
Employment Status	0.0233	Employment Status	0.0829
Time Since Last Checkup	0.0126	Kidney Disease	0.0641
Income	0.0107	Income	0.0368
Kidney Disease	0.0104	Personal Provider	0.0313
Source of Health Insurance	0.0086	Heart Disease	0.0303
Heart Disease	0.0074	Heart Attack	0.0296
Race	0.0062	Time Since Last Checkup	0.0292
Heart Attack	0.0059	Race	0.0207
Sex	0.0045	State of Residence	0.0186
Education Level	0.0045	Education Level	0.0136
Stroke History	0.0017	Sex	0.0084

5.2. Analysis and Discussion

Across varying levels of SMOTE oversampling, five of the six models consistently achieved accuracies of approximately 85%, with Naïve Bayes slightly underperforming at 79%. Precision scores averaged around 82%, while recall scores remained at 85% for most models, with Naïve Bayes again exhibiting lower performance. The F1-scores were consistently 81-82% across most models. AUROC scores ranged from 79% to 81%, with boosting algorithms XGBoost, AdaBoost, and LightGBM demonstrating slightly superior performance. Notably, the application of SMOTE did not yield significant improvements in model performance.

To assess feature importance, SHAP and built-in feature importance modules were applied to rank the top 15 features for the highest-performing models: XGBoost, LightGBM, and Random Forest. The most influential risk factors across rankings were blood pressure, BMI, cholesterol, alcohol consumption, and time since last checkup. While slight variations in ranking were observed across models, these features consistently remained within the top 5–7 most influential attributes.

In comparing the prevalence of biomedical and social determinant risk factors, blood pressure, cholesterol, and BMI emerged as the most dominant predictors, both in ranking and measured importance. However, a substantial and nearly balanced representation of social determinants was observed among the most influential features. Key social determinants included time since last checkup, employment status, income, education level, personal provider, source of health insurance, and state of residence. Additionally, race and sex may be considered social determinants in certain contexts, further highlighting the relevance of non-biomedical factors in diabetes prediction.

6. Conclusion

This study highlights the effectiveness of machine learning models in predicting diabetes using a combination of biomedical and social determinants of health. The consistent performance across key metrics accuracy, F1-score, and AUROC exceeding 80% underscores the reliability of these models in distinguishing between diabetes and non-diabetes cases. The findings also reinforce the predictive significance of biomedical attributes, particularly blood pressure, cholesterol, and BMI, which consistently ranked among the most influential features. However, the strong presence of social determinants, including income, education level, healthcare access, and employment status among the top predictive factors suggests their relevance in diabetes risk assessment.

Future research in diabetes predictive modeling should aim to integrate both biomedical and social determinants to enhance accuracy and provide a more holistic approach to patient analysis. Additionally, policymakers should further investigate the causal relationships and prevalence of diabetes in vulnerable populations, ensuring that healthcare interventions address both medical and socioeconomic risk factors.

7. References

[1] T. Sharma and M. Shah, "A Comprehensive Review of Machine Learning Techniques on Diabetes Detection," *Vis. Comput. Ind. Biomed. Art.*, vol. 4, no. 1, p. 30, Dec. 3, 2021, DOI: 10.1186/s42492-021-00097-7.

[2] Q. Sun, X. Cheng, K. Han, Y. Sun, H. Ren, and P. Li, "Machine Learning-Based Assessment of Diabetes Risk," *Appl. Intell.*, vol. 55, no. 2, p. 106, Dec. 2024, DOI: 10.1007/s10489-024-05912-1.

[3] M. Javaid, A. Haleem, R. Pratap Singh, R. Suman, and S. Rab, "Significance of Machine Learning in Healthcare: Features, Pillars and Applications," *Int. J. Intell. Netw.*, vol. 3, pp. 58–73, 2022, DOI: 10.1016/j.ijin.2022.05.002.

[4] Z. Cooper and O. Mowbray, *Social Determinants of Health and Diabetes: Using a Nationally Representative Sample to Determine Which Social Determinant of Health Model Best Predicts Diabetes*, 2023, DOI: 10.2139/ssrn.4463538.

[5] I. Kavakiotis, O. Tsave, A. Salifoglou, N. Maglaveras, I. Vlahavas, and I. Chouvarda, "Machine Learning and Data Mining Methods in Diabetes Research," *Comput. Struct. Biotechnol. J.*, vol. 15, pp. 104–116, Jan. 8, 2017, DOI: 10.1016/j.csbj.2016.12.005.

[6] F. J. Horestani and M. M. Owrang O, "Machine Learning for Diabetes Prediction," *Comput. Sci. Inf. Technol.*, vol. 14, pp. 137–154, Apr. 2024, DOI: 10.5121/csit.2024.140711.

[7] D. Tanner, Y. Zhang, J. E. Chang, P. Speyer, E. Adamson, A. Aerts, et al., "Machine Learning to Evaluate the Relationship Between Social Determinants and Diabetes Prevalence in New York City," *BMJ Public Health*, vol. 2, no. 2, p. e001394, Sep. 24, 2024, DOI: 10.1136/bmjph-2024-001394.

[8] Md. M. Islam et al., "Identification of the Risk Factors of Type 2 Diabetes and Its Prediction Using Machine Learning Techniques," *Health Syst.*, vol. 12, no. 2, pp. 243–254, Nov. 2022, DOI: 10.1080/20476965.2022.2141141.

[9] J. M. Arockiasamy, "Proactive Healthcare Analytics: Early Detection of Diabetes with SDOH Insights and Machine Learning," *Eur. J. Comput. Sci. Inf. Technol.*, vol. 13, no. 2, pp. 64–74, Feb. 2025, DOI: 10.37745/ejcsit.2013/vol13n26474.

[10] Centers for Disease Control and Prevention, "CDC - 2021 BRFSS Survey Data and Documentation.". Available: https://www.cdc.gov/brfss/annual_data/annual_2021.html.

[11] N. V. Chawla, K. W. Bowyer, L. O. Hall, and W. P. Kegelmeyer, "SMOTE: Synthetic Minority Over-Sampling Technique," *J. Artif. Intell. Res.*, vol. 16, pp. 321–357, Jun. 2002, DOI: 10.1613/jair.953.

[12] M. Alghamdi, M. Al-Mallah, S. Keteyian, C. Brawner, J. Ehrman, and S. Sakr, "Predicting Diabetes Mellitus Using SMOTE and Ensemble Machine Learning Approach: The Henry Ford ExercIse Testing (FIT) Project," *PLoS One*, vol. 12, no. 7, p. e0179805, Jul. 24, 2017, DOI: 10.1371/journal.pone.0179805.

[13] M. Kıvrak, et al., "The Impact of the SMOTE Method on Machine Learning and Ensemble Learning Performance Results in Addressing Class Imbalance in Data Used for Predicting Total Testosterone Deficiency in Type 2 Diabetes Patients," *Preprints*, Oct. 2024, DOI: 10.20944/preprints202410.1324.v1.

[14] S. Sadeghi, D. Khalili, A. Ramezankhani, M. A. Mansournia, and M. Parsaeian, "Diabetes Mellitus Risk Prediction in the Presence of Class Imbalance Using Flexible Machine Learning Methods," *BMC Med. Inform. Decis. Mak.*, vol. 22, no. 1, p. 36, Feb. 10, 2022, DOI: 10.1186/s12911-022-01775-z.

[15] R. Kohavi, "A Study of Cross-Validation and Bootstrap for Accuracy Estimation and Model Selection," in *Proc. 14th Int. Joint Conf. Artif. Intell. (IJCAI)*, Montreal, QC, Canada, 1995, pp. 1137–1145.

[16] T. Hastie, R. Tibshirani, and J. Friedman, *The Elements of Statistical Learning: Data Mining, Inference, and Prediction*, 2nd ed. New York, NY, USA: Springer, 2009, DOI: 10.1007/978-0-387-84858-7.

[17] S. M. Lundberg and S.-I. Lee, "A Unified Approach to Interpreting Model Predictions," in *Adv. Neural Inf. Process. Syst.*, Long Beach, CA, USA: Neural Inf. Process. Syst., 2017, pp. 4765–4774.

[18] T. Chen and C. Guestrin, "XGBoost: A Scalable Tree Boosting System," in *Proc. 22nd ACM SIGKDD Int. Conf. Knowl. Discov. Data Min.*, San Francisco, CA, USA, 2016, pp. 785–794, DOI: 10.1145/2939672.2939785.

[19] L. Breiman, "Random Forests," *Mach. Learn.*, vol. 45, no. 1, pp. 5–32, 2001, DOI: 10.1023/A:1010933404324.

[20] J. Wu, et al., "Dual Instance and Attribute Weighting for Naïve Bayes Classification," in *Proc. Int. Joint Conf. Neural Netw. (IJCNN)*, Beijing, China, 2014, DOI: 10.1109/IJCNN.2014.6889572.

[21] D. W. Hosmer, S. Lemeshow, and R. X. Sturdivant, *Applied Logistic Regression*, 3rd ed. Hoboken, NJ, USA: Wiley, 2013, DOI: 10.1002/9781118548387.

[22] Y. Freund and R. E. Schapire, "A Decision-Theoretic Generalization of On-Line Learning and an Application to Boosting," *J. Comput. Syst. Sci.*, vol. 55, no. 1, pp. 119–139, 1997, DOI: 10.1006/jcss.1997.1504.

[23] G. Ke, et al., "LightGBM: A Highly Efficient Gradient Boosting Decision Tree," in *Adv. Neural Inf. Process. Syst. (NeurIPS)*, Long Beach, CA, USA, 2017, pp. 3146–3154.

The STRIDE Database: Workers' Compensation Claims and Adjuster Notes

Chelsea M. Zuvieta*, Richard Bauder*, Brian White*, and Taghi M. Khoshgoftaar*
*Florida Atlantic University
Email: czuvieta2016@fau.edu, rbauder2014@fau.edu, whiteb2022@fau.edu, khoshgof@fau.edu

***Abstract*—The Structured and Textual Records for Injury Data Exploration (STRIDE) database consists of two datasets, tabular and text, detailing workers' compensation claims that were compiled, cleaned, and anonymized for analysis of workplace injuries. The database provides insights into work-related injury types, costs, and outcomes, with the potential to inform safety improvements, cost reduction strategies, and fair workers' compensation practices. Additionally, the repository includes notes documented by insurance adjusters. The tabular data encompasses 230,833 workers' compensation claims, and the text data contains notes for 25,691 of those claims. We present the baseline results of a medical cost classification model, which shows promise for future machine learning experiments. Primary research outcomes of the STRIDE database should include predictions on different costs, injury severity, claim length, and legal involvement.**

***Index Terms*—Workplace Injury, Workers' Compensation, Machine Learning, Dataset, Data Analysis, Natural Language Processing**

I. Introduction

Work-related injuries are a significant threat to the health and safety of employees. Depending on injury severity, businesses and insurers may face lengthy legal proceedings and be required to provide monetary support for the injured employee. As defined by the U.S. Bureau of Labor Statistics (BLS), workplace injuries include any wound or damage to an employee's body because of an event in their work environment [1]. Injuries may range from minor, requiring minimal medical expenses, to severe, causing permanent disability or even death. Workplace injury claims affect several parties, including employees, employers, workers' compensation insurance companies, attorney representation, and state and federal agencies, such as the BLS and Occupational Safety and Health Administration (OSHA). In 2023, the BLS reported that there were nearly 2.6 million nonfatal injuries and illnesses within private industry [2]. In the same year, work injuries cost a total of $176.5 billion according to the NSC [3]. This total mainly includes, but is not limited to, wage and productivity losses, medical expenses, and administrative costs [3]. Research looking into risk factors based on employee, injury, and claim details can help determine what predictors are most informative.

The STRIDE database consists of two datasets, which can provide insights into workplace injury patterns, costs, and outcomes, and may direct future safety improvements, cost reduction strategies, and fair compensation practices. Analyzing workplace injuries is critical for assessing risks associated with specific occupational tasks, equipment, or areas. Organizations, such as the Workers' Compensation Research Institute, conduct several studies specifically looking at claim cost drivers and injury outcomes [4]. Such research can help ensure fair workers' compensation premiums for employers while also guaranteeing equitable compensation for employees.

In this paper, we will describe the STRIDE database, its features, and applications. Section II provides an overview on each dataset in the database. Section III describes a simple classification task performed on the database to establish a baseline performance. Section IV discusses potential future research areas and questions which can be explored using one or both of the datasets, and Section VI finally concludes the work.

We note that the STRIDE database is currently unavailable to the public.

II. Data Files

The STRIDE database is made up of a tabular and a text dataset. Additionally, both datasets include a data dictionary describing each feature and a README file providing a summary of the dataset. Matching claim ID numbers may merge the tabular and text datasets for the 25,691 overlapping cases.

A. *Tabular Dataset*

The tabular data file has 48 features that describe claim dates, costs, injury details, demographic data, geographic data, and employer information. The features represent both structured and unstructured data types, including dates, categorical variables, text, and numerical values. The claims consist of injuries dating from January 2002 to December 2020. Only 0.6% of the claims were still open at the end of the collection date. The dataset has records for 230,833 claims, which may be defined as either Lost Time (LT) or Medical Only (MO). The injury severity may be defined as MO, Temporary Partial Disability (TPD), Temporary Total Disability (TTD), Permanent Partial Disability (PPD), Permanent Total Disability (PTD), or Death Benefits (DB). MO makes up nearly 77% of the claims, while TTD, TPD, and PPD each constitute around 7%. Only 0.1% of claims identify injury severity as either PTD or DB. The remaining $\sim$2% of instances do not have a specified injury severity. The National Council on Compensation Insurance (NCCI) provides a set of standardized injury descriptions

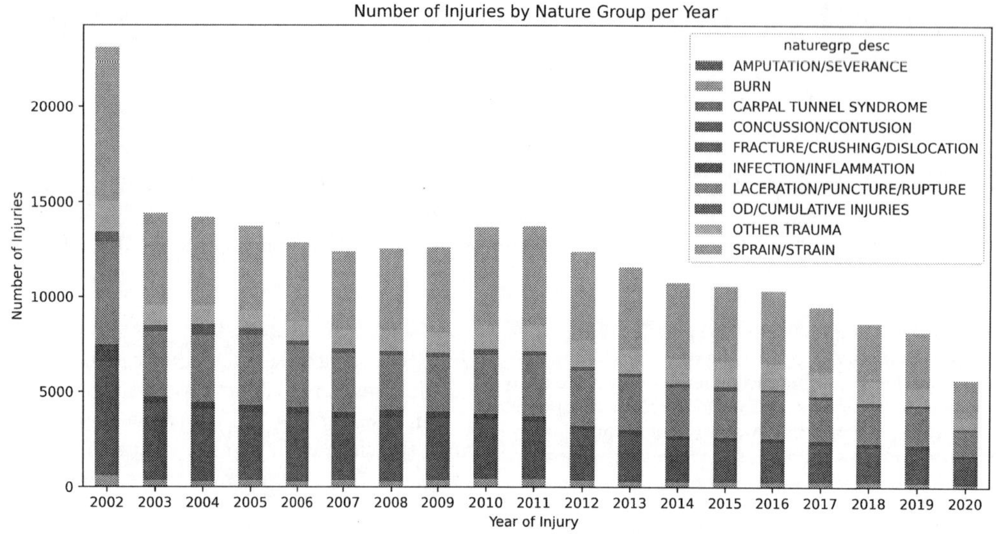

Fig. 1. Stacked bar chart of the number of injuries per nature group based on the feature 'naturegrp_desc' from 2002 to 2020.

for workers' compensation claims: cause of injury, nature of injury, and part of body [5]. We have several features based on these classifications. Figure 1 shows the annual number of injuries grouped by the ten categories of the nature of injury feature. The overall number of injuries generally declines with a peak at 2002. This downward trend may be supported by future findings derived from the diverse feature set of the dataset. The following bullets list details on the main groups of features within the tabular dataset:

- Claim details: ID number, injury date, first report of injury date, open date, close date, number of days open to close, return-to-work date, waiting period for wage-loss benefits, legal or attorney indicator, attorney name, claim status, indemnity costs, medical costs, Defense and Cost Containment (DCC) expenses, indication of whether multiple employees were injured in the same incident
- Injury details: Claim type, cause or cause group description, nature or nature group description, body part or body part group description, NCCI body severity group
- Employee demographics: Age at injury, age at hiring, length of tenure at injury, gender, marital status, number of dependents, employee's weekly wage, NCCI occupation class code and description
- Geography: Jurisdiction county and state
- Employer details: Standard Industrial Classification (SIC) code, age of business, employer's credit score, employer's payroll

A comprehensive description of each feature is provided in Table II in Appendix A. When addressing a claim's overall cost, we are referring to the combined total of indemnity, medical care, and DCC costs. It is worth noting that indemnity costs are zero for 76.7% of the claims. This is because MO claims involve injuries that do not keep employees away from work as long as they receive immediate medical care. Hence, there are no wages lost to compensate. Meanwhile, medical and DCC costs are only zero for less than 16% of the claims, since most injuries would require medical attention and insurance records. Given that the claims range from 2002 to 2020, we created a second version of the tabular dataset that has cost-related features, including the employee's weekly wage, adjusted for inflation based on consumer price index [6].

B. Text Dataset

An insurance adjuster acts as an intermediary between an injured worker, employer, and attorney if applicable. They primarily investigate a workplace injury claim by reviewing medical records, interviewing the affected individuals, and ensuring compliance in accordance with workers' compensation rules. Their role requires extensive documentation throughout the claim process. The text dataset consists of adjuster's notes for 25,691 LT claims that were opened from September 2010 to December 2020. The entries of these records are made up of two features: the unique claim ID and anonymized text. Each claim may contain multiple notes over multiple days as one text block. Each entry is separated in the text by day starting from the opening date, which is indicated as "<Day 0:>". Each claim has an average of 53 days of notes. Each text instance ends with "<EON>" to signify that there were no additional notes for the claim.

The raw format of the adjuster's notes included private information, such as the names of involved individuals, and spelling errors. In addition, the original notes were already pre-processed to remove punctuation, numeric values, and stop words. To preserve anonymity, we used Python, specifically the spaCy and nltk packages, to mask all names in the notes [7], [8]. The names are replaced with "<PROPN>" in the text. While it is unlikely that any proper nouns were missed, this process tends to produce false positives where

Fig. 2. Word cloud of the most common words in the anonymized text dataset, excluding single letters and artificial tokens.

some words were mistakenly included in the masking. Despite careful review, the magnitude of text in the data file makes it difficult to verify if masking mistakes still remain. Otherwise, no corrections have been made to the misspelled words, abbreviations, or acronyms. The data dictionary also provides a list of abbreviations and acronyms associated with medical and insurance terms that were common in the adjusters' notes. These include, but are not limited to, "IW" for injured worker, "PT" for physical therapy, "RTW" for return to work, and "MMI" for maximum medical improvement.

Figure 2 shows a word cloud of the most frequently used words in the text dataset. This excludes single letters and the artificial tokens, "PROPN", "EON", and "DAY", since these are largely common due to the masking and note formatting. From the word cloud, we can observe that the text likely contains useful information such as medical recommendations, treatment plans, and specific pain descriptions. These types of details can be lacking from the tabular dataset. The anonymized text can support around 11% of the claims in the tabular dataset to develop deeper insights.

III. Baseline Cost Prediction

As a baseline performance to demonstrate the STRIDE database's potential for machine learning tasks, we ran a simple cost classification model using the gradient-boosting framework CatBoost [9]. Due to space limitations, we only utilized the tabular dataset; CatBoost was chosen for its strong performance [10] and its ability to internally and automatically handle categorical data. We engineered the target feature *medical_cost* from the numeric *medical_amt* feature. Of the 230,833 claims, 11.8% have a medical cost equal to or higher than $10,000; these claims were labeled as "high", and all other claims were classified as "low". For the data preprocessing, we converted all categorical features to strings and decomposed the date features into year, month, and day components. We dropped 10 features that contained information that would not be known until a claim closes. The discarded features were *close_date*, *days_open_to_close*, *rtw_date*, *indemnity_amt*, *medical_amt*, *dcc_amt*, *indwochkamt*, *medwochkamt*, *claim_status*, and *close_year*. Rather than removing instances with missing values, these values were instead filled with an empty string or converted into a float type. The data was randomly split for training and testing at a ratio of 80:20.

TABLE I
Summary of Baseline Performance

	High	Low
Precision	0.7306	0.9450
Recall	0.5723	0.9721
F1 Score	0.6418	0.9584
AUC	0.9545	

The test dataset consisted of 5,392 "high" claims and 40,775 "low" claims. Table I shows the precision, recall, and F1-score when either "high" or "low" is assigned as the positive class, as well as the AUC score, which is the same in both cases. In practical applications, "high" (the minority class) would be the positive class, but we include the second set of results to highlight the performance gaps between the labels. Of all the instances predicted as "high", the precision value shows that only 73.06% of those were actually "high". The recall is worse in comparison, because only 57.23% of all the actual "high" samples are correctly predicted. Since F1-score is calculated using both precision and recall, its value of 0.6418 is weighed down by the suboptimal recall.

On the other hand, the model did very well across all three metrics when the "low" class is regarded as the positive class. This difference in performance indicates that the model

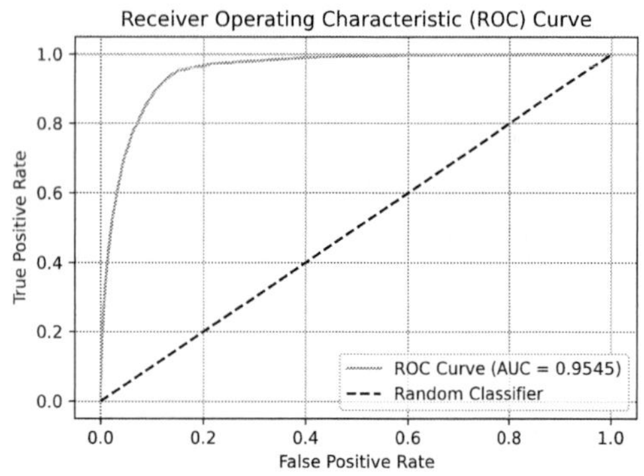

Fig. 3. ROC Curve of the medical cost classification

is biased towards the "low" label and that the "high" label likely suffered due to class imbalance. The Receiver Operating Characteristic (ROC) curve, plotting the model's true positive rate and false positive rate across different thresholds, is shown in Figure 3. The model produced a strong Area Under the ROC Curve (AUC) score of 0.9545, which shows the model is good at distinguishing between the two classes. However, it is worth noting that AUC scores can be misleadingly high when working with imbalanced datasets. This baseline performance shows that the tabular dataset can provide accurate predictions for workplace injury claims. Future work can consider alternative performance metrics [11], as well as machine learning methods that address class imbalance, such as data sampling [12], [13], [14].

IV. Future Applications

Below, we suggest four promising areas of interest for an initial exploration of the STRIDE database.

- Claim costs: There are three main costs associated with workplace injury claims: indemnity, medical, and DCC. The tabular dataset contains features that represent each. Relevant research questions may focus on predicting a single cost type or the combined total. The consulting firm Milliman developed a private model built on adjusters' notes and found that health factors, such as comorbidities, were significant [15]. Researchers may apply a similar approach by utilizing the text dataset within the STRIDE database.
- Injury severity: As previously stated, there are six levels of injury severity. Researchers may look into how features related to an employee and employer, such as age of business or tenure, correlate with this feature. If available, the adjuster's notes may provide extra details, such as preexisting medical conditions. Using a distinct dataset, a 2022 paper by Khairuddin et al. demonstrated the performance of five machine learning models for predicting injury severity in terms of an employee's chance of hospitalization and amputation [16]. The dataset used in this prior study shares common features with ours, namely nature of injury and affected body part, indicating the STRIDE database's potential for this research area.
- Number of days: Researchers could either predict the number of days that a claim is open, or that an employee is away from work. These values heavily influence claim costs and likely correlate with injury severity. Multiple studies have proven that machine learning models can predict the probability an employee returns to work after injury-related leave [17], [18], [19].
- Attorney representation: Researchers could explore how claim variables affect the likelihood of legal involvement in a workplace injury case. A 2022 article by Milliman detailed that that claims with attorney representation take around twice as long to close and cost over twice as much compared to claims that do not [20]. Thus, it may be worthwhile to investigate whether the STRIDE database can support these findings, or help to avoid costly claims.

Most research topics would primarily rely on the tabular dataset, since it contains the target variables for predictions and provides specific claim and employee details. However, the text dataset may possess valuable supplementary information, especially if the notes mention alcohol and drug use, preexisting conditions, and insurance details that are not addressed by the tabular features. We intend to use Natural Language Processing (NLP) methods to analyze the text dataset. Through this, we may gain insights through sentiment analysis of a LT claim through the adjuster notes. Additionally, we may look into the frequency of key words to determine which most affect the cost of the claim, such as "surgery", "hospital", "opioids", etc. Both datasets include diverse data types, namely free-form text descriptions, categorical variables, and integer values, which allows for a wide range of research approaches. If a research question can benefit from both datasets, we may merge them to enhance the scope of the analysis. Overall, we aim to apply machine learning algorithms with both datasets to support studies to predict workplace injury factors.

V. Contributors

All 230,833 claims in the STRIDE database were collected thanks to an anonymous insurance company.

VI. Conclusion

Workplace injuries represent a major area of concern for the occupational safety of employees and impose a significant financial burden on an employer's insurance. The STRIDE database offers two datasets with substantial potential for exploring risk factors to predict cost, injury classifications, and work loss. By utilizing NLP and machine learning models, future research can analyze both the structured and unstructured data of the workplace injury cases to access their effects on different target variables, such as claim costs, injury severity, time away from work, and the likelihood of attorney involvement. While we examine these topics through distinct research questions, it is important to consider when reviewing outcomes that these variables are deeply interconnected. Although there are no published studies based on the STRIDE database yet, its research prospects are extensive, and it will prove to be a valuable resource for enhancing workplace safety, supporting fair workers' compensation practices, and improving claim processes for all involved parties.

REFERENCES

[1] U. B. of Labor Statistics, "BLS OSH Definitions," Jun. 2023. [Online]. Available: https://www.bls.gov/iif/definitions/occupational-safety-and-health-definitions.htm

[2] ——, "Employer-Reported Workplace Injuries and Illnesses (Annual) News Release - 2023 A01 Results," U.S. Bureau of Labor Statistics, Tech. Rep., Nov. 2024. [Online]. Available: https://www.bls.gov/news.release/archives/osh_11082024.htm

[3] N. S. Council, "Work Injury Costs." [Online]. Available: https://injuryfacts.nsc.org/work/costs/work-injury-costs/

[4] W. C. R. Institute, "About - WCRI." [Online]. Available: https://www.wcrinet.org/about/

[5] N. C. on Compensation Insurance, "Injury Characteristics & Insights." [Online]. Available: https://www.ncci.com/SecureDocuments/Injury_Severities_Dashboard.html

[6] U. B. of Labor Statistics, "How to Use the Consumer Price Index for Escalation," Jun. 2023. [Online]. Available: https://www.bls.gov/cpi/factsheets/escalation.htm

[7] I. Montani, M. Honnibal, M. Honnibal, A. Boyd, S. V. Landeghem, and H. Peters, "explosion/spaCy: v3.7.2: Fixes for APIs and requirements," Oct. 2023. [Online]. Available: https://zenodo.org/records/10009823

[8] S. Bird, K. Ewan, and E. Loper, *Natural Language Processing with Python*. O'Reilly Media, Inc., Jun. 2009, iSBN: 9780596516499. [Online]. Available: https://www.oreilly.com/library/view/natural-language-processing/9780596803346/

[9] L. Prokhorenkova, G. Gusev, A. Vorobev, A. V. Dorogush, and A. Gulin, "CatBoost: unbiased boosting with categorical features," in *Proceedings of the 32nd International Conference on Neural Information Processing Systems*, ser. NIPS'18. Red Hook, NY, USA: Curran Associates Inc., Dec. 2018, pp. 6639–6649.

[10] J. T. Hancock and T. M. Khoshgoftaar, "CatBoost for big data: an interdisciplinary review," *Journal of Big Data*, vol. 7, no. 1, p. 94, Nov. 2020. [Online]. Available: https://doi.org/10.1186/s40537-020-00369-8

[11] N. Seliya, T. M. Khoshgoftaar, and J. Van Hulse, "A Study on the Relationships of Classifier Performance Metrics," in *2009 21st IEEE International Conference on Tools with Artificial Intelligence*, Nov. 2009, pp. 59–66, iSSN: 2375-0197. [Online]. Available: https://ieeexplore.ieee.org/abstract/document/5364367

[12] J. Van Hulse, T. M. Khoshgoftaar, and A. Napolitano, "Experimental perspectives on learning from imbalanced data," in *Proceedings of the 24th international conference on Machine learning*, ser. ICML '07. New York, NY, USA: Association for Computing Machinery, Jun. 2007, pp. 935–942. [Online]. Available: https://doi.org/10.1145/1273496.1273614

[13] J. M. Johnson and T. M. Khoshgoftaar, "Survey on deep learning with class imbalance," *Journal of Big Data*, vol. 6, no. 1, p. 27, Mar. 2019. [Online]. Available: https://doi.org/10.1186/s40537-019-0192-5

[14] C. Seiffert, T. M. Khoshgoftaar, J. Van Hulse, and A. Napolitano, "RUSBoost: A Hybrid Approach to Alleviating Class Imbalance," *IEEE Transactions on Systems, Man, and Cybernetics - Part A: Systems and Humans*, vol. 40, no. 1, pp. 185–197, Jan. 2010. [Online]. Available: https://ieeexplore.ieee.org/abstract/document/5299216

[15] M. Paczolt, "Using predictive modeling to forecast large workers' compensation costs: A case study," Mar. 2019. [Online]. Available: https://www.milliman.com/en/insight/using-predictive-modeling-to-forecast-large-workers-compensation-costs-a-case-study

[16] M. Z. F. Khairuddin, P. Lu Hui, K. Hasikin, N. A. Abd Razak, K. W. Lai, A. S. Mohd Saudi, and S. S. Ibrahim, "Occupational Injury Risk Mitigation: Machine Learning Approach and Feature Optimization for Smart Workplace Surveillance," *International Journal of Environmental Research and Public Health*, vol. 19, no. 21, p. 13962, Jan. 2022, number: 21 Publisher: Multidisciplinary Digital Publishing Institute. [Online]. Available: https://www.mdpi.com/1660-4601/19/21/13962

[17] K.-S. Na and E. Kim, "A Machine Learning-Based Predictive Model of Return to Work After Sick Leave," *Journal of Occupational and Environmental Medicine*, vol. 61, no. 5, p. e191, May 2019. [Online]. Available: https://journals.lww.com/joem/abstract/2019/05000/a_machine_learning_based_predictive_model_of.14.aspx

[18] H. Van Deynse, W. Cools, V.-J. De Deken, B. Depreitere, I. Hubloue, E. Kimpe, M. Moens, K. Pien, E. Tisseghem, G. Van Belleghem, and K. Putman, "Predicting return to work after traumatic brain injury using machine learning and administrative data," *International Journal of Medical Informatics*, vol. 178, p. 105201, Oct. 2023. [Online]. Available: https://www.sciencedirect.com/science/article/pii/S1386505623002198

[19] C. J. Yuan, K. D. Varathan, A. Suhaimi, and L. W. Ling, "Predicting Return to Work after Cardiac Rehabilitation using Machine Learning Models," *Journal of Rehabilitation Medicine*, vol. 55, pp. jrm00348–jrm00348, Jan. 2023. [Online]. Available: https://medicaljournalssweden.se/jrm/article/view/2432

[20] M. Paczolt, "How does attorney involvement impact workers' compensation claims?" Apr. 2022. [Online]. Available: https://www.milliman.com/en/insight/how-does-attorney-involvement-impact-workers-compensation-claims

APPENDIX A

TABLE II: Summary of Tabular Dataset Features

Feature Name	Description	Value
ui_claim	Unique claim identifier	1 to 230,833
injury_date	Date of injury incident	MM/DD/YYYY
froi_date	Date when the First Report of Injury was filed by the employer	MM/DD/YYYY
open_date	Date when the insurer opened the claim	MM/DD/YYYY
close_date	Date when the insurer closed the claim	MM/DD/YYYY
days_open_to_close	Number of days the claim was open	close_date – open_date
rtw_date	Date when the employee returned to work	MM/DD/YYYY
waiting_period	Number of days until wage-loss benefits began	3, 5, or 7 days
clm_type	Type of claim	MO or LT
injury_severity	Severity level of injury	MO, TPD, TTD, PPD, PTD, or DB
indemnity_amt	Total indemnity costs paid	\$0 to \$1.5 million
medical_amt	Total medical costs paid	\$0 to \$10.3 million
dcc_amt	Total DCC expenses paid	\$0 to \$645k
indwochkamt	Portion of indemnity costs paid at time of claim settlement	\$0 to \$1.3 million
medwochkamt	Portion of medical costs paid at time of claim settlement	\$0 to \$6 million
claim_status	Status of claim by end date of data collection	Closed With Payment, Closed No Payment, or Open
legal_ind	Indicator of internal legal involvement in the claim	True or False
attorney_name	Name of the employee's attorney if applicable	Free-form text
legal_or_attorney_ind	Indicator of legal involvement in the claim	True or False
injury_desc	Description of injury	Free-form text
cause_desc	Description of the cause of injury provided by the NCCI	Free-form text
causegrp_desc	Grouping for the cause of injury provided by the NCCI	10 labels, including strain, burn, etc.
nature_desc	Description of the nature of injury provided by the NCCI	45 labels, including contusion, sprain, etc.
naturegrp_desc	Grouping for the nature of injury provided by the NCCI	10 labels, including concussion/contusion, sprain/strain, etc.
bdyprt_desc	Description of injured body part provided by the NCCI	Free-form text
bdyprtgrp_desc	Grouping for the injured body part provided by the NCCI	16 labels, including face, leg, arm/shoulder, etc.
ncci_pob_grp	Grouping for expected injury complexity based on injured body part	0.0 or 1.0
cat_ind	Indicator on whether multiple employees were injured in the same incident	True or False
gender	Gender of the injured employee	M or F
martial_status	Marital status of the injured employee	Married, Single, Divorced, or Widowed
dependents	Number of dependents that the injured employee has if applicable	0 to 23
occupation	Description of the injured employee's occupation	Free-form text
class_code	4-digit class code assigned based on occupation and provided by the NCCI	5 to 9812
cc_desc	Description of assigned class code provided by the NCCI	Free-form text
haz_grp	Class code for hazard group provided by the NCCI	A to G
employ_grp	Grouping for the injured employee's type of employment	Employee, Subcontractor, or Owner/officer
age_at_hire	Age of the injured employee at hiring	14 to 91
age_at_injury	Age of the injured employee at injury incident	14 to 107
tenure_at_injury	Number of days employee worked for the employer at the date of injury	0 to 22,320
wkly_wage	Weekly wage of the injured employee at the date of injury	0.24 to 140,000
juris_cnty	County that govern the jurisdiction of the claim	Free-form text
juris_st	State that govern the jurisdiction of the claim	32 labels, including AL, GA, etc.
juris_st_cnty	Concatenated state and county that govern the jurisdiction of the claim	Free-form text
sic_code	4-digit SIC code of the employer	111 to 9721
payroll	Payroll of the employer	4 to ∼257 million
employer_credit_score	Credit score of the employer	0 to 100
age_of_business	Age of employer's business	0 to 235
close_year	The year the claim closed	2002 to 2020

Demand Forecasting in the Aviation Aftermarket: A Gradient-Boosting Approach

Joffrey L. Leevy*, Chelsea M. Zuvieta*, and Taghi M. Khoshgoftaar*
*College of Engineering and Computer Science
Florida Atlantic University
Boca Raton, FL 33431
Email: jleevy2017@fau.edu, czuvieta2016@fau.edu, khoshgof@fau.edu,

***Abstract*—This study investigates advanced gradient-boosting approaches to improve demand forecasting for used aircraft parts in the aviation aftermarket. Irregular demand patterns, high costs, and stringent service-level requirements make accurate forecasting a significant operational challenge. We utilized over 13,000 monthly aggregated data points and applied two gradient-boosting algorithms, CatBoost and XGBoost, to predict spare parts demand. Parts with more unstable demand patterns were excluded by applying *Average Demand Interval* (ADI) and *Coefficient of Variation Squared* (CV^2) thresholds, and the data was augmented with engineered features. Our experimental results indicate that CatBoost, especially the CV^2 filtering model, achieves the lowest *Mean Absolute Error* (MAE), outperforming XGBoost models. The proposed framework can integrate seamlessly into existing systems, providing a cost-effective, data-driven solution for improved supply-chain management in the aviation aftermarket.**

***Index Terms*—demand forecasting, aviation, CatBoost, XGBoost, feature selection, machine learning**

1. Introduction

The aviation aftermarket is essential for ensuring operational readiness and cost efficiency across global aircraft fleets. Unlike industries with stable demand patterns, the aviation sector faces significant volatility due to fluctuating maintenance schedules, unexpected operational needs, and varying regulatory requirements [1]. Accurate demand forecasting in this sector is both crucial and highly complex. Inaccurate predictions typically lead to costly stockouts or overstock conditions. While overstock ties up capital and wastes resources, stockouts can cause maintenance delays or even canceled flights, disrupting business operations and profitability.

Traditional forecasting methods, such as *Autoregressive Integrated Moving Average* (ARIMA) [2] models, rely heavily on assumptions of consistent trends and seasonality. However, they often struggle with intermittent demand, which is marked by long periods without orders followed by sudden spikes. Early efforts to address intermittent demand focused on adapting exponential smoothing methods, leading to specialized techniques such as Croston's method [3] and its variants. These traditional methods improved forecasting but often depended on restrictive assumptions and did not fully utilize available granular data such as historical quotes and route details.

With the growing complexity of data in the aviation aftermarket, machine learning algorithms such as CatBoost [4], [5] and XGBoost [6], [7], which are based on gradient boosting, offer promising solutions. These models can efficiently manage non-linear relationships, feature interactions, categorical variables, and imbalanced data. Nevertheless, their effectiveness relies on careful data curation and domain-specific feature engineering.

Our study emphasizes features capturing intermittent demand characteristics, focusing on two key metrics:

- ***Average Demand Interval* (ADI):** Average time interval between successive part demands, indicating regularity.
- ***Coefficient of Variation Squared* (CV^2):** Squared ratio of standard deviation to mean, quantifying demand variability.

Demand is traditionally classified based on thresholds (ADI = 1.32, CV^2 = 0.49) defined by Syntetos et al. [3] into four types:

- **Smooth:** ADI $\leq$ 1.32, $CV^2 \leq 0.49$
- **Erratic:** ADI $\leq$ 1.32, $CV^2 > 0.49$
- **Intermittent:** ADI $>$ 1.32, $CV^2 \leq 0.49$
- **Lumpy:** ADI $>$ 1.32, $CV^2 > 0.49$

These classifications enable tailored forecasting techniques, enhancing predictive accuracy.

This paper investigates the use of advanced gradient-boosting models to forecast monthly aggregated demand for used aircraft parts. Our approach combines targeted data filtering via ADI and CV^2, along with an engineered feature set that includes cyclical transformations, route-based aggregations, and lag variables. Our experimental findings show that CatBoost, applied to a suitably filtered and augmented dataset, yields more accurate predictions as measured by *Mean Absolute Error* (MAE).

The paper is structured as follows: Section 2 reviews relevant literature; Section 3 details our data collection, preprocessing, and feature engineering methods; Section 4 presents our experimental findings; and Section 5 summarizes key points and suggests directions for future research.

2. Related Work

This literature review covers four key studies on demand forecasting. Each focuses on forecasting methods suited to intermittent or non-smooth demand patterns, common in service parts.

Amirkolaii et al. [8] evaluated forecasting techniques for business aircraft spare parts using data from Dassault Aviation, covering 23,646 *Stock Keeping Units* (SKUs) across 22 locations from 2012 to 2015. Based on ADI and CV^2 thresholds, 65% of SKUs showed intermittent demand, 31% lumpy, and 4% smooth or erratic. Forecasts were performed on 30 SKUs using 12 rolling windows of 36 periods to predict the final 12, allowing one-month inventory adjustments aligned with business needs. Their research compared six classical methods: Croston, Croston *Syntetos-Boylan Approximation* (SBA), Croston *Teunter-Syntetos-Babai* (TSB), Croston *Shale-Boylan-Johnston* (SBJ), moving average, and single exponential smoothing. These were tested against four multi-layer perceptron [9] variants (M-S1, M-S2, M-S3, M-S4), which differed in input features and whether demand was forecasted for individual SKUs or all SKUs collectively. All approaches were benchmarked against Dassault Aviation's commercial forecasting model, with performance evaluated using *Mean Squared Error* (MSE) and total inventory cost based on overstocking and understocking. Models M-S1 and M-S3, which predicted demand for individual SKUs, outperformed others in 90% of cases. In contrast, M-S2 and M-S4, which forecast all SKUs simultaneously, performed the worst. Among the classical methods, Croston TSB, moving average, and the commercial model delivered the strongest results in the remaining cases. The findings demonstrate that artificial intelligence models can enhance forecasting accuracy when feature relevance is well aligned with SKU-level behavior.

Dodin et al. [10] proposed two machine learning-based frameworks to improve forecasting for Bombardier Aftermarket's business aircraft spare parts, where 90% of parts exhibit intermittent demand. The inventory consists of 97.14% expendable and 2.86% rotable parts, with greater intermittency among expendables. The company previously used a regional adaptation of Croston's method to forecast monthly demand across 15 locations within three global regions. To enhance forecast performance, the authors developed the *Rotable Machine Learning* (RML) framework for rotable parts, built using *Light Gradient Boosting Machine* (LGBM) [11] and Elastic Net [12], and the *Intermittent Machine Learning* (IML) framework for expendable parts, which combined LGBM with a machine learning-enhanced Croston variant. Both frameworks used data from 2015–2019 and incorporated features including flight activity, customer data, and rolling demand statistics. Evaluation on a test set from May 2018 to December 2019 showed that both frameworks outperformed the legacy method by at least 7% in *Root Mean Squared Scaled Error* (RMSSE) and *Normalized Forecasting Bias* (NFB), while also reducing runtime from 30 to 8 hours. Following deployment from January to July 2021, forecast accuracy improved by 5.3%, resulting in lower costs, greater operational flexibility, and improved customer satisfaction.

Kannan et al. [13] investigated demand forecasting for spare parts using over one million transaction records from 28,344 SKUs provided by an anonymous original equipment manufacturer. After filtering to include only parts with at least four months of positive demand, 25,789 SKUs were retained for analysis. Intermittent and lumpy demand were identified using adjusted ADI and CV^2 thresholds, allowing for more targeted forecasting strategies. Experiments on 6,415 SKUs from early 2020 evaluated forecasting accuracy using the Forecast Economic Gain function. Surprisingly, baseline methods such as Naïve Forecasting [14] and the Zero Forecast Method [15] outperformed others, with Naïve Forecasting achieving the highest overall gain. Although machine learning models like XGBoost and Random Forest [16] outperformed time series methods overall, they were top performers for only 14% of SKUs. In subsequent quarterly forecasts using the full test set, LightGBM with quotation activity features (LGBMq) produced the best results across all demand types. For smooth demand, Facebook Prophet performed comparably. Overall, machine learning models showed stronger performance in final evaluations, especially when enriched with relevant features.

Kaya et al. [17] evaluated Croston's method and three of its variants: Syntetos-Boylan Approximation (SBA), Levén and Segerstedt, and Vinh. The study used synthetic and real-world datasets. The real-world data came from Turkish Airlines and included 500 SKUs, with 131,000 demand instances from January 2009 to December 2013. In this dataset, 92.6% of the time series were intermittent and 7.4% were lumpy. The synthetic experiment involved 400 datasets generated in R, each with 300 instances evenly split across four demand types. Forecast accuracy was measured using the geometric mean of the absolute scaled error (*Geometric Mean of the Mean Squared Error Average* (GMAMSE/A)) [18]. In both experiments, the Levén and Segerstedt variant consistently performed best. Vinh's method ranked second in most cases, while the original Croston and SBA variants generally performed worst. These results were consistent across both datasets. The findings support the continued relevance of Croston-based forecasting techniques, particularly refined variants. The authors recommend comparing these with newer models developed for irregular or sparse demand.

Although these existing studies make notable strides in forecasting intermittent demand for spare parts, they often rely on classical methods with limited feature integration or machine learning frameworks that lack key domain-specific variables. These prior studies neglect advanced feature engineering, such as cyclical time variables or route-based aggregations, despite their operational relevance. In addition, some of the proposed solutions remain constrained by small, highly filtered datasets or rely heavily on exponential smoothing approaches. This prevents full use of diverse transactional and operational data. Our work fills these gaps by applying CatBoost and XGBoost with tailored feature engineering (e.g., route-based aggregations, cyclical time variables), while rigorously evaluating the role of ADI and CV^2 filtering.

3. Methodology

A. Data Collection and Preprocessing

The dataset for this study was sourced from a proprietary Snowflake database, comprising aviation aftermarket sales orders and customer quotes from January 2022 to June 2024. These records include detailed information on aircraft parts, customer interactions, and relevant transactional details. Because the demand patterns are intermittent, monthly aggregation was chosen to capture broader cycles and reduce noise from daily fluctuations.

B. Feature Calculation and Data Filtering

A key step in preprocessing involved computing the ADI and CV^2 for each part number:

- **ADI:** Calculated by averaging the intervals between non-zero demand occurrences. It identifies parts with more consistent demand patterns.
- **CV^2:** Obtained by squaring the coefficient of variation of demand quantities, emphasizing demand variability. A lower CV^2 points to more stable demand, beneficial for forecasting.

Based on ADI and CV^2, the dataset was divided into three groups to focus on parts with varying demand characteristics:

1) **ADI Only Filter:** Parts with ADI < 1.32 were selected, indicating relatively consistent intervals between demand occurrences.
2) **CV^2 Only Filter:** Parts with $CV^2 \leq 0.49$ were chosen for their lower variability in demand.
3) **Combined ADI + CV^2 Filter:** Parts satisfying both ADI ≤ 1.32 and $CV^2 \leq 0.49$ were grouped, highlighting parts with stable and regular demand patterns.

C. Dataset Sizes After Filtering

TABLE 1: Dataset sizes after applying each filter

Filter	Training Set	Test Set
ADI Only	883	319
CV^2 Only	10,706	2,258
Combined ADI + CV^2	549	221

Notably, the combined ADI + CV^2 filter in Table 1 yielded a substantially smaller dataset, potentially limiting the learning capacity of certain models.

D. Data Splitting

To preserve temporal order, the data was divided into training and testing sets based on time periods:

- **Training Set:** The first **26 months** (January 2022 to February 2024).
- **Test Set:** The most recent **4 months** (March 2024 to June 2024).

This split mirrors real-world scenarios in which models forecast future demand using only historical data.

E. Model Selection

Two gradient-boosting models were chosen:

- **CatBoost:** Known for its native handling of categorical variables and robust performance on imbalanced data, CatBoost often excels in cases with complex feature interactions [19].
- **XGBoost:** A powerful framework recognized for its scalability and efficiency. XGBoost requires explicit encoding of categorical variables but can model intricate relationships effectively [20].

F. Model Configuration

Both models were tuned to balance predictive accuracy and computational cost:

- **Iterations:** 2,000 rounds of boosting.
- **Learning Rate:** 0.05 for gradual convergence.
- **Depth:** Tree depth of 6 to capture interactions without overfitting.
- **Categorical Features:** Used natively in CatBoost; for XGBoost, an explicit encoding process is required.

G. Feature Engineering

Additional features were constructed to capture temporal, cyclical, and behavioral patterns in the data, resulting in six engineered attributes:

1) Date-Based Features: Month and year were extracted from each record's entry date to capture seasonal and yearly trends.

- **Month:** An integer value from 1 to 12 indicating the transaction month.
- **Year:** The transaction year (e.g., 2022, 2023) to account for long-term trends.

2) Cyclical Time Features: Months form a natural cycle, so sine and cosine transformations were applied:

- **Month_Sin:** $\sin\left(\frac{2\pi \times \text{Month}}{12}\right)$
- **Month_Cos:** $\cos\left(\frac{2\pi \times \text{Month}}{12}\right)$

These transformations help the model detect cyclical demand patterns.

3) Route-Based Aggregation: A route record refers to the historical demand along a particular service route. The aggregation combines part number and customer information, capturing usage patterns across routes:

- **Route_Customer_Count:** The number of unique customers per route, indicating overall route diversity.

4) Lag Feature: A lag feature incorporates historical insights and is essential for capturing temporal dependencies in time series data:

- **Lag_1_Condition_Simple**: The condition of the parts sold on the same route in the prior month.

5) Summary of Engineered Features:

a) **Month**
b) **Year**
c) **Month_Sin**
d) **Month_Cos**
e) **Route_Customer_Count**
f) **Lag_1_Condition_Simple**

H. Handling Missing Values

For `Lag_1_Condition_Simple`, the first record of each route has no prior-month data, leading to a missing value. Missing values in Lag_1_Condition_Simple were filled using the next valid observation (backward fill).

4. Results and Discussion

This section reports and analyzes the outcomes of our demand forecasting approach.

A. Initial Model Performance (Without Feature Engineering)

We evaluated the performance of CatBoost and XGBoost across three filtered datasets: **ADI only**, **CV^2 only**, and the **combined ADI + CV^2**, using the MAE metric.

1) Definition and Benefits of MAE: ***Mean Absolute Error* (MAE)** quantifies the average magnitude of errors between predicted and actual demand:

$$\text{MAE} = \frac{1}{n}\sum_{i=1}^{n}\left|\hat{y}_i - y_i\right| \quad (1)$$

- $\hat{y}_i$: Predicted demand quantity
- y_i: Actual demand quantity
- n: Number of observations

Advantages of MAE:

- **Interpretability:** Errors remain in the same units as the target variable, simplifying analysis.
- **Robustness to Outliers:** Less sensitive to extremes than metrics like Mean Squared Error.
- **Simplicity:** Straightforward to compute and understand.

2) Initial Results: As shown in Table 2, CatBoost was tested on datasets filtered by ADI only, CV^2 only, and ADI + CV^2 without feature engineering.

TABLE 2: CatBoost Results for Different Filters (Without Feature Engineering)

Metric	ADI Only	CV^2 Only	ADI + CV^2
Mean Absolute Error (MAE)	4.3389	2.1250	4.3337
Minimum Error	0.00197	0.00017	0.0046
Maximum Error	108.46	137.59	68.57
Std. Dev. of Errors	9.03	8.11	10.32

Table 3 presents the XGBoost results for the same three filters without feature engineering.

TABLE 3: XGBoost Results for Different Filters (Without Feature Engineering)

Metric	ADI Only	CV^2 Only	ADI + CV^2
Mean Absolute Error (MAE)	4.4272	2.3721	9.6327
Minimum Error	0.00082	0.00005	0.00119
Maximum Error	343.66	194.71	387.04
Std. Dev. of Errors	20.30	10.72	51.57

3) Analysis of Initial Model Performance:

a) CatBoost vs. XGBoost:

- **Consistent Superiority for CatBoost:** Table 2 shows lower MAE and smaller standard deviations for CatBoost, indicating more stable predictions than XGBoost (Table 3) across all filters.
- **Increased Variability for XGBoost:** XGBoost exhibited higher maximum errors and greater variance, especially under the ADI + CV^2 filter.

b) Impact of Filtering Methods:

- **CV^2 Only Filter:** Both models performed best with this filter, suggesting that demand variability (*i.e.,* CV^2) is a key factor in forecasting intermittent demand.
- **Combined ADI + CV^2 Filter:** Performance dropped when both filters were applied, likely due to:
  - **Reduced Dataset Size:** Fewer data points hampered model learning.
  - **Loss of Potentially Valuable Data:** Some parts with useful patterns may have been excluded.

B. Feature Engineering and Model Performance

Having established baseline performance, we next evaluated the impact of the engineered features described in Section 3. We re-trained the CatBoost models using these features but only on the **ADI Only** and **CV^2 Only** datasets, since they already showed superior baseline performance.

1) Feature Selection for CatBoost Models: Our experiments identified specific feature subsets that produced optimal results:

a) ADI Only Filter:

1) **Average_Unit_Price**
2) **ADI**
3) **Month_Sin**
4) **Month_Cos**

b) CV^2 Only Filter:

1) **Average_Unit_Price**
2) **CV^2**
3) **Route_Customer_Count**

TABLE 4: CatBoost Performance after Feature Engineering

Metric	ADI Only Filter	CV^2 Only Filter
Mean Absolute Error (MAE)	3.4099	1.8349
Minimum Error	0.0241	0.00052
Maximum Error	124.09	159.35
Std. Dev. of Errors	8.62	7.86

2) Analysis of Feature Engineering Impact:

a) Improved Performance: Table 4 shows a notable drop in MAE for both filters compared to initial results (Table 2), indicating that additional features enriched the model's predictive capacity.

b) CV^2 Filter Advantage: With feature engineering, the CV^2 dataset's MAE of 1.83 significantly outperforms the ADI filter's 3.41, likely reflecting the predictive importance of demand variability and the benefit of a larger dataset.

c) Practical Implications: An MAE of around 1.83 allows for tighter control over spare-part inventory in an environment marked by lumpy or intermittent demand. This level of accuracy can help reduce holding costs and mitigate stockouts.

C. Interpreting MAE in Context

To assess whether the MAE is acceptable, it should be compared with the actual scale of demand.

Table 5 summarizes descriptive statistics for the target variable (*Total_Qty_Requested*) under both ADI and CV^2 filtering.

TABLE 5: Target Variable Statistics in Test Sets

Statistic	ADI Only Filter	CV^2 Only Filter
Mean Demand	3.64 units	2.78 units
Median Demand	1.0 unit	1.0 unit
Standard Deviation	8.74 units	10.01 units
Maximum Demand	124 units	189 units

a) Scale of Predictions: For the ADI filter, mean demand is 3.64 units, while for CV^2 it is 2.78 units. Achieving an MAE in the 1.83–3.41 range places predictions well within typical monthly demand variations.

b) Business Impact: From an inventory standpoint, these error rates are likely acceptable for most spare parts. More critical or higher-cost items may warrant even tighter forecasts to avoid overstocking or service disruptions.

TABLE 6: Sample Demand Predictions for Selected Part Numbers

Part No.	Actual	Predicted
X1	3.00	1.94
X2	1.00	2.25
X3	1.00	2.00
X4	2.00	1.51
X5	1.00	1.11

c) Predictions by Part: Table 6 highlights how predictions align relatively closely with actual values for several test instances, demonstrating the model's ability to handle varying levels of demand complexity. Overall, these results highlight the potential of a data-driven, machine learning approach to handle intermittent demand effectively.

5. Conclusion

This study demonstrates that advanced gradient-boosting models, particularly CatBoost, can significantly enhance demand forecasting in the aviation aftermarket, where intermittent demand is a major challenge. Focusing on demand variability (CV^2) yielded the most accurate predictions, especially when combined with well-engineered features. In contrast, using both ADI and CV^2 reduced dataset size and weakened model performance. Our results show that CV^2 filtering and domain-specific features are critical for accurate forecasts, enabling tighter inventory control.

Future work should explore larger, more diverse datasets and integrate external indicators like maintenance schedules or economic signals to improve contextual understanding. Continued refinement of features and modeling strategies can further reduce forecast error, minimize inventory costs, prevent stockouts, and improve overall operational efficiency in the aviation sector.

6. Acknowledgments

We would like to thank the reviewers in the Data Mining and Machine Learning Laboratory at Florida Atlantic University.

References

[1] C.-L. Wu and R. E. Caves, "Aircraft operational costs and turnaround efficiency at airports," *Journal of Air Transport Management*, vol. 6, no. 4, pp. 201–208, 2000.

[2] R. H. Shumway, D. S. Stoffer, R. H. Shumway, and D. S. Stoffer, "Arima models," *Time series analysis and its applications: with R examples*, pp. 75–163, 2017.

[3] A. A. Syntetos, J. E. Boylan, and J. D. Croston, "On the categorization of demand patterns," *Journal of the Operational Research Society*, vol. 56, no. 5, pp. 495–503, 2005.

[4] J. L. Leevy, T. M. Khoshgoftaar, and J. Hancock, "Evaluating performance metrics for credit card fraud classification," in *2022 IEEE 34th International Conference on Tools with Artificial Intelligence (ICTAI)*. IEEE, 2022, pp. 1336–1341.

[5] Q. Liang, R. A. Bauder, and T. M. Khoshgoftaar, "Enhancing medicare fraud detection: Random undersampling followed by shap-driven feature selection with big data," in *2024 IEEE 36th International Conference on Tools with Artificial Intelligence (ICTAI)*. IEEE, 2024, pp. 256–263.

[6] J. Hancock, J. M. Johnson, and T. M. Khoshgoftaar, "A comparative approach to threshold optimization for classifying imbalanced data," in *2022 IEEE 8th International Conference on Collaboration and Internet Computing (CIC)*. IEEE, 2022, pp. 135–142.

[7] R. K. Kennedy, J. M. Johnson, and T. M. Khoshgoftaar, "The effects of class label noise on highly-imbalanced big data," in *2021 IEEE 33rd International Conference on Tools with Artificial Intelligence (ICTAI)*. IEEE, 2021, pp. 1427–1433.

[8] K. N. Amirkolaii, A. Baboli, M. Shahzad, and R. Tonadre, "Demand forecasting for irregular demands in business aircraft spare parts supply chains by using artificial intelligence (ai)," *IFAC-PapersOnLine*, vol. 50, no. 1, pp. 15 221–15 226, 2017.

[9] T. M. Khoshgoftaar, J. Van Hulse, and A. Napolitano, "Supervised neural network modeling: an empirical investigation into learning from imbalanced data with labeling errors," *IEEE Transactions on Neural Networks*, vol. 21, no. 5, pp. 813–830, 2010.

[10] P. Dodin, J. Xiao, Y. Adulyasak, N. E. Alamdari, L. Gauthier, P. Grangier, P. Lemaitre, and W. L. Hamilton, "Bombardier aftermarket demand forecast with machine learning," *INFORMS Journal on Applied Analytics*, vol. 53, no. 6, pp. 425–445, 2023.

[11] C. M. Zuvieta, J. L. Leevy, and T. M. Khoshgoftaar, "A survey on statistical and ml-based demand forecasting methods for spare parts in aviation," *IEEE Access*, 2025.

[12] H. Zou and T. Hastie, "Regularization and variable selection via the elastic net," *Journal of the Royal Statistical Society Series B: Statistical Methodology*, vol. 67, no. 2, pp. 301–320, 2005.

[13] B. Adur Kannan, G. Kodi, O. Padilla, D. Gray, and B. C. Smith, "Forecasting spare parts sporadic demand using traditional methods and machine learning-a comparative study," *SMU Data Science Review*, vol. 3, no. 2, p. 9, 2020.

[14] C. P. Dhakal, "A naïve approach for comparing a forecast model," *International Journal of Thesis Projects and Dissertations (IJTPD)*, vol. 5, no. 1, pp. 1–3, 2017.

[15] D. C. Chatfield and J. C. Hayya, "All-zero forecasts for lumpy demand: a factorial study," *International Journal of Production Research*, vol. 45, no. 4, pp. 935–950, 2007.

[16] T. M. Khoshgoftaar, M. Golawala, and J. Van Hulse, "An empirical study of learning from imbalanced data using random forest," in *19th IEEE international conference on tools with artificial intelligence (ICTAI 2007)*, vol. 2. IEEE, 2007, pp. 310–317.

[17] G. O. Kaya, M. Sahin, and O. F. Demirel, "Intermittent demand forecasting: a guideline for method selection," *Sādhanā*, vol. 45, pp. 1–7, 2020.

[18] G. O. Kaya, O. F. Demirel, and O. F. Beyca, "Forecasting intermittent demand using the cox process." *Journal of Multiple-Valued Logic & Soft Computing*, vol. 31, 2018.

[19] J. T. Hancock and T. M. Khoshgoftaar, "Catboost for big data: an interdisciplinary review," *Journal of big data*, vol. 7, no. 1, p. 94, 2020.

[20] P. Zhang, Y. Jia, and Y. Shang, "Research and application of xgboost in imbalanced data," *International Journal of Distributed Sensor Networks*, vol. 18, no. 6, p. 15501329221106935, 2022.

Perturbation Strategies for the Component Assignment Problem in Three-Dimensional Consecutive-k Systems

Taishin NAKAMURA[1], Tomoaki AKIBA[2], Koji SHINGYOCHI[3]

[1]Department of Applied Computer Engineering, Tokai University,
4-1-1 Kitakaname, Hiratsuka, Kanagawa, Japan.

[2]Department of Business System Design and Management, Chiba Institute of Technology,
2-17-1 Narashino, Chiba, Japan.

[3]Department of Social and Information Design, Jumonji University,
2-1-28 Sugasawa, Niiza, Saitama, Japan.

Keywords: Three-dimensional Consecutive-k System, Component Assignment Problem, Iterated Local Search, Optimization

Abstract - This paper addresses the component assignment problem in linear connected-$(1,1,2)$!-out-of-(n_1,n_2,n_3):F systems, where system failure occurs if and only if a pair of adjacent failed components is arranged along any of the three coordinate axes. We propose an iterated local search algorithm incorporating five different perturbation methods specifically designed for this system. Computational experiments on various system sizes reveal that the effectiveness of these perturbation methods depends on the system's size parameters. Notably, the parity (even or odd) of these parameters influences the optimal component arrangement, as certain advantageous patterns are more easily achieved in systems with odd parameters. The proposed perturbation strategies can also serve as mutation operators in genetic algorithms and other metaheuristics.

1 Introduction

Consecutive-k systems are models where clusters of failed components can cause system failure. Three-dimensional consecutive-k systems comprise components arranged in a three-dimensional grid. These systems have applications in various fields, including medical diagnostic systems that process three-dimensional imaging data [1], and environmental monitoring networks in cold storage facilities [2].

Among these, the three-dimensional consecutive-(r_1,r_2,r_3)-out-of-(n_1,n_2,n_3):F system (abbreviated as $(r_1,r_2,r_3)/(n_1,n_2,n_3)$:F), comprising $n_1 \times n_2 \times n_3$ components in an (n_1,n_2,n_3) rectangular solid, fails if and only if (iff) a $r_1 \times r_2 \times r_3$ block of failed components exists. Yi *et al.* [2] further introduced the linear connected-(r_1,r_2,r_3)!-out-of-(n_1,n_2,n_3):F system (abbreviated as $(r_1,r_2,r_3)!/(n_1,n_2,n_3)$:F), where $r_1 \leq r_2 \leq r_3$. This system also comprises $n_1 \times n_2 \times n_3$ components and fails iff there exist $r_1 \times r_2 \times r_3$, $r_1 \times r_3 \times r_2$, $r_2 \times r_1 \times r_3$, $r_2 \times r_3 \times r_1$, $r_3 \times r_1 \times r_2$, or $r_3 \times r_2 \times r_1$ consecutive failed components. For example, in the $(r_1,r_2,r_3)!/(n_1,n_2,n_3)$:F system with $(r_1,r_2,r_3) = (1,1,2)$, i.e., the $(1,1,2)!/(n_1,n_2,n_3)$:F system, failure occurs iff a pair of adjacent failed components is arranged along any of the three coordinate axes.

Previous studies focused on calculating the reliability of three-dimensional consecutive-k systems. Two effective approaches have been developed for this purpose, the recursive equation approach (REA) and the finite Markov chain imbedding approach (FMCIA). Akiba *et al.* [3] proposed an REA for computing the reliability of $(r_1,r_2,r_3)/(n_1,n_2,n_3)$:F systems.

Conversely, Gharib *et al.* [4] applied the FMCIA to calculate the reliability of a simple $(1,1,2)!/(n_1,n_2,n_3)$:F system with $n_2 = n_3 = 2$. Yi *et al.* [2] employed FMCIA to evaluate several types of three-dimensional consecutive-k systems, including $(r_1,r_2,r_3)/(n_1,n_2,n_3)$:F and $(r_1,r_2,r_3)!/(n_1,n_2,n_3)$:F systems. Recently, Akiba *et al.* [5] discussed the similarities and differences between REA and FMCIA in computing the reliability of $(r_1,r_2,r_3)/(n_1,n_2,n_3)$:F systems.

The reliabilities of components in real-world systems may exhibit non-negligible differences due to factors such as manufacturing variations, usage history, or procurement from different suppliers. Thus, determining the optimal arrangement of components is crucial for improving overall system reliability. The component assignment problem (CAP) seeks to determine the optimal arrangement of components with different reliabilities to maximize overall system reliability. Although exhaustive enumeration can, theoretically, yield optimal solutions, it is computationally impractical for real-world applications.

This difficulty is particularly acute in three-dimensional consecutive-k systems, where the solution space grows exponentially with system size, necessitating the use of metaheuristic algorithms to efficiently find high-quality solutions. For $(r_1,r_2,r_3)/(n_1,n_2,n_3)$:F systems, Akiba and Nakamura [6] proposed a genetic algorithm (GA) to obtain near-optimal solutions. However, no specific algorithm has yet been reported for solving the CAP in $(1,1,2)!/(n_1,n_2,n_3)$:F systems.

This study aimed to construct an iterated local search (ILS) algorithm to address the CAP in $(1,1,2)!/(n_1,n_2,n_3)$:F systems. The ILS framework incorporates perturbation to introduce mod-

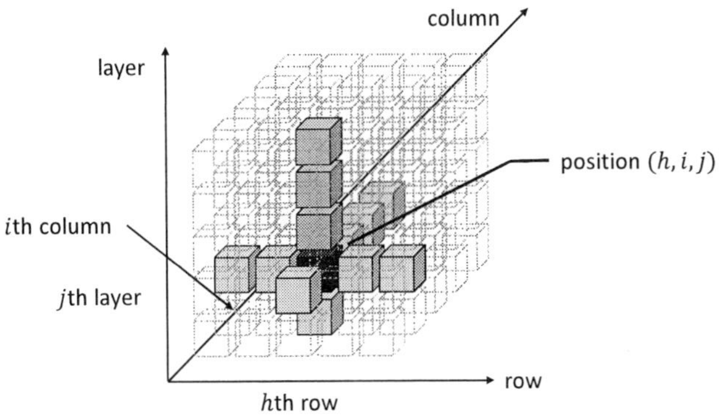

Figure 1: Position in row h, column i, and layer j of the system.

erate modifications to the current solution to escape local optima and explore new regions of the search space. Our algorithm uses perturbation mechanisms tailored to the structural properties of the system. These schemes effective within the ILS framework can also be adapted as mutation operators in GA and other meta-heuristic approaches.

2 Formulations

We first present the formulation of the CAP for $(1,1,2)!/(n_1,n_2,n_3)$:F systems. The following assumptions are adopted in this work:

(a) Each component and the system can exist in only two states: working or failed.
(b) All components fail independently of one another.
(c) Reliabilities of all components are known.
(d) Components are functionally exchangeable.

Assumption (d) indicates that any component can be assigned to any position in the system.

For $h = 1,2,\dots,n_1$, $i = 1,2,\dots,n_2$, and $j = 1,2,\dots,n_3$, let (h,i,j) denote the position located at row h, column i, and layer j of the system (Figure 1). Let $\pi(h,i,j)$ $(\in \{1,2,\dots,n_1n_2n_3\})$ be the index of the component assigned to position (h,i,j). Then, the arrangement of $n_1 \times n_2 \times n_3$ components is expressed as

$$\Pi = \Big(\pi(h,i,j)\Big)_{1\le h\le n_1, 1\le i\le n_2, 1\le j\le n_3}. \tag{1}$$

Let p_τ denote the reliability of component τ $(\in \{1,2,\dots,n_1n_2n_3\})$. Without loss of generality, we assume that

$$p_1 < p_2 < \dots < p_{n_1n_2n_3}, \tag{2}$$

which implies that p_τ represents the τ-th lowest reliability among all components. Define the vector of component reliabilities as $\boldsymbol{p} = (p_1, p_2, \dots, p_{n_1n_2n_3})$. Let $R((n_1,n_2,n_3),\boldsymbol{p};\Pi)$ denote the system reliability of the $(1,1,2)!/(n_1,n_2,n_3)$:F system under component reliabilities $\boldsymbol{p}$ and arrangement Π.

Using these notations, the CAP for $(1,1,2)!/(n_1,n_2,n_3)$:F system is formulated as follows:

$$\Pi^* = \underset{\Pi\in\Omega}{\arg\max}\, R((n_1,n_2,n_3),\boldsymbol{p};\Pi), \tag{3}$$

where Ω represents the set of all possible arrangements Π.

3 Iterated Local Search for CAP

Here, we present an ILS algorithm to solve the CAP for the $(1,1,2)!/(n_1,n_2,n_3)$:F system.

ILS is a metaheuristic that systematically combines local search with perturbation mechanisms to effectively explore the solution space. It balances intensification (through local search) and diversification (through perturbation) to escape local optima and explore promising regions of the solution space. **Algorithm 1** presents our ILS framework.

Algorithm 1 Iterated local search for CAP.

Generate initial solution Π randomly
Apply local search (**Algorithm 2**) to Π
$\Pi_{\text{best}} \leftarrow \Pi$
while termination criteria not met **do**
    $\Pi \leftarrow \Pi_{\text{best}}$
    Apply a perturbation to Π
    Apply local search (**Algorithm 2**) to Π
    if reliability(Π) $\ge$ reliability(Π_{best}) **then**
        $\Pi_{\text{best}} \leftarrow \Pi$
    end if
end while
return Π_{best}

The following subsections describe the key components of the proposed algorithm.

3.1 Local Search

The local search procedure explores the neighborhood of a current solution by swapping pairs of components. A first-improvement strategy is employed: the search accepts the first swap that does not reduce the system reliability. **Algorithm 2** outlines this process.

Algorithm 2 Local search for CAP.

Initialize solution Π
while termination criteria not met **do**
    Select two distinct positions $\pi^{(a)}$ and $\pi^{(b)}$ randomly
    $\Pi' \leftarrow$ the solution obtained by swapping the components at $\pi^{(a)}$ and $\pi^{(b)}$ in Π
    Compute reliability of Π'
    if reliability(Π') $\ge$ reliability(Π) **then**
        $\Pi \leftarrow \Pi'$
    end if
end while
return Π

3.2 Perturbation Methods

For clarity, we define a "slice" as a two-dimensional cross-section of the three-dimensional (n_1,n_2,n_3) grid. A slice can take one of the following forms:

- an $n_2 \times n_3$ grid at a fixed h,
- an $n_1 \times n_3$ grid at a fixed i, or
- an $n_1 \times n_2$ grid at a fixed j.

Figure 2 illustrates a slice represented by an $n_1 \times n_2$ grid at a fixed j.

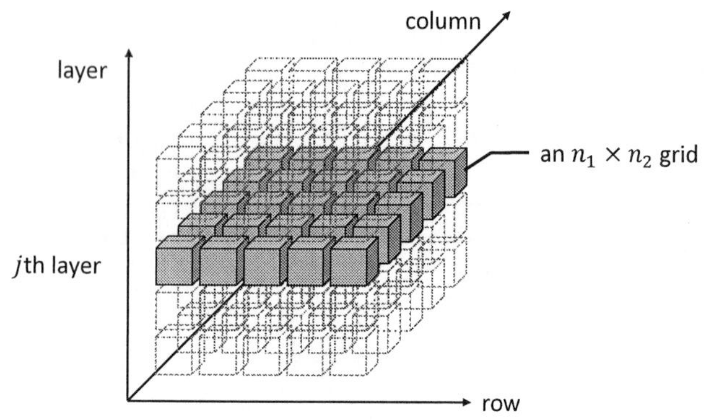

Figure 2: Slice represented as an $n_1 \times n_2$ grid at a fixed j.

Perturbation methods escape local optima and encourage exploration of diverse solution regions. The perturbation strength directly affects this balance. Excessive perturbation may destroy beneficial structural characteristics, reducing the discovery of improved solutions. Conversely, insufficient perturbation risks returning to previously visited local optima, thereby limiting diversification. To address this balance, we propose five tailored perturbation methods for the $(1,1,2)!/(n_1,n_2,n_3)$:F system:

(A) **Random Shuffle Perturbation**:
The entire component arrangement is randomized by shuffling all component positions in the system.

(B) **Component Swap Perturbation**:
Pairs of components are randomly selected and swapped. The number of swaps is controlled by a parameter (default: three swaps).

(C) **Slice Swap Perturbation**:
Pairs of randomly chosen slices are selected and exchanged. The number of slice swaps is controlled by a parameter (default: one swap).

(D) **Slice Rotation Perturbation**:
Randomly selected slices are rotated by 180 degrees.

(E) **Slice Reflection Perturbation**:
Randomly selected slices are reflected along either the horizontal or vertical axis.

4 Computational Experiments

Computational experiments were performed to evaluate the effectiveness of the proposed perturbation methods. We examined the performance of the methods across different system sizes and analyzed the structural characteristics of high-quality solutions.

4.1 Experimental Setup

The ILS algorithm was implemented in Python 3.10. All experiments were conducted on a machine equipped with an Intel(R) Core(TM) i9-11900K processor (3.50 GHz), 64.0 GB of RAM, and Windows 11 Pro operating system.

Here, we categorize system sizes based on the total number of components, $n_1 \times n_2 \times n_3$, as follows:

- Small: $(n_1,n_2,n_3) = (3,3,3)$, with 27 components
- Medium-1: $(n_1,n_2,n_3) = (3,3,4)$, with 36 components
- Medium-2: $(n_1,n_2,n_3) = (3,4,4)$, with 48 components
- Large: $(n_1,n_2,n_3) = (4,4,4)$, with 64 components

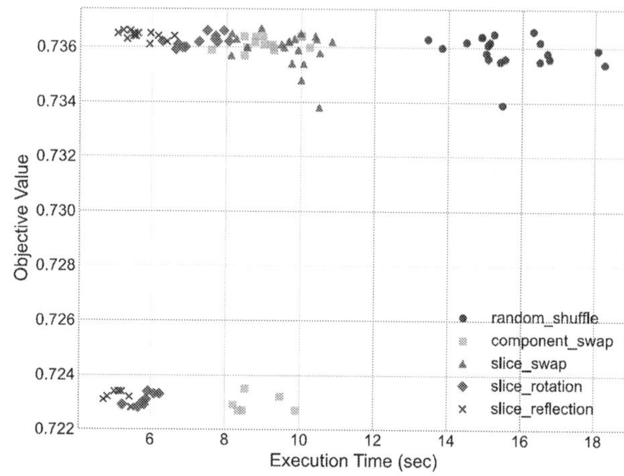

Figure 3: Scatter plot in the $(n_1,n_2,n_3) = (3,3,3)$ case.

It should be noted that this classification does not correspond to the actual sizes of real-world systems, but was introduced to facilitate the evaluation of the proposed perturbation methods. For each instance, component reliabilities were independently sampled from a uniform distribution over the interval $[0.80, 1.00]$; the resulting values were sorted in ascending order according to Eq. (2).

The ILS algorithm (**Algorithm 1**) was configured to terminate after 30 iterations. Additionally, the local search procedure (**Algorithm 2**) was terminated if no improvement in solution quality was observed over 30 consecutive iterations.

4.2 Results

Figures 3–6 show scatter plots of the relationship between system reliability (objective function value) and execution time (in seconds) for each instance. Each perturbation method was executed 20 times, using different random seeds.

A common pattern was observed in these results. Method (A), random shuffle, generally yields solutions of high quality but incurs a longer execution time. This method provides maximum diversification, which is particularly beneficial when the search is trapped in a deep local optimum. However, it entirely disrupts the beneficial solution structures accumulated during previous iterations, necessitating additional computational effort to rebuild them during subsequent local search phases.

Several noteworthy patterns were revealed regarding the suitability of each perturbation method across various system sizes.

- **Small systems** $(n_1,n_2,n_3) = (3,3,3)$: All methods except method (A) achieved solutions in relatively shorter time frames. This is primarily because these methods preserve good solution structures. However, methods (B) component swap, (D) slice rotation, and (E) slice reflection occasionally become trapped in strong local optima because of their relatively weak perturbation strengths.

- **Medium-sized systems** $(n_1,n_2,n_3) = (3,3,4)$ and $(n_1,n_2,n_3) = (3,4,4)$: Methods (B), (C), (D), and (E) showed relatively similar behavior. However, method (D) showed a recurring tendency to become trapped in local

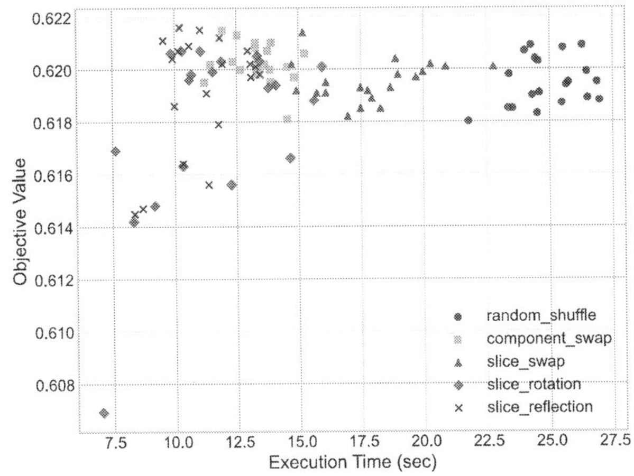

Figure 4: Scatter plot in the $(n_1, n_2, n_3) = (3, 3, 4)$ case.

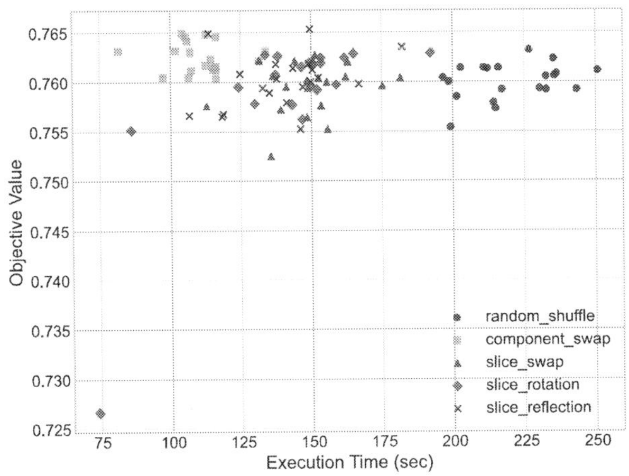

Figure 5: Scatter plot in the $(n_1, n_2, n_3) = (3, 4, 4)$ case.

optima, indicating insufficient diversification in certain cases.

- **Large systems** $(n_1, n_2, n_3) = (4, 4, 4)$: Methods (B) and (D) are recommended. These methods successfully balance the preservation of favorable structures with sufficient diversification to escape local optima.

4.3 Factors Influencing Perturbation Performance

Within the scope of our experiments, we observed that the performance of the perturbation methods depends on the parameters n_1, n_2, and n_3. From the results, we identified two key factors that influence performance.

4.3.1 Search Space Size

Parameters n_1, n_2, and n_3 determine the space size for the CAP. The search space increases exponentially with increase in system size. For larger systems, highly diversifying perturbation methods (e.g., Methods (A)) may severely disrupt promising solution structures, requiring more iterations to recover them. In contrast, methods that preserve structural integrity (e.g., Method (B)) tend to perform better on larger systems.

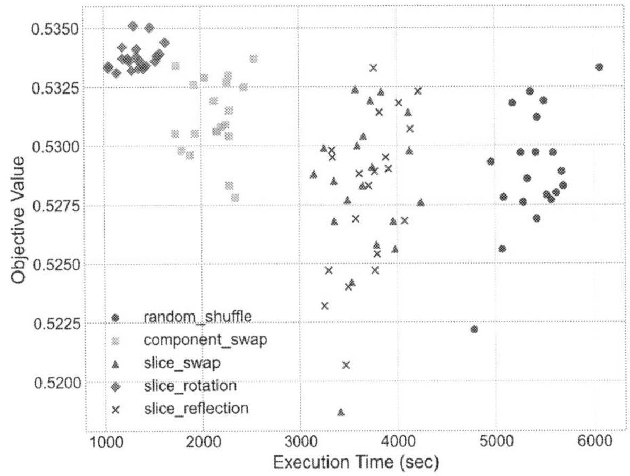

Figure 6: Scatter plot in the $(n_1, n_2, n_3) = (4, 4, 4)$ case.

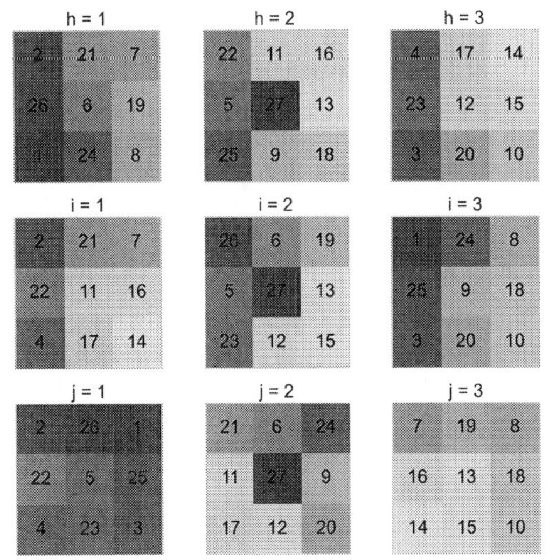

Figure 7: Heatmaps of the best component arrangement found for the $(n_1, n_2, n_3) = (3, 3, 3)$ case.

4.3.2 Impact of Parity in Parameters n_1, n_2, n_3

The $(1, 1, 2)!/(n_1, n_2, n_3)$:F system fails if a pair of adjacent components along any of the three coordinate axes fail. To reduce this risk, the following structural patterns are desirable:

(i) **Alternating high- and low-reliability components**: This pattern reduces the likelihood of adjacent failures by ensuring that low-reliability components are neighbored by high-reliability ones.

(ii) **High-reliability components placed interior and low-reliability components at the exterior**: Interior positions are typically involved in more minimal cut sets and have a greater influence on system reliability.

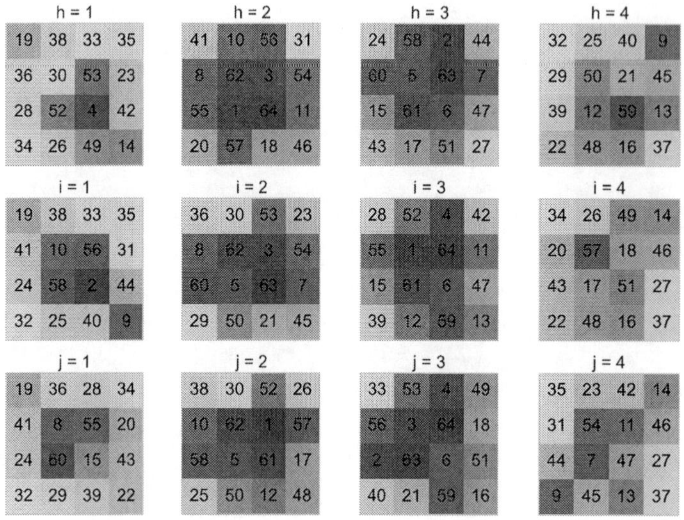

Figure 8: Heatmaps of the best component arrangement found for $(n_1,n_2,n_3) = (4,4,4)$ case.

When all parameters are odd, both patterns can be fulfilled simultaneously. However, if at least one parameter is even, maintaining both patterns simultaneously is impossible.

Figures 7 and 8 present heatmaps of slices (two-dimensional cross-sections) of the best solutions obtained in our experiments for the $(3,3,3)$ and $(4,4,4)$ cases, respectively. Each figure shows slices from multiple perspectives (rows, columns, and layers). Each cell contains a component index, with lower numbers indicating components of lower reliability. Colors range from blue (high reliability) to red (low reliability).

In the $(3,3,3)$ case, where all parameters are odd, an alternating arrangement of high- and low-reliability components is observed, with high-reliability components assigned to interior positions. By contrast, the $(4,4,4)$ case, with even parameters, exhibits more complex patterns, reflecting the algorithm's attempt to balance both structural goals. Overall, Figures 7 and 8 support our analysis of the effect of parameter parity on optimal component arrangements.

5 Concluding Remarks

In this study, we constructed an iterated local search algorithm to address the component assignment problem in $(1,1,2)!/(n_1,n_2,n_3)$:F systems. We evaluated five perturbation methods across various system sizes, finding their effectiveness influenced by size parameters. Specifically, the parity of the parameters, whether even or odd, affects component arrangements and the perturbation method performance. Future research will focus on designing adaptive perturbation strategies that consider system characteristics and the dynamic state of the search process.

6 Acknowledgement

This work was supported by Grant-in-Aid for JSPS KAKENHI Grant Numbers 25K17796.

7 References

[1] Anthony A. Salvia and William C. Lasher. "2-dimensional consecutive-k-out-of-n:F models,". *IEEE Transactions on Reliability*, 39(3):382–385, 1990. ISSN 0018-9529. doi: 10.1109/24.103023.

[2] H. Yi, N. Balakrishnan, and X. Li. "Reliability of three-dimensional consecutive-k-type systems,". *Reliability Engineering & System Safety*, 233:109131, 2023. doi: 10.1016/j.ress.2023.109131.

[3] T. Akiba, N. Takahashi, and H. Yamamoto. "Reliability of a 3-dimensional consecutive-k system,". In *Proceedings of the 9th International Conference on Mathematical Methods in Reliability*, pages 1144–1151, 2015.

[4] M. Gharib, E. M. El-Sayed, and I. Nashwan. "Reliability of connected $(1,1,2)$ or $(1,2,1)$ or $(2,1,1)$-out-of-$(n,2,2)$:F lattice systems,". *Journal of Advanced Research in Statistics and Probability*, 3(1):47–56, 2011. doi: 10.3844/jmssp.2010.261.264.

[5] T. Akiba, T. Nakamura, and H. Yamamoto. "Reliability expression of three-dimensional consecutive-k systems,". In *Reliability Analysis and Maintenance Optimization of Complex Systems*, pages 3–19. Springer, 2025.

[6] T. Akiba and T. Nakamura. "Method for obtaining quasi-optimal arrangement of the 3-dimensional consecutive-(r_1,r_2,r_3)-out-of-(n_1,n_2,n_3):F lattice system with GA,". In *Proceedings of the 24th Asia Pacific Industrial Engineering and Management Systems Conference*, pages 1154–1156, November 2024.

Investigation on the Improvement of Optimization Model for Consecutive-k-out-of-n: G Systems

Lei ZHOU
Department of Information and
Management System Engineering
Nagaoka University of Technology
Nagaoka, Niigata, Japan
zhoulei@vos.nagaokaut.ac.jp

Keywords: Consecutive-k-out-of-n:G system, number of failed components, optimization model

Abstract - A consecutive-k-out-of-n:G system consists of n components which are arranged in a line or a circle and the system works if and only if at least k consecutive components work. We once discussed maintenance policy for the consecutive-k-out-of-n:G system. Only failed components were considered to be maintained when the policies are carried out. As a result, the distributions and expected values of the number of failed components when system is failed or working at a particular time t was also evaluated. The expected cost rates were considered as the objective function to be minimized. However, the maintenance cost for the working components was assumed to be ignored and the proposed maintenance policy was ineffective in some cases. As a result, in this paper, we will improve the optimization model and verify the effectiveness of the model through numerical experiments.

1. Introduction

A consecutive-k-out-of-n:G system consists of n components which are arranged in a line or in a circle and the system works if and only if at least k consecutive components work [1]. Fig. 1 illustrates an example of the consecutive-k-out-of-n:G system. In this figure, whenever more than 2 consecutive components work, the signal transmission from the initial to the end will not be interrupted and the system becomes working. Zhang et al. [2] explained a typical application of consecutive-k-out-of-n:G systems to a railroad operation. Other examples are given by Kuo and Zuo [3], such as a photographing of a nuclear accelerator.

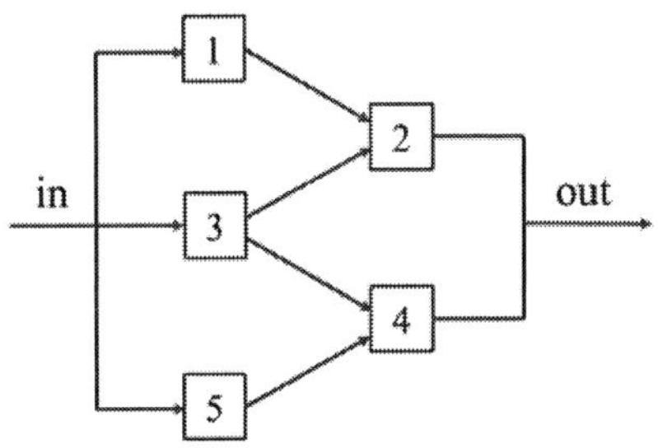

Figure 1. A consecutive-2-out-of-5:G system.

Considerable research on the reliability and the application to the optimal assignment of the consecutive-k-out-of-n:G system have been done by a few papers. Tong [4] reported the first study on the consecutive-k-out-of-n:G system and gave the definition of it. Navarro et al. [5] studied the failure rate of this system and proved that when $2k \geq n$, the system has IFR (increasing failure rate) if all components are independent and identical with IFR. Furthermore, Zuo and Kuo [6] derived the invariant optimal assignment of a circular consecutive-k-out-of-n:G system when $2k \geq n$. The more results can be found in [7–9].

In addition, several optimization problems have been well studied. Nakagawa [10] considered the k-out-of-n system (such the system works if and only if at least k components work) and proposed the model of the expected cost rate per renewal cycle. He also derived the optimal number of components in system design and the optimal replacement time in system maintenance analytically, by minimizing the expected cost rate. Zhou et al. [11] first studied the optimization problems for the consecutive-k-out-of-n:G system. They discussed the optimal number of components and the optimal replacement time respectively, by considering to replace all components in objective functions. It would be reasonable because the life of the working components at the time of maintenance may be damaged and will not be as new as ones at the next operation cycle. From an economical view, it is reasonable to replace failed components only. As a result, it is interesting to study the number of failed components when maintenance occurs. Recently, the number of failed or working components for different types of systems have been well studied and the study is considered to be useful to understand the behavior of the system. Papastavridis [12] first discussed the number of failed components at the moment when system failure occurs for a consecutive-k-out-of-n:F system (such the system failed if and only if at least k consecutive components failed). Eryilmaz [13, 14] studied the k-out-of-n:G system and obtained the expected number of working or failed components under the condition that the system is working or failed. He also used the results to propose the optimal replacement policies. Furthermore, for the consecutive-k-out-of-n system,

Eryilmaz [15] studied the number of working components under the condition that system is working at time t. Zhou et al. [16] then gave the expressions of the expected number of failed components under two situations where system is failed or working for a coherent system. Furthermore, Zhou and Yamamoto [17] used the results in [16] to improve the replacement policy by replacing failed components only from an economical view. However, they found out that when component lifetime follows Weibull distribution where $F(t) = 1 - \exp[-t^m]$ and m>1, the optimization model becomes ineffective.

As a result, in this paper, according to the optimization model in [17], we will consider the maintenance cost for working components and improve the effectiveness of the model.

2. Expected Number of Failed Components and the Proposed Optimization Model

In this section, we first briefly review the previously derived expected number of failed components and the proposed preventive maintenance model in [17].

Preventive maintenance is always applied to improve the system availability. We try to replace the components before system failure in order to decrease the maintenance cost of a failed system. However, the maintenance cost will be high if components are replaced frequently. Therefore, it is necessary to determine the economic maintenance time of the system. We considered a typical age-based replacement policy. In Fig. 2, the failed components will be replaced at the planned time t or the time of system failure, whichever occurs first. Thus, it is necessary to obtain the expected number of failed components under these two conditions. Case 1 is that system is working at time t and the expected number of failed components under the condition that system is still working was obtained. Case 2 is that system is failed before time t and the expected number of failed components under the condition that system failed before time t was obtained.

2.1 Expected number of failed components at a particular time t

Before introducing the expected number of failed components, we first give the definition of signature which is necessary for the calculation. Samaniego [18] gave the definition of the system signature $\mathbf{s}$, where $\mathbf{s} = (s_1, \ldots, s_n)$. It

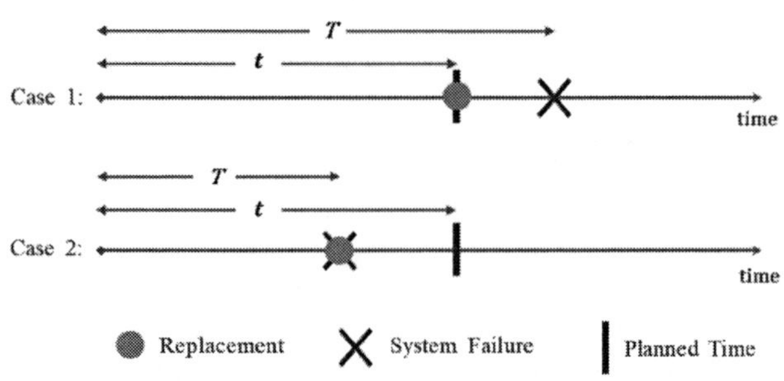

Figure 2. Process of age-based replacement.

is an n-dimensional probability vector whose ith element s_i is equal to the probability that the ith component failure causes the system failure. Here, s_i is expressed as

$$s_i = \Pr\{T = T_{[i]}\},$$

where T is the lifetime of the system and $T_{[i]}$ is the ith order statistic of the n component failure times, that is, the time of the ith component failure. Boland [19] defined the vector $\mathbf{A} = (a_1, \ldots, a_n)$, where a_j represents the proportion of component subsets of size j which are path sets for the system and it is expressed as

$$a_j = \frac{\#\text{ path sets of size } j \text{ for the system}}{\binom{n}{j}}.$$

Then the calculation formula of system signature is expressed as

$$s_{n-j} = a_{j+1} - a_j,$$

where $j = 0, \ldots, n-1$.

We then proposed the signature-based expression of the reliability for the consecutive-k-out-of-n:G system. Denote that $F(t)$ is the lifetime distribution of each component and $\bar{F}(t)$ is the survival function of each component, then

$$\Pr\{T > t\} = \sum_{i=1}^{n-k+1} s_i \Pr\{T_{[i]} > t\}$$
$$= \sum_{i=1}^{n-k+1} s_i \sum_{j=n-i+1}^{n} \binom{n}{j} \bar{F}(t)^j F(t)^{n-j}, \qquad (1)$$

where

$$s_i = \frac{N_{n-i+1}}{\binom{n}{i-1}} - \frac{N_{n-i}}{\binom{n}{i}},$$

and N_{n-i} is the number of path sets with $(n-i)$ working components of the consecutive-k-out-of-n:G system, which is expressed as

$$N_{n-i} = \binom{n}{i} - \sum_{q=0}^{\lfloor (n-i)/k \rfloor} (-1)^q \binom{i+1}{q} \binom{n-qk}{i}.$$

Case 1: system is working at time t

We first give the number of failed components while system is working at time t. Denote that $X(t)$ is the number of failed components until time t, then the conditional distribution of the number of failed components at a particular time t when a consecutive-k-out-of-n:G system is working is

$$\Pr\{X(t) = i | T > t\} = \frac{\Pr\{X(t) = i, T > t\}}{\Pr\{T > t\}}$$
$$= \frac{\Pr\{T > t | X(t) = i\} \Pr\{X(t) = i\}}{\Pr\{T > t\}}$$

$$= \frac{\binom{n}{i} \bar{F}(t)^{n-i} F(t)^i}{\Pr\{T > t\}} \sum_{j=i+1}^{n-k+1} s_j, \quad (2)$$

and the expected number of failed components under this condition is

$$E[X(t)|T > t] = \frac{\sum_{i=0}^{n-k} i\left(\sum_{j=i+1}^{n-k+1} s_j\right) \binom{n}{i} \bar{F}(t)^{n-i} F(t)^i}{\Pr\{T > t\}}. \quad (3)$$

Case 2: system is failed before time t

We then give the number of failed components when system is failed before time t. Denote that $\{X(T) = i|T \le t\}$ denotes the number of failed components under the condition that system failure occurs before time t, then the conditional distribution of the number of failed components at the time when the system is failed before time t is

$$\Pr\{X(T) = i|T \le t\} = \frac{\Pr\{T = T_{[i]}, T \le t\}}{\Pr\{T \le t\}} = \frac{\Pr\{T \le t|T = T_{[i]}\}\Pr\{T = T_{[i]}\}}{\Pr\{T \le t\}} = \frac{\Pr\{T = T_{[i]}\}\Pr\{T_{[i]} \le t\}}{\Pr\{T \le t\}} = \frac{s_i \sum_{j=0}^{n-i} \binom{n}{j} \bar{F}(t)^j F(t)^{n-j}}{\Pr\{T \le t\}}. \quad (4)$$

and the expected number of failed components under this condition is

$$E[X(T)|T \le t] = \frac{\sum_{i=1}^{n-k+1} i s_i \sum_{j=0}^{n-i} \binom{n}{j} \bar{F}(t)^j F(t)^{n-j}}{\Pr\{T \le t\}}. \quad (5)$$

2.2 Expected cost rate and the optimal replacement time

Under the age-based replacement policy, the expected time of a renewal cycle includes the time to system failure before the planned replacement time t, or the time t while system is still working. Then the expected replacement time of a renewal cycle is estimated as

$$E[\min(t, T)] = \int_0^t \Pr\{T > u\} du. \quad (6)$$

We then applied the results of the expected number of failed components to the preventive maintenance problems. As mentioned in [17], we gave the following assumptions in previous study: a. the components and system are either working or failed; b. the time of replacement activity is negligible; c. the maintenance cost for the working components is small to be ignored. To build the model of the cost rate, we considered two cost factors, where c_1 is the acquisition cost for each failed component, and c_R is the maintenance cost for the failed system. Using the renewal reward theory, we obtained the expected cost rate by a signature-based expression as

$$C_A(t; k, n) = \frac{\left[\begin{matrix} c_1 E[X(t)|T > t] \cdot \Pr\{T > t\} + \\ (c_R + c_1 E[X(T)|T \le t]) \cdot \Pr\{T \le t\} \end{matrix}\right]}{\int_0^t \Pr\{T > u\} du} = \frac{\left[\begin{matrix} c_1 \sum_{i=1}^{n-k+1}\left(\sum_{j=i}^{n-k+1} s_j\right)\Pr\{T_{[i]} \le t\} + \\ c_R \cdot \Pr\{T \le t\} \end{matrix}\right]}{\int_0^t \Pr\{T > u\} du}. \quad (7)$$

Then, we focused on the optimal replacement time t^* which minimizes the expected cost rate in Eq. (7). We also gave the results of the numerical experiments for the optimal replacement time with given k and n. Assumed that all components have the independent and identical Weibull lifetime distribution $F(t) = 1 - \exp[-t^m]$. According to the results, we found out that when $m > 1$, the expected cost rate increases strictly with t, which means that the proposed maintenance policy is ineffective. This outcome is likely due to the assumption made in our maintenance model that the cost associated with working components is negligible. However, when $m > 1$, the lifetime of normally working components also degrade over time during maintenance, which was not accounted for in the initial optimization model. As a result, we will improve the model by taking into account the maintenance cost associated with working components.

3. Improvement of the Optimization Model

As mentioned in Section 2, in this paper, we consider three cost factors, where c_1 and c_R are the same in Section 2, and c_2 is the maintenance cost for each working component. Then we give the new expected cost rate as

$$C_B(t; k, n) = \frac{\left[\begin{matrix} (c_1 E[X(t)|T > t] + c_2(n - E[X(t)|T > t])) \cdot \Pr\{T > t\} + \\ (c_R + c_1 E[X(T)|T \le t] + c_2(n - E[X(T)|T \le t])) \cdot \Pr\{T \le t\} \end{matrix}\right]}{\int_0^t \Pr\{T > u\} du} = \frac{c_1 G(t) + c_2(n - G(t)) + c_R \cdot \Pr\{T \le t\}}{\int_0^t \Pr\{T > u\} du}, \quad (8)$$

where $G(t) = \sum_{i=1}^{n-k+1}\left(\sum_{j=i}^{n-k+1} s_j\right)\Pr\{T_{[i]} \le t\}$. As a special case, when $t \to \infty$ in Eq. (8), the expected cost rate becomes

$$C_B(\infty; k, n) = \frac{\left(c_1 \sum_{i=1}^{n-k+1}(i \cdot s_i) + c_2\left(n - \sum_{i=1}^{n-k+1}(i \cdot s_i)\right)\right) + c_R \cdot \Pr\{T \le t\}}{\int_0^\infty \Pr\{T > u\} du}. \quad (9)$$

Taking the derivative of Eq. (8) with respect of t and setting it equal to 0, we have

$$\left[\frac{c_1 - c_2}{c_R} U(t) + H(t)\right] \int_0^t R(u) du - \frac{c_1 - c_2}{c_R} G(t) - \bar{R}(t) = \frac{c_2}{c_R} n, \quad (10)$$

where $R(t) = \Pr\{T > t\}$, $\bar{R}(t) = 1 - R(t)$, $U(t) = G'(t)/R(t)$, and $H(t) = -R'(t)/R(t)$. Letting the left-hand side of

Eq. (10) as $L(t)$, where $L(0) = 0$. Differentiating $L(t)$ with respect to t, we have

$$\frac{\mathrm{d}L(t)}{\mathrm{d}t} = \left[\frac{c_1 - c_2}{c_R} U'(t) + H'(t)\right] \int_0^t R(u)\mathrm{d}u. \tag{11}$$

As a result, we consider the following cases. (1) If the value of $\mathrm{d}L(t)/dt$ is always less than 0, then the expected cost rate $C_B(t;k,n)$ decreases strictly with t and system is considered to be maintained when system failure occurs, which corresponding the expected cost rate Eq. (9). (2) If $\mathrm{d}L(t)/\mathrm{d}t$ is greater than 0, then there exists a unique and finite $t^*(0 < t^* < \infty)$ which satisfies $L(t^*) = 0$, and t^* is the optimal maintenance time which minimizes the expected cost rate in Eq. (8).

4. Numerical Experiments

To verify the effectiveness of the improved optimization model in preventive maintenance of the system, we conduct numerical experiments and compare the results. We give the same assumption that all components have the independent and identical Weibull lifetime distribution $F(t) = 1 - \exp[-(\lambda t)^m]$. Furthermore, different values of n have different values of minimum expected cost rate, and we try to determine the optimal n^* and t^* simultaneously, which can give the most minimum value of the expected cost rate. For the given k, c_1, c_2, c_R and m, we check the expected cost rate by the given sufficient large number of n and find the optimal n^* and t^*. In Table 1, we give the results of the optimal n^*, t^* and the corresponding $C_B(t^*;k,n^*)$. To facilitate comparative analysis, the results of $C_A(t^*;k,n^*)$ obtained from the previous model were also presented. The symbol ∞ means that the optimal replacement time is infinity, where the expected cost rate decreases strictly with t and the system is considered to be maintained when system failure occurs. Then, we find out that although $m = 0.8$ and system has the decrease failure rate, the optimal replacement time t^* is not infinite when c_R is small for both $C_B(t^*;k,n^*)$ and $C_A(t^*;k,n^*)$, which is against the classical age replacement result. We explain it that according to the replacement policy, the optimal replacement time is not only related to the system reliability $R(t)$, but also related to the values of the expected number of failed components. Finally, we confirmed that when m>1, the minimal expected cost rate $C_B(t^*;k,n)$ exists, and the proposed improved optimization model is effective.

5. Conclusion

In this paper, a consecutive-k-out-of-n:G system is considered where the system is working if and only if at least k consecutive components work. We focused on the improvement of the optimization model for the optimal replacement time by minimizing the expected cost rate. The numerical experiments were conducted and the effectiveness of the new model was confirmed.

In this paper, when the optimal replacement time was studied, we only considered a simple preventive maintenance, the standard age replacement. However, the complicated maintenance, such as first age replacement or last age replacement, may be more practical during the preventive maintenance policies. It is interesting to discuss the differences between these replacement models.

6. References

[1] Y.L. Tong, "A rearrangement inequality for the longest run, with an application to net-work reliability," J. Appl. Probab., vol.22, pp.386–393, 1985.

[2] W.X. Zhang, C. Miller, and W. Kuo, "Application and analysis for a consecutive-k-out-of-n:G structure," Reliab. Eng. Syst. Safe., vol.33, pp.189–197, 1991.

[3] W. Kuo and M.J. Zuo, Optimal Reliability Modeling, Wileys, 2003.

[4] F. K. Hwang, "A Rearrangement Inequality for the Longest Run, with an Application to Net-Work Reliability," Journal of Applied probability, vol. 22, pp. 386–393, 1985.

[5] J. Navarro, A. Guillamón, and M.C. Ruiz, "Generalized mixtures in reliability modelling: Applications to the construction of bathtub shaped hazard models and the study of systems," Appl. Stochastic Models Bus. Ind., vol.25, pp.323–337, 2009.

[6] M. J. Zuo, and W. Kuo, "Design and Performance Analysis of Consecutive-k-out-of-n Structure," Nav. Res. Logist., vol. 37, pp. 203–230, 1990.

[7] S. Eryilmaz, "Conditional lifetimes of consecutive k-out-of-n systems," IEEE Trans. Rel., vol.59, no.1, pp.178–182, 2010.

[8] S. Eryilmaz, "Circular consecutive k-out-of-n systems with exchangeable dependent components," J. Stat. Plan. Inference, vol.141, pp.725–733, 2011.

[9] S. Eryilmaz and J. Navarro, "Failure rates of consecutive-k-out-of-n systems," J. Korean Statistical Society, vol.41, pp.1–11, 2012.

[10] T. Nakagawa, "Optimization Problems in k-out-of-n Systems," IEEE Transactions on Reliability, vol. R-34, no. 3, pp. 248–250, 1985.

[11] L. Zhou, H. Yamamoto, T. Nakamura, and X. Xiao, "Optimization problems for consecutive-k-out-of-n:G systems," IEICE Trans. Fund., vol.E103–A, no.5, pp.741–748, 2020.

[12] S. Papastavridis, "The Number of Failed Components in a Consecutive-k-of-n:F System," IEEE Transactions on Reliability, vol. 38, no. 3, pp. 338–340, 1989.

[13] S. Eryilmaz, "Dynamic Behavior of k-out-of-n:G Systems," Operations Research Letters, vol. 39, pp. 155–159, 2011.

TABLE 1 OPTIMAL REPLACEMENT TIME AND THE CORRESPONDING EXPECTED COST RATE FOR THE CONSECUTIVE-K-OUT-OF-N:G SYSTEM.

m	k	$c_1=1, c_2=0.1, c_R=5$			$c_1=1, c_R=5$			$c_1=1, c_2=0.1, c_R=10$			$c_1=1, c_R=10$			$c_1=1, c_2=0.1, c_R=20$			$c_1=1, c_R=20$		
		n	t^*	$C_B(t;k,n)$	n	t^*	$C_A(t;k,n)$	n	t^*	$C_B(t;k,n)$	n	t^*	$C_A(t;k,n)$	n	t^*	$C_B(t;k,n)$	n	t^*	$C_A(t;k,n)$
		11	∞	13.409	11	∞	12.869	17	∞	17.922	17	∞	17.395	26	∞	24.975	26	∞	24.437
	3	**12**	**∞**	**13.363**	**12**	**∞**	**12.828**	**18**	**∞**	**17.907**	**18**	**∞**	**17.380**	**27**	**∞**	**24.962**	**27**	**∞**	**24.424**
		13	∞	13.371	13	∞	12.839	19	∞	17.920	19	∞	17.393	28	∞	24.966	28	∞	24.425
		14	∞	24.211	14	∞	22.746	21	∞	32.259	21	∞	30.801	31	∞	44.825	31	∞	43.313
0.5	4	**15**	**∞**	**24.173**	**15**	**∞**	**22.714**	**22**	**∞**	**32.257**	**22**	**∞**	**30.796**	**32**	**∞**	**44.814**	**32**	**∞**	**43.295**
		16	∞	24.200	16	∞	22.746	23	∞	32.291	23	∞	30.826	33	∞	44.823	33	∞	43.298
		17	∞	38.520	17	∞	35.432	24	∞	51.159	24	∞	48.061	36	∞	70.812	37	∞	67.533
	5	**18**	**∞**	**38.495**	**18**	**∞**	**35.414**	**25**	**∞**	**51.129**	**25**	**∞**	**48.022**	**37**	**∞**	**70.801**	**38**	**∞**	**67.532**
		19	∞	38.546	19	∞	35.469	26	∞	51.147	26	∞	48.029	38	∞	70.816	39	∞	67.557
		8	∞	14.175	8	∞	13.601	10	0.347	19.064	8	0.083	16.276	12	0.254	22.997	8	0.382	19.073
	3	**9**	**∞**	**14.132**	**9**	**∞**	**13.560**	**11**	**0.392**	**18.943**	**9**	**0.117**	**15.884**	**13**	**0.286**	**22.928**	**9**	**0.060**	**18.010**
		10	∞	14.208	10	∞	13.633	12	0.440	18.980	10	0.161	16.014	14	0.318	22.994	10	0.088	18.065
		10	∞	20.806	10	0.164	19.420	13	0.288	28.344	11	0.067	22.848	16	0.207	34.456	11	0.033	26.362
0.8	4	**11**	**∞**	**20.739**	**11**	**0.198**	**19.306**	**14**	**0.313**	**28.196**	**12**	**0.087**	**22.604**	**17**	**0.225**	**34.397**	**12**	**0.046**	**25.500**
		12	∞	20.797	12	0.241	19.407	15	0.339	28.202	13	0.111	22.794	18	0.243	34.462	13	0.061	25.593
		12	∞	28.145	12	0.115	25.735	17	0.270	38.551	14	0.056	29.900	20	0.177	47.474	14	0.028	34.172
	5	**13**	**∞**	**28.057**	**13**	**0.134**	**25.526**	**18**	**0.287**	**38.534**	**15**	**0.068**	**29.764**	**21**	**0.188**	**47.422**	**15**	**0.036**	**33.460**
		14	∞	28.097	14	0.155	25.541	19	0.304	38.629	16	0.083	30.001	22	0.200	47.4842	16	0.046	34.172
		6	0.230	12.193	--	--	--	8	0.204	14.398	--	--	--	9	0.168	16.585	--	--	--
	3	**7**	**0.279**	**12.002**	**9**	**0.052**	**8.890**	**9**	**0.237**	**14.242**	**9**	**0.024**	**8.947**	**10**	**0.198**	**16.509**	**9**	**0.012**	**8.974**
		8	0.321	12.028	10	0.104	9.741	10	0.273	14.443	10	0.054	9.863	11	0.226	16.610	10	0.028	9.928
		9	0.249	16.984	--	--	--	11	0.189	20.442	--	--	--	12	0.147	23.888	--	--	--
1	4	**10**	**0.274**	**16.963**	**11**	**0.002**	**10.999**	**12**	**0.208**	**20.366**	**12**	**0.016**	**11.954**	**13**	**0.166**	**23.752**	**12**	**0.008**	**11.977**
		11	0.298	17.113	12	0.034	11.904	13	0.230	20.564	13	0.030	12.901	14	0.183	23.779	13	0.016	12.949
		11	0.233	22.298	--	--	--	14	0.175	27.035	--	--	--	16	0.145	31.7133	--	--	--
	5	**12**	**0.249**	**22.254**	**14**	**0.005**	**13.995**	**15**	**0.189**	**27.015**	**15**	**0.011**	**14.959**	**17**	**0.157**	**31.681**	**15**	**0.005**	**14.980**
		13	0.264	22.362	15	0.024	14.915	16	0.203	27.214	16	0.019	15.923	18	0.169	31.791	16	0.010	15.961
		5	0.213	4.509	--	--	--	5	0.173	5.553	--	--	--	5	0.135	7.162	--	--	--
	3	**6**	**0.251**	**4.126**	--	--	--	**6**	**0.220**	**4.466**	--	--	--	**6**	**0.190**	**4.928**	--	--	--
		7	0.278	4.533	--	--	--	7	0.249	4.802	--	--	--	7	0.219	5.180	--	--	--
		7	0.220	5.959	--	--	--	7	0.182	7.158	--	--	--	7	0.146	9.001	--	--	--
2	4	**8**	**0.244**	**5.615**	--	--	--	**8**	**0.212**	**6.115**	--	--	--	**8**	**0.183**	**6.787**	--	--	--
		9	0.263	6.007	--	--	--	9	0.233	6.434	--	--	--	9	0.204	7.022	--	--	--
		9	0.222	7.446	--	--	--	9	0.185	8.801	--	--	--	9	0.150	10.863	--	--	--
	5	**10**	**0.238**	**7.144**	--	--	--	**10**	**0.206**	**7.820**	--	--	--	**10**	**0.177**	**8.720**	--	--	--
		11	0.253	7.527	--	--	--	11	0.222	8.126	--	--	--	11	0.193	8.941	--	--	--

[14] S. Eryilmaz, "The Number of Failed Components in a k-out-of-n System Consisting of Multiple Types of Components," Reliability Engineering and System Safety, vol. 175, pp. 246–250, 2018.

[15] S. Eryilmaz, "Number of Working Components in Consecutive k-out-of-n System while It Is Working," Communications in Statistics-Simulation and Computation, vol. 39, pp. 683–692, 2010.

[16] L. Zhou, T.Nakamura, H.Yamamoto, and X. Xiao, "Number of failed components in a consecutive-k-out-of-n:G system," in Proceedings of the 20th Asia Pacific Industrial Engineering and Management System Conference, 2019.

[17] L. Zhou and H. Yamamoto, "Number of Failed Components in consecutive-k-out-of-n: G systems and Their Applications in Optimization Problems," IEICE Trans. Fund., vol.E105–A, no.6, pp.943–951, 2022.

[18] F. J. Samaniego, System Signature and Their Applications in Engineering Reliability, Springer, 2007.

[19] P. J. Boland, "Signatures of Indirect Majority Systems," Applied Probability, vol. 38, pp. 597–603, 2001.

An Algorithm for Obtaining the Pareto-Optimal Solutions of the Reservation Frame Allocations in a Complete Reservation System

HIROYUKI ICHIHARA
Department of Management Synthesis,
Chubu University
1200 Matsumoto-cho, Kasugai-shi,
Aichi 487-8501, Japan.

SATOSHI MIZUTANI
Department of Business Administration,
Aichi Institute of Technology
1247 Yachigusa, Yakusa-cho,
Toyota 470-0392, Japan.

MITSUTAKA KIMURA
Faculty of Business Administration,
Aichi University
4-60-6 Hiraike-cho, Nakamura-ku,
Nagoya, Aichi, 453-8777, Japan.

Key Words: Scheduling, Multi-Objective Optimization, Pareto-Optimal Solutions, Simulation.

Abstract

We propose an algorithm for obtaining the Pareto-optimal solutions for the optimization problem of [3]. In [3], we discuss an optimization model to obtain a reservation frame allocation which minimizes the waiting times for all customers and the idle times for all frames in a complete reservation system. The optimization model can be formulated as the multi-objective optimization problem. The typical solutions of the problem are listed as Pareto-optimal solutions. In this paper, we give the definitions of Pareto-dominance and of Pareto-optimal solutions in the reservation frame allocation problem, and we propose an algorithm for obtaining the Pareto-optimal solutions based on these definitions. In addition, we show the effectiveness of the Pareto-optimal solution by comparing with the solution in [3].

1. Introduction

Many hospitals progress in introducing service reservation systems, mainly to reduce waiting times for customers. In the hospital that introduces the service reservation systems, each patient reserves at a time frame in advance, and the patient visits at the time reserved. In each time frame, the available number for reservation is decided, therefore in case that the reservation frame is full, the patient cannot reserve at that time frame. In addition, in case that the all the frames are full with reservations, which leads to longer waiting times and increases patient dissatisfaction.

In order to relieve the above situation, we have formulated the model that optimizes the available reservations (the upper bound of reservations) and the length of the time frame in terms of reducing the waiting time for each customer, and have implemented that problem. The way to consider this problem is as follows. We suppose that the hospital is sufficiently overflowing with patients, we calculate the patients' waiting times under this setting. We formulate the optimization problem whose decision variables are the available numbers for reservation, and by solving this problem, we get the optimal available numbers for reservation in each reservation frame. As we solve this optimization problem under the assumption that the system is overflowing with patients, the waiting times for customers are considered so as to be reduced under the case that the system is not overflowing with patients, too.

As an example of this study, we cite the optimization model in [3]. In [3], we treat the model that optimize the available numbers for reservation in each frame in terms of minimization of the waiting times for customers and idle times in a complete reservation system. In this paper, we propose a concise formulation in [3] and an algorithm to solve this problem. The formulation in [3] is devided into minimax problem and minisum problem by parameter settings. In this paper, we formulate the optimization problem that minimizes the estimations of the probabilities that waiting times are more than a threshold for all frames, and we propose an algorithm for solving the Pareto-optimal solutions of this problem. In addition, we generalize the arrival law of patients [5]. An advantage of the algorithm of the study is that the formulation is concise because there is no need to classify cases by parameter settings.

In addition, this study is an application of the repairman problem, considering the doctor as the repairman and the customer as the faulty part [1]. There are extended studies of the Repairman Problem. For example, there are extensions such as an analysis using the discrete event simulation and Traveling Repairman Problem [4].

We show a list of the most important notations and abbreviations in the rest of Sect.1. In addition, in order to do this we briefly describe the queueing model. The model in this paper is based on the FCFS queueing model in [3] where we assume that the number of doctors is one, and that the service starts at time 0. The reservation frame is set as the time span. Furthermore, for generalization of the customer arrival law, we divide each reservation frame as the short time span which is called as slot [5].

The details for the queueing model are descirbed in the next section. At first, we show main notations and abbreviations in advance as follows.

Notations and Abbreviations

T	The length for one frame
$\mathscr{L} := \{1, 2, \ldots, l_{\max}\}$	The index set for reservation frames, where $l_{\max}$ represents the number of frames
$\mathscr{T} := \{1, 2, \ldots, t_{\max}\}$	The index set for slots, where $t_{\max}$ represents the number of slots
The reservation frame l (frame l)	The time span $[(l-1)T, lT)$ $(l \in \mathscr{L})$(Fig. 1)
The reservation frame l slot t (frame l slot t)	The time span $\left[(l-1)T + \frac{(t-1)T}{t_{\max}}, (l-1)T + \frac{tT}{t_{\max}}\right)$ $(l \in \mathscr{L}, t \in \mathscr{T})$ (Fig. 1)
$p_{\text{no-show}}$	No-show probability for each customer

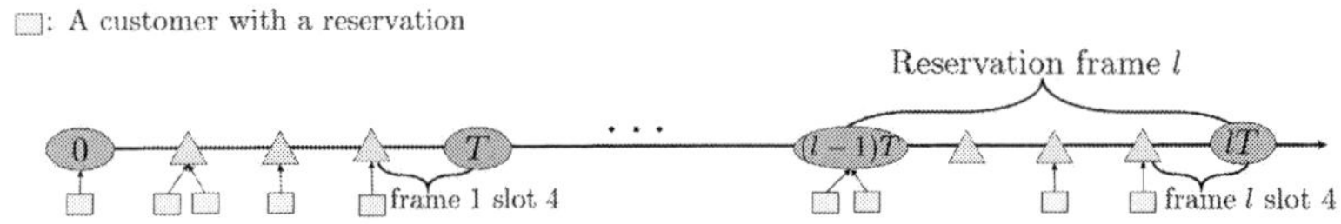

Figure 1: Illustration for reservation frames (e.g. $t_{\max} = 4, N_1 = 5, N_l = 4$)

$\boldsymbol{p} = (p_1, \ldots, p_{t_{\max}})$ Probability distribution for each customer with a reservation selecting his/her own arrival slot (Arrival time distribution)

N_l The available number for reservations in frame l ($l \in \mathscr{L}$)

B_l The lower bound of available number in frame l ($l \in \mathscr{L}$)

U_l The upper bound of available number in frame l ($l \in \mathscr{L}$)

N The total number of available number for reservations in consultation hours ($N = \sum_{l \in \mathscr{L}} N_l$)

$N_{l,t}$ Random variable representing the number of customers who chose to visit in frame l slot t among those who made a reservation in frame l ($l \in \mathscr{L}, t \in \mathscr{T}$)

$J_{l,t}$ Random variable representing the service order for the attention-customer who visits in frame l slot t ($l \in \mathscr{L}, t \in \mathscr{T}$)

$A^k_{l,t}$ Random variable that takes 0 if the k-th cutomer in frame l slot t does not show up, 1 if he/she appears ($k \in \{1,2,\ldots,N_{l,t}\}, l \in \mathscr{L}, t \in \mathscr{T}$)

$S^k_{l,t}$ Random variable respresenting the service time for the k-th customer in frame l slot t ($k \in \{1,2,\ldots,N_{l,t}\}, l \in \mathscr{L}, t \in \mathscr{T}$)

$E_{l,t}$ Random variable respresenting the ending time for all services of customers who arrive in frame l slot t ($l \in \mathscr{L} \cup \{0\}, t \in \mathscr{T} \cup \{0\}$)

2. Queueing Model

We explain a queueing model based on a complete reservation system for obtaining indicators playing the important roles in optimization problems.

At first, we discuss the reservation situation to be assumed. Each customer can make a reservation at time $(l-1)T$ up to N_l customers. In addition, as the situation is assumed to be overflowing with customers in all frames, all frames are assumed to be full with reservations (Fig. 1).

Attention-Custmer and Customer's Arrival Law

In this model, we use the waiting time for the attention-customer whose arrival slot number is given. The waiting time for the attention-customer is calculated as the average waiting time for customers who visit in any frames and slots. Even if we don't use the waiting times for all customers in any frames and slots, we can set the index for the waiting time by the use of attention-customers' waiting time. From this, we can reduce the computational complexity by numerical simulation, and thus the description for an optimization model becomes clear.

At first, all customers except for the attention-customer are assumed to be homogeneous. We set the customer who arrives in the frame whose index number is given higher priority as it is smaller. Next, we set the arrival law for each customer as follows:

- An attention-customer arrives at the start time of a slot t given in advance
- Each customer with a reservation in frame l except for the attention-customer selects the arrival slot following the arrival time distribution $\boldsymbol{p}$, respectively. He/She arrives at the start time of the slot.

In addition, the order of service for customers arriving at the same time is determined at random. As the attention-customer in each frame is assumed to be given predefined arrival slot number, $(N_{l,1}, N_{l,2}, \ldots, N_{l,t_{\max}})$ is an allocation of $N_l - 1$ as $\sum_{t \in \mathscr{T}} N_{l,t} = N_l - 1$. Furthermore, the distribution of $A^k_{l,t}$ introduced to discuss the case that each customer does not show up is given by,

$$P(A^k_{l,t} = 0) = p_{\text{no-show}},\ P(A^k_{l,t} = 1) = 1 - p_{\text{no-show}},\quad k \in \{1,2,\ldots,N_{l,t}\}, l \in \mathscr{L}, t \in \mathscr{T}. \tag{1}$$

If the customer who arrives in a same slot does not show up, the service for the next customer immediately starts.

2.1 Waiting Time for an Attention-Customer

We define the wating time for each customer as the time span from arrival time to service beginning time. We discuss the structure of $E_{l,t}$, as $E_{l,t}$ is closely related to the waiting time in this model. For convenience, we set $E_{0,t} = 0$ ($t \in \mathscr{T}$), and to to simplify the notations, $E_{l,0} = E_{l-1,t_{\max}}$ ($l \in \mathscr{L}$).

At first, the beginning time of the service for the first customer in frame l slot t is given by

$$\max\left\{E_{l,t-1}, (l-1)T + \frac{(t-1)T}{t_{\max}}\right\},\ t \in \mathscr{T},\ l \in \mathscr{L}. \tag{2}$$

The ending time for all services of customers who arrive in frame l slot t is the sum of the total service times in frame l slot t and the beginning time of the service for the first customer in frame l slot t, i.e.,

$$E_{l,t} = \max\left\{E_{l,t-1}, (l-1)T + \frac{(t-1)T}{t_{\max}}\right\} + \sum_{i=1}^{N_{l,t}} A^i_{l,t} S^i_{l,t},\quad t \in \mathscr{T}, l \in \mathscr{L}. \tag{3}$$

The waiting time for the attention-customer in frame l slot t is given by the following equation using $E_{l,t}$ and the order of

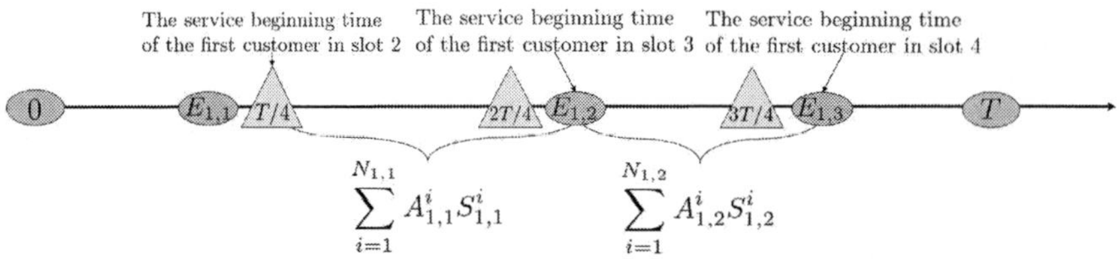

Figure 2: An example of the sequence of services (e.g. $l = 1, t_{\max} = 4$)

examination of the attention-customer in frame l slot t, $J_{l,t}$,

$$\begin{aligned} W_{l,t} &= \max\left\{E_{l,t-1}, (l-1)T + \frac{(t-1)T}{t_{\max}}\right\} + \sum_{i=1}^{J_{l,t}-1} A^i_{l,t}S^i_{l,t} \\ &\quad - (l-1)T - \frac{(t-1)T}{t_{\max}} \\ &= \left(E_{l,t-1} - (l-1)T - \frac{(t-1)T}{t_{\max}}\right)^+ + \sum_{i=1}^{J_{l,t}-1} A^i_{l,t}S^i_{l,t}, \\ &\quad t \in \mathscr{T},\ l \in \mathscr{L}, \end{aligned} \tag{4}$$

where $(x)^+ = \max\{x, 0\}$. In addition, $J_{l,t}$ is determined uniformly at random among $N_{l,t}$ people, so its distribution is given by,

$$\begin{aligned} P(J_{l,t} = j) &= \sum_{k=j}^{N_l} P(J_{l,t} = j | N_{l,t} + 1 = k) P(N_{l,t} = k-1) \\ &= \sum_{k=j-1}^{N_l-1} \frac{1}{k+1} \binom{N_l - 1}{k} p_t^k (1-p_t)^{N_l-k-1}. \end{aligned} \tag{5}$$

We perform Montecarlo simulation based on the above model, and compute the value of the waiting time for the attention-customer in each frame l slot t, $W_{l,t}$. We use the value to define the indicator for the optimization problem in Sect.3.

3. Optimization Problem

In this section, we explain the outline of the optimization problem and its formulation. At first, the purpose of this problem is as follows:

- Find the allocation that minimizes the waiting times for the attention-customers for all frames

In order to do this, we adopt the estimation of the probability for the waiting time of the attention-customer as the index. The decision variable in the optimization problem is the available number of reservations, x_l in frame $l \in \mathscr{L}$. Note that the variable x_l satisfies the following equation:

$$x_l - 1 = \sum_{t \in \mathscr{T}} N_{l,t}, \tag{6}$$

where the left side of the above equation represents x_l minus the number of attention-customer in frame l. Also, set $\boldsymbol{x} = (x_1, x_2, \ldots, x_{l_{\max}}) \in \mathbb{N}^{l_{\max}}$, where $\mathbb{N}^n$ is the set of n dimensional vectors whose elements are positive integers.

x_l is supposed to be between B_l and U_l to avoid biased allocations, such as an extreme number of customers in one frame. Let $\mathscr{F}$ be the set of reservation frame allocations (the set of feasible solutions). Using the above notations, the set $\mathscr{F}$ is expressed as

$$\mathscr{F} = \left\{\boldsymbol{x} \in \mathbb{N}^{l_{\max}} \middle| \sum_{l=1}^{l_{\max}} x_l = N, B_l \le x_l \le U_l \right\}. \tag{7}$$

Next we define the objective function. We denote the index as the proportion that the real value $w^i_{l,t}$ in the i-th simulation of the waiting time $W_{l,t}$ for the attention-customer in frame l slot t for the allocation $\boldsymbol{x}$ is more than the threshold, T_0. Using indicator function

$$\mathbb{1}_{\{W_{l,t} \ge T_0\}}(w^i_{l,t}) = \begin{cases} 1, \text{ if } w^i_{l,t} \in \{W_{l,t} \ge T_0\}, \\ 0, \text{ otherwise,} \end{cases} \tag{8}$$

the above index is expressed as the following equation.

$$\tilde{P}_{\boldsymbol{x}}(W_{l,t} \ge T_0) = \frac{1}{n} \sum_{i=1}^{n} \mathbb{1}_{\{W_{l,t} \ge T_0\}}(w^i_{l,t}), \tag{9}$$

where n is the number of the simulations. In the left side of Eq. (9), we emphasize that the value is given at allocation $\boldsymbol{x}$ by adding a subscript $\boldsymbol{x}$. We formulate the multi-objective optimization problem to minimize Eq. (9) for all frames $l \in \mathscr{L}$ as follows.

$$\min_{\boldsymbol{x} \in \mathscr{F}} \tilde{P}_{\boldsymbol{x}}(W_{l,t} \ge T_0) \quad l = 1, 2, \ldots, l_{\max}. \tag{10}$$

The typical solutions of the problem are listed as Pareto-optimal solution. In this paper, to solve the set of Pareto-optimal solutions of the problem (10), we give definitions of the Pareto-dominance (Definition 1) and of the Pareto-optimal solution (Definition 2).

Definition 1 *The allocation $\boldsymbol{x}' \in \mathscr{F}$ Pareto-dominating the $\boldsymbol{x} \in \mathscr{F}$ means that, for some ε and for all $l \in \mathscr{L}$,*

$$\tilde{P}_{\boldsymbol{x}'}(W_{l,t} \ge T_0) \le \tilde{P}_{\boldsymbol{x}}(W_{l,t} \ge T_0) \text{ or } \left| \frac{\tilde{P}_{\boldsymbol{x}'}(W_{l,t} \ge T_0) - \tilde{P}_{\boldsymbol{x}}(W_{l,t} \ge T_0)}{\tilde{P}_{\boldsymbol{x}}(W_{l,t} \ge T_0)} \right| \le \varepsilon \tag{11}$$

holds, and for some $l' \in \mathscr{L}$,

$$\tilde{P}_{\boldsymbol{x}'}(W_{l',t} \ge T_0) < \tilde{P}_{\boldsymbol{x}}(W_{l',t} \ge T_0) \text{ and } \left| \frac{\tilde{P}_{\boldsymbol{x}'}(W_{l',t} \ge T_0) - \tilde{P}_{\boldsymbol{x}}(W_{l',t} \ge T_0)}{\tilde{P}_{\boldsymbol{x}}(W_{l',t} \ge T_0)} \right| > \varepsilon \tag{12}$$

holds, where ε is a sufficiently small number.

In Definition 1, the inequality including the absolute value means that the relative error between $\tilde{P}_{\boldsymbol{x}}(W_{l,t} \ge T_0)$ and

$\tilde{P}_{\boldsymbol{x}'}(W_{l,t} \geq T_0)$ is smaller than ε. This means the proportion of the error between $\tilde{P}_{\boldsymbol{x}}$ and $\tilde{P}_{\boldsymbol{x}'}$. If this is less than ε, these values are judged to be equal. By Definition 1, Pareto-optimal solution is defined as follows:

Definition 2 *The allocation* $\boldsymbol{x} \in \mathscr{F}$ *to be a Pareto-optimal solution means that the allocation* $\boldsymbol{x} \in \mathscr{F}$ *is not Pareto-dominated by for all* $\boldsymbol{x}' \in \mathscr{F} \setminus \{\boldsymbol{x}\}$.

We solve the set of Pareto-optimal solutions $\mathscr{O}$ based on Definition 2 by brute force.

Next, to obtain the optimal solution $\boldsymbol{x}^*$ from the set of Pareto-optimal solutions $\mathscr{O}$, we solve the following problem.

$$\min_{\boldsymbol{x} \in \mathscr{O}} \sum_{l \in \mathscr{L}} \tilde{P}_{\boldsymbol{x}}(W_{l,t} \geq T_0). \tag{13}$$

From now on, we call the allocation obtained by the above problem Pareto-optimal solution.

4. Numerical Examples

In this section, we verify the Pareto-optimal solution obtained by the algorithm of this paper. We compare obtained above with the allocations given in [3] under the following each parameter setting:

- Parameter1: $N = 18$, $p_{\text{no-show}} = 0$, $n = 2000$, $B_l = 2$, $\boldsymbol{p}_{30} = (1/3, 1/3, 1/3)$, $T_0 = 30$ (minutes), $S^i_{l,t}$: (i) Following Gamma distribution with mean of 11.5 minutes and variance of 11, (ii) Constant 11.5 minutes
- Parameter2: $N = 15$, $p_{\text{no-show}} = 0$, $n = 2000$, $B_l = 1$, $\boldsymbol{p}_{30} = (1/3, 1/3, 1/3)$, $T_0 = 20$ (minutes), $S^i_{l,t}$: (i) Following Gamma distribution with mean of 10.5 minutes and variance of 10 (ii) Constant 11.5 minutes

In addition, in [3], the idle time in each frame is taken into consideration, however, note that in the formulation of [3] for comparison, the index as Eq.(9) is referred, and the idle times are not considered.

Under Parameter1, the formulation in [3] is expressed as a minimax problem. When the service times follow Gamma distribution with mean of 11.5 minutes and variance of 11, the allocations obtained by [3] and Pareto-optimal solution are $\hat{\boldsymbol{x}}_1 = (3,3,2,2,2,6)$ and $\boldsymbol{x}^*_1 = (2,3,2,2,2,7)$, respectively. When we set the reservation frame allocations by $\hat{\boldsymbol{x}}_1$ and $\boldsymbol{x}^*_1$, the probabilities that the attention-customers' waiting times are more than 30 minutes, and the average waiting times for reservation frames are shown in Fig. 3 and Table 1, respectively. Also, the distributions of the doctor's overtime hour are shown in Fig. 4.

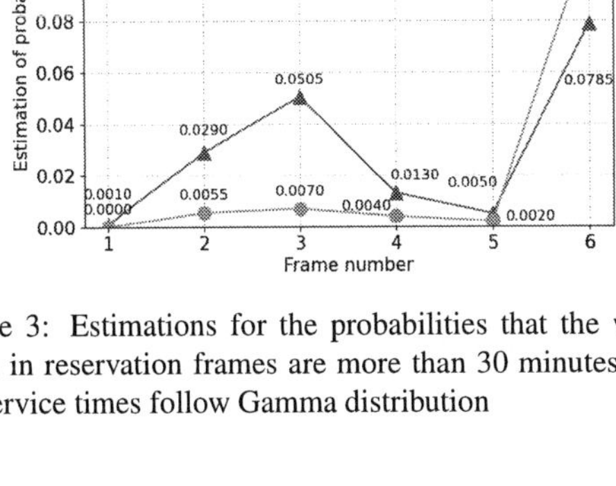

Figure 3: Estimations for the probabilities that the waiting times in reservation frames are more than 30 minutes where the service times follow Gamma distribution

Table 1: The average waiting times in reservation frames where the service times follow Gamma distribution (minutes)

No.	$\hat{\boldsymbol{x}}_1$	$\boldsymbol{x}^*_1$
1	3.87	1.96*
2	10.25	4.66*
3	13.18	8.81*
4	8.23	4.96*
5	5.27	3.68*
6	11.22*	12.07
Total	52.02	36.13*

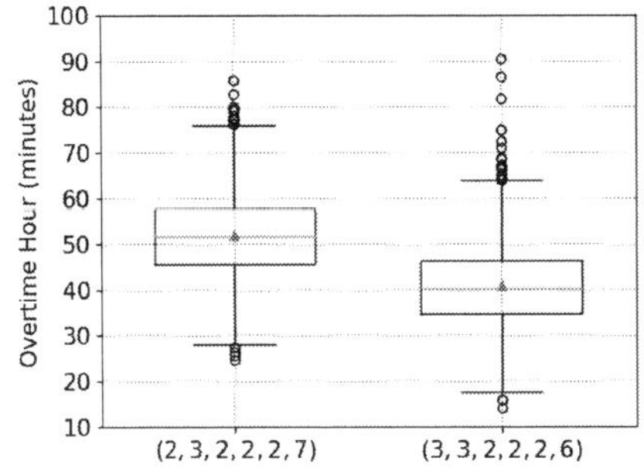

Figure 4: The distributions of the doctor's overtime hour

From Fig. 3, we find that, of the probabilities that the waiting times are more than 30 minutes, those for $\boldsymbol{x}^*_1$, except for frame 6, are smaller than for $\hat{\boldsymbol{x}}_1$. From Table 1, the average waiting times for $\boldsymbol{x}^*_1$, except for frame 6, also become smaller than for $\hat{\boldsymbol{x}}_1$. The total of the average waiting times from frame 1 to 6 for $\boldsymbol{x}^*_1$ also becomes smaller than for $\hat{\boldsymbol{x}}_1$. On the other hand, from Fig. 4, as for the distribution of the doctor's overtime hour, that for $\boldsymbol{x}^*_1$ is about 10 minutes longer than for $\hat{\boldsymbol{x}}_1$. Thus, if we can accept overtime hour for about 10 minutes, $\boldsymbol{x}^*_1$ is more advantageous than $\hat{\boldsymbol{x}}_1$.

Under Parameter2, the problem in [3] is formulated as minisum problem. When the service times follow Gamma distribution with a mean of 10.5 minutes and a variance of 10, the allocation solving this problem and Pareto-optimal solution in this paper are $\hat{\boldsymbol{x}}_2 = (3,2,2,2,2,4)$ and $\boldsymbol{x}^*_2 = (2,2,2,2,2,5)$, respectively. When we set the reservation frame allocations by $\hat{\boldsymbol{x}}_2$ and $\boldsymbol{x}^*_2$, the probabilities that attention-customers' waiting times are more than 20 minutes, and average waiting times for reservation frames are shown in Fig. 5 and Table 2, respectively.

From Fig. 5, we find that, of the probabilities that the waiting times are more than 20 minutes, those for $\boldsymbol{x}^*_2$ are, except for frame 6, smaller than for $\hat{\boldsymbol{x}}_2$. In addition, from Table 2, the average waiting times for $\boldsymbol{x}^*_2$, except for frame 6, also become smaller than for $\hat{\boldsymbol{x}}_2$. The total of average waiting times from frame 1 to 6 for $\boldsymbol{x}^*_2$ also becomes smaller than for $\hat{\boldsymbol{x}}_2$.

Then numerical calculations are performed with a constant service time of 11.5 minutes under Parameter1 and a constant service time of 10.5 minutes under Parameter2. Under Param-

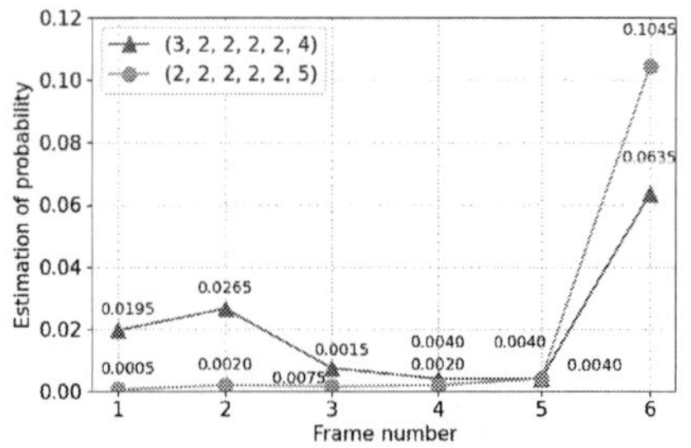

Figure 5: Estimations for the probabilities that the waiting times in reservation frames are more than 20 minutes where the service times follow Gamma distribution

Table 2: The average waiting times in reservation frames where the service times follow Gamma distribution (minutes)

No.	$\check{x}_2$	x_2^*
1	3.65	1.96*
2	5.82	2.29*
3	3.36	2.36*
4	2.66	2.40*
5	2.40	2.27*
6	5.98*	7.99
Total	23.87	19.26*

eter1, the reservation frame allocation solving minimax problem and the Pareto-optimal solution are $\check{x}_1 = (4,2,2,3,2,5)$ and $x_1^\dagger = (3,3,2,3,2,5)$, respectively. The average waiting times for attention-customers for $\check{x}_1$ and $x_1^\dagger$ are shown in Table 3a, respectively. In addition, under Parameter2, the reservation frame allocation solving minisum problem and the Pareto-optimal solution are $\check{x}_2 = (3,2,2,2,3,3)$ and $x_2^\dagger = (2,3,2,2,2,4)$, respectively. The waiting times for attention-customers for $\check{x}_2$ and $x_2^\dagger$ are shown in Table 3b.

Table 3: The average waiting times in reservation frames for constant service times (minutes)

(a) Parameter 1

No.	$\check{x}_1$	$x_1^\dagger$
1	5.65	3.77*
2	18.14	9.29*
3	11.16*	12.32
4	6.48*	7.37
5	9.22*	10.30
6	9.16*	9.75
Total	59.81	52.8*

(b) Parameter 2

No.	$\check{x}_2$	$x_2^\dagger$
1	3.54	1.67*
2	4.37	3.55*
3	2.24*	4.50
4	1.78*	2.10
5	3.64	1.82*
6	6.13	5.60*
Total	21.72	19.25*

Table 3a exhibits that the average waiting times in frames 1 and 2 for $x_1^\dagger$ are shorter than for $\check{x}_1$. In addition, the average waiting time in frame 2 for $x_1^\dagger$ is about 9 minutes shorter than for $\check{x}_1$. In frames 3, 4, 5 and 6, the waiting times for $x_1^\dagger$ are a little longer than for $\check{x}_1$, but the total average waiting times for $x_1^\dagger$ is shorter than for $\check{x}_1$. Table 3b exhibits that the average waiting times in frames 1, 2, 5 and 6 for $x_2^\dagger$ are shorter than for $\check{x}_2$. Furthermore, the total average waiting time for $x_2^\dagger$ is shorter than for $\check{x}_2$.

Thus, if we adopt Pareto-optimal solutions as the reservation frame allocations, these are likely to be more advantageous than other allocations, from the point of view of minimizing the waiting time for each customer. As there is no need to change formulations by changing parameters, it is relatively easy to implement the algorithm. However, the number of customers in the final frame tends to increase somewhat. The average waiting time for customers arriving in the last frame is not much longer, although the waiting time for the last service could be longer.

5. Concluding Remarks

In this paper, we have proposed an algorithm for obtaining the Pareto-optimal solutions based on the optimization model in [3]. Through the numerical examples, we verified the advantage of Pareto-optimal solutions. Under two parameter settings, we compared the Pareto-optimal solution in terms of average waiting times with the allocation given by the algorithm in [3].

When the service times follow Gamma distribution, the average waiting times for the Pareto-optimal solution were often shorter than for the allocation by the algorithm in [3], and similar results were obtained for the total average waiting time from frame 1 to 6. When the service times were given by constants, we became aware that the average waiting times for Pareto-optimal solution got a little longer than these for the allocation given by Algorithm in [3]. However, the total average waiting time from frame 1 to 6 for Pareto-optimal solution got shorter.

Note that the number of customers in the last frame for Pareto-optimal solution tends to increase. Thus, if we can accept overtime hour for about 10 minutes in advance, the allocation is likely to be more advantageous than other allocations.

References

[1] Barlow, R. E. and Proschan, F., *Mathematical theory of reliability*, Society for Industrial and Applied Mathematics (1996).

[2] Gomi, Y., Nogawa, H., "Reliability Concepts in Medical Field(⟨Special feature⟩Simulation and reliability)", Journal of Reliability Engineering Association of Japan Reliability, Vol.31, No.4, pp.287-290 (2009), in Japanese.

[3] Ichihara, H., "Optimization of the Reservation Frame Allocation in a Complete Reservation System by Estimation of Customer Waiting Times", Applied Reliability and Statistical Modeling: Their Applications, Springer, 12 pages (2025), in press.

[4] Pei, J. and Mladenović, N. and Urošević, D. and Brimberg, J. and Liu, X., "Solving the traveling repairman problem with profits: A novel variable neighborhood search approach", Information Sciences, Vol.507, pp.108-123 (2020).

[5] Sakuma, Y. and Masuyama, H. and Fukuda, E., "A discrete-time single-server Poisson queueing game: Equilibria simulated by an agent-based model", European Journal of Operational Research, Vol.283, No. 1, pp.253-264 (2020).

Improving Optimal Strategies Search for Maximum Flow Network Interdiction

TAKAHASHI Natsumi[1], YUGE Tetsushi[2]

[1,2]Department of Electrical and Electronic Engineering, National Defense Academy, Japan, 1-10-20 Hashirimizu, Yokosuka, Kanagawa 239-8686, Japan
[1]ntaka@nda.ac.jp, [2]yuge@nda.ac.jp

Keywords: Flow, Network Interdiction Problem, Stochastic Network

Abstract -Network Interdiction Problems are related to identifying components that should be interdicted. This study considers the network interdiction problem whose objective is the maximum network flow. This interdiction problem is between two parties known as an evader and an interdictor. An evader aims to maximize the expected flows which are transmitted from a source to a sink without being detected. In this study, flows are detected stochastically at each arc. On the other hand, an interdictor seeks to minimize the maximum expected flows of evader by interdicting arcs. In this situation, we need to effectively obtain the flows that maximize the expected flows considering the detection probability, and determine which arcs are the best to interdict.

1. Introduction

There are many kinds of network systems in our world. These networks (especially distribution network) rapidly developed and are becoming internationalized in recent years. On the other hand, there are negative effects; for instance, illegal drugs are smuggled, and infectious diseases spread. In this situation, we consider setting up checkpoints and sensors reduce network performance for mitigating negative effects. Network interdiction deals with decision making problem that whether each arc and node is to be interdicted or not. In general, an object of this problem is reduction of network performance by interdicting these components. This problem is applied in various field such as military planning[1,2], interdiction of smuggling drugs and weapons[3,4], and robustness evaluation of networks.

This study considers interdiction problems whose objective is maximum flow between two specific nodes. Stochastic network indicates that the network is given the probability of successful flow detection on each arc. Sadeghi et al.[5] formulated this interdiction problem as maximum flow network interdiction with endogenous uncertainty, and applied to drug trafficking network. For the uncertain version of the interdiction problem, they supposed that the flow detection for any arc may be successful with the given probability measure initially and the interdictor can increase this probability measure by interdiction action. Then, they showed the evaluation measure of flow, and proposed the solution method for stochastic maximum flow network interdiction problem.

This paper deals with the model of Sadeghi et al. To decide interdicted arcs, optimal flow needs to be searched with given detection probabilities. Their algorithm needs more memory area and computation time to obtain optimal strategies (flows). Therefore, we consider efficient algorithm to search for the flows that maximize the expected profits. This problem needs to find the optimal flow strategy for each interdictor strategy. To discard of no possibility of the optimal interdiction strategy, the examine order of interdicted arcs is considered. We conduct numerical experiments, and the effectiveness of our proposed algorithm is evaluated.

2. Maximum Flow Network Interdiction Problem

2.1. Notations and Assumptions

We consider the maximum flow network interdiction problem that aims to minimize the maximum flow by interdicting arcs. Interdictor can interdict arcs within budget and minimizes the maximum flow from source to sink. For describing our problem, we define some notations as follows.

$G(N, A)$: weighted graph with set of nodes N, and set of arcs A
n: number of nodes
$a_{i,j}$: arc from node i to node j
$u(a_{i,j})$: capacity of arc $a_{i,j}$
$c(a_{i,j})$: cost of interdicting arc $a_{i,j}$
$s_{i,j}$: binary variable that is 1 if the evader being interdicted while transmitting flow in the arc k and 0 otherwise.
B: budget for interdiction
C: penalty cost
$f(a_{i,j})$: flow through arc $a_{i,j}$
$p(a_{i,j})$: probability of detection on arc $a_{i,j}$
x: interdictor strategy such that the set of interdicted arcs $a_{i,j}$
y: evader flow strategy

The following assumptions are considered for the study.

- Network has source s and sink t node. Capacity $u(a_{i,j})$ and detect probability $p(a_{i,j})$ are given to each arc as shown in Figure 1.
- Detection by interdictor disables flows and impose penalty cost on evader.
- Interdictor can interdict arcs by using cost $c(a_{i,j})$ and this strategy increases detection probabilities $p(a_{i,j})$.

In Figure1, vector $(u(a_{i,j}), p(a_{i,j}))$ means a capacity and a detection probability of arc. This study searches for the maximum flows which maximize the expected profits of evader and decides optimal interdiction strategy.

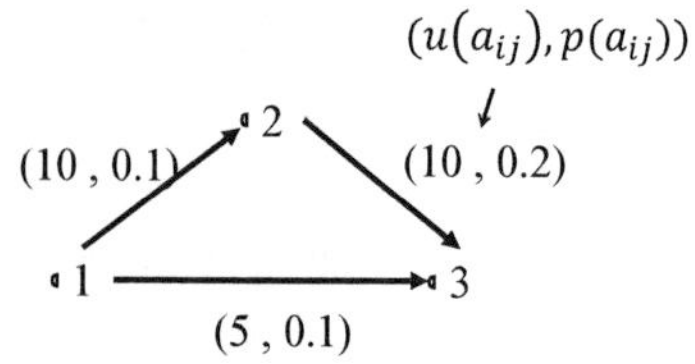

Figure 1. Example of a network

2.2. Formulation of Maximum Flow Network Interdiction

Maximum flow network interdiction problem is formulated by Sadeghi et al[5] as follows.

$$\min_{x} a(x) \tag{1}$$

$$a(x) = \max_{y} e_n(y) \tag{2}$$

$$e_n(y) = \sum_{s} \pi_n^s(x)\{(1-\gamma^s)f_n(y) - \gamma^s C\} \tag{3}$$

$$\pi_n^s(x) = \sum_{a_{ij}\in A} [(1-s_{ij})(1-p(a_{ij})) + s_{ij}p(a_{ij})] \tag{4}$$

$$p(a_{ij}) = \begin{cases} p_1(a_{i,j}) & \text{for } a_{i,j} \in A\backslash x \\ p_1(a_{i,j}) + p_2(a_{i,j}) & \text{for } a_{i,j} \in A \end{cases} \tag{5}$$

$$\sum_{a_{ij}\in x} c(a_{ij}) \le B \tag{6}$$

π_n^s is the state probability measure related to detect pattern s. γ^s is a binary variable where $\gamma^s = 1$ if flow is detected under detect pattern s and $\gamma^s = 0$ if not. Detect pattern s is a vector and consists of binary variable s_{ij}.Figure 1 is an example of the network with three arcs $A = \{a_{12}, a_{13}, a_{23}\}$. The detect pattern $s = (0, 0, 0)$ means that flow is not detected on all arcs, and $s = (1, 1, 1)$ means that flow is detected on all arcs. Therefore, there are $|A|$ patterns of detection. Penalty cost C is imposed on evader when $a_{ij} \in y$ and $s_{ij} = 1$. This paper refers $e_n(y)$ to expected profits of flow y. For example, when evader flow strategy $y = \{a_{12}, a_{23}\}$, detect pattern $(s_{12}, s_{13}, s_{23}) = (0, 0, 0)$ induces $\gamma^s = 0$ because flow is not detected. On the other hand, detect pattern $(0, 0, 1)$ induces $\gamma^s = 1$ because flow is detected on an arc a_{23}. $p_1(a_{i,j})$ means a detection probability with the condition that arc $a_{i,j}$ is not interdicted. If $a_{i,j}$ is interdicted, then detection probability of $a_{i,j}$ increases by $p_2(a_{i,j})$. Interdictor can interdict arcs within budget B.

Under such circumstances, an evader seeks the maximum flow y to maximize the expected profits. An interdictor's goal is to find critical arcs x for interdiction to minimize the evader's expected profits.

3. Proposed Algorithm

Formulation by Sadeghi et al.[5] needs to divide detect patterns into two cases even about arcs where flows do not traverse. As an example, suppose flow is $y = \{a_{12}, a_{23}\}$ in Figure 1. They considered detect patterns (s_{12}, s_{13}, s_{23}) such as $(0, 0, 0)$ and $(0, 1, 0)$. However, a_{13} isn't included in flow y and γ^s does not vary in these detect patterns. That is, taking account of s_{13} is irrelevant to expected profits $e_n(y)$. Therefore, our study reduces the number of detect patterns by considering only arcs included in flow. Equation (3) and (4) that are about an expected profit $e_n(y)$ of flow y can be reformulated as follows.

$$e_n(y) = f_n(y) \prod_{a_{ij}\in y} (1 - p(a_{ij})) - C\left\{1 - \prod_{a_{ij}\in y} (1 - p(a_{ij}))\right\} \tag{7}$$

Equation (7) calculates expected profit of flow y by division into two cases, that flow is not detected in any arcs and its complementary event. Therefore, flows seem to be efficiently evaluated. Assuming flow $y = \{a_{12}, a_{23}, a_{13}\}$, the amount of flow $f_n(y) = 15$ and $C = 6$, the expected profit is $e_n(y) = 15 \cdot 0.9 \cdot 0.8 \cdot 0.9 - 6 \cdot (1 - 0.9 \cdot 0.8 \cdot 0.9) = 5.808$.

3.1. Approach for Evader Strategy

An evader's object is finding the flows y that maximize the expected profits. This section describes the way to search for the flow y. Previous study[5] needed to consider all flows which are from s to t for evaluations of expected profits. However, computation time is expected to expand with increasing number of arcs This study obtains optimal flows by augmenting path algorithm and augmenting paths are searched based on Dijkstra's algorithm.

For considering augmenting paths, rhe key concept is the residual network, denoted as $G_f(N, A_f)$ for the current flow f. For each arc $a_{i,j}$ with capacity $u(a_{i,j})$ and flow $f(a_{i,j})$, A_f contains two arcs with following residual capacity $u_f(a_{i,j})$.

- $u_f(a_{i,j}) = u(a_{i,j}) - f(a_{i,j})$
- $u_f(a_{j,i}) = f(a_{i,j})$

In the residual network, augmenting paths are searched, based on the expected profits and reachable rate from source node to each node. This way enables to make the optimal flow in terms of the expected profits.

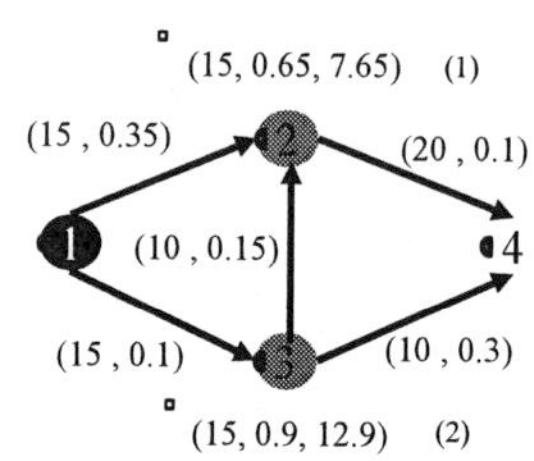

Figure 2. Process of searching an augmenting path

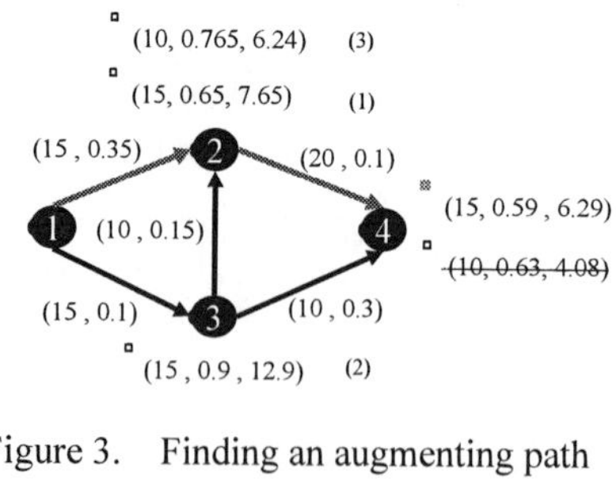

Figure 3. Finding an augmenting path

In Figure 2, vector labels on nodes 2, 3 show (upper bound of flow, reachable rate, expected profit). Here, $e(i)$ means the expected profit to node i and $C = 6$. Node 1 is a start node, and node 1 and arcs connecting to node 1 induce upper bound of flow, reachable rate and expected profits $e(i)$ to adjacent nodes 2 and 3. As an example, a flow can be transmitted to node 3 up to 15, and then $e(3) = 15 \cdot 0.9 - 6 \cdot 0.1 = 12.9$. Expected profits are compared among labels, and the node 3 with maximum expected profit node 3 is next start node. Augmenting path is searched by repeating this operation until all nodes are explored. Then, augmenting path $P_1 = \{a_{12}, a_{24}\}$ is found as shown in Figure 3, and this path maximizes expected profit. After a flow is augmented by 15 along a path P_1, find augmenting path in residual network. Repeat same operations until there is no augmenting path in residual network.

As a result, two augmenting paths $P_2 = \{a_{13}, a_{34}\}$ and $P_3 = \{a_{13}, a_{32}, a_{34}\}$ are found. A flow y is made by combining searched augment paths. Compared expected profits of augmenting path combinations, decide the flow that maximizes expected profits.

3.2. Approach for Interdictor Strategy

An interdictor can interdict arcs within budget and increase detect probabilities of arcs. The interdictor seeks to find critical arcs x to minimize the evader's expected profits. Previous study needs to consider $|A|$ interdiction strategies in the worst case. For each interdiction strategy, finding the maximum flow of expected profits is required. Therefore, large number of arcs cause an increase in computational time.

To discard of no possibility of the optimal interdiction strategy, we first consider an enumeration order of interdiction arcs. This study applies detection probabilities to the enumeration of interdictor strategies. In addition, we search for a certain solution in advance and use it as the upper bound of expected profits. First, obtain the flow y which maximizes expected profits with the condition that no arc is interdicted. Next focus on arcs that have the largest flow and interdict arcs in descending order of flow within budget.

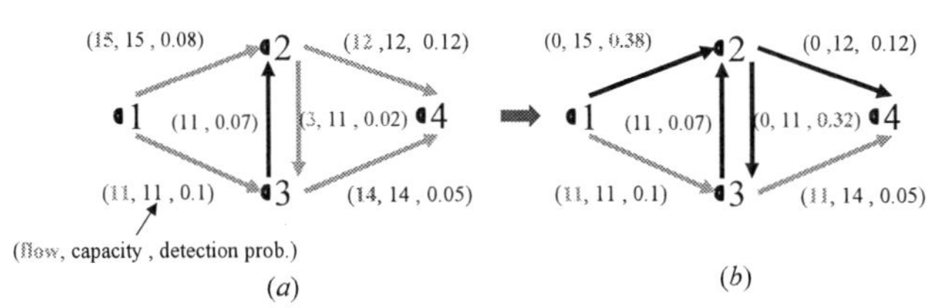

Figure 4. Image of the upper bound of expected profits

Figure 4 describes the upper bound of expected profits. Assume that penalty cost $C = 6$, interdiction budget $B = 2$, and each interdiction arc cost $c(a_{ij}) = 1$. Figure 4(a) shows a flow that achieves maximum expected profit with the condition that no arc is interdicted. Here, flow $y = \{a_{12}, a_{24}, a_{23}, a_{13}, a_{34}\}$, $f_n(y) = 26$. Then, expected profit is $e_n(y) = 8.924$. In this flow, arcs $\{a_{12}, a_{34}\}$ have the largest flow within budget. The maximum expected profit under this strategy that arcs $\{a_{12}, a_{34}\}$ are interdicted is set as an upper bound of expected profits. This maximum expected profit $e_n(y) = 8.102$. The process of finding the interdictor strategy enumerates combinations of interdicted arcs within budget. Assume that arcs $\{a_{12}, a_{23}\}$ are interdicted as shown in Figure 4(b) in this process. In this interdiction strategy, an augmenting path $\{a_{13}, a_{34}\}$ is first obtained. The expected profit by this augment path is calculated as 9.405. At this time, it suggests that the maximum expected profit is more than upper bound 8.102. Searching augmenting paths can be stopped here, though there is some augmenting paths in residual network. If a better solution (interdictor strategy) than the upper bound is found, the upper bound is updated.

4. Numerical Experiments

This section compares proposed algorithm to the previous algorithm[5]. Numerical examples are conducted to evaluate the effect of reducing the number of considered flows by weighted graph with 8 nodes and 15 arcs presented in Figure 5.

As the results of each algorithm are shown in table I. Related parameters are set as $C = 6$, $B = 1, 2, 3, 4$. Detection probabilities of each arc increase by $p_2(a_{i,j}) = 0.3, 0.5$ after interdiction. Interdiction costs of each arc are set as $c(a_{ij}) = 1$.

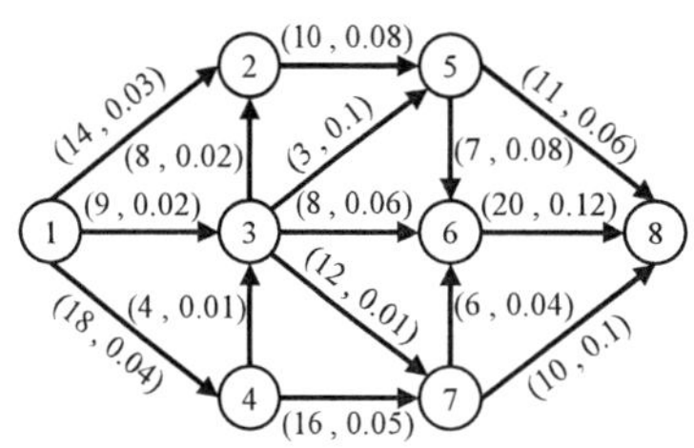

Figure 5. mage of the upper bound of expected profits

Table 1. Expected Profits and Update frequency of Optimal Solution

p_2	B	$e_n(y)$	flowbb	flowbb_s
0.3	1	10.918	1	1
	2	7.133	4	2
	3	3.801	5	5
	4	2.755	2	2
0.5	1	10.918	1	1
	2	7.098	2	3
	3	0.415	2	4
	4	-0.163	2	4

Table 2. Comparison of Computing Time[ms]

p_2	B	flowbb	flowbb_s	previous
0.3	1	10.937	12.725	12221.130
	2	32.426	28.450	18889.960
	3	82.390	78.233	22115.660
	4	180.965	180.006	-
0.5	1	11.792	15.220	12222.201
	2	33.620	30.017	18892.426
	3	84.385	78.924	22120.370
	4	198.920	194.275	-

Table1 shows expected profits $e_n(y)$ and update frequency of optimal solutions of proposed algorithms. “flowbb” means an algorithm that upper bound solution has been used in the process of finding interdictor strategy. “flowbb_s” is an algorithm that upper bound solution has been used, and interdictor strategies have been enumerated in descending order of detection probabilities. Comparing two algorithms, update frequency of “flowbb” is lower than “flowbb_s”.

Table2 is comparisons of computing time with each algorithm. “Previous” means an algorithm of Sadeghi et al. The result shows proposed algorithms reduces more computing time than previous algorithm. The effect of restricting the number of considered flows and interdicted arcs seems to reduce computing time. Compared “flowbb” with “flowbb_s”, computing time of “flowbb_s” tends to be lower. In terms of update frequencies of optimal solutions, “flowbb” is lower than “flowbb_s”. It seems that “flowbb_s” finds the better upper bound solution in the upstream process. But, “flowbb_s” has an additional procedure of finding an upper bound solution. This may affect the effectiveness of computing time.

5. Conclusion

We focused on the maximum flow network interdiction problem that aims to minimize the maximum flow by interdicting arcs. For this problem, reformulation was described. We proposed the algorithm that effectively search for optimal strategies. Evader strategies were found by replacing distance in Dijkstra’s algorithm with expected flow value. For interdictor strategies, an enumeration order of interdiction arcs was considered. In addition, we search for a certain solution in advance and use it as the upper bound of expected profits.

Numerical experiments showed that proposed algorithms reduced computing times. However, an additional procedure of finding an upper bound may reduce the effectiveness of computing time a little.

6. References

[1] A. W. McMasters and T. M. Mustin. “Optimal interdiction of a supply”, Naval Research Logistics Quarterly, vol.17, no.13, 261-268, Sept. 1970

[2] P. M. Ghare, D. C. Montgomery and W. C. Turner. “Optimal Interdiction Policy for a Flow Network”, Naval Research Logistics Quarterly, vol.18, no.1, 37-45, Mar. 1971

[3] N. O. Bakir. “A Stackelberg game model for resource allocation in cargo container security”, Annals of Operations Research, vol.187, no.1, 5-22, Jul. 2011.

[4] J. P. Caulkins. “G. Crawford and P. Reuer. Simulation of Adaptive Response: A Model of Drug Interdiction”, Mathematical and Computer Modeling, vol.17, no.2, 37-52, Jan. 1993.

[5] S. Sadeghi and A. Seifi. “Stochastic Maximum Flow Network Interdiction with Endogenous Uncertainty”, International Journal of Supply and Operations Management, vol.6, no.3, 200-212, Aug. 2019.

Constructing Reliability Models for State-dependent Resilient Systems Using Continuous-time Markov Chain

Yu-Cheng CHANG, Ruey-Huei YEH*, Pei-Chen CHENG

Department of Industrial Management, National Taiwan University of Science and Technology, Taiwan
* rhyeh@mail.ntust.edu.tw

Keywords: Reliability, random shocks, resilience, continuous-time Markov chain

Abstract - The failure of most products or systems typically arises from two main aspects: internal degradation and random impacts from the external operating environment. In recent years, system resilience has gained increasing attention, as technological advancements enable many systems to recover from external shocks partially. However, resilience is still rarely integrated into reliability modeling and maintenance analysis. This paper aims to construct a reliability model incorporating internal degradation, external shocks, and resilience-based recovery mechanisms. A discrete-state continuous-time Markov chain (CTMC) is proposed to describe the system's state transitions, where internal degradation occurs gradually and shocks cause jumps in states with state-dependent resilience. This modeling approach enables the analysis of reliability behavior over time and allows for evaluating how resilience mechanisms affect system reliability. The framework serves as a foundation for future integration with maintenance policies or cost-based decision-making in resilient system design.

1. Introduction

Resilient systems operate under conditions where both gradual internal degradation and sudden external shocks can contribute to system failures. Traditional reliability models often focus on either degradation or shock effects separately, overlooking their combined impact and the system's capacity to recover (resilience). This study develops a reliability modeling framework based on a continuous-time Markov chain (CTMC), integrating internal degradation, random shocks, and resilience-based recovery mechanisms. The proposed model distinguishes between various failure causes and captures the dynamic transitions among operational, degraded, and failure states. Through comparative simulations of three progressively complex models, the study demonstrates how external shocks accelerate reliability decay and how resilience mechanisms can mitigate this damage caused by the random shocks. The findings underscore the importance of incorporating system resilience in reliability assessment, particularly for modern systems designed with resilient or self-healing features.

2. Mathematical model

This study proposes a reliability model for a resilient system using a continuous-time Markov chain to simulate state transitions under internal degradation and external random shocks. The model incorporates various failure scenarios and a probabilistic recovery mechanism to reflect the system's resilience, enabling effective reliability analysis and supporting future maintenance decision-making.

2.1. System description

This study establishes a model for a resilient system whose condition evolves through discrete state transitions following a continuous-time Markov chain [1, 2]. The system's condition is discretized into N operational states, indexed from State 1 (the healthiest state) to State N (the most degraded but still functioning condition) [3]. And, the state $N+1$ is the failure state in which the system is not functioning.

To reflect increasing levels of environmental uncertainty and control strategies, three reliability models are constructed:

Model 1 considers only internal degradation. The system deteriorates gradually over time, transitioning sequentially from State 1 to State $N+1$ at a constant degradation rate λ.

Model 2 adds external random shocks to the degradation process. Shocks arrive according to a Poisson process with rate β [4, 5]. When a shock arrives, the system in state i will jump to state $i+J$, where $J>1$ is the size of the random shock. For highly degraded states (States $N-J$, ..., $N-2$, $N-1$), any shock leads directly to a system failure. In order to distinguish various failures caused by degradation or random shocks, this paper introduces some fictitious failure states, $N+2$, $N+3$, ..., $N+J$. In other words, they are shock-induced failure states, and only $N+1$ is the degradation-induced failure state.

Model 3 introduces resilience into Model 2 by allowing partial recovery after random shocks. Again, to distinguish various transitions caused by degradation or random shocks, this paper introduces some fictitious states, i', which represent the system entering state i by random shocks. Upon entering the fictitious state (denoted as i'), the system may recover itself back to the $i-j$ state with probability P_j, where $P_0 + P_1 + \ldots + P_{J-1} = 1$.

Using the fictitious states, we may construct a reliability model incorporating internal degradation, external shocks, and resilience-based recovery into the continuous-time Markov chain. This model architecture allows for a progressive reliability analysis under increasing real-world complexity, from purely degradation-driven systems to those affected by random shocks and designed with resilience features [6].

2.2. Notations

N Number of operational states
i Operational state, i=1, 2, …, N
i' Fictitious state after a random shock
S Set of operational states: {1, 2, …, N}
J Jump size caused by a random shock
F Set of absorbing failure states: {N+1, N+2, …, N+J }
$R(t)$ System reliability at time t
T System lifetime (time to first entry into any failure state)
$\pi(t)$ Row vector of state probabilities at time t
λ Internal degradation rate
β External shock arrival rate
P_0 Probability of no recovery
P_j, Probability of recovering by j state after entering a fictitious state, j=1, 2, …, J-1
Q Transition rate matrix of the Markov process

2.3. Model formulation

The system states are partitioned into three categories [7]:

1. Operational states i=1, 2, …, N, represent the healthy levels of the system, from fully functional to severely degraded but still operating.
2. Fictitious operational states i': temporary states entered after a shock in a relatively healthy condition. A shock causes a fixed jumps of J levels (e.g., $i \rightarrow (i+J)'$).
3. Absorbing failure states:
   - N+1: failure due to internal degradation
   - N+2, N+3, ..., N+J: fictitious failure due to a random shock

The subsequent sections define the transition logic between these states, construct the full generator matrix **Q**, and lay the foundation for computing the system reliability $R(t)$.

The state space of this model is separated into three distinct layers — operational states, fictitious (shock-affected) states, and absorbing failure states — offers both structural and analytical advantages. By assigning a dedicated set of fictitious states to capture the system's condition immediately after external random shocks, the model allows resilience-based recovery mechanisms to be precisely modeled. This avoids ambiguity in transition paths and enables more realistic post-shock behavior to be represented.

Additionally, the definition of multiple absorbing failure states serves to differentiate failure induced by various causes. For instance, failures due to internal degradation and those triggered by external random shocks from different degraded states are assigned to distinct absorbing states (e.g., States N+1, N+2, ..., N+J). This facilitates clear attribution of system failures, which is essential in applications requiring detailed failure diagnostics or cause-based maintenance planning.

Moreover, the separation of fictitious and absorbing states enables layered evaluation of system performance. Analysts can not only measure overall reliability but also decompose failure probability by sources, which provides insights into how much of the risk is contributed by wear versus sudden impacts. This clarity supports further integration with maintenance cost models, risk prioritization, and resource allocation strategies in resilient system management.

Overall, this structured formulation enhances the model's interpretability, supports downstream decision-making, and strengthens its applicability to complex reliability scenarios.

2.3.1. Internal degradation

The system deteriorates over time due to internal factors such as mechanical fatigue or aging. This process is modeled as sequential transition between adjacent operational states in a continuous-time Markov chain. Specifically, when the system is in state $i \in \{1, 2, ..., N\}$, it transitions to state $i+1$ at a constant degradation λ.

Once the system reaches the final operational state N, any further degradation leads to failure, represented by a transition to the absorbing state $N+1$, also occurring at rate λ.

The transition structure for internal degradation can be described as follows:

$$i \xrightarrow{\lambda} i+1, \quad \text{for } i = 1,2,\dots,N-1$$
$$N \xrightarrow{\lambda} N+1$$

All transitions are unidirectional and occur at a uniform rate λ, reflecting a homogeneous internal degradation mechanism across all operational stages as depicted in Figure 1.

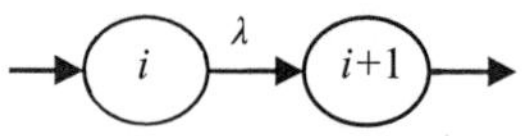

Figure 1. System degradation

2.3.2. External random shocks

External random shockss are assumed to arrive according to a Poisson process with a constant rate β. The effect of a shock depends on the system's current operational state and is classified into two types of transitions.

(1) Transitions to fictitious (shock-induced) states
If the system is in a relatively healthy state $i \in S_R = \{1, 2, ..., N-J\}$, an external random shock causes an immediate degradation of J levels. Instead of transitioning directly to state $i+J$, the system enters a fictitious state $(i+J)'$, which captures the system's condition immediately after the shock and before any potential resilience-based recovery. The transition rule is defined as:

$$i \xrightarrow{\beta} (i+j)', \quad \text{for } i \in S_R$$

Here, J represents the fixed jump size due to a random shock, and the prime symbol (') is used to distinguish states from regular operational states as depicted in Figure 2.

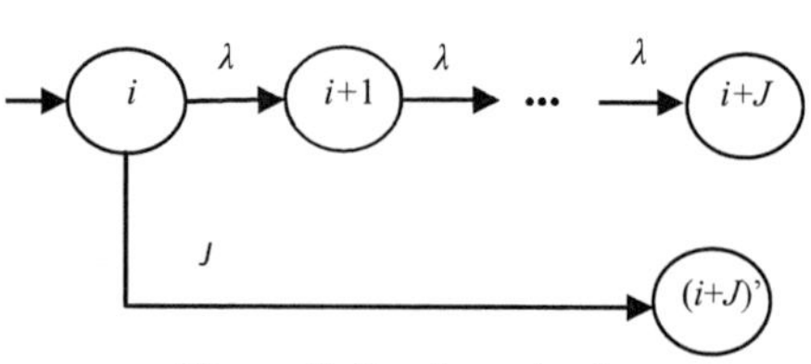

Figure 2. Random shocks

(2) Direct transition to failure states
If the system is in a severely degraded state $i \in S_F = \{N-J+1, \dots, N\}$, an external shock results in immediate failure. To differentiate failure induced by random shocks, the transition leads to a distinct fictitious absorbing state F_i specific to the pre-failure state i.

In this study, these fictitious absorbing states are defined as $N+1, N+2, \ldots, N+J$, corresponding to shock-induced failures. The transition rule is described in Figure 3 when $J=3$.

$$i \xrightarrow{\beta} F_i, \quad \text{for } i \in S_F$$

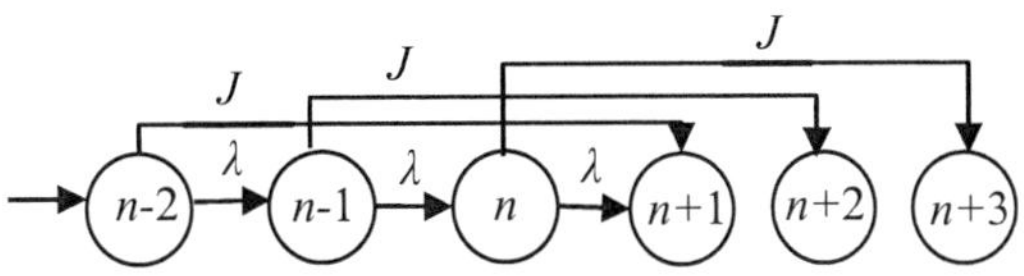

Figure 3. Fictitious failure states

These transitions are unidirectional and represent the structural response of the system under external random shocks, either entering a transient recoverable state or leading to direct failure [8]. The shock-induced degradation magnitude J remains a model parameter and will be specified during the numerical phase. For the purposes of model tractability and transition structure clarity, we set $J=3$ in this study from this point forward.

The shock transition mechanism in Model 2 introduces abrupt state changes that deviate from the linear progression seen in internal degradation. By modeling a fixed shock impact of $J=3$ states, the system captures significant damage caused by unexpected external events. The introduction of fictitious states $(i+J)'$ provides a structural placeholder for post-shock conditions and separates the moment of shock impact from any subsequent behavior. Although no recovery occurs in Model 2, this fictitious structure anticipates the resilience mechanisms of Model 3 and maintains consistency in state definitions. Additionally, directing shocks from severely degraded states to distinct absorbing states (e.g., $N+2$, $N+3$) enables failure sources differentiation, which is essential for downstream analysis such as failure attribution or cause-specific maintenance policies.

2.3.3. Resilience

When the system enters a shock-fictitious state $(i+j)'$, with a fixed shock size J, it undergoes an immediate resilience-based recovery transition to one of the nearby operational states. The recovery is probabilistic and defined by the following outcomes [9]: the system may recover itself from state i' back to the state $(i-j)$ with probability P_j, where $P_0 + P_1 + \ldots + P_{J-1} = 1$.

This mechanism applies to all fictitious states resulting from shocks, where $i \in \{1, 2, \ldots, N-j\}$, and can be expressed as Figure 4 when $J=3$.

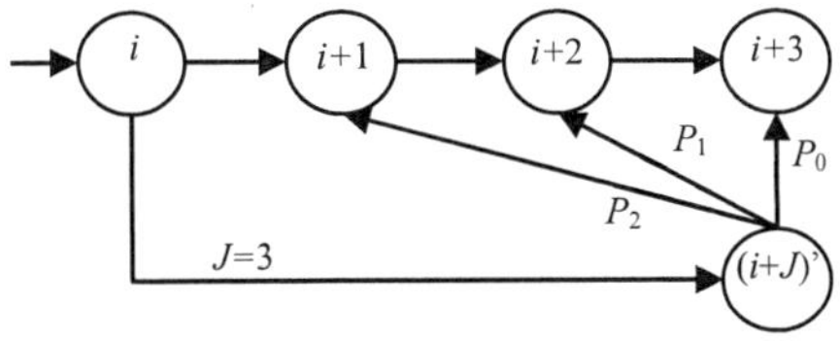

Figure 4. Resilience when $J=3$

All transitions occur instantaneously, with no residence time in the fictitious states, reflecting a prompt resilience response of the system.

The transition diagram for Model 3 illustrates the system's behavior following an external random shock. After a shock occurs in operational state i, the system undergoes an immediate jump of three levels, moving to the fictitious state $(i+3)'$. From this shock-affected state, the system can probabilistically recover by two states $(i+1)$ with probability P_2, by one state $(i+2)$ with probability P_1, or remain in the degraded state $(i+3)$ with probability P_0. This structure clearly separates the post-shock condition from subsequent resilience-based transitions and allows the system to return to different operational levels depending on its recovery capability.

2.3.4. Transition probabilities

The goal of this paper is to evaluate how internal degradation, external random shocks, and resilience-based recovery influence the system's reliability behavior over time. The models are analyzed using continuous-time Markov chains. For each model, a transition rate matrix $\mathbf{Q}$ is constructed according to the degradation and shock mechanisms, whose entries q_{ij} is the transition rate from state i to state j for $i \neq j$ and $q_{ii} = -\sum_{k \neq i} q_{ik} = -v_i$. Then, the transition probability matrix P(t) at any time t satisfies the Chapman-Kolmogorov Equations.

$$p_{ij}(t+s) = \sum_{k=0}^{\infty} p_{ik}(t) p_{kj}(s) \text{ for all } t \geq 0, s \geq 0 \tag{1}$$

Hence, the transition probability matrix P(t) at any time t can be computed via Kolmogorov's Backward Equations

$$\frac{d}{dt} p_{ij}(t) = \sum_{k \neq i} q_{ik} p_{kj}(t) - v_i p_{ij}(t) \rightarrow \frac{d}{dt} \mathbf{P}(t) = \mathbf{QP}(t) \tag{2}$$

The solution of Equation (2) is $\mathbf{P}(t) = \mathbf{P}(0) e^{\mathbf{Q}t}$

where $e^{\mathbf{Q}t} = \sum_{n=0}^{\infty} \mathbf{Q}^n \frac{t^n}{n!} = \mathbf{I} + \mathbf{Q}t + \frac{\mathbf{Q}^2 t^2}{2!} + \frac{\mathbf{Q}^3 t^3}{3!} + \cdots$.

Furthermore, the system reliability function $R(t)$ is defined as the probability that the system remains within operational states S at time t, calculated by:

$$R(t) = \sum_{j \in S} P_{1j}(t) \tag{3}$$

where $P_{1j}(t)$ denotes the probability of transitioning from the initial state 1 to operational state j at time t.

3. Numerical examples

This section conducts a numerical comparison of three reliability models to numerically evaluate how internal degradation, external random shocks, and resilience-based recovery affect system performance over time. By computing reliability functions using Kolmogorov's Backward Equations, the results demonstrate that resilience mechanisms significantly mitigate the impact of shocks and enhance system reliability. A sensitivity analysis further illustrates how varying recovery probabilities influence the extent of performance improvement in resilient systems.

3.1. Comparisons

In this section, three different system models are compared under a fixed set of baseline parameters as given in Table 1.

Table 1. Baseline parameter setting for numerical analysis

N	λ	β	J	P_0	P_1	P_2
10	0.05	3	3	0.3	0.4	0.3

The baseline parameters in Table 1 are consistently used throughout Section 3.1 to observe the impact of different system assumptions on reliability performance. A detailed sensitivity analysis on the recovery probabilities will be presented in Section 3.2.

Recall that these three models are constructed in a layered structure to progressively incorporate additional system features.

Model 1 Internal degradation only.

Model 2 Internal degradation + external shocks.

Model 3 Internal degradation + external shocks + resilience

The reliability functions $R(t)$ for each model are computed based on the transition probability given in Equation (3). Under the same baseline parameter settings given in Table 1, the reliability curves exhibit the expected trend as given in Figure 5.

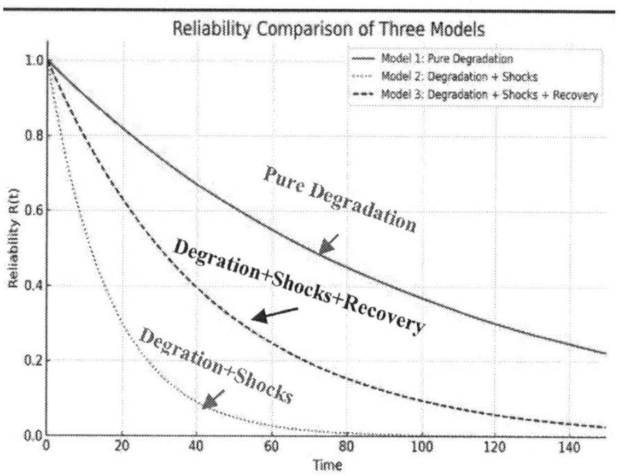

Figure 5. Reliability functions $R(t)$ for various models

As we can observe from Figure 5, the reliability function of Model 1 displays a slower and smoother degradation trajectory under pure internal degradation. Since there are no external random shocks, the Model 1 with pure degradation has the highest reliability at any time t among these three models. When there are external random shocks, the reliability of Model 2 shows the fastest decline due to the presence of external shocks. However, if the system has resilient capability, the reliability of Model 3 demonstrates that resilience mechanisms significantly mitigate the impact of shocks and enhance system reliability. The reliability of Model 3 is somewhere between Model 1 and Model 2 at any time t. This comparison also highlights the effects of random shocks and resilience mechanisms on system performance.

3.2. Sensitivity analysis

To further explore the influence of resilience mechanisms within Model 3, this section conducts a sensitivity analysis by varying the recovery probabilities P_0, P_1, and P_2 in Model 3. The extreme resilient scenarios are considered as given in Table 2.

Table 2. Various resilient Scenarios when J=3

Scenario	P_0	P_1	P_2
Case A	1	0	0
Case B	0	1	0
Case C	0	0	1

In Case A, the system has no resilience and cannot recover after shocks, which is a special case of Model 3. In fact, this is the Model 2 mentioned before. In Case B, the system recovers by one state after each shock. Similarly, in Case C, the system fully recovers by two states, representing the highest level of resilience.

The reliability functions $R(t)$ are computed using the the transition probability given in Equation (3), with the shock arrival rate set to β=0.6 and the maximum observed time set to T=50.

The results, as shown in Figure 6, reveal clear differences among the three scenarios. Without any recovery (Case A), the system reliability declines most rapidly. Allowing recovery by one state (Case B) moderately improves reliability, while full recovery by two states (Case C) significantly extends the system's operational lifetime and maintains a higher reliability level throughout the observed period. This result highlights the critical role of resilience in enhancing system reliability, especially under severe external shock conditions.

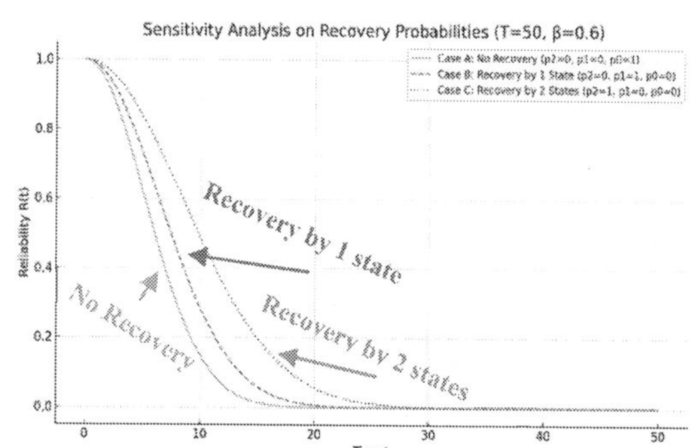

Figure 6. Reliability functions $R(t)$ for various resilience

The above analysis indicates that resilience has a substantial effect on system reliability, especially when the recovery capability closely compensates for shock-induced damage. While this may seem intuitive, the implication is practically important. Instead of treating recovery probabilities as fixed design parameters, a system can be improved through targeted maintenance actions. For example, predictive maintenance or post-shock inspections may help restore partial system functionality or recalibrate degraded components. In future research, these recovery probabilities could be modeled as dynamic variables influenced by maintenance strategies, environmental conditions, or resource allocation policies. This opens the possibility of integrating resilience optimization into system-level maintenance planning.

4. Conclusion

This study proposed a continuous-time Markov chain model to systematically evaluate the system reliability of resilient systems under both internal degradation and external random shocks. By constructing three progressively mathematical models and conducting numerical simulations, the results show that the external random shocks (Model 2) significantly reduce the reliability of a system. When a system suffers severe external random shocks, incorporating system resilience capability (Model 3) can effectively mitigate the damage and enhance overall system reliability.

These findings highlight the importance of considering resilience when evaluating the reliability of real-world engineering systems. The layered modeling approach used in this study provides a structural framework to isolate and assess the individual and combined effects of degradation, random shocks, and resilience, allowing system designers to better understand the trade-offs involved.

Moreover, the results offer practical implications for reliability engineering, such as systems equipped with effective resilience capability or supported by targeted maintenance actions, including post-shock inspections or real-time reconfiguration, can significantly reduce the likelihood of failure under uncertain environments. This emphasizes the value of designing not just robust systems, but resilient ones.

Future work may extend this model by integrating preventive maintenance strategies, cost considerations, or optimal replacement policies to improve its practical applicability [4]. Additionally, the recovery probabilities may be modeled as dynamic variables influenced by maintenance effort or environmental factors, further linking system resilience with operational decisions.

5. Acknowledgement

This research is partly supported by a grant (NSTC-113-2221-E-011-125) from the Ministry of Science and Technology, Taiwan.

6. References

[1] Lin, Y.-Y. (2023). Constructing a failure model for degrading systems under random shocks using continuous-time Markov chains (Master's thesis, National Taiwan University of Science and Technology, Taipei, Taiwan).

[2] Chen, H.-Y. (2024). Constructing a reliability model for resilient systems using continuous-time Markov chains (Master's thesis, National Taiwan University of Science and Technology, Taipei, Taiwan).

[3] Gut, A. (1990). Stopped random walks: Limit theorems and applications. Springer.

[4] Noortwijk, J. M. (2009). A survey of the application of gamma processes in maintenance modeling. Reliability Engineering & System Safety, 94(1), 2–21.

[5] Gut, A. (2001). Mixed shock models in reliability. Statistical Papers, 42(1), 57-72.

[6] Hoang Pham, (2005). Reliability modeling of multi-state degraded systems with multi-competing failures and random shocks, IEEE Transactions on Reliability.

[7] Li, W., & Kong, L. (2007). Failure models under cumulative and extreme shocks. Reliability Engineering & System Safety, 92(1), 28-36.

[8] Ahmad, R. (1995). Fatigue analysis in structural materials. International Journal of Fatigue, 17(4), 245-251.

[9] Eryilmaz, S. (2015). Discrete-time shock models with Markovian environment. European Journal of Operational Research, 255(2), 363–372.

Optimal scheduling problem for a single machine with preventive maintenance constraints

Lu-Wen Liao, Tsang-Chuan Chang*, Yen-Chia Chen

Department of Intelligent Production Engineering, National Taichung University of Science and Technology, Taichung City, Taiwan
* Corresponding author: pigsmallchang@gmail.com

Keywords: Machine scheduling; Preventive maintenance; MIP model; Branch and Bound

Abstract - With the rapid advancement of information technology and the rise of Industry 4.0, automated machines and intelligent equipment are increasingly being utilized in manufacturing. These technologies have significantly enhanced production capacity and efficiency across production lines. However, the substantial investment required for such equipment makes preventive maintenance a critical strategy for manufacturers. Preventive maintenance ensures machinery operates at optimal performance, minimizing malfunctions and maintaining production stability. This approach helps prevent disruptions to production schedules and avoids unnecessary costs.

This study focuses on incorporating preventive maintenance periods into scheduling plans to optimize machine utilization. The goal is to schedule independent jobs within a planning horizon while minimizing the makespan. A mixed-integer programming model is proposed to address this scheduling problem, alongside a branch-and-bound method designed to optimize solutions based on machine maintenance and job characteristics. Data analysis reveals that the branch-and-bound method can solve up to 40 jobs within a reasonable timeframe, while the genetic algorithm effectively handles larger instances, providing high-quality approximate solutions.

1. Introduction

With the rise of Industry 4.0 and the emergence of automated factories, advancements in production technologies and manufacturing processes have become increasingly refined. Companies face the ongoing challenge of addressing production issues while reducing costs. There are numerous strategies to lower production costs, such as saving raw materials, improving labor productivity, enhancing equipment utilization, increasing product quality, reducing waste, and cutting manufacturing expenses. Among these, production scheduling has proven to be a critical tool in modern industries, as effective scheduling can significantly reduce production costs [1]. Scheduling involves allocating limited resources—such as machines, personnel, and materials—within a factory to transform orders or production plans into actionable arrangements [2]. This process requires balancing three often conflicting objectives: efficiency, inventory, and service levels [3]. A well-constructed scheduling plan ensures that resources, capacity, and time are optimized to minimize costs while meeting production goals.

In machine scheduling, Stevenson & William [4] categorize scheduling into five types: single machine, parallel machine, flow shop, job shop, and open shop scheduling. Among these, single machine scheduling serves as the foundation for more complex scheduling problems. It focuses on efficiently sequencing tasks on a single machine, considering constraints such as processing time, release time, and downtime for maintenance or testing [5]. For example, in semiconductor manufacturing, a single machine may process various parts with differing processing times. The goal is to determine the optimal sequence to minimize total processing time or costs.

This study focuses on single machine scheduling under realistic conditions, where machines are not continuously available due to maintenance, testing, or breakdowns [6]. Unlike traditional assumptions of continuous machine availability, this research addresses the challenges posed by intermittent machine availability, aiming to minimize completion time. By reviewing existing literature, this study identifies gaps in current single machine scheduling research and proposes solutions tailored to real-world industrial scenarios.

Single machine scheduling serves as the foundation for other scheduling types [4] and is classified as an NP-hard problem [7]. Its applications have been widely studied, particularly in Taiwan's advanced semiconductor industry. [8] reviewed single machine scheduling literature from 2010 to 2022, highlighting that most studies assume machines are continuously available. However, real-world scenarios often involve interruptions due to factors like material changes, preventive maintenance, or unexpected breakdowns. This study focuses on a single machine scheduling problem in the metal processing industry, where heating and cooling treatments are required. Heating time is treated as release time, while cooling time represents machine unavailability. The study assumes non-resumable jobs, meaning once a job starts, it must be completed without interruption. A mixed-integer programming model is developed to minimize makespan by optimizing job sequences based on processing and release times. For large-scale problems, algorithms are employed to efficiently find optimal solutions. This research addresses single machine scheduling under non-resumable conditions, aiming to minimize makespan while considering machine availability constraints.

2. Literature review

The problem of minimizing total completion time in single machine scheduling has been a key focus in scheduling theory. Wilkerson & Irwin [9] introduced methods to minimize total tardiness, reducing costs effectively. Holsenback & Russell [10] proposed an algorithm to determine job sequences for minimizing total tardiness. Sbihi & Varnier [11] incorporated periodic maintenance into scheduling, while Tseng et al. [12] and Yin et al. [13] developed mixed-integer programming models and heuristic algorithms for large-scale problems.

In practical scenarios, machine operations are often non-continuous due to factors such as breakdowns, maintenance to extend machine lifespan, or component replacements. Scheduling assumptions must account for machine availability, as highlighted in studies like Feitelson and Rudolph [14]. Lee & Liman [15] classified single machine scheduling problems, particularly those minimizing flow time affected by maintenance, as NP-hard. Adiri et al. [16] optimized this problem, introducing error bounds for Shortest Processing Time (SPT) sequences. These studies underscore the importance of addressing non-continuous machine availability in scheduling research. The literature review reveals that single machine scheduling with machine availability constraints has been insufficiently explored. Existing studies typically address either a single unavailable time period or non-continuous processing but rarely consider both simultaneously. In practice, however, production planners often encounter both scenarios on the production line. Additionally, unavailable time periods may arise from various controllable or uncontrollable factors, and workpieces often have differing specifications and processing times. This study aims to address these gaps by investigating single machine scheduling under machine availability constraints, incorporating at least one unavailable time interval, with the objective of minimizing makespan.

3. Problem description and mathematical model

This study focuses on single machine scheduling with machine availability constraints, aiming to minimize makespan. Unlike traditional scheduling problems, this research incorporates greater generality, as outlined in the literature review. The problem involves *n* independent jobs, each with a processing time and release time, where processing can only begin after the release time. The machine operates within specified availability intervals. This study investigates scheduling strategies under these constraints to achieve the objective of minimizing makespan.

There are some assumptions given as follows.

- Each job is independent.
- The machine can process only one job at a time, and each job can be executed only once.
- During the processing of any job, the machine will not experience breakdowns or malfunctions.
- The processing time, release time for each job, and the machine's unavailable intervals are all known.
- Once a job starts on the machine, it must be completed without interruption, with no pauses for maintenance or other activities.

In addition, we briefly state symbols used in the mathematical model as follows.

- j: the index of the jobs, where $j=1,\ldots,n$.
- k: the index of the position in machine.
- r: the index of the machine's available time intervals.
- p_j: the processing time of job j.
- r_j: the release time of job j.
- $[B^r, F^r]$: the rth available time interval of the machine, where B^r is the start time and F^r is the end time of the interval.
- X^r_{jk}: if job j is assigned to the rth available time interval and kth position of the machine
- C^r_k: the completion time of rth available time interval in the kth position on the machine
- C_{max}: the makespan.

The mathematical model for the studied problem is shown in the following Figure 1.

$$Minimze \quad C_{max} \qquad (1)$$

s.t.

$$\sum_{r=1}^{U}\sum_{k=1}^{N} X^r_{jk} = 1 \qquad \forall j \in J \qquad (2)$$

$$\sum_{r=1}^{U}\sum_{j=1}^{N\times U} X^r_{jk} \le 1 \qquad \forall k \in K \qquad (3)$$

$$\sum_{k=1}^{N} C^r_k \le F^r - B^r \qquad \forall r \in (U-1) \qquad (4)$$

$$C^1_1 = \sum_{j=1}^{N} X^1_{j1}(p_j + r_j) \qquad (5)$$

$$C^r_k = C^r_{k-1} + \sum_{j=1}^{N} X^r_{jk} p_j + h^r_k \left(\sum_{j=1}^{N} X^r_{jk} r_j - C^r_{k-1}\right) \qquad \forall r \in U \quad \forall k \in K \quad K > 2 \qquad (6)$$

$$C^2_1 = B^2 + \sum_{j=1}^{N} X^2_{j1} p_j + h^2_1 \left(\sum_{j=1}^{N} X^2_{j1} r_j - B^2\right) \qquad (7)$$

$$C^r_{k-1} - \sum_{j=1}^{N} X^r_{jk} r_j + M h^r_k \le M \qquad \forall r \in U \quad \forall k \in K \quad K > 2 \qquad (8)$$

$$C^r_{k-1} - \sum_{j=1}^{N} X^r_{jk} r_j + M h^r_k \ge 0 \qquad \forall r \in U \quad \forall k \in K \quad K > 2 \qquad (9)$$

$$X^r_{jk}, h^r_k \text{ is binary} \qquad \forall j \in J \quad \forall k \in K \quad \forall r \in U \qquad (10)$$

$$C^r_k, F^r, B^r, p_j, r_j, C_{max} \ge 0 \qquad \forall j \in J \quad \forall k \in K \quad \forall r \in U \qquad (11)$$

Figure 1 Mathematical model for the studied problem

(1) is the objective function and aims to minimize the maximum completion time. Constraint (2) ensures that each job can only be assigned to specific available time intervals for processing, while constraint (3) guarantees that only one job can be processed at a time in each position. Constraint (4) represents the machine's available time constraints. Constraints (5), (6), and (7) define the cumulative completion time for jobs processed at each position on the machine. Constraints (8) and (9) use the maximum value and the release time of the preceding position to determine h, which is a binary variable.

4. Branch and bound algorithm

This section presents a Branch and Bound algorithm to find the optimal solution for minimizing machine availability in single-machine scheduling. The branching rule is that each node in the search tree signifies the jobs that are scheduled on the machine. The upper bound of each branching node is defined by using the SPT rule to find the schedule for the studied problem. On the other hand, the lower bound of each branching node is calculated by setting that each job can be split and resumed. The branch and bound algorithm is shown as follows:

Step 1: Set initial values and categorize jobs into arranged and unarranged groups.

- Level 1: For each job, create a set of remaining jobs that have not been scheduled.
- Level 2: For each combination of two jobs, create a set of remaining jobs that have not been scheduled.
  Continue this process until all jobs are included in the unarranged set.

Step 2: Refer to the jobs in the arranged set from Step 1.

- For each job in the arranged set, find its processing time and add it to the schedule.
- Then, based on the arranged jobs, find their release times and add them in order.

Step 3: Arrange the jobs based on the order in the arranged set.

- Identify the job with the minimum processing time.
- Determine the corresponding release time for that job.
- Move the arranged job into a completed set.
- Define the start and end points of the earliest available processing interval.
- Store the cumulative values of the sorted jobs.

After completing the calculations, place the job with the minimum processing time into the completed set. Return to Step 3 until there are no jobs left in the arranged set.

5. Computational analysis

Based on the research methodology outlined, this study establishes a mixed-integer programming model and a Branch and Bound algorithm for minimizing machine availability in single-machine scheduling. This section concentrates on the computational analysis. The experiment starts by generating processing times, release times, and machine downtime. Next, a mixed-integer programming model is constructed using Lingo, and the Branch and Bound algorithm is implemented in Python to evaluate the results and solution times.

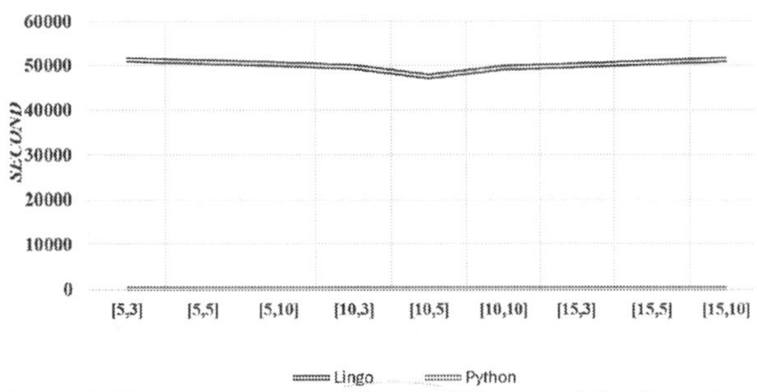

Figure 1 The computational times of Lingo and the Branch and Bound algorithm

Table 1 The computational analysis result

Job	p_{max}	r_{max}	method	number	C_{max}	Time(s)	average
20	5	3	Lingo	1	-	51723.61	51384.19
				2	64	51507.71	
				3	59	51373.78	
				4	-	51201.6	
				5	62	51114.23	
			BB	1	75	0.0011	0.00318
				2	64	0.0015	
				3	59	0.0051	
				4	66	0.003	
				5	62	0.0052	
		5	Lingo	1	51	51030.92	50870.8
				2	-	50952.73	
				3	-	50875.25	
				4	61	50777.92	
				5	61	50717.17	
			BB	1	51	0.0015	0.00724
				2	62	0.001	
				3	72	0.001	
				4	61	0.017	
				5	61	0.0157	
		10	Lingo	1	62	50588.96	50284.7
				2	45	50378.3	
				3	-	50206.12	
				4	-	50173.52	
				5	60	50076.62	
			BB	1	62	0.0021	0.00398
				2	45	0.011	
				3	62	0.0023	
				4	52	0.0017	
				5	60	0.0028	

6. Conclusion

This study focuses on scheduling for a single machine in the metal processing industry. Before processing sheet metal, preheating is essential to prepare the materials for further treatment. To prevent overheating, the machine must be allowed to rest and cool down at appropriate intervals. To address this issue, the project defines preheating time as the release time, working time as the processing time, and downtime for cooling as the unavailable period. This approach simulates real factory conditions, which not only reduces machine costs but also enhances overall efficiency and extends the machine's lifespan.

To tackle these challenges, the study reviews various literature on single-machine scheduling, mixed-integer programming, and the Branch and Bound algorithm. After analyzing the problem characteristics, an integer programming model is constructed. This model is then solved using Lingo. However, since the study is an NP-hard problem, the solution time for large-scale issues significantly increases, and some instances may remain unsolved with these methods. Therefore, the study develops a Branch and Bound algorithm tailored to the problem's characteristics for solving larger instances.

In this algorithm, upper and lower bounds are established. The upper bound uses the Shortest Processing Time priority rule, while the lower bound relaxes job characteristics by allowing for job splitting. These two rules are employed to find the optimal solution. Experimental designs are conducted, and the results show that the solution efficiency is significantly faster than that of the mathematical programming model.

7. Acknowledgement

The authors gratefully acknowledge the financial support provided by the National Science and Technology Council of Taiwan under Grants NSTC 112-2221-E-025-010 and 112-2221-E-025-011-MY2.

8. References

[1] Herrmann, J. W. (2006). A history of production scheduling. Handbook of production scheduling, 1-22.

[2] Lin I-Cong (1994) "Research on the Establishment of On-site Scheduling Expert System Using Individual Technology" Information Industry Policy Society

[3] Zeng Yuk-wen (2001) Information and Computer Press "Research on Non-Related Parallel Machine Scheduling Using Systematic Simulation and Genetic Algorithms", Taipei University of Science and Technology Master's thesis in Production Systems Engineering and Management

[4] Stevenson, William J. (2002) Operations management, McGraw-Hill Education, Seventh Edition.

[5] Arunarani, A., Manjula, D., & Sugumaran, V. (2019). Task scheduling techniques in cloud computing: A literature survey. Future Generation Computer Systems, 91, 407–415.

[6] He, C., Leung, J. Y. T., Lee, K., & Pinedo, M. L. (2016). Scheduling a single machine with parallel batching to minimize makespan and total rejection cost. Discrete Applied Mathematics, 204, 150-163.

[7] Brucker, Peter, et al. "Scheduling a batching machine." Journal of scheduling 1.1 (1998): 31-54.

[8] Martinelli, R., Mariano, F. C. M. Q., & Martins, C. B. (2022). Single machine scheduling in make to order environments: A systematic review. Computers & Industrial Engineering, 169, 108190.

[9] Wilkerson, L. J., and J. D. Irwin. "An improved method for scheduling independent tasks." AIIE transactions 3.3 (1971): 239-245.

[10] Holsenback, J. Edward, and Randolph M. Russell. "A heuristic algorithm for sequencing on one machine to minimize total tardiness." Journal of the Operational Research Society 43 (1992): 53-62.

[11] Sbihi, Mohammed, and Christophe Varnier. "Single-machine scheduling with periodic and flexible periodic maintenance to minimize maximum tardiness." Computers & Industrial Engineering 55.4 (2008): 830-840.

[12] Tseng, Chao-Tang, Ching-Jong Liao, and Kuo-Ling Huang. "Minimizing total tardiness on a single machine with controllable processing times." Computers & Operations Research 36.6 (2009): 1852-1858.

[13] Yin, Yunqiang, T. C. E. Cheng, and Chin-Chia Wu. "Scheduling with time-dependent processing times." Mathematical Problems in Engineering 2014 (2014)

[14] Feitelson, D. G., & Rudolph, L. (Eds.). (1995). Job Scheduling Strategies for Parallel Processing: IPPS'95 Workshop, Santa Barbara, CA, USA, April 25, 1995. Proceedings (Vol. 949). Springer Science & Business Media.

[15] Lee, C. Y., & Liman, S. D. (1992). Single machine flow-time scheduling with scheduled maintenance. Acta Informatica, 29, 375-382.

[16] Adiri, I., Bruno, J., Frostig, E., & Rinnooy Kan, A. H. G. (1989). Single machine flow-time scheduling with a single breakdown. Acta Informatica, 26, 679-696.

Reliability Evaluation of a Stochastic-Flow Production Network with Automatic and Manual Production Lines

Chieh Lee[1], Chen-Yu Yeh[2], Ping-Chen Chang[2,*]

[1]Department of Information Management, National Sun Yat-sen University, Kaohsiung, Taiwan
[2]Department of Industrial Engineering and Management, National Taipei University of Technology, Taipei 106, Taiwan
*pcchang@ntut.edu.tw

Keywords: stochastic-flow hybrid production network (SFHPN), automatic and manual, system reliability, reworking action

Abstract - Previous studies on stochastic-flow production networks are often considered fully automatic or fully manual workstations. However, real-world production lines typically combine both machines and workers. Different production phases may adopt various modes to meet diverse product demands and large-scale orders. Rework is also common, and in some sectors, such as surface mount technology (SMT), it remains manual due to complexity and flexibility needs for small-batch order production of small and medium enterprises. This study adopts a stochastic-flow hybrid production network (SFHPN) model to analyze a two-phase hybrid production line. In phase one, each workstation can operate in either automatic or manual mode. In phase two, one workstation is fully automatic and the other manual, with all rework performed on the manual line. The study proposes an algorithm to compute minimal capacities for each workstation under two phases and evaluates satisfaction probability, representing the system reliability. This helps production managers improve decision-making, operational performance, and system stability.

1. Introduction

Production systems play a crucial role in modern industry, directly influencing a company's production efficiency, product quality, and customer satisfaction. As today's markets demand increasing product diversity and higher volumes, managers must strike a balance between the high efficiency of automation and the flexibility of manual operations. Typical production systems may include either automatic or manual workstations. Workstations composed of machines usually offer high speed and precision [11], but they come with higher setup and maintenance costs, and may lack flexibility in situations requiring specialized skills [12]. On the other side, manual workstations operated by manual workers provide greater flexibility [9] and lower costs, but their efficiency depends heavily on the workers' skill levels. As a result, large-volume orders are generally handled by automated equipment, while small-batch orders are completed by manual labor [5, 8]. Recent trends in the manufacturing industry are increasingly shifting toward high-mix, high-volume production, which demands greater collaboration and flexible production solutions [2]. To achieve such flexibility, various system architectures and configurations can be employed to meet operational needs. However, conventional single-mode production systems comprised solely of either machines or human workers are no longer economically sustainable and fail to accommodate the growing diversity in market demands. As a result, hybrid production systems have emerged as a promising alternative. A hybrid production system refers to a configuration that combines at least two distinct organizational structures [3]. In this context, systems that integrate both manual and automated operations can be classified as hybrid systems. To address this, Krüger, et al. [6] proposed a method that optimizes assembly performance through strategic task allocation between machines and human labor. Similarly, Botti, et al. [1] conducted a case study involving the assembly process of hard-shell tool cases at an Italian manufacturer, demonstrating the effectiveness of their proposed mathematical model in designing hybrid assembly lines that balance manual labor and automation.

In a stochastic-flow hybrid production network (SFHPN), each arc can be regarded as a workstation composed of both machines and workers, while nodes represent inspection points. Due to potential machine failures, maintenance requirements, and variability in worker performance, the capacities of these workstations are stochastic. As such, the hybrid production network can be constructed as a stochastic-flow network [4]. The operational mode and efficiency of each workstation significantly impact the overall production capacity, especially in cases where defective WIPs are generated. Although these products are classified as defective, they still retain recoverable value. Through an effective rework process, defective WIPs can be transformed back into "normal" condition [10]. Reworking operations may occur at the same workstation, resulting in two production sources in the network: the general production path and the reworking path [7]. However, in an SFHPN, the characteristics of rework and scrapping violate the traditional flow conservation, as the input of raw materials may exceed the output of qualified products.

To consider for two production phases under different operational scenarios, where in the first phase, each workstation can choose to operate using either machines or manual workers, and in the second phase, the system consists of one fully automatic line and one fully manual line, with rework operations carried out on the manual line, this study models the production system as an SFHPN. An algorithm is developed to calculate the flow transitions between the two production phases and to evaluate the minimal capacity for each workstation. Based on these minimal capacity vectors, the probability that the production system can meet the demand, which is referred to as the system reliability, is computed. Production managers can use this system's reliability as a key indicator to assess whether customer demands can be fulfilled.

2. Problem description and assumption

Let $G = (\mathbf{N}, \mathbf{A}, \mathbf{M}, \mathbf{C}, \mathbf{U})$ be an SFHPN with two production phases, where $\mathbf{N}$ is the set of nodes to represent inspection points and $\mathbf{A} = \{a_1, a_2, \ldots, a_{\pi_1}, a_{\pi_1+1}, \ldots, a_{\pi_2}\}$ is the set of arcs to represent workstations, and π_1 and π_2 are the number of workstations before the production phases E_1 and E_2, where in production phase E_1, workstations can choose to operate in either automatic mode or manual mode based on production demand. In E_2, one line is automatic and the other is manual, with rework operations being performed on the manual line of E_2. In practice, the workstations of E_2 include both automatic and manual workstations, represented as $a_i^{(0)}$ and $a_i^{(1)}$; workstations of E_1 include two production modes: automatic and manual modes. In particular, $\mathbf{C}$ is a $2^h \times \pi_1$ matrix of the operation modes of the workstation composed of $s_{c,i}$, where $s_{c,i} = \{0, 1\}$, 0 represents the automatic machine and 1 represents manual worker. $\mathbf{U} = (u_i \mid i = 1, 2, \ldots, \pi_1)$ represents the automation proportion vector, where u_i denotes opting for the automatic machine proportion for each workstation and $0 \le u_i \le 1$. If a_i only has only one automatic mode, which means $s_{c,i} = \{0\}$, then $u_i = 1$ for all c. The capacity vector ($x_i^{(s_{c,i})}$, $x_i^{(s)} \mid i$ such that $a_i \in E_1$ and i such that $a_i \in E_2$), where $x_i^{(s_{c,i})}$ denotes the (current) capacity of workstation $a_i \in E_1$ and $x_i^{(s)}$ denotes the (current) capacity of workstation $a_i \in E_2$. The success rate of the $a_i \in E_1$ is $p_i^{(s_{c,i})}$ and $a_i \in E_2$ in the s mode line P_s is $p_i^{(s)}$, where $0 \le p_i^{(s_{c,i})}, p_i^{(s)} \le 1$. Such a G is studied based on the assumptions 1-5.

1. Each defective WIP is reworked at most once by the same workstation.
2. The capacity of each workstation (arc) is a random variable according to a given probability distribution.
3. The capacities of different workstations (arcs) are statistically independent.
4. Each node (inspection point) is perfectly reliable.
5. In this production process, the tasks at each workstation can be performed either by automatic machines or manual operations.

2.1. Determination of production combination matrix

The $\mathbf{C}$ matrix is used to represent the setting of different operational mode combinations on the production system. Each row of the matrix corresponds to a combination of operational modes, with each workstation's operating mode defined as $s_{c,i}$. The $\mathbf{C}$ matrix consists of 0 and 1, where 0 represents automatic mode and 1 represents manual mode. The size of the $\mathbf{C}$ matrix is determined by the number of workstations in E_1 and the number of combinations as equation (1), where the number of combinations is 2^h, with "2" representing the two operational modes (automatic and manual) available for each adjustable workstation (i.e., $s_i = \{0, 1\}$), and "h" being the number of workstations with non-fixed modes. The remaining workstations have fixed modes (i.e., $s_i = \{0\}$ or $s_i = \{1\}$), and these fixed-mode workstations remain unchanged in the matrix.

$$\mathbf{C} = \begin{bmatrix} s_{1,1} & s_{1,2} & \cdots & s_{1,\pi_1} \\ s_{2,1} & s_{2,2} & \cdots & s_{2,\pi_1} \\ \vdots & \vdots & & \vdots \\ s_{2^h,1} & s_{2^h,2} & \cdots & s_{2^h,\pi_1} \end{bmatrix}. \tag{1}$$

2.2. Determination of input amount

In this production network, the capacity between the automatic and manual lines in E_2 will be allocated based on the demand. First, the capacity of the automatic line will be fully utilized; if the capacity of the automatic line cannot meet the demand, the remaining demand will be fulfilled by the manual line. It is assumed that I_c units of raw materials can produce O_c units of products, and the relationship between I_c and O_c should satisfy $O_c \ge d$. The product O_c is determined as $O_c = I_c \cdot \prod_{a_t \in E_1} p_t^{(s_{c,t})} \cdot \lambda$, where the term of $I_c \cdot \prod_{a_t \in E_1} p_t^{(s_{c,t})}$ is produced by the E_1, and the output of E_1 is the input of E_2. To evaluate the output of the cth combination, I_c is multiplied by the success probability of the workstations in E_2. For convenience, let λ be the product of the success probabilities of the workstations in E_2. There are two forms of λ: 1. The capacity of the automatic line can meet the demand; 2. The capacity of the automatic line cannot meet the demand, and the remaining demand will be fulfilled by the manual line. This is determined by $O_{2,\max}^{(0)}/d$. When $O_{2,\max}^{(0)}/d \ge 1$, it indicates that the capacity of the automatic line can meet the demand, then λ can be determined as $\lambda = \frac{O_{2,\max}^{(0)}}{d} \cdot \left(\prod_{t=\pi_1+1}^{\pi_2} p_t^{(0)} + \prod_{t=\pi_1+1}^{r-1} p_t^{(0)} \cdot q_r^{(0)} \cdot \prod_{t=r-k}^{\pi_2} p_t^{(1)}\right) + \left(1 - \frac{O_{2,\max}^{(0)}}{d}\right) \cdot \left(\prod_{t=\pi_1+1}^{\pi_2} p_t^{(1)} + \prod_{t=\pi_1+1}^{r-1} p_t^{(1)} \cdot q_r^{(1)} \cdot \prod_{t=r-k}^{\pi_2} p_t^{(1)}\right)$. On the contrary, if $O_{2,\max}^{(0)}/d < 1$, it indicates that the capacity of the automatic line cannot meet the demand, and the remaining demand will be fulfilled by the manual line. We treat $O_{2,\max}^{(0)}/d$ as the proportion of the demand that the automatic line can meet, and ($1 - O_{2,\max}^{(0)}/d$) as the proportion of the demand that the manual line fulfills, as $\lambda = \prod_{t=\pi_1+1}^{\pi_2} p_t^{(0)} + \prod_{t=\pi_1+1}^{r-1} p_t^{(0)} \cdot q_r^{(0)} \cdot \prod_{t=r-k}^{\pi_2} p_t^{(1)}$.

It is necessary that $O_c \ge d$, such as $I_c \ge d \Big/ \left(\prod_{a_t \in E_1} p_t^{(s_{c,t})} \cdot \lambda\right)$, for obtaining sufficient output O_c that satisfies the demand d. To ensure that the I_c derived from the SFHPN can produce output O_c equal to the given demand d, $I_c = d \Big/ \left(\prod_{a_t \in E_1} p_t^{(s_{c,t})} \cdot \lambda\right)$ can be used for calculation.

2.3. Determination of input flows for each production phase

After the raw materials input in the E_1, each workstation has a corresponding input flow, and the input flow of each workstation in every combination is different, determined as $f_{c,i}^{(G)} = I_c \cdot \prod_{t=1}^{i-1} p_t^{(s_{c,t})}$ for i such that $a_i \in E_1$. Before the flow inputs the E_2 from the E_1, it should first be determined whether the demand can be met by the automatic line alone in the E_2. That is, if $O^{(0)}_{2,\max}/d \geq 1$, the input flow of workstations in E_2 can be determined $f^{(G_0)}_{c,i} = f^{(G_{s_{c,\pi_1}})}_{c,\pi_1} \cdot p^{(s_{c,\pi_1})}_{\pi_1} \cdot \prod_{t=\pi_1+1}^{i-1} p^{(0)}_t$ for i such that $a_i \in E_2$ and $f^{(R_0|r,r-k)}_{c,i} = f^{(G_{s_{c,\pi_1}})}_{c,\pi_1} \cdot p^{(s_{c,\pi_1})}_{\pi_1} \cdot \prod_{t=\pi_1+1}^{r-1} p^{(0)}_t \cdot q^{(0)}_r \cdot \prod_{t=r-k}^{i-1} p^{(1)}_t$ for $i = r-k, r-k+1, \ldots, \pi_2$, where $f^{(G_0)}_{c,i}$ represents the input flow of the general production path of the automatic line, and $f^{(R_0|r,r-k)}_{c,i}$ represents the input flow of the reworking path of the automatic line. It is particularly important to note that in these two equations, the terms of $f^{(G_{s_{c,\pi_1}})}_{c,\pi_1} \cdot p^{(s_{c,\pi_1})}_{\pi_1}$ is the input flow of the last workstation in E_1 multiplied by the success rate of that workstation (i.e., the input flow of the first workstation in E_2). On the contrary, when $O^{(0)}_{2,\max}/d < 1$, it indicates that the manual line must also be included in the general production process. Therefore, the input flow of workstations in E_2 can be redetermined by equation (11)-(14), where equations (12) and (14) represent the input flow of workstations for the general production path and rework path of the manual line, respectively. $O^{(0)}_{2,\max}/d$ is treated as the proportion of production using the automatic line in the demand, while $(1 - O^{(0)}_{2,\max}/d)$ is the proportion of production using the manual line.

3. Algorithm to generate the minimal capacity vectors

Given two production phases, in the first phase $E_1 = \{a_1, a_2, \ldots, a_{\pi_1}\}$, the workstations on the production line can choose between automated or manual production. The second phase $E_2 = \{a_{\pi_1+1}, a_{\pi_1+2}, \ldots, a_{\pi_2}\}$ consists of an automated line and a manual line, with rework operations performed on the manual line in the E_2. Defective WIP output from the rth workstation is reworked from the previous k workstation. Given the success rates of each station is set as $p^{(s)}_i$, the minimal capacity vectors for d can be derived by the following steps.

Step 1. Determine all possible production combinations for E_1.

$$\mathbf{C} = \begin{bmatrix} s_{1,1} & s_{1,2} & \cdots & s_{1,\pi_1} \\ s_{2,1} & s_{2,2} & \cdots & s_{2,\pi_1} \\ \vdots & \vdots & & \vdots \\ s_{2^h,1} & s_{2^h,2} & \cdots & s_{2^h,\pi_1} \end{bmatrix}. \quad (2)$$

Step 2. Find the maximum output for E_2.

2.1) Find the maximum output for automatic line.

$$\Phi^{(0)}_i = M^{(0)}_i p^{(0)}_i \left(\prod_{t=i+1}^{\pi_2} p^{(0)}_t\right) \text{ for } i \text{ such that } a_i \in E_2, \quad (3)$$

$$O^{(0)}_{2,\max} = \min\{\Phi^{(0)}_i \mid i = \pi_1+1, \pi_1+2, \ldots, \pi_2\}. \quad (4)$$

2.2) Find the maximum output for manual line.

$$\Phi^{(1)}_i = M^{(1)}_i p^{(1)}_i \left\{\left(\prod_{t=i+1}^{\pi_2} p^{(1)}_t\right) + \mu^{(1)}_i \left(\prod_{t=i+1}^{r-1} p^{(1)}_t\right) \cdot p^{(1)}_r \cdot \left(\prod_{t=r-k}^{\pi_2} p^{(1)}_t\right)\right\} \text{ for } i \text{ such that } a_i \in E_2, \quad (5)$$

$$O^{(1)}_{2,\max} = \min\{\Phi^{(1)}_i \mid i = \pi_1+1, \pi_1+2, \ldots, \pi_2\}. \quad (6)$$

Step 3. For each production combination, do the following steps.

3.1) The operation mode matrix $C = [s_{c,1}, s_{c,2}, \ldots, s_{c,\pi_1}]$ for E_1 under the cth combination.

3.2) Determine if E_2 requires production solely by the automated line and calculate the λ value.

If $d \leq (O^{(0)}_{2,\max} + O^{(1)}_{2,\max})$,

If $\left(O^{(0)}_{2,\max}/d\right) < 1$,

$$\lambda = \frac{O^{(0)}_{2,\max}}{d} \cdot \left(\prod_{t=\pi_1+1}^{\pi_2} p^{(0)}_t + \prod_{t=\pi_1+1}^{r-1} p^{(0)}_t \cdot q^{(0)}_r \cdot \prod_{t=r-k}^{\pi_2} p^{(1)}_t\right) + \left(1 - \frac{O^{(0)}_{2,\max}}{d}\right) \cdot \left(\prod_{t=\pi_1+1}^{\pi_2} p^{(1)}_t + \prod_{t=\pi_1+1}^{r-1} p^{(1)}_t \cdot q^{(1)}_r \cdot \prod_{t=r-k}^{\pi_2} p^{(1)}_t\right), \quad (7)$$

Else

$$\lambda = \prod_{t=\pi_1+1}^{\pi_2} p^{(0)}_t + \prod_{t=\pi_1+1}^{r-1} p^{(0)}_t \cdot q^{(0)}_r \cdot \prod_{t=r-k}^{\pi_2} p^{(1)}_t. \quad (8)$$

Else $R_{sys} = 0$.

3.3) Determine the amount of combination input materials.

$$I_c = d \Big/ \left(\prod_{a_t \in E_1} p^{(s_{c,t})}_t \cdot \lambda\right). \quad (9)$$

3.4) Determine the input flows for each combination.

$$f^{(G)}_{c,i} = I_c \cdot \prod_{t=1}^{i-1} p^{(s_{c,t})}_t \text{ for } i \text{ such that } a_i \in E_1. \quad (10)$$

If $O^{(0)}_{2,\max}/d < 1$,

$$f^{(G_0)}_{c,i} = f^{(G_{s_{c,\pi_1}})}_{c,\pi_1} \cdot p^{(s_{c,\pi_1})}_{\pi_1} \cdot \frac{O^{(0)}_{2,\max}}{d} \cdot \prod_{t=\pi_1+1}^{i-1} p^{(0)}_t \quad (11)$$

for i such that $a_i \in E_2$,

$$f^{(G_1)}_{c,i} = f^{(G_{s_{c,\pi_1}})}_{c,\pi_1} \cdot p^{(s_{c,\pi_1})}_{\pi_1} \cdot \left(1 - \frac{O^{(0)}_{2,\max}}{d}\right) \cdot \prod_{t=\pi_1+1}^{i-1} p^{(1)}_t \quad (12)$$

for i such that $a_i \in E_2$,

$$f^{(R_0|r,r-k)}_{c,i} = f^{(G_{s_{c,\pi_1}})}_{c,\pi_1} \cdot p^{(s_{c,\pi_1})}_{\pi_1} \cdot \frac{O^{(0)}_{2,\max}}{d} \cdot \prod_{t=\pi_1+1}^{r-1} p^{(0)}_t \cdot q^{(0)}_r \cdot \prod_{t=r-k}^{i-1} p^{(1)}_t \text{ for } i = r-k, r-k+1, \ldots, \pi_2, \quad (13)$$

$$f^{(R_1|r,r-k)}_{c,i} = f^{(G_{s_{c,\pi_1}})}_{c,\pi_1} \cdot p^{(s_{c,\pi_1})}_{\pi_1} \cdot \left(1 - \frac{O^{(0)}_{2,\max}}{d}\right) \cdot \prod_{t=\pi_1+1}^{r-1} p^{(1)}_t \cdot q^{(1)}_r \cdot \prod_{t=r-k}^{i-1} p^{(1)}_t \text{ for } i = r-k, r-k+1, \ldots, \pi_2. \quad (14)$$

Else

$$f^{(G_0)}_{c,i} = f^{(G_{s_{c,\pi_1}})}_{c,\pi_1} \cdot p^{(s_{c,\pi_1})}_{\pi_1} \cdot \prod_{t=\pi_1+1}^{i-1} p^{(0)}_t, \quad (15)$$

for i such that $a_i \in E_2$,

$$f^{(R_0|r,r-k)}_{c,i} = f^{(G_{s_{c,\pi_1}})}_{c,\pi_1} \cdot p^{(s_{c,\pi_1})}_{\pi_1} \cdot \prod_{t=\pi_1+1}^{r-1} p^{(0)}_t \cdot q^{(0)}_r \cdot \prod_{t=r-k}^{i-1} p^{(1)}_t \quad (16)$$

for $i = r-k, r-k+1, \ldots, \pi_2$.

3.5) Then check the amount of input flows and calculate the probability of each combination occurring.

For $a_i \in E_1$

If $f^{(G)}_{c,i} \leq M^{(s_{c,i})}_i$,

If $s_{c,i} = 0$,

$u_c = u_c \cdot u_i$.

Else

$u_c = u_c \cdot (1 - u_i)$.

Else $R_c = 0$.
Next i

For $a_i \in E_2$
If $f_{c,i}^{(G_0)} \le M_i^{(0)}$ and $f_{c,i}^{(G_1)} + f_{c,i}^{(R_1|r,r-k)} + f_{c,i}^{(R_0|r,r-k)} \le M_i^{(1)}$,
continue
Else $R_c = 0$.
Next i

3.6) Transform input flows from general processing path and reworking path into workstation' loading vector L_c.

$$l_{c,i}^{(s_{c,i})} = f_{c,i}^{(G_{s_{c,i}})} \text{ for } i \text{ such that } a_i \in E_1, \quad (17)$$

$$l_{c,i}^{(0)} = f_{c,i}^{(G_0)} \text{ for } i \text{ such that } a_i \in E_2, \quad (18)$$

$$l_{c,i}^{(1)} = f_{c,i}^{(G_1)} + f_{c,i}^{(R_1|r,r-k)} + f_{c,i}^{(R_0|r,r-k)} \text{ for } i \text{ such that } a_i \in E_2. \quad (19)$$

3.7) For each workstation, find the minimal capacity vector such that $x_{ij}^{(s_{c,i})} \ge l_{c,i}^{(s_{c,i})} > x_{i(j-1)}^{(s_{c,i})}$ and $x_{ij}^{(s)} \ge l_{c,i}^{(s)} > x_{i(j-1)}^{(s)}$. Then $Y_c = (y_{c,1}^{(s_{c,1})}, \ldots, y_{c,\pi_1}^{(s_{c,\pi_1})}, y_{c,\pi_1+1}^{(0)}, \ldots, y_{c,\pi_2}^{(0)}, y_{c,\pi_1+1}^{(1)}, \ldots, y_{c,\pi_2}^{(1)})$ is the lower boundary vector for d where $y_{c,i}^{(s_{c,i})} = x_{ij}^{(s_{c,i})}$ and $y_{c,i}^{(s)} = x_{ij}^{(s)}$ for all c, i, and s.

3.8) Those Y_c obtained in 3.7 are the minimal capacity vectors for d. Then apply disjoint subset method to compute combination reliability $R_c = \Pr\{X_c \mid X_c \ge Y_c\}$.

3.9) Next combination

Step 4. Determine the amount of system input materials and system reliability.

$$I_{sys} = \sum_{c=1}^{2^h} (u_c \cdot I_c), \quad (20)$$

$$R_{sys} = \sum_{c=1}^{2^h} (u_c \cdot R_c). \quad (21)$$

4. Example

An SMT production process to demonstrate a production network with two phases E_1 and E_2. The raw material is bare printed circuit board (PCB), and the production process and sequence may vary depending on the product type. The SMT production network consists of five workstations (n = 5), as shown in Figure 1. The first phase only has one board loading workstation ($E_1 = \{a_1\}$), which loads the bare PCB one by one into various processes. This workstation can be operated by either an automatic loader or a manual worker. The second phase consists of four workstations $E_2 = \{a_2, a_3, a_4, a_5\}$, the PCB first passes through the printing workstation (a_2), where solder paste quality is stabilized, followed by component placement using the pick-and-place tool (a_3). Then, the PCB is sent into the reflow oven (a_4) to melt the solder paste, using high temperatures to solder the components onto the PCB. Finally, the completed PCB is sequentially sent one by one to the unload workstation (a_5). The proportion of automatic loader in a_1 is 0.8 ($u_1 = 0.8$). In the SMT production network, defective components installed on the PCB will be detected as anomalies before entering the board unload workstation at a_4 ($r = 4$), then reworking from the printing station a_2 ($k = 2$). This SMT production network must satisfy the demand required as d = 500 units per unit time. The success rates $p_i^{(s)}$ and capacity distributions for each workstation are shown in Table 1.

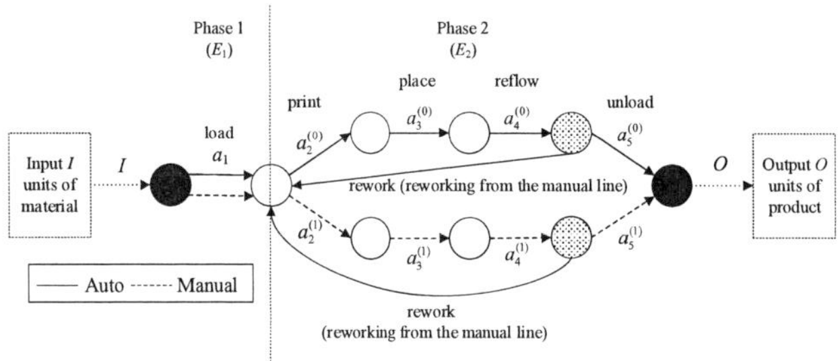

Figure 1. The partial SMT production process.

Table 1. The workstation data of example.

E_v	$a_i^{(0)}$	$p_i^{(0)}$	$x_{ij}^{(0)}$	prob.	$a_i^{(1)}$	$p_i^{(1)}$	$x_{ij}^{(1)}$	prob.
E_1	$a_1^{(0)}$	0.99	0	0.001	$a_1^{(1)}$	0.95	0	0.001
			800	0.002			240	0.003
			1600	0.002			480	0.003
			2400	0.005			720	0.008
			3200	0.990			960	0.007
							1200	0.978
E_2	$a_2^{(0)}$	0.97	0	0.002	$a_2^{(1)}$	0.93	0	0.001
			750	0.002			250	0.002
			1500	0.004			500	0.005
			2250	0.004			750	0.007
			3000	0.988			1000	0.985
	$a_3^{(0)}$	0.97	0	0.001	$a_3^{(1)}$	0.94	0	0.004
			560	0.003			190	0.004
			1120	0.003			380	0.005
			1680	0.005			570	0.005
			2240	0.007			760	0.011
			2800	0.981			950	0.971
	$a_4^{(0)}$	0.98	0	0.004	$a_4^{(1)}$	0.91	0	0.002
			750	0.005			250	0.002
			1500	0.010			500	0.015
			2250	0.010			750	0.020
			3000	0.971			1000	0.961
	$a_5^{(0)}$	0.99	0	0.002	$a_5^{(1)}$	0.96	0	0.002
			950	0.002			300	0.002
			1900	0.002			600	0.003
			2850	0.994			900	0.005
							1200	0.988

Step 1. Determine all possible production combinations for E_1.

$$\mathbf{C} = \begin{bmatrix} 0 \\ 1 \end{bmatrix}.$$

Step 2. Find the maximum output for E_2.

$$O_{2,\max}^{(0)} = \{2738.58, 2635.06, 2910.60, 2821.50\} - 2635.06$$

$$O_{2,\max}^{(1)} = \{763.70, 780.12, 873.60, 1152.00\} = 763.70$$

Step 3. After the calculations in Step 1, two combinations are obtained. Using those combinations can find out the results in Step 3.1-3.4, as shown in the Table 2.

3.5) Then check the amount of input flows and calculate the probability of each combination occurring. Then transform input flows from general processing path and reworking path into workstations' loading vector L_c, as shown in the Table 3.

Table 2. Result of Step 3.1-3.4.

c	mode	I_c	flow	$i=1$	$i=2$	$i=3$	$i=4$	$i=5$
1	0	544.69	$f_{1,i}^{(G)}$	544.69	0.00	0.00	0.00	0.00
			$f_{1,i}^{(G_0)}$	0.00	539.24	523.06	507.37	497.22
			$f_{1,i}^{(R_0\|4,2)}$	0.00	10.15	9.44	8.87	8.07
2	1	567.62	$f_{2,i}^{(G)}$	567.62	0.00	0.00	0.00	0.00
			$f_{2,i}^{(G_0)}$	0.00	539.24	523.06	507.37	497.22
			$f_{2,i}^{(R_0\|4,1)}$	0.00	10.14	9.43	8.87	8.07

Since this example requires only the automatic line for production in E_2, $f_{c,i}^{(G_1)}$ and $f_{c,i}^{(R_1|4,2)}$ omitted here.

Table 3. Result of Step 3.5-3.6.

c	u_c	loading	$i=1$	$i=2$	$i=3$	$i=4$	$i=5$
1	0.8	$l_{1,i}^{(0)}$	544.69	539.24	523.06	507.37	497.22
		$l_{1,i}^{(1)}$	0.00	10.15	9.44	8.87	8.07
2	0.2	$l_{2,i}^{(0)}$	567.62	539.24	523.06	507.37	497.22
		$l_{2,i}^{(1)}$	0.00	10.15	9.44	8.87	8.07

3.7) For each combination, find the minimal capacity vectors and combination reliability (Step 3.8), as shown in
3.8) Table **4**.

Table 4. Result of Step 3.7-3.8.

c	Y_c	R_c
1	(800, 750, 560, 750, 950, 250, 190, 250, 300)	0.9812
2	(720, 750, 560, 750, 950, 250, 190, 250, 300)	0.9753

Step 4. Determine the amount of system input materials and system reliability.

$$I_{sys} = \sum_{c=1}^{2} (I_c \cdot u_c)$$
$$= (544.69 \cdot 0.8) + (567.62 \cdot 0.2) = 549.2728.$$

$$R_{sys} = \sum_{c=1}^{2} (R_c \cdot u_c)$$
$$= (0.9812 \cdot 0.8) + (0.9753 \cdot 0.2) = 0.9800.$$

The proposed algorithm generates the corresponding minimal capacity vectors for different production combinations, enabling the evaluation of the combined reliability associated with each production combination. In the sample production system with $d = 500$, two production combinations were obtained, and their corresponding combined reliabilities are listed in the

Table **4**. Among them, the combination with $c = 1$, represented by the state [0], has a higher reliability of 0.9812 and is considered a better production strategy. By calculating the system reliability based on the occurrence probabilities and combined reliabilities of these combinations, the overall system reliability is 0.9800, indicating a high likelihood that the system can meet the demand.

5. Conclusion

This paper investigates a stochastic-flow hybrid production network (SFHPN) consisting of two production phases. In the first phase, each workstation can operate in either automatic or manual mode. The second phase includes one fully automatic workstation and one fully manual workstation, with all rework operations executed exclusively on the manual line in the second phase. To better reflect real production scenarios, the system first evaluates whether the demand can be met solely by the automatic line before proceeding to the second phase. Accordingly, this study proposes an SFHPN model that handles two production phases and develops an algorithm to calculate the system's minimal capacity vector. Based on such a vector, the system reliability is computed. A surface-mount technology (SMT) case is used to demonstrate the effectiveness of the proposed network model and algorithm. With this approach, managers can assess whether the current production system can meet customer demand and select the most appropriate production combination based on the reliability of each combination. Future research can extend the model to production networks with more than two phases, where each phase may follow a different sequence of production scenarios.

6. References

[1] Botti, L., C. Mora, and A. Regattieri, "Integrating ergonomics and lean manufacturing principles in a hybrid assembly line"; *Computers & Industrial Engineering*, 111, 481-491, 2017.

[2] Deniša, M., et al., "Technology Modules Providing Solutions for Agile Manufacturing"; *Machines*, 11(9), 877, 2023.

[3] ElMaraghy, H.A., "Changeable and reconfigurable manufacturing systems". Springer Science & Business Media, 2008.

[4] Forghani-elahabad, M. and N. Mahdavi-Amiri, "An improved algorithm for finding all upper boundary points in a stochastic-flow network"; *Applied Mathematical Modelling*, 40(4), 3221-3229, 2016.

[5] Hu, S.J., et al., "Assembly system design and operations for product variety"; *CIRP annals*, 60(2), 715-733, 2011.

[6] Krüger, J., T.K. Lien, and A. Verl, "Cooperation of human and machines in assembly lines"; *CIRP annals*, 58(2), 628-646, 2009.

[7] Lin, Y.K. and P.C. Chang, "System reliability of a manufacturing network with reworking action and different failure rates"; *International Journal of Production Research*, 50(23), 6930-6944, 2012.

[8] Miqueo, A., M. Torralba, and J.A. Yagüe-Fabra, "Lean Manual Assembly 4.0: A Systematic Review"; *Applied Sciences*, 10(23) 2020.

[9] Reinhart, G. and J. Werner, "Flexible automation for the assembly in motion"; *CIRP annals*, 56(1), 25-28, 2007.

[10] Song, W.T. and P. Lin, "System reliability of stochastic networks with multiple reworks"; *Reliability Engineering & System Safety*, 169, 258-268, 2018.

[11] Ting, K.C., P. Ling, and G. Giacomelli, "Research on flexible automation and robotics for plant production at Rutgers University"; *Advances in Space Research*, 18(1-2), 175-180, 1996.

[12] Viswanadham, N. and Y. Narahari, "Performance modeling of automated systems". PHI Learning Pvt. Ltd., 2015.

Modeling Quickest Path Reliability in Networks with Random Transmission Time

Ding-Hsiang Huang[1], Cheng-Fu Huang[2]

[1]Department of Industrial Engineering and Enterprise Information, Tunghai University, Taichung 407, Taiwan, dhhuang@thu.edu.tw
[2]Department of Business Administration, Feng Chia University, Taichung 407, Taiwan, cfuhuang@fcu.edu.tw

Keywords: multi-state flow networks (MSFNs), quickest path (QP), quickest path reliability, random transmission time, Monte Carlo-based simulation.

Abstract - Modern computer systems, such as IoT, cloud platforms, and wireless sensor networks, are often modeled as multi-state flow networks (MSFNs) to capture uncertainties in arc capacities caused by failures and bandwidth variability. The quickest path (QP) problem seeks to identify a path that transmits a required demand within the shortest time under time and capacity constraints. However, computing the quickest path reliability, the probability that the required flow is successfully delivered within a time limit, is NP-hard due to the exponential number of minimal paths (MPs) in large-scale networks. To address this challenge, this study develops a Monte Carlo-based simulation algorithm that simultaneously generates random arc capacities and stochastic transmission time to approximate quickest path reliability. Unlike prior methods assuming fixed transmission time, the proposed framework better reflects real-world conditions. Extensive experiments on a practical network, NSFNET, demonstrate the algorithm's effectiveness and efficiency. Across six test scenarios with varying arc capacities, the estimated reliabilities closely match exact values, with average deviation less than 0.1% and average CPU time of only 0.0013 seconds. These results confirm the proposed method's accuracy and scalability for evaluating quickest path reliability in complex, time-sensitive systems.

1. Introduction

Due to their inherently distributed architecture and complex communication requirements, modern computer systems—such as the Internet of Things (IoT), cloud computing platforms, and wireless sensor networks—are commonly represented using network topologies consisting of nodes (e.g., processors, storage units, or sensors) and transmission arcs (e.g., communication links). This modeling approach facilitates efficient performance evaluation, reliability analysis, and system simulation. However, in real-world applications, the capacity of each arc is subject to uncertainty arising from various sources such as random failures, scheduled maintenance, degradation, and bandwidth fluctuations. To effectively characterize these uncertainties, such systems are modeled as multi-state flow networks (MSFNs) [1, 2]. In MSFNs, each arc can operate at multiple discrete capacity levels rather than a simple binary (working/failed) state, and these capacity levels are treated as stochastic variables. This multi-state modeling framework provides a more realistic and flexible means to capture the partial functionality of network components and enables comprehensive reliability analysis under varying flow demands and system conditions.

Building upon this modeling foundation, the quickest path (QP) problem has emerged as a fundamental topic in the study of flow-based systems, particularly in MSFNs. In MSFNs, each arc is characterized not only by a stochastic capacity, which reflects the uncertain availability of resources, but also by a deterministic lead time, representing the time required to transmit flow across the arc. The QP problem aims to determine the path or set of paths that enable the minimum transmission time while satisfying a predefined flow across such an MSFN. The importance of the QP problem is especially pronounced in computer systems, where nodes act as transmitters or receivers, and arcs correspond to communication channels whose bandwidths fluctuate over time due to operational uncertainties [3, 4]. As a result, identifying the quickest reliable path becomes essential for ensuring timely data delivery and system responsiveness.

Given its wide range of applications, from data routing in sensor networks to traffic engineering in cloud infrastructures, the QP problem has garnered significant academic interest. Over the past decades, numerous algorithms have been developed to solve the QP problem and its various extensions. These algorithms typically aim to determine either the single most time-efficient path or to rank feasible paths in terms of their ability to meet both time and capacity constraints under uncertainty [5-8]. Moreover, research has expanded to include the all-pairs QP problem, which involves computing the shortest transmission times between all node pairs in the network. Such advancements further enhance the analytical depth and practical relevance of QP-related methods in MSFNs [9, 10].

Within the MSFN framework, while the transmission time along a given path is treated as deterministic, the ability of the network to fulfill a transmission request within a specified time constraint remains uncertain due to the stochastic nature of arc capacities. This uncertainty gives rise to the concept of quickest path reliability [11-13], which is defined as the probability that a given amount of flow can be successfully transmitted from a designated source to a terminal node within a predefined time limit. To address this issue, Lin [12] extended the classical QP problem to MSFNs by focusing on the computation of this time-constrained transmission probability, which serves as a quantitative measure of quickest path reliability. This metric plays a critical role in time-sensitive applications such as real-time data delivery and emergency communication systems.

Prior research has investigated various approaches to evaluate quickest path reliability in MSFNs [11-13]. A prominent contribution by Lin [12] introduced a two-phase algorithm grounded in the notion of minimal paths (MPs). In the first phase, all MPs that can potentially satisfy the required flow are enumerated. In the second phase, each MP is tested against the given time constraint. This verification step is computationally efficient, as the condition for time feasibility can be checked in polynomial time. However, a significant computational challenge arises due to the exponential growth in the number of MPs as the network size increases. The sheer volume of MPs leads to considerable overhead in identifying and eliminating infeasible paths, thereby impacting the scalability and efficiency of the method. To enhance transmission reliability under time constraints, several studies have proposed methods that consider the simultaneous use of multiple non-intersecting MPs [14-16]. These approaches evaluate the joint probability that multiple independent MPs, each satisfying the time constraint, can concurrently support the required flow. In this context, researchers aim to identify the optimal combination of non-overlapping MPs that maximizes overall quickest path reliability.

However, this direction introduces considerable computational complexity, as determining the most reliable pair or set of MPs often necessitates exhaustive enumeration and combinatorial analysis, which significantly increases CPU run time and limits practical applicability in large-scale networks. In parallel, exact methods have been developed to assist decision-makers in assessing quickest path reliability by focusing on a single-path transmission scenario [13-20]. These methods evaluate the probability that a multi-state flow network (MSFN) can transmit a specified volume of flow from a source to a sink node via a single feasible path within a given time constraint. In addition to flow and time feasibility, these studies often incorporate practical limitations, such as cost or resource budgets, into their evaluation models. However, in large-scale networks, the number of possible MPs grows rapidly. The process of identifying feasible QPs becomes increasingly time-consuming, as each candidate path must be evaluated against multiple constraints. This repeated checking imposes a substantial computational burden, further highlighting the scalability challenges of exact approaches when applied to complex real-world networks.

A significant challenge in evaluating the quickest path reliability lies in its NP-hard nature. As the network scale and structural complexity increase, obtaining exact reliability measures through exhaustive enumeration becomes computationally infeasible within a reasonable time frame. This computational bottleneck has driven the development of alternative and more scalable solution methods. Among these, Monte Carlo-based algorithms have emerged as an effective class of approximation techniques that can generate reliable estimates of network reliability without the need to enumerate all possible minimal paths or system states. Monte Carlo simulation has been extensively applied in traditional network reliability evaluations and has demonstrated strong adaptability to flow-based and multi-state network environments [21-24]. In the context of QP problems, Monte Carlo-based approaches assess the probability that a given amount of flow can be transmitted from a source to a terminal within a specified time constraint by randomly generating capacity scenarios and simulating the network's behavior under each. This strategy significantly reduces computational complexity and enhances scalability, making it particularly suitable for large and complex MSFNs where exact methods become impractical.

To improve the efficiency and applicability of evaluating network reliability, numerous studies have adopted simulation-based approaches, particularly those based on Monte Carlo simulation, to estimate network reliability in complex systems [23, 25, 26]. These methods have proven effective in approximating reliability metrics without the need for exhaustive enumeration. However, most existing approaches were developed for general flow or connectivity reliability problems and do not explicitly incorporate time constraints, which are central to the QP problem.

Furthermore, they typically assume fixed transmission times for arcs, limiting their ability to reflect the stochastic and dynamic characteristics of real-world systems. To address these limitations, this study proposes a Monte Carlo-based algorithm specifically designed for quickest path reliability analysis in multi-state flow networks (MSFNs). In contrast to exact methods, which become computationally infeasible for large-scale systems, the proposed simulation-based method offers a scalable and efficient approximation framework capable of handling stochastic variability in both capacity and time. This research further enhances realism by jointly simulating arc capacities and transmission times as random variables. In each simulation iteration, a random capacity vector is generated to reflect the current state of arc capacities, and a corresponding random time vector is produced to simulate variability in transmission delays. These time values can be drawn from various distributions, such as exponential, uniform, or empirical, depending on network-specific characteristics.

This proposed simulation framework captures the interdependent effects of stochastic capacity and non-deterministic transmission delays, providing a more accurate and practical assessment of quickest path reliability. It is especially applicable to environments such as wireless sensor networks, cloud infrastructures, and time-critical communication systems, where uncertainties in both resource availability and delay are common. By incorporating these uncertainties, the proposed method delivers more realistic, relevant, and decision-supportive insights for managing large-scale, time-sensitive networked systems. The remainder of this paper is organized as follows. Section 2 introduces the multi-state flow network (MSFN) model, along with the formulation of flow under time constraints and the definition of quickest path reliability. Section 3 presents the proposed Monte Carlo-based algorithm for estimating quickest path reliability. In Section 4, a set of experiments based on a large-scale practical network is conducted to demonstrate the effectiveness and efficiency of the proposed method. Finally, Section 5 concludes the paper with a summary of findings.

2. Model Construction

Let $G \equiv (A, N, M, P, L)$ be an MSFN (multi-state flow network) with source s and terminal t. In a G, $A = \{a_1, a_2, \ldots, a_n\}$ represents the set of n arcs, N represents the set of perfectly reliable nodes, and $M = \{m_1, m_2, \ldots, m_n\}$ represents the set of components for each a_i. Because of failure, maintenance, operation requirement, and unexpected reasons, the number of the workable components y_i in a_i would vary in the different periods such that y_i are presented as random variables that can take values from $\{0, 1, 2, \ldots, m_i\}$ to reflect the real-world scenarios. The number of the working components y_i in every arc can follow any arbitrary statistical distribution that derives from historical data such that p_{ik} in the set P means the probability of k available components in the a_i for $i = 1, 2, \ldots, n$ and $k = 1, 2, \ldots, m_i$.

Furthermore, $\mathbf{L} = \{l_1, l_2, \ldots, l_n\}$ denotes the lead time set for each arc a_i in the G. Every lead time is presented as a random variable following any (continuous and discrete) distributions (such as normal distributions and Poisson distributions). Specifically, we can define the probability function as

where .

with representing the parameter space of the distribution. The distribution followed can be approximated using specific statistical hypothesis testing such as the Kolmogorov-Smirnov test and Anderson-Darling Test by inputting historical lead time data. The MSFN model is constructed based on the following assumptions:

1. The flow in the MSFN G adheres to the principle of flow conservation [27].
2. All nodes in the MSFN G are characterized by complete reliability. For the unreliable node case, the nodes are also treated as components in the quickest paths (QP).

2.1. Flow with time constraints

Suppose that $QP_1, QP_2, \ldots, QP_k$ are QPs in the MSFN, where each QP_j is a sequence of arcs in an MSFN but contains no cycle. The data can be transmitted from source s to terminal t through any QP_j. In order to learn and analyze the data transmission on QP_j, a flow vector $F = (f_1, f_2, \ldots, f_k)$ to represent the flow of all QP_j is defined. In addition to the flow vectors, a capacity vector is denoted as $X = (x_1, x_2, \ldots, x_n)$ where x_i corresponds to the capacity state of a_i to represent the complete network state such that the capability of the network can be detected and evaluated.

The objective of the data transmission is to transmit a given amount of demand d from source s to terminal t in an MSFN G within a time constraint T. When selecting P_j to transmit the given amount of d under the current capacity vector (network status) X, the transmission time can be denoted by . From the literature [12], it is known that is calculated:

for $j = 1, 2, \ldots m$.

for $j = 1, 2, \ldots m$.

The ceiling function generates the smallest integer such that and is presented as the maximal flow of P_j. The jth minimal path contradicts the time constraint if . Note that every lead time is considered stochastic in this study instead of determined values (assumed in the references).

2.2. Quickest path reliability

The MSFN performance can be judged based on the quickest path reliability, which is defined as the probability that the given amount of demand d can be transmitted from s to t within a time constraint T. Quickest path reliability can be mathematically represented as follows.

.

To evaluate the quickest path reliability , the first intuitive but time-consuming approach is to enumerate all possible capacity vectors X and calculate the transmission time for $j = 1, 2, \ldots, m$. While collecting all the feasible X (i.e., there exists $\leq$ T for any one of QP_j under X), quickest path reliability can be calculated by summing the probability of the feasible X.

3. Proposed Simulation Approach

In order not to enumerate all capacity vectors satisfying under the stochastic lead time, a simulation approach is developed in the study. The Monte-Carlo simulation approach is developed, which involves randomly generating one of the capacity vectors X and a stochastic lead time set to present the current network states and lead time for all the arcs. Quickest path reliability can be approximated by assessing whether the generated x_i and l_i for all i can satisfy the given amount of d within the time constraint T via (1) QP_j for $j = 1, 2, \ldots, m$. Therefore, quickest path reliability can be obtained immediately for monitoring and managing related networks such as intelligent computer systems.

3.1 Capacity vector and lead time simulation

First, we have to consider multiple simulations for every trial $t = 1, 2, \ldots, \psi$. A roulette wheel selection method is used under p_{ik} (the probability of k available components in the a_i) The method assigns a probability proportional to p_{ik} to each possible value for $i = 1, 2, \ldots, n$ and $k = 1, 2, \ldots, m_i$ by the cumulative probabilities c_{ik}:

$c_{ik} =$ for $i = 1, 2, \ldots, n$ and $k = 1, 2, \ldots, m_i$.

such that current available capacity tuple is termed $X_t = (x_{1t}, x_{2t}, \ldots, x_{nt})$. Random numbers $s_{it} \sim$ U(0, 1) for $i = 1, 2, \ldots, n$ are generated to find the current maximal capacity of a_{it}:

$x_{it} = k$ if $c_{i(k-1)} \leq s_{it} < c_{ik}$ for $i = 1, 2, \ldots, n$, $k = 1, 2, \ldots, m_i$, and $t = 1, 2, \ldots, \psi$.

For the trail t, a lead time set $\mathbf{L}_t = \{l_{1t}, l_{2t}, \ldots, l_{nt}\}$ can be simulated according to the following sampling formula:

$l_{it} \sim$ for $t = 1, 2, \ldots \psi$.

3.2 Quickest path reliability approximation

Based on one of the simulated capacity vectors termed $X_t = (x_{1t}, x_{2t}, \ldots, x_n)$, the maximal flow for P_j is restricted by the minimal capacity state for $a_i \in P_j$ such that

for $j = 1, 2, \ldots, m$ and $t = 1, 2, \ldots, \psi$.

With all the maximal flows: , , …, and the simulated lead time set $\mathbf{L}_t = \{l_{1t}, l_{2t}, \ldots, l_{nt}\}$, the transmission time for the demand d via QP_j using Equation (8):

for $j = 1, 2, \ldots m$ and $t = 1, 2, \ldots, \psi$.

(2)

According to the definition of the quickest path reliability, success or failure can be confirmed if the demand d can be successfully transmitted within the time constraint T, resulting in a fact that $\leq T$ for any one of QP_j. Hence, we can determine a binary state as

(3)

Through multiple iterations, the number of successful trials such that quickest path reliability is then estimated by dividing the number of successful trials by the total number of iterations conducted during the simulation. That is, the quickest path reliability under the demand d and time constraint T is able to be approximated via

. (4)

3.3 Simulation algorithm

Suppose an MSFN $G \equiv (\mathbf{A}, \mathbf{N}, \mathbf{M}, \mathbf{P}, \mathbf{L})$ with the QPs: $QP_1, QP_2, \ldots, QP_k$. Suppose that there are d demand units from the source to the terminal of the MSFN is transmitted within T

time units. To estimate quickest path reliability, the number of trails ψ is needed for the following steps.

For $t = 1, 2, \ldots, \psi$

Step 1. Generate a simulated capacity vector $X_t = (x_{1t}, x_{2t}, \ldots, x_{nt})$ for the trail t.

Step 1.1. Calculate cumulative probabilities c_{ik} for every state of the arcs:

$c_{ik} =$ for $i = 1, 2, \ldots, n$ and $k = 1, 2, \ldots, m_i$.

Step 1.2. Generate random numbers $s_{it} \sim U(0, 1)$ for $i = 1, 2, \ldots, n$ to find the current simulated capacity x_{it}:

$x_{it} = k$ if $c_{i(k-1)} \leq s_{it} < c_{ik}$ for $i = 1, 2, \ldots, n$, $k = 1, 2, \ldots, m_i$.

Step 2. Generate a simulated lead time set $\mathbf{L}_t = \{l_{1t}, l_{2t}, \ldots, l_{nt}\}$ for the trail t as follows.

$l_{it} \sim$.

Step 3. Calculate the maximal flow for P_j to restrict the flow of P_j such that

for $j = 1, 2, \ldots, m$.

Step 4. Calculate the transmission time for the demand d via P_j

for $j = 1, 2, \ldots m$.

Step 5. Determine the status of the trial t as Z_t as follows.

Step 6. After finishing all the trails, approximate quickest path reliability under the demand d and time constraint T via

.

4 Experiments for NSFNET

In this section, experiments for NSFNET (National Science Foundation Network) is provided to substantiate the effectiveness and efficiency of the proposed Monte Carlo-based algorithm. Finally, in the following examples, the proposed algorithm is implemented in Python 3.11 on a personal computer with an Intel Core™ i7-11600H processor clocked at 3.2 GHz and 32 GB of RAM. The NSFNET consists of 35 arcs with 30 MP, as shown in Fig. 1. All MP can be efficiently gained from the references [28, 29]. To assess the ability of the proposed Monte Carlo-based algorithm to accommodate different maximal capacities and demands, a series of experiments is conducted on the NSFNET. These experiments include six different scenarios, each involving the assignment of maximal capacity to each arc at 5, 6, 7, 8, 9 and 10 transmission units, The objective was to estimate the quickest path reliability under specific demand levels and time constraints. To evaluate the performance of the proposed Monte Carlo-based algorithm, ten iterations for each experiment are run, corresponding to different maximum capacity values (m_i = 5, 6, 7, 8, 9, 10). In each iteration, lead times (l_i) and component reliabilities (r_i) are randomly generated for all arcs, with the demand level (d) set to $9m_i$ and the time constraint (T) set to $5m_i$. These random values were generated according to uniform distributions, with r_i drawn from U(0.90, 0.95) and l_i from U(3, 5). Ten thousand trials are run for each iteration using the proposed Monte Carlo-based algorithm.

The results of experiments are summarized in Table1, where $\gamma_{d,T}$ and $R_{d,T}$ represent the estimated and exact quickest path reliability, respectively. Γ represents the ratio of the difference between the estimated and the exact values to the exact value itself. The proposed Monte Carlo-based algorithm's average CPU execution time over six experimental runs is recorded as 0.0013 seconds. According to findings, these experiments have demonstrated the achievement of a reasonably slight deviation, approximately 0.1%, between estimated and exact quickest path reliability.

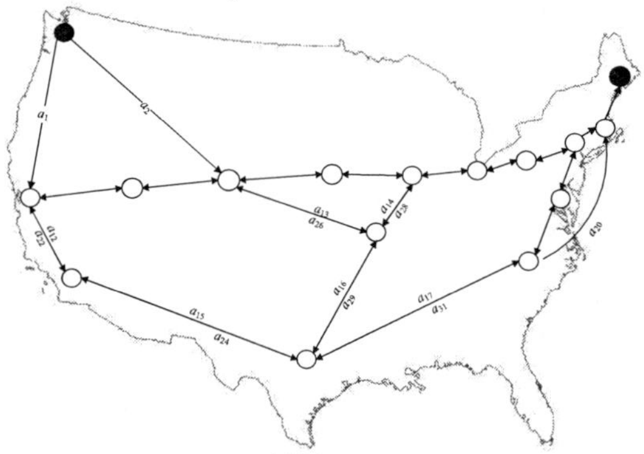

Fig. 1. A practical MSFN for NSFNET.

Table 1. Experiment results for NSFNET experiments.

m_i	5	6	7	8	9	10	Average
$\gamma_{d,T}$	0.4006	0.9936	1.0000	1.000	0.9984	1.000	
$R_{d,T}$	0.3982	0.9927	0.9997	0.9995	0.9981	0.9998	
Γ	0.0059	0.0008	0.0003	0.00045	0.0003	0.0002	0.0013

5 Conclusions

This study addresses the quickest path reliability in multi-state flow networks (MSFNs) by considering both random arc capacities and stochastic transmission times—a modeling feature often neglected in prior research. The major contribution lies in the development of a Monte Carlo-based simulation algorithm that approximates the probability of successfully transmitting a specified demand from source to terminal within a predefined time constraint. The proposed method incorporates a dual-random framework that simulates the current capacity and lead time states for each arc, allowing for a realistic evaluation of time-constrained flow reliability under uncertainty. The algorithm avoids exhaustive enumeration of all possible minimal paths (MPs), significantly reducing computational complexity. Experimental evaluations conducted on the NSFNET demonstrate that the algorithm achieves high accuracy with an average deviation of less than 0.1% from exact reliability values, while maintaining very low CPU execution time (0.0013 seconds) across multiple scenarios. These results confirm that the proposed approach provides a practical, efficient, and scalable solution for assessing quickest path reliability in large-scale, time-sensitive, and dynamically uncertain systems.

References

1. Huang, C.-F., D.-H. Huang, and Y.-K. Lin, *Network reliability evaluation for multi-state computing networks considering demand as the non-integer type.* Reliability Engineering & System Safety, 2022. **219**: p. 108226.

2. Kozyra, P.M., *A parallel algorithm for reliability assessment of multi-state flow networks based on simultaneous finding of all multi-state minimal paths and performing state space decomposition.* Reliability Engineering & System Safety, 2024. **251**: p. 110376.
3. Chen, Y.L. and Y.H. Chin, *The quickest path problem.* Computers & Operations Research, 1990. **17**(2): p. 153-161.
4. Chen, G.-H. and Y.-C. Hung, *On the quickest path problem.* Information Processing Letters, 1993. **46**(3): p. 125-128.
5. Rosen, J.B., S.-Z. Sun, and G.-L. Xue, *Algorithms for the quickest path problem and the enumeration of quickest paths.* Computers & Operations Research, 1991. **18**(6): p. 579-584.
6. Martins, E.d.Q.V. and J.L.E. Dos Santos, *An algorithm for the quickest path problem.* Operations Research Letters, 1997. **20**(4): p. 195-198.
7. Calvete, H.I., L. del-Pozo, and J.A. Iranzo, *Algorithms for the quickest path problem and the reliable quickest path problem.* Computational Management Science, 2012. **9**(2): p. 255-272.
8. Calvete, H.I., *The quickest path problem with interval lead times.* Computers & Operations Research, 2004. **31**(3): p. 383-395.
9. Young-Cheol, B., C. Hyunseung, and M. Youngsong. *Reliability problem on all pairs quickest paths.* in *Computational Science—ICCS 2003: International Conference, Melbourne, Australia and St. Petersburg, Russia, June 2–4, 2003 Proceedings, Part IV 3.* 2003. Springer.
10. Lee, D. and E. Papadopoulou, *The all-pairs quickest path problem.* Information Processing Letters, 1993. **45**(5): p. 261-267.
11. Yeh, W.-C., *A fast algorithm for quickest path reliability evaluations in multi-state flow networks.* IEEE Transactions on Reliability, 2015. **64**(4): p. 1175-1184.
12. Lin, Y.-K., *Extend the quickest path problem to the system reliability evaluation for a stochastic-flow network.* Computers & Operations Research, 2003. **30**(4): p. 567-575.
13. Jane, C.-C. and Y.-W. Laih, *Algorithms for the quickest time distribution of dynamic stochastic-flow networks.* RAIRO-Operations Research, 2017. **51**(4): p. 1317-1330.
14. Lin, Y.-K., *Calculation of minimal capacity vectors through k minimal paths under budget and time constraints.* European Journal of Operational Research, 2010. **200**(1): p. 160-169.
15. Lin, Y.-K., *Spare routing reliability for a stochastic flow network through two minimal paths under budget constraint.* IEEE transactions on reliability, 2010. **59**(1): p. 2-10.
16. Forghani-elahabad, M. and N. Mahdavi-Amiri, *A New Algorithm for Generating All Minimal Vectors for the $ q $ SMPs Reliability Problem With Time and Budget Constraints.* IEEE Transactions on Reliability, 2015. **65**(2): p. 828-842.
17. Lin, Y.-K., *System reliability for quickest path problems under time threshold and budget.* Computers & Mathematics with Applications, 2010. **60**(8): p. 2326-2332.
18. Lin, Y.-K., *Stochastic flow networks via multiple paths under time threshold and budget constraint.* Computers & Mathematics with Applications, 2011. **62**(6): p. 2629-2638.
19. El Khadiri, M., W.-C. Yeh, and H. Cancela, *An efficient factoring algorithm for the quickest path multi-state flow network reliability problem.* Computers & Industrial Engineering, 2023. **179**: p. 109221.
20. Forghani-elahabad, M. and O.M. Alsalami, *Using a Node–Child Matrix to Address the Quickest Path Problem in Multistate Flow Networks under Transmission Cost Constraints.* Mathematics, 2023. **11**(24): p. 4889.
21. Liu, X., et al., *Research on a seismic connectivity reliability model of power systems based on the quasi-Monte Carlo method.* Reliability Engineering & System Safety, 2021. **215**: p. 107888.
22. Chen, X.G., *A novel reliability estimation method of complex network based on Monte Carlo.* Cluster Computing, 2017. **20**: p. 1063-1073.
23. Chang, P.-C., *Simulation approaches for multi-state network reliability estimation: Practical applications.* Simulation Modelling Practice and Theory, 2022. **115**: p. 102457.
24. Cancela, H., L. Murray, and G. Rubino, *Efficient estimation of stochastic flow network reliability.* IEEE Transactions on Reliability, 2019. **68**(3): p. 954-970.
25. Ramirez-Marquez, J.E. and D.W. Coit, *A Monte-Carlo simulation approach for approximating multi-state two-terminal reliability.* Reliability Engineering & System Safety, 2005. **87**(2): p. 253-264.
26. Chang, P.-C., *MC-based simulation approach for two-terminal multi-state network reliability evaluation without knowing d-MCs.* Reliability Engineering & System Safety, 2022. **220**: p. 108289.
27. Ford, L. and D. Fulkerson, *Flows in networks princeton university press.* Princeton, New Jersey, 1962. **276**: p. 22.
28. Lin, Y.-K. and S.-G. Chen, *A merge search approach to find minimal path vectors in multistate networks.* International Journal of Reliability, Quality and Safety Engineering, 2017. **24**(01): p. 1750005.
29. Chen, S.-G. and Y.-K. Lin, *Search for all minimal paths in a general large flow network.* IEEE Transactions on Reliability, 2012. **61**(4): p. 949-956.

Expanded Optimal Visit Suspension Policy Corporate Sale using Reliability Model

Takahiro NAKAMURA
Department of Management of Social Systems and Civil Engineering, Graduate school of Engineering, Tottori University,Japan, nak1124tak196@gmail.com,
Kodo ITO
Faculty of Science and Engineering, Yamato University,Japan, ito.kodo@yamato-u.ac.jp
Toshio NAKAGAWA
Department of Business Administration Aichi Institute of Technology,Japan, toshi-nakagawa@aitech.ac.jp

Keywords: Closing strategy, Weibull distribusiton, Corporate sales, Financial institution.

Abstract

The environment surrounding corporate organizations, whether for-profit or non-profit, has changed significantly, and the outlook remains difficult to predict. In this environment, the financial base of some organizations has weakened, and some corporate organizations are unable to respond to the growing need to address social issues. In Japan, the reform of the public interest incorporated foundation and incorporated association system, effective April 2025, will provide greater freedom to strengthen their financial base and simplify the procedures for transferring their operations to other corporations to continue their public interest activities.

Nonprofit organizations are expected to respond to changes in the business environment by acquiring information from external organizations.

On the other hand, sales representatives of financial institutions secure contact opportunities by providing useful information to corporate clients, and profit by proposing financial services.

In this paper, we determine the optimal policy for deciding whether to continue visits, taking into account the costs of visits over a certain period, the benefits of the visit proposal, and the risk of the target corporation suddenly suspending operations. The age replacement of the reliability model is used to formulate the policy.

1 Introduction

The global economy is becoming increasingly uncertain, as seen in the trend towards forming blocs of countries. According to the Global Debt Monitor report [1] released by the Institute of International Finance on February 25, the global debt balance reached a record high of \$318 trillion as of December 2024. It is worth noting that government departments are the most common type of entity, followed by households, financial institutions, and non-financial institutions. Elizabeth et al. [2] note that nonprofit organizations are exposed to business cycle risk, and that public sector organizations are characterized by a decrease in income during economic downturns, while demand increases. Furthermore, it is also mentioned that nonprofit organizations can expect to continue their operations by increasing their income from donations, and it is indicated that nonprofit organizations need to have contact with external organizations to continue their operations.

In Japan, the system of public interest incorporated foundations and incorporated associations was reformed in April 2025 to allow for more flexible fund management, business development, and improved autonomous governance. The government and regulatory authorities are planning to make the public aware of the details of the system through study sessions and seminars during the period up to April 2028. While nonprofit organizations are expected to adapt to the external environment, such as economic fluctuations, Therefore, it is thought that financial institutions will increase their proposals for strengthening the financial base while observing the status of efforts by nonprofit organizations to reform. On the other hand, nonprofit organizations that are unable to respond to changes in the external environment must now assume that they may suddenly have to suspend their operations due to the transfer of operations to a simplified other corporation to continue their public interest activities. Nakamura et al.[3] considered a model in which sales representatives of financial institutions regularly secure effective contact opportunities with corporate clients.

In this paper, we extend the model to consider the

risk of a nonprofit organization suddenly ceasing operations.

2 Model 1 : Fundamental model

Figure 1 shows an example of a financial institution's site visits with a corporate client of Model 1. We make the following assumptions:

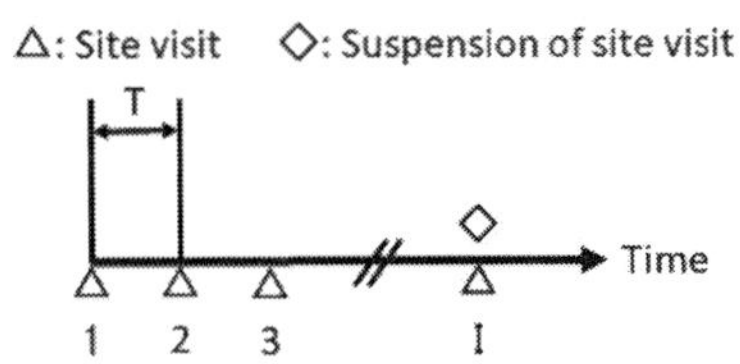

Figure 1: Financial institution's site visits with corporate client of Model 1

1) Sales representatives of the financial institution visit corporate client sites at a prespecified time $iT\,(i = 1, 2, \ldots, I)$ and suspends the visit at IT.

2) The financial institution obtains profit when it can close deals with corporate clients. Let $s_i\,(i = 1, 2, \ldots)$ denote the probability of corporate clients taking profitable action at the i-th visit with the financial institution's sales representatives.

3) The average profit per sales visit which is the profit obtained until IT divided by time period IT, is b_1. The average cost per visit in sales is $c_1\,(< b_1)$ and the average cost of sales which is independent of the financial institution's visit is $c_2\,(< b_1)$.

The expected time from the start of site visit to the suspension is

$$\sum_{i=1}^{I} iTs_i + \overline{S}_I IT = T\sum_{i=0}^{I-1}\overline{S}_i, \tag{1}$$

where $S_j \equiv \sum_{i=1}^{j} s_i$ $(S_0 = 0)$ and $\overline{\Phi} \equiv 1 - \Phi$, The expected profit is

$$\sum_{i=1}^{I}(b_1 - c_1 i - c_2)s_i - (c_1 I + c_2)\overline{S}_I$$
$$= b_1 S_I - c_1\sum_{i=0}^{I-1}\overline{S}_i - c_2. \tag{2}$$

Therefore, by dividing (2) by (1), the expected profit rate $P_1(I)$ is

$$TP_1(I) = \frac{b_1 S_I - c_1\sum_{i=0}^{I-1}\overline{S}_i - c_2}{\sum_{i=0}^{I-1}\overline{S}_i} = \frac{b_1 S_I - c_2}{\sum_{i=0}^{I-1}\overline{S}_i} - c_1. \tag{3}$$

Letting $P_1(I+1) < P_1(I)$,

$$S_{I+1} - \alpha_{I+1}\sum_{i=0}^{I}\overline{S}_i > \frac{c_2}{b_1}, \tag{4}$$

where $\alpha_j \equiv s_j/\overline{S}_{j-1}$. Letting denote the left-hand side of (4) by $L_1(I)$,

$$L_1(I) - L_1(I-1) = (\alpha_I - \alpha_{I+1})\sum_{i=0}^{I-1}\overline{S}_i \geq 0,$$
$$L_1(1) = s_1 - \frac{s_2}{1 - s_1}, \qquad L_1(\infty) = 1.$$

Therefore, we have the following optimal policy:

i) There exists a finite and unique I_1^* which satisfies (4) when $L_1(1) \leq c_2/b_1$.

ii) $I_1^* = 1$ when $L_1(1) > c_2/b_1$.

3 Model2

Figure 2 shows an example of a financial institution's site visits with a corporate client of Model 1. We make assumption 1) and 2) of Model 1, add 3), and rewrite 3) of Model 1 as 4).

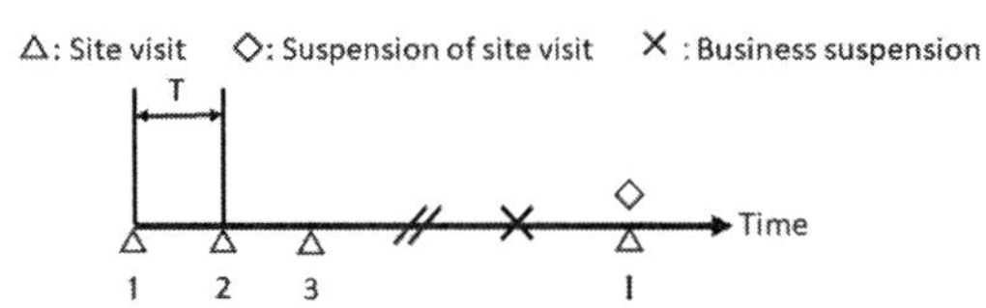

Figure 2: Financial institution's site visits with corporate client of Model 2

3) There is a possibility that corporate clients stop their business suddenly due to their circumstances. For simplicity, we assume that such stop occurs at t, but the post-stop process is performed at the next visit. Let $F(T)$ be the probability that a client stops its business at time T.

4) The average profit per sales visit which is the profit obtained until IT divided by time period IT, is b_1. The average cost per visit in sales is $c_1\,(< b_1)$ and the average cost of sales which is independent of the financial institution's visit is $c_2\,(< b_1)$. The average loss cost due to business suspension is d_1.

The expected time from the start of site visit to the suspension is

$$\sum_{i=1}^{I} iTs_i\overline{F}(iT)$$
$$+\sum_{i=1}^{I} iT\overline{S}_{i-1}[F(iT) - F((i-1)T)] + IT\overline{S}_I\overline{F}(IT)$$
$$= T\sum_{i=0}^{I-1}\overline{S}_i\overline{F}(iT). \tag{5}$$

The expected profit is

$$\begin{aligned}
&\sum_{i=1}^{I}(b_1 - c_1 i - c_2)s_i\overline{F}(iT) \\
&-(c_1 I + c_2)\sum_{i=I+1}^{\infty} s_i\overline{F}(iT) \\
&+\sum_{i=1}^{I}(b_1 - c_1 i - c_2 - d_1)s_i F(iT) \\
&-(c_1 I + c_2 + d_1)\sum_{i=I+1}^{\infty} s_i F(iT) \\
= \;& b_1 S_I - c_1\sum_{i=0}^{I-1}\overline{S}_i - c_2 - d_1\sum_{i=1}^{\infty} s_i F(iT). \quad (6)
\end{aligned}$$

The expected profit rate $P_2(I)$ is,

$$TP_2(I) = \frac{b_1 S_I - c_1\sum_{i=0}^{I-1}\overline{S}_i - c_2 - d_1\sum_{i=1}^{\infty} s_i F(iT)}{T\sum_{i=0}^{I-1}\overline{S}_i\overline{F}(iT)}. \quad (7)$$

Forming the inequality $P_2(I+1) < P_2(I)$,

$$\begin{aligned}
&S_{I+1} - \alpha_{I+1}\sum_{i=0}^{I}\overline{S}_i\frac{\overline{F}(iT)}{\overline{F}(IT)} \\
&> \frac{c_1}{b_1}\sum_{i=0}^{I-1}\left[1 - \frac{\overline{F}(iT)}{\overline{F}(IT)}\right]\overline{S}_i + \frac{c_2}{b_1} + \frac{d_1}{b_1}\sum_{i=1}^{\infty} s_i F(iT). \quad (8)
\end{aligned}$$

When $\overline{F} = 1$, (8) is equal to Eq. (4) in [3].

4 Model3

Next, we make assumption 3) and 4) of Model 2 and rewrite assumptions 1) and 2) as follows:

1') Sales representatives of the financial institution visit corporate client sites at prespecified times $iT\,(i = 1, 2, \cdots, I)$, $IT + mjT\,(j = 1, 2, \cdots, J)$ and suspends the visit at $(I + mJ)T$.

2') The financial institution obtains profit when it can close deals with corporate clients. Let $s_i\,(i = 1, 2, \cdots, I)$ and $u_j\,(j = 1, 2, \cdots, J)$ denote the probability of corporate clients taking profitable action at the i-th and $(I+j)$-th visit with the financial institution's sales representatives, respectively.

The expected time from the start of site visit to the suspension is

$$T\left[\sum_{i=0}^{I-1}\overline{S}_i\overline{F}(iT) + m\overline{S}_I\sum_{j=0}^{J-1}\overline{U}_j\overline{F}((I+jm)T)\right], \quad (9)$$

where $U_j \equiv \sum_{i=1}^{j} u_i$. The expected profit is

$$\begin{aligned}
&b_1(1 - \overline{S}_I\overline{U}_J) - c_1\left(\sum_{i=0}^{I-1}\overline{S}_i + \overline{S}_I\sum_{j=0}^{J-1}\overline{U}_j\right) - c_2 \\
&-d_1\left[\sum_{i=1}^{I} s_i F(iT) + \sum_{i=I+1}^{\infty} s_i\sum_{j=1}^{\infty} u_j F((i+jm)T)\right]. \quad (10)
\end{aligned}$$

The expected profit rate $P_3(I, J)$ is,

$$TP_3(I,J) = \frac{\left\{\begin{aligned}&b_1(1 - \overline{S}_I\overline{U}_J) - c_1\left(\sum_{i=0}^{I-1}\overline{S}_i + \overline{S}_I\sum_{j=0}^{J-1}\overline{U}_j\right) - c_2\\ &-d_1\left[\sum_{i=1}^{I} s_i F(iT) + \sum_{i=I+1}^{\infty} s_i\sum_{j=1}^{\infty} u_j F((i+jm)T)\right]\end{aligned}\right\}}{\sum_{i=0}^{I-1}\overline{S}_i\overline{F}(iT) + m\overline{S}_I\sum_{j=0}^{J-1}\overline{U}_j\overline{F}((I+jm)T)}. \quad (11)$$

4.1 Optimal policy 1

Forming the inequality $P_3(I+1, J) < P_3(I, J)$,

$$\begin{aligned}
&\left(b_1\overline{U}_J + c_1\sum_{j=0}^{J-1}\overline{U}_j\right)(\overline{S}_I A_{I+1} - \overline{S}_{I+1}A_I) \\
&\quad -c_1\left(A_I\sum_{i=0}^{I}\overline{S}_i - A_{I+1}\sum_{i=0}^{I-1}\overline{S}_i\right) \\
&< (b_1 - c_2)(A_{I+1} - A_I) \\
&-d_1\left\{\left[\sum_{i=1}^{I} s_i F(iT) + \sum_{i=I+1}^{\infty} s_i\sum_{j=1}^{\infty} u_j F((i+jm)T)\right]A_{I+1}\right. \\
&\left. -\left[\sum_{i=1}^{I+1} s_i F(iT) + \sum_{i=I+2}^{\infty} s_i\sum_{j=1}^{\infty} u_j F((i+jm)T)\right]A_I\right\}, \quad (12)
\end{aligned}$$

where $A_I \equiv \sum_{i=0}^{I-1}\overline{S}_i\overline{F}(iT) + m\overline{S}_I\sum_{j=0}^{J-1}\overline{U}_j\overline{F}((I + jm)T)$. When $\overline{F} = 1$, (12) is equal to Eq. (8) in [3].

4.2 Optimal policy 2

Forming the inequality $P_3(I, J+1) < P_3(I, J)$,

$$\begin{aligned}
&\beta_{J+1}\sum_{i=0}^{I-1}\overline{S}_i\overline{F}(iT) \\
&\quad + m\overline{S}_I\left[\overline{U}_J\overline{F}((I+jm)T) + \beta_{J+1}\sum_{j=0}^{J-1}\overline{U}_j\overline{F}((I+jm)T)\right] \\
&< \frac{1}{b_1}\left\{b_1 - c_2 - d_1\left[\sum_{i=0}^{I} s_i F(iT) + \sum_{i=I+1}^{\infty} s_i\sum_{j=1}^{\infty} u_j F((i+jm)T)\right]\right\} \\
&\quad \times m\overline{F}((I+Jm)T) \\
&\quad -\frac{c_1}{b_1}\left\{m\overline{F}((I+Jm)T)\sum_{i=0}^{I-1}\overline{S}_i - \sum_{i=0}^{I-1}\overline{S}_i\overline{F}(iT)\right. \\
&\quad \left. -m\overline{S}_I\sum_{j=0}^{J-1}\overline{U}_j\left[\overline{F}((I+jm)T) - \overline{F}((I+Jm)T)\right]\right\}, \quad (13)
\end{aligned}$$

where $\beta_j \equiv u_j/\overline{U}_{j-1}$. When $\overline{F} = 1$,(13) is equal to Eq.(9) in [3].

5 Model4

Then we make assumption 3) and 4) of Model 2 and rewrite assumptions 1) and 2) as follows:

1") Sales representatives of the financial institution visit corporate client sites at prespecified times $iT\,(i = 1, 2, \cdots, I)$, $IT + mjT\,(j = 1, 2, \cdots, J)$, $IT + mJT + nkT\,(k = 1, 2, \cdots, K)$ and suspends the visit at $(I + mJ + nK)T$.

2") The financial institution obtains profit when it can close deals with corporate clients. Let $s_i\,(i = 1, 2, \cdots, I)$, $u_j\,(j = 1, 2, \cdots, J)$ and $v_k\,(k = 1, 2, \cdots, K)$ denote the probability of corporate clients taking profitable action at the i-th, $(I+j)$-th and $(I+J+k)$-th visit with the financial institution's sales representatives, respectively.

The expected time from the start of site visit to the suspension is

$$T\left\{\sum_{i=0}^{I-1}\overline{S}_i\overline{F}(iT)+m\overline{S}_I\sum_{j=0}^{J-1}\overline{U}_j\overline{F}((I+jm)T)\right.$$
$$\left.+n\overline{S}_I\overline{U}_J\sum_{k=0}^{K-1}\overline{V}_k\overline{F}((I+Jm+kn)T)\right]\Bigg\}, \quad (14)$$

where $V_j \equiv \sum_{i=1}^{j} v_i$. The expected profit is

$$b_1(1-\overline{S}_I\overline{U}_J\overline{V}_K)$$
$$-c_1\left(\sum_{i=0}^{I-1}\overline{S}_i+\overline{S}_I\sum_{j=0}^{J-1}\overline{U}_j+\overline{S}_I\overline{U}_J\sum_{k=0}^{K-1}\overline{V}_k\right)-c_2$$
$$-d_1\left[\sum_{i=1}^{I}s_iF(iT)+\sum_{i=I+1}^{\infty}s_i\sum_{j=1}^{J}u_jF((i+jm)T)\right.$$
$$\left.+\sum_{i=I+1}^{\infty}s_i\sum_{j=J+1}^{\infty}u_j\sum_{k=1}^{\infty}v_kF((i+mj+nk)T)\right]. \quad (15)$$

The expected profit rate $P_4(I, J, K)$ is,

$$TP_4(I,J,K)$$
$$=\frac{\begin{pmatrix} b_1(1-\overline{S}_I\overline{U}_J\overline{V}_K) \\ -c_1\left(\sum_{i=0}^{I-1}\overline{S}_i+\overline{S}_I\sum_{j=0}^{J-1}\overline{U}_j+\overline{S}_I\overline{U}_J\sum_{k=0}^{K-1}\overline{V}_k\right) \\ -c_2-d_1\Big\{\sum_{i=1}^{I}s_iF(iT) \\ +\sum_{i=I+1}^{\infty}s_i\Big[\sum_{j=1}^{J}u_jF((i+jm)T) \\ +\sum_{j=J+1}^{\infty}u_j\sum_{k=1}^{\infty}v_kF((i+mj+nk)T)\Big]\Big\}\end{pmatrix}}{\begin{pmatrix}\sum_{i=0}^{I-1}\overline{S}_i\overline{F}(iT)+m\overline{S}_I\sum_{j=0}^{J-1}\overline{U}_j\overline{F}((I+jm)T) \\ +n\overline{S}_I\overline{U}_J\sum_{k=0}^{K-1}\overline{V}_k\overline{F}((I+Jm+kn)T)\end{pmatrix}}. \quad (16)$$

5.1 Optimal policy 1

Forming the inequality $P_4(I+1, J, K) < P_4(I, J, K)$,

$$b_1\overline{U}_J\overline{V}_K\left(\overline{S}_IB_{I+1}-\overline{S}_{I+1}B_I\right)-c_1\left(B_ID_{I+1}-B_{I+1}D_I\right)$$
$$< \;(b_1-c_2)(B_{I+1}-B_I)-d_1(B_{I+1}E_I-B_IE_{I+1}), \quad (17)$$

where $B_I \equiv \sum_{i=0}^{I-1}\overline{S}_i\overline{F}(iT) + m\overline{S}_I\sum_{j=0}^{J-1}\overline{U}_j\overline{F}((I + jm)T) + n\overline{S}_I\overline{U}_J\sum_{k=0}^{K-1}\overline{V}_k\overline{F}((I + Jm + kn)T)$, $D_I \equiv \sum_{i=0}^{I-1}\overline{S}_i + \overline{S}_I\sum_{j=0}^{J-1}\overline{U}_j + \overline{S}_I\overline{U}_J\sum_{k=0}^{K-1}\overline{V}_k$, and $E_I \equiv \sum_{i=1}^{I}s_iF(iT) + \sum_{i=I+1}^{\infty}s_i\big[\sum_{j=1}^{J}u_jF((i + jm)T) + \sum_{j=J+1}^{\infty}u_j\sum_{k=1}^{\infty}v_kF((i + jm + kn)T)\big]$.

When $\overline{F} = 1$, (17) is equal to Eq. (21) in [3].

5.2 Optimal policy 2

Forming the inequality $P_4(I, J+1, K) < P_4(I, J, K)$,

$$\left(b_1-c_2-c_1\sum_{i=0}^{I-1}\overline{S}_i\right)n(H_J-H_{J+1}+\beta_{J+1}H_{J+1})$$
$$+b_1\left\{\overline{V}_K\beta_{J+1}\sum_{i=0}^{I-1}\overline{S}_i\overline{F}(iT)+\overline{S}_I\overline{V}_K\left[m\overline{U}_J\overline{F}((I+Jm)T)\right.\right.$$
$$\left.\left.+m\beta_{J+1}\sum_{j=0}^{J-1}\overline{U}_j\overline{F}((I+jm)T)-n\overline{U}_{J+1}(H_J-H_{J+1})\right]\right\}$$
$$-c_1\left\{\left(1-\beta_{J+1}\sum_{k=0}^{K-1}\overline{V}_k\right)\left[\sum_{i=0}^{I-1}\overline{S}_i\overline{F}(iT)\right.\right.$$
$$\left.+m\overline{S}_I\sum_{j=0}^{J-1}\overline{U}_j\overline{F}((I+jm)T)+n\overline{S}_I\overline{U}_JH_J\right]$$
$$+\overline{S}_I\left(\sum_{j=0}^{J-1}\overline{U}_j+\overline{U}_J\sum_{k=0}^{K-1}\overline{V}_k\right)$$
$$\left.\times\left[n\left(H_J-H_{J+1}+\beta_{J+1}H_{J+1}\right)-m\overline{F}((I+Jm)T)\right]\right\}$$
$$<\;\left(b_1-c_2-c_1\sum_{i=0}^{I-1}\overline{S}_i\right)m\overline{F}((I+Jm)T), \quad (18)$$

where $H_J \equiv \sum_{k=0}^{K-1}\overline{V}_k\overline{F}((I + Jm + kn)T)$. When $\overline{F} = 1$, (18) is equal to Eq. (14) in [3].

5.3 Optimal policy 3

Forming the inequality $P_4(I, J, K+1) < P_4(I, J, K)$,

$$(b_1\gamma_{K+1}-c_1)\left[\sum_{i=0}^{I-1}\overline{S}_i\overline{F}(iT)+m\overline{S}_I\sum_{j=0}^{J-1}\overline{U}_j\overline{F}((I+jm)T)\right]$$
$$+b_1n\overline{S}_I\overline{U}_J\left[\gamma_{K+1}\sum_{k=0}^{K-1}\overline{V}_k\overline{F}((I+Jm+kn)T)\right.$$
$$\left.+\overline{V}_K\overline{F}((I+Jm+Kn)T)\right]$$

$$-c_1 n\overline{S}_I\overline{U}_J\sum_{k=0}^{K-1}\overline{V}_k\Big[\overline{F}((I+Jm+kn)T)$$
$$-\overline{F}((I+Jm+Kn)T)\Big]$$
$$<\Bigg\{b_1-c_2-c_1\left(\sum_{i=0}^{I-1}\overline{S}_i+\overline{S}_I\sum_{j=0}^{J-1}\overline{U}_j\right)$$
$$-d_1\sum_{i=1}^{I}s_iF(iT)$$
$$-d_1\sum_{i=I+1}^{\infty}s_i\Bigg[\sum_{j=1}^{J}u_jF((i+jm)T)$$
$$+\sum_{j=J+1}^{\infty}u_j\sum_{k=1}^{\infty}v_kF((i+jm+kn)T)\Bigg]\Bigg\}$$
$$\times n\overline{F}((I+Jm+Kn)T)\,. \tag{19}$$

When $\overline{F}=1$, (19) is equal to Eq. (15) in [3].

6 Numerical Calculations

We assume that $F(t)$ is an exponential distribution and S_i, U_j and V_k are discrete Weibull distributions[4] and

$$S_i = 1-(1-p_1)^{i^{\omega_1}}(i=0,1,2,\cdots,I;0<p_1<1,\omega_1>0)\,,$$
$$U_j = 1-(1-p_2)^{j^{\omega_2}}(j=0,1,2,\cdots,J;0<p_2<1,\omega_2>0)\,,$$
$$V_k = 1-(1-p_3)^{k^{\omega_3}}(k=0,1,2,\cdots,K;0<p_3<1,\omega_3>0)\,. \tag{20}$$

(3), (7), (11), and (16) are rewritten as, respectively,

$$TP_1(I)=\frac{b_1\left[1-(1-p_1)^{I^{\omega_1}}\right]-c_2}{\sum_{i=0}^{I-1}(1-p_1)^{i^{\omega_1}}},$$
$$TP_2(I)=\frac{\begin{array}{c}b_1\left[1-(1-p_1)^{I^{\omega_1}}\right]-c_2\\ -d_1\sum_{i=1}^{\infty}\left[(1-p_1)^{(i-1)^{\omega_1}}-(1-p_1)^{i^{\omega_1}}\right](1-e^{-i\lambda T})\end{array}}{\sum_{i=0}^{I-1}(1-p_1)^{i^{\omega_1}}}, \tag{21}$$

$TP_3(I,J)$ and $TP_4(I,J,K)$ are omitted due to the number of report pages.

Table 1: Optimal I^* and resulting profit rate $TP_2(I^*)$ when $c_1=c_2=1$, $b_1=10$, $T=1$, $p_1=0.8$, $\omega_1=0.8$ and $\lambda=0.01$.

d_1	I^*	$TP_2(I^*)$
1	4	0.258
5	6	0.178
10	9	0.096

7 Conclusion

The properties of $TP_1(I)$ do not include d_1 due to Eq. (21), and therefore, we obtain the same results as the original model [3]. For $TP_2(I)$, the optimal I^* increases and the expected profit rate $TP_2(I^*)$ decreases

Table 2: Optimal I^*,J^* and resulting profit rate $TP_3(I^*,J^*)$ when $c_1=c_2=1$, $b_1=10$, $T=1$, $p_1=0.8$, $p_2=0.81$, $\omega_1=\omega_2=0.8$, $m=1$ and $\lambda=0.01$.

d_1	I^*	J^*	$TP_3(I^*,J^*)$
1	2	2	0.383
5	3	3	0.251
10	6	5	0.140

Table 3: Optimal I^*,J^*,K^* and resulting profit rate $TP_4(I^*,J^*,K^*)$ when $c_1=1$, $c_2=1$, $b_1=10$, $T=1$ $p_1=0.8$, $p_2=0.81$, $p_2=0.82$, $\omega_1=\omega_2=\omega_3=0.8$, $m=n=1$ and $\lambda=0.01$.

d_1	I^*	J^*	K^*	$TP_4(I^*,J^*,K^*)$
1	1	1	1	0.436
5	3	3	2	0.274
10	5	4	4	0.150

as d_1 increases from table1. For $TP_3(I,J)$, the optimal I^*,J^* are both increase and the expected profit rate $TP_3(I^*,J^*)$ decreases as d_1 increases from table2. For $TP_4(I,J,K)$, the optimal I^*,J^*,K^* both increase and the expected profit rate $TP_4(I^*,J^*,K^*)$ decreases as d_1 increases from table3. Also, as d_1 increases, $TP_2(I^*) < TP_3(I^*,J^*) < TP_4(I^*,J^*,K^*)$ results are obtained at the optimal I^*,J^*,K^* in each. When variables other than d_1 were changed, the results were the same as for the original model [3]. In this paper, it was derived in a way that is consistent with the actual situation of first visit planning, revised visit planning, and re-revised visit planning in actual operations, including the average loss cost d_1. In addition, the average loss cost d_1 can be used in a more practical way if the following method is set up. 1)d_1 is set higher when the program operation plan period, etc. for public interest purpose programs, etc. is short, based on financial statements. 2)d_1 will be adjusted based on the corporate client information obtained through contact, taking into account the likelihood of obtaining donations and the stability of revenue-generating businesses.

References

[1] Institute of International Finance, Return of the Bond Vigilantes - Dangerous Dynamics in Debt Markets, *Global Debt Monitor*, (2025).

[2] E. A.M.Searing, T. St. Clair, Nonprofit Revenue Portfolios and Exposure to Business Cycle Risk, *Sage Journal Nonprofit and Voluntary Sector Quarterly*, (2025) (23 pages).

[3] T. Nakamura, A. Tokuoka, K. Ito, T. Nakagawa, Optimal Visit Suspension Policy of Corporate Sale using Reliability Model, *International Journal of Reliability, Quality and Safety Engineering*, **31**(6) (2024) 2450049(17 pages).

[4] T. Nakagawa and S. Osaki, The Discrete Weibull Distribution, *IEEE Trans. Reliab.* **24**(5) (1975) 300-301.

Considering for the Forecasting Method of the Nikkei Stock Average using Deep Learning with Natural Language Processing

Ryota NEKOMOTO[1], Tomoaki AKIBA[1]

[1]Graduate School of Social Systems Science, Chiba Institute of Technology, Tsudanuma 2-17-1 Narashino, Chiba 275-0016, Japan

Keywords: Forecasting Nikkei Stock Average, Data Collection and Analysis, Data Mining, Deep Learning, Algorithms, Optimization

Abstract – This study aims to improve the prediction accuracy of the Nikkei Stock Average thereby facilitating the determination of financial products to optimize asset building. We considered a prediction method for the Nikkei Stock Average using Long Short Term Memory (LSTM) and Convolution Neural Network (CNN) among deep learning techniques. The LSTM learns the open, high, low, and close (OHLC) values for x days and predicts the closing price for $x + 1$ days. In the CNN, one value on day $x + 1$ is added to the data trained in the LSTM and trained again. The Nikkei Stock Average data were obtained between 1988 to 2024 using yfinance, an open-source tool that uses Yahoo's public API. As a result, all LSTM models, except the one using Adaptive Moment Estimation with Weight decay (AdamW), achieved accuracy rates higher than the chance rate. The LSTM models using all optimization algorithms, except Stochastic Gradient Descent (SGD) and AdamW, showed the highest accuracy. In the CNN model, the prediction accuracy decreased for all algorithms except AdamW when compared with the LSTM model. These results indicate that it is possible to make predictions that can be used to assess economic conditions to a certain extent.

1. Introduction

Recently in Japan, the necessity of accumulating personal assets has increased owing to social problems such as the "20-million-yen problem for retirement" [1] and low bank interest rates. The main means of accumulating personal assets are fin ancial products, such as savings and stock investments. Therefore, this study aims to verify the accuracy of a method to predict the Nikkei Stock Average, an important indicator for assessing trends of the Japanese economy, using natural language processing and deep learning. This will serve as a guide to evaluate the future direction of the Japanese economy and identify the financial products that should be used for asset building.

In Previous studies, Ishige's research [2], which used deep learning for prediction with daily data as training data, Komatsu's research [3], which predicted the Nikkei Stock Average using Long Short Term Memory (LSTM), known for its excellent handling of time-series data and Miyazaki et al.'s research [4], which applied Convolution Neural Network (CNN) to the prediction of the Nikkei Stock Average. Based on these studies, we aimed to reduce the random walk phenomenon in prediction and improve prediction accuracy by adding further optimization algorithms and introducing mini-batch learning [5]. The introduction of mini-batch learning confirmed a decrease in the random walk of prediction in the learning process, as well as an increase in prediction accuracy and stability. However, issues such as the validity of the correct answer criterion of prediction error within ± 10 yen, the inability to obtain sufficient prediction accuracy, and the difficulty of prediction during rapid stock price fluctuations persisted. Therefore, in this study, we aimed to improve prediction accuracy by changing the correct answer criterion to match the predicted and actual price fluctuation directions compared to the previous day. Furthermore, we aimed to develop a model that can cope with rapid stock price fluctuations by obtaining distributed representations of overseas news articles using the Sentiment Sparse Composite Document Vectors (SSCDV) algorithm [6] and learning them together with the open, high, low and close (OHLC) values of the Nikkei Stock Average. Consequently, we were able to achieve prediction accuracy that exceeded the chance rate.

2. Nikkei Stock Average

2.1. What is the Nikkei Stock Average

The Nikkei Stock Average is a stock price index calculated by Nikkei Inc., which carefully selects 225 stocks from approximately 2,000 listed on the Tokyo Stock Exchange Prime Market, focusing on stocks with high market liquidity and considering the balance between industries. It is calculated by adjusting the stock prices of each constituent stock with a stock price conversion factor, summing the adjusted stock prices, and dividing by a divisor [7]. It is calculated and distributed every 5 s during the Tokyo Stock Exchange's trading hours of 9:00 a.m. to 11:30 a.m. and from 12:30 p.m. to 3:30 p.m.

2.2. Nikkei Stock Average movements and trends

Investors predict Nikkei Stock Average using fundamental and technical analysis. Fundamental analysis involves predicting stock prices using external influencing factors such as global events and occurrences [8]. External factors include the collapse of the Lehman Brothers collapse and the Great East Japan Earthquake. It also includes predictions based on global stock market indices and exchange-rate trends. Technical analysis involves predicting stock prices using internal factors such as past stock price fluctuations and events [8]. Examples of internal factors include moving averages and OHLC values for stocks. For example, one technique uses the property of stock prices to return to their original values after deviating significantly from the moving average line in a short period of time. This study predicts fluctuations in the Nikkei Stock Average using past stock price data, news article topics and sentiment data. Therefore, it uses an analytical method that combines the elements of both methods.

3. Previous Research

3.1. Prediction method using stock price data

Komatsu [3] aimed to predict stock prices using a neural network with an intermediate LSTM layer, trained on daily opening and closing prices, and evaluated using Mean Absolute Percentage Error (MAPE). The training data consisted of the Nikkei Stock Average obtained from Yahoo Finance between March 13, 2000, and March 19, 2018, while learning data were generated using a rolling method. Separate networks were trained to predict the opening and closing prices using the past consecutive x days of stock prices as inputs to predict the price for the following day. The Mean Squared Error (MSE) function was used as the loss function, and a mini-batch gradient descent was used for optimization. The number of LSTM memory units was varied to examine their impact. To evaluate the predictive capability of the model, a 5-day consecutive stock price series was fed into the trained model using the final portion of the training data as input, and the closing price of the output series was considered as the predicted value. In the computer simulations, the stock price data underwent min-max normalization. Under the specific computational conditions of 2000 epochs, a mini-batch size of 5, an Adam optimizer, an initial learning rate of 0.002, and one LSTM layer, three experiments were conducted by varying the number of training data points, number of input days, and number of LSTM blocks. The results showed a tendency for higher prediction accuracy with a larger amount of training data. However, the optimal values for the number of input days and LSTM blocks varied based on the prediction target and market conditions. Furthermore, the impact of sharp stock price fluctuations on the learning curves was observed during the learning process.

Miyazaki et al. [4] examined the applicability of CNNs to financial time series by formulating a binary classification problem to predict whether the Nikkei Stock Average would rise or fall. Specifically, a model was developed to predict whether the Nikkei Stock Average would rise or fall the following day using past data from the Nikkei Stock Average and TOPIX Core30, a stock index of 30 major Japanese companies, as input. To evaluate prediction accuracy, metrics such as accuracy and F-score were used. The stock price data for a 30 min interval was fed into a 100-step window as the input, which predicted the price fluctuations one step ahead of the window. The prediction period covered six months, from January to June 2016, and data corresponding to each month served as the test data. The training data used were from the year before the prediction month. The final accuracy evaluation used the average of the six predictions. Two methods were used to input stock price data into the CNN: a method that treats the input data as images and a method that uses principal components equal to the number of stocks as input data. Other statistical and machine learning models, such as rand, logistic regression, random forest, Multi-layer Perceptron (MLP), and LSTM, were also used as comparison methods, and their respective accuracies were compared. As a result, the LSTM showed the highest accuracy. While simple CNNs had a prediction accuracy lower than the chance rate, Principal Component Analysis-CNN (PCA-CNN) had a prediction accuracy higher than the chance rate. This study shows an improvement in prediction accuracy over random prediction, indicating the potential for using CNNs in financial data.

3.2. Prediction method using stock price and text data

Takahashi et al. [9] conducted a comparative verification of the prediction accuracy using Root Mean Squared Error (RMSE) and Mean Absolute Error (MAE) for a model that learned only past logarithmic returns of stock prices with LSTM, a model that learned only news data with Bidirectional Encoder Representations from Transformers (BERT), and a composite model that integrated these two base models using Light Gradient Boosting Machine (LightGBM) using an ensemble learning technique called stacking. The stock price data used were the logarithmic returns of the Nikkei Stock Average closing prices from September 1, 2012, to September 1, 2021. Reuters business news was used as news data for the same period as stock price data. Notably, for the news data, one article was randomly selected from the data on the day before the prediction date to predict the stock price change rate. For all base models, the data were divided chronologically into 80% training data and 20% test data. The Adam optimizer was used as the optimal algorithm, and each base model provided data for five consecutive days as input values, with the stock price change rate for the sixth day begin the prediction value. The results showed that the composite model, which integrated predictions from different information sources (stock prices and news) through stacking, outperformed the individual base models in terms of accuracy.

Ueda et al. [6] aimed to develop an algorithm for social media text embeddings that could effectively handle contextual information, overcome noise-induced performance degradation, and richly capture both topic and sentiment information. This study used the Nikkei Stock Average and the Nikkei Volatility Index (VI) from November 26, 2012, to September 30, 2020, as financial time series data, as well as bulletin board posts from Yahoo! Finance as text data. They proposed the SSCDV algorithm, an extension of the Sparse Composite Document Vectors (SCDV) algorithm, which allows the joint use of topic and sentiment information by generating vectors associated with mixed topic-sentiment clusters using pre-defined sentiment dictionaries (both domain-dependent and domain-independent). The input features included the opening price, difference from the previous day, and rate of change from the previous day for stock price data. For the text data, the distributed representation of the day's posts, as well as their difference and rate of change from the previous day, were used to set up a binary classification task that predicted whether the Nikkei VI would rise above a certain threshold in the next five days. A random forest classifier was used for prediction, and learning and evaluation were done using a rolling window approach with a fixed learning period and a test period that was shifted by one day at a time. The evaluation metrics included the accuracy, precision, recall, F1-score, and the Matthews Correlation Coefficient (MCC). The results demonstrated that the proposed SSCDV method achieved higher precision, recall, and MCC than the historical only method, Latent Dirichlet Allocation (LDA), Joint sentiment/topic model (JST), Simple Word-Embedding Model (SWEM-aver), Distributed Memory Model of Paragraph Vectors(PV-DM), BERT, Efficiently Learning an Encoder that Classifies Token Replacements Accurately (ELECTRA), and the baseline SCDV.

4. Experimental Overview

4.1. Usage data

The collected data were obtained daily (on a 1-day basis) from yfinance [10], an open-source tool that uses Yahoo's public API. In this study, data spanning approximately 36 years, from April 8, 1988, to February 9, 2024, for a total of 8801 days. In this study, the OHLC values were used as learning data.

4.2. Prediction Methodology

We used the LSTM, which excels at handling time-series data. We input the OHLC values for x days and predicted the closing price for the $x + 1$ day. In addition, for convolution, we used a two-stage training method, where the $x + 1$ predicted value was added to the original data and the model was retrained. We compared and analyzed the prediction accuracy of three combinations: a, before tuning, b, after tuning, and c, after introducing mini-batch learning using optimization algorithms such as SGD, RMSprop, Radam, Adam, AdamW and Adadelta. PyTorch was used as the framework, and Python was used as the programming language.

It is worth noting that the actual source code is similar to that used for predicting sine waves, as it inputs a series of x time-series data points to predict the single $x + 1$ value. While it may be a stretch to strictly consider the Nikkei Stock Average as a sine wave, we determined it to be predictable because of its characteristic of repeatedly rebounding at specific values (bottom or ceiling) and exhibiting upward or downward trends outside of those rebounding periods.

4.3. Parameter tuning and module configuration

MSELoss was used as the loss function. Parameter tuning was performed using Optuna; following the research of Ishige [2] and Komatsu [3], we conducted 100 trials with the items and ranges listed in Table 1, using the parameters that resulted in the lowest loss function value.

Table 1. Tuning parameters and rages

	Training days	Learning rate	LSTM layers	Epoch	Batch size
LSTM	5 - 50	0.01 - 0.1	1 - 4	500	2 - 50
CNN	5 - 50	0.01 - 0.1	1 - 8	500	2 - 50

4.4. Correct Answer condition

In previous research [5], a prediction was considered correct if the error between the prediction and the correct label was less than ±10 yen. However, in this study, a prediction is considered correct if the direction of stock price movement between the prediction date and the previous day's stock price matches. Specifically, the following conditions must be satisfied:

Let $direction_{pred}$ be the predicted direction of change in the stock price on the prediction date, and $direction_{actual}$ be the actual direction of change in the stock price on the prediction date. These are calculated using equations (1) and (2) as follows:

$$direction_{pred} = Output - Close_x \quad (1)$$

$$direction_{actual} = Label - Close_x \quad (2)$$

where $Output$ is the stock price for prediction date $x + 1$ calculated by the prediction model, $Label$ is the actual stock price for prediction date $x + 1$, and $Close_x$ is the closing price on the day before prediction date $x + 1$. The prediction is considered correct when either equation (3) or (4) is satisfied as follows:

$$direction_{pred} \geq 0 \text{ and } direction_{actual} \geq 0 \quad (3)$$

$$direction_{pred} < 0 \text{ and } direction_{actual} < 0 \quad (4)$$

This method, in contrast to the prediction error-based evaluation method used in previous research [5], focuses on the rise and fall of stock prices, resulting in an evaluation that is more closely aligned with actual market conditions.

5. Results

5.1. Accuracy of LSTM

Table 2 lists the highest accuracy values recorded during the learning process for each optimization algorithm using LSTM in the three combinations described in 4.2. No differences in accuracy rates were observed between the various optimization algorithms and the three combinations shown in 4.2. However, AdamW yielded a lower accuracy rate lower than the chance rate.

Table 2. Peak accuracy of LSTM

	a	b	c
SGD	62.0%	62.0%	62.0%
RMSprop	62.1%	62.1%	61.9%
Radam	62.1%	62.0%	62.1%
AdamW	40.4%	40.4%	40.4%
Adam	62.1%	57.1%	62.0%
Adadelta	62.1%	62.0%	62.0%

We output the loss function value; the training accuracy, which indicates the accuracy of the training data; and the test accuracy, which indicates the accuracy of the test data. In addition, we generated graphs with the X-axis representing the number of epochs and the Y-axis representing each output data. Figures 1-3 show the prediction trends for pattern a, which exhibited particularly high accuracy. First, we evaluated the loss fuction value. In SGD, the loss function values became scattered, and in AdamW, the learning stopped at a certain stage. In contrast, the other four methods showed a decrease in the loss values as learning progressed. However, the loss oscillations are larger than those observed in previous study [5].

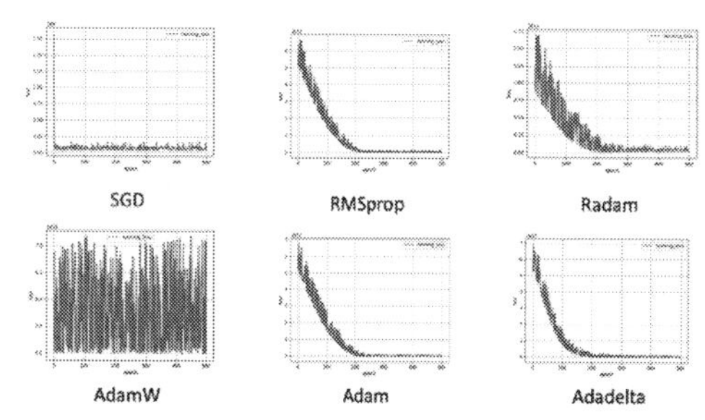

Figure 1. LSTM's loss function transition

Subsequently, we evaluated the training accuracy. Although there was a dispersion in the prediction accuracy as an overall trend, AdamW outperformed the previous study [5]. However, there was no improvement in accuracy because of learning progression, as observed in other algorithms. Similarly, SGD showed high accuracy but did not improve in accuracy owing learning progression.

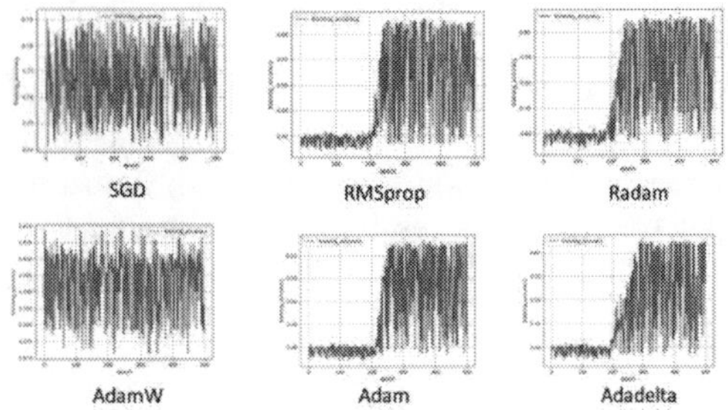

Figure 2. LSTM's training accuracy transition

Finally, the accuracy was evaluated. SGD exhibited a dispersed accuracy rate. In contrast to the training accuracy in a previous study [5], AdamW made correct predictions; however, the prediction accuracy did not improve beyond approximately 40%. Other algorithms showed a significant increase in prediction accuracy after exceeding 100 epochs, but the increase in prediction accuracy plateaued after exceeding 200 epochs.

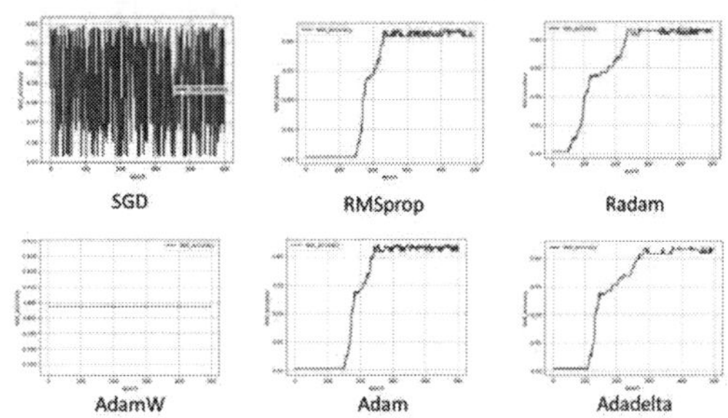

Figure 3. LSTM's accuracy transition

5.2. Accuracy of CNN

Table 3 lists the highest accuracy values recorded during the learning process for each optimization algorithm using the CNN, in the three combinations described in 4.2. All of the optimization algorithms showed accuracy rates that exceeded the chance rate. However, except for AdamW, the accuracy rates were generally lower than those achieved using LSTM. When comparing each optimization algorithm, only SGD showed a noticeable decrease in accuracy, whereas AdamW showed a significant increase. Furthermore, of the three combinations shown in 4.2, pattern a exhibited the highest accuracy, with accuracy decreasing when parameter tuning or mini-batch learning was performed.

Table 3. Peak accuracy of CNN

	a	b	c
SGD	51.3%	51.3%	51.3%
RMSprop	58.4%	58.4%	57.9%
Radam	57.9%	51.3%	51.4%
AdamW	56.8%	56.8%	56.8%
Adam	58.4%	58.4%	58.2%
Adadelta	58.5%	58.4%	58.4%

Figures 4-6 show the prediction trends for pattern a, which exhibited particularly high accuracy, using output data and graphs similar to those presented in 5.1. First, we evaluated the loss function value. The loss trends were similar when CNN was used as compared with LSTM. However, it can be observed from the graph that the learning progression speed is approximately twice as fast for CNN compared to LSTM.

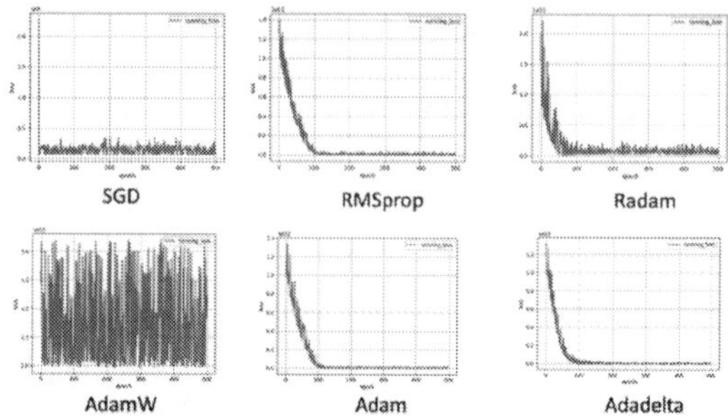

Figure 4. CNN's loss function transition

Subsequently, we evaluated training accuracy. Similar to the loss, we observed an increase in the learning progression speed for the training accuracy. However, in all other aspects, there were no changes compared to the results obtained using the LSTM.

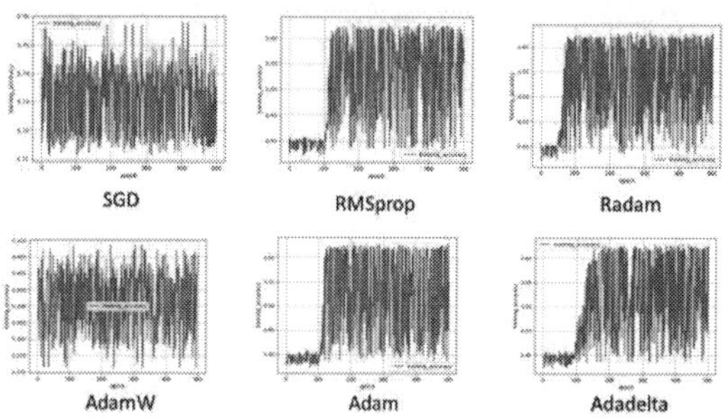

Figure 5. CNN's training accuracy transition

Finally, the accuracy rate is evaluated. For SGD and AdamW, the accuracy rate trends were similar to those observed when the LSTM was used. However, for the other algorithms, the trends were significantly different when comparing the LSTM and CNN. In the CNN, the initial accuracy was significantly improved compared to the LSTM, showing a slight improvement from the initial accuracy in the first half of learning. However, the prediction accuracy began to deteriorate significantly at approximately 100 epochs, with no further improvement in prediction accuracy observed.

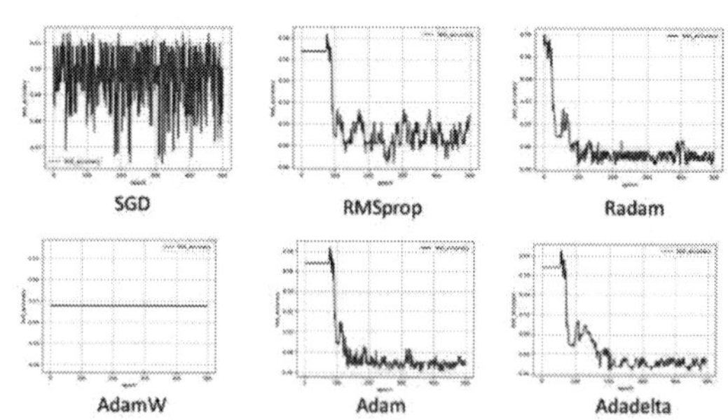

Figure 6. CNN's accuracy transition

6. Conclusion

We conducted experiments by changing the correct prediction criteria from those used in previous studies. Similar to previous studies [5], when SGD and AdamW were used as optimization algorithms, the loss function failed to escape the local minimum, resulting in learning failure. However, the other four algorithms succeeded in learning with the loss function values that escaped the local minima. By changing the method for calculating the accuracy rate, which measures prediction accuracy, we achieved a significantly higher prediction accuracy. This study's best result was 62.1% accuracy, surpassing the chance rate, using the LSTM model with the optimization functions RMSprop, Radam, Adam, and Adadelta, which differs from previous research [5]. Conversely, while CNN, which recorded higher accuracy than LSTM in previous research [5], contributed to improving the learning speed as in previous research [5], it showed a tendency for prediction accuracy to decrease compared to the four successful learning algorithms by approximately 4 and 11% for SGD. However, AdamW exhibited a 15% increase in prediction accuracy. Furthermore, regarding the accuracy rate transition, while LSTM showed an improvement in accuracy as learning progressed, CNN reached its peak accuracy in the early stages of learning and subsequently declined below the chance rate. Furthermore, parameter tuning and mini-batch learning, which were previously shown to improve learning speed, accuracy, and learning stability, had no effect in this study. Considering the possibility of overfitting caused by these trends, it is necessary to visualize the appropriate range for selecting tuning parameters using a new method based on learning and validation curves.

Considering the loss transitions in Figures 1 and 4, even for the algorithms that succeeded in learning, the prediction of random walks fluctuated significantly. In addition to tuning reviews, there is another improvement method that uses textual data. Considering the general behavior of investors who gather information from various media such as newspapers, television, and company press releases, it is possible to create a more accurate model by using not only numerical information, such as past stock prices, but also textual information. Specifically, in the Tokyo Stock Exchange Prime Market, which requires listing as a condition for the selection of the Nikkei Stock Average, the trading ratio of overseas investors reaches 60% [11], and data from the Japan Exchange Group show that approximately 80% of market funds originate in Europe [12]. Therefore, identifying the information sources used by European institutional investors, such as the Financial Times, Bloomberg, and Reuters, and analyzing textual data that match these sources are expected to improve prediction accuracy. We aimed to obtain distributed text representations by extending the SSCDV algorithm developed by Ueda et al. [6] to suit overseas news sources, using the Loughran-McDonald Master Dictionary [13], a financial sentiment dictionary. Furthermore, we extended the algorithm to include emotions other than negative and positive, which was not possible in Ueda et al.'s study [6]. Furthermore, we aim to improve the prediction accuracy by developing a prediction model that integrates the obtained distributed representations with the four daily prices of the Nikkei Stock Average, considers time lags, and trains the model with the generated new features.

7. References

[1] Financial Services Agency, the Working Group on Capital Market Regulations of the Financial System Council, Asset building and its management in the aging society, 2019

[2] Koutarou Ishige, Tomoaki Akiba, Proposal for the Forecasting Method of Nikkei Stock Average by Using Deep Learning, graduation thesis, Chiba institute of technology, 2022

[3] Takayuki Komatsu, Experimental study on Stock Price Prediction using Deep Learning, Bulletin of Hokkaido University of science, No.46, Research Report pp.27~34, 2018

[4] Kunihiro Miyazaki, Yutaka Matsuo, Stock Prediction Analysis using Deep Learning Technique, The 31st Annual Conference of the Japanese Society for Artificial Intelligence, 2017

[5] Ryota Nekomoto, Tomoaki Akiba, Improvement for the Forecasting Method of the Nikkei Stock Average using Deep Learning Adopting for Minibatch Learning, The Japa Industrial Management Association Annual Conference, 2024, spring

[6] Kentaro Ueda, keiichi Yasumoto, Proposal and evaluation of a Method to Obtain Distributed Representations of Documents Posted on Web Financial Discussion Boards for Financial Market Forecasting, master's Thesis, Graduate School of Science and Technology, Nara Institute of Science and Technology, March 17 2022

[7] Nikkei.Inc, https://indexes.nikkei.co.jp/nkave/archives/faq/faq_nikkei_stock_average_en.pdf, (Accessed : 2025 April 11)

[8] Yoshihiro Yanase, Tomohiro Odaka, Jousuke Kuroiwa, Haruhiko Shirai, Use of Big Data in Stock Price, Mem. Grad. Eng. Univ.Fukui, Vol.66, pp.59~66, March, 2018

[9] Kenta Takahashi, Shion Fujito, Takayuki Furukawa, Hiroyuki Goto, Stock price change prediction model using stock prices and news data, graduation theis, Housei university, 2022 (in Japanese)

[10] yfinance, https://pypi.org/project/yfinance/, (Accessed : 2025 March 13)

[11] JPX, Trading by Type of Investors Equities Annual, https://www.jpx.co.jp/english/markets/statistics-equities/investor-type/00-02.html, (Accessed :2025 March 27)

[12] JPX, Trading by Investor Category, https://www.jpx.co.jp/markets/statistics-equities/investor-type/04-01.html,(Accessed:2025 April 9)

[13] Loughran Timothy, McDonald Bill, Loughran-McDonald Master Dictionary (1993-2023), 2023, https://sraf.nd.edu/loughranmcdonald-master-dictionary/,(Accessed: 2025 March 27)

Optimizing Reliability and Quality in AI-Based Manufacturing Diagnostics: Machine Learning and Risk Assessment Perspectives

Kuo-Yi Lin[1], Ying-Hong Yang[1], Meng-Hua Li [2,3], Ming-Lang Tseng [4]

[1]Department of Industrial Engineering and Management, National Kaohsiung University of Science and Technology, No. 415, Jiangong Road, Sanmin District, Kaohsiung City, Taiwan, kylin@nkust.edu.tw

[2] Department of Industrial Management, National Formosa University, Taiwan

[3] Smart Machinery and Intelligent Manufacturing Research Center, National Formosa University, Taiwan

[4] Institute of innovation of circular economy, Asia University, Taiwan

Keywords: UNISON, Reliability Modeling, Risk Assessment, Quality Optimization, Intelligent Diagnostic System, Industry 4.0, Industry, Innovation and Infrastructure

Abstract

In response to the increasing demand for intelligent transformation in manufacturing, this study proposes a machine learning-driven diagnostic framework that integrates risk assessment models to enhance reliability, quality, and operational efficiency. Leveraging real enterprise diagnostic data, key AI-driven application scenarios—including process failure prediction, quality optimization, and cost reduction—are systematically constructed. To achieve a data-driven reliability assessment, this framework incorporates Failure Mode and Effects Analysis (FMEA) and predictive reliability modeling, enabling the identification of critical failure risks and guiding robust design decisions. Additionally, it utilizes structured and unstructured production process data to train AI models for anomaly detection, defect classification, and predictive optimization. The integration of machine learning algorithms with probabilistic risk modeling allows for continuous system adaptation and uncertainty quantification, improving overall diagnostic accuracy. Empirical validation demonstrates that the proposed approach enhances equipment reliability, reduces unplanned downtime, shortens production cycles, and improves decision quality. By providing a scalable and AI-enabled intelligent diagnostic consultation system, this research contributes to the advancement of reliability engineering and quality-driven decision-making in modern manufacturing.

1. Introduction

With the rapid development of Industry 4.0 technologies, the manufacturing industry is experiencing rapid digital transformation [1]. Manufacturers aim to enhance efficiency, reduce costs, and improve quality [2]. AI plays a key role in driving productivity and reliability. Traditional diagnostics lack predictive capability and cannot proactively manage risks, which should be measurable and objective [3]. AI frameworks can integrate diverse data to improve decision accuracy [4]. This study proposes a machine learning-based diagnostic system combined with risk models to enhance quality and reliability.

Despite AI's potential, many companies struggle to adopt intelligent diagnostics. Most tools lack integration with risk assessment, limiting their ability to prevent failures [5]. AI is often applied in isolated processes without system-wide impact. A unified framework combining machine learning, risk evaluation, and reliability modeling is needed [6]. This study fills the gap by supporting failure prediction and robust decision-making.

The proposed framework integrates analytics, FMEA, and the UNISON model to identify key risks and guide design decisions [7]. It aims to reduce failures, improve quality, shorten cycles, and enhance efficiency while supporting scalable deployment in manufacturing.

This study is divided into five chapters: background, literature review, methodology, empirical analysis, and conclusion.

2. Literature Review

2.1 Research Topic

In recent years, driven by Industry 4.0, intelligent diagnostic systems have become core technologies in manufacturing [8]. These systems integrate machine learning and analytics for real-time monitoring, anomaly detection, and decision support [9]. By analyzing sensor and process data, they identify risk patterns and suggest improvements. Compared to static, experience-based methods, AI provides higher accuracy and self-learning [10], enhancing stability and enabling industrial upgrades.

Recent research focuses on improving prediction accuracy and expanding applications. Deep learning is widely used for defect detection and quality prediction using complex data. Despite promising results, most studies lack integration with risk and reliability frameworks, limiting system-wide improvement [11].

This study develops a framework that combines machine learning, FMEA, and reliability modeling to improve decision-making and resilience. Unlike isolated applications, it aims for practical use in manufacturing and forms the foundation for applying the UNISON decision model.

2.2 Research Questions

Most existing AI diagnostic studies focus heavily on technical aspects, such as improving model accuracy or algorithm efficiency, but pay less attention to holistic and practical integration of AI in manufacturing environments. A truly effective system must integrate multiple elements—especially risk assessment and reliability-oriented decision support—to help users make the best possible decisions [12]. This study explores how diagnostics can assist not only in failure prediction but also in design and quality decision-making.

Although AI has demonstrated great potential in predictive maintenance and quality control, recent research is still mostly limited to specific scenarios, such as equipment anomaly detection or process monitoring. Most studies use cleaned datasets that lack real-world noise and complexity, and often ignore operational uncertainty—limiting AI's value as a core decision-making tool.

To address these issues, this study proposes an integrated diagnostic framework combining prediction, risk, and reliability analysis. By incorporating FMEA and UNISON, the system prioritizes risks and supports uncertainty handling to improve decision quality in design and manufacturing.

2.3 UNISON Framework

UNISON is a multi-criteria decision analysis framework designed to assist in making decisions under complex or uncertain conditions. It helps decision-makers integrate diverse viewpoints, clarify problems, evaluate options, and identify optimal solutions through structured analysis [13]. It is especially valuable in diagnostics, where AI lacks subjective judgment and collaboration mechanisms.

In recent years, UNISON has been applied to process design, product development, and quality improvement, proving its value in complex engineering tasks. However, few diagnostic systems use UNISON for risk assessment or decision support. As a result, many AI projects lack structured decision-making paths and fail to incorporate user insights, limiting practical outcomes.

This study incorporates UNISON into intelligent diagnostics as a human-machine decision platform. Combined with FMEA, the framework prioritizes risks, defines goals, and generates solutions. It addresses subjectivity gaps, improves decision transparency, and offers a clear structure for practical validation and future system implementation.

3. Research Methodology

This study constructs a decision-making process based on the UNISON framework, including six steps: problem understanding, niche identification, influence mapping, perception description, integrated judgment, and decision-making. A seventh step—decision evaluation and knowledge integration—is added, forming the extended UNISONE model [14].

Table 1. UNISON Decision Analysis Framework

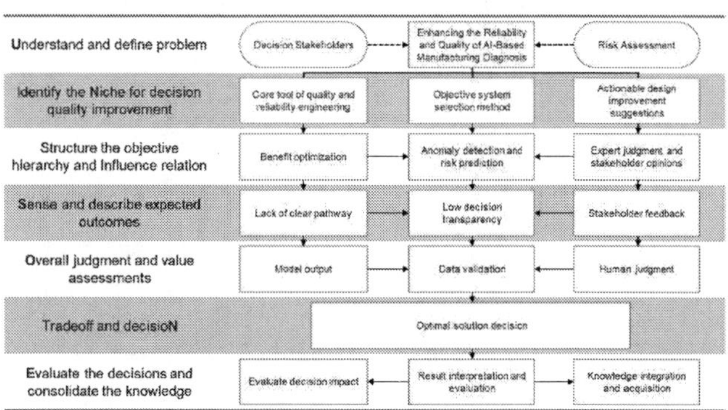

3.1 Understand and define problem

This study analyzes real issues faced by manufacturers using intelligent diagnostics. Most lack integrated decision systems. AI outputs risks but cannot link to actionable design feedback, so quality improvements still depend on human experience and remain inconsistent.

3.2 Identify the Niche for decision quality improvement

This research aims to build a structured, adaptive framework that improves diagnostic accuracy and translates AI predictions into design actions. Unlike existing approaches, it connects prediction, understanding, and decision-making into a complete and usable improvement process.

3.3 Structure the objective hierarchy and Influence relation

In this study, an influence relationship map is constructed to demonstrate how predictive results are quantified into risk levels through FMEA, and how such quantification feeds into decision-making processes for anomaly detection and risk prediction.

3.4 Sense and describe expected outcomes

Initial implementation revealed users are confident in AI predictions but unsure how they lead to actual improvements. There's a lack of clear linkage to actions. Users expect a system that balances technical accuracy with transparent, cross-department decision-making.

3.5 Overall judgment and value assessments

This phase integrates AI outputs with field experience through multi-criteria evaluation. It uses risk indicators and expert opinions to create decisions grounded in both objective data and practical judgment, improving decision relevance and acceptance.

3.6 Tradeoff and decisioN

All inputs are analyzed to compare improvement

options. Recommendations are produced and compiled into structured reports. These reports serve as clear guides for implementation and ensure decisions are traceable and aligned with system logic.

3.7 Evaluate the decisions and consolidate the knowledge

The last step evaluates decision outcomes and captures knowledge. Lessons learned are structured into a reusable knowledge base, supporting future risk cases and allowing continual improvement through organizational knowledge reuse.

4. Empirical Study

Based on the UNISONE framework, this study investigated various manufacturing companies. Company interviews and descriptions were collected, analyzed, and categorized to support the following empirical validation process.

4.1 Understand and define problem

Most companies had basic early warning functions but relied on experience for action. AI could predict risks, but results rarely translated into improvements. Lack of systematic prioritization and traceable decisions weakened diagnostic effectiveness.

4.2 Identify the Niche for decision quality improvement

Many AI applications focused on technical predictions but lacked structured risk handling. This study introduces an FMEA-based diagnostic process that links prediction, evaluation, decision, and action—aiming to enhance reliability and efficiency.

4.3 Structure the objective hierarchy and Influence relation

A risk analysis axis was built using AI diagnostics and FMEA to categorize failure modes and causes. This structure defines logical information flow across functions, promoting consistent understanding and cross-departmental decision alignment.

4.4 Sense and describe expected outcomes

Survey analysis showed past risk evaluations were mostly for audits, rarely guiding strategy. After adopting this framework, users clearly saw how risks linked to actions, enabling better discussions on priorities and resource allocation.

4.5 Overall judgment and value assessments

A multi-criteria tool was designed to evaluate options based on cost, expected impact, and feasibility. Some high-risk items were delayed due to cost, while high-value medium-risk actions were prioritized, showing structured evaluation value.

4.6 Tradeoff and decisioN

After comparing options, the team chose a mid-risk, mid-cost improvement plan with quick deployment as a demo. All logic from risk to decision was retained to ensure transparency, consistency, and traceability of actions.

4.7 Evaluate the decisions and consolidate the knowledge

All decisions and feedback were recorded in the system. In future similar risk cases, past decisions and suggestions can be reused, forming a knowledge base to support continuous learning and better future decisions.

5. Conclusion and Suggestions

This study proposes a smart diagnostic framework integrating FMEA and UNISONE to enhance process reliability and quality improvement. Empirical results confirm it bridges the gap between AI outputs and practical decision-making with traceable, structured, and transparent logic.

Future research can refine FMEA by integrating AI and statistical data to reduce bias. The method could be extended to more industries through multi-criteria analysis. Knowledge modules are also recommended to support system learning and long-term decision quality.

Acknowledgements

This research was funded by the Ministry of Science and Technology of Taiwan (MOST 113-2622- E-992-024-, 114-2622-8-150 -001 -TE3) and NKUST Industry-Academic Cooperation Project (20241129170433, 20241209141747, 20250420145108).

References

[1] Hofmann E., Rüsch M. "Industry 4.0 and the current status as well as future prospects on logistics"; *Computers in Industry* (Elsevier), Vol. 89, pp. 23–34, 2017.

[2] Duman M. C., Akdemir B. "A study to determine the effects of industry 4.0 technology components on organizational performance"; *Technological Forecasting and Social Change* (Elsevier), Vol. 167, Article ID 120615, 2021.

[3] Rane S. B., Potdar P. R., Rane S. "Development of project risk management framework based on industry 4.0 technologies"; *Benchmarking: An International Journal* (Emerald), Vol. 28, No. 5, pp. 1451–1481, 2021.

[4] Chen T., Sampath V., May M. C., Shan S., Jorg O. J., Aguilar Martín J. J., et al. "Machine learning in manufacturing towards industry 4.0"; *[Journal Name Missing]*, [Incomplete Reference].

[5] Wu Z., Liu W., Nie W. "Literature review and prospect of the development and application of FMEA in manufacturing industry"; *The International Journal of Advanced Manufacturing Technology* (Springer), Vol. 112, pp. 1409–1436, 2021.

[6] Soori M., Arezoo B., Dastres R. "Virtual manufacturing in industry 4.0: A review"; *Data Science and Management* (Elsevier), Vol. 7, No. 1, pp. 47–63, 2024.

[7] Hong T. Y., Chien C. F., Chen H. P. "UNISON framework of system dynamics-based technology acquisition decision for semiconductor manufacturing and an empirical study"; *Computers & Industrial Engineering* (Elsevier), Vol. 177, Article ID 109012, 2023.

[8] Jan Z., Ahamed F., Mayer W., Patel N., Grossmann G., Stumptner M., Kuusk A. "Artificial intelligence for industry 4.0: Systematic review of applications, challenges, and opportunities"; *Expert Systems with Applications* (Elsevier), Vol. 216, Article ID 119456, 2023.

[9] Angelopoulos A., Michailidis E. T., Nomikos N., Trakadas P., Hatziefremidis A., Voliotis S., Zahariadis T. "Tackling faults in the industry 4.0 era—a survey of machine-learning solutions and key aspects"; *Sensors* (MDPI), Vol. 20, No. 1, Article ID 109, 2019.

[10] Mohamed N., Al-Jaroodi J., Lazarova-Molnar S. "Leveraging the capabilities of industry 4.0 for improving energy efficiency in smart factories"; *IEEE Access* (IEEE), Vol. 7, pp. 18008–18020, 2019.

[11] Peres R. S., Jia X., Lee J., Sun K., Colombo A. W., Barata J. "Industrial artificial intelligence in industry 4.0—systematic review, challenges and outlook"; *IEEE Access* (IEEE), Vol. 8, pp. 220121–220139, 2020.

[12] Yang T., Yi X., Lu S., Johansson K. H., Chai T. "Intelligent manufacturing for the process industry driven by industrial artificial intelligence"; *Engineering* (Elsevier), Vol. 7, No. 9, pp. 1224–1230, 2021.

[13] Chien C. F., Kuo H. A., Lin Y. S. "Smart semiconductor manufacturing for pricing, demand planning, capacity portfolio and cost for sustainable supply chain management"; *International Journal of Logistics Research and Applications* (Taylor & Francis), Vol. 27, No. 1, pp. 193–216, 2024.

[14] Lin K. Y. "Circular supply chain for smart production in Industry 4.0"; *Computers & Industrial Engineering* (Elsevier), Vol. 198, Article ID 110682, 2024.

On the Consistency and Variety of Automated C Source Code Generation for Training Software Defect Detectors

OHARA Mamoru[1], SUGAWA Yuto[2], MURAKAMI Chisato[2]

[1]Tokyo Metropolitan Industrial Technology Research Institute, Japan, ohara.mamoru@iri-tokyo.jp
[2]Nihon University, Japan

Keywords: Machine learning, Software defect detection, Software defect injection, C language, LLVM IR, Sequence to sequence

Abstract - In recent years, machine learning (ML) techniques have become popular for detecting software bugs. However, a common challenge in ML-based bug detection arises from the unequal distribution of correct and incorrect training data. Specifically, there is a scarcity of incorrect data (containing bugs) compared to the abundance of correct data, negatively impacting ML model performance. To address this issue, researchers suggest artificially injecting bugs into correct samples. In addition to the equal distribution of samples, the diversity of training data significantly affects ML performance. Our work focuses on generating various incorrect samples stemming from a single root cause (bug). Specifically, we plan to inject bugs into LLVM IR codes and translate them into source codes written in high-level programming languages. For diversity, we use probabilistic language models in the translator. In this paper, we present an IR-to-C translator using seq2seq and explore the resulting consistency and diversity of generated samples by learning real-world software codes.

1. Introduction

Machine learning (ML) techniques have recently become popular for detecting software defects (bugs). These techniques learn features of bugs that appear in source codes [1], assembly codes [2], or binary codes [3]. More specifically, the state of the art of such techniques leverages deep-learning (DL) based natural language processing (NLP) models. While NLP techniques were developed originally for handling natural languages, since high-level programming languages resemble natural languages by design, NLP models can also learn features of programming languages.

A common challenge in ML-based bug detection arises from the unequal distribution of correct and incorrect training data. Specifically, there is a scarcity of incorrect data (containing bugs) compared to the abundance of correct data [4]. This is because everyone expects software to work correctly, and developers try to make it so. Although we can collect a huge number of correct samples from open-source repositories such as GitHub, it is rather difficult to collect enough incorrect buggy codes. This inequality of training data distribution leads to a negative impact on ML model performance.

In addition to the unequal distribution of training samples, the diversity of training data significantly affects ML model performance. This is also true for bug detection. In high-level programming languages, we can write codes in several ways to achieve the same software behavior. For example, in C language,

```
int i, x[] = {1, 2, 3, 4, 5};
for (i=0; i<6; ++i)
    x[i] *= 2;
```

and

```
int index=0, array[] = {1, 2, 3, 4, 5};
while (index<6)
    array[index++] *= 2;
```

behave in the exact same manner; both codes have bugs resulting from the single root cause (array indices overflow). To handle such diversity of codes in the same semantics by ML models, it is required that several similar expressions of codes are learned equally frequently by the models.

To address the former sample distribution issue, researchers suggest artificially injecting bugs into correct samples. For example, to learn security vulnerabilities, Pewny et al. focused on injecting security-critical bugs into source codes in software systems [5]; Zheng et al. developed an automatic vulnerability injection system [6]. Alternatively, without generating new samples, the imbalance in distribution can be mitigated through data sampling methods such as over-sampling and under-sampling [4]. Our approach to resolving this issue involves the injection of bugs.

In this paper, we focus on the latter diversity issue, with the eventual objective of developing a comprehensive ML-based bug detection technique that incorporates bug injection. We hypothesize that probabilistic language models, commonly employed in translation tasks within NLP, will introduce variability in code expressions. Liu et al. investigated the impact of ChatGPT's non-determinism on code generation and concluded that code generation may be affected by this non-determinism [7]. Based on the non-deterministic characteristics, we have designed our bug injection technique to include a translation process from intermediate representation of a program (IR) to a high-level language. Specifically in this paper we translate LLVM IR to C language.

LLVM IR is a kind IR used in LLVM, which is an infrastructure for developing compilers [8]. We can obtain LLVM IR by compiling source codes written in several high-level languages by using, e.g., Clang (for C/C++/Objective-C), Jlang (for Java), llgo (for Go). Recently, the text information contained in LLVM IR has also been attracting attention. Both text information and graph structure information can be obtained from LLVM IR. The advantages of LLVM IR are as follows:

- It contains hardware information that the source code does not.
- It is independent of the programming languages.
- Although it is composed of lower-level information than source code, it contains sufficient program semantics information.

In this study, we aim to develop a technique for automatically generating bug samples written in several different ways in a high-level programming language from a single root cause. The specific process of our proposed proposing method applying C language is shown in Fig. 1. We convert C source codes to LLVM IR codes and then reversely generate C codes by passing the converted LLVM IR codes through the IR-C translation generator. We can inject a bug into the LLVM IR codes. Then correct and buggy LLVM IR codes pass through the IR-C translation generator, therefore we get correct/buggy C codes. The correct C code must be equivalent to the original C source code (consistency in Fig. 1). In addition, to evaluate code diversity, it is also important that multiple C codes generated from a single LLVM IR code have the equivalent behavior, which can be confirmed by that they pass the same unit tests for the original code (variety in Fig. 1).

For our first step, we used the sequence-to-sequence (seq2seq) model to construct an IR-C translation generator using supervised learning in our previous work [9]. However in [9], the training dataset was collected from Codeflaws [10], which is based on educational programming competition, and we simplified the C source codes for ease of training; thus the codes included are relatively small and impractical ones (about 40 lines and 80 words in a C source file on average). In this paper, we again collect the dataset from real-world software projects published on GitHub. For example, C source files of curl [11] have about 440 lines and 1 450 words on average. This paper applies the model parameters, which showed the best performance in our former work [9], and trains the model with real-world software source codes. Then we observe the consistency and variety of the generated C source codes.

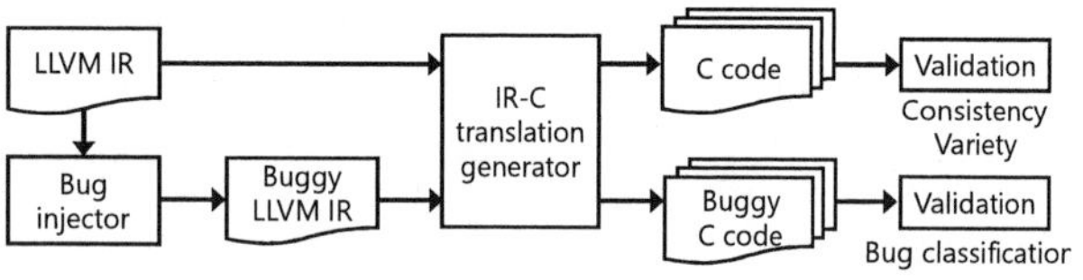

Figure 1. The eventual architecture of the proposed technique that injects bugs in LLVM IR codes

2. Related work

In this section, we introduce several works on ML-based bug detection and injection. For example, a method for automatic learning-based creating realistic bugs that consider semantics has been proposed [12]. Phan et al. proposed a method to automatically learn defect features from assembly instruction sequences for software defect prediction [2]. Recently, deep learning have been also utilized in several studies about software defect prediction. A survey was conducted on several recent studies [13]. In particular, many existing studies that use abstract syntax trees (ASTs) are introduced, and numerical vectors are constructed from the ASTs. In many research, machine learning has been used in for ASTs that transform source code rather than the source code itself.

In this study, we use LLVM IR as the input of the code generator. LLVM IR is composed of lower-level information than source code, however it contains sufficient program semantic information [14]. Recently, the text information contained in IR has also attracted attention. Yu et al. used both pieces of information to develop a code similarity analysis technique [15]. Fault analysis techniques that utilize the features of LLVM IR have been also proposed. Liang et al. developed a static program analysis tool using LLVM IR, independent of programming languages, to analyze programs written in multiple programming languages [16].

Meulen et al. confirmed no difference in software metrics between correct and incorrect programs in programs of 30-200 lines of C or C++ code [17]. This study focused on C programs with LOCs comparable to one in the research of Meulen et al. as the first step of developing an IR to C translation generator. Moreover, the characteristics of the translation that resulted in this study should apply to C source codes after bug injection because there is no difference in software metrics between correct and incorrect programs.

In our former work, we used the seq2seq model for translating LLVM IR codes to C codes [9]. From the perspective of the code variation, intuitively, we should collect datasets from several human-written codes rather than artificial codes. Therefore, we used the dataset obtained from Codeflaws, which is designed as a benchmark of programming competitions. Moreover, we simplified the C source codes to ease training for our first step, therefore the programs included in our dataset were small and naïve. In this paper we collect datasets from some real-world software projects provided in GitHub, such as curl [11], and examine again the effectiveness of our approach practically.

3. LLVM IR-to-C translation model

3.1. Sequence-to-sequence model

The seq2seq model [18] converts a sequence of data (input data) to another sequence of data (target data). The model consists of two components: an encoder and a decoder. The encoder converts the input data sequence to a hidden vector. Then the decoder again converts the encoded hidden vector into another expression. In our study, an LLVM IR sequence is input to the encoder, and corresponding C source codes are generated by the decoder.

In this study, we use only the hidden vectors from the forward RNN. LLVM IR codes are usually too long to represent the code with only one hidden vector practically. To provide more information to the decoder, we adopted a seq2seq model with attention [19] as the generator model.

In addition, we apply the teacher forcing method in decoder training. In contrast to the normal RNN training process, in which the output of the encoder at the previous time step is input to the decoder and it is usually difficult to train a model only with long texts and extensive vocabulary training, in the teacher forcing, the decoder inputs accept the target sequence (ground truth) with a certain probability in the training process. The teacher forcing enables efficient learning of syntactic relationships while preventing error accumulation, especially in the early stage of the training. Fig. 2 illustrates the model architecture we used in this study.

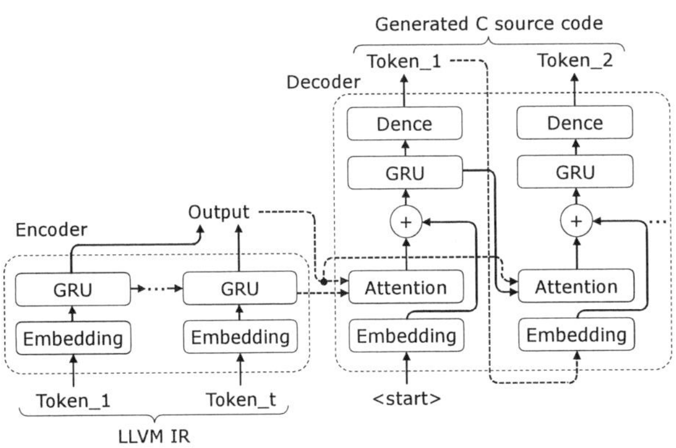

Figure 2. Our model architecture

3.2. Dataset

We used a subset of defects4C [20], a defect dataset of practical software. Defects4C includes several C/C++ projects. We adopt only C projects, such as curl [11] and AWS C Common (aws-c-common) [21].

For obtaining LLVM IR by Clang (by providing '-emit-llvm' option to Clang), the projects were built with the procedures given by their documentation. In these build procedures, C source files (*.c) are translated into *.i files by C preprocessor, by which preprocessor commands such as #include and #define are expanded.

The bodies of functions were extracted from the preprocessed C source codes (*.i) and then the bodies were rewritten so that identifiers, including variable names, user-defined function names, function arguments, struct members, and enum constants, were renamed meaningless index-based ones like b_1, b_2, ... for block scope variables, g_1, g_2, ... for global variables, f_1, f_2, ... for user-defined functions, and _1, _2, ... for function arguments. For instance, a C function shown in Fig. 3(a) was translated into Fig. 3(b). In this example, a function call to "free" was replaced with a pointer variable to function, "Curl_cfree", by C preprocessor macro expansion and then identifiers (the function argument "info", the field name "buf" in "info", and "Curl_cfree") were renamed to index-based names.

In this paper, we train the translation model by input pairs of the preprocessed C functions and the corresponding IR sequences. The number of tokens in functions included in the datasets distributed as shown in Fig. 4. We can observe that LLVM IR codes are longer than C source codes. We classified the C & IR pairs by the token lengths in IR codes. The number of IR codes having more than 50 and fewer than 100 tokens is the greatest in this dataset. From curl and aws-c-common, we collected datasets including IR functions of 1-50, 51-100, and 101-200 tokens, respectively, and the corresponding preprocessed C functions.

(a) original C codes	(b) dataset
(curl_memory.h) #define free(ptr) Curl_cfree(ptr)	

(fileinfo.h)
struct fileinfo {
  struct curl_fileinfo info;
  struct Curl_llist_node list;
  struct dynbuf buf;
};	

(fileinfo.c)
#include "fileinfo.h"
 	
extern curl_free_callback
  Curl_cfree;
 	
void Curl_fileinfo_cleanup(
  struct fileinfo *finfo)
{
  if(!finfo)
    return;
 	
  Curl_dyn_free(&finfo->buf);
  free(finfo);
}
	if (!_1) {
	  return;
	};
	f_2882(&_1->m_3);
	g_352(_1);

Figure 3. Example of preprocessed C function code (in curl/lib/fileinfo.c)

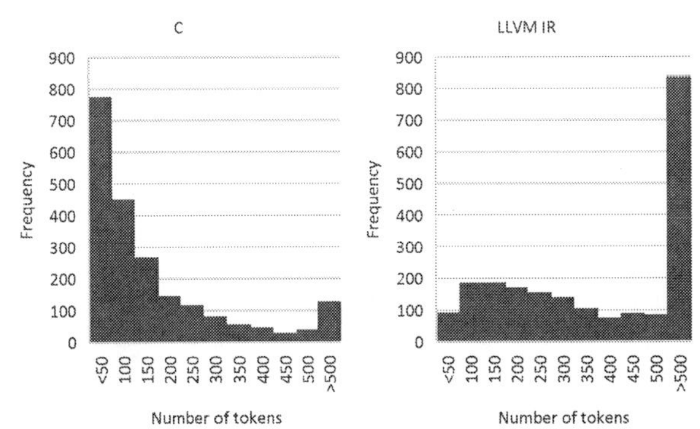

Figure 4. Distribution of token lengths in curl

3.3. Configuration

We trained the seq2seq model using LLVM IR code as the input data and C source code as the target data. The parameters were set as follows: epochs = 1 000 and batch size = 16. We used the cross-entropy loss as the loss function and the Adam optimizer. We saved the model and recorded the loss every 100 epochs. The model was built using GRU. We set the GRU units to 1 024 and the embedding size to 64.

In our previous work [9], we observed that: 1) pre-padding is better for the input sequences (LLVM IR) while post-padding is better for target sequences (C); 2) teacher forcing effectively works for the translation task. Therefore, in this paper, we used these settings for training models.

3.4. Evaluation

In this paper, we evaluate the consistency of generated codes with the ground truth by the Gestalt pattern matching algorithm, which measures the similarity of two strings. The Gestalt similarity is 1 when the two strings are the same and the lower value when the strings are the more different.

To evaluate the variety of the generated codes, we should consider not only lexical points but also the behaviors of the codes; that is, for our eventual purpose, we need to obtain several versions of codes having the same buggy behavior. An approach for examining the code's behavior is unit testing. However, in this paper, we have not yet validated the behavioral (in)correctness of the generated codes because, unlike educational datasets like Codeflaws, real-world software projects do not always provide unit test codes for every function. Collecting real-world unit tests or constructing another approach for behavioral evaluation are some of our future challenges.

4. Results

4.1. Consistency

We selected the model that provided the minimum loss for each dataset. Table 1 shows the similarity measured by Gestalt pattern matching between the ground truth and the source codes generated by the minimum-loss model. Table 2 presents some examples of the similarity, the ground truth, and the predicted codes, which are generated by the model trained with the curl's 1-50 dataset. We observed the trend in failing predictions such as:

1) The names of user defined functions, which are renamed like f_1, are difficult to predict because their definitions cannot be seen from function scopes; Also, predicting the names of global variables, struct members, and enum fields are difficult.

2) Longer IR codes are more difficult to learn.

Intuitively speaking, generated codes with a similarity of 0.6 or higher often have correct syntax but a couple of name errors for the function call or an incorrect index of struct field members. From this observation and Table 1, our models are expected to be useful for datasets with less than 100 tokens by using additional techniques supporting the translation of names.

Table 1. Mean Gestalt similarity

Dataset	*Range of IR token number*		
	1-50	***51-100***	***101-200***
curl	0.672	0.640	0.477
aws-c-common	0.722	0.635	0.530

Table 2. Examples of similarity and true/generated codes

Simi-larity	True code	Generated code
1.0	memset(_1, 0, sizeof(*_1));	memset(_1, 0, sizeof(*_1));
0.96	return _1->m_2;	return _1->m_16;
0.67	return f_3227(((void*)0), _1);	return f_3227(_1, 328);
0.23	g_89 = g_89;	(void)_1;

In addition, we trained a model using both curl and aws-c-common having 1-50 tokens as a preliminary study for cross-project translation. Contrary to expectations, the generated codes from the model showed a Gestalt similarity of 0.764 on average, which was better than those consisting of the single projects. Although it is promising for our model to learn the joint datasets consisting of multiple projects, learning the joint datasets takes a longer time, therefore, a comprehensive survey of the joint dataset will be addressed in our future work.

4.2. Variety

By adopting predicted codes other than one with the maximum likelihood, we obtained several versions of C source codes based on a single LLVM IR code. We repeatedly (100 times) input the IR codes to the best model for the dataset of curl's 1-50 tokens, and obtained 26 different variants of a C function from a single LLVM IR at most (for curl_multi_init()); while for a couple of LLVM IR sequences, we always obtained the same output, we had around 10 variants for a single IR sequence on average.

We tried to compile these variants of C source codes in the same manner as the original ones. Only a few variants succeeded in compiling. The reasons for failures were, e.g., unclosed parentheses, reference to undefined global variables, user-defined functions, and struct fields. The mistranslations of global variables and functions, which are not seen from the function scope, would be improved by learning not functions but files. Learning files, which are longer than functions, require models with longer memories, e.g., transformer-based ones. Such models are also expected to improve syntactic mistranslations.

5. Concluding remarks

In this paper, we extend the dataset to include real-world software projects for training our ML-based LLVM IR-to-C translator. Although the source codes consisting of these projects have much more complex functions than those used in our previous work, our converter showed good consistency performance, especially for relatively short functions.

Validating the codes generated by the translator will be one of our future works. In our previous work, we can validate the generated codes by running unit tests, however, in real-world software, unit tests are not always prepared for every function. Moreover, it can be expected to improve the translator's performance by feeding back the validation results to the training process.

Moreover, cross-project bug prediction is widely regarded as significantly more challenging than single-project prediction. Despite observing countertrends in this study, cross-project prediction is desirable to leverage the programming language independence of LLVM IR. This is another challenge for us in the future.

6. Acknowledgement

This work was partially supported by JSPS KAKENHI Grant Number JP23K11355.

7. References

[1] Z. Bilgin, M. A. Ersoy, E. U. Soykan, E. Tomur, P. Comak, and L. Karacay, "Vulnerability Prediction from Source Code Using Machine Learning," IEEE Access, Vol. 8, pp. 150672–150684, 2020.

[2] A. V. Phan and M. L. Nguyen, "Convolutional Neural Networks on Assembly Code for Predicting Software Defects," Proc. 2017 21st Asia Pacific Symp. Intell. and Evolutionary Syst. (IES), pp. 37–42, Dec. 2017.

[3] S. Arakelyan, S. Arasteh, C. Hauser, E. Kline, and A. Galstyan, "Bin2vec: Learning Representations of Binary Executable Programs for Security Tasks," Cybersecurity, Vol. 4, No. 1, Dec. 2021.

[4] Z. Li, X. Zhang, J. Guo, and Y. Shang, "Class Imbalance Datadata-Generation for Software Defect Prediction," Proc. 2019 26th Asia-Pacific Softw. Eng. Conf. (APSEC), pp. 276–283, Dec. 2019.

[5] J. Pewny and T. Holz, "EvilCoder: Automated Bug Insertion," Proc. 32nd Annu. Conf. Comput. Secur. Appl., pp. 214–225, Dec. 2016.

[6] T. Zheng, Z. Tong, P. Yi, and Y. Wu, "Automated Generation of Bug Samples Based on Source Code Analysis," Proc. 2022 29th Asia-Pacific Softw. Eng. Conf. (APSEC), pp. 51–60, Dec. 2022.

[7] Z. Liu, Y. Tang, X. Luo, Y. Zhou and L. F. Zhang, "No Need to Lift a Finger Anymore? Assessing the Quality of Code Generation by ChatGPT," IEEE Trans. Softw. Eng., Vol. 50, No. 6, pp. 1548-1584, June 2024.

[8] C. Lattner and V. Adve, "LLVM: A Compilation Framework for Lifelong Program Analysis & Transformation," Proc. Int. Symp. Code Gener. Optim. 2004 (CGO 2004), pp. 75–86, 2004.

[9] Y. Sugawa, C. Murakami, and M. Ohara, "C Source Code Generation from IR towards Making Bug Samples to Fluctuate for Machine Learning," Proc. 2024, Oct. 2024.

[10] S. H. Tan, J. Yi, Yulis, S. Mechtaev, and A. Roychoudhury, "Codeflaws: A Programming Competition Benchmark for Evaluating Automated Program Repair Tools," Proc. 2017 IEEE/ACM 39th Int. Conf. Softw. Eng. Companion (ICSE-C), pp. 180–182, May 2017.

[11] D. Stenberg, everything curl, available at https://everything.curl.dev/.

[12] J. Patra and M. Pradel, "Semantic Bug Seeding: A Learning-Based Approach for Creating Realistic Bugs," Proc. 9th ACM Joint Meeting on Eur. Softw. Eng. Conf. and Symp. Found. Softw. Eng., pp. 906–918, Aug. 2021.

[13] G. Giray, K. E. Bennin, Ö. Köksal, Ö. Babur, and B. Tekinerdogan, "On the Use of Deep Learning in Software Defect Prediction," J. Syst. Softw., Vol. 195, Jan. 2023.

[14] E. Liu, S. Xu, and D. Lie, "FLUX: Finding Bugs ith LLVM IR Based Unit Test Crossovers," Proc. 2023 38th IEEE/ACM Int. Conf. Automated Softw. Eng. (ASE), pp. 1061–1072

[15] Z. Yu, W. Zhang, and T. Xu, "Leveraging IR Based Sequence and Graph Features for Source-Binary Code Alignment," Proc. 2024 4th Int. Conf. Neural Netw., Inf. Commun. (NNICE), pp. 175–180, Jan. 2024.

[16] H. Liang, L. Wang, D. Wu, and J. Xu, "MLSA: A Static Bugs Analysis Tool Based on LLVM IR," Proc. 2016 17th IEEE/ACIS Int. Conf. Softw. Eng., Artif. Intell., Netw. and Parallel/Distrib. Comput. (SNPD), pp. 407–412, May 2016.

[17] M. A. Revilla, "Correlations between Internal Software Metrics and Software Dependability in a Large Population of Small C/C++ Programs," Proc. 18th IEEE Int. Symp. Softw. Rel. (ISSRE '07), pp. 203–208, Nov. 2007.

[18] I. Sutskever, O. Vinyals, and Q. V. Le, "Sequence to Sequence Learning with Neural Networks," arXiv:1409.3215, Dec. 2014.

[19] D. Bahdanau, K. Cho, and Y. Bengio, "Neural Machine Translation by Jointly Learning to Align and Translate," arXiv:1409.0473, May 2016.

[20] Defects4C Benchmarking C/C++ Faults to Assess LLM-Based Program Repairs, available at https://sites.google.com/view/anonymous-defects4c/.

[21] AWS C Common, available at https://github.com/awslabs/aws-c-common.

Assessing multistate production system ability via network reliability considering product classification and rework action

Hsuan-Yu CHEN[1*], Yi-Kuei LIN[2]

[1*] Department of Industrial Engineering and Management, National Yang Ming Chiao Tung University Hsinchu, 300, Taiwan, shanec5229@gmail.com

[2] Department of Industrial Engineering and Management, National Yang Ming Chiao Tung University Hsinchu, 300, Taiwan, yklin@nycu.edu.tw

Keywords: network reliability, product classification, rework, order acceptance

Abstract - Product classification has become a strategic approach for manufacturers to increase orders and reduce waste by allocating products of varying quality, generally called coproducts, to orders with varying customer requirements. As a manufacturer receives more orders, it is necessary to evaluate the capability and uncertainty of a production system in fulfilling all received orders; the system is modeled as a multi-state production network considering rework action (MPNR) that incorporates the possible capacities of each manufacturing process and their associated probabilities. An algorithm is developed to assess the probability of meeting demand for different product quality levels under rework actions. This probability, defined as network reliability, serves as a performance metric for manufacturers in order acceptance decision-making. A jumper cable manufacturing system with a rework process is presented as a case study to demonstrate the applicability of the proposed algorithm.

1. Introduction

As global environmental and social challenges intensify, sustainability has become a key priority for governments and businesses. To address issues such as climate change and resource depletion, an increasing number of policies and business strategies emphasize environmental protection, social responsibility, and economic sustainability. In response, companies are focusing on optimizing resource utilization, such as classifying resources according to different acceptable standards [1, 2]and converting defects into conforming items through rework [3, 4]. As a result, manufacturers are able to accept more orders. Orders from different customers often come with varying quality requirements and delivery schedules. Therefore, the ability to complete these orders within the specified time while minimizing resource waste is crucial for making informed order acceptance decisions.

A product may have multiple quality characteristics, but only a few of them directly affect its core function. These characteristics are referred to as key quality characteristics (KQCs) and are of particular concern to customers. Due to the tradeoff between cost and quality, customers may place orders for the same product with different quality requirements for the KQC, with the differences reflected in the tolerances for the KQC. Additionally, certain industries have recognized classification standards or standards set by national authorities [5, 6]. Based on these tolerances or standards, the produced products can be classified into several classes and defects. As a result, lower-quality products can be sold to customers with less strict quality requirements for the KQC.

Moreover, not all products categorized as defective need to be scrapped; some can be reworked to meet the required specifications. Instead of starting with raw material at the first workstation, rework actions involve returning defective products to the workstation where the KQC is formulated. Rework actions have been considered in numerous studies [2, 7, 8] due to their advantages in reducing material waste and costs. For example, Gupta and Khanna [2] investigated the profit optimization problem involving green technology, carbon control policies, and rework strategies. They found that rework actions significantly reduce carbon emissions and enhance profits. By incorporating rework and product classification into manufacturing system assessments, manufacturers can improve production flexibility, optimize resource allocation, and better align with sustainability goals.

A manufacturing system typically consists of multiple predefined processes that transform raw materials into products with desired quality characteristics. Each process is performed by a machine or a group of identical machines. However, machines are not always operational, as downtime may occur due to maintenance, malfunctions, or interruptions in the supply of electricity. To model the machine uncertainty, the capacity of each process can be represented as a multi-state variable, with the probability of each capacity state estimated using a probability distribution or historical data [9-12]. Network analysis is an effective tool for analyzing a complex system by modeling it as a network topology with nodes and arcs for straightforward visualization [13, 14]. Many studies [9, 12, 15-17] have employed network-based models to analyze the flows of work-in-progress (WIP) with rework actions of each production process and used network reliability as a key performance index to evaluate the performance of the production system. Network reliability is defined as the probability that the production system can successfully output the required amount of conforming products. Additionally, the concept of minimal path (MP) and lower capacity vector (LCV) satisfying demand [10, 12-14, 18]has been widely adopted to analyze the flow of improve the efficiency of network reliability calculations. This study utilizes d-LCV to compute network reliability.

In the context of product classification, rework actions can convert defective products into different classes or remain as defects, affecting the workload for the production process and the need for additional raw materials. The objective of this research is to evaluate the feasibility of meeting the requirements for products of all classes while considering the rework actions. Network reliability, defined as the probability that the manufacturing system can meet the demands of all classes, is utilized as a performance index to assess such feasibility. The production system is modeled as a multistate production network considering rework action (MPNR). By using the calculated network reliability, managers can make more informed decisions on order acceptance and production planning.

2. Model formulation

In this section, the multistate network model and assumption are first formulated. Then, the method of product classification is introduced. Then, the required amount of raw material and corresponding workload is determined; the approach for generating the LCV that meets the demands of all classes and evaluating network reliability is introduced. Finally, an algorithm is proposed.

2.1. Multistate production network and assumptions

Activity on node (AON) diagram is utilized to formulate the multi-state production network with rework actions (MPNR). Let **(V, A, M)** be an MPNR, $\mathbf{V} = \{v_i \mid i = 1, 2, \ldots, n\}$ represents the set of vertices representing the production processes, **A** represents other facilities including buffers between workstations are denoted by arcs workstation), $\mathbf{M} = \{m_i \mid i = 1, 2, \ldots, n\}$ is the set of the maximal capacity of v_i. To compute the network reliability, MPNR abides by the assumptions:

I. Multiple quality requirements of a specific KQC that have a substantial impact on the main function of the product are used for product classification.
II. The rework process for the KQC is conducted on the production process that forms the KQC. Each product can only be reworked one time. If the products are still defective after rework, they are scrapped.
III. The specification of the KQC is expressed as a random variable X that follows a normal distribution, $X \sim N(\hat{\mu}_x, \hat{\sigma}_x)$
IV. All production processes are statistically independent in terms of the capacity they provide.

The vector operation abides by the following rules:

- $B \le C$ $(b_1, b_2, \ldots, b_n) \le (c_1, c_2, \ldots, c_n)$: $b_i \le c_i$ for each $i = 1, 2, \ldots, n$.
- $B < C$ $(b_1, b_2, \ldots, b_n) < (c_1, c_2, \ldots, c_n)$: $B \le C$ and $b_i < c_i$ for at least one i.

2.2. Product classification based on a KQC

Larger-the-better (LTB), nominal-the-better (NTB), and smaller-the-better (STB) are three types for KQC whose target values are zero, specified target value, and infinity, respectively. The acceptable quality is defined by the specification limits including a lower specification limit (LSL) and upper specification limit (USL). In general, the KQC with closer specification to the target value is considered as product with better quality. As different orders may specify distinct specification limits, products are therefore categorized into several classes based on these specification intervals. The LSL and USL that define class α are denoted as L_α and U_α where $\alpha = 1, 2, \ldots, \beta$. A classification example that categorizes products into β classes for each type of KQC is demonstrated in Figure 1. Any product with a specification of the specific KQC that falls outside the widest specification limits of L_β and U_β is considered a defective product that may be reworked. The proportion for class α products can be calculated as

$$\lambda_1 = \int_{L_1}^{U_1} \frac{1}{\sqrt{2\pi} \cdot \hat{\sigma}_x} e^{-\frac{(X-\hat{\mu}_x)}{2\hat{\sigma}_x}} dx \tag{1}$$

$$\lambda_\alpha = \int_{L_\alpha}^{U_\alpha} \frac{1}{\sqrt{2\pi} \cdot \hat{\sigma}_x} e^{-\frac{(X-\hat{\mu}_x)}{2\hat{\sigma}_x}} dx - \lambda_{\alpha-1},\ \alpha = 2, \ldots, \beta. \tag{2}$$

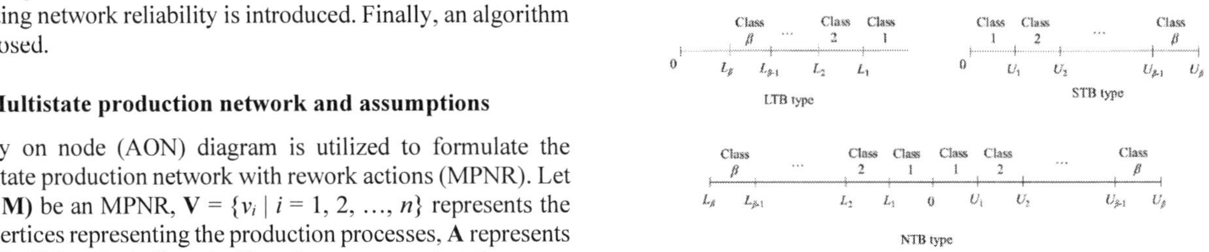

Figure 1. Illustration of product classification.

2.3. Determination of required raw material and workloads at workstations

The demand of class α is expressed as d_α, $\alpha = 1, 2, \ldots, \beta$. Generally, the amount of output O_α of each class α can be calculated as the amount E of raw material multiplied by the total yield rate and the proportion of class α. As the rework action is implemented, the output of grade α output can be divided into the amount O_α^{WR} of output without rework, and the amount O_α^{R} of output by rework. The output of each class without rework can be calculated as

$$O_\alpha^{WR} = E \times \prod_{i=1}^{n} p_j \times \lambda_\alpha,\ \alpha = 1, 2, \ldots, \beta. \tag{3}$$

Defective products can only be detected at θth production process, then sent back to ζth production process to rework the output of the product without rework action is represented as

$$O_\alpha^{R} = E \times \prod_{j=1}^{\theta-1} p_j \cdot (1 - p_\theta) \cdot \prod_{j=\theta-\zeta}^{n} p_j \times \lambda_\alpha,\ \alpha = 1, 2, \ldots, \beta. \tag{4}$$

The total amount O_α of class α products produced by the production system can be calculated as

$$O_\alpha = O_\alpha^{WR} + O_\alpha^{R}. \tag{5}$$

O_α should be no less than the demand d_α of class α to meet the demand d_α of class α, namely $O_\alpha \ge d_\alpha$. The amount E_α of input that meets the demand d_α of class α can be calculated as

$$E_{\alpha} = d_{\alpha} \Big/ \left(\prod_{i=1}^{n} p_j + \prod_{j=1}^{\theta-1} p_j \cdot (1-p_{\theta}) \cdot \prod_{j=\theta-\zeta}^{n} p_j \right) \times \lambda_{\alpha} . \quad (6)$$

The amount E_α of raw material input may only satisfy the demand of class α product but not guarantee the fulfillment of demands for other classes. The required amount E of raw material input to satisfy the demands of all classes can be obtained via

$$E = \max\left(E_1, E_2, \ldots, E_\beta\right) \quad (7)$$

The workload of each production process with the determined amount E of raw material can be obtained as

$$w_i = E \times \prod_{i=1}^{\zeta-1} p_i \text{, where } i = 2, \ldots, \zeta\text{-}1. \quad (8)$$

$$w_{\zeta} = E \times \prod_{i=1}^{\eta-1} p_i + E \times \prod_{i=1}^{\theta\text{-}1} p_j \cdot (1-p_{\theta}). \quad (9)$$

$$w_{\eta} = E \times \prod_{i=1}^{\eta-1} p_i + E \times \prod_{i=1}^{\theta\text{-}1} p_j \cdot (1-p_{\theta}) \cdot \prod_{j=\zeta}^{\eta\text{-}1} p_j \text{ where } \eta = \zeta+1, \ldots, n$$

(10)

The workload of the workstations without any rework WIPs can be calculated via equation (8).The workload caused by the rework WIP at the workstation which is responsible for rework action is calculated via Equation (9); the workload caused by rework WIP of subsequent workstation can be obtained via equation (10). The an example of network diagram with rework action is illustrated in Figure 2.

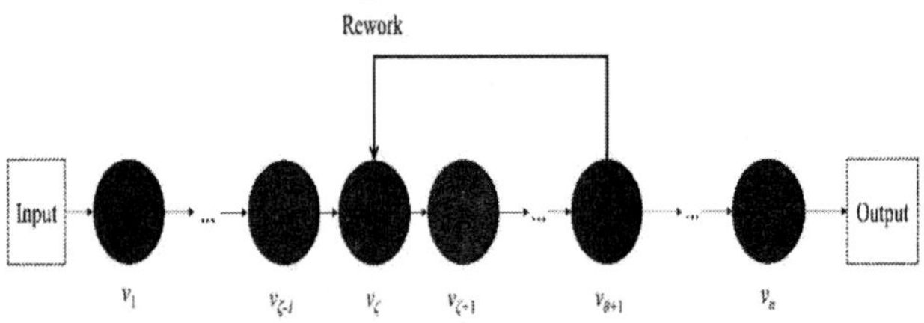

Figure 2. An example of a manufacturing network diagram with a rework action.

All workloads cannot exceed the maximal capacity that each production process can provide, namely

$$w_i \leq m_i,\ i = 1, 2, \ldots, n. \quad (11)$$

If any workload w_i is greater than its maximal capacity m_i, it is impossible for the production system to output sufficient products to meet all demands.

2.4. Network reliability evaluation

In this research, network reliability is defined as the success probability that an MPNR can produce enough products to satisfy the demands of all classes, denoted as R_D. $Q_\alpha(C, E)$ is defined as the output of class α products under capacity vector $C = (c_1, c_2, \ldots, c_n)$ with raw material input equals E. Let Ξ be a set consisting of all capacity vectors satisfying demands of all classes, namely $\Xi = \{C \mid Q_\alpha(C', E) \geq d_\alpha, \alpha = 1, 2, \ldots, \beta\}$. An intuitive approach to compute network reliability is to list all capacity vectors. Then, calculate the probability that all production processes can provide the capacity specified by the capacity vectors in Ξ; finally, sum all the calculated probabilities. Nevertheless, finding LCV that satisfies the demand of all classes, denoted as D-LCV, is a more efficient approach to compute network reliability instead. Let $C' = (c'_1, c'_2, \ldots, c'_3)$ be a D-LCV in Ξ if and only if (*i*) $Q_\alpha(C', E) \geq d_\alpha$ and (*ii*) $Q_\alpha(B, E) < d_\alpha$ for at least one α and for any capacity vector B such that $B < C'$. Then, the network reliability can be determined with the D-LCV C' as follows:

$$\begin{aligned} R_{d_1, d_2, \ldots, d_\beta} &= Pr\{C \mid C \geq C'\} \\ &= Pr\{C \mid (c_1, c_2, \ldots, c_n) \geq (c'_1, c'_2, \ldots, c'_n)\} \\ &= \Pr\{c_1 \geq c'_1\} \times \Pr\{c_2 \geq c'_2\} \times \ldots \times \Pr\{c_n \geq c'_n\}. \end{aligned}$$

The capacity of a machine in each production process is denoted as k_i, $i = 1, 2, \ldots, n$. The LCV can be obtained by determining the minimal amount of machines at the ith production process required to be in operation providing sufficient capacity to handle the workload of w_i, such that $c'_i = l_i k_i \geq w_i > (l_i\text{-}1)\, k_i$. Then, the LCV, $C' = (c'_1, c'_2, \ldots, c'_3)$, is be obtained.

2.5. Proposed Algorithm

The steps for computing network reliability is demonstrated as below:

Algorithm: network reliability evaluation considering rework action

INPUT: (V, A, M), $d_1, d_2, \ldots, d_\beta$, $\hat{\mu}_x = 0.3$, $\hat{\sigma}_x = 0.07$.

Step 1. Calculate the proportion of each class via

$$\lambda_1 = \int_{L_1}^{U_1} \frac{1}{\sqrt{2\pi} \cdot \hat{\sigma}_x} e^{-\frac{(X-\hat{\mu}_x)}{2\hat{\sigma}_x}} dx \quad (12)$$

$$\lambda_\alpha = \int_{L_\alpha}^{U_\alpha} \frac{1}{\sqrt{2\pi} \cdot \hat{\sigma}_x} e^{-\frac{(X-\hat{\mu}_x)}{2\hat{\sigma}_x}} dx - \lambda_{\alpha-1},\ \alpha = 2, \ldots, \beta. \quad (13)$$

Step 2. Determine the required amount E to meet demands of all classes via:

$$E_{\alpha} = d_{\alpha} \Big/ \left(\prod_{i=1}^{n} p_j + \prod_{j=1}^{\theta-1} p_j \cdot (1-p_{\theta}) \cdot \prod_{j=\theta-\zeta}^{n} p_j \right) \times \lambda_{\alpha} . \quad (14)$$

$$E = \max\left(E_1, E_2, \ldots, E_\beta\right) \quad (15)$$

Step 3. Calculate the workload of each workstation via

$$w_i = E \times \prod_{i=1}^{\zeta-1} p_i \text{, where } i = 2, \ldots, \zeta\text{-}1. \quad (16)$$

$$w_{\zeta} = E \times \prod_{i=1}^{\eta-1} p_i + E \times \prod_{i=1}^{\theta\text{-}1} p_j \cdot (1-p_{\theta}). \quad (17)$$

$$w_{\eta} = E \times \prod_{i=1}^{\eta-1} p_i + E \times \prod_{i=1}^{\theta\text{-}1} p_j \cdot (1-p_{\theta}) \cdot \prod_{j=\zeta}^{\eta\text{-}1} p_j \text{ where } \eta = \zeta+1, \ldots, n. \quad (18)$$

Step 4. Check all workstation loadings do not exceed their maximal capacity via

$w_i \le m_i$, $i = 1, 2, \ldots, n$. (19)

If any w_i exceeds the maximal capacity, terminate the algorithm. The network reliability is zero.

Step 5. Determine the LCV via $c'_i = l_i k_i \ge w_i > (l_i-1)\, k_i$.

Step 6. Evaluate the network reliability as follows:

$$R_{d_1,d_2,\ldots,d_\beta} = Pr\{C \mid C \ge C'\}$$
$$= Pr\{C \mid (c_1, c_2, \ldots, c_n) \ge (c'_1, c'_2, \ldots, c'_n)\}$$
$$= \Pr\{c_1 \ge c'_1\} \times \Pr\{c_2 \ge c'_2\} \times \ldots \times \Pr\{c_n \ge c'_n\}.$$

3. Illustrative case

The MPNR of a jumper cable production system is shown in Figure 3. There are six processes for producing a jumper cable, which are cable cutting (v_1), kits assembling and stripping (v_2), fiber insertion and curing (v_3), polishing (v_4), end-face inspection (v_5), and function testing (v_6). The multistate capacity and probability of all workstations are shown in Table 1. The insertion loss is a KQC of the jumper cable, which is an STB-type characteristic that has a great impact on the main function. The jumper cable is categorized into two classes based on the specification limits shown in Table 2.

All cables are tested at the last process for product classification. Any cable with an insertion loss greater than the upper limit of the Class 2 specification will be sent back to the polishing process (v_4). Suppose the demands of class 1 and class 2 from all orders being 15000 and 10500, $\hat{\mu}_x$=0.3, $\hat{\sigma}_x$=0.07; the proportion of two classes is first calculated as

$$\lambda_1 = \int_0^{0.3} \frac{1}{\sqrt{2\pi}\cdot 0.07} e^{-\frac{(X-0.29)}{2\times 0.07}} dx = 0.5567,$$

$$\lambda_2 = \int_{0.3}^{0.5} \frac{1}{\sqrt{2\pi}\cdot 0.07} e^{-\frac{(X-0.29)}{2\times 0.07}} dx = 0.3851.$$

Then, the amount E of raw material required to meet each class is calculated as follows:

$E_1 = 15000 / ((0.8759+0.0492) \times 0.5567) = 29124.3653$,

$E_2 = 10500 / ((0.8759+0.0492) \times 0.3851) = 29471.4981$

The amount E of raw material that simultaneously meets the demands of both two classes is determined as

$E = \max(28829.0191, 29173.5986) = 29173.5986$.

Then, the workload for each production process can be obtained as

$w_1 = 29471.4981$,
$w_2 = 29462.6566$,
$w_3 = 29126.7823$,
$w_4 = 28293.7564 + 1595.2015 = 29888.9579$,
$w_5 = 27722.2225 + 1577.1757 = 29299.3983$,
$w_6 = 27408.9614 + 1485.3841 = 28894.3455$.

Table 1. Multi-state capacity and probability

Production Process	Success rate	Machine availability	Capacity	Probability
v_1	0.9997	0.9523	0	0.0000
			12000	0.0004
			24000	0.0124
			36000	0.1648
			48000	0.8224
v_2	0.9986	0.9645	0	0.0000
			10000	0.0002
			20000	0.0070
			30000	0.1274
			40000	0.8654
v_3	0.9714	0.9732	0	0.0000
			9000	0.0000
			18000	0.0004
			27000	0.0097
			36000	0.1404
			45000	0.8496
v_4	0.9798	0.9179	0	0.0000
			4500	0.0000
			9000	0.0000
			13500	0.0000
			18000	0.0003
			22500	0.0037
			27000	0.0278
			31500	0.1332
			36000	0.3723
			40500	0.4625
v_5	0.9887	0.9897	0	0.0000
			12000	0.0000
			24000	0.0006
			36000	0.0399
			48000	0.9594
v_6	0.9418	0.9762	0	0.0000
			6000	0.0000
			12000	0.0000
			18000	0.0003
			24000	0.0077
			36000	0.1266
			42000	0.8654

Table 2. Specification limits of insertion loss for two classes.

specification limits		(mean, standard deviation)
Class 1	Class 2	
(0,0.3)	(0.3, 0.4)	(0.25, 0.01)

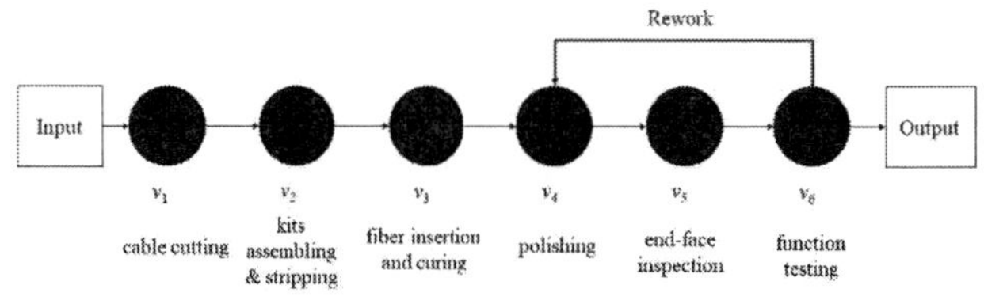

Figure 3. MPNR of jumper cable production system

The workloads of the first three production processes are directly equal to the output of the previous production process. However, the workload of each process, from polishing (v_4) to function testing (v_6), is the sum of the workload without rework and the workload with rework. Since all the workloads do not exceed the maximal capacity of the corresponding workstation, it implies that all workstations can provide enough capacity to handle the calculated workload. The capacity of the minimal amount of operational machines that can handle the workload. For example, the lowest capacity to process the workload is determined as follows:

$c'_1 = 36000 \geq \mathbf{29471.4981} > 24000.$

Then, the LCV C' equals (36000, 30000, 36000, 31500, 36000, 36000). The network reliability can be computed with LCV C' as

$$R_{15000,10500} = Pr\{C \mid C \geq C'\}$$
$$= \Pr\{c_1 \geq 36000\} \times \Pr\{c_2 \geq 30000\} \times \ldots \times \Pr\{c_6 \geq 36000\}$$
$$= 0.9342.$$

The calculated network reliability indicates that there is an approximate 93.5% success probability that the MPNR can meet the demands of two classes of jumper cable. If the minimum acceptable network reliability threshold is 95%, it is necessary for the decision-maker to reduce the number of received orders. To understand their order fulfillment capability, decision-makers can also evaluate the network reliability for different demand scenarios of the two classes, as shown in Table 3.

Table 3. Network reliability results from different demands.

Demand for two classes (d_1, d_2)	Network reliability (R_{d_1,d_2})
(14000, 10000)	0.8143
(13000, 12000)	0.7023
(12000, 13000)	0.2735
(11000, 14000)	0.2386
(10000, 15000)	0

Conclusion

This study primarily aims to evaluate the capability of a production system to fulfill orders for products classified into different classes, taking rework actions into account. Network reliability—defined as the probability that the system can produce enough items to meet the demands of all classes across all orders—is assessed and provided to decision-makers as a performance index. The production system is modeled as a multi-state production network with rework actions (MPNR) to capture machine uncertainty and analyze the workload at each process. We evaluate the network reliability, incorporating both product classification and rework. By evaluating the network reliability of given demands of all classes, production managers can obtain valuable information for making order acceptance decisions.

4. References

[1] Arora R, Chauhan D, Singh AP, Sayal A. Smart manufacturing system with rework and partial outsourcing for battery industry. Cleaner Engineering and Technology. 2025;24.

[2] Gupta A, Khanna A. A holistic approach to sustainable manufacturing: Rework, green technology, and carbon policies. Expert Systems with Applications. 2024;244.

[3] Kim J, Lee JY. Development of a Quality Prediction Algorithm for an Injection Molding Process Considering Cavity Sensor and Vibration Data. International Journal of Precision Engineering and Manufacturing. 2023;24:901-14.

[4] Liu M, Liu C, Xing L, Mei F, Zhang X. Study on a tolerance grading allocation method under uncertainty and quality oriented for remanufactured parts. The International Journal of Advanced Manufacturing Technology. 2013;87:1265-72.

[5] Dai D, Hui G, Zhang Y, Ye C, Zhang Y, Xiao Y, et al. Study of brown sugar grade discrimination method based on electrochemical scanning techniques. Food Chem. 2025;465:142112.

[6] Wang X, Li X, Ma X, Li W, Yang S. Advance on surface finishing technology of precision bearing cylindrical rollers. The International Journal of Advanced Manufacturing Technology. 2023;131:2341-63.

[7] Das S, Akhtar F, Shaikh AA, Manna AK, Konstantaras I. Reduction of emission efforts and rework on optimal policy for products meeting the specific absorption rate via equilibrium optimiser algorithm. International Journal of Systems Science: Operations & Logistics. 2025;12.

[8] Singh SK, Chauhan A, Sarkar B. Resilience of sustainability for a smart production system to produce biodiesel from waste animal fat. Journal of Cleaner Production. 2024;452.

[9] Chang P-C, Huang C-F, Fiondella L. Reliability evaluation for time-based stochastic manufacturing networks with time-dependent reliability. Quality Technology & Quantitative Management. 2023;21:1025-41.

[10] Huang C-F, Huang D-H, Lin Y-K, Chen Y-F. Network reliability evaluation of manufacturing systems by using a deep learning approach. Annals of Operations Research. 2022.

[11] Liao R, He Y, Feng T, Yang X, Dai W, Zhang W. Mission reliability-driven risk-based predictive maintenance approach of multistate manufacturing system. Reliability Engineering & System Safety. 2023;236.

[12] Lin Y-K, Chang P-C. System reliability of a manufacturing network with reworking action and different failure rates. International Journal of Production Research. 2012;50:6930-44.

[13] Niu Y-F, He C, Fu D-Q. Reliability assessment of a multi-state distribution network under cost and spoilage considerations. Annals of Operations Research. 2021;309:189-208.

[14] Yeh C-T, Lyu S-H, Fiondella L. Power supply reliability assessment for a multistate electrical power network with line loss rates. Annals of Operations Research. 2024.

[15] Yeh C-T, Lin Y-K, Yeng LC-L, Chao Y-L. Hybrid flow-shop manufacturing network reliability optimization using genetic algorithm and absorbing Markov chain. Applied Mathematical Modelling. 2023;120:595-611.

[16] Hao Z, Yeh W-C, Tan S-Y. One-batch preempt deterioration-effect multi-state multi-rework network reliability problem and algorithms. Reliability Engineering & System Safety. 2021;215.

[17] Huang C-H, Lin Y-K. Manufacturing system evaluation in terms of system reliability via long short-term memory. Reliability Engineering & System Safety. 2024;251.

[18] Yang X, He Y, Liao R, Cai Y, Ai J. Integrated mission reliability modeling based on extended quality state task network for intelligent multistate manufacturing systems. Reliability Engineering & System Safety. 2022;223.

Reliability evaluation for identifying critical infrastructure in a multistate power grid

Ting-Hau SHIH[1*], Yi-Kuei LIN[2].

[1*] Department of Industrial Engineering and Management, National Yang Ming Chiao Tung University
Hsinchu, 300, Taiwan, andy890830@gmail.com
[2] Department of Industrial Engineering and Management, National Yang Ming Chiao Tung University
Hsinchu, 300, Taiwan, yklin@nycu.edu.tw

Keywords: multistate power grid (MPG); grid reliability; lower capacity vector; infrastructure importance measurement.

Abstract - A reliability-based evaluation method developed in this study for assessing the grid reliability of the power grid (PG) and identifying critical infrastructure. Given that the infrastructures in the PG, including power plants, substations, and transmission lines, operate at multiple capacity levels, the PG is constructed as a multistate power grid (MPG).The grid reliability is defined as a performance index to measure the capability of the MPG to meet demand. To calculate grid reliability, an algorithm is proposed based on the concept of lower capacity vectors, which enables an effective determination of the probability that the MPG can satisfy demand. Additionally, an infrastructure importance measurement method is introduced to systematically evaluate the impact of individual infrastructure failures on grid reliability by considering the scenario of complete infrastructure failures. The proposed method is applied to a real instance in southeastern Taiwan, providing feasibility for the system manager to evaluate the MPG grid reliability and identify the critical infrastructures that significantly influence MPG performance.

1. Introduction

The rapid development of modern society increasingly relies on the continuous and reliable operation of the power grid (PG). As a complex system composed of generation, transformation, and transmission infrastructures, including generators, transformers, and transmission lines [1], the PG plays a fundamental role in ensuring stable power supply. However, it faces challenges such as infrastructure failures and extreme natural disasters (e.g., earthquakes, tsunamis) intensified by climate change, which compromises its reliability. To address these threats, it is essential for the system manager to adopt accurate and practical reliability assessment methods [2] that support decision-making for maintaining uninterrupted power supply.

Selecting appropriate performance indices is key to evaluating PG reliability. Previous studies have assessed PG performance from various angles, such as economic efficiency [3], voltage stability [4], and reliability [5-7]. Reliability indices are typically classified into customer-oriented and energy-oriented types. The former, including indices like SAIDI, SAIFI, and CAIDI, measure the frequency and duration of service interruptions. Amarasinghe et al. [5] proposed methods to optimize these indices through improved protection system design and failure sampling. Energy-oriented indices, such as loss of load probability and expected energy not supplied, focus on system capacity and energy shortfalls. Notably, Pantoš & Lukas [6], and Zhao et al. [7] have developed models and algorithms to enhance the computational efficiency and accuracy of reliability evaluations. These studies confirm the practicality and value of using diverse indices to assess PG performance.

Another applicable method to evaluate reliability is network analysis. Many practical systems can be modeled as multistate flow networks (MFNs), including computing [8], manufacturing [9], and supply chains [10], where each arc has multiple capacity states. In the field of power system [11-14], Lin et al. [11,12] modeled the PG as an MFN, accounting for multistate transmission line capacity and correlated failures. Other works [13,14] extended MFN applications by incorporating maintenance strategies, insurance, and multistate components such as generators and substations. These approaches validate the feasibility of MFN modeling for PG reliability assessment.

Beyond performance evaluation, identifying critical infrastructure (CI) is vital for maintaining PG stability. CI can significantly affect system reliability, especially during extreme events [15]. Studies like O'Neil et al. [16] and Zhang et al. [17] introduced optimization and modeling techniques to improve CI resilience and recovery. However, most models simplify infrastructure to binary states (fully functional or failed), ignoring partial failures or degraded capacity. Infrastructure components often operate at multiple capacity levels [14], which should be reflected in reliability assessments for more accurate evaluations.

This study thus proposes a method to assess PG reliability and identify CI by considering infrastructures with multistate capacities. The PG is modeled as a multistate power grid (MPG), where grid reliability is defined as the probability that electricity demand in each region is satisfied. An algorithm is developed to compute grid reliability based on the MPG, and infrastructure importance is measured by its impact on reliability. The remainder of this paper is structured as follows: **Section 2** introduces the MPG model; **Section 3** describes the reliability evaluation algorithm; **Section 4** presents the CI identification method; **Section 5** applies the approach to a case study in southeastern Taiwan; and Section 6 concludes the study.

2. Multistate power grid model construction

In **Section 2.1**, the MPG model is constructed to represent the power transmission process. Subsequently, the relationship between power flow and capacity is addressed in **Section 2.2**.

2.1. The representation of an MPG

Let (**G**, **S**, **T**) denotes an MPG, where **G** = $\{c_i \mid i = 1, 2, \ldots, u\}$ denotes the set of p power plants (sources), **S** = $\{c_i \mid i = u + 1, u + 2, \ldots, u + v\}$ denotes the set of q substations (vertices), and **T** = $\{c_i \mid i = u + v + 1, u + v + 2, \ldots, u + v + w\}$ denotes the set of r transmission lines (arcs). Each infrastructure c_i exist ω_i states, i =

1, 2, …, $u + v + w$, representing available capacities. The value m_i is the maximal capacity of the infrastructure c_i, and $0 = \theta_{i,1} \leq \theta_{i,2} \leq \ldots \leq \theta_{i,\omega_i} = m_i$ for $i = 1, 2, \ldots, u + v + w$ where $\theta_{i,k}$ is the kth capacity of c_i with $k = 1, 2, \ldots, \omega_i$. In the MPG, the generated power is delivered to the user (sink) through several transmission lines and substations. Therefore, the power transmission route (PTR) can be represented as a minimal path within the MPG for power delivery, including a power plant, multiple transmission lines and substations, and the user. For clarity, let $P_{i,j}$ denotes the jth PTR linking a power plant to the user, where $i = 1, 2, \ldots, u$, $j = 1, 2, \ldots, \lambda_j$, with λ_j representing the number of PTR s linking to power plant c_i to the user. The MPG is necessary to satisfy the following assumptions,

1) The capacities of different sources and arcs are statistically independent.
2) The power flow in the MPG satisfies the flow-conservation law.

The notation $f_{i,\mu}$ denotes the power flow passing through the jth PTR connecting power plant c_i to the user, for $i = 1, 2, \ldots, u$, $j = 1, 2, \ldots, \lambda_j$. The vector of power flow is thus represented as $F = (f_{1,1}, f_{1,2}, \ldots, f_{1,\lambda_1}, f_{2,1}, \ldots, f_{u,\lambda u})$. To meet the demand d exactly, the power flow vector P must fulfill the following equation for each PTR $P_{i,j}$:

$$\sum_{i=1}^{u}\sum_{j=1}^{\lambda_i} f_{i,j} = d, \tag{1}$$

where $\sum_{i=1}^{u}\sum_{j=1}^{\lambda_i} f_{i,j}$ is the total amount of power flow.

Let $M \equiv (m_1, m_2, \ldots, m_{u+v+w})$ represents the maximal capacity vector. Any power flow vector F is said to be feasible under M if it meets the following constraint:

$$\sum_{i=1}^{u}\sum_{j:\, c_i \in P_{i,j}} f_{i,j} \leq m_i \text{ for } i = 1, 2, \ldots, u + v + w. \tag{2}$$

where $\sum_{i=1}^{u}\sum_{j:\, c_i \in P_{i,j}} f_{i,j}$ is the total power flow transmitted through the infrastructure c_i. For convenience, let F_M denotes the set of power flow vectors feasible under M. Let $X = (x_1, x_2, \ldots, x_{u+v+w})$ be a current capacity vector, where x_i denotes the current capacity, $i = 1, 2, \ldots, u + v + w$. Similarly, any F satisfying the following is called feasible under X,

$$\sum_{i=1}^{u}\sum_{j:\, c_i \in P_{i,j}} f_{i,j} \leq x_i \text{ for } i = 1, 2, \ldots, u + v + w, \tag{3}$$

and F_X is the set of all power flow vectors feasible under X.

3. Grid reliability evaluation for an MPG

If there exists a power flow vector $F \in F_X$ which meets the demand d under M, then the capacity vector X fulfills d. Let $\boldsymbol{\Gamma}$ represent the set of all X satisfying the demand d, therefore $\boldsymbol{\Gamma} \equiv \{X \mid X \text{ meets the demand } d\}$. The grid reliability GR_d is defined as the probability that the MPG can successfully meet the demand d from multiple power plants to the user, which is calculated as $\sum_{X \in \Gamma} \Pr\{X\}$. Searching all of $X \in \boldsymbol{\Gamma}$ then summing the corresponding probability of these vectors will generate the grid reliability GR_d, which becomes increasingly computationally expensive as the network scale grows. To address this challenge, Zuo et al. [18] demonstrated that this probability can be efficiently computed in terms of the lower vectors in the set $\boldsymbol{\Gamma}$, which is the lower capacity vector (LCV) to meet the demand d. To apply the concept of LCV, some useful rules are described as follows:

Definition 1: $X \leq Y$: $(x_1, x_2, \ldots, x_n) \leq (y_1, y_2, \ldots, y_n)$ if and only if $x_i \leq y_i$ for each i.

Definition 2: $X < Y$: $(x_1, x_2, \ldots, x_n) < (y_1, y_2, \ldots, y_n)$ if and only if $X \leq Y$ and $x_i < y_i$ for at least one i.

Definition 3: An LCV is a lower capacity vector in Γ, then $Y \notin \Gamma$ for any capacity vector Y with $Y < X$.

Suppose there are a total of θ LCVs: $X_1, X_2, \ldots, X_\theta$, the electric power grid reliability can be rewritten as:

$$GR_d = \sum_{X \in \Gamma} \Pr\{X\} = \Pr\left(\bigcup_{i=1}^{\theta}\{X \mid X \geq X_i\}\right). \tag{4}$$

To calculate GR_d, various approaches can be utilized, and the RSDP method [19] has been demonstrated to offer better computational efficiency, particularly for large-scale networks. Therefore, the RSDP method is adopted in this study. Next, to generate all LCVs, each $F \in F_M$ satisfying the demand such that the X can be converted from F by the following equation:

$$\begin{cases} x_i = 0, \ if \ \sum_{i=1}^{u}\sum_{j:\, c_i \in P_{i,j}} f_{i,j} = 0 \\ x_i = \theta_{i,k}, \ if \ \theta_{i,k} \geq \sum_{i=1}^{u}\sum_{j:\, c_i \in P_{i,j}} f_{i,j} > \theta_{i,k-1}, \ k \in \{2, 3, \ldots, \omega_i\}, \text{ for } i = 1, 2, \ldots, u+v+w. \end{cases} \tag{5}$$

Thus, any X transformed via Eq. (5) is treated as an LCV candidate X. To clarify the situation, let $\boldsymbol{\rho}$ be a set to contain all LCV candidates and $\boldsymbol{\rho}_{\min}$ be the set of the minimal ones in $\boldsymbol{\rho}$. For finding all LCV, suppose there are h LCV candidates, the **Comparison Procedure** shown as the following is used to verify LCV candidate is an LCV or not.

Comparison Procedure

```
Set ρmin ← ∅
Set ψ ← ∅. // ψ stores the indices of non-LCVs.
FOR i ← 1 to h - 1 & i ∉ ψ
  FOR j ← i + 1 to h & j ∉ ψ
    IF Xi > Xj // Xi does not belong to ρmin.
      ψ ← ψ ∪ {i}
    BREAK // next i
    ELSE IF Xi ≤ Xj // Xj does not belong to ρmin.
      ψ ← ψ ∪ {j}
    END IF
  END FOR
  ρmin ← ρmin ∪ Xi
END FOR
```

4. The proposed algorithm to evaluate the grid reliability

Based on the MPG model, an algorithm is developed to evaluate grid reliability as follows.

INPUT: An MPG (**G**, **S**, **T**), a demand d, a set of PTRs $\{P_{1,1}, P_{1,2}, \ldots, P_{u,\lambda_u}\}$.

Step 1. Find all power flow vectors F feasible under the following constraint:

$$\sum_{i=1}^{u}\sum_{j=1}^{\lambda_i} f_{i,j} = d \text{ for } i = 1, 2, \ldots, u. \tag{6}$$

Step 2. Check whether the F derived from **Step 1** is a feasible power flow vector by following constraint:

$$\sum_{i=1}^{u}\sum_{j:\, c_i \in P_{i,j}} f_{i,j} \le m_i \text{ for } i = 1, 2, \ldots, u+v+w. \tag{7}$$

Step 3. Transform each F into current capacity vector $X \equiv (x_1, x_2, \ldots, x_{u+v+w})$ via the following equation:

$$\begin{cases} x_i = 0, \text{ if } \sum_{i=1}^{u}\sum_{j:\, c_i \in P_{i,j}} f_{i,j} = 0 \\ x_i = \theta_{i,k}, \text{ if } \theta_{i,k} \ge \sum_{i=1}^{u}\sum_{j:\, c_i \in P_{i,j}} f_{i,j} > \theta_{i,k-1},\ k \in \{2, 3, \ldots, \omega_i\}, \text{ for } i = 1, 2, \ldots, u+v+w. \end{cases} \tag{8}$$

Step 4. Suppose there are h LCV candidates: $X_1, X_2, \ldots, X_h$ obtained from **Step 3**, use the **Comparison Process** to obtain all LCVs.

Step 5. Suppose there are θ LCV: $X_1, X_2, \ldots, X_\theta$ obtained from **Step 4**, apply the RSDP method to calculate the grid reliability GR_d:

$$GR_d = \Pr\left(\bigcup_{i=1}^{\theta}\{X \mid X \ge X_i\}\right). \tag{9}$$

Output: Grid reliability GR_d.

5. Infrastructure importance measurement

From a reliability perspective, major disruptions can significantly compromise the ability of the MPG to supply electricity, such as natural disasters, equipment failures, or human errors. To support effective system management, it is essential to assess how individual infrastructure failures impact overall grid reliability. Thus, a reliability-based infrastructure importance measurement (IIM) is introduced to quantify the effect of each infrastructure by completing failure on grid reliability GR_d.

The IIM process is as follows:

Step 1. Assume all infrastructures are operational and compute the baseline grid reliability, GR_0.

Step 2. For each infrastructure c_i, simulate a complete failure by setting its capacity to zero and compute the resulting reliability, GR_i.

Step 3. Calculate the difference between GR_0 and GR_i to evaluate the impact of c_i.

Step 4. Repeat for all infrastructures. The one with the largest reduction in GR_d is deemed the most critical.

6. An instance of the MPG

In this study, the MPG in Taiwan is utilized as a benchmark to illustrate the proposed algorithm of grid reliability evaluation. The MPG in Taiwan is crucial for providing a reliable power supply to support the demands of over 23 million residents, spanning industrial and residential demands. The system structure of the MPG in Taiwan is illustrated in Figure 1, consisting of 11 power plants, 25 substations, and 47 transmission lines, which collectively interconnect all users across Taiwan. Additionally, its topological representation is illustrated in Figure 2.

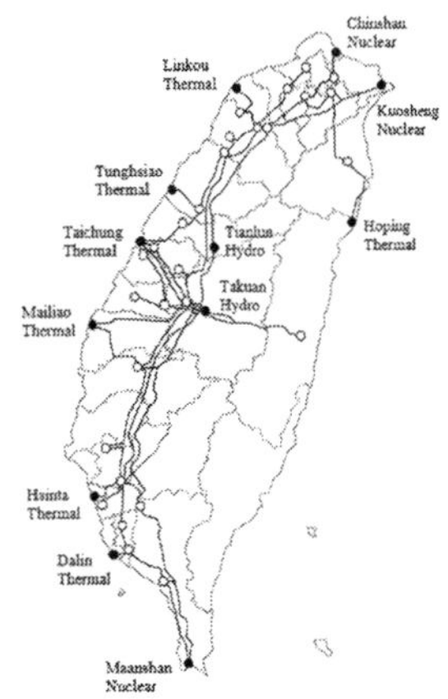

Figure 1. System structure of the MPG in Taiwan.

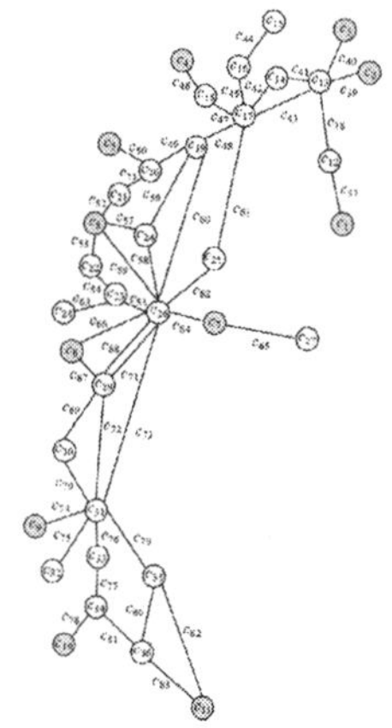

Figure 2. Network topology for the MPG.

6.1. The power supply in southwestern Taiwan

In recent years, rising electricity demand has led to more frequent power shortages, significantly impacting daily life and the economy. A notable case is the 303 Power Outage on March 3, 2022, which affected over 5.49 million households in southern Taiwan, with outages lasting up to 12 hours. This incident underscores the urgent need for stable infrastructure and effective PG management to ensure reliability. To assess the ability of the MPG to meet demand in southern Taiwan, grid reliability must be evaluated. Electricity in this region primarily comes from three power plants: Takuan Hydroelectric (c_7), Hsinta Thermal (c_9), and Maanshan Nuclear (c_{11}), and is transmitted through 8 substations ($c_{26}, c_{29}, c_{30}, c_{31}, c_{33}, c_{34}, c_{35}, c_{36}$) and 14 transmission lines ($c_{64}, c_{68}, c_{69}, c_{70}, c_{71}, c_{72}, c_{74}, c_{76}, c_{77}, c_{79}, c_{80}, c_{81}, c_{82}, c_{83}$), ultimately reaching substation c_{29} for distribution. The capacity and reliability of each component are detailed in Table 1, based on historical data from the power company.

Table 1. Capacity (Unit: MW) and reliability of a single component in the infrastructure

	component 1		component 2		component 3		component 4	
	capacity	reliability	capacity	reliability	capacity	reliability	capacity	reliability
c_7	250	0.9797	250	0.8019	250	0.8504	250	0.9369
c_9	500	0.9480	500	0.9772	550	0.8504	550	0.7990
c_{11}	950	0.9910	950	0.9850	0[a]	0[a]	0	0
c_{26}	200	0.8901	200	0.9205	200	0.8873	200	0.9478
c_{29}	250	0.9312	250	0.8802	250	0.8377	0	0
c_{30}	300	0.8553	300	0.7956	300	0.9488	300	0.9517
c_{31}	100	0.9604	100	0.9219	100	0.9711	100	0.9044
c_{33}	150	0.9542	150	0.8827	0	0	0	0
c_{34}	150	0.8977	150	0.9012	0	0	0	0
c_{35}	300	0.9655	300	0.9578	300	0.8843	300	0.8966
c_{36}	250	0.9122	250	0.9743	250	0.8879	0	0
c_{64}	50	0.9832	50	0.9832	50	0.9832	50	0.9832
c_{68}	50	0.9591	50	0.9591	0	0	0	0
c_{69}	50	0.9433	50	0.9433	50	0.9433	50	0.9433
c_{70}	50	0.9564	50	0.9564	0	0	0	0
c_{71}	50	0.9822	50	0.9822	0	0	0	0
c_{72}	50	0.9577	50	0.9577	50	0.9577	50	0.9577
c_{74}	50	0.9773	50	0.9773	50	0.9773	50	0.9773
c_{76}	50	0.9649	50	0.9649	0	0	0	0
c_{77}	50	0.9738	50	0.9738	0	0	0	0
c_{79}	50	0.9557	50	0.9557	0	0	0	0
c_{80}	50	0.9811	50	0.9811	50	0.9811	50	0.9811
c_{81}	50	0.9837	50	0.9837	50	0.9837	50	0.9837
c_{82}	50	0.9535	50	0.9535	0	0	0	0

c_{83}	50	0.9862	50	0.9862	50	0.9862	50	0.9862

a. The infrastructure does not provide the component.

In the MPG, each infrastructure is composed of multiple components, with the capacity of these components following a probability. As a result, the capacity of each infrastructure is multistate, and the probability of each capacity state is determined by a multivariate Bernoulli distribution. For example, consider a hydroelectric power plant with three electrical generators, each having electricity capacities of 800 MW, 500 MW, and 550 MW, with corresponding reliability values of 0.8302, 0.9137, and 0.9605, respectively. The possible capacity states for this plant would be 0 MW, 500 MW, 550 MW, 800 MW, 1050 MW, 1300 MW, 1350 MW, and 1850 MW, determined by the various combinations of operational generators. To further clarify the calculation method for the probability under each state, consider the following example: The probability of the capacity state being 1050 MW, which occurs when the 800 MW generator fails while the other two remain operational, can be calculated as $(1 - 0.8302) \times 0.9137 \times 0.9605 = 0.149018$. By inputting the data provided in Table 1, the state distribution of each infrastructure c_i can be calculated using the multivariate Bernoulli distribution. We suppose that d=450 (MW), the following steps describe the procedures to obtain all the LCV for calculating grid reliability GR_d.

Step 1. Identify all the power flow vectors $F = (f_{1,1}, f_{1,2}, f_{2,1}, f_{2,2}, f_{3,1}, f_{3,2}, f_{3,3}, f_{3,4}, f_{3,5}, f_{3,6})$ that satisfy the constraint (10):

$$f_{1,1} + f_{1,2} + f_{2,1} + \ldots + f_{3,6} = 450. \tag{10}$$

In this step, a total of 16,235 power flow vectors are generated.

Step 2. Under the maximal capacity vector M=(1000, 2100, 1900, 800, 750, 1200, 400, 300, 300, 1200, 750, 200, 100, 200, 100, 100, 200, 200, 100, 100, 100, 200, 200, 100, 200), power flow vectors that violate the following constraints are eliminated:

$$\begin{aligned} & f_{1,1} + f_{1,2} \leq 1000, \\ & f_{2,1} + f_{2,2} \leq 2100, \\ & \vdots \\ & f_{3,1} + f_{3,3} + f_{3,4} + f_{3,6} \leq 200 \end{aligned} \tag{11}$$

This filtering step reduces the set of feasible power flow vectors from 16,235 to 1,191.

Step 3. Each feasible power flow vector G from **Step 2** is converted into a corresponding LCV candidate $X = (x_1, x_2, \ldots, x_{25})$. For example, the power flow vector F_1 = (0, 150, 0, 0, 0, 0, 100, 100, 100, 0) transforms into the capacity vector X_1 = (250, 0, 950, 200, 500, 300, 300, 150, 150, 300, 250, 150, 0, 150, 100, 100, 200, 0, 100, 100, 100, 200, 100, 100, 200).

$$\begin{cases} x_1 = 0, \ if \ \sum_{i=1}^{u} \sum_{j: c_i \in P_{i,j}} f_{i,j} = 0 \\ x_1 = \theta_{1,k}, \ if \ \theta_{1,k} \geq \sum_{i=1}^{u} \sum_{j: c_i \in P_{i,j}} f_{i,j} > \theta_{1,k-1}, \ k \in \{2, 3, 4, 5\} \end{cases} = 250,$$

$$\begin{cases} x_2 = 0, \ if \ \sum_{i=1}^{u} \sum_{j: c_i \in P_{i,j}} f_{i,j} = 0 \\ x_2 = \theta_{2,k}, \ if \ \theta_{2,k} \geq \sum_{i=1}^{u} \sum_{j: c_i \in P_{i,j}} f_{i,j} > \theta_{2,k-1}, \ k \in \{2, 3, \ldots, 9\} \end{cases} = 0, \tag{12}$$

$$\vdots$$

$$\begin{cases} x_{25} = 0, \ if \ \sum_{i=1}^{u} \sum_{j: c_i \in P_{i,j}} f_{i,j} = 0 \\ x_{25} = \theta_{25,k}, \ if \ \theta_{25,k} \geq \sum_{i=1}^{u} \sum_{j: c_i \in P_{i,j}} f_{i,j} > \theta_{25,k-1}, \ k \in \{2, 3, 4, 5\} \end{cases} = 200.$$

As a result, a total of 1,191 capacity vectors, denoted as X_1, X_2, …, X_{1191}, are obtained. These capacity vectors are also the LCV candidates.

Step 4. The **Comparison Algorithm** is applied to the 1,191 capacity vectors obtained in **Step 3** to identify the LCVs or not. After eliminating the non-minimal X, a total of 288 LCVs are identified.

Step 5. Utilize the RSDP method to calculate the following probability GR_d = 0.901403.

In this instance, the probability of successfully meeting the demand d is calculated as GR_d = 0.901403, indicating that the MPG have a 90% possibility of supplying sufficient electricity to satisfy the demand.

6.2. Infrastructure importance measurement in the MPG

After determining the grid reliability GR_d of the MPG, the IIM is further applied to analyze the MPG. The objective of the IIM is to assess the impact of infrastructure failures (i.e., when the capacity of an infrastructure is reduced to zero) on the overall GR_d. To illustrate this, the capacity of each infrastructure in the MPG was taking turns to set to zero, and the resulting changes in GR_d are presented in Table 2. As expected, infrastructure c_{29}, which is directly connected to the user, results in a complete loss of GR_d upon failure. Additionally, infrastructure c_{31} also causes a complete failure of the MPG, indicating its importance in maintaining GR_d of the MPG. These results highlight that infrastructure c_{31} and c_{29} are the most CIs within the MPG. Therefore, the system manager should prioritize the maintenance and reinforcement of these infrastructures to mitigate potential reliability risks and ensure the capacity to meet the deman0d of the MPG.

Table 2. Results of executing the IIM for infrastructure failure.

Infrastructure (c_i)	MEM GR_d	Change in GR_d	Ranking
c_7	0.886167	-0.015236	9
c_9	0.859265	-0.042138	6
c_{11}	0.868255	-0.033148	8
c_{26}	0.886167	-0.015236	9
c_{29}	**0**	**-0.901403**	**1**
c_{30}	0.866035	-0.035368	7
c_{31}	**0**	**-0.901403**	**1**
c_{33}	0.901124	-0.000279	12
c_{34}	0.901124	-0.000279	12
c_{35}	0.901102	-0.000301	11
c_{36}	0.856094	-0.045309	5
c_{64}	0.886167	-0.015236	9
c_{68}	0.847465	-0.053938	2
c_{69}	0.866035	-0.035368	7
c_{70}	0.866035	-0.035368	7
c_{71}	0.854484	-0.046919	4
c_{72}	0.849322	-0.052081	3
c_{74}	0.859265	-0.042138	6
c_{76}	0.901124	-0.000279	12
c_{77}	0.901124	-0.000279	12
c_{79}	0.901124	-0.000279	12
c_{80}	0.856094	-0.045309	5
c_{81}	0.900767	-0.000636	10
c_{82}	0.901402	-0.000001	13
c_{83}	0.901102	-0.000301	11

To further evaluate the relative importance of each infrastructure within the MPG, the IIM method is further applied to analyze the cascading effects of infrastructure failures following the initial failure of CIs. Given that the failure of either

c_{29} or c_{31} results in a complete failure of the MPG, the analysis proceeds by examining the impact of the next CI, c_{68}. The results reveals that the failure of both c_9 and c_{74} leads to the most significant reduction in GR_d when c_{68} is also complete failure. Notably, while infrastructure c_{72} ranked third in Table 2, its failure does not result in the most significant decrease in GR_d after c_{68} has failed. This observation highlights the dynamic nature of the MPG, which means that if there is a particular infrastructure failing, the state of MPG will be changed, potentially altering the relative importance of other infrastructures. Thus, it is essential to apply the proposed algorithm iteratively under different failure scenarios to accurately assess the shifting importance of infrastructures within the MPG. By continuously applying the IIM to identify and rank infrastructure failures based on their cumulative impact on GR_d, a deeper understanding of the interdependencies and relative importance of different infrastructures within the MPG can be achieved.

7. Conclusion

To identify critical infrastructure (CI) in a practical power grid (PG), a reliability evaluation method is developed based on a multistate power grid (MPG) model. Grid reliability (GR_d) is used as the performance index, calculated using an algorithm that identifies minimal vectors, referred to as lower capacity vectors, and computes the union of their associated probabilities. This approach estimates the likelihood that the MPG can meet electricity demand. To assess the impact of individual failures, the infrastructure importance measurement method is developed by assuming complete failure scenarios and evaluating the resulting reduction in GR_d. This allows the system manager to identify CIs and prioritize maintenance to enhance grid reliability. By incorporating multistate infrastructure capacities, the proposed method offers a practical and accurate framework for reliability assessment and CI identification.

8. Acknowledgement

This paper is partially supported by the National Science and Technology Council, Taiwan, under Grant No. NSTC 112-2221-E-A49 -110 -MY3.

9. References

[1] Chen, M.-S., & Dillon, W. E. (1974). Power system modeling. Proceedings of the IEEE, 62(7), 901-915.

[2] Kamel, R. M., Hashem, M., Ebeed, M., & Ali, A. (2024). Enhancing the reliability and security of distribution networks with plug-in electric vehicles and wind turbine generators considering their stochastic natures. Sustainable Energy, Grids and Networks, 39, 101439.

[3] Zhou, J., Weng, Z., Li, J., & Song, X. (2024). Reliability evaluation, planning, and economic analysis of microgrid with access to renewable energy and electric vehicles. Electric Power Systems Research, 230, 110252.

[4] Martinez, G., Rodríguez, F., Sanchez-Guardamino, I., Urnieta, M., & Echeverría, J. M. (2024). Improving the reliability of a future more electric aircraft DC power system through a novel topology and software combination. International Journal of Electrical Power & Energy Systems, 157, 109795.

[5] Amarasinghe, P., Abeygunawardane, S., & Singh, C. (2025). Reliability evaluation of solar integrated power distribution systems using an Evolutionary Swarm Algorithm. Engineering Applications of Artificial Intelligence, 149, 110464.

[6] Pantoš, M., & Lukas, L. (2025). Enhancing power system reliability through demand flexibility of Grid-Interactive Efficient Buildings: A thermal model-based optimization approach. Applied Energy, 381, 125045.

[7] Zhao, Y., Hu, J., Xie, K., & Tang, J. (2025). Improved cross-entropy-based power system reliability evaluation using GMM with highly-efficient closed-form parameter updating. International Journal of Electrical Power & Energy Systems, 166, 110535.

[8] Huang, D.-H., Huang, C.-F., & Lin, Y.-K. (2024). A reliability prediction model for a multistate cloud/edge-based network based on a deep neural network. Annals of Operations Research, 340(1), 271-287.

[9] Huang, C.-H., & Lin, Y.-K. (2024). Manufacturing system evaluation in terms of system reliability via long short-term memory. Reliability Engineering & System Safety, 251, 110365.

[10] Lin, K.-Y., & Lin, Y.-K. (2025). A Novel Two-Stage Algorithm for Assessing System Reliability of a Multistate Sustainable Supply Chain. IEEE Transactions on Reliability.

[11] Lin, Y.-K., & Yeh, C.-T. (2011). Maximal network reliability with optimal transmission line assignment for stochastic electric power networks via genetic algorithms. Applied Soft Computing, 11(2), 2714-2724.

[12] Lin, Y.-K., Chang, P.-C., & Fiondella, L. (2012). A study of correlated failures on the network reliability of power transmission systems. International Journal of Electrical Power & Energy Systems, 43(1), 954-960.

[13] Tsao, Y.-C., & Vu, T.-L. (2023). Electricity pricing, capacity, and predictive maintenance considering reliability. Annals of Operations Research, 322(2), 991-1011.

[14] Yeh, C.-T., Lyu, S.-H., & Fiondella, L. (2024). Power grid reliability assessment for a multistate electrical power network with line loss rates. Annals of Operations Research, 1-22.

[15] Hafeznia, H., & Stojadinović, B. (2023). ResQ-IOS: An iterative optimization-based simulation framework for quantifying the resilience of interdependent critical infrastructure systems to natural hazards. Applied Energy, 349, 121558.

[16] O'Neil, R., Diallo, C., Khatab, A., & Rezg, N. (2025). Enhancing critical network infrastructure resilience through optimal post-disruption maintenance and routing decisions. Reliability Engineering & System Safety, 257, 110717.

[17] Zhang, J., Bagtzoglou, Y., Zhu, J., Li, B., & Zhang, W. (2023). Fragility-based system performance assessment of critical power infrastructure. Reliability Engineering & System Safety, 232, 109065.

[18] Zuo, M. J., Tian, Z., & Huang, H.-Z. (2007). An efficient method for reliability evaluation of multistate networks given all minimal path vectors. IIE transactions, 39(8), 811-817.

3D Convolutional Network-Based Monitor Flicker Defect Detection: A Structured Approach for Real-World Application

Jia-Hong Chou[1,*], Fu-Kwun Wang[1], Alfian Nur Hidayat[1], Chin-Chung Wu[2], Tao-Peng Chu[2]

[1]National Taiwan University of Science and Technology, Taipei City 10633, Taiwan,
*d11201006@mail.ntust.edu.tw, fukwun@mail.ntust.edu.tw, m11201843@mail.ntust.edu.tw
[2]Dell Taiwan Branch, Taipei City 106335, Taiwan, Rick.Cc.Wu@dell.com, Darcy.Chu@dell.com

Keywords: Flicker detection, real-time detection, temporal CNN-based model, product reliability, frames per second

Abstract - The reliability and quality control of consumer electronics are crucial in both the production process and outgoing quality control. Laptops, widely used for gaming and video streaming, are particularly affected by monitor issues such as flashing, lines, points, and flickering, which significantly impact user experience. This research proposes a novel framework integrating You Only Look Once version 8 (YOLOv8) to identify the monitor's location from image frames captured by an extended webcam and send the focused region to a well-trained Convolutional 3D (C3D) Network for flicker detection. Frames per second (FPS) and model accuracy are key factors in determining real-world applicability. Through experimental analysis, the C3D model is selected for its high FPS and superior performance compared to other existing 3D convolutional-based models. The proposed framework achieves high accuracy in flicker detection and has been successfully tested in real-time within an industrial environment at a well-known company.

1. Introduction

Information and Communication Technology (ICT) refers explicitly to a broad range of technological tools, components, or devices that enable communication, data sharing, and global connectivity between humans and between humans and machines. The Advancement of ICT in recent years has revolutionized industries, including consumer electronics. Enebeli [1] also mentions the increase in information technology (IT) expenditure on devices, including PCs, laptops, mobile phones, data centers, and software, which reached 4.7 trillion U.S. dollars in 2023. With the increase in demand and rapid advancement of ICT, it proves challenging for the industry to comply with the demand while necessitating high-quality production of electronic devices [2]. One critical area of focus is the inspection of liquid crystal displays (LCDs) in laptops and monitors, ensuring they are free of defects for consumers [3].

During manufacturing, defects such as lines, points, flickering, and flashing can occur in LCDs due to microscopic debris in the environment, inconsistencies in production equipment, and human error [4]. The study conducted by Bi et al. [5] mentioned that most LCD detections are conducted artificially, resulting in high costs and low productivity. Moreover, the objective functions, such as environment, time, and subjective factors of the observer, have a significant impact on the detection result. Based on the development and critical challenge in the consumer electronic industry, it is inevitable that the industry will shift toward computer vision to replace manual inspection.

Computer vision is a method that automatically processes and interprets images of real-world objects through optical devices, such as cameras, to obtain desired information, bypassing the need for human inference [6]. Over the past few years, computer vision has gained significant attention for a solution in the LCD defect detection in the manufacturing. For example, Kang et al. [7] developed a model-based approach to defect inspection of thin-film-transistor liquid-crystal display (TFT-LCD) panels for an actual manufacturing process using an automatic optical inspection (AOI) system that combined air floating stage and multi-line scan cameras enhanced with an adjacent pattern comparison algorithm for pattern elimination to extract the defected image of TFT-LCD panels, which resulted in acceptable performance and introduce effective processing time in the manufacture.

However, the aforementioned methods require a strictly controlled environment, limited flexibility, rigorous methodologies, and strong physical modeling. To overcome this challenge, recent researcher leverages machine learning (ML) and deep learning (DL) which are based on learning data representation rather than task-specific algorithms. Thus, they are more robust, flexible and exhibit stronger generalization due to their scalability [8-9].

While existing methods have proven effective, most previous studies primarily focus on defects when the LCD is not operating, analyzing only a single still image. However, in real-world scenarios, defects can occur during specific color transitions or while the LCD is in use, as images change sequentially, for example in videos or gaming. The following Section 2 will introduce DL model uses for computer vision in video inference.

This research evaluates the applicability of the Convolutional 3D (C3D) Network with You Only Look Once version 8 (YOLOv8) in real-world scenarios, specifically for detecting flickering monitor LCD defects in sequence of images (videos). To simulate diverse video conditions, flicker videos were generated using downloaded videos from YouTube to train the 3D convolutional network (3D ConvNets) based model. The results demonstrate reliable flicker defect detection with minimal human effort, enhancing industrial productivity. This approach is now being used by a major technology company in a real-time scenario.

The remainder of this paper is organized as follows: Section 2 provides an overview of literature review. Section 3 provides an overview of data collection. Section 4 outlines the proposed method and presents the analysis flowchart. Section 5 discusses the experimental analysis for each experimental scenario, and Section 6 concludes the study with final remarks.

2. Literature review

With advancements in computer vision techniques for DL models, researchers are increasingly interested in video recognition and object detection. One such model, YOLOv8, a Convolutional Neural Network (CNN) based model which leverages an advanced version of the Cross-Stage Partial Network (CSPNet) as its backbone, combined with a Feature Pyramid Network (FPN) in its neck and a decoupled head architecture. This design enables YOLOv8 to achieve high accuracy and excellent object detection performance, even with a small training dataset [10-12]. Although YOLOv8 achieves high accuracy and supports real-time video detection, it operates at the spatial level only, without incorporating temporal information, which is crucial for defect detection in video sequences.

Compared to individual image classification, the temporal aspect of videos provides important cues for defect detection, as many defects rely on motion patterns for accurate recognition. Simonyan et al. [13] proposed a two-stream CNN model that incorporates both spatial and temporal networks, where the spatial stream processes single RGB frames and the temporal stream leverages multi-frame optical flow to enhance video action recognition. Another study by Tran et al. [14] proposed a method for extending 2D convolutional network into a 3D ConvNets, enabling the model to learn spatio-temporal features from videos. This approach, known as C3D, improves the model's ability to process the initial frames while effectively tracking salient motion in the subsequent frames. Carreira et al. [15] proposed a two-stream Inflated 3D ConvNet (I3D) based on the 2D convolutional network, turning it into a spatio-temporal domain by inflating the 2D filter and polling kernel into 3D. While leveraging two stream inputs of RGB and optical flow, resulting a significant improvement in action recognition performance.

Based on the survey of previous studies, relatively few have utilized the 3D ConvNets-based for monitoring LCD flicker detection in real-time applications. This type of study can significantly contribute to improving real-time flicker detection.

2.1. Experimental setup

Since the application in this research is relatively new, finding an open-source dataset for DL model training is challenging. Therefore, in this study, the dataset was collected using a webcam in a real-world laboratory environment. The experimental setup includes three main components: the system under test (SUT), a main PC, and an extended webcam. After multiple trials, to prevent light contamination from affecting detection performance, a black box was ultimately added to mitigate the issue. Figure 1 illustrates the experimental setup for data collection.

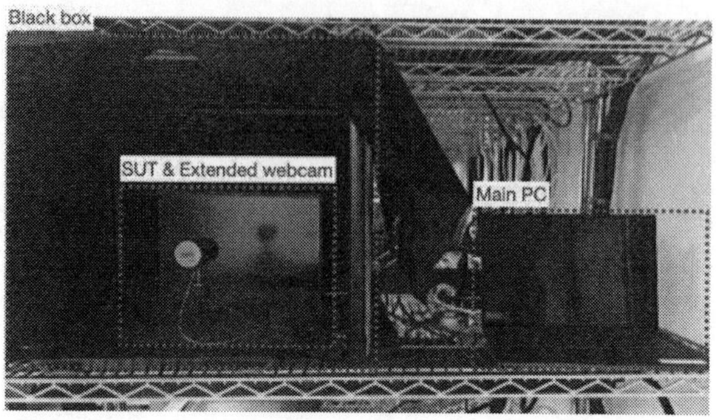

Figure 1. The experimental setup for data collection

2.2. Training data generation

The goal of this research is to use a DL model to detect flicker on the laptop monitor, referred to as the SUT in this study. Therefore, the dataset must include both flickering and non-flickering videos to train the DL model for recognizing flicker defects. To generate a suitable amount of flicker in each clip, with each consisting of 16 concatenated frames for training the 3D ConvNets-based model, various methods were tested for model training. Finally, videos with flicker were generated in advance using a specific rule that introduces flickers in each frame. After that, the extended webcam was used to capture the frames, which were then concatenated into clips with the focus area identified using YOLOv8. The collected frames are presented in Figure 2.

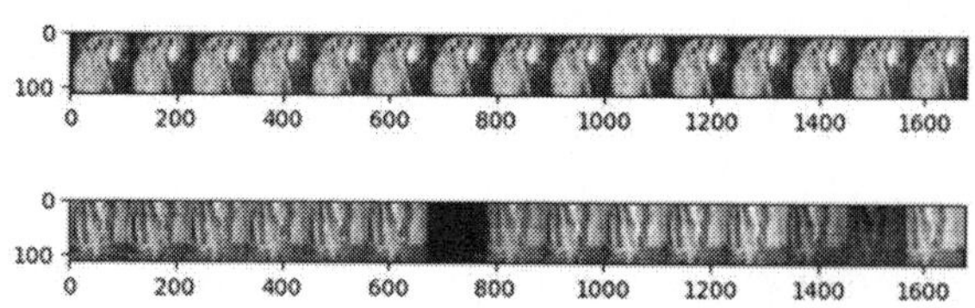

Figure 2. The illustration of the collected clip (The upper clip represents a non-flickering sequence, while the lower clip represents a flickering sequence)

Based on Figure 2, even if the video contains flickers in each frame, the clips captured by the webcam may not always include flickers in every frame. This is the main reason why, in this research, flickers are generated in each frame to ensure that the webcam can capture them when the webcam frames per second (FPS) is lower than that of the video playback FPS. This research considers only full-screen, horizontal line, and vertical line flickers.

3. Proposed flicker detection framework

This research proposes a comprehensive framework for detecting flicker on the SUT monitor. The proposed framework has already been verified in a real-world setting at a well-known company. Additionally, the input video for the framework is captured by the extended webcam connected to the main PC. Furthermore, the trained DL model is deployed on the main PC,

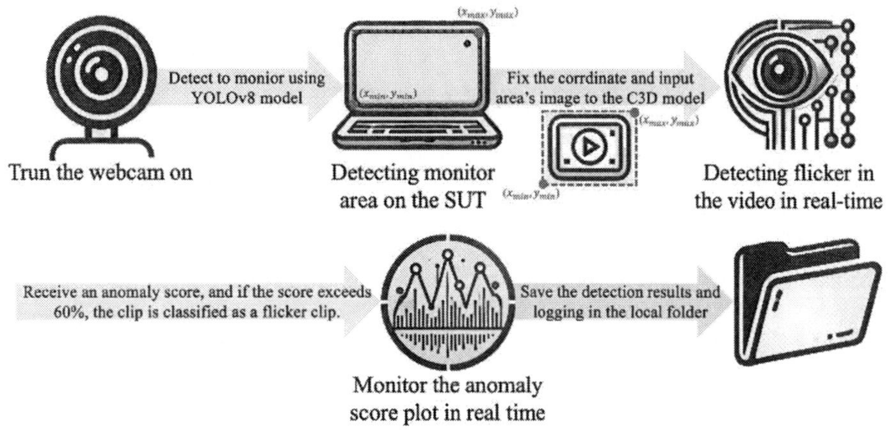

Figure 3. The illustration of the proposed flicker detection framework

where the detection results with log files are also stored. Figure 3 illustrates the proposed flicker detection framework within the real-world experimental setup.

At the start of the framework, a trained YOLOv8 model detects the monitor area, filtering out noise from surrounding regions. This detection is performed once at initialization. A well-trained C3D-based model conducts real-time flicker detection using the obtained coordinates, focusing on the identified regions. The results include clip images of detected flickers, locally saved log files, and detection information presented to the user.

3.1. C3D model

This study employs the C3D model, as the research problem involves detecting flickers in sequential images (videos). Thus, traditional 2D convolution cannot effectively address temporal problems such as motion recognition. Recognizing motion based on a single image frame is challenging because there is no information about the preceding or subsequent frames. The input to the C3D model is a clip consisting of 16 stacked frames. The C3D model includes 3D convolutional layers that not only extract features by convolving along the two spatial dimensions are width and height but also along the channel dimension, enabling it to learn temporal information from the 16 frames. Figure 4 illustrates the operation of 3D convolution.

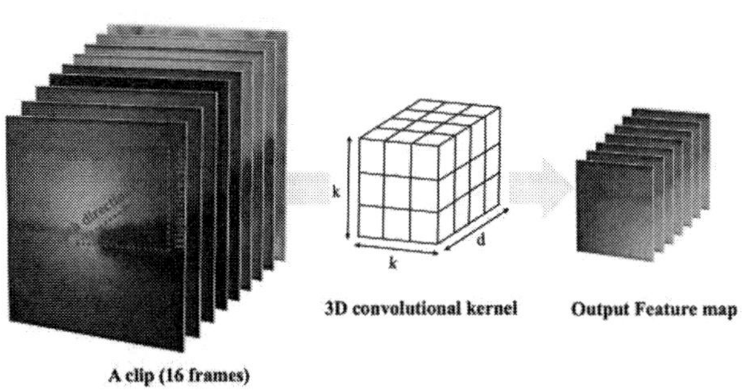

Figure 4. The operation of 3D convolution

As shown in Figure 4, the clip serves as the input to the 3D convolution, where a 3D convolutional kernel of size k × k and depth d is used to extract features. The black dotted line represents the transition from the 2D spatial path to the 3D depth path, enabling the extraction of temporal features.

The C3D model used in this research consists of eight 3D convolutional layers and three 3D max pooling layers as the feature extractor to learn features from 34 normal videos and 34 abnormal videos. Finally, three fully connected layers are used to classify the feature maps extracted from the convolutional layers. The C3D model structure used in this research can refer in [14].

Since this research problem is a binary classification task, the Sigmoid function is applied at the end of the three fully connected layers to transform the output into a probability ranging from 0 to 1, which is then used as input for the Binary Cross-Entropy (BCE) loss function. The calculations for the Sigmoid function and BCE loss function are shown below.

$$Sigmoid(x) = \frac{1}{1+e^{-x}} \tag{1}$$

$$BCE\ loss = -\frac{1}{N}\sum_{i=1}^{N}[y_{true_i} log(p_i) + (1 - y_{true_i}) log(1-p_i)] \tag{2}$$

Where N is the total number of clips and y_{true} represents the ground truth. If the number i clip contains a flicker, the ground truth is 1; otherwise, it is 0. p_i is the output probability of the Sigmoid function of the i clip.

The C3D model in this research was trained from scratch using initialized weights, rather than pre-trained weights. After training the C3D model, the probability value from the Sigmoid function represents the anomaly score. If the score exceeds 60%, the clip is classified as abnormal, indicating the presence of flickers.

4. Experimental analysis and discussion

The experimental analysis is conducted using the laboratory setup shown in Figure 1. The collected clips are split into training (80%) and validation (20%) datasets. Real-time detection experiments are performed using the test dataset within the experimental setup. Table 1 presents the distribution of collected clip data and the training and validation datasets.

The hyperparameters for the output channels of the 3D convolutional layers in the C3D model are 64, 128, 256, 256, 512, 512, 512, and 512, serving as the feature extractor with a kernel size of 3 × 3 × 3 (k × k × d). The hyperparameters for the fully connected layers in the C3D model are 512, 32, and 1. The training parameters of the C3D model are set as follows: epoch = 1000, learning rate = 0.0001, and batch size = 128. To prevent overfitting, an early stopping rule is applied when the validation performance does not improve within 10 consecutive epochs. The performance metrics used include accuracy to evaluate the training and validation performance during the training process. For testing, video-based accuracy is used to assess the model's performance. This means that if a video is detected as abnormal and it is indeed a flicker video, the model is considered to have correctly identified the flicker in this video.

Table 1. The data distribution of the collected clips

Dataset	Types of videos	
	Normal	*Abnormal*
Total	5622 clips	5560 clips
Training	4503 clips	4444 clips
Validation	1119 clips	1116 clips

4.1. C3D model real-time detection performance

Based on the hyperparameters used to train the C3D model, the training process takes approximately 8 hours, with early stopping applied due to the large dataset. Figure 5 presents the accuracy and BCE loss of the validation dataset for each epoch.

As shown in Figure 6, the C3D model performs well on the validation dataset, achieving approximately 99.70% accuracy. The model converges by epoch 25, which is the early stopping point. However, validation performance alone cannot guarantee real-time detection performance in the experimental setup due to the computational limitations of the main PC. In the experimental setup, the main PC is connected to an external webcam and must simultaneously process the C3D model. If the FPS is too low, the webcam may fail to detect flickers, as frames containing flickers could be skipped. Finally, the well-trained C3D model test in the experimental setup using the flowchart shown in Figure 3. Three generated videos with flickers are used to test the trained C3D model. Figure 6 presents one of the test results from these three videos.

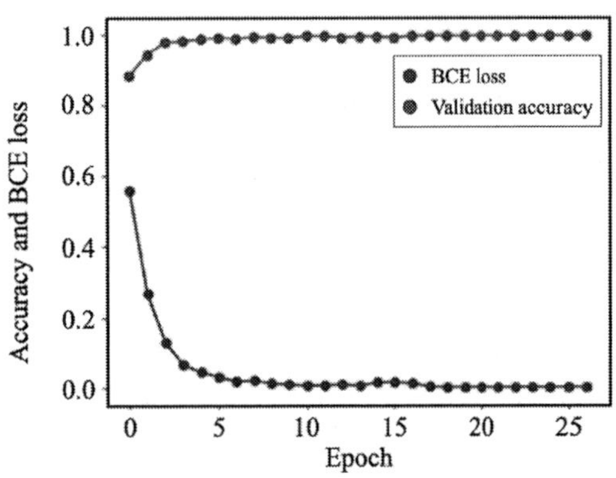

Figure 5. The performance of the validation dataset at each epoch

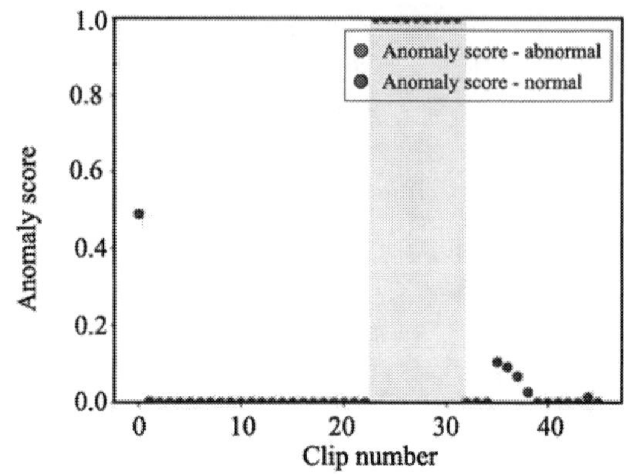

Figure 6. Real-time detection performance

The flickers in these three videos are generated during the middle period of each video and are marked in red in Figure 6. The results in Figure 6 demonstrate that the proposed real-time detection framework outperforms existing methods and successfully detects flickers in real-world scenarios. During detection testing, the FPS dynamically fluctuates between 26 and 30. Additionally, all three videos are correctly identified as abnormal.

In the experiment, a real-world case is used to evaluate the model's performance. The results, shown in Figure 7, demonstrate that the proposed framework effectively detects flickers in real-world scenarios, even when the video was not used for model training.

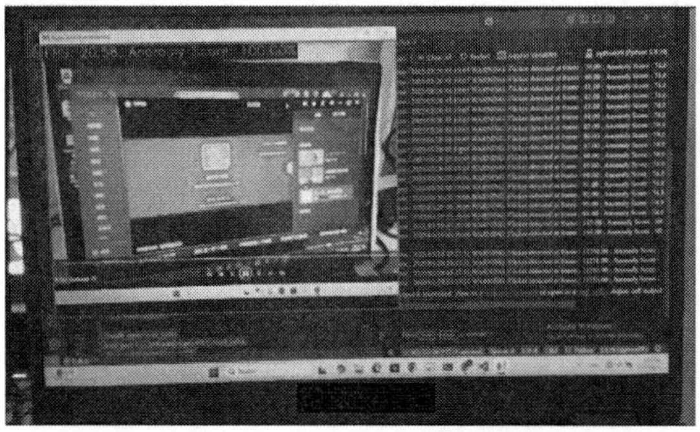

Figure 7. C3D detection results in real case

4.2. Comparison of 3D convolutional-based model

Since many 3D convolutional-based models have been proposed, this research also compares the performance of the C3D model with the I3D model [15]. In this comparison, both accuracy and FPS are considered to determine whether the model is suitable for real-time detection in real-world scenarios.

Before deployment, an offline test is conducted to evaluate the model's performance. Pre-recorded webcam videos are stored locally and processed by the models to compare performance and assess FPS. Table 2 presents the comparison of existing 3D convolutional-based models.

Table 2. Comparsion between each exsiting 3D convolutional-based model

performance	3D convolutional-based model			
	C3D	*I3D – RGB*	*I3D – optical*	*I3D – two streams*
FPS	26	23	4	3
Overkill	0	2	5	0
Underkill	0	0	0	0

Table 2 shows that both the two-stream I3D (RGB + optical flow) and C3D models achieve zero overkill and underkill rates. However, I3D's low FPS around 3 in offline detection makes it impractical for real-time use, risking missed flicker frames.

5. Conclusion

This research proposes a real-time flicker detection framework for laptop monitors in a real-world experimental setup. A structured data collection method is introduced, and four 3D ConvNets-based DL models are compared for offline detection using pre-recorded videos from an extended webcam. These models are trained from scratch with initialized weights. Given the need for real-time inference on a connected main PC, FPS and accuracy are key factors in model selection.

The C3D model is ultimately chosen for online prediction. In the proposed method, YOLOv8 focuses on the monitor area while C3D detects flickers. The framework achieves a process FPS of around 26, with zero overkill and underkill rates, demonstrating strong real-world performance. It has been validated at a well-known company using videos with generated flickers and real-case scenarios.

However, this study focuses on detecting vertical, horizontal, and full-screen flickers. Future work will expand the label set to include additional defects such as flashing and distortion, enhancing the framework's generalization and reliability.

6. References

[1] John Paul Enebeli. "Information and Communication Technology (ICT), Globalization and Inpeneding Challenges"; Global Journal of Pure and Applied Sciences, Vol. 30., No. 1., 95—100, Mar 2024.

[2] Jeferson Spiering Böes and Jeferson Ost Patzlaff. "Information and Communication Technology (ICT) Applied to Quality Control to Secure Performance and Compliance in Project Lifespan"; Journal of Building Pathology and Rehabilitation, Vol. 1., No. 14., Nov 2016.

[3] Heeyeon Jo and Jeongtae Kim. "Regularized Auto-encoder-based Separation of Defects from Backgrounds for Inspecting Display Devices"; Electronics, Vol. 8., No. 533., May 2019.

[4] Aslı Çelik, Ayhan Küçükmanisa, Aydın Sümer, Aysun Ta¸syapı Çelebi, and Oğuzhan Urhan. "A Real-time Defective Pixel Detection System for LCDs Using Deep Learning Based Object Detectors"; Journal of Intelligent Manufacturing, Vol. 33., 985—994, Nov 2022.

[5] Xin Bi, Xiaoping Xu, and Jinhua Shen. "An Automatic Detection Method of Mura Defects for Liquid Crystal Display Using Real Gabor Filters"; 2015 8th International Congress on Image and Signal Processing (CISP), 871—875, Feb 2016.

[6] Anil Bharath and Maria Petrou. "Next Generation Artificial Vision Systems : Reverse Engineering The Human Visual System"; Artech House, 2008.

[7] Kang Sung Bum, Lee, Myung Sun, and Pahk Heui Jae. "Development of AOI (Automatic Optical Inspection) System for Defect Inspection of Patterned TFT-LCD Panels Using Adjacent Pattern Comparison and Border Expansion Algorithms "; Journal of Institute of Control, Robotics and Systems, Vol. 14., Issue. 1., 444—452, May 2008.

[8] Haidi Zhu, Jingchang Huang, Huawei Liu, Qianwei Zhou, Jianqing Zhu, and Baoqing Li. "Deep-Learning-Enabled Automatic Optical Inspection for Module-Level Defects in LCD"; IEEE Internet of Things Journal, Vol. 9., Issue. 2., 1122—1135, May 2021.

[9] Sourav Dutta. "An Overview on The Evolution and Adoption of Deep Learning Applications Used in The Industry"; WIREs Data Mining and Knowledge Discovery, Vol. 15., Issue. 1., Apr 2018.

[10] Frouke Hermens. "Automatic Object Detection for Behavioural Research Using YOLOv8"; Journal of Behavior Research Methods, Vol. 56., 7307—7330, May 2024.

[11] Murat Bakirci. "Advanced Aerial Monitoring and Vehicle Classification for Intelligent Transportation Systems with YOLOv8 Variants"; Journal of Network and Computer Applications, Vol. 237., No. 104134., May 2025.

[12] Glenn Jocher, Ayush Chaurasia, and Jing Qiu. Ultralytics Yolov8. Retrieved from https://github.com/ultralytics/ultralytics.

[13] Karen Simonyan and Andrew Zisserman. "Two-Stream Convolutional Networks for Action Recognition in Videos"; arXiv:1406.2199, Nov 2014.

[14] Du Tran, Lubomir Bourdev, Rob Fergus, Lorenzo Torresani, and Manohar Paluri. "Learning Spatiotemporal Features with 3D Convolutional Networks"; 2017 IEEE International Conference on Computer Vision (ICCV), 4489—4497, Feb 2016.

[15] Joao Carreira and Andrew Zisserman. "Quo Vadis, Action Recognition? A New Model and The Kinetics Dataset"; 2017 IEEE Conference on Computer Vision and Pattern Recognition (CVPR), 4724—4733, Nov 2017.

Optimal Production and Quality Policy Consider Rework and Carbon Emission

Pei-Hsuan Hsu[1*], Yu-Chung Tsao[1,2], Tsung-Hui Chen[3]

[1]Department of Industrial Management, National Taiwan University of Science and Technology, Taipei, Taiwan, pei88625@gmail.com
[2]Artificial Intelligence for Operations Management Research Center, National Taiwan University of Science and Technology, Taipei, Taiwan, yctsao@mail.ntust.edu.tw
[3]Department of Industrial Engineering and Management, National Yunlin University of Science and Technology, Yunlin, Taiwan, chenth@yuntech.edu.tw

Keywords: Quality, rework, carbon emission, production, inventory

Abstract - This study investigates how manufacturers can optimize production costs, enhance product quality, and reduce carbon emissions through quality investment. We develop an Economic Production Quantity model incorporating quality investment, remanufacturing, and carbon emission costs to analyze how these factors influence overall production costs.
Defective products are inevitable in manufacturing, but reworking them instead of scrapping them helps minimize resource waste and reduce environmental impact. While quality investment increases initial production costs, it reduces defect rates, thereby decreasing rework demand and carbon emissions. This study developed mathematical modeling that considers a supply chain system comprising suppliers, manufacturers, and consumers. Analyze the effects of production, defect, and rework rates on total costs. This paper's findings indicate that as quality investment increases, carbon emission costs exhibit an exponential decline while defect rates and rework requirements also decrease. Furthermore, numerical analysis reveals that a higher production rate helps allocate fixed costs more effectively, lowering per-unit production costs and improving operational efficiency. This study provides a viable approach to balancing production costs, quality control, and carbon emission management, enabling firms to achieve economic and environmental goals amid increasingly stringent regulations.

1. Introduction

Sustainability concerns reshape manufacturing, particularly in addressing defective products caused by deterioration or production flaws. Many companies adopt remanufacturing to rework such items before sale. The Economic Production Quantity (EPQ) model optimizes production while minimizing costs [1] and has been extended to account for scrap, rework, and stochastic demand as referenced in [2] and [3].

Industry 4.0 technologies, such as AI, IoT, and cloud computing, enhance efficiency by reducing defects and optimizing resource utilization [4]. However, high investment costs remain a significant barrier to widespread adoption.

With net-zero targets set for 2050, governments enforce stricter regulations, driving research on balancing economic and environmental objectives as referenced in [5] and [6]. However, the relationship between quality investment and carbon reduction remains underexplored.

This study assumes manufacturers invest in quality-enhancing technologies to reduce carbon emissions and improve product quality. While these investments may increase initial costs, they can ultimately lower overall environmental expenditures and stimulate greater consumer demand for eco-friendly products.

2. Literature review

Quality management plays a crucial role in industrial engineering, ensuring product quality while directly impacting company costs. Zhu et al. [7] highlight that although green technology investments enhance customer satisfaction, they also introduce additional expenses. However, companies can alleviate financial burdens through government subsidies or technological innovation. Moreover, smart manufacturing is evolving into Social Smart Manufacturing Systems (SSMS). Bao et al. [8] emphasize that promoting data sharing and collaboration enhances interoperability and resilience across supply chains. In reliability engineering, Zheng et al. [9] propose an intelligent identification method that integrates Simulated Annealing (SA) with Harris Hawks Optimization (HHO). This approach improves defect prediction in product design, enhancing quality control and reducing production costs. For internal logistics, Büyüközkan et al. [10] develop a hybrid model combining the Genetic Algorithm (GA) with the Best Synchronized Material Allocation Technique (BSMATE). Their model optimizes scheduling, inventory, and transportation, leading to a 15% increase in operational efficiency. In Engineering-Procurement-Construction (EPC) projects, Chen et al. [11] establish cost-sharing and incentive mechanisms that mitigate moral hazards while improving project quality and timeliness.

Fan et al. [12] introduced a Vision Transformer (ViT) based augmentation technique in semiconductor supply chain management, significantly improving wafer defect classification. This method effectively addresses data imbalance issues, resulting in a 12% increase in accuracy. Regarding integrating Lean Manufacturing and Industry 4.0, Frank et al. [13] demonstrate substantial operational benefits, with moderate automation increasing productivity by 25%. However, excessive automation may create adaptation challenges for workers, ultimately reducing production flexibility. Organizational learning also plays a crucial mediating role in lean production and digital transformation. Prashar [14] highlights that leveraging digitalization as a strategic resource for lean transformation enhances competitiveness and ensures long-term sustainability.

In sustainability, Niu and Wang [15] employed a game-theoretic modeling approach to compare green transition strategies under recycling uncertainty. Their results indicate that establishing a new production line is optimal when carbon emissions are moderate, and recycling efficiency is high, leading to environmental and economic benefits. Ahmadi et al. [16] developed a framework based on the Best-Worst Method (BWM) to evaluate social sustainability in manufacturing supply chains, with empirical validation conducted in Iran providing practical insights for sustainable supply chain management. Kannan et al. [17] applied BWM and the Weighted Aggregated Sum Product Assessment method to rank key sustainable manufacturing challenges and align them with appropriate innovative manufacturing technologies. The study highlighted governmental support as the most significant challenge and proposed a strategic framework connecting Industry 4.0 solutions to these barriers.

Therefore, this paper utilizes the Economic Production Quantity (EPQ) model to examine the relationship between production cycle optimization, quality efforts, and carbon emission reduction in a remanufacturing context. By developing a model, manufacturers can effectively minimize defect rates, enhance product quality, and reduce carbon emissions to minimize cost.

3. Model

This study has a supplier, a manufacturer, and customers in a supply chain system. The manufacturer produces products, orders raw materials from the supplier, and invests in quality efforts to increase product quality and reduce carbon emissions.

3.1 Assumptions and Environment Settings

This study develops an Economic Production Quantity (EPQ) model under the following assumptions: The demand and production rates and the proportion of imperfect items are known and constant. In this system, all defective items undergo remanufacturing and are added back to inventory, ensuring a stable supply without shortages from the supplier or the manufacturer.

The manufacturer's cost increases with the level of investment in quality effort, represented as $I(\theta) = a + b\theta$. During a production cycle, the total number of items produced is given by $Q(T) = [t_r(D - p_r)]/[p(1-\alpha)]$. This investment also reduces carbon emissions following an exponential pattern, expressed as $E(\theta, Q) = b[F + p \cdot Q(T) + p_r \cdot (1-\alpha) \cdot Q(T)]$. Additionally, all imperfect items are remanufactured rather than scrapped. The remanufacturing rate decreases as quality effort increases, formulated as $R(\theta) = r\left[p_r(1-\alpha) \cdot Q(T) \cdot g^{-\theta}\right]$ by integrating these assumptions. Overall, the cost $I(\theta)$ will increase with the degree of investment in quality effort, but $E(\theta, Q)$ and $R(\theta)$ will reduce.

3.2 Mathematical model

This paper divides the production cycle time into four distinct periods. As illustrated in Figure 1, this segmentation helps model the cost function component. The total annual cost includes production and raw material costs $(m+u)D$, remanufacturing cost $r \cdot \alpha \cdot D$, and setup cost $\frac{s}{T}$. Holding costs consist of two parts (Taleizadeh et al.[18]): (1) perfect items, given by $h(\frac{H_1}{2}t_m + \frac{H_1+H}{2}t_r + \frac{H}{2}t_d)$; and (2) imperfect items during uptime and remanufacturing, represented as $h(\frac{p \cdot \alpha \cdot t_m^2}{2} + \frac{p_r \cdot t_r^2}{2})$ so annual holding cost equal $h_t = h\left(\frac{H_1}{2}t_m + \frac{H_1+H}{2}t_r + \frac{H}{2}t_d\right) + h(\frac{p \cdot \alpha \cdot t_m^2}{2} + \frac{p_r \cdot t_r^2}{2})$. Therefore, the total cost function is given by TC as follows: $TC = (m+u)D + r \cdot \alpha \cdot D + \frac{s}{T} + h_t + I(\theta) + E(\theta, Q) + R(\theta)$

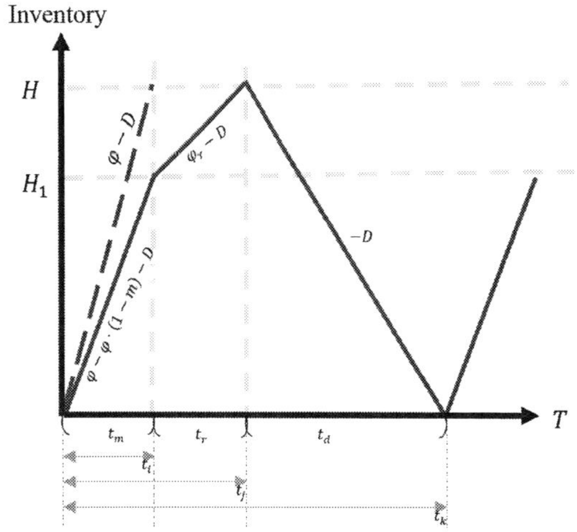

Figure 1. The production cycle and inventory of the EPQ model

The first-order differential equation within the total cost model was solved to derive the optimal quality effort.

$$\theta^* = \frac{r \cdot D \cdot \alpha^2 \cdot p_r \cdot t_r - r \cdot D \cdot \alpha \cdot p_r \cdot t_r + r \cdot m \cdot p_r^2 - b\alpha + b}{r \cdot \alpha \cdot p_r(D \cdot \alpha \cdot t_r - D \cdot t_r + p_r)}$$

Lemma: The total cost, TC, was convexity in θ.

Proof: The following equation can be obtained by taking the second-order derivative of the cost with respect to:

$$\frac{d^2TC}{d\theta^2} = \frac{r \cdot \alpha \cdot p_r[D \cdot t_r(\alpha - 1) + p_r]}{\alpha - 1} > 0$$

Because the parameters r,t_r,p_r, D are positive integers, and the value of α is between 0 to 1, the convexity property was satisfied.

4.1 Numerical example

A manufacturing system produces a product with an annual demand of 200 units at a selling price of $180 per unit. The production facility operates at a rate of 145 units per year. Due to imperfections, 15% of the produced items require remanufacturing, resulting in 45 units annually. The unit production cost, including inspection, is $42, while each remanufactured item costs an additional $15. The carbon emission cost is $8 per unit, and raw materials cost $64 per unit. Each production cycle incurs a fixed setup cost of $800. The investment in quality improvement consists of a fixed cost of 0.7 and a variable cost of 0.3. The carbon emission reduction function allows for a maximum reduction of 500 units. The remanufacturing rate depends on quality effort, with a defective rate of 0.15 and an associated coefficient of 15.

Under these conditions, the optimal cost function is given by $TC(T^*|\theta) = 2.4007$, resulting in a total cost of $17,025.29.

4.2 Numerical analysis

This section explores how the production rate (p), imperfect production rate (p_r), and the percentage of defective items (α) impact overall costs. The parameters calculated in Table 1 and Figure 2 were up to ±50%, providing key managerial insights.

- Defect rate impact: A higher defect rate increases the total cost, while a lower defect rate significantly reduces it. It highlights the need for stringent quality control to minimize defects and lower costs.
- Production rate impact: A higher production rate reduces the total cost for two main reasons. First, fixed costs are distributed over more product units, lowering the price per unit. Second, more high-quality products can be produced within the same time frame, increasing efficiency.
- Rework production rate impact: An increase in the rework rate raises the total cost, whereas a decrease leads to substantial cost savings. Controlling rework is crucial for cost reduction.

Overall, to optimize cost efficiency, management should prioritize defect and rework rate reductions, as these have the most significant cost impact since efforts should focus on enhancing quality control and minimizing rework by investment quality efforts.

Table 1. Effects of TC on total cost

	α	p	p_r
+50%	20,637.00	11,434.38	20,730.53
+25%	18,867.86	14,229.83	19,142.33
0%	17,025.29	17,025.29	17,025.29
-25%	15,116.54	19,820.74	14,379.42
-50%	13,147.95	22,616.20	11,204.71

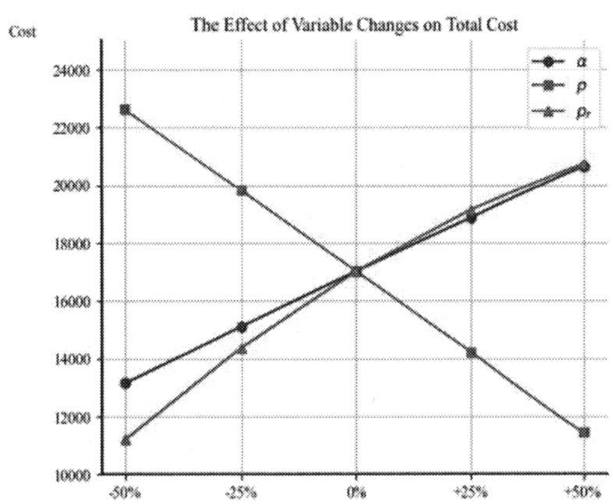

Figure 2. Impact of parameters on total costs

5. Conclusion

This study develops an Economic Production Quantity (EPQ) model that integrates quality investment, remanufacturing, and carbon emission costs to examine how manufacturers can improve quality, reduce carbon emissions, and optimize costs. This paper findings that increasing quality investment significantly reduces defect rates, thereby decreasing rework demand and carbon emission costs, ultimately lowering total production costs. Additionally, numerical analysis demonstrates that higher production rates help distribute fixed costs more effectively, reducing per-unit production costs and improving overall economic efficiency.

Furthermore, numerical analysis of carbon emission costs confirms that quality investment can effectively mitigate environmental impacts while enhancing long-term business performance. Therefore, firms should incorporate quality investment into their production strategies to improve product quality, achieve carbon neutrality, and increase market demand.

Future research could explore the differences in quality investment strategies and carbon reduction effects across various industries or incorporate uncertainty factors such as market demand fluctuations or changes in environmental regulations to develop more flexible decision-making models.

6. References

[1] E. W. Taft. "The Most Economical Production Lot"; The Iron Age, Vol. 101, 1410-1412, May 1918.

[2] Chiu, Singa Wang, Shan-Ling Wang, and Yuan-Shyi Peter Chiu. "Determining the optimal run time for EPQ model with scrap, rework, and stochastic breakdowns"; European Journal of Operational Research, Vol. 180, Issue 2, 664-676, July 2007.

[3] Pal, Brojeswar, Shib Sankar Sana, and Kripasindhu Chaudhuri. "A mathematical model on EPQ for stochastic demand in an imperfect production system"; Journal of Manufacturing Systems, Vol.32, Issue 1,260-270, Jan 2013.

[4] Cohen, B. "Blockchain Cities and the Smart Cities Wheel"; Medium, 2018.

[5] Liu, Biyu, et al. "Effects of carbon emission regulations on remanufacturing decisions with limited information of demand distribution"; International Journal of Production Research, Vol.53, Issue 2, 532-548, Sep 2014.

[6] Watari, Takuma, Keisuke Nansai, and Kenichi Nakajima. "Review of critical metal dynamics to 2050 for 48 elements"; Resources, Conservation and Recycling, Vol.155, 104669, Apr 2020.

[7] Zhu, Yuan, et al. "Customer-centric policies for environmentally sustainable manufacturing of deteriorating items with varying quality control practices under disruptions"; Computers & Industrial Engineering,Vol.189, 109895, Mar 2024.

[8] Bao, Yuguang, et al. "Further expansion from smart manufacturing system (SMS) to social smart manufacturing system (SSMS) based on industrial internet"; Computers & Industrial Engineering, Vol.191, 110119, May 2024.

[9] Zheng, Xin, et al. "Built-in reliability-oriented R-KQC intelligent identification based on SA-HHO and proactive reliability assurance strategy"; Computers & Industrial Engineering, Vol.200, 110817, Feb 2025.

[10] Büyüközkan, Kadir, et al. "An optimization model and customized solution approaches for in-plant logistic problem within the context of lean management"; Computers & Industrial Engineering, Vol.200, 110832, Feb 2025.

[11] Chen, Zhenzhen, Wanshan Zhu, and Pascale Crama. "Subcontracting and rework cost sharing in engineering–procurement–construction projects"; International Journal of Production Economics, Vol.262, 108901, Aug 2023.

[12] Fan, Shu-Kai S., and Shang-Hao Chiu. "A new ViT-Based augmentation framework for wafer map defect classification to enhance the resilience of semiconductor supply chains"; International Journal of Production Economics, Vol.273, 109275, Jul 2024.

[13] Frank, Alejandro G., et al. "How Lean and Industry 4.0 affect worker outcomes and operational performance: A quantitative assessment of competing models"; International Journal of Production Economics, Vol.279, 109475, Jan 2025.

[14] Prashar, Anupama. "The interplay of lean practices and digitalization on organizational learning systems and operational performance"; International Journal of Production Economics, Vol.270, 109192, Apr 2024.

[15] Niu, Baozhuang, and Lingfeng Wang. "How does green manufacturing promote the recycling of renewable solid waste and carbon reduction?. "; Resources, Conservation and Recycling, Vol.203, 107410, Apr 2024.

[16] Ahmadi, Hadi Badri, Simonov Kusi-Sarpong, and Jafar Rezaei. "Assessing the social sustainability of supply chains using Best Worst Method. "; Resources, Conservation and Recycling, Vol.126, 99-106, Nov 2017.

[17] Kannan, Devika, Parvaneh Gholipour, and Chunguang Bai. "Smart manufacturing as a strategic tool to mitigate sustainable manufacturing challenges: a case approach. "; Annals of Operations Research, Vol.331, 543-579, Sep 2023.

[18] Taleizadeh, Ata Allah, et al. "Imperfect economic production quantity model with upstream trade credit periods linked to raw material order quantity and downstream trade credit periods"; Applied Mathematical Modelling, Vol.40, Issue19-20, 8777-8793, Oct 2016.

Decision-making process for improved sustainable maintenance strategies of naval systems

Silvia Carpitella[1], Antonella Certa[2,3], Cinzia Muriana[2,3] and Costanza Laura Parlapiano[2]
[1]Department of Manufacturing Systems Engineering and Management, California State University, Northridge; 18111 Nordhoff St, CA 91330, US
[2]Department of Engineering, University of Palermo; Viale delle Scienze, 90128, Italy
[3]National Sustainable Mobility Center (Centro Nazionale per la Mobilità Sostenibile—CNMS)

Keywords: Multi-Criteria Decision-Making, FMECA, Risk Assessment, Naval Systems

Abstract - This paper formalizes a decision-making process to efficiently prioritize failure modes for naval sub-systems. This work of research extends the results obtained in a previous paper [1] concerning a framework aimed at formalizing guidelines in failure analysis and risk prioritization for an autonomous ship navigation system. The assignment of significant failure modes to ordered risk classes was an important result reached in the mentioned paper. The focus is now on the highest risk class to explore the increment of new criteria while contemplating different weight scenarios. Specifically, the present research proposes a combined approach to identify the most critical failure mode requiring management under resource and time constraints, involving different experts with conflicting interests. The approach is based on Multi-Criteria Decision-Making (MCDM) methods, in particular the Analytic Hierarchy Process (AHP) and the ELimination Et Choix Traduisant la REalité I (ELECTRE I). In addition to the criteria typically considered within the framework of the Failure Mode, Effects and Criticality Analysis (FMECA), that are occurrence, detection, and severity, the additional sub-set of criteria characterizing the decision-making process is herein represented by Economic Factors (EC), Sustainability Maintenance Strategies (SMS), and Management and Data Security (MDS).

1. Introduction

The maritime industry faces growing challenges in maintaining naval sub-systems, particularly for Maritime Autonomous Surface Ships (MASS). Particularly, selecting an optimal maintenance strategy is essential for risk mitigation, reliability and efficiency, since modern naval systems exhibit complex and deep interdependencies. In this context, the present study proposes a Multi-Criteria Decision-Making (MCDM) framework to support risk evaluation on complex systems in the naval industry. This procedure suggested the use of the Analytic Hierarchy Process (AHP) [2] to assign the relative priority to a set of criteria, herein extended with respect to the typical one considered by Failure Mode, Effects and Criticality Analysis (FMECA). The use of the ELimination Et Choix Traduisant la REalité I (ELECTRE I) has been integrated in order to detect the most critical failure mode and promptly intervene under resource constrains and severe conditions.

This hybrid multi-criteria approach ensures a structured decision-making process. Furthermore, the proposed framework has been validated through a case study, demonstrating its effectiveness. The paper is structured as follows. Section 2 reports the literature review, section 3 details the proposed methodological approach, section 4 presents the case study and section 5 discusses key findings and future development.

2. Literature review

Over the last decades, the maritime sector has experienced remarkable technological advancements such as the introduction of satellite systems and automation technologies. Nevertheless, MASS systems represent a disruptive innovation offering outstanding improvements in terms of safety as well as reduction of operational costs and environmental impact. This marks a radical transformation for management and operation, with fully autonomous ships capable of making real-time decisions, processing vast amounts of data and relying on an interconnected and synchronizable network of subsystems. The integration of these cutting-edge subsystems enables an optimized navigation management, ensuring efficient routes, preventing collisions with other maritime transportations while dynamically adapting to weather conditions [1]. Nonetheless, these advanced technologies require continuous improvements. This is the reason why balancing their development within the environment in which they operate is necessary [3]. As showcased in [4], several development drivers and opportunities exist, as well as significant barriers. The three main aspects related to sustainability (economic, environmental and social), which are depicted as the main drivers for such innovation, are hindered by such factors as business acceptance, public perception of this new mode of transportation and legal and regulatory barriers. In addition, the uncertainty characterizing the operational context is linked to challenges of cargo management, ship control, security and failure recovery and repairs. Nevertheless, by leveraging real-time data analysis, it seems that these autonomous ships have the strong potential to increase the profitability through reduced capital and operational costs, while improving supply chain efficiency with the integration of advanced technological innovations [5], [6].

However, for large-scale adoption to become a reality, these ships must demonstrate a level of safety equal to or greater than the one of traditional ships [7]. Moreover, safety is not only about physical protection but also security and resilience of Information Technology (IT) systems: MASS are complex cyber-physical systems integrating advanced navigation technologies, such as Integrated Navigation Systems (INS) and real-time monitoring technologies [8]. This increasing digitalization exposes them to cyber threats that could compromise maritime operations. The interconnection between IT systems, which manage data and communications through software and databases, and Operational Technology (OT) systems, which monitor and control physical processes through hardware and software, has expanded the attack surface for cybercriminals. They can indeed exploit vulnerabilities in onboard networks to compromise systems. The consequences of such attacks may include the theft of sensitive data, operational system shutdowns, ship hijacking and even its use for terrorist purposes [7].

In [9] is showed how, according to Lloyd's of London, cyberattacks in the maritime sector have caused economic losses of up to 200 billion dollars per year, highlighting the vulnerability of the global economy's interconnectedness. Later, it is also emphasized how a cyberattack in 2017 rendered a ship's navigation system unusable for over ten hours, while spoofing incidents have been linked to maritime collisions, including one between a U.S. Navy ship and a South Korean fishing vessel. While cybersecurity remains a critical concern, it is equally important to consider another crucial challenge for MASS, linked to its environmental sustainability. It is well known that the global maritime industry is responsible for 2.5% of total greenhouse gas emissions, with a projected increase over time [9]. In this context, MASS have the potential to reduce the environmental impact compared to the current one, due to the design solutions proposed so far [10].

Despite the optimistic perspective largely considered, the high level of uncertainty in the scientific field challenges the current legal framework on ship-source pollution. It is fundamental to think over that the existing regulations were designed for traditional ships; therefore, it is necessary to reflect on the challenges strictly related to the usage of the MASS. Thus, it is not known yet whether these rules can be applied regardless the kind of vessel. For this reason, it is not possible to provide stakeholders with clear and predictable legal regulations concerning environmental standards using the current legal instruments. Nonetheless, tests are currently run in order to evaluate how these ships can operate safely, and the International Maritime Organization (IMO) and its Member States are working to update existing laws to support the widespread implementation of these new technologies [11]. Given the imminent implementation of autonomous ships, which is inevitable in the near future, supporting their development is crucial by ensuring system reliability and effective risk management, as well as a dedicated regulatory code, or continuous and precise update of the existing one.

This enables to warrant the compliance with environmental requirements [12]. To conclude, the existing literature indicates that MASS may offer considerable opportunities in terms of efficiency, safety and sustainability. However, their large-scale implementation is subjected to vulnerabilities, for which addressing several challenges is required. To make initial steps toward the resolution of the raised issues, it is necessary to consider such factors as environmental impact and data security, since these aspects permit a broader analysis for the evolution of the marine system in the digital age. The requested integrated approach must provide a strategy seeking to prioritize interventions for a set of critical failures on the basis of time and resource constraints, while guaranteeing the achievement of security and sustainability objectives. This study aims, in such way, to integrate new criteria into FMECA analyses, providing a more precise approach to contemporary challenges and ensuring a safe and sustainable development of MASS, guiding the maritime industry toward a more resilient future.

3. Proposed methodological approach

The present research first suggests the application of the Analytical Hierarchy Process, developed by Saaty [2], to prioritize the diverse evaluation criteria representing the set of drivers for the decision makers group. Second, ELECTRE I [13] is suggested to select the most critical failure mode to be managed through limited resources and time in extreme conditions, potentially characterizing the analyzed system. These two specific methods, although not described in detail here for the sake of brevity, have been selected due to their well-established scientific validity, as widely acknowledged in the literature. Their selection is based on a set of methodological and practical considerations, explained in the following.

a) AHP is a structured method of measurement designed for formulating and analyzing decisions. It serves as a powerful decision support tool, particularly useful for addressing complex decision-making problems that involve multiple and often conflicting criteria. AHP supports decision makers in incorporating their experience, knowledge, and intuition into the decision-making process. This makes it especially valuable in scenarios where expert opinions play a critical role [14].

b) ELECTRE methods are mostly based on the so called outranking approach [13]. In other terms, they seek to establish outranking relations by pairwise comparing alternatives, that in this research are represented by failure modes. Different versions of ELECTRE methods have been proposed in literature. Among these versions, the ELECTRE I aims to select a single alternative belonging to a wider set, representing the best trade-off on the basis of the different evaluation criteria taken into account. For this reason, this method is proposed as decision-making tool in integration with the AHP, whose scientific validity has been widely proven with relation to different research fields and practical applications [15].

4. Practical Application

By observing the results produced in [1], the failure modes that result to have been sorted to class A (high risk priority) are: FM_2, inadequate lookout; FM_5, inappropriate/ ineffective maintenance; FM_6, ineffective use of technology; FM_8, mishandling; FM_9, poor management of voyage plan; FM_{10}, rule violation; FM_{11}, overloading; FM_{13}, under-manning; FM_{14}, failure in communication. The evaluations reported in Table 1 are expressed as numerical scores on a scale of 1 to 10, according to each criterion. The data collection process involved expert opinions and collaborative discussions with a maritime professional. It incorporates his extensive knowledge and experience, by continuing the elicitation process undertaken in [1] to extend the analysis to the other previously cited criteria (EC, SMS, MDS). The other criteria already considered in the analysis conducted in [1] are: S (the estimate of how strongly the failure mode will affect the system), O (the frequency of occurrence of the failure mode within a determined period of time) and D (the probability of detecting the failure).

Table 1. FMs evaluations

Failure Mode (FM)	*S*	*O*	*D*	*EC*	*SMS*	*MDS*
FM_2 - Inadequate lookout	4	2	8	7	6	5
FM_5 - Inappropriate/ ineffective maintenance	4	7	5	9	10	3
FM_6 - Ineffective use of technology	2	8	6	5	7	9
FM_8 - Mishandling	5	2	9	5	4	7
FM_9 - Poor management of voyage plan	7	5	8	2	8	6
FM_{10} - Rule violation	9	7	7	10	4	2
FM_{11} - Overloading	8	6	4	6	7	3
FM_{13} - Under manning	7	8	2	8	3	4
FM_{14} - Failure in communication	5	5	8	6	9	3

Table 2 shows the aggregated matrix and criteria weights, obtained through the average geometry of the pairwise comparison judgments of the decision makers (Tables 3, 4, 5), for which the same decisional weight is assumed. Table 6 shows the weights of criteria and Consistency Ratio (CR) and Consistency Index (CI) for each decision maker matrix. Indeed, as stressed in [16], one of the key strengths of the AHP lies in its ability to measure the consistency of decision makers' judgments. Moreover, AHP proves particularly valuable in group decision-making contexts, as it allows for the assessment of relative values while ensuring consistency across different participants' evaluations. As asserted in the referenced study [16], the use of the Weighted Geometric Mean Method (WGMM) for aggregation, the Row Geometric Mean Method (RGMM) for prioritization, and the geometric consistency index as the inconsistency measure provides a robust and coherent framework for group decision-making within the AHP methodology. The inconsistency of the group is smaller than the largest individual inconsistency.

Table 2. Aggregated matrix

	S	*O*	*D*	*EC*	*SMS*	*MDS*	*Weights*
S	1	1.14	0.79	0.55	0.43	0.48	0.12
O	0.87	1	1.25	0.23	0.38	0.40	0.13
D	1.25	0.79	1	1.18	1.44	0.55	0.13
EC	1.81	4.21	0.84	1	0.79	0.50	0.20
SMS	2.28	2.62	0.69	1.25	1	0.55	0.23
MDS	2.08	2.46	0.69	2	1.81	1	0.19

Table 3. Decision maker 1-matrix

	S	*O*	*D*	*EC*	*SMS*	*MDS*
S	1	3	1	2	0.50	0.33
O	0.33	1	2	0.33	0.50	0.33
D	1	0.50	1	5	1	0.33
EC	0.50	3	0.20	1	0.33	0.13
SMS	2	2	1	3	1	0.50
MDS	3	3	3	8	2	1

Table 4. Decision maker 2-matrix

	S	*O*	*D*	*EC*	*SMS*	*MDS*
S	1	2	2	0.33	1	2
O	0.50	1	0.50	0.20	0.33	1
D	0.50	2	1	0.33	1	2
EC	3	5	3	1	0.50	2
SMS	1	3	1	2	1	2
MDS	0.50	1	0.50	0.50	0.50	1

Table 5. Decision maker 3-matrix

	S	*O*	*D*	*EC*	*SMS*	*MDS*
S	1	0.25	0.25	0.25	0.17	0.17
O	4	1	2	0.20	0.33	2
D	4	0.50	1	1	3	0.25
EC	4	5	1	1	3	0.50
SMS	6	3	0.33	0.33	1	0.17
MDS	6	5	4	2	6	1

Table 6. CR and CI indexes

	CR	***CI***
Decision maker 1	0.089	0.111
Decision maker 2	0.083	0.102
Decision maker 3	0.087	0.108

With regard to the ELECTRE I method, only a selection of key outputs characterizing the approach will be presented, for the sake of brevity. Specifically, these include:

- the matrix of concordance indices (Table 7);
- the matrix of discordance indices (Table 8);
- the matrix of outranking indices (Table 9).

These matrices provide insights about the degree of agreement and disagreement among the alternatives and their respective ranking.

The input values are the FMs evaluations, normalized by the following expression:

$$\frac{FM_i - worst\ value\ of FM_i}{best\ value\ of FM_i - worst\ value\ of FM_i}\ \forall_i$$

The normalized evaluation enables a consistent and objective comparison among the various failure modes through pre-defined concordance threshold C^* and discordance threshold D^*. These parameters act as key drivers in the decision-making process carried out by ELECTRE I. In the present analysis, C^* and D^* have been set to 0.5 and 0.7, respectively.

The ELECTRE I identifies the most critical failure mode as FM_{10} (Rule violation), since its associated row in Table 9 presents all the values equal to 1, that is FM_{10} outranks all the other failure modes. Furthermore, a sensitivity analysis was performed by adjusting the weight of the criteria within the same set, confirming the robustness of the results.

By narrowing the analysis to the classical criteria, S, O, and D, a comparison was conducted between the results obtained using the proposed approach and those derived from the traditional method based on the Risk Priority Number (RPN) [17]. The ELECTRE I has been applied by comparing the alternatives (FM_i) evaluated based on the S, O, and D criteria (as showed in Table 1), while maintaining the same threshold values for concordance (C^*) and discordance (D^*) as previously defined.

The ELECTRE I method identifies FM_{10} (rule violation) as the most critical failure mode, confirming the previous result. In contrast, the traditional RPN-based approach highlights FM_9 (poor management of voyage plan) as the most critical.

Table 7. Matrix of concordance indices

	FM₂	***FM₅***	***FM₆***	***FM₈***	***FM₉***	***FM₁₀***	***FM₁₁***	***FM₁₃***	***FM₁₄***
FM_2	-	0.48	0.87	0.52	0.75	0.13	0.56	0.13	0.56
FM_5	0.64	-	0.51	0.52	0.52	0.13	0.65	0.52	0.52
FM_6	0.13	0.49	-	0.33	0.56	0.13	0.49	0.26	0.36
FM_8	0.61	0.48	0.87	-	0.56	0.36	0.36	0.13	0.48
FM_9	0.38	0.48	0.44	0.44	-	0.13	0.13	0.25	0.61
FM_{10}	0.87	1.0	0.87	0.87	0.87	-	1.0	0.64	0.87
FM_{11}	0.44	0.54	0.74	0.64	0.87	0.0	-	0.44	0.87
FM_{13}	0.87	0.48	0.87	0.87	0.87	0.36	0.56	-	0.68
FM_{14}	0.57	0.67	0.64	0.64	0.65	0.13	0.52	0.32	-

Table 8. Matrix of discordance indices

	FM_2	***FM_5***	***FM_6***	***FM_8***	***FM_9***	***FM_{10}***	***FM_{11}***	***FM_{13}***	***FM_{14}***
FM_2	-	0.83	1.00	0.29	0.5	0.83	0.67	1.00	0.50
FM_5	0.57	-	0.43	0.86	0.43	0.86	0.57	1.00	0.43
FM_6	0.57	0.86	-	0.43	0.71	1.00	0.86	0.71	0.86
FM_8	0.29	0.83	1.00	-	0.50	0.83	0.67	1.00	0.57
FM_9	0.63	0.88	0.50	0.57	-	1.00	0.50	0.75	0.50
FM_{10}	0.14	0.00	0.17	0.29	0.14	-	0.00	0.17	0.14
FM_{11}	0.57	0.38	0.33	0.71	0.57	0.50	-	0.57	0.57
FM_{13}	0.86	0.43	0.57	1.00	0.86	0.71	0.29	-	0.86
FM_{14}	0.43	0.38	0.50	0.71	0.29	0.71	0.43	0.86	-

Table 9. Matrix of outranking indices

	FM_2	***FM_5***	***FM_6***	***FM_8***	***FM_9***	***FM_{10}***	***FM_{11}***	***FM_{13}***	***FM_{14}***
FM_2	-	0	0	1	1	0	1	0	1
FM_5	1	-	1	0	1	0	1	0	1
FM_6	0	0	-	0	0	0	0	0	0
FM_8	1	0	0	-	1	0	0	0	0
FM_9	0	0	0	0	0	0	0	0	1
FM_{10}	1	1	1	1	1	-	1	1	1
FM_{11}	0	1	1	0	1	0	-	0	1
FM_{13}	0	0	1	0	0	0	1	-	0
FM_{14}	1	1	1	0	1	0	1	0	-

5. Conclusion

The proposed study focuses on a combined approach, based on the AHP and ELECTRE I methodologies, in the operative systems failure management. Based on different decision-makers' evaluations with conflictual opinions, the first method generates consistent weights related to specific criteria, which concern not only the traditional FMECA parameters (occurrence, severity and detection), but also new ones, including EC, SMS and MDS. Based on the outranking approach, ELECTRE I compares different alternatives in order to determine which is dominant over others, allowing the evaluation of failure modes in a multi-criteria and multi-decision-makers approach. The combined approach reveals the importance of FM_{10} (rule violation) as the highest-risk failure mode, indicating that it should be the top priority in failure management. The sensitivity analysis reinforced the robustness of the model and, therefore, of the result as, even by changing the weights, FM_{10} remained the most critical failure mode.

The results of this research highlight the importance of formalization, in terms of structuring and defining standards for the fundamental procedures related to naval subsystems. This aspect is essential to ensure compliance with the rules and leads to an overall improvement in the reliability and safety of the systems. Therefore, a future development is proposed, based on the design of artificial intelligence-driven systems capable of monitoring compliance with protocols, thereby enhancing their security and reliability. Furthermore, in order to improve the generalizability of the proposed approach, additional case studies across various naval setting will be conducted.

Acknowledgement
This research has been partially supported by the European Union – Next Generation EU - National Sustainable Mobility Center CN00000023, Italian Ministry of University and Research Decree n. 1033- 17/06/2022, Spokes 3 and 12, CUP B73C22000760001.

References

[1] Carpitella, S., Certa, A., & Muriana, C. (2024, August). Risk Assessment Framework for Autonomous Ship Navigation Systems. In Proceedings of the 29th ISSAT International Conference on Reliability and Quality in Design 2024.

[2] Saaty, T. L. (1990). Multicriteria decision making: The analytic hierarchy process: Planning, priority setting. Resource Allocation, 2, 1-20.

[3] International Maritime Organization, (2023). Report of the MSC-LEG-FAL Joint Working Group on Maritime Autonomous Surface Ships (MASS) on its second session.

[4] Alamoush, A. S., Ölçer, A. I., & Ballini, F. (2024). Drivers, opportunities, and barriers, for adoption of Maritime Autonomous Surface Ships (MASS). Journal of International Maritime Safety, Environmental Affairs, and Shipping, 8(4), 2411183.

[5] Rødseth, Ø. J., Kvamstad, B., Porathe, T., & Burmeister, H. C. (2013, June). Communication architecture for an unmanned merchant ship. In 2013 MTS/IEEE OCEANS-Bergen (pp. 1-9). IEEE.

[6] Bratić, K., Pavić, I., Vukša, S., & Stazić, L. (2019). A review of autonomous and remotely controlled ships in maritime sector. Transactions on maritime science, 8(02), 253-265.

[7] Rivkin, B. S. (2023). Maritime cybersecurity. navigational aspect. Gyroscopy and Navigation, 14(4), 386-400.

[8] Akpan, F., Bendiab, G., Shiaeles, S., Karamperidis, S., & Michaloliakos, M. (2022). Cybersecurity challenges in the maritime sector. Network, 2(1), 123-138.

[9] Li, Z., Zhang, D., Han, B., & Wan, C. (2023). Risk and reliability analysis for maritime autonomous surface ship: A bibliometric review of literature from 2015 to 2022. Accident Analysis & Prevention, 187, 107090.

[10] Wright, R. G. (2020). Unmanned and autonomous ships: an overview of mass. Routledge.

[11] Xing, W. (2024). Contemplating Maritime Autonomous Surface Ships (MASS) under the international law on ship-source pollution. Marine Pollution Bulletin, 207, 116884.

[12] Fan, C., Wróbel, K., Montewka, J., Gil, M., Wan, C., & Zhang, D. (2020). A framework to identify factors influencing navigational risk for Maritime Autonomous Surface Ships. Ocean Engineering, 202, 107188.

[13] Roy, B. (1991). The outranking approach and the foundations of ELECTRE methods. Theory and decision, 31, 49-73.

[14] Berrittella, M., Certa, A., Enea, M., & Zito, P. (2008). Transport policy and climate change: How to decide when experts disagree. environmental science & policy, 11(4), 307-314.

[15] Khan, A. U., & Ali, Y. (2020). Analytical hierarchy process (AHP) and analytic network process methods and their applications: a twenty year review from 2000-2019: AHP & ANP techniques and their applications: Twenty years review from 2000 to 2019. International Journal of the Analytic Hierarchy Process, 12(3).

[16] Escobar, M. T., Aguarón, J., & Moreno-Jiménez, J. M. (2004). A note on AHP group consistency for the row geometric mean priorization procedure. European Journal of Operational Research, 153(2), 318-322.

[17] IEC 60812. Analysis techniques for system reliability – procedure for failure mode and effects analysis (FMEA). International Electrotechnical Commission, Switzerland; 2006.

ACSA: A Hybrid Approach for Designing Smart Building Maintenance Strategies

Anas HOSSINI[1,2], Leïla KLOUL[2], Maël GUIRAUD[1,2], Benjamin COHEN BOULAKIA[2]

[1]Lineact CESI Laboratory, Nanterre, France
{ahossini, mguiraud}@cesi.fr
[2]DAVID Laboratory, Paris Saclay University, Versailles, France
{leila.kloul, benjamin.cohen-boulakia}@uvsq.fr

Keywords: Smart Buildings, Predictive Maintenance, Reinforcement Learning, Simulated Annealing

Abstract - Effective Predictive Maintenance is essential for ensuring the reliability of Smart Building systems while minimizing maintenance costs. This paper explores maintenance optimization by modeling system interactions using a Fault Tree and characterizing component failures with Weibull distributions. We evaluate two optimization techniques to enhance decision-making in this complex environment: Reinforcement Learning and Simulated Annealing. We propose ACSA, a hybrid algorithm that integrates reinforcement learning (Actor-Critic) with stochastic optimization (Simulated Annealing) to adjust maintenance strategies dynamically. Experimental results show that ACSA achieves a superior balance between system reliability and intervention costs while meeting Quality of Service constraints. This hybrid approach leverages adaptive decision-making to efficiently manage maintenance in non-stationary environments, making it a scalable solution for interconnected systems or any system of systems.

1. Introduction

Recent progress in sensing technologies, connectivity, and IoT architectures has been instrumental in advancing smart buildings (SB), enabling the integration of systems to enhance efficiency, sustainability, and scalability. A System of Systems (SoS) is a complex architecture of independent or semi-independent systems working together to achieve a given objective. SoS has four key features: autonomy [1], heterogeneity [2], connectivity [3], and emergence. Understanding these dynamics is essential for analyzing such systems. SB exemplifies the SoS concept, showcasing how interconnected systems collaborate to create dynamic and adaptive environments. SB resources can be optimized by leveraging real-time data from sensors and meters. Although subsystems operate autonomously, their integration improves adaptability, scalability, and supports predictive maintenance (PdM) [4], which enables early detection of potential failures.

Several models have been introduced to predict failures in general systems, as summarized in [5, 6]. PdM techniques are generally divided into three main categories: physical models, knowledge-based approaches, and data-driven methods [7]. In SBs, PdM predominantly relies on data-driven approaches, which use machine learning (ML) algorithm advancements [8, 9]. Despite their potential, these methods encounter significant challenges, including high instrumentation costs and a lack of sufficient failure data in newly constructed SBs, making their implementation more difficult. Most proposed solutions for PdM in SBs focus on maintenance strategies designed to maximize system reliability and availability, typically relying on predictive failure models, such as traditional ML approaches and heuristics [10, 11]. The integration of reinforcement learning (RL) algorithms into PdM strategies marks a significant advancement, offering the potential for greater efficiency and cost-effectiveness in SB maintenance operations. This approach has attracted considerable interest in recent research. As highlighted in [12], RL-based multi-agent systems and optimization techniques from Operations Research [13] are widely applied in the industrial context, aiming to reduce the financial costs of managing multiple machines or enhance machine availability. RL empowers systems to learn from experience autonomously, enabling dynamic adaptation of maintenance strategies based on real-time building performance data and cost considerations [14].

In our previous works [15, 16], we developed a PdM approach for the lighting system of a SB case study (NR3) [17], considering only its interaction with the network system. A Fault Tree (FT) modeled the system's component interactions. Due to the lack of failure data, we relied solely on manufacturer-provided data to characterize the failure probability distributions of each component that we assume follows a Weibull distribution (α, β, γ). A RL model based on the FT structure was then employed to optimize maintenance decisions while ensuring a given quality of service (QoS). However, this approach was limited to analyzing the impact of network subsystem failures on the lighting subsystem. In this paper, we address these limitations by developing concurrent maintenance strategies for all interconnected subsystems of this SB, thereby introducing greater algorithmic complexity. We also compare the RL model with an optimization-based approach -Simulated Annealing (SA) algorithm- and propose a novel hybrid algorithm, ACSA, which combines the strengths of both algorithms.

2. Predictive Maintenance Methodology

We introduce a PdM methodology for a given system. This methodology requires knowledge of:

- The operating status of each component in the system.
- The impact of each component on the system.
- The operating status after a maintenance operation.

We follow the methodology summarized in Figure 1 to meet the above requirements. It consists of two main steps:

Step 1: First, the user's QoS is defined in critical safety metrics, such as reliability, failure rate, and adherence to safety standards. Subsequently, each system component's Weibull parameters (α, β, γ) are determined based on the initial manufacturer data, notably the Mean Time to Failure (MTTF). Using these parameters, the system's failure probability is calculated using the FT. These steps collectively enable the computation of essential safety metrics, including reliability and the hazard function.

Step 2: We adapt the RL model to find the best maintenance decision according to the calculated metrics and user-defined QoS constraints. This decision is obtained using RL algorithms (Value-Based or Policy-based), depending on each component's (β, γ) parameters.

The Weibull distribution parameters for each component may change based on the maintenance action performed. Once again, a computation is performed to obtain the new system failure probability and metrics values. This process is repeated until the end of the defined simulation interval.

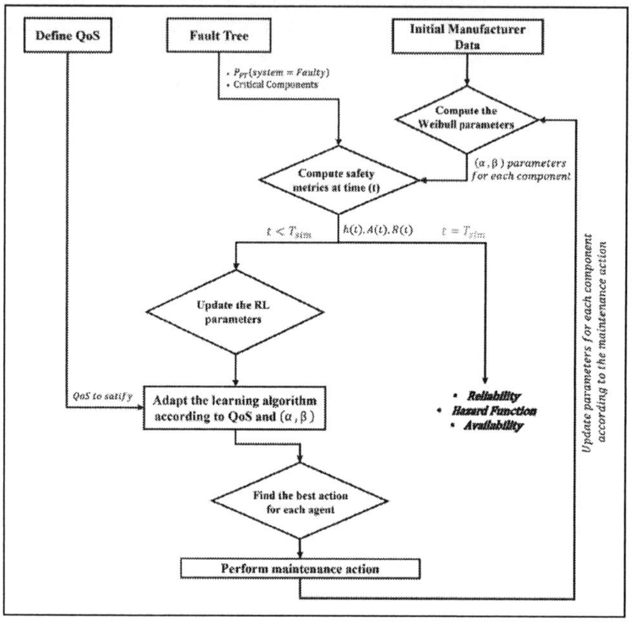

Figure 1. PdM Methodology

2.1. Case study: NR3 Smart Building

The NR3 Smart Building, part of CESI-Nanterre in Paris, France, is a two-story structure featuring an electrical room, a server room, and five multipurpose rooms. Each room has a lighting and an HVAC system comprising physical and logical components with interconnected sensors that enable interaction across rooms. The general architecture of the Nobel room is detailed in [16]. Figure 2 illustrates the system's interactions in the SB. A failure in the network system directly impacts both the lighting and Monitoring (IT) systems, while the IT system also affects the lighting system. These interactions represent the propagation of failures; for example, a power failure in the network system can disrupt data flow in the IT system and cut off the Power over Ethernet (PoE) supply to the lighting system.

In the following, we examine the Nobel room lighting system, considering all its interactions.

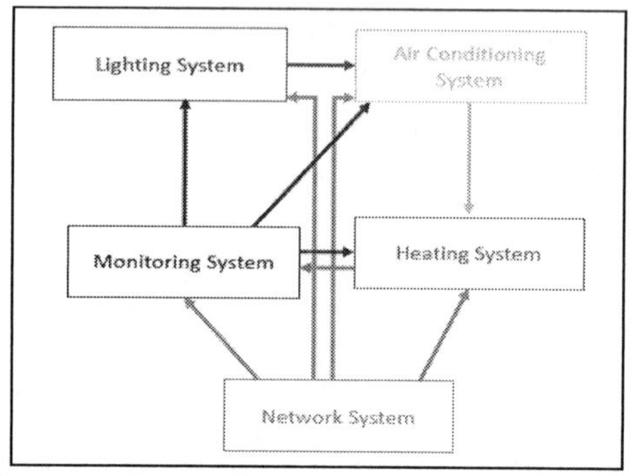

Figure 2. Interactions in the NR3 Smart Building

2.1.1. Systems description

The lighting system in the Nobel Room includes Light Fixtures and an Internal Switch (Cisco 3650CX). There are six light fixtures, each containing 12 bulbs, a temperature sensor (°C), an infrared (IR) sensor, and a Lux meter sensor (Lux). Moreover, the Internal Switch interacts with all the room's sensors and supplies PoE to the light fixtures.

The network system and the lighting system interact through several components, which include the Floor Switch (Cisco 2950X), essential for communication with the room's internal switch, the server, and the electrical system. The Cisco's MicroGrid LT consists of the power cables that connect the Cisco 3650CX and the Cisco 2950X, ensuring efficient power distribution, and the MicroGrid for Low Voltage (MicroGrid LT) that comprises six units, each linked to a light fixture, enabling PoE functionality.

Finally, the IT and lighting systems interact via a Virtual Machine of the Lighting System (VM-LS), which manages and controls the lighting functions.

2.1.2. From FT to FT-CE

We introduce the concept of a *connection event (CE)* to represent the other system's impacts in the FT model. Unlike the system's component failures, a *connection event* represents an external event or a logical combination of failures impacting the lighting system.

Figure 3 illustrates the FT with the Nobel room lighting system's *connection events* (FT-CE). Further details on light fixture failure events are provided in [18]. The events shown in bold highlight critical failures that led to the complete failure of the room's lighting system, identified through the application of the Minimum CutSet method [19].

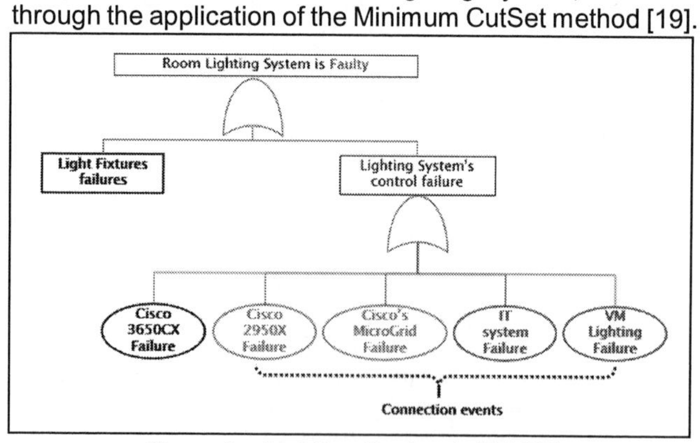

Figure 3. Lighting System's FT-CE

2.2. Design of a maintenance action

Due to the lack of failure data, we assume that component failures follow a Weibull distribution (α, β, γ) [20], a widely used model in reliability analysis for its flexibility in representing real-world failure behaviors. The shape and location parameters (β, γ) identify the three phases of a component's life cycle [21]. The β parameter influences whether the failure rate is increasing, decreasing, or constant over time, and the γ parameter represents a minimum threshold before no failure can occur. Adjusting these parameters allows different failure patterns corresponding to various stages of a component's lifecycle to be accurately modeled. In our approach, we use the MTTF value provided by the manufacturer to construct the Weibull distribution. Component aging is modeled by gradually increasing the β parameter, reflecting the progressive deterioration associated with the wear-out phase. This method has the advantage of simulating aging without requiring extensive failure data. It also incorporates the effects of maintenance interventions, where an improvement in the component's condition following a maintenance action is modeled as a reduction in the β value and an update of the γ parameter.

Figure 4 illustrates the characterization of a maintenance action and the Weibull parameter update process.

When **no maintenance** operation is performed for a component *i* in a simulation interval [0, T_{sim}], we suppose at $t = 0$ the component is new $\beta_0^i = 1$ and $\gamma_0^i = 0$:

$$\beta_{t+1}^i = \beta_t^i + \delta_t^i \quad where\ \delta_t^i = \frac{\beta_{t=MTTF_0^i}^i - \beta_0^i}{MTTF_0^i} \tag{1}$$

At time $t = MTTF_0^i$, component *i* is in the wear-out phase, and we suppose its probability density distribution follows a normal distribution ($\beta_{t=MTTF_i}^i = 3{,}6$).

When a **replacement** operation is performed at a given time T_{int} , component *i* is new. This means $\beta_{t=T_{int}}^i = 1$ and $MTTF_{T_{int}}^i = MTTF_0^i$. Thus, this component is at the beginning of a new cycle ($\gamma_{T_{int}}^i = T_{int}$), and its density distribution is updated:

$$f(t) = \frac{\beta_t^i}{\alpha_0^i}\left(\frac{t - T_{int}}{\alpha_0^i}\right)^{\beta_t^i - 1} e^{-\left(\frac{t-T_{int}}{\alpha_0^i}\right)^{\beta_t^i}} \tag{2}$$

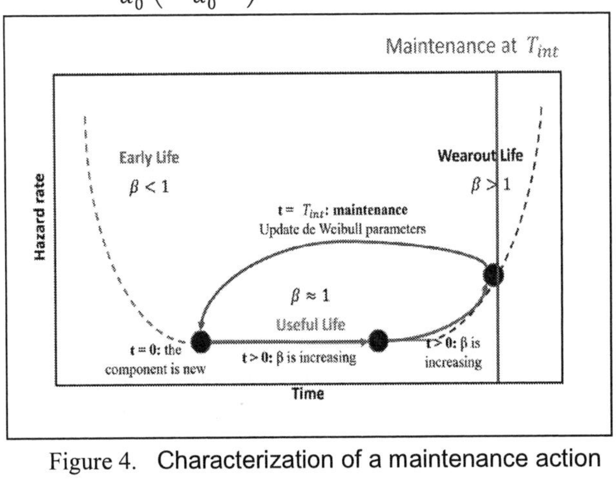

Figure 4. Characterization of a maintenance action

3. The proposed ACSA algorithm

In the proposed methodology, the RL model aims to find the best maintenance action that minimizes maintenance costs and satisfies a defined QoS.

3.1. RL model description

The RL model is described as follows:

- The *agents* are all the basic events in the FT-CE.
- The set of *states* for a given agent is represented by $S = \{Functional\ (F), Faulty\ (\bar{F})\}$.
- The agent's possible *actions* refer to the possible maintenance operations that can be taken when the agent is in state $s \in S$. The agents can choose whether to perform a replacement or not.

We aim to determine the most effective strategies for reducing maintenance costs while ensuring the QoS constraint. To achieve this goal, all agents must work together in a coordinated and cooperative manner. We define G_t^{sys} as the lighting system's global reward, considering all the interactions with other systems:

$$G_t^{sys} = \delta_{sys} \sum_{k=1}^{N} \frac{R_k(t)}{\sum_{j=1}^{N} R_j(t)} . r_k^a + (1 - \delta_{sys}). \psi_{QoS} \tag{3}$$

Such that:

- N: Total number of agents in the system.
- $R_k(t)$: Reliability at time *t* for agent $k \in \{1, \dots N\}$.
- r_k^a: The immediate reward of agent k according to the maintenance action a chosen at time *t*.
- ψ_{QoS}: A penalty if the QoS is unsatisfied.
- $\delta_{sys} = 1$ if the QoS is satisfied; otherwise, 0.

Using Equation 3, we can formulate the *reward* value obtained by an agent $k \in \{1, \dots N\}$ for the chosen action a, noted $G_{s_i^k \to s_j^k}^{a,k}$ as follows:

$$G_{s_i^k \to s_j^k}^{a,k} = \rho_1 . r_k^a + \rho_2 . G_t^{sys} \tag{4}$$

Such that ρ_1 $(resp. \rho_2)$ represents the importance factor ≥ 0 for the immediate (resp. system) reward.

3.2. When Actor-Critic meets Simulated Annealing

The Actor-Critic (AC) algorithm is adopted because it effectively handles exploration-exploitation trade-offs in complex environments [22]. Unlike purely value-based or policy-based methods, the AC combines the strengths of both approaches. The Actor is responsible for selecting actions based on a policy and updating this policy by following the gradients derived from the Critic's feedback. The Critic evaluates the actions taken by estimating the value function and computing the temporal difference error (TD error) to guide the Actor's updates. Finding an optimal policy using the AC algorithm is based on a gradient descent that depends on the TD error, as highlighted in Figure 5.

The main challenge in a non-stationary environment is that the agent's estimated value might be significantly biased when he chooses to perform an action [23]. To minimize this bias and improve the estimation, we adjust it using the predicted value obtained by the SA algorithm. Indeed, SA is a metaheuristic that optimizes complex problems by effectively exploring the solution space. The algorithm offers several advantages, making it an appealing choice for optimization problems. One of its key strengths is the ability to escape local optima, as the algorithm allows for the acceptance of worse solutions with a certain probability, enabling broader exploration of the solution space [24]. SA provides a maintenance policy for each agent with an optimal reward G^{SA}.

Algorithm 1 ACSA algorithm in a Non-Stationary Environment

Initialize critic θ^V and actor θ^π network parameters
Initialize target networks $\theta^{V'} \leftarrow \theta^V$, $\theta^{\pi'} \leftarrow \theta^\pi$
Initialize environment with initial state s
for episode $= 1$ to M **do**
  Initialize episode reward $R \leftarrow 0$
  Observe initial state s
  for timestep $(t) = 1$ to T **do**
    Simulated Annealing policy and reward: $\pi^{SA}, G^{SA} \leftarrow SA(\beta, \gamma)$
    Select action $a \sim \pi_{\theta^\pi}(a|s)$
    Execute action a, observe reward r and new state s'
    Compute TD error $\delta_i = r_i + \gamma V_{\theta^{V'}}(s_i') - V_{\theta^V}(s_i)$
    Update critic network: $\theta^V \leftarrow \theta^V + \alpha^V \nabla_{\theta^V} \delta_i^2$
    Update actor network using policy gradient:

$$\nabla_{\theta^\pi} J(\theta^\pi) \approx \frac{1}{|\mathcal{D}|} \sum_i \nabla_{\theta^\pi} \log \pi_{\theta^\pi}(a_i|s_i) \cdot \delta_i$$

    Update target networks:

$$\theta^{V'} \leftarrow \tau\theta^V + (1-\tau)\theta^{V'}, \quad \theta^{\pi'} \leftarrow \tau\theta^\pi + (1-\tau)\theta^{\pi'}$$

    $s \leftarrow s'$
    $R \leftarrow R + r$
    $score_{reliability} \leftarrow \frac{R_{sys}(t)}{R_{ideal}}$, $score_{reward} \leftarrow \frac{G^{AC}(t)}{G^{SA}(t)}$
    if $score_{reliability} \geq 1$ and $score_{reward} \leq 1$ **then**
      Update (β, γ) using the Simulated Annealing policy π^{SA}
    else
      Update (β, γ) using the Actor-Critic policy π_{θ^π}
    end if
  end for
end for

Figure 5. ACSA algorithm

The proposed ACSA algorithm is designed for non-stationary environments. The algorithm initializes actor and critic networks, along with target networks. An agent interacts with the environment over multiple time steps. A Simulated Annealing policy is applied at each step to generate an alternative policy π^{SA} and a reward estimate G^{SA}. The agent selects an action based on its current Actor-Critic policy π^{θ^π}, executes it, and observes the reward and the new state. The critic network uses TD learning, while the actor-network is updated using policy gradient optimization.

The algorithm includes an adaptive mechanism based on system reliability and reward scores. The Simulated Annealing policy updates the agent's Weibull parameters (β, γ) when the system's reliability exceeds a predefined target R_{ideal} set by the user and when the reward associated with this policy surpasses the Actor-Critic approach. Otherwise, the parameters are updated using the Actor-Critic policy.

Another advantage of the ACSA framework is its ability to balance QoS and maintenance cost. In this context, each maintenance action selected by an agent updates the system's degradation profile, typically modeled through a change in the Weibull parameters.

When the optimal maintenance decision, based on both cost and QoS criteria, is identified by the Simulated Annealing algorithm, the agent *i* is rewarded accordingly through immediate reward r_i.

This reward, in turn, influences the Temporal Difference (TD) error, which updates the value function and the policy estimates within the Actor-Critic algorithm. This process contributes to improved learning dynamics and overall performance of the AC algorithm.

Conversely, when the Actor-Critic determines the optimal maintenance decision at a given time, the resulting change in Weibull parameters is incorporated into the SA algorithm. This algorithm will then use the updated degradation information to refine its search for an improved maintenance policy at the next decision epoch.

This hybrid approach enables the agents to balance exploration and exploitation, ensuring improved adaptability in dynamic environments.

4. Numerical Results

The proposed model is tested on an NR3 Nobel room lighting subsystem. Using the manufacturer's $MTTF_0$ values of each component at the beginning of the simulation, we obtain by simulation the initial Weibull parameters $(\alpha_0, \beta_0) = (MTTF_0, 1)$ based on the relation that links these parameters to the MTTF ($MTTF_0 = \alpha_0.\Gamma(1 + 1/\beta_0)$ where Γ is the Gamma function). Over time, the (β, γ) parameters are updated based on the maintenance actions performed. We consider a simulation interval $[0, T_{sim}]$ where $T_{sim} = 3650\ days$ and a defined reliability QoS to satisfy the lighting system fixed at $R_{QoS} = 70\%$ and $R_{ideal} = 80\%$.

We calculate and display the reliability $R_{sys}(t)$ and the system reward evolution. Table 1 summarizes the simulation parameters.

Table 1. Simulation Parameters

Actor and Critic learning rate	(0.01,0.01)
Discount factor (Future rewards importance)	0.99
(ρ_1, ρ_2)	(0.9, 0.1)
Initial temperature	500
Cooling rate	0.99

Figure 6 illustrates the evolution of the lighting system's reliability when applying the algorithms presented in Section 3. A common feature among these algorithms is the collaborative behavior of agents to maintain the required QoS. Although the ACSA algorithm occasionally deviates from this objective, it generally aligns well with the expected performance. A key distinction among the algorithms lies in the efficiency of maintenance actions: the Simulated

Annealing approach achieves the desired QoS with fewer interventions than the other methods. Additionally, minor improvements in reliability observed correspond to the replacement of non-critical components, such as bulbs, which are highly abundant in the system.

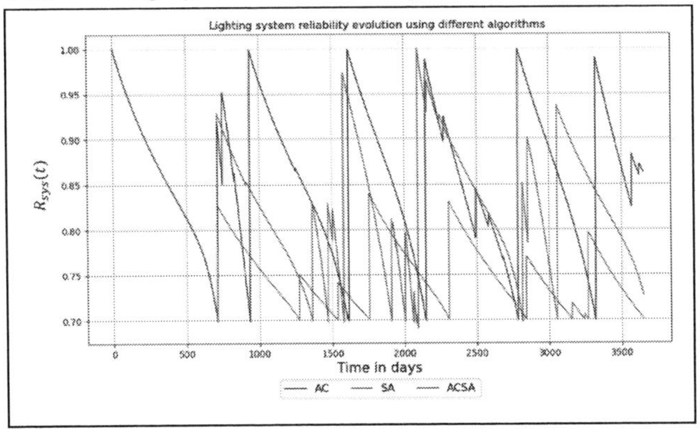

Figure 6. Lighting system reliability $R_{sys}(t)$

Figure 7 illustrates the evolution of the system's reward obtained through the AC algorithm. The reward is directly linked to the system's reliability, capturing the inherent trade-off between maintenance costs and benefits. Positive rewards are assigned when the system operates above the QoS, incentivizing agents who proactively initiate maintenance actions. Conversely, significant drops in reward correspond to replacement events, reflecting the increased costs required to restore system reliability. Additionally, the reward G^{AC} obtained using the ACSA algorithm exhibits a slight improvement compared to the standard AC approach, highlighting the benefits of integrating SA in optimizing maintenance strategies.

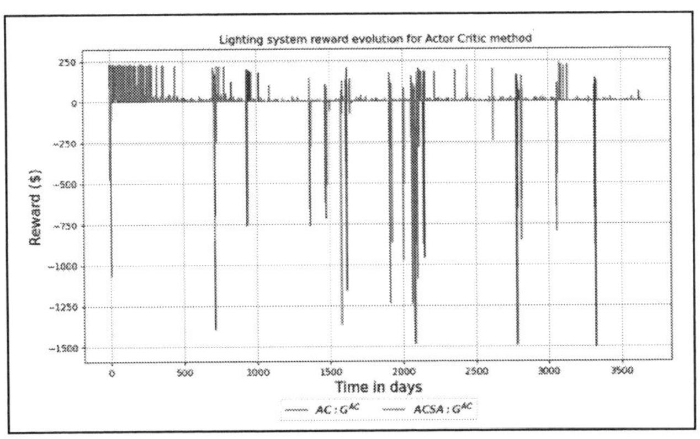

Figure 7. Reward comparison between AC and ACSA

Figure 8 illustrates the evolution of the reward G^{SA} obtained using the SA algorithm. The results indicate that the ACSA algorithm improves the cumulative reward over time, demonstrating its ability to enhance long-term performance. This improvement highlights the impact of the AC policy on the SA algorithm, showing that integrating RL mechanisms helps refine maintenance decisions by balancing exploration and exploitation.

Figure 9 presents a comparative analysis of the performance of the proposed algorithms, evaluating both average reliability and average reward in the simulation interval $[0, T_{sim}]$. The AC algorithm achieves the highest average reliability (86%) but at the cost of a negative reward (-1.32), indicating frequent maintenance actions that ensure system stability but increase costs. In contrast, the SA algorithm maintains a lower average reliability (77%) while achieving a significantly higher average reward (228.71), suggesting a more cost-effective yet less reliable maintenance strategy.

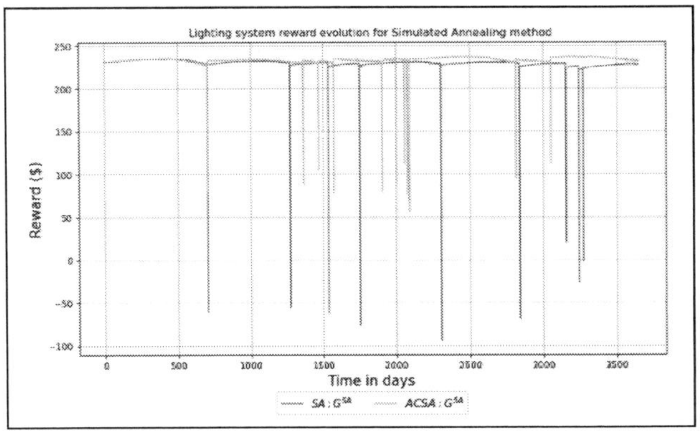

Figure 8. Reward comparison between SA and ACSA

The ACSA algorithm reaches an average reliability of 83% and an improved reward of 232.25, surpassing both standalone approaches regarding reward efficiency. This highlights the advantage of ACSA in optimizing maintenance decisions, effectively mitigating costs while ensuring high system reliability.

Thus, the Simulated Annealing algorithm provides maintenance decisions that are primarily cost-effective while ensuring compliance with the required QoS. In parallel, the Actor-Critic algorithm continuously improves maintenance actions over time, enhancing the system's average reliability. The ACSA framework combines the strengths of both approaches, yielding a balanced performance that optimizes cost-efficiency and long-term system dependability.

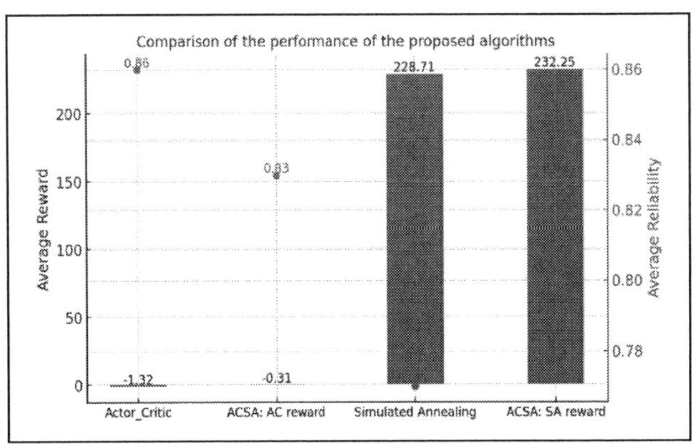

Figure 9. Algorithms performance comparison

5. Conclusion

The proposed ACSA algorithm, which combines reinforcement learning (AC) with stochastic optimization

(SA), exhibits superior performance by achieving a well-balanced trade-off between reliability and maintenance costs. This approach demonstrates that policy-based learning with adaptive optimization techniques can enhance decision-making in non-stationary environments. The results highlight the potential of hybrid Reinforcement Learning approaches for predictive maintenance, providing a scalable and adaptive solution for smart building management.
In our future work, we aim to design maintenance plans for each smart building system based on the obtained predictions and integrate them into a general framework adapted to any complex system.

6. References

[1] M. Jamshidi, System of Systems - *the Third International Conference on Industrial and Information Systems*, India, pp. 6-7, 2008.

[2] W. C. Baldwin and B. Sauser, Modeling the Characteristics of System of Systems, *IEEE International Conference on SoSE* pp. 1-6, 2009.

[3] G. Fortino, C. Savaglio, G. Spezzano, and M. Zhou, Internet of Things as System of Systems: A Review of Methodologies, Frameworks, Platforms, and Tools, *IEEE Transactions on Systems*, pp. 223-236, 2021

[4] S. Petersen and M. D. Knudsen, Optimization of Energy Consumption in Smart Buildings Using a System of Systems Framework, *Energy and Buildings*, vol. 251, article 111384, 2022

[5] Muthumani. A survey on failure prediction methods. *ACM Computing Surveys*, 42(3), 2010.

[6] D. Pagano. A predictive maintenance model using long short-term memory neural networks and bayesian inference. *Decision Analytics Journal, ELSEVIER*, 2023.

[7] Zonta, Costa, Righi, de Lima, Trindade, and Li. Predictive maintenance in the industry 4.0: A systematic literature review. *Comput. Ind. Eng.,* 150, 106889, 2020.

[8] Susto, Schirru, Pampuri, McLoone, and Beghi. Machine learning for predictive maintenance: A multiple classifiers approach. *IEEE Transactions on Industrial Informatics,* 11, 2015.

[9] Bouabdallaoui, Lahfaj, Yim, Ducoulombier, and Bennadji. Predictive maintenance in building facilities: A machine learning-based approach. *Sensors, ISSN*, 1424-8220, 2021.

[10] Y. Ran, X. Zhou, P. Lin, Y. Wen, and R. Deng. A survey of predictive maintenance: Systems, purposes and approaches. *IEEE Communication Survey Tutorials*, 2019.

[11] K. Alanne and S. Sierla. An overview of ML applications for smart buildings. *ELSEVIER*, 2022.

[12] M. L. R. Rodriguez, S. Kubler, A. de Giorgio, M. Cordy, J. Robert, and Y. Le Traon. Multi-agent deep reinforcement learning-based predictive maintenance on parallel machines. *Robotics and Computer–Integrated Manufacturing, ELSEVIER*, 2022.

[13] O. Pisacane, D. Potena, S. Antomarioni, M. Bevilacqua, F. E. Ciarapica, and C. Diamantini. Data-driven predictive maintenance policy based on multi-objective optimization approaches for the component repairing problem. *Engineering Optimization*; Volume 53,- Issue 10, 2021.

[14] D. Vamvakas, P. Michailidis, C. Korkas, and E. Kosmatopoulos. Review and evaluation of reinforcement learning frameworks on smart grid applications. *Energies* 2023, 16(14), 5326, 2023.

[15] A. Hossini, L. Kloul, B. C. Boulakia, Fault Prediction in a Smart Building Lighting System, *European Safety and Reliability Conference*, 2023.

[16] A. Hossini, L. Kloul, M. Guiraud, B. C. Boulakia, Adaptive Reinforcement Learning Approach for Predictive Maintenance of a Smart Building Lighting System, *IEEE International Conference on Industrial Informatics*, 2024.

[17] CESI Demonstrators - Research & Innovation CESI demonstrators – CESI, 2025.

[18] A. Hossini, L. Kloul, M. Guiraud, B. C. Boulakia. Modeling the lighting system of the Nanterre 3 smart building. *https://hal.science/CESI/hal-04693839v1*.

[19] Ladislav Rosenberg, Algorithm for finding minimal cut sets in a fault tree, *Reliability Engineering & System Safety*, Volume 53, Issue 1,1996,

[20] HALLINAN JR, Arthur J. A review of the Weibull distribution. *Journal of quality technology*, 1993, vol. 25, no 2, p. 85-93.

[21] Xie, M., & Lai, C. D. Reliability analysis using an additive Weibull model with bathtub-shaped failure rate function. *Reliability Engineering & System Safety*, 52(1), 87-93-1996.

[22] C. Banerjee, Z. Chen, and N. Noman, Improved Soft Actor-Critic: Mixing Prioritized Off-Policy Samples With On-Policy Experiences, *IEEE Transactions on Neural Networks and Learning Systems*, vol. 35, no. 3, pp. 3121-3129, 2024.

[23] Sutton, R. S., & Barto, A. G. Reinforcement learning: An introduction (2nd ed.). *MIT Press,* 2018.

[24] Rutenbar, R. A. Simulated annealing algorithms: An overview. *IEEE Circuits and Devices magazine*, 5(1), 19-26, 1989.

Potentiating forecasting capabilities in the retail business

Nachiket Pusadkar[1], Silvia Carpitella[1] and Sepideh Abolghasem[1]

[1]California State University, Northridge; 18111 Nordhoff Street, CA 91330, US

Abstract

In the current business environment, particularly in sectors characterized by high market volatility, improving forecasting accuracy has become a critical industrial priority. The retail sector plays a crucial role within the industry, where inaccurate forecasts can significantly impact the entire supply chain. Retail serves as a bridge between manufacturers and customers while managing the distribution of diverse product types. Due to this complexity and potential limitations in existing forecasting models, acquiring incorrect quantities of goods often leads to higher costs and ineffective demand predictions. One of the primary challenges in the retail sector is that, despite the availability of various forecasting models, they often struggle to deliver reliable predictions due to the impact of product seasonality. This study aims to compare different models from the current literature and identify the best suited to specific data samples, with the goal of enhancing forecast accuracy in the retail sector.

1 Introduction

In the modern retail landscape, where consumers have an abundance of choices, the shopping experience often begins with a visit to a physical store or an online platform. Whether searching for everyday essentials or specialty items, customers expect to find what they need without difficulty. However, encountering an out-of-stock product can be a frustrating experience that may lead to abandoned purchases or a shift to competing brands. One of the main reasons for these stock shortages is inaccurate demand forecasting [1]. Retailers must anticipate consumer needs to ensure that products are available when and where they are needed. This specific task is particularly complex due to the vast number of brands and product variations in the retail sector [2].

Consumer preferences, seasonal trends, supply chain disruptions, and unpredictable shifts in demand further complicate the accuracy of forecasts [3]. As a result, retailers face the challenge of balancing inventory levels to minimize shortages while avoiding excess stock that leads to financial losses. In this context, effective forecasting methods and data-driven strategies are essential for improving product availability and enhancing the overall shopping experience. While some companies have adopted advanced demand forecasting techniques that leverage data analytics, many other organizations still rely on qualitative assessments from senior management or other expert stakeholders, often based on intuition and past experiences.

This approach can be effective in some areas [4], but the transition to data-driven decision-making requires a fundamental shift in organizational mindset, with executives playing a critical role in steering this transformation [5]. In today's increasingly volatile market, subjective methods carry indeed higher risks of inaccurate predictions, resulting in inefficiencies in sales and operations, either through overallocation or underuse of resources [6]. On the contrary, data-driven forecasting offers more precise and reliable insights into future demand trends [7]. With the rapid advancement of Artificial Intelligence (AI) and Machine Learning (ML), predictive analytics is becoming increasingly prevalent across various industries. In the supply chain domain [8], not only are ML models proving to be highly effective in ensuring smooth business operations, but also in driving overall business growth and efficiency.

This study focuses on sales forecasting for a retail store by evaluating and comparing various predictive models applied to daily sales data across popular product categories. The goal is to assess the accuracy of these models, identifying the one with the lowest standard deviation in forecasted values. To explore the most effective approach for predicting intermittent demand, the research will examine the Croston model, which is widely used for items with fluctuating demand patterns [9]. Additionally, ensemble regression models such as XGBoost, LightGBM, Histogram Gradient Boosting, and Random Forest will be analyzed for their ability to handle complex data. The performance of these models will be evaluated based on key metrics such as Mean Absolute Percentage Error (MAPE), Root Mean Squared Error (RMSE) and R-squared (R^2) with the aim of identifying the most accurate model for demand forecasting. The findings improve data-driven decision-making and operational efficiency.

This paper is organized as follows. Section 2 offers a literature review on current forecasting techniques. Section 3 describes and compares different methods. Section 4 reports a case study along with practical discussions. Section 5 closes the paper by highlighting areas for future research.

2 Literature Review

Demand planning and forecasting have long been integral practices within business operations [10]. In their most traditional view, these processes may be predominantly driven by expert judgment and qualitative approaches, including the Delphi method, historical analogies, and executive consensus.

As previously touched, while these methods provide subjective insights, they lack the precision of data-driven decision models, often leading to inaccuracies, financial losses, and inefficient resource allocation. The transition to Industry 4.0 has marked a shift toward fact-based analyses [7], leveraging historical data and quantitative analytics to enhance predictive accuracy. This transformation enables organizations to analyze market trends, assess product performance, and proactively adjust inventory levels rather than reacting to demand fluctuations [11]. The application of ML models originally focused on specific areas like forecasting stock prices, financial analysis, and recommendation systems. For instance, e-commerce companies used ML algorithms to predict user preferences and recommend products based on past behaviors or purchasing history. However, with the advent of Industry 4.0, ML has increasingly become an integral part of supply chain optimization and inventory planning. Many industries have now incorporated ML into their demand forecasting strategies [12], something that enables them to optimize stock levels while reducing overstocking, with a general improvement of customer retention rates.

Specifically, the introduction of AI in demand forecasting has revolutionized predictive analytics [13], enabling businesses to transition from such traditional time-series models as, for instance, the Autoregressive Integrated Moving Average (ARIMA) [14], to more sophisticated ML approaches. As industries continue to pursue more accurate demand forecasting, many companies have also adopted hybrid models [15] aiming at integrating multiple forecasting techniques suited to their specific business requirements.However, demand forecasting remains a challenging task due to the inherent variability in demand patterns over time, which can be influenced by numerous external factors [16]. To address this challenge, researchers have developed frameworks that incorporate uncertainty modeling [17], which helps to account for the unpredictable nature of demand fluctuations. This ongoing development has led to an active debate in the field regarding the best forecasting methods that can consistently deliver the highest level of accuracy [18].

This research aims to contribute to this discussion by exploring and comparing various forecasting techniques. Given the complexity of intermittent demand, one of the primary models herein investigated is the Croston model [19]. This method is specifically designed for sporadic demand patterns, where products do not follow a regular consumption trend. Xu et al. [20] have extensively covered the theoretical aspects of the Croston model, demonstrating how it applies exponential smoothing techniques to update forecasts only after positive demand occurrences. In addition to the Croston model, the present study incorporates the Extreme Gradient Boosting (XGBoost) [21], a robust ML-based model that has gained popularity due to its ability to handle complex datasets [22]. In this regard, XGBoost has demonstrated significant predictive performance in various domains, particularly in financial risk assessment, where this approach was successfully applied to classify company financial data and predict e-commerce risk levels [23]. Considering its importance in current literature, we are going to apply XGBoost in demand forecasting to evaluate its ability to improve prediction accuracy and model efficiency.

Lastly, the Light Gradient Boosting Machine (LightGBM) is included in this study due to its high computational efficiency and interpretability [24]. Unlike XGBoost, which grows trees by expanding them level by level, LightGBM grows trees by focusing on individual leaves. This approach speeds up training and improves efficiency, particularly when working with large datasets [25]. Prior research [26] demonstrates effectiveness of LightGBM in customer retention analysis, particularly in assessing customer loyalty factors with a high degree of accuracy, the last one evaluated via key metrics. We aim to further contribute to the existing literature by evaluating LightGBM's performance in demand forecasting.

3 Methodology

The methodological comparison presented in this section employs two primary datasets, which will be examined in the case study section: a sales dataset and a calendar dataset. Both are key for developing an accurate demand forecasting model. In detail, the sales dataset contains historical daily sales records for multiple products across different stores and categories, while the calendar dataset provides with contextual information such as dates, weekdays, months, years, special events, and state-level Supplemental Nutrition Assistance Program (SNAP) eligibility.

The first step in our approach involves data preprocessing, ensuring that the datasets are clean and structured for consequent analysis. The sales dataset is merged with the calendar dataset by aligning sales data with actual dates and corresponding calendar attributes. Missing values, particularly in event-related columns, are going to be imputed by using prior trends or filled with "No Event" to ensure consistency. Several features are created to enhance forecasting capabilities [27], including time-related variables like the day of the week, month, year, and whether it is a weekend. Lag features are added to capture past sales trends, and moving averages for different time periods are used to reduce fluctuations. Event-based features are incorporated to measure the impact of special promotions or holidays, while SNAP-related columns are analyzed to assess economic influences on sales. Exploratory Data Analysis (EDA) is then performed to uncover important trends and patterns in the data.

Particularly, sales trends are analyzed across different product categories (e.g., hobbies, foods, household) to identify seasonal changes and fluctuations in demand. The effects of holidays and promotional events are assessed to understand how they impact sales. Additionally, sales patterns between weekdays and weekends are examined to spot trends specific to different store locations. Products with irregular sales patterns are identified, as they may require specialized forecasting methods, since traditional time-series models might not be effective in such cases.

For the implementation and training of the model, the dataset is divided into two sets: 80% for training and 20% for validation. This split allows for the model to be trained on the majority of the data while still being tested on a smaller portion to assess its performance. To ensure the predictions are reliable and not overly specific to the training data, cross-validation techniques are employed. This approach helps in minimizing the risk of overfitting, ensuring the model generalizes well to unseen data.

Additionally, feature importance analysis is carried out to pinpoint the key variables that play a crucial role in driving demand fluctuations [28]. This helps in understanding which factors most significantly influence the forecasted outcomes. Once the models are trained, their performance is evaluated on validation data, and the most effective model is selected based on its ability to minimize forecasting errors while capturing underlying demand patterns. The final model is then suggested to be used to generate future demand forecasts, supporting improved inventory planning and decision-making in the retail sector.

The Croston model forecasts intermittent demand by updating demand level and periodicity using exponential smoothing. When demand occurs $[d(t) > 0]$, both are updated; otherwise, the forecast remains unchanged. Although both XGBoost and LightGBM are gradient boosting models, their architectural differences impact performance, as we discussed in the literature review section. LightGBM is faster due to its leaf-wise tree growth and histogram-based learning, while XGBoost's depth-wise growth allows for more detailed feature analysis, though it requires more memory and takes longer to train. In the next case study, we aim to find the model that best balances computational efficiency with predictive accuracy. MAPE, RMSE and R^2 are the key metrics that will be used to evaluate performance. MAEP and RMSE respectively measure the average absolute error and the standard deviation of prediction errors, with lower values suggesting higher accuracy. R^2 measures how well predictions match actual demand trends, with higher values indicating a better fit. Through these analyses, the most effective forecasting method for retail demand prediction will be identified in the next section.

4 Case Study

The present case study focuses on the retail industry due to the complex challenges faced by this sector in demand forecasting. As reported in [29], forecasting inaccuracies are considered a critical issue for the 73% of corporate retail professionals, leading to increased storage costs, missed sales and decreased customer satisfaction. To address these challenges, this study analyzes historical sales data across multiple product categories with contextual calendar data, available here [30]. We are now going to evaluate the effectiveness of the forecasting models previously discussed, that are the Croston model for intermittent demand and ensemble ML models (XGBoost and LightGBM), demonstrating how AI-powered forecasting solutions can help retailers mitigate overstocking and understocking risks.

Figure 1 reports the total sales trend over time, showing a clear seasonal pattern with fluctuations in demand. Periodic drops in sales typically indicate holidays, supply chain disruptions, either anomalies in data recording. Despite these fluctuations, there is a general increasing trend in sales over the years, emphasizing the importance of forecasting models that can adapt to seasonal and long-term trends. The dataset contains sales data categorized into three main groups: Foods, Hobbies, and Household. The Foods category leads in sales, significantly exceeding the Household and Hobbies categories, which follow at moderate and low levels, respectively.

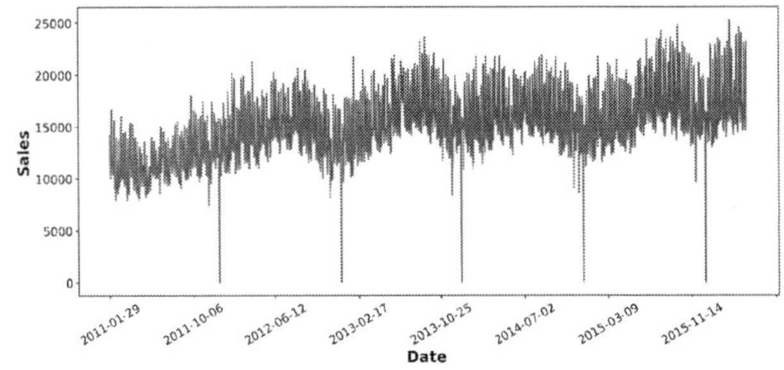

Figure 1. Total sales over time

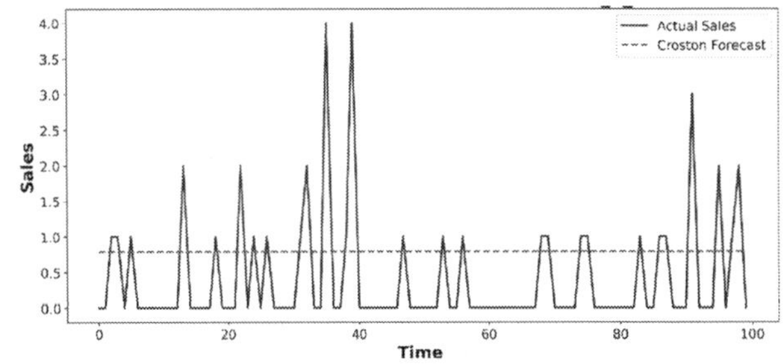

Figure 2. Actual vs. Croston predicted sales

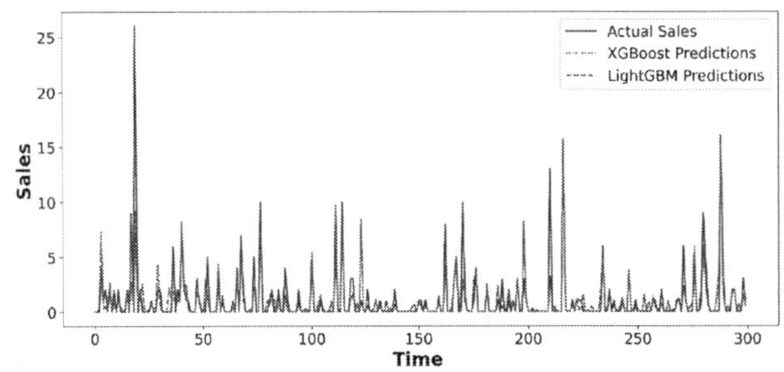

Figure 3. Actual vs. ML-based predicted sales

The statistical summary reveals fluctuating sales patterns, with low average sales per product but occasional spikes in demand. A high standard deviation indicates significant variability, highlighting intermittent demand. This variability justifies the use of the Croston model, which effectively handles such patterns. Overall, these insights emphasize the need for a robust forecasting approach that accounts for seasonality, differences in product categories, and intermittent demand fluctuations to improve inventory management and reduce forecast errors.

Retail products often experience sporadic demand with frequent zero-sales periods, making accurate forecasting challenging. To classify such products, we calculated the Coefficient of Variation Squared (CV^2) to measure demand variability and the Average Demand Interval (ADI) to assess sales frequency, identifying items as intermittent if ADI ≥ 1.32 and $CV^2 < 0.49$. Based on this classification, the Croston's method was applied to the top 10 most intermittent products, as it effectively models non-zero demand occurrences and their intervals separately. The model generated 50-period forecasts, providing a more stable and reliable prediction, ensuring better inventory control for products with irregular sales patterns.

Figure 2 compares actual vs. Croston predicted sales for a sample product from the Foods category. The blue line represents real sales data and the red dashed line represents the Croston forecast, offering a more consistent baseline. By smoothing demand fluctuations, the Croston method enables better inventory planning and prevents unnecessary stock replenishment. In such a direction, Croston forecast provides a solution for managing intermittent demand products, allowing retailers to optimize inventory levels and mitigate overstocking or stockout risks.

We also employed XGBoost and LightGBM, both of them using historical sales trends, time-based features (month, year, weekday), lagged sales (7-day and 14-day), and rolling mean sales (7-day and 14-day) to capture demand patterns. XGBoost has been configured with 150 estimators, a learning rate of 0.3, and a max depth of 20, while LightGBM has been set with 150 estimators, a learning rate of 0.1, and a max depth of 25.

A comparison between actual sales (blue line) and predicted sales (red dashed line for XGBoost and green dashed line for LightGBM) is offered in Figure 3. Both models closely follow the actual sales trend, demonstrating their ability to capture fluctuations in demand. While some deviations are visible, particularly in extreme sales spikes, the overall alignment indicates that the models effectively predict sales patterns, supporting their application in demand forecasting for inventory optimization.

As explained in Section 3, we are now going to use MAPE, RMSE, and R^2 as key evaluation metrics fro comparing model performance. More in detail, MAPE assesses the average percentage error, indicating model accuracy in relative terms. RMSE measures prediction error magnitude, penalizing larger deviations for better precision assessment [31]. R^2 evaluates how well the model explains variance in sales, with values closer to 1 indicating stronger predictive capability [32]. These metrics collectively ensure a balanced evaluation of accuracy, precision, and explanatory power, aiding in selecting the best forecasting approach for retail demand optimization. Table 1 reports the values obtained for these metrics with relation to each of the model analyzed in this case study.

We can derive various practical considerations from the values reported in Table 1. These results highlight the importance of selecting the right forecasting model for inventory and procurement planning. For sporadic demand, Croston model, despite its high error (MAEP: 2184.14%) and low accuracy (R^2: 0.5%), helps set minimum stock levels to prevent shortages. However, for regularly selling products, more accurate models like LightGBM (R^2: 78%) and XGBoost (R^2: 74%) provide better predictions, with LightGBM reducing forecast errors the most (RMSE: 1.93). LightGBM is particularly effective for high-volume products, where small inaccuracies can lead to costly overstocking or shortages. Using the right model improves stock control, purchasing decisions, and overall supply chain efficiency by balancing inventory costs, reducing waste, and ensuring reliable order fulfillment.

TABLE 1. Model performance evaluation

Model/Parameter	MAPE	RMSE	R^2
Croston	2184.14%	0.86	0.5%
XGBoost	60.10%	2.09	74%
LightGBM	59.72%	1.93	78%

5 Conclusions

The present paper explores the fundamental topic of demand forecasting in the retail sector with relation to specific models used in literature to enhance inventory management, procurement, and capacity planning. By analyzing historical sales data and time-based features, we have applied the Croston method to model sales of products characterized by intermittent demand, enabling decision-makers to determine minimum stock levels for low-frequency sales items. We then implemented both the XGBoost and LightGBM models for regularly selling products, with results indicating that LightGBM (R^2: 78%) outperforms XGBoost (R^2: 74%), delivering more accurate and stable forecasts for optimizing inventory levels. The findings of this study highlight that AI-driven forecasting models improve supply chain efficiency by minimizing stockouts, reducing excess inventory, and enhancing procurement strategies. However, future improvements can focus on hybrid modeling approaches aimed at integrating the Croston method with ML techniques to capture long-term trends. Additionally, incorporating external factors such as economic indicators, competitor pricing, and real-time sales data could further refine forecasting accuracy, making inventory planning even more resilient in dynamic retail environments.

References

[1] Y. Tadayonrad and A. B. Ndiaye, “A new key performance indicator model for demand forecasting in inventory management considering supply chain reliability and seasonality,” *Supply Chain Analytics*, vol. 3, p. 100026, 2023.

[2] M. G. Dekimpe, “Retailing and retailing research in the age of big data analytics,” *International Journal of Research in Marketing*, vol. 37, no. 1, pp. 3–14, 2020.

[3] L. Ye, N. Xie, J. E. Boylan, and Z. Shang, “Forecasting seasonal demand for retail: A Fourier time-varying grey model,” *International Journal of Forecasting*, vol. 40, no. 4, pp. 1467–1485, 2024.

[4] N. G. Shepherd, B. Lou, and J. M. Rudd, “Going with the gut: Exploring top management team intuition in strategic decision-making,” *Journal of Business Research*, vol. 181, p. 114740, 2024.

[5] P. Korherr, D. K. Kanbach, S. Kraus, and P. Mikalef, “From intuitive to data-driven decision-making in digital transformation: A framework of prevalent managerial archetypes,” *Digital Business*, vol. 2, no. 2, p. 100045, 2022.

[6] S. K. R. Malikireddy, “Transforming SME cloud cost management with artificial intelligence,” *International Journal of Cloud Computing and Services Science*, vol. 9, no. 3, pp. 112–124, 2020.

[7] A. R. Muthukalyani, “Unlocking accurate demand forecasting in retail supply chains with AI-driven predictive analytics,” *Information Technology and Management*, vol. 14, no. 2, pp. 48–57, 2023.

[8] M. Selvaraju and L. Arokiasamy, "Inaccurate forecasting planning nurture inventory wastage (perishable items) in the hypermarket retail.," *Global Business & Management Research*, vol. 11, no. 1, 2019.

[9] X. Tian, H. Wang, and E. Erjiang, "Forecasting intermittent demand for inventory management by retailers: A new approach," *Journal of Retailing and Consumer Services*, vol. 62, p. 102662, 2021.

[10] C. Crum and G. E. Palmatier, *Demand management best practices: process, principles, and collaboration*. J. Ross Publishing, 2003.

[11] Ö. Turgut, F. Taube, and S. Minner, "Data-driven retail inventory management with backroom effect," *OR Spectrum*, vol. 40, no. 4, pp. 945–968, 2018.

[12] H. Kagalwala, G. Radhakrishnan, I. A. Mohammed, R. R. Kothinti, and N. Kulkarni, "Predictive analytics in supply chain management: The role of AI and machine learning in demand forecasting," *Advances in Consumer Research*, vol. 2, pp. 142–149, 2025.

[13] Y. K. Dwivedi, A. Sharma, N. P. Rana, M. Giannakis, P. Goel, and V. Dutot, "Evolution of artificial intelligence research in technological forecasting and social change: Research topics, trends, and future directions," *Technological Forecasting and Social Change*, vol. 192, p. 122579, 2023.

[14] S. Jaipuria and S. S. Mahapatra, "An improved demand forecasting method to reduce bullwhip effect in supply chains," *Expert Systems with Applications*, vol. 41, no. 5, pp. 2395–2408, 2014.

[15] S. Jaipuria and S. Mahapatra, "A hybrid forecasting technique to deal with heteroskedastic demand in a supply chain," *Operations and Supply Chain Management: An International Journal*, vol. 14, no. 2, pp. 123–132, 2021.

[16] M. Abolghasemi, E. Beh, G. Tarr, and R. Gerlach, "Demand forecasting in supply chain: The impact of demand volatility in the presence of promotion," *Computers & Industrial Engineering*, vol. 142, p. 106380, 2020.

[17] R. Fildes and B. Kingsman, "Incorporating demand uncertainty and forecast error in supply chain planning models," *Journal of the Operational Research Society*, vol. 62, no. 3, pp. 483–500, 2011.

[18] H. Ahaggach, L. Abrouk, and E. Lebon, "Systematic mapping study of sales forecasting: Methods, trends, and future directions," *Forecasting*, vol. 6, no. 3, pp. 502–532, 2024.

[19] J. D. Croston, "Forecasting and stock control for intermittent demands," *Journal of the Operational Research Society*, vol. 23, no. 3, pp. 289–303, 1972.

[20] Q. Xu, N. Wang, and H. Shi, "Review of Croston's method for intermittent demand forecasting," in *2012 9th International Conference on Fuzzy Systems and Knowledge Discovery*, pp. 1456–1460, IEEE, 2012.

[21] D. Nielsen, "Tree boosting with XGBoost-why does XGBoost win "every" machine learning competition?," Master's thesis, NTNU, 2016.

[22] D. Tarwidi, S. R. Pudjaprasetya, D. Adytia, and M. Apri, "An optimized XGBoost-based machine learning method for predicting wave run-up on a sloping beach," *MethodsX*, vol. 10, p. 102119, 2023.

[23] T. S. Ho and S. B. Lee, *The Oxford Guide to financial modeling: Applications for capital markets, corporate finance, risk management and financial institutions*. Oxford university press, 2004.

[24] L. Bian, X. Qin, C. Zhang, P. Guo, and H. Wu, "Application, interpretability and prediction of machine learning method combined with lstm and lightgbm-a case study for runoff simulation in an arid area," *Journal of Hydrology*, vol. 625, p. 130091, 2023.

[25] C. Bentéjac, A. Csörgő, and G. Martínez-Muñoz, "A comparative analysis of gradient boosting algorithms," *Artificial Intelligence Review*, vol. 54, pp. 1937–1967, 2021.

[26] G. Ke, Q. Meng, T. Finley, T. Wang, W. Chen, W. Ma, Q. Ye, and T.-Y. Liu, "LightGBM: A highly efficient gradient boosting decision tree," *Advances in neural information processing systems*, vol. 30, 2017.

[27] S. Makridakis, E. Spiliotis, and V. Assimakopoulos, "The M4 competition: 100,000 time series and 61 forecasting methods," *International Journal of Forecasting*, vol. 36, no. 1, pp. 54–74, 2020.

[28] R. Fildes, P. Goodwin, M. Lawrence, and K. Nikolopoulos, "Effective forecasting and judgmental adjustments: an empirical evaluation and strategies for improvement in supply-chain planning," *International journal of forecasting*, vol. 25, no. 1, pp. 3–23, 2009.

[29] M. Leonard, "A majority of retailers struggle with inventory forecasting," *Featured Prediction Competition*, 2019.

[30] U. of Nicosia · Featured Prediction Competition, "M5 forecasting - accuracy estimate the unit sales of walmart retail goods," *Featured Prediction Competition*, vol. 450.47, 2023.

[31] T. Chai and R. R. Draxler, "Root mean square error (RMSE) or mean absolute error (MAE)?–Arguments against avoiding RMSE in the literature," *Geoscientific model development*, vol. 7, no. 3, pp. 1247–1250, 2014.

[32] A. Akossou and R. Palm, "Impact of data structure on the estimators R-square and adjusted R-square in linear regression," *Int. J. Math. Comput*, vol. 20, no. 3, pp. 84–93, 2013.

An efficient inverse solution for MIMO dynamic systems by a Moving Least Squares meta-model

Gordon J. Savage[1], Young Kap Son[2]

[1]Department of Systems Design Engineering, University of Waterloo, Waterloo, ON, Canada, gjsavage@uwaterloo.ca

[2]Department of Smart Mobility Engineering, Reliability Education & Research Center, Gyeongkuk National University, South Korea, ykson@gknu.ac.kr

Keywords: Inverse problem, Dynamic systems, Moving least-squares meta-model, Distance metric, Singular value decomposition.

Abstract - In the inverse problem, the component parameters and excitations (e.g. inputs), are to be determined given corresponding system query responses (e.g. outputs). Most model-based solutions to the inverse problem involve optimization using the so-called forward model - typically a mechanistic model in some form. Recently, data-based approaches, or model-free methods, have been invoked whereby feature extraction methods such as Support Vector Machines (SVM) and artificial neural networks (ANN) are used. Alternatively, in this paper, we develop an inverse solution for dynamic systems through simple least-squares methodology. More importantly, this paper develops a Moving Least Squares (MLS) approach that permits larger design space and greatly improved accuracy. Once the training has been completed (in the normal fashion) the input and output training data are interchanged to provide a new causal relationship. Now, the inputs can be found for given query outputs. To do this, the pertinent closest responses to the query data are found by using a novel distance metric created primarily from the integral of squared error. Singular-value decomposition (SVD) makes any matrix inversion tractable. A nonlinear dynamic mechanical system is invoked to demonstrate both parameter design and excitation allocation. The new inverse MLS meta-model is compared to the original least squares models using data from mechanistic models for fidelity. The results show significant error mitigation with acceptable computation effort.

1. Introduction

Let an engineering system comprise a set of interconnect components that are energized by excitations to provide useful responses. Then the forward problem predicts the responses based on selected component parameters and system excitations. The inverse problems either predict the component parameters based on both known responses and excitations, or, determine the excitations using previously obtained responses and component parameters. Inverse problems have garnered significant attention in recent years [1-3]. Parameter identification, crucial in designing mass-spring-damper systems (e.g., optimizing stiffness and damping for driver comfort in smart truck seats), is a prime example. Similarly, excitation identification is vital for improving engineering structural designs by determining large loads and displacements. Direct excitation measurements are often impractical due to sensor limitations or inaccessibility. Consequently, estimating system inputs from observed responses is essential for reliability analysis, fault diagnosis, and health monitoring across various sectors, including automotive, aerospace, mechatronics, and civil engineering [4].

Inverse problems are generally addressed using two primary approaches: model-based and data-based. Model-based methods are suitable when system dynamics are well-defined or partially known. Conversely, data-based approaches are employed when system structures are largely unknown, offering the significant advantage of model independence. Data-based methods utilize various regression techniques, ranging from simple linear, polynomial, or exponential models to complex machine learning algorithms. In particular, support vector regression (SVR) [5] and artificial neural networks (ANNs) [6] have been applied to identify input excitations. However, these machine learning techniques typically demand extensive response datasets for effective training. The application of artificial intelligence to excitation identification is still a developing area. Beyond excitation identification, data-based inverse problem solutions are also prevalent in image processing, encompassing tasks such as image reconstruction, denoising, super-resolution, and deblurring.

Inverse problems could be classified into *static* and *dynamic* problems. To date, research has predominantly focused on static problems. This approach typically involves developing a model that predicts system responses for different parameters. Subsequently, an optimization process is used to determine the parameters that best match a measured real response. Employing a meta-model of the underlying mechanistic model can speed up the optimization. Huang et al constructed a Kriging meta-model to model the relationship between material parameters and the objective function value representing the error between the experimental data and FEM simulation results, and then obtained material parameters through the optimization procedure using the meta-model [7].

Dynamic input identification for systems is now a growing area of inverse problem research. In model-based approaches, solving the inverse problem requires distinct methodologies compared to the forward problem. Specifically, while forward problems are often formulated as solvable differential equations, inverse problems typically involve matrix inversion and deconvolution techniques. These inverse problems are inherently challenging due to ill-conditioned matrices, sensitivity to noise, and overall uncertainty.

Inverse problems can be formulated in both the frequency and time domains. In the frequency domain, input excitation estimation has been achieved using the inverse Fourier transform as a model-based approach [8]. In the time domain, two primary methods are commonly employed: convolution and Kalman filtering. Convolution relationships between input excitations and system responses have been applied in Refs [9, 10]. Alternatively, Kalman filter-based recursive identification methods have been used to estimate the input as a state variable [11]. Recently, Least Squares method have been used as data driven method. Therein excitation allocation and parameter design have been performed simultaneously based only on the responses [12].

Herein we present a data-based approach to the inverse dynamic problem based on a Moving Least Squares formulation. The so-called moving nature of the method helps mitigate errors associated with meta-models [13 – 16]. The proposed approach would be a useful design tool for either reliability-based or robust designs of system parameters and system inputs for dynamic systems. The training data takes the form of matrices: one for the inputs, comprising excitations and component parameters, and one for the outputs comprising the responses. Then, the outputs and inputs are mathematically interchanged to provide a new causal system. To enable the Moving Least Squares regime, the selection of the training sets closest to the query response is accomplished via a distance metric based on the integral of squared error.

2. Matrices for a Meta-Model

2.1 The Input Matrix

First, let us consider the excitation type of inputs. In continuous time, let there be N excitation functions denoted as $f_n(\boldsymbol{\theta}_n, t)$ where $n = 1, 2 \ldots N$ and where $\boldsymbol{\theta}_n$ represents, typically, a list of physical and dimensional properties, or shape and scale factors. Next, let time run from initial time t_0 to final time t_L and be discretized into instances with uniform spacing and stored as a vector $\mathbf{t}$. The spacing depends on the sampling rate which in turn depends on the band limit of the spectrum of the excitation. Let l be the time instant index where herein $l = 1, 2 \ldots L$. Finally, the discrete time excitation vector for the nth excitation is denoted as $\mathbf{a}_n = f_n(\boldsymbol{\theta}_n, \mathbf{t})$. The elements of the Euclidian vector $\mathbf{a}_n$ may have units of length, amplitude, etc. A series of training excitation vectors may be formed as follows: let there be δ samples of the properties $\boldsymbol{\theta}_n$ with each sample set denoted as $\boldsymbol{\theta}_n^{(k)}$ $k = 1, 2 \ldots \delta$. Hence, for the nth excitation, we end up with δ training vectors $\mathbf{a}_n^{(k)} = f_n^{(k)}(\boldsymbol{\theta}_n^{(k)}, \mathbf{t})$: these are assembled into a training sub-matrix of the form

$$[\mathbf{A}_n] = \begin{bmatrix} \left[\mathbf{a}_n^{(1)}\right]^T \\ \left[\mathbf{a}_n^{(2)}\right]^T \\ \vdots \\ \left[\mathbf{a}_n^{(k)}\right]^T \\ \vdots \\ \left[\mathbf{a}_n^{(\delta)}\right]^T \end{bmatrix}_{\delta \times L} \quad (1)$$

Then for all N excitations

$$\bar{\mathbf{A}} = [\mathbf{A}_1 \quad \mathbf{A}_2 \cdots \mathbf{A}_n \quad \cdots \mathbf{A}_N]_{\delta \times (N \times L)} \quad (2)$$

Note, the kth complete excitation training vector has the form

$$\left[\bar{\mathbf{a}}^{(k)}\right]^T = \left[\left[\mathbf{a}_1^{(k)}\right]^T \quad \left[\mathbf{a}_2^{(k)}\right]^T \quad \ldots \quad \left[\mathbf{a}_j^{(k)}\right]^T \quad \ldots \quad \left[\mathbf{a}_N^{(k)}\right]^T\right]_{1 \times (N \times L)} \quad (3)$$

Secondly, let us consider the parameter type of inputs. Let there be R parameters with index $r = 1, 2, \ldots R$. The kth parameter training set for all R parameters is the row vector

$$[\mathbf{p}^{(k)}]^T = \left[p_1^{(k)} \quad \cdots p_r^{(k)} \quad \cdots p_R^{(k)}\right]_{1 \times R} \quad (4)$$

For all R parameters, and all δ parameter training sets we have the parameter matrix, in terms of columns, written as

$$[\mathbf{P}] = [\mathbf{p}_1 \quad \cdots \mathbf{p}_r \quad \cdots \mathbf{p}_R]_{\delta \times R} \quad (5)$$

The rth parameter, produces the column

$$\mathbf{p}_r = \begin{bmatrix} p_{1,r} \\ p_{2,r} \\ \vdots \\ p_{k,r} \\ \vdots \\ p_{\delta,r} \end{bmatrix}_{\delta \times 1} \quad (6)$$

Finally, combining both excitations and parameters, the kth system training set has the combined form

$$[\mathbf{x}^{(k)}]^T = \left[\bar{\mathbf{a}}^{(k)}\right]^T [\mathbf{p}^{(k)}]^T \quad (7)$$

The input matrix $\mathbf{X}$ comprises all δ system training sets and has the structure

$$\mathbf{X} = [\mathbf{A}_1 \quad \mathbf{A}_2 \cdots \mathbf{A}_n \quad \cdots \mathbf{A}_N \ \mathbf{P}]_{\delta \times (N \times L + R)} \quad (8)$$

The individual columns of $\mathbf{X}$ are denoted as

$$\mathbf{X} = [\mathbf{x}_1 \ \mathbf{x}_2 \ \ldots \ \mathbf{x}_j \ \ldots \ \mathbf{x}_{(N \times L + R)}] \quad (9)$$

2.2 The Output Matrix

Let the output comprise M responses with index $m = 1, 2, \ldots, M$. Now then, for each system training set, the mth related sampled output (response) can be obtained, typically from a simulation with the mechanistic model. The complete output for the kth system training input is

$$\left[\mathbf{y}^{(k)}\right]^T = \left[\left[\mathbf{z}_1^{(k)}\right]^T \quad \left[\mathbf{z}_2^{(k)}\right]^T \quad \ldots \quad \left[\mathbf{z}_m^{(k)}\right]^T \quad \ldots \quad \left[\mathbf{z}_M^{(k)}\right]^T\right]_{1 \times (M \times L)} \quad (10)$$

For all δ experiments, the mth corresponding response is placed into its output matrix $[\mathbf{Z}_m]_{\delta \times L}$. The complete output matrix for all M responses is

$$[\mathbf{Y}] = [\mathbf{Z}_1 \quad \mathbf{Z}_2 \quad \cdots \mathbf{Z}_m \cdots \ \mathbf{Z}_M]_{\delta \times (M \times L)} \quad (11)$$

with the mth response providing all δ row vectors

$$[\mathbf{Z}_m] = \begin{bmatrix} \left[\mathbf{z}_m^{(1)}\right]^T \\ \left[\mathbf{z}_m^{(2)}\right]^T \\ \vdots \\ \left[\mathbf{z}_m^{(k)}\right]^T \\ \vdots \\ \left[\mathbf{z}_m^{(\delta)}\right]^T \end{bmatrix}_{\delta \times L} \quad (12)$$

The individual columns of $\mathbf{Y}$ are denoted as

$$\mathbf{Y} = [\mathbf{y}_1 \ \mathbf{y}_2 \ \ldots \ \mathbf{y}_j \ \ldots \ \mathbf{y}_{(M \times L)}] \quad (13)$$

3. Least Squares Developments

3.1 The Inverse Least-squares (ILS) Meta Model

Let us start with the development of the usual least-squares approach but with the inverse formulation. Now, the rows of the output matrix (responses) are treated as the experimental data and the rows of the input matrix (excitations and component parameters) are treated as the results. Thus, consider any column of $\mathbf{X}$, say $\mathbf{x}_j$, and then define a weight vector $\mathbf{w}_j$ that transforms each row of $\mathbf{Y}$ into the corresponding entry in vector $\mathbf{x}_j$ or

$$\mathbf{Y}\mathbf{w}_j = \mathbf{x}_j \quad (14)$$

Then for a best fit by least-squares, we write symbolically

$$\mathbf{w}_j = (\mathbf{Y}^T\mathbf{Y})^{-1}\mathbf{Y}^T\mathbf{x}_j \quad (15)$$

To provide weights for all ($N \times L + R$) columns of $\mathbf{X}$ we expand (15) to get

$$\mathbf{W} = [\mathbf{w}_1 \quad \cdots \mathbf{w}_j \quad \cdots \mathbf{w}_{(N \times L + R)}]_{(M \times L) \times (N \times L + R)} = (\mathbf{Y}^T\mathbf{Y})^{-1}\mathbf{Y}^T\mathbf{X} \quad (16)$$

It follows from an expansion of (14) that we have the meta-model to provide the approximate row input for the arbitrary query responses $[\mathbf{y}^{(q)}]^T$ as

$$[\mathbf{x}^{(q)}]^T = [\mathbf{y}^{(q)}]^T\mathbf{W} \quad (17)$$

3.2 A distance metric for Inverse Moving Least-Squares

The idea behind the Inverse Moving Least-Squares (IMLS) approach is simple: Given an arbitrary query output (responses for the inverse meta-model), find a small set of close neighbors to be used to replace the original meta-model. Since the responses are vectors of time-sampled data, usually with different units, some method of evaluating the closeness of the vectors to the query vector is needed. That is, we need to compute in some way the difference between the query vector and each of the training vectors.

Herein, for our distance metric, we adopt the nature of performance indexes that come from control theory and signal analysis. There are many indexes available, and the choice is difficult to make without analysis. Herein we tried three indexes for consideration. The *integral of absolute error* (IAE) which seems appropriate for under-damped systems, the *integral-of-time-multiplied absolute error* (ITAE) which seems best for mainly oscillatory systems, and the *integral of squared error* (ISE) which has its roots in energy matching. Experience has shown that the ISE index is the most selective and the easiest to calculate.

The individual *distance measure* from the *integral of squared error* has the form

$$d_{k,m} = \sum_{l=1}^{L}\left(z_{m,l}^{(q)} - z_{m,l}^{(k)}\right)^2 \Delta t \tag{18}$$

The errors from each training set can be stored as the vector $\mathbf{d_m}$. Because of different units and ranges for the responses, it is convenient to have the simple differences for each response scaled to a common 0 - 1 range. Hence, let the lowest and highest values of $d_{k,m}$ be d_m^L and d_m^H respectively. Now the *scaled distance measure* for each response is

$$s_{k,m} = \frac{d_{k,m} - d_m^L}{d_m^H - d_m^L} \tag{19}$$

All errors can be stored as the vector $\mathbf{s_m}$. We next find the *system distance metric* for each response vector in turn. The 2-Norm seems appropriate, hence we write, for the kth system response

$$S_k = \sqrt{\sum_{n=1}^{M}(s_{k,m})^2} \tag{20}$$

All indexes, S_k for $k = 1, 2 \ldots \delta$, can be stored in a vector **S** and ranked from smallest to largest.

Let us define a so-called *critical distance* as S_C. This value helps divide the training responses into those close by and those farther away from the query responses. The value can be selected by some suitable formula, such as median or percentile. To subdivide the responses, first consider a square ($\delta \times \delta$) binary selection matrix **H** with entries

$$h_{k,k} = \begin{cases} 1 & if S_k \leq S_C \\ 0 & otherwise \end{cases} \tag{21}$$

Then, the matrix **H** is used to produce the localized least squares set of equations by simply multiplying both matrix **X** and matrix **Y** by **H**. Now, let $\mathbf{B} = \mathbf{HY}$ and $\mathbf{C} = \mathbf{HX}$, then the MLS normal equations become

$$(\mathbf{B^T})(\mathbf{B})\mathbf{W_M} = (\mathbf{B^T})\mathbf{C} \tag{22}$$

Finally, we have the solution as

$$\mathbf{W_M} = [(\mathbf{B^T})(\mathbf{B})]^{-1}(\mathbf{B^T})\mathbf{C} \tag{23}$$

where $\mathbf{W_M}$ is the new weight matrix and is different from **W**.

3.3 The Matrix Solution

Consider a matrix **B** of dimensions $m \times n$, then Singular Value Decomposition (SVD), keeping only the dominant singular values, gives [17]

$$\mathbf{B} \approx \mathbf{USV^T} \tag{24}$$

The matrices **U** and **V** are each orthogonal, thus $\mathbf{U^T U} = \mathbf{I_U}$ and $\mathbf{V^T V} = \mathbf{I_V}$ and the singular value matrix **S** is diagonal. From (24), we write

$$\mathbf{B^T B} = \mathbf{VS^2V^T} \tag{25}$$

Then, to get an identity matrix to satisfy an inverse, we must have

$$(\mathbf{B^T B})^{-1} = \mathbf{V\,S^{-2}\,V^T} \tag{26}$$

It follows from (24) and (26) that

$$(\mathbf{B^T B})^{-1}\mathbf{B^T} = \mathbf{VS^{-2}V^T(VSU^T)} = \mathbf{VS^{-1}U^T} \tag{27}$$

And from (23), our new weight matrix becomes

$$\mathbf{W_M} = \mathbf{VS^{-1}U^T C} \tag{28}$$

Finally, the MLS input prediction for an arbitrary output query is

$$[\mathbf{x}^{(q)}]^T = [\mathbf{y}^{(q)}]^T \mathbf{W_M} \tag{29}$$

4. Examples

4.1 MIMO Dynamic Example

A schematic of a nonlinear, lumped-parameter, mechanical system with two masses, three springs and two dampers is shown in Fig. 1. The two specified excitations are the displacement $w(t)$ and the force $f(t)$ and they are specified via general harmonic functions in terms of variable amplitude and variable period. Such functions model many natural phenomena and are easy to create.

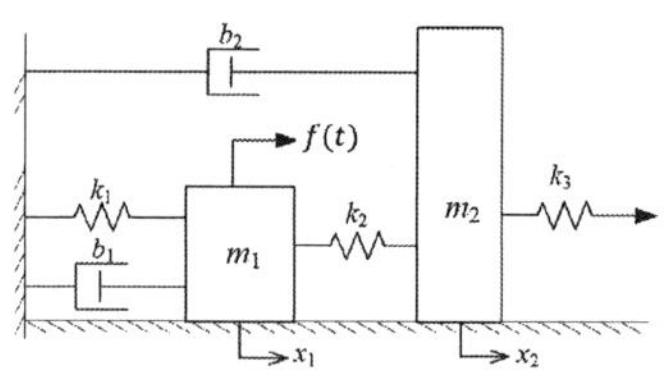

Fig. 1. Coupled spring-mass-damper system with two excitations.

The two responses are the displacements of the masses, labelled correspondingly as, x_1 and x_2. Each of the two linear dampers follows the viscous damping law. The damper force has a magnitude $|bv|$, (where v is the velocity of the mass) and has a direction that opposes the motion of the mass. The springs may be linear or nonlinear. For a spring with small deformation, the elastic coefficient is k and the displacement is Δx. From Hooke's law, the force is $|k\Delta x|$ with a direction opposing the deformation. Herein spring k_3 is linear. However, for a spring undergoing a large deformation, the force relation becomes nonlinear. For our system, springs k_1 and k_2 are nonlinear. We use the form given in Ref. [18] and thus the magnitude of the force, with parameters k and μ, is

$$F = k\Delta x + \mu\Delta x^3$$

4.2 The mechanistic model

The two, coupled, nonlinear equations of motion are

$$m_1\ddot{x}_1 = -b_1\dot{x}_1 - k_1x_1 - \mu_1x_1^3 + k_2(x_2 - x_1) + \mu_2(x_2 - x_1)^3 + f(t) \tag{30}$$
$$m_2\ddot{x}_2 = -b_2\dot{x}_2 - k_2(x_2 - x_1) - \mu_2(x_2 - x_1)^3 + k_3(w(t) - x_2)$$

where x_1 and x_2 are the displacements of the corresponding masses measured from their at-rest positions. For a state-space format, first we introduce two new variables via the extra equations $\dot{x}_1 = x_3$ and $\dot{x}_2 = x_4$, and then rewrite (30) as

$$\begin{bmatrix}\dot{x}_1\\ \dot{x}_2\\ \dot{x}_3\\ \dot{x}_4\end{bmatrix} = \begin{bmatrix}0 & 0 & 1 & 0\\ 0 & 0 & 0 & 1\\ -(k_1+k_2)/m_1 & k_2/m_1 & -b_1/m_1 & 0\\ k_2/m_2 & -(k_2+k_3)/m_2 & 0 & -b_2/m_2\end{bmatrix}\begin{bmatrix}x_1\\ x_2\\ x_3\\ x_4\end{bmatrix} + \begin{bmatrix}0\\ 0\\ 1/m_1\\ 1\end{bmatrix} f(t) + \begin{bmatrix}0\\ 0\\ 0\\ k_3/m_2\end{bmatrix} w(t) + \begin{bmatrix}0\\ 0\\ -\mu_1 x_1^3/m_1 + \mu_2(x_2-x_1)^3/m_1\\ -\mu_2(x_2-x_1)^3/m_2\end{bmatrix} \quad (31)$$

4.3 Example with two responses

Let us now combine a variable displacement excitation and a variable force excitation with three variable parameters to show excitation allocation and parameter design for the displacements of m_1 and m_2 denoted as $x_1(t)$ and $x_2(t)$ respectivley. The variation in the system follows. The displacement input is a step function $w(\boldsymbol{\theta},t) = \theta_1 u(t)$ where θ_1 is the amplitude with range: $\theta_1 \in [4, 6]$ m or about 20% of the mean. Also, the force input is a step function $f(\boldsymbol{\theta},t) = \theta_2 u(t)$ where θ_2 is the amplitude with range: $\theta_2 \in [0.8, 1.2]$ N or about 20% of the mean. The three variable component parameters have the following ranges: $m_2 \in [175, 325]$, $b_2 \in [7, 13]$, and $k_2 \in [35, 65]$ – all at 30% variation. The fixed component parameters are fixed as follows: $m_1 = 250$ kg, $b_1 = 10$ N-s/m, $\mu_1 = 6$ N/m^3 and $\mu_2 = 10$ N/m^3. $k_1 = k_3 = 50$ N/m. The life-time of the simulation is $t_L = 60$ s and the sampling interval is $\Delta t = 0.1$ s. All initial conditions of the masses (displacement and velocity) are fixed to zero.

For the meta-model building we use $\delta = 50$ experiments (ten per parameter). Some output responses from the training data are shown in Fig. 2. To test our work, query responses are set from known excitations and component parameters. In this example, we set the five parameters to be $[\theta_1, \theta_2, m_2, b_2, k_2] = [4.5, 1.1, (185, 11, 60)]$. First, the two excitations and the three component parameters were estimated using the inverse Least Squares meta-model. In Table 1, the true inputs and the estimated inputs from the inverse LS are compared. The stated times include both training data computation and estimation computation.

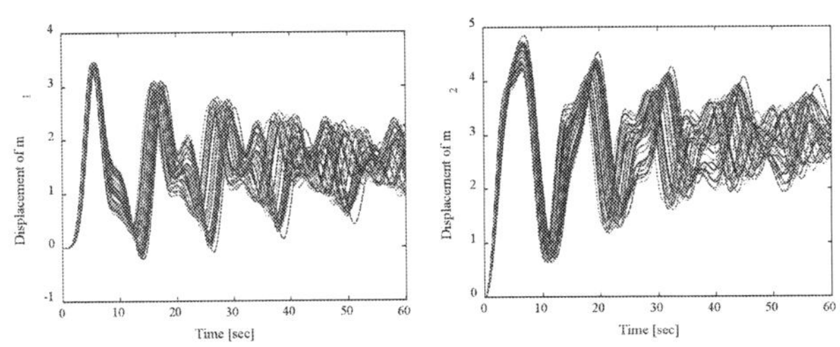

(a) Output of m_1 (b) Output of m_2

Fig. 2. Some training data for the MIMO system

Table 1. Comparison of results and times.

Method/Result	$[m_2, b_2, k_2]$, $[w(t), f(t)]$	Time [sec]
True	[185, 11, 60], [4.5$u(t)$, 1.1$u(t)$]	
Inverse (LS)	[189.2296, 10.8199, 59.6960], [4.5072$u(t)$, 1.0893$u(t)$]	1.1817
Inverse (MLS ISE)	[186.2408, 10.9766, 60.0997], [4.5077$u(t)$, 1.1068$u(t)$]	1.1909

For the MLS meta-model, the distance matrix, the scaled distance matrix and the system distance metric from eqns. (18, 19 and 20) become:

$$[\mathbf{d}_1\ \mathbf{d}_2] = \begin{bmatrix}30.3050 & 41.9213\\ 50.6455 & 66.5840\\ \vdots & \vdots\\ 1.6555 & 2.6232\\ \vdots & \vdots\\ 60.6233 & 88.3045\\ \vdots & \vdots\\ 53.8556 & 90.5580\\ \vdots & \vdots\\ 13.8175 & 31.5736\end{bmatrix} \quad (32)$$

$$[\mathbf{s}_1\ \mathbf{s}_2] = \begin{bmatrix}0.5876 & 0.4469\\ 0.8308 & 0.7274\\ \vdots & \vdots\\ 0.0000 & 0.0000\\ \vdots & \vdots\\ 1.0000 & 0.9744\\ \vdots & \vdots\\ 0.8852 & 1.0000\\ \vdots & \vdots\\ 0.2062 & 0.3292\end{bmatrix} \quad [S] = \begin{bmatrix}0.7382\\ 1.1042\\ \vdots\\ 0.0000\\ \vdots\\ 1.3962\\ \vdots\\ 1.3355\\ \vdots\\ 0.3884\end{bmatrix}$$

The critical distance S_c is the median value of all entries in vector $\mathbf{S}$, so about half of the training responses are used. The results are shown in Table 1. Note that the MLS method provides a superior design with similar computation time. To show the benefits of MLS more clearly, the displacements of the masses are compared to the true values and the differences are shown in Fig. 3.

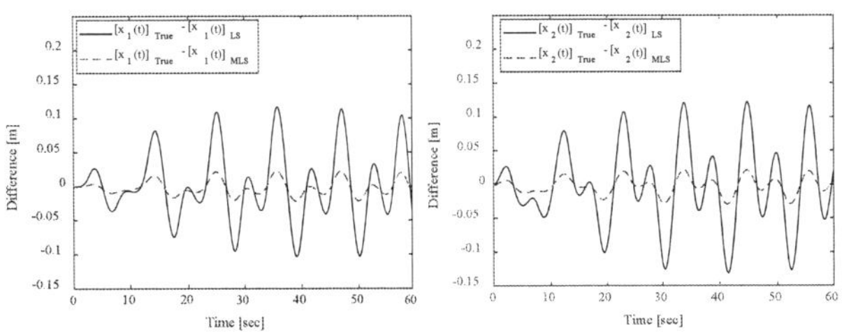

(a) m_1 (b) m_2

Fig. 3. Difference in outputs of masses for the true inputs and estimated inputs.

The MLS method shows a marked improvement over the standard LS method.

4.4 Example with Four responses

Let us now consider a fixed sinusoidal displacement excitation and a fixed sinusoidal force excitation along with three variable component parameters to show parameter design for now four responses: these include the displacements of m_1 and m_2 denoted as $x_1(t)$ and $x_2(t)$ respectively and their velocities denoted as $v_1(t)$ and $v_2(t)$ respectively. We let the displacement input be the function $w(t) = 0.1\sin(2\pi t/10)$, and the force input be the function $f(t) = 0.05\sin(2\pi t/10)$. The three variable component parameters give $\mathbf{p}^T = [m_2, b_2, k_2]$ with ranges of $m_2 \in [175, 325]$, $b_2 \in [7, 13]$, and $k_2 \in [35, 65]$. The fixed component parameters areas above: $m_1 = 250$ kg, $b_1 = 50$ N-s/m, $\mu_1 = 6$ N/m^3 and $\mu_2 = 10$ N/m^3, $k_1 = k_3 = 50$ N/m.

For the Least Squares meta-model building, we use $\delta = 30$ experiments (ten for each parameter) and 0.1 sec time increments. The query responses for the system parameters $[m_2, b_2, k_2] = [210, 12, 50]$ are generated from (31) and shown for reference in Fig 4. The approximated query parameters from the inverse LS and MLS meta-models are compared in Table 2. Again we see the improved selection of the paramters from the MLS method. The differences in the approximate responses are shown in Fig. 5 and Fig. 6. The MLS results show a 30 – 40% difference reduction compared to the standard LS method.

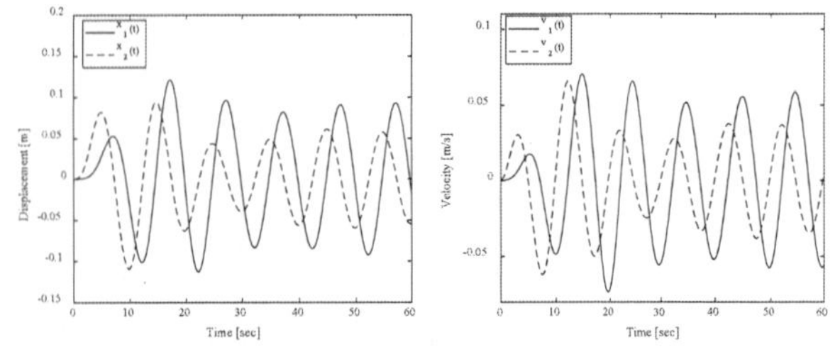

(a) Displacement (b) Velocity

Fig. 4. Query responses for the MIMO system.

Table 2. Comparison of results and computation times.

Method/Result	m_2	b_2	k_2	Time [sec]
True	210	12	50	
Inverse (LS)	210.7132	10.2977	49.9241	1.20619
Inverse (MLS ISE)	211.0468	11.5912	49.9187	1.21171

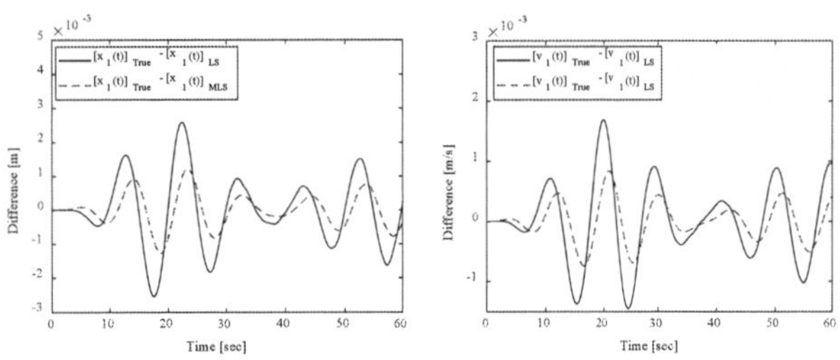

(a) Displacement (b) Velocity

Fig. 5. Differences in responses of m_1 for the true inputs and estimated inputs.

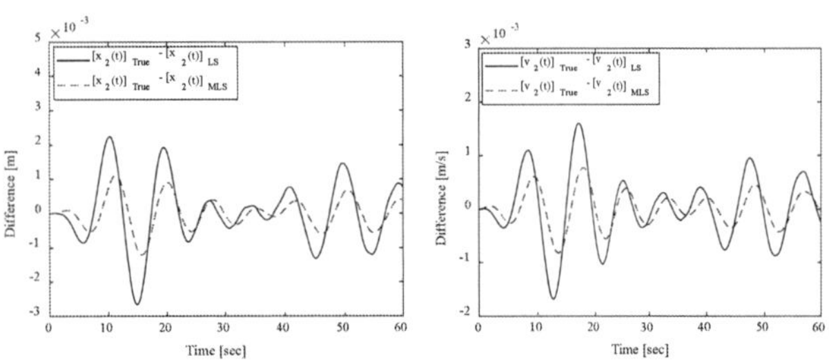

(a) Displacement (b) Velocity

Fig. 6. Differences in responses of m_2 for the true inputs and estimated inputs.

5. Conclusions

In this paper, we have presented a data-based, inverse, Moving Least-Squares meta-model that performs simultaneous parameter design and excitation allocation for dynamic engineering systems. Herein, the output data and the input data, derived from the training process, are mathematically interchanged. Now, the same least-squares fitting regime that is used for the forward model has been invoked to relate the inputs to the outputs, thus forming an inverse meta-model. Moreover, a Moving Least Squares methodology has been invoked to provide better accuracy with broad parameter ranges. The range of parameter variation has been set as high as 30%. To select the closest training responses to the query responses, the Integral of Squared Errors has been used as the first part of the distance metric. A normalization process and the 2-norm complete the metric. Singular-value decomposition (SVD) makes any matrix inversion tractable.

The efficacy of the approach has been demonstrated with a nonlinear, mechanical, system with multiple excitations, multiple component parameters and multiple responses. Time excitations have been applied with both two and four responses to consider. In both cases the errors found in the standard least squares method have been mitigated by the new approach by 80% to 30% respectively with computation time in the range of one or two seconds.

References

[1] J. Sanchez, and H. Benaroya, 2014, "Review of force reconstruction techniques," Journal of sound and vibration, 333 (14), pp. 2999-3018

[2] R. Liu, E. Dobriban, Z. Hou, and K. Qian, 2021, "Dynamic Load Identification for Mechanical Systems: A Review," Archives of Computational Methods in Engineering

[3] X. Guo and S. Fang, 2023, "Structural parameter identification using physics-informed neural networks," Measurement, 220, 113334.

[4] H. Li, J. Jiang, W. Cui, J. Zhao, and M.S. Mohamed 2022, "One Novel Dynamic-Load Time-Domain Identification Method Based on Function Principle," Appl. Sci., 12, 9623.

[5] W. J. Staszewski, K. Worden, R. Wardle, and G. R. Tomlinson, 2000, "Fail-safe sensor distributions for impact detection in composite materials," Smart Mater Struct, 9(3), pp. 298 - 303

[6] B. Qiu, M. Zhang, Y. Xie, X. Qu, and X. Li, 2019, "Localisation of unknown impact loads on a steel plate using a pattern recognition method combined with the similarity metric via structural stress responses in the time domain," Mech Syst Signal Process. 128 (1), pp. 429 - 445

[7] C. Huang, A. El Hami, and B. Radi, 2017, "Metamodel-based inverse method for parameter identification: elastic–plastic damage model," Engineering optimization, 49 (4), pp. 633–653

[8] J.M. Starkey, and G.L. Merrill, 1989, "On the ill-conditioned nature of indirect force measurement techniques," Int. J. Anal. Exp. Modal Anal. 4 (3), pp. 103–105.

[9] S.Q. Wu, and S.S. Law, 2011, "Vehicle axle load identification on bridge deck with irregular road surface profile," Engineering Structures, 33 (2), pp. 591-601

[10] C. Wang, C. Du, and S. Jiang, 2018, "Simultaneous identification of the load and unknown parameters of the structure based on the perturbation method," Advances in Mechanical Engineering, 10 (10), pp. 1–12

[11] L. Guo, Y. Ding, Z. Wang, G. Xu, and B. Wu, 2018, "A dynamic load estimation method for nonlinear structures with unscented Kalman filter," Mech Syst Signal Process, 101 (15), pp. 254 – 273.

[12] Son, Y. K. and Savage, Gordon J., 2023, "Combined Excitation and System Parameter Identification of Dynamic Systems by an Inverse Meta-Model", International Journal of Reliability, Quality and Safety Engineering, 30 (5), 2350017.

[13] D. W. Aha, Editorial - Lazy Learning. Artificial Intelligence, 11, 1-6, 1997.

[14] M. Birattari, G. Bontempi, and H. Bersini, 1999, "Lazy learning meets the recursive least squares algorithm", Advances in Neural Information Processing Systems 11, eds. M.S. Keens, A. Solla and D. A. Cohn, MIT Cambridge MA. pp. 375-381.

[15] P. Lancaster and K. Salkauskas, 1981, "Surfaces generated by moving least squares methods'', Mathematics of Computation, 37, 141-168.

[16] T. Most and C. A. Bucher, 2005, "A moving least squares weighting function for the element free Galerkin method which almost fulfils essential boundary conditions", Structural Engineering and Mechanics, 21 (3), 315-332.

[17] S. J. Leon, 1998, "Linear Algebra with Applications," Prentice-Hall, Inc., Upper Saddle River, New Jersey, 07458.

[18] T. H. Fay and S. D. Graham, 2003, "Coupled Spring Equations," Int. J. Math. Educ. Sci. Technol., 34 (1), pp. 65–79.

Analyzing the impact of economic, social and technical objectives on the optimal selection of EVCS locations

Jayesh Girdhar[1], Bhushan Choudhari[1], Silvia Carpitella[1], Xudong Jia[1], Rasoul Narimani[1], Daisy Lemus[1] and Crist Khachikian[1]

[1]California State University, Northridge; 18111 Nordhoff Street, CA 91330, US

Abstract

The growing adoption of Electric Vehicles (EVs) emphasizes the need for optimal Electric Vehicle Charging Station (EVCS) placement. This paper develops a methodological framework based on Multi-Criteria Decision-Making (MCDM) to first identify and categorize important objectives in this field, and to then evaluate their mutual degrees of importance. To such an aim, we integrate economic, social, and technical considerations by categorizing critical objectives through literature review, and successively weighting these objectives within their respective categories using the Analytic Network Process (ANP). The developed model offers various stages of sensitivity analysis visualized through a dedicated dashboard, offering adaptation to different geographical needs. The findings highlight the importance of balanced decision-making to prioritize user convenience while ensuring infrastructure cost efficiency.

1 Introduction and Objectives

The ongoing accelerated transition to Electric Vehicles (EVs) is essential for addressing current environmental sustainability challenges within the global transport sector [1]. With their potential to cut emissions and reduce reliance on fossil fuels, EVs have become a key focus of both policy and technological innovation. However, the effective adoption of EVs is still hindered by the need for accessible and efficient charging infrastructure. The optimal placement of Electric Vehicle Charging Stations (EVCS) aims to mitigate concerns about insufficient charging infrastructure for users while also supporting broader goals of urban mobility and grid stability [2, 3].

Recent studies emphasize the importance of multi-objective approaches to EVCS planning, which enable taking into account multiple factors like travel distance to charging sites, infrastructure costs, and reliability of local energy grids, among others. With this regard, Chen et al. [2] developed a model focused on grid constraints to maximize the economic benefits of operators while maintaining grid safety, ultimately demonstrating the value of considering both grid and operator perspectives in EVCS placement. Another study led by Cenedese et al. [4] integrated genetic algorithms and neural networks to address the issue of traffic mitigation by strategically designing EV service stations, demonstrating how optimized station locations can alleviate traffic and improve EV access within congested urban centers. Furthermore, Multi-Criteria Decision-Making (MCDM) techniques have proven to be an effective tool in determining optimal EVCS locations in urban environments. As showed by Morocho-Chicaiza et al. [5], these methods enable planners to weigh multiple factors, including proximity to urban activity hubs and population density, in order to find locations that maximize accessibility and user convenience. Additionally, Çelik and Ok [6] integrated simulation techniques to forecast demand, ensuring EVCS capacities meet future growth in EV usage while minimizing queuing and wait times for users. In this context, it is evident that, given the evolving nature of the EVCS placement problem, further research is needed to comprehensively address the diverse objectives that influence it, ensuring that charging infrastructure development and the updated transport infrastructure align with environmental, economic, and urban mobility goals [7] while meeting the growing demands of EV adoption.

The objective of the present paper is to formalize and categorize a comprehensive list of objectives critical to the selection of optimal EVCS locations. Building on a previous research work [8], the objectives will be grouped into three main categories, economic, social, and technical, with each being rigorously identified through an extensive literature review. This paper will then propose the Analytic Network Process (ANP) to assign weights to the formalized objectives, accounting for the relations of interdependence existing between them. In the initial analysis, the weights will be computed assuming equal importance across the three categories. To enhance the precision of the model, various iterations of sensitivity analysis will be conducted by varying the importance of each category and examining the resulting changes in the objective weights. This approach aims to provide a comprehensive understanding of how varying the weights of different factors can lead to different impacts on the optimal selection of EVCS locations.

This paper is structured as follows. Section 2 develops a literature review aimed at identifying the main objectives as drivers of analysis. Section 3 describes the proposed methodological approach based on ANP. Section 4 reports the practical application while discussing results from a practical point of view. Section 5 reports the conclusions along with potential future lines of development for the proposed research.

2 Literature Review

The optimal EVCS placement is critical to the broader transition toward transportation electrification, which is a key element in achieving sustainability goals. As mentioned before, EVs play a crucial role in reducing greenhouse gas emissions, improving air quality, and decreasing dependence on fossil fuels. Transformative approaches are essential for sustainable transportation strategies [9], as EV adoption heavily depends on the availability and accessibility of charging infrastructure. As EV use increases, efficient and strategic EVCS placement is crucial, supported by robust policies of sustainable transportation to drive stakeholders in refining strategies aimed at ensuring that the infrastructure is capable of supporting the growing fleet of electric vehicles [10]. The role of EVs in transportation electrification extends beyond environmental benefits to include economic and societal advantages [11]. As cities and countries invest in electric mobility, the need for a well-established charging network becomes increasingly important. Efficient siting of EVCS can help promote the widespread adoption of electric vehicles by addressing user convenience, enhancing the driving experience, and ensuring equitable access to charging infrastructure. Research has focused on optimizing EVCS placement to balance these factors, providing data-driven solutions that can optimize infrastructure impact while minimizing costs [12].

Methodologies currently available in literature to address the problem of EVCS location are diverse and vary in their approach. Gönül et al. [13] used a weighted sum method to optimize the placement of charging stations along highways, focusing on accessibility in high-traffic areas. The proposed approach considered various factors such as population density, traffic patterns, and accessibility, allowing for strategic placement that caters to both high-volume areas and long-distance travel needs. Other methods aim to minimize the distance that users must travel to access a charging station, an essential factor in encouraging the adoption of electric vehicles. For instance, Nazari-Heris et al. [14] highlighted the need of placing EVCSs at regular spatial intervals along major routes to ensure easy access for drivers, thereby reducing detour times and increasing the convenience of owning an EV. Their approach involved geographic considerations, aiming to achieve a balance between station placement and user convenience. In the same research, the authors also emphasized as social equity is another key consideration in the placement of EVCS. EVCSs should be equitably distributed across different socio-economic regions to ensure that all communities, regardless of income or geographic location, have access to EV charging infrastructure. The same issue has been raised by several other authors [15, 16, 17], making this approach particularly relevant in urban planning, where disadvantaged areas may otherwise be overlooked in the deployment of EV infrastructure.

The integration of new EVCS with existing infrastructure is another important aspect explored by such authors as Singh et al. [7]. Their work focused on aligning new charging stations with existing power grids and transportation networks to optimize the performance and efficiency of the charging infrastructure. This integration aims to minimize disruptions to the existing infrastructure while leveraging it to improve the overall network's sustainability and cost-effectiveness [18].

Cost minimization is another essential objective to be pursued for addressing the problem of EVCS placement. Ray et al. [19] focused on optimizing the siting of charging stations to reduce the costs associated with land acquisition, construction, and ongoing maintenance. Their work of research outlined various optimization models that consider factors such as proximity to existing infrastructure and the potential for cost savings in construction and operational processes. Furthermore, the optimization of EVCS density is crucial in high-demand areas, where the number of EVs on the road may outpace the available charging infrastructure. With this regard, Pal et al. [20] applied Particle Swarm Optimization (PSO) to determine the optimal density and placement of charging stations. This methodology aimed to ensure adequate support to areas with high EV demand, while avoiding the over-saturation of charging stations in lower-demand regions. Balancing the distribution of EVCS certainly ensures that EV owners have reliable access to charging points without overwhelming any particular area [21].

Table 1 presents a formalized and comprehensive list of key objectives identified through this literature review that should be prioritized when addressing the EVCS location problem.

TABLE 1. Objectives for optimal EVCS placement

ID	Objective	Description	Ref.
O_1	Accessibility	Locating EVCS in high-traffic and popular areas, such as shopping centers, highways and public transit hubs, aims to promote EV adoption ensuring easy access for a broad user base.	[13]
O_2	Distance traveled	Strategically placing EVCS at even intervals along major routes and urban areas aims to minimize the distance EV drivers need to travel to charge, enhancing convenience and reducing range anxiety (the fear of depleting battery power before reaching a station).	[14]
O_3	Social equity	Ensuring the equitable distribution of EVCS across different socioeconomic areas aims to provide all communities with access to inclusive adoption of EV technology.	[14]
O_4	Integration with existing infrastructure	Aligning new EVCSs with current EV infrastructure, such as existing charging networks and grid capabilities, aims to enhance efficiency and avoid redundant installations.	[7]
O_5	General costs	Optimizing EVCS locations aims to reduce expenses related to land acquisition, construction and maintenance, balancing costs with coverage for a financially sustainable network.	[19]
O_6	EVCS density	Optimizing the number of EVCSs in high-demand areas aims to prevent overcrowding or underutilization, maximizing resource use while meeting user demand effectively.	[20]

The objectives outlined in Table 1 are related with each other and may vary in their levels of importance depending on the context [8]. This highlights the value of employing MCDM methods to calculate their relative weights effectively. As underlined by Morocho-Chicaiza et al. [5], results derived from MCDM analyses support the evaluation of citywide electrical systems and improve EV accessibility. In particular, the Analytic Network Process (ANP) proves to be a highly effective approach for this task, as it not only accounts for the dependencies and feedback between criteria but also provides a structured framework for evaluating complex interrelationships [22, 23]. By doing so, ANP will enable a more precise prioritization of the diverse and often conflicting factors involved in the EVCS location problem.

3 Methodology

The methodological approach detailed in the following is based on ANP and integrates sensitivity analysis and visualization techniques providing a systematic framework for evaluating and prioritizing the factors influencing EVCS placement.

- Define the problem goal and main criteria. This phase establishes the decision goal and clearly defines the main categories as economic, social, and technical, herein denoted with E, S, and T, respectively. These categories will be assumed as main criteria for the decision-making process.
- Formalizing sub-criteria. At this stage, objectives from Table 1 will be treated as sub-criteria, organized into clusters. These sub-criteria will be linked to the main criteria, and the existence of relationships will be established between criteria and the goal, between sub-criteria and the goal, between sub-criteria and their corresponding criteria, as well as between the sub-criteria themselves.
- Pairwise comparing the decision-making elements. According to the relationships established during the previous stage, criteria and sub-criteria will be pairwise compared in relation to each level of the hierarchy. A [1-9] scale will be used to assess their relative importance based on expert judgment.
- Building the supermatrix. The supermatrix will incorporate the weights derived from the pairwise comparisons defined during the previous stage, computed via traditional Analytic Hierarchy Process (AHP). This matrix will reflect how the importance of criteria and sub-criteria may influence or depend on another.
- Normalizing the supermatrix and calculating the final weights. The previously obtained supermatrix will be normalized by raising it to higher powers until reaching convergence, ensuring that the influence of all interdependencies stabilizes. This process generates the relative weights of each criterion and sub-criterion, reflecting their overall importance.
- Analyzing results and iterating sensitivity analysis. Results will be assessed to identify the most important sub-criterion within each category assumed as criterion. A final sensitivity analysis will be performed by adjusting the relative importance of the main criteria and observing how these changes impact the weights of the sub-criteria.
- Visualizing results through a dedicated dashboard. The outcomes of the various iterations of sensitivity analysis are going to be presented via an interactive dashboard, enabling dynamic exploration and clear presentation of the the research findings.

In the next section, we present the practical application of the methodology, where the input data derived from the ANP process have been carefully formalized and double-checked. To ensure accuracy and reliability, we sought the external support of an expert in the field of transportation infrastructure planning, who assisted in validating the data and confirming its relevance for the EVCS placement analysis.

4 Case Study

This section focuses on the practical application, with the primary goal of determining the weights assigned to the objectives relevant to the problem of EVCS placement within their respective categories. The process begins by identifying and establishing the relationships among the decision-making elements involved. Figure 1 illustrates the network of relations identified within the framework of the analysis. Solid arrows represent direct relationships between pairs of criteria, i.e., the economic (E), social (S) and technical (T) categories, highlighting their interdependencies. Dotted thicker arrows indicate the hierarchical connections between criteria and their corresponding sub-criteria, i.e., the objectives formalized from the literature review and described in Table 1. Lastly, dotted weaker arrows depict the associations between pairs of sub-criteria within the network. This visual representation provides a comprehensive overview of the structured relationships, supporting a deeper understanding of the existing interactions and in which direction the factors under analysis may influence each other.

After identifying the relationships, the next step is to organize all the elements into a matrix, grouping them into appropriate clusters. Pairwise comparisons are then conducted for each level of the hierarchy. These comparisons, processed using the traditional AHP method, are used to derive the weights for each cluster, which are then used to construct the ANP unweighted supermatrix. For conciseness, the unweighted supermatrix is not reported. The weighted supermatrix, presented in Table 2, has been obtained by normalizing the columns of the unweighted supermatrix. As a result, the sum of each column in the weighted supermatrix is equal to 1, ensuring consistency in the relative weights across the decision-making elements.

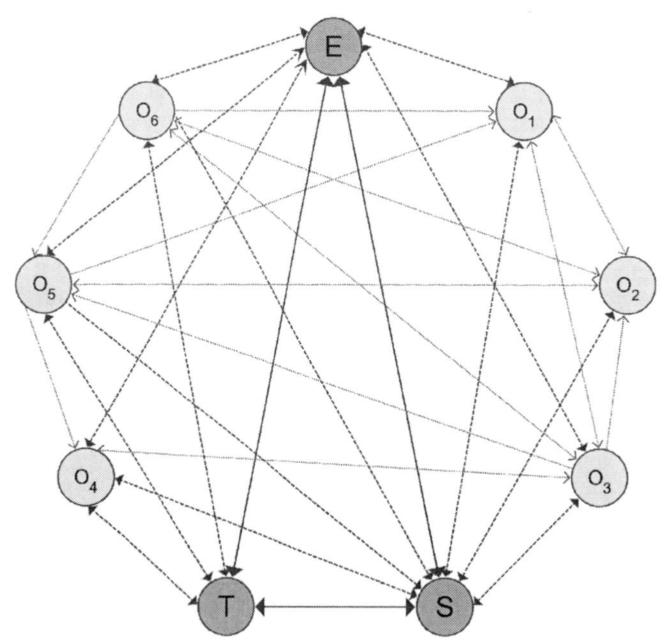

Figure 1. ANP weighted supermatrix

TABLE 2. ANP weighted supermatrix and extraction of weights for categories and objectives

	Goal	E	T	S	O_1	O_2	O_3	O_4	O_5	O_6	Resulting Values	Weights
Goal	0.0000	0.0000	0.0000	0.0000	0.0000	0.0000	0.0000	0.0000	0.0000	0.0000	—	—
E	**0.1667**	0.0000	0.2500	0.2500	0.1500	0.0000	0.1000	**0.1000**	**0.3000**	**0.1500**	0.1625	32.5014 %
T	**0.1667**	0.2500	0.0000	0.2500	0.0000	0.0000	0.0000	**0.3000**	**0.1250**	**0.1500**	0.1329	26.5742 %
S	**0.1667**	0.2500	0.2500	0.0000	0.3500	0.5000	0.4000	**0.1000**	**0.0750**	**0.2000**	0.2046	40.9244 %
O_1	0.0670	0.1080	0.0000	0.2355	0.0000	0.1040	0.1050	0.0000	0.0000	0.0000	0.0824	16.4818 %
O_2	0.0190	0.0000	0.0000	0.1240	0.0660	0.0000	0.0475	0.0000	0.3335	0.1250	0.0923	18.4532 %
O_3	0.0800	0.0350	0.0000	0.0870	0.1740	0.0000	0.0000	0.1000	0.0000	0.3750	0.0674	13.4740 %
O_4	0.1030	0.0770	0.1090	0.0535	0.0000	0.0000	0.0430	0.0000	0.0000	0.0000	0.0408	8.1680 %
O_5	0.1520	0.1275	0.3455	0.0000	0.2150	0.3305	0.2680	0.4000	0.0000	0.0000	0.1492	29.8459 %
O_6	0.0790	0.1525	0.0455	0.0000	0.0450	0.0655	0.0365	0.0000	0.1665	0.0000	0.0679	13.5771 %

As shown in Table 2, E, S, and T initially received equal weights under the goal. However, after applying ANP, S emerges as the most prominent category due to its stronger interdependencies, particularly its connection with the objectives O_5 (general costs), O_2 (distance traveled) and O_1 (accessibility), essential to ensure equitable access, minimize financial burdens, and improve user convenience in the placement of EVCS.

We proceed by considering the obtained results as baseline scenario and implementing three different iterations of sensitivity analysis by varying entries in the unweighted supermatrix [24], specifically those corresponding to the normalized values highlighted in bold in Table 2. We progressively increased the weights of each category under the goal by 20% and applied the same adjustment within the corresponding row of the block comparing categories and objectives when relationships existed across all analyzed categories. The remaining values in the affected columns were then proportionally reduced by 10% each to maintain balance within the ANP framework. The results obtained per each iterated scenario are reported in the following and displayed in Figure 2, demonstrating the robustness of obtained solutions, as weights attributed to objectives are very similar even with considerable changes in weights of categories.

- I Scenario, categories have been weighted under the goal as: $w_E = 53.33\%$, $w_S = 23.33\%$, $w_S = 23.33\%$.
- II Scenario, categories have been weighted under the goal as: $w_E = 23.33\%$, $w_S = 53.33\%$, $w_S = 23.33\%$.
- III Scenario, categories have been weighted under the goal as: $w_E = 23.33\%$, $w_S = 23.33\%$, $w_S = 53.33\%$.

When the weight of category S is further increased (III Scenario), the weight assigned to objective O_3 (social equity) exceeds that of objective O_6 (EVCS density), due to the heightened emphasis on equitable distribution and fair access.

5 Conclusions

This research presents a comprehensive analysis of the main factors for the optimal EVCS placement. We integrate economic, social, and technical considerations into a unified ANP-based framework, designed to prioritize and weight as set of objectives identified as the most relevant in the literature, facilitating informed decision-making in the placement of EVCS. The findings highlight the strong interconnections among these objectives and emphasize the importance of balancing them to develop a sustainable and efficient charging infrastructure, with particular attention to social considerations. The results of this study will inform future research aimed at developing a deep learning-based MCDM approach for EVCS location. This approach will first predict optimal new EVCS locations by incorporating the herein analyzed objectives and subsequently prioritize these locations while considering the obtained objectives' weights.

Acknowledgement

This research is part of the project "Climate Action - Community-driven eLectric vEhicle chArging solutioN (CA-CLEAN)", funded by Climate Action University of California.

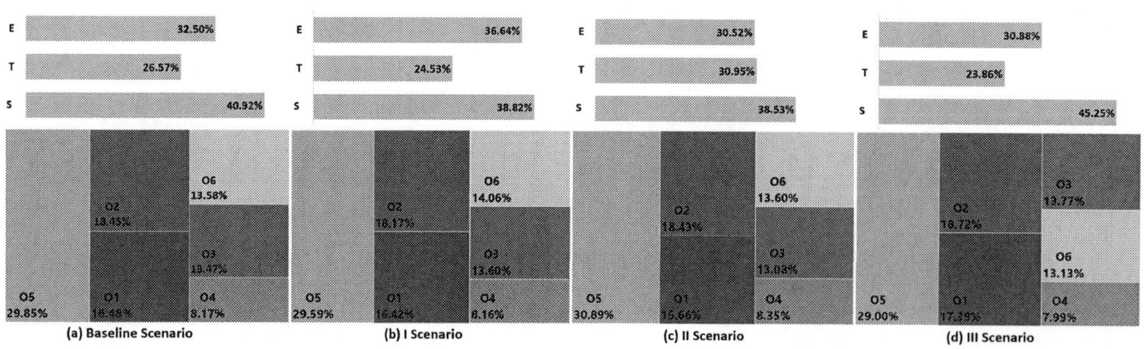

Figure 2. Dashboard visualizing sensitivity analysis results

References

[1] A. Ramanath, "Sustainability and environmental impacts of electric vehicles," in *Handbook of Power Electronics in Autonomous and Electric Vehicles*, pp. 337–351, 2024.

[2] Z. Chen, C. Li, X. Chen, and Q. Yang, "Towards optimal planning of EVCS under grid constraints," *IFAC-PapersOnLine*, vol. 53, no. 2, pp. 14103–14108, 2020.

[3] A. Mohammed, O. Saif, M. Abo-Adma, A. Fahmy, and R. Elazab, "Strategies and sustainability in fast charging station deployment for electric vehicles," *Scientific Reports*, vol. 14, no. 1, p. 283, 2024.

[4] C. Cenedese, M. Cucuzzella, A. C. Ramusino, D. Spalenza, J. Lygeros, and A. Ferrara, "Optimal service station design for traffic mitigation via genetic algorithm and neural network," *IFAC-PapersOnLine*, vol. 56, no. 2, pp. 1528–1533, 2023.

[5] W. Morocho-Chicaiza, A. Barragán-Escandón, E. Zalamea-León, D. Ochoa-Correa, J. Terrados-Cepeda, and X. Serrano-Guerrero, "Identifying locations for electric vehicle charging stations in urban areas through the application of multicriteria techniques," *Energy Reports*, vol. 12, pp. 1794–1809, 2024.

[6] S. Çelik and Ş. Ok, "Electric vehicle charging stations: Model, algorithm, simulation, location, and capacity planning," *Heliyon*, vol. 10, no. 7, 2024.

[7] A. R. Singh, P. Vishnuram, S. Alagarsamy, M. Bajaj, V. Blazek, I. Damaj, R. S. Rathore, F. N. Al-Wesabi, and K. M. Othman, "Electric vehicle charging technologies, infrastructure expansion, grid integration strategies, and their role in promoting sustainable e-mobility," *Alexandria Engineering Journal*, vol. 105, pp. 300–330, 2024.

[8] S. Carpitella, X. Jia, and R. Narimani, "A review on current trends on optimal EVCS location," in *Proceedings of the 12th International Workshop on Simulation for Energy, Sustainable Development Environment SESDE, Tenerife, Spain, September 18-20*, 2024.

[9] N. Tilly, T. Yigitcanlar, K. Degirmenci, and A. Paz, "How sustainable is electric vehicle adoption? insights from a PRISMA review," *Sustainable Cities and Society*, p. 105950, 2024.

[10] S. A. Qadir, F. Ahmad, A. M. A. Al-Wahedi, A. Iqbal, and A. Ali, "Navigating the complex realities of electric vehicle adoption: A comprehensive study of government strategies, policies, and incentives," *Energy Strategy Reviews*, vol. 53, p. 101379, 2024.

[11] D. Singh, U. K. Paul, and N. Pandey, "Does electric vehicle adoption (EVA) contribute to clean energy? bibliometric insights and future research agenda," *Cleaner and Responsible Consumption*, vol. 8, p. 100099, 2023.

[12] A. Loni and S. Asadi, "Data-driven equitable placement for electric vehicle charging stations: Case study San Francisco," *Energy*, vol. 282, p. 128796, 2023.

[13] Ö. Gönül, A. C. Duman, and Ö. Güler, "A comprehensive framework for electric vehicle charging station siting along highways using weighted sum method," *Renewable and Sustainable Energy Reviews*, vol. 199, p. 114455, 2024.

[14] M. Nazari-Heris, S. Asadi, and B. Mohammadi-Ivatloo, "Review on techno-socio-economic studies of electric vehicles in electrical energy systems," *e-Prime-Advances in Electrical Engineering, Electronics and Energy*, vol. 10, p. 100782, 2024.

[15] C.-W. Hsu and K. Fingerman, "Public electric vehicle charger access disparities across race and income in California," *Transport Policy*, vol. 100, pp. 59–67, 2021.

[16] A. Roy and M. Law, "Examining spatial disparities in electric vehicle charging station placements using machine learning," *Sustainable cities and society*, vol. 83, p. 103978, 2022.

[17] M. Nazari-Heris, A. Loni, S. Asadi, and B. Mohammadi-ivatloo, "Toward social equity access and mobile charging stations for electric vehicles: A case study in Los Angeles," *Applied Energy*, vol. 311, p. 118704, 2022.

[18] M. Kumar, K. P. Panda, R. T. Naayagi, R. Thakur, and G. Panda, "Comprehensive review of electric vehicle technology and its impacts: Detailed investigation of charging infrastructure, power management, and control techniques," *Applied Sciences*, vol. 13, no. 15, p. 8919, 2023.

[19] S. Ray, K. Kasturi, S. Patnaik, and M. R. Nayak, "Review of electric vehicles integration impacts in distribution networks: Placement, charging/discharging strategies, objectives and optimisation models," *Journal of Energy Storage*, vol. 72, p. 108672, 2023.

[20] K. Pal, K. Verma, and R. Gandotra, "Optimal location of FACTS devices with EVCS in power system network using PSO," *e-Prime-Advances in Electrical Engineering, Electronics and Energy*, vol. 7, p. 100482, 2024.

[21] H. ElHussini, C. Assi, B. Moussa, R. Atallah, and A. Ghrayeb, "A tale of two entities: Contextualizing the security of electric vehicle charging stations on the power grid," *ACM Transactions on Internet of Things*, vol. 2, no. 2, pp. 1–21, 2021.

[22] I. Mzougui, S. Carpitella, A. Certa, and J. Izquierdo, "A strategic approach to safeguard global supply chains against covid-19 disruptions," *Mathematical Methods in the Applied Sciences*, 2023.

[23] S. Carpitella, I. Mzougui, J. Benítez, F. Carpitella, A. Certa, J. Izquierdo, and M. La Cascia, "A risk evaluation framework for the best maintenance strategy: The case of a marine salt manufacture firm," *Reliability Engineering & System Safety*, vol. 205, p. 107265, 2021.

[24] B. Adams, "ANP row sensitivity," in *International Symposium on The Analytical Hierarchy Process*, 2011.

Improving Software Dependability by AI Agents

ALBEANU Grigore[1], POPENȚIU-VLĂDICESCU Florin[2], MADSEN Henrik[3]

[1]"Spiru Haret" University, Bucharest, Romania, g.albeanu.mi@spiruharet.ro
[2]National University of Science and Technology "Politehnica" of Bucharest & Academy of Romanian Scientists, Romania, popentiu@imm.dtu.dk
[3]Danish Technical University, Lyngby, Denmark, hmad@dtu.dk

Keywords: software agent, artificial intelligence based agent, software testing, LLM, DevSecOps

Abstract – Integrating Software Engineering (SE) and Artificial Intelligence (AI) impacted the current practice in software development and its dependability assurance. In this paper the agentic approach is considered as evolved from classical software agent to AI agents and agentic AI systems. The usage of AI agents separate or belonging to an agentic AI system is analyzed to discover how the software dependability can be improved, and what new challenges appear due to AI integration in SE practices. The coding and testing processes have benefitted from AI, the automation degree being increased. However, many failure modes both from safety and security points of view already have been identified in agentic AI systems increasing the effort of risk mitigation.

1. Introduction

In Software Engineering (SE) the practice evolved along years from traditional models (Waterfall, V-model, Spiral, Incremental), to iterative (Agile, Scrum), modern (DevSecOps, CI/CD), and AI-driven methodology (Machine Learning (ML), Artificial Intelligence (AI), Multi Agent Systems (MAS), AI-agents, Large Language Models (LLM))). This evolution starts with linear/sequential style and moved step by step to automated coding, testing and maintenance [1].

As mentioned by Alenezi & Akour in [1], integrating AI and SE is the newest approach that promotes automated steps from customer requirements to validated software artifacts, but new complexities have emerged, such as those for "ensuring the reliability and robustness of AI-based tools", "managing the ethical implications of AI applications", and "adapting SE methodologies to cope with the dynamic nature of AI technologies".

In this paper the agentic approach is considered as evolved from classical software agent to AI-agents and agentic AI systems. The main objective is to analyze how the software dependability can be improved based on the current SE practice and AI integration.

2. Software Agents

The concept of software agent has evolved over time with the contributions of many researchers [2, 4, 6, 8, 16, 25, 27]. Kay, discussing about computers in 1984 [10], says that the idea of software agent belongs to John McCarthy, but the term was introduced by Selfridge [2, 10]. However, the developments of intelligent agents gained popularity in the 1980s, in the context of multi-agent systems implemented for concurrent, parallel, or distributed environments.

Mainly, the term "software agent" refers to a computer procedure, providing a "service", acting autonomously on behalf of a user or a piece of software under supervision of an "agency". Nowadays, software agents are widely used in applications such as virtual assistants including those for learning, collaborative learning and "intelligent assistance", and multi-agent applications for energy management [5], autonomous driving [22], healthcare [19], and many other real life domains [16]. Recently, various AI based methodologies, including agentic AI approaches, have been involved in software development [1, 7, 8, 9, 13, 14, 17, 18, 20, 21, 23, 24].

According to [2], a software agent can be seen from some points of view:

- *ascription* (having expertise and able to understand the "user" calls),
- *description* (react, be proactive and have "self-starting behavior", collaborate, have both strong "communication ability" and "inferential capability", assure "temporal continuity", behave like a person/human, and migrate through mobility opportunities), and
- *agency based strong orientation*.

Some researchers divide software agents into classes like *intelligent agents*, *autonomous agents*, *distributed agents*, and *mobile agents* according to their strongest features [6]: "pro-activeness", "adaptiveness", "mobility", "collaboration", "veracity", and "disposition".

The *adaptiveness* describes an agent's ability to modify its behavior over time by continuously learning, working under constraints, or extending its tasks by new software layers (assured by software developer).

Mobility is an interesting feature. *Physical mobility* in Internet environment is mostly known due to computer viruses, a special type of software agents. *Logical mobility* is possible by visiting various nodes of the network like a *web spider*.

Communicative agents make use of messages sent/received during solving a task according to a *collaborative protocol.*

Through *veracity* is observed the TRUTHFUL/ UNTRUTHFUL flagship for a software agent. Such a flag can be raised by negotiation among agents.

Finally, the *disposition* is measured by the agent attitude in relation with other collaborators: benevolent, malevolent, and self-interested.

The architecture of software agents depends on data streams to acquire and process. From scientific point of view, the agents should have a "logical" behavior, which means symbolic logic for expert systems is necessary.

For *knowledge representation*, software agents use logical expressions to store and reason about information, enabling them to make decisions based on facts and rules.

By applying *rules of inference*, symbolic logic allows software agents to obtain new information or provide logical results. This helps software agents to be skilled for problem-solving and planning. Also, using symbolic logic is a mean to facilitate the communication between agents mediated by a structured language. In this manner, software agents can exchange information and negotiate using logical propositions about data to provide a number of results (NR). They can use logical operators like: ***and*** (to decrease NR), ***or*** (to increase NR), and ***not*** (to exclude some results)). More advanced operators can be used as **nand** (*NOT* (A *AND* B)), **nor** (*NOT* (A *OR* B)), **xor** (eXclusive *OR*) etc.

Other inferences are based on best practices used in the domain of software agent and will be used during life cycle of agent development:

- *Domain Understanding* (identifying domain artifacts),
- *Reference Architecture Development* (components and relationship flowchart),
- *Reference Architecture Validation* (based on a comparison analysis method), and
- *Domain Oriented Agent Implementation* (taking into account the future specialty of agent).

In *Software Engineering* agents are viewed as systems that require more or less formal means for their development, verification, testing and maintenance. According to [15], software agents are used in SE to help the development of software or to explain and communicate changes in software.

3. Artificial Intelligence Agents

The interest on software agents increased and also for their applications, with the advancement of Artificial Intelligence (AI). Now, terms as PAI (parallel artificial intelligence), and DAI (distributed artificial intelligence) are applied for the new software agents.

Techniques such as *collaborative learning* and *multi-actor reinforcement learning* promise to create agents that can continuously adapt and improve their performance through shared experiences.

According to [16], multi-agent systems (MAS) are very important both for healthcare and industrial automation. Moreover, the intelligence based on *language* (LLM – Large Language Models), or *vision* (Convolution Networks) opened new vistas for agents. In [27] the architecture of MAS for "smart city traffic management with vehicle-to-everything (V2X) communication" is presented.

Process control, manufacturing control, air traffic control, commercial information management, commercial transactions, business process management, patient monitoring, games, interactive theater and cinema are supplementary applications of intelligent agents as described in [8], [19], and [22].

According to [26], an AI agent can be described as a system that is able to acquire information like sound, text, image, pressure etc., making use of sensors and is able to respond (by effectors) to the proper environment. Following [27], advances in AI made possible the development of systems able to handle big datasets and manage uncertainty by ML/deep learning.

Nowadays, the architecture of current AI agents uses LLMs in many configuration ways. The agent begins by presenting the user (caller), which is directed to the agency. The user request could be a prompt (in the new LLM language) given to execute an instruction. The agency directs the user request to the model that represents the algorithmic basis of the agent. This model can be an LLM or another machine learning algorithm, depending on the agent's domain. The model applies the data received from the user/caller to determine the result/output.

The core of the architecture is represented by the agency (control center), a basic component that manages the logic of the entire system. For example, an autonomous vehicle may use an AI agent system that includes code for perception, route planning, and localization to find a specific location on the road, and steering and braking control. The interoperability of AI agents is assured by common communication protocols based on a specific language under a dedicated ontology permitting to learn in future depending on new events and knowledge.

In [21], some actual software is labeled as static and lifeless even fulfilling the client requirements in real time. Moreover, the author claims: "*our current software systems have little to no ability to incorporate context into them.*"

Such a vision has been created by the new transformative mechanisms for LLM and their power of translation. However, more time is required to test the correctness of results provided by generative machines at users' prompts indicated some context of problem to be solved [12].

For SE, the "Human-in-the-loop" (HIL) approach is necessary: an LLM-based agent interacts with a developer/tester, to follow a hybrid approach combining the agent's computational power and the expert knowledge of the engineer.

4. Agentic AI for Improving Software Dependability

Agentic AI refers to systems capable of making independent decisions and taking action to achieve certain long-term goals sensing and acting on their environment. For instance Microsoft uses artificial intelligence to monitor IT systems, predict failures, and automate support requests, ensuring smooth, reliable and secure operations [11].

AI agents can work both independently and in teams. Agentic AI always works as a team. For example, an agentic AI-powered system for IT help desk can understand a user's problem using natural language, identify the affected systems, find the best solution, and then act in order to change passwords and modify the policy access for security reason.

Agentic systems can use *simple reflex* agents (responding to immediate triggers), *model based* agents (for searching/processing repositories), *goal-based* agents (including those priority oriented) and *utilitarian* agents (to support other agents). These agents can offer reaction in real time (for instance: anomaly detection in networks, malfunction, value out over interval, etc.), may plan various actions (like preventive maintenance) by analyzing historical data, or combine both styles by learning from data and provides recommendations [25].

In [4], has been identified the agentic AI *capabilities* (autonomy, limited or no human intervention, decision-making, adaptability, language understanding and workflow optimization) and their *core pillars*: perception, reasoning, optimal planning, continuous learning, verify before executing, and active execution. For example, in a DevSecOps approach, the agentic AI-powered system is able to understand the customer requirements (using LLM [7, 13] or image identification tools), annotate them, create UML diagrams, convert diagrams to code or create code directly from customer requirements by Generative AI, test the code, debug code if necessary, revised the code and repeat from testing, validate code and repeat from beginning if the code is not valid, deploy the final code for integration.

The mentioned pillars give rise to a layered implementation of agents embedded in an agentic system.

Implementing AI-powered systems using Generative AI (GenAI) can benefit by existing and new APIs to translate user's goal into code, as mentioned in [21]. However, according to [18] there are some challenges like: almost correct code generation and the introduction of bugs by GenAI, including "malware code". The authors of [24] investigated how LLM can be used for Automated Program Repair.

AutoCodeRover [24] will retrieve the context by *stratified search* and generate the patch along *repetitive iterations* in both stages. Other LLM agents for software engineering have been discussed in [1] and [17].

Viswanathan in [20], presented a layered architecture for AI-driven agentic "scriptless" automation. Starting from text written in English, three AI-agents responsible for analyzing, data abstraction, and test generation for execution, under orchestration of an agent driver and LLM interpretation the final test will be integrated in a CI/CD DevOps pipeline.

Automated Test Case Generation with AI is also discussed in [9] from the following points of view: improvement of the test coverage, increasing the software reliability by reduction of errors/bugs number, and automation of the regressing testing in a CI/CD pipeline.

Paduraru et al [14] considered the usage of Behavior-Driven Development (BDD) Testing in order to improve the quality of software artifacts produced according to DevSecOps approach. They extended BDD testing by integrating LLM. Moreover, the usage of HIL approach, and agentic AI methods integrating LLM, make possible the automated BDD test creation as reported in [14].

To establish trust for AI-Agent SE is necessary to solve the following challenges:

- cross-checking for cross-validation of generated test to assure the consistency of the testing process;
- pre/post-assertions about a generated test should be inferred and explained according to the proof-oriented programming paradigm;
- promoting LLM-based secure programming to discover malicious/ vulnerable generated code/ tests, and develop secure communication protocols inter-agents.

Some ideas on these aspects have been considered in [3, 17], but more efforts are necessary for building trustable agentic AI systems.

Recently, Microsoft AI Red Team updated the list of failure modes of agentic systems. The first list was published in 2019. The new failure modes are unique to agentic AI systems, and affect both safety and security of agentic systems [3]. These can produce impact outside of agent environment, knowledge loss, user harm and user erosion trust. Moreover, the agents will make incorrect decisions, will be misaligned, or act deficiently.

In this case the developers of frameworks based on agentic AI, software developers using such frameworks, and organizations have to mitigate the risk of failure.

5. Conclusion

Modern applications of software agents span various fields, such as virtual assistants, autonomous driving, energy management, healthcare, and AI-driven software development. In this paper the agentic approach has been considered as evolved from classical software agent to AI-agents and agentic AI systems.

The main aim of the work was to analyze how the software dependability can be improved based on the current SE practice and AI integration. Generative AI (through LLM) plays a growing role in enabling agentic AI systems, translating user goals into executable code through APIs.

However, challenges such as near-accurate code generation, bug introduction, and security risks (e.g., potential malware) remain. Safety and security remain as crucial aspects of agentic AI systems. The coding and testing processes have benefitted from AI, the automation degree being increased, but many failure modes both from safety and security points of view already have been identified in agentic AI systems increasing the effort of risk mitigation. Addressing the risks generated by various failure modes in agentic AI systems is essential for ensuring robust and trustworthy AI-powered solutions and increase de software artifact dependability.

6. References

[1] M. Alenezi & M. Akour. "AI-Driven Innovations in Software Engineering: A Review of Current Practices and Future Directions"; *Appl. Sci.* 2025, 15, 1344, doi.org/10.3390/app15031344.

[2] J.M. Bradshaw. "An Introduction to Software Agents". In "Software Agents", J. M. Bradshaw (ed.), pp. 3 – 46. Cambridge. The MIT Press, 1997.

[3] P. Bryan, G. Severi, J. de Gruyter ... & R.S.S. Kumar. "Taxonomy of Failure Mode in Agentic AI Systems", https://cdn-dynmedia-1.microsoft.com/is/content/microsoftcorp/microsoft/final/en-us/microsoft-brand/documents/Taxonomy-of-Failure-Mode-in-Agentic-AI-Systems-Whitepaper.pdf, Accessed April 27, 2025.

[4] S. Ghonge & A. Gosavi, "Agentic AI - An Executive's Guide to In-depth Understanding of Agentic AI", Konverge.ai, https://konverge.ai/pdf/Ebook-Agentic-AI.pdf, Accessed April 27, 2025.

[5] D.E. Hafiane, A.E. Magri, H.E. Chakir, R. Lajouad & S. Boudoudouh. "A multi-agent system approach for real-time energy management and control in hybrid low-voltage microgrids"; *Results in Engineering*, Vol. 24, doi.org/10.1016/j.rineng.2024.103035, 2024.

[6] A. Hector & V.L. Narasimhan. "A New Classification Scheme for Software Agents". In Proceedings of the Third International Conference on Information Technology and Applications (ICITA'05), IEEE, 2005.

[7] X. Hou, Y. Zhao, Y. Liu, Z. Yang, K. Wang, L. Li, X. Luo, D. Lo, J. Grundy & H. Wang. "Large Language Models for Software Engineering: A Systematic Literature Review"; *ACM Transactions on Software Engineering and Methodology*, 33 (8), pp. 1 - 79, doi.org/10.1145/ 3695988, 2024.

[8] N.R. Jennings & M. Wooldridge. "Applications of Intelligent Agents". In: Jennings, N.R., Wooldridge, M.J. (eds) "Agent Technology". Springer, Berlin, Heidelberg, 1998. doi.org/10.1007/978-3-662-03678-5_1

[9] G. Kathiresan. "Automated Test Case Generation with AI: A Novel Framework for Improving Software Quality and Coverage"; doi.org/10.30574/wjarr.2024.23.2.2463, 2024.

[10] A. Kay. "Computer software"; *Scientific American*, 251(3), 53-59, 1984.

[11] J. Kellington. "Rethinking device management internally at Microsoft with AI", https://www.microsoft.com/insidetrack/blog/rethinking-device-management-internally-at-microsoft-with-ai/, April 17, 2025.

[12] A. Osmany. "The 70% problem: Hard truths about AI-assisted coding - A field guide and why we need to rethink our expectations". Dec. 2024, https://addyo.substack.com/p/the-70-problem-hard-truths-about. Accessed April 3, 2025.

[13] I. Ozkaya, A. Carleton, J. Robert & D. Schmidt. "Application of Large Language Models (LLMs) in Software Engineering: Overblown Hype or Disruptive Change?" Carnegie Mellon University, Software Engineering Institute's Insights (blog), 2023, doi.org/10.58012/6n1p-pw64. Accessed April 3, 2025.

[14] C. Paduraru, M. Zavelca & A. Stefanescu. "Agentic AI for Behavior-Driven Development Testing Using Large Language Models". In Proceedings of the 17th International Conference on Agents and Artificial Intelligence (ICAART 2025) – Vol. 2, pp. 805-815, SCITEPRESS, 2025.

[15] J. Rech, K.-D. Althoff. "Artificial Intelligence and Software Engineering: Status and Future Trends"; https://www.dfki.de/fileadmin/user_upload/import/9622_KI_AI-SE-Survey.pdf, 2004.

[16] A. De Ridder. "Exploring the Applications of Multi-Agent Systems in Real-World Scenarios", https://smythos.com/ai-agents/multi-agent-systems/applications-of-multi-agent-systems/, 2024, Accessed April 3, 2025.

[17] A. Roychoudhury, C. Păsăreanu, M. Pradel, B. Ray. "Agentic AI Software Engineer: Programming with Trust"; arXiv:2502.13767v2 [cs.SE] 26 Mar 2025.

[18] F. V. Ruiz. "Agent-Driven Automatic Software Improvement". EASE '24: Proceedings of the 28th International Conference on Evaluation and Assessment in Software Engineering, Pages 470 – 475, doi.org/10.1145/3661167.3661171, 2024.

[19] E. Shakshuki & M. Reid. "Multi-Agent System Applications in Healthcare: Current Technology and Future Roadmap"; *Procedia Computer Science,* 52, pp. 252 – 261, 2015.

[20] G. Viswanathan, "AI Agentic Scriptless Automation in Software Testing"; *IJCTT*, 72(9), 120-125, 2024, https://www.ijcttjournal.org/archives/ijctt-v72i9p118.

[21] J. White. "Building Living Software Systems with Generative & Agentic AI"; https://arxiv.org/pdf/2408.01768, Aug 2024.

[22] Y. Wu, D. Li, Y. Chen, R. Jiang, H. P. Zou, L. Fang, Z. Wang, P.S. Yu. "Multi-Agent Autonomous Driving Systems with Large Language Models: A Survey of

Recent Advances", arXiv:2502.16804v1 [cs.MA] 24 Feb 2025.

[23] Q. Zhang, C. Fang, Y. Xie, Y. Zhang, Y. Yang, W. Sun, S. Yu & Z. Chen, "A Survey on Large Language Models for Software Engineering". arXiv: 2312.15223v2 [cs.SE] 8 Sep 2024.

[24] Y. Zhang, H. Ruan, Z. Fan & A. Roychoudhury. "AutoCodeRover: Autonomous Program Improvement". In Proceedings of the 33rd ACM SIGSOFT International Symposium on Software Testing and Analysis (ISSTA '24). ACM. https://doi.org/10.1145/3650212.3680384, 2024.

[25] ***, "Agentic AI the new frontier in GenAI"; https://www.pwc.com/m1/en/publications/documents/2024/agentic-ai-the-new-frontier-in-genai-an-executive-playbook.pdf, PWC, Accessed April 3, 2025.

[26] ***, ISO/IEC 22989:2023: *Information technology – artificial intelligence – artificial intelligence concepts and terminology*, 2023.

[27] ***, "Navigating the AI Frontier: A Primer on the Evolution and Impact of AI Agent"; WEF, 2024, https://reports.weforum.org/docs/WEF_Navigating_the_AI_Frontier_2024.pdf, Accessed April 3, 2025.

Reliability Calculations of Square and Cube Redundant Systems

Syouji NAKAMURA[1], Kazunori IWATA[2], Toshio NAKAGAWA[3]

[1]Kinjo Gakuin University, Nagoya, Japan,snakam@kinjo-u.ac.jp
[2]Aichi University, Nagoya, Japan, kazunori@vega.aichi-u.ac.jp
[3]Aichi Institute of Technology, Toyota, Japan, toshi-nakagawa@aitech.ac.jp

Keywords: Square System, Cube System, Reliability, Failure Rate, Replacement.

Abstract - This paper considers square and cube redundant systems with 12 units and obtains their reliabilities, making tables of each unit with two states of on and off. MTTF, failure rate, median and complexity of two systems are computed explicitly and numerically. Furthermore, these results are applied to age replacement and optimal policies are derived. With the advancement of information and technology, objective systems have grown in size, complexity, randomness and vastness, methods and tools obtained in this paper would be useful and effective for designing and analyzing such systems.

1. Introduction

Most systems contain significant redundancies as technology advances, making risk and reliability management increasingly important. Reliabilities of many redundant systems were calculated and summarised [1-3], and their optimization problems were discussed extensively [1,4,5].

As examples of redundant systems, we take square and cube network systems with 12 units and try to calculate their reliabilities. However, it might be much trouble to compute explicitly reliabilities of such complex systems by the standard reliability method. Using a general personal computer, we consider every combination of units with two states of on and off, and compute reliabilities of systems.

We consider a square network system with $n = 12$ units and make a table of N_k of paths which represent the number that the system is operable when k units are operable, and $P_k = N_k/\binom{n}{k}$ which is the rate that the system is operable when k units are operable. Using this table, we obtain reliability, MTTF, failure rate and complexity of the system. Similarly, we obtain such reliability measures of a cubic system. Furthermore, we apply these results to age replacement and derive their optimal times numerically.

2. General Redundant System

Consider a general redundant system with n units ($n = 2, 3, \ldots$), each of which is independent, and has an identical failure distribution $F(t)$ with mean $\mu \equiv \int_0^\infty \overline{F}(t)\mathrm{d}t$ and failure rate $h(t) \equiv f(t)/\overline{F}(t)$, where $f(t)$ is a density function $f(t) \equiv \mathrm{d}F(t)/\mathrm{d}t$ and $\overline{\Phi}(t) \equiv 1-\Phi$ for a general function $\Phi(t)$.

Reliability of the system at time t is [3, 6, 7]

$$R_n(t) = \sum_{k=1}^{n} P_k \binom{n}{k} \overline{F}(t)^k F(t)^{n-k}, \tag{1}$$

where P_k represents the probability or rate that the system is operable when k units are operable, and $R_n(t)$ decreases with t from 1 to 0. Furthermore, letting N_k be a path number of the system when k units are operable, P_k is given by $P_k = N_k/\binom{n}{k}$, and (1) is

$$R_n(t) = \sum_{k=1}^{n} N_k \overline{F}(t)^k F(t)^{n-k}. \tag{2}$$

Mean time to failure (MTTF) is

$$\mu_n \equiv \int_0^\infty R_n(t)\mathrm{d}t = \sum_{k=1}^{n} P_k \binom{n}{k} \int_0^\infty \overline{F}(t)^k F(t)^{n-k}\mathrm{d}t. \tag{3}$$

In particular, when $F(t) = 1 - \mathrm{e}^{-\lambda t}$,

$$\mu_n \equiv \sum_{k=1}^{n} P_k \binom{n}{k} \int_0^\infty \mathrm{e}^{-k\lambda t}(1-\mathrm{e}^{-\lambda t})^{n-k}\mathrm{d}t = \frac{1}{\lambda}\sum_{k=1}^{n}\frac{P_k}{k}. \tag{4}$$

Failure rate is, when $p_k \equiv P_k - P_{k-1}$,

$$h_n(t) = -\frac{R_n'(t)}{R_n(t)} = \frac{nh(t)\sum_{k=1}^{n} p_k \binom{n-1}{k-1}\overline{F}(t)^k F(t)^{n-k}}{\sum_{k=1}^{n} P_k \binom{n}{k}\overline{F}(t)^k F(t)^{n-k}}$$

$$= \frac{nh(t)\sum_{k=1}^{n} p_k \binom{n-1}{k-1}[\overline{F}(t)/F(t)]^k}{\sum_{k=1}^{n} P_k \binom{n}{k}[\overline{F}(t)/F(t)]^k}. \tag{5}$$

Furthermore, it was shown [3] that if kp_k/P_k for $P_k > 0$ decreases with k, then failure rate $h_n(t)$ increases with t, where $kp_k/P_k \equiv \infty$ for $P_k = 0$.

Median M_n of a general system is given by

$$\sum_{k=1}^{n} P_k \binom{n}{k}\overline{F}(t)^k F(t)^{n-k} = \frac{1}{2}. \tag{6}$$

Furthermore, letting P_a be a minimal path number of the system, complexities of the system are [3, 5]

$$P_e \equiv \log_2 P_a,$$
$$P_H = -\sum_{k=1}^{n} p_k \log_2 p_k. \tag{7}$$

3. Square Network System with 12 Units

We consider a square network system with 12 units in Fig. 1, and obtain its reliability $R_S(q)$.

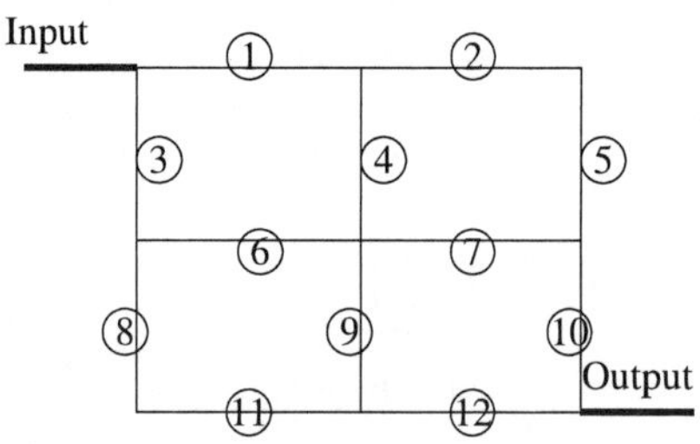

Figure 1: Square network system with 12 units

To compute $R_S(q)$, we make tables in which the system is operable when $k(k = 1, 2, \ldots, 12)$ units are operable. For example, Table 1 presents the number N_k of paths and $P_k = N_k / \binom{12}{k}$ when $k = 4$ as follows:

$$N_k = 6, \quad P_k = 6 \Big/ \binom{12}{4} = \frac{6}{495} = \frac{2}{165}.$$

Using these similar tables for $k = 1, 2, \ldots, 12$, we present Table 2 for obtaining reliability $R_S(q)$. Properties $p_k = P_k - P_{k-1}$ are:

$$\sum_{k=1}^{12} p_k = 1,$$
$$\sum_{k=1}^{12} k p_k = \frac{8}{165} + \frac{8}{33} + \frac{5}{7} + \frac{3}{2} + \frac{1112}{495} + \frac{98}{55} + \frac{32}{33} + \frac{1}{3} \approx 7.8365,$$

mode is 8 and median is 8, and kp_k/P_k decreases with k from ∞ to 0. Furthermore, Table 3 presents $R_S(q)$ for q.

From (1) and (2), when $q \equiv \overline{F}(t)$, reliability is

$$\begin{aligned} R_S(t) = {} & 6\overline{F}(t)^4 F(t)^8 + 48\overline{F}(t)^5 F(t)^7 + 166\overline{F}(t)^6 F(t)^6 \\ & + 312\overline{F}(t)^7 F(t)^5 + 334\overline{F}(t)^8 F(t)^4 + 192\overline{F}(t)^9 F(t)^3 \\ & + 64\overline{F}(t)^{10} F(t)^2 + 12\overline{F}(t)^{11} F(t) + \overline{F}(t)^{12}, \end{aligned} \tag{8}$$

Table 1: Path number of a square system with 12 units when $k = 4$

1	2	3	4	5	6	7	8	9	10	11	12	S
○	○	○	○	×	×	×	×	×	×	×	×	×
○	○	○	×	○	×	×	×	×	×	×	×	×
○	○	○	×	×	○	×	×	×	×	×	×	×
○	○	○	×	×	×	○	×	×	×	×	×	×
○	○	○	×	×	×	×	○	×	×	×	×	×
○	○	○	×	×	×	×	×	○	×	×	×	×
○	○	○	×	×	×	×	×	×	○	×	×	×
○	○	○	×	×	×	×	×	×	×	○	×	×
○	○	○	×	×	×	×	×	×	×	×	○	×
						≀						
○	○	×	×	○	×	×	×	×	○	×	×	○
○	×	×	○	×	×	○	×	×	○	×	×	○
○	×	×	○	×	×	×	×	○	×	×	○	○
×	×	○	×	×	○	○	×	×	○	×	×	○
×	×	○	×	×	○	×	×	○	×	×	○	○
×	×	○	×	×	○	×	○	×	×	○	○	○
						≀						
○	×	×	×	×	×	×	×	×	○	○	○	×
×	○	×	×	×	×	×	×	×	○	○	○	×
×	×	○	×	×	×	×	×	×	○	○	○	×
×	×	×	○	×	×	×	×	×	○	○	○	×
×	×	×	×	○	×	×	×	×	○	○	○	×
×	×	×	×	×	○	×	×	×	○	○	○	×
×	×	×	×	×	×	○	×	×	○	○	○	×
×	×	×	×	×	×	×	○	×	○	○	○	×
×	×	×	×	×	×	×	×	○	○	○	○	×

○:Operation ×: Failure S:System

and failure rate is, from (5),

$$\begin{aligned} h_S(t) = \frac{nh(t)}{R_S(t)} \Big[& 2\overline{F}(t)^4 F(t)^8 + 16\overline{F}(t)^5 F(t)^7 + 55\overline{F}(t)^6 F(t)^6 \\ & + 99\overline{F}(t)^7 F(t)^5 + \frac{278}{3}\overline{F}(t)^8 F(t)^4 + \frac{98}{3}\overline{F}(t)^9 F(t)^3 \\ & + \frac{16}{3}\overline{F}(t)^{10} F(t)^2 + \frac{1}{3}\overline{F}(t)^{11} F(t) \Big]. \end{aligned}$$

When $F(t) = 1 - e^{-\lambda t}$, MTTF is, from (4),

$$\mu_s = \frac{1}{\lambda}\left[\frac{1}{330} + \frac{2}{165} + \frac{83}{2772} + \frac{13}{231} + \frac{167}{1980} + \frac{16}{165} + \frac{16}{165} + \frac{1}{11} + \frac{1}{12}\right] \approx \frac{0.5539}{\lambda}.$$

Table 2: Path number N_k and P_k for k

k	1	2	3	4	5	6	7	8	9	10	11	12
N_R	0	0	0	6	48	166	312	334	192	64	12	1
P_k	0	0	0	$\frac{2}{165}$	$\frac{2}{33}$	$\frac{83}{462}$	$\frac{13}{33}$	$\frac{334}{495}$	$\frac{48}{55}$	$\frac{32}{33}$	1	1
p_k	0	0	0	$\frac{2}{165}$	$\frac{8}{165}$	$\frac{5}{42}$	$\frac{3}{14}$	$\frac{139}{495}$	$\frac{98}{495}$	$\frac{16}{165}$	$\frac{1}{33}$	0
kp_k	0	0	0	$\frac{8}{165}$	$\frac{8}{33}$	$\frac{5}{7}$	$\frac{3}{2}$	$\frac{1112}{495}$	$\frac{98}{55}$	$\frac{32}{33}$	$\frac{1}{3}$	0
$\frac{P_k}{k}$	0	0	0	$\frac{1}{330}$	$\frac{2}{165}$	$\frac{83}{2772}$	$\frac{13}{231}$	$\frac{167}{1980}$	$\frac{16}{165}$	$\frac{16}{165}$	$\frac{1}{11}$	$\frac{1}{12}$
$\frac{kp_k}{P_k}$	∞	∞	∞	4	4	$\frac{330}{83}$	$\frac{99}{26}$	$\frac{556}{167}$	$\frac{49}{24}$	1	$\frac{1}{3}$	0
$\binom{n-1}{k-1}P_k$	0	0	0	2	16	55	99	$\frac{278}{3}$	$\frac{98}{3}$	$\frac{16}{3}$	$\frac{1}{3}$	0

Table 3: Reliability $R_S(q)$ for $q = 0.99 \sim 0.50$

q	0.99	0.95	0.90	0.80	0.70	0.60	0.50
$R_S(q)$	0.9998	0.9940	0.9725	0.8695	0.6914	0.4767	0.2771

Median M_S satisfies

$$
\begin{aligned}
&6e^{-4\lambda t}(1-e^{-\lambda t})^8 + 48e^{-5\lambda t}(1-e^{-\lambda t})^7 \\
&+ 166e^{-6\lambda t}(1-e^{-\lambda t})^6 + 312e^{-7\lambda t}(1-e^{-\lambda t})^5 \\
&+ 334e^{-8\lambda t}(1-e^{-\lambda t})^4 + 192e^{-9\lambda t}(1-e^{-\lambda t})^3 \\
&+ 64e^{-10\lambda t}(1-e^{-\lambda t})^2 + 12e^{-11\lambda t}(1-e^{-\lambda t}) + e^{-12\lambda t} = \frac{1}{2},
\end{aligned}
$$

i.e., $M_S \approx \dfrac{0.4930}{\lambda}$.

Failure rate is, from (5),

$$
h_S(t) = \frac{12\lambda B}{A}, \tag{9}
$$

which increases strictly with t from 0 to 4λ, where

$$
\begin{aligned}
A \equiv 6 &+ \frac{48}{e^{\lambda t}-1} + \frac{166}{(e^{\lambda t}-1)^2} + \frac{312}{(e^{\lambda t}-1)^3} \\
&+ \frac{334}{(e^{\lambda t}-1)^4} + \frac{192}{(e^{\lambda t}-1)^5} + \frac{64}{(e^{\lambda t}-1)^6} \\
&+ \frac{12}{(e^{\lambda t}-1)^7}. + \frac{1}{(e^{\lambda t}-1)^8}, \\
B \equiv 2 &+ \frac{16}{e^{\lambda t}-1} + \frac{55}{(e^{\lambda t}-1)^2} + \frac{99}{(e^{\lambda t}-1)^3} \\
&+ \frac{278}{3(e^{\lambda t}-1)^4} + \frac{98}{3(e^{\lambda t}-1)^5} + \frac{16}{3(e^{\lambda t}-1)^6} \\
&+ \frac{1}{3(e^{\lambda t}-1)^7}.
\end{aligned}
$$

Complexity is

$$
\begin{aligned}
P_e &= \log_2 16 = 4, \\
P_H &= -\frac{2}{165}\log_2\frac{2}{165} - \frac{8}{165}\log_2\frac{8}{165} - \frac{5}{42}\log_2\frac{5}{42} \\
&\quad - \frac{3}{14}\log_2\frac{3}{14} - \frac{139}{495}\log_2\frac{139}{495} - \frac{98}{495}\log_2\frac{98}{495} \\
&\quad - \frac{16}{165}\log_2\frac{16}{165} - \frac{1}{33}\log_2\frac{1}{33} \approx 2.5870.
\end{aligned}
$$

4. Cube Network System with 12 Units

We consider a cube network system with 12 units in Fig. 2 and obtain its reliability $R_C(q)$.

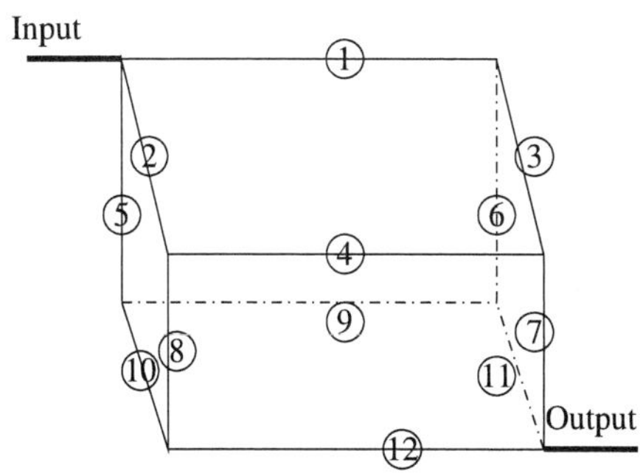

Figure 2: Cube network system with 12 units

Table 4 presents path number N_k and rate P_k. Using Table 4,

Table 4: Path number N_k and P_k for k

k	1	2	3	4	5	6	7	8	9	10	11	12
N_k	0	0	6	54	216	483	636	468	218	66	12	1
P_k	0	0	$\frac{3}{110}$	$\frac{6}{55}$	$\frac{3}{11}$	$\frac{23}{44}$	$\frac{53}{66}$	$\frac{52}{55}$	$\frac{109}{110}$	1	1	1
p_k	0	0	$\frac{3}{110}$	$\frac{9}{110}$	$\frac{9}{55}$	$\frac{1}{4}$	$\frac{37}{132}$	$\frac{47}{330}$	$\frac{1}{22}$	$\frac{1}{110}$	0	0
kp_k	0	0	$\frac{9}{110}$	$\frac{36}{110}$	$\frac{45}{55}$	$\frac{6}{4}$	$\frac{259}{132}$	$\frac{188}{165}$	$\frac{9}{22}$	$\frac{1}{11}$	0	0
$\frac{P_k}{k}$	0	0	$\frac{1}{110}$	$\frac{3}{110}$	$\frac{3}{55}$	$\frac{23}{264}$	$\frac{53}{462}$	$\frac{13}{110}$	$\frac{109}{990}$	$\frac{1}{10}$	$\frac{1}{11}$	$\frac{1}{12}$
$\frac{kp_k}{P_k}$	∞	∞	3	3	3	$\frac{66}{23}$	$\frac{259}{106}$	$\frac{47}{39}$	$\frac{45}{109}$	$\frac{1}{11}$	0	0
$\binom{n-1}{k-1}p_k$	0	0	$\frac{3}{2}$	$\frac{27}{2}$	54	$\frac{231}{2}$	$\frac{259}{2}$	47	$\frac{15}{2}$	$\frac{1}{2}$	0	0

Table 5: Reliability $R_C(q)$ for $q = 0.99 \sim 0.50$

q	0.99	0.95	0.90	0.80	0.70	0.60	0.50
$R_C(q)$	1.0000	0.9997	0.9970	0.9698	0.8864	0.7323	0.5273

$$\sum_{k=1}^{12} p_k = 1,$$

$$\mu_C = \sum_{k=1}^{12} kp_k = \frac{9}{110} + \frac{36}{110} + \frac{45}{55} + \frac{3}{2} + \frac{259}{132} + \frac{188}{165} + \frac{9}{22} + \frac{1}{11} = \frac{697}{110} \approx 6.3364, \tag{10}$$

mode is 7, median is 6, and kp_k/P_k decreases with k from ∞ to 0. Furthermore, Table 5 presents $R_C(q)$ for q.

From (1) and (2), reliability is

$$\begin{aligned} R_C(t) =& 6\overline{F}(t)^3F(t)^9 + 54\overline{F}(t)^4F(t)^8 + 216\overline{F}(t)^5F(t)^7 \\ &+ 483\overline{F}(t)^6F(t)^6 + 636\overline{F}(t)^7F(t)^5 + 468\overline{F}(t)^8F(t)^4 \\ &+ 218\overline{F}(t)^9F(t)^3 + 66\overline{F}(t)^{10}F(t)^2 + 12\overline{F}(t)^{11}F(t) \\ &+ \overline{F}(t)^{12}, \end{aligned} \tag{11}$$

and failure rate is, from (5),

$$\begin{aligned} h_C(t) =& \frac{nh(t)}{R_C(t)}\left[\frac{3}{2}\overline{F}(t)^3F(t)^9 + \frac{27}{2}\overline{F}(t)^4F(t)^8 + 54\overline{F}(t)^5F(t)^7 \right. \\ &+ \frac{231}{2}\overline{F}(t)^6F(t)^6 + \frac{259}{2}\overline{F}(t)^7F(t)^5 + 47\overline{F}(t)^8F(t)^4 \\ &\left. + \frac{15}{2}\overline{F}(t)^9F(t)^3 + \frac{1}{2}\overline{F}(t)^{10}F(t)^2\right]. \end{aligned}$$

Noting that kp_k/P_k decreases with k, failure rate increases strictly with t when $F(t) = 1 - e^{-\lambda t}$. MTTF is, from (4),

$$\mu_C = \frac{1}{\lambda}\left[\frac{1}{110} + \frac{3}{110} + \frac{3}{55} + \frac{23}{264} + \frac{53}{462} + \frac{13}{110} + \frac{109}{990} + \frac{1}{10} + \frac{1}{11} + \frac{1}{12}\right] \approx \frac{0.7953}{\lambda}.$$

Median M_C which satisfies $R_C(t) = 1/2$ is, when $\lambda = 1$, $M_C = 0.7187/\lambda$. Failure rate is , from (5),

$$h_C(t) = \frac{12\lambda B}{A}, \tag{12}$$

which increases strictly with t from 0 to 3λ, where

$$\begin{aligned} A \equiv& 6 + \frac{54}{e^{\lambda t} - 1} + \frac{216}{(e^{\lambda t} - 1)^2} + \frac{483}{(e^{\lambda t} - 1)^3} + \frac{636}{(e^{\lambda t} - 1)^4} \\ &+ \frac{468}{(e^{\lambda t} - 1)^5} + \frac{218}{(e^{\lambda t} - 1)^6} + \frac{66}{(e^{\lambda t} - 1)^7} + \frac{12}{(e^{\lambda t} - 1)^8} \\ &+ \frac{1}{(e^{\lambda t} - 1)^9}, \end{aligned}$$

$$\begin{aligned} B \equiv& \frac{3}{2} + \frac{27}{2(e^{\lambda t} - 1)} + \frac{54}{(e^{\lambda t} - 1)^2} + \frac{231}{2(e^{\lambda t} - 1)^3} + \frac{259}{2(e^{\lambda t} - 1)^4} \\ &+ \frac{47}{(e^{\lambda t} - 1)^5} + \frac{15}{2(e^{\lambda t} - 1)^6} + \frac{1}{2(e^{\lambda t} - 1)^7}. \end{aligned}$$

Complexity is

$$P_e = \log_2 30 \approx 4.9069,$$

$$P_H = -\frac{3}{110}\log_2\frac{3}{110} - \frac{9}{110}\log_2\frac{9}{110} - \frac{9}{55}\log_2\frac{9}{55} - \frac{1}{4}\log_2\frac{1}{4} - \frac{37}{132}\log_2\frac{37}{132} - \frac{47}{330}\log_2\frac{47}{330} - \frac{1}{22}\log_2\frac{1}{22} - \frac{1}{110}\log_2\frac{1}{110} \approx 2.5437. \quad (13)$$

Comparing square and cube systems, $R_C(q) > R_S(Q)$, $\mu_C > \mu_S$, $M_C > M_S$ which indicates that cube system is much better than square system from the viewpoint of reliability. However, both complexities P_H are almost the same. After that, cube system should be used in practical fields more than square system in designing a redundant system.

5. Application to Age Replacement Policy

Suppose that the system is replaced at time T or at failure, whichever occurs first, which is called age replacement policy. Then, the expected cost rate is

$$C(T) = \frac{c_1 - (c_1 - c_2)R(T)}{\int_0^T R(t)\mathrm{d}t}, \quad (14)$$

where c_1 =cost of replacement at failure and c_2 =cost of preventive replacement at time T, where $c_1 > c_2$. Optimal T^* to minimize $C(T)$ satisfies

$$h(T)\int_0^T R(t)\mathrm{d}t - [1 - R(T)] = \frac{1}{c_1/c_2 - 1}, \quad (15)$$

and the resulting cost rate is

$$\frac{C(T^*)}{c_2} = \left(\frac{c_1}{c_2} - 1\right)h(T^*). \quad (16)$$

We compute optimal policies for square and cube systems when $F(t) = 1 - e^{-t}$, where note that both failure rates increase strictly with t from 0.

For a square system, reliability $R_S(t)$ is given in (8) when $F(t) = 1 - e^{-t}$ and failure rate $h_S(t)$ is given in (9), and for a cube system, reliability $R_C(t)$ is given in (11) when $F(t) = 1 - e^{-t}$ and failure rate $h_C(t)$ is given in (12). Substituting $R_i(t)$ and $h_i(t)(i = S, C)$ into (15), we can compute T_i^* and the resulting cost rates $C_i(T_i^*)$ numerically. Table 6 presents optimal T_i^* and $C_i(T_i^*)$ when $F(t) = 1 - e^{-t}$. This indicates that $T_S^* < T_C^*$ and $C_S(T_S^*) > C_C(T_C^*)$, which means that reliability of cube system is much better than that of square system.

Table 6: Optimal T_S^*, $C_S(T_S^*)$ and T_c^*,$C_c(T_c^*)$ when $F(t) = 1 - e^{-t}$.

$\frac{c_1}{c_2}$	T_s^*	$C_s(T_s^*)/c_2$	T_c^*	$C_c(T_c^*)/c_2$
2	0.2817	4.5877	0.9400	2.4780
3	0.1898	6.4598	0.5427	3.2521
5	0.1343	8.9449	0.3835	4.1882
10	0.0916	13.0071	0.2758	5.5353
15	0.0746	15.9479	0.2345	6.4098
20	0.0648	18.3701	0.2106	7.0828

References

[1] Balow RE, Proschan F (1965) Mathematical theory of reliability. Wiley, New York.

[2] Ushakov IA (1994) Handbook of reliability engineering. Wiley, New York.

[3] Zhao X, Feng HS, Qian CH, Nakamura S (2024) Reliability structures of general redundant systems. In: Nakamura S, Sawaki S, Nakagawa T (eds) Probability and statistical models in operations research, computer and management sciences. Springer Nature, Switzerland, pp.352-371.

[4] Pham H (2003) Handbook of reliability engineering. Springer, London.

[5] Nakagawa T (2008) Advanced reliability models and maintenance policies. Springer, London.

[6] Nakagawa T (2014) Random maintenance policies. Springer, London.

[7] Ito K, Nakagawa T (2023) Optimal inspection models with their applications. Springer Nature, Switzerland.

OSS Performability Analysis Based on Deep Multitask Learning as Multi-Objective Optimization

Yoshinobu Tamura[†], Adarsh Anand[††], Pramod Kumar Kapur[†††], and Shigeru Yamada[††††]

[†]Yamaguchi University, Japan, tamuray@yamaguchi-u.ac.jp
[††]University of Delhi, India, adarsh.anand86@gmail.com
[†††]Amity University, India, pkkapur1@gmail.com
[††††]Tottori University, Japan, bex2yama@muse.ocn.ne.jp

Keywords: Open source software, deep multitask learning, performability, software reliability

Abstract

Recently, many deep learning methods have been used in various research areas. In particular, we will be able to obtain new knowledge by using the large scale data. We focus on the method of reliability assessment based on the deep learning. Then, this paper proposes the deep multitask learning by using the fault big data. Moreover, we propose the performability as the OSS assessment measure obtained from the deep multitask learning. Several numerical illustrations based on the proposed method are shown in this paper.

1 Introduction

The cloud computing has been used in various areas as the main network computing technology [1]. Recently, the cloud computing is changing to the edge computing because of the distributed network structure. Also, many open source software (OSS) have been used in many social areas. Various OSS's play a major role in terms of the cloud and edge computing. The reliable OSS is important for the users to provide the safe society.

In the past, many methods of software reliability assessment have been proposed by many resesrchers [2–5]. On the other hand, the OSS development style is similar to the agile paradigm. Therefore, it is difficult to apply the conventional software reliability assessment methods to the development paradigm of OSS. The edge computing by using OSS becomes popular because of cost reduction [6–9]. Then, it will be important to assess the reliability of edge computing based on the OSS. Our research group has been proposed the method of OSS reliability assessment in the past [10,11]. In particular, our research group has been proposed several methods of OSS reliability assessment based on the deep learning [12,13]. Also, several research papers have been proposed in terms of the deep multitask learning [14–16].

We have proposed the OSS reliability assessment methods based on the deep single-task learning. The single-task deep learning has several problems such as the overtraining and the findless of feature values. By using the deep multitask learning, we will be able to solve these problems. Many fault categories have been recorded on the bug tracking system of OSS. In particular, the huge fault data sets are obtained from the distributed network OSS. This paper proposes new reliability assessment measure based on the deep multitask learning. In particular, the performability is important to understand the current situation of edge computing. This paper proposes the performability as new reliability assessment measure. Generally, the performability of system has existed in the past. Considering the OSS operation, the definitions of operation time and the repair one are different from the OSS operation. Therefore, we define the performability of OSS in this paper. Moreover, we show several numerical examples based on the proposed method.

2 OSS Reliability Assessment Based on Deep Multitask Learning

2.1 Objective functions for deep multitask learning model

This paper focuses on the fault detection time and the fault modification one. Then, we consider the following objective functions.

$$\alpha(i) = p_i(o_i - o_{i-1}), \quad (1)$$

$$\beta(i) = q_i(c_i - c_{i-1}), \quad (2)$$

where o_i is the opened time interval between OSS faults of i-th and $i-1$-th. p_i is the appearance frequency of fault reporter. Then, $\alpha(i)$ is the opened time interval between OSS faults weighted by the appearance frequency of fault reporter. Also, c_i is the changed time interval between OSS faults of i-th and $i-1$-th. qi is the appearance frequency of fault assignee. Then, $\beta(i)$ is the changed time interval between OSS faults weighted by the appearance frequency of fault assignee.

Therefore, the OSS reliability grows when $\alpha(i)$ becomes large. Also, the efficiency of OSS debugging grows when $\beta(i)$ becomes small.

2.2 Performability based on the proposed deep multitask learning model

By using the output values of objective variable in above mentioned results, we can obtain the performability as the OSS reliability assessment measure as follows:

$$\gamma(i) \approx \frac{\alpha(i)}{\alpha(i)+\beta(i)}, \tag{3}$$

$$\delta(i) = \frac{\gamma(i)-\gamma_{max}}{\gamma_{max}-\gamma_{min}}, \tag{4}$$

where $\delta(i)$ is approximately defined as the performability based on our deep multitask learning model.

2.3 Model structure of our deep multitask learning

The structure of our deep multitask learning model is shown in Fig. 1.

We have used the sequential API in our existing researches. Then, the part of the sequential API is shown as the following source code.

```
# An example of the sequential API

model.add(tf.keras.layers.Dense(100, activation
    ='relu', input_shape=(10,)))
model.add(tf.keras.layers.Dropout(0.1))
model.add(tf.keras.layers.Dense(100, activation
    ='relu'))
model.add(tf.keras.layers.Dropout(0.1))
model.add(tf.keras.layers.Dense(100, activation
    ='relu'))
model.add(tf.keras.layers.Dropout(0.1))
model.add(tf.keras.layers.Dense(100, activation
    ='relu'))
model.add(tf.keras.layers.Dropout(0.1))
model.add(tf.keras.layers.Dense(100, activation
    ='relu'))
model.add(tf.keras.layers.Dropout(0.1))
model.add(tf.keras.layers.Dense(100, activation
    ='relu'))
model.add(tf.keras.layers.Dropout(0.1))
```

The deep multitask learning model proposed in this paper is implemented by using the functional API of the following source code.

```
# An example of the functional API

input = tf.keras.Input(shape=(10,))
x = tf.keras.layers.Dense(10,activation='relu')(
    input)
x = tf.keras.layers.Dense(10,activation='relu')(
    x)
x = tf.keras.layers.Dropout(0.1)(x)
x = tf.keras.layers.Dense(10,activation='relu')(
    x)
x = tf.keras.layers.Dense(10,activation='relu')(
    x)
output1 = tf.keras.layers.Dense(3,activation='
    relu')(x)
output2 = tf.keras.layers.Dense(3,activation='
    relu')(x)
output3 = tf.keras.layers.Dense(2,activation='
    relu')(x)
output4 = tf.keras.layers.Dense(2,activation='
    relu')(x)
x1 = tf.keras.layers.Dense(100,activation='relu
    ')(output1)
x2 = tf.keras.layers.Dense(100,activation='relu
    ')(output2)
x3 = tf.keras.layers.Dense(100,activation='relu
    ')(output3)
x4 = tf.keras.layers.Dense(100,activation='relu
    ')(output4)
x1 = tf.keras.layers.Dense(100,activation='relu
    ')(x1)
x2 = tf.keras.layers.Dense(100,activation='relu
    ')(x2)
x3 = tf.keras.layers.Dense(100,activation='relu
    ')(x3)
x4 = tf.keras.layers.Dense(100,activation='relu
    ')(x4)
x1 = tf.keras.layers.Dropout(0.1)(x1)
x2 = tf.keras.layers.Dropout(0.1)(x2)
x3 = tf.keras.layers.Dropout(0.1)(x3)
x4 = tf.keras.layers.Dropout(0.1)(x4)
x1 = tf.keras.layers.Dense(100,activation='relu
    ')(x1)
x2 = tf.keras.layers.Dense(100,activation='relu
    ')(x2)
x3 = tf.keras.layers.Dense(100,activation='relu
    ')(x3)
x4 = tf.keras.layers.Dense(100,activation='relu
    ')(x4)
output5 = tf.keras.layers.Dense(1,activation='
    relu')(x1)
output6 = tf.keras.layers.Dense(1,activation='
    relu')(x2)
output7 = tf.keras.layers.Dense(1,activation='
    relu')(x3)
output8 = tf.keras.layers.Dense(1,activation='
    relu')(x4)
model = tf.keras.Model(inputs=input, outputs=[
    output5, output6, output7, output8])
```

The sequential API cannot define the deep multitask learning. Therefore, we define the deep multitask learning by using the functional API.

3 Numerical Examples

We focus on the OSS fault big data set of *OpenStack* Project [17] including several edge components.

We show the estimated opened time interval between OSS faults in Fig. 2. Also, the estimated changed time

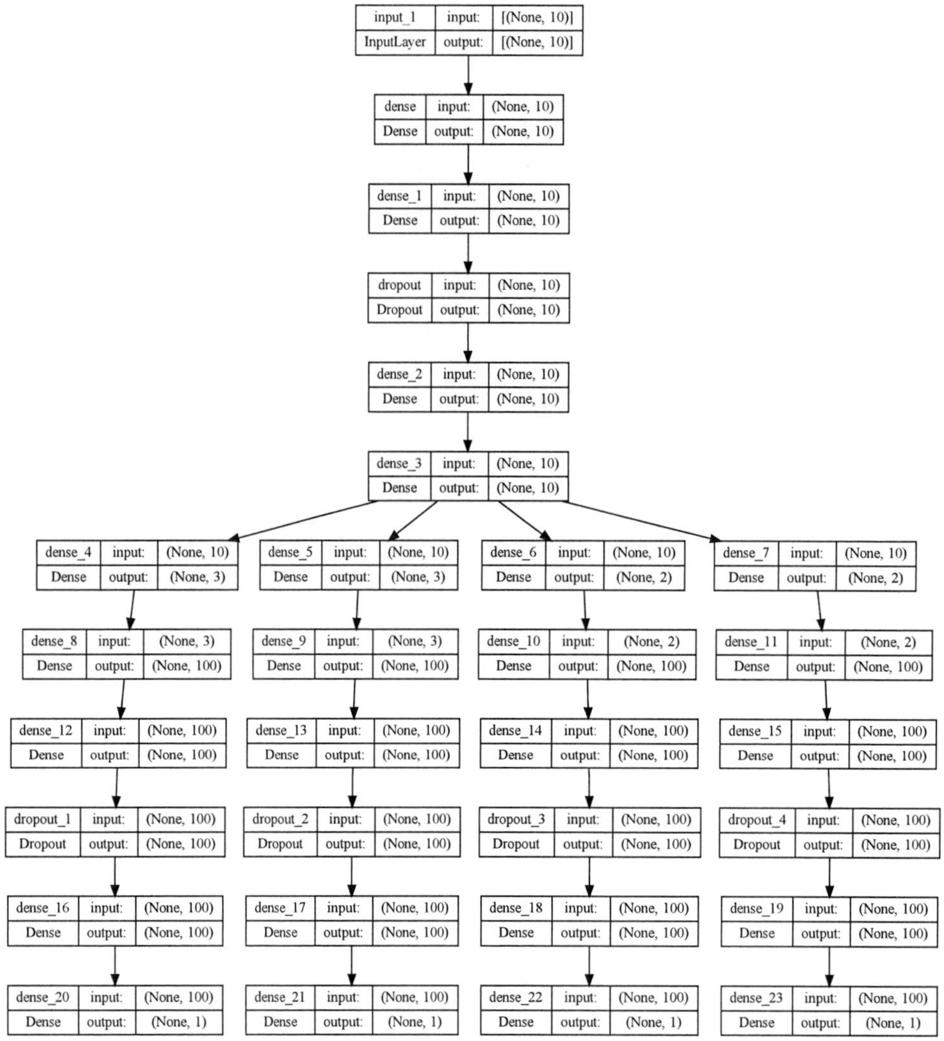

Fig. 1: The structure of our deep multitask learning model.

interval between OSS faults is shown in Fig. 3. Moreover, we show the estimated frequency rate of the reporter for time interval between OSS faults in Fig. 4. Similarly, the estimated frequency rate of the assignee for time interval between OSS faults in Fig. 5.

Finally, the estimated OSS performability in Eq. (3) is shown in Fig. 6. The estimated OSS performability becomes large according to the operation procedures go on.

Considering the fault detection and correction phenomena of OSS, the opened time interval between OSS faults overlaps to the changed time interval between OSS faults. In this case, we cannot use the existing definition of the system performability to the fault detection and correction phenomena of OSS, because the estimate performability deviates from the definition of probability, i.e., the estimate performability exceeds the value of 1. Therefore, we have define the performability by using the data normalization.

4 Conclusion

Many fault data sets are recorded on the bug tracking system of OSS. We will be able to obtain new knowledge in terms of the OSS reliability by using the fault big data. Especially, we have approximately defined the performa-

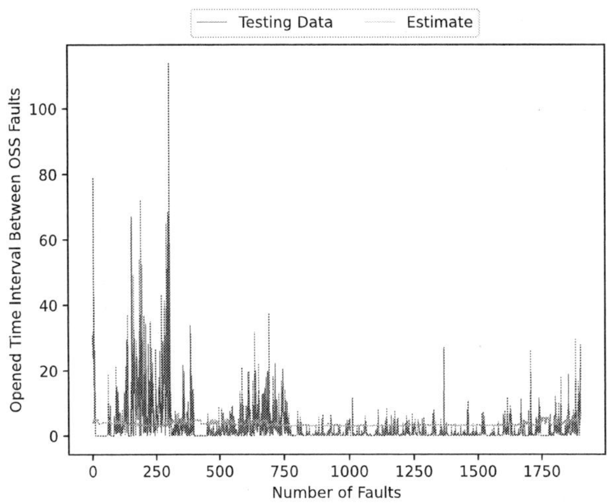

Fig. 2: The estimated opened time interval between OSS faults.

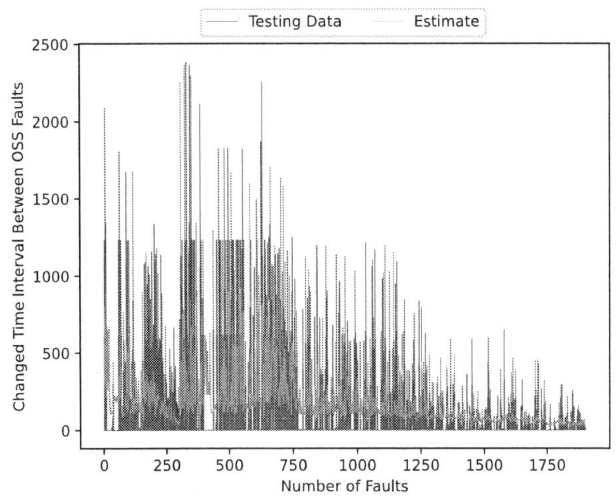

Fig. 3: The estimated changed time interval between OSS faults.

bility based on our deep multitask learning model.

In the case estimated Figs. 2∼6 by using the conventional stochastic model, we can estimate the expected value. However, the expected value only show the curve based on the mathematical model. On the other hand, the machine learning such as the deep multitask learning can show more detailed value than the curve based on the mathematical model. In this point, the proposed deep multitask learning model is better than the conventional stochastic model.

There is no research paper in terms of the deep multitask learning for OSS reliability assessment. The deep

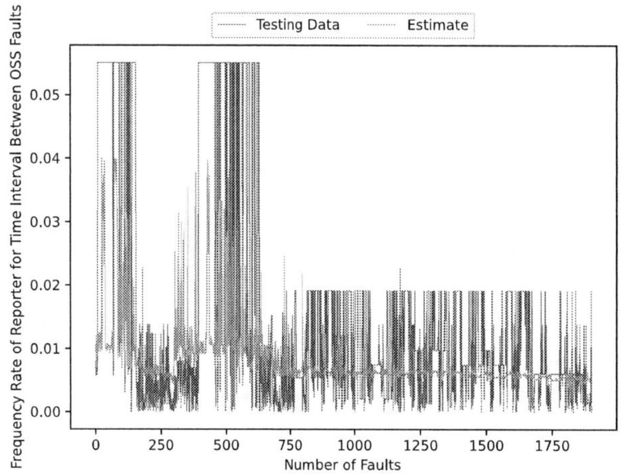

Fig. 4: The estimated frequency rate of reporter for time interval between OSS faults.

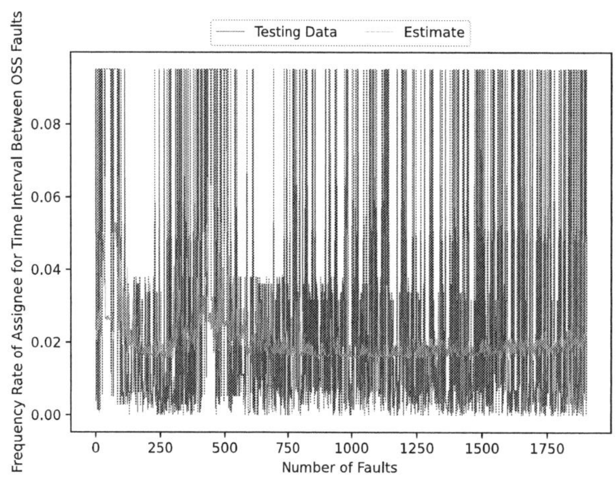

Fig. 5: The estimated frequency rate of assignee for time interval between OSS faults.

multitask learning takes advantage of simultaneously assessing several tasks as the output values. Also, the deep multitask learning can avoid the overtraining. Moreover, the features are easily obtained from the data by using the deep multitask learning. The proposed deep multitask model will be helpful as the useful method for the OSS reliability assessment for edge OSS service in the edge computing operation.

Acknowledgments

This work was supported in part by the JSPS KAKENHI Grant No. 23K11066 in Japan.

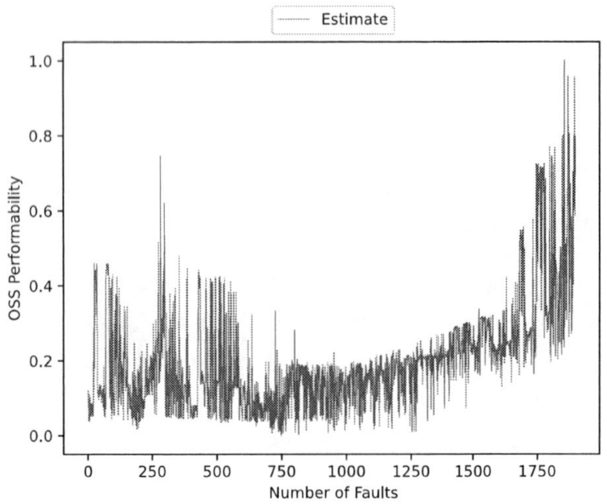

Fig. 6: The estimated OSS performability.

References

[1] I.M. Ibrahim et al., "A robust generic multi-authority attributes management system for cloud storage services," *IEEE Transactions on Cloud Computing*, 10.1109/TCC.2018.2867871, 30 Aug. 2018.

[2] S. Yamada, *Software Reliability Modeling: Fundamentals and Applications*, Springer–Verlag, Tokyo/Heidelberg, 2014.

[3] M.R. Lyu, ed., *Handbook of Software Reliability Engineering*, IEEE Computer Society Press, Los Alamitos, CA, U.S.A., 1996.

[4] J.D. Musa, A. Iannino, and K. Okumoto, *Software Reliability: Measurement, Prediction, Application*, McGraw–Hill, New York, 1987.

[5] P.K. Kapur, H. Pham, A. Gupta, and P.C. Jha, *Software Reliability Assessment with OR Applications*, Springer–Verlag, London, 2011.

[6] A.A. Ahmad et al., "Scalability analysis comparisons of cloud-based software services," *Journal of Cloud Computing: Advances, Systems and Applications*, 10.1186/s13677-019-0134-y, 23 Jul. 2019.

[7] M.O. Ozcan, F. Odaci and I. Ari, "Remote debugging for containerized applications in edge computing environments," Proceedings of the 2019 IEEE International Conference on Edge Computing (EDGE), Milan, Italy, 2019, pp. 30-32, doi: 10.1109/EDGE.2019.00021.

[8] Y. Ngoko and C. Cérin, "An edge computing platform for the detection of acoustic events," Proceedings of the 2017 IEEE International Conference on Edge Computing (EDGE), Honolulu, HI, USA, 2017, pp. 240-243, doi: 10.1109/IEEE.EDGE.2017.44.

[9] M. Caprolu, R. Di Pietro, F. Lombardi and S. Raponi, "Edge computing perspectives: architectures, technologies, and open security issues," Proceedings of the 2019 IEEE International Conference on Edge Computing (EDGE), Milan, Italy, 2019, pp. 116-123, doi: 10.1109/EDGE.2019.00035.

[10] S. Yamada and Y. Tamura, *OSS Reliability Measurement and Assessment*, Springer International Publishing, Switzerland, 2016.

[11] Y. Tamura and S. Yamada, *Applied OSS Reliability Assessment Modeling, AI and Tools*, Springer Series in Reliability Engineering, Springer, 2024.

[12] Y. Tamura, R. Ueki, A. Anand, and S. Yamada, "Estimation and comparison of mean time between failures based on deep learning for OSS fault big data," *International Journal of System Assurance Engineering and Management*, Springer, Latest Articles, https://doi.org/10.1007/s13198-023-01907-2, pp. 1-16, April 2023.

[13] Y. Tamura and S. Yamada, "Prototype of 3D reliability assessment tool based on deep learning for edge OSS computing," *Mathematics*, vol. 10, no. 9, Multidisciplinary Digital Publishing Institute, Switzerland, DOI: 10.3390/math10091572, pp. 1-12, May 2022.

[14] X. Gibert, V.M. Patel and R. Chellappa, "Deep multitask learning for railway track inspection," *IEEE Transactions on Intelligent Transportation Systems*, vol. 18, no. 1, pp. 153-164, Jan. 2017.

[15] S. Vandenhende, S. Georgoulis, W. Van Gansbeke, M. Proesmans, D. Dai and L. Van Gool, "Multi-task learning for dense prediction tasks: A survey," *IEEE Transactions on Pattern Analysis and Machine Intelligence*, vol. 44, no. 7, pp. 3614-3633, 1 July 2022.

[16] R. Ranjan, V.M. Patel and R. Chellappa, "Hyperface: A deep multi-task learning framework for face detection, landmark localization, pose estimation, and gender recognition," *IEEE Transactions on Pattern Analysis and Machine Intelligence*, vol. 41, no. 1, pp. 121-135, 1 Jan. 2019.

[17] The OpenStack project, Build the future of Open Infrastructure, https://www.openstack.org/

Reliability evaluation of multimodal humanitarian logistics in disaster response

NGUYEN Thi-Phuong[1]

[1]Department of Industrial Engineering and Management, National Chin-Yi University of Technology, Taichung 411, Taiwan, phuongnt@gm.ncut.edu.tw

Keywords: multistate air travel network, reliability, group demands, budgets, time window

Abstract - Reliability becomes an essential performance measure of several practical networks. This paper evaluates the reliability of multimodal humanitarian logistics to indicate the ability to distribute all relief demands under specific constraints of time. The MHLN model is constructed, and the process to determine the minimal paths feasible within the time constraint is provided. Then, reliability is calculated by employing the concept of lower boundary points and the recursive sum of the disjoint products method. Through an illustrative example, this study indicates how the main algorithm assesses reliability in practice and proves the implications of this research.

1. Introduction

Natural disasters like floods, earthquakes, and forest fires have increased [1]. Focusing on disaster recovery, humanitarian logistics delivers essential aid such as food, water, medicine, healthcare, shelter, and supplies to affected areas. This support helps mitigate the impact of natural disasters on people's lives and health. Given the importance of humanitarian logistics (HL) in disaster response, most research in recent years has focused on designing humanitarian logistics that can effectively and stably mitigate the impact of disasters [2]. Hong et al. introduced a stochastic model for humanitarian logistics networks ensuring reliable relief goods supply under local self-sufficiency constraints [3]. Ahmadi et al. proposed a model accounting for network failures, multiple vehicles, and standard relief times to determine warehouse locations and distribution routes post-earthquake. Ni et al. created a robust min-max model to optimize facility location and emergency inventory prepositioning for disaster relief [4]. Liu et al. optimized ambulance locations, numbers, and health care service allocation at minimal cost for emergency medical services [5]. Sheikholeslami and Zarrinpoor proposed a possibilistic location-allocation model using fuzzy chance constraint programming to maximize network coverage while minimizing costs [6].

Along with optimizing efficiency, it is very crucial to learn about the current and future performance of humanitarian logistics. . By examining historical data, various aspects such as logistics efficiency, cost, timeliness of response, and suitability of service providers can be analyzed. Consequently, several theoretical and practical approaches have been proposed to evaluate the performance of the humanitarian logistics (HL) network. Key performance factors that have been extensively studied include responsiveness, cost savings, flexibility, government coordination, and reliability [7]–[12].

Although reliability is widely used in evaluating network performance [13]–[18], there have been few studies examining the reliability of humanitarian logistics networks. Roh et al. considered reliability as the ability to deliver materials at the appropriate time, quantity, and quality when investigating the overall performance of international humanitarian relief organizations in Taiwan [19]. The authors calculated through historical completion rates, irrespective of differences between each relief operation. Considering the time factor, Günneç and Salman (2011) evaluated several probabilistic measures of connectivity and the expected time/distance to travel between critical origin-destination pairs, assessing the effective emergency response capability of the transportation network in disaster situations [20]. Note that, even with fully connected links, vulnerable or severely damaged areas may still lack relief goods due to varying levels of damage among beneficiaries [21], [22]. Thus, network connectivity and rapid response alone do not sufficiently indicate the reliability of humanitarian logistics, To address these gaps, this study provides an algorithm to effectively assess the reliability of humanitarian logistics for prompt disaster response considering multi-state delivery capacity. Reliability is defined as the probability of successfully distributing all relief demands under specific constraint of time.

In humanitarian logistics, suppliers and donors provide relief. When catastrophic earthquakes occur, people may need to be moved from affected areas to safe locations like care centers [23].]. Care centers and disaster-affected areas are the beneficiaries, while warehouses and distribution centers facilitate efficient logistics. Routes connecting relief sources, transit places, and beneficiaries are called transport routes. Fig. 1 illustrates the structure of humanitarian logistics.

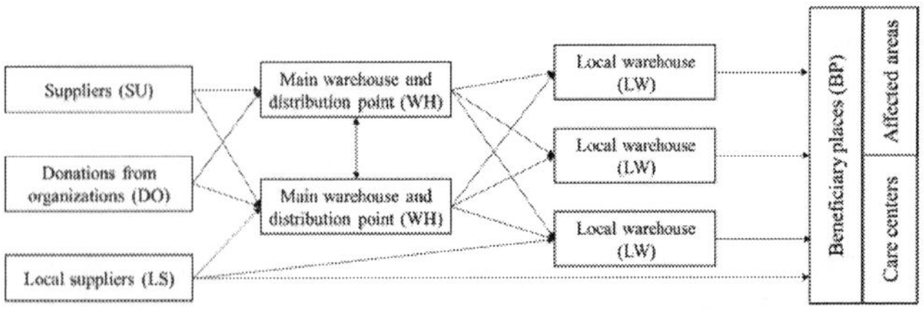

Fig. 1. Modified structure of humanitarian logistics [24]

As the capacity of each transport route in the humanitarian logistics is regarded as multi-state and statistically independent [25]–[27], a multi-state humanitarian logistic network (MHLN) comprising nodes and arcs is constructed. Nodes denote suppliers, donations, warehouses and distribution centers, care centers, and disaster-affected areas, and arcs denote the transport routes connecting a pair of vertices and delivering by a specific means of transport. Each edge may be operational or inactive after a disaster. Different disaster levels lead to varied degrees of damage and relief demands [21], [22], referring to Table 1. The probability of transport time and capacity on each route is calculated through historical data.

Table 1. Damage at each level of disaster [21], [22]

Damaged level	High	Moderate	Low
Description of earthquake magnitude	7.8 above	7.1 -7.7	6.5 - 7.1
Percentage of closed route	30 %	15 %	5 %
Estimated beneficiary/ Area population	4 – 10 %	3 – 10 %	1.5 – 2 %
Standard necessities/ person	1.18 kg of food, 3 liters of water, 91 gram of medical supplies, 2.044 kg of hygiene kit		

Employing the concept of minimal paths [28]–[32], this study first identifies all possible minimal paths (MPs) from sources of relief to beneficiary locations. The processing time for each MP, including transport and handling time, is calculated. Then, all lower boundary points, which are the minimal capacity vectors meeting the demands given within time constraint, are determined. The reliability of the MHLN is computed as the probability of disjointed unions. The remaining of this study is organized as follows. Section 2 first models the MHLN then constructs the framework for reliability assessment. In section 3, the main algorithm is accordingly presented. A numerical example is provided in section 4 to indicate how the main algorithm works in practice. Some remarks and future research are discussed in the conclusion section.

2. MHLN and Reliability evaluation

Frist, an MHLN is represented as a graph **H** = (**A**, **E**, U, b, **T**, t^*). **A** consists of n nodes $\{a_1, a_2, \ldots, a_n\}$ including relief sources, beneficiary places, and transit points. **E** contains m edges (e_j) connecting pairs of nodes in **A** with transport capacity v_j, measured in vehicles. The transport capacity vector $V = (v_1, v_2, \ldots, v_m)$ is bounded by the maximal transport capacity vector $U = (U_1, U_2, \ldots, U_m)$. Vehicles hold up to b_j boxes of relief goods. Relief must be loaded/unloaded at relief sources or beneficiary places, and both at transit points. Transport time for each arc t_j is stored in $\mathbf{T} = (t_1, t_2, \ldots, t_m)$. The unloading/loading time per box is assumed to be fixed, t^* (mins). Other assumptions include:

(i) MHLN follows the conservation law.
(ii) The capacity is statistically independent.
(iii) All vehicles will carry the maximum load possible.

2.1. Search for all minimal paths to beneficiary places

Suppose that there are r care centers and disaster-affected areas and the set of demands at all beneficiary places are $D = (d_1, d_2, \ldots, d_r)$. The reliability of the MHLN (R_H) is defined as the probability that all given demands D can be fulfilled within the time constraint T. Let transport capacity vectors (V) that meet these requirements are stored in Δ. The MHLN's reliability is then calculated based on capacity vector V in Δ as below.

$$R_{\mathrm{H}} = \sum_{V \in \Delta} \Pr(V) \tag{1}$$

Enumerating and summing the probability of numerous V is inefficient. Instead, this study uses minimal paths to find all lower boundary points of Δ. A lower boundary point is in Δ but not greater than any other capacity vectors. Any transport capacity vector in Δ must meet the following conditions to be a lower boundary point:

a. Successfully transport reliefs from sources to sinks within the time constraint T.
b. Fulfill the set of demands D.
c. It is not greater than any transport capacity vectors in Δ.

Assume that there are ∂ lower boundary points (L_k) found, the MHLN's reliability can be derived as:

$$R_{\mathrm{H}} = \Pr\Big(\bigcup_{k=1}^{\partial} \{V | V \geq L_k\}\Big) \tag{2}$$

This section employs the backtrack method to identify all possible minimal paths (MPs), then calculates processing times. An MP is a set of routes from source to sink without loops, meeting time constraint. Processing time depends on the number of relief boxes in a vehicle. MPs are represented as P_i^{α} for $\alpha = 1, 2, \ldots, \omega_i$, where i represents the ith beneficiary place (sink) and ω_i is the total number of MPs to that sink.

2.2. Lower boundary points

This stage aims to deal with the conditions of a lower boundary point. All conditions are presented as follows.

- Let any V whose flow vector F = ($f_1^1, f_1^2, \ldots, f_1^{\omega_1}, f_2^1, \ldots f_i^{\alpha}, \ldots, f_r^{\omega_r}$) represent the maximum flow under a transport capacity vector V. Any V will successfully fulfill the set of demands D (i.e., the condition b) if its F satisfies two equations (3) and (4).

$$\sum_{\alpha=1}^{\omega_i} f_i^{\alpha} = d_i \quad \text{for } i = 1, 2, \ldots, r. \tag{3}$$

$$\sum_{P_i^{\alpha} \subset e_j} \left\lceil \frac{f_i^{\alpha}}{b_j} \right\rceil \le U_j \quad \text{for } j = 1, 2, \ldots, m. \tag{4}$$

- Since the processing time for each MP encompasses both the transport time on the respective routes and the handling time, condition a is satisfied if:

$$\begin{cases} \sum_{P_i^{\alpha} \subset e_j} (t_j + 2.t^*.f_i^{\alpha}) \le T \mid b_j > f_i^{\alpha} > 0 \\ \sum_{P_i^{\alpha} \subset e_j} (t_j + 2.t^*.b_j) \le T \mid b_j \le f_i^{\alpha} \end{cases} \quad \text{for all } P_i^{\alpha}. \tag{5}$$

- In terms of the condition c, any V is an exact lower boundary point (L_k) if it meets equation (6) and qualifies the following vector comparison procedure:

$$v_j = \sum_{P_i^{\alpha} \subset e_j} \left\lceil \frac{f_i^{\alpha}}{b_j} \right\rceil \quad \text{for } j = 1, 2, \ldots, m. \tag{6}$$

2.3. Reliability assessment

This stage explains the computation process of the MHLN's reliability, referring to the formula below.

$$R_{\mathrm{H}} = \Pr(\bigcup_{k=1}^{\partial} \{V | V \ge L_k\}). \tag{7}$$

According to equation (7), the reliability of MHLN is the probability of disjointed unions. Various methods, such as state-space decomposition [33], [34], inclusion-exclusion [32], [35], and the sum of disjoint products [29], [36], [37] can be used in this case. However, this study utilizes the recursive sum of the discrete product method for efficient computation.

3. Main algorithm

The main algorithm containing 5 steps to assess reliability (R_{H}) is presented as follows.

Input: $\mathbf{H} = (\mathbf{A}, \mathbf{E}, U, b, \mathbf{T}, t^*)$, D, and T

Step 1: Find all MPs that are feasible under time constraint T.

Step 2: (1) Determine all flow vectors F meeting the following constraints.

$$\sum_{\alpha=1}^{\omega_i} f_i^{\alpha} = d_i \quad \text{for } i = 1, 2, \ldots, r. \tag{8}$$

$$\sum_{P_i^{\alpha} \subset e_j} \left\lceil \frac{f_i^{\alpha}}{b_j} \right\rceil \le U_j \quad \text{for } j = 1, 2, \ldots, m. \tag{9}$$

(2) Remove any flow vector which does not satisfy for all P_i^{α} that:

$$\begin{cases} \sum_{P_i^{\alpha} \subset e_j} (t_j + 2.t^*.f_i^{\alpha}) \le T \mid b_j > f_i^{\alpha} > 0 \\ \sum_{P_i^{\alpha} \subset e_j} (t_j + 2.t^*.b_j) \le T \mid b_j \le f_i^{\alpha} \end{cases} \tag{10}$$

Step 3: From each flow vector, gain a candidate of lower boundary point V via Equation (11), and store in $\boldsymbol{\theta}$.

$$v_j = \sum_{P_i^{\alpha} \subset e_j} \left\lceil \frac{f_i^{\alpha}}{b_j} \right\rceil \quad \text{for } j = 1, 2, \ldots, m. \tag{11}$$

Step 4: Compare all candidates in $\boldsymbol{\theta}$ to obtain the set Δ of ∂ exact lower boundary points $\mathbf{y}$.

Step 5: Using the RSDP method, compute the MHLN's reliability as follows:

$$R_{\mathrm{H}} = \Pr(\bigcup_{k=1}^{\partial} \{V | V \ge L_k\}) \tag{12}$$

Output R_{H}

4. Illustrative example

To demonstrate how to assess the reliability that the MHLN meets the set of relief demands within the given time constraint, this section takes a humanitarian logistics in Table 2 as an illustrative example. A MHNL consists of two relief sources (a_1, a_2), two beneficiary places (a_5, a_6), and two transit points (a_3, a_4). All vehicles can hold up 2500 boxes of reliefs, t^* = 30 mins for 2500 boxes.

Table 2. Relevant information about the MHLN.

Arc	From node	To node	Transport time	Probability				
				0	1	2	3	4
v_1	a_1	a_3	4.5	0.04	0.02	0.03	0.02	0.89
v_2	a_1	a_4	6	0.04	0.02	0.05	0.89	
v_3	a_2	a_3	6	0.05	0.04	0.01	0.01	0.89
v_4	a_2	a_4	4.5	0.04	0.02	0.01	0.93	
v_5	a_3	a_5	4	0.05	0.03	0.02	0.02	0.88
v_6	a_3	a_6	5	0.05	0.03	0.02	0.01	0.89
v_7	a_4	a_5	5	0.05	0.01	0.01	0.93	
v_8	a_4	a_6	4	0.04	0.01	0.95		

Note that rapid response, i.e. the ability to transport relief goods from local warehouses to the affected area within 24 hours (standard relief time), is one of the requirements of effective humanitarian logistics [21]. Considering a low level of disaster, the assessment of MHLN's reliability to distribute a set of relief demands D = (5000, 2500) boxes within T = 12 hours is presented as follows.

Step 1: Find all MPs that are feasible under time constraint T.

$$P_5^1=(e_1,e_5)\quad P_6^1=(e_1,e_6)$$
$$P_5^2=(e_2,e_7)\quad P_6^2=(e_2,e_8)$$
$$P_5^3=(e_3,e_5)\quad P_6^3=(e_3,e_6)$$
$$P_5^4=(e_4,e_7)\quad P_6^4=(e_4,e_8)$$

Step 2: (1) Determine 40 flow vectors Fs meeting the following constraints.

$$\begin{cases} f_5^1+f_5^2+f_5^3+f_5^4=5000 \\ f_6^1+f_6^2+f_6^3+f_6^4=2500 \end{cases} \tag{13}$$

$$\begin{cases} \left\lceil \frac{f_5^1+f_6^1}{2500} \right\rceil \le 4; & \left\lceil \frac{f_5^2+f_6^2}{2500} \right\rceil \le 3 \\ \left\lceil \frac{f_5^3+f_6^3}{2500} \right\rceil \le 4; & \left\lceil \frac{f_5^4+f_6^4}{2500} \right\rceil \le 3 \\ \left\lceil \frac{f_5^1+f_5^3}{2500} \right\rceil \le 4; & \left\lceil \frac{f_6^1+f_6^3}{2500} \right\rceil \le 4 \\ \left\lceil \frac{f_5^2+f_5^4}{2500} \right\rceil \le 3; & \left\lceil \frac{f_6^2+f_6^4}{2500} \right\rceil \le 2 \end{cases} \tag{14}$$

(2) Remove 16 flow vectors which do not satisfy for 8 P_i^{α} that:

$$\begin{cases} \sum_{P_i^{\alpha}\subset e_j} (t_j+2.t^*.f_i^{\alpha}) \le T \mid b_j > f_i^{\alpha} > 0 \\ \sum_{P_i^{\alpha}\subset e_j} (t_j+2.t^*.b_j) \le T \mid b_j \le f_i^{\alpha} \end{cases} \tag{15}$$

Step 3: From each flow vector, gain a candidate of lower boundary point V via Equation (16), and store in $\boldsymbol{\theta}$.

$$\begin{cases} \left\lceil \frac{f_5^1+f_6^1}{2500} \right\rceil \le v_1; & \left\lceil \frac{f_5^2+f_6^2}{2500} \right\rceil \le v_2 \\ \left\lceil \frac{f_5^3+f_6^3}{2500} \right\rceil \le v_3; & \left\lceil \frac{f_5^4+f_6^4}{2500} \right\rceil \le v_4 \\ \left\lceil \frac{f_5^1+f_5^3}{2500} \right\rceil \le v_5; & \left\lceil \frac{f_6^1+f_6^3}{2500} \right\rceil \le v_6 \\ \left\lceil \frac{f_5^2+f_5^4}{2500} \right\rceil \le v_7; & \left\lceil \frac{f_6^2+f_6^4}{2500} \right\rceil \le v_8 \end{cases} \tag{16}$$

Step 4: Compare 24 candidates to obtain the set Δ of 18 exact lower boundary points **y**.

Step 5: Using the RSDP method, compute the MHLN's reliability as follows:

$$R_{\mathrm{H}}=\Pr\left(\bigcup_{k=1}^{\partial}\{V \mid V\ge L_k\}\right)=0.988389 \tag{12}$$

Output R_{H}

With the reliability R_{H} = 0.988389, MHLN can successfully deliver the reliefs to 7500 beneficiaries within 12 hours in 988 times out of 1000. It means that the MHLN has a high ability to successfully relief in low-level disasters. Thus, the MHLN is said to be reliable. However, it does not guarantee against all low-level disasters and higher levels of disasters.

5. Conclusions

This paper assesses the reliability of a multimodal humanitarian logistics network in meeting disaster relief demands within time constraints at specific level of disaster. The algorithm uses lower boundary points to evaluate reliability. A numerical example is provided to demonstrate the algorithm and validate the study's applicability. Future research should extend the problem to include multistate transport time for realistic findings.

6. References

[1] IFRC, "World Disasters Report 2020," 2020. [Online]. Available: https://www.ifrc.org/document/world-disasters-report-2020.

[2] L. N.VanWassenhove, "Humanitarian aid logistics: supply chain management in high gear," *J. Oper. Res. Soc.*, vol. 57, no. 5, pp. 475–489, May2006, doi: 10.1057/palgrave.jors.2602125.

[3] X.Hong, M. A.Lejeune, andN.Noyan, "Stochastic network design for disaster preparedness," *IIE Trans.*, vol. 47, no. 4, pp. 329–357, Apr.2015, doi: 10.1080/0740817X.2014.919044.

[4] W.Ni, J.Shu, andM.Song, "Location and Emergency Inventory Pre-Positioning for Disaster Response Operations: Min-Max Robust Model and a Case Study of Yushu Earthquake," *Prod. Oper. Manag.*, vol. 27, no. 1, pp. 160–183, Jan.2018, doi: https://doi.org/10.1111/poms.12789.

[5] K.Liu, Q.Li, andZ.-H.Zhang, "Distributionally robust optimization of an emergency medical service station location and sizing problem with joint chance constraints," *Transp. Res. Part B Methodol.*, vol. 119, pp. 79–101, 2019, doi: https://doi.org/10.1016/j.trb.2018.11.012.

[6] M.Sheikholeslami andN.Zarrinpoor, "Designing an integrated humanitarian logistics network for the preparedness and response phases under uncertainty," *Socioecon. Plann. Sci.*, vol. 86, p. 101496, 2023, doi: https://doi.org/10.1016/j.seps.2022.101496.

[7] N.Sahebjamnia, S. A.Torabi, andS. A.Mansouri, "A hybrid decision support system for managing humanitarian relief chains," *Decis. Support Syst.*, vol. 95, pp. 12–26, Mar.2017, doi: 10.1016/j.dss.2016.11.006.

[8] W.Wang, L.Huang, andX.Liang, "On the Simulation-Based Reliability of Complex Emergency Logistics Networks in Post-Accident Rescues," *Int. J. Environ. Res. Public Health*, vol. 15, no. 1, p. 79, Jan.2018, doi: 10.3390/ijerph15010079.

[9] R.Oloruntoba andG.Kovács, "A commentary on agility in humanitarian aid supply chains," *Supply Chain Manag. An Int. J.*, vol. 20, no. 6, pp. 708–716, Sep.2015, doi: 10.1108/SCM-06-2015-0244.

[10] S.Fathalikhani, A.Hafezalkotob, andR.Soltani, "Government intervention on cooperation, competition, and coopetition of humanitarian supply chains," *Socioecon. Plann. Sci.*, vol. 69, p. 100715, Mar.2020, doi: 10.1016/j.seps.2019.05.006.

[11] Q.Lu, M.Goh, andR.DeSouza, "A SCOR framework to measure logistics performance of humanitarian organizations," *J. Humanit. Logist. Supply Chain Manag.*, vol. 6, no. 2, pp. 222–239, Aug.2016, doi: 10.1108/JHLSCM-09-2015-0038.

[12] O.Larrea, "Key performance indicators in humanitarian logistics in Colombia," *IFAC Proc. Vol.*, vol. 46, no. 24, pp. 211–216, Sep.2013, doi: 10.3182/20130911-3-BR-3021.00089.

[13] P.Peng, L.V.Snyder, A.Lim, andZ.Liu, "Reliable logistics

networks design with facility disruptions," *Transp. Res. Part B Methodol.*, vol. 45, no. 8, pp. 1190–1211, 2011, doi: 10.1016/j.trb.2011.05.022.

[14] M.Mohammadi, R.Tavakkoli-Moghaddam, A.Siadat, andJ.-Y.Dantan, "Design of a reliable logistics network with hub disruption under uncertainty," *Appl. Math. Model.*, vol. 40, no. 9–10, pp. 5621–5642, May2016, doi: 10.1016/j.apm.2016.01.011.

[15] Y.-K.Lin andC.-T.Yeh, "Optimal carrier selection based on network reliability criterion for stochastic logistics networks," *Int. J. Prod. Econ.*, vol. 128, no. 2, pp. 510–517, Dec.2010, doi: 10.1016/j.ijpe.2010.07.001.

[16] T.-P.Nguyen andY.-K.Lin, "Investigation of the influence of transit time on a multistate transportation network in tourism," *Eksploat. i Niezawodn. - Maint. Reliab.*, vol. 23, no. 4, pp. 670–677, Sep.2021, doi: 10.17531/ein.2021.4.9.

[17] Y.-K.Lin, C.-T.Yeh, andC.-F.Huang, "Reliability evaluation of a stochastic-flow distribution network with delivery spoilage," *Comput. Ind. Eng.*, vol. 66, no. 2, pp. 352–359, 2013, doi: https://doi.org/10.1016/j.cie.2013.06.019.

[18] A.Chen, H.Yang, H. K.Lo, andW. H.Tang, "Capacity reliability of a road network: An assessment methodology and numerical results," *Transp. Res. Part B Methodol.*, vol. 36, no. 3, pp. 225–252, 2002, doi: 10.1016/S0191-2615(00)00048-5.

[19] S.Roh, H. H.Lin, andH.Jang, "Performance indicators for humanitarian relief logistics in Taiwan," *Asian J. Shipp. Logist.*, vol. 38, no. 3, pp. 173–180, Sep.2022, doi: 10.1016/j.ajsl.2022.06.002.

[20] D.Günneç andF. S.Salman, "Assessing the reliability and the expected performance of a network under disaster risk," *OR Spectr.*, vol. 33, no. 3, pp. 499–523, 2011, doi: 10.1007/s00291-011-0250-7.

[21] M.Ahmadi, A.Seifi, andB.Tootooni, "A humanitarian logistics model for disaster relief operation considering network failure and standard relief time: A case study on San Francisco district," *Transp. Res. Part E Logist. Transp. Rev.*, vol. 75, pp. 145–163, 2015, doi: https://doi.org/10.1016/j.tre.2015.01.008.

[22] A.Ghavamifar, S. A.Torabi, andM.Moshtari, "A hybrid relief procurement contract for humanitarian logistics," *Transp. Res. Part E Logist. Transp. Rev.*, vol. 167, p. 102916, 2022, doi: https://doi.org/10.1016/j.tre.2022.102916.

[23] A.Kaveh, S. M.Javadi, andR. M.Moghanni, "Emergency management systems after disastrous earthquakes using optimization methods: A comprehensive review," *Adv. Eng. Softw.*, vol. 149, p. 102885, Nov.2020, doi: 10.1016/j.advengsoft.2020.102885.

[24] B.Balcik, B. M.Beamon, C. C.Krejci, K. M.Muramatsu, andM.Ramirez, "Coordination in humanitarian relief chains: Practices, challenges and opportunities," *Int. J. Prod. Econ.*, vol. 126, no. 1, pp. 22–34, Jul.2010, doi: 10.1016/j.ijpe.2009.09.008.

[25] C. F.Huang, D. H.Huang, andY. K.Lin, "Network reliability evaluation for a distributed network with edge computing," *Comput. Ind. Eng.*, vol. 147, no. July, p. 106492, 2020, doi: 10.1016/j.cie.2020.106492.

[26] Y.-K.Lin, T.-P.Nguyen, andL. C.-L.Yeng, "Reliability evaluation of a multi-state air transportation network meeting multiple travel demands," *Ann. Oper. Res.*, vol. 277, no. 1, pp. 63–82, Jun.2019, doi: 10.1007/s10479-018-2843-x.

[27] E.Zio andL.Podofillini, "Importance measures of multi-state components in multi-state systems," *Int. J. Reliab. Qual. Saf. Eng.*, vol. 10, no. 3, pp. 289–310, 2003, doi: 10.1142/S0218539303001159.

[28] S.-G.Chen, "Study on the Covering Problem in Network Reliability for Precision Business Management," *Int. J. Reliab. Qual. Saf. Eng.*, vol. 29, no. 02, Apr.2022, doi: 10.1142/S0218539321500492.

[29] S. K.Chaturvedi, G.Khanna, andS.Soh, "Reliability evaluation of time evolving Delay Tolerant Networks based on Sum-of-Disjoint products," *Reliab. Eng. Syst. Saf.*, vol. 171, no. November 2017, pp. 136–151, 2018, doi: 10.1016/j.ress.2017.11.007.

[30] T.-P.Nguyen andY.-K.Lin, "Assess reliability of a tourism transport network considering limited-budget and late arrivals," *Proc. Inst. Mech. Eng. Part O J. Risk Reliab.*, vol. 236, no. 5, pp. 828–840, Oct.2022, doi: 10.1177/1748006X211037137.

[31] J.MALINOWSKI, "A LOWER BOUND FOR THE NODE-PAIR RELIABILITY OF NETWORK SYSTEMS WITH SMALL DISTANCES BETWEEN ADJACENT NODES," *Int. J. Reliab. Qual. Saf. Eng.*, vol. 13, no. 01, pp. 73–84, Feb.2006, doi: 10.1142/S0218539306002100.

[32] M.ElKhadiri andW. C.Yeh, "An efficient alternative to the exact evaluation of the quickest path flow network reliability problem," *Comput. Oper. Res.*, vol. 76, pp. 22–32, 2016, doi: 10.1016/j.cor.2016.06.010.

[33] C.Zhang, T.Liu, andG.Bai, "An improved algorithm for reliability bounds of multistate networks," *Commun. Stat. - Theory Methods*, vol. 49, no. 15, pp. 3772–3791, 2020, doi: 10.1080/03610926.2020.1752728.

[34] D. H.Huang, C. F.Huang, andY. K.Lin, "Exact project reliability for a multi-state project network subject to time and budget constraints," *Reliab. Eng. Syst. Saf.*, vol. 195, no. May 2019, p. 106744, 2020, doi: 10.1016/j.ress.2019.106744.

[35] L.Schäfer, S.García, andV.Srithammavanh, "Simplification of inclusion–exclusion on intersections of unions with application to network systems reliability," *Reliab. Eng. Syst. Saf.*, vol. 173, pp. 23–33, May2018, doi: 10.1016/j.ress.2018.01.003.

[36] W. C.Yeh, "An Improved Sum-of-Disjoint-Products Technique for Symbolic Multi-State Flow Network Reliability," *IEEE Trans. Reliab.*, vol. 64, no. 4, pp. 1185–1193, 2015, doi: 10.1109/TR.2015.2452573.

[37] G.Bai, M. J.Zuo, andZ.Tian, "Ordering Heuristics for Reliability Evaluation of Multistate Networks," *IEEE Trans. Reliab.*, vol. 64, no. 3, pp. 1015–1023, 2015, doi: 10.1109/TR.2015.2430491.

Renewal Function of Weibull Distribution Using Gamma Distribution

Toshio NAKAGAWA[1], Kazunori IWATA[2]

[1]Aichi Institute of Technology, Toyota, Japan, toshi-nakagawa@aitech.ac.jp
[2]Aichi University, Nagoya, Japan, kazunori@vega.aichi-u.ac.jp

Keywords: Renewal function, Hazard rate, Weibull distribution, Gamma distribution, Replacement

Abstract - In the analysis of optimal policies for reliability and maintenance models, we have to know the properties of renewal and hazard rate functions. However, it is quite difficult to compute explicitly a renewal function of Weibull distribution. This paper makes an attempt to obtain approximate renewal functions of Weibull distribution, using gamma distribution. When mean, variance, median and mode of both distributions are equal, we compare their hazard rate functions, and propose approximate renewal functions of Weibull distribution. Finally, we apply such results to two periodic replacement policies.

1 Introduction

Many studies on maintenance polices in reliability have been done extensively and summarized widely [1–4]. It has been usually assumed in such models that the failure time has Weibull and gamma distributions [5–7]. In analyzing such models and obtaining their optimal policies, we have to investigate and know statistically the properties of renewal functions and cumulative hazard rates of the two distributions. In general, it is quite difficult to obtain explicitly a renewal function of Weibull distribution, and is not easy either to compute a cumulative hazard rate of gamma distribution.

This paper has a main object of computing numerically a renewal function of Weibull distribution using gamma distribution. In Sect. 2, we investigate the properties of two distributions and obtain their mean, failure rate, median and mode. In Sect. 3, when mean, variance, median and mode are equal in three cases, we compute the parameters of Weibull and gamma distributions. Using such results, we compute asymptotic values of renewal functions of Weibull distribution in Sect. 4. It is of interest that some numerical tables give lower and upper bounds of renewal functions. Furthermore, in Sect. 5, using these results, we apply them to two periodic replacement policies and obtain their optimal replacement times. Some methods and tools used in this paper would be useful for discussing maintenance policies when failure times have Weibull distribution and other distributions.

2 Properties of Weibull and Gamma Distributions

Suppose that for $m \geq 1$, a random variable X has Weibull distribution

$$f(t) = m\lambda(\lambda t)^{m-1} \mathrm{e}^{-(\lambda t)^m}, \qquad F(t) = 1 - \mathrm{e}^{-(\lambda t)^m}. \quad (1)$$

Then, the following properties are given: Moments are

$$\mathrm{E}(X^n) = \frac{1}{\lambda^n}\Gamma\left(1 + \frac{n}{m}\right) \quad (n = 1, 2, \dots), \quad (2)$$

and mean μ and σ^2 are

$$\mu = \mathrm{E}(X) = \frac{1}{\lambda}\Gamma\left(1 + \frac{1}{m}\right),$$

$$\sigma^2 = \mathrm{E}\left(X^2\right) - \mathrm{E}(X)^2 = \frac{1}{\lambda^2}\left[\Gamma\left(1 + \frac{2}{m}\right) - \Gamma\left(1 + \frac{1}{m}\right)^2\right]. \quad (3)$$

Failure rate $h(t)$ and cumulative hazard rate $H(t)$ are

$$H(t) = (\lambda t)^m, \quad h(t) = H'(t) = m\lambda(\lambda t)^{m-1}, \quad (4)$$

which increases strictly with t from 0 to ∞ for $m > 1$. Median $\widetilde{\mu}$ is given:

$$F(t) = \frac{1}{2}, \quad \text{i.e.,} \quad \widetilde{\mu} = \frac{1}{\lambda}(\ln 2)^{1/m}, \quad (5)$$

which increases strictly with m from $\ln 2/\lambda$ to $1/\lambda$. Mode $\widehat{\mu}$ is given:

$$f'(t) = 0, \quad \text{i.e.,} \quad \widehat{\mu} = \frac{1}{\lambda}\left(\frac{m-1}{m}\right)^{1/m}, \quad (6)$$

which increases strictly with m from 0 to $1/\lambda$.

Table 1 presents mean μ, standard deviation σ, median $\widetilde{\mu}$ and mode $\widehat{\mu}$ for m = 1, 1.1, 1.5, 2.0, 2.5 and 3.0 when $1/\lambda = 10$. It is of interest that $\widetilde{\mu}$ and $\widehat{\mu}$ increase with m, and σ decreases with m, however, μ takes a minimum 8.856 at $m = 2.166$, and after that, increases with m to 10.000. Furthermore, when $m = 3.4395$, $\mu = \widetilde{\mu} = 8.9892$.

Table 1: Values of μ, σ, $\widetilde{\mu}$ and $\widehat{\mu}$ when $\lambda = 0.1$

m	μ	σ	$\widetilde{\mu}$	$\widehat{\mu}$
1.0	10.000	10.000	6.9315	0.0000
1.1	9.6491	8.7828	7.1663	1.1305
1.5	9.0275	6.1294	7.8322	4.8075
2.0	8.8623	4.6325	8.3255	7.0711
2.5	8.8726	3.7967	8.6363	8.1519
3.0	8.9298	3.2455	8.8500	8.7358

Next, suppose that for $\alpha \geq 1$, a random variable Y has gamma distribution

$$g(t) = \frac{\beta(\beta t)^{\alpha-1}}{\Gamma(\alpha)} \mathrm{e}^{-\beta t}, \quad G(t) = \int_0^t \frac{\beta(\beta x)^{\alpha-1}}{\Gamma(\alpha)} \mathrm{e}^{-\beta x} \, \mathrm{d}x. \quad (7)$$

Clearly, when $m = \alpha = 1$ and $\beta = \lambda$, $F(t) = G(t) = 1 - \mathrm{e}^{-\lambda t}$. The following properties are given: Moments are

$$\mathrm{E}(Y^n) = \frac{1}{\beta^n} \frac{\Gamma(\alpha+n)}{\Gamma(\alpha)}, \quad (n = 1, 2, \dots), \quad (8)$$

and mean μ and σ^2 are

$$\mu = \mathrm{E}(Y) = \frac{\alpha}{\beta}, \quad \sigma^2 = \mathrm{E}(Y^2) - \mathrm{E}(Y)^2 = \frac{\alpha}{\beta^2}. \quad (9)$$

Failure rate $h(t)$ and cumulative hazard rate $H(t)$ are:

$$h(t) = \frac{(\beta t)^{\alpha-1} \mathrm{e}^{-\beta t}}{\int_t^\infty (\beta x)^{\alpha-1} \mathrm{e}^{-\beta x} \, \mathrm{d}x} = \frac{t^{\alpha-1} \mathrm{e}^{-\beta t}}{\int_t^\infty x^{\alpha-1} \mathrm{e}^{-\beta x} \, \mathrm{d}x},$$

$$H(t) = \int_0^t h(x) \, \mathrm{d}x = -\ln\left[\int_t^\infty \frac{\beta(\beta x)^{\alpha-1}}{\Gamma(\alpha)} \mathrm{e}^{-\beta x} \, \mathrm{d}x\right], \quad (10)$$

where $h(t)$ increases strictly with t from 0 to β. Median $\widetilde{\mu}$ is given by a solution of the equation

$$\int_0^{\widetilde{\mu}} \frac{\beta(\beta x)^{\alpha-1}}{\Gamma(\alpha)} \mathrm{e}^{-\beta x} \, \mathrm{d}x = \frac{1}{2}. \quad (11)$$

Mode $\widehat{\mu}$ is given:

$$g'(t) = 0, \quad \text{i.e.,} \quad \widehat{\mu} = \frac{\alpha - 1}{\beta} < \frac{\alpha}{\beta} = \mu. \quad (12)$$

In particular, when $\alpha = k$ $(k = 1, 2, \dots)$,

$$g(t) = \frac{\beta(\beta t)^{k-1}}{(k-1)!} \mathrm{e}^{-\beta t}, \quad G(t) = \sum_{j=k}^{\infty} \frac{(\beta t)^j}{j!} \mathrm{e}^{-\beta t},$$

$$\mathrm{E}(Y^n) = \frac{1}{\beta^n} \frac{(k+n-1)!}{(k-1)!}, \quad \mu = \frac{k}{\beta}, \quad \sigma^2 = \frac{k}{\beta^2},$$

$$h(t) = \frac{\beta(\beta t)^{k-1} / (k-1)!}{\sum_{j=0}^{k-1} \left[(\beta t)^j / j!\right]}, \quad H(t) = -\ln\left[\sum_{j=0}^{k-1} \frac{(\beta t)^j}{j!} \mathrm{e}^{-\beta t}\right],$$

$$\widehat{\mu} = \frac{k-1}{\beta},$$

and median $\widetilde{\mu}$ is a solution of the equation

$$\sum_{j=0}^{k-1} \frac{(\beta t)^j}{j!} \mathrm{e}^{-\beta t} = \frac{1}{2}. \quad (13)$$

3 Approximations of Weibull to Gamma Distributions

Let $\Phi_W(t)$ and $\Phi_G(t)$ be the respective functions of Weibull and gamma distributions for a general function $\Phi(t)$. Then, cumulative hazard rates of Weibull and gamma distributions are given by

$$H_W(t) = (\lambda t)^m, \quad H_G(t) = -\ln\left[\int_t^\infty \frac{\beta(\beta x)^{\alpha-1}}{\Gamma(\alpha)} \mathrm{e}^{-\beta x} \, \mathrm{d}x\right].$$

We compare $H_i(t)$ $(i = W, G)$ in three cases where (i) $\mu_W = \mu_G$, $\sigma_W = \sigma_G$, (ii) $\mu_W = \mu_G$, $\widetilde{\mu}_W = \widetilde{\mu}_G$ and (iii) $\sigma_W = \sigma_G$, $\widehat{\mu}_W = \widehat{\mu}_G$:

(i) Case of $\mu \equiv \mu_W = \mu_G$ and $\sigma \equiv \sigma_W = \sigma_G$
Set that

$$\mu = \frac{1}{\lambda}\Gamma\left(1 + \frac{1}{m}\right) = \frac{\alpha}{\beta},$$

$$\sigma = \frac{1}{\lambda}\sqrt{\Gamma\left(1 + \frac{2}{m}\right) - \Gamma\left(1 + \frac{1}{m}\right)^2} = \frac{1}{\beta}\sqrt{\alpha}.$$

We compute α and β for given λ and m to compare $H_i(t)$ $(i = W, G)$. Table 2 presents α and β for m when $\lambda = 0.1$. This indicates that both α and β increases with m.

Table 2: Parameters α and β when $\lambda = 0.1$

m	α	β
1.1	1.2070	0.1251
1.5	2.1692	0.2403
2.0	3.6598	0.4130
2.5	5.4614	0.6155
3.0	7.5704	0.8478

Using Table 2, we compute $H_i(t)$ $(i = W, G)$ for m and $1 \leq t \leq 30$ when $\lambda = 0.1$ in Table 3. This indicates that $H_W(t)$ are almost the same as $H_G(t)$ when m is small or when m is large and $10 \leq t \leq 15$.

(ii) Case of $\mu \equiv \mu_W = \mu_G$ and $\widetilde{\mu}_W = \widetilde{\mu}_G$
Set that

$$\frac{1}{\lambda}\Gamma\left(1 + \frac{1}{m}\right) = \frac{\alpha}{\beta},$$

$$\frac{1}{\lambda}(\ln 2)^{1/m} = \widetilde{\mu},$$

where $\widetilde{\mu}$ is a solution of

$$\int_0^{\widetilde{\mu}} \frac{\beta(\beta x)^{\alpha-1}}{\Gamma(\alpha)} \mathrm{e}^{-\beta x} \, \mathrm{d}x = \frac{1}{2}.$$

Table 4 presents α and β for m when $\lambda = 0.1$. This indicates that both α and β increase with m.

Table 4: Parameters α and β when $\lambda = 0.1$

m	α	β
1.1	1.2139	0.1258
1.5	2.4475	0.2711
2.0	5.4399	0.6138
2.5	12.4553	1.4038
3.0	37.2293	4.1691

Using Table 4, we compute $H_i(t)$ $(i = W, G)$ for m and $1 \leq t \leq 30$ when $\lambda = 0.1$ in Table 5. This indicates that both $H_W(t)$ and $H_G(t)$ are almost the same when $m = 1.1, 1.5$ and 2.0.

Table 3: Cumulative hazard rate $H_W(t)$ and $H_G(t)$ when $\mu_W = \mu_G$ and $\sigma_W = \sigma_G$

t	$m = 1.1$		$m = 1.5$		$m = 2.0$		$m = 2.5$		$m = 3.0$	
	$H_W(t)$	$H_G(t)$	$H_W(t)$	$H_G(t)$	$H_W(t)$	$H_G(t)$	$H_W(t)$	$H_G(t)$	$H_W(t)$	$H_G(t)$
1	0.07943282	0.0712021	0.03162278	0.01652943	0.01	0.00195714	0.003162278	0.00015682	0.001	0.00000837
2	0.17026798	0.1606848	0.08944272	0.06490183	0.04	0.01817519	0.017888544	0.00415943	0.008	0.00076218
3	0.26597045	0.25725808	0.16431677	0.13865411	0.09	0.05999562	0.04929503	0.02328783	0.027	0.00796808
4	0.36497741	0.35818274	0.25298221	0.23229023	0.16	0.13136238	0.101192885	0.07009287	0.064	0.03487737
5	0.4665165	0.4621515	0.35355339	0.34175521	0.25	0.23172936	0.176776695	0.15234684	0.125	0.09648592
10	1	1.00840905	1	1.04389499	1	1.07541107	1	1.09455151	1	1.10633085
12	1.22207925	1.23440235	1.31453414	1.37172605	1.44	1.52656103	1.577440966	1.66726332	1.728	1.80101771
15	1.56206962	1.57827218	1.83711731	1.8951688	2.25	2.28310602	2.755675961	2.66933132	3.375	3.06392522
20	2.14354693	2.16049402	2.82842712	2.82707038	4	3.69439362	5.656854249	4.60934181	8	5.58594406
25	2.73989557	2.75045337	3.95284708	3.80943866	6.25	5.23264068	9.882117688	6.77602407	15.625	8.45647642
30	3.34836952	3.34574971	5.19615242	4.82636283	9	6.85703394	15.58845727	9.09529358	27	11.56001489

Table 5: Cumulative hazard rate $H_W(t)$ and $H_G(t)$ when $\mu_W = \mu_G$ and $\widetilde{\mu}_W = \widetilde{\mu}_G$

t	$m = 1.1$		$m = 1.5$		$m = 2.0$		$m = 2.5$		$m = 3.0$	
	$H_W(t)$	$H_G(t)$	$H_W(t)$	$H_G(t)$	$H_W(t)$	$H_G(t)$	$H_W(t)$	$H_G(t)$	$H_W(t)$	$H_G(t)$
1	0.07943282	0.07033608	0.03162278	0.01085333	0.01	0.00016247	0.00316228	0.00000001	0.001	0
2	0.17026798	0.15937109	0.08944272	0.0500603	0.04	0.00425336	0.01788854	0.0000191	0.008	0
3	0.26597045	0.25570595	0.16431677	0.11612176	0.09	0.02365199	0.04929503	0.00083709	0.027	0.00000001
4	0.36497741	0.35652874	0.25298221	0.2048302	0.16	0.07088957	0.10119289	0.00861964	0.064	0.00000997
5	0.4665165	0.46049426	0.35355339	0.31229346	0.25	0.15364596	0.1767767	0.04095554	0.125	0.00076183
10	1	1.00761803	1	1.03980178	1	1.0973246	1	1.20396771	1	1.49519294
12	1.22207925	1.2342129	1.31453414	1.38964431	1.44	1.66987845	1.57744097	2.18619259	1.728	21.907796
15	1.56206962	1.57915326	1.83711731	1.95449344	2.25	2.6710349	2.75567596	4.07596519	3.375	29.93608576
20	2.14354693	2.16347424	2.82842712	2.97127932	4	4.60819602	5.65685425	8.00708112	8	44.35749221
25	2.73989557	2.75580079	3.95284708	4.05198286	6.25	6.77089119	9.88211769	20.32755223	15.625	59.74210172
30	3.34836952	3.35364921	5.19615242	5.17639028	9	9.08540496	15.58845727	25.84448145	27	75.83762635

(iii) Case of $\sigma = \sigma_W = \sigma_G$ and $\widetilde{\mu}_W = \widetilde{\mu}_G$
Set that

$$\sigma = \frac{1}{\lambda}\sqrt{\Gamma\left(1+\frac{2}{m}\right) - \Gamma\left(1+\frac{1}{m}\right)^2} = \frac{1}{\beta}\sqrt{\alpha},$$

$$\frac{1}{\lambda}\left(\frac{m-1}{m}\right)^{1/m} = \frac{\alpha-1}{\beta}.$$

Table 6 presents α and β for m when $\lambda = 0.1$. This indicates that the values of α and β are almost the same as those in Table 2.

Table 6: Parameters α and β when $\lambda = 0.1$

m	α	β
1.1	1.1373	0.1214
1.5	2.1501	0.2392
2.0	4.0851	0.4363
2.5	6.4553	0.6692
3.0	9.1356	0.9313

Using Table 6, we compute $H_i(t)$ $(i = W, G)$ for m and $1 \leq t \leq 30$ when $\lambda = 0.1$ in Table 7. This shows similar tendencies to Table 3.

4 Renewal Functions of Weibull Distribution

We compute renewal function $M(t)$ of failure distribution $F(t)$. It is denoted that $F^{(n)}(t)$ is the n-fold Stieltjes convolution of $F(t)$ with itself, i.e., $F^{(n)}(t) \equiv \int_0^t F^{(n-1)}(t-u)\,\mathrm{d}F(u)$ $(n = 1, 2, \dots)$ and $F^{(0)}(t) \equiv 1$ for $t \geq 0$. Suppose that the unit begins to operate at time 0 and is replaced with a new one and operates immediately. Letting $N(t)$ be the number of failures in $[0, t]$,

$$\Pr\{N(t) = n\} = F^{(n)}(t) - F^{(n+1)}(t),$$

and the expected number of failures in $[0, t]$ is

$$M(t) \equiv \mathrm{E}\{N(t) = n\} = \sum_{n=1}^{\infty} F^{(n)}(t), \tag{14}$$

which is called *renewal function*.

4.1. Approximate Renewal Functions

When the failure time has Weibull distribution $F(t)$ in (1), we try to compute numerically renewal function $M(t)$ in (14). However, it is very difficult to compute the n-fold Stieltjes convolution $F^{(n)}(t)$ for large n. It is possible to compute $F^{(n)}(t)$ for $n \leq 7$ by using a usual personal computer. Table 8 presents $F^{(n)}(t)$ $(n = 1, 2, \dots, 7)$ and their sum $\widetilde{M}_7(t) \equiv \sum_{n=1}^{7} F^{(n)}(t)$ when $m = 2.0$ and $\lambda = 0.1$. This indicates that $\widetilde{M}_7(t)$ would be less than $M(t)$, however, they are almost the same for $t \leq 20$ because $F^{(n)}(t)$ for $n \geq 8$ takes small values.

It is assumed that a random variable Y_k $(k = 1, 2, \dots)$ are independent and have an identical distribution $G(t)$ in (7). Then, the sum $S_n = \sum_{k=1}^{n} Y_k$ has mean $n\alpha/\beta$ and variance $n\alpha/\beta^2$, and from the reproductive property of gamma distri-

Table 7: Cumulative hazard rate $H_W(t)$ and $H_G(t)$ when $\sigma_W = \sigma_G$ and $\widehat{\mu}_W = \widehat{\mu}_G$

t	$m = 1.1$		$m = 1.5$		$m = 2.0$		$m = 2.5$		$m = 3.0$	
	$H_W(t)$	$H_G(t)$	$H_W(t)$	$H_G(t)$	$H_W(t)$	$H_G(t)$	$H_W(t)$	$H_G(t)$	$H_W(t)$	$H_G(t)$
1	0.07943282	0.08336865	0.03162278	0.01717045	0.01	0.00087364	0.00316228	0.00002451	0.001	0.00000046
2	0.17026798	0.18059581	0.08944272	0.06664612	0.04	0.01057708	0.01788854	0.00121752	0.008	0.00011281
3	0.26597045	0.28283258	0.16431677	0.14152335	0.09	0.04015923	0.04929503	0.00954965	0.027	0.00202197
4	0.36497741	0.38808146	0.25298221	0.23618276	0.16	0.09605058	0.10119289	0.03562626	0.064	0.01253553
5	0.4665165	0.49541323	0.35355339	0.34653645	0.25	0.18003891	0.1767767	0.08966259	0.125	0.0440535
10	1	1.04992389	1	1.05127074	1	0.96148468	1	0.88759312	1	0.83696101
12	1.22207925	1.27674672	1.31453414	1.37947719	1.44	1.40027119	1.57744097	1.42527138	1.728	1.46988606
15	1.56206962	1.62022976	1.83711731	1.90299159	2.25	2.14960102	2.75567596	2.40145782	3.375	2.68214778
20	2.14354693	2.19874692	2.82842712	2.83405899	4	3.57177558	5.65685425	4.354344	8	5.21095945
25	2.73989557	2.78239042	3.95284708	3.81476612	6.25	5.14106986	9.88211769	6.58362647	15.625	8.16961341
30	3.34836952	3.36956505	5.19615242	4.82945591	9	6.81046593	15.58845727	8.99978685	27	11.4170775

bution,

$$G^{(n)}(t) \equiv \Pr\{S_n \leq t\} = \int_0^t \frac{\beta(\beta x)^{n\alpha-1}}{\Gamma(n\alpha)} e^{-\beta x} \, dx, \qquad (15)$$

and

$$M_G(t) \equiv \sum_{n=1}^{\infty} G^{(n)}(t) = \sum_{n=1}^{\infty} \int_0^t \frac{\beta(\beta x)^{n\alpha-1}}{\Gamma(n\alpha)} e^{-\beta x} \, dx. \qquad (16)$$

Using the approximate method in Sect. 3, we define the following approximate renewal function $M_k(t)$ of Weibull distribution:

$$M_k(t) \equiv F(t) + F^{(2)}(t) + \cdots + F^{(k)}(t) + \sum_{n=k+1}^{\infty} G^{(n)}(t) \qquad (17)$$

$$(k = 0, 1, 2, \dots),$$

where note that

$$M_0(t) = M_G(t) = \sum_{n=1}^{\infty} \int_0^t \frac{\beta(\beta x)^{n\alpha-1}}{\Gamma(n\alpha)} e^{-\beta x} \, dx,$$

$$M_1(t) = F(t) + \sum_{n=2}^{\infty} \int_0^t \frac{\beta(\beta x)^{n\alpha-1}}{\Gamma(n\alpha)} e^{-\beta x} \, dx. \qquad (18)$$

Table 9 presents $M_0(t)$, $M_1(t)$ and $M_7(t)$ when $F(t) = 1 - e^{-(\lambda t)^m}$, $m = 2.0$ and $\lambda = 0.1$, i.e., $\alpha = 3.6598$ and $\beta = 0.4130$ from Table 2. This indicates that all of $M_0(t)$, $M_1(t)$ and $M_7(t)$ are almost the same for $1 \leq t \leq 10$, and $M_0(t) < M_1(t) < M_7(t)$ for $11 \leq t \leq 30$.

Next, comparing $M_7(t)$ in Table 9 with $H_G(t)$ in Table 3, it is noted that when $m = 2.0$, $M_7(t) < H_G(t)$ for all t, however, two differences are very small. In addition, when $\alpha = 3.6598$ and $\beta = 0.4130$, Table 9 presents $H_G(t)$ in (10). This indicates that for $t \geq 5$,

$$M_7(t) < M(t) < H_G(t).$$

We expect that this shows good lower and upper bounds of renewal function $M(t)$ except for the small t.

5 Applications to Periodic Replacements

We consider the following two periodic replacement policies in which the unit is replaced at periodic times $kT (k = 1, 2, \dots)$ for a specified $T (0 < T < \infty)$ [1,4]:

(1) Replacement with minimal repair: The unit undergoes minimal repair at failures.

(2) Block replacement: The unit is replaced with a new one at failures. In case of **(1)**, the expected cost rate is

$$C_H(T) = \frac{c_H H(T) + c_T}{T}, \qquad (19)$$

optimal T_H^* to minimize $C_H(T)$ satisfies

$$T h(T) - H(T) = \frac{c_T}{c_H}, \qquad (20)$$

and the resulting cost rate is

$$C_H(T_H^*) = c_H h(T_H^*), \qquad (21)$$

where c_H = cost of minimal repair at each failure and c_T = replacement cost at time T.

In case of **(2)**, the expected cost rate is

$$C_M(T) = \frac{c_M M(T) + c_T}{T}, \qquad (22)$$

optimal T_M^* to minimize $C_M(T)$ satisfies

$$T m(T) - M(T) = \frac{c_T}{c_B}, \qquad (23)$$

and the resulting cost rate is

$$C_M(T_M^*) = c_M m(T_M^*), \qquad (24)$$

where c_M = replacement cost at each failure.

5.1. Periodic Replacement with Minimal Repair

Assume that the failure time has Weibull distribution $F(t) = 1 - e^{-(\lambda t)^m}$ for $m > 1$. Then, from (19), the expected cost rate is

$$C_H(T) = \frac{c_H (\lambda T)^m + c_T}{T}, \qquad (25)$$

and from (20), optimal T_H^* is given by

$$T_H^* = \frac{1}{\lambda} \left[\frac{c_T}{(m-1) c_H} \right]^{1/m}. \qquad (26)$$

Table 8: $F^{(n)}(t)$ and sum $\widetilde{M}_7(t)$ when $m = 2.0$ and $\lambda = 0.1$

t	$F(t)$	$F^{(2)}(t)$	$F^{(3)}(t)$	$F^{(4)}(t)$	$F^{(5)}(t)$	$F^{(6)}(t)$	$F^{(7)}(t)$	$\widetilde{M}_7(t)$
1	0.00995	0.00002	0.00000	0.00000	0.00000	0.00000	0.00000	0.00997
2	0.03921	0.00026	0.00000	0.00000	0.00000	0.00000	0.00000	0.03948
3	0.08607	0.00130	0.00005	0.00000	0.00000	0.00000	0.00000	0.08742
4	0.14786	0.00400	0.00025	0.00001	0.00000	0.00000	0.00000	0.15212
5	0.22120	0.00943	0.00089	0.00007	0.00001	0.00000	0.00000	0.23159
6	0.30232	0.01873	0.00224	0.00027	0.00003	0.00000	0.00000	0.32358
7	0.38737	0.03300	0.00577	0.00084	0.00013	0.00002	0.00000	0.42701
8	0.47271	0.05313	0.01174	0.00220	0.00044	0.00009	0.00002	0.53990
9	0.55514	0.07975	0.02152	0.00499	0.00124	0.00030	0.00007	0.66185
10	0.63212	0.11316	0.03305	0.00921	0.00300	0.00087	0.00026	0.78893
11	0.70180	0.15323	0.05691	0.01876	0.00649	0.00221	0.00076	0.93442
12	0.76307	0.19948	0.08235	0.03054	0.01209	0.00499	0.00197	1.08437
13	0.81548	0.25110	0.11882	0.05140	0.02303	0.01020	0.00454	1.25608
14	0.85914	0.30697	0.16042	0.07767	0.03871	0.01913	0.00948	1.44229
15	0.89460	0.36581	0.20861	0.11159	0.06111	0.03324	0.01812	1.65009
16	0.92270	0.42625	0.26250	0.15334	0.09126	0.05403	0.03204	1.88291
17	0.94442	0.48690	0.32087	0.20256	0.12975	0.08279	0.05289	2.14332
18	0.96084	0.54647	0.35554	0.23127	0.14929	0.12033	0.08208	2.37860
19	0.97295	0.60378	0.44512	0.31936	0.23108	0.16686	0.12056	2.74918
20	0.98168	0.65788	0.50319	0.37465	0.29203	0.22182	0.16855	3.07632
21	0.98784	0.70804	0.56911	0.45018	0.35771	0.28395	0.22546	3.45004
22	0.99209	0.75373	0.60966	0.51628	0.42608	0.35142	0.28988	3.80294
23	0.99496	0.79467	0.68218	0.58050	0.49505	0.42200	0.35977	4.19383
24	0.99685	0.83077	0.72771	0.62924	0.55728	0.49334	0.43265	4.54319
25	0.99807	0.86211	0.77731	0.69773	0.62690	0.56317	0.50594	4.91027
26	0.99884	0.88893	0.81711	0.74880	0.68661	0.62954	0.57721	5.23764
27	0.99932	0.91154	0.85169	0.79412	0.74073	0.69088	0.64440	5.53636
28	0.99961	0.93033	0.88122	0.83356	0.78866	0.74616	0.70594	5.80277
29	0.99978	0.94575	0.90605	0.86725	0.83023	0.79477	0.76083	6.03525
30	0.99988	0.95822	0.92473	0.89093	0.86046	0.83657	0.80857	6.22746

Table 9: Approximations $M_0(t)$, $M_1(t)$, $M_7(t)$ and $H_G(t)$ in (10)

t	$M_0(t)$	$M_1(t)$	$M_7(t)$	$H_G(t)$
1	0.00196	0.00995	0.00997	0.00196
2	0.01803	0.03922	0.03948	0.01818
3	0.05841	0.08624	0.08742	0.06001
4	0.12410	0.14883	0.15212	0.13139
5	0.21038	0.22470	0.23159	0.23178
6	0.31083	0.31171	0.32358	0.35874
7	0.41968	0.40796	0.42701	0.50933
8	0.53271	0.51170	0.53990	0.68067
9	0.64729	0.62131	0.66185	0.87017
10	0.76203	0.73525	0.78893	1.07560
11	0.87637	0.85207	0.93442	1.29502
12	0.99018	0.97048	1.08437	1.52681
13	1.10356	1.08944	1.25608	1.76957
14	1.21663	1.20814	1.44229	2.02213
15	1.32953	1.32606	1.65009	2.28345
16	1.44235	1.44292	1.88291	2.55268
17	1.55515	1.55864	2.14332	2.82906
18	1.66795	1.67330	2.37860	3.11192
19	1.78076	1.78706	2.74918	3.40071
20	1.89358	1.90012	3.07632	3.69491
21	2.00642	2.01269	3.45004	3.99409
22	2.11926	2.12496	3.80294	4.29785
23	2.23211	2.23706	4.19383	4.60585
24	2.34496	2.34912	4.54319	4.91777
25	2.45781	2.46121	4.91027	5.23333
26	2.57066	2.57338	5.23765	5.55230
27	2.68351	2.68563	5.53636	5.87443
28	2.79635	2.79799	5.80278	6.19953
29	2.90920	2.91044	6.03527	6.52741
30	3.02205	3.02298	6.22749	6.85791

Next, assume that the failure time has gamma distribution $g(t) = [\beta(\beta t)^{\alpha-1}/\Gamma(\alpha)]\mathrm{e}^{-\beta t}$ for $\beta > 1$. Then, from (19), the expected cost rate is

$$C_H(t) = \frac{-c_H \ln\left\{\int_T^\infty \left[\beta(\beta x)^{\alpha-1}/\Gamma(\alpha)\right]\mathrm{e}^{-\beta x}\,\mathrm{d}x\right\} + c_T}{T}, \quad (27)$$

and optimal T_H^* satisfies

$$\frac{T^\alpha \mathrm{e}^{-\beta T}}{\int_T^\infty x^{\alpha-1}\mathrm{e}^{-\beta x}\,\mathrm{d}x} + \ln\left\{\int_T^\infty \frac{\beta(\beta x)^{\alpha-1}}{\Gamma(\alpha)}\mathrm{e}^{-\beta x}\,\mathrm{d}x\right\} = \frac{c_T}{c_H}. \quad (28)$$

Table 10 presents optimal T_H^* of periodic replacement policies for Weibull and gamma distributions when $m = 2.0$, $1/\lambda = 10$ and $\alpha = 3.6598$, $\beta = 0.4130$. This indicates that both T_H^* are almost the same for $c_T/c_H \leq 1.00$.

Similarly, we can compute optimal T_B^* of block replacement for both distributions.

Table 10: Optimal T_H^* of Weibull and gamma distributions

c_T/c_H	Weibull T_H^*	Gamma T_H^*
0.01	1.00000	1.27986
0.02	1.41421	1.60897
0.05	2.23607	2.22004
0.10	3.16228	2.89443
0.20	4.47214	3.88389
0.50	7.07107	6.16261
1.00	10.00000	9.63255
2.00	14.14214	17.67720

Acknowledgments

This research was partially supported by the joint research project "Modeling and Analyzing Information Security Measures for Server Systems" of the Institute of Managerial Research, Aichi University.

References

[1] Barlow RE, Proschan F. *Mathematical Theory of Reliability.* John Wiley & Sons, New York, 1965.

[2] Pham H. *Handbook of Reliability Engineering.* Springer, London, 2023.

[3] Rausand M, Hoyland A. *System Reliability Theory.* John Wiley & Sons, Ltd, New York, 2004.

[4] Nakagawa T. *Maintenance Theory of Reliability.* Springer, London, 2005.

[5] Johnson NL, Kotz S. *Distributions in Statistics*, volume I, II, III. John Wiley & Sons, New York, 1972.

[6] Murthy DNP, Xie M, Jiang R. *Weibull Models.* John Wiley & Sons, New York, 2003.

[7] Forbes C, Evans M, Hastings N, Peacock B. *Statistical Distributions, 4th Edition.* John Wiley & Sons, New York, 2010.

Optimal replacement policy of a mission-oriented system under additive damage

Jiajia Cai
Business School
Yangzhou University, China
cai_jiajia@yeah.net

Keywords: Maintenance, Preventive replacement, Shock, Damage model

Abstract - Mission-oriented systems are generally designed to perform critical missions under variable operational environments. When it suffers random shocks and additive damage, preventive replacement policies should integrate the damage level, mission reliability, and maintenance costs. However, few of the related works have taken the mission duration into account, which will lead to the overestimation or underestimation of preventive replacement variables. In this study, we propose an optimal replacement policy of a mission-oriented system under additive damage, where a system is replaced preventively at a planned time, at a shock number, or at mission end time, whichever occurs first. Optimal variables are given in analytical and numerical ways to verify the effectiveness of the proposed policies.

1 Introduction

Mission-oriented systems, designed to perform critical missions under variable operational environments, inevitably experience performance degradation due to aging, usage, and external shocks. Such degradation not only escalates maintenance costs but also reduces the mission success probability by amplifying the risk of failures [1]. Consequently, making an optimal replacement policy by balancing mission reliability with cost efficiency remains a pivotal challenge in reliability engineering [2].

Most degradation models of mission-oriented systems are two types: deterioration-based type and shock-based type. For the first type, the system deteriorates due to internal factors such as aging, overload, wear, or corrosion. Then, preventive maintenance (PM) policies are adopted when it reaches a predetermined age T, a failure/repair number n, or a consecutive working cycle N. For another type, the system suffers external shock damage in different environments. Then, the number of experienced shocks and the damage threshold should be considered as parameters for PM policies. Next, PM policies subject to shock and damage are extended by categorizing the shocks into fatal and non-fatal ones [3, 4]. Non-fatal shocks are rectified by minimal repairs, and fatal shocks are removed by replacement. Moreover, the fusion of the above two types of degradation models has been recently discussed in order to describe the degradation mechanism more accurately [5]. In this study, we investigate the shock-based degradation models for mission-oriented systems.

Additive damage, characterized by the cumulative effect of successive shocks, further exacerbates system vulnerability, necessitating timely maintenance interventions. Zhao et al. [6] proposed replacement policies with cumulative damage where PM activities are scheduled before failure at planned time T, at shock number N, or at damage level Z, whichever occurs first. Mathematical analysis for optimal policies with one variable and two variables was given, respectively. Dui et al. [7] introduced a system performance efficiency and the budget surplus rate model for multi-state systems. Sun et al. [8] provided a tailored advantage actor-critic algorithm to address the dynamic maintenance optimization problem.

When a system executed multiple missions, it would be better to do PM activities after completing its missions [9]. Zhao et al. [10] considered the cumulative damage caused by each job and discussed optimal PM policies for cumulative damage models. When a system executes random projects, Sheu et al. [11] extended preventive replacement models with shocks that bring fatal or non-fatal failures. Levitin et al. [12] assumed that the operating component may be preventively replaced by a standby component during the mission, and optimized the maintenance schedule by minimizing the mission cost while satisfying a certain mission success probability. In summary, it becomes an interesting problem to plan replacement policies for mission-oriented systems according to their damage level, mission reliability, and maintenance costs, as the reliability is required at mission time.

However, few of the related works have considered mission durations in damage models. Different from general systems, PM for mission-oriented systems can not be carried out during the mission execution. From [13, 14, 15], mission durations play a critical role in planning preventive replacement time. Optimal variables of PM policies may be overestimated or underestimated if the mission duration is not taken into account. In this study, we propose an optimal replacement policy of a mission-oriented system under additive damage, where a system is replaced preventively at a planned time, at a shock number, or at mission end time, whichever occurs first. Next, we construct cost models by considering the mission duration. Optimal variables are given in analytical and numerical ways.

We outline the rest of this paper as follows. The next section gives a detailed description and cost models of the preventive replacement policy. Analysis of optimal variables in the above models is represented in Section 3. In Section 4, we provide numerical examples to highlight the properties of our policy. Finally, the conclusions of this research and future work are drawn.

2 Expected cost rate

The system progressively accumulates damage from an initial state of 0 to a critical level x under external shocks. A system failure occurs when the accumulated damage x exceeds a predetermined threshold K. The model assumptions are specified as follows:

1. The inter-arrival times of shocks form a *renewal process*, where the intervals are independent and identically distributed (i.i.d.) random variables with cumulative distribution function (CDF) $F(t)$, probability density function (PDF) $f(t) = \mathrm{d}F(t)/\mathrm{d}t$, and finite mean $\mu = \int_0^\infty tf(t)\mathrm{d}t$. Let $F^{(j)}(t)$ denote the *j-fold convolution* of $F(t)$, which represents the probability that at least number j of shocks occurs in $[0, t)$.

2. Let W_j denote the damage caused by the jth shock, which follows a i.i.d. distribution $G(x) = P(W_j \le x)$ with a PDF $g(x) = \mathrm{d}G(x)/\mathrm{d}x$ and finite mean $1/\omega = \int_0^\infty xg(x)dx$. Define $G^{(j)}(x)$ as the *j-fold convolution* of $G(x)$, which characterizes the probability that $\sum_{i=0}^{j} W_i \le x$. Then, the distribution of additive damage $W(t)$ at time t is

$$\Pr\{W(t) \le x\} = \sum_{j=0}^{\infty}[F^{(j)}(t) - F^{(j+1)}(t)]G^{(j)}(X).$$

3. We consider a system should be in operating state during the mission duration $[T_0, T_0 + t_x]$ $(0 \le t_x < \infty)$, where T_0 is a random variable and has a general distribution $Y(t) \equiv \Pr\{T_0 \le t\}$. t_x is the duration of the mission, during which, the system provides reliability and no replacement can be done preventively.

Different from other studies, we discuss preventive maintenance policies by taking mission duration into account. Suppose that a mission-oriented system under additive damage is replaced at planned time T, at shock number N, or at mission end time $T_0 + t_x$, *whichever occurs first*. During the mission duration $[T_0, T_0 + t_x]$, only corrective replacement is permitted upon failures, with preventive replacement activities prohibited to prevent mission interruptions. Then, the probability of a system replaced preventively at T is

$$P_T(T, N; t_x) = \overline{Y}(T) \sum_{j=0}^{N-1} \left[F^{(j)}(T) - F^{(j+1)}(T)\right] G^{(j)}(K). \tag{1}$$

The probability of a system replaced preventively at N is

$$P_N(T, N; t_x) = G^{(N)}(K) \int_0^T \overline{Y}(t)\mathrm{d}F^{(N)}(t). \tag{2}$$

The probability of a system replaced preventively at $T_0 + t_x$ is

$$P_x(T, N; t_x) = \sum_{j=0}^{N-1} \int_0^T \left[F^{(j)}(t) - F^{(j+1)}(t)\right] \mathrm{d}Y(t) * \sum_{i=0}^{\infty} \left[F^{(i)}(t_x) - F^{(i+1)}(t_x)\right] G^{(i+j)}(K). \tag{3}$$

The probability of a system replaced at failure is

$$P_f(T, N; t_x) = \sum_{j=0}^{N-1} \sum_{i=0}^{\infty} \int_0^T \left[F^{(j)}(t) - F^{(j+1)}(t)\right] \mathrm{d}Y(t) * \left[F^{(i)}(t_x) - F^{(i+1)}(t_x)\right] \left[G^{(j)}(K) - G^{(i+j)}(K)\right] + \sum_{j=0}^{N-1} \left[G^{(j)}(K) - G^{(j+1)}(K)\right] \int_0^T \overline{Y}(t)\mathrm{d}F^{(j+1)}(t). \tag{4}$$

From Appendix 1, it can be proved that $P_T(T, N; t_x) + P_N(T, N; t_x) + P_x(T, N; t_x) + P_f(T, N; t_x) = 1$. Then, the mean time to replacement is

$$MT(T, N; t_x) = \sum_{j=0}^{N-1} \sum_{i=0}^{\infty} \int_0^T \left[F^{(j)}(t) - F^{(j+1)}(t)\right] \mathrm{d}Y(t) * \int_0^{t_x} \left[F^{(i)}(x) - F^{(i+1)}(x)\right] \mathrm{d}x \left[G^{(j)}(K) - G^{(i+j)}(K)\right] + \sum_{j=0}^{N-1} [G^{(j)}(K) - G^{(j+1)}(K)] \int_0^T \overline{F}^{(j+1)}(t)\overline{Y}(t)\mathrm{d}t. \tag{5}$$

Therefore, the expected cost rate is

$$C_F(T, N; t_x) = \frac{c_K - (c_K - c_T)P_T(T, N; t_x) - (c_K - c_N) * P_N(T, N; t_x) - (c_K - c_x)P_x(T, N; t_x)}{MT(T, N; t_x)}$$

$$= \frac{\begin{array}{c} c_K - (c_K - c_N)G^{(N)}(K) \int_0^T \overline{Y}(t)\mathrm{d}F^{(N)}(t) \\ -(c_K - c_T)\overline{Y}(T) \sum_{j=0}^{N-1}[F^{(j)}(T) - F^{(j+1)}(T)]G^{(j)}(K) \\ -(c_K - c_x) * \sum_{j=0}^{N-1} \int_0^T [F^{(j)}(t) - F^{(j+1)}(t)]\mathrm{d}Y(t) \\ * \sum_{i=0}^{\infty}[F^{(i)}(t_x) - F^{(i+1)}(t_x)]G^{(i+j)}(K) \end{array}}{\begin{array}{c} \sum_{j=0}^{N-1}[G^{(j)}(K) - G^{(j+1)}(K)] \int_0^T \overline{F}^{(j+1)}(t)\overline{Y}(t)\mathrm{d}t \\ + \sum_{j=0}^{N-1} \sum_{i=0}^{\infty} \int_0^T [F^{(j)}(t) - F^{(j+1)}(t)]\mathrm{d}Y(t) \\ * \int_0^{t_x} [F^{(i)}(x) - F^{(i+1)}(x)]\mathrm{d}x[G^{(j)}(K) - G^{(j+i)}(K)] \end{array}}. \tag{6}$$

When a system is replaced preventively only at time $T_0 + t_x$, i.e., $T \to \infty$, $N \to \infty$, the cost rate becomes

$$C_S(t_x) = \lim_{T\to\infty, N\to\infty} C_F(T, N; t_x) \tag{7}$$

$$= \frac{\begin{array}{c} c_K - (c_K - c_x) \sum_{j=0}^{\infty} G^{(j)}(K) \\ * \int_0^\infty [F^{(j)}(t + t_x) - F^{(j+1)}(t + t_x)]\mathrm{d}Y(t) \end{array}}{\sum_{j=0}^{\infty} G^{(j)}(K) \int_0^\infty \int_0^{t+t_x} [F^{(j)}(u) - F^{(j+1)}(u)]\mathrm{d}u\mathrm{d}Y(t)}. \tag{8}$$

Especially, when we do not take the mission duration into account, putting $t_x = 0$ in (6), the cost rate becomes

$$C_F(T,N;0) = \frac{\begin{array}{c} c_K - (c_K - c_N)G^{(N)}(K)\int_0^T \overline{Y}(t)\mathrm{d}F^{(N)}(t) \\ -(c_K - c_T)\overline{Y}(T)\sum_{j=0}^{N-1}[F^{(j)}(T) - F^{(j+1)}(T)]G^{(j)}(K) \\ -(c_K - c_x)\sum_{j=0}^{N-1}G^{(j)}(K)\int_0^T[F^{(j)}(t) - F^{(j+1)}(t)]\mathrm{d}Y(t)\end{array}}{\sum_{j=0}^{N-1}G^{(j)}(K)\int_0^T[F^{(j)}(t) - F^{(j+1)}(t)]\overline{Y}(t)\mathrm{d}t}. \tag{9}$$

3 Optimization

When $c_N = c_T = c_x$, the expected cost rate becomes

$$C_F(T,N;t_x) = \frac{\begin{array}{c} c_T + (c_K - c_T)\sum_{j=0}^{N-1}\sum_{i=0}^{\infty}\int_0^T[F^{(j)}(t) - F^{(j+1)}(t)]\mathrm{d}Y(t) \\ *[F^{(i)}(t_x) - F^{(i+1)}(t_x)][G^{(j)}(K) - G^{(i+j)}(K)] \\ +\sum_{j=0}^{N-1}[G^{(j)}(K) - G^{(j+1)}(K)]\int_0^T \overline{Y}(t)\mathrm{d}F^{(j+1)}(t)\end{array}}{\begin{array}{c}\sum_{j=0}^{N-1}[G^{(j)}(K) - G^{(j+1)}(K)]\int_0^T \overline{F}^{(j+1)}(t)\overline{Y}(t)\mathrm{d}t \\ +\sum_{j=0}^{N-1}\sum_{i=0}^{\infty}\int_0^T[F^{(j)}(t) - F^{(j+1)}(t)]\mathrm{d}Y(t) \\ *\int_0^{t_x}[F^{(i)}(x) - F^{(i+1)}(x)]\mathrm{d}x[G^{(j)}(K) - G^{(j+i)}(K)]\end{array}} \tag{10}$$

We find optimal T_f^* and N_f^* to minimize $C_F(T,N;t_x)$ in (10). Differentiating $C_F(T,N;t_x)$ with respect to T and setting it equal to zero,

$$\begin{aligned} &Q_T(T,N)\sum_{j=0}^{N-1}\sum_{i=0}^{\infty}\int_0^T\left[F^{(j)}(t) - F^{(j+1)}(t)\right]\mathrm{d}Y(t) \\ &*\int_0^{t_x}\left[F^{(i)}(x) - F^{(i+1)}(x)\right]\mathrm{d}x\left[G^{(j)}(K) - G^{(i+j)}(K)\right] \\ &+\sum_{j=0}^{N-1}[G^{(j)}(K) - G^{(j+1)}(K)]\int_0^T \overline{F}^{(j+1)}(t)\overline{Y}(t)\mathrm{d}t \\ &-\sum_{j=0}^{N-1}\sum_{i=0}^{\infty}\int_0^T\left[F^{(j)}(t) - F^{(j+1)}(t)\right]\mathrm{d}Y(t) \\ &*\left[F^{(i)}(t_x) - F^{(i+1)}(t_x)\right]\left[G^{(j)}(K) - G^{(i+j)}(K)\right] \\ &+\sum_{j=0}^{N-1}\left[G^{(j)}(K) - G^{(j+1)}(K)\right]\int_0^T \overline{Y}(t)\mathrm{d}F^{(j+1)}(t) = \frac{c_T}{c_K - c_T}, \end{aligned} \tag{11}$$

where

$$Q_T(T,N) = \frac{\begin{array}{c}\sum_{j=0}^{N-1}\sum_{i=0}^{\infty}[F^{(j)}(T) - F^{(j+1)}(T)]r(T) \\ *[F^{(i)}(t_x) - F^{(i+1)}(t_x)][G^{(j)}(K) - G^{(i+j)}(K)] \\ +\sum_{j=0}^{N-1}[G^{(j)}(K) - G^{(j+1)}(K)]f^{(j+1)}(T)\end{array}}{\begin{array}{c}\sum_{j=0}^{N-1}[G^{(j)}(K) - G^{(j+1)}(K)]\overline{F}^{(j+1)}(T) \\ +\sum_{j=0}^{N-1}\sum_{i=0}^{\infty}[F^{(j)}(T) - F^{(j+1)}(T)]r(T) \\ *\int_0^{t_x}[F^{(i)}(x) - F^{(i+1)}(x)]\mathrm{d}x[G^{(j)}(K) - G^{(j+i)}(K)]\end{array}}$$

and $r(t) = y(t)/\overline{Y}(t)$.

When $F(t) = 1 - \mathrm{e}^{-t}$, $G(x) = 1 - \mathrm{e}^{-\omega x}$, and $y(t) = t\mathrm{e}^{-t}$, Figure 1 shows the curve of $Q_T(T,N)$ with respect to T when $N = 1,3,5$. It implies that $Q_T(T,N)$ increases strictly with T. Therefore, there exists a finite and unique T_f^* which satisfies (11).

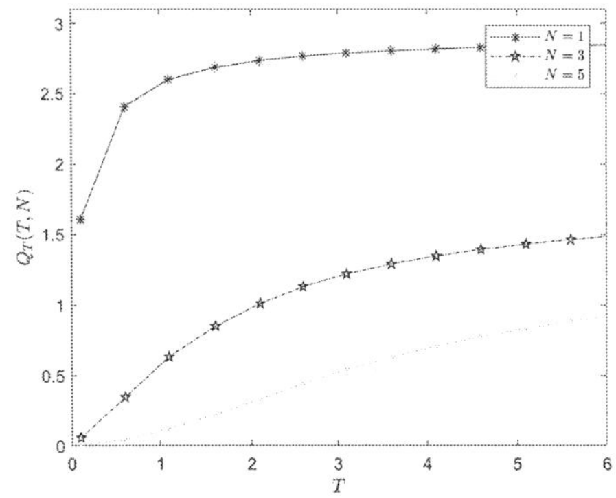

Figure 1: The curve of $Q_T(T,N)$ with respect to T when $N = 1,3,5$.

Forming the inequality $C_F(T,N+1;t_x) - C_F(T,N;t_x) \geq 0$,

$$\begin{aligned} &Q_N(T,N)\sum_{j=0}^{N-1}\sum_{i=0}^{\infty}\int_0^T\left[F^{(j)}(t) - F^{(j+1)}(t)\right]\mathrm{d}Y(t) \\ &*\int_0^{t_x}\left[F^{(i)}(x) - F^{(i+1)}(x)\right]\mathrm{d}x\left[G^{(j)}(K) - G^{(i+j)}(K)\right] \\ &+\sum_{j=0}^{N-1}[G^{(j)}(K) - G^{(j+1)}(K)]\int_0^T \overline{F}^{(j+1)}(t)\overline{Y}(t)\mathrm{d}t \\ &-\sum_{j=0}^{N-1}\sum_{i=0}^{\infty}\int_0^T\left[F^{(j)}(t) - F^{(j+1)}(t)\right]\mathrm{d}Y(t) \\ &*\left[F^{(i)}(t_x) - F^{(i+1)}(t_x)\right]\left[G^{(j)}(K) - G^{(i+j)}(K)\right] \\ &+\sum_{j=0}^{N-1}\left[G^{(j)}(K) - G^{(j+1)}(K)\right]\int_0^T \overline{Y}(t)\mathrm{d}F^{(j+1)}(t) \geq \frac{c_T}{c_K - c_T}, \end{aligned} \tag{12}$$

where

$$Q_N(T,N) = \frac{\begin{array}{c}\int_0^T[F^{(N)}(t) - F^{(N+1)}(t)]\mathrm{d}Y(t) \\ *\sum_{i=0}^{\infty}[F^{(i)}(t_x) - F^{(i+1)}(t_x)][G^{(N)}(K) - G^{(i+N)}(K)] \\ +[G^{(N)}(K) - G^{(N+1)}(K)]\int_0^T \overline{Y}(t)\mathrm{d}F^{(N+1)}(t)\end{array}}{\begin{array}{c}[G^{(N)}(K) - G^{(N+1)}(K)]\int_0^T \overline{F}^{(N+1)}(t)\overline{Y}(t)\mathrm{d}t \\ +\int_0^T[F^{(N)}(t) - F^{(N+1)}(t)]\mathrm{d}Y(t) \\ *\sum_{i=0}^{\infty}\int_0^{t_x}[F^{(i)}(x) - F^{(i+1)}(x)]\mathrm{d}x[G^{(N)}(K) - G^{(N+i)}(K)]\end{array}}$$

When $F(t) = 1 - \mathrm{e}^{-t}$, $G(x) = 1 - \mathrm{e}^{-\omega x}$, and $y(t) = t\mathrm{e}^{-t}$, Figure 2 shows the curve of $Q_N(T,N)$ with respect to N when $T = 1,3,5$. It implies that $Q_N(T,N)$ increases strictly with N. Therefore, there exists a finite and unique N_f^* which satisfies

(12).

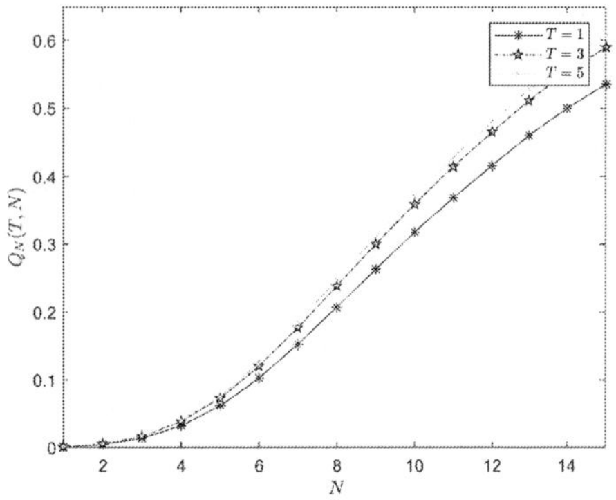

Figure 2: The curve of $Q_N(T,N)$ with respect to N when $T = 1, 3, 5$.

4 Numerical Examples

When $F(t) = 1 - \mathrm{e}^{-t}$, $F^{(j)}(t) = \sum_{i=j}^{\infty} t^i \mathrm{e}^{-t}/i!$, $G(x) = 1 - \mathrm{e}^{-\omega x}$, $G^{(j)}(x) = \sum_{i=j}^{\infty} (\omega x)^i \mathrm{e}^{-\omega x}/i!$, and $y(t) = t\mathrm{e}^{-t}$, Table 1 presents optimum N_f^* and $C_F(T, N_f^*; t_x)/c_T$ for c_K/c_T and t_x when $c_T : c_x : c_N = 1 : 2 : 3$, $\omega K = 10$, and $T = 5$.

Figures 1 and 2 show the curves of $C_F(T_f^*, N; t_x)$ with respect to N and T, respectively. Clearly, approximate shock numbers and planned replacement times can be found from Figures 3 and 4, whose exact values are presented in Tables 1 and 2.

From Table 1 and Table 2, N_f^* and T_f^* decreases with c_K/c_T and t_x, $C_F(T, N_f^*; t_x)/c_T$ and $C_F(T_f^*, N; t_x)/c_T$ increases strictly with c_K/c_T and t_x. It indicates that a system should be replaced with a smaller shock number, an earlier replacement time, or a lower per-unit failure cost when a longer mission duration is required. For instance, under specified parameters $T = 5$ and $c_K/c_T = 30$, the system requires preventive replacement at the 7th shock when $t_x = 0$, compared to the 5th shock at $t_x = 2$. This marked reduction demonstrates that maintenance policies neglecting the mission duration t_x overestimate optimum replacement times. Hence, it is proved that the proposed models in this study are more effective and reasonable.

Table 1: optimum N_f^* and $C_F(T, N_f^*; t_x)/c_T$ for c_K/c_T and t_x when $c_T : c_x : c_N = 1 : 2 : 3$, $\omega K = 10$, and $T = 5$.

$\frac{c_K}{c_T}$	$t_x = 0$		$t_x = 1$		$t_x = 2$	
	N_f^*	$\frac{C_F(T,N_f^*;t_x)}{c_T}$	N_f^*	$\frac{C_F(T,N_f^*;t_x)}{c_T}$	N_f^*	$\frac{C_F(T,N_f^*;t_x)}{c_T}$
5	∞	1.027	∞	1.041	∞	1.062
10	∞	1.054	∞	1.097	9	1.171
15	∞	1.081	8	1.151	6	1.268
20	9	1.108	7	1.198	6	1.349
30	7	1.156	6	1.274	5	1.480
40	6	1.196	5	1.333	4	1.587
50	6	1.230	5	1.386	4	1.678

Table 2: optimum T_f^* and $C_F(T_f^*, N; t_x)/c_T$ for c_K/c_T and t_x when $c_T : c_x : c_N = 1 : 2 : 3$, $\omega K = 10$, and $N = 3$.

$\frac{c_K}{c_T}$	$t_x = 0$		$t_x = 1$		$t_x = 2$	
	T_f^*	$\frac{C_F(T_f^*,N;t_x)}{c_T}$	T_f^*	$\frac{C_F(T_f^*,N;t_x)}{c_T}$	T_f^*	$\frac{C_F(T_f^*,N;t_x)}{c_T}$
5	1.939	1.442	1.932	1.444	1.914	1.451
10	1.932	1.445	1.911	1.451	1.853	1.473
15	1.926	1.447	1.891	1.458	1.798	1.494
20	1.920	1.450	1.872	1.464	1.747	1.516
30	1.907	1.455	1.835	1.477	1.658	1.557
40	1.895	1.460	1.801	1.490	1.582	1.597
50	1.883	1.465	1.768	1.503	1.516	1.636

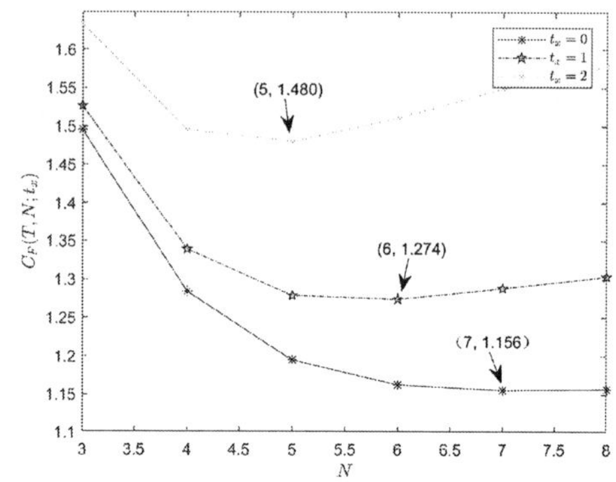

Figure 3: The curve of $C_F(T_f^*, N; t_x)$ with respect to N when $T = 3.0$ and $t_x = 0, 1, 2$.

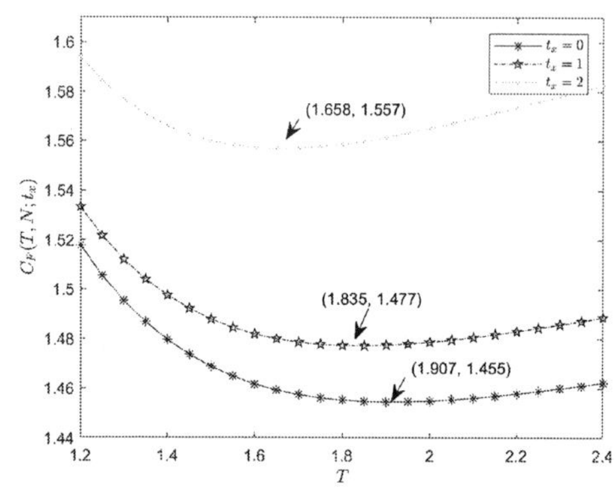

Figure 4: The curve of $C_F(T_f^*, N; t_x)$ with respect to T when $N = 3$ and $t_x = 0, 1, 2$.

5 Conclusions

In this study, we propose an optimal replacement policy of a mission-oriented system under additive damage, where a system is replaced preventively at a planned time T, at a shock number N, or at mission end time $T_0 + t_x$, whichever occurs first. During the duration $[T_0, T_0 + t_x]$, only corrective replacement is permitted upon failures, with preventive replacement activities prohibited to prevent mission interruptions. Via numerical examples, it can be found that the planned replacement time and the shock number are overestimated if we do not consider the mission duration, which further causes a high risk of failure. Hence, it is proved that the proposed models in this study are more effective and reasonable.

References

[1] Sheu, S. H., Tsai, H. N., Wang, F. K., & Zhang, Z. G. (2015). An extended optimal replacement model for a deteriorating system with inspections. Reliability Engineering & System Safety, 139, 33-49.

[2] Nakagawa, T. (2007), Shock and Damage Models in Reliability Theory, Springer, London.

[3] Cha, J. H., & Finkelstein, M. (2011). On new classes of extreme shock models and some generalizations. Journal of Applied Probability, 48, 258-270.

[4] Sheu, S. H., Liu, T. H., Sheu, W. T., Ke, J. C., & Zhang, Z. G. (2023). Optimal replacement policy for a two-unit system subject to shocks and cumulative damage. Reliability Engineering & System Safety, 238, 109420.

[5] Zhou, X., Wu, C., Li, Y., & Xi, L. (2016). A preventive maintenance model for leased equipment subject to internal degradation and external shock damage. Reliability Engineering & System Safety, 154, 1-7.

[6] Zhao, X., & Nakagawa, T. (2018). Advanced maintenance policies for shock and damage models. Springer International Publishing, Switzerland.

[7] Dui, H., Lu, Y., Gao, Z., & Xing, L. (2023). Performance efficiency and cost analysis of multi-state systems with successive damage and maintenance in multiple shock events. Reliability Engineering & System Safety, 238, 109403.

[8] Sun, Y., & Yin, J. (2025). Dynamic condition-based maintenance for shock systems based on damage evolutions using deep reinforcement learning. Reliability Engineering & System Safety, 111095.

[9] Nakagawa, T. (2005). Maintenance Theory of Reliability. Springer, London.

[10] Zhao, X., Nakamura, S., & Nakagawa, T. (2013). Optimal maintenance policies for cumulative damage models with random working times. Journal of Quality in Maintenance Engineering, 19, 25-37.

[11] Sheu, S. H., Liu, T. H., Zhang, Z. G., Zhao, X., & Chien, Y. H. (2021). A generalized age-dependent minimal repair with random working times. Computers & Industrial Engineering, 156, 107248.

[12] Levitin, G., Xing, L., & Dai, Y. (2025). Optimal operation and maintenance scheduling in generalized repairable m-out-of-n standby systems with common shocks. Reliability Engineering & System Safety, 260, 110967.

[13] Zhao, X., Cai, J., Mizutani, S., & Nakagawa, T. (2021). Preventive replacement policies with time of operations, mission durations, minimal repairs and replacement triggering approaches. Journal of Manufacturing Systems, 61, 819-829.

[14] Zhang, Q., Fang, Z., & Cai, J. (2021). Preventive replacement policies with multiple missions and maintenance triggering approaches. Reliability Engineering & System Safety, 213, 107691.

[15] Zhang, Q., Fang, Z. (2025). Optimal age replacement policies for k-out-of-n systems considering mission durations. Reliability Engineering & System Safety, 254, 110625.

Appendix 1. To prove that $P_T(T,N;t_x) + P_N(T,N;t_x) + P_x(T,N;t_x) + P_f(T,N;t_x) = 1$.

Proof

$$\begin{aligned}
&P_x(T,N;t_x) + P_f(T,N;t_x) = \\
&\sum_{j=0}^{N-1}\left[G^{(j)}(K) - G^{(j+1)}(K)\right]\int_0^T \overline{Y}(t)\mathrm{d}F^{(j+1)}(t) \\
&+\int_0^T \sum_{j=0}^{N-1}\left[F^{(j)}(t) - F^{(j+1)}(t)\right]G^{(j)}(K)\mathrm{d}Y(t).
\end{aligned}$$

Next,

$$\begin{aligned}
&P_x(T,N;t_x) + P_f(T,N;t_x) + P_T(T,N;t_x) = \\
&\sum_{j=0}^{N-1}\left[G^{(j)}(K) - G^{(j+1)}(K)\right]\int_0^T \overline{Y}(t)\mathrm{d}F^{(j+1)}(t) \\
&+\sum_{j=0}^{N-1} G^{(j)}(K)\int_0^T \overline{Y}(t)\mathrm{d}\left[F^{(j)}(t) - F^{(j+1)}(t)\right] \\
&=\sum_{j=0}^{N-1} G^{(j)}(K)\int_0^T \overline{Y}(t)\mathrm{d}F^{(j)}(t) \\
&-\sum_{j=0}^{N-1} G^{(j+1)}(K)\int_0^T \overline{Y}(t)\mathrm{d}F^{(j+1)}(t) \\
&= 1 - G^{(N)}(K)\int_0^T \overline{Y}(t)\mathrm{d}F^{(N)}(t) \\
&= 1 - P_N(T,N;t_x).
\end{aligned}$$

Thus, we complete the proof that $P_T(T,N;t_x)+P_N(T,N;t_x)+P_x(T,N;t_x)+P_f(T,N;t_x) = 1$.

Condition-based replacement and spare management under stochastic ordering for three-state competition failure system

WANG Jiantai[1], ZHAO Yu[1*], ZHOU Shihan[1]

[1] School of Reliability and Systems Engineering, Beihang University, China, wjt2114@buaa.edu.cn
[1] School of Reliability and Systems Engineering, Beihang University, China, 04404@buaa.edu.cn
[1] School of Reliability and Systems Engineering, Beihang University, China, zsh1220@buaa.edu.cn

Keywords: maintenance management, hybrid spare provision, competing failure, three-state system

Abstract –the integrated replacement and spare parts provision strategies can significantly enhance maintenance efficiency and operational applicability. This paper develops a maintenance decision-making framework for three-state competing failure systems, incorporating a stochastic ordering mechanism that better reflects practical resource constraints. The proposed approach features a dynamic selection mechanism integrating stochastic ordering with defect-triggered ordinary and failure-induced urgent orders to satisfy spare requirements for both preventive and corrective replacements. Specifically, key operational principles include: 1) stochastic ordering is placed at a random time, 2) defect identification initiates an ordinary ordering unless preceded by a stochastic ordering, and 3) the unexpected degradation failure or shock failure, without prior defect identification or stochastic ordering, activates an urgent ordering. We establish and optimize the long-run expected cost rate through inspection interval optimization. The effectiveness of this integrated management strategy is validated through numerical experiments on railway bearings, demonstrating significant advantages over the conventional maintenance approach.

1. Introduction

Maintenance plays a pivotal role in ensuring operational availability, reliability, and cost-effectiveness of industrial systems[1-5]. Practical maintenance operations typically account for approximately 70% of total lifecycle expenditures [6-8], driving substantial research interest in cost-efficient optimization strategies. An effective maintenance policy must consider the operational and failure mechanisms comprehensively. Quantities of modern industrial systems, frequently exhibit three-state degradation patterns[9-11], which can be effectively modeled via delay time model (DTM) initially proposed by Christer et al [12]. It characterizes system evolution through sequential normal, defective, and failed states prior to complete degradation failure[13-15].

However, complex operational environments and inherent system mechanisms often induce competing failure modes[16, 17], necessitating more appropriate maintenance approaches. Recent studies by Peng et al. [18] and Han et al. [19] have demonstrated the importance of considering competing failures in maintenance optimization, particularly for critical systems wherein single-failure-mode assumptions represent oversimplifications. Among the competition failure modes, the degradation-based failure (soft failure) and shock-induced failure (hard failure) represents a fundamental classification. As for three-state competition failure system, the degradation-based failure mechanism implies the normal, defective and failed states, while the shock-induced failure encompasses only the normal and failed states. Wherein the shock-induced failure time can be modelled by a stochastic variable.

The maintenance policy has developed from the breakdown maintenance, time-based maintenance to condition-based maintenance (CBM), based on the rapid development and sensors as well as signal processing technologies [20-22]. CBM demonstrates superior efficiency through real-time condition monitoring or predictive capabilities. For instance, Wang et al. [23] developed a CBM framework for three-state continuous degradation systems incorporating both real-time monitoring data and remaining useful life predictions. Zhang et al. [24] produced the strategies for three-state discrete deterioration systems captured by DTM while accounting for inspection inaccuracies and imperfect maintenance effects. While these studies highlight CBM's effectiveness for critical assets, they predominantly assume immediate spare part availability-an idealization rarely encountered in practice [25-27].

Existing correlated studies predominantly assume perfect spare availability—an unrealistic premise[28-32]. This drives research integrating maintenance with spare provision, wherein the spare supports the implementation of maintenance action, and the maintenance acquirement might guide the ordering of spare[33]. While CBM typically initiates orders at defect detection in three-state systems, practical capacity constraints during procurement remain unaddressed. As such, stochastic ordering effectively models these dynamic resource limitations (e.g., budget/logistical fluctuations), yet remains understudied in maintenance-spare collaborative research.

To Address these research gaps in competing failure modes and stochastic ordering, this paper proposes a condition-based replacement and spare management framework for three-state competing failure systems. The methodology features: 1) stochastic ordinary ordering for preventive replacement, superseded by defect-triggered orders if defect identification precedes stochastic ordering, and 2) corrective replacement implementation through spare parts sourced from either stochastic ordering, defect-initiated ordinary ordering, or failure-induced urgent ordering. This multi-layered decision framework optimizes maintenance efficiency through dynamic resource allocation.

The principal contributions of this research are threefold:

- A joint optimization of replacement and spare policy is conducted for three-state competition failure system, attached with multi-layer design;

- The stochastic ordering mode is incorporated, reflecting the real-world economic constraints;
- The dynamic selection mechanism between stochastic and defect/failure-induced ordering is devised for enhancing the robustness and efficiency.

PR	Preventive replacement
CR	Corrective replacement
DBF	Degradation-based failure
SBF	Shock-based failure
Notations	
X	Sojourn time of normal stage in DBF
Y	Sojourn time of defective stage in DBF
Z	Arising time of SBF
T_S	The stochastic ordering time
$f_X(x)$	Probability density function of X
$f_Y(y)$	Probability density function of Y
$f_Z(z)$	Probability density function of Z
$f_S(t_s)$	Probability density function of T_S
τ	Cycle length of inspection
$\tau_h = h\tau$	h-th inspection instant
T_f	Failure time
l_1	Lead time of ordinary ordering
l_2	Lead time of urgent ordering
C_I	The unit cost of inspection
C_P	The unit cost of PR
C_S	The unit time cost of downtime penalty
C_{F_1}	The unit cost of CR with ordinary order
C_{F_2}	The unit cost of CR with urgent order
$EC(\tau)$	Expected cost for one renewal cycle
$EL(\tau)$	Expected length for one renewal cycle
$E\bar{C}(\tau)$	Expected long run cost rate

The arrangement of the rest paper is as follows. Section 2 introduces the studied system and proposed collaborative maintenance policy. Section 3 conducts the renewal scenarios analysis. Section 4 establishes the maintenance cost model and presents the calculation approach. Section 5 conducts a numerical experiment for verifying the superiority of the proposed policy. Section 6 concludes the whole work of this paper.

2. Problem statement

2.1. System description

A single-component system whose failure mode follows three-state competition is studied, wherein degradation-based failure (DBF) and shock-based failure (SBF) are competitive. As for three states, it implies that the system experiences normal and defective states orderly before the failed time within DBF mode. The normal and defective states can be obtained via inspection channel, and failed state (whatever DBF or SBF) is self-announcing due to the noticeable failure symptom. Such failure mode is ordinary in industrial systems, such as mechanical, electrical, petrochemical systems. The cost-efficiency is employed to serve as the optimization objective of maintenance decision-making.

2.2. Replacement and spare management policy

Maintenance encompasses replacement and spare provision in this paper. The replacement accomplishes the renewal of system, while the spare supports the implementation of preventive replacement (PR) or corrective replacement (CR) actions. Both the replacement and spare provision policies interact each other to promote the maintenance efficiency.

■ **Replacement policy**

The preventive replacement (PR) will be triggered by the defect identification at $\tau_j, j=1,2,\cdots,\infty$ time, which contains two situations:1) no spare has been ordered before τ_j and the ordinary order will be placed simultaneously, wherein the PR is executed at $\tau_j + l_1$;2) the PR is executed once the spare is accessible wherein the spare has been stochastically ordered prior to τ_j.

The corrective replacement (CR) is triggered by DBF or SBF, and an urgent order will be placed at T_f once no spare has been ordered before the failed time. By contrast, CR will be postponed executed for waiting for pre-ordered spare, or it is implemented immediately with arrived spare at T_f.

■ **Spare provision policy**

Spare provision contains the ordering as well as lead of spare, which mainly encompasses three modes.

- **Stochastic ordinary ordering.** The spare is ordered at T_s following a stochastic variable with lead time l_1. This mode is a realistic setting since not all times possess the ability to make an ordering.
- **Defective-driven ordinary ordering.** The spare is ordinary ordered at defect identification time τ_j with lead time l_1.
- **Failed-driven urgent ordering.** An urgent order will be placed at failure time once no other order has been placed before T_f with lead time $l_2 (l_1 > l_2)$.

■ **Collaborative replacement-spare management**

The spare policy and replacement policy interact each other and co-promote the system maintenance efficiency.

- **PR with stochastic ordering.** PR is executed at $T_s + l_1$ time when the spare arrives.
- **PR with defective-driven ordinary ordering.** PR is executed at $\tau_j + l_1$ wherein the defect identification occurs at τ_j and no stochastic ordering arises before τ_j.
- **CR with stochastic ordering.** The failure lies between T_s and $T_s + l_1$, wherein no defect identification arises before T_s.
- **CR with defective-driven ordinary ordering.** The failure lies in $(\tau_j, \tau_j + l_1)$ and CR is executed at $\tau_j + l_1$ with C_{F_1} cost.
- **CR with failed-driven urgent ordering.** CR is executed at $T_f + l_2$ supported by urgent ordering with C_{F_2} cost.

3. Renewal scenario analysis

3.1. PR with stochastic ordering

The stochastic order is placed at T_s and the system is renewed at $T_s + l_1$ wherein no defect identification before T_s. It contains that 1) no defect occurs before T_s, 2) the defect arises before T_s while the identification time is later than T_s. The probability satisfies:

$$\begin{aligned} P_{pr1}(\tau,i) &= P(\tau_i < T_s < \tau_{i+1}, X > T_s, T_s + l_1 < \min(X+Y,Z)) + \\ &P(X < T_s < \tau_{i+1}, \tau_i < X < \tau_{i+1}, T_s + l_1 < \min(X+Y,Z)) \\ &= \int_{\tau_i}^{\tau_{i+1}} \int_{T_s}^{\infty} f_S(t_s) f_X(x)[1 - F_Y(T_s + l_1 - x)][1 - F_Z(T_s + l_1)] dx dt_s + \\ &\int_{\tau_i}^{\tau_{i+1}} \int_{x}^{\tau_{i+1}} f_S(t_s) f_X(x)[1 - F_Y(T_s + l_1 - x)][1 - F_Z(T_s + l_1)] dt_s dx, \end{aligned} \tag{1}$$

where $f_X(x)$ and $f_S(t_s)$ denote the probability density functions (PDF) of X and T_s, respectively. $F_Y(y)$ and $f_S(t_s)$ denote the probability density functions of X and T_s, respectively. represents the lead time of ordinary ordering. $i = 0,1,2,\cdots,\infty$ holds.

3.2. PR with defect-driven ordinary ordering.

The defect identification occurs at $\tau_j, j = 1,2,\cdots,\infty$ time, and no stochastic order has been placed before that time. As such, the defect-driven ordinary order is placed at τ_j immediately, and the system is preventive replaced at $\tau_j + l_1$. The probability is:

$$\begin{aligned} P_{pr2}(\tau,j) &= P(T_s > \tau_j, \tau_{j-1} < X < \tau_j, \tau_j + l_1 < \min(X+Y,Z)) \\ &= \int_{\tau_{j-1}}^{\tau_j} \int_{\tau_j}^{\infty} f_S(t_s) f_X(x)[1 - F_Y(\tau_j + l_1 - x)][1 - F_Z(\tau_j + l_1)] dt_s dx. \end{aligned} \tag{2}$$

3.3. CR with stochastic ordering

No defect identification occurs before the T_s time, and the DBF or SBF occurs between T_s and $T_s + l_1$.

Case 1. The DBF occurs, whose probability satisfies:

$$\begin{aligned} P_{cr1}^{1}(\tau,i) &= P(\tau_i < T_s < \tau_{i+1}, X > T_s, T_s + l_1 > X+Y, Z > X+Y) + \\ &P(X < T_s < \tau_{i+1}, \tau_i < X < \tau_{i+1}, T_s + l_1 > X+Y, Z > X+Y) \\ &= \int_{\tau_i}^{\tau_{i+1}} \int_{T_s}^{\infty} \int_0^{T_s + l_1 - x} f_S(t_s) f_X(x) f_Y(y)[1 - F_Z(x+y)] dy dx dt_s + \\ &\int_{\tau_i}^{\tau_{i+1}} \int_{x}^{\tau_{i+1}} \int_0^{T_s + l_1 - x} f_S(t_s) f_X(x) f_Y(y)[1 - F_Z(x+y)] dy dt_s dx, \end{aligned} \tag{3}$$

where $f_Y(y)$ denotes the PDF of Y, and $i = 0,1,2,\cdots,\infty$ holds.

Case 2. The SBF happens, whose probability satisfies:

$$\begin{aligned} P_{cr1}^{2}(\tau,i) &= P(\tau_i < T_s < \tau_{i+1}, X > T_s, T_s + l_1 > Z, Z < X+Y) + \\ &P(X < T_s < \tau_{i+1}, \tau_i < X < \tau_{i+1}, T_s + l_1 > Z, Z < X+Y) \\ &= \int_{\tau_i}^{\tau_{i+1}} \int_{T_s}^{\infty} \int_0^{T_s + l_1} f_S(t_s) f_X(x) f_Z(z)[1 - F_Y(z-x)] dz dx dt_s + \\ &\int_{\tau_i}^{\tau_{i+1}} \int_{x}^{\tau_{i+1}} \int_0^{T_s + l_1} f_S(t_s) f_X(x) f_Z(z)[1 - F_Y(z-x)] dz dt_s dx, \end{aligned} \tag{4}$$

where $f_Z(z)$ denotes the PDF of Z, and $i = 0,1,2,\cdots,\infty$ holds.

3.4. CR with defective-driven ordinary ordering

The defect identification occurs at $\tau_j, j = 1,2,\cdots,\infty$ and no stochastic ordering has been placed before that time. The DBF or SBF happens between τ_j and $\tau_j + l_1$, wherein maintainers select to await for the pre-ordered spare rather than performing an urgent ordering.

Case 1. The DBF occurs, whose probability satisfies:

$$\begin{aligned} P_{cr2}^{1}(\tau,j) &= P(T_s > \tau_j, \tau_{j-1} < X < \tau_j, \min(\tau_j + l_1, Z) > X+Y) \\ &= \int_{\tau_{j-1}}^{\tau_j} \int_{\tau_j}^{\infty} \int_0^{\tau_j + l_1 - x} f_S(t_s) f_X(x) f_Y(y)[1 - F_Z(x+y)] dy dt_s dx. \end{aligned} \tag{5}$$

Case 2. The SBF happens, whose probability satisfies:

$$\begin{aligned} P_{cr2}^{2}(\tau,j) &= P(T_s > \tau_j, \tau_{j-1} < X < \tau_j, \min(\tau_j + l_1, X+Y) > Z) \\ &= \int_{\tau_{j-1}}^{\tau_j} \int_{\tau_j}^{\infty} \int_0^{\tau_j + l_1} f_S(t_s) f_X(x) f_Z(z)[1 - F_Y(z-x)] dz dt_s dx. \end{aligned} \tag{6}$$

3.5. CR with failed-driven urgent ordering

The system fails at T_f, before which no defect identification or stochastic ordering happens. As such, an urgent order will be placed at T_f and CR is executed at $T_f + l_2$. Notably, no defect identification contains two conditions: 1) no defect occurs before SBF, 2) both the defect and failure (DBF or SBF) happen in the identical inspection interval.

Case 1. The DBF occurs in $(\tau_k, \tau_{k+1}), k = 0,1,\cdots,\infty$ and the defect happens in this interval as well. The stochastic ordering time T_s is later than T_f. The probability satisfies:

$$\begin{aligned} P_{cr3}^{1}(\tau,k) &= P(T_s > X+Y, \tau_k < X < \tau_{k+1}, \\ &\qquad \tau_k < X+Y < \tau_{k+1}, X+Y < Z) \\ &= \int_{\tau_k}^{\tau_{k+1}} \int_0^{\tau_{k+1} - x} \int_{x+y}^{\infty} f_S(t_s) f_X(x) f_Y(y)[1 - F_Z(x+y)] dt_s dy dx. \end{aligned} \tag{7}$$

Case 2. The SBF occurs in (τ_k, τ_{k+1}) wherein no defect occurs

$$\begin{aligned} P_{cr3}^{2}(\tau,k) &= P(T_s > Z, \tau_k < Z < \tau_{k+1}, X > \tau_k, X+Y > Z) \\ &= \int_{\tau_k}^{\infty} \int_{\tau_k}^{\tau_{k+1} - x} \int_z^{\infty} f_S(t_s) f_X(x) f_Z(z)[1 - F_Y(z-x)] dt_s dy dx. \end{aligned} \tag{8}$$

4. Maintenance cost model and calculation

The maintenance cost model is established based on the pre-stated renewal scenarios, and the calculation as well as optimization are presented as well.

4.1. Maintenance cost model

We list the corresponding renewal cost and length of each renewal scenarios referring to the section 3, shown in Table 1.

Table. 1 The corresponding renewal length and cost of all scenarios

Scenario	Renewal cost	Renewal length	Probability
Section 3.1	$iC_I + C_P$	$T_s + l_1$	$P_{pr1}(\tau,i)$, $i \ge 0$
Section 3.2	$jC_I + C_P$	$\tau_j + l_1$	$P_{pr2}(\tau,j)$, $j \ge 1$
Section 3.3	$iC_I + C_{F_1} + C_S(T_s + l_1 - T_f)$	$T_s + l_1$	$P_{cr1}^{1}(\tau,i), P_{cr1}^{2}(\tau,i)$ $i \ge 0$
Section 3.4	$jC_I + C_{F_1} + C_S(\tau_j + l_1 - T_f)$	$\tau_j + l_1$	$P_{cr2}^{1}(\tau,j), P_{cr2}^{2}(\tau,j)$ $j \ge 1$
Section 3.5	$kC_I + C_{F_2} + C_S l_2$	$T_f + l_2$	$P_{cr3}^{1}(\tau,k), P_{cr3}^{2}(\tau,k)$, $k \ge 0$

Consequently, the expected renewal length and cost of the system can be established as follows:

$$
\begin{aligned}
EC(\tau) = & \sum_{i=0}^{\infty} P_{pr1}(\tau,i)(iC_I + C_P) + \sum_{j=1}^{\infty} P_{pr2}(\tau,j)(jC_I + C_P) + \\
& \sum_{i=0}^{\infty} \begin{matrix} P_{cr1}^{1}(\tau,i)[iC_I + C_{F_1} + C_S(T_s + l_1 - X - Y)] + \\ P_{cr1}^{2}(\tau,i)[iC_I + C_{F_1} + C_S(T_s + l_1 - Z)] \end{matrix} + \\
& \sum_{j=1}^{\infty} \begin{matrix} P_{cr2}^{1}(\tau,j)[jC_I + C_{F_1} + C_S(\tau_j + l_1 - X - Y)] + \\ P_{cr2}^{2}(\tau,j)[jC_I + C_{F_1} + C_S(\tau_j + l_1 - Z)] \end{matrix} \\
& \sum_{k=0}^{\infty} [P_{cr3}^{1}(\tau,k) + P_{cr3}^{2}(\tau,k)](kC_I + C_{F_2} + C_S l_2),
\end{aligned}
\tag{9}
$$

$$
\begin{aligned}
EL(\tau) = & \sum_{i=0}^{\infty} P_{pr1}(\tau,i)(T_s + l_1) + \sum_{j=1}^{\infty} P_{pr2}(\tau,j)(\tau_j + l_1) + \\
& \sum_{i=0}^{\infty} [P_{cr1}^{1}(\tau,i) + P_{cr1}^{2}(\tau,i)](T_s + l_1) + \\
& \sum_{j=1}^{\infty} [P_{cr2}^{1}(\tau,j) + P_{cr2}^{2}(\tau,j)](\tau_j + l_1) + \\
& \sum_{k=0}^{\infty} P_{cr3}^{1}(\tau,k)(X + Y + l_2) + P_{cr3}^{2}(\tau,k)(Z + l_2).
\end{aligned}
\tag{10}
$$

As derived above, the long run expected cost rate satisfies:

$$\overline{EC}(\tau) = EC(\tau) / EL(\tau). \tag{11}$$

Notably, the random variables arising in equations (9) and (10) are for convenient expression, which should be attached with the corresponding PDF and the integral when calculating these two equations.

4.2. Calculation and optimization

The maintenance optimization of the proposed policy is seeking for the optimal inspection cycle length τ^*. As for the calculation of $\overline{EC}(\tau)$ when fixing the variable τ, the Monte Carlo simulation algorithm can be employed to substitute the complicated integral calculation. The similar simulation solution can be obtained based on the references [34, 35]. Furthermore, the optimization of $\overline{EC}(\tau)$ can be conducted utilizing the enumeration optimization algorithm, and the optimal decision variable τ^* as well as minimum cost rate $\overline{EC}(\tau^*)$ can be obtained.

5. Numerical experiments

Numerical experiments are conducted on railway bearings, which can be seen as a typical three-state competition system. As for the DTF, the durations of normal and defective states can be modelled by Weibull distribution and exponential distribution, respectively. The SBF time can be expressed by exponential distribution[18, 19]. The stochastic ordering time is featured by Weibull distribution. The initial parameters of maintenance model are shown in Table.2, wherein m_1 and η_1 denote the parameters of X, λ_1 and λ_2 represent the parameters of Y and Z, respectively. m_2 and η_2 denote the parameters of T_s.The cost unit is USD and the time unit is day.

Table. 2 The initial parameters of maintenance model

m_1	η_1	λ_1	λ_2	l_1	l_2	
1.81	56	0.037	0.015	4	2	
C_I	C_P	C_S	C_{F_1}	C_{F_2}	m_2	η_2
15	100	30	1500	1600	1.56	78

A comparative policy is proposed to verify the necessity of stochastic ordering, which can be released via setting a large value regarding T_s based on the proposed policy. Within the comparative policy, the τ^* and $\overline{EC}(\tau^*)$ are 9 and 31.8, respectively. By contrast, the τ^* and $\overline{EC}(\tau^*)$ are 7 and 34.7, respectively, in proposed policy. The above phenomenon demonstrates that the difference between ideal and practical spare provision settings is significant, and proves the necessity of stochastic ordering as well.

6. Conclusion

Aimed at promoting the applicability as well as practicality of the maintenance strategy, this paper conducts the joint decision-making of replacement and spare provision, especially devising the dynamic selection between stochastic ordering and state-driven ordering. Furthermore, the competition failure between three-state DBF and SBF avoids the oversimplification of practical industrial assets, under complicated and extreme operational environment. The superiority of dynamic selection and condition-based replacement mechanism is verified via numerical experiments on the train bearings, wherein the necessity of practical considerations are demonstrated as well.

As for the prospect, three directions can be explored furtherly: 1) the multiple components system is valuable to be studied[36-42], 2) the predictive information can be integrated into the replacement and spare ordering[43-45], 3) the imperfect inspection can be modelled for enhancing the strategy practicality[46-49].

7. Acknowledgement

This work is supported partially by National Natural Science Foundation of China (Grant No. 72101010) and Fundamental Research Funds for the Central Universities (Grant No. ZG216S21C3).

8. References

[1] L. Yang, F. Wei, and Q. Qiu, "Mission risk control via joint optimization of sampling and abort decisions," *Risk Anal.*, vol. 44, no. 3, pp. 666-685, 2024.

[2] R. Zheng, "Structured replacement policies for a system subject to random mission types," *Nav. Res. Logist.*, vol. 71, no. 7, pp. 1055-1069, 2024.

[3] L. Yang, F. Wei, X. Ma, and Q. Qiu, "Controlling mission hazards through integrated abort and spare support optimization," *Risk Anal.*, 2025.

[4] L. Yang, Y. Chen, and X. Ma, "A state-age-dependent opportunistic intelligent maintenance framework for wind turbines under dynamic wind conditions," *IEEE Trans. Ind. Inf.*, vol. 19, no. 10, pp. 10434-10443, 2023.

[5] D. Wu, R. Han, Y. Ma, L. Yang, F. Wei, and R. Peng, "A two-dimensional maintenance optimization framework balancing hazard risk and energy consumption rates," *Comput.Ind.Eng.*, vol. 169, 2022, Art no. 108193.

[6] C. Cavalcante, R. Lopes, and P. Scarf, "Inspection and replacement policy with a fixed periodic schedule," *Rel.Eng.Syst.Saf.*, vol. 208, 2021, Art no. 107402.

[7] W. Wang, "An overview of the recent advances in delay-time-based maintenance modelling," *Rel.Eng.Syst.Saf.*, vol. 106, pp. 165-178, 2012.

[8] J. Wang, S. Zhou, R. Peng, Q. Qiu, and L. Yang, "An inspection-based replacement planning in consideration of state-driven imperfect inspections," *Rel.Eng.Syst.Saf.*, vol. 232, 2023, Art no. 109064.

[9] Z. Chen, Z. Chen, D. Zhou, C. Shao, and E. Pan, "Optimal replacement policy for multi-state manufacturing system with economic and resource dependence under epistemic uncertainty," *Int J Prod Res*, vol. 61, no. 20, pp. 6772-6790, 2023.

[10]Z. Chen, Z. Chen, D. Zhou, and E. Pan, "Joint optimization of fleet-level sequential selective maintenance and repairpersons assignment for multi-state manufacturing systems," *Comput.Ind.Eng.*, vol. 182, 2023, Art no. 109411.

[11]G. Levitin, L. Xing, and Y. Dai, "Optimizing corrective maintenance for multistate systems with storage," *Rel.Eng.Syst.Saf.*, vol. 244, 2024, Art no. 109951.

[12]A. Christer and W. Waller, "Reducing production downtime using delay-time analysis," *J. Oper. Res. Soc.*, vol. 35, no. 6, pp. 499-512, 1984.

[13]P. Scarf, C. Cavalcante, and R. Lopes, "Delay-time modelling of a critical system subject to random inspections," *Eur.J.Oper.Res.*, vol. 278, no. 3, pp. 772-782, 2019.

[14]L. Yang, Y. Zhao, and X. Ma, "Multi-level maintenance strategy of deteriorating systems subject to two-stage inspection," *Comput.Ind.Eng.*, vol. 118, pp. 160-169, 2018.

[15]L. Yang, Z. Ye, C. Lee, S. Yang, and R. Peng, "A two-phase preventive maintenance policy considering imperfect repair and postponed replacement," *Eur.J.Oper.Res.*, vol. 274, no. 3, pp. 966-977, 2019.

[16]L. Yang, X. Ma, R. Peng, Q. Q. Zhai, and Y. Zhao, "A preventive maintenance policy based on dependent two-stage deterioration and external shocks," (in English), *Rel.Eng.Syst.Saf.*, vol. 160, pp. 201-211, Apr 2017.

[17]H. Xiao, Y. Yan, G. Kou, and S. Wu, "Optimal Inspection Policy for a Single-Unit System Considering Two Failure Modes and Production Wait Time," *IEEE Trans.Rel.*, vol. 72, no. 1, pp. 395-407, 2023.

[18]R. Peng, X. He, C. Zhong, G. Kou, and H. Xiao, "Preventive maintenance for heterogeneous parallel systems with two failure modes," *Rel.Eng.Syst.Saf.*, vol. 220, p. 108310, 2022, Art no. 108310.

[19]M. Han, Z. Ma, S. Ma, W. Li, and J. Yang, "Joint Optimization of Condition-Based Maintenance and Spare Ordering Strategy for a Multistate Competing Failure System," *IEEE Acc.*, vol. 11, pp. 37006-37020, 2023.

[20]L. Yang, Y. Chen, Q. Qiu, and J. Wang, "Risk Control of Mission-Critical Systems: Abort Decision-Makings Integrating Health and Age Conditions," *IEEE Trans. Ind. Inf.*, vol. 18, no. 10, pp. 6887-6894, 2022.

[21]C. A. V. Cavalcante, R. S. Lopes, and P. A. Scarf, "Inspection and replacement policy with a fixed periodic schedule," *Rel.Eng.Syst.Saf.*, vol. 208, 2021, Art no. 107402.

[22]B. de Jonge and P. A. Scarf, "A review on maintenance optimization," *Eur.J.Oper.Res.*, vol. 285, no. 3, pp. 805-824, 2020.

[23]J. Wang, L. Tan, X. Ma, K. Gao, H. Jia, and L. Yang, "Prognosis-driven reliability analysis and replacement policy optimization for two-phase continuous degradation," *Rel.Eng.Syst.Saf.*, vol. 230, 2023, Art no. 108909.

[24]F. Zhang, J. Shen, and Y. Ma, "Optimal maintenance policy considering imperfect repairs and non-constant probabilities of inspection errors," *Rel.Eng.Syst.Saf.*, vol. 193, 2020, Art no. 106615.

[25]Z. Zhang and L. Yang, "Postponed maintenance scheduling integrating state variation and environmental impact," *Rel.Eng.Syst.Saf.*, vol. 202, 2020, Art no. 107065.

[26]Z. Zhang and L. Yang, "State-Based Opportunistic Maintenance With Multifunctional Maintenance Windows," (in English), *IEEE Trans.Rel.*, vol. 70, no. 4, pp. 1481-1494, Dec 2021.

[27]H. Jia, R. Peng, L. Yang, T. Wu, D. Liu, and Y. Li, "Reliability evaluation of demand-based warm standby systems with capacity storage," *Rel.Eng.Syst.Saf.*, vol. 218, 2022, Art no. 108132.

[28]W. Wang and H. Wang, "Preventive replacement for systems with condition monitoring and additional manual inspections," *Eur.J.Oper.Res.*, vol. 247, no. 2, pp. 459-471, 2015.

[29]W. Wang, F. Zhao, and R. Peng, "A preventive maintenance model with a two-level inspection policy based on a three-stage failure process," *Rel.Eng.Syst.Saf.*, vol. 121, pp. 207-220, 2014.

[30]X. Tang, H. Xiao, G. Kou, and R. Peng, "Optimal Inspection Policy for a Three-Stage System With Imperfect Inspection and Repair," *IEEE Trans.Rel.*, vol. 73, no. 3, pp. 1669-1683, 2024.

[31]M. Han, J. Yang, and X. Zhao, "Joint optimization of inspection, maintenance, and spare ordering policy considering defective products loss," *J. Syst. Eng. Electron.*, vol. 32, no. 5, pp. 1167-1179, 2021.

[32]L. Shang, B. Liu, Q. Qiu, and L. Yang, "Three-dimensional warranty and post-warranty maintenance of products with monitored mission cycles," *Rel.Eng.Syst.Saf.*, vol. 239, 2023, Art no. 109506.

[33]J. Wang, L. Yang, X. Ma, and R. Peng, "Joint optimization of multi-window maintenance and spare part provisioning policies for production systems," *Rel.Eng.Syst.Saf.*, vol. 216, 2021, Art no. 108006.

[34]J. Wang, X. Ma, K. Gao, Y. Zhao, and L. Yang, "Condition-based maintenance management for two-stage continuous deterioration with two-dimensional inspection errors," *Qual.Rel.Eng.Int.*, vol. 40, no. 7, pp. 3691-3708, 2024.

[35]J. Wang, X. Ma, L. Yang, Q. Qiu, L. Shang, and J. Wang, "A hybrid inspection-replacement policy for multi-stage degradation considering imperfect inspection with variable probabilities," *Rel.Eng.Syst.Saf.*, vol. 241, 2024, Art no. 12901.

[36]F. Zhang, H. Liao, J. Shen, and Y. Ma, "Optimal Maintenance of a System With Multiple Deteriorating Components Served by Dedicated Teams," *IEEE Trans.Rel.*, vol. 72, no. 3, pp. 900-915, 2023.

[37]L. Yang, S. Zhou, X. Ma, Y. Chen, H. Jia, and W. Dai, "Group machinery intelligent maintenance: Adaptive health prediction and global dynamic maintenance decision-making," *Rel.Eng.Syst.Saf.,* vol. 252, 2024, Art no. 110426.

[38]L. Yang, G. Li, Z. Zhang, X. Ma, and Y. Zhao, "Operations & Maintenance Optimization of Wind Turbines Integrating Wind and Aging Information," (in English), *IEEE Trans. Sustain. Energ.,* vol. 12, no. 1, pp. 211-221, 2021.

[39]Y. Chen, X. Ma, F. Wei, L. Yang, and Q. Qiu, "Dynamic Scheduling of Intelligent Group Maintenance Planning under Usage Availability Constraint," *Mathematics-Basel,* vol. 10, no. 15, 2022, Art no. 2730.

[40]Y. Chen, T. Wu, X. Ma, J. Wang, R. Peng, and L. Yang, "System Maintenance Optimization Under Structural Dependency: A Dynamic Grouping Approach," *IEEE Syst. J.,* vol. 18, no. 3, pp. 1605-1616, 2024.

[41]T. Wu, F. Wei, L. Yang, X. Ma, and L. Hu, "Maintenance Optimization of k -Out-of- n Load-Sharing Systems Under Continuous Operation," *IEEE Transactions on Systems, Man, and Cybernetics: Systems,* pp. 1-13, 2023.

[42]Z. Chen, Z. Chen, D. Zhou, and E. Pan, "Energy-oriented opportunistic maintenance optimization of continuous process manufacturing systems with two types of stochastic durations," *Rel.Eng.Syst.Saf.,* vol. 237, 2023, Art no. 109385.

[43]L. Wang, Y. Chen, X. Zhao, and J. Xiang, "Predictive Maintenance Scheduling for Aircraft Engines Based on Remaining Useful Life Prediction," *IEEE IoT J.,* vol. 11, no. 13, pp. 23020-23031, 2024.

[44]L. Yang, Y. Chen, X. Ma, and C. Qian, "A Prognosis-centered Intelligent Maintenance Optimization Framework under Uncertain Failure Threshold," *IEEE Trans.Rel.,* vol. 73, no. 1, pp. 115-130, 2024.

[45]F. Wei *et al.*, "A hybrid prognostic framework: Stochastic degradation process with adaptive trajectory learning to transfer historical health knowledge," *Mech. Syst. Signal Process.,* vol. 224, p. 112171, 2025.

[46]Z. Chen, Z. Chen, D. Zhou, and E. Pan, "Joint optimization of opportunistic maintenance and speed control for continuous process manufacturing systems considering stochastic imperfect maintenance," *Comput.Ind.Eng.,* vol. 198, 2024, Art no. 110685.

[47]Z. Chen, Z. Chen, D. Zhou, T. Xia, and E. Pan, "Opportunistic maintenance optimization of continuous process manufacturing systems considering imperfect maintenance with epistemic uncertainty," *J Manuf Syst,* vol. 71, pp. 406-420, 2023.

[48]F. Zhang, J. Shen, H. Liao, and Y. Ma, "Optimal preventive maintenance policy for a system subject to two-phase imperfect inspections," *Rel.Eng.Syst.Saf.,* vol. 205, 2021, Art no. 107254.

[49]X. Zhao, J. Cai, S. Mizutani, and T. Nakagawa, "Preventive replacement policies with time of operations, mission durations, minimal repairs and maintenance triggering approaches," *J Manuf Syst,* vol. 61, pp. 819-829, 2021.

Optimal Switching Decisions in a Degrading Standby System with Switching Time Redundancy

Rongchi Sun, Cuicui Pei, Bosen Liu, Qingan Qiu*
School of Management, Beijing Institute of Technology, Beijing 100081, China.
Email: qiu_qingan@bit.edu.cn

Keywords: Standby systems, Switching decision, Time redundancy, Degradation modelling

Abstract - Switching time redundancy plays a critical role in optimizing standby systems, as it can enhance both system reliability and economic performance. After the failure of the primary component, a redundancy time window exists during which the standby component does not need to be activated immediately, as long as the switch occurs within this window. Such systems are commonly observed in engineering applications such as power supply systems and reconnaissance unmanned aerial vehicles (UAVs). This paper develops a two-component warm standby system model that incorporates switching time redundancy. Based on this model, we propose an integrated strategy that combines preventive shutdown and delayed switching. This strategy takes full advantage of the redundancy time to reduce wear on the standby component and extend the overall system lifetime. Furthermore, the expected operating cost—a key performance indicator—is derived, and an optimization framework is established to determine the optimal switching threshold. Finally, the limitations of this study are discussed, and future work will include comparisons with existing strategies and numerical experiments to evaluate the superiority of the proposed approach.

1. Introduction

In modern engineering systems, reliability is a critical factor in ensuring safety, performance, and economic viability. Standby redundancy strategies have long been employed to enhance system reliability by introducing standby components that take over operations upon the failure of primary components. Traditionally, such strategies rely on immediate or predetermined switching mechanisms to minimize downtime and prevent system-level failures. However, in various real-world systems, such as urban residential water supply networks [1], electrical power distribution infrastructures [2], and virtual machines supporting cloud computing services [3, 4], a brief period of failure tolerance is often inherent following the malfunction of a critical component. Consider a scenario in which a residential water supply pipeline experiences a failure but is recovered promptly. If the restoration occurs within a short duration, end users may remain unaware that the system ever entered a failed state[5]. This phenomenon introduces the opportunity to adopt delayed switching strategies, where the transition to a standby component is not immediate but occurs within a failure time threshold.

Several researchers have recognized the significance of systems exhibiting failure tolerance, where a complete functional collapse does not occur immediately upon component failure. Qiu et al. [6] conducted an availability analysis of inspected Markov systems with a downtime threshold, suggesting that the system can continue to operate normally within a certain period following failure, as long as the downtime does not exceed the specified threshold. Rodrigues et al. [7] observed that catastrophic consequences arising from system failures often do not manifest instantaneously but are instead triggered upon external inspections or demand occurrence. Accordingly, they developed a novel two-phase (inspection and replacement) policy tailored for protective systems in power supply applications. Du et al. [2] proposed a modeling framework based on aggregated stochastic process theory to capture the history-dependent dynamics and the impact of undetected failures in Markovian repairable systems. Wu et al. [8] evaluated the reliability for subsea oil and gas production facilities considering delayed restoration . These studies demonstrate that failure-tolerant behavior is prevalent in a variety of practical systems and has attracted growing scholarly attention. However, limited research has focused on modeling such behavior in the context of standby systems, particularly in the design of switching strategies. To address this gap, this paper introduces a two-component standby system that incorporates a switching time redundancy, allowing the standby component to be activated at any point within the redundancy window following the failure of the working component.

Switching strategies play a critical role in the performance and reliability of standby redundant systems. The timing and conditions under which a standby component is activated directly influence system availability, maintenance costs, and overall operational efficiency. In conventional standby systems, two primary switching policies are commonly employed: immediate switching, where the standby unit is activated instantaneously upon failure of the primary component, and scheduled or preventive switching, where the transition occurs at a predetermined time or condition regardless of the primary component's status [9, 10]. Nevertheless existing switching strategies maybe suboptimal when applied to failure-tolerant systems, as they do not exploit the available redundancy time following the failure of the primary component. To address this limitation, this paper proposes a delayed switching strategy, wherein the activation of the standby component is intentionally postponed. This approach aims to reduce unnecessary wear and tear on standby units and optimize system performance. For example, in battlefield scenarios involving unmanned aerial vehicles performing a reconnaissance mission, delaying the activation of a backup drone can reduce its exposure to electromagnetic interference, thereby increasing the likelihood of mission success [3]. This delayed activation framework lays the foundation for modeling optimal switching decisions under uncertainty and mission-critical constraints.

2. Integrated strategy combining preventive shutdown and delayed switching

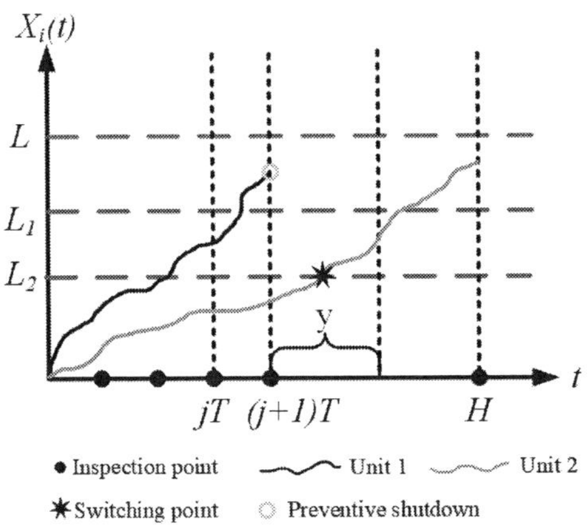

(a) Preventive shutdown and delayed switching

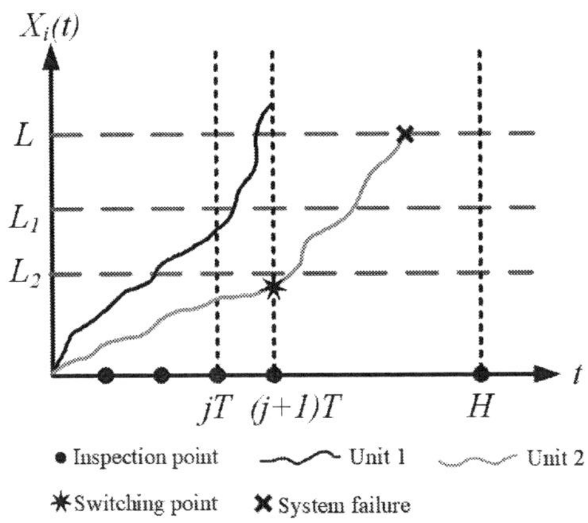

(b) Absence of preventive shutdown

Figure 1: Integrated strategy combining preventive shutdown and delayed switching

This paper considers a two-component warm standby system with switching redundancy time, motivated by the power supply system described in [2]. A power system supplies electricity to a factory through a primary transformer, with a backup transformer configured in a warm standby mode. With the advancement of distributed energy systems, the factory is also equipped with a photovoltaic (PV) generation system to provide supplemental power. However, the PV system can only be activated when the factory is already operational, as its control center requires electricity to issue control commands. If the factory experiences a power outage, the PV system cannot function. To address this limitation, one potential strategy is to proactively shut down the primary transformer while it is still operating and initiate the PV system. Once the PV power supply is nearly exhausted, the backup transformer can be activated at an appropriate time to ensure continuous power delivery.

To model the proposed system, and without loss of generality, we consider the Wiener process as an example and assume that the primary and standby components follow two distinct degradation processes. At the initial time, the primary component $Unit$ 1 is active, while the standby component $Unit$ 2 is in a warm standby state. To be specific, the degradation behavior of the primary component is represented by a Wiener process $\{X_1(t),\ t > 0\}$ with drift parameter μ_1 and diffusion parameter σ_1, while the degradation of the standby unit under standby state is modeled by another Wiener process $\{X_2(t),\ t > 0\}$ with drift parameter μ_2 and diffusion parameter σ_2. It is assumed that $\mu_1 > \mu_2$ and $\sigma_1 > \sigma_2$, reflecting the harsher operational conditions experienced by the primary unit. The system under investigation is designed to perform a mission lasting for a fixed duration H.

Degradation levels of the two components are monitored through inspections conducted every T time units. During the entire mission, a total of N inspections can be performed, i.e., $H = NT$. These inspections are assumed to be instantaneous, perfect and nondestructive. Component failure is assumed to occur when the degradation level reaches a specified threshold L. Besides, if a failure occurs, we assume it is not self-announcing, and could only be detected by inspections. This study proposes a preventive shutdown strategy, in which the primary unit is proactively terminated before failure occurs, particularly when degradation approaches a critical threshold. We define the preventive shutdown threshold of the primary component as L_1, where $L_1 < L$. At each inspection point, if the degradation level of the primary component reaches L_1, its operation is preemptively terminated. If the degradation level exceeds L_1 and directly reaches the failure threshold L, the primary component is considered to have failed. After the primary component is preemptively shut down, a redundancy period Y is available for the standby component to switch in. In the power supply system example, this redundancy period is supported by the PV power system. The standby transformer does not need to be activated immediately; it only needs to be activated within this redundancy window to ensure system continuity. A switching threshold L_2 is introduced; if the degradation level of $Unit$ 2 reaches L_2 before the redundancy period expires, it is then activated. Such delayed switching can help mitigate component degradation and wear, as well as reduce the excessive operational costs associated with premature activation, such as electricity expenses.

The decision-making process of the proposed integrated strategy combining preventive shutdown and delayed switching is illustrated as an example in Figure 1. In Figure 1a, the degradation level of $Unit$ 1 at observation point jT does not reach the threshold L_1, and thus the early termination condition is not satisfied. At time $(j+1)T$, the degradation level exceeds L_1 but remains below L, triggering a preventive shutdown. Following the shutdown of $Unit$ 1, the system operates within a redundant delay period y. During this interval, the standby unit successfully reaches the switching threshold L_2, switches to the active state, and continues operating until the mission horizon H. In contrast, Figure 1b depicts a scenario where a preventive shutdown fails to occur. At $(j+1)T$, $Unit$ 1's degradation level exceeds L, resulting in failure. As the failure of $Unit$ 1 results in the absence of a redundancy period y—for instance, due to a blackout in the plant's power control room preventing the activation of photovoltaic power—the system can only activate the standby component even if its degradation level doesn't reach the switching threshold L_2. $Unit$ 2 then switches to the operating state, but fails after reaching its failure threshold L, leading to overall system failure before the mission is completed. This paper jointly optimizes the shutdown threshold L_1 and the switching threshold L_2 to minimize the expected operational cost (EOC).

3. Deriving expected operating cost

The two-component warm standby system considered in this study is assumed to perform a mission of fixed duration H. Let c_1 denote the unit operating cost when a component is in the active working state. During the standby period, the backup component incurs a lower unit cost c_2, where $c_2 < c_1$. If a component fails during active operation, a failure cost A_f is incurred, encompassing repairs and labor reallocation. The system failure cost, denoted by A_t , captures the total loss resulting from complete system breakdown, including economic losses from service disruption, customer compensation, safety hazards, and possible post-failure remediation. If the primary component is shutdown prematurely before completing the mission (e.g., as part of the preventive shutdown strategy), a penalty cost A_s is imposed, where $A_s < A_f$. Furthermore, let c_3 denote the unit time cost during periods of system inactivity, which primarily reflects the opportunity loss borne by the company due to the unavailability of normal operations. We model the redundancy time Y as a random variable, characterized by the PDF of $g(y)$ and CDF of $G(y)$. In practice, Y reflects external uncertainties such as the factory's PV unit's power supply duration, which is influenced by generation capacity, weather fluctuations, and equipment wear. It is noteworthy that during the post-failure redundancy time—a short interval after the primary component fails and before the standby unit is switched in—the system is assumed to incur no operating cost. For example, in a power supply system, this period might be sustained by low-cost photovoltaic backup, which contributes negligible cost to the system.

Assume that both $Unit$ 1 and $Unit$ 2 start with an initial degradation level of zero. Their degradation processes $X_i(t)$ $(i=1,2)$ follow the Wiener process given below:

$$X_1(t) = \mu_1 t + \sigma_1 B_1(t), \tag{1}$$

$$X_2(t) = \begin{cases} X_{21}(t) = \mu_2 t + \sigma_2 B_2(t), \quad 0 \le t \le z, \\ X_{22}(t) = X_{21}(z) + \mu_1(t-z) + \sigma_1 B_1(t-z), \\ \qquad z < t \le H, \end{cases} \tag{2}$$

where $B_1(t)$ and $B_2(t)$ are two independent standard Brownian motion processes and z denotes the time at which $Unit$ 2 switches from standby state to active state.

Given the Wiener processes with drift terms, the probability density function (PDF) of the degradation level of $Unit$ 1 at time t, $f_1(x|t)$, is

$$f_1(x|t) = \frac{1}{\sqrt{2\pi\sigma_1^2 t}} e^{\frac{(x-\mu_1 t)^2}{-2\sigma_1{}^2 t}}, \tag{3}$$

and the PDF of the degradation level of $Unit$ 2 at time t, $f_2(x|t)$, is

$$f_2(x|t) = \frac{1}{\sqrt{2\pi\sigma_2^2 t}} e^{\frac{(x-\mu_2 t)^2}{-2\sigma_2{}^2 t}}. \tag{4}$$

The survival function of $Unit$ 1, $\overline{F}_1(t,L)$, is

$$\overline{F}_1(t,L) = \Pr\{X_1(t) < L\} = \Phi(\tfrac{L-\mu_1 t}{\sigma_1\sqrt{t}}), \tag{5}$$

where $\Phi(\cdot)$ represents the cumulative distribution function (CDF) of the standard normal distribution. Similarly, the survival function of $Unit$ 2 under standby state, $\overline{F}_2(t,L)$, is

$$\overline{F}_2(t,L) = \Pr\{X_2(t) < L\} = \Phi(\tfrac{L-\mu_2 t}{\sigma_2\sqrt{t}}), \quad 0 \le t \le z. \tag{6}$$

Let $T_{L,1}$ denote the first passage time at which the $Unit$ 1's degradation process first reaches the threshold L. Then, $T_{L,1}$ follows an inverse Gaussian distribution with PDF given by Equation 7

$$f_{T_{L,1}}(t) = \frac{L}{\sqrt{2\pi\sigma_1^2 t^3}} \exp(-\frac{(L-\mu_1 t)^2}{2\sigma_1^2 t}),\ t > 0. \tag{7}$$

Similarly, we define the following first passage times: $T_{l,1}$ as the time when $Unit$ 1 first reaches the threshold l; $T_{l,2}$ as the time when $Unit$ 2 first reaches the threshold l. Their corresponding probability density functions are denoted by $f_{T_{l,1}}(t)$ and $f_{T_{l,2}}(t)$ respectively. It should be emphasized that l is not fixed and may correspond to any degradation level in this setting.

Assume that the preventive shutdown is triggered at $(j+1)T$, $j = 0,1,2...$, only if the system remains in a normal state at that moment, i.e., $Unit$ 1's degradation level lies within (L_1, L), and the degradation level at time jT is below L_1. The probability of this situation can be derived as

$$\begin{aligned} P_s(j) &= \Pr\{X_1(jT) < L_1, L_1 < X_1((j+1)T) < L\} \\ &= \int_{-\infty}^{L1} f_1(x|jT)[\overline{F}_1(T, L-x) - \overline{F}_1(T, L_1 - x)]dx. \end{aligned} \tag{8}$$

Since the Wiener process is a stochastic process with independent and stationary increments, the degradation increment over the interval $[jT,(j+1)T]$ can be represented by the increment over $[0,T]$, which leads to Equation 8. In a similar manner, the probability that $Unit$ 1 is detected to have failed at $(j+1)T$ is derived and presented in Equation 9

$$\begin{aligned} P_f(j) &= \Pr\{X_1(jT) < L_1, L < X_1((j+1)T)\} \\ &= \int_{-\infty}^{L1} f_1(x|jT)[1 - \overline{F}_1(T, L-x)]dx. \end{aligned} \tag{9}$$

Deriving EOC was developed mathematically by constructing probabilities for 12 different operating scenarios.

Scenario 1: $Unit$ 1 remains in a functional state throughout the mission time H, as its degradation level stays below the shutdown threshold L_1 without failure. Under this circumstance, the expected cost is given by Equation 10

$$E_1 = \Phi(\frac{L_1 - \mu_1 H}{\sigma_1 \sqrt{H}})[c_1 H + c_2 H \Phi(\frac{L - \mu_2 H}{\sigma_2 \sqrt{H}}) + \int_0^H (c_2 t + A_f) f_{T_{L,2}}(t) dt], \tag{10}$$

where the right-hand side of the equation represents three types of costs and their associated probabilities: the operating cost of $Unit$ 1 functioning for a duration of H, the operating cost of $Unit$ 2 functioning for H, and the operating cost incurred when the component operates for less than H.

Scenario 2: At time $(j+1)T$, $Unit$ 1 is detected to have failed, and the standby component has also failed by that time. The expected operating cost under this scenario is calculated as follows

$$E_2 = \sum_{j=0}^{N-1} \int_0^{(j+1)T} P_f(j)[c_1(j+1)T + c_2 t + c_3(H - (j+1)T) + 2A_f + A_t] f_{T_{L,2}}(t) dt. \tag{11}$$

Scenario 3: At time $(j+1)T$, $Unit$ 1 is detected to have failed, while the standby component (i.e., $Unit$ 2) is still functioning properly. $Unit$ 2 is immediately switched to the active state and continues operating until the end of the mission. The expected operating cost in this scenario is calculated as follows

$$E_3 = \sum_{j=0}^{N-1} \int_0^{H-(j+1)T} \int_0^L P_f(j)[c_1((j+1)T + u) + c_2(j+1)T + c_3(H - (j+1)T - u) + 2A_f + A_t] f_{T_{L-x,1}}(u) f_2(x|(j+1)T) dx du. \tag{12}$$

Scenario 4: At time $(j+1)T$, $Unit$ 1 is detected to have failed, while $Unit$ 2 is still functioning properly. $Unit$ 2 is immediately switched to the active state but it fails before the mission is completed. Under this circumstance, the expected cost is given by Equation 13

$$E_4 = \sum_{j=0}^{N-1} \int_{H-(j+1)T}^{\infty} \int_0^L P_f(j)[c_1 H + c_2(j+1)T + A_f] f_{T_{L-x,1}}(u) f_2(x|(j+1)T) dx du. \tag{13}$$

Scenario 5: At time $(j+1)T$, the degradation level of $Unit$ 1 exceeds L_1 but remains below L, indicating a planned preventive shutdown. However, since $Unit$ 2 has already failed, the switch cannot be performed, and $Unit$ 1 continues to operate. It survives until the end of the mission at time H. The expected operating cost in this scenario is calculated as follows

$$E_5 = \sum_{j=0}^{N-1} \int_{H-(j+1)T}^{\infty} \int_0^{L-x} \int_{-\infty}^{L_1} \int_0^{(j+1)T} \cdot [c_1 H + c_2 t + A_f] f_{T_{L-x-v,1}}(u) f_1(v|T) \cdot f_1(x|jT) f_{T_{L,2}}(t) dt dx dv du. \tag{14}$$

Scenario 6: At time $(j+1)T$, the degradation level of $Unit$ 1 exceeds L_1 but remains below L, indicating a planned preventive shutdown. However, since $Unit$ 2 has already failed, the switch cannot be performed, and $Unit$ 1 continues to operate and eventually fails before the mission completion time H. The expected operating cost in this scenario is calculated as follows

$$E_6 = \sum_{j=0}^{N-1} \int_0^{H-(j+1)T} \int_0^{L-x} \int_{-\infty}^{L_1} \int_0^{(j+1)T} \cdot [c_1((j+1)T + u) + c_2 t + c_3(H - (j+1)T - u) + 2A_f + A_t] f_{T_{L-x-v,1}}(u) f_1(v|T) \cdot f_1(x|jT) f_{T_{L,2}}(t) dt dx dv du. \tag{15}$$

Scenario 7: If $Y + (j+1)T < H$, $Unit$ 1 is shut down preventively at time $(j+1)T$, while $Unit$ 2 successfully reaches the switching threshold L_2 within the redundancy period Y and takes over the operation. Nevertheless, it fails before the mission is achieved due to reaching the degradation threshold L. The expected operating cost under this scenario is calculated as follows

$$E_7 = \sum_{j=0}^{N-1} \int_{-\infty}^{H-(j+1)T} \int_0^{H-(j+1)T-\lfloor y \rfloor} \int_0^{L-L_2} \int_{(j+1+\lfloor \frac{y}{T} \rfloor)T}^{(j+2+\lfloor \frac{y}{T} \rfloor)T} \cdot [c_1((j+1)T + u) + c_2((j+1)T + \lfloor y \rfloor) + c_3(H - (j+1)T - \lfloor y \rfloor) + A_s + A_f + A_t] \cdot P_s(j) g(y) f_{T_{L-x-L_2},1}(u) f(x|(j+1)T + \lfloor y \rfloor - t) \cdot f_{T_{L_2},2}(t) dt dx du dd y. \tag{16}$$

Scenario 8: If $Y + (j+1)T < H$, $Unit$ 1 is shut down preventively at time $(j+1)T$, while $Unit$ 2 successfully reaches the switching threshold L_2 within the redundancy period Y and takes over the operation. It continues functioning successfully until the mission ends at time H. The expected operating cost under this scenario is calculated as follows

$$E_8 = \sum_{j=0}^{N-1} \int_{-\infty}^{H-(j+1)T} \int_{H-(j+1)T-\lfloor y \rfloor}^{\infty} \int_0^{L-L_2} \int_{(j+\lfloor \frac{y}{T} \rfloor)T}^{(j+1+\lfloor \frac{y}{T} \rfloor)T} \cdot [c_1(H - \lfloor y \rfloor) + c_2((j+1)T + \lfloor y \rfloor) + A_s] \cdot P_s(j) g(y) f_{T_{L-x-L_2},1}(u) f(x|(j+1)T + \lfloor y \rfloor - t) \cdot f_{T_{L_2},2}(t) dt dx du dy. \tag{17}$$

Scenario 9: If $Y + (j+1)T < H$, $Unit$ 1 is shut down preventively at time $(j+1)T$, but $Unit$ 2 fails to reach the switching threshold L_2 by the end of the redundancy period Y, resulting in overall system failure. The expected operating cost under this scenario is calculated as follows

$$E_9 = \sum_{j=0}^{N-1} \int_{-\infty}^{H-(j+1)T} \int_{(j+1+\lfloor \frac{y}{T} \rfloor)T}^{\infty} \cdot[c_1(j+1)T + c_2((j+1)T+y) + c_3(H-(j+1)T-y) + A_s + A_f]P_s(j)g(y)f_{T_{L_2},2}(t)dtdy. \tag{18}$$

Scenario 10: If $Y + (j+1)T > H$, $Unit$ 1 is shut down preventively at time $(j+1)T$, while $Unit$ 2 successfully reaches the switching threshold L_2 within H and takes over the operation. But it fails before the mission horizon H. The expected operating cost under this scenario is calculated as follows

$$E_{10} = \sum_{j=0}^{N-1} \int_{H-(j+1)T}^{\infty} \int_{0}^{H-\lceil \frac{t}{T} \rceil T} \int_{0}^{L-L_2} \int_{(j+1)T}^{H} \cdot[c_1((j+1)T+u) + c_2 \lceil \tfrac{t}{T} \rceil T + c_3(H - \lceil \tfrac{t}{T} \rceil T - u) + A_s + A_f + A_t] \cdot P_s(j)g(y)f_{T_{L-x-L_2},1}(u)f(x| \lceil \tfrac{t}{T} \rceil T - t) \cdot f_{T_{L_2},2}(t)dtdxdudy. \tag{19}$$

Scenario 11: If $Y + (j+1)T > H$, $Unit$ 1 is shut down preventively at time $(j+1)T$, while $Unit$ 2 successfully reaches the switching threshold L_2 within H and takes over the operation. It continues functioning successfully until the mission ends at time H. The expected operating cost under this scenario is calculated as follows

$$E_{11} = \sum_{j=0}^{N-1} \int_{H-(j+1)T}^{\infty} \int_{H-\lceil \frac{t}{T} \rceil T}^{\infty} \int_{0}^{L-L_2} \int_{(j+1)T}^{H} \cdot[c_1(H - \lceil \tfrac{t}{T} \rceil T + (j+1)T) + c_2 \lceil \tfrac{t}{T} \rceil T + A_s] \cdot P_s(j)g(y)f_{T_{L-x-L_2},1}(u)f(x| \lceil \tfrac{t}{T} \rceil T - t) \cdot f_{T_{L_2},2}(t)dtdxdudy. \tag{20}$$

Scenario 12: If $Y + (j+1)T > H$, $Unit$ 1 is shut down preventively at time $(j+1)T$, but $Unit$ 2 fails to reach the switching threshold L_2 by the end of the mission. The system completes the task within the redundancy period, meaning that at the end of the task, it is still operating under PV power in the factory case. The expected operating cost under this scenario is calculated as

$$E_{12} = \sum_{j=0}^{N-1} \int_{H-(j+1)T}^{\infty} \int_{H}^{\infty} \cdot[c_1(j+1)T + c_2 H + A_s]P_s(j)g(y)f_{T_{L_2},2}(t)dtdy. \tag{21}$$

According to Equations 10-21, EOC is calculated as the sum of the expected operating costs under all scenarios, as given by the following expression

$$EOC(L_1, L_2) = \sum_{i=1}^{12} E_i. \tag{22}$$

4. Conclusion

This paper presents a novel reliability optimization framework for a two-component warm standby system that incorporates a random redundancy period following the failure of the main component. We introduce a unified switching strategy that comprehensively accounts for the costs of component failure, system downtime, and switching, as well as the operating benefit during the redundancy period. By constructing a cost model that integrates these factors, we analytically derive an expected operational cost (EOC) function that serves as the basis for determining the optimal switching time.

Acknowledgment

This research is supported by National Natural Science Foundation of China (72371030 and 72001026).

References

[1] Xinzhuo Bao and Lirong Cui. An analysis of availability for series markov repairable system with neglected or delayed failures. *Ieee Transactions on reliability*, 59(4):734–743, 2010.

[2] Shijia Du, Zhiguo Zeng, Lirong Cui, and Rui Kang. Reliability analysis of markov history-dependent repairable systems with neglected failures. *Reliability Engineering & System Safety*, 159:134–142, 2017.

[3] Gregory Levitin, Liudong Xing, and Yuanshun Dai. Optimal task aborting policy and component activation delay in consecutive multi-attempt missions. *Reliability Engineering & System Safety*, 238:109482, 2023.

[4] Sa Meng, Liudong Xing, and Gregory Levitin. Activation delay and aborting policy minimizing expected losses in consecutive attempts having cumulative effect on mission success. *Reliability Engineering & System Safety*, 247:110078, 2024.

[5] Qingan Qiu and Lirong Cui. Availability analysis for general repairable systems with repair time threshold. *Communications in Statistics-Theory and Methods*, 48(3):628–647, 2019.

[6] Qingan Qiu, Lirong Cui, and Jingyuan Shen. Availability analysis and maintenance modelling for inspected markov systems with down time threshold. *Quality Technology & Quantitative Management*, 16(4):478–495, 2019.

[7] Augusto JS Rodrigues, Cristiano AV Cavalcante, and Chi-Guhn Lee. A general inspection and replacement policy for protection systems subject to shocks with state dependent effect. *Reliability Engineering & System Safety*, 251:110397, 2024.

[8] Shengnan Wu, Laibin Zhang, Wenpei Zheng, Yiliu Liu, and Mary Ann Lundteigen. Reliability modeling of subsea siss partial testing subject to delayed restoration. *Reliability Engineering & System Safety*, 191:106546, 2019.

[9] Li Yang, Xiaobing Ma, and Yu Zhao. A condition-based maintenance model for a three-state system subject to degradation and environmental shocks. *Computers & Industrial Engineering*, 105:210–222, 2017.

[10] Xian Zhao, Rong Li, He Han, and Qingan Qiu. Condition-based switching, loading, and age-based maintenance policies for standby systems. *European Journal of Operational Research*, 321(2):565–585, 2025.

Optimal Preventive Replacement Policy for Repairable Products with Multiple Repair Attempts under Free-repair Warranty

DONG Wenjie
College of Economics and Management, Nanjing University of Aeronautics and Astronautics, China, Email: dongwenjie@nuaa.edu.cn
ZHANG Meixuan
College of Economics and Management, Nanjing University of Aeronautics and Astronautics, China, Email: 269183341@qq.com
XIE Naiming
College of Economics and Management, Nanjing University of Aeronautics and Astronautics, China, Email: xienaiming@nuaa.edu.cn
SHEU Shey-Huei
Department of Business Administration, Asia University, Taiwan, Email: shsheu@mail.ntust.edu.tw

Keywords: periodic replacement, multiple repair attempts, free-repair warranty, expected cost rate

Abstract - **This paper explores the optimal preventive replacement policy for a repairable product with multiple repair attempts under free-repair warranty (FRW). Specifically, under the FRW policy provided with a particular warranty period, a repairable product undergoes preventive replacement at periodic times. In case of unexpected failure during two successive replacement cycles, repairs will be made to rectify the failures, free of charge to the customer during the warranty period. Taking the practical factor that a repair is imperfect due to various reasons, the effect of a repair may be successful but worse than minimal repair or unsuccessful. The optimal preventive replacement cycles for the situations whether the product is provided with or without a warranty in minimizing the expected cost rates are respectively analyzed and compared analytically. Finally, detailed numerical examples and computation results are addressed to illustrate the conclusion that the preventive replacement policy for the product with a FRW is more cost-effective than the case without a warranty.**

1. Introduction

A warranty serves as a post-sales guarantee by manufacturers, ensuring repairs or maintenance when products fail to meet specified performance standards. As can be seen from the definition of product warranty, maintenance and warranty are two strongly interlinked aspects as they both aim to deal with product failures, directly or indirectly [10]. There are usually two general types of warranties, expressed and implied [8]. For the expressed warranty, two types of basic warranty schemes are often provided by the manufacturer, i.e., free-repair warranty (FRW) policy and pro-rata warranty (PRW) policy [7]. A FRW policy is a strategy where the manufacturer will bear all the repair costs within the warranty period and no fees are charged to the customer, while a PRW policy provides product maintenance at a proportional cost to the customer during the warranty time window [12].

As to the maintenance strategy in the warranty service, periodic replacement or periodic maintenance is one of the most frequently adopted policies [19, 13]. A periodic replacement policy refers to that a product is preventively maintained or planned replaced at periodic times, and any product is as good as new (AGAN) after the periodic maintenance. Commonly used repair actions to rectify failures during two successive replacement periods are minimal repair, which restores the product to be "as bad as old" (ABAO). A non-homogeneous Poisson process (NHPP) whose intensity function corresponds with product failure rate function is often introduced to model the minimal repair process, in which a cost optimization framework incorporating minimal repair cost and preventive replacement cost is increasingly established to seek the optimal replacement cycle [2].

However, as described in Lee and Cha [17], although minimal repair which is based on NHPP has many advantages, it also has practical limitations. For example, the failure of a specific unit in a complex system may lead to a more severe working environment through increased pressure, temperature, humidity, etc., causing instantaneous stress or damage to the adjacent non-failed components [1, 6]. This eventually results in more serious system degradation, increasing the level of system failure rate in the subsequent repair process [9, 14]. As a result, a new repair type, called as GPP repair, which is based on the Generalized Polya Process (GPP) and whose effect is worse than minimal repair is more suitable to describe the successful repair with degenerative effectiveness [6].

On the other aspect, it can happen in practice that a minimal repair is unsuccessful and should be executed repeatedly [11]. This occurs due to a number of reasons [16]. For example, if a spare part used in the repair process is faulty or with lower quality, an unsuccessful repair may happen and multiple repair attempts should be taken into account [3]. Based on the non-homogeneous

Polya-Aeppli process (NHPAP), a multi-attempt minimal repair model is proposed, where the effect of repairing a system after failure can be unsuccessful and therefore, it should be executed repeatedly [4, 5]. The NHPAP is in fact a compound Poisson process, in which the successful repair process is described with an NHPP and the unsuccessful repair process is defined with another counting process, associated with the NHPP and the NHPAP. Over the past years, the research on the properties of NHPAP and its applications in warranty and maintenance policies has diverse results [11, 15, 16, 20].

The multi-attempt repair model in Cha and Finkelstein [4, 5], like many others mentioned, is built under the assumption that the successful repairs are minimal and described with NHPP. In fact, this assumption is too restrictive to fully describe the underlying process [18]. At some instances, it may be more realistic to consider the successful repairs as worse than minimal due to the adverse effects of the previous repair attempts, external and internal shocks to the system, insufficient quality of a successful repair attempt, and so on. A more general multiple repair attempt process describing the successful repairs that are worse than minimal repair based on the GPP and the unsuccessful repair with another counting process is proposed in Langston and Finkelstein [15].

To the best of our knowledge, the general multiple repair attempt models for repairable products under the FRW policy have not yet been sufficiently considered. In this paper, the optimal preventive replacement policy for a repairable product with multiple repair attempts under FRW is studied. To be specific, under the FRW policy provided with a particular warranty period, a repairable product is preventively replaced at periodic times. When an unexpected failure occurs during two successive replacement cycles, repairs will be made to rectify the failures, free of charge to the customer during the warranty period. Taking the practical factor that a repair is imperfect due to various reasons, the effect of a repair may be successful but worse than minimal repair or unsuccessful. The optimal preventive replacement cycles for the situations whether the product is provided with or without a warranty in minimizing the expected cost rates are respectively analyzed and compared. It is shown that the preventive replacement policy for the product with a FRW is more cost-effective than the case without a warranty and the proposed model offers a generalized application in warranty service.

The remainder of this paper is structured as follows. Section 2 briefly states some preliminaries and useful properties of GPP, GPP repair and the point process of multiple repair attempts. Section 3 presents the mathematical approaches to derive the expected cost rate for the situation where the warranty period is considered or not. In Section 4, we derive the optimal preventive replacement cycles for different situations as well as the corresponding expected cost rates. The theoretical comparisons of the effect of a FRW policy on the optimal preventive replacement cycle are addressed analytically in Section 5. Section 6 concludes the whole research and points out some potential research interests in the future.

2. Preliminaries

Consider a repairable product whose lifetime X is subject to a general distribution $F(t) = P\{X \leq t\}$ and the survival function $\overline{F}(t) = 1 - F(t)$. When $F(t)$ has a probability density function (PDF) $f(t) = \frac{\mathrm{d}F(t)}{\mathrm{d}t}$, the failure rate function $\gamma(t)$ is given by $\gamma(t) = \frac{f(t)}{\overline{F}(t)}$ and is assumed to increase from $\gamma(0)$ to $\gamma(\infty) = \lim_{t\to\infty} \gamma(t)$. The maintenance of the product is characterized by a periodic replacement policy, where it is preventively replaced at periodical times nT $(n = 1, 2, \cdots)$, independent of its age X.

When the repairable product is failed between two successive replacement periods, it is repaired by the repairman to restore its functionality. It is commonly seen that an unsuccessful repair may occur for a number of reasons, for example, if a spare part used in the repair attempt is faulty or with lower quality. This makes the possibility of unsuccessful repair attempts a practical consideration when trying to modeling real-life repair problem in product maintenance [15]. Therefore, we assume that there are two possible results of a repair, i.e., successful and unsuccessful. Meanwhile, due to the adverse effects of the previous repair attempts, external and internal shocks to the product, and so on, even though a successful repair cannot recover the system's condition to the state as it was before the failure, but to a "weaken" state [16]. In this paper, the point process GPP and its associated GPP repair are defined to describe the above successful repair behavior.

Definition 1 (GPP [17]) A counting process $\{M(t), t \geq 0\}$ is called the GPP with parameter set $(\gamma(t), \alpha, \beta)$, where $\alpha \geq 0$ and $\beta \geq 0$ if

(1) $M(0) = 0$;

(2) $\gamma_t = (\alpha M(t_-) + \beta)\gamma(t)$.

In **Definition 1**, $M(t_-)$ is the number of the point events in $(0, t)$, $\gamma(t)$ is the baseline intensity function of $\{M(t), t \geq 0\}$, and γ_t is the stochastic intensity. It is clear that a GPP with parameter set $(\gamma(t), \alpha = 0, \beta = 1)$ reduces to an NHPP with the intensity function $\gamma(t)$, and therefore, a GPP is in fact a generalized version of the NHPP.

It is widely acknowledged that the NHPP is appropriate to describe the stochastic behavior of the minimal repair, where the intensity function $\gamma(t)$ is undisturbed by a repair, i.e., system condition after repair is the same as that before failure. For the effect of a successful repair which weakens the system's condition after repair, the GPP is more suitable to describe the phenomenon of worse than minimal repair as the stochastic intensity increases with the number of repairs. Under the assumption that the repair time is negligible, a mathematically tractable parameterization of the GPP was presented to define a new type of repair process, whose definition is given in **Definition 2**.

Definition 2 (GPP repair) For a system with failure rate $\gamma(t)$, a repair type is called the "GPP repair" with parameter α if the counting process $\{M(t), t \geq 0\}$ is a GPP with parameter set $(\gamma(t), \alpha, 1)$.

It is clear that the GPP repair can sufficiently describe a successful repair with degenerative effectiveness as the intensity function γ_t increase with t. In this paper, the counting process $\{M(t), t \geq 0\}$ is denoted as the number of successful repairs in the time interval $[0, t]$. According to the characteristic of GPP, the expected number of successful repairs in a replacement cycle

$[0, T]$ is characterized as

$$E[M(T)] = \int_0^T \gamma(t) e^{\alpha\Lambda(t)} dt = \frac{1}{\alpha}\left[e^{\alpha\Lambda(T)} - 1\right], \quad (1)$$

in which $\Lambda(t) = \int_0^t \gamma(u) du$.

Let $N(t)$ represent the total number of repairs including successful repairs and unsuccessful repair attempts in $[0, t]$ and $X_1, X_2, \cdots$ be iid geometric random variables with parameter ρ ($\rho > 0$), independent of $M(t)$, in which $\{M(t), t \geq 0\}$ is a GPP with parameter set $(\gamma(t), \alpha, 1)$. Denote $\{N(t), t \geq 0\}$ as a counting process describing the multiple repair attempts, i.e.,

$$N(t) = X_1 + X_2 + \cdots + X_{M(t)}. \quad (2)$$

Then, the parameter ρ of the geometrically distributed random variables $X_1, X_2, \cdots$ can be viewed as the probability of a successful repair when a repair is performed at system failure. In practice, as a product is aging and it is more and more difficult to execute a successful repair, it is a reasonable assumption that the successful probability is decreasing with time [4]. Under such circumstance that a repair is successfully executed with the probability $\rho(t)$ $(0 < \rho(t) \leq 1)$, the expected number of the total repairs in a replacement cycle $[0, T]$ is

$$E[N(T)] = \int_0^T \frac{\gamma(t)}{\rho(t)} e^{\alpha\Lambda(t)} dt. \quad (3)$$

Let $\{L(t), t \geq 0\}$ be the number of unsuccessful repair attempts in $[0, t]$, and therefore, the expected number of unsuccessful repair attempts in a replacement cycle $[0, T]$ is

$$E[L(T)] = \int_0^T \left(\frac{1 - \rho(t)}{\rho(t)}\right) \gamma(t) e^{\alpha\Lambda(t)} dt. \quad (4)$$

3. Model formulation

Define c_d ($c_d > 0$) and c_{du} ($c_{du} > 0$) as downtime costs for the customer due to each product failure and an unsuccessful repair attempt, respectively. It is clear that the customer will bear the downtime costs whether or not the product is offered with a warranty policy due to some inconvenience caused by a failure. For the product provided with a FRW policy, the manufacturer will cover the repair fees to rectify the failure within the warranty period W ($W > 0$), free of charge to the customer if the failure occurs during the warranty period and charging to customers if the failure occurs beyond the warranty period W. Assume c_m ($c_m > 0$) and c_{mu} ($c_{mu} > 0$) as the repair costs for implementing successful repair and unsuccessful repair attempt, respectively. Furthermore, the fixed cost for preventively replacing the product at the periodic times is c_p. The times to any repair and replacement are negligible.

3.1. Expected cost rate without warranty

To investigate the effects of product warranty on the optimal preventive replacement policy as well as the corresponding expected cost rate, the expected cost rate for the product without warranty needs to be derived first. Based on the renewal reward theorem, the expected cost rate for the product without warranty is

$$C_0(T) = \frac{Q_A(T) + c_p}{T}, \quad (5)$$

in which

$$Q_A(T) = (c_d + c_m)E[M(T)] + (c_{du} + c_{mu})E[L(T)]. \quad (6)$$

When $\alpha = 0$, the counting process for the successful repairs $\{M(t), t \geq 0\}$ degrades into an NHPP, and the result in Tsai and Chien [20] becomes a special case of the model in (5). Therefore, the model constructed in this paper is more practical and generalized.

3.2. Expected cost rate with warranty

3.2.1. Case I: $T \geq W$

For the case $T \geq W$, the customer will bear the downtime costs in the whole replacement cycle T and only the repair costs if the failure time is beyond the warranty period W. Therefore, the expected cost rate for the product with warranty is

$$C_1(T) = \frac{Q_A(T) + [c_p - Q_B(W)]}{T}, \quad (7)$$

in which

$$Q_B(W) = c_m E[M(W)] + c_{mu} E[L(W)]. \quad (8)$$

3.2.2. Case II: $T < W$

For the case $T < W$, the manufacturer will cover all repair costs and only downtime costs will occur to the customer. Therefore, the expected cost rate for the product with warranty is

$$C_2(T) = \frac{Q_C(T) + c_p}{T}, \quad (9)$$

in which

$$Q_C(T) = c_d E[M(T)] + c_{du} E[L(T)]. \quad (10)$$

Observe that $Q_A(T) = Q_B(T) + Q_C(T)$ from (6), (8), and (10). When the replacement cycle T equals to the warranty period W, i.e., $T = W$, we have

$$C_1(W) = C_2(W). \quad (11)$$

4. Optimization

4.1. Optimal replacement period without warranty

Theorem 1 Given that $\gamma(t)$ is an increasing failure rate (IFR) function and $\rho(t)$ is a decreasing function in t, then the following results hold for the case the product is sold without warranty:

(1) If $\lim_{T\to\infty} \eta_0(T) > c_p$, there exists a finite and unique $0 < T_0^* < \infty$ such that $\eta_0(T_0^*) = c_p$, and the corresponding optimal expected cost rate is

$$C_0(T_0^*) = (c_d + c_m)\gamma(T_0^*) e^{\alpha\Lambda(T_0^*)} + (c_{du} + c_{mu}) \left(\frac{1 - \rho(T_0^*)}{\rho(T_0^*)}\right) \gamma(T_0^*) e^{\alpha\Lambda(T_0^*)}. \quad (12)$$

(2) Otherwise, if $\lim_{T\to\infty} \eta_0(T) \le c_p$, $T_0^* = \infty$, in which

$$\eta_0(T) = (c_d + c_m)\left[T\gamma(T)\mathrm{e}^{\alpha\Lambda(T)} - \int_0^T \gamma(t)\mathrm{e}^{\alpha\Lambda(t)}\mathrm{d}t\right] + (c_{du} + c_{mu})\left[\left(\frac{1-\rho(T)}{\rho(T)}\right)\gamma(T)\mathrm{e}^{\alpha\Lambda(T)} - \int_0^T \left(\frac{1-\rho(t)}{\rho(t)}\right)\gamma(t)\mathrm{e}^{\alpha\Lambda(t)}\mathrm{d}t\right]. \tag{13}$$

From **Theorem 1**, the result show that when a product deteriorates with age (the failure rate function $\gamma(t)$ is increasing in t) or it is more and more difficult to repair (the execution probability of a successful repair $\rho(t)$ is decreasing in t), it makes sense to perform a preventive replacement, i.e., $0 < T_0^* < \infty$. Otherwise, a preventive replacement is unnecessary.

4.2. Optimal replacement period with warranty

4.2.1. Local optimization for the case $T \ge W$

Theorem 2 Given that $\gamma(t)$ is an IFR function and $\rho(t)$ is a decreasing function in t, then the following results hold for $T \ge W$:

(1) If $\eta_0(W) \ge c_p - Q_B(W)$, then the optimal preventive replacement cycle is $T_1^* = W$, and the corresponding optimal expected cost rate is given in (11).

(2) If $\eta_0(W) < c_p - Q_B(W) < \lim_{T\to\infty} \eta_0(T)$, then there exists a finite and unique $W < T_1^* < \infty$ satisfying $\eta_0(T_1^*) = c_p - Q_B(W)$, and the corresponding optimal expected cost rate is

$$C_1(T_1^*) = (c_d + c_m)\gamma(T_1^*)\mathrm{e}^{\alpha\Lambda(T_1^*)} + (c_{du} + c_{mu})\left(\frac{1-\rho(T_1^*)}{\rho(T_1^*)}\right)\gamma(T_1^*)\mathrm{e}^{\alpha\Lambda(T_1^*)}. \tag{14}$$

(3) If $\lim_{T\to\infty} \eta_0(T) \le c_p - Q_B(W)$, then $T_1^* = \infty$.

4.2.2. Local optimization for the case $T < W$

Theorem 3 Given that $\gamma(t)$ is an IFR function and $\rho(t)$ is a decreasing function in t, then the following results hold for $T < W$:

(1) If $\eta_1(W) \ge c_p$, then the optimal preventive replacement cycle is $T_2^* = W$, and the corresponding optimal expected cost rate is given in (11).

(2) If $\eta_1(W) > c_p$, then there exists a finite and unique $0 < T_2^* < W$ satisfying $\eta_1(T_2^*) = c_p$, and the corresponding optimal expected cost rate is

$$C_2(T_2^*) = c_d\gamma(T_2^*)\mathrm{e}^{\alpha\Lambda(T_2^*)} + c_{du}\left(\frac{1-\rho(T_2^*)}{\rho(T_2^*)}\right)\gamma(T_2^*)\mathrm{e}^{\alpha\Lambda(T_2^*)}, \tag{15}$$

in which

$$\eta_1(T) = c_d\left[T\gamma(T)\mathrm{e}^{\alpha\Lambda(T)} - \int_0^T \gamma(t)\mathrm{e}^{\alpha\Lambda(t)}\mathrm{d}t\right] + c_{du}\left[\left(\frac{1-\rho(T)}{\rho(T)}\right)\gamma(T)\mathrm{e}^{\alpha\Lambda(T)} - \int_0^T \left(\frac{1-\rho(t)}{\rho(t)}\right)\gamma(t)\mathrm{e}^{\alpha\Lambda(t)}\mathrm{d}t\right]. \tag{16}$$

4.2.3. Global optimization with warranty

Combining the results in **Theorem 2** and **Theorem 3**, the following theorem can be obtained to seek an optimal preventive replacement cycle T_w^* for the product provided with warranty W.

Theorem 4 Under the FRW policy for the repairable product with warranty W, given that $\gamma(t)$ is an IFR function and $\rho(t)$ is a decreasing function in t, then the following results hold for seeking an optimal T_w^*:

(1) If $\eta_0(W) < c_p - Q_B(W)$, then $T_w^* = T_1^* > W = T_2^*$.

(2) If $\eta_0(W) \ge c_p - Q_B(W)$ and $\eta_1(W) \le c_p$, then $T_w^* = T_1^* = T_2^* = W$.

(3) If $\eta_1(W) > c_p$, then $T_w^* = T_2^* < W = T_1^*$.

5. Comparisons

In this section, the impact of the FRW on the optimal preventive replacement policy is evaluated by comparing the expected cost rate and the optimal replacement cycle.

Corollary 1 (Cost Savings under FRW) Given the warranty period W, the expected cost rate for the repairable product without warranty is always greater than the case for the product provided with a FRW.

Furthermore, to further quantify the cost saving of the FRW policy, the difference between the optimal expected cost rates $C_0(T_0^*)$ and $C(T_w^*)$ is defined as

$$\Delta C = \frac{C_0(T_0^*) - C(T_w^*)}{C_0(T_0^*)} \times 100\%, \tag{17}$$

where $C(T_w^*) = C_1(T_1^*)$ for $T_w^* \ge W$ and $C(T_w^*) = C_2(T_2^*)$ for $T_w^* < W$.

Corollary 2 (Replacement Cycle Relationships) Under the FRW policy for the repairable product with warranty W, given that $\gamma(t)$ is an IFR function and $\rho(t)$ is a decreasing function in t, the optimal preventive replacement cycles T_0^* and T_w^* have the following properties:

(1) If $\eta_0(W) < c_p - Q_B(W)$, then $W < T_w^* < T_0^*$.

(2) If $c_p - Q_B(W) \le \eta_0(W) < c_p$, then $W = T_w^* < T_0^*$.

(3) If $\eta_0(W) = c_p$, then $W = T_w^* = T_0^*$.

(4) If $\eta_1(W) \le c_p < \eta_0(W)$, then $T_0^* < T_w^* = W$.

(5) If $\eta_1(W) > c_p$, then $T_0^* < T_w^* < W$.

6. Conclusions

In this paper, a generalized preventive replacement policy for repairable products with multiple repair attempts under FRW is proposed. The optimal preventive replacement cycles for the situations where FRW is considered or not are analyzed and compared in minimizing their respective expected cost rate. The comparison result that the optimal expected cost rate for the product without warranty is greater than the case with warranty shows that a FRW policy is more profitable for the customers. It should also be noted that the proposed model in this paper is more general and many existing models are special cases.

In the future study, the fixed warranty period can be more flexible and dynamically adjusted by the manufacturer. In addition, though preventive maintenance (PM) is widely adopted to reduce product failures, more numbers of preventive replacement increase the cost pressure to the customers. Therefore, the joint optimization on the preventive replacement cycle and the PM number under a warranty policy will be the next emphasis.

Acknowledgement

This work was supported by the National Natural Science Foundation of China under Grant numbers 72401132 and 72371128, China Postdoctoral Science Fundation under Grant number 2022M721596, the Natural Science Foundation of Jiangsu Province under Grant number BK20230870, and Jiangsu Funding Program for Excellent Postdoctoral Talent under Grant number 2022ZB222.

References

[1] Badia, F. G., Berrade, M. D., Cha, J. H., & Lee, H. (2018). Optimal replacement policy under a general failure and repair model: Minimal versus worse than old repair. *Reliability Engineering & System Safety*, 180, 362-372.

[2] Barlow, R., & Hunter, L. (1960). Optimum preventive maintenance policies. *Operations Research*, 8(1), 90-100.

[3] Cha, J. H. (2022). An extended class of univariate and multivariate generalized Polya processes. *Advances in Applied Probability*, 54(3), 974-997.

[4] Cha, J. H., & Finkelstein, M. (2024a). On the multiattempt minimal repair and the corresponding counting process. *Applied Stochastic Models in Business and Industry*, 40(1), 206-215.

[5] Cha, J. H., & Finkelstein, M. (2024b). Preventive maintenance for the constrained multi-attempt minimal repair. *Reliability Engineering & System Safety*, 243, 109899.

[6] Cha, J. H., & Finkelstein, M. (2025). On the fixed and evolving frailties in some survival models. *Metrika*. https://doi.org/10.1007/s00184-025-00993-5.

[7] Chang, C. C. (2021). Optimal preventive replacement policy for operating products with renewing free-replacement warranty. *Communications in Statistics-Theory and Methods*, 50(18), 4255-4270.

[8] Chang, C. C. (2022). Optimal renewing free-maintenance warranty period and preventive replacement age for repairable products. *Journal of the Operational Research Society*, 73(12), 2602-2613.

[9] Chien, Y. H. (2019a). Optimal periodic replacement policy for a GPP repairable product under the free-repair warranty. *Quality Technology & Quantitative Management*, 16(3), 347-354.

[10] Chien, Y. H. (2019b). The optimal preventive-maintenance policy for a NHPBP repairable system under free-repair warranty. *Reliability Engineering & System Safety*, 188, 444-453.

[11] Chien, Y. H., & Zhang, Z. G. (2024). Optimal replacement policy based on number of failures for a system with multiple attempt minimal repairs. *Reliability Engineering & System Safety*, 251, 110366.

[12] Chien, Y. H., Zhang, Z. G., & Yin, X. (2019c). On optimal preventive-maintenance policy for generalized Polya process repairable products under free-repair warranty. *European Journal of Operational Research*, 279(1), 68-78.

[13] Finkelstein, M., & Cha, J. H. (2024). On a new point process approach to reliability improvement modeling for repairable systems. *Applied Stochastic Models in Business and Industry*. https://doi.org/10.1002/asmb.2906.

[14] Hashemi, M., & Asadi, M. (2021). Optimal preventive maintenance of coherent systems: A generalized Polya process approach. *IISE Transactions*, 53(11), 1266-1280.

[15] Langston, A., & Finkelstein, M. (2024a). A general multiple-repair-attempt process and its application to optimal age replacement. *South African Statistical Journal*, 58(2), 81-98.

[16] Langston, A., Finkelstein, M., & Cha, J. H. (2024b). A bathtub pattern for repairable systems: From better-than-minimal to minimal and worse-than-minimal repairs. *Proceedings of the Institution of Mechanical Engineers, Part O: Journal of Risk and Reliability*. https://doi.org/10.1177/1748006X241306.

[17] Lee, H., & Cha, J. H. (2016). New stochastic models for preventive maintenance and maintenance optimization. *European Journal of Operational Research*, 255(1), 80-90.

[18] Lee, H., & Cha, J. H. (2019). A bivariate optimal replacement policy for a system subject to a generalized failure and repair process. *Applied Stochastic Models in Business and Industry*, 35(3), 637-650.

[19] Sheu, S. H., Liu, T. H., Sheu, W. T., Ke, J. C., & Zhang, Z. G. (2024). Bivariate replacement policy for a system subject to shocks. *Quality Technology & Quantitative Management*, 21(1), 54-71.

[20] Tsai, H. N., & Chien, Y. H. (2024). Optimal replacement policy for repairable products with multi-attempt minimal repair under the free-repair warranty. *Quality Technology & Quantitative Management*. https://doi.org/10.1080/16843703.2024.2425894.

Assessing Transportation Network Reliability and Carbon Emissions Under Stochastic Capacity Degradation

Mingyang Yue[1], Yifeng Niu[2], Xiuzhen Xu[3]

[1] School of Economics and Management, Chongqing University of Posts and Telecommunications, Chongqing, China, yuemingyang2020@163.com
[2] School of Modern Posts, Chongqing University of Posts and Telecommunications, Chongqing, China, ifeng021@gmail.com
[3] School of Modern Posts, Chongqing University of Posts and Telecommunications, Chongqing, China, 164456936@qq.com

Keywords: carbon emissions; travel time reliability; Monte Carlo simulation; degradable network

Abstract - Transportation networks serve as critical hubs in city operations, facilitating the movement of people and goods. However, transportation networks are inherently susceptible to random events like weather or accident, which causes nodes or links within the network to deteriorate at varying degrees, ultimately resulting in degradable capacities. Capacity degradation due to deteriorated roads could increase congestion, and thus significantly influence travel time reliability and carbon emission. This study employs the Dirichlet distribution to model stochastic capacity degradation and introduces Monte Carlo simulation to simultaneously assess both travel time reliability and carbon emission. A numerical example indicates that as network degradation intensifies, travel time reliability (TTR) declines while carbon emissions increase, yet they exhibit distinct evolutionary patterns.

1. Introduction

The transportation network is a vital infrastructure that ensures the normal movement of people and logistics across different locations, thereby playing an indispensable role in the normal functioning of the economy and society [1]. However, as urban areas continue to expand, the negative externalities associated with transportation networks have become increasingly pronounced, including traffic congestion, air pollution, and public health risks. Furthermore, both natural and human factors, such as adverse weather conditions, traffic accidents, and mass gatherings, can disrupt the normal operation of transportation systems, leading to reduced network efficiency and resulting in traffic congestion. Traffic congestion, on one hand, leads to unreliable travel conditions, and on the other, significantly increases vehicle emissions. Therefore, enhancing the reliability of transportation networks and reducing transportation-related carbon emissions have long been key priorities in transportation system planning.

The existing research on transportation network reliability has primarily focused on three aspects: connectivity reliability, travel time reliability and capacity reliability. Among these, travel time reliability (TTR) is the most intuitive and easily understood by both network users and service providers. It serves as a key indicator of transportation network performance and service quality, defined as the probability of completing a trip within the specified time [2]. TTR has a significant impact on all stakeholders, including users, service providers, planners, and managers [3]. However, focusing solely on TTR cannot provide a comprehensive assessment of the performance of a transportation network.

The transport sector accounts for more than one third of total carbon emissions [4], which play a vital role in emission reduction. Numeral studies have focused extensively on the calculation of transportation carbon emissions, as well as on identifying the key factors that influence these emissions [5-8], which is crucial for developing effective mitigation strategies. In terms of theoretical modelling, Yin et al [9] addressed the issue of internalizing traffic emission externalities in road networks with fixed traffic demand. They provided an upper bound on the potential reduction in traffic emissions achievable through any charging scheme and proposed methods for computing charges that balance the conflicting objectives of alleviating congestion and reducing emissions. Building on this work, Nagurney et al [10] introduced environmental impact assessment indices and environmental link importance indicators in degradable transportation networks. A key limitation of these studies is their assumption of uniform network degradation rates, which does not reflect reality, as the degradation of road networks is random in practice.

Transportation reliability and carbon emissions are two important metrics in urban transportation systems. The highlight of this paper is the presentation of a Monte Carlo simulation-based method for simultaneously calculating carbon emissions indicator and TTR in degradable network. Specifically, the method employs a particular distribution as a tool to represent the stochastic degradation of road networks. A new carbon emission stability indicator is proposed to reflect the carbon emission status of the network. The proposed method is validated through numerical experiments, revealing that carbon emissions indicator and TTR all decreases during network degradation.

The remainder of this article is structured as follows. In section 2, the modeling process for the degraded network is detailed. Section 3 presents a numerical example to illustrate the application of the proposed methodology and includes a sensitivity analysis of key parameters. Finally, the article concludes with a concise summary.

2. Model construction

2.1. Multi-state transportation network

Some scholars consider a transportation system as a degradable transportation system (DTS) [11] or a degradable transportation network (DTN) [12-14]. In such systems, the performance of the network and the state of its components (e.g., link capacity) can deteriorate due to various events, including adverse weather conditions, traffic accidents, and roadworks. Nicholson et al [15] categorize these causes into two main factors: supply-side and demand-side. Furthermore, a network in which each link has multiple possible capacity levels is referred to as a multi-state flow network [16]. Given that each road in a degradable transportation network may experience multiple capacity states due to above random events, a DTS is essentially a multi-state network or multi-state transportation network. Therefore, the multi-state network model is one of the effective tools for analyzing degradable transportation networks.

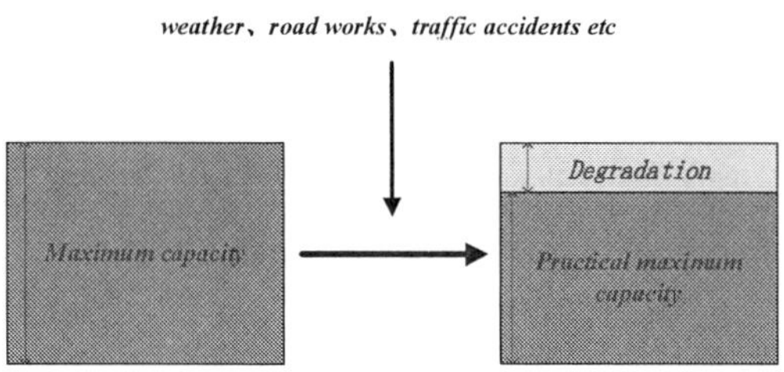

Figure 1. Changes in network capacity

We assume that flow conservation holds for each origin-destination (O-D) pair and across links and paths. Additionally, we assume that the total cost of using a path is the sum of the costs of the individual links that constitute it. Furthermore, the cost functions for links are assumed to be continuous and increase monotonically. We focus on the transportation network in the short term, where travel demand is considered fixed.

Let G (N, A, C) denote a multi-state transportation network with n nodes and m links, where $N=\{1, 2,..., n\}$ is the set of nodes, $A=\{e_1, e_2,..., e_m\}$ is the set of links, $C= (C_1, C_2,..., C_m)$ is the set of maximum capacity of each link, $F = (f_1, f_2,..., f_m)$ represents flow vector of links. As transportation networks are prone to degradation caused by random factors, the practical capacity of each link is often reduced below its maximum capacity. Consequently, transportation networks can be characterized as multi-state flow networks. Let d_i be the degraded capacity of link e_j, then $D = (d_1, d_2, ..., d_m)$ denotes the vector of degraded capacities of all links. Let $U = (u_1, u_2, ..., u_m)$ denotes the vector of reserve capacity of each links, where

$$u_i = C_i - d_i, \text{ for } i = 1, 2, ..., m \tag{1}$$

2.2. UE model

In order to simulate traffic flow distribution patterns on real road networks, the help of traffic assignment model is needed. We use the most classic user equilibrium (UE) model. The UE model follows Wardrop's first principle of equilibrium [17]. That is, when the network reaches equilibrium, the travel time of all used paths are equal and minimized. Its specific form is as follows

$$\text{Min} \sum_{i\in A} \int_0^{f_i} t_i(w)\,dw \tag{2a}$$

Subject to

$$\sum_{k\in K_{rs}} f_k^{rs} = q_{rs}, \forall r\in R, s\in S \tag{2b}$$

$$f_i = \sum_{r\in R}\sum_{s\in S}\sum_{k\in K_{rs}} f_k^{rs}\delta_{ik}^{rs}, \forall i\in A \tag{2c}$$

$$f_k^{rs} \geq 0, \forall k\in K_{rs}, r\in R, s\in S \tag{2d}$$

where $t_i(w)$ is the link cost function; f_k^{rs} is the flow on the k-th path between OD pair r-s; q_{rs} is the demand of OD pair r-s; $\delta_{ik}^{rs}=1$ if path k uses link i, 0 otherwise.

Once the traffic flow across the network is determined, the travel time of each link can be calculated. The link travel time is represented using a modified BPR [18] function to model the link cost. That is,

$$t_i(f_i) = t_{i0}[1 + \alpha\,(\frac{f_i}{u_i})^{\beta}] \tag{3}$$

where t_{i0} is the free travel time of link i; f_i denotes the traffic flow of link i; u_i denotes the practical capacity of link i; α and β are the parameters of the model, taken as 0.15 and 4, respectively.

2.3. Description of link capacity degradation

Early studies on network degradation only considered extreme scenarios, it only allows for two operating states: operating at full capacity or complete failure with zero capacity. This type of degradation modeling may be appropriate for abnormal situations, such as earthquakes. Moreover, this situation also contradicts the characteristics of multi-state transportation networks. This binary-state approach fails to account for everyday scenarios in which links typically operate at varying levels between full capacity and complete failure.

Note that several existing studies have also addressed the degradation of transportation networks during daily operations. Nagurney et al [10][19] assume that the link capacities are degraded by a uniform proportion. That is, given a ratio γ ($\gamma \in (0, 1]$), the new capacities of all links are γC (i.e. all links follow the same degree of capacity degradation). If we use $(1 - \eta)$ to denote γ, the new capacities of the link are represented as $(1 - \eta)C$. A metric is defined to represent the total degradation of the network, which is calculated by summing the degradation of each link. The specific form is as follows:

$$TD_\eta = \eta \sum_{i=1}^{m} C_i \tag{4}$$

where TD_η denotes the total degradation of the network.

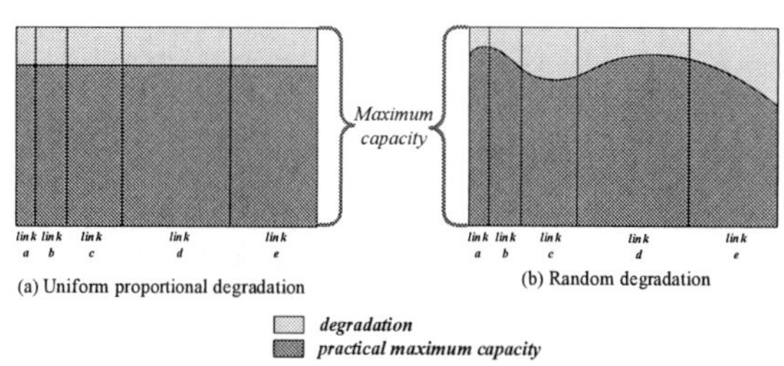

Figure 2. A graphical comparison of two degradation models

However, this scenario does not accurately reflect practical conditions because links are subject to different degrees of degradation due to certain factors. The figure below illustrates the degradation of the road network in real-world scenarios.

To accurately represent the randomness of network degradation, we can use a random variable to depict the degree of capacity degradation of each link. After calculating the total degradation TD_η of the network, the Dirichlet distribution is used to randomly distribute these degradation levels across the links, effectively simulating the degradation patterns in real-world transportation networks.

The Dirichlet distribution is a multivariate probability distribution widely applied in fields such as Bayesian statistics, machine learning, and bioinformatics. It serves as a generalization of the Beta distribution to multidimensional spaces. Suppose that the vector $X = (X_1, X_2, \ldots, X_n)$denotes an n-dimensional vector, if X obeys the Dirichlet distribution, its probability density function (PDF) can be expressed as:

$$f(x_1, x_2, \ldots, x_n; \alpha_1, \alpha_2, \ldots, \alpha_n) = \frac{1}{B(\alpha)} \prod_{i=1}^{n} x_i^{\alpha_i - 1} \tag{5}$$

where $\alpha = (\alpha_1, \alpha_2, \ldots, \alpha_n)$ is parameter vector and $\alpha_i > 0$, for $i = 1, 2, \ldots, n$; $B(\alpha)$ is a multivariate Beta function.

The specific form of the $B(\alpha)$ as follow:

$$B(\alpha) = \frac{\prod_{i=1}^{n} \Gamma(\alpha_i)}{\Gamma\left(\sum_{i=1}^{n} \alpha_i\right)} \tag{6}$$

where Γ is Gamma function.

Property 1： $\sum_{i=1}^{n} x_i = 1$ and $x_i \geq 0$, for $i = 1, 2, \ldots, n$.

Suppose there is already a set of intermediary vectors $x = (x_1, x_2, \ldots, x_m)$ and $\sum_{i=1}^{m} x_i$. We allocate the total degradation TD_η described in the previous section according to the corresponding proportions to get the new degradation for each link.

$$d_i = TD_\eta x_i, \text{ for } i = 1, 2, \ldots, m \tag{7}$$

It is essential to ensure that the degradation observed in the process remains within reasonable limits. Therefore, the following constraints apply.

$$0 \leq \frac{d_i}{C_i} \leq 1, \text{ for } i = 1, 2, \ldots, m \tag{8}$$

The above approach ensures that the total allocated degradation across all links is equal to TD_η. The relationship between the newly derived parameter and the original one can also be represented by an equation.

$$\sum_{i=1}^{m} d_i = TD_\eta \sum_{i=1}^{m} x_i = TD_\eta, \text{ for } i = 1, 2, \ldots, m \tag{9}$$

$$y_i = \frac{TD_\eta x_i}{C_i} = \frac{(\eta \sum_{i=1}^{m} C_i) x_i}{C_i}, \text{ for } i = 1, 2, \ldots, m \tag{10}$$

where y_i is a randomized degenerate parameter for each link.

2.4. Travel time reliability in a degradable transportation network

Asakura [20] and Chen [21] defined the TTR of a degraded network as the probability that the ratio of the OD travel time in the degraded network to that in the normal network is maintained within an acceptable level. This paper considers the second case as well, given that C and U represent the maximum state vector and the practical state vector, respectively, TTR can be expressed as the following formula:

$$R_{rs}(c) = P\left\{\frac{t_{rs}(U)}{t_{rs}(C)} \leq c\right\} \tag{11}$$

where $R_{rs}(c)$ is the TTR of the OD pair from r-s under the threshold c; $t_{rs}(C)$ and $t_{rs}(P)$ are the travel time between the OD pair from r-s before and after network degradation, respectively. The value of c serves as an input. This threshold value is typically specified by the decision-making body that invests in the network.

Chen et al [21] have given three possible metrics for calculating network reliability, minimum, average and weighted average, respectively. A transportation network is composed of multiple OD pairs, each with a specific traffic demand. Since OD pairs with higher traffic demand are more crucial to the overall network, this paper calculates the TTR of the entire network using a weighted average, as follows:

$$R_{wa} = \frac{\sum_{r \in R} \sum_{s \in S} R_{rs}(c) \cdot d^{rs}}{\sum_{r \in R} \sum_{s \in S} d^{rs}} \tag{12}$$

where R_{wa} is theTTR of the whole network; d^{rs} is the traffic demand between the OD pair r-s.

2.5. A new carbon emission indicator

It is well known that carbon monoxide is a highly toxic gas that poses significant risks to human health. In this paper, CO emissions are used as a representation of carbon emissions. According to Yin et al [9], carbon emissions can be calculated according to the following equation:

$$e_i(f_i) = 0.2038 \times t_i(f_i) \times e^{0.7962 \times \left(\frac{l_i}{t_i(f_i)}\right)} \tag{13}$$

$$E_i(f_i) = e_i(f_i) \times f_i \tag{14}$$

where l_i is the length (in kilometers) of link i; $t_i(f_i)$ is the link cost function, i.e., travel time; $E_i(f_i)$ is the total emissions of link i.

Using the above equation, the total CO emissions of the road network can be obtained by summing the CO emissions from each individual road:

$$TE = \sum_{i=1}^{m} E_i(f_i) \tag{15}$$

To unify the dimensional consistency with TTR and improve the computational accuracy, we adopted a probabilistic indicator similar to TTR to represent the carbon emission service level of the network. We call it the carbon emission stability index (CESI). Its specific definition is the probability that the ratio of total carbon emissions before and after network degradation satisfies a certain service level. The closer the value of this indicator is to 1, the more stable the carbon emission level of the network; conversely, a lower value indicates a more deteriorated carbon emission condition. That is,

$$CESI = \mathrm{P}\left\{\frac{TE_\eta}{TE_0} \leq s\right\} \tag{16}$$

where TE_0 and TE_ηdenote the total carbon emissions before and after network degradation, respectively; s is the given threshold value.

3. Algorithm

This study employs a Monte Carlo simulation-based approach to effectively model the operational conditions of real-world networks. This method not only eliminates the complexities of data collection and streamlines the research process but also enhances the estimation of TTR. Furthermore, the Monte Carlo simulation integrates carbon emission calculations with network reliability assessments, providing a robust tool for comprehensive performance analysis of transportation networks. The specific steps are as follows:

Step1. Predefine the variable η. Set the number of samples to i = 10,000 and define the link characteristics. Initialize counters k, m and j to 0.

Step2. Calculate the travel time for each OD pairs r-s $t_{rs}(C), \forall r \in R, s \in S$ and TE_0 before degradation.

Step3. Generate a set of Dirichlet distributions sample. Compute the total degradation TD_η using Eq. (4). Subsequently, determine the stochastic degradation vector $D = (d_1, d_2, \ldots, d_m)$ based on Eq. (7) and Eq. (8), utilizing the calculated TD_η as input. Finally, calculate the reserve capacity vector $U = (u_1, u_2, \ldots, u_m)$ using Eq. (1).

Step4. Solve the UE model with the Method of Successive Average (MSA) to get the flow of each link, i.e. $F = (f_1, f_2, \ldots, f_m)$.

Step5. Calculate the carbon emissions TE_η and path travel time $t_{rs}(U)$ under this flow allocation. If $\frac{t_{rs}(U)}{t_{rs}(C)} \leq c$, let $m = m + 1$.If $\frac{TE_\eta}{TE_0} \leq s$, let $j = j + 1$. If $k \leq i$, let $k = k + 1$ and return to the Step3. Otherwise, proceed to the next step.

Step6. The calculated values of CESI and $R_{rs}(c)$ under current degradation are m/i and j/i, respectively. Then the reliability of the whole network is obtained by Eq. (12).

Through the above steps, the values of carbon emissions and time reliability corresponding to different values of the variable η can be obtained. A clear flow chart of the calculation is given below.

4. Numerical examples

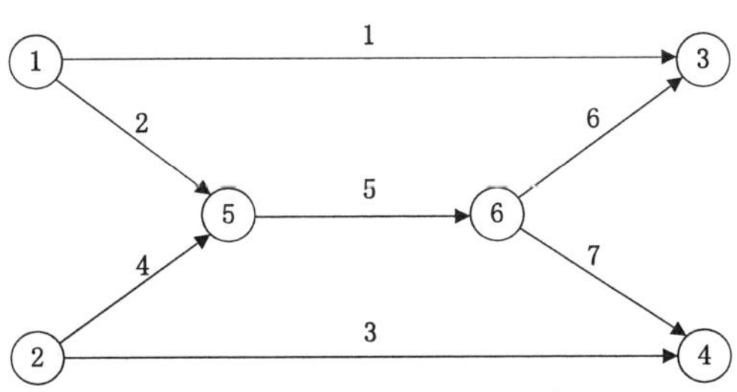

Figure 3. Test network

The test network, depicted in Figure 3, comprises six nodes, seven links, and four origin-destination (O-D) pairs. The fixed traffic demand for the O-D pairs (1-3), (1-4), (2-3), and (2-4) is 1000, 400, 400, and 1000 units, respectively. Table 1 summarizes the characteristics of the network links. Link degradation is modeled using a predefined probability distribution, where the c and s are defined as 1.08 and 1.05, respectively. The parameters of the Dirichlet distribution are set to $\alpha = (1, 1, 1, 1, 1, 1, 1)$. The values of the degradation variable η range from 10% to 50%, increasing in steps of 5%.The calculations are performed using the method introduced in Section 3.

Table 1. Link characteristics for the test network

Link	1	2	3	4	5	6	7
l_a	16	6	16	6	4	7	7
t_{a0}	16	6	16	6	4	7	7
C_a	1500	1200	1500	1200	2000	1300	1300

Table 2 presents the values of TTR and CESI throughout the degradation process, while Figure 6 visually illustrates their respective trends. It is evident that both TTR and CESI generally decline as degradation progresses, indicating that the deterioration of the transportation network reduces service levels, leading to decreased reliability and increased carbon emissions. This finding aligns with intuitive expectations, as degraded systems typically experience simultaneous declines in performance and environmental quality. However, notable differences exist between TTR and CESI. Specifically, TTR exhibits an almost linear decline, whereas CESI initially decreases at a slower rate, accelerates as degradation intensifies, and eventually stabilizes. This nonlinear pattern suggests that carbon emissions are relatively insensitive to minor degradation but become more pronounced once the network reaches a critical threshold. In real-world scenarios, road degradation often prompts travelers to adjust their routes to minimize travel time. However, the rerouted paths are typically longer than the original ones, reducing the probability of reaching the destination within the expected time and leading to higher carbon emissions due to increased travel distances. Consequently, as network degradation progresses, both TTR and environmental impact deteriorate, underscoring the importance of proactive interventions to mitigate adverse effects on transportation efficiency and sustainability.

Table 2. Results of the test network

η	**TTR**	**CESI**
0.10	0.9754	1
0.15	0.9026	0.9963
0.20	0.8078	0.9571
0.25	0.7006	0.8276
0.30	0.5775	0.5975
0.35	0.4539	0.3541
0.40	0.3551	0.1667
0.45	0.2742	0.0568
0.50	0.2090	0.0143

These findings highlight the complex relationship between network degradation, reliability, and environmental impacts. Specifically, the nonlinear behavior of CESI suggests that carbon emissions may be less sensitive to lower levels of degradation, but as the network approaches a critical threshold, emissions become more significant. This has important implications for transportation network management. Identifying the degree of degradation is crucial, as targeted interventions at specific levels can prevent abrupt performance declines and minimize environmental impacts. By understanding these dynamic changes, policymakers and urban planners can better prioritize maintenance efforts and optimize interventions to ensure both operational efficiency and sustainability in the long term.

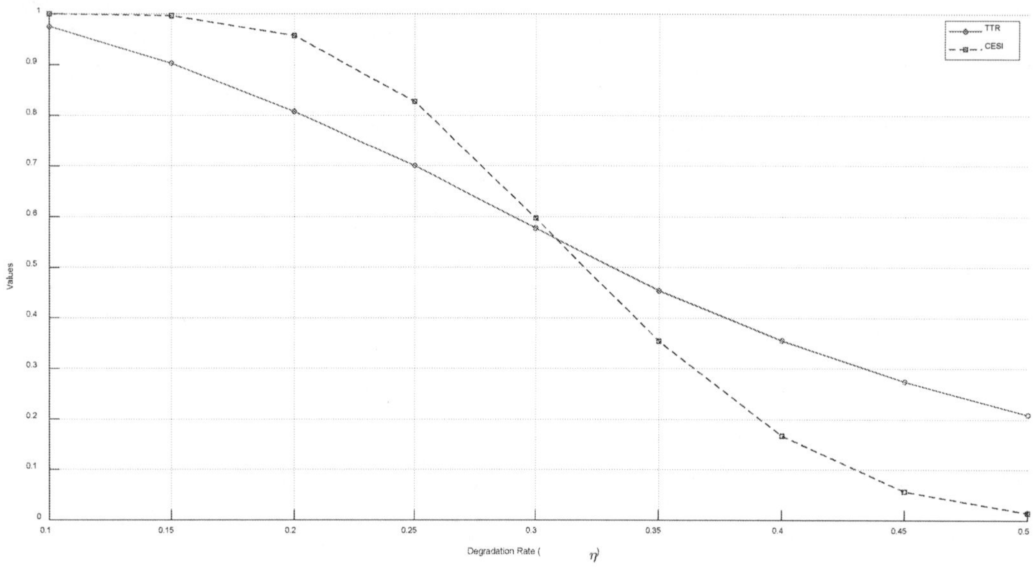

Figure 4. Trends of TTR and CESI

5. Conclusion

Reliability and carbon emissions have long been key concerns in the transportation sector. Since the former is a probabilistic measure and the latter is a specific quantitative value, few studies have analyzed both concepts quantitatively in conjunction. Despite being two distinct concepts, they are both key elements of urban transportation systems. This paper presents a Monte Carlo-based simulation approach for simultaneously evaluating time reliability and carbon emissions. The model accounts for daily random fluctuations in traffic networks, i.e., degradable networks, and simulates the random degradation of road capacity using the Dirichlet distribution, rather than the uniform degradation model typically used in previous studies. This approach better aligns with actual traffic conditions. Through numerical experiments, we validate the feasibility of the method. Additionally, sensitivity analyses are conducted on several key variables. The novelty of this article mainly lies in two aspects. First, it provides valuable insights into exploring the relationship between reliability and carbon emissions in transportation networks. Second, it considers the stochastic degradation of link capacity, which better reflects actual traffic conditions.

6. Acknowledgement

7. References

[1] Nie YH, Li JP , Liu GY , Zhou P. "Cascading failure-based reliability assessment for post-seismic performance of highway bridge network", Reliability engineering & system safety, Vol. No. 238, 109457, Oct 2003.

[2] Asakura Y, M Kashiwadani. "Road network rebiability caused by daily fluctuation of traffic flow", Proceddings of the 19th Summer Annual Meeting in Brighton, Vol. No. 347, 73—84, 1991.

[3] Zang Z, Xu X, Qu K, Chen R, Chen, A. "Travel time reliability in transportation networks: A review of methodological developments" , Transportation Research Part C, Vol. No. 143, 103866, Oct 2022.

[4] International Energy Agency (IEA). Transport, Available online at: https://www.iea.org/energy-system/transport, 2024.

[5] Zhang N, Xiao W. "Dynamic total factor carbon emissions performance changes in the Chinese transportation industry", Applied Energy, Vol. No. 146, 409—420, May 2015.

[6] Xie R, Fang JY, Liu CJ. "The effects of transportation infrastructure on urban carbon emissions", Applied Energy, Vol. No. 196, 199—207, Jun 2017.

[7] Bai CQ, Zhou L, Xia ML, Feng C. "Analysis of the spatial association network structure of China's transportation carbon emissions and its driving factors", Journal of environmental management, Vol. No. 253, 109765, Jan 2020.

[8] Liu JM, Li JY, Chen Y, Lian S, Zeng JQ, Geng MS, ... Chen XQ. "Multi-scale urban passenger transportation CO2 emission calculation platform for smart mobility management", Applied Energy, Vol. No. 331, 120407, Feb 2023.

[9] Yin YF, Lawphongpanich S. "Internalizing emission externality on road networks", Transportation Research Part D, Vol. No.11, Issue. No. 4, 292—301, Jul 2006

[10] Nagurney A, Qiang Q, Nagurney LS. "Environmental impact assessment of transportation networks with degradable links in an era of climate change", International Journal of Sustainable Transportation, Vol. No.4, Issue. No. 3, 154—171, Jul 2010.

[11] Du ZP, Nicholoson A. "Degradable transportation systems: sensitivity and reliability analysis", Transportation Research Part B, Vol. No. 33, Issue. No. 3, 225—237, Jun 1997.

[12] Chen A, Yang C, Kongsomsaksakul S, Lee, M. "Network-based accessibility measures for vulnerability analysis of degradable transportation networks". Networks and Spatial Economics, Vol. No. 7, 241—256, Sep 2007.

[13] Liu BQ, Huang CC. "Multi-class time reliability-based congestion pricing model based on a degradable transportation nctwork", Applied Mathematical Modelling, Vol. No.40, Issue. No. 5—6, 3483-3497, Mar 2016.

[14] Zhao L, Guan HZ, Zhu JZ, Wei YF. "A reliability-based network equilibrium model with adaptive risk-averse travelers", Journal of Advanced Transportation, Vol. No. 2018, 5294185, Dec 2018.

[15] Nicholson A, Schmöcker JD, Bell MGH, Iida Y. "Assessing transport reliability: malevolence and user knowledge", In The network reliability of transport,Vol. No. 1, 1-22, May 2003.

[16] Niu YF. "Performance measure of a multi-state flow network under reliability and maintenance cost considerations", Reliability Engineering & System Safety, Vol. No. 215, 107822, Nov 2021.

[17] Wardrop JG. "Road paper. Some theoretical aspects of road traffic reselinkh", Proceedings of the Institution of Civil Engineers, Vol. No. 1, Issue. No.3, 325—378, 1952.

[18] Bureau of Public Roads. Traffic Assignment Manual. Washington, DC: U.S. Department of Commerce, 1964.

[19] Nagurney A, Qiang Q. "A relative total cost index for the evaluation of transportation network robustness in the presence of degradable links and alternative travel behavior", International Transaction in Operation Reselinkh ,Vol. No. 16, Issue. No. 1, 4967, Jan 2009.

[20] Asakura Y. "Reliability measures of an origin and destination pair in a deteriorated road network with variable flows", Selected Proceedings of the 4th EURO Transportation Meeting, 273—287, Jan 1999.

[21] Chen A, Yang H, Lo HK, Tang WH. "Capacity reliability of a road network : an assessment methodology and numerical results", Transportation Research Part B, Vol. No. 36, Issue. No. 3, 225—252, Mar 2002.

Hybrid Cumulative Backup Policies in Reliability Theory

Hongshuang Feng
Nanjing University of Aeronautics and Astronautics
Nanjing, China
fengshuang0518@163.com

Xufeng Zhao
Nanjing University of Aeronautics and Astronautics
Nanjing, China
zx.peak@outlook.com

Yilei Bu
Jiangsu Provincial Administration for Market Regulation Data Center
210036, Nanjing, China

Wendi Pang
Jiangsu Provincial Administration for Market Regulation Data Center
210036, Nanjin, China

Keywords: Cumulative backup, full backup, database failure, reliability theory.

Abstract - This paper addresses the operational dilemma faced by 24/7 transactional databases characterized by stochastic update-intensive workloads, where traditional pause-and-backup approaches often result in significant resource underutilization during peak periods. We propose two adaptive hybrid cumulative backup policies: 1) A time-triggered policy executing full backups at periodic intervals KT while performing cumulative backups immediately after each data update; 2) An event-driven policy initiating full backups after N data updates with intermediate cumulative backups. Through a stochastic cost-benefit framework incorporating reliability theory, we derive explicit formulations for expected cost rates that account for system downtime penalties, storage overhead, and recovery complexity. The optimization landscape is systematically explored, yielding closed-form solutions for optimal trigger thresholds K^*, K_F^*, and N_F^* that achieve Pareto efficiency between backup frequency and operational disruption. In addition, analytical derivations are rigorously validated through numerical simulations modeling.

1 Introduction

With the significant advancement of computer systems in today's highly data-driven society, database security has become a critical issue [1]. The rapid growth of data volume and the deep dependence of business on data have exposed databases to internal and external threats, including malicious attacks, data breaches, system failures, and human errors. These threats can result in severe economic losses and security risks. In this case, data backup has emerged as a critical policy, by copying data to other storage locations, data backup effectively guarantee the security of data and the continuity of business operations, ensuring the efficient and reliable operation of the system. Consequently, there is growing academic interest in the development of efficient and rational data backup policies [2, 3, 4, 5].

For instance, Qian applied the cumulative damage model in reliability theory to solve backup problems. Full backups were performed periodicly at time intervals of NT or when the total updated files exceeded a threshold level K, and cumulative backups were performed at periodic times of iT $(i = 1, 2, \cdots, N-1)$ [6]. Zhao extended these incremental backup policies by introducing failure-obvious computing, planning full backups either at time T or after N bulk-data updates [7]. Additionally, zhao proposed periodic and random backup policies, where the incremental backup is implemented randomly right after data updates in large volumes [8].

To the best of our knowledge, few works have addressed the periodic and random cumulative backup policies with periodic times KT and update number N. This scenario differs from traditional periodic backup policies, as it is inefficient to pause a running system for backups during times of heavy application activity. For a 24/7 database system, it is essential to implement backups promptly following substantial data updates. Accordingly, in this study, we propose a backup policy that is triggered immediately after significant updates, ensuring that the backup process captures the latest changes and preserves system integrity. Moreover, we aim to schedule these backups during non-peak periods to minimize the impact on system performance and user experience. By combining various backup policies, we have developed a flexible approach that strikes an effective balance between backup efficiency and recovery speed.

In this study, we focus on full backup and cumulative backup policies [9, 10]: Full backup, a basic and complete backup operation that copies all of the data since the last full backup. When recovery after database failure is required, data restoration needs only the last full backup. In contrast, a cumulative backup copies only the data updated since the most recent full or cumulative backup. While cumulative backups are more time-efficient than full backups, their recovery process is more complex, requiring the combination of the latest full backup and the most recent cumulative backups. We will demonstrate that a hybrid of full and cumulative backup policies can achieve a balance between backup efficiency, storage space utilization, and recovery speed, while ensuring data integrity and consistency.

The remainder of this paper is organized as follows: In Sect. 2, we firstly describe the stochastic processes of updates, failures, and give some assumptions of the costs involved in the data backup process. Sect. 3 develops a time-triggered optimization modeling where full backups are scheduled at deterministic intervals KT. Using stochastic calculus, we derive closed-form expressions for both total operational costs and normalized expected cost rates. Based on Sect. 3, Sect. 4 proposed an integrated models of the backup polices implemented at time KT or after N data updates, using the triggering approaches of which occurs first. Finally, conclusions are given in Sect. 5.

2 Assumptions

The following assumptions for data failure, cumulative backups, full backups, and recoveries are given:

(1) Data updates randomly at a renewal process according to an identical distribution $F(t)$ with a density function $f(t) \equiv \mathrm{d}F(t)/\mathrm{d}t$ and finite mean $1/\lambda \equiv \int_0^\infty \overline{F}(t)\mathrm{d}t$, where $\Phi(t) \equiv 1 - \Phi(t)$ for any function $\Phi(t)$.

(2) A volume W_j $(j = 1, 2, \cdots)$ of updated data due to the jth update has an identical distribution $G(x) \equiv \Pr\{W_j \le x\}$ with finite mean $1/\omega \equiv \int_0^\infty \overline{G}(x)\mathrm{d}x$.

(3) Database failure occurs randomly with a general distribution $D(t)$ with a density function $d(t) \equiv \mathrm{d}D(t)/\mathrm{d}t$, finite mean $1/\mu \equiv \int_0^\infty \overline{D}(t)\mathrm{d}t$ The failure rate $r(t) \equiv \mathrm{d}t/\overline{D}(t)$ is supposed to be increasing with t strictly to $r(\infty)$ that might be infinity.

(4) Suppose that an cumulative backup is conducted immediately right after data updating and a full backup is implemented when the database failure occurs.

(5) Suppose that c_F is the constant full backup cost, $c_B + c_0 x$ is the cumulative backup cost when a total volume x of data has been updated, $c_R + c_0 x$ is recovery cost for database failure when a total volume x of data has been updated. We denote that for $j = 1, 2, \cdots, N$ that

$$M_j \equiv \int_0^\infty (c_K + c_0 x)\mathrm{d}G^{(j)}(x) = c_B + \frac{jc_0}{\omega},$$

$$N_j \equiv \int_0^\infty (c_R + c_0 x)\mathrm{d}G^{(j)}(x) = c_R + \frac{jc_0}{\omega}.$$

3 Stand backup at time KT

We plan that a full backup is performed at periodic times KT $(K = 1, 2, \cdots, 0 < T < \infty)$. Then, the probability that a full backup is performed at planned time KT is

$$\overline{D}(KT)\sum_{j=0}^{\infty}[F^{(j)}(KT) - F^{(j+1)}(KT)] = \overline{D}(KT), \quad (1)$$

the probability that it is implemented at database failure is

$$\sum_{j=0}^{\infty}\int_0^{KT}[F^{(j)}(t) - F^{(j+1)}(t)]\mathrm{d}D(t) = D(KT), \quad (2)$$

where $F^{(j)}(t) \equiv \int_0^t F^{(j-1)}(t-u)\mathrm{d}F(u)$ $(j = 1, 2, \cdots)$ is the j-fold convolution of $F(t)$, and $F^{(0)}(t) \equiv 1$ for any $t \ge 0$. The mean time to full backup is

$$KT\overline{D}(KT) + \int_0^{KT} t\mathrm{d}D(t) = \int_0^{KT}\overline{D}(t)\mathrm{d}t. \quad (3)$$

Thus, the expected cost until full backup is

$$\begin{aligned}
&\sum_{j=0}^{\infty}\left\{c_F + \sum_{i=1}^{j} M_i + N_j\right\}\int_0^{KT}[F^{(j)}(t) - F^{(j+1)}(t)]\mathrm{d}D(t) \\
&+ \overline{D}(KT)\sum_{j=0}^{\infty}\left\{c_F + \sum_{i=1}^{j} M_i\right\}[F^{(j)}(KT) - F^{(j+1)}(KT)] \\
&= c_F + c_R D(KT) + \left(c_B + \frac{c_0}{\omega}\right)\int_0^{KT}\overline{D}(t)\mathrm{d}M_F(t) \\
&+ \frac{c_0}{\omega}\left[-\overline{D}(KT)M_F(KT) + \sum_{j=1}^{\infty} j\int_0^{KT}\overline{D}(t)\mathrm{d}F^{(j)}(t)\right], \\
&= c_F + c_R D(KT) + c_B\int_0^{KT}\overline{D}(t)\mathrm{d}M_F(t) \\
&+ \frac{c_0}{\omega}\left[\int_0^{KT} M_F(t)\mathrm{d}D(t) + \sum_{j=1}^{\infty} j\int_0^{KT}\overline{D}(t)\mathrm{d}F^{(j)}(t)\right],
\end{aligned} \quad (4)$$

where $M_F(t) \equiv \sum_{j=1}^{\infty} F^{(j)}(t)$. Therefore, the expected cost rate is

$$C(K) = \frac{c_F + c_R D(KT) + c_B\int_0^{KT}\overline{D}(t)\mathrm{d}M_F(t) + c_0/\omega[\int_0^{KT} M_F(t)\mathrm{d}D(t) + \sum_{j=1}^{\infty} j\int_0^{KT}\overline{D}(t)\mathrm{d}F^{(j)}(t)]}{\int_0^{KT}\overline{D}(t)\mathrm{d}t}. \quad (5)$$

When $F(t) = 1 - \mathrm{e}^{-\lambda t}$, (5) becomes

$$C(K) = \frac{c_F + c_R D(KT) + (\lambda c_0/\omega)[\int_0^{KT}\lambda t\overline{D}(t)\mathrm{d}t + \int_0^{KT} t\mathrm{d}D(t)]}{\int_0^{KT}\overline{D}(t)\mathrm{d}t} + \lambda(c_B + c_0/\omega). \quad (6)$$

We find optimum K^* to minimize $C(K)$ in (6). Forming the equality $C(K+1)-C(K)\geq 0$,

$$Q(K)\int_0^{KT}\overline{D}(t)\mathrm{d}t - c_R D(KT) - \frac{\lambda c_0}{\omega}\left[\int_0^{KT}\lambda t\overline{D}(t)\mathrm{d}t + \int_0^{KT} t\mathrm{d}D(t)\right] \geq c_F, \quad (7)$$

where

$$Q(K) \equiv \frac{(\lambda c_0/\omega)[\int_{KT}^{(K+1)T}\lambda t\overline{D}(t)\mathrm{d}t + \int_{KT}^{(K+1)T} t\mathrm{d}D(t)] + c_R[D((k+1)T)-D(KT)]}{\int_{KT}^{(K+1)T}\overline{D}(t)\mathrm{d}t}.$$

In partiular, when $D(t)=1-\mathrm{e}^{-\mu t}$, (7) becomes,

$$q(K)[1-\mathrm{e}^{-\mu KT}] - [1-\mathrm{e}^{-\mu KT}(1+\mu KT)] \geq \frac{c_F}{c_0/\omega}, \quad (8)$$

where

$$q(K) \equiv \frac{1+\mu KT - \mathrm{e}^{-\mu T}[1+\mu(K+1)T]}{1-\mathrm{e}^{-\mu T}}.$$

Therefore, if $q(K)$ increases strictly with K to ∞, then the left-hand side of (8) increases strictly with K to ∞, and there exists a finite and unique minimum K^* ($1\leq K^*<\infty$) which satisfies (8).

When $D(t)=1-\mathrm{e}^{-t/100}$, $F(t)=1-\mathrm{e}^{-t}$, $c_B=1$, $c_R=1$ and $T=0.5$, Table 1 presents optimum K^* and its cost rate $C(K^*)$ in (5).

Table 1: Optimal K^* and $C(K^*)$.

$\frac{c_0}{\omega}$	$c_F=5$		$c_F=10$	
	K^*	$C(K^*)$	K^*	$C(K^*)$
0.1	20	2.132	29	2.565
0.2	14	2.648	20	3.254
0.3	12	3.068	17	3.807
0.4	10	3.437	14	4.287
0.5	9	3.774	13	4.722
0.6	8	4.089	12	5.127
0.7	8	4.390	11	5.505
0.8	7	4.669	10	5.864
0.9	7	4.945	9	6.213
1.0	6	5.209	9	6.538

4 First backup policies

We plan that a full backup is implemented at time KT ($K=1,2,\cdots,0<T\leq\infty$), or at a number N ($N=1,2,\cdots$) of data updates, whichever takes place first. Then, the probability that a full backup is implemented at time KT is

$$\overline{D}(KT)\sum_{j=0}^{N-1}[F^{(j)}(KT)-F^{(j+1)}(KT)] = \overline{D}(KT)[1-F^{(N)}(KT)], \quad (9)$$

the probability that a full backup is implemented at update N is

$$\int_0^{KT}\overline{D}(t)\mathrm{d}F^{(N)}(t), \quad (10)$$

the probability that it is implemented at database failure is

$$\int_0^{KT}[1-F^{(N)}(t)]\mathrm{d}D(t). \quad (11)$$

The mean time to full backup is

$$KT\overline{D}(KT)[1-F^{(N)}(KT)] + \int_0^{KT} t\overline{D}(t)\mathrm{d}F^{(N)}(t) + \int_0^{KT} t[1-F^{(N)}(t)]\mathrm{d}D(t) = \int_0^{KT}\overline{D}(t)[1-F^{(N)}(t)]\mathrm{d}t. \quad (12)$$

The expected cost until full backup is

$$\overline{D}(KT)\sum_{j=0}^{N-1}(c_F+\sum_{i=1}^{j}M_i)[F^{(j)}(KT)-F^{(j+1)}(KT)] + (c_F+\sum_{i=1}^{N}M_i)\int_0^{KT}\overline{D}(t)\mathrm{d}F^{(N)}(t) + \sum_{j=0}^{N-1}(c_F+\sum_{i=1}^{j}M_i+N_j)\int_0^{KT}[F^{(j)}(t)-F^{(j+1)}(t)]\mathrm{d}D(t)$$
$$= c_F + \sum_{j=1}^{N}(c_B+jc_0/\omega)\int_0^{KT}\overline{D}(t)\mathrm{d}F^{(j)}(t) + \sum_{j=0}^{N-1}(c_R+jc_0/\omega)\int_0^{KT}[F^{(j)}(t)-F^{(j+1)}(t)]\mathrm{d}D(t). \quad (13)$$

Therefore, the expected cost rate is

$$C(K,N) = \frac{c_F+\sum_{j=1}^{N}(c_B+jc_0/\omega)\int_0^{KT}\overline{D}(t)\mathrm{d}F^{(j)}(t) + \sum_{j=0}^{N-1}(c_R+jc_0/\omega)\int_0^{KT}[F^{(j)}(t)-F^{(j+1)}(t)]\mathrm{d}D(t)}{\int_0^{KT}\overline{D}(t)[1-F^{(N)}(t)]\mathrm{d}t}. \quad (14)$$

We find optimum K_F^* and N_F^* to minimize $C(K,N)$. For given N, Forming the inequality $C(K+1,N)-$

$C(K,N) \geq 0$,

$$Q(K,N)\int_0^{KT}\overline{D}(t)[1-F^{(N)}(t)]\mathrm{d}t - \sum_{j=1}^{N}(c_B+jc_0/\omega)\int_0^{KT}\overline{D}(t)\mathrm{d}F^{(j)}(t) - \sum_{j=0}^{N-1}(c_R+jc_0/\omega)\int_0^{KT}[F^{(j)}(t)-F^{(j+1)}(t)]\mathrm{d}D(t) \geq c_F, \tag{15}$$

where

$$Q(K,N) \equiv \frac{\sum_{j=1}^{N}(c_B+jc_0/\omega)\int_{KT}^{(K+1)T}\overline{D}(t)\mathrm{d}F^{(j)}(t) + \sum_{j=0}^{N-1}(c_R+jc_0/\omega)\int_{KT}^{(K+1)T}[F^{(j)}(t)-F^{(j+1)}(t)]\mathrm{d}D(t)}{\int_{KT}^{(K+1)T}\overline{D}(t)[1-F^{(N)}(t)]\mathrm{d}t}.$$

Furthermore, forming the inequality $C(K-1,N) - C(K,N) < 0$,

$$Q(K-1,N)\int_0^{KT}\overline{D}(t)[1-F^{(N)}(t)]\mathrm{d}t - \sum_{j=1}^{N}(c_B+jc_0/\omega)\int_0^{KT}\overline{D}(t)\mathrm{d}F^{(j)}(t) - \sum_{j=0}^{N-1}(c_R+jc_0/\omega)\int_0^{KT}[F^{(j)}(t)-F^{(j+1)}(t)]\mathrm{d}D(t) < c_F, \tag{16}$$

Forming the inequality $C(K,N+1) - C(K,N) \geq 0$,

$$H(K,N)\int_0^{KT}\overline{D}(t)[1-F^{(N)}(t)]\mathrm{d}t - \sum_{j=1}^{N}(c_B+jc_0/\omega)\int_0^{KT}\overline{D}(t)\mathrm{d}F^{(j)}(t) - \sum_{j=0}^{N-1}(c_R+jc_0/\omega)\int_0^{KT}[F^{(j)}(t)-F^{(j+1)}(t)]\mathrm{d}D(t) \geq c_F, \tag{17}$$

where

$$H(K,N) \equiv \frac{[c_B+(N+1)c_0/\omega]\int_0^{KT}\overline{D}(t)\mathrm{d}F^{(N+1)}(t) + (c_R+Nc_0/\omega)\int_0^{KT}[F^{(N)}(t)-F^{(N+1)}(t)]\mathrm{d}D(t)}{\int_0^{KT}\overline{D}(t)[F^{(N)}(t)-F^{(N+1)}(t)]\mathrm{d}t}.$$

In order to find (K_F^*, N_F^*), substituting (16) for (17),

$$H(K,N) > Q(K-1,N), \tag{18}$$

which does not hold for any K, i.e., $K_F^* = \infty$. Thus, optimum polies to minimize $C(K,N)$ is $(K_F^* = \infty, N_F^* = N^*)$, where N^* is given in [8].

In particular, when $F(t) = 1-\mathrm{e}^{-\lambda t}$, $D(t) = 1-\mathrm{e}^{-\mu t}$, (15) becomes

$$q(K,N)\sum_{j=0}^{N-1}\int_0^{KT}[(\lambda t)^j/j!]\mathrm{e}^{-(\lambda+\mu)t}\mathrm{d}t - \sum_{j=0}^{N-1}(j+1)\int_0^{KT}\lambda\mathrm{e}^{-(\lambda+\mu)t}[(\lambda t)^j/j!]\mathrm{d}t - \sum_{j=0}^{N-1}j\int_0^{KT}\mu\mathrm{e}^{-(\lambda+\mu)t}[(\lambda t)^j/j!]\mathrm{d}t \geq \frac{c_F}{c_0/\omega}, \tag{19}$$

where

$$q(K,N) \equiv \frac{\sum_{j=0}^{N-1}(j+1)\int_{KT}^{(K+1)T}\lambda\mathrm{e}^{-(\lambda+\mu)t}[(\lambda t)^j/j!]\mathrm{d}t + \sum_{j=0}^{N-1}j\int_{KT}^{(K+1)T}\mu\mathrm{e}^{-(\lambda+\mu)t}[(\lambda t)^j/j!]\mathrm{d}t}{\sum_{j=0}^{N-1}\int_{KT}^{(K+1)T}[(\lambda t)^j/j!]\mathrm{e}^{-(\lambda+\mu)t}\mathrm{d}t}.$$

(17) becomes

$$h(K,N)\sum_{j=0}^{N-1}\int_0^{KT}\mathrm{e}^{-(\lambda+\mu)t}[(\lambda t)^j/j!]\mathrm{d}t - \sum_{j=0}^{N-1}(j+1)\int_0^{KT}\lambda\mathrm{e}^{-(\lambda+\mu)t}[(\lambda t)^j/j!]\mathrm{d}t - \sum_{j=0}^{N-1}j\int_0^{KT}\mu\mathrm{e}^{-(\lambda+\mu)t}[(\lambda t)^j/j!]\mathrm{d}t > \frac{c_F}{c_0/\omega}, \tag{20}$$

where

$$h(K,N) \equiv \frac{(N+1)\int_0^{KT}\lambda\mathrm{e}^{-(\lambda+\mu)t}[(\lambda t)^N/N!]\mathrm{d}t \; N\int_0^{KT}\mu\mathrm{e}^{-(\lambda+\mu)t}[(\lambda t)^N/N!]\mathrm{d}t}{\int_0^{KT}[(\lambda t)^N/N!]\mathrm{e}^{-(\lambda+\mu)t}\mathrm{d}t\mathrm{d}t}.$$

When $D(t) = 1-\mathrm{e}^{-t/100}$, $F(t) = 1-\mathrm{e}^{-t}$, $c_B = 1$, $c_R = 1$, $c_F = 5$ and $T = 0.5$, Table 2 presents optimum K_F^* and its cost rate $C(K_F^*, N)$.

5 Conclusion

To ensure data integrity during backups while minimizing the impact on system performance, this paper has proposed periodic and random backup policies, where the cumulative backup is implemented randomly right after data updates in large volumes, and the full backup is performed at periodic times KT, or at a number N of data updates. Using the maintenance theory in reliability theory, we have obtained the expected cost rates of data backup and data recovery for cumulative backup. Optimum K^* for $C(K)$ and K_F^* N_F^* for $C(K,N)$ are obtained analytically and numerically. For future research, we will compare backup first policies with last policies, in which, a full backup is implemented at time

Table 2: Optimal K_F^* and $C(K_F^*, N)$ for given N.

$\frac{c_0}{\omega}$	$N=5$		$N=10$	
	K_F^*	$C(K_F^*, N)$	K_F^*	$C(K_F^*, N)$
0.1	∞	2.340	∞	2.084
0.2	∞	2.640	18	2.611
0.3	∞	2.940	12	3.049
0.4	∞	3.240	10	3.427
0.5	∞	3.540	9	3.767
0.6	∞	3.840	8	4.085
0.7	18	4.139	8	4.385
0.8	13	4.431	7	4.667
0.9	11	4.715	7	4.943
1.0	9	4.990	6	5.208

Table 3: Optimal N_F^* and $C(K, N_F^*)$ for given K.

$\frac{c_0}{\omega}$	$K=5$		$K=10$	
	N_F^*	$C(K, N_F^*)$	N_F^*	$C(K, N_F^*)$
0.1	16	3.261	14	2.386
0.2	12	3.487	8	2.730
0.3	8	3.712	6	3.051
0.4	7	3.937	5	3.346
0.5	6	4.159	5	3.620
0.6	5	4.376	4	3.872
0.7	5	4.591	4	4.111
0.8	4	4.795	4	4.349
0.9	4	4.997	3	4.575
1.0	4	5.199	3	4.771

KT ($K = 1, 2, \cdots, 0 < T \leq \infty$), or at a number N ($N = 1, 2, \cdots$) of data updates, whichever takes place last. It is believed that system resources will be maximally utilized.

6 Acknowledgement

This work was supported by the National Natural Science Foundation of China under Grant 72471116, T2441003, National Foreign Expert Project under Grant H20240454, Aeronautical Science Foundation of China Aviation Academy under Grant 2022Z057052002, and Jiangsu Provincial Administration for Market Regulation Science and Technology Plan Project KJ2025044.

References

[1] Qian C , Huang Y , Zhao X ,et al. Optimal Backup Policies for a Database System with Periodic Incremental Backup, 2009.

[2] Levitin G, Xing L, Dai Y. Optimal Distribution of Nonperiodic Full and Incremental Backups; IEEE Transactions on Systems, Man, and Cybernetics: Systems, 2017.

[3] Nakamura S, Zhao X, Qian C. Optimum Backup Policies with Update Failure at Random Times; World Scientific Publishing Company, 2019.

[4] Qian C, Nakamura S, Nakagawa T. Optimal Backup Policies for a Database System with Incremental Backup; Electronics & Communications in Japan, 2010.

[5] Zhao X, Nakamura S , Nakagawa T. Constant and Random Full Backup Models with Incremental and Differential Backup Schemes; International journal of reliability, quality and safety engineering, 2017.

[6] Qian C, Pan Y, Nakagawa T. Optimal policies for a database system with two backup schemes; EDP Sciences, 36(3), 227-235 2002.

[7] Zhao X, Wang D, Mizutani S, et al. Data backup policies with failure-oblivious computing in reliability theory; Annals of Operations Research, 1-30, 2022.

[8] Zhao X, Bu Y, Pang W, et al. Periodic and random incremental backup policies in reliability theory; Software Quality Journal, 32(3), 1325-1340, 2024.

[9] Nakamura S, Qian C, Nakagawa T. Cumulative Backup Policies for Database Systems, 10.1142/10559, 235-254, 2017.

[10] Levitin G, Xing L, Dai Y. Optimal work distribution and backup frequency for two non-identical work sharing elements; Reliability Engineering & System Safety, 2018.

Enhancing Cloud Security via Joint Optimization of Backup and Mission Abort Policies

Cuicui Pei, Bosen Liu, Rongchi Sun, Qingan Qiu*
School of Management, Beijing Institute of Technology, Beijing 100081, China.
Email: qiu_qingan@bit.edu.cn

Keywords: Mission Abort Policy, Periodic Backup, Cyber-Physical Security, Mission Success Probability, Shock Process

Abstract -
In cyber-physical systems subject to cumulative random shocks, potential data loss pose critical operational risks. To enhance data security and mission resilience, this paper proposes a hybrid strategy that integrates periodic data backup with a shock-triggered mission abortion policy. The system gradually degrades under stochastic shock arrivals, modeled as a Poisson process, affecting data upload efficiency. A recursive probabilistic model is developed to derive the Mission Success Probability (MSP), incorporating both backup interval and abort threshold as decision variables. Simulation results reveal that properly balancing backup frequency and abort timing significantly improves system robustness under attack conditions. This study provides a novel framework for proactive data protection in mission-critical IoT applications.

1. Introduction

With the rapid advancement of Internet of Things (IoT) technologies, billions of terminal devices have been globally deployed across critical domains including industrial automation, intelligent transportation, telemedicine, and urban management. These devices continuously collect environmental parameters, equipment statuses, and user-generated data, facilitating centralized data management and intelligent analytics through cloud-server interactions. Within this framework, reliable data transmission and cloud backup mechanisms constitute fundamental prerequisites for ensuring IoT system stability and data integrity.

In practical implementations, while real-time data streaming remains the primary transmission mode, periodic backup protocols have been widely adopted to address energy efficiency, storage optimization, and security hierarchy requirements[1]. Specifically, terminal devices persistently upload acquired data to edge nodes or primary servers, while the system executes batch archiving or encrypted snapshots at predetermined intervals, storing processed datasets in trusted cloud platforms or distributed storage systems. This hybrid architecture, characterized by "continuous streaming and periodic backups," effectively balances communication resource utilization and computational overhead, while ensuring controllable and adjustable backup operations.

In mission-critical IoT ecosystems, domain-specific threats amplify systemic security challenges. For instance, telemedicine systems face acute risks from unauthorized interception of real-time electrocardiogram data streams, which could compromise patient confidentiality through privacy breaches. These application-layer vulnerabilities intersect with overarching cybersecurity threats in large-scale, high-concurrency IoT environments. While modern encryption protocols elevate attack barriers, adaptive hacking collectives persistently develop advanced penetration techniques capable of bypassing conventional safeguards. Particularly concerning are multi-vector attacks targeting communication infrastructure – service denials may cause irreversible data loss in unbacked systems, whereas channel hijacking exploits could paralyze entire networks through coordinated payload injections.

Traditional reactive defense strategies prove inadequate in such scenarios, necessitating the integration of proactive protection frameworks that enable pre-attack phase interventions[2]. Compared to traditional reactive mechanisms, proactive defense strategies offer a strategic edge by shifting the system's response point ahead of the actual breach, thereby enabling risk mitigation at significantly lower cost and with greater operational flexibility.

This background highlights the key challenge of developing an active risk control policy in a cyclical backup architecture. In particular, developing preventive defense strategies becomes critical when external attacks can be monitored. This study considers two risk control strategies that include periodic data backup and mission abort. In particular, the processed data are proactively backed up to ensure data safety. The core principle of strategically aborting ongoing data transfer missions when a certain number of external attacks are detected, thereby isolating potential intrusion paths and reinitializing encryption protocols before the channel is fully compromised, effectively reduces large-scale data leakage and systemic damage.

2. Literature review

The Mission Abort Policy (MAP) enables the initiation of a rescue procedure by interrupting an ongoing primary mission, which reduces the risk of system failure and significantly boosts operational safety. Decision-makers are enabled to avert catastrophic failures by leveraging real-time condition data, predictive analytics, and pre-established parameters, thanks to the explicit criteria set forth by MAPs for triggering early mission abortions.Decision-makers can setting appropriate thresholds to balance the relationship between mission continuation and abortion, thereby preventing the escalation of losses caused by delayed abort decision.

Since Myers [3] advanced the modeling of abort policies by studying parallel systems in 2009, MAP have been receiving increasing attention as an emerging proactive defense paradigm. Existing research not only focuses on risk assessment but also explores the optimal timing for abortion through optimization models and algorithms, thereby enhancing the overall performance of missions and systems[4].

In environments subject to external hazards, mission abort policies have been extensively explored through models designed for stochastic operating conditions, with shock models being among the most widely adopted approaches. These models typically consider decision variables such as the total number of accumulated shocks and the count of consecutive shocks [5, 6, 7, 8, 9]. For systems where safety is critical, environmental shocks originating from adverse external conditions represent a significant contributor to failure risk. Structural shock modeling has proven to be a powerful analytical tool for investigating failure behavior and assessing system reliability under uncertain conditions. To represent the inherent randomness in external environments, researchers often adopt stochastic processes to describe shock events, including homogeneous Poisson processes [10], non-homogeneous Poisson processes [11], and renewal processes [12]. These modeling approaches allow for a realistic depiction of the influence of external shocks on system performance and provide a solid theoretical basis for evaluating failure risks and informing mission abort decisions.

Beyond external shocks, the inherent degradation mechanisms of systems also play a critical role in explaining how performance evolves under varying workload demands and stress conditions as a mission progresses. The degradation level of a system is essential for assessing operational risks and informing mission abort decisions [13, 14, 15]. For systems experiencing performance deterioration, mission abort criteria often incorporate metrics such as the duration of the defective stage and the total mission time [16, 17].

As real-world systems and mission requirements grow increasingly complex, relying on a single decision variable may not adequately capture the dynamic nature of mission execution. Consequently, an increasing number of studies have integrated multiple decision variables into MAPs to enhance their effectiveness[18]. A lot of researchers [19, 20, 21] proposed dual-parameter policies that jointly consider system age or operational time and the number of shocks. Yang et al. [21] further extended this by incorporating system health and aging into the abort decision-making process. While most of these studies focus on single-attempt scenarios, numerous researchers[22] explored a more general framework allowing for multiple rescue attempts, where each attempt incrementally influences the overall probability of mission completion.

While a large body of literature has investigated data backup policies and MAP separately, a review of existing studies shows that no studies have investigated the joint optimization of data backup and MAP policies. Therefore, incorporating a mission abort policy as a proactive defense mechanism into a regular backup policy for IoT systems can interrupt vulnerable missions in a timely manner and mitigate potential threats before they escalate into critical failures.

To this end, this study proposes a joint optimization policy for "when to start backup" and "when to stop uploading" by introducing two key decision variables: periodic backup interval and abort threshold. In order to verify the effectiveness of the proposed joint optimization policy, the mission success probability (MSP) and system survival probability (SSP) are derived from the probabilistic model and the optimization algorithm, which are important indicators for evaluating the effectiveness of the policy.

3. Problem modeling

This study focuses on IoT systems subject to uncertain cyber-attacks during continuous data uploading missions. During mission execution, the system is required to complete the upload and backup of a specified data volume W , while maintaining adaptability and resilience against external attacks. The data uploading process operates continuously, yet its efficiency deteriorates progressively due to cumulative shock impacts. Specifically, each attack imposes a random impact on system performance. The shock arrival is modeled as a Poisson process with intensity λ, resulting in a decreasing upload efficiency g_k as the cumulative number of shocks k increases. This degradation effect prolongs the time required for mission completion and significantly increases the risk of failure under frequent attacks.

Once data is uploaded, it is backed up to the cloud in parallel with the uploading process. The system can thus be abstracted as a two-component structure. Unlike the uploading component, which is subject to performance degradation, the backup system operates at a constant rate and is unaffected by external shocks. According to the decision variable τ, the backup mechanism is triggered after each continuous upload interval, transferring uploaded but unbacked data to a secure cloud storage. Illustration of periodic backup activation triggered by consecutive shocks is given in Fig. 1, and periodic activation of backup states in combination with mission abort policies is shown in Fig. 2.

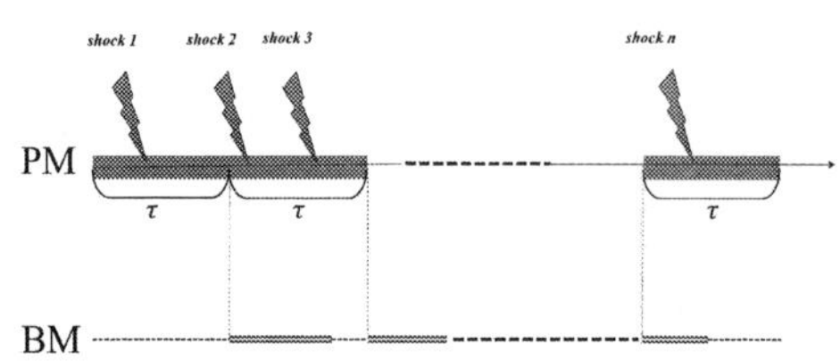

Figure 1: Illustration of periodic backup activation triggered by consecutive shocks.

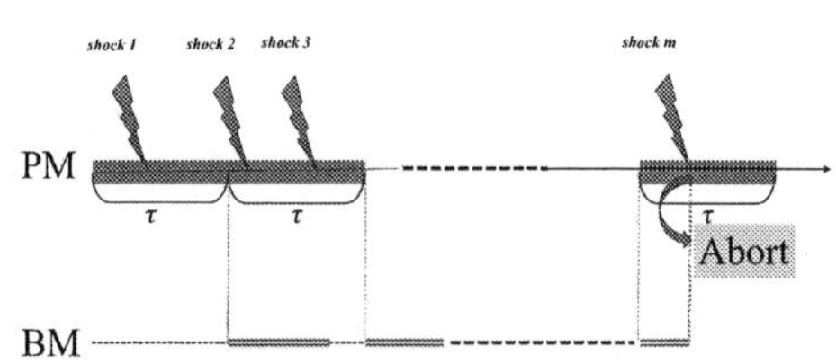

Figure 2: Periodic activation of backup states in combination with mission abort policies.

If the backup interval τ is set too small, the system will frequently switch to backup mode, potentially interrupting the uploading process and lowering overall efficiency. Conversely, a large τ may result in a prolonged duration during which uploaded data remains unprotected; if the system fails during this time, the unbacked data may be irrecoverably lost. Therefore, the optimal τ should be determined to strike a balance between upload continuity and timely data protection.

In addition to data backup decision, to mitigate catastrophic losses from attack escalation, the system incorporates a proactive termination mechanism. Once the cumulative number of shocks reaches a predefined threshold m, the mission is immediately aborted, and the system enters an emergency phase to back up any remaining unprotected data at a fixed rate. The threshold m represents a trade-off: a small m may lead to premature termination and a low success rate, while a large m risks exposing the system to fatal damage before protective measures are enacted. Thus, the determination of m must balance tolerance to shocks and timely response.

A mission is considered successful if the entire data volume is uploaded and backed up, and the number of shocks does not exceed threshold m. In summary, this study aims to jointly optimize the backup interval τ and the termination threshold m to maximize the MSP under stochastic shock environments. The appropriate configuration of these two parameters not only enhances data security and operational efficiency but also contributes to the overall robustness and stability of the system in the presence of unpredictable threats.

4. MSP derivation

Based on the established system framework, this section employs a recursive approach to derive key performance metrics, particularly the mission success probability. Let the system state upon the arrival of the k-th shock be denoted by the triplet$(w_k, v_k, s_k \mid i)$, where:s_k is the cumulative execution time;w_k is the total uploaded data;v_k is the total backed-up data. Let $f_k(w_k, v_k, s_k \mid i)$ be the joint probability density function that the system is in state $(w_k, v_k, s_k \mid i)$ at the k-th shock. The initial condition assumes zero upload, backup, and execution time:$f_0(w, v, s) = 1$.

Given that the shock arrivals follow a homogeneous Poisson process with rate λ, the inter-arrival time t between shocks is exponentially distributed: $p(t) = \lambda e^{-\lambda t}, \quad t \geq 0$.

During each interval τ, data uploading and backup are carried out concurrently. The upload rate is not constant, but gradually deteriorates as shocks accumulate, capturing the system's declining performance under sustained attacks. Specifically, upon the arrival of the k-th shock, the upload rate attenuates to g_k. The backup process runs continuously at a fixed rate *alpha*. All parameters are shown in Table. 1.

The model is categorized into the following four scenarios. As shown in Fig. 3, when the (k)th and $(k-1)$th shocks arrive, the primary system (PM) continuously uploads data while the backup system (BM) is in standby.Under this condition, the cumulative uploaded data increases proportionally to the upload rate and elapsed time, while the backup data remains constant. Accordingly, the state transitions follow:$w_k = w_{k-1} + g_{k-1} \cdot t, v_k = v_{k-1}$.

Table 1: Notation Summary

Symbol	Definition
W	Total volume of data to be uploaded and backed up
k	Cumulative number of shocks encountered
g_k	Upload efficiency after k shocks
α	Constant backup rate of the system
w_k	Cumulative uploaded data at the k-th shock
v_k	Cumulative backed-up data at the k-th shock
s_k	Elapsed system time at the k-th shock
τ	Backup interval period
m	Shock threshold for mission abortion
$S(m, \tau)$	Probability of successful mission

$$f_k(w, v, s \mid i) = \int_0^{\min\left(\frac{w}{g_{k-1}}, s\right)} f_{k-1}(w - g_{k-1} \cdot t, v, \; s - t \mid i) \, p(t) dt \quad (1)$$

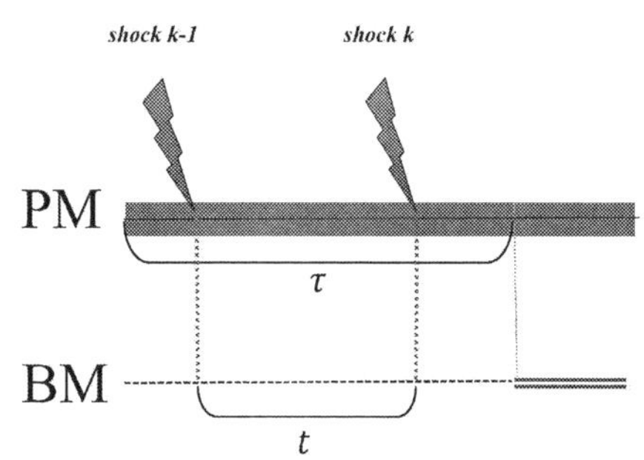

Figure 3: Backup activation within overlapping PM and BM phases.

When the kth shock arrives when both the primary system and the backup system are in operation. During a given interval of duration t, the system continues to operate by uploading and backing up data concurrently in Fig. 4. Accordingly, the state variables evolve as follows: the uploaded data increases by $g_{k-1} \cdot t$, the backed-up data increases by $\alpha \cdot t$, and the total mission time extends by t. That is,$w_k = w_{k-1} + g_{k-1} \cdot t, v_k = v_{k-1} + \alpha \cdot t$.

$$f_k(w, v, s \mid i) = \int_0^{\min\left(\frac{w}{g_{k-1}}, s\right)} f_{k-1}(w - g_{k-1} \cdot t, v - \alpha \cdot t, \; s - t \mid i) \, p(t) dt \quad (2)$$

During the interval between two consecutive shocks, the backup system transitions from a standby state to an active working state. Specifically, after the $(k-1)$th shock has occurred, the system enters a normal data processing phase where both uploading and backup operations proceed simultaneously in Fig. 5.

In this phase, the system state evolves as follows:$w_k = w_{k-1} + g_{k-1} \cdot t, v_k = v_{k-1} + \alpha \cdot [s - (i-1) \cdot \tau]$, where t denotes the

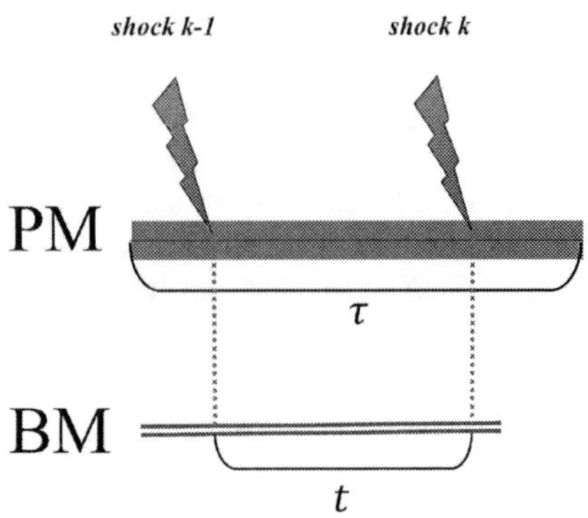

Figure 4: Backup Activation within Overlapping PM and BM Phases.

time interval between the $(k-1)$th and kth shocks, g_{k-1} is the degraded upload rate after experiencing $(k-1)$ shocks, and α is the fixed backup rate. The term $[s-(i-1)\cdot\tau]$ captures the duration during which the backup system remains active within the ith interval, starting from the transition point $(i-1)\cdot\tau$ when the system reactivates backup functionality.

$$f_k(w, v, s \mid i) = \int_0^{\min\left(\frac{w}{g_{k-1}}, s\right)} f_{k-1}(w - g_{k-1}\cdot t, v - \alpha\cdot[s-(i-1)\cdot\tau],\ s-t \mid i)\, p(t)dt \quad (3)$$

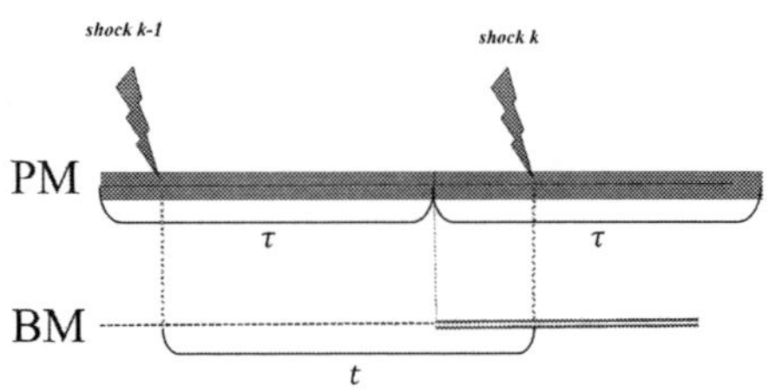

Figure 5: Backup system has a standby state to a working state beyond PM period.

In contrast, during certain intervals between consecutive shocks, the backup system may switch from an active working state to a standby mode, depending on the current mission status and elapsed time in Fig. 6. Specifically, if the backup activity terminates before the next shock arrives, the state transitions follow:$w_k = w_{k-1} + g_{k-1}\cdot t, v_k = v_{k-1} + \alpha\cdot[t+(i-1)\cdot\tau - s]$,where t is the inter-arrival time between the $(k-1)$th and kth shocks, and the expression $[t+(i-1)\cdot\tau - s]$ denotes the effective backup time before the system enters the standby state. This situation typically occurs when the current elapsed mission time s falls short of the expected activation time $(i-1)\cdot\tau + t$, causing the backup process to suspend prematurely.

$$f_k(w, v, s \mid i) = \int_0^{\min\left(\frac{w}{g_{k-1}}, s\right)} f_{k-1}(w - g_{k-1}\cdot t, v - \alpha\cdot[t+(i-1)\cdot\tau - s], s-t \mid i)\, p(t)dt \quad (4)$$

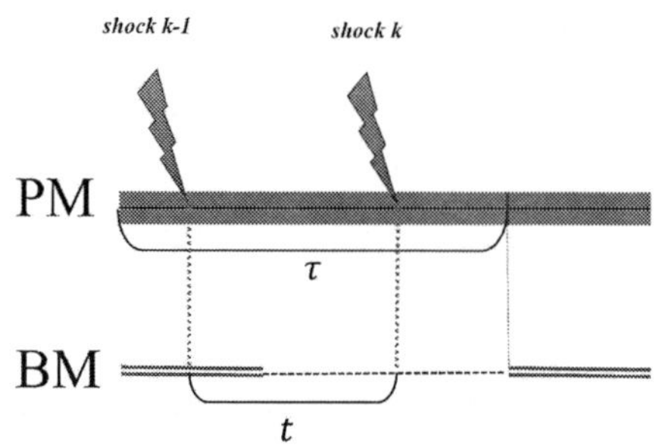

Figure 6: Backup system has active to a standby status beyond the PM period.

A mission is considered successful if, before the number of shocks exceeds the abort threshold m, both the uploaded and backed-up data reach the required volume W and the total time s_k remains. The success probability is computed by integrating $f_k(w_k, v_k, s_k \mid i)$ over all such admissible states.

$$S(m,\tau) = \sum_{k=0}^{m-1}\sum_{i=1}^{\infty}\int_0^{i\tau}\int_0^{W}\int_0^{w} f_k(w, v, s \mid i)dvdwds$$

This ensures that the mission is both completed and not aborted. The recursive computation terminates either upon successful data protection or when the abort threshold m is exceeded, marking mission failure.

5. Conclusion

This paper proposes a hybrid data protection policy that integrates continuous uploading with shock-triggered periodic backups, aiming to balance data security and task completion efficiency in uncertain and adversarial environments. A mathematical modeling framework is established to evaluate the MSP under varying abortion thresholds, enabling a quantitative trade-off between data preservation and task risk. The results demonstrate that a properly tuned abort strategy can significantly reduce expected data loss and overall system cost. The analysis characterizes complex interactions among shock frequency, backup effectiveness, and mission parameters that influence the optimal threshold policy.

Future research will further investigate detailed cost modeling—including abort, switching, and data loss costs—and develop adaptive algorithms to compare and optimize termination strategies under stochastic conditions. These efforts are expected to improve the robustness and real-world applicability of mission planning frameworks. In light of recent advances, where many researchers have developed dynamic optimization strategies[23, 24], future work will also consider integrating dynamic policies that can adaptively adjust abortion thresholds based on real-time system states and evolving threat levels. Additionally, it is worth exploring dynamic threshold policies that adjust in real time according to observed shock patterns, degradation trends, and task progress.

Acknowledgment

This research is supported by National Natural Science Foundation of China (72371030 and 72001026).

References

[1] Umesh Hodeghatta Rao and Umesha Nayak. Data backups and cloud computing. In *The InfoSec Handbook: An Introduction to Information Security*, pages 263–288. 2014.

[2] Jianhui Chen, Hongda Gao, and Chen Fang. Optimal two-stage abort policy considering performance-based missions. *Reliability Engineering System Safety*, 257:110803, 2025.

[3] A. Myers. Probability of loss assessment of critical k-out-of-n:g systems having a mission abort policy. *IEEE Transactions on Reliability*, 58(4):694–701, 2009.

[4] Qingan Qiu, Meng Kou, Ke Chen, Qiao Deng, Fengming Kang, and Cong Lin. Optimal stopping problems for mission oriented systems considering time redundancy. *Reliability Engineering & System Safety*, 205:107226, 2021.

[5] Gregory Levitin, Maxim Finkelstein, and Yuanshun Dai. Mission abort policy optimization for series systems with overlapping primary and rescue subsystems operating in a random environment. *Reliability Engineering & System Safety*, 193:106590, 2020.

[6] Xian Zhao, Xiaofei Chai, Jinglei Sun, and Qingan Qiu. Optimal bivariate mission abort policy for systems operate in random shock environment. *Reliability Engineering & System Safety*, 205:107244, 2021.

[7] Gregory Levitin, Maxim Finkelstein, and Yuanshun Dai. State-based mission abort policies for multistate systems. *Reliability Engineering & System Safety*, 204:107122, 2020.

[8] Li Yang, Yuhan Ma, Fanping Wei, and Qingan Qiu. Optimal condition-based parameter learning and mission abort decisions. *Naval Research Logistics (NRL)*, 2024.

[9] Qingan Qiu, Rong Li, and Xian Zhao. Failure risk management: adaptive performance control and mission abort decisions. *Risk Analysis*, 45(2):421–440, 2025.

[10] Xian Zhao, Xinlei Wang, Ying Dai, and Qingan Qiu. Joint optimization of loading, mission abort and rescue site selection policies for UAV. *Reliability Engineering & System Safety*, 244:109955, 2024.

[11] Gregory Levitin, Maxim Finkelstein, and Yuanshun Dai. Mission abort and rescue for multistate systems operating under the poisson process of shocks. *Reliability Engineering & System Safety*, 202:107027, 2020.

[12] Gregory Levitin, Maxim Finkelstein, and Yanping Xiang. Optimal aborting rule in multi-attempt missions performed by multicomponent systems. *European Journal of Operational Research*, 283(1):244–252, 2020.

[13] Qingan Qiu and Lirong Cui. Gamma process based optimal mission abort policy. *Reliability Engineering & System Safety*, 190:106496, 2019.

[14] Gregory Levitin, Maxim Finkelstein, and Yanping Xiang. Optimal inspections and mission abort policies for multistate systems. *Reliability Engineering & System Safety*, 214:107700, 2021.

[15] Xian Zhao, Yu Fan, Qingan Qiu, and Ke Chen. Multi-criteria mission abort policy for systems subject to two-stage degradation process. *European Journal of Operational Research*, 295(1):233–245, 2021.

[16] Qingan Qiu, Lisa M. Maillart, Oleg A. Prokopyev, and Lirong Cui. Optimal condition-based mission abort decisions. *IEEE Transactions on Reliability*, 72(1):408–425, 2023.

[17] Gregory Levitin, Maxim Finkelstein, and Hong-Zhong Huang. Optimal abort rules for multiattempt missions. *Risk Analysis*, 39(12):2732–2743, 2019.

[18] Li Yang, Fanping Wei, Xiaobing Ma, and Qingan Qiu. Controlling mission hazards through integrated abort and spare support optimization. *Risk Analysis*, 2025.

[19] Gregory Levitin and Maxim Finkelstein. Optimal mission abort policy for systems in a random environment with variable shock rate. *Reliability Engineering & System Safety*, 169:11–17, 2018.

[20] Gregory Levitin, Maxim Finkelstein, and Yuanshun Dai. Mission abort policy balancing the uncompleted mission penalty and system loss risk. *Reliability Engineering & System Safety*, 176:194–201, 2018.

[21] Li Yang, Yi Chen, Qingan Qiu, and Jiantai Wang. Risk control of mission-critical systems: Abort decision-makings integrating health and age conditions. *IEEE Transactions on Industrial Informatics*, 18(10):6887–6894, 2022.

[22] Gregory Levitin, Maxim Finkelstein, and Yanping Xiang. Optimal multi-attempt missions with cumulative effect. *Reliability Engineering & System Safety*, 203:107091, 2020.

[23] Qingan Qiu, Lirong Cui, and Bei Wu. Dynamic mission abort policy for systems operating in a controllable environment with self-healing mechanism. *Reliability Engineering & System Safety*, 203:107069, 2020.

[24] Xian Zhao, Haoran Liu, Yaguang Wu, and Qingan Qiu. Joint optimization of mission abort and system structure considering dynamic tasks. *Reliability Engineering System Safety*, 234:109128, 2023.

A Deep Reinforcement Learning Approach to Dynamic Extravehicular Maintenance Policy in Space Stations

Haochen Luo, Qin Zhang, Yu Liu*

School of Mechanical and Electrical Engineering
University of Electronic Science and Technology of China
Chengdu, Sichuan, 611731, P.R. China
yuliu@uestc.edu.cn

Keywords: Extravehicular Maintenance, multi-agent system, deep reinforcement learning, dynamic maintenance policy

Abstract - The long-term stable operation of space stations is critical for advancing space research and technology validation, making efficient extravehicular maintenance a pivotal concern. This article proposes a multi-agent collaborative model for extravehicular maintenance, optimized using deep reinforcement learning (DRL), handle risk constraints, and adapt to dynamic environments in space environment. Utilizing Deep Q-Networks (DQN), the model integrates hierarchical maintenance planning and reactive execution agents, coupled with dynamic state transition models for device degradation, environmental hazards, and personnel stamina decay. This framework optimizes maintenance policy for cost efficiency and safety under constraints of limited spare parts, restricted extravehicular maintenance duration, and environmental risks. These insights highlight the model's potential for cost reduction and rapid response to stochastic failures of components, ensuring astronaut safety and providing decision support for extravehicular maintenance.

1. Introduction

Space stations serve as critical platforms for space exploration, relying on effective on-orbit maintenance to ensure operational stability [1]. Extravehicular maintenance tasks involve multiple astronauts collaborating on complex operations [2], such as device repair, working condition monitoring and robotic arm manipulation. These tasks are constrained by limited spacesuit performance, astronaut fatigue, and environmental risks like solar storms [3]. Traditional rule-based strategies struggle to adapt to these dynamic conditions, and existing multi-agent coordination models often fail to integrate heterogeneous agent interactions or comprehensively handle risk constraints. The collaborative nature of extravehicular maintenance, involving coordinated decision-making among ground control, station commanders, and astronauts, highlights the potential of a multi-agent framework to optimize maintenance decisions under dynamic conditions. However, the intricate interactions among these heterogeneous agents present significant challenges in designing effective coordination mechanisms.

This article introduces a multi-agent collaborative framework based on DQN to optimize extravehicular maintenance policies. By modeling planning and execution agents within a dynamic environment, the proposed approach enhances decision-making efficiency and safety, addressing the limitations of prior methods.

2. Problem descriptions

In this section, we first present the definition and main properties of the proposed multi-agent system model for space station extravehicular maintenance tasks. The motivation of proposing this multi-agent system model is also discussed.

2.1 System model description

The multi-agent system models a space station maintenance scenario with devices subject to degradation, managed by an astronaut team supported by the ground commander team. The model includes two agent classes: planning agents and execution agents, alongside non-intelligent entities. Factors considered include device degradation, environmental hazards, and astronaut stamina decay. Costs comprise device failure losses, astronaut physical exertion, ground operations, and space operations. The objective is to minimize total maintenance cost while ensuring device functionality and astronaut safety. Figure 1 illustrates the multi-team architecture.

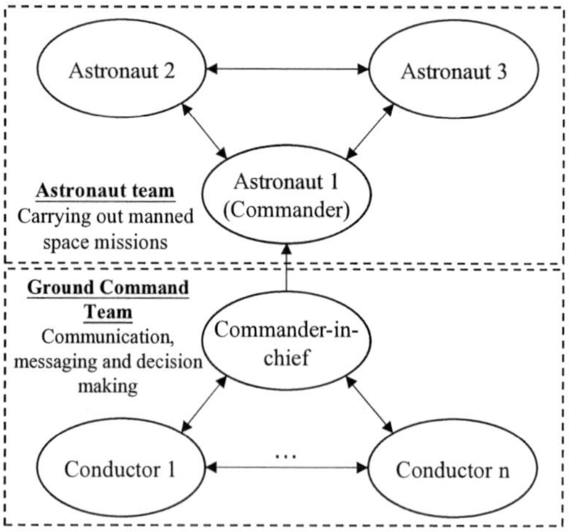

Figure 1. Multi-team system architecture in manned space missions

Some assumptions of the studied multi-agent system are summarized as follows.

(1) The activities of the ground command team are simplified to cosmic environment monitoring, space station device monitoring, and release of device repair or replacement tasks.

(2) A simplified astronaut working state assessment model and extravehicular maintenance operation process is used without considering the details of specific actions for extravehicular maintenance.

(3) The extreme events that may occur in the space environment are simplified, and only one extreme environmental disaster, i.e., the "solar storm", is considered.

2.2 Motivation of the system model

The complexity of extravehicular maintenance tasks, driven by dynamic device degradation and environmental uncertainties, necessitates advanced decision-making models. Current multi-agent extravehicular maintenance models are limited, failing to fully address inter-agent collaboration and risk constraints. This study develops a DRL-based framework to optimize maintenance strategies, enhancing efficiency and safety through coordinated multi-agent interactions and dynamic state modeling.

3. DQN-Based Multi-Agent modeling method

Deep Q-network combines deep learning and reinforcement learning to approximate the Q-value function by constructing a neural network to realize efficient decision-making in complex environments [4]. Compared with traditional reinforcement learning methods, DQN can handle high-dimensional state spaces, effectively improving the learning ability and decision-making level of intelligent bodies. In the space station outbound maintenance scenario of this study, DQN is applied to the multi-agent model to achieve the optimization of maintenance strategies.

3.1 Extravehicular Maintenance Process Modeling

The extravehicular maintenance process involves four steps: (1) astronauts exit with tools, (2) move to the repair site via spacewalk or robotic arm, (3) repair or replace device, and (4) return to the cabin. The multi-agent model, as shown as Fig.2, assigns planning agents to monitor states and allocate tasks, while execution agents perform repairs based on instructions.

In this model, the planning agents include the ground commander team and the space station commander temporarily assigned for each mission, which are mainly responsible for device and environment status monitoring, task assignment, planning and personnel supervision; the executing agents are the astronauts, who carry out the specific operation or maintenance processes according to the instructions of the planning agents. Each agent plays a specific role in the system through different decision logic and action capabilities.

3.2 Dynamic State Transition Models

This section describes the mathematical formulations governing the evolution of device, environmental, and personnel states over time, integrating stochastic processes and physical constraints to simulate realistic maintenance dynamics.

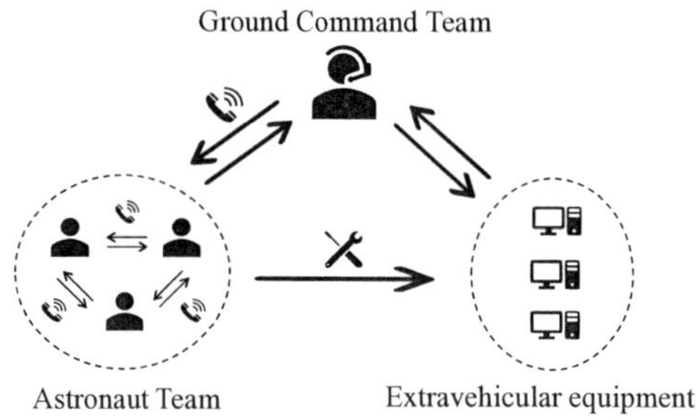

Figure 2. Multi-agent model architecture for extravehicular maintenance

(1) **Device Model:** The device states D_s^i are discretized into three categories: normal, degraded, and failed. The degradation process of device i is modeled using a Gamma distribution. The formula for the degradation increment in a single time step is as follows:

$$D_t^i = D_{t-1}^i + \Delta D_t^i,\ \ \Delta D_t^i \sim \Gamma(\alpha_i + \Delta\alpha \cdot R_i, \beta_i) \quad (1)$$

where D_t^i is defined as the degradation level of device i at time t, and Gamma distribution parameters α_i and β_i are initialized based on empirical settings. After each repair, the repair count R_i is incremented and the device's Gamma distribution shape parameter α_i is incremented by $\Delta\alpha$ to reflect increased degradation resistance. The initial degradation time of the device follows a Weibull distribution:

$$T_d^i = \theta\left(-\ln(1-U)\right)^{1/\beta},\ U \sim U(0,1) \quad (2)$$

where θ is the scale parameter, reflecting the characteristic life of the product, β is the shape parameter and U is a random variable uniformly distributed in the interval $[0,1]$.

Device repair and replacement actions are modeled to restore device functionality. For repair, the degradation level D_t^i of device i at time t is reduced based on the astronaut's stamina and a repair effect coefficient. The repair update is defined as:

$$D_{t+1}^i = \max(0, D_t^i - \eta \cdot \frac{W_j(t)}{100}) \quad (3)$$

where η is the repair effect coefficient, and $W_j(t)$ is the stamina of astronaut j performing the repair, normalized to $[0,100]$. The stamina of astronaut impacts repair effectiveness, as higher $W_j(t)$ yields greater degradation reduction during repairs. For replacement, the device is restored to its initial state, resetting D_t^i, α_t, β_i and R_i. The replacement action is only feasible if spare parts inventory S_i is enough, ensuring inventory limitations are respected.

(2) Environment Model: The space environment E_s is discretized into normal, warning, or storm states, with solar storms modeled as a Poisson process:

$$P(N(t)=k) = \frac{(\lambda t)^k}{k!} e^{-\lambda t} \quad (4)$$

where $N(t)=k$ is the number of solar storm events in the time interval $[0,t]$, and λ is the storm intensity parameter. During solar storms, the additional degradation increment of device i

follows a truncated normal distribution (TN), defined as $TN(\mu=0,\sigma=0.01,a=0,b=\infty)$, where truncation ensures nonnegative increments.

(3) Personnel Model: Astronaut stamina, denoted $W_j(t)$ for astronaut j at time t, is a critical factor influencing maintenance performance. During extravehicular activities, stamina decays exponentially based on task duration and intensity:

$$W_j(t)=W_j(t-1)\cdot e^{-k\cdot\Delta t} \tag{5}$$

where k is the decay rate, and Δt is the discrete time step. Specific extravehicular actions (e.g., moving to repair sites, performing repairs) incur additional stamina costs. If $W_j(t)$ falls below a certain value during a mission, an emergency return is triggered. When resting in the cabin, astronauts' stamina can gradually recover, and the degree of recovery is related to the rest time.

3.3 Markov Decision Process Modeling

In the Markov Decision Process (MDP) formulation for extravehicular maintenance tasks, the state space serves as the foundation for agent decision-making.

3.3.1 State Space

Building upon the dynamic state transition models described in section 3.2, we define the observable state space to comprehensively capture the status of devices, the space environment, and astronaut attributes. This state space integrates both discrete and continuous variables to reflect the evolving dynamics of the maintenance scenario, formalized as:

$$S_{obs}=\{D_s^i,D_t^i,R_i,S_i,E_s,A_{info}\} \tag{6}$$

where the discrete device status D_s^i is used for high-level decision-making, such as determining repair or replacement needs, while the continuous degradation level D_t^i provides detailed information for fine-grained control of maintenance actions, capturing subtle changes in device health. R_i is the frequency of repairs performed on device i, influencing its subsequent degradation behavior. S_i is the spare parts inventory of device i, critical for replacement decisions. E_s describes the space environment. A_{info} is all astronaut information, including identity (ID, role), position and stamina $W_j(t)$, which directly affect task execution capabilities.

This hybrid state space , including the discrete and continuous state space, enables agents to base decisions on comprehensive environmental and operational information.

3.3.2 Action Space

The action space represents the set of actions available to agents at each decision step, tailored to their roles in the maintenance process. It is defined as:

$$A_{act}=\{A_g,A_a^1,A_a^2,A_a^3\} \tag{7}$$

where A_g are ground control actions, representing check device status, issue repair task, issue replacement task, suspend task check environment and standby, respectively. A_a^j : Actions for astronaut j represent rest, execute repair or replacement, and emergency return.

The action space facilitates coordinated decision-making, with ground control directing tasks and astronauts executing operations under dynamic constraints.

3.3.3 Reward Function

The reward function guides the training of the DRL model by balancing maintenance efficiency, safety, and cost. It comprises three components: device state improvement, astronaut safety, and operational cost penalties, defined as:

$$R(s,a)=R_{device}+R_{safety}-C_{total} \tag{8}$$

where R_{device} is reward for improving device state, calculated as the improvement in device status (e.g., from failed to normal yields +1, degraded to normal +0.5), while the reward for astronaut safety R_{safety} is based on maintaining stamina a high level or penalizing low stamina. C_{total} represents the penalty for costs, including device failure cost, ground operations, space operations, and human costs.

This reward function incentivizes timely repairs, safe operations, and cost minimization, aligning with mission objectives.

3.3.4 Constraints and Objectives

During the extravehicular maintenance process, due to numerous objective reasons and uncertainties, relatively safe, conservative, and convenient maintenance strategies are often adopted. Constraints include limited spare parts in space station, restricted extravehicular maintenance duration, and risk penalties. The optimization objective minimizes total cost:

$$\min C_{total}=\min(C_d+C_h+C_g+C_s)$$
$$=\min\begin{cases}C_d=\sum_{t=1}^{T}\sum_{i=1}^{n}\left(s_i(t)\cdot cost_{degraded}+\delta_{s_i(t)=2}\cdot cost_{broken}\right)\\ C_h=\sum_{t=1}^{T}\left(\sum_{j=1}^{n}\delta_{storm}(t)\cdot\delta_{pos_j(t)\neq 0}\cdot cost_{storm}\right)\\ C_g=\sum_{t=1}^{T}\left(\delta_{check\_0}\cdot cost_{check\_device}+\delta_{check\_1}\cdot cost_{check\_spcae}\right)\\ C_s=\sum_{t=1}^{T}\left(\delta_{repair}(t)\cdot cost_{repair}+\delta_{replace}(t)\cdot cost_{replace}\right)\end{cases} \tag{9}$$

where the device failure loss C_d is calculated based on the failure state of the device and its duration. The astronaut physical exertion cost C_h is related to factors such as physical fatigue and the handling of abnormal conditions. The ground operation cost C_g covers the costs of operations like device inspection and environmental monitoring. The in-space operation cost C_s includes the costs of device repair and replacement. By optimizing the decision-making process and satisfying various constraint conditions, the cost of the maintenance task can be optimized, thereby enhancing the overall effectiveness of extravehicular maintenance tasks in the space station.

3.4 DQN Algorithm

DRL combines reinforcement learning's decision-making with deep learning's perception capabilities. DQN approximates the Q-value function using a neural network, enabling efficient handling of high-dimensional state spaces. The Q-function is approximated using a neural network with three fully connected layers, where the input is the flattened state vector, and the output is the Q-values for each action, optimized via experience replay and target network updates. The DQN structure employs a multi-layer perceptron (MLP) with shared environment encoders and independent Q-networks for each agent, as shown in Fig. 3.

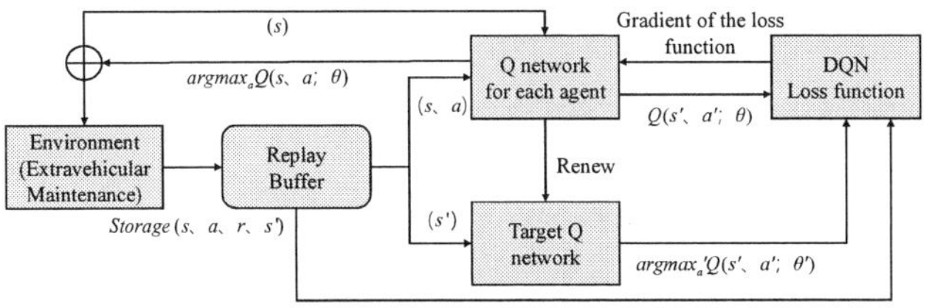

Figure 3. DQN algorithm structure

The DQN training process uses an ϵ-greedy policy for action selection, balancing exploration and exploitation. The loss function is defined as:

$$L = E\left[\left(r + \gamma \max_{a'} Q(s',a';\theta^{-}) - Q(s,a;\theta)\right)^2\right] \quad (10)$$

where r is the reward, γ is the discount factor, s' is the next state, and θ^{-}, θ are the target and online network parameters, respectively.

4. Case study

4.1 Experimental Settings

Experiments were conducted on a Windows 10 system (Intel Core i5-12500, 24GB RAM) using Visual Studio Code with PyTorch in a SpaceStationEnv environment. Three devices were modeled, each with $\Gamma(1.0,0.01)$ degradation, $\Delta\alpha = 0.1$, initial stamina $W_j = 100$, and $k = 0.05$. Solar storms occur with $\lambda = 0.1$, lasting 10 steps, with a minimum interval of 150 steps.

The DQN model used a learning rate of 10^{-4}, batch size 256, experience buffer size 500,000, and 20,000 training episodes, with epsilon decaying from 1.0 to 0.001 with a decay factor of 0.999. Target network updates occurred every 10 episodes, and the discount factor $\gamma = 0.99$ was is used to balance the importance of immediate and future rewards. The rule-based and threshold-based strategies were evaluated over 100 episodes, each with a maximum of 800 steps, to align with the DQN's evaluation phase. All strategies operated in the same environment, with same costs structures consistent across models. Experiments were repeated 10 times, and results were averaged to ensure statistical robustness.

4.2 Strategy Descriptions

The DQN model learns optimal actions through experience replay, optimizing the Q-value function to balance device status, safety, and costs. It dynamically selects actions based on the full state space, adapting to degradation and environmental changes.

Scheduled maintenance strategy follows a fixed schedule, checking the environment every 50 steps or upon storm warnings, checking device status every 40 steps, and issuing repair for degraded devices or replacement for failed devices with available spares. Tasks are paused during solar storms, and post-storm checks are mandated.

The Condition-Based maintenance strategy monitors devices at each step, issuing replacement tasks for failed devices or repair tasks for devices with degradation $D_d^i > 0.8$. It checks the environment every 50 steps or on storm warnings and pauses tasks during storms.

4.3 Results and Comparative Analysis

Performance was evaluated using cumulative cost, extravehicular maintenance frequency, device status durations, and storm detection times. Results were averaged over 10 runs, with standard deviations reported to assess stability.

Table 1. Performance Comparison of Maintenance Strategies

Metric	DQN	Scheduled	Condition-Based
Cumulative Cost	1963.3	6563.9	2249.5
Repair Count	27.8	9.1	41.3
Replace Count	7.8	12.6	4.3
EVA Total	35.6	21.7	45.6
Storm Avoidance Rate (%)	81.6	72.5	56.8
Normal Status Duration (steps)	439.7	322.4	394.2
Degraded Status Duration	338.8	288.4	382.4
Failed Status Duration	21.5	189.2	24.2

Table 1 summarizes the results, comparing the DQN-based, Scheduled, and Condition-Based strategies across cumulative cost, extravehicular maintenance frequency (repair count, replace count, EVA total), storm avoidance rate, and device status durations (normal, degraded, failed). Results were averaged over 10 runs to ensure statistical robustness.

The DQN-based strategy outperforms both baselines, achieving the lowest cumulative cost, approximately 70% lower than the Scheduled one and 13% lower than the Condition-Based one. DQN's high repair count and moderate replace count reflect a balanced approach, favoring cost-effective repairs over replacements. Its superior storm avoidance rate indicates effective responses to solar storms, leveraging adaptive action selection based on comprehensive state information.

As observed in Figs. 4, the Scheduled strategy exhibits the highest cost and failed duration, driven by low repair frequency and excessive replacements. Its rigid schedule fails to prevent degradation, incurring substantial failure penalties. The Condition-Based strategy, with a moderate cost, achieves the highest EVA total, driven by frequent repairs triggered by degradation thresholds. However, its lower storm avoidance rate and higher degraded duration suggest limited adaptability to environmental dynamics.

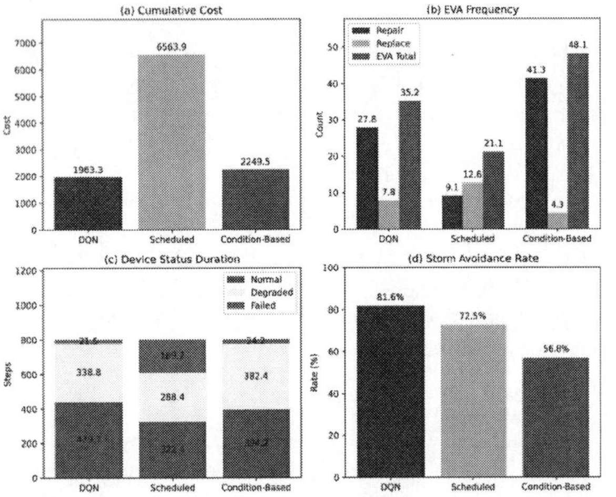

Figure 4. Illustrates the comparative performance: (a) Cumulative cost, (b) EVA frequency, (c) Device status durations, (d) Storm avoidance rate.

These findings validate the DQN-based model's suitability for extravehicular maintenance, offering superior cost efficiency and reliability under complex, stochastic conditions.

5. Conclusion

This study presents a DQN-based multi-agent framework for optimizing extravehicular maintenance in space stations. Comparative evaluations demonstrate its superiority in cost efficiency and device management over rule-based and threshold-based baselines. Despite minor reward stability challenges observed during training, the framework's adaptability to dynamic conditions significantly enhances safety and cost efficiency. The DQN-based model reduces maintenance costs by 70% compared to Scheduled and 13% compared to Condition-Based strategies, ensuring reliable device operation and astronaut safety.

6. Acknowledgement

The authors greatly acknowledge grant support from the National Natural Science Foundation of China under contract number 72271044.

7. References

[1] Ge X, Zhou Q, Liu Z. "Assessment of space station on-orbit maintenance task complexity"; Reliability Engineering & System Safety, Vol.193, 2020.

[2] Zhang, Jia-cheng, Yue-he Zhu, and Ya-zhong Luo. "Many-objective optimization and decision-making for overall allocation of space station on-orbit activities."; Acta Astronautica, Vol.177, 202-216, 2020.

[3] Shen, Liang, et al. "Extending ISS Life Beyond 2030."; 75th International Astronautical Congress (IAC), No. IAC-24-B3, July 2024.

[4] Mnih V, Kavukcuoglu K, Silver D, et al. "Playing atari with deep reinforcement learning"; arXiv preprint arXiv:1312.5602, 2013.

Robust parameter design of multiple functional responses based on transfer learning and its application in additive manufacturing

Mingyue Chu[1,2], Jianjun Wang[1,2].

[1]Department of Management Science and Engineering, Nanjing University of Science and Technology, Nanjing 210094, China
[2]Jiangsu Province Engineering Research Center of Quality Improvement for High-end Equipment, Nanjing University of Science and Technology, Nanjing, China

Keywords: multiple functional responses, robust parameter design, transfer learning, additive manufacturing

Abstract – Robust parameter design (RPD) plays an important role in the quality control of additive manufacturing (AM) processes. However, with the advancement of sensor technology, the quality characteristics of AM parts have evolved from traditional independent scalar values to high-dimensional curves, also referred to as functional responses. Additionally, only limited data is available for each product due to the relatively high cost of AM. These factors pose significant challenges in building accurate predictive models for the AM process. To address these issues, this article proposes a transfer learning method based on the tensor regression algorithm, which can build predictive models and optimize parameters for multiple functional quality responses of AM products under data-scarce conditions. The performance of the proposed method is evaluated using real data from Jiangsu Province High-end Equipment Quality Improvement Engineering Center. The experimental results demonstrate that the proposed method can more accurately model and optimize high-dimensional quality characteristics, even with limited training data.

1. Introduction

Additive manufacturing (AM), also known as 3D printing, is a cost-effective and flexible method for producing 3D parts by adding material layer by layer. However, a significant barrier to the broader industrial adoption of extrusion-based AM is its limited fabrication quality, particularly in dimensional accuracy and mechanical strength[1-3]. To address this issue, researchers commonly apply quality control methods to ensure that the quality characteristics of interest meet the desired standards. For instance, Kechagias et al.[4] conducted 125 orthogonal experiments to examine the effects of six 3D printing parameters on part strength, printing time, and weight. Their results indicated that the raster deposition angle, nozzle temperature, printing speed, and infill density had the most significant impact on the mechanical properties of the printed parts. Saad et al.[5] developed a response surface model linking key 3D printing process parameters to the surface roughness of printed parts. They then applied a novel optimization algorithm to identify parameter settings that minimize surface roughness. Their studies consistently demonstrate that predictive modeling and subsequent optimization of process parameters enable 3D-printed products to achieve the desired quality characteristics.

However, with advancements in sensor technology, product quality characteristics are no longer limited to independent scalar data but increasingly take the form of high-dimensional functional data[6, 7]. Feng et al.[8] developed a novel additive GP model capturing the relationship between key 3D printing process parameters (such as layer height, infill density, etc.) and the resulting functional responses (creep rate and rupture time), and used this model to optimize the target quality. Their study indicates that selecting an appropriate predictive model for RPD in functional multi-response problems remains a viable approach in the context of 3D printing. Moreover, tensor regression methods are widely applied in modeling high-dimensional data structures. Lock[9] proposed a general tensor-on-tensor regression framework for predicting one multi-dimensional array from another, and validated its effectiveness on simulated and facial image datasets. The framework has demonstrated applicability across multiple prediction scenarios, including methods to predict a scalar outcome from a tensor, a matrix from a matrix, or a tensor from a scalar. Subsequently, Huang et al.[10] pointed out that currently available tensor regression models are sensitive to arbitrary outliers within the tensors. To address the issue, they proposed a Robust Tensor-On-Tensor (RTOT) regression approach, which has the capability of modeling high-dimensional data when outliers corrupt the data. Wang C. and Wang[11] developed a predictive model using the RTOT method to capture multiple functional responses—such as force–time and deformation–time curves—for AM products based on densely sampled data. This model was then used to formulate an optimization objective using the Euclidean distance metric, enabling the identification of a set of 3D printing parameters that allows all functional responses to achieve their target simultaneously. Their research offers a valuable method for developing high-dimensional functional response models.

Although predictive methods for multiple functional quality characteristics of AM products have seen considerable development, most existing statistical models depend on extensive training datasets to ensure predictive accuracy. This assumption is often inconsistent with the limited data available in practical additive manufacturing settings[12]. Currently, the modeling of different AM products is conducted in isolation. Specifically, when faced with a new AM product or a new engaged 3D printer, data must be collected through experiments or simulations before machine learning (ML)-based modeling can be performed. This process is time-consuming, as AM experiments or simulations often require several hours or even days to complete[13]. Leveraging prior data and knowledge from a source printer with abundant historical quality information effectively addresses this limitation. Therefore, many scholars are increasingly exploring the application of transfer learning (TL) methods to quality modeling in AM. TL facilitates knowledge transfer across distinct yet related products or printers by leveraging historical data from previous processes, thereby reducing the time, material, and computational costs of new products or machines. Cheng et al.[14, 15] integrated feature-based and model-based transfer learning approaches to predict in-plane shape deviations of 3D-printed parts with varying geometries. Their study demonstrated that data from geometrically distinct products can be effectively leveraged to predict shape deviations under similar printing conditions. Sabbaghi et al.[16] propose an adaptive Bayesian methodology that integrates empirical in-plane deviation data with corresponding predictive models, derived from limited sets of previously fabricated and heterogeneous shapes, to support the specification of in-plane deviation models for a broader class of novel geometries. Subsequently, A. Sabbaghi and Q. Huang [17] develop a novel effect equivalence framework and a Bayesian approach that facilitates the transfer of deviation models across processes within additive manufacturing systems under constraints of limited experimental runs. Zhang et al.[18] proposed a novel transfer learning approach for predicting stress-strain curves of parts fabricated with different materials. They integrated Optimal Transport (OT) into the transfer learning framework by aligning the source and target label spaces, enhancing knowledge transferability across diverse material composites. Their studies demonstrate the efficacy of transfer learning for predicting shape deviations and mechanical properties in AM components.

Despite recent advances, research on the modeling and optimization of multiple functional responses in AM products remains limited, particularly under data-scarce conditions. To address this gap, this study proposes a transfer learning-based method for modeling and optimizing multiple functional responses and validates its effectiveness through empirical experiments. Using a limited sample size, the proposed method can accurately predict multiple functional responses of 3D-printed products.

2. Proposed methodology

2.1. Tensor regression model

In this paper, we employ the robust tensor-on-tensor (RTOT) method proposed by Lee et al.[10], to model the multifunctional responses of sufficient sampled source printers. In contrast, this paper aims to model a tensor-on-scholar regression problem. In the context of AM, we consider the influencing factors to be scalar variables. Accordingly, we adapt the RTOT model and apply minor modifications to it so that we can derive the RTOS model, which is expressed as:

$$\mathcal{Y}_i = (\boldsymbol{x}_i \times_1 \mathcal{B}) + \mathcal{S}_i + \mathcal{E}_i \tag{1}$$

where $\mathcal{Y}_i \in \mathbb{R}^{Q_1 \times Q_2}$ denotes the tensor response output from the i th experimental, and the response from each trial in this study is a two-dimensional tensor with dimensions $Q_1 \times Q_2$. Also, in Equation (1), $\boldsymbol{x}_i$ is a $p \times 1$ vector representing the scholar influencing factors, $\mathcal{B} \in p \times Q_1 \times Q_2$ is the tensor of parameters, $\mathcal{S}_i$ is a sparse tensor representing the outliers, and $\mathcal{E}_i$ is the tensor of errors. And then we build a linear model for all the training data. That is, we construct the response tensor $\mathcal{Y} \in \mathbb{R}^{N \times Q_1 \times Q_2}$ to be estimated by the input tensor $\mathcal{X} \in \mathbb{R}^{N \times p}$, and the model is as follows:

$$\mathcal{Y} = (\mathcal{X} \times_1 \mathcal{B}) + \mathcal{S} + \mathcal{E} \tag{2}$$

where $\mathcal{S}$ and $\mathcal{E}$ represent the outlier sparse tensor and the error tensor containing all the training datasets, respectively. In this paper, the tensor of parameters are estimated using the method proposed by Lee et al.[10], and the effectiveness of this method in the prediction of multifunctional responses of AM products is also confirmed by Wang C. and Wang[11].

2.2. Model-based transfer learning

Zhang et al.[19] state that if a model has been well developed on the source domain, transferring the common process knowledge to the target domain can be achieved utilizing parameter transfer or model migration. Inspired by them, we believe the 3D printing process follows a similar material deposition mechanism under different printing conditions. In this paper, we suppose that a structural similarity exists between the quality prediction model of the newly engaged 3D printer and that of the source printer. Parameter fine-tuning based on the source model enables the development of a predictive model that performs well in the target 3D printer.

It is known that the parameter tensor $\mathcal{B} \in p \times Q_1 \times Q_2$ is a third-order tensor, and it can be regarded as a collection of p matrices of size $Q_1 \times Q_2$, each characterizing the influence of the corresponding factor on the tensor response. For the target predictive model, we suppose it shares the same structure as that of the source model, but its parameters are obtained by scaling the source model parameters by a certain multiple. That is:

$$\mathcal{B}_{tar} = \mathcal{B}_{src} \times_3 D \tag{3}$$

where $\mathcal{B}_{tar}$ and $\mathcal{B}_{src}$ respectively denote the parameter tensor of the target and source models, and

$D = \mathrm{diag}(\lambda_1, \lambda_2, \ldots, \lambda_{(p\cdot Q_2)}) \in \mathbb{R}^{(p\cdot Q_2)\times(p\cdot Q_2)}$ is a diagonal matrix that represents the relative scaling between the target and the source model parameters. Subsequently, a genetic algorithm (GA), together with limited training data from the target printer, is employed to estimate the scaling factor D. The predictive model of the target 3D printer is expressed as:

$$\mathcal{Y}_{tar} = \{\mathcal{X} \times_1 (\mathcal{B}_{src} \times_3 D)\} + \mathcal{S} + \mathcal{E} \tag{4}$$

3. Case study

Force-time and deformation-time curves play an important role in evaluating the mechanical properties of AM products. In practice, researchers must optimize the parameters of the 3D printing process to ensure product quality and meet desired specifications. However, this process typically involves extensive experimentation and simulation, resulting in considerable time and materials consumption. In this case study, we apply our proposed method to predict force-time and deformation-time curves under conditions of limited sample size.

3.1. Experimental design and data collection

Wang C. and Wang[11] developed predictive models for the force-time and deformation-time profiles of cylindrical parts using data collected from Jiangsu Province Engineering Research Center of Quality Improvement for High-end Equipment. This paper uses the data from their study as the source domain. Our study aims to predict and optimize two functional responses (force-time and deformation-time curves) of products made by a newly engaged 3D printer with a small sample size.

To create a data-poor environment, this study designs 20 experiments using Latin hypercube sampling and fabricates samples using the target printer. Among them, 5 data sets were allocated to the training set, and the remaining 15 were used to evaluate the predictive performance of the target model. The source and target printers are shown in Figure 1 and represent two different 3D printers.

Figure 1. The two 3D printers used in this case/ (a) Source printer, (b) Target printer

Furthermore, to more accurately simulate the diversity of 3D printed products in practical applications, square samples are fabricated using the target printer instead of the cylindrical ones made in the source domain. The specimens fabricated by the target printer are presented in Figure 2.

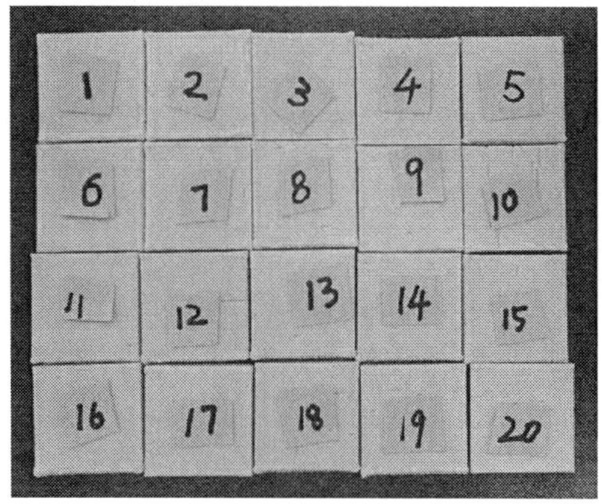

Figure 2. Specimens made by the target printer

The samples were subjected to compression tests using a multifunctional testing machine at the Research Center, to obtain force–time and deformation–time curves for each specimen. The test results of the 20 samples fabricated by the target printer are presented in Figure 3.

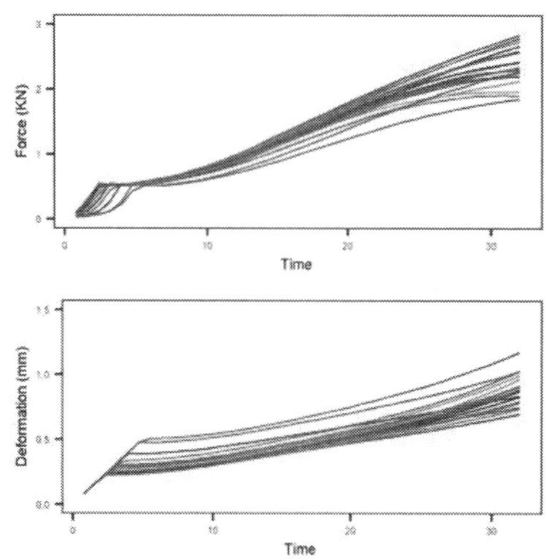

Figure 3. Experimental results for all samples from the target printer

In this case, the corresponding curve is characterized by taking 40 fixed points along each curve. Thus, the two output curves for each sample are discretized into a second-order tensor. Therefore, the next objective is to develop a predictive model between the second-order tensor response and four scalar influencing factors, namely, a tensor-on-scalar regression model, and to optimize its parameters.

3.2. Modeling for the target 3-D printer based on transfer learning

Before building the target model, we first develop a reliable source model using abundant source domain data.

The RTOS regression model proposed in Chapter 2 was employed to construct it. Among the 40 source domain data sets, 32 were divided into the training set, and the remaining eight were reserved for testing. The training data were used to estimate the parameters of the RTOS model.

To accurately evaluate the performance of the predictive model, we employ Relative Prediction Error (RPE), the Root Mean Square Error (RMSE), and the Mean Absolute Error (MAE) as evaluation metrics, where lower values indicate better predictive performance. The calculation procedures for these metrics are presented in Equations (5)-(7).

$$RPE = \frac{\| \mathcal{Y} - ((\mathcal{X} \times_1 \mathcal{B}) + \mathcal{S}) \|_F}{\| \mathcal{Y} \|_F} \tag{5}$$

$$RMSE = \sqrt{\frac{1}{N} \Sigma (vec(\mathcal{Y}) - vec((\mathcal{X} \times_1 \mathcal{B}) + \mathcal{S}))^2} \tag{6}$$

$$MAE = \frac{1}{N} \Sigma | vec(\mathcal{Y}) - vec((\mathcal{X} \times_1 \mathcal{B}) + \mathcal{S}) | \tag{7}$$

In this study, the three metrics of the source model were, respectively, 0.0337, 0.0764, and 0.0580. They are consistent with the results in the study of Wang C. and Wang[11] who have demonstrated the superiority of the model.

Following the development of a reliable source model, the target model is constructed using the model-based transfer learning method presented in Equation (4). The scaling matrix D can be estimated by optimizing the following equation together with the representative dataset $(\mathcal{Y}_{tar}, \mathcal{X}_{tat})$ collected from the target domain.

$$arg \ \min L(D) = \frac{\| \mathcal{Y}_{tar} - ((\mathcal{X}_{tar} \times_1 (\mathcal{B}_{src} \times_8 D) + \mathcal{S}) \|_F}{\| \mathcal{Y}_{tar} \|_F} \tag{8}$$

where D is a matrix with a diagonal size of 8×8, and each diagonal entry represents the scaling applied to a model parameter by a corresponding influence factor. In this study, we obtain the scaling matrix D by GA, expressed as Equation (9).

$$D = diag(0.5163, 0.5142, 0.5653, 0.6061, \\ 0.5587, 0.5987, 0.3662, 0.3531) \tag{9}$$

Then, the target prediction model is derived from the scaled source model. The proposed transfer learning method achieves an RPE of 0.1686 on the target domain test set, representing a 10.6% improvement in predictive performance compared to the RPE of 0.1886 obtained using the direct RTOS method without transfer learning. This result further demonstrates the superiority of the modeling approach that incorporates a priori knowledge.

3.3. Determination of optimal process parameters

After establishing the predictive model for the target printer, it is employed to identify the optimal parameter setting that drives multiple functional responses toward their target values. In this case study, the target force–time and deformation–time curves were discretized into a 40×2 matrix denoted T, where each column represents one type of curve and each row corresponds to a sampled time point. As shown in Equation (10), the Frobenius norm is then constructed as the objective function,

$$\min \ Loss = \frac{\| \mathcal{Y} - T \|_F}{\| T \|_F} \tag{10}$$

Where the tensor $\mathcal{Y}$ denotes the predicted values from the target domain model. The optimal parameter setting that minimize the quality loss are obtained through GA.

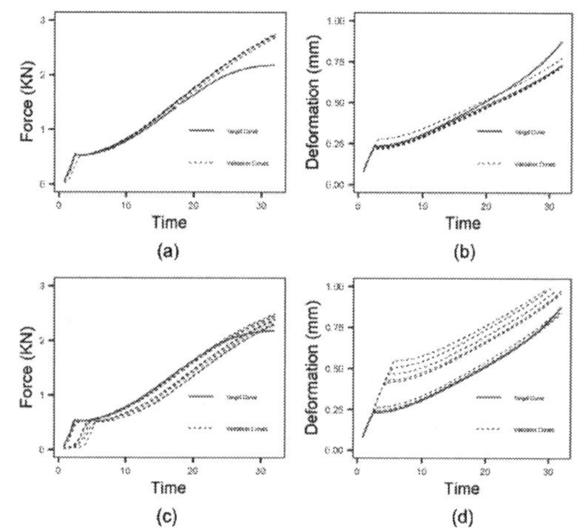

Figure 4. Validation results of the parameters under the two modeling approaches.

Table 1. Comparison results for different methods

Method	Parameters	Loss
With transfer learning	(229.35, 0.13, 19.16, 60.05)	0.1204
Without transfer learning	(220.57, 0.1964, 30, 67.15)	0.1712

After obtaining the optimal parameter settings from the two prediction models, we conducted eight validation tests under these settings. The corresponding test results are presented in Figure 4 and Table 1. Figure 4(a) and (b) illustrate the results of validation experiments based on the proposed approach, where red solid lines represent the target curves and blue dashed lines represent the actual experimental results. In contrast, Figure 4(c) and (d) show the results of the validation experiments conducted by the direct modeling approach. As shown in Figure 4, the proposed method demonstrates superior performance compared to the direct modeling approach. The results in Table 1 also indicate that the loss between the target and resulting curves of the functional responses is small when using the optimized parameters obtained by the proposed method.

4. Conclusion

Monitoring and optimizing profiles characterizing their mechanical properties for AM products are essential to ensure product reliability in service. However, current research on the analysis of multiple target curves remains limited. In addition, the AM process is characterized by product variety and small batch sizes, making data collection for analyzing a specific product both time-consuming and labor-intensive. To address these challenges, this paper proposes a tensor regression method combined with a transfer learning approach. The goal is to predict multiple functional quality characteristics of AM products using limited data by leveraging a priori information to newly engaged printers with scarce data. The experimental results demonstrate that the proposed method significantly enhances prediction and optimization performance compared to the direct modeling approach.

The transfer learning process proposed in this paper is limited to a single source-target domain pair. However, in practice, multiple processes or products may provide helpful information for modeling the target domain. Therefore, future research should focus on extending transfer learning to information systems involving various source domains.

5. Acknowledgements

This work is supported by the National Natural Science Foundation of China [Grant Number 72171118]

6. References

[1] J. Ren, A.-T. Wei, Z. Jiang, H. Wang, and X. Wang, "Improved Modeling of Kinematics-Induced Geometric Variations in Extrusion-Based Additive Manufacturing Through Between-Printer Transfer Learning," *IEEE Transactions on Automation Science and Engineering,* vol. 19, no. 3, pp. 2310-2321, 2022.

[2] A. Dey, and N. Yodo, "A Systematic Survey of FDM Process Parameter Optimization and Their Influence on Part Characteristics," *Journal of Manufacturing and Materials Processing,* vol. 3, no. 3, pp. 64, 2019.

[3] K. He, Q. Zhang, and Y. Hong, "Profile monitoring based quality control method for fused deposition modeling process," *Journal of Intelligent Manufacturing,* vol. 30, no. 2, pp. 947-958, 2019.

[4] J. Kechagias, N. Vidakis, M. Petousis, and N. Mountakis, "A multi-parametric process evaluation of the mechanical response of PLA in FFF 3D printing," *Materials and Manufacturing Processes,* vol. 38, no. 8, pp. 941-953, 2023.

[5] M. S. Saad, A. M. Nor, M. E. Baharudin, M. Z. Zakaria, and A. Aiman, "Optimization of surface roughness in FDM 3D printer using response surface methodology, particle swarm optimization, and symbiotic organism search algorithms," *The International Journal of Advanced Manufacturing Technology,* vol. 105, pp. 5121-5137, 2019.

[6] B. Palumbo, F. Centofanti, and F. Del Re, "Function-on-function regression for assessing production quality in industrial manufacturing," *Quality and Reliability Engineering International,* vol. 36, no. 8, pp. 2738-2753, 2020.

[7] R. D. Guevara, and J. A. Vargas, "Process capability analysis for nonlinear profiles using depth functions," *Quality and Reliability Engineering International,* vol. 31, no. 3, pp. 465-487, 2015.

[8] Z. Feng, J. Wang, X. Zhou, C. Zhai, and Y. Ma, "Robust optimization for functional multi-response in 3D printing process," *Simulation Modelling Practice and Theory,* vol. 126, 2023.

[9] E. F. Lock, "Tensor-on-tensor regression," *Journal of Computational and Graphical Statistics,* vol. 27, no. 3, pp. 638-647, 2018.

[10] H. Y. Lee, M. Reisi Gahrooei, H. Liu, and M. Pacella, "Robust tensor-on-tensor regression for multidimensional data modeling," *IISE Transactions,* vol. 56, no. 1, pp. 43-53, 2024.

[11] C. Wang, and J. Wang, "Functional multi-response robust optimization for additive manufacturing process." pp. 1314-1320.

[12] Y. Yao, and G. Doretto, "Boosting for transfer learning with multiple sources," *2010 IEEE Computer Society Conference on Computer Vision and Pattern Recognition*, 2010, pp. 1855-1862.

[13] Y. Tang, M. Rahmani Dehaghani, and G. G. Wang, "Review of transfer learning in modeling additive manufacturing processes," *Additive Manufacturing,* vol. 61, pp. 103357 2023.

[14] L. Cheng, F. Tsung, and A. Wang, "A Statistical Transfer Learning Perspective for Modeling Shape Deviations in Additive Manufacturing," *IEEE Robotics and Automation Letters,* vol. 2, no. 4, pp. 1988-1993, 2017.

[15] L. Cheng, K. Wang, and F. Tsung, "A hybrid transfer learning framework for in-plane freeform shape accuracy control in additive manufacturing," *IISE Transactions,* vol. 53, no. 3, pp. 298-312, 2020.

[16] A. Sabbaghi, Q. Huang, and T. Dasgupta, "Bayesian Model Building From Small Samples of Disparate Data for Capturing In-Plane Deviation in Additive Manufacturing," *Technometrics,* vol. 60, no. 4, pp. 532-544, 2018.

[17] A. Sabbaghi, and Q. Huang, "Model transfer across additive manufacturing processes via mean effect equivalence of lurking variables," *The Annals of Applied Statistics,* vol. 12, no. 4, pp. 2409-2429, 2018.

[18] Z. Zhang, Q. Liu, and D. Wu, "Predicting stress–strain curves using transfer learning: Knowledge transfer across polymer composites," *Materials & Design,* vol. 218, pp. 110700, 2022.

[19] H. Zhang, J. P. Choi, S. K. Moon, and T. H. Ngo, "A knowledge transfer framework to support rapid process modeling in aerosol jet printing," *Advanced Engineering Informatics,* vol. 48, pp. 101264, 2021.

Mission risk control strategy via joint optimization of information acquisition and parameter learning

Li Yang[1]

[1]Reliability and Systems Engineering, Beihang University, Beijing, China

Keywords: Risk control, mission reliability, Bayesian parameter learning, mission abort

Abstract - Conventional mission risk control policies typically rely on fixed inspection intervals and deterministic degradation models. These approaches, however, fail to account for system uncertainties, which can result in delayed failure detection and suboptimal decision-making. To address these challenges, we introduce an innovative dynamic decision framework that combines non-periodic information acquisition with Bayesian parameter learning. This novel framework mitigates the significant limitations of traditional models by allowing decision-makers to select optimal time intervals for information acquisition, thereby minimizing unnecessary inspections and ensuring system safety. The proposed framework incorporates a real-time parameter learning mechanism that adapts to the uncertainty in system degradation, and we demonstrate that non-periodic information acquisition does not compromise the accuracy of parameter estimation. We thoroughly explore the model's structural characteristics, proving the monotonicity of the value function and the existence of a mission abort control threshold. These insights are crucial for developing a threshold-based control policy that dynamically balances the need for information acquisition and the decision to abort a mission. To implement this policy efficiently, we propose a computationally lightweight algorithm that minimizes decision model complexity, ensuring both timely and precise decision-making.

1. Introduction

Modern mission-critical systems in industries like energy, aerospace, and industrial automation face the dual challenge of maintaining continuous operation while preventing failures [1-6]. Effective risk management for such systems is vital, with preventive maintenance being the most common strategy. However, advancements in sensor technology now make condition-based maintenance more feasible, offering real-time health monitoring of systems [7-11]. Despite these advancements, systems requiring continuous mission execution present unique challenges, as mid-operation maintenance is often impractical. To address this, mission abort strategies have been introduced as a risk-control method that weighs the risks of completing a mission against the potential for catastrophic failure. These strategies aim to minimize overall losses by calculating the risk of continuing operations versus the risk of aborting a mission [12-15].

Research on mission abort strategies has primarily focused on two categories: single-unit and multi-component systems [16-21]. In single-unit systems, the most common approach is based on binary-state models, where random shocks or system defects trigger an abort decision once a predefined threshold is exceeded [21, 22]. These strategies are often enhanced by advances in sensor technology, which allows for more accurate real-time monitoring of system conditions and better-informed mission abort decisions [23-27]. Another approach centers around systems in defective states, where the risk criterion is based on the duration of system defects or failures. This category also includes work on utilizing early warning signals and considering the effects of repairable and irreparable failures on mission abort decisions [28-32]. Stochastic models such as Gamma processes are also employed to describe continuous degradation, helping to determine when to abort a mission based on the system's level of degradation [33, 34].

In contrast, multi-component systems, where the failure of one or more components triggers an abort decision, introduce additional complexity [35-40]. Early work on multi-component systems focused on optimizing abort strategies based on the number of failed components, while later studies incorporated non-identical components, cooperative UAVs, and failure propagation effects [41]. The impact of task distribution among components and its relationship to the abort decision has also been explored [42]. However, most research on mission abort focuses on discrete system states or shock numbers, while continuous degradation models have shown more potential for strategy development [43]. Despite the potential of continuous models, such stochastic processes have been underutilized in mission abort studies.

Despite the progress made in mission abort research, two key gaps remain [44-46]. First, most existing studies rely on fixed inspection cycles. While periodic inspection schemes offer simplicity, they often result in delayed failure detection or unnecessary inspections in systems subject to stochastic variations [47-50]. Second, the majority of research assumes deterministic degradation paths, which fail to capture real-world uncertainties in system degradation and environmental factors. These limitations highlight a need for a unified framework that integrates non-periodic information acquisition strategies and dynamic parameter learning techniques.

This paper seeks to bridge these gaps by proposing an innovative risk management framework that integrates non-periodic information acquisition with Bayesian parameter learning. This new approach enables decision-makers to determine when to acquire health data, optimizing inspection intervals to reduce unnecessary data collection while maintaining system safety. Unlike traditional models, our framework allows for dynamic and adaptive decisions on information acquisition, accounting for variations in system degradation caused by heterogeneity or environmental uncertainties.

A key feature of this framework is its real-time parameter learning mechanism, which is effective even when information acquisition occurs on an aperiodic basis. This mechanism ensures the accuracy of updated system parameters, even when information is not collected at regular intervals. Furthermore, our framework addresses the uncertainties in system degradation by combining non-periodic data collection with Bayesian learning, creating a more robust and flexible system for risk management.

In addition to improving decision-making accuracy, this approach introduces a threshold-based control policy to balance information acquisition with mission abort decisions. The policy ensures that decisions are made at the right time, considering the trade-offs between the cost of inspections, the potential risks of system failure, and the need for mission completion. To implement this policy, we propose a computationally efficient algorithm that reduces the complexity of solving the decision model. This algorithm ensures fast and cost-effective decision-making, allowing for the timely execution of inspection and abort decisions.

In summary, this paper makes several contributions to the field of mission abort strategies. First, we propose a joint framework that integrates non-periodic information acquisition with parameter learning, offering a more flexible and cost-effective approach to system health monitoring and risk management. Second, we provide an in-depth analysis of the structural properties of the proposed model, demonstrating that non-periodic data acquisition does not compromise parameter accuracy and that the value function of the decision model is monotonic. Third, we introduce a computationally efficient algorithm for decision-making, improving the system's overall performance while minimizing computational complexity.

The remainder of this paper is structured as follows. Section 2 formulates the mission risk management framework, combining non-periodic information acquisition with parameter learning. Section 3 presents the analytical properties of the optimal control policy. Section 4 introduces numerical experiments to demonstrate the model's effectiveness and its superior performance compared to traditional heuristic policies. Section 5 concludes with a discussion of the findings and potential directions for future research.

2. Problem Formulation

We propose a novel mission risk management framework that tightly integrates non-periodic information acquisition with Bayesian parameter learning which allows to adaptively decide when to collect health information based on the current degradation state and mission context. A distinguishing feature of the framework compared to existing research on mission abort is flexibility, which allows decision-makers to evaluate the necessity of information acquisition, preventing unnecessary data collection costs while maintaining system security.

2.1. Degradation model and parameter learning

Define $\{X(t), t \geq 0\}$ as a parametric stochastic process to describe the evolution of the degraded level. It is set as an equation with transformed time scale and Brownian error terms for specific exploration. The specific degradation process can be expressed as

$$X(t) = v\Lambda(t) + \sigma B(\Lambda(t)), \tag{1}$$

where $\Lambda(t) = \int_0^t \alpha(u;\boldsymbol{\theta})du$ is the transformed time scale which can take different forms depending on the system type, such as linear, exponential, or polynomial, determines the shape of its degradation trajectory. $\boldsymbol{\theta}$ is the set of fixed degradation parameters of the system itself. Heterogeneous parameter v captures unit-to-unit heterogeneity, which has an impact on the degradation trajectory of the system through the form of acceleration factor. It is not a fixed parameter, but a random variable that follows a distribution. $B(\cdot)$ represents Brownian motion with mean 0, and σ is the drift parameter.

The stochastic acceleration factor v can be inferred with increasing accuracy by observing the degradation level of system in a Bayesian manner. The prior distribution is a Gaussian distribution with parameters μ and κ. Parameter learning can be performed based on the set of information collection time $\mathbf{t} = \{t_1, t_2, \cdots, t_n\}$ and collected degradation level set $\mathbf{X} = \{X_1, X_2, \cdots, X_n\}$. The updated hyperparameters are denoted as $\langle \tilde{\mu} \mid \mathbf{X}, \mathbf{t} \rangle$ and $\langle \tilde{\sigma} \mid \mathbf{X}, \mathbf{t} \rangle$, and abbreviated as $\tilde{\mu}$ and $\tilde{\kappa}$.

The prior probability density function of drift parameter v is given as

$$f_V(v \mid \mu, \kappa) = \frac{1}{\sqrt{2\pi\kappa^2}} \exp\left[-\frac{(v-\mu)^2}{2\kappa^2}\right]. \tag{2}$$

For a fixed drift parameter v, the probability density of obtaining this information is

$$p(\mathbf{X}, \mathbf{t} \mid v) = \prod_{i=1}^{n} \frac{\exp\left\{-\frac{\left(X_i - X_{i-1} - v\left(\Lambda(t_i) - \Lambda(t_{i-1})\right)\right)^2}{2\sigma^2\left(\Lambda(t_i) - \Lambda(t_{i-1})\right)}\right\}}{\sigma\sqrt{2\pi\left(t_i - t_{i-1}\right)}}. \tag{3}$$

There is

$$\begin{aligned} f(v \mid \mathbf{X}, \mathbf{t}) &\propto f_V(v) p(\mathbf{X}, \mathbf{t} \mid v) \\ &\propto \exp\left\{-\frac{1}{2}\left[\frac{(v-\mu)^2}{\kappa^2} + \sum_{i=1}^{n} \frac{\left(\begin{array}{c} X_i - X_{i-1} \\ -v\left(\Lambda(t_i) - \Lambda(t_{i-1})\right) \end{array}\right)^2}{\sigma^2\left(\Lambda(t_i) - \Lambda(t_{i-1})\right)}\right]\right\} \\ &\propto \exp\left\{\frac{v^2 - 2\mu v}{\kappa^2} + \frac{v^2\Lambda(t_n) - 2vX_n}{\sigma^2}\right\} \\ &\propto \exp\left\{\frac{v^2 - 2v\frac{\mu\sigma^2 + \kappa^2 X_n}{\kappa^2\Lambda(t_n) + \sigma^2}}{\frac{\kappa^2\sigma^2}{\kappa^2\Lambda(t_n) + \sigma^2}}\right\}. \end{aligned} \tag{4}$$

Since the conjugate distribution of the Gaussian distribution is also Gaussian distribution, it can be obtained that the posterior distribution of drift parameter v corresponds to a Gaussian distribution with hyperparameters $\tilde{\mu}$ and $\tilde{\kappa}$, which can be given as

$$\tilde{\mu}=\frac{\kappa^2 X_n+\mu\sigma^2}{\kappa^2\Lambda_n+\sigma^2};\tilde{\kappa}=\frac{\sigma^2\kappa^2}{\kappa^2\Lambda_n+\sigma^2}. \tag{5}$$

According to equation (4), it can be seen that the updated hyperparameters only depend on the initial hyperparameters μ, κ, the last collection time t_n and corresponding degradation level X_n.

2.2. Decision model

Consider a safety-critical system that is responsible for continuously performing a mission of duration τ. During the entire process, the system is subjected to continuous degradation due to the combined effect of external environmental and endogenous degradation of components. The health information of system can be obtained by monitoring the cumulative amount of degradation.

Let δ be a sufficiently small-time unit, denoting the minimum interval between information acquisition. There is $N\delta=\tau$. Let $\mathbf{S}=\{\mathbf{N},\mathbf{R}\}$ be the state space, where $\mathbf{N}=\{1,2,\cdots,N\}$ represents the set of possible decision epoch and $\mathbf{R}$ is the set of all real numbers. The information acquisition point $n\in\mathbf{N}$ and degradation level $x\in\mathbf{R}$ can constitute the system state $(n,x)\in\mathbf{S}$, which represents the two basic information for the decision. Decision can perform action $a\in A=\{0,1,2,\cdots,N\}$, where $a=1,\cdots,N$ represents that the next information collection is performed at $a\delta$, and $a=0$ represents that mission abort is performed.

If no abort action is performed and health indicator of the system meets $X(t)>L,\ t<\tau$, the system fails. Then both mission failure loss c_m and system failure loss c_f will be incurred. If no failure is inspected at an inspection point and the mission is aborted, only mission failure loss is incurred. In addition, the cost of each inspection is c_i. To minimize the expected total costs of the mission, the integrated problem of information acquisition and mission abort is investigated utilizing a finite horizon MDP model.

Let $V(n,x)$ represent the minimal expected cost after performing acquisition at $n\delta$. For $n=1,2,\cdots,N-1$ and $x<L$, the optimal value function can be expressed as

$$V(n,x)=\min\{V(n,x,a),a\in A\}. \tag{6}$$

$V(n,x,0)\equiv c_m$ represents the expected cost of aborting the mission. $V(n,x,a),\ a>n$ represents the expected cost of continuing the mission and is given as

$$V(n,x,a)=c_i+(c_m+c_f)\cdot[1-R(n,x,a)] + \int_x^L V(a,x')f(x'\mid n,x,a)dx', \tag{7}$$

where $R(n,x,a)$ is the reliability of the system under state (n,x) and action a, (a,x') is the next state and $f(x'\mid n,x,a)$ is the transition probability density. $V(n,x,a),\ 1\le a\le n$ is meaningless action that can be ignored. Thus, it is given as $V(n,x,a)\to\infty,\ 1\le a\le n$. $f(x'\mid n,x,a)$ can be given as

$$f(x'\mid n,x,a)=\frac{\exp\left[-\frac{\left[x'-x-\tilde{\mu}(\Lambda(a\delta)-\Lambda(n\delta))\right]^2}{2\left[\tilde{\kappa}^2(\Lambda(a\delta)-\Lambda(n\delta))^2+\sigma^2(\Lambda(a\delta)-\Lambda(n\delta))\right]}\right]}{\sqrt{2\pi\left[\tilde{\kappa}^2(\Lambda(a\delta)-\Lambda(n\delta))^2+\sigma^2(\Lambda(a\delta)-\Lambda(n\delta))\right]}}, \tag{8}$$

and $R(n,x,a)$ can be given as

$$R(n,x,a)=\Pr\{x'<L\mid n,x,a\} =\Phi\left(\frac{L-x-\tilde{\mu}(\Lambda(a\delta)-\Lambda(n\delta))}{\sqrt{\tilde{\kappa}^2(\Lambda(a\delta)-\Lambda(n\delta))^2+\sigma^2(\Lambda(a\delta)-\Lambda(n\delta))}}\right). \tag{9}$$

If no system failure occurs and no abort action is performed over the mission, then a reward c_r is obtained. The boundary equation at the N-th epoch is given as

$$V(n,x\mid n=N)=\begin{cases}-c_r, & x<L,\\ c_m+c_f, & x\ge L.\end{cases} \tag{10}$$

3. Structural Properties

This section investigates the structural properties of the optimal decision model, and then proposes algorithmic improvements to reduce the computational complexity. We establish the monotonicity of the value function, which allows us to verify the existence of control limits for mission abort. These properties promote the understandings of dynamic risk control decisions, which facilitates fast decision-making and efficient analytical computation.

■ **Definition 1.** A stochastic variable X is said to be stochastically smaller than a stochastic Y in the stochastic order, denoted by $X\prec Y$, if $\Pr\{X\le z\}\ge\Pr\{Y\le z\}\ \forall z$.

■ **Lemma 1.** For any fixed action $a\in A$ and $\Lambda(t)$ with arbitrary concave-convex characteristics, the stochastic variable $\langle X_a\mid X_n\rangle$ is stochastically non-decreasing in X_n, i.e., $\langle X_a\mid X_n=x\rangle\prec\langle X_a\mid X_n=x^+\rangle$ provided $x<x^+$.

■ **Lemma 2.** For any fixed action $a\in A$ and $\Lambda(t)$ with arbitrary concave-convex characteristics, the value function $V(n,x,a)$ is non-decreasing in x and non-increasing in n.

The proofs of Lemma 1 and Lemma 2 can be found in Appendix. Lemma 1 and Lemma 23 prove the monotonicity of the value function of the system with respect to two crucial variables. When the inspection reveals the system's degradation level, it is intuitive that higher degradation levels are associated with higher expected subsequent costs for a given epoch. Conversely, for the same degradation level, delaying the inspection leads to lower expected costs. Based on Lemma 1 and

Lemma 2, Theorem 1 establishes the control limit and proves its structural properties.

■ **Theorem 1.** For each possible decision epoch n, there exists a control limit $\xi(n)$ such that the optimal decision is mission abort if and only if $X_n > \xi(n)$. $\xi(n)$ is non-decreasing in n.

Proof. According to Lemma 3, $V(n,x,a)$ is a non-decreasing in x. Therefore, $V(n,x,a)-c_m$ is a non-decreasing in x. So clearly there is a control limit $\xi_a(n)$, such that for $x \ge \xi_a(n)$, it's better to abort the mission than to perform acquisition at $a\delta$. Then, there is a control limit $\xi(n) = \max\{\xi_a(n), a \in A\}$, such that for $x \ge \xi(n)$, it is optimal to abort the mission.

For $\forall n_1 > n_2$, it follows from Lemma 2:

$$V(n_2, \xi(n_1), a) \ge V(n_1, \xi(n_2), a) \ge c_m. \quad (11)$$

Therefore, $\xi(n)$ satisfies that $\xi(n_1) \ge \xi(n_2)$. □

Theorem 1 establishes the existence of a control limit for every inspection epoch, beyond which it is optimal to choose mission abort. Moreover, it demonstrates that this control limit consistently increases as the mission advances. Intuitively, as the mission approaches its conclusion, higher levels of degradation can be adopted before aborting a mission. Through Theorem 1, a control limit risk control policy can be established: at each inspection epoch, when the degradation level of the system is higher than a specific control limit, mission abort is performed, otherwise the system continues to perform the mission.

4. Case Study

We demonstrate the application of the proposed solution to bearings, a critical component in ensuring the safe and efficient operation of high-speed trains. Bearings are essential for reducing friction and enabling smooth rotation of wheels, and any failure can lead to severe disruptions in service, safety risks, and substantial economic losses. Therefore, effective monitoring of bearing health, early detection of degradation, and efficient risk management are vital to prevent failure during operations. High-speed train bearing degradation is influenced by multiple factors, such as mechanical wear, thermal stress, and external environmental conditions. Advances in sensor technology, such as vibration analysis and acoustic emission sensors, have enabled real-time monitoring of bearing conditions, helping to detect early signs of degradation. Page numbering

We evaluated the initial parameters of the model by selecting the actual vibration signal monitoring data of 30 groups of failed bearings during the mission. To facilitate the subsequent optimal strategy solution and case comparison, we scaled the degenerate parameters. The amount of degradation at the beginning is set to 0, and the failure threshold is set to $L = 10$. The degradation related parameters of the battery can be converted. For models considering parameter learning, the drift parameter is $v \sim N(\mu, \kappa^2)$ where $\mu = 0.714, \kappa = 0.341$. The diffusion parameter is $\sigma = 0.09$.

A mission with a duration of 20 days was selected for this case validation. During the mission, it cannot be replaced or repaired directly, otherwise it will cause the vehicle to shut down and will not be able to continue the mission for the following days. There is a window for bearing health status assessment only at the end of each day's mission. That is, the minimum detection unit interval is 1 day. Thus, the unit time is set as $\delta = 1$. For ease of calculation, the costs of system failure and mission failure are quantified in equal scale as $c_m = 3000$, $c_f = 5000$, $c_r = 4000$. Each time a bearing is inspected and evaluated for its health condition, it will result in non-negligible time, equipment and labor costs, which are denoted as $c_i = 200$.

According to the above data, combined with equations (5)-(10), we calculate the value function under the proposed policy and model. Fig. 1 shows the overall trend of the value function across different decision epochs. This visual representation captures the relationship between the system's degradation level and the associated optimal costs. The monotonic decrease in the value function as time progresses aligns with our earlier structural property findings, particularly the conclusion that the value function is non-increasing with respect to the decision epoch n for any given degradation level.

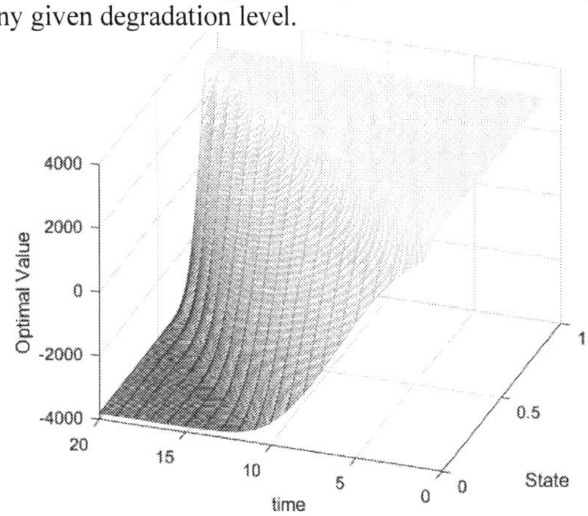

Figure 1. Optimal value function trend graph.

Fig. 2 illustrates how the control limit varies under different cost parameters. This figure reflects the behavior predicted in Theorem 1, where the control limit is shown to increase as the mission progresses, confirming that higher levels of degradation can be tolerated as time elapses. The graph also highlights the dependency of the control limit on different cost parameters, validating the structural property that the control limit is non-decreasing with respect to time and degradation level. By comparing the impact of varying cost parameters, this figure emphasizes the importance of the cost structure in shaping mission abort decisions.

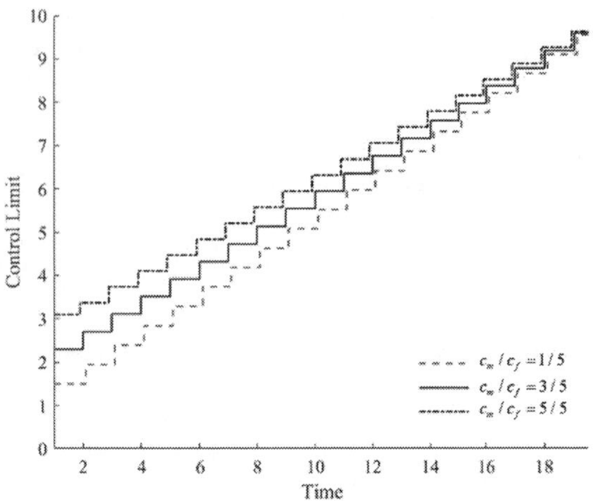

Figure 2. Control limit of different cost.

5. Conclusion

This paper introduces an innovative mission risk management framework that integrates non-periodic information acquisition with Bayesian parameter learning to optimize decision-making. By relaxing fixed inspection intervals, the framework reduces unnecessary data collection and inspection costs while ensuring system safety. The real-time learning method enhances the model's ability to manage product heterogeneity and environmental uncertainties. We demonstrate that reducing information acquisition frequency does not compromise parameter accuracy, and a threshold-based mission abort policy is proposed. A computationally efficient algorithm ensures the solvability of the model. The framework's practical value is validated through its application to high-speed train bearings, outperforming traditional policies and delivering superior economic benefits and risk control efficiency.

Future research could extend this framework to consider multiple uncertainties, such as environmental and operational variations, for a more robust decision-making model. Investigating detection and maintenance strategies for individual components in complex systems would further enhance the framework's adaptability. Additionally, integrating operational constraints, such as resource availability and time limitations, could optimize mission outcomes and resource usage, improving the applicability of mission abort strategies in diverse critical systems.

6. Acknowledgement

This work is supported by the National Natural Science Foundation of China (Grant No. 72101010), and the Basic Technical Research Project of China (Grant No. JSZL2018601B004).

7. Appendix

Proof of Lemma 1. The conditional distribution of v can be obtained as $\langle v \mid \mathbf{X}, \mathbf{t}\rangle \sim N(\tilde{\mu}, \tilde{\kappa}^2)$. According to Proposition 1, $\tilde{\mu}$ is an increasing function of X_n and $\tilde{\kappa}^2$ is constant in X_n.

For $\forall x_1 \ge x_2$ and $\forall z \ge 0$, it follows that

$$\begin{aligned}\Pr\{v \le z \mid X_n = x_1\} &= \Phi\left(\frac{z - \dfrac{\kappa^2 x_1 + \mu\sigma^2}{\kappa^2\Lambda(n\delta)+\sigma^2}}{\tilde{\kappa}}\right)\\ &\le \Phi\left(\frac{z - \dfrac{\kappa^2 x_2 + \mu\sigma^2}{\kappa^2\Lambda(n\delta)+\sigma^2}}{\tilde{\kappa}}\right)\\ &= \Pr\{v \le z \mid X_n = x_2\}.\end{aligned} \tag{12}$$

It can be obtained that $\langle v \mid X_n = x^+\rangle \succ \langle v \mid X_n = x\rangle$.

For $\forall v^1 \ge v^2$ and $\forall z \ge 0$, there is

$$\begin{aligned}\Pr\left\{X_a - X_n \le z \mid v^1\right\} &= \Phi\left(\frac{z - v^1\left(\Lambda(a\delta) - \Lambda(n\delta)\right)}{\sigma\sqrt{\Lambda(a\delta) - \Lambda(n\delta)}}\right)\\ &\le \Phi\left(\frac{z - v^2\left(\Lambda(a\delta) - \Lambda(n\delta)\right)}{\sigma\sqrt{\Lambda(a\delta) - \Lambda(n\delta)}}\right)\\ &= \Pr\left\{X_a - X_n \le z \mid v^2\right\}.\end{aligned} \tag{13}$$

It can be obtained that $\langle X_a - X_n \mid v^1\rangle \succ \langle X_a - X_n \mid v^2\rangle$.

Combining above, it can be concluded that

$\langle X_a - X_n \mid X_n = x^+\rangle \succ \langle X_a - X_n \mid X_n = x\rangle$. Finally, it can be noted that

$$\begin{aligned}\langle X_a \mid X_n = x^+\rangle &= \langle X_a - X_n \mid X_n = x^+\rangle + x^+\\ &\succ \langle X_a - X_n \mid X_n = x^+\rangle + x\\ &\succ \langle X_a - X_n \mid X_n = x\rangle + x\\ &= \langle X_a \mid X_n = x\rangle.\end{aligned} \tag{14}$$

Proof completed. □

Proof of Lemma 2. To prove the monotonicity of value functions, a Proposition is derived from Shaked and Shanthikumar (2007): Consider a family of distributions $\{G_\theta(x)\}$, indexed by θ, if $G_\theta(x) \prec G_{\theta'}(x)$ whenever $\theta \le \theta'$, and if $F_1(\theta) \prec F_2(\theta)$ are two distribution of θ, then $\int G_\theta(x)dF_1(\theta) \prec \int G_\theta(x)dF_2(\theta)$.

By equation (9), it clearly that $V(n, x \mid n = N)$ is non-decreasing in x.

Suppose that $V(a, x)$ is non-decreasing in x for all $a > n$. According to Lemma 1, $\langle X_a \mid X_n\rangle$ is stochastically non-decreasing in X_n. There is

$$\begin{aligned} V(n,x,a) &= c_i + (c_m + c_f)\cdot[1 - R(n,x,a)] \\ &\quad + \int_x^L V(a,x') f(x' \mid n,x,a)\,dx' \\ &\le c_i + (c_m + c_f)\cdot[1 - R(n,x^+,a)] \\ &\quad + \int_{x^+}^L V(a,x') f(x' \mid n,x^+,a)\,dx' \\ &= V(n,x^+,a). \end{aligned} \tag{15}$$

$V(n,x,0) \equiv c_m$ is constant in x. It can be proved that $V(n,x)$ is also non-decreasing in x if $V(a,x)$ is non-decreasing in x for all $a > n$. Furthermore, we can recursively get that for each possible decision epoch n, $V(n,x)$ is non-decreasing in x.

There exists $x < x^+ < L$ that makes

$$\begin{aligned} V(n,x,a) &= c_i + (c_m + c_f)\cdot[1 - R(n,x,a,a)] \\ &\quad + \int_x^L V(a,x') f(x' \mid n,x,a)\,dx' \\ &= c_i + (c_m + c_f)\cdot[1 - R(n,x,a)] \\ &\quad + R(n,x,a) V(a,x^+) \\ &\ge V(a,x^+) \\ &\ge V(a,x). \end{aligned} \tag{16}$$

Therefore, $V(n,x,a)$ is non-increasing in n can be proved. □

8. References

[1] Levitin G, Finkelstein M, Huang H. Optimal mission abort policies for multistate systems. Reliability Engineering & System Safety, 2020, 193: 106671.

[2] Peng R, Zhai Q, Xing L, Yang J. Reliability analysis and optimal structure of series-parallel phased-mission systems subject to fault-level coverage. IISE Transactions, 2016, 48(8): 736-746.

[3] Jardine A, Lin D, Banjevic D. A review on machinery diagnostics and prognostics implementing condition-based maintenance. Mechanical Systems and Signal Processing, 2006, 20(7): 1483-1510.

[4] Shang L, Liu B, Qiu Q, et al. Three-dimensional warranty and post-warranty maintenance of products with monitored mission cycles, Reliability Engineering & System Safety, 2023, 239:109506.

[5] Zhang Z, Yang L. State-Based Opportunistic Maintenance with Multifunctional Maintenance Windows, IEEE Transactions on Reliability, 2021, 70(4): 1481-1494.

[6] Zhang Z, Yang L. Postponed maintenance scheduling integrating state variation and environmental impact, Reliability Engineering & System Safety, 2020, 202: 107065.

[7] Kim MJ, Makis V. Joint optimization of sampling and control of partially observable failing systems. Operations Research, 2013, 61(3): 777-790.

[8] Jafari L, Makis V. Optimal production and maintenance policy for a partially observable production system with stochastic demand. International Journal of Industrial and Systems Engineering, 2019, 13(7): 449-456.

[9] Xiao H, Zhang Y, Xiang Y, Peng R. Optimal design of a linear sliding window system with consideration of performance sharing. Reliability Engineering & System Safety, 2020, 198: 106900.

[10] Wei F, Tan L, Ma X, et al. A hybrid prognostic framework: Stochastic degradation process with adaptive trajectory learning to transfer historical health knowledge, Mechanical System & Signal Processing, 2025, 224: 112171.

[11] Yang L, Chen Y, Qiu Q, et al. Risk Control of Mission-Critical Systems: Abort Decision-Makings Integrating Health and Age Conditions, IEEE Transactions on Industrial Informatics, 2022, 18(10): 6887-6894.

[12] Levitin G, Finkelstein M, Xiang Y. Optimal aborting rule in multi-attempt missions performed by multicomponent systems. European Journal of Operational Research, 2020, 283(1): 244-252.

[13] Yang L, Ye ZS, Lee CG, et al. A two-phase preventive maintenance policy considering imperfect repair and postponed replacement, European Journal of Operational Research, 2019, 274: 966-977.

[14] Yang L, Peng R, Li G, Lee CG. Operations management of wind farms integrating multiple impacts of wind conditions and resource constraints, Energy Conversion and Management, 2020, 205: 112162.

[15] Myers A. Probability of loss assessment of critical k-out-of-n: G systems having a mission abort policy. IEEE Transactions on Reliability, 2009, 58(4): 694-701.

[16] Levitin G, Finkelstein M. Optimal mission abort policy for systems operating in a random environment. Risk Analysis, 2018, 38(4): 795-803.

[17] Qiu Q, Cui L. Gamma process based optimal mission abort policy. Reliability Engineering & System Safety, 2019, 190: 106496.

[18] Peng R, Zhai Q, Xing L, Yang J. Reliability of demand-based phased-mission systems subject to fault level coverage. Reliability Engineering & System Safety, 2014, 121: 18-25.

[19] Wei F, Wang J, Ma X, et al. An Optimal Opportunistic Maintenance Planning Integrating Discrete- and Continuous-State Information, Mathematics, 2023, 11(15): 3322.

[20] Shang L, Liu B, Gao K, et al. Random Warranty and Replacement Models Customizing from the Perspective of Heterogeneity, Mathematics, 2023, 11(15): 3330.

[21] Wang L, Song L, Qiu Q, et al. Warranty Cost Analysis for Multi-State Products Protected by Lemon Laws. Applied Sciences, 2023, 13(3): 1541.

[22] Qu L, Liao J, Gao K, et al. Joint Optimization of Production Lot Sizing and Preventive Maintenance Threshold Based on Nonlinear Degradation, Applied Sciences, 2022, 12(17): 8638.

[23] Qiu Q, Maillart LM, Prokopyev OA, et al. Optimal condition-based mission abort decisions. IEEE Transactions on Reliability, 2022, 72(1): 408-425.

[24] Levitin G, Finkelstein M. Optimal mission abort policy for systems operating in a random environment. Risk Analysis, 2018, 38(4): 795-803.

[25] Xiao H, Yi K, Kou G, Xing L. Reliability of a two-dimensional demand-based networked system with multistate components. Naval Research Logistics, 2020, 67(6): 453-468.

[26] Qiu Q, Cui L. Optimal mission abort policy for systems subject to random shocks based on virtual age process. Reliability Engineering & System Safety, 2019, 189: 11-20.

[27] Cha J, Finkelstein M, Levitin G. Optimal mission abort policy for partially repairable heterogeneous systems. European Journal of Operational Research, 2018, 271(3): 818-825.

[28] Zhao X, Sun J, Qiu Q, Chen K. Optimal inspection and mission abort policies for systems subject to degradation. European Journal of Operational Research, 2021, 292(2): 610-621.

[29] Levitin G, Xing L, Dai Y. Mission abort policy for systems with observable states of standby components. Risk Analysis, 2020, 40(10): 1900-1912.

[30] Levitin G, Finkelstein M, Xiang Y. Optimal inspections and mission abort policies for multistate systems. Reliability Engineering & System Safety, 2021, 214: 107700.

[31] Levitin G, Finkelstein M, Xiang Y. Optimal mission abort policies for repairable multistate systems performing multi-attempt mission. Reliability Engineering & System Safety, 2021, 209: 107497.

[32] Liu X, Sun Q, Ye ZS, et al. Optimal multi-type inspection policy for systems with imperfect online monitoring. Reliability Engineering & System Safety, 2021, 207: 107335.

[33] Zheng R, Wang J, Zhang Y. A hybrid repair-replacement policy in the proportional hazards model. European Journal of Operational Research, 2023, 304(3): 1011-1021.

[34] Peng R, He X, Zhong C, et al. Preventive maintenance for heterogeneous parallel systems with two failure modes. Reliability Engineering & System Safety, 2022, 220: 108310.

[35] Levitin G, Xing L, Dai Y. Optimal activation of components exposed to individual and common shock processes in asynchronous multi-phase missions. Reliability Engineering & System Safety, 2025, 256: 110789.

[36] Levitin G, Xing L, Dai Y. Optimal scheduling, loading and aborting in additive missions performed by multiple components in shock environment. Reliability Engineering & System Safety, 2025, 256: 110750.

[37] Yang L, Wei F, Qiu Q, et al. Controlling Mission Hazards through Integrated Abort and Spare Support Optimization, Risk Analysis, 2024, DOI: 10.1111/risa.17696.

[38] Yang L, Wei F, Qiu Q. Mission Risk Control via Joint Optimization of Sampling and Abort Decisions, Risk Analysis, 2024, 44(3): 666-685.

[39] Yang L, Zhou S, Ma X, et al. Group machinery intelligent maintenance: Adaptive health prediction and global dynamic maintenance decision-making, Reliability Engineering & System Safety, 2024: 110426.

[40] Wang J, Yang L, Ma X, et al. Joint optimization of multi-window maintenance and spare part provisioning policies for production systems, Reliability Engineering & System Safety, 2021, 216: 108006.

[41] Wang J, Tang L, Ma X, et al. Prognosis-driven reliability analysis and replacement policy optimization for two-phase continuous degradation, Reliability Engineering & System Safety, 2023, 230:108909.

[42] Jia H, Peng R, Yang L, et al. Reliability evaluation of demand-based warm standby systems with capacity storage, Reliability Engineering & System Safety, 2022, 218: 108132.

[43] Wu D, Han R, Ma Y, et al. A two-dimensional maintenance optimization framework balancing hazard risk and energy consumption rates, Computers & Industrial Engineering, 2022, 169, 108193.

[44] Chen Y, Ma X, Wei F, et al. Dynamic Scheduling of Intelligent Group Maintenance Planning under Usage Availability Constraint, Mathematics, 2022, 10 (15): 2730.

[45] Wang J, Peng R, Qiu Q, et al. An inspection-based replacement planning in consideration of state-driven imperfect inspections, Reliability Engineering & System Safety, 2023, 232(6): 109064.

[46] Ma X, Liu B, Yang L, et al. Reliability analysis and condition-based maintenance optimization for a warm standby cooling system, Reliability Engineering & System Safety, 2020, 193: 106588.

[47] Wang J, Ma X, Qiu Q, et al. A hybrid inspection-replacement policy for multi-stage degradation considering imperfect inspection with variable probabilities, 2023, 241: 109629.

[48] Yang L, Sun Q, Ye Z. Designing mission abort strategies based on early-warning information: Application to UAV, IEEE Transactions on Industrial Informatics, 2020, 16 (1): 277-287.

[49] Chen Y, Wu T, Ma X, et al. System Maintenance Optimization Under Structural Dependency: A Dynamic Grouping Approach, IEEE Systems Journal, 2024, DOI: 10.1109/JSYST.2024.3422284.

[50] Wang J, Ma X, Zhao Y, et al. Condition-based maintenance management for two-stage continuous deterioration with two-dimensional inspection errors, Quality and Reliability Engineering International, 2024, DOI: 10.1002/qre.3613.

Joint Optimization of Mission Abort and Learning Strategies in Cloud Computing Environments

Bosen Liu, Cuicui Pei, Rongchi Sun, Qingan Qiu*
School of Management, Beijing Institute of Technology, Beijing 100081, China.
Email: qiu_qingan@bit.edu.cn

Keywords: Bayesian learning; adaptive decision-making; risk control; mission abort strategies

Abstract -
When operating in dynamic uncertain environments, safety-critical systems are often threatened by unknown stochastic shock damages, where traditional risk control strategies with known model parameters struggle to address the coupled challenges of parameter uncertainty and dynamic risks. This paper proposes an adaptive first learning and then optimize framework based on Bayesian inference, which enhances system survivability by jointly optimizing learning duration and risk-sensitive termination decisions. First, a learning duration is set and Bayesian parameter learning strategy is developed to address the unknown shock arrival rate, enabling online learning of shock rates through observed number of shocks. Second, the mission abort decision is optimized based on the updated parameter distribution. Furthermore, a multi-objective optimization model that integrates observation costs, failure losses, and termination penalties is established to determine the optimal observation time. The quantitative trade-off between information acquisition accuracy and risk exposure duration is studied. Theoretical analysis demonstrates that the proposed adaptive strategy dynamically balances the exploration-exploitation dilemma through the synergy of Bayesian sequential updating and risk-sensitive decision-making. This study provides a novel methodological framework for reliable operation of safety-critical systems such as drones and industrial robots in unknown environments.

1 Introduction

Mission abort mechanisms are one of the key operational strategies for ensuring system stability, enabling organizations to monitor performance in real-time and respond quickly to potential risks. These mechanisms terminate tasks under specific conditions, such as when resource utilization becomes critical or when security alarms are triggered[1, 2, 3, 4]. Mission abort strategies are widely used in industrial fields with high safety requirements, such as aerospace [5], reactor operations[6], and drone missions[7, 8]. Levitin et al. [9, 10] established optimization algorithm framework based on stochastic shock processes to balance mission success probability (MSP) and system survival probability (SSP). Subsequent studies have expanded into multi-state systems, exploring optimal abort-and-rescue methods that consider system degradation over time and allow for multiple attempts at recovery, achieving a balance between MSP and SSP[11, 12, 13, 14]. As research advances, significant efforts have been focused on mitigating failure risks through mission abort strategies.

From the perspective of system structure, mission abort policies can be divided into two categories: single-component systems and multi-component systems. The optimal task termination decisions for single-component systems are fundamental and have received considerable attention in recent literature [15, 16, 17, 18, 12]. Building upon these studies, research on multi-component systems highlights the complexity of task execution and termination decisions, which are influenced by a variety of factors. For example, Chai [19]used Markov chain embedding to examine multiple criteria, providing valuable insights into optimizing abort strategies and related probabilities to minimize expected costs. Wang [20] optimized the abort thresholds within multi-state balanced systems. Other studies have developed joint optimization models for multi-phase component reallocation and maintenance cost balancing, offering decision-making support for engineers. Research findings indicate the necessity for tailored strategies to enhance performance and efficiently manage risks in various engineering systems [21, 22, 23].

The operational risk of safety-critical systems commonly comes external damage and internal degradation. In hazardous external environments, the formulation of mission abort policies has predominantly relied on shock-based frameworks. These models typically track variables such as the cumulative number of shocks and the length of shock sequences, employing stochastic processes like homogeneous and non-homogeneous Poisson models, as well as renewal processes, to accurately capture the randomness of external shock [24, 25, 26, 27, 28, 29]. Such approaches are vital for characterizing failure mechanisms and evaluating system reliability amid external uncertainties in safety-sensitive systems. Besides external shocks, the progressive internal degradation of components driven by operational stress and workload also influences the timing of mission termination. Risk assessments often incorporate measurement metrics like degradation level and total mission time to inform abort decisions [30, 31, 32, 33].

In mission abort decision modeling, missions are typically classified based on whether they involve a single attempt or multiple attempts. The optimization of abort strategies for single-attempt missions has been addressed in studies such as [24, 26, 27, 34]. Recently, research has shifted focus toward multi-attempt missions, with advanced models developed to evaluate critical performance metrics such as mission success probability, system survivability, and expected component losses. For example, Meng et al. [35] proposed a model that optimizes activation delays and abort strategies to minimize expected mission loss. Levitin et al.[36]designed parallel models focusing on component activation delays and abort strategies, emphasizing the importance of timing in task execution. Other studies have built multi-attempt models to evaluate different activation delays, highlighting the necessity to coordinate the activation order. Hu and Chen[1]introduced a dual abort strategy that considers imperfect alarms and dynamically adjusts decision thresholds. Levitin et al. [37] explored task abort and sequencing in multi-task, multi-attempt missions constrained by time, providing insights into joint optimization challenges.

Due to their practical relevance, mission abort policies are often combined with various optimization issues such as system load distribution [15, 36, 27], component activation policies [38], sequencing of tasks [39], implementation of protective strategies [40], adjustments to mission plans [41], management of spare parts [13], and protocols for switching components [42].

Despite significant progress in mission abort strategies, substantial research gaps remain in systematic solutions for parameter-unknown scenarios under dynamic uncertain environments [43]. Existing literature predominantly focuses on risk decision-making in static environments, lacking adaptive mechanisms for uncertain degradation process and shock environment. Furthermore, current methods often employ single risk control thresholds, failing to adequately distinguish between system-level catastrophic failures and task-level routine failures, resulting in insufficient conservatism in safety-critical decision models.

To address these limitations, this paper introduces a novel framework for learning and mission abort strategies, featuring three key innovations: (1) A novel age-based learning strategy is developed. To be specific, a parameter learning phase is employed utilizing conjugate priors, enabling real-time estimation and quantification of uncertainty for time-varying shock rates. (2) Based on the accumulated data on shock occurrences during the learning phase, the decision-maker updates the unknown parameters and subsequently determines whether to abort the mission. (3) The optimal length of learning phase and mission abort decisions are jointly studied to minimize the expected total cost. This framework effectively bridges the gap between dynamic environment modeling, enhanced risk assessment, and practical engineering implementation, offering decision support tools that are both theoretically rigorous and readily applicable to safety-critical systems.

2 Problem Formulation

2.1 Model Description

We consider a safety-critical system operating in dynamic uncertain environments and is required to complete predetermined workload W within total duration T. The system initiates with operational speed v that decays exponentially upon each external shock according to the mechanism: $v_i = v \cdot a^i$ where $a \in (0,1)$ is the speed decay factor. For instance, when $a = 0.9$, the speed reduces to 59% of its initial value after the 5th shock. This multiplicative degradation model effectively captures progressive performance deterioration caused by component wear-out and sensor accuracy decline in real-world systems.

During mission execution, external shocks arrive following a Poisson process with unknown rate λ, where the number of shocks in time interval $[0, t]$ is modeled as $N(t) \sim \text{Poisson}(\lambda t)$. The failure probability at the k-th shock follows a progressive pattern: $p(k) = 1 - (1-q)^k$ with $q \in (0,1)$ as baseline failure probability, which ensures monotonically increasing failure risk from shock damage accumulation. The survival probability after k shocks is analytically expressed as:

$$S(k) = \prod_{i=1}^{k}(1 - p(i)) = (1-q)^{k(k+1)/2} \tag{1}$$

where the triangular number summation $\sum_{i=1}^{k} i = k(k+1)/2$ simplifies computational complexity through exponential transformation.

2.2 Learning and Mission Abort Strategies

This section proposes a first learning and then optimize framework to address the problem of mission abort decision-making in uncertain shock environment. The operational process features risk control through learning and decision phases. Specifically, to address the unknown shock arrival rate in the abort decision-making, the decision-maker sets a learning phase with length of $t(t < T)$. During the learning phase, the decision-maker actively monitors shock events to collect data of the number of shocks $n = N(t)$. Based on the collected data, a Bayesian learning framework is employed that enables real-time estimation of the unknown λ. To ensure computational efficiency, we set Gamma prior $\lambda \sim \text{Gamma}(\alpha_0, \beta_0)$ with α_0 as prior virtual shocks and β_0 as prior "virtual observation time". Using the monitored number of shocks, posterior parameter updates can be conducted as $\alpha = \alpha_0 + n$, $\beta = \beta_0 + t$. That is, posterior distribution can be updated to $\lambda | n, t \sim \text{Gamma}(\alpha_0 + n, \beta_0 + t)$ after observing (n, t).

Following the finite learning phase, the decision-maker then updates the distribution of remaining shocks as $m \sim \text{NB}(\alpha, \frac{\beta}{\beta+T'})$ over $T' = T - t$, and then calculates system survival probability in decision-phase as $S_2(m|n) = (1-q)^{(2n+m+1)m/2}$. The optimal mission abort decision should be made to balance the cost of system failure and mission failure.

This study considers three types of cost including the observation cost $c_1 t$, which is linear in observation time, reflecting resource consumption; catastrophic failure cost c_2 and task failure cost c_3. On one hand, a longer learning phase allows for a more comprehensive understanding of the uncertain environment, but it also incurs higher observation costs. On the other hand, shortening the learning period may lead to less accurate estimation of the shock arrival rate, resulting in less reliable abort decisions. Therefore, the optimal duration of the learning phase should be determined in conjunction with the abort decision to minimize the expected total cost. Given decision variable t, the optimal learning and mission abort problem can be formulated as

$$\begin{aligned} \min_t \quad & \mathbb{E}[C_{\text{total}}] = c_1 t + \sum_{n=0}^{\infty} P(n|t) \cdot \min\{R_{\text{continue}}(n,t), c_4\} \\ \text{s.t.} \quad & T - t \geq t_{\min} \\ & S_{\text{total}} \geq S_{\min} \\ & W_{\text{remain}} \geq 0 \end{aligned}$$

where conditional risk value R_{continue} integrates dual risks:

$$R_{\text{continue}} = c_2[1 - S_{\text{total}}] + c_3[1 - P_{\text{complete}}] \quad (2)$$

The optimal learning and stopping decisions can be determined by minimizing the expected total cost.

3 Cost Analysis and Optimization Model

Given the posterior parameter distribution$\lambda|n,t \sim \text{Gamma}(\alpha_0 + n, \beta_0 + t)$, the survival probability after n shocks in the observation phase, $S_1(n)$, and the survival probability after n shocks in the decision phase, $S_2(m|n)$ can be given as follows

$$S_1(n) = (1-q)^{n(n+1)/2} \quad (3)$$

$$S_2(m|n) = (1-q)^{(2n+m+1)m/2} \quad (4)$$

The term $(2n + m + 1)m/2$ corresponds to the cumulative sum from shock $n + 1$ to $n + m$. Then the probability of m shocks occurring in remaining time $T' = T - t$ during the decision phase is

$$P(m|n,t) = \binom{\alpha_0 + n + m - 1}{m} \left(\frac{\beta_0 + t}{\beta_0 + t + T'}\right)^{\alpha_0 + n} \left(\frac{T'}{\beta_0 + t + T'}\right)^m \quad (5)$$

Here, the combination number $\binom{\alpha_0+n+m-1}{m}$ represents success-failure permutations. $\frac{\beta_0+t}{\beta_0+t+T'}$ is the posterior success probability reflecting historical data weight. $\frac{T'}{\beta_0+t+T'}$ is the posterior failure probability proportional to T'. $\alpha_0 + n$ denotes the posterior success count combining prior belief and observations.

Linearizing the speed decay constraint $va^{n+m}T' \geq W'$ via logarithmic transformation, we have

$$m_{\max} = \left\lfloor \frac{\ln(W'/(vT'))}{\ln a} - n \right\rfloor, \quad W' = W - vt\frac{1-a^{n+1}}{1-a} \quad (6)$$

where W' represents remaining workload considering cumulative speed decay effects. The overall success probability is given as

$$P_{\text{success}} = \sum_{n=0}^{\infty} \text{NB}(n; \alpha_0, \tfrac{\beta_0}{\beta_0+t}) S_1(n) \sum_{m=0}^{m_{\max}} P(m|n,t) S_2(m|n) \quad (7)$$

Here, $\text{NB}(n; \alpha_0, \frac{\beta_0}{\beta_0+t})$ denotes the negative binomial distribution for observation-phase shocks. Outer summation covers all possible observation outcomes n. Inner summation calculates allowable shocks $m_{\max}$ for each n. $S_2(m|n) = (1-q)^{(2n+m+1)m/2}$ denotes the survival probability during the decision phase.

$$R_{\text{continue}}(n,t) = c_2 \left[1 - S_1(n) \sum_{m=0}^{m_{\max}} P(m|n,t) S_2(m|n)\right] + c_3 S_1(n) \left[1 - \sum_{m=0}^{m_{\max}} P(m|n,t) \mathbf{1}_{\text{complete}}\right] \quad (8)$$

Here, the first term corresponds to the cost associated with catastrophic failure risk. The second term is the expected cost of task failure. The indicator function $\mathbf{1}_{\text{complete}}$ represents the speed constraint satisfaction.

The expected total cost combining direct observation cost $c_1 t$, mission failure and system failure and can be given as

$$\mathbb{E}[C_{\text{total}}] = c_1 t + \sum_{n=0}^{\infty} \text{NB}(n; \alpha_0, \tfrac{\beta_0}{\beta_0+t}) \cdot \min\{R_{\text{continue}}(n,t), c_4\} \quad (9)$$

Combining the optimization constraints, the optimal learning strategy, i.e., the optimal length of learning phase, can be determined by minimizing the expected total cost,

$$t^* = \arg\min_{t\in[0,T]} \mathbb{E}[C_{\text{total}}], \quad \text{s.t. } T - t \geq t_{\min}, \ S_1(n) \geq S_{\min} \ \forall n \quad (10)$$

where $t_{\min}$ denotes the minimum decision-phase operation time and $S_{\min}$ is the lower bound of the survival probability.

4 Conclusions and Future Perspectives

This study introduces an innovative learning-optimization framework for mission abort decisions in uncertain stochastic shock environments, marking significant advances in both theory and methodology. First, we develop an adaptive approach to parameter learning and mission decision-making. The process begins with a fixed-length observation phase to monitor shock occurrences. Using observed data, the uncertain shock rate parameter λ is updated via the Gamma-Poisson conjugate model, with the posterior distribution given by $\lambda|n,t \sim \text{Gamma}(\alpha_0 + n, \beta_0 + t)$. This formulation allows real-time Bayesian estimation of λ, where the prior parameters—namely the "virtual shock count" α_0 and "virtual observation time" β_0 are designed to ensure a probabilistic foundation for adaptive decisions. Second, the framework assesses the expected total cost, integrating the learning and optimization strategies. Lastly, a multi-objective constrained optimization model uncovers quantitative trade-offs between observation duration t and associated risk costs, providing a mathematically rigorous and verifiable foundation for reliability assessment and decision-making in industrial systems.

While demonstrating significant advantages in theoretical derivation and numerical simulation, the model's application boundaries and improvement potential require objective recognition. Regarding modeling assumptions, the current homogeneous Poisson process assumption fails to consider prevalent real-world scenarios with time-varying shock rates and shock intensity heterogeneity, potentially leading to decision biases in sudden shock cluster events. Computational efficiency-wise, despite reduced complexity through closed-form solutions, the state space dimensionality still suffers combinatorial explosion with increasing shock counts, necessitating approximate simplification strategies for high-dimensional problems. Fixed failure probability parameter q overlooks dynamic multi-physics coupling effects from temperature and vibration. Moreover, practical engineering constraints like sensor latency and communication noise remain unaddressed, potentially affecting algorithm deployment in real hardware platforms.

The fundamental framework established in this work creates a new methodological paradigm for decision-making in safety-critical systems. Future research will focus on enhancing environmental robustness, computational real-time performance, and engineering practicality to transform theoretical advantages into industrial value. To be specific, future research can broaden this framework by incorporating advanced theoretical models and engineering techniques. In complex environments, Hawkes processes could be used to model spatiotemporal shock clustering, developing self-exciting failure models that adapt to new risks. Additionally, as multiple sources of uncertainty exist, exploring optimal learning strategies and mission abort decisions amid multi-parameter uncertainty is essential. In multi-agent systems, designing distributed abort protocols that leverage information sharing and resource management is necessary. Engineering efforts should focus on creating efficient parameter estimation algorithms to facilitate industrial application. Ultimately, deploying online learning modules, such as Kalman filter-based multi-sensor data fusion, will enable real-time environmental parameter estimation, improving dynamic reliability assessment and adaptive control.

Acknowledgment

This research is supported by National Natural Science Foundation of China (72371030 and 72001026).

References

[1] Jiawen Hu and Piao Chen. Mission abort policy considering imperfect alarms and two abort options. *Naval Research Logistics (NRL)*, 2025.

[2] Chen Fang, Jianhui Chen, and Daizhen Qiu. Reliability modeling for balanced systems considering mission abort policies. *Reliability Engineering System Safety*, 243:109853, 2024.

[3] Lujie Liu and Jun Yang. A dynamic mission abort policy for the swarm executing missions and its solution method by tailored deep reinforcement learning. *Reliability Engineering & System Safety*, 234:109149, 2023.

[4] Gregory Levitin, Maxim Finkelstein, and Yuanshun Dai. Mission abort policy optimization for series systems with overlapping primary and rescue subsystems operating in a random environment. *Reliability Engineering & System Safety*, 193:106590, 2020.

[5] Li Yang, Qiuzhuang Sun, and Zhi-Sheng Ye. Designing mission abort strategies based on early-warning information: Application to UAV. *IEEE Transactions on Industrial Informatics*, 16(1):277–287, 2020.

[6] Guoqing Cheng, Ling Li, Chunxia Shangguan, Nan Yang, Bo Jiang, and Ningrong Tao. Optimal joint inspection and mission abort policy for a partially observable system. *Reliability Engineering System Safety*, 229:108870, 2023.

[7] Qingan Qiu, Meng Kou, Ke Chen, Qiao Deng, Fengming Kang, and Cong Lin. Optimal stopping problems for mission oriented systems considering time redundancy. *Reliability Engineering & System Safety*, 205:107226, 2021.

[8] Xian Zhao, Ying Dai, Qingan Qiu, and Yaguang Wu. Joint optimization of mission aborts and allocation of standby components considering mission loss. *Reliability Engineering & System Safety*, 225:108612, 2022.

[9] Gregory Levitin, Maxim Finkelstein, and Yuanshun Dai. State-based mission abort policies for multistate systems. *Reliability Engineering & System Safety*, 204:107122, 2020.

[10] Gregory Levitin, Liudong Xing, and Yuanshun Dai. Optimal attempt scheduling and aborting in heterogenous system performing asynchronous multi-attempt mission. *Reliability Engineering & System Safety*, 251:110335, 11 2024.

[11] Qinglai Dong and Pin Liu. Optimal mission abort policy for a balanced system with a restricted mechanism. *Quality and Reliability Engineering International*, 39(6):2385–2397, 2023.

[12] Li Yang, Fanping Wei, and Qingan Qiu. Mission risk control via joint optimization of sampling and abort decisions. *Risk Analysis*, 44(3):666–685, 2024.

[13] Li Yang, Fanping Wei, Xiaobing Ma, and Qingan Qiu. Controlling mission hazards through integrated abort and spare support optimization. *Risk Analysis*, 2025.

[14] Li Yang, Yi Chen, Qingan Qiu, and Jiantai Wang. Risk control of mission-critical systems: Abort decision-makings integrating health and age conditions. *IEEE Transactions on Industrial Informatics*, 18(10):6887–6894, 2022.

[15] Qingan Qiu, Rong Li, and Xian Zhao. Failure risk management: Adaptive performance control and mission abort decisions. *Risk Analysis*, 45(2):421–440, 2025.

[16] Qingan Qiu, Lirong Cui, and Bei Wu. Dynamic mission abort policy for systems operating in a controllable environment with self-healing mechanism. *Reliability Engineering & System Safety*, 203:107069, 2020.

[17] Xian Zhao, Haoran Liu, Yaguang Wu, and Qingan Qiu. Joint optimization of mission abort and system structure considering dynamic tasks. *Reliability Engineering System Safety*, 234:109128, 2023.

[18] Qingan Qiu, Lisa M Maillart, Oleg A Prokopyev, and Lirong Cui. Optimal condition-based mission abort decisions. *IEEE Transactions on Reliability*, 72(1):408–425, 2023.

[19] Xiaofei Chai, Boyu Chen, and Xian Zhao. Optimal Mission Abort Decisions for Multi-Component Systems Considering Multiple Abort Criteria. *Mathematics*, 11(24):4922, December 2023.

[20] Siqi Wang, Xian Zhao, Zhigang Tian, and Ming J. Zuo. Optimal mission abort policy with multiple abort criteria for a balanced system with multi-state components. *Computers & Industrial Engineering*, 160:107544, October 2021.

[21] Xian Zhao, Jinglei Sun, Qingan Qiu, and Ke Chen. Optimal inspection and mission abort policies for systems subject to degradation. *European Journal of Operational Research*, 292(2):610–621, 2021.

[22] Xian Zhao, Ying Dai, Qingan Qiu, and Yaguang Wu. Joint optimization of mission aborts and allocation of standby components considering mission loss. *Reliability Engineering & System Safety*, 225:108612, 2022.

[23] Xian Zhao, Zuheng Lv, Qingan Qiu, and Yaguang Wu. Designing two-level rescue depot location and dynamic rescue policies for unmanned vehicles. *Reliability Engineering & System Safety*, 233:109119, 2023.

[24] Xian Zhao, Xiaofei Chai, Jinglei Sun, and Qingan Qiu. Optimal bivariate mission abort policy for systems operate in random shock environment. *Reliability Engineering & System Safety*, 205:107244, 2021.

[25] Li Yang, Yuhan Ma, Fanping Wei, and Qingan Qiu. Optimal condition-based parameter learning and mission abort decisions. *Naval Research Logistics (NRL)*, 2024.

[26] Qingan Qiu, Rong Li, and Xian Zhao. Failure risk management: adaptive performance control and mission abort decisions. *Risk Analysis*, 45(2):421–440, 2025.

[27] Xian Zhao, Xinlei Wang, Ying Dai, and Qingan Qiu. Joint optimization of loading, mission abort and rescue site selection policies for UAV. *Reliability Engineering & System Safety*, 244:109955, 2024.

[28] Gregory Levitin, Maxim Finkelstein, and Yuanshun Dai. Mission abort and rescue for multistate systems operating under the poisson process of shocks. *Reliability Engineering & System Safety*, 202:107027, 2020.

[29] Gregory Levitin, Maxim Finkelstein, and Yanping Xiang. Optimal aborting rule in multi-attempt missions performed by multicomponent systems. *European Journal of Operational Research*, 283(1):244–252, 2020.

[30] Qingan Qiu and Lirong Cui. Gamma process based optimal mission abort policy. *Reliability Engineering & System Safety*, 190:106496, 2019.

[31] Gregory Levitin, Maxim Finkelstein, and Yanping Xiang. Optimal inspections and mission abort policies for multistate systems. *Reliability Engineering & System Safety*, 214:107700, 2021.

[32] Xian Zhao, Yu Fan, Qingan Qiu, and Ke Chen. Multi-criteria mission abort policy for systems subject to two-stage degradation process. *European Journal of Operational Research*, 295(1):233–245, 2021.

[33] Gregory Levitin, Maxim Finkelstein, and Hong-Zhong Huang. Optimal abort rules for multiattempt missions. *Risk Analysis*, 39(12):2732–2743, 2019.

[34] Qingan Qiu. Managing system failure risk: Performance control and mission abort decisions. In *2023 9th International Symposium on System Security, Safety, and Reliability (ISSSR)*, pages 55–61. IEEE, 2023.

[35] Sa Meng, Liudong Xing, and Gregory Levitin. Activation delay and aborting policy minimizing expected losses in consecutive attempts having cumulative effect on mission success. *Reliability Engineering & System Safety*, 247:110078, July 2024.

[36] Gregory Levitin, Liudong Xing, and Yuanshun Dai. Optimal system loading and aborting in additive multi-attempt missions. *Reliability Engineering & System Safety*, 251:110315, 2024.

[37] Gregory Levitin, Liudong Xing, and Yanshun Dai. Joint optimal mission aborting and replacement and maintenance scheduling in dual-unit standby systems. *Reliability Engineering & System Safety*, 216:107921, 2021. Publisher: Elsevier.

[38] Gregory Levitin, Liudong Xing, and Yuanshun Dai. Optimal task aborting policy and component activation delay in consecutive multi-attempt missions. *Reliability Engineering & System Safety*, 238:109482, 2023.

[39] Gregory Levitin, Liudong Xing, and Yuanshun Dai. Optimal task sequencing and aborting in multi-attempt multi-task missions with a limited number of attempts. *Reliability Engineering & System Safety*, 236:109309, 2023.

[40] Xian Zhao, Xiaofei Chai, Jinglei Sun, and Qingan Qiu. Joint optimization of mission abort and protective device selection policies for multistate systems. *Risk Analysis*, 42(12):2823–2834, 2022.

[41] Faizanbasha A. and U. Rizwan. Deep learning-stochastic ensemble for rul prediction and predictive maintenance with dynamic mission abort policies. *Reliability Engineering System Safety*, 259:110919, 2025.

[42] Xian Zhao, Xiaofei Chai, Jinglei Sun, and Qingan Qiu. Joint optimization of mission abort and component switching policies for multistate warm standby systems. *Reliability Engineering & System Safety*, 212:107641, 2021.

[43] Qingan Qiu. Joint optimization of learning and project abandonment decisions. In *2024 10th International Symposium on System Security, Safety, and Reliability (ISSSR)*, pages 363–370. IEEE, 2024.

A Bayesian deep neural network model for remaining useful life prediction using a multi-point active query strategy

Ying Chen
College of Economics and Management
Nanjing University of
Aeronautics and Astronautics
Nanjing, China
yingchen@nuaa.edu.cn

Taofeng Fan
College of Aeronautics
Nanjing University of
Aeronautics and Astronautics
Nanjing, China
fantaofeng@nuaa.edu.cn

Mingchih Chen
College of Management
Fu Jen Catholic University
New Taipei City, Taiwan
081438@mail.fju.edu.tw

Xufeng Zhao
College of Economics and Management
Nanjing University of
Aeronautics and Astronautics
Nanjing, China
zx.peak@outlook.com

Keywords:Remaining useful life; Active learning; Bayesian deep neural network; Multi-point active query

Abstract - Accurate remaining useful life (RUL) prediction is critical for ensuring the reliability and safety of mechanical systems, particularly in aerospace and industrial applications where unexpected failures can lead to severe consequences. While deep learning (DL) has shown promise in RUL prediction, its performance heavily relies on large amounts of labeled training data, which are often scarce in real-world scenarios due to high acquisition costs and operational constraints. Active learning (AL) offers a potential solution by strategically selecting the most informative samples for annotation, thereby improving model efficiency with limited data. However, existing AL-based RUL prediction methods primarily focus on single-point query strategies, which may limit learning efficiency and generalization. To address this gap, this paper proposes a novel multi-point active query strategy that enhances sample selection by simultaneously acquiring multiple high-value data points in each query cycle. Furthermore, we integrate this approach with a Bayesian deep neural network to quantify prediction uncertainty, enabling more robust and interpretable RUL estimation. Extensive experiments on the C-MAPSS dataset demonstrate that the proposed method significantly outperforms conventional AL strategies and baseline models, achieving higher prediction accuracy with fewer labeled samples. This work provides a promising direction for data-efficient RUL prediction in practical industrial applications.

1 Introduction

Remaining useful life (RUL) prediction of aircraft engines has emerged as a critical research focus in prognostics and health management (PHM), with substantial implications for aviation safety, operational efficiency, and maintenance optimization [1]. In commercial and military aviation, where engine failures can lead to severe safety incidents and costly unscheduled maintenance, accurate RUL estimation enables condition-based maintenance strategies that prevent catastrophic failures while minimizing unnecessary part replacements. The complex degradation patterns of modern turbofan engines, influenced by varying operational conditions and material wear mechanisms, make RUL prediction particularly challenging yet indispensable for modern PHM systems. This challenge has driven extensive research into data-driven approaches that can effectively model nonlinear degradation processes from multivariate time-series sensor data.

The advent of deep learning has revolutionized data-driven RUL estimation, offering superior capability in capturing complex temporal degradation patterns compared to traditional machine learning approaches. Convolutional neural networks (CNNs) have demonstrated exceptional performance in extracting spatial features from multivariate sensor data, as evidenced by their application in NASA's C-MAPSS benchmark studies [2]. Recurrent architectures, particularly Long short-term memory (LSTM) networks and their bidirectional variants, have become prevalent for modeling temporal dependencies in engine sensor time series, achieving state-of-the-art results on prognostic benchmarks [3]. More recently, hybrid models combining attention mechanisms with 1D-CNNs (e.g., Transformer-based approaches) have shown promise in handling long-range dependencies while maintaining computational efficiency. These advancements collectively address critical aspects of engine degradation modeling, including nonlinear feature interactions, operational condition variability, and noise robustness.

Although deep learning models have achieved success in RUL prediction, their actual deployment faces a fundamental limitation: the demand for a large amount of high-quality labeled training data [4]. Unlike a large number of available benchmark datasets running to fault trajectories, real-world aircraft engine monitoring scenarios typically generate a limited number of fault examples for the following reasons: (1) the high reliability of modern engines, (2) the high cost of destructive testing, and (3) the operational variability that requires specific conditional models. This data scarcity limits the generalization capability of deep learning models, leading to suboptimal predictions when deployed in practical settings.

Active learning emerges as a particularly effective solution to this data scarcity problem when combined with deep learning architectures. Unlike passive learning approaches that treat all data points equally, active learning employs intelligent query strategies to identify and prioritize the most informative samples for annotation. This approach is especially powerful in RUL prediction because it can focus labeling resources on critical degradation phases where the model exhibits high uncertainty or where failure progression becomes nonlinear. The iterative nature of active learning allows the model to progressively refine its understanding of the failure dynamics, with each newly labeled sample providing maximum information gain. When integrated with deep neural networks, this strategy enables the model to achieve comparable accuracy with significantly fewer labeled samples while simultaneously reducing overfitting through strategic coverage of the input space.

However, existing AL-based RUL prediction methods in the aerospace domain remain underexplored and predominantly rely on single-point query strategies, where only one sample is selected for annotation in each iteration. While effective in some scenarios, this approach may suffer from inefficiency in high-dimensional, time-series data, where multiple informative samples could be acquired simultaneously to accelerate model convergence. Moreover, most existing methods do not account for prediction uncertainty, which is crucial for reliable decision-making in safety-critical applications.

To address these limitations, this paper proposes a novel multi-point active query strategy combined with a Bayesian deep neural network for RUL prediction. The key innovations of our approach include:

(i) We establish a Bayesian hybrid deep neural network -CNN-BiLSTM-AM to improve the RUL prediction accuracy of the model.

(ii) We propose a multi-point query strategy with deep learning model framework, which selects multiple high-value samples in each query cycle to improve data efficiency;

(iii) We utilize Bayesian inference and the Monte Carlo dropout method to quantify the prediction uncertainty and improve the reliability of the model;

The remainder of this paper is organized as follows: Section 2 introduces Bayesian deep learning model including Bayesian deep neural networks and CNN-BiLSTM-AM model. Section 3 details the proposed multi-point query strategy. Section 4 presents experimental results on the C-MAPSS dataset, demonstrating the superiority of our approach. Finally, Section 5 concludes the paper and discusses future research directions.

2 Bayesian deep learning model

2.1 Bayesian deep neural networks

Bayesian deep learning treats neural networks probabilistically, quantifying uncertainty through Bayesian inference. A Bayesian neural network assigns a prior to the weights and computes posterior distributions from observed data.

Consider a dataset with N instances, each having degradation measurements at T_n time intervals, represented by $\boldsymbol{x}_n^t$. The RUL at the last time point is Y_n. The complete dataset is $\mathcal{X} = \{X_1, X_2, \ldots, X_N\}$ and $\mathcal{Y} = \{Y_1, Y_2, \ldots, Y_N\}$. The posterior distribution of the parameters Θ is:

$$p(\Theta \mid \mathcal{X}, \mathcal{Y}) = \frac{p(\mathcal{Y} \mid \mathcal{X}, \Theta)p(\Theta)}{p(\mathcal{Y} \mid \mathcal{X})}. \tag{1}$$

The marginal likelihood is:

$$p(\mathcal{Y} \mid \mathcal{X}) = \int p(\Theta)p(\mathcal{Y} \mid \mathcal{X}, \Theta)\, d\Theta. \tag{2}$$

The posterior is updated as:

$$p(\Theta \mid \mathcal{X}, \mathcal{Y}) = \frac{p(\mathcal{Y} \mid \mathcal{X}, \Theta)p(\Theta)}{\int p(\Theta)p(\mathcal{Y} \mid \mathcal{X}, \Theta)\, d\Theta}. \tag{3}$$

The Bayesian model estimates the conditional probability for a new RUL prediction:

$$p(Y^* \mid X^*, \mathcal{X}, \mathcal{Y}) = \int p(Y^* \mid X^*, \Theta)p(\Theta \mid \mathcal{X}, \mathcal{Y})\, d\Theta. \tag{4}$$

As computing the integral is intractable, variational inference approximates the posterior with a simpler distribution $q_\phi(\Theta)$. The optimal variational distribution is found by minimizing the Kullback-Leibler (KL) divergence:

$$\mathrm{KL}(q_\phi(\Theta) \| p(\Theta \mid \mathcal{X}, \mathcal{Y})) = \int q_\phi(\Theta) \log \frac{q_\phi(\Theta)}{p(\Theta \mid \mathcal{X}, \mathcal{Y})}\, d\Theta. \tag{5}$$

This simplifies to:

$$\mathrm{KL}(q_\phi(\Theta) \| p(\Theta)) - \mathbb{E}_{q_\phi(\Theta)} \log p(\mathcal{Y} \mid \mathcal{X}, \Theta) + \log p(\mathcal{Y} \mid \mathcal{X}). \tag{6}$$

The optimal ϕ^* is found by minimizing:

$$\phi^* = \arg\min_\phi \left\{ \mathrm{KL}(q_\phi(\Theta) \| p(\Theta)) - \mathbb{E}_{q_\phi(\Theta)} \log p(\mathcal{Y} \mid \mathcal{X}, \Theta) \right\}. \tag{7}$$

Monte Carlo dropout, viewed as a variational inference instance, introduces stochasticity during training and inference. It serves as a regularization technique to prevent overfitting and enhances the model's robustness to noise, offering a simpler, computationally efficient alternative for uncertainty quantification.

2.2 CNN-BiLSTM-AM model

For aero-engine RUL prediction, this study uses a baseline deep learning model combining CNN, BiLSTM, and AM networks, as proposed by Wang et al. [5]. The CNN extracts local features,

BiLSTM captures long-term temporal relationships, and the AM network highlights key temporal segments, improving attention to the most relevant data. Together, these components enable the model to handle complex time-series data, providing more reliable RUL estimates for aero-engines. While CNNs are effective at feature extraction, they struggle with capturing temporal relationships. To overcome this, we integrate a BiLSTM network, which is better at modeling sequential patterns and capturing both past and future temporal dependencies.

LSTM is a specialized variant of the recurrent neural network specifically developed to handle sequential data, especially in tasks requiring the model to capture long-range dependencies. It consists of a cell state and three gates including forget, input, and output gates. A single LSTM only processes data in one direction (from past to future), which limits the ability to capture future context. BiLSTM unit incorporates two LSTM networks, addressing this limitation by analyzing input sequences in both forward and reverse directions. By employing this bidirectional approach, the model can capture dependencies from both the past and future contexts within the data. At each time step, the BiLSTM updates its hidden state h_t using the current input x_t and the previous hidden state h_{t-1}.

The AM enables the model to dynamically prioritize the most relevant segments of a sequence during prediction. Certain time steps in the sensor data may be more informative than others, and the AM assigns weights to different segments of the sequence according to their relevance. The AM assigns a weight α_t to each time step t, indicating its importance. The weighted sum of hidden states h_t from the BiLSTM layer is used as the final representation of the sequence. Let h_t represent the hidden state at time step t from the BiLSTM layer, and let W_a and b_a denote the learnable weight matrix and bias vector, respectively. In the Bayesian framework, these parameters are regarded as random variables with prior distributions.

3 multi-point active query strategy based RUL prediction

3.1 Maximum uncertainty-based multi-point active query strategy

We propose a BMAL method that selects a batch of samples for labeling by maximizing uncertainty, which accelerates model convergence compared to traditional single-sample active learning. In traditional methods, the most informative sample is selected in each iteration, leading to suboptimal use of labeling resources in multi-annotator scenarios. By choosing a batch of samples, annotators can process multiple samples simultaneously, improving labeling efficiency and consistency.

The acquisition function guides the sample selection, where uncertainty maximization is the core principle. High uncertainty indicates regions where the model's knowledge is insufficient, thus maximizing learning efficiency. We define the acquisition function as:

$$AF(X_i, f) = \mathrm{Var}(f(X_i)) = \frac{1}{M}\sum_{t=1}^{M}\left(f_t(X_i) - \hat{f}(X_i)\right)^2, \tag{8}$$

where $f_t(X_i)$ is the prediction for the t-th sample, and $\hat{f}(X_i)$ is the average prediction.

Let $U = \{X_1, X_2, \cdots, X_{n_1}\}$ be the unlabeled dataset, and we aim to select the top q units based on the acquisition function. A candidate subset $S \subseteq S_a$ is selected based on:

$$S^* = \arg\max_{S \subseteq S_a} \sum_{X_i \in S} AF(X_i, f), \tag{9}$$

with the assumption that X_1^* has the highest acquisition function value, so:

$$AF(X_1^*, f) \geq AF(X_2^*, f) \geq \cdots \geq AF(X_q^*, f). \tag{10}$$

3.2 The pseudocode of the multi-point active query strategy

The multi-point active query strategy algorithm outlined in Algorithm 1 aims to enhance model performance by selecting the most uncertain data points from an unlabeled dataset for labeling. The algorithm operates iteratively, where in each iteration, the model is trained on the labeled dataset L, and the most uncertain data points from the unlabeled dataset U are identified. These data points are then labeled through experiments and added to the labeled dataset, while the unlabeled dataset is updated.

The inputs to the algorithm include an initial labeled dataset L, an unlabeled dataset U, a model f, the total number of iterations N, and the batch size q for selecting uncertain data points. In each iteration, the uncertainty of data points is quantified by a function $\sum_{X_i \in S} AF(X_i, f)$, and the most uncertain points are selected. These points are labeled, and the datasets L and U are updated accordingly. The model is retrained using the updated labeled dataset, and the process is repeated for N iterations.

The final model f^*, after N iterations, is expected to be highly accurate, as it has been trained with the most informative data points, maximizing labeling efficiency and reducing uncertainty.

Algorithm 1 Maximum uncertainty-based multi-point active query strategy algorithm

Input: Labeled dataset L, unlabeled dataset U, the number of iteration rounds N, the number of units to be selected in each round q, and the model f.
for $i = 1, 2, \ldots, N$ **do**
  Train the hybrid model f with an initial labeled dataset L.
  Identify the update dataset $S_j^* = (X_{j1}^*, X_{j2}^*, \cdots, X_{jq}^*)$ by maximizing $\sum_{X_i \in S} AF(X_i, f)$.
  Obtain the run-to-failure labels values $Y_j^* = (Y_{j1}^*, Y_{j2}^*, \cdots, Y_{jq}^*)$ in S_j^* parallelly by the degenerate fault experiments.
  Update the labeled dataset $L = L \cup (S_j^*, Y_j^*)$.
  Update the unlabeled dataset $U = U \setminus S_j^*$.
  Retrain the model f with the updated labeled dataset L.
end for
Output: The trained Bayesian deep learning model f^*

4 Experimental validation

4.1 Data description and preprocessing details

In this study, we use the C-MAPSS aero-engine simulation dataset [6] for RUL prediction. The dataset includes 26 multivariate time series, 21 of which are sensor data. The FD001 subset is selected, which contains training and test sets, both with 100 engines. The training set spans from normal operation to failure, while the test set ends at a random time before failure, providing true RUL labels. Seven sensors with constant values throughout the lifecycle are excluded, leaving 14 sensors as effective features. Min-max normalization is applied for preprocessing. Multi-time-step data, which better captures degradation trends, is segmented using a sliding window of length 25.

In the early engine lifecycle, degradation is minimal (healthy phase), while later, it follows a linear degradation pattern. A piecewise linear function models this process, with RUL set to 125 during the healthy phase.

RUL prediction is evaluated using RMSE and a custom scoring function. The RMSE is defined as:

$$\text{RMSE} = \sqrt{\frac{1}{N}\sum_{i=1}^{N}(y_i^{pred} - y_i^{true})^2}, \tag{11}$$

where N is the test set size, and y_i^{pred} and y_i^{true} are the predicted and true RUL values, respectively.

Additionally, the scoring function penalizes overpredictions more heavily, defined as:

$$\text{Score} = \begin{cases} \sum_{i=1}^{N}(e^{-\frac{y_i^{pred} - y_i^{true}}{13}} - 1), & \text{if } y_i^{pred} - y_i^{true} < 0, \\ \sum_{i=1}^{N}(e^{\frac{y_i^{pred} - y_i^{true}}{10}} - 1), & \text{if } y_i^{pred} - y_i^{true} \geq 0. \end{cases} \tag{12}$$

4.2 Experiment results

This section compares the proposed maximum uncertainty-based multi-point active query approach with two baseline strategies: random selection and batch selection based on minimizing uncertainty. The random selection strategy chooses a batch of engine units randomly for labeling in each iteration. The batch selection strategy based on minimizing uncertainty selects the batch with the smallest uncertainty values. The proposed strategy, in contrast, maximizes uncertainty during batch selection. All strategies start with an initial training set of 20 engine units.

The comparison results, shown in Fig. 1 and 2, include RMSE and Score plots for the three strategies. To account for experimental randomness, each strategy was trained ten times, and the average values were used. In each iteration, five engine units were selected for updates. The results reveal that the maximum uncertainty-based strategy achieved the fastest reduction in RMSE and score. As seen in Fig. 1, the proposed strategy significantly outperformed the others, with lower RMSE values up to the 10th iteration. The random selection strategy performed second, while the minimizing uncertainty strategy showed the slowest improvement, only matching the other two strategies after the 12th iteration. The Score plot in Fig. 2 follows a similar trend, indicating that the proposed method is particularly effective when training samples are limited, as it selects more informative samples to enhance model predictions.

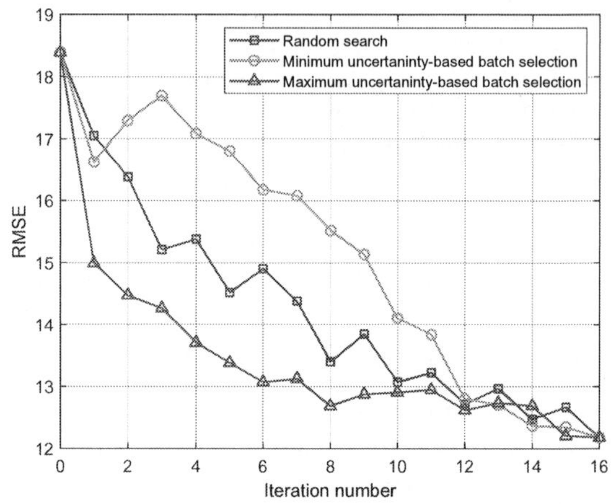

Figure 1: The RMSE results of three selection strategies on FD001 dataset.

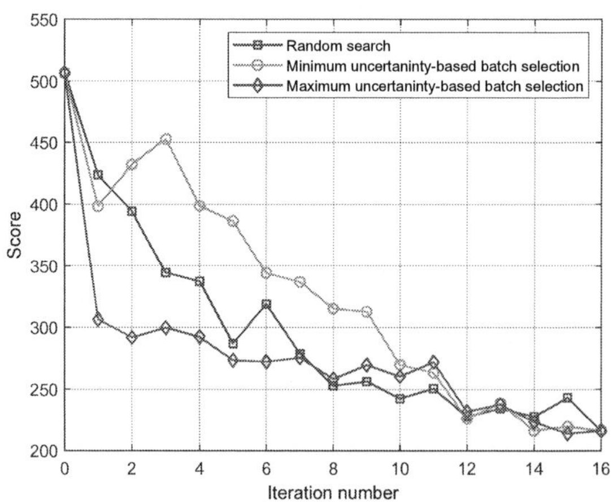

Figure 2: The Score results of three selection strategies on FD001 dataset.

Table 1 compares RUL estimation performance on the FD001 dataset across various models, including Bi-LSTM-ED, Attention-LSTM, and the proposed Bayesian hybrid model with multi-point active query strategy. The hybrid Bayesian CNN-BiLSTM-AM model is tested with different training data proportions (60%, 80%, 90%, 95%, 100%). Results show consistent improvement as more training data is used. With only 60% of the data, the model achieves an RMSE of 11.90 and a Score of 202.06, outperforming several full-data models. As the training data increases to 80% and 90%, performance improves with RMSE values of 11.44 and 11.34, and Scores of 195.60 and 179.49. At 95% data utilization, the model reaches its best performance with an RMSE of 11.17 and a Score of 165.29, the lowest among all models. Even with 100% data, it maintains strong performance with an RMSE of 11.28 and a Score of 177.21. These

Table 1: Comparison of RUL prediction performance on FD001 dataset.

Method	Evaluation metrics	
	RMSE	Score
Bi-LSTM-ED [7]	14.74	273.00
Attention-LSTM [8]	14.53	322.44
MCLSTM [9]	13.71	315.00
CATA-TCN [10]	12.80	234.31
BiGRU-TSAM [11]	12.56	213.35
AGCNN [12]	12.42	225.51
SCTA-LSTM [13]	12.10	207.00
BGT [1]	12.09	262.67
Proposed model (60%)	11.90	202.06
Proposed model (80%)	11.44	195.60
Proposed model (90%)	11.34	179.49
Proposed model (95%)	**11.17**	**165.29**
Proposed model (100%)	11.28	177.21

results highlight the model's ability to maximize data utility and achieve superior predictive accuracy with less training data, reducing deep learning networks' data dependency.

5 Conclusion

This paper introduces a new multi-point active query strategy framework for predicting the RUL of aero-engines, addressing the challenge of limited fault data. The proposed strategy selects the most informative samples for labeling using MC dropout inference, improving model performance while reducing labeling efforts. By combining CNN, BiLSTM networks, and attention mechanisms, we create a strong Bayesian hybrid deep learning model for RUL prediction. The approach selects multiple informative instances per iteration, minimizing both labeling effort and computational cost, making it efficient for RUL prediction with limited data. Experiments on the NASA C-MAPSS dataset show that our method outperforms traditional approaches in prediction accuracy and data efficiency. The iterative process and comparison with other selection strategies confirm the advantages of our framework, especially under limited data conditions.

Future research will focus on using transfer learning to improve the model's ability to generalize across different operational conditions and engine types. Combining transfer learning with multi-point active query strategy is expected to boost model performance in data-scarce environments. Additionally, new batch selection strategies that better utilize sample information will be explored, possibly by developing hybrid methods that balance uncertainty and representativeness metrics. Finally, dynamic maintenance strategies based on RUL predictions will be studied, with an emphasis on cost-benefit analysis to optimize the trade-off between sample size, prediction accuracy, and maintenance costs for better predictive maintenance outcomes.

Acknowledgement This work was supported by the National Natural Science Foundation of China under Grant 72471116, T2441003, the National Foreign Expert Project under Grant H20240454, and the Aeronautical Science Foundation of China Aviation Academy under Grant 2022Z057052002.

References

[1] F. Xiang, Y. Zhang, S. Zhang, Z. Wang, L. Qiu, J.-H. Choi, Bayesian gated-transformer model for risk-aware prediction of aero-engine remaining useful life, *Expert Systems with Applications* 238 (2024) 121859.

[2] L. Liu, X. Song, Z. Zhou, Aircraft engine remaining useful life estimation via a double attention-based data-driven architecture. *Reliability Engineering & System Safety* 221 (2022) 108330.

[3] Y. Wu, M. Yuan, S. Dong, L. Lin, Y. Liu, Remaining useful life estimation of engineered systems using vanilla LSTM neural networks. *Neurocomputing* 275 (2018) 167–179.

[4] X. Zhao, Y. Chen, M. Yang, J. Xiang, Fault diagnosis of rolling bearing using convolutional denoising autoencoder and siamese neural network with small sample, *IEEE Internet of Things Journal* (2024) 1–12.

[5] L. Wang, B. Li, X. Zhao, Multi-objective predictive maintenance scheduling models integrating remaining useful life prediction and maintenance decisions, *Computers & Industrial Engineering* 197 (2024) 110581.

[6] A. Saxena, K. Goebel, D. Simon, N. Eklund, Damage propagation modeling for aircraft engine run-to-failure simulation, in: *2008 international conference on prognostics and health management*, IEEE, 2008, pp. 1–9.

[7] W. Yu, I. Y. Kim, C. Mechefske, Remaining useful life estimation using a bidirectional recurrent neural network based autoencoder scheme, *Mechanical Systems and Signal Processing* 129 (2019) 764–780.

[8] Z. Chen, M. Wu, R. Zhao, F. Guretno, R. Yan, X. Li, Machine remaining useful life prediction via an attention-based deep learning approach, *IEEE Transactions on Industrial Electronics* 68 (3) (2020) 2521–2531.

[9] S. Xiang, Y. Qin, J. Luo, H. Pu, B. Tang, Multicellular LSTM-based deep learning model for aero-engine remaining useful life prediction, *Reliability Engineering & System Safety* 216 (2021) 107927.

[10] L. Lin, J. Wu, S. Fu, S. Zhang, C. Tong, L. Zu, Channel attention & temporal attention based temporal convolutional network: A dual attention framework for remaining useful life prediction of the aircraft engines, *Advanced Engineering Informatics* 60 (2024) 102372.

[11] L. Yang, Y. Liao, R. Duan, T. Kang, J. Xue, A bidirectional recursive gated dual attention unit based RUL prediction approach, *Engineering Applications of Artiffcial Intelligence* 120 (2023) 105885.

[12] H. Liu, Z. Liu, W. Jia, X. Lin, Remaining useful life prediction using a novel feature-attention-based end-to-end approach, *IEEE Transactions on Industrial Informatics* 17 (2) (2020) 1197–1207.

[13] H. Tian, L. Yang, B. Ju, Spatial correlation and temporal attention-based lstm for remaining useful life prediction of turbofan engine, *Measurement* 214 (2023) 112816.

Comparison of Fatigue Characteristics of Single Shear Lap Joints with Two Types of Hi-lock Bolts

Lei WANG [1,2*], Jianfeng YANG [3], Jun LI[1], Ruijin ZHANG [1], Wenxue QIAN[1]

[1] School of Mechanical Engineering & Automation, Northeastern University, Shenyang 110819, China
[2]Key Laboratory of Vibration and Control of Aero-Propulsion Systems of Ministry of Education, Northeastern University, Shenyang 110819, China
[3] Suzhou Nuclear Power Research Institute Co., Ltd., Suzhou 215004, China
*leiwang@mail.neu.edu

Keywords: Hi-Lock Bolt, Internal Cone Bushing, Lap Joint, Fatigue Behavior, Finite Element

Abstract - This paper presents a comprehensive analysis of the fatigue characteristics of the conventional high-lock bolt (HLB) joints and internal cone bushing high-lock bolt (ICB-HLB) joints. Through experimental testing and finite element (FE) simulation, the installation behavior, fatigue life, fracture locations, and stress-strain distributions of the two configurations were systematically evaluated. The results show that the ICB-HLB joint exhibits superior installation integrity with negligible protrusion formation. Its fatigue life is significantly improved compared to conventional HLB joint, particularly under low-amplitude loading. FE simulation reveal that the design of ICB-HLB achieves more uniform stress distribution after installation, which alleviating residual stress concentration. After loading, the maximum stress amplitude at critical location is further shifted away from the borehole wall, which effectively delaying crack initiation. These findings highlight the ICB-HLB's potential as an optimized fastener solution for aerospace applications requiring enhanced structural reliability.

1. Introduction

In high-tech manufacturing fields, such as aerospace, high-lock bolts serve as critical fastening components, whose fatigue performance directly impacts overall equipment safety and reliability. Conventional HLBs, while widely used, often suffer from connection plate damage and bolt fracture during installation, compromising fatigue life. To address these limitations, the ICB-HLB fastener system was developed as showed in Figure 1. The outer wall of the bushing forms a transition or small clearance fit with the connection plate hole, while the bolt and bushing utilize a large interference fit with a tapered interface between the stud and inner wall of the bushing. During installation, the bushing is firstly inserted into the plate hole, followed by bolt pressing to expand the bushing and create interference with the hole. This design retains HLB's advantages while effectively avoiding installation damage, reducing protrusion defects, and ensuring stable installation to enhance joint performance.

Many scholars have studied the characteristics of HLB joint. Khairi [1] used 3D finite element analysis to predict the stress of single-row multi-bolted single-shear lap joint, validating FE analysis effectiveness. Chakherlou [2-9] did a lot of experiments and finite element simulation, and analyzed the factors affecting the joint life. They used the up and down plates as fixture and the middle plate of the double shear joint as fatigue specimen, but the influence of inter-plate contact on fatigue life is ignored. Some domestic scholars [10-15] took the single-shear lap joints as the research object, but they did not conduct an in-depth study on the location of crack initiation. However, limited research exists on ICB-HLB structures. This paper compares fatigue characteristics of conventional HLBs and ICB-HLBs under different conditions to explore performance differences, providing practical significance for improving joint fatigue resistance.

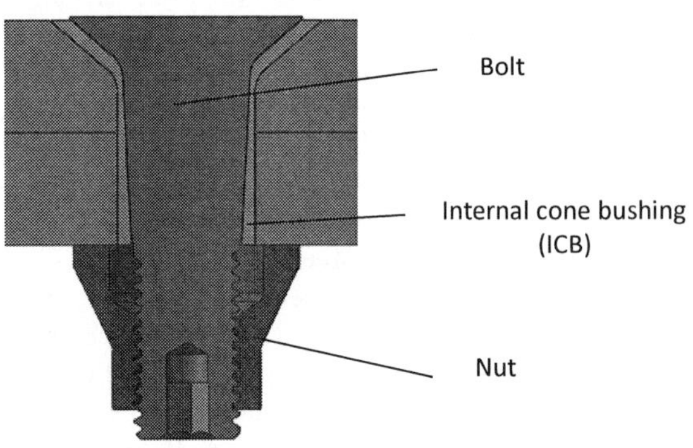

Figure 1. Internal cone bushing Hi-lock bolt joint

2. Fatigue Test

2.1. Specimen and Test Conditions

The nominal diameter of the ICB-HLB is designed as M6, and the outer diameter of the bushing is 8 millimeters. The specimen was designed referring to the standard named Fastener Test Method-Shear Joint Fatigue. Figure 2 shows the structure of the ICB-HLB specimen. The specimen consists of two main joint plates, four bolts, four bushings, four nuts, and two backing plates. Among them, the main joint plate and backing plate are made of Al alloy7075-T6, the material of Hi-lock bolt is titanium alloy Ti-6Al-4V, the material of Hi-lock nut is stainless steel A286, and the material of bushing is stainless steel 0Cr18Ni9. Table 1 lists the fatigue loading conditions, specimen quantity, and fatigue life results. The nominal diameter of the conventional HLB is taken as M8, the size of mounting holes of two types of joints are all 8 millimeters, and the loading of both ICB-HLB and HLB specimen have the same nominal stress at the hole edge.

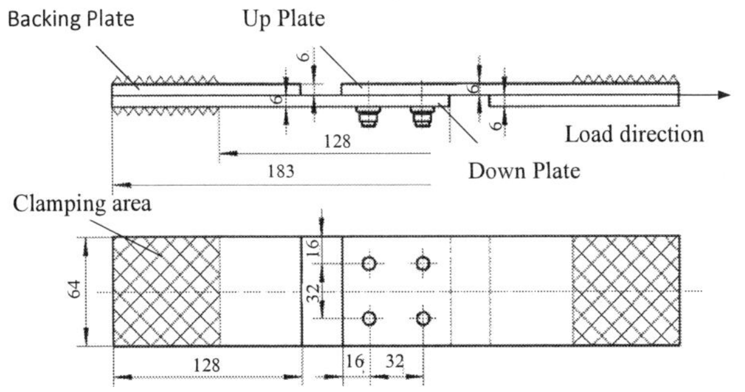

Figure 2. Diagram of specimen

Table 1. Fatigue Test Conditions and Results

No.	Bolt Type	Nominal Stress of Fatigue Load		Number of the Specimen	Fatigue Life /cycle
		Maximum cycle stress /MPa	*stress ratio*		
1	M8 HLB	122	0.1	6	3.28× 10^4
2	M8 HLB	244	0.1	3	7.98× 10^3
3	M6 ICB-HLB	122	0.1	5	2.46× 10^5
4	M6 ICB-HLB	244	0.1	2	1.45× 10^4

2.2. Analysis of Test Results

Through the fatigue test, it is found that under low loading conditions, the fatigue life of the ICB-HLB joint is significantly improved compared to the conventional HLB joint, and the fatigue life of former is 7.5-fold that of the latter. This is mainly due to the optimization of the distribution of the bushing structure on the stress of the hole edge and the effective suppression of installation damage. Under high loading conditions, although the fatigue life of the ICB-HLB joint is also improved, but the incremental effect is relatively limited to 1.82-fold compared to the low loading conditions. This may be due to the relaxation of residual stresses under high loads and the higher maximum value of actual stresses at the hole edge, which partially offset the interference strengthening effect. Overall, the ICB-HLB joints show better fatigue life characteristics than conventional HLB joints under different load levels, particularly under low loading conditions, which is more obvious. It is offering great significance for prolonging the service life of the equipment and reducing maintenance costs.

2.3. Macro Fracture Section Analysis

Figure 3 and Figure 4 respectively show the fracture section diagrams of conventional HLB joints and ICB-HLB joints. It can be seen that the fatigue cracks propagate through the hole under high loading, and the fracture position deviates from the hole under low loading. Further, the deviation distance increases in the case of ICB-HLB joints. The fatigue cracks of the conventional HLB joint initiate at the lap interface between two plates of the joint, with a certain regularity, when the crack source appears in the up plate, it is biased toward the load-bearing side, and when it appears in the down plate, it is biased toward the clamping end. As well as, the fatigue cracks of the ICB-HLB joint initiate at the mounting hole wall and the two-plate joint surface off the edge of the hole for a distance, which is characterized by multi-source fatigue. This difference in fracture section location reflects the distinct in the stress distribution and crack initiation and expansion mechanism between the two types of joints. Through the strutureal optimization, the design of the ICB-HLB joints modifies the stress concentration regions, thus effectively delaying the fatigue crack initiation and expansion to improve the fatigue resistance of the joint.

(a) Under high load

(b) Under low load

Figure 3. Diagrams of fatigue fracture for HLB specimen

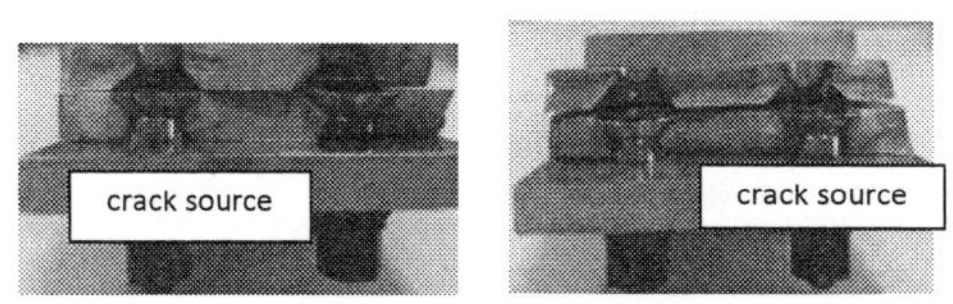

(a) Under high load

(b) Under low load

Figure 4. Diagrams of fatigue fracture for ICB-HLB specimen

3. Finite Element Simulation

Abaqus is used to model the two kinds of bolted joints and simulate the installation process and fatigue loading process. The unit types, material performance parameters, constraints and load steps used in the simulation process are described in the Literature [16]. The stresses and strains of the two kinds of Hi-lock bolt joints after installation and loading are analyzed comparatively in the following.

3.1. Stress Distribution after Installation

As shown in Figure 5, the maximum Mises stress at the hole edge after installation of HLB joint is 595MPa, while the maximum Mises stress at the hole edge after installation of ICB-HLB joint is 493MPa. The stress of ICB-HLB is reduced by 16% with the same amount of interference, and the distribution is more uniform. Figure 6 and Figure 7 show the changes of circumferential stress and radial stress along the thickness direction, respectively. It can be seen that the edge of the hole for ICB-HLB specimen generates higher circumferential compressive stress and radial compressive stress. The existence of these compressive stresses helps to inhibit the initiation and expansion of fatigue cracks, which providing a better fatigue performance foundation for the joint.

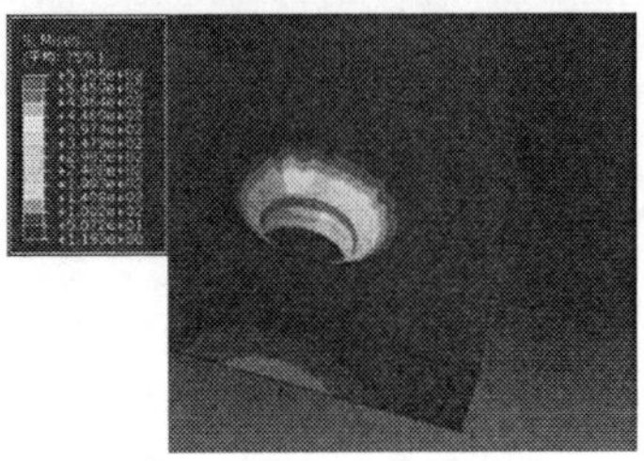

(a) For HLB specimen

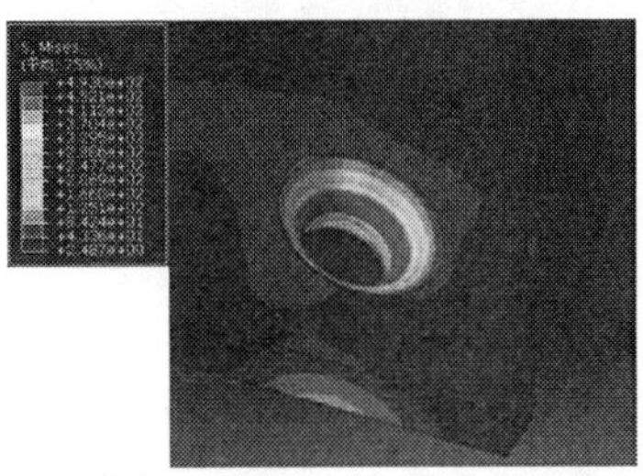

(b) For ICB-HLB specimen

Figure 5. Mises Stress diagram of upper plate

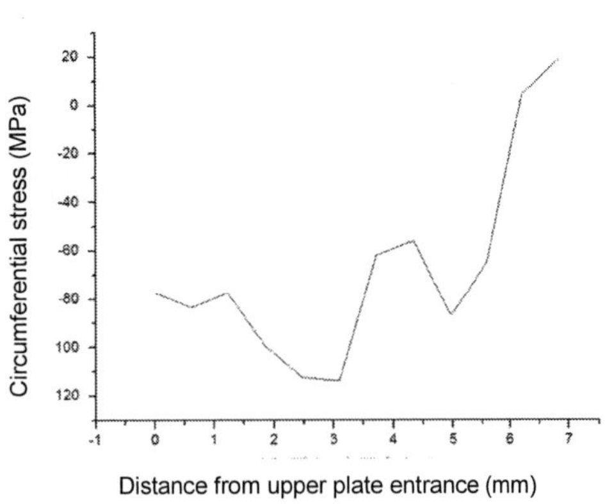

(a) For HLB specimen

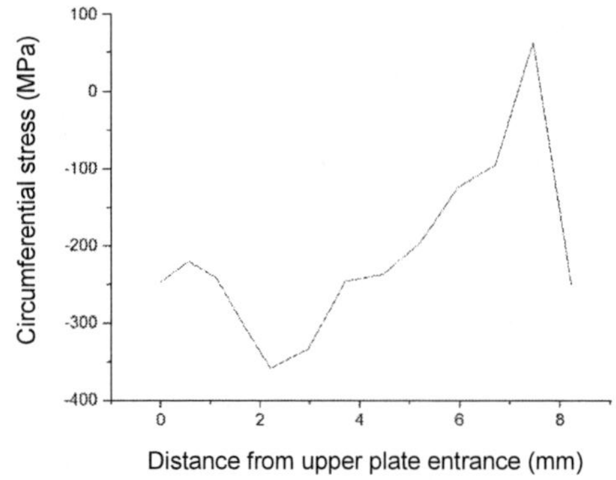

(b) For ICB-HLB specimen

Figure 6. Circumferential stress varying in the thickness direction

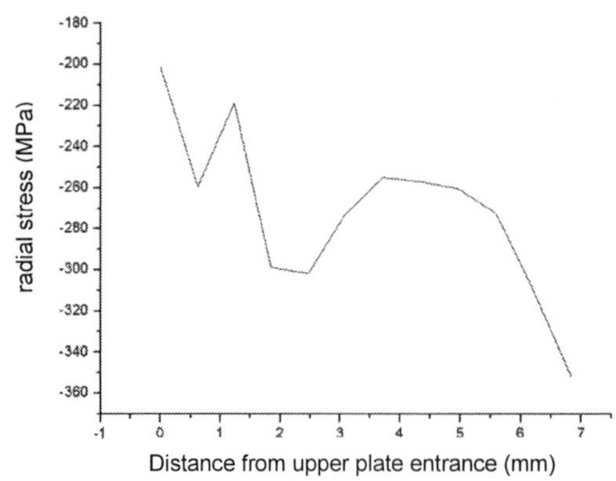

(a) For HLB specimen

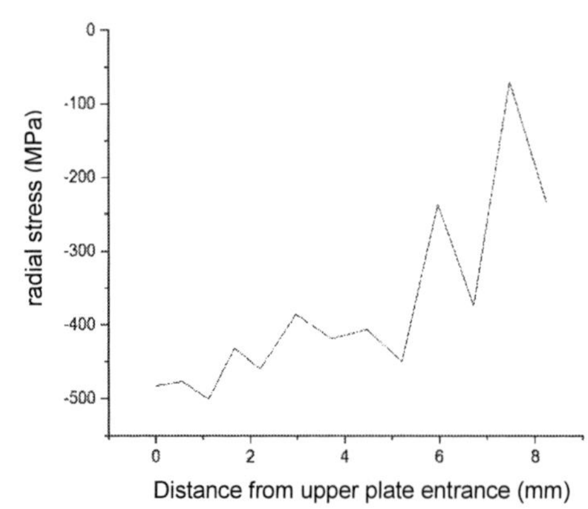

(b) For ICB-HLB specimen

Figure 7. Radial stress varying in the thickness direction

3.2. Strain and Displacement after Installation

Figure 8 shows the strain distribution diagram of the hole edge for two types of specimen. The maximum strain after installation of conventional HLB joint is 1.4%, while the maximum strain after installation of ICB-HLBs is 0.6%. The strain is reduced by 57% with the same amount of interference. Figure 9 displays the displacement along the hole edge thickness direction. It can be seen, the conventional HLB installation process is easy to produce convex tumor. The production of convex tumor will not only lead to local stress concentration, but also may be triggered fatigue cracks in the subsequent loading process. For the new ICB-HLB, due to the moderate effect of the bushing, the displacement distribution after installation is more uniform, almost no obvious convex tumor, which significantly reduces the risk of fatigue performance degradation caused by installation defects.

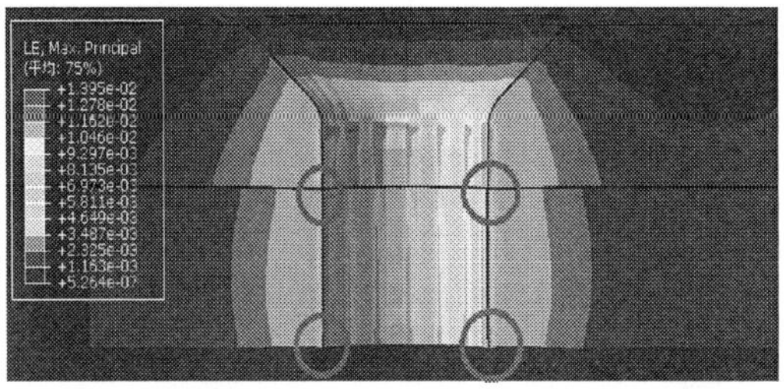

(a) For HLB specimen

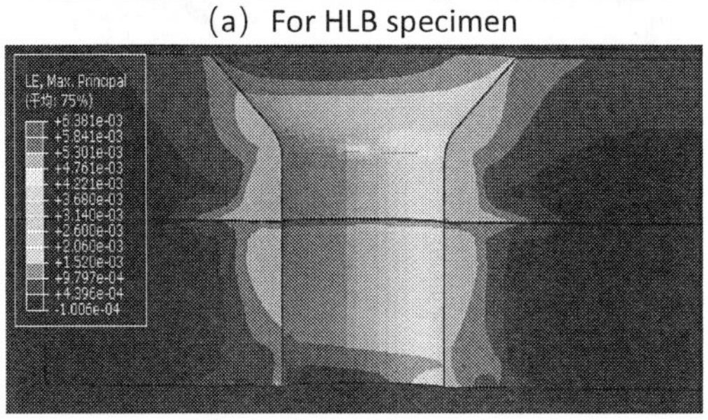

(b) For ICB-HLB specimen

Figure 8. Strain diagram of the hole edge

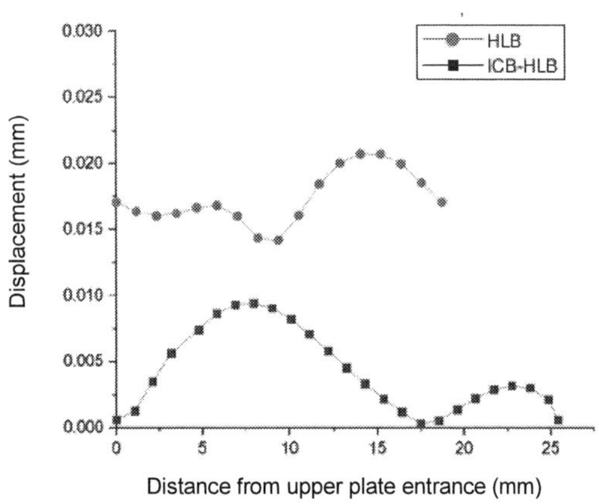

Figure 9. Radial stress varying in the thickness direction

3.3. Stress amplitude under fatigue loading

Figures 10 shows the fatigue stress amplitude of two types of joints under low loading. It can be seen that for the conventional HLB joints, the fatigue stress amplitude of the lap structure can be reduced during interference fit installation compared to clearance fit installation. After loading, the stress amplitude at the dangerous position of the new ICB-HLB joints is lower than that of the conventional HLB joints, which is atributed to the larger residual compressive stresses obtained during the installation process. Furthermore, the most dangerous position is further away from the hole wall, which further reduces the probability of fatigue cracks initiation at the hole edge, and improves the fatigue resistance of the joint structure under the cyclic loading . This simulation result is consistent with the fatigue life observed in the fatigue test, which fully verifies the advantages of the new ICB-HLB connection structure in fatigue performance.

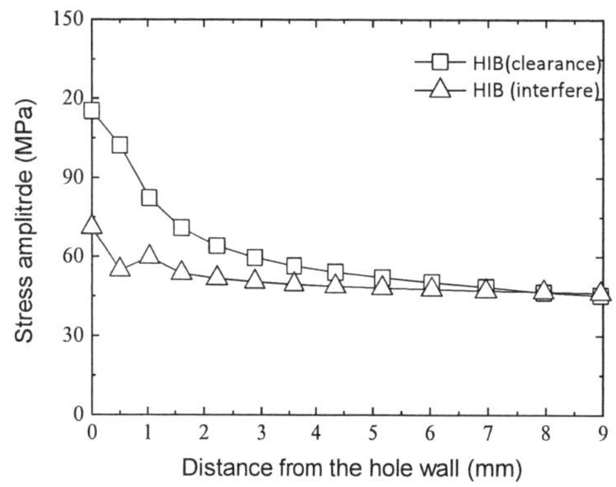

(a) For HLB specimen

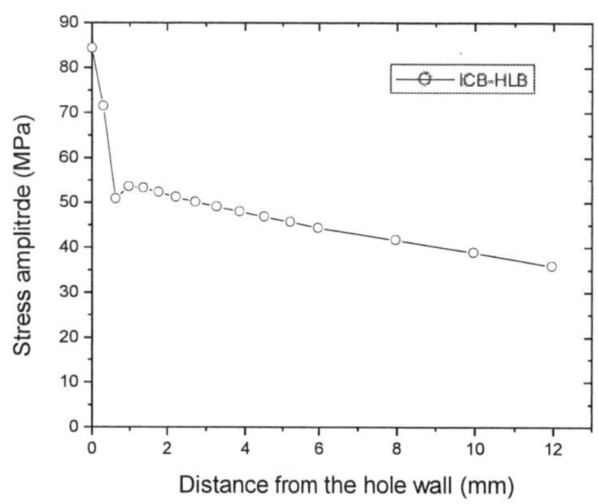

(b) For ICB-HLB specimen

Figure 10. Fatigue stress amplitude

4. Conclusion

In this paper, through the fatigue test and finite element simulation analysis of the conventional HLB joint and the ICB-HLB joint, the following conclusions are obtained:

(1) The ICB-HLB joint is not easy to produce convex tumor and other damages in the installation process, the installation characteristics are more excellent, and can effectively avoid the fatigue performance degradation caused by installation defects.

(2) In terms of fatigue life, the ICB-HLB joint has a significant improvement compared with the conventional HLB joint, especially in the low load conditions the advantage is more prominent.

(3) The difference in fatigue fracture location reflects the difference in stress distribution and crack initiation and expansion mechanism between two types of joints. By optimizing the structural design of the ICB-HLB, the stress concentration area is changed, which effectively slows down the fatigue crack initiation and expansion.

(4) Finite element simulation results show that the ICB-HLB installation stress distribution is more uniform, the residual stress concentration phenomenon has been alleviated. Further, the stress amplitude at the dangerous location can be farther away from the hole wall during loading, and these characteristics make it have better fatigue performance during cyclic loading.

In summary, the ICB-HLB joint shows significant advantages in fatigue performance, which can be used as the optimization choice of Hi-lock bolt joint in aerospace and other fields. It has important application value for improving the safety and reliability of equipment.

Acknowledgement

This work was partially supported by the National Natural Science Foundation of China (Grant No. 52175131).

References

[1] S. Khairi, A. Hilton. "3-D modelling of single-lap multi-bolted joints under quasi-static conditions", American Institute of Physics, 2017, vol. 1885, pp. 1-8.

[2] T. N. Chakherlou, M. Mirzajanzadeh, and B. Abazadeh, "An investigation about interference fit effect on improving fatigue life of a holed single plate in joints", European Journal of Mechanics - A/Solids, 2010, vol. 29, pp. 675-682.

[3] T. N. Chakherlou, M. Mirzajanzadeh, and J. Vogwell, "Experimental and numerical investigations into the effect of an interference fit on the fatigue life of double shear lap joints", Engineering Failure Analysis, 2009, vol. 16, pp. 2066-2080.

[4] T. N. Chakherlou and B. Abazadeh, "Experimental and numerical investigations about the combined effect of interference fit and bolt clamping on the fatigue behavior of Al 2024-T3 double shear lap joints", Materials & Design, 2012, vol. 33, pp. 425-435.

[5] T. N. Chakherlou, H. Taghizadeh, and A. B. Aghdam, "Experimental and numerical comparison of cold expansion and interference fit methods in improving fatigue life of holed plate in double shear lap joints", Aerospace Science & Technology, 2013, vol. 29, pp. 351-362.

[6] B. Abazadeh, T. N. Chakherlou, and R. C. Alderliesten, "Effect of interference fitting and/or bolt clamping on the fatigue behavior of Al alloy 2024-T3 double shear lap joints in different cyclic load ranges", International Journal of Mechanical Sciences, 2013, vol. 72, pp. 2-12.

[7] H. Taghizadeh, T. N. Chakherlou, and H. Ghorbani, "Prediction of fatigue life in cold expanded fastener holes subjected to bolt tightening in Al alloy 7075-T6 plate", International Journal of Mechanical Sciences, 2015, vol. 90, pp. 6-15.

[8] T. N. Chakherlou, M. J. Razavi, and B. Abazadeh, "Finite element investigations of bolt clamping force and friction coefficient effect on the fatigue behavior of aluminum alloy 2024-T3 in double shear lap joint", Engineering Failure Analysis, 2012, vol. 29, pp. 62-74.

[9] T. N. Chakherlou, T. N. Chakherlou, M. Mirzajanzadeh, and J. Vogwell, "Investigation of the fatigue life and crack growth in torque tightened bolted joints", Aerospace Science and Technology, 2011, vol. 15, pp. 304-313.

[10] X. Liu, H. Cui, and S. Z. Zhang, et al, "Experimental and numerical investigations on fatigue behavior of aluminum alloy 7050-T7451 single lap four-bolted joints", Journal of Materials Science & Technology, 2018, vol. 34, pp.1205-1213.

[11] H. Cui, "Fatigue Properties of 7050 High Strength Aluminum Alloy Plate joints", Yantai University Dissertation, 2017.

[12] J. F. Jiang, "Hi-lock bolt interference installation and its effect on the mechanical properties of bolt connected structure", Zhejiang University Dissertation, 2014.

[13] N. X. Wu, F. Cheng, and D. H. Liao, "Experimental Study on the Relationship Between the Mechanical Parameters of Hi-lock Bolt Connection", Machine Tool & Hydraulics, 2017, vol. 45, pp77-80.

[14] C. Rans, P. V. Straznicky, and R. Alderlisten, "Riveting process induced residual stresses around solid rivets in mechanical joints", Journal of Aircraft, 2007, vol. 44, pp. 323-329.

[15] D. Z. Yu, Y. L. Chen, and Z. H. Jia, "Parametric Analysis Mechanical Properties of Bolted Joints", Advanced Materials Research, 2010, vol. 97-101, pp. 3924-3927.

[16] L. Wang, R.J. Zhang and W.X. Qian, et al., "Fatigue testing and simulation of Hi-Lock bolted single shear lap joints", Internatioanl Symposium on System Security, safety, and Reliability, ISSSR 2024, 10th, pp291-302.

Research on Seismic Failure Correlation Analysis Methods for Redundant Nuclear Power Systems

HE Zhaokai [1*], ZHANG Ruijin [1*], YANG Jianfeng [2], QIAN Wenxue [1], XIE Liyang [1]

[1]School of Mechanical Engineering and Automation, Northeastern University, Shenyang, China
[2]Suzhou Nuclear Power Research Institute Co., Ltd., Suzhou, China
*2370133@stu.neu.edu.cn, *rjzhang@mail.neu.edu.cn

Keywords: Seismic Hazard Analysis, Seismic Fragility Assessment, System Failure Probability, Failure Correlation

Abstract- As a typical external disaster, earthquakes not only can trigger the failure of individual nuclear power equipment but may also lead to common-cause failures, thereby significantly increasing the risk of systemic failure. To fully reflect the seismic risk of common cause failures of multiple equipment, this paper constructs an integrated probabilistic analysis framework of "ground motion parameter-equipment response-system failure." Based on a system failure probability modeling approach that considers failure dependencies, probabilistic risk parameters derived from seismic hazard analysis and seismic fragility assessments are integrated to achieve accurate quantification of multi-equipment failures. Quantitative analysis of failure dependencies under varying ground motion intensities is conducted based on the α-factor model, revealing a significant nonlinear evolutionary pattern of failure correlation coefficients with respect to ground motion intensity. The rationality of the framework and methodology is validated through practical case studies. This research provides an analytical tool with both theoretical rigor and engineering applicability for seismic risk assessment in the nuclear engineering field, effectively enhancing the precision of probabilistic safety analysis for complex redundant systems.

1 Introduction

Since the occurrence of the Fukushima Daiichi nuclear disaster, there has been a remarkable increase in global attention towards the analysis of external hazard risks for nuclear power plants (NPPs). Earthquakes, as a natural disaster with immense destructive power, have emerged as one of the primary external risk factors confronting NPPs. The quantitative assessment of seismic risks for NPPs utilizing probabilistic safety analysis (PSA) methods has gradually been integrated into the design, construction, and operational phases of NPPs. Since the 1970s, the U.S. Nuclear Regulatory Commission (NRC) has issued a series of guidance documents and technical specifications for seismic PSA, while the International Atomic Energy Agency (IAEA) has also promulgated multiple guidance documents on seismic PSA, providing a systematic elaboration of the methodology. [1] In recent years, with the deepening of relevant research and the accumulation of practical experience, China has successively published a series of technical guidelines for seismic PSA, offering guidance for its development and application. [2] However, current seismic PSA efforts in China are predominantly in the research and exploration stage, with room for improvement in technical maturity, and a comprehensive standard system has yet to be established.

In contrast to internal event PSA, seismic PSA exhibits two distinct characteristics: Firstly, the failure probability of structures, systems, and components (SSCs) is directly correlated with earthquake intensity, necessitating a comprehensive consideration of the range of potential seismic events that the NPP may encounter and their underlying impacts. Secondly, earthquakes may simultaneously damage multiple redundant or similar SSCs; therefore, during the quantitative analysis of seismic PSA, it is imperative to scientifically and rationally account for such failure correlation. [3] In reality, failure correlation among system units are ubiquitous and objective phenomena. [4] Disregarding the correlation in system reliability analysis and adopting simplistic assumptions of mutual independence among unit failures would significantly undermine the reliability of seismic PSA results.

Building upon existing research on seismic PSA, this paper focuses on analytical methods for system failure dependencies under seismic conditions. It delves into how to more accurately reflect the impact of SSC failure correlation and systematically discusses their specific applications in seismic PSA. The aim is to provide theoretical support and technical references for enhancing the accuracy and credibility of seismic PSA.

2. System Failure Probability Modeling Considering Failure Correlation

2.1 Failure Correlation in Engineering

In practical engineering systems during service, the load environment typically exhibits uncertainty, leading to varying degrees of correlation in components failures within the system. This failure correlation significantly diminishes the reliability gains achieved through redundancy design and constitutes an important aspect of system reliability research.

From the perspective of the load-strength interaction mechanism, component failure is essentially a stochastic event where load exceeds strength. However, the uncertainties in load and strength play distinct roles in influencing failure correlation among components, necessitating differentiated treatment in system failure probability analysis. The degree of failure correlation among system components is jointly determined by the load distribution characteristics and the strength distribution characteristics. For systems where components are subjected to the identical or correlated environmental loads, load randomness serves as the root cause of failure correlation.

Research indicates that the scenarios of completely independent or fully correlated component failures in a system only occur under extreme conditions:

- Independent Failures: This occurs if and only if the environmental load is a deterministic constant while component performances are random variables, with each component's failure depending solely on its performance.
- Fully Correlated Failures: This occur if and only if component performances are deterministic constants while the service load is random variables, resulting in either all components failing or none failing simultaneously.

In practical situations, both the environmental load and component performance are random variables, therefore, component failures in a system are neither completely independent nor fully correlated. System failure correlation arises from the randomness of the load, while the dispersion of component performance helps mitigate the degree of failure correlation among components.

2.2 System Failure Probability Model

2.2.1 System Failure Probability Model under Independent Failure Assumption: Contemporary scientific analysis typically evaluates system performance based on component behavior. The conventional methodology for system failure probability analysis proceeds as follows: Initially, determine the failure probability of individual components, then derive the system failure probability based on the logical configuration (series, parallel, voting, etc.) of the system, under the assumption of mutually independence among component failures.

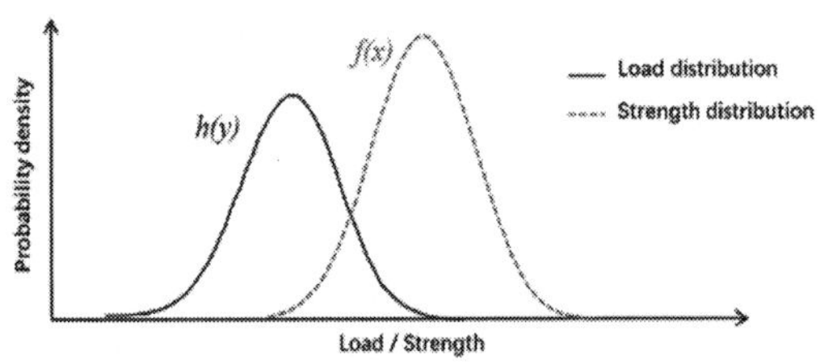

Figure 1 Interference relationship diagram of environmental load and component strength

The component failure probability p can be calculated using the load-strength interference model. Load y and strength x are fundamental random variables in reliability analysis, with failure essentially being the result of load exceeding strength. Let $h(y)$ denote the load probability density function (PDF) and $f(x)$ the component strength probability density function (see Figure 1 for the load-strength interference diagram). The component failure probability can be expressed as:

$$p = \int_0^{\infty} h(y)[\int_0^{y} f(x)\,dx]dy \quad (1)$$

Under the independent failure assumption, the parallel failure probability can be expressed as:

$$p^{n/n} = \{\int_0^{\infty} h(y)\left[\int_0^{y} f(x)\,dx\right]dy\}^n \quad (2)$$

Engineering practices demonstrate that traditional probability models based on independent failure assumptions fail to couple load randomness with failure event interdependencies, limiting their accuracy in characterizing system reliability.

2.2.2 Failure Probability Model Based on System-Level Load-Strength Interference Analysis: This paper, based on system-level probability interference analysis, considers both environmental load and component performance while treating their roles differently, establishing a system failure probability model that can reflect the influence of correlated failures.

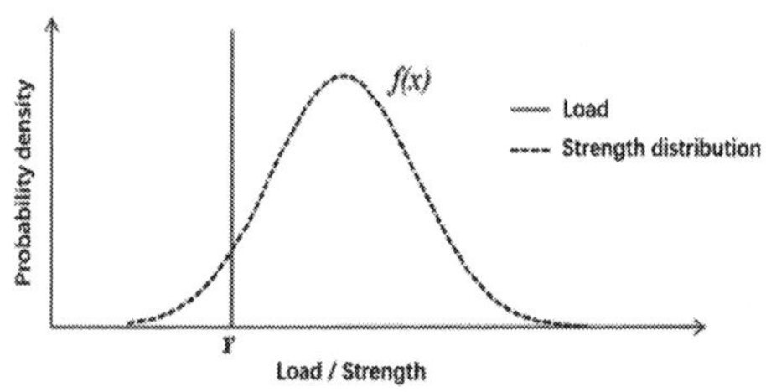

Figure 2 Interference relationship diagram of deterministic load and random strength

First, consider the case of deterministic load (denoted as Y). Under deterministic load Y, the conditional failure probability of a component is entirely determined by its strength distribution, i.e., the conditional failure probability that the component performance (strength) is less than the deterministic environmental load Y can be expressed as:

$$p(Y) = \int_0^{Y} f(x)dx \quad (3)$$

Since the strengths of components in a system typically satisfy the independent and identically distributed assumption, under a given load, the failure events of components are conditionally independent. Therefore, the conditional failure probability of an n-component parallel system can be expressed as:

$$[p(Y)]^n = \left[\int_0^{Y} f(x)dx\right]^n \quad (4)$$

Next, considering the randomness of the load y, the failure probability of each component in the system is a function of the load y, so the failure probability of an n-component parallel system should be the statistical average over the entire load space:

$$P_s^{n/n}=\int_0^{\infty} h(y)[p(y)]^n\, dy = \int_0^{\infty} h(y)[\int_0^{y} f(x)dx]^n dy \quad (5)$$

By comparing with the traditional model based on the independent failure assumption, it can be found that the parallel system failure probability model constructed based on system-level load-strength interference analysis does not introduce the "independent component failure" assumption and can naturally characterize failure correlation.

This method can be extended to calculate failure probabilities of various orders in redundant systems. That is, the probability of k-out-of-n components failures in redundant systems is formulated as:

$$P_s^{k/n}=C_n^k \int_0^{\infty} h(y)[\int_0^{y} f(x)dx]^k[\int_y^{\infty} f(x)dx]^{n-k} dy \quad (6)$$

This model provides a more precise theoretical framework for failure probability analysis of complex systems by strictly distinguishing the contributions of load and strength randomness.

3 Seismic Hazard Analysis

3.1 Purpose of Analysis

Seismic hazard analysis aims to quantify the exceedance probability of ground motion parameters (e.g., peak ground acceleration, PGA) of varying intensities at a site over a specified time interval, providing foundational load data support for system failure probability assessment.

3.2 Construction of Seismic Hazard Curves

Due to the stochastic nature of earthquake generation mechanisms, the complexity of seismic wave propagation paths, and the nonlinear characteristics of site conditions, among other uncertainties, the spatial-temporal distribution of seismic activity is difficult to predict precisely. Consequently, the probabilistic analysis method is widely adopted as the mainstream framework in engineering practice. Probabilistic seismic hazard analysis (PSHA) integrates all potential seismic sources and their activity parameters within a region to compute the probability of ground motion parameters exceeding specific thresholds at a site. The final result is presented in the form of seismic hazard curves (also known as exceedance probability curves), which map seismic risk characteristics through probabilistic space.

In probabilistic seismic risk assessments, seismic hazard curves are typically expressed as the relationship between annual exceedance probability and peak ground acceleration (PGA). Based on the stationary Poisson assumption of spatiotemporal independence of seismic events, the exceedance probability of ground motion parameter $A \geqslant a$ at a site over t years can be calculated using Equation (7):

$$P\{A \geq a\} = 1 - e^{-\lambda(a)t} \quad (7)$$

Here, a is defined as the specified peak ground acceleration (unit: g), and $\lambda(a)$ represents the annual occurrence frequency of earthquakes with ground motion exceeding a (unit: events/year).

Based on Equation (7), discrete calculations are performed to obtain annual exceedance probabilities corresponding to different values of a, representing the seismic hazard of the site. A series of discrete points $\{(a_1,P\{A \geq a_1\})\ldots(a_n,P\{A \geq a_n\})\}$ are typically interpolated to form a continuous curve, known as the seismic hazard curve. This curve uses PGA as the horizontal axis and annual exceedance probability as the vertical axis, exhibiting a typical negative exponential decay characteristic. As ground motion intensity increases, its exceedance probability decreases exponentially, reflecting the non-uniform distribution of seismic risk.

Figure 3 presents the seismic hazard curves for a specific site. Multiple curves in the figure illustrate analytical uncertainties. Each hazard curve is assigned a weighting factor based on the analyst's judgment, representing the degree of confidence in the curve's portrayal of actual seismic hazard likelihood. For any given PGA, the mean exceedance probability is obtained by weighted summation of exceedance probabilities from different hazard curves at that acceleration level.

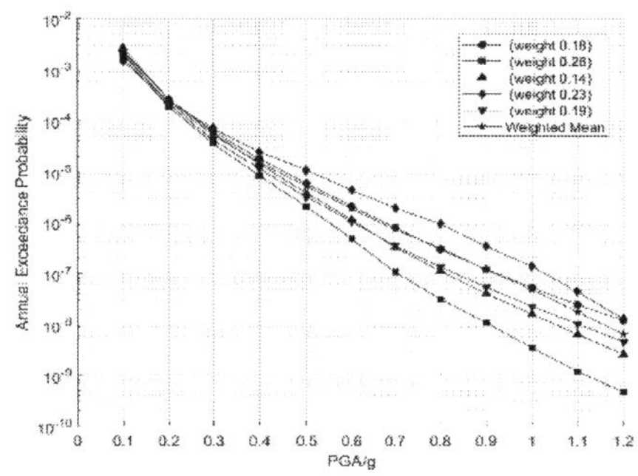

Figure 3 Seismic Hazard Curves for a Specific Site

After defining seismic initiating event intervals based on specific ground motion parameters, the probability of seismic initiating events within corresponding intervals can be calculated by taking the difference between exceedance probabilities associated with adjacent ground motion parameters on the same curve. The probability H of an earthquake occurring within the PGA interval (a_1,a_2) can be calculated using Equation (8):

$$H = H(a_1) - H(a_2) \quad (8)$$

4 Seismic Fragility Assessment

4.1 Purpose of Assessment

The core objective of seismic fragility assessment is to quantify the seismic resistance capacity of structures, systems, and components (SSCs) under specific ground motion parameters (such as PGA and response spectrum values) and establish a mapping relationship for conditional failure probability. This assessment provides critical failure probability parameters for subsequent system risk assessment and seismic design optimization.

4.2 Seismic Fragility Model

The seismic resistance capacity A of an SSC can be represented using the median seismic resistance capacity A_m and two random variables with a median of 1:

$$A = A_m e_R e_U \tag{9}$$

Here, e_R represents inherent randomness (also referred to as aleatory uncertainty) in the median seismic resistance capacity, assumed to follow a lognormal distribution with a logarithmic standard deviation of β_R, and e_U reflects epistemic uncertainty (also referred to as cognitive uncertainty), assumed to follow a lognormal distribution with a logarithmic standard deviation of β_U.

4.2.1 Family of Seismic Fragility Curves: When both aleatory and epistemic uncertainties are considered, fragility is expressed as a probability distribution. For any given acceleration a, the subjective probability Q (also known as the confidence level) and the conditional failure probability threshold f'satisfy the following relationship:

$$f' = \phi\left[\frac{\ln\left(\frac{a}{Am}\right)+\beta_U\phi^{-1}(Q)}{\beta_R}\right] \tag{10}$$

Here, $Q = \mathrm{P}[f < f'|a],$) represents the subjective probability (confidence level) that the conditional failure probability does not exceed f' under a given PGA, $\emptyset^{-1}[\cdot]$ represents the inverse of the standard normal cumulative Gaussian distribution function.

After determining the failure modes of the SSC and parameters of its seismic fragility model, the fragility curves of the SSC under different confidence levels can be derived based on the bivariate logarithmic normal distribution model (10). Figure 4 displays seismic fragility curves with the horizontal axis representing PGA and the vertical axis representing the conditional failure probability of the SSC.

4.2.2 Mean Seismic Fragility Curve: When only inherent randomness is considered, the mean fragility curve can be derived as:

$$f_0 = \phi\left[\frac{\ln\left(\frac{a}{Am}\right)}{\beta_C}\right] \tag{11}$$

Where β_R in Equation (10) is replaced by the combined standard deviation $\beta_C = \sqrt{{\beta_R}^2 + {\beta_U}^2}$. The mean fragility curve is also shown in Figure 4.

4.3 Analysis of Seismic Fragility Curves

According to Equation (10), for an SSC with a median seismic capacity A_m=0.68, random uncertainty standard deviation β_R=0.25 and epistemic uncertainty standard deviation β_U=0.35. The seismic fragility curves at different confidence levels are shown in Figure 4

It can be seen, when the PGA is 0.6g and considering a 95% confidence level (Q=95%), the conditional failure probability f' reaches 0.96 (as shown in the 95% confidence level fragility curve in Figure 4). Further analysis indicates that under PGA = 0.6g, the range of conditional failure probabilities corresponding to the 5%–95% confidence interval is from 0 to 0.96. This result clearly defines the relationship between ground motion intensity and structural failure through a probabilistic framework, where:

- The Q=95% curve defines the upper limit of failure probability predictions;
- The width of the confidence interval reflects epistemic uncertainty;
- The gradient of the fragility curve reflects the nonlinear response characteristics between PGA and failure probability.

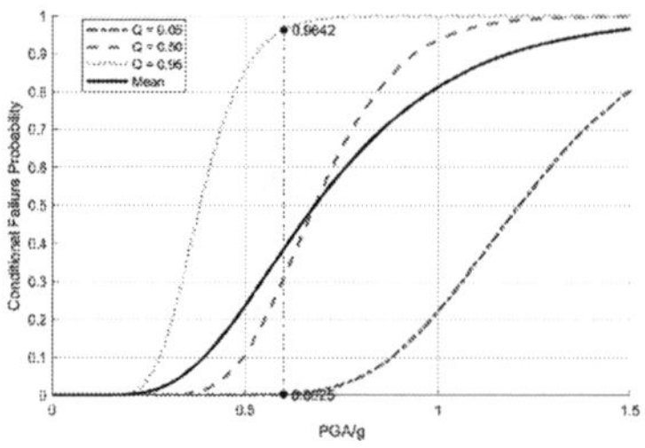

Figure 4 SSC Seismic Fragility Curves Example

5 Quantitative Analysis Methods for System Seismic Failure

5.1 Quantitative Analysis Framework for Redundant System Failure Probability

By constructing a system probability model that considers failure correlation, this study achieves explicit quantitative characterization of the failure correlation mechanism in redundant systems. Based on this model, by integrating probabilistic risk parameters provided by seismic hazard analysis and seismic vulnerability assessment, a comprehensive probabilistic analysis framework of "ground motion parameters - equipment response - system failure" is established.

5.1.1 Continuous Probability Convolution Model: Based on the redundant system failure model described in Equation (6), using the site-specific seismic hazard curve and equipment fragility curve as input parameters. The k-out-of-n system failure probability under seismic conditions is derived using the continuous full-probability convolution formula:

$$P_s^{k/n} = C_n^k \int_0^\infty \left[-\frac{dH(a)}{da}\right][f'(a)]^k[1 - f'(a)]^{n-k}da \tag{12}$$

Here, $-\frac{\mathrm{d}H(a)}{da}$ represents the annual probability density function of PGA derived from hazard curves, and $f'(a)$ represents the equipment failure probability corresponding to seismic acceleration a, derived from the fragility curve.

5.1.2 Discretized Numerical Integration: The annual exceedance probability of different ground motion parameters (i.e., load occurrence probability) can be obtained from the seismic hazard curve. It should be noted that the "load" here refers to the peak ground acceleration (PGA). On the other hand, the conditional failure probability of equipment under specific PGA values can be determined through the seismic fragility curve.

Considering that Equation (12) represents the continuous form of the full-probability formula, but given that both the hazard curve *H*(*a*) and the seismic fragility function *f*′(*a*) are expressed in discrete forms, numerical computation is conducted using the discretized full-probability formula in Equation (13):

$$P_s^{k/n} = C_n^k \sum_{i=1}^{q} H(i)\,[f'(i)]^k[1-f'(i)]^{n-k} \tag{13}$$

Here, q represents the total number of discrete ground motion parameter intervals, $H(i)$ represents the annual occurrence probability of the i-th acceleration interval (a_i- $\Delta a/2$,a_i+$\Delta a/2$), $f'(i)$ represents the equipment failure probability corresponding to the interval midpoint a_i.

5.1.3 Convergent Qualitative Analysis of Discrete Computation: It can be easily observed that when calculating the failure probability of a system under earthquake action based on the aforementioned analytical model, the calculation accuracy is significantly influenced by the granularity of discretization intervals. Specifically, as the parameter q defining the number of discretization intervals increases, the calculation accuracy for system failure probabilities is enhanced. In the subsequent section, a detailed examination of the interplay between the q-value and convergence characteristics of computational outcomes is conducted, with the objective of identifying the optimal q-parameter configuration that satisfies the predetermined precision criteria.

5.1.4 Definition of Engineering Applicable Interval: Theoretically, it is necessary to consider the effects of different levels of ground motion, and Equation (12) should be convolved over the range (0~∞). However, in practice, engineering seismic design codes commonly adopt 0.1g as the benchmark for functional verification, below which ground motions have negligible impact on structural integrity for most nuclear equipment. For ground motions exceeding 1.0g, the annual exceedance probability is generally below the 10^{-7} order of magnitude, representing extremely rare events. Furthermore, 1.0g intensity earthquakes exceed the site's disaster-resistant design limit states, necessitating no refined quantitative assessment. Based on these considerations, the integration interval can be simplified to [0.1g, 1g] in practical engineering calculations, which is deemed to cover the full probabilistic range of engineering concern. In the subsequent section, a practical example is also used to verify the definition of the applicable range

5.2 Uncertainty Analysis of System Failure Probability

In practice, due to uncertainties in seismic occurrence frequencies, the seismic hazard curve is generally represented by multiple curves with different weight values. Similarly, the seismic fragility curve has multiple versions with varying confidence levels. Therefore, a more precise expression for Equation (13) is:

$$P_s^{k/n} = C_n^k \sum_{i=1}^{q} H_j(i)\,[f'(i|Q)]^k[1-f'(i|Q)]^{n-k} \tag{14}$$

Here, $H_j(i)$ represents the annual occurrence probability of interval i on the j-th seismic hazard curve, $f'(i|Q)$ represents the failure probability for interval i on the fragility curve with confidence level Q.

To comprehensively consider the influence of weight coefficients of seismic hazard curves, it is recommended to adopt the weighted mean hazard curve H_0 and the fragility curve with confidence level Q to obtain the weighted solution of system failure probability:

$$P_s^{k/n} = C_n^k \sum_{i=1}^{q} H_0(i)\,[f'(i|Q)]^k[1-f'(i|Q)]^{n-k} \tag{15}$$

Here, H_0 represents the seismic hazard curve.

Furthermore, adopting both the weighted mean hazard curve H_0 and the mean fragility curve f_0 yields a robust solution for the system failure probability:

$$P_s^{k/n} = C_n^k \sum_{i=1}^{q} H_0(i)\,[f_0(i)]^k[1-f_0(i)]^{n-k} \tag{16}$$

Here, f_0 represents the Mean seismic fragility curve.

5.3 Quantitative Analysis Methods of Failure Correlation

In the current framework of seismic probabilistic safety assessment, the handling of correlation among system safety components typically adopts simplified assumptions: for analogous equipment located in the same position (e.g., within the same building, at the same elevation, or within the same system) and mutually redundant, their correlation is set to 1, while for other scenarios, the correlation is set to 0. Evidently, this approach has significant flaws—its theoretical foundation solely considers spatial positional correlation and overlooks the fundamental source of failure correlation: load uncertainty. For seismic conditions, the magnitude of failure correlation is closely related to ground motion intensity.

Currently, there are many Common cause failure (CCF) models applied in nuclear power safety analysis. Among them, the α-factor model, characterized by its clear physical significance and concise mathematical expression, has become one of the mainstream methods. The model quantifies system failure correlation through parameter α_k, defined as the ratio between the probability of exactly k units failing (kth-order failure) and the total probability of all possible failure orders in an n-unit system. Drawing on the concept of the α-factor model, this paper, based on existing research, obtains the failure probabilities of various orders of the system under different seismic initiating events and then conducts quantitative analysis of failure correlation under different ground motion intensities:

$$\alpha_k(i) = \frac{C_n^k H_0(i)[f_0(i)]^k[1-f_0(i)]^{n-k}}{\sum_{k=1}^{n} C_n^k H_0(i)[f_0(i)]^k[1-f_0(i)]^{n-k}} \tag{17}$$

Here, $\alpha_k(i)$ represents the *k*-th order correlation coefficient of seismic initiation event *i*.

Equation (17) computes the failure correlation coefficient based on the mean seismic vulnerability curve. To obtain more conservative results, the fragility curve corresponding to a high confidence level *Q*=95% can be adopted instead.

$$\alpha_k(i) = \frac{C_n^k H_0(i)\left[f'(i|Q=95\%)\right]^k\left[1-f'(i|Q=95\%)\right]^{n-k}}{\sum_{k=1}^{n} C_n^k H_0(i)[f'(i|Q=95\%)]^k[1-f'(i|Q=95\%)]^{n-k}} \quad (18)$$

6 Case Studies on Validation and Application of the Proposed Method

6.1 Quantitative Convergence Analysis of Discretization Parameters

Here, utilizing existing seismic hazard data and equipment seismic fragility data, the PGA range is set from 0.1 to 1.0g, and n=4 is taken. A case study is carried out based on Equation (16). By gradually increasing the parameter *q*, the changes in the calculation results of the system failure probability are observed. As shown in Figure 5, with the incremental increase of parameter *q*, the calculation results exhibit a clear convergence trend. In particular, when *q* reaches 200, the failure probabilities have stabilized, indicating that the calculation results have good robustness.

Based on the above analysis, it is recommended to set the parameter $q \geq 200$ in practical applications to ensure the stability of the calculation results.

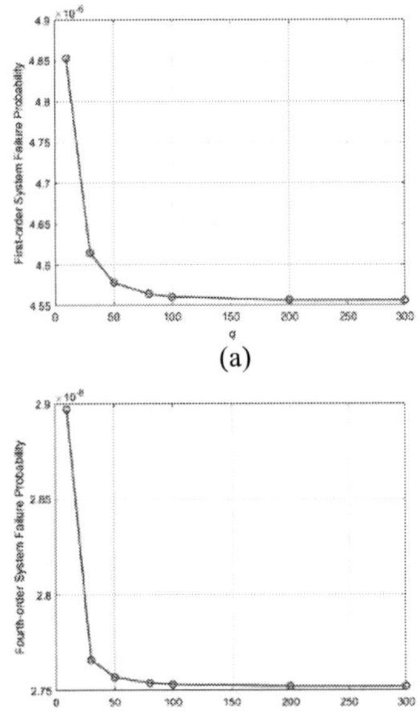

(a)

(b)

Figure 5 (a) Relationship between the first-order failure probability and the parameter *q*, (b) Relationship between the fourth-order failure probability and the parameter *q*

6.2 Examination and Confirmation of Interval Definition

Furthermore, in order to verify the rationality of the previously defined engineering applicable intervals, the parameter *q* is fixed at 200, and the PGA range is expanded to calculate the system failure probability. Table 1 shows the calculation results under different earthquake PGA ranges. From these data, it can be seen that the failure probability results across the three earthquake ranges are largely consistent. This indicates that the previous definition of the engineering applicable intervals is reasonable. Meanwhile, it can be observed that even when the analysis range is expanded to 0–1.5g, the set values of discrete interval numbers can still ensure the accuracy and stability requirements of calculations, which also further validates the rationality of the discrete interval numbers.

Table 1 Calculation Results of System Failure Probability under Different Earthquake PGA Ranges

PGA range	First-order system failure probability	Second-order system failure probability	Third-order system failure probability	Fourth-order system failure probability
0.1~1.0g	4.5564×10^{-6}	6.1656×10^{-7}	1.3990×10^{-7}	2.7522×10^{-8}
0~1.0g	4.5573×10^{-6}	6.1659×10^{-7}	1.3991×10^{-7}	2.7523×10^{-8}
0~1.5g	4.5596×10^{-6}	6.1722×10^{-7}	1.4189×10^{-7}	2.9907×10^{-8}

6.3 Analysis of Correlation Coefficients of Various Failure Orders

The failure correlation coefficients were further calculated based on the system failure probabilities under varying seismic intensities. As shown in Figure 6, the correlation coefficients for different orders of failure exhibit a significant dependency on ground motion intensity:

- First-Order Failure: The correlation coefficient decreases monotonically with increasing ground motion intensity, indicating that under weak seismic conditions, unit failure primarily exhibits independent characteristics.
- Fourth-Order Failure: The correlation coefficient increases monotonically with increasing ground motion intensity, reflecting significant system-level coupling effects during strong earthquakes.
- Second- and Third-Order Failures: The correlation coefficients exhibit a single-peak distribution that first rises and then falls, suggesting optimal coupling intervals for collective failures.

This evolution pattern has clear physical significance: in the low seismic intensity region (PGA < 0.2g), failure events are mainly dominated by independent unit failures, and the contribution of high-order common cause failures is negligible. When the ground motion intensity exceeds the 0.5g threshold, the system failure mode undergoes a qualitative change, with multi-unit coupled failure becoming the dominant mechanism. This nonlinear evolution characteristic essentially reflects the regulatory effect of load level on failure mechanisms—strong earthquakes not only increase the probability of unit failure but also exacerbate the correlation of system-level failure through dynamic response coupling.

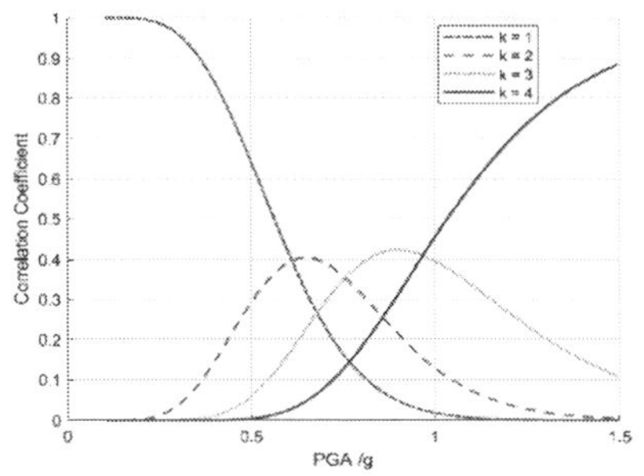

Figure 6 Variation of Failure Correlation Coefficient with Ground Motion Intensity

7 Conclusion

By constructing a system failure probability model that incorporates failure correlations, research was conducted on the system failure probability and correlation coefficients under seismic conditions. The following conclusions were drawn:

1) Based on a system failure probability model considering failure correlation, combined with seismic hazard analysis and seismic fragility assessment, a comprehensive probability analysis framework integrating " seismic motion parameters - equipment response - system failure" was constructed. It provides an operational method for quantitatively studying the failure probability and correlation of redundant systems under seismic excitation.

2) By using discretization methods to transform complex quantitative integration calculations into discrete sum numerical solving problems, the model is more convenient for practical application in engineering, which provides a reliable basis for system risk assessment. The practicality of the method has been verified through engineering examples

3) Drawing on the concept of the α-factor model, this paper proposes an estimation method for failure correlation coefficients under different ground motion intensities, and unveils the nonlinear evolution characteristics of failure correlation coefficients with respect to ground motion intensity.

8 Acknowledgements

This work was partially supported by the National Natural Science Foundation of China (Grant NO.52175131).

9 References

[1] IAEA-TECDOC-1937: 'Probabilistic Safety Assessment for Seismic Events', 2020

[2] NB/T 20037.5-2021: ' Level 1 Probabilistic Safety Assessment for Nuclear Power Plants - Part 5: Seismic at-power', 2021

[3] Bingchen F., Jianfeng Y., Xiaoming Z., et al.: 'Research on Correlation Analysis Method for Seismic PSA Based on Separation of Variables[J]', Atomic Energy Science and Technology, 2021, 55(03), pp 488-493

[4] Liyang X., Jinyu Z., Cuiling L., et al.: 'Common Cause Failure Analysis and Discretely Modeling for System Probability Prediction [J]', Journal of Mechanical Engineering, 2006, (01), pp 62-68

Research on hybrid redundancy allocation for multi-level repairable heterogeneous systems with interval valued reliability of components

Xu Han[1], Ilhan Chung[2], Qian Qian Zhao*

[1]School of Management, Zhengzhou University, Henan, China, hanx@gs.zzu.edu.cn

[2] Department of Integrated Safety Engineering, Ulsan College, Ulsan, 44550, South Korea

*[1]School of Management, Zhengzhou University, Henan, China, qianqianzhao@zzu.edu.cn

Keywords: multi-level heterogeneous systems; hybrid redundancy allocation; interval valued reliability; availability simulation; memetic algorithm

Abstract –This paper studies a hybrid redundancy allocation problem (HRAP) for multi-level repairable heterogeneous systems (MLRHS) with interval valued reliability of components. The redundancy design for the units involves heterogenous units of different performance but the same type. For each failure path, assume that only one level (component or module) could be selected as the redundant object. This study focuses on the HRAP to optimize the steady-state availability (SSA) interval over a finite time span under the constraint of the mean cost. Firstly, we propose a steady-state availability simulation model of MLRHS based on the discrete event simulation method to obtain the interval value of steady-state availability of the MLRHS. Secondly, a memetic algorithm (MA) that combines particle swarm optimization (PSO) with local search (LS) strategy is developed to address HRAP. Next, we discussed the order relations of the interval valued numbers. To validate the effectiveness and efficiency of the proposed method, numerical case studies are conducted.

1. Introduction

Reliability metrics serve as key indicators for measuring the quality of industrial systems during the design and production phases. There are three methods to optimize the reliability metrics of the system: improving the inherent reliability of components, implementing redundancy allocation, and reassigning the location of units in the system. Among them, redundancy allocation is considered the most cost-effective and easily implementable method[1]. Generally, RAP is designed with units in parallel, cold standby, k-out-of-N and other configurations to either maximize the system reliability or availability under constraints such as cost, weight, and volume or minimize system cost while satisfying system reliability, availability, weight, and other design constraints. For repairable systems, the system availability is a more suitable performance metric[2]. This study considers the SSA, defined as the ratio of the system's operational time within a finite lifetime, is adapted as the performance evaluation criterion for MLRHS.

In practice, industrial equipment is typically structured hierarchically (modular structure) from a physical perspective. At the highest level is the system, while components reside at the lowest level, with subsystems (modules) positioned in between[3]. Collectively, the system, modules, and components are referred to as units. With advancements in technology, each unit at different levels may have alternative units that perform the same functionality but differ in inherent reliability, cost, and other characteristics. Such a system is referred to as a multi-level heterogeneous system (MLHS). Han[4] studied a reliability redundancy allocation problem (RRAP) for the MLHS. Amirhossein[5] considered redundancy strategy as a decision variable and studied the RRAP of heterogeneous systems through reliability simulation.

Since RAP is classified as NP-hard[1], many evolutionary algorithms(EA) have been proposed to address such issues, including genetic algorithm(GA)[7], PSO[8], and simulated annealing (SA)[9] *et al.* However, the EA often struggle with exploring the neighborhood of solutions, leading to a tendency to get trapped in local optima. To address this issue, Wang and Tang[10] enhanced the GA by incorporating a LS strategy. They implemented a $(-1,+1)$ strategy, which involves removing a component with low reliability and adding one with high reliability to explore the neighborhood of solutions generated by the genetic algorithm. This approach led to the development of an MA to solve the RRAP under cost constraints. Udvardy *et al.*[11] proposed the Bacterial Memetic Algorithm (BMA) as a solution to the storage location allocation problem. Ying *et al.*[12] demonstrated the effectiveness of the MA in solving real-world dynamic programming problems. Most of the research focuses on the optimization of the system structure in the design stage, but do not consider the performance change of the system in the operation stage. Du and Li[13] introduced the system availability as a metric to evaluate the performance over the system's lifetime. The RAP is addressed by minimizing system design cost under the constraint of availability, which was calculated using the universal generating function (UGF) method. Building on the Quantum Evolutionary Algorithm (QEA), they incorporated local search strategies of $(-all,+x)$ and $(-x,+y)$ to develop the MA. In real life, the failure rate of some components at a certain moment is not a fixed value, but a uniformly distributed interval, which results in the SSA of the system being a uniformly distributed interval. Gupta *et al.*[6] have researched the RRAP with interval valued reliability of components by penalty function technique.

The contributions of this paper are as follows. (1) The redundancy design incorporates not only the original units but also the corresponding alternative units for the MLRHS to improve the SSA of the system. (2) This study considers the case where some components have a uniformly distributed failure rate at a certain moment and uses penalty function technique to construct a comparison model between two SSA intervals.

In this study, the system aging over time, with maintenance times following a general distribution. Because of the redundancy structure, the system may contain hidden failures after each maintenance. Additionally, we consider the HRAP, where the redundancy design incorporates not only the original units but also the corresponding alternative units for the MLRHS with interval valued reliability of components at a certain moment. Moreover, the component types in this study are non-identical. To address this problem, we propose an MA that integrates PSO and LS strategy. The remainder of this study is organized as follows: the system definition and system model are proposed in Section 2. Section 3 introduces the optimization model. Section 4 presents a numerical case study. Finally, Section 5 concludes the study and discusses directions for future research.

2. Problem definition

2.1. Multi-level heterogeneous systems

A multi-level system typically consists of multiple hierarchical levels: the system, subsystems (modules), and components. A basic structure of three-level system discussed in this study is illustrated in Fig. 1[14].

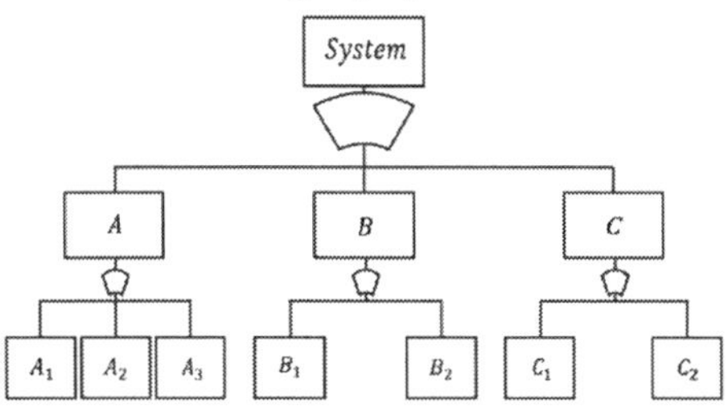

Fig. 1. An example of basic structure for three-level system

For convenience, the system, modules and components within the system are defined as units, and each unit, along with its corresponding alternative units, is defined as a set. Modules are composed of components arranged in series. In the RAP, simultaneously configuring redundancy for both a module and its child components within a failure path (e.g., component A_1 and module A in the failure path System-A-A_1 in Fig.1) could lead to increased design costs, unnecessary resource waste, and greater structural complexity. Therefore, in each failure path, only one level (either component or a module) is assumed to be selected as the redundant object in this study.

Once redundancy is established for a decided set, it can be implemented using any combination of the alternative units within that set. Fig. 2 gives an example of component A_1 and its alternative unit A_{1s1}, applied in the HRAP studied in this paper. When redundancy is designed for this set, it may involve any parallel combination of component A_1 and its alternative unit.

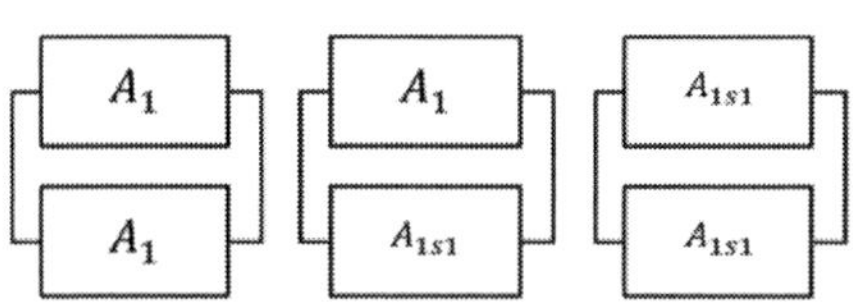

Fig. 2. An example of redundancy set in the HRAP

This structure gives rise to a heterogeneous hierarchical system, in which redundant modules are composed of functionally equivalent components that differ in reliability characteristics, design parameters, or physical attributes. Although the components within a redundancy set perform the same function, their structural and reliability differences must be accounted for in system modeling and optimization. The assumptions for this study are as follows:

- Each unit has alternative units, and each alternative unit of the modules is composed of several components in the series. The time to failure of each component follows the Exponential distribution or Weibull distribution.
- System level is not considered for redundancy.
- Assuming the scale parameters of components that the time to failure follow Weibull distribution are uniformly distributed intervals.
- The failure of the components could be identified and maintained at the system failure. Replacement is considered for each faulty component.
- During the system operation, the redundant units designed are not replaced during maintenance.
- All faulty units are replaced simultaneously, with the maintenance time for each component following a lognormal distribution.
- The resources for maintenance are available.

The notations for the optimization and simulation models are shown in **错误!未找到引用源。** 1.

Table. 1. Notations for simulation and optimization models.

Notation	Description
NC	Number of components in the heterogeneous system
K	Number of system failures in n-th simulation
N	Number of availability simulations for each hybrid redundancy solution
Q	Number of hybrid redundant solutions
T	Maximum lifetime of the system
A_q	Availability of the q-th hybrid redundancy solution
C_q	Mean cost of the q-th hybrid redundancy solution
c_f	Fixed cost
c_v	Variable cost
t_c	Failure time of all components
dwt	The downtime of the system
upt	The uptime of the system
NF^k	Number of failure components at the k-th failure of the system
NF_c^k	Number of failures of the c-th component at the k-th failure of the system
t_{wj}	The failure time of the j-th component that follows the Weibull distribution
T_m^k	Maintenance time for the k-th failure of the system
T_{op}^k	Normal operation time from the $(k-1)$-th maintenance to the k-th failure of the system
$T_R^{f,k}$	Replacement time of the f-th failure component at the k-th failure of the system
$MC_{q,n}$	Maintenance cost of the n-th simulation of the q-th hybrid redundancy solution

2.2. Mathematical model

This study addresses the HRAP for MLRHS, aiming to maximize the SSA of MLRHS under the constraints of cost by determining redundancy objects and their corresponding quantities. A SSA simulation model is developed for MLRHS based on discrete event simulation methods to evaluate the upper and lower limits of the SSA for system. The detailed steps are presented below.

Step 1: Set the number of redundant solutions as $q = 1$

Step 2: Set the number of simulation iterations as $n = 1$. Set the system lifetime is T.

Step 3: Initialize the simulation statistics $uptime$, $downtime$, and $MC_{q,n}$ to 0. Set the number of the failures $k = 1$, and initialize the simulation time $t = 0$.

Step 4: Generate the time to failure t $(m = 1,2,\dots,M)$ for each component and generate the time to failure $T_k(k = 1,2,\dots K)$ of system based on the reliability structure. When the system fails, the scale parameter α_j of the Weibull distribution for components j is updated as follows:

$$\alpha_j = \begin{cases} \alpha_j & t_{wj} \leq T_k \\ \alpha_j \times \left(1 - T_{1k}/t_{wj}\right) & t_{wj} > T_k \end{cases} \tag{6}$$

update $uptime = uptime + T_{1k}$, $t = t + T_k$. If $t < T$, proceed to Step 5, Otherwise, calculate the results of the simulation and proceed to step 8:

$$A_{q,n} = \frac{T - dwt}{T} \tag{7}$$

where $A_{q,n}$ refers to the steady-state availability of the system for the n-th$(n = 1,2,\dots N)$ simulation of the q-th $(q = 1,2,\dots,Q)$ hybrid redundancy solution.

Step 5: Determine the failure number for each component $NF_c^k(c = 1,2,\dots,NC)$, and estimate the total number of components that failed by $NF^k = \sum_{c=1}^{C} NF_c^k$. Generate the replacement time for each failed component $T_R^{f,k}(f = 1,2,\dots,NF_k)$, and calculate the maintenance time for the system $T_m^k = \max(T_R^{f,k})$, Update $downtime = dowmtime + T_m^k$, and update $t = t + T_m^k$. Determine whether the simulation runtime t is greater than the maximum system lifetime T. If $t < T$, proceed to step 6, Otherwise, calculate the results of this simulation and proceed to step 8:

$$A_{q,n} = \frac{upt}{T} \tag{8}$$

Step 6: Update the maintenance cost with by:

$$MC_{q,n} = MC_{q,n} + \sum_{c=1}^{C} NF_c^k \cdot C_v \tag{9}$$

where C_v represents the variable cost of each component.

Step 7: Update $k = k + 1$, and repeat steps 4-6 until the simulation runtime $t \geq T$.

Step 8: Record the steady-state availability obtained from the simulation and update the cost by $C_{qn} = c_f + MC_{qn}$. Update $n = n + 1$.

Step 9: Repeat steps 3-8 until $n > N$. Calculate the expected steady-state availability $A_q = \sum_{n=1}^{N} A_{qn}/N$ and the expected cost $C_q = \sum_{n=1}^{N} C_{qn}/N$ for the q-th hybrid redundant solution.

Step 10: Repeat steps 2-9 to simulate the availability of each hybrid redundant solution. Update $q = q + 1$.

After calculating the upper and lower limits of SSA for each MLRHS, we obtain the interval value of expected SSA and expected cost for each hybrid redundant solution. After removing the hybrid redundant solutions that the minimum cost did not satisfy the cost constraint, we need to find the optimal SSA interval, the interval comparison model in this study is given.

Firstly, define the evaluation and penalty functions:

$$E_{q_1} = (E_{q_1}^{min}, E_{q_1}^{max}) = \begin{cases} E_{q_1}^{max} = SSA_{q_1}^{max} - \text{Penalty}_{q_1} \\ E_{q_1}^{min} = SSA_{q_1}^{min} - \text{Penalty}_{q_1} \end{cases} \tag{10}$$

$$\text{Penalty}_{q_1} = \begin{cases} 0 & C_{q_1}^{max} \leq T_c \\ \dfrac{C_{q_1}^{max} - T_c}{T_c} & C_{q_1}^{max} > T_c \end{cases} \tag{11}$$

where $q_1 = 1,2,\dots,Q_1$. To distinguish the notation Q defined in the previous text, we use Q_1 to represent the number of solutions that the minimum cost satisfies cost constraint among all hybrid redundant solutions, $C_{q_1}^{max}$ represents the maximum cost of the q_1-th hybrid redundant solution that the minimum cost meets cost constraint.

We assume that the evaluation function intervals for two hybrid redundant solutions are $E_1(\alpha_1,\beta_1)$, $E_2(\alpha_2,\beta_2)$. If $P(E_1 \leq E_2) \geq 0.5$, we can determine that interval E_2 is better than interval E_1, and we calculate this probability under the following three cases:

Case1: The two intervals are independent of each other (If $\alpha_1 < \alpha_2, \beta_1 < \beta_2$ and $\alpha_2 > \beta_1$).

$$P(E_1 \leq E_2) = 1 \tag{12}$$

Case2: Two intervals have a containment relationship (If $\alpha_1 \leq \alpha_2$ and $\beta_1 \geq \beta_2$).

$$\begin{aligned} P(E_1 \leq E_2) &= P\big((\alpha_1,\beta_1) \leq (\alpha_2,\beta_2)\big) \\ &= \int_{\alpha_2}^{\beta_2} P(E_1 \leq e_2 | E_2 = e_2) * P(e_2) de_2 \\ &= \int_{\alpha_2}^{\beta_2}\int_{\alpha_1}^{e_2} \frac{1}{\beta_1 - \alpha_1} de_1 * \frac{1}{\beta_2 - \alpha_2} de_2 \\ &= \frac{\beta_2 + \alpha_2}{2(\beta_1 - \alpha_1)} - \frac{\alpha_1}{\beta_1 - \alpha_1} \end{aligned} \tag{13}$$

Case3: The two intervals intersect but do not completely contain each other (If $\alpha_1 \leq \alpha_2$ and $\beta_1 < \beta_2$). Same as equation (21):

$$\begin{aligned} P(E_1 \leq E_2) &= \int_{\alpha_2}^{\beta_2} P(E_1 \leq e_2 | E_2 = e_2) * P(e_2) de_2 \\ &= \frac{\frac{1}{2}(\beta_1^2 - \alpha_2^2) + \alpha_1(\alpha_2 - \beta_1)}{(\beta_1 - \alpha_1)(\beta_2 - \alpha_2)} + \frac{\beta_2 - \beta_1}{\beta_2 - \alpha_2} \end{aligned} \tag{14}$$

3. Memetic algorithm for hybrid redundancy allocation

To address the HRAP for multi-level repairable heterogeneous systems, a MA based on PSO and LS strategies is designed, incorporating an LS strategy to enhance the local search capability of the PSO. The specific steps of the memetic algorithm are as follows:

Step 1: Input the system information and algorithm parameters to generate N_A initial solutions, each initial solution includes the redundancy quantity for each set, which is the sum of the redundancy quantities of each unit and its alternative units. Initialize the algorithm iteration number as $eps = 1$.

Step 2: Initialize $n_A = 1$.

Step 3: Generate all possible hybrid redundancy solutions for the n_A-th initial solution, that is, the redundancy quantity of each unit and its alternative units.

Step 4: Evaluate the availability interval and mean cost interval of the generated hybrid redundancy solutions using the availability simulation model provided in Section 2.2. Select the hybrid redundancy solution with the optimal availability interval under the cost constraint and update the local best solution (pbest) for the n_A-th initial solution.

Step 5: Periodically perform the $(-x, +y)$ local search strategy on the n_A-th initial solution to get a new initial solution, generate all possible hybrid redundancy solutions for this new initial solution and execute Step 4 again. If the availability interval of pbest improves, replace the initial solution with the one obtained from the LS, otherwise the n_A-th initial solution will unchanged. Update $n_A = n_A + 1$.

Step 6: Repeat Steps 3 to 5 until $n_A > N_A$. Update the global best solution (gbest).

Step 7: Update the position of each initial solution by: $V_{id} = \omega * V_{id} + c_1 r_1(\text{pbest} - x_{id}) + c_2 r_2(\text{gbest} - x_{id})$, where $x_{id} = x_{id} + V_{id}$. Update $eps = eps + 1$.

Step 8: Repeat Steps 2-7 until the $eps > EPS$. Output the initial solution, hybrid redundancy solution with optimal availability interval and mean cost interval of gbest.

4. Numerical study

The numerical experiments are designed to demonstrate the effectiveness of the constructed availability simulation model, interval comparison model and the memetic algorithm. The maximum lifetime of the system is set to T=2000, with a target mean cost of T_c=800. In this experiment, each component has one alternative unit that serves the same function but differs in inherent reliability and cost, each module has two alternative units. The information of failure distribution and cost of each component are listedin Table. 2. The time-to-failure distribution and cost of alternative units of each inherent component are shown in Table. 3, where $E(\lambda)$ means this component follows an Exponential distribution with a failure rate of λ, and $W(\alpha_1 \sim \alpha_2, \beta)$ means the component follows a Weibull distribution with interval scale parameter $\alpha_1 \sim \alpha_2$ and shape parameter β. The size of initial solutions is set to $N_A = 100$. Iteration times of algorithm $EPS = 120$. Maximum redundancy for every set is 4. The experiments are accomplished in Matlab 2023 on the computer processor AMD Ryzen 7 5800H with Radeon Graphics 3.20 GHz.

Table. 2. Parameter setting in heterogeneous system

Parent unit	Time-to-failure distribution	Cost
A	$Exp(0.0022)Exp(0.002)Wei(420 \sim 450,2.5)$	15,15,17
A_{s1}	$Exp(0.0019)Exp(0.0018)Wei(440 \sim 470,2.5)$	17,18,20
A_{s2}	$Exp(0.0025)Exp(0.002)Wei(390 \sim 420,2.5)$	13,13,14
B	$Wei(440 \sim 470,2.5)Exp(0.0024)$	16,15
B_{s1}	$Wei(460 \sim 490,2.5)Exp(0.0022)$	20,18
B_{s2}	$Wei(420 \sim 450,2.5)Exp(0.0027)$	12,11
C	$Wei(380 \sim 410,2.5)Exp(0.0026)$	16,17
C_{s1}	$Wei(410 \sim 440,2.5)Exp(0.0023)$	19,20
C_{s2}	$Wei(360 \sim 390,2.5)Exp(0.0029)$	12,12

Table. 3. Parameter setting in heterogeneous system

Alternative unit	Time-to-failure distribution	Cost
A_{1s1}	$Exp(0.0027)$	14
A_{2s1}	$Exp(0.0017)$	16
A_{3s1}	$Wei(390 \sim 420,2.5)$	16
B_{1s1}	$Wei(420 \sim 450,2.5)$	14
B_{2s1}	$Exp(0.0019)$	17
C_{1s1}	$Wei(360 \sim 390,2.5)$	15
C_{2s1}	$Exp(0.0030)$	15

To get a reasonable number N of availability simulations for each hybrid redundancy solution, this study conducted the following experiment, a hybrid redundancy solution was randomly generated, and the change trend of the availability, obtained through the simulation model proposed in this paper, was recorded as N varies from 1 to 1000 in steps of 1. The results are presented in Fig. 3.

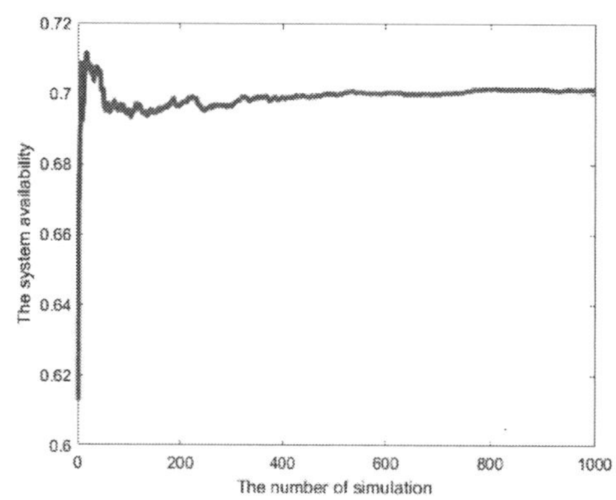

Fig. 3. The trend of system availability as $\boldsymbol{N}$ varies.

It can be seen from Fig. 3 that when $n \geq 500$, the system availability tends to converge, so in this study, N is set to 500. To verify the effectiveness of the proposed availability simulation model, the interval comparison model and memetic algorithm, the results obtained after inputting the data listed above are presented in Table. 4, where SR means the redundancy of each set, and UR means the redundancy of each unit and its alternative units. It can be seen that when the target mean cost is set to 800, according to the availability simulation model, the interval comparison model and memetic algorithm set in this paper, the availability interval of the optimal solution is $[0.6764, 0.7094]$, and the mean cost interval of the optimal solution is $[791.992, 797.102]$.

Table. 4. Experimental results when $\boldsymbol{T_c}$=800 for HRAP

Availability interval	Cost interval	Set	SR	UR
0.6764 ~ 0.7094	791.992 ~ 797.102	A	4	0,2,2
		B	0	0,0,0
		C	0	0,0,0
		A_1	0	0,0
		A_2	0	0,0
		A_3	0	0,0
		B_1	3	1,2

		B_2	3	1,2
		C_1	4	2,2
		C_2	2	2,0

To demonstrate the improvement of system SSA by the HRAP, we consider implementing redundancy for only one of the units and its corresponding alternative units. System information and algorithm information remain unchanged, when the target cost $T_c = 800$, the results are shown in Table. 5.

Table. 5. Experimental results when T_c=800

Availability interval	Cost interval	Set	SR	UR
0.6363 ~ 0.6806	777.992 ~ 782.102	A	3	0,3,0
		B	3	3,0,0
		C	0	0,0,0
		A_1	0	0,0
		A_2	0	0,0
		A_3	0	0,0
		B_1	0	0,0
		B_2	0	0,0
		C_1	4	0,4
		C_2	3	3,0

According to the interval comparison model proposed in this paper, $P\big((0.6363,0.6806) \leq (0.6764,0.7094)\big) \approx 0.9394 \gg 0.5$. In other words, for MLRHS, considering both the units and their corresponding alternative units for redundancy may significantly enhance its SSA interval.

5. Conclusions

This research solves the HRAP in MLRHS with interval valued reliability of components. The expected steady-state availability and expected total maintenance cost are considered to evaluate the system performance, which is estimated by the discrete event simulation. The MA which improves the LS ability of the PSO is used to solve the problem. An interval comparison model is proposed to deal with the comparison among the interval values of the objective function of feasible solutions. Finally, a numerical example is used to verify that the proposed models can effectively solve the problem. For future studies, we can consider the multi-objective optimization of MLHS, such as the reliability of the system at a certain time, the volume of the system, etc. can be used as the optimization objectives or constraints of the system. Secondly, we can consider different redundancy strategies to optimize the MLHS.

6. Acknowledgment

This research was supported by the National Natural Science Foundation of China (Grant No. 72101240), and the International Science and Technology Cooperation Project of Henan Province (Grant No. 242102521030).

7. References

[1] Chern M S. "On the computational complexity of reliability redundancy allocation in a series system". Operations research letters, Vol.11(5): 309-315(1992).

[2] Mani S, Sharareh T. "Redundancy allocation problem with a mix of components for a multi-state system and continuous performance level components". Reliability Engineering and System Safety 241(2024).

[3] Kumar R, Izui K, & Yoshimura M. "Optimal multilevel redundancy allocation in series and series–parallel systems". Computers & Industrial Engineering, Vol.57(1): 169-180(2009).

[4] Han I C. "Optimization of Redundancy Allocation in Multi-Level System considering Alternative Units". Journal of the Korean society for quality management, Vol.43(1):31-42(2015).

[5] Amirhossein C, Parham A, & Abbas A N. "Redundancy allocation of heterogeneous components by simulation-based optimization". Proceedings of the Institution of Mechanical Engineers, Part O: Journal of Risk and Reliability, Vol.235(6):1090-1101(2021).

[6] Gupta R, Bhunia A, Roy D. "A GA based penalty function technique for solving constrained redundancy allocation problem of series system with interval valued reliability of components". Journal of Computational and Applied Mathematics, Vol.232(2):275-284(2009).

[7] Kayedpour F, Amiri M, & Rafizadeh M. "A Markov chain-based genetic algorithm for solving a redundancy allocation problem for a system with repairable warm standby components". Journal of Risk and Reliability, Vol.238(4): 853-872(2024).

[8] Yeh W C. "A two-stage discrete particle swarm optimization for the problem of multiple multi-level redundancy allocation in series systems". Expert Systems with Applications, Vol.36(5): 9192-9200(2009).

[9] Borhani H, Sharifi M. "Solving a Joint Availability-Redundancy Optimization Model with Multistate Components and Metaheuristic Approach". Vol.1:59-70(2020).

[10] Wang Z, Tang K, & Yao X. "A memetic algorithm for multi-level redundancy allocation". IEEE Transactions on reliability, Vol.59(4): 754-765(2010).

[11] Udvardy K, Görbe P, & Bódis T. "Conceptual Framework for Adaptive Bacterial Memetic Algorithm Parameterization in Storage Location Assignment Problem". Mathematics, Vol.12(23):3688-3688(2024).

[12] Ying Z, Ling J K, & Li J Y. "A memetic algorithm for a real-world dynamic pickup and delivery problem". Memetic Computing, Vol. 16(2):203-217(2024).

[13] Du M, Li Y F. "An investigation of new local search strategies in memetic algorithm for redundancy allocation in multi-state series-parallel systems". Reliability Engineering & System Safety, Vol.195: 106703(2020).

[14] Yun W Y, Song Y M, & Kim H G. "Multiple multi-level redundancy allocation in series systems". Reliability Engineering & System Safety, Vol. 92(3): 308-313(2007).

Research on Failure Probability Analysis Method of Nuclear Power Equipment Based on Failure Data

ZHANG Ruijin[1,*], YANG Jianfeng [2], HE Zhaokai [1,*], XIE Liyang [1]
[1] School of Mechanical Engineering and Automation, Northeastern University, Shenyang, China
[2] Suzhou Nuclear Power Research Institute Co. Ltd., Suzhou, China
rjzhang@mail.neu.edu.cn, 2370133@stu.neu.edu.cn

Keywords: Nuclear Power Equipment; CCF; System Failure Probability; Parameterized Model; Correlation Coefficient

Abstract—The safe and reliable operation of nuclear power equipment is crucial for the stable development of nuclear power plants, and accurately analyzing its failure probability is a key link in ensuring nuclear power safety. In this paper, due to the scarcity of CCF (Common-Cause Failure) data of nuclear power equipment, it is difficult to conduct CCF analysis using empirical models. Based on the generalized stress-strength interference analysis at the system level, a failure probability model for a parallel system that can reflect the influence of failure correlation is established. The model is discretized, and a parameterized model of the system failure probability is established. The statistical method for CCF data based on the parameterized model is determined and is carried out on the on-site failure data records of the SEC pumps in nuclear power equipment. The parameterized model of the system failure probability is applied to conduct failure probability analysis and failure correlation analysis of the SEC pumps. The results show that this model can well predict the occurrence probability of high-order failure events according to the occurrence times of low-order failure events and reasonably calculate the CCF coefficients of each order of the system according to the occurrence times of failure events of each order of the system.

1. Introduction

Common Cause Failure (CCF) is a type of Dependent Failure, which is manifested as multiple redundant units failing simultaneously or within a short time interval due to a common cause [1-2]. In the design of safety-related systems in nuclear power plants, to ensure that the systems meet the requirements of safety and reliability, redundant design is usually adopted. Only when multiple identical units performing the same function in the system all fail will the system fail.

In the early days of reliability engineering, when calculating the reliability of systems with redundant designs, it was usually assumed that the failures of redundant units were independent of each other. However, based on the long-term experience accumulation in the engineering field, it was later found that if only independent failures were considered in the PSA model, the failure probability of the system would be severely underestimated, resulting in analysis results that were dangerously biased. Therefore, in the probabilistic safety assessment of nuclear power plants, common cause failure analysis, as an important technical topic in probabilistic safety assessment, has received full attention.

Due to the relatively small amount of common cause failure data for nuclear power equipment, currently, the common practice of common cause analysis at home and abroad is to analyze in combination with the empirical data from different countries and different nuclear power plants [3-4]. This is a feasible approach for analysis. However, sometimes the data from enterprises in other countries cannot represent the actual operation situation in China. Therefore, it is very necessary to collect and analyze the operation data of domestic nuclear power plants and establish a common cause failure analysis method based on failure data.

2. Establishment of a Parameterized Model for System Failure Probability

2.1. System Failure Probability Model Based on Independent Failure

In the reliability problem, a system in which each unit fails independently is called an independent failure system. In an independent failure system, the failures of each "unit" (components of the system, such as subsystems, parts, etc.) are independent random events. The traditional system failure probability model is established under the assumption that each component fails independently.

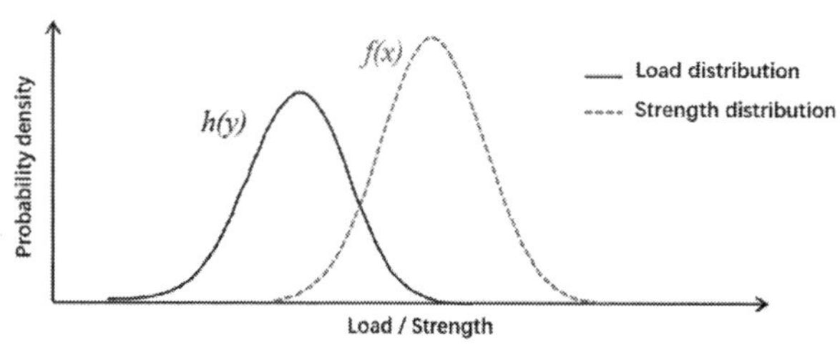

Figure 1. Diagram of the interference relationship between environmental loads and unit strength

In short, a system is composed of units. In a deterministic sense, it can be said that the state of the system completely depends on the state of its units. The traditional method of system failure probability analysis is to calculate the system failure probability based on the unit failure probabilities. To use the traditional method of calculating the system failure probability, it is necessary to first calculate the failure probability of the unit according to the stress-strength interference analysis method (the load-strength interference relationship diagram is shown in Figure 1), and then, under the assumption that "the failures of each unit are independent of each other", calculate the system failure probability from the unit failure probabilities.

Load (stress) and strength are the fundamental random variables in reliability analysis. Essentially, failure is the result of the load (stress) exceeding strength. The load y is a random variable, and its probability density function is denoted as $g(y)$; the strength x of a unit is also a random variable, and its probability density function is denoted as $f(x)$. The failure probability p of a unit is the probability that the strength x of the unit is less than the load y. The load-strength interference model for calculating the failure probability of a unit is shown in Equation (1).

$$p = \int_0^{\infty} g(y)[\int_0^{y} f(x)\,dx]dy \tag{1}$$

Under the assumption of "independent failure of each unit", the model for calculating the failure probability of a parallel system from the failure probabilities of unit are expressed by Equation (2).

$$P^{n/n} = \{\int_0^{\infty} g(y) \int_0^{y} f(x)dxdy\}^n \tag{2}$$

Similarly, the probability, that any k out of n units of the system fail, can be expressed as

$$P^{k/n} = \frac{n!}{k!(n-k)!} p^k (1-p)^{n-k} \tag{3}$$

2.2. Establishment of System Failure Probability Model Considering Failure Correlation

In most cases, both environmental loads and unit performance are random variables, and the failures of each unit in the system have statistical correlations. The failure probability of the system is not only related to the failure probabilities of its units, but also related to the magnitude of the failure correlation between the units. Therefore, the failures of each unit in the system are generally neither independent of each other nor completely correlated. The system failure probability model under the assumption of independent unit failure often has a large error.

The failure probability p of a unit is defined as the probability that the unit performance (strength) x is less than the environmental load y and can be expressed as p=P(x<y).

The reliability of a unit can be regarded as a function of stress. When both stress and strength are random variables, the conditional failure probability of the unit (conditional on the stress) can be defined as follows

$$p(y) = \int_0^{y} f(x)\,dx \tag{4}$$

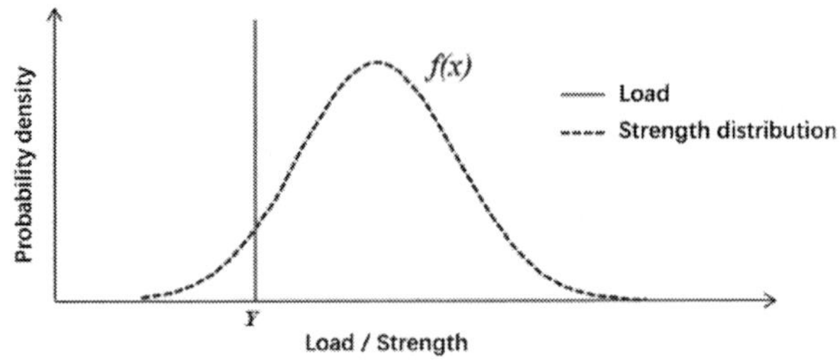

Figure 2. Interference relationship diagram between deterministic load and random strength

Obviously, under a certain stress y, the conditional failure probability of the unit is completely determined by its strength distribution. Since the strengths of each unit in the system can generally be regarded as independent and identically distributed random variables, the failures of each unit are independent of each other under a deterministic stress. For a specified stress y, the probability that all units fail simultaneously in a parallel system is

$$[p(y)]^n = [\int_0^{y} f(x)\,dx]^n \tag{5}$$

Here, $[p(y)]^n$ is equivalent to the conditional failure probability of an n-order parallel system. The probability that the n units of the system fail simultaneously under the action of the random stress y is the mathematical expectation of its conditional failure probability function $[p(y)]^n$, which can be interpreted as the statistical average value of the "system conditional failure probability" over the entire possible stress interval $0<s<+\infty$, and its expression is

$$P_s^{\frac{n}{n}} = \int_0^{\infty} [p(y)^n] h(y)\,dy = \int_0^{\infty} h(y)[\int_0^{y} f(x)dx]^n dy \tag{6}$$

This model is a failure probability model of a parallel system established through the stress-strength interference analysis at the system level, which can reflect the influence of failure correlation. It can be easily seen from the difference between Equation (6) and Equation (2), which Equation (2) is the traditional failure probability model of a parallel system based on the independent failure assumption.

3. DISCRETIZATION OF SYSTEM FAILURE PROBABILITY MODEL

3.1. Principle of Model Discretization

Considering that the system failure probability models established above are all presented in the form of integral equations, it is difficult to directly apply them to the calculation of the failure probability of engineering systems, because there are few conditions such as known load distributions or strength distributions. To apply the system failure probability model above to actual engineering systems, it is necessary to discretize it so that the model parameters can be determined from the failure data of the system or components.

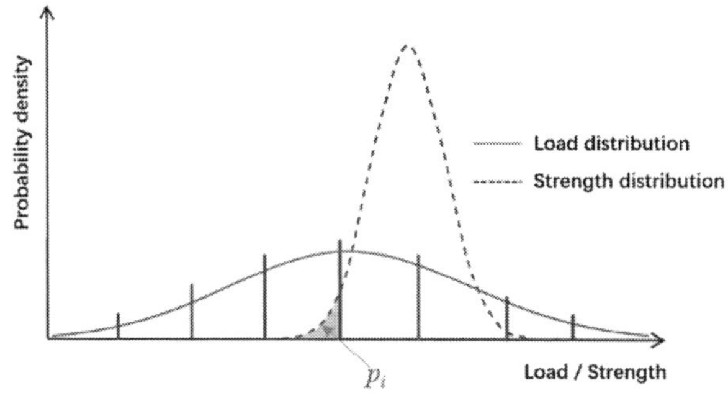

Figure 3. Discretization of the Load-Strength Interference Model

Integration is a limiting state of the summation of polynomials. Therefore, integration can be approximately expressed in the form of the sum of polynomials, which is the mathematical basis for the discretization of the system failure probability model. Therefore, the failure probability model of the voting system considering failure correlation in Equation (7) can be expressed by the following polynomial sum formula.

$$p_s^{k/n} = \binom{n}{k} \sum_i \{H(y_i)[p(y_i)]^k[1-p(y_i)]^{n-k}\} \qquad (7)$$

Here, $p(y_i) = \int_0^{y_i} f(x)\,dx$ is the conditional failure probability of unit when the load value is y_i. $H(y_i)=h(y_i)\Delta y_i$ is the probability that the load value appears in the interval $(y_i - \Delta y_i/2, y_i + \Delta y_i/2)$.

According to the meaning of each term in Equation (7), the specific values of its parameters can be determined from the known system failure data. For example, consider an n-order redundant system and conduct m independent tests. In the j-th test, k_j components fail (k_j ranges from 0, 1, 2,... n, j=0,1,...m). The different numbers of failed components in each test mean that the magnitudes of the loads appearing in each test are different. For these m tests, all possible results can be represented by a set $K\{k_j \mid k_j = 0,1,...,n\}$. According to statistical theory, in such tests, the cumulative distribution (conditional failure probability) corresponding to the failure number of the i-th (i=0,1,2,...n) order rank is exactly the estimate of the conditional failure probability of the component under the condition that the load value is y_i (for a certain test, the number of failed components directly depends on the magnitude y_i of the load that appears in a statistical sense). Therefore, the occurrence probability (conditional failure probability) of a failure event (a certain order of failure) can be expressed as

$$p(y_i) = \frac{i-0.3}{n+0.4} \qquad (8)$$

The occurrence frequency of the corresponding load y_i can be estimated by the following formula

$$H(y_i)=h(y_i)\,\Delta y_i = \frac{\text{number of } i\text{–order failure}}{\text{test number of system}} \qquad (9)$$

3.2. Verification of the Parameterized Model

To better describe the application of the discretization processing of the system failure probability model, a typical example is given here. This example conducts the prediction of the system failure probability based on the failure event data that occurred during 34 tests of a redundant system composed of 10 valves (a 10-order redundant system). The failure events include the "valve cannot open normally" failure events with different failure orders, among which there are 5 single-unit failures, 2 second-order failures (two units fail simultaneously), 1 third-order failure (three units fail simultaneously), and 26 successful events. In other words, among the 340 (34×10) tests of the units, a total of 12 (5×1 + 2×2 + 1×3) units failed. Obviously, these data contain not only the failure probability information of the units but also the system correlation failure information.

For this system failure probability prediction, the common-cause failure probabilities of all orders of this system can be uniformly calculated according to the Equation (7-9).

TABLE I. CCF EVENTS DATA AND PARAMETERS OF THE PARAMETRIC MODEL

Failure order	Number of events	$H(y_i)$	$p(y_i)$
0	26	0.765	
1	5	0.147	0.067
2	2	0.059	0.162
3	1	0.029	0.259

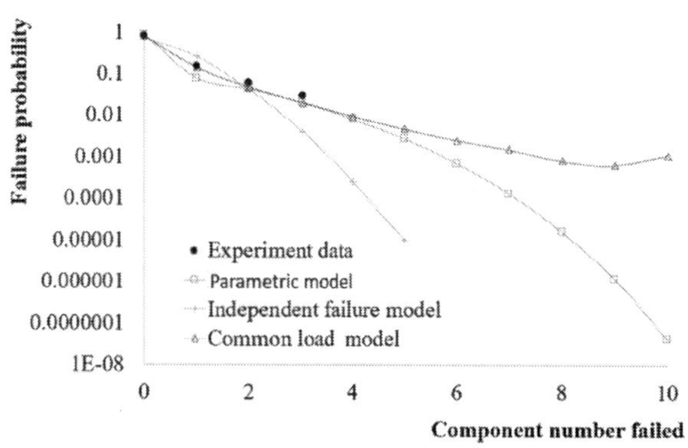

Figure 4. Comparison between the Model and the Observed Values

Figure 4 shows the comparison between the failure probabilities of each order of the system estimated by different models and the observed data. Compared with the directly observed data, the independent failure model's estimation of the failure probabilities of the first two orders is also consistent with the observed values. However, when it comes to the third-order failure, there is an obvious deviation between its estimation result and the observed value. This error trend reflects that the higher the failure order is, the greater the influence of CCF will be, and of course, the error of the independent failure model will also be larger. When the CLM model in the common-cause failure model is adopted, the estimated values of the failure probabilities in the first three orders match the observed values very well. However, there is a significant increase in the common-cause failure probability of the tenth order, which goes against the actual engineering situation. The model of the failure probabilities of the first three orders of the system obtained by using the parametric model is relatively close to the observed values, and the prediction of the failure of higher orders conforms to the expected trend in engineering.

4. PROBABILITY ANALYSIS OF NUCLEAR POWER EQUIPMENT FAILURE BASED ON FAILURE DATA

4.1. Collection of CCF Data for Nuclear Power Equipment

Common cause failure (CCF) refers to the dependent failures of two or more identical or similar equipment caused by the same common cause that cannot be explicitly expressed at the same time or within a very short time interval.

It is pointed out in NUREG/CR-6268 that the equipment failures included in a CCF event need to meet the following four criteria simultaneously:

① It includes two or more independent equipment failures, degradations, or defects (defects will cause standby failures of the equipment);

② The equipment group fails within a selected time period;

③ The equipment group fails due to a common cause and coupling mechanism;

④ The equipment failures occur within the established boundary range.

The plant-specific data source refers to the information on the common cause failure data of equipment accumulated during the actual operation of the power plant. The accumulation and preservation of the CCF data of the power plant involve multiple departments such as operation, maintenance, and testing. Therefore, these data sources must be fully utilized during the collection of common cause failure data.

The data sources for the collection of the CCF data of equipment mainly include the operator's logbook, the experience feedback system, the production process management system, the power plant operation event report (IOE/LOE), etc.

The historical data of 759 items related to the pumps of the SEC system at a certain enterprise's site were collected and analyzed. After removing duplicate records, there were a total of 193 event records involving equipment failure or degradation. Among them, there were 179 independent failure or degradation events, 7 groups of 2-order CCF events, and 1 group of 4-order CCF events, listed in Table 2 .

4.2. Statistical of CCF Data Based on Parametric Model

When applying the CCF parametric model, it is necessary to first accurately count the number of CCF events from the failure data, and at the same time determine the total number of tests. Then, the parameters required by the CCF parametric model should be obtained according to Equations (8-9).

In order to ensure the accuracy of the number of tests, the primary task is to define a single test. Here, the time is selected as the measurement standard. The determination method is as follows: For the SEC pump system with four units, the independent working period of one pump is 2 weeks, and running in turn of four pumps constitutes a working cycle, that is 8 weeks (nearly equivalent to 2 months). Therefore, 2 months of running is regarded as one test period for SEC pump system.

The determination of total number of tests requires a comprehensive analysis of the operation time data of all units in power plants. The number of tests for each unit is calculated by dividing its operation time by the single test period. By summing up the number of tests for each unit, the total number of tests is determined to be 1,172. Then, the data of common cause failure events are statistically analyzed, and listed in Table 2.

TABLE II. STATISTICS RESULTS OF CCF EVENTS FOR SEC PUMP

Equipment	CCCG	Failure Mode	Total test number	Statistics of CCF Events	
SEC pump system	4	Starting failure Running failure	1172	n_1	179
				n_2	7
				n_3	0
				n_4	1

4.3. CCF Probability and Correlation Analysis of Nuclear Power Equipment

By using the parametric model and the statistical values of the failure data of SEC pumps as tabulated in Table 2, the failure probabilities of each order of SEC system can be calculated (seen in Table 3). The failure probability of CCCG of SEC pumps shows a downward trend as the order of failure increases. Although no failure data on 3-order CCF were collected during the on-site data collection, the parametric model proposed in this paper can effectively predict the high-order failure probabilities of the CCCG of SEC pumps.

TABLE III. FAILURE PROBABILITIES OF SEC PUMP SYSTEM BASED ON THE PARAMETRIC MODEL

Equipment	CCCG	Unit failure probability	Failure order	Failure probability
SEC pump system	4	0.04202	1	0.05994
			2	0.01851
			3	0.0324
			4	0.0066

Currently, there are many CCF models applied in nuclear power safety analysis, and the α-factor model is one of the most widely used CCF models. In the α-factor model, the parameter α_k is used to quantitatively characterize the degree of each order CCF, and its value is the ratio of the probability of a k-unit ($k = 1, 2, \ldots, n$) failure event (k-order failure) to the sum of probabilities of failure events of all orders among n units. In this paper, the concept of the α-factor model is used for reference, and the correlation coefficient based on parametric model of the nuclear power equipment system is calculated as follows

$$\alpha_k = \frac{p_s^{k/n}}{\sum_{k=1}^{n} p_s^{k/n}} \tag{10}$$

TABLE IV. COMPARISON OF A FACTOR MODEL AND PARAMETRIC MODEL ON SEC PUMP SYSTEM

Equipment	CCCG	Correlation coefficient	α-factor model	parametric model
SEC pump system	4	α_1	0.957219	0.72794
		α_2	0.037433	0.22476
		α_3	0	3.931e-2
		α_4	0.0053476	7.986e-3

Table 4 shows the analysis of the common cause failure data of the SEC water pumps by using the α-factor model and the parameterized model method respectively, and the correlation coefficients of failures of all orders of the SEC pump system are obtained. The comparison of the analysis results is shown in Figure 5. The analysis results of the correlation coefficients of the α-factor model completely depend on the test data. When the amount of test data is insufficient or the distribution of test data is unreasonable, the correlation coefficients of the α-factor model may be inconsistent with the actual engineering situation. For example, the 4-order correlation coefficient $\alpha_4 = 0.0053476$ of the CCCG is higher than the 3-order correlation coefficient $\alpha_3 = 0$. While using the parameterized model established in this paper, the analysis results are different from those of the α-factor model, but its tendency is more reasonable.

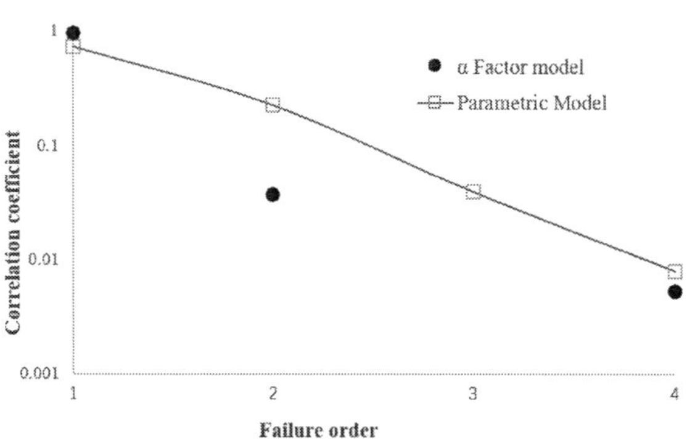

Figure 5. Comparison of correlation analyses of the α Factor Model and the Parametric Model

5. CONCLUSION

This paper conducts research on the problem that there is extremely little CCF data of nuclear power equipment, making it difficult to calculate the failure probability and failure correlation coefficient through empirical formulas, and the following conclusions are obtained:

1) Based on the generalized stress-strength interference analysis at the system level, a failure probability model for parallel systems that can reflect the influence of failure correlation is established. Further, the model is discretized, and the quantitative integral calculation is transformed into a numerical solution problem of discrete summation, making the model more convenient for engineering applications.
2) The relationship between the parameters in the system failure probability model and the records of system failure events was established, and a parameterized model of system failure probability was established. This model can calculate the failure probability of each order of the system based on the number of failure events at each order.
3) A statistical analysis is carried out on on-site failure data records of SEC pumps, and the CCF statistical data of SEC pumps are obtained. The parameterized model is applied, and the failure probability results show that it can well predict the occurrence probability of high-order failure events according to the occurrence times of low-order failure events.

ACKNOWLEDGMENT

This work was partially supported by the National Natural Science Foundation of China (Grant No. 52175131).

REFERENCES

[1] RASMUSON D M, MOSLEH A, MARSHALL F M. Guidelines on modeling common-cause failures in probabilistic risk assessment: NUREG/CR-5485[R]. University of Maryland: Idaho National Engineering and Environment Laboratory, 1998.

[2] WIERMAN T E, RASMUSON D M, MOSLEH A. Common-cause failure database and analysis system: event data collection, classification, and coding: NUREG/CR-6268[R]. University of Maryland: Idaho National Engineering and Environment Laboratory, 2007.

[3] An Jin, Yan Lin. Application of Bayesian Estimation Method in Parameter Estimation of Alpha Factor Model[J]. Nuclear Power Engineering, 2021, 42(2): 157-160

[4] Bing Zhang, Shanqi Chen, Zhixian Lin, etc. A rapid modeling method and accuracy criteria for common-cause failures in Risk Monitor PSA model[J]. Nuclear Engineering and Technology, 2021, 53:103-110

Motion Trajectory Planning and Motion Accuracy Reliability Analysis of Welding Robot

Wenxue Qian[1], Jianfeng Yang[2], Xiaowei Yin[3*], Ruijin Zhang[1], Ningxiang Wu[1], and Liyang Xie[1]

[1] School of Mechanical Engineering and Automation, Northeastern University, Shenyang 110819, China
[2] Suzhou Nuclear Power Research Institute Co., Ltd., Suzhou 215004, China
[3] Department of Mechanical Engineering, Shenyang Institute of Engineering, Shenyang 110136, China

Keywords: Welding robot, trajectory planning, pose accuracy reliability, mechanism analysis.

Abstract - Welding robots are widely used in engineering practice, and their positional accuracy has an important impact on welding quality; in addition, welding trajectory planning affects welding quality. In order to achieve the high-quality work requirements of welding robots, based on the actual working conditions, a six-degree-of-freedom serial welding robot is taken as the research object, relevant technical parameters are designed, and a kinematic model of the welding robot under the D-H coordinate system is established. The Monte Carlo analysis method is introduced to analyze the working space of the welding robot, and the trajectory planning of the welding robot is carried out by using the fifth-degree polynomial interpolation method, and its reasonableness is verified. Based on the micro-displacement synthesis method, and established the static position error model and reliability calculation model of the robot, the influencing factors of the position accuracy of the welding robot were analyzed, and the sensitivity of the influencing factors was derived, finally, based on the Monte Carlo method, the reliability of the position and accuracy of the welding robot was verified with the connecting rod parameters of the welding robot as an example, and the relevant results were obtained. The research work in this paper has certain reference significance for the design of welding robot and the improvement of welding quality.

1. Introduction

Welding robots have been widely used in engineering practice, which can effectively improve the welding quality and reduce the labor intensity of welders. The high accuracy of welding robot end-effectors is extremely important for weld quality[1, 2]. The accuracy of these robots is affected by a variety of factors, including raw rod errors, kinematic pair clearance errors, and joint angle errors. High precision work for welding robots requires that the tasks performed by welding robots require extremely high levels of accuracy, particularly in the positioning and movement of the end-effector, which is the component that interacts directly with the workpiece to perform the weld[3-5]. This high standard of precision is essential to ensure weld quality and to meet industry standards. Specifically, there are several factors that can affect the accuracy of a welding robot[6-8]. 1. Linkage length error. This refers to deviations or errors in the dimensions of the length of the linkage that make up the structure of the robot. Each linkage has precise dimensions, but manufacturing tolerances may introduce small errors that cumulatively affect the overall accuracy of the robot. 2. Kinematic pair clearance error. This error arises in the joints of the robot. Joints are pairs of moving parts, and any gaps or clearances in these kinematic pairs can result in inaccurate position and motion of the robot's end-effectors. 3. Joint angle errors. This involves errors in the angles achieved by the robot's joints compared to their commanded positions. These errors can originate from original dimensional errors, control system limitations, mechanical wear, or other factors. Within the overall framework of the robot, different links and joints have different effects on the accuracy of the robot's motion[9]. Understanding which components have the greatest impact on accuracy is critical to future designs. Engineers can prioritize improvements to these critical components to improve the overall performance of the robot[10, 11]. At the same time, the trajectory of the welding robot's end-effector has an important influence on the quality of the weld. Reasonable trajectory planning can reduce the influence of movement speed and acceleration, etc. on welding quality[12]. Carrying out the reliability analysis of the motion accuracy of the welding robot can adequately take into account the uncertainty of various influencing parameters and ensure sufficient welding quality[13-15]. Kumar et al. first introduced the concept of positional error in operating robots. They used the Denavit-Hartenberg (D-H) coordinate transformation to establish a mathematical expression for end position error, which has been the basis of the methodology used in robot kinematics[16]. Hraiech et al. proposed a new algorithm that estimates the motion error of the end-effector and the force error of the actuator as a function of the uncertainty of the design parameters by means of interval analysis. The results show that the kinematic error at the center of the workspace is minimal. Furthermore, these errors increase as the platform moves along the vertical axis. The results also show that the kinematic error of the actuator joints is the parameter that has the greatest impact on the accuracy of the manipulator. Therefore, the use of more accurate actuators can significantly reduce the motion errors of the platform[17]. Wang et al. introduced an intelligent optimization algorithm for welding robot path optimization. In addition, obstacle avoidance strategies were studied and multi-objective path optimization for welding robots was given. The optimization results show the effectiveness of the intelligent path optimization strategy[18]. Wu et al. analyzed the error model of position and pose based on non-probabilistic interval theory considering the effects of link size deviation and joint clearance on the robot end operator. Then the time-varying motion reliability evaluation model of the robot was established using the non-probabilistic interval theory, and the motion reliability variation of the robot at trajectory points was obtained[19]. Li et al. investigated a real-time robot trajectory error compensation method using a laser tracker to measure the robot end position in real-time. After compensation, the absolute positioning error of the robot is less than 0.06 mm, and the trajectory position error is less than 0.15 mm, which greatly improves the positional accuracy of the robot[20]. Tang et al. established a kinematic model for industrial robots considering the influence of joint clearance on the motion reliability of industrial robots, deduced the kinematic equations of the robots, and carried out positive kinematic solutions. A non-probabilistic positioning accuracy reliability measure for the robot end-effector is proposed, and the displacement error interval of the end-effector under a preset motion path is analyzed. It is argued that the reliability of the end-effector changes in different working regions under the influence of uncertain joint clearance parameters[21].

In this paper, the focus is on two aspects of the study. Firstly, the kinematic analysis of the welding robot was established based on the D-H coordinate system method. Analyzing the workspace, the range of positions and orientations reachable by the robot's end-effectors, and modeling the robot's kinematics helps to understand how different factors affect the robot's kinematic performance. Welding robot motion trajectory planning was carried out, where the correct planning of the end effector trajectory is essential for performing accurate welding tasks. Secondly, based on the principle of precision reliability, Monte Carlo simulation is applied to analyze the effects of connection parameter errors and kinematic clearance errors on kinematic precision and reliability. By conducting a large number of simulation experiments using different input parameters, the Monte Carlo method helps to understand the probability distribution of the errors and to determine the reliability of the robotic system under different conditions. This work contributed to a deeper understanding of error propagation in robotic systems. Such analyses are essential for the design of more reliable and accurate robotic systems, which can ultimately improve the reliability of welding robots in industrial applications.

2. Welding robot structure and kinematics modeling

In this paper, a six-degree-of-freedom series welding robot is used as the research object. The robotic mechanical system consists of a base, a waist, a big arm, a forearm, a wrist, and an end portion. The design of the robot starts from both the arm and the wrist, the first four joints are used to control the change of the position of the end effector, and the rear three joints control the change of the end effector posture. The structural schematic diagram is shown in Figure 1.

In order to meet the actual work requirements and refer to the technical characteristics of similar products, the basic technical requirements of the welding robot are determined, as shown in Table 1 below.

The forward kinematics of the welding robot is based on the establishment of the D-H model to obtain the parameters of each link, the two links matrix transformation is used to obtain the posture of the end link coordinate system for the base coordinates. The D-H method is a 4×4 homogeneous transformation matrix that establishes the relationship with the previous member coordinate system for the coordinate system at each joint. This paper will model with the STD-DH parameter method and obtain the D-H coordinate system of the welding robot, as shown in Figure 2.

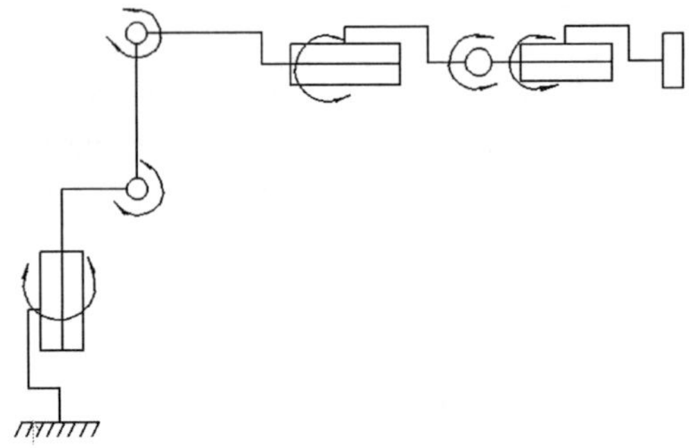

Figure 1 The mechanism of the robot

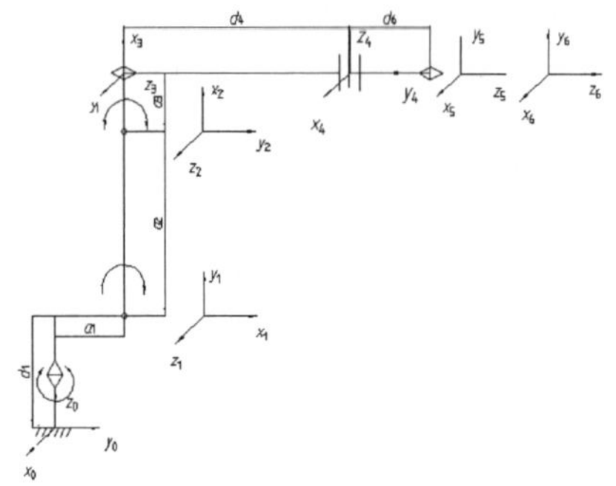

Figure 2 D-H coordinate system of welding robot

Table 1 Basic design parameters

axis	Maximum rotation range（°）	Maximum velocity（m/s）	Allowable moment（Nm）	Allowable inertia (kg·m^2)	Number of degrees of freedom	Payload（kg）
1	-170~170	110	-	-		
2	-70~148	100	-	-		
3	-175~150	110	-	-	6	50
4	-150~150	205	8.8	0.27		
5	-45~180	205	8.8	0.27		
6	-200~200	305	2.9	0.03		

The length dimension information of each connecting rod is shown in Table 2. As shown in Table 3 is the welding robot link parameter table. The connecting links 1, 2, 3, 4, 5, and 6 are all rotating joints, and the variables are θ_i.

Table 2 Table of design variables for bar size

Link	Length mean value/mm	Range/mm
1	384	383,385
2	234	233,235
3	686	685,687
4	232	231,233
5	675	674,676
6	90	89,91

Table 3 Parameters of link for welding robot

Link i	θ_i	a_i	α_i	d_i
1	θ_1	108	+π/2	383.5
2	θ_2	686	+π/2	0
3	θ_3	232	0	0
4	θ_4	0	+π/2	675
5	θ_5	0	0	0
6	θ_6	0	0	189

Using the STD-DH parameter method, the kinematic equation of the position and posture of the end effector of the welding robot, the transformation relationship between the two links is:

$$T_i = Rot(z, \theta_i)Trans(0,0,d_i)Trans(a_i,0,0)Rot(x,\alpha_i) \tag{1}$$

After the transformation of the rotation matrix and the displacement matrix, the transformation formula of the link can be obtained as follows:

$$\begin{bmatrix} c\theta_i & -s\theta_i c\alpha_i & s\theta_i c\alpha_i & a_i c\theta_i \\ s\theta_i & c\theta_i c\alpha_i & -c\theta_i c\alpha_i & a_i s\theta_i \\ 0 & s\alpha_i & c\alpha_i & d_i \\ 0 & 0 & 0 & 1 \end{bmatrix} \tag{2}$$

The transformation matrix of the welding robot end coordinate system relative to the base coordinate system can be obtained:

$$\begin{bmatrix} r_{11} & r_{12} & r_{13} & p_x \\ r_{21} & r_{22} & r_{23} & p_y \\ r_{31} & r_{32} & r_{33} & p_z \\ 0 & 0 & 0 & 1 \end{bmatrix} \tag{3}$$

The expression of r_{ij} in the formula is the attitude of the welding robot end effector coordinate system relative to the base coordinate system, and p_i is the position of the welding robot end effector coordinate system relative to the base coordinate system.

Then, the welding robot end position coordinate, that is, the motion function expression is:

$$\begin{bmatrix} x = a_1c1 + a_2c2c1 + d_6(c5(c1c2s3 + c1c3s2) - s5(s1s4 + c4(c1c2c3 - \\ \quad c1s2s3))) + d_4(c1c2s3 + c1c3s2) + a_3c3c1c2 - a_3s3c1s2] \\ y = a_1s1 + a_2c2s1 + d_6(c5(c2s1s3 + c3s1s2) + s5(c1s4 - c4(c2c3s1 - \\ \quad s1s2s3))) + d_4(c2s1s3 + c3s1s2) + a_3c3c2s1 - a_3s3s1s2] \\ z = a_2s2 + d_1 + a_3s3c2 + a_3c3s2 - d_4(c2c3 - s2s3) - d_6(c5(c2c3 - s2s3) + \\ \quad c4s5(c2s3 + c3s2)) \end{bmatrix} \tag{4}$$

In the formula, $c\theta_i$ is $\cos\theta_i$, $s\theta_i$ is $\sin\theta_i$.

(1) When the X-Y-Z fixed coordinate system (α, β, γ) is the attitude coordinate system, the attitude coordinate of the end effector of the welding robot according to equation (3), that is, the motion function expression is obtained by the following formula:

$$\begin{cases} \beta = Atan2\left(-r_{11}, \sqrt{r_{11}^2 + r_{21}^2}\right) \\ \alpha = Atan2(r_{21}/c\beta, r_{11}/c\beta) \\ \gamma = Atan2(r_{32}/c\beta, r_{33}/c\beta) \end{cases} \tag{5}$$

(2) When the Z-Y-X Euler angle (α, β, γ) is the attitude coordinate system, the end of the welding robot's attitude coordinate according to equation (3), that is the motion function expression is obtained from the following equation:

$$\begin{cases} \beta = Atan2\left(\sqrt{r_{31}^2 + r_{32}^2}, r_{33}\right) \\ \alpha = Atan2(r_{23}/s\beta, r_{12}/s\beta) \\ \gamma = Atan2(r_{32}/s\beta, -r_{31}/s\beta) \end{cases} \tag{6}$$

Therefore, the motion function expression of the end position and posture of the welding robot relative to the base coordinate is obtained.

3. Welding robot workspace analysis and trajectory planning

3.1 Welding robot workspace analysis

The Monte Carlo method is used to generate the random number of each joint of the welding robot, and the value is brought into the forward kinematics equation of the welding robot. The random number range of the reference point on the end effector is the working space. The plane and the three-dimensional space diagram are shown in Figure 3- 6.

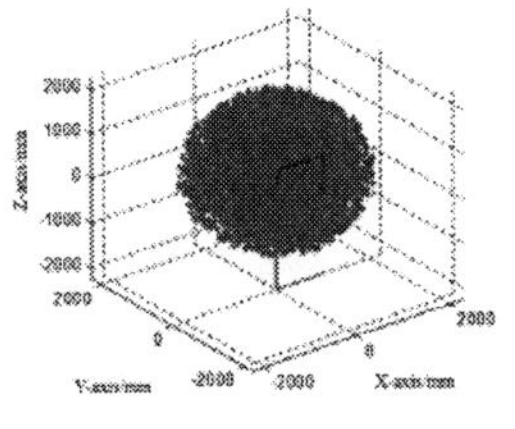

Figure 3 Point cloud of welding robot workspace

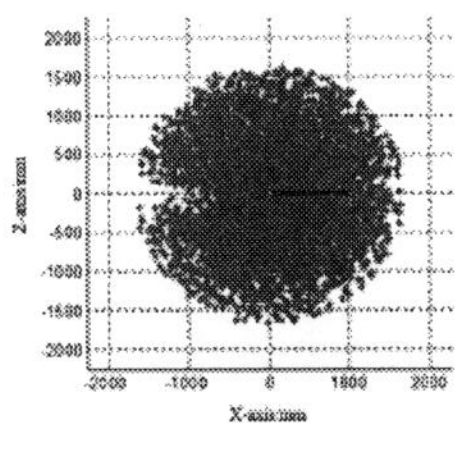

Figure 4 Projection of workspace in the XOY plane

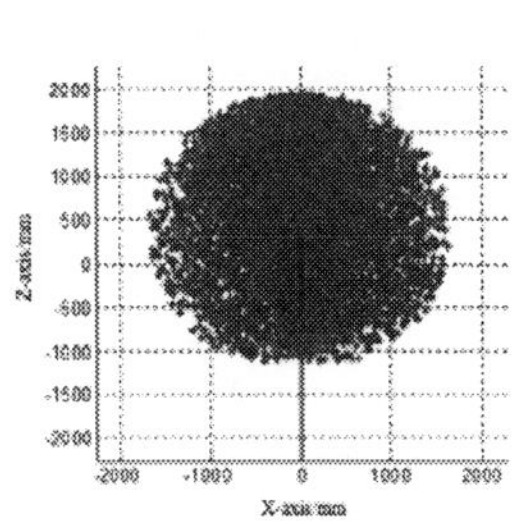

Figure 5 Projection of workspace in the YOZ plane

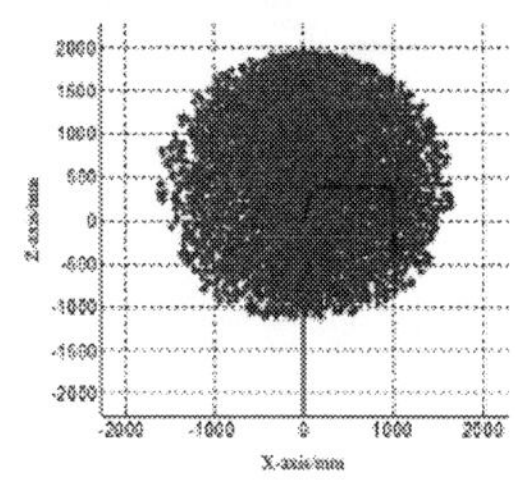

Figure 6 Projection of workspace in the XOZ plane

The working space of the welding robot is $3650 \times 3300 \times 3100$ mm, which can cover the space occupied by the required welding, and there is no vacant part in the figure, which proves that the simulation result conforms to the actual working space.

3.2 Welding robot working track planning

In this paper, the trajectory planning of the welding robot is using the quintic polynomial interpolation. According to the D-H parameters of the welding robot in Table 2.12, the kinematics simulation model of the welding robot was established by using the LINK function in MATLAB Robotic Toolboox using STD-DH parameter method. Its kinematic model is shown in Figure 7.

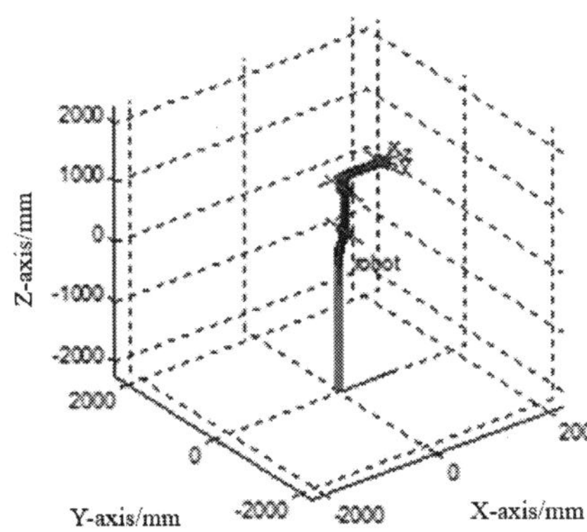

Figure 7 Welding robot simulation control panel and model

In the welding process, the path is set to avoid obstacles, so the planning of the path can not be made in the form of direct arrival. As shown in Table 4, the complete path of the welding process is divided into five segments, the path planning is implemented on each segment, and finally the complete path planning is implemented.

Table 4 Values of Key Points Corresponding to Joint Variables

Key points i	θ_1	θ_2	θ_3	θ_4	θ_5	θ_6
1	0	pi/2	0	0	0	0
2	pi/15	24pi/45	-4pi/45	4pi/45	pi/30	pi/10
3	2pi/15	51pi/90	-8pi/45	8pi/45	pi/15	pi/5
4	pi/5	27pi/50	-12pi/45	12pi/45	pi/10	9pi/30
5	4pi/15	57pi/90	-16pi/45	16pi/45	6pi/45	2pi/5
6	pi/3	2pi/3	-2pi/3	2pi/3	pi/6	pi/2

After the planning of the overall path is completed, the motion of the welding robot is obtained, and the changes of the joint variables during the movement are also observed. Using MATLAB's Robotic Toolbox, the displacement, velocity, and acceleration of each joint of the welding robot during the motion can be obtained through simulation. The changes are shown in Figure 8 to Figure 10. By comparing the curves, it can be judged whether the planning of the trajectory is reasonable and feasible.

During the movement of the welding robot from the initial position to the end position, the displacement of each joint changes continuously and steadily, and the angular velocity and angular acceleration change continuously and without a phase step phenomenon, so the welding robot trajectory planning from the initial position to the end position is reasonable, and can ensure the smoothness of the welding robot movement.

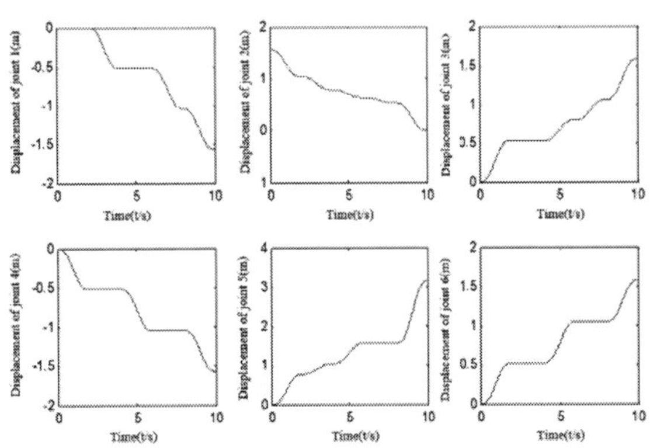

Figure 8 Displacement-time curve

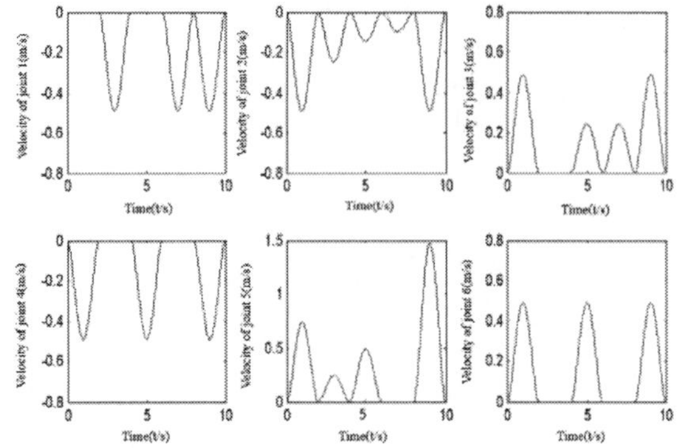

Figure9 Speed-time curve

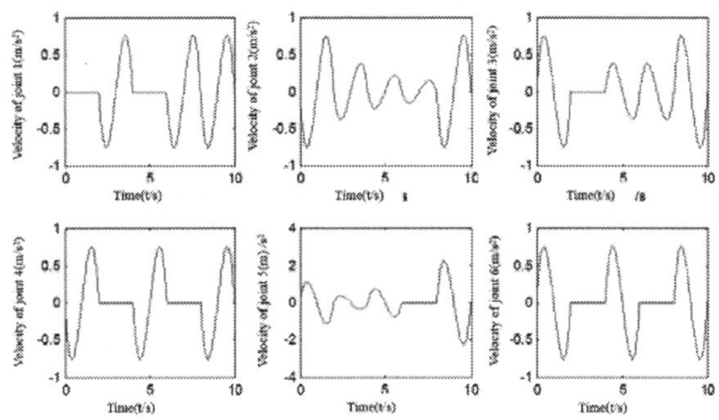

Figure 10 Acceleration-time curve

4. Reliability Analysis of Welding Robot Motion Accuracy

There are many factors affecting the reliability of welding robots. In the process of production design, assembly, and actual work, the accuracy error will be caused and the accuracy reliability will be affected. Considering that these errors are random and it is difficult to determine the specific values, this paper applies the method of probability and statistics to estimate the possible range of values of the motion position error of the working members of the mechanism. The mechanism motion error of welding robot generally includes the end pose error, velocity error, and acceleration error. In this paper, it is assumed that the kinematic output parameter of the mechanism is Y(t), and the allowable limit range is $[Y_{min}, Y_{max}]$. The probability of the event $[Y_{min} < \mathrm{Y(t)} < Y_{max}]$ of mechanism motion reliability is:

$$\mathrm{R} = \mathrm{P}(Y_{min} < \mathrm{Y(t)} < Y_{max}) \quad (7)$$

In this paper, on the basis of establishing the kinematics equation of welding robot by D-H method and using STD-DH parameter method, according to the working requirements of the research object, the transformation relation between the two rods is:

$$T_i = Rot(z,\theta_i)Trans(0,0,d_i)Trans(a_i,0,0)Rot(x,\alpha_i) \tag{8}$$

After the transformation of rotation matrix and displacement matrix, the general formula of connecting rod transformation is:

$$T_i = \begin{bmatrix} c\theta_i & -s\theta_i c\alpha_i & s\theta_i c\alpha_i & a_i c\theta_i \\ s\theta_i & c\theta_i c\alpha & -c\theta_i c\alpha_i & a_i s\theta_i \\ 0 & s\alpha_i & c\alpha_i & d_i \\ 0 & 0 & 0 & 1 \end{bmatrix} \tag{9}$$

MATLAB was used to program and calculate the end pose coordinates, and the transformation matrix of the end coordinate system of the welding robot relative to the base coordinate system was obtained:

$$T = \begin{bmatrix} r_{11} & r_{12} & r_{13} & p_x \\ r_{21} & r_{22} & r_{23} & p_y \\ r_{31} & r_{32} & r_{33} & p_z \\ 0 & 0 & 0 & 1 \end{bmatrix} \tag{10}$$

where r_{ij} represents the attitude of the end-effector coordinate system of the welding robot relative to the base coordinate system based on the coordinate transformation between the two links, and P represents the position of the end-effector coordinate system of the welding robot relative to the base coordinate system.

In order to model the pose error of the welding robot end, the sensitivity of each influencing factor was analyzed by using the method of micro-displacement synthesis. The motion reliability calculation model and the end motion trajectory model of welding robot mechanism were established mainly from the two aspects of connecting rod parameters and motion pair clearance. The Monte Carlo method was used to analyze the influence of the error of connecting rod parameters on the pose accuracy of welding robot.

Posture Error Model Considering Connecting Rod Parameter Error

The pose error of the end-effector of the robot was calculated by using the micro-displacement synthesis method [12], and the transfer matrix error T obtained by the D-H parameter method is:

$$\Delta T = \sum_{i=1}^{n}\left(\frac{\partial T}{\partial \theta_i}\Delta\theta_i + \frac{\partial T}{\partial d_i}\Delta d_i + \frac{\partial T}{\partial a_i}\Delta a_i + \frac{\partial T}{\partial \alpha_i}\Delta\alpha_i\right) \tag{11}$$

where $\partial_T/\partial_{\theta i}, \partial_T/\partial_{di}, \partial_T/\partial_{ai}, \partial_T/\partial_{\alpha i}$ is the error transfer matrix of connecting rod parameters.

It is assumed that $V_{ij}(j = 1,2,3,4)$ is the connecting rod parameters d_i, θ_i, a_i, and α_i, According to formula (3), the partial derivative of the matrix with respect to each parameter is:

$$\frac{\partial T_i}{\partial V_{i1}} = \frac{\partial T_i}{\partial \theta_i}, \frac{\partial T_i}{\partial V_{i2}} = \frac{\partial T_i}{\partial d_i}, \frac{\partial T_i}{\partial V_{i4}} = \frac{\partial T_i}{\partial \alpha_i}, \frac{\partial T_i}{\partial V_{i3}} = \frac{\partial T_i}{\partial a_{i-1}}.$$

According to formula (2), the partial derivatives of the pose matrix T_i of the robot end-effector to joint $d_i, \theta_i, a_i, \alpha_i$ of each link is:

$$\frac{\partial T_i}{\partial V_{ij}} = \begin{bmatrix} r'_{11} & r'_{12} & r'_{13} & p'_x \\ r'_{21} & r'_{22} & r'_{23} & p'_y \\ r'_{31} & r'_{32} & r'_{33} & p'_z \\ 0 & 0 & 0 & 1 \end{bmatrix}. \tag{12}$$

where $i = 1,2,\cdots n,\ j = 1,2,3,4$.

Therefore, the end position error of the welding robot is the partial derivative of the position coordinate with the connecting rod parameters, and the following formula can be obtained:

$$\frac{\partial p}{\partial V_{ij}} = \left[\frac{\partial p_x}{\partial V_{ij}}, \frac{\partial p_y}{\partial V_{ij}}, \frac{\partial p_z}{\partial V_{ij}}\right]^T = \left[p'_x, p'_y, p'_z\right]^T \tag{13}$$

The attitude error is the partial derivative of the position coordinates with the connecting rod parameters, the following formula can be obtained:

$$\frac{\partial \emptyset}{\partial V_{ij}} = \left[\frac{\partial \alpha}{\partial V_{ij}}, \frac{\partial \beta}{\partial V_{ij}}, \frac{\partial \gamma}{\partial V_{ij}}\right]^T \tag{14}$$

Posture Error Model Considering the Clearance of Motion Pairs

Because of the high welding speed of the welding robot and the close contact between the axle and the hole at the joint, the contact model of the moving pair is continuous, so that the pin always moves along the inner wall of the sleeve. When the clearance error of the pair was considered, the effective length model theory was adopted. The pin axle moves continuously on the sleeve. Point C is always on the error circle and point P is randomly distributed. The theoretical model of effective connection of motion pairs is shown in Figure 11 and Figure 12.

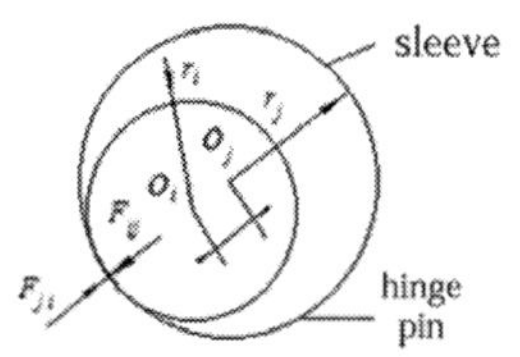

Figure 11 Contact model of

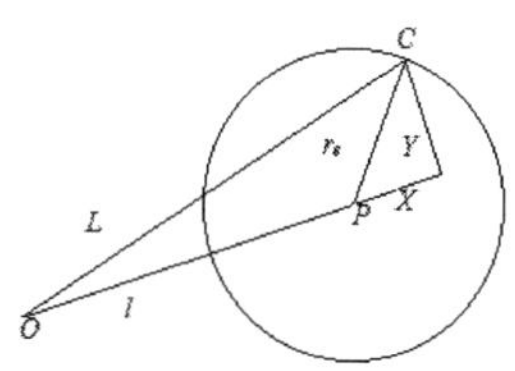

Figure 12 Effective

motion pair connection model

Point P is the geometric center of the sleeve, and the connecting rod OP length is L. Point O is the geometric center of the pin shaft. Due to the existence of clearance, point P and point C do not coincide, so the actual rod length includes the radial clearance of the hinge motion pair, which is called the effective length and set as L. The relationship between effective length and actual rod length is:

$$L^2 = (l + x)^2 + y^2 \tag{15}$$

Where x, y is the local coordinate of the pin center.

The dimension error of welding robot bar is $\Delta l = L - l$, From the geometric relationship, it can be seen that the maximum size of effective rod length is $L_{max} = l + r_e$, and the minimum size is $L_{min} = l - r_e$.

Sensitivity Analysis of Various Errors

The most significant factors affecting the motion error of the welding robot end can be found by sensitivity analysis of the influencing factors. The sensitivity is to derive the partial derivative of the output function F(x) to the input variable x_i:

$$S_i = \frac{\partial F}{\partial x_i} \tag{16}$$

The sensitivity reflects the sensitivity of the output variable to the input variable. Through the influence of connecting rod parameter error, joint clearance, and joint Angle error on terminal pose error, the most sensitive input error factor was analyzed. In order to compare objectively, the input error ranges and intervals were the same, and the errors were 0.02, 0.04, 0.06, 0.08 and 0.1, in units (mm or degree). The input errors were brought into the model error to obtain the change of the end position error of the welding robot under different errors, and the end position error of the welding robot under different errors was analyzed. As shown in Figure 13, Figure 13(a), (b) and (c) respectively represent the displacement and position-sensitive curves in the X and Z directions obtained under the influence of parameter errors of the connecting rod. Figure 13 (d) is the terminal position-sensitive curve under the influence of clearance error of the motion pair.

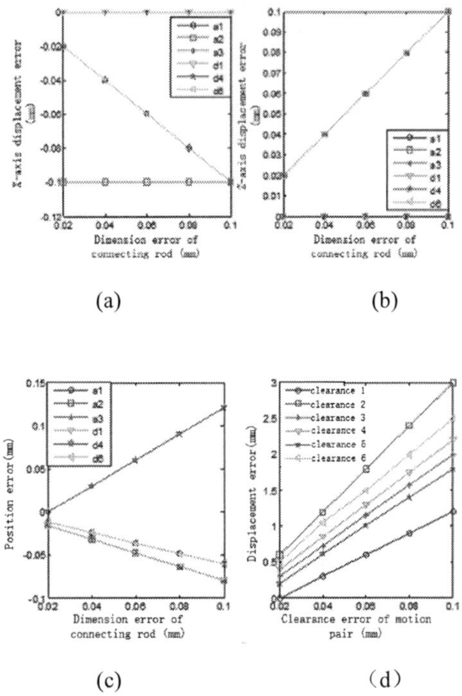

Figure 13 Sensitive response curve of rod parameters error

There is a linear relationship between input error and pose error of welding robot.

5. Reliability Analysis of Static Pose Accuracy of Welding Robot

Samples of the rod parameters were sampled by Monte Carlo, and the values were brought into the mathematical expression of the pose error of the end effector of the welding robot to obtain a sample value of the pose error. The position error formula is

$$\Delta P_i = P_i - P_c \tag{17}$$

The attitude error formula is

$$\begin{cases} \Delta\alpha_i = \alpha_i - \alpha_c \\ \Delta\beta_i = \beta_i - \beta_c \\ \Delta\gamma_i = \gamma_i - \gamma_c \end{cases} \tag{18}$$

where $P_i, \alpha_i, \beta_i, \gamma_i$ is the attitude coordinate value calculated by the i th sampling of the link parameters, and $p_c, \alpha_c, \beta_c, \gamma_c$ is the ideal pose coordinate value of the welding robot.

Assuming that the given position error and attitude error are R and $T = (T_\alpha, T_\beta, T_\gamma)^T$ respectively, the number of samples within the error range are λ_P and $\lambda_{\phi_i} = (\lambda_\alpha, \lambda_\beta, \lambda_\gamma)^T$ respectively. The pose reliability of welding robot mechanism is:

$$\begin{cases} P(|\Delta P_i| < R) = \lambda_P/\lambda \\ P(|\Delta \phi_i| < R) = \lambda_{\phi_i}/\lambda \end{cases} \tag{19}$$

Assuming that the parameter error of the connecting rod is normally distributed, and taking each parameter as the mean value, and the standard deviation of d_i, θ_i, a_i and α_i was 0.03mm,0.5°,0.03mm and 0.5°respectively. The joint angles of the initial position are $0, \pi/2, 0, 0, 0$ and 0 respectively, and the positions of the end positions are $\pi/3, 2*\pi/3, -4*\pi/9, 4*\pi/9, \pi/6$ and $\pi/2$ respectively. The parameters of the connecting rod of the welding robot were sampled 10000 times, and the number extracted each time was substituted into formula (3) to obtain the mean value, standard deviation, and extreme value of each error. The results are shown in Table 5 below. A frequency histogram is made for the calculated pose error and attitude error, as shown in Figure 14 below.

Table 5 Digital character of end posture error of welding robot

Error	Desire value	Mean value	Standard deviation	Maximum value	Minimum value
ΔP(mm)	0	0.0110	3.5764	10.2645	-10.0032
Δα (fixed angular coordinate system / rad)	0	-0.0001	0.0221	0.00812	-0.0801
Δβ (fixed angular coordinate system / rad)	0	0.0001	0.0199	0.0724	-0.0718
Δγ (fixed angular coordinate system / rad)	0	0.0001	0.0316	0.0997	-0.0991
Δα（Eulerian angles / rad）	0	-1.6801	0.0283	0.0998	-0.0997
Δβ（Eulerian angles / rad）	0	0	0.0346	0.0812	-0.0809
Δγ（Eulerian angles /rad）	0	0	0.0339	0.1254	-0.9134

It can be known from the above table that the parameters of each link have the greatest influence on the Euler Angle.

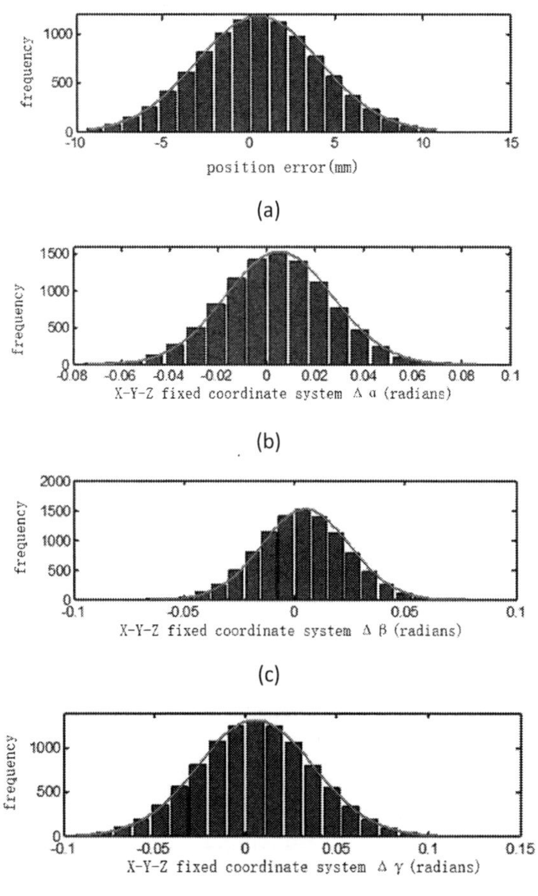

Figure 14 Frequency histogram of pose error

The reliability of the robot end-effector is:

$$\begin{cases} P(|\Delta P_i| < R) = 0.7035 \\ P(|\Delta \phi_i| < R) = (0.7647, 0.8352, 0.7012) \end{cases}$$

6. Conclusion

The forward kinematics equation established in this paper based on the D-H coordinate system and the analysis of the sensitivity of each error can be concluded as follows: When there is a dimensional error in the linkage, the factor influencing the error in the X direction is a_1, d_4, d_6, the maximum displacement error in the X direction is 0.1mm, and the input error sensitivity is the same; It has no effect on the Y-direction displacement. The influence of the Z direction error is a_2, a_3, d_1, the maximum displacement error is 0.1 mm, and the error sensitivity is the same; The maximum influence on position error is d_4, and the maximum position error is 0.12mm. Under the influence of motion pair error, the maximum comprehensive displacement error is 3mm, and the most sensitive factors are clearance of motion pair 2, clearance of motion pair 6 and clearance of motion pair 4. The sensitivity is arranged from high to low. Through the Monte Carlo method, the position error of the end of the welding robot is 0.7035 and the error of the three attitude angles is 0.7647, 0.8352 and 0.7012 respectively under the influence of the link parameter and the clearance parameter of the motion pair, and the link parameter has the greatest influence on the Euler Angle Δα.

Acknowledgments

This work was partially supported by the National Natural Science Foundation of China (Grant No. 52175131), and Key Research Projects of Liaoning Provincial Department of Education (Grant No. LJKZZ20220139).

References

[1] T. Zhang, S. B. Chen, M. H. Wu, Y. Z. Zhao, and X. Q. Chen, "Optimal Motion Planning of All Position Autonomous Mobile Welding Robot System for Fillet Seams," *IEEE Transactions on Automation Science and Engineering,* vol. 10, no. 4, pp. 1147-1151, Oct 2013, doi: 10.1109/tase.2013.2252462.

[2] D. W. Kim, J. S. Choi, and B. O. Nnaji, "Robot arc welding operations planning with a rotating/tilting positioner," *International Journal of Production Research,* vol. 36, no. 4, pp. 957-979, Apr 1998, doi: 10.1080/002075498193471.

[3] C. Yang, W. Z. Lu, and Y. Q. Xia, "Positioning Accuracy Analysis of Industrial Robots Based on Non-Probabilistic Time-Dependent Reliability," *Ieee Transactions on Reliability,* 2023 Jul 2023, doi: 10.1109/tr.2023.3292089.

[4] W. Qian, S. Song, K. Liu, X. Zeng, X. Yin, and L. Xie, "Motion error analysis of a shield machine tool-changing robot based on a screw-vector method," *Sci Rep-Uk,* vol. 12, no. 1, p. 20484, 2022/11/28 2022, doi: 10.1038/s41598-022-24847-6.

[5] M. Hafezipour and S. Khodaygan, "An uncertainty analysis method for error reduction in end-effector of spatial robots with joint clearances and link dimension deviations," *International Journal of Computer Integrated Manufacturing,* vol. 30, no. 6, pp. 653-663, 2017, doi: 10.1080/0951192x.2016.1187298.

[6] D. Y. Shang, Y. Li, Y. Liu, and S. W. Cui, "Research on the Motion Error Analysis and Compensation Strategy of the Delta Robot," *Mathematics,* vol. 7, no. 5, May 2019, Art no. 411, doi: 10.3390/math7050411.

[7] Y. Li, D. Y. Shang, and Y. Liu, "Kinematic modeling and error analysis of Delta robot considering parallelism error," *International Journal of Advanced Robotic Systems,* vol. 16, no. 5, Sep 2019, Art no. 1729881419878927, doi: 10.1177/1729881419878927.

[8] W. X. Qian, S. Song, J. H. Zhao, J. Q. Hou, L. Wang, and X. W. Yin, "A Study of the Effect of a Kinematic Pair Containing Clearance on the Dynamic Characteristics of a Tool-Changing Robot," (in English), *Appl Sci-Basel,* Article vol. 12, no. 21, p. 17, Nov 2022, Art no. 11041, doi: 10.3390/app122111041.

[9] Q. F. Zeng, X. M. Liu, and Z. R. Liu, "Error allocation model and coordination control for stringer-skin T-shape structure welding robot with multiple manipulators," *International Journal of Advanced Robotic Systems,* vol. 19, no. 4, Jul 2022, Art no. 17298806221109706, doi: 10.1177/17298806221109706.

[10] J. D. Qi, B. Chen, and D. H. Zhang, "Compensation for absolute positioning error of industrial robot considering the optimized measurement space," *International Journal of Advanced Robotic Systems,* vol. 17, no. 2, Mar 2020, Art no. 1729881420921644, doi: 10.1177/1729881420921644.

[11] R. Shan, P. Sun, S. Y. Wang, and H. B. Chang, "Each step time-limited iterative learning control for a cushion robot with motion velocity constraints," *T I Meas Control,* vol. 46, no. 6, pp. 1105-1119, Apr 2024, doi: 10.1177/01423312231190446.

[12] J. Dong, B. He, M. Ming, C. H. Zhang, and G. Li, "Design of Open-Closed-Loop Iterative Learning Control With Variable Stiffness for Multiple Flexible Manipulator Robot Systems," *Ieee Access,* vol. 7, pp. 23163-23168, 2019, doi: 10.1109/access.2019.2898266.

[13] P. Huang, H. Li, Y. K. Gu, and G. Q. Qiu, "An extended moment-based trajectory accuracy reliability analysis method of robot manipulators with random and interval uncertainties," *Reliab Eng Syst Safe,* vol. 246, Jun 2024, Art no. 110082, doi: 10.1016/j.ress.2024.110082.

[14] M. H. Korayem and A. Iravani, "Improvement of 3P and 6R mechanical robots reliability and quality applying FMEA and QFD approaches," *Robotics and Computer-Integrated Manufacturing,* vol. 24, no. 3, pp. 472-487, Jun 2008, doi: 10.1016/j.rcim.2007.05.003.

[15] B. Yang and W. Y. Yang, "Modular approach to kinematic reliability analysis of industrial robots," *Reliab Eng Syst Safe,* vol. 229, Jan 2023, Art no. 108841, doi: 10.1016/j.ress.2022.108841.

[16] A. Kumar and K. J. Waldron, "Numerical plotting of surfaces of positioning accuracy of manipulators," *Mechanism and Machine Theory,* vol. 16, no. 4, pp. 361-368, 1981/01 1981, doi: 10.1016/0094-114x(81)90010-0.

[17] S. El Hraiech, A. H. Chebbi, Z. Affi, and L. Romdhane, "Error estimation and sensitivity analysis of the 3-UPU translational parallel robot due to design parameter uncertainties," *Proceedings of the Institution of Mechanical Engineers Part C-Journal of Mechanical Engineering Science,* vol. 233, no. 8, pp. 2713-2727, Apr 2019, doi: 10.1177/0954406218793673.

[18] X. W. Wang, X. Zhou, Z. L. Xia, and X. S. Gu, "A survey of welding robot intelligent path optimization," *Journal of Manufacturing Processes,* vol. 63, pp. 14-23, Mar 2021, doi: 10.1016/j.jmapro.2020.04.085.

[19] H. M. Wu, G. H. Cui, P. Chen, and H. J. Hou, "Motion reliability evaluation of six-axes robot based on non-probability interval theory," *International Journal of Vehicle Design,* vol. 84, no. 1-4, pp. 238-257, 2020. [Online]. Available: <Go to ISI>://WOS:000669935600012.

[20] R. Li, N. Ding, Y. Zhao, and H. Liu, "Real-time trajectory position error compensation technology of industrial robot," *Measurement,* vol. 208, Feb 2023, Art no. 112418, doi: 10.1016/j.measurement.2022.112418.

[21] Z. P. Tang, J. Peng, J. P. Sun, and X. Meng, "Non-Probabilistic Reliability Analysis of Robot Accuracy under Uncertain Joint Clearance," *Machines,* vol. 10, no. 10, Oct 2022, Art no. 917, doi: 10.3390/machines10100917.

A General Analytical Framework for Preventive Replacement Models in Discrete Time

Jing Wu, Liqu Lin, Jie Cui, Tadashi Dohi
Faculty of Management Engineering, Huaiyin Institute of Technology, China, 12024049@hyit.edu.cn;
College of Economics and Management, Nanjing University of Aeronautics and Astronautics, China, 00132005@wzu.edu.cn;
Faculty of Management Engineering, Huaiyin Institute of Technology, China, cuijie@hyit.edu.cn;
Gradauate School of Advanced Science and Engineering, Hiroshima University, Japan, dohi@hiroshima-u.ac.jp

Keywords: Analytical framework, Preventive replacement, Discrete time, Replacement priority

Abstract -
In this paper, we propose a general analyzing framework for optimizing preventive replacement models in discrete time. We formulate the discrete time framework by replacement option priority and characterize the optimal preventive replacement policies minimizing the associated expected cost in steady state. Then, we reformulate the several important discrete time preventive replacement models, including age replacement models, minimal repair models and block replacement models, under this framework.

1. Introduction

Maintenance optimization ensures that the equipment and systems operate reliably and cost-effectively by improving the effectiveness and efficiency of maintenance activities. Generally, maintenance optimization activities include preventive maintenance, predictive maintenance, total productive maintenance, spare parts management, and key performance indicators. Over the past several decades, many researchers have focused on maintenance optimization by analyzing general models, methods, and frameworks [1-4]. Essentially, many mathematical models have been studied and selected due to the variety and complexity of systems and the ways chosen actions. A useful general analytical framework can contain a set of preventive maintenance models. In addition, it can simplify the derivation process of optimal preventive maintenance policies and explain the models from an economic perspective. This allows readers to understand the complex mathematical models more easily.

The study objectives in early related works were simple. The analyzing framework models mainly focused on single-unit, single-state and single-objective system. More concretely, the most researchers formulated the preventive maintenance models by optimizing a single decision variable, such as working time, the times of usage and shock, and the damage level. With the advancement of modelling techniques and solving tools, preventive maintenance models with two-time dimensions were extensively studied. These important results in theory and applications are systematically collected. For example, Cho and Parlar [5] overviewed maintenance models for multiunit systems. Keizer et al. [6] summarized condition-based maintenance policies with multiunit dependent components systems.

The mentioned study on maintenance optimization primarily concentrated on studying continuous time preventive maintenance models. However, these analyzing methods, such as the marginal cost, are not suitable to the discrete time ones. In this study, we purpose a useful framework to analyze some basic discrete time models. The discrete time preventive replacement models were dealt with as trivial analogies of the continuous time ones in 1980s. Many real industry problems indicate the discrete time preventive maintenance models can work more effective in some special scenarios. For instance, the failure time data of pole air switches are recorded as group data such as month or year. For another example, the lifetime of a piston pump can be measured as the number of no failure cycles with "compression/release" actuations [7]. Hence, the continuous time preventive replacement polices may not have satisfied effective on long-lifetime equipment. On the latest study also support the above opinion. The methodical book [8] comprehensively analyze the reliability modellings in discrete time. A lot of basic reliability concepts, such as multivariable reliability, multivariate age and multivariate lifetime models are defined.

The study of discrete time preventive replacement models has a challenge in the formulation, when compared the continuous time ones. It is due to the fact that two more replacement options may occur at the same time point. For instance, in the discrete time age replacement model, preventive replacement and failure (corrective) replacement may come simultaneously. In this case, the early model, such as Nakagawa and Osaki [9], implicitly thought that the failure replacement is always has priority to the preventive replacement. This assumption may not be right, because the cost of preventive replacement is less than that of failure replacement. Hence, when dealing with the discrete time models, we should clarify the priority of replacement options in advance. For such challenge problem in discrete time replacement models, Wu et al. [10] firstly introduced the concept of replacement option priority and reformulated two age-based opportunistic replacement models.

In this paper, we propose a general analyzing framework for formulating maintenance replacement policies in discrete time. To deal with two more replacement options occurring as a simultaneous event, we introduce the definition of replacement option priority in sense of Wu et al. [10]. First, we propose a general analyzing framework model by preventive option priority and formulate the optimal preventive replacement policies minimizing the expected cost rate function. Then, we reformulate the age replacement models, minimal repair models and block replacement models under this analyzing framework. We briefly introduce the contributions as follows:

- A general analyzing framework for optimal preventive replacement models is genialized in discrete time.
- Several basic preventive replacement models are reformulated under this analytical framework.

The structure of the paper is organized as follows. In Section 2, we propose the analytical framework and derive optimal preventive replacement policies aimed at minimizing the relevant expected costs in the steady state. Section 3 applies this framework to age replacement models. Section 4 reformulates minimal repair models. In Section 5, we extend the analysis to block replacement models. Finally, Section 6 concludes the paper with some remarks.

2. Analytical Framework

Let us consider a single-unit system in discrete time. We assume that the interval-arrival times between consecutive opportunities for replacements, X, are independent and identically distributed (i.i.d.) integer-valued random variables, with the probability mass function $\Pr\{X = x\} = g_X(x)$ $(x = 1, 2, \cdots)$ and cumulative function $\Pr\{X \leq x\} = G_X(x)$. The failure times (lifetimes) of the item, Y, follow i.i.d. integer-valued random variables having the common probability mass function $\Pr\{Y = y\} = f_Y(y)$ $(y = 1, 2, \cdots)$ and cumulative distribution function $\Pr\{Y \leq y\} = F_Y(y)$. It is convenient to introduce the shifted failure rate function $R_Y(y) = f_Y(y)/\overline{F}_Y(y)$ and failure rate function $r_Y(n) = f_Y(y)/\overline{F}_Y(y-1)$. Without any loss of generality, we assume that $g_X(0) = f_Y(0) = 0$, where in general $\overline{G}_X(x) = 1 - G_X(x)$ and $\overline{F}_Y(y) = 1 - F_Y(y)$.

The cost components in our modelling as follows:
c_F: corrective (failure) replacement cost;
c_P: preventive replacement cost made at prescheduled time;
c_Y: preventive replacement cost made at a random opportunity;
c_M: minimal repair cost;

Assumption 1: $c_F > c_P \geq c_Y$.

It would be valid to assume that the failure replacement cost is most expensive, and that the opportunistic replacement cost is less than or equals to the preventive replacement one, because the opportunity means that a spare part of an item is available with a cheaper cost at a random (unscheduled) timing. Note that the above discrete time models must be treated carefully. At an arbitrary discrete point of time, suppose that one of two options; failure replacement F_a or prescheduled replacement S_c (or opportunistic replacement O_p), may occur as a simultaneous event. We introduce the following symbol for the priority relationship.

Definition 1: The replacement option P has a priority to the replacement option Q, if $P \succ Q$.

We consider a one-unit system and a decision variable N (> 0), which affects the timing of maintenance action(s) renewing the system. In the simplest case of this framework, N is the time at which the system is replaced preventively. Alternatively, N may also be a critical time after which the first suitable moment (opportunity) is awaited to renew the system. The aim is to determine the value of N which optimizes a given objective function. We consider expected cost per unit time at steady state. As the execution of the action(s) implies a renewal of the system, we can apply renewal theory [11] and obtain for the long-term average costs for Model j

$$EC_j(N) = \frac{C_j(N)}{L_j(N)}, \tag{1}$$

where $C_j(N)$ and $L_j(N)$ denote the expected costs and time length during one cycle, respectively. We make the following two definitions:

Definition 2: Both $C_j(N)$ and $L_j(N)$ are absolute discrete time functions of N, i.e., $C_j(N) = C_j(0) + \sum_{n=1}^{N} c_j(n)$ and $L_j(N) = L_j(0) + \sum_{n=1}^{N} l_j(n)$ for some functions $c_j(n)$ and $l_j(n)$.

Definition 3: $L_j(0) \geq 0$, $l_j(n) \geq 0$ for all $n > 0$ and $c_j(n) = 0$ if $l_j(n) = 0$.

From above definitions, it follows that there exists a function $a_j(n)$ such that $c_j(n) = a_j(n)l_j(n)$, $n > 0$. To simplify notation, we rewrite c_j for $C_j(0)$ and l_j for $L_j(0)$. Accordingly, we can rewrite $EC_j(N)$ as

$$EC_j(N) = \frac{c_j + \sum_{n=1}^{N} a_j(n)l_j(n)}{l_j + \sum_{n=1}^{N} l_j(n)}. \tag{2}$$

The above equation plays a central role in this paper. Notice that for $N = 0$, the expected cost during one cycle is c_j, and typically this represents the cost of preventive replacement c_P. The quantity $a_j(n)$ can be interpreted as the expected deterioration cost rate and $l_j(n)$ commonly denotes a survival function. This general framework covers quite some important models.

The analysis of the framework follows similar the continuous time model. First, taking the difference of $EC_j(N)$ with respect to N, we have

$$\begin{aligned} EC_j(N+1) - EC_j(N) &= \frac{[a_j(N+1) - EC_j(N)]\, l_j(N+1)}{L_j(N+1)} \\ &= \frac{[\Psi_j(N) - c_j]\, l_j(N+1)}{L_j(N+1)L_j(N)}, \end{aligned} \tag{3}$$

where $\Psi_j(N) = a_j(N+1)L_j(N) - \sum_{n=1}^{N} a_j(n)l_j(n)$. Hence, if $a_j(N+1) - EC_j(N) \geq 0$, then $EC_j(N+1) - EC_j(N) \geq 0$. Alternatively, if $\Psi_j(N) - c_j \geq 0$, then $EC_j(N+1) - EC_j(N) \geq 0$. We give the following theorem.

Theorem 1
Suppose $a_j(N+1) > 0$ for all $N > 0$,

(i) If $a_j(N+1)$ is non-increasing on $\left[\underline{N}, \overline{N}\right]$ and $\Psi_j(\underline{N}) < b_j$, then $EC_j(N)$ is decreasing on $\left[\underline{N}, \overline{N}\right]$.
(ii) If $a_j(N+1)$ increases strictly for $N > \underline{N}$, and $\Psi_j(\underline{N}) < c_j$ while $\Psi_j(\overline{N}) > c_j$, then $EC_j(N)$ has at least one (or at most two) minimal values, denoted by $EC_j(N^*)$, where the optimal preventive replacement time N^* satisfies

$$\Psi_j(N^*-1) < c_j \quad \text{and} \quad \Psi_j(N^*) \geq c_j.$$

Furthermore, the following inequalities hold:

$$\begin{aligned} &a_j(N^*) - EC_j(N^*-1) < 0 \\ &\text{and} \quad a_j(N^*+1) - EC_j(N^*) \geq 0. \end{aligned} \tag{4}$$

$$\begin{aligned} &a_j(N) - EC_j(N-1) < 0, \quad \text{for} \quad \underline{N} < N \leq N^*-1, \\ &\text{and} \\ &a_j(N+1) - EC_j(N) \geq 0, \quad \text{for} \quad N^* < N \leq \overline{N}. \end{aligned} \tag{5}$$

$$\begin{aligned} &a_j(N) - EC_j(N^*-1) < 0, \quad \text{for} \quad \underline{N} < N \leq N^*-1, \\ &\text{and} \\ &a_j(N+1) - EC_j(N^*) \geq 0, \quad \text{for} \quad N^* < N \leq \overline{N}. \end{aligned} \tag{6}$$

(iii) If $\Psi_j(N) < c_j$ for all $N > \underline{N}$, then $EC_j(N)$ is decreasing for $N > \underline{N}$.
(iv) Suppose that $a_j(N)$ is increasing for $N > \underline{N}$, and that $\Psi_j(\underline{N}) < c_j$ and $\Psi_j(\overline{N}) > c_j$, if one of the following conditions hold

1. $\lim_{N\to\infty} a_j(N) = \infty$.
2. $\lim_{N\to\infty} a_j(N) > \lim_{N\to\infty} EC_j(N)$.
3. $\lim_{N\to\infty} L_j(N) = \infty$, $\lim_{N\to\infty} a_j(N) = a$, for $a > 0$, and $\lim_{N\to\infty} \sum_{n=1}^{N} \left[a - a_j(n)\right] l_j(n) > c_j - a l_j$.

Theorem 1 implies that for optimization one only needs to consider those regions where $a_j(N)$ is increasing. Furthermore, it says that a basic criterion in which at every moment we consider whether to delay the replacement or not, is average optimal. That is, the expected cost of delay the replacement to level $N+1$, being $a(N+1)l(N+1)$, should be compared to the minimal average costs over an interval of the same time length, being $EC_j(N^*)l(N+1)$. Hence, if $a(N+1)$ is larger than or equals $EC_j(N^*)$, the deferment costs are larger and we should replace. This result gives a structure of the optimal policy, and it gives an explanation of reason that a policy is optimal.

3. Age Replacement Models

3.1 Standard Age Replacement Model

In the discrete time age replacement model, we suppose that there are two options for replacement. If the item fails, it is replaced immediately; otherwise, a non-failed item is replaced at a prescheduled preventive replacement time N. Its objective is to determine the optimal preventive replacement time N^* which minimizes the expected cost per unit time in the steady state. According to definition 1, if failure replacement and preventive replacement come at the same time instant, we select the preventive option with higher priority. In our model setting, it is possible to totally consider two different models as follows:
Model 1: $S_c \succ F_a$,
Model 2: $F_a \succ S_c$.

The mean time lengths of one cycle, $L_j(N)$ $(j = 1, 2)$, in two cases are exactly same, where

$$\begin{aligned} L_j(N) &= \sum_{n=1}^{N-1} n f_Y(n) + N\overline{F}_Y(N-1) \\ &= \sum_{n=1}^{N} \overline{F}_Y(n-1). \end{aligned} \tag{7}$$

We compute the expected costs of one cycle:

$$C_1(N) = c_F \sum_{n=1}^{N-1} f_Y(n) + c_P \overline{F}_Y(N-1), \tag{8}$$

$$C_2(N) = c_F \sum_{n=1}^{N} f_Y(n) + c_P \overline{F}_Y(N). \tag{9}$$

Then, the long-run costs per unit time in the steady state are denoted as $EC_j(N)$ for Model j $(= 1, 2)$, from the renewal reward theory [11],

$$EC_j(N) = \frac{C_j(N)}{L_j(N)}, \tag{10}$$

and our interest is to find the optimal N^* minimizing $EC_j(N)$.

According to Theorem 1, the cost parameters c_j are both preventive replacement c_P in Model 1 and 2. The functions $a_j(n)$ are $(c_F - c_P) R_Y(n)$ in Model 1 and $(c_F - c_P) r_Y(n+1)$ in Model 2. The functions $l_j(n)$ are the survival function $\overline{F}_Y(n-1)$ with $l_j = 0$.

Here, we take the Model 1 as an example. $R_Y(n)$ is an increasing function, if $r_Y(n)$ is an increasing function (see the related works [12]). We know that if $R_Y(n)$ is an increasing function, $a_1(\infty) = (c_F - c_P) R_Y(\infty)$ and $EC_1(\infty) = c_P / \sum_{n=1}^{\infty} \overline{F}_Y(n-1)$. Therefore, we can confirm that the condition $a_1(\infty) > EC_1(\infty)$ is equivalent to

$$R_Y(\infty) \sum_{n=1}^{N} \overline{F}_Y(n-1) > \frac{c_F}{c_F - c_P}. \tag{11}$$

It is clear that the above analysis process is exactly same as Theorem 2.1 in [12].

3.2 Dekker and Dijkstra's Model [13]

We analyze an important opportunity-age replacement model in Dekker and Dijkstra [13]. We consider a unit with discrete time lifetime Y. When the system fails, the unit is replaced with corrective cost c_F. A preventive replacement of the unit with cost c_Y is only carried out at first opportunity after the prescheduled time N. In discrete time setting, we supposed that the interarrival of opportunities is generated according to geometric distribution with parameter p. The problem is to determine a strategy which minimizes the expected cost per unit of time in the steady state.

According to definition 1, we can consider two following models:

Model 1: $O_p \succ F_a$,
Model 2: $F_a \succ O_p$.

In this model, $L_j(N)$ is the mean time lengths of one cycle for Model j $(= 1, 2)$:

$$L_j(N) = \sum_{n=1}^{N} \overline{F}_Y(n-1) + \sum_{n=N+1}^{\infty} \overline{F}_Y(n-1)(1-p)^{n-N-1}. \tag{12}$$

We also can compute the expected costs of one cycle, $C_j(N)$, for Model j $(= 1, 2)$:

$$C_1(N) = c_F \sum_{n=1}^{N} f_Y(n) + c_F \sum_{n=N+1}^{\infty} f_Y(n)(1-p)^{n-N} + c_Y \sum_{n=N+1}^{\infty} \overline{F}_Y(n-1)p(1-p)^{n-N-1}, \tag{13}$$

$$C_2(N) = c_F \sum_{n=1}^{N} f_Y(n) + c_F \sum_{n=N+1}^{\infty} f_Y(n)(1-p)^{n-N-1} + c_Y \sum_{n=N+1}^{\infty} \overline{F}_Y(n)p(1-p)^{n-N-1}. \tag{14}$$

Then, the expected costs per unit time in the steady state are formulated as $EC_j(N)$ for Model j $(= 1, 2)$:

$$EC_j(N) = \frac{C_j(N)}{L_j(N)}, \tag{15}$$

and our objective is to determine the optimal preventive replacement time N^* minimizing $EC_j(N)$.

In the general framework, the cost parameters c_j are the preventive replacement cost $c_Y + (c_F - c_Y)\sum_{n=1}^{\infty} f_Y(n)(1-p)^n$ in Model 1 and $c_Y + (c_F - c_Y)\sum_{n=1}^{\infty} f_Y(n)(1-p)^{n-1}$ in Model 2. $c_j(n)$ are $(c_F - c_Y)\sum_{n=N+1}^{\infty} \overline{F}_Y(n)(1-p)^{n-N-1}$ in Model 1 and $p(c_F - c_Y)\sum_{n=N+1}^{\infty} \overline{F}_Y(n+1)(1-p)^{n-N-1}$ in Model 2. $a_j(n)$ are $(c_F - c_Y)H(n)$ in Model 1 and $(c_F - c_Y)h(n+1)$ in Model 2, where $H(n)$ and $h(n+1)$ are the shifted failure rate function and failure rate function in opportunity-based age replacement models (see the related works [13]). Finally, $l_j(n) = p\sum_{n=N+1}^{\infty} f_Y(n)(1-p)^{n-N-1}$ and $l_j = \sum_{n=1}^{\infty} \overline{F}_Y(n-1)(1-p)^{n-1}$.

4. Minimal Repair Models

4.1 Standard Minimal Repair Model

We consider that a new unit begins at time $n = 0$. When it fails, only minimal repair is made. Also, a unit is replaced at periodic times kN $(k = 1, 2 \cdots)$ and the failure rate does not change after replacement. We assume that the times of repair and replacement are negligible. We suppose that a system which is subject to failures appearing according to a general distribution with the mass function probability $p(1), p(2), \cdots, p(n)$ and $E[Y] = \sum_{i=1}^{n} ip(i)$. Then, the expected cost of one cycle in steady state is

$$EC(N) = \frac{c_M \sum_{n=1}^{N-1} p(n) + c_P}{\sum_{1}^{N} 1}. \tag{16}$$

In the general framework, the function $a(n)$ is $c_M p(n-1)$. $l(n)$ is 1 with $l = 0$. Cost parameter $c(n)$ is $c_M p(n-1)$ with $c = c_P$.

4.2 Modified Minimal Repair Model

Muth [14] formulated somewhat different minimal repair model in continuous time. In this model, the system can either be minimally repaired with costs c_M or be replaced preventively with costs c_P. Furthermore, the optimal policy is of the form: 'replace the system preventively at the first failure after periodic time kN $(k = 1, 2, \cdots)$'. The problem is to decide the optimal prescheduled preventive replacement time N, when to replace the system preventively. In discrete-time setting, we suppose that failures appears following a general distribution with the mass function probability $p(1), p(2), \cdots, p(n)$ and $E[Y] = \sum_{i=1}^{n} ip(i)$. The expected costs in steady state is given by

$$EC(N) = \frac{c_P + c_M \sum_{n=1}^{N} p(n)}{N + E[W_N]}, \tag{17}$$

where $E[W_N]$ denotes the expected time to the first failure after time N. It can be calculated by

$$E[W_N] = \sum_{k=1}^{\infty} kp(N+k). \tag{18}$$

Hence it easily follows that $l(n) = p(n)E[W_n]$. In a similar way, we obtain that $c(n) = c_M p(n)$ and $a(n) = c_M / [W_n]$. Finally, we remark that $l = E[W_0]$.

5. Block Replacement Models

5.1 Standard Block Replacement Model

A new unit begins at time $n = 0$. When it fails, it is replaced by new one. Also, a unit is replaced at periodic times kN $(k = 1, 2 \cdots)$ and any unit becomes 'as good as new after replacement'. It is assumed that the replacement time is negligible. We consider one cycle with discrete time N from the predetermined replacement to the next one. According to definition 1, we should totally consider two different models as follows:

Model 1: $S_c \succ F_a$,
Model 2: $F_a \succ S_c$.

Then, the expected costs per unit in the steady state are given by

$$EC_1(N) = \frac{c_P + c_F \sum_{n=1}^{N-1} m(n)}{\sum_{1}^{N} 1}, \tag{19}$$

$$EC_2(N) = \frac{c_F + c_F \sum_{n=1}^{N-1} m(n)}{\sum_{1}^{N} 1}. \tag{20}$$

In general framework, the functions $a_j(n)$ are both $c_F m(n-1)$ in Model 1 and 2, where $m(n)$ is the renewal density function. $l_j(n)$ is 1 in Model 1 and 2, with $l_j = 0$ in both models. The cost parameters $c_j(n)$ are both $c_F m(n-1)$, with $c_j = c_P$ in Moel 1 and $c_j = c_F$ in Model 2.

5.2 'No Replacement at Failure'
Finally, we consider another system which is always replaced at times kN $(k = 1, 2\cdots)$, but it is not replaced at failure. Hence, it remains in failed state for the time interval from a failure to its detection. This can be applied to the maintenance model where a unit is not monitored continuously, and its failures can be detected only at times and some maintenance is done [15]. We calculate the mean times of failure from a failure to its detection

$$\sum_{i=1}^{N}(N-n)f_Y(n) = \sum_{i=1}^{N} F_Y(n). \tag{21}$$

The expected costs in steady state for each model are

$$EC_1(N) = \frac{c_P + c_F\sum_{i=1}^{N-1} F_Y(n)}{\sum_{n=1}^{N} 1}, \tag{22}$$

$$EC_2(N) = \frac{c_F + c_F\sum_{i=1}^{N-1} F_Y(n)}{\sum_{n=1}^{N} 1}. \tag{23}$$

In general framework, the functions $a_j(n)$ are both $c_F F_Y(n-1)$ in Model 1 and 2. $l_j(n)$ is 1 in Model 1 and 2, with $l_j = 0$ in both models. The cost parameters $c_j(n)$ are both $c_F F_Y(n-1)$, with $c_1 = c_P$ in Model 1 and $c_2 = c_F$ in Model 2.

6. Conclusions

In this paper, a general analyzing framework for optimal preventive replacement models in discrete time is proposed. First, we develop a discrete time framework based on replacement option priority and derive the optimal preventive replacement policies. Since the general analyzing framework encompasses various preventive replacement models, we analyze several important discrete time preventive replacement models, including age replacement models, minimal repair models, and block replacement models.

In future, we will reformulate the discrete time preventive replacement model with discounting in this framework. We take the discrete time age replacement model with discounting as an example. We denote α as discount factor. In general framework, it can be calculated as: the parameters c_j are 0 in Model 1 and preventive replacement c_P in Model 2. The functions $a_j(n)$ are $[(c_F - c_P)\, R_Y(n)/(1-\alpha)] - c_P$ in Model 1 and $[\alpha\,(c_F - c_P)\, r_Y(n+1)/(1-\alpha)] - c_P$ in Model 2. The function $l_j(n)$ is $(1-\alpha)\alpha^n \overline{F}_Y(n-1)$ with $l_j = 0$. Besides, other preventive replacements models with discounting will be analyzed in the framework.

Reference

[1] McCall, J. J. Maintenance policies for stochastically failing equipment: a survey . *Manage. Sci.* **1965**, *11*, 1493–524.

[2] Pierskalla, W. P.; Voelker, J. A. A survey of maintenance models: the control and surveillance of deteriorating systems. *Nav. Res. Logist.* **1979**, *23*, 353–388.

[3] Sherif, Y. S.; Smith, M. L. Optimal maintenance models for systems subject to failure-a review . *Nav. Res. Logist.* **1981**, *28*, 47–74.

[4] Valdez-Flores, C.; Feldman, R. M. A survey of preventive maintenance models for stochastically deteriorating single-unit systems. *Nav. Res. Logist.* **1979**, *23*, 419–446.

[5] Cho, D. I.; Parlar, M. A survey of maintenance models for multi-unit systems. *Eur. J. Oper. Res.* **1991**, *51*, 1–23.

[6] Keizer, M. C. O.; Flapper, S. D. P.; Teunter, R. H. Condition-based maintenance policies for systems with multiple dependent components: A review. *Eur. J. Oper. Res.* **2017**, *261*, 405–420.

[7] Eryilmaz, S. Age based preventive replacement policy for discrete time coherent systems with independent and identical components. *Reliab. Eng. Syst. Saf.* **2023**, *240*, 109544.

[8] Nair, U.; Sankaran, P. G.; Balakrishnan, N. Reliability modelling and analysis in discrete time. **2018**, Academic Press.

[9]Nakagawa, T.; Osaki, S. Discrete time age replacement policies. *J. Oper. Res. Soc.* **1977**, *28*, 881–885.

[10] Wu, J.; Qian, C.; Dohi, T. Optimal opportunity-based age replacement policies in discrete time. *Reliab. Eng. Syst. Saf.* **2024**, *241*, 109587.

[11] Ross, S. M. Applied probability models with optimization applications. **2013**, Courier Corporation.

[12] Wu, J.; Qian, C.; Tadashi, D. Two discrete-time age-based replacement problems with/without discounting. *Int. J. Math. Eng. Manag. Sci.* **2024**, *9*, 385–410.

[13] Dekker, R.; Dijkstra, M.C. Opportunity-based age replacement: Exponentially distributed times between opportunities. *Nav. Res. Logist.* **1992**, *39*, 175–190.

[14] Muth, E. J. An optimal decision rule for repair vs replacement. *IEEE Trans. Reliab.* **1977**, *26*, 179—81.

[15] Nakagawa, T. Maintenance Theory of Reliability. **2005**, Springer Science & Business Media

Proportional Hazards Model-Based Global Dynamic Maintenance Optimization for Multi-Component Degradation System

CHEN Yi[1], KANG Zijian[1], ZHAO Yu[1*].

[1] School of Reliability and Systems Engineering, Beihang University, China, chenyi1118@buaa.edu.cn
[1] School of Reliability and Systems Engineering, Beihang University, China, kangzijian@buaa.edu.cn
[1] School of Reliability and Systems Engineering, Beihang University, China, zhaoyu@buaa.edu.cn

Keywords: Maintenance grouping, Dynamic maintenance, Degradation system, Proportional hazards model.

Abstract – This paper proposes a global dynamic maintenance-optimization framework for multi-component systems based on a Proportional Hazards Model (PHM) that integrates real-time condition monitoring to update component hazard rates and remaining useful life. Maintenance decision - making is formulated as a global optimization problem where updated PHM parameters determine optimal preventive maintenance (PM) intervals and group scheduling captures economic dependencies and shared setup costs. The total expected cost rate, comprising preventive, corrective, and group - setup costs, is analytically expressed and minimized via a simulation - based algorithm combining grid search and stochastic degradation sampling. A numerical case study of a four - component pumping station demonstrates that the proposed method reduces long - run maintenance costs compared with static, component - by - component policies by coordinating PM actions, adapting to evolving degradation states, and exploiting economic coupling. The results confirm that PHM - driven group maintenance scheduling enhances cost efficiency. Future work can extend this framework by incorporating multi - state degradation models, stochastic inspection effects, and real-world field validation in industrial settings.

1. Introduction

In modern industrial operations, ensuring the reliability and availability of complex systems is paramount. Multi-component systems, prevalent in sectors such as aerospace, manufacturing, and energy, are subject to various degradation mechanisms over time [1]-[7]. Effective maintenance strategies are essential to mitigate unexpected failures, optimize operational efficiency, and reduce life-cycle costs [8]-[12].

Traditional maintenance approaches, including time-based and reactive maintenance, often fall short in addressing the dynamic nature of component degradation and the interdependencies among system components [13]-[21]. Condition-Based Maintenance (CBM) has emerged as a proactive strategy that leverages real-time condition monitoring data to inform maintenance decisions. Central to CBM is the ability to accurately model the degradation process and predict the remaining useful life (RUL) of components.

The Proportional Hazards Model (PHM), introduced by Cox in 1972, has been widely adopted in reliability engineering for modeling the hazard rate of components as a function of covariates, such as environmental conditions and operational stresses [22]-[25]. PHM's flexibility allows it to incorporate various influencing factors, making it a powerful tool for RUL prediction and maintenance optimization [26]-[28]. While PHM has been extensively applied to single-component systems, its extension to multi-component systems presents additional challenges due to the complexities arising from component interactions and economic dependencies [29]-[31].

Recent studies have explored PHM-based CBM policies for multi-component systems, considering factors such as shared maintenance costs and the benefits of simultaneous component replacements [32]-[37]. These approaches aim to develop maintenance strategies that minimize the total expected cost by accounting for the stochastic nature of component degradation and the economic interdependencies among components [38]-[42]. However, existing models often rely on static optimization frameworks that may not fully capture the dynamic evolution of system conditions and the need for adaptive decision-making [43]-[47].

In this paper, we propose a global dynamic maintenance optimization framework for multi-component degradation systems based on the Proportional Hazards Model. Our approach integrates real-time condition monitoring data to dynamically update the degradation models of individual components. By formulating the maintenance decision-making process as a global optimization problem, we aim to determine optimal maintenance schedules that minimize the total expected cost over a planning horizon, considering both the degradation states of components and the economic dependencies among them.

The innovations presented in this paper can be summarized as follows:

- We propose a global dynamic optimization framework that incorporates real-time condition monitoring data to dynamically update degradation models for each component. This allows for more accurate and timely maintenance decisions.
- We introduce a novel approach that integrates the economic dependencies between components, accounting for shared maintenance costs of joint replacements, which enhances the cost-effectiveness of the maintenance strategy.
- We develop an efficient optimization algorithm that reduces the computational complexity of solving the maintenance scheduling problem while ensuring the accuracy of decision-making for systems with a large number of components and stochastic degradation behaviors.

The remainder of this paper is organized as follows: Section 2 presents the proposed global dynamic maintenance optimization framework. Section 3 details the modeling of component reliability, cost structures, and the maintenance optimization. Section 4 provides a numerical example to demonstrate the effectiveness of the proposed approach. Finally, Section 5 concludes the paper and discusses potential directions for future research.

2. Global dynamic maintenance framework

In this section, we present the proposed global dynamic maintenance framework for multi-component degradation systems. The framework aims to optimize maintenance decisions dynamically by integrating degradation monitoring, reliability modeling, and cost evaluation into a unified decision-making process. The framework is composed of three main components: system definition, dynamic maintenance decision process, and PHM-based integration.

2.1. System Description

The system under consideration is a multi-component engineering asset widely encountered in industries such as manufacturing, transportation, and energy. Each component within the system is subject to degradation over time due to operational and environmental stressors such as load, temperature, vibration, and corrosion. These degradation processes are monitored through a network of embedded sensors that provide real-time condition data, including physical indicators like wear depth, crack length, or fluid contamination levels.

The components operate in parallel or in functional groups, contributing collectively to system performance. Failures in individual components can lead to partial or complete system shutdowns, resulting in costly downtime and safety risks. To ensure high reliability and cost-efficiency, the system requires a maintenance strategy that can dynamically adapt to each component's evolving health state.

Maintenance actions for each component include both preventive maintenance (PM), carried out before failure based on condition assessments, and corrective maintenance (CM), performed after a failure occurs. These actions incur different levels of cost, downtime, and resource consumption. In practical operations, it is often more economical to service multiple components simultaneously during planned maintenance windows, making the coordination of component-level decisions a key element in overall maintenance planning.

Moreover, the system is typically subject to periodic inspections or maintenance planning cycles (e.g., daily, weekly, or monthly), during which decisions are made based on the latest degradation data. This forms the basis for a global, dynamic optimization approach that continuously updates maintenance plans across all components, balancing reliability, availability, and economic efficiency.

2.2. Maintenance Framework

The maintenance framework in this paper integrates real-time monitoring data, degradation models, and cost structures to optimize the maintenance decisions for a multi-component degradation system. The framework is designed to operate dynamically, allowing for continuous updates to the maintenance schedule based on the evolving health states of each component.

The framework is composed of the following key modules:

- **Dynamic Reliability Assessment**: The degradation process for each component is modeled using the Proportional Hazards Model (PHM), which estimates the hazard rate of failure as a function of component age and operating conditions. This allows for continuous updates to the reliability assessment.
- **Maintenance Decision Process**: Based on the real-time degradation data and reliability estimates, each component is assigned a specific PM interval, optimized through a cost rate minimization approach. Components whose remaining time to their PM interval falls within a predefined PM window are eligible for group maintenance.
- **Global Optimization for Maintenance Scheduling**: The dynamic optimization approach is based on a given horizon, where decisions are updated periodically over the planning horizon. The optimization algorithm determines the best maintenance schedule that minimizes the total expected cost.
- **Dynamic Update for Maintenance Scheduling**: As new data is collected from the sensors, the framework continuously updates the degradation models and maintenance schedules. This feedback loop ensures that the system adapts to changes in component health and operational conditions, leading to more accurate predictions and optimized decisions over time.

3. Cost modeling and optimization

3.1. PHM-based reliability model

In this study, we utilize the PHM to model the reliability of individual components within a multi-component system. The PHM allows us to express the failure risk of components in a way that accounts for the influence of time, degradation indicators, and operational/environmental conditions. The model is continuously updated with real-time sensor data to refine the estimation of failure probabilities.

The PHM is a survival analysis technique often used to analyze failure data. In the context of component reliability, the PHM estimates the hazard rate—the instantaneous failure rate—of a component as a function of time and degradation factors. The basic form of the model is given by:

$$\lambda_i(t) = \lambda_{0,i}(t) \exp\left(\boldsymbol{\beta}_i^{\top} \boldsymbol{X}_i(t)\right), \tag{1}$$

where $\lambda_{0,i}(t)$ is the baseline hazard function, modeling the time-dependent risk in the absence of external factors; $\boldsymbol{X}_i(t)$ is the vector of real-time degradation covariates obtained from sensors (e.g., vibration, temperature, pressure); $\boldsymbol{\beta}_i$ is a vector of coefficients representing the effect of each covariate on the hazard rate.

In this work, we assume the baseline hazard $\lambda_{0,i}(t)$ follows a Weibull form:

$$\lambda_{0,i}(t) = \frac{\gamma_i}{\alpha_i}\left(\frac{t}{\alpha_i}\right)^{\gamma_i - 1}, \tag{2}$$

with shape parameter $\gamma_i > 1$ and scale parameter $\alpha_i > 0$, capturing the intrinsic aging characteristics of the component. Combining this with the PHM structure yields the total hazard:

$$\lambda_i(t) = \frac{\gamma_i}{\alpha_i}\left(\frac{t}{\alpha_i}\right)^{\gamma_i - 1} \exp\left(\boldsymbol{\beta}_i^{\top} \boldsymbol{X}_i(t)\right). \tag{3}$$

Given the hazard rate, the reliability function $R_i(t) = P(T_i > t)$ is expressed as:

$$R_i(t) = \exp\left(-\int_0^t \lambda_i(s)ds\right) = \exp\left(-\int_0^t \frac{\gamma_i}{\alpha_i}\left(\frac{t}{\alpha_i}\right)^{\gamma_i-1} \exp\left(\boldsymbol{\beta}_i^T \boldsymbol{X}_i(s)\right) ds\right). \quad (4)$$

The model parameters $\boldsymbol{\theta}_i = (\alpha_i, \gamma_i, \boldsymbol{\beta}_i)$ are estimated via maximum likelihood estimation (MLE) using historical failure data.

Assume we have a dataset with n historical component samples. Each sample is represented by a triplet $\{T_j, \delta_j, \boldsymbol{X}_j(t)\}$, where T_j is the failure time of the j-th component (or the censoring time if the component has not failed); $\delta_j \in \{0,1\}$ is a failure indicator that $\delta_j = 0$ if right-censored and $\delta_j = 1$ if component failed; $\boldsymbol{X}_j(t)$ is the covariate vector representing the component's degradation or condition data over time (e.g., sensor readings).

For each sample j, its contribution to the likelihood depends on whether it is failed or censored. If the component failed at time T_j, $f_i(T_j) = \lambda_i(T_j)R_i(T_j)$; else if the component is right-censored at time T_j, $P(T_i > T_j) = R_i(T_j)$. Thus, the full likelihood function is:

$$L(\boldsymbol{\theta}_i) = \prod_{j=1}^{n} [\lambda_i(T_j) \cdot R_i(T_j)]^{\delta_j} \cdot [R_i(T_j)]^{1-\delta_j} = \prod_{j=1}^{n} [\lambda_i(T_j) \cdot R_i(T_j)]^{\delta_j}. \quad (5)$$

Taking the logarithm gives the log-likelihood:

$$\ln L(\boldsymbol{\theta}_i) = \sum_{j=1}^{n} \delta_j \ln \lambda_i(T_j) + \sum_{j=1}^{n} \ln R_i(T_j) = \sum_{j=1}^{n} \left[\delta_j \ln \lambda_i(T_j) - \int_0^{T_j} \lambda_i(s)ds\right]. \quad (6)$$

This is the expression used to estimate the parameters $\boldsymbol{\theta}_i = (\alpha_i, \gamma_i, \boldsymbol{\beta}_i)$ through numerical optimization.

3.2. Component cost model

To optimize the preventive maintenance (PM) strategy for each component i, we aim to determine the optimal PM interval $\mathcal{T}_i$ that minimizes the long-run expected cost rate. The cost rate model integrates the PHM-based reliability of the component and distinguishes between preventive and corrective maintenance outcomes.

Assuming a periodic PM strategy, where the component is either preventively maintained at interval $\mathcal{T}_i$, or replaced upon failure if failure occurs earlier, the expected cost per cycle is:

$$E[C(\mathcal{T}_i)] = C_{PM}^{(i)} \cdot R_i(\mathcal{T}_i) + C_{CM}^{(i)} \cdot (1 - R_i(\mathcal{T}_i)) + C_{SET}^{(i)}, \quad (7)$$

where $C_{PM}^{(i)}$ is the cost of performing PM; $C_{CM}^{(i)}$ is the cost of CM upon failure, where typically $C_{CM}^{(i)} \gg C_{PM}^{(i)}$; C_{SET} is the setup cost for maintenance preparation, which can be shared by all components.

Likewise, the expected renewal cycle length is formulated as:

$$E[L(\mathcal{T}_i)] = \int_0^{\mathcal{T}_i} R_i(s)ds. \quad (8)$$

Thus, the expected cost rate is:

$$g_i(\mathcal{T}_i) = \frac{E[C(\mathcal{T}_i)]}{E[L(\mathcal{T}_i)]} = \frac{C_{PM}^{(i)} R_i(\mathcal{T}_i) + C_{CM}^{(i)}(1 - R_i(\mathcal{T}_i)) + C_{SET}}{\int_0^{\mathcal{T}_i} R_i(s)ds}. \quad (9)$$

The optimal PM interval $\mathcal{T}_i^*$ can be determined by minimizing the expected cost rate

$$\mathcal{T}_i^* = \mathrm{argmin}_{\mathcal{T}_i}[g_i(\mathcal{T}_i)]. \quad (10)$$

Given that $R_i(t)$ is derived from the PHM with estimated parameters $\boldsymbol{\theta}_i$ and that $\lambda_i(t)$ can be evaluated numerically, the optimization problem in (10) is typically solved using numerical methods such as: Golden section search or Brent's method (for 1D optimization). Since $g_i(\mathcal{T}_i)$ is typically unimodal for reasonable reliability models, these methods converge efficiently.

3.3. System maintenance schedule

In complex systems composed of multiple monitored components, individual component-level preventive maintenance (PM) decisions may result in suboptimal system-wide costs due to frequent interventions and ignored coordination opportunities. To address this, we propose an opportunistic PM framework where maintenance decisions are made periodically based on system-wide condition assessments. At each inspection point, components are considered for grouped PM based on how close their current age is to their PHM-based optimal PM interval.

The key idea is to jointly optimize two critical decision variables:

1. System inspection interval Δ, which determines how frequently component health is assessed;
2. Group PM window ω, which defines the allowable deviation from each component's optimal PM interval $\mathcal{T}_i^*$ to qualify for coordinated PM.

This section presents the modeling framework and cost-based optimization method to minimize the expected long-run system maintenance cost rate.

Let the system consist of N components indexed by $i = 1,2,\dots,N$. Each component is continuously monitored via PHM, and its degradation profile is modeled with time-varying covariates $\boldsymbol{X}_i(t)$. From Section 3.2, we obtain the optimal PM interval $\mathcal{T}_i^*$ for component i, based on its current PHM parameters.

To coordinate PM actions, the system is periodically inspected at discrete times:

$$t_k = k\Delta, k = 1,2,\dots,K, \qquad \text{where } K = \left\lfloor \frac{T}{\Delta} \right\rfloor. \quad (11)$$

At each inspection t_k, the following steps are executed:

1. All components' PHM models are updated using the latest sensor data;
2. The updated optimal PM interval $\mathcal{T}_i^*$ is computed for each component;
3. The working age of component i, denoted $a_i(t_k)$, is recorded (time since last maintenance);
4. A component is selected for PM if its working age is close enough to $\mathcal{T}_i^*$, i.e., component $i \in \{\mathcal{T}_i^* - a_i(t_k) \le \omega\}$ and component $j \in \{a_j(t_k) - \mathcal{T}_j^* \ge 0\}$ are selected for PM.

For each component i, we compute the expected maintenance cost rate over horizon T, accounting for both PM and failure scenarios. At each inspection time t_k, the probability of PM is:

$$P_{PM}^{(i)}(t_k) = \begin{bmatrix} P(\mathcal{T}_i^* - a_i(t_k) \le \omega) \\ +P(a_i(t_k) - \mathcal{T}_i^* \ge 0) \end{bmatrix} R_i(a_i(t_k)). \quad (12)$$

If the component is not selected for PM, it may fail before the next inspection, incurring CM cost. The expected maintenance cost for component i is then:

$$E[C_i(\Delta,\omega)] = \sum_{k=1}^{K} \begin{bmatrix} C_{SET} + P_{PM}^{(i)}(t_k) C_{PM}^{(i)} \\ + \left(1 - P_{PM}^{(i)}(t_k)\right) P_{CM}^{(i)}(t_k) C_{CM}^{(i)} \end{bmatrix}, \quad (13)$$

where $P_{CM}^{(i)}(t_k)$ denotes the conditional failure probability of component i between inspections if no PM was performed.

$$P_{CM}^{(i)}(t_k) = P(T_i \in [a_i(t_k), a_i(t_k) + \Delta] | T_i > a_i(t_k))$$
$$= \frac{R_i(a_i(t_k)) - R_i(a_i(t_k) + \Delta)}{R_i(a_i(t_k))} = 1 - \frac{R_i(a_i(t_k) + \Delta)}{R_i(a_i(t_k))}. \quad (14)$$

Every time the system conducts PM on at least one component, the shared group cost C_{SET} is incurred. The amortized group PM cost is:

$$S(\Delta,\omega) = C_{SET} \sum_{k=1}^{K} [\max(|i \cup j|_k - 1, 0)], \quad (15)$$

where $|i \cup j|_k$ the number of components selected for group PM at each inspection t_k.

Combining all cost components, the expected total system maintenance cost rate over the planning horizon T is:

$$E[C_G(\Delta,\omega)] = \sum_{i=1}^{N} E[C_i(\Delta,\omega)] - S(\Delta,\omega). \quad (16)$$

Our optimization problem is then to find the inspection interval Δ and group PM window ω that minimize the system cost rate:

$$(\Delta^*, \omega^*) = \text{argmin}_{\Delta>0,\omega>0}\{E[C_G(\Delta,\omega)]\}. \quad (17)$$

The minimization of $E[C_G(\Delta,\omega)]$ can be approached through a simulation-based optimization process:

Initialize a candidate pair (Δ,ω);

Simulate component's reliability over $[0,T]$ using PHM models;

At each inspection t_k:

Update each $\mathcal{T}_i^*$ and $a_i(t_k)$;

Determine $|i \cup j|_k$ based on step 4;

Record maintenance actions and associated costs;

Compute $E[C_i(\Delta,\omega)]$ and $|i \cup j|_k$;

Evaluate the objective $E[C_G(\Delta,\omega)]$;

Search for the optimal (Δ^*,ω^*) using a grid search algorithm.

4. Numerical example

Consider a pumping station consisting of four critical components, each monitored by condition sensors. The system must remain operational to ensure stable water supply in an industrial zone. The components are: electric motor, water pump, pressure valve, and control sensor module.

All components degrade over time, and their degradation processes are monitored using condition-based sensor signals. Preventive maintenance (PM) and corrective maintenance (CM) costs vary by component type. Due to operational constraints, maintenance can only be performed during scheduled inspections, which occur at fixed intervals Δ. At each inspection, components whose current age is within a certain window ω of their individually optimal PM interval $\mathcal{T}_i^*$ are considered for group PM.

The goal is to determine the optimal inspection interval Δ and group PM window ω that minimize the total expected system maintenance cost over a 5-year planning horizon.

4.1. Initial data and assumptions

In our PHM-based reliability model, we take vibration amplitude as the sole degradation indicator for each component. A Cox proportional-hazards fit on historical field data yields a hazard coefficient of $\beta = 1.13$, with the degradation process of vibration amplitude is modeled as $x(t) = x(0) + vt = 0.22t$.

The failure time of each component follows a Weibull distribution, which is commonly used for modeling failure rates in industrial systems.

Each component incurs costs for preventive and corrective maintenance actions, with corrective maintenance generally being more expensive due to the risk of system disruption or collateral damage. Additionally, each group PM action (involving at least one component) triggers a fixed system-level overhead cost, representing labor, shutdown, and setup costs.

The following parameter values are assumed for the four components at the beginning of the simulation:

Table I. Distribution and maintenance cost parameters.

Component	Distribution parameters		Maintenance cost ($)		
	Scale parameter (month)	Shape parameter	PM	CM	SET
#1 Electric motor	50	2.5	400	1200	1000
#2 Water pump	40	2.0	500	1500	
#3 Pressure valve	45	3.0	300	1000	
#4 Sensor module	30	1.8	200	800	

The total planning horizon is set to $T = 60$ months, representing a five-year operational period. Preventive maintenance is only allowed at scheduled system inspections, which occur at fixed intervals Δ (to be optimized). At each inspection point, components whose working age is sufficiently close to their individual optimal PM interval $\mathcal{T}_i^*$ may be included in a group PM action if they satisfy the condition: component $i \in \{\mathcal{T}_i^* - a_i(t_k) \le \omega\}$ and component $j \in \{a_j(t_k) - \mathcal{T}_j^* \ge 0\}$. The candidate ranges for decision variables are:

1. Inspection interval: $\Delta \in [3,12]$ months;
2. Group PM window: $\omega \in [1,4]$ months.

The following assumptions govern the simulation process:

1. Preventive maintenance can only be performed during scheduled inspections;
2. Corrective maintenance is triggered upon component failure and executed immediately;

3. All PM and CM actions reset the component's age to zero;
4. Inspection itself is assumed to be costless and perfectly accurate.

4.2. Simulation results

In this section, we evaluate the time-dependent reliability of four critical components using the PHM degradation model and proportional-hazards coefficient defined in Section 4.1.

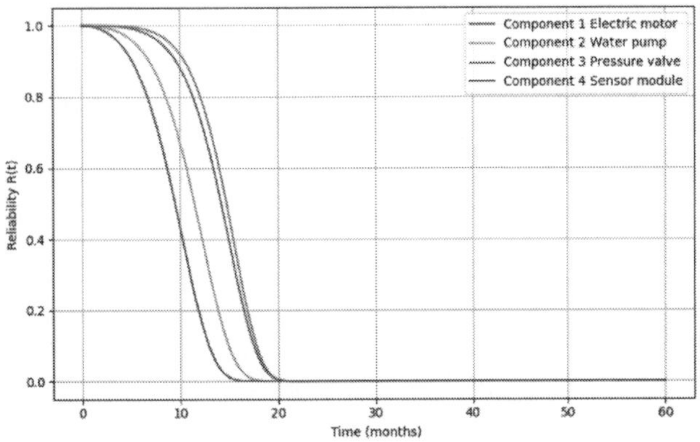

Fig. 1. Reliability curves of four components.

As shown in Fig.1, each component's reliability decays over time due to the combined effect of its Weibull-modeled baseline hazard and the exponential increase from the vibration-based degradation metric. Components with higher shape or scale parameters exhibit slower initial decline, but all ultimately approach zero reliability by the end of the planning horizon. These reliability profiles form the basis for the cost-rate calculations and preventive maintenance interval optimization presented in the following context.

Using the reliability profiles and the cost-rate formula, we compute each component's long-run average maintenance cost over PM intervals $\mathcal{T}_i$ ranging from 0 to 60 months. The maintenance cost-rate curves in Fig.2 were generated by numerically integrating the reliability function and evaluating $g_i(\mathcal{T}_i)$ on a fine grid of $\mathcal{T}_i$. From these curves we extract each component's minimum cost rate and the corresponding optimal PM interval $\mathcal{T}_i^*$ in Table II.

Table II. Optimal PM intervals and minimum cost rates.

Component	Optimal PM interval (month)	Minimum cost rate ($/month)
#1 Electric motor	13.0	138.82
#2 Water pump	10.7	196.80
#3 Pressure valve	13.4	120.71
#4 Sensor module	10.0	182.72

Building on the component-level analyses, we now determine the optimal inspection interval Δ and grouping window ω that minimize the total maintenance cost over the 60-month planning horizon.

We performed a fine-grid search over $\Delta \in [3,12]$ months and $\omega \in [1,4]$ months, Fig.3 shows the contour of total maintenance cost. The global minimum occurs at $\Delta \approx 11.5$ months and $\omega \approx 1.5$ months, with the minimum total maintenance cost is 8912.57 ($). This interior solution demonstrates that allowing moderate inspection spacing combined with a sufficiently wide grouping window strikes the best balance between inspection overheads and failure-avoidance savings.

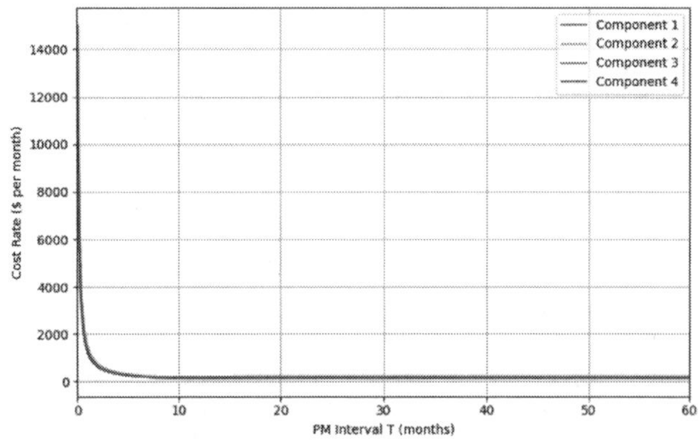

Fig. 2. Maintenance cost rate vs. PM interval.

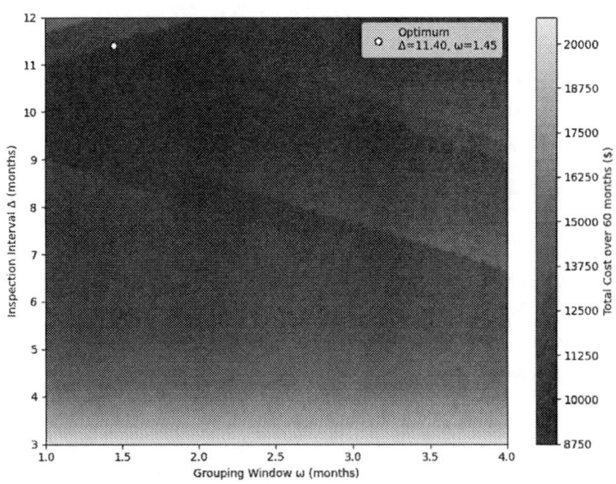

Fig. 3. Contour of total maintenance cost over 60 months.

4.3. Strategy comparison

We now compare our PHM-driven, grouping-based PM strategy (dynamic) against a conventional static calendar-based policy in which all four components are preventive-maintained every 12 months regardless of condition.

Table III. Dynamic grouping vs. static 12-month PM.

Metric	Dynamic Grouping Strategy	Static 12-Month Strategy
Inspection interval	11.5 months	12.0 months
Grouping window	1.5 months	—
Number of inspections	$\lceil 60/11.5 \rceil = 6$	$60/12 = 5$

Total maintenance cost ($)	8912.57	12000.00
Average cost rate ($/month)	8912.57/60 ≈ 148.54	12000/60 = 200.00

1. **Lifecycle cost reduction:** The dynamic strategy cuts total 5-year maintenance cost by 25.7%;
2. **Inspection efficiency improvement:** Although it schedules one extra inspection, grouping ensures only components whose age lies within 1.5 months of their individual optimal PM ages are serviced each time—avoiding unnecessary PMs.

Overall, by tailoring PM to real-time degradation and synchronizing components within a modest window, the dynamic grouping strategy delivers significant cost savings over a fixed-interval calendar policy, while preserving system reliability.

5. Conclusion

In this work, we developed a proportional hazards model-based global dynamic maintenance optimization for multi-component degradation system. By modeling component degradation through a proportional-hazards framework, we derived analytical reliability functions that inform maintenance decision-making.

Our key innovations include:

1. **Component-level optimization**: Estimation of optimal individual PM intervals based on the trade-off between preventive and corrective costs, rather than relying on fixed calendar schedules.
2. **Flexible grouping mechanism**: Introduction of a grouping window that allows components with similar residual lifetimes to be serviced together, amortizing setup overhead and reducing redundant downtime.
3. **System-level scheduling**: Joint selection of inspection interval and grouping window through a computationally efficient grid search, minimizing total maintenance cost over the planning horizon.

Application of this framework demonstrated substantial lifecycle cost savings and improved maintenance efficiency compared with a traditional static PM policy. Future work can extend this framework by incorporating multi-state degradation models, stochastic inspection effects, and real-world field validation in industrial settings.

6. Acknowledgement

This work is supported partially by National Natural Science Foundation of China (Grant No. 72101010), National Key Laboratory Foundation (Grant No. KZ42004001), Fundamental Research Funds for the Central Universities (Grant No. ZG216S21C3), and Basic Technical Research Project of China (Grant No. JSZL2018601B004).

7. References

[1] Shang L, Liu B, Qiu Q, et al. Three-dimensional warranty and post-warranty maintenance of products with monitored mission cycles, *Reliability Engineering & System Safety*, 2023, 239:109506.

[2] George Williams H, Patelli E. Maintenance strategy optimization for complex power systems susceptible to maintenance delays and operational dynamics, *IEEE Transactions on Reliability*, 2017, 66(4): 1309-1330.

[3] Wang J, Yang L, Ma X, et al. Joint optimization of multi-window maintenance and spare part provisioning policies for production systems, *Reliability Engineering & System Safety*, 2021, 216: 108006.

[4] Wang J, Tang L, Ma X, et al. Prognosis-driven reliability analysis and replacement policy optimization for two-phase continuous degradation, *Reliability Engineering & System Safety*, 2023, 230:108909.

[5] Shen J, Cui L, Ma Y. Availability and optimal maintenance policy for systems degrading in dynamic environments. *European Journal of Operational Research*, 2019, 276(1): 133-143.

[6] Zhou S, Ma X, Wang J, et al. Global-dynamic maintenance management of multi-component degrading plants with non-immediate replacement: a self-adaptive grouping approach, *Eksploatacja i Niezawodność – Maintenance and Reliability*, 2024. DOI: 10.17531/ein/193132.

[7] Yang L, Wei F, Qiu Q, et al. Controlling Mission Hazards through Integrated Abort and Spare Support Optimization, *Risk Analysis*, 2024, DOI: 10.1111/risa.17696.

[8] Wang L, Zhu Z, Zhao X. Dynamic predictive maintenance strategy for system remaining useful life prediction via deep learning ensemble method, *Reliability Engineering & System Safety*, 2024, 245: 110012.

[9] Wang L, Chen Y, Zhao X, et al. Predictive maintenance scheduling for aircraft engines based on remaining useful life prediction, *IEEE Internet of Things Journal*, 2024, 11(13), 23020-23031.

[10] Wang L, Li B, Zhao X. Multi-objective predictive maintenance scheduling models integrating remaining useful life prediction and maintenance decisions, *Computers & Industrial Engineering*, 2024, 197: 110581.

[11] Wang J, Wang L, Zhao X, et al. Optimization problems and maintenance policy for a parallel computing system with dependent components, *Annals of Operations Research*, 2024. DOI:10.1007/s10479-024-06065-7.

[12] Do P, Vu H C, Barros A, et al. Maintenance grouping for multi-component systems with availability constraints and limited maintenance teams, *Reliability Engineering & System Safety*, 2015, 142: 56-67.

[13] Yang L, Chen Y, Ma X. A State-age-dependent Opportunistic Intelligent Maintenance Framework for Wind Turbines Under Dynamic Wind Conditions, *IEEE Transactions on Industrial Informatics*, 2023, 19(10): 10434-10443.

[14] Chen Y, Ma X, Wei F, et al. Dynamic Scheduling of Intelligent Group Maintenance Planning under Usage Availability Constraint, *Mathematics*, 2022, 10 (15): 2730.

[15] Zhang Z, Yang L. Postponed maintenance scheduling integrating state variation and environmental impact, *Reliability Engineering & System Safety*, 2020, 202: 107065.

[16] Jia H, Peng R, Yang L, et al. Reliability evaluation of demand-based warm standby systems with capacity storage, *Reliability Engineering & System Safety*, 2022, 218: 108132.

[17] Wang J, Peng R, Qiu Q, et al. An inspection-based replacement planning in consideration of state-driven imperfect inspections, *Reliability Engineering & System Safety*, 2023, 232(6): 109064.

[18] Wang J, Ma X, Zhao Y, et al. Condition-based maintenance management for two-stage continuous deterioration with two-dimensional inspection errors, *Quality and Reliability Engineering International*, 2024, DOI: 10.1002/qre.3613.

[19] Yang L, Ye ZS, Lee CG, et al. A two-phase preventive maintenance policy considering imperfect repair and postponed replacement, *European Journal of Operational Research*, 2019, 274: 966-977.

[20] Vu H C, Do P, Barros A. A study on the impacts of maintenance duration on dynamic grouping modeling and optimization of multicomponent systems. *IEEE Transactions on Reliability*, 2018, 67(3): 1377-1392.

[21] Huynh KT, Grall A, Bérenguer C. A parametric predictive maintenance decision-making framework considering improved system health prognosis precision, *IEEE Transactions on Reliability*, 2018, 68(1): 375-396.

[22] Zhang Q, Hua C, Xu G. A mixture Weibull proportional hazard model for mechanical system failure prediction utilising lifetime and monitoring data, *Mechanical Systems & Signal Processing*, 2014, 43(1-2): 103-112.

[23] Liu B, Liang Z, Parlikad A K, et al. Condition-based maintenance for systems with aging and cumulative damage based on proportional hazards model, *Reliability Engineering & System Safety*, 2017, 168: 200-209.

[24] Zheng H, Kong X, Xu H, et al. Reliability analysis of products based on proportional hazard model with degradation trend and environmental factor, *Reliability Engineering & System Safety*, 2021, 216: 107964.

[25] Zheng R, Zhou Y, Gu L, et al. Joint optimization of lot sizing and condition-based maintenance for a production system using the proportional hazards model, *Computers & Industrial Engineering*, 2021, 154: 107157.

[26] Yang L, Chen Y, Ma X, et al. A Prognosis-centered Intelligent Maintenance Optimization Framework under Uncertain Failure Threshold, *IEEE Transactions on Reliability*, 2024, 73(1): 115-130.

[27] Zheng R, Chen B, Gu L. Condition-based maintenance with dynamic thresholds for a system using the proportional hazards model, *Reliability Engineering & System Safety*, 2020, 204: 107123.

[28] Man J, Zhou Q. Prediction of hard failures with stochastic degradation signals using Wiener process and proportional hazards model, *Computers & Industrial Engineering*, 2018, 125: 480-489.

[29] Hu J, Chen P. Predictive maintenance of systems subject to hard failure based on proportional hazards model, *Reliability Engineering & System Safety*, 2020, 196: 106707.

[30] Compare M, Baraldi P, Bani I, et al. Industrial equipment reliability estimation: A Bayesian Weibull regression model with covariate selection, *Reliability Engineering & System Safety*, 2020, 200: 106891.

[31] Duan C, Makis V, Deng C. An integrated framework for health measures prediction and optimal maintenance policy for mechanical systems using a proportional hazards model, *Mechanical Systems & Signal Processing*, 2018, 111: 285-302.

[32] Yang L, Wei F, Qiu Q. Mission Risk Control via Joint Optimization of Sampling and Abort Decisions, *Risk Analysis*, 2024, 44(3): 666-685.

[33] De Jonge B, Scarf P A. A review on maintenance optimization. *European journal of operational research*, 2020, 285(3): 805-824.

[34] Wei F, Tan L, Ma X, et al. A hybrid prognostic framework: Stochastic degradation process with adaptive trajectory learning to transfer historical health knowledge, *Mechanical System & Signal Processing*, 2025, 224: 112171.

[35] Yang L, Zhou S, Ma X, et al. Group machinery intelligent maintenance: Adaptive health prediction and global dynamic maintenance decision-making, *Reliability Engineering & System Safety*, 2024: 110426.

[36] Chen Y, Wu T, Ma X, et al. System Maintenance Optimization Under Structural Dependency: A Dynamic Grouping Approach, *IEEE Systems Journal*, 2024, 18(3): 1605-1616.

[37] Qiu Q, Liu B, Lin C, et al. Availability analysis and maintenance optimization for multiple failure mode systems considering imperfect repair, *Proceedings of the Institution of Mechanical Engineers, Part O: Journal of Risk and Reliability*, 2021, 235(6): 982-997.

[38] Yang L, Chen Y, Qiu Q, et al. Risk Control of Mission-Critical Systems: Abort Decision-Makings Integrating Health and Age Conditions, *IEEE Transactions on Industrial Informatics*, 2022, 18(10): 6887-6894.

[39] Papadopoulos P, Coit D W, Ezzat A A. Seizing Opportunity: Maintenance Optimization in Offshore Wind Farms Considering Accessibility, Production, and Crew Dispatch. *IEEE Transactions on Sustainable Energy*, 2021, 13(1): 111-121.

[40] Wang J, Ma X, Qiu Q, et al. A hybrid inspection-replacement policy for multi-stage degradation considering imperfect inspection with variable probabilities, *Reliability Engineering & System Safety*, 2023, 241: 109629.

[41] Zhang Z, Yang L. State-Based Opportunistic Maintenance with Multifunctional Maintenance Windows, *IEEE Transactions on Reliability*, 2021, 70(4): 1481-1494.

[42] Wu D, Han R, Ma Y, et al. A two-dimensional maintenance optimization framework balancing hazard risk and energy consumption rates, *IEEE Transactions on Reliability*, 2022, 169, 108193.

[43] Yang L, Zhao Y, Ma X. Multi-level maintenance strategy of deteriorating systems subject to two-stage inspection, *IEEE Transactions on Reliability*, 2022, 118:160-169.

[44] Chalabi N, Dahane M, Beldjilali B, et al. Optimisation of preventive maintenance grouping strategy for multi-component series systems: Particle swarm based approach, *Computers & Industrial Engineering*, 2016, 102: 440-451.

[45] Yang L, Li G, Zhang Z, et al. Operations & maintenance optimization of wind turbines integrating wind and aging information, *IEEE Transactions on Sustainable Energy*, 2021, 12(1): 211-221.

[46] Dong E, Cheng Z, Wang R. Two-dimensional extended warranty strategy for an economic dependence multi-component series system with grid search algorithm, *IEEE Access*, 2022, 10: 26876-26894.

[47] Yang L, Peng R, Li G, et al. Operations management of wind farms integrating multiple impacts of wind conditions and resource constraints, *Energy Conversion and Management*, 2020, 205: 112162.

Risk-aware task termination strategy for mission-critical systems with preventive inspection scheduling

MA Yuhan[1], WEI Fanping[1], QIU Qingan[2], YANG Li[1*]

[1]School of Reliability and Systems Engineering, Beihang University, Beijing, China
[2]School of Management, Beijing Institute of Technology, Beijing, China
mayuhan@buaa.edu.cn, WeiFP@buaa.edu.cn, qiu_qingan@bit.edu.cn, yanglirass@buaa.edu.cn

Keywords: Risk management, Abort strategy, Markov decision process, Security planning, Mission reliability.

Abstract –Modern safety-critical systems often face a critical trade-off between mission completion and failure prevention during mission execution. To address this challenge, this paper proposes a novel risk-aware decision-making strategy for systems governed by Gamma process degradation with an unknown scale parameter. The system performs a mission with fixed duration, undergoing periodic inspections at preventive intervals to assess the degradation level. The parameter estimation is continuously updated during mission execution via the maximum likelihood method. By formulating the problem as a finite-horizon Markov decision process, we derive a state-dependent control limit policy that achieves an optimal balance between operational risk and mission security. Theoretical analysis reveals state-dependent control limits associated with degradation levels that vary monotonically with the inspection phase. Numerical studies demonstrate the framework's applicability, providing a principled solution for preventive risk management in condition monitoring systems, ensuring both mission reliability and system safety.

1. Introduction

Safety-critical systems in aerospace, and energy equipment face severe consequences when failures occur during mission execution [1-4]. While preventive maintenance can improve reliability [5-9], it is often not feasible for time-sensitive operations where mission interruptions compromise mission objectives [10-14]. Mission termination policies are therefore an important safeguard, balancing mission completion with the potential failure risk through timely termination decisions [15-19].

Research on mission termination methodologies has progressed significantly, evolving from early studies of abrupt failures using discrete event counts as termination triggers [20-22] to modern degradation modeling through Wiener and Gamma processes [23-26]. In addition, the Markov Decision Process has become the main framework for optimizing sequential termination decisions [27-30]. Contemporary studies have further extended the task abort problem to complex scenarios involving multi-component systems and phased mission profiles, where adaptive policies must dynamically account for resource constraints and changing operating conditions [31-34].

The advent of high-precision sensor networks has enabled real-time degradation monitoring with unprecedented temporal resolution. Modern condition monitoring systems are now able to capture degradation signals at configurable sampling intervals, providing a rich data set for dynamic abort decisions [35-38]. While existing task abort studies often assume fixed inspection schedules, the optimization of these intervals remains largely unexplored, despite its significant impact on decision accuracy and operational costs [39-41]. Meanwhile, the current literature focuses on fixed degradation parameter settings, ignoring the important interplay between adaptive sensing and real-time decision making [42-44].

This paper proposes an integrated task termination framework that simultaneously solves the adaptive decision-making problems of inspection interval optimization, parameter estimation, and optimal task abort. The proposed method is oriented towards the Gamma degradation process with an unknown scale parameter, and utilizes maximum likelihood estimation to continuously update the unknown scale parameter based on real-time degradation measurements. By formulating the problem as a finite horizon Markov decision process, we derive an optimal control limit policy that adapts to both the changing system state and the progressively better parameter estimate. The framework uniquely incorporates inspection interval optimization at mission initialization, establishing a closed-loop relationship between inspection frequency and decision quality. Theoretical analysis characterized the structural properties of the optimal policy, while numerical simulations demonstrate the applicability of the optimal policy.

The main theoretical contributions can be summarized as follows:

1) The framework jointly optimizes the monitoring frequency and termination time to minimize fault-induced damage.

2) The maximum likelihood estimation is integrated with termination decision-making to address mission-critical issues in the degradation process with an unknown parameter.

3) Through a rigorous analysis of the MDP formulation, we prove that the optimal policy follows a state-dependent control limit structure.

2. Mission abort problem formulation

We consider a system executing a mission with a fixed duration of T_m. The system's degradation process $\{X(t), t \geq 0\}$

follows a Gamma process with the following characteristic: for any $s>0$, the increment $X(t+s)-X(t)$ follows a Gamma distribution $Ga(\alpha s,\beta)$, where α is the known shape parameter and β is the unknown scale parameter. System failure occurs immediately when the degradation level exceeds a predetermined failure threshold L.

The system is inspected at equally spaced intervals δ, where the total number of inspections M satisfies $(M-1)\delta < T_m \le M\delta$ and the last inspection occurs at moment T_m. Each inspection reveals the exact degradation level x_n. Since the parameter β is unknown, we employ maximum likelihood estimation (MLE) to update its value after each inspection n, i.e., the MLE estimate $\hat{\beta}_n$ after the n-th inspection is $\hat{\beta}_n = n\alpha\delta / x_n$.

Based on the independent increment property of Gamma process, the conditional distribution of the degradation level at the $(n+1)$-th inspection given the current state (n,x_n) follows:

$$f\left(X_{n+1}=x \mid X_n=x_n\right) = \frac{(n\alpha\delta)^{\alpha\delta}}{\Gamma(\alpha\delta)x_n}\left(\frac{x-x_n}{x_n}\right)^{\alpha\delta-1}\exp\left(-n\alpha\delta\frac{x-x_n}{x_n}\right) \tag{1}$$

where $\Gamma(m)=\int_0^\infty y^{m-1}e^{-y}dy$ is the Gamma function. Eq. (1) indicates that the future degradation state depends only on the current state (n,x_n). Thereby the degradation process of this system has Markovian property and the number of inspections n and the degradation level x_n form a discrete-time continuous state Markov chain with state space $\{(n,x_n) \mid n\in\{1,2,\cdots,M\}, x_n\in[0,L)\}$.

Thus, the transition probability density function from state (n,x_n) to $(n+1,x_{n+1})$ is given by:

$$\begin{aligned} f\left((n+1,x_{n+1}) \mid (n,x_n)\right) &= P\left(X_{n+1}=x_{n+1} \mid X_n=x_n\right) \\ &= \frac{(n\alpha\delta)^{\alpha\delta}}{\Gamma(\alpha\delta)x_n}\left(\frac{x_{n+1}-x_n}{x_n}\right)^{\alpha\delta-1}\exp\left(-n\alpha\delta\frac{x_{n+1}-x_n}{x_n}\right) \end{aligned} \tag{2}$$

And the probability of surviving until the next inspection, i.e., the system reliability, can be expressed as:

$$\begin{aligned} R(n,x_n) &= P\left(X_{n+1}<L \mid X_n=x_n\right) \\ &= \int_0^{L-x_n}\frac{\hat{\beta}_n^{\alpha\delta}}{\Gamma(\alpha\delta)}x^{\alpha\delta-1}e^{-\hat{\beta}_n x}dx \\ &= 1-\frac{\Gamma\left(\alpha\delta, n\alpha\delta(L-x_n)/x_n\right)}{\Gamma(\alpha\delta)} \end{aligned} \tag{3}$$

where $\Gamma(m,y)=\int_y^\infty z^{m-1}e^{-z}dz$ is the incomplete Gamma function.

The Markovian nature of the Gamma degradation process enables the mission abort problem to be rigorously formulated within the Markov decision process (MDP) framework. Let c_I, c_m and c_f denote the inspection cost, mission failure cost and system failure cost, respectively. At any inspection point, if the observed degradation level x_n surpassed L, the system is considered failed and incurs combined costs of c_m+c_f. When the observed degradation remains below than the threshold L, the decision-maker faces two alternatives: either abort the mission immediately with cost c_m, denoted as $A_\delta(n,x_n)=c_m$, or continue operation with expected cost:

$$\begin{aligned} C_\delta(n,x_n) &= E\left[V_\delta(n+1,X_{n+1}) \mid (n,x_n)\right] \\ &= c_I+(c_m+c_f)\left(1-R(n,x_n)\right)+ \\ &\int_{x_n}^{L} V_\delta(n+1,x_{n+1})f\left((n+1,x_{n+1}) \mid (n,x_n)\right)dx_{n+1} \end{aligned} \tag{4}$$

where the reliability function $R(n,x_n)$ can be obtained from Eq. (3), the state transition probability density function $f\left((n+1,x_{n+1}) \mid (n,x_n)\right)$ can be obtained from Eq. (2), and $V_\delta(n+1,x_{n+1})$ denotes the expected minimum cost at the next inspection moment.

The Bellman equation yields the minimum expected total cost when the system is in state (n,x_n):

$$V_\delta(n,x_n)=\begin{cases}\min\{C_\delta(n,x_n),A_\delta(n,x_n)\}, x_n<L \\ c_m+c_f, x_n\ge L\end{cases} \tag{5}$$

where $A_\delta(n,x_n)=c_m$ and $C_\delta(n,x_n)$ can be obtained from Eq. (4).

For boundary condition, if the system survives all inspections until mission completion, it can be rewarded with a value of R. Thus, the terminal value function is

$$V_\delta(M,x_M)=\begin{cases}-R, x_M<L \\ c_m+c_f, x_M\ge L\end{cases} \tag{6}$$

3. Structural properties

In this section, we investigate some structural properties of optimal mission abort policy. We start by proving monotonicity of the random variable X_{n+1}.

Lemma 1. The random variable X_{n+1} is stochastically non-decreasing in x_n, and stochastically non-increasing in n.

Proof. From Eq. (1), the predicted cumulative distribution function of the degradation level of the system for the next inspection X_{n+1} when given the state of the system for the n-th inspection is

$$P\left(X_{n+1}>x_{n+1} \mid X_n=x_n\right)=\frac{\Gamma\left(\alpha\delta, n\alpha\delta(x_{n+1}/x_n-1)\right)}{\Gamma(\alpha\delta)} \tag{7}$$

It is clear that $\Gamma(m,y)$ is a monotonically non-increasing function of y, and therefore Eq. (7) is monotonically non-decreasing on x_n. Thus, by the definition of random order [45], we have that X_{n+1} is stochastically non-decreasing in x_n.

Similarly, we can show that X_{n+1} is stochastically non-increasing with respect to n. □

Theorem 1. For a given δ, the optimal value function $V_\delta(n,x_n)$

is a non-decreasing function of x_n, and a non-increasing function of *n*.

Proof. The monotonic properties of the value function are established through recursive algorithm. Lemma 1 establishes that the random variable X_{n+1} is stochastically non-decreasing in x_n, which forms the basis for our proof.

Obviously, the terminal value function $V_\delta(M, x_M)$ satisfies the monotonicity property. Assuming that $V_\delta(n, x_n)$ is non-decreasing in x_n for any $n < M$. Then for $x < \tilde{x} < L$, we have

$$\begin{aligned} V_\delta(n-1,x) &= \min\{C_\delta(n-1,x), A_\delta(n-1,x)\} \\ &= \min\{E[V_\delta(n,X_n)|(n-1,x)], c_m\} \\ &\le \min\{E[V_\delta(n,X_n)|(n-1,\tilde{x})], c_m\} \\ &= V_\delta(n-1,\tilde{x}) \end{aligned} \tag{8}$$

Thus the non-decreasing property of $V_\delta(n-1, x_{n-1})$ with respect to x_{n-1} is still satisfied. By a recursive process one can propagate forward to all inspection stages, i.e., for any $n \le M$, $V_\delta(n, x_n)$ is a non-decreasing function with respect to x_n.

Regarding the monotonicity of the number of inspections *n*, we can obtain that $V_\delta(n, x_n)$ is a non-increasing function with respect to *n* by using the same recursive method. □

Theorem 2. For a given δ, the optimal mission abort policy is a control limit policy. Specifically, at each inspection moment *n*, there exists a threshold $\xi_\delta(n)$ such that, for $x_n > \xi_\delta(n)$, the optimal action is to abort the mission, otherwise, the optimal is to continue the mission. And the control limit $\xi_\delta(n)$ is non-decreasing with *n*.

Proof. Lemma 1 proves that for a given δ, $V_\delta(n, x_n)$ is non-decreasing in x_n, and hence $C_\delta(n, x_n)$ is non-decreasing in x_n as well. Since the cost function of aborting the mission is constant, i.e., $A_\delta(n, x_n) = c_m$, we have that the cost function $C_\delta(n, x_n) - A_\delta(n, x_n)$ remains non-decreasing about x_n. This means that for any two degradation states $x < \tilde{x} < L$, we have

$$C_\delta(n,x) - A_\delta(n,x) \le C_\delta(n,\tilde{x}) - A_\delta(n,\tilde{x}) \tag{9}$$

Thus, for a given δ, at the *n*-th inspection moment, there exists a control limit $\xi_\delta(n)$ such that, when $x_n < \xi_\delta(n)$, it satisfies $C_\delta(n, x_n) - A_\delta(n, x_n) \le 0$, i.e., the optimal action is to continue the mission, and when $x_n > \xi_\delta(n)$, the optimal action at this point is to abort the mission.

Next prove the monotonicity property of the control limit $\xi_\delta(n)$ with respect to *n*. At the *n*-th inspection moment we have $C_\delta(n, \xi_\delta(n)) = A_\delta(n, \xi_\delta(n))$. By Lemma 1 we have that $C_\delta(n, x_n)$ is non-increasing with respect to *n*. Thus, for any $i < n$ we have

$$\begin{aligned} C_\delta(i,\xi_\delta(n)) &\ge C_\delta(n,\xi_\delta(n)) \\ &= A_\delta(n,\xi_\delta(n)) = C_\delta(i,\xi_\delta(i)) \end{aligned} \tag{10}$$

i.e., $C_\delta(i,\xi_\delta(n)) \ge C_\delta(i,\xi_\delta(i))$, and given that $C_\delta(n, x_n)$ is monotonically non-decreasing with respect to x_n, we have $\xi_\delta(n) \ge \xi_\delta(i)$, i.e., the control restriction $\xi_\delta(n)$ is non-decreasing with respect to *n*. □

Theorem 2 shows that the optimal mission abort policy follows a control-limit structure, where at each inspection stage *n*, there exists a critical threshold $\xi_\delta(n)$ such that continuation is optimal when $x_n < \xi_\delta(n)$, while abort becomes optimal when $x_n > \xi_\delta(n)$. This threshold exists because higher degradation increases near-term failure risk, justifying termination to avoid severe penalties. Moreover, the threshold $\xi_\delta(n)$ exhibits a non-decreasing trend as *n* increases, as fewer remaining inspections reduce the accumulated failure risk, allowing for more lenient degradation limits later in the mission.

To minimize the total expected cost, the inspection interval δ can be optimized. For any fixed inspection interval δ, the value iteration algorithm can compute the corresponding optimal value function. Subsequently, the optimal inspection interval δ^* can be determined using derivative free search techniques [46]:

$$\delta^* = \arg\min_{\delta} V_\delta(0,0) \tag{11}$$

4. Numerical examples

To validate the theoretical results, we conduct numerical experiments using a Gamma degradation with shape parameter $\alpha = 0.75$. The duration of the mission is set at 10 days, denoted as $T_m = 10$. Cost parameters are configured as follows: inspection cost $c_I = 2$, mission failure penalty $c_m = 400$, and system failure cost $c_f = 1000$.

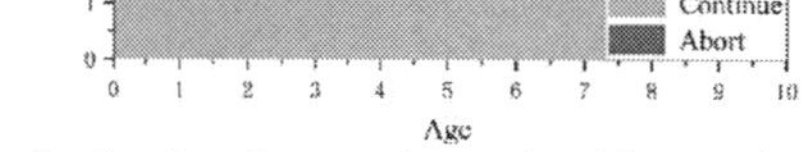

Figure 1. Optimal actions under optimal inspection interval

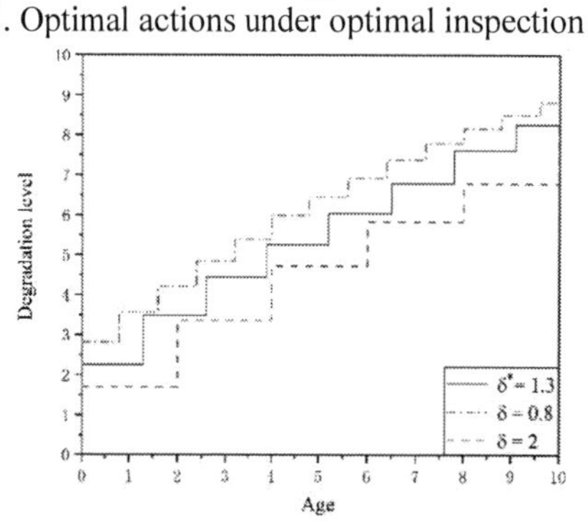

Figure 2. Optimal actions under different values of δ

Figure 1 demonstrates the control-limit policy's key features. The optimal action switches from continuation to abort when degradation exceeds the optimal threshold $\xi_\delta(n)$. The threshold increases with inspection count n, as fewer remaining periods reduce failure risk exposure. Early stages maintain stricter thresholds to mitigate long-term risks, while later phases tolerate higher degradation levels. This is the same conclusion as theorems we obtained above.

Figure 2 illustrates the control-limit policy under different inspection intervals δ. The results confirm the threshold structure where mission abort becomes optimal when degradation exceeds the state-dependent limit $\xi_\delta(n)$. The threshold exhibits increasing trends with mission progress due to diminishing failure risks. Notably, sub-optimal intervals affect policy conservatism: longer intervals yield lower thresholds for safety, while frequent inspections allow higher tolerance due to better monitoring.

5. Conclusion

This paper investigates the optimal mission abort policy for systems subject to the degradation of Gamma process with an unknown scale parameter. By formulating the problem within the framework of a Markov decision process, we develop an adaptive control limit strategy that integrates parameter maximum likelihood estimation with real-time decision making. The proposed approach uniquely optimizes both the inspection interval and abort threshold while taking into account parameter uncertainty. Theoretical analysis shows that the optimal policy exhibits a monotonic threshold structure that depends on the observed degradation level and the system operating time. Numerical experiments demonstrate the feasibility of the optimal policy in a variety of situations. Future research directions could consider extending the framework to online parameter learning based on Bayesian learning or multi-stage mission environments.

6. Acknowledgement

Funding: The authors gratefully acknowledge that funding for this work was provided by Basic Technical Research Project of China under Grant JSZL2018601B004.

7. References

[1] Yang L, Zhou S, Ma X, et al. Group machinery intelligent maintenance: Adaptive health prediction and global dynamic maintenance decision-making, Reliability Engineering & System Safety, 2024: 110426.

[2] Chen Y, Ma X, Wei F, et al. Dynamic Scheduling of Intelligent Group Maintenance Planning under Usage Availability Constraint, Mathematics, 2022, 10 (15): 2730.

[3] Wang J, Ma X, Qiu Q, et al. A hybrid inspection-replacement policy for multi-stage degradation considering imperfect inspection with variable probabilities, Reliability Engineering & System Safety, 2023, 241: 109629.

[4] Wu D, Han R, Ma Y, et al. A two-dimensional maintenance optimization framework balancing hazard risk and energy consumption rates, Computers & Industrial Engineering, 2022, 169, 108193.

[5] Yang L, Wei F, Qiu Q, et al. Controlling Mission Hazards through Integrated Abort and Spare Support Optimization, Risk Analysis, 2024, DOI: 10.1111/risa.17696.

[6] Qiu Q, Li R, Zhao X. Failure risk management: adaptive performance control and mission abort decisions. Risk Analysis, 2025, 45(2), 421-440.

[7] Zhao X, Sun J, Qiu Q, Chen K. Optimal inspection and mission abort policies for systems subject to degradation. European Journal of Operational Research, 2021, 292(2): 610-621.

[8] Yang L, Wei F, Qiu Q. Mission Risk Control via Joint Optimization of Sampling and Abort Decisions, Risk Analysis, 2024, 44(3): 666-685.

[9] Kim M J, Makis V. Joint optimization of sampling and control of partially observable failing systems, Operations Research, 2013, 61(3) : 777-790.

[10] Shang L, Liu B, Qiu Q, et al. Three-dimensional warranty and post-warranty maintenance of products with monitored mission cycles, Reliability Engineering & System Safety, 2023, 239:109506.

[11] Chen Y, Wu T, Ma X, et al. System Maintenance Optimization Under Structural Dependency: A Dynamic Grouping Approach, IEEE Systems Journal, 2024, 18(3): 1605-1616.

[12] Yang L, Zhao Y, Ma X. Multi-level maintenance strategy of deteriorating systems subject to two-stage inspection, Computers & Industrial Engineering, 2022, 118:160-169.

[13] Zhang Z, Yang L. State-Based Opportunistic Maintenance with Multifunctional Maintenance Windows, IEEE Transactions on Reliability, 2021, 70(4): 1481-1494.

[14] Wang J, Yang L, Ma X, et al. Joint optimization of multi-window maintenance and spare part provisioning policies for production systems, Reliability Engineering & System Safety, 2021, 216: 108006.

[15] Qiu Q, Kou M, Chen K, Deng Q, Lin C. Optimal stopping problems for mission oriented systems considering time redundancy, Reliability Engineering & System Safety, 2021, 205: 107226.

[16] Zhao X, Wang X, Dai Y, et al. Joint optimization of loading, mission abort and rescue site selection policies for UAV. Reliability Engineering & System Safety, 2024, 244: 109955.

[17] Levitin G, Xing L, Dai Y. Expected losses minimization in missions with multi-phase rescue procedure, Reliability Engineering and System Safety,2025, 256: 110780.

[18] Yang L, Peng R, Li G, Lee CG. Operations management of wind farms integrating multiple impacts of wind conditions and resource constraints, Energy Conversion and Management, 2020, 205: 112162.

[19] Jia H, Peng R, Yang L, et al. Reliability evaluation of demand-based warm standby systems with capacity

storage, Reliability Engineering & System Safety, 2022, 218: 108132.

[20] Zhao X, Fan Y, Qiu Q, Chen K. Multi-criteria mission abort policy for systems subject to two-stage degradation process. European Journal of Operational Research, 2021, 295:233-245.

[21] Qiu Q, Cui L. Optimal mission abort policy for systems subject to random shocks based on virtual age process. Reliability Engineering & System Safety, 2019, 189: 11-20.

[22] Zhao X, Li Rong, Chao S, Qiu Q. Joint optimization of loading and mission abort policies for production systems operating in dynamic environments. Reliability Engineering & System Safety,2023,108948.

[23] Yang L, Chen Y, Qiu Q, et al. Risk Control of Mission-Critical Systems: Abort Decision-Makings Integrating Health and Age Conditions, IEEE Transactions on Industrial Informatics, 2022, 18(10): 6887-6894.

[24] Wang J, Tang L, Ma X, et al. Prognosis-driven reliability analysis and replacement policy optimization for two-phase continuous degradation, Reliability Engineering & System Safety, 2023, 230:108909.

[25] Qiu Q, Cui L. Gamma process based optimal mission abort policy. Reliability Engineering & System Safety, 2019, 190: 106496.

[26] Ma X, Liu B, Yang L, et al. Reliability analysis and condition-based maintenance optimization for a warm standby cooling system, Reliability Engineering & System Safety, 2020, 193: 106588.

[27] Yang, L., Ma, Y., Wei, F., Qiu, Q. Optimal Condition-based Parameter Learning and Mission Abort Decisions. Naval Research Logistics, 2024, DOI: 10.1002/nav.22225.

[28] Levitin G, Xing L, Dai Y. Optimal attempt scheduling and aborting in heterogenous system performing asynchronous multi-attempt mission, Reliability Engineering and System Safety, 2024, 251: 110335.

[29] Qiu Q, Maillart L M, Prokopyev O A, et al. Optimal condition-based mission abort decisions. IEEE Transactions on Reliability, 2023, 72(1): 408-425.

[30] Yang L, Sun Q, Ye Z. Designing mission abort strategies based on early-warning information: Application to UAV, IEEE Transactions on Industrial Informatics, 2020, 16 (1): 277-287.

[31] Wei F, Wang J, Ma X, et al. An Optimal Opportunistic Maintenance Planning Integrating Discrete- and Continuous-State Information, Mathematics, 2023, 11(15): 3322.

[32] Zhao X, Lv Z, Wu Y, Qiu Q. Optimal abort and selective replacement policies for multi-attempt missions. Reliability Engineering & System Safety,2023,109119.

[33] Qiu Q, Cui L, Wu B. Dynamic mission abort policy for systems operating in a controllable environment with self-healing mechanism. Reliability Engineering & System Safety, 2020, 203: 107069.

[34] Zhao X, Liu H, Wu Y, Qiu Q. Joint optimization of mission abort and system structure considering dynamic tasks. Reliability Engineering & System Safety, 2023, 109128.

[35] Wei F, Tan L, Ma X, et al. A hybrid prognostic framework: Stochastic degradation process with adaptive trajectory learning to transfer historical health knowledge, Mechanical System & Signal Processing, 2025, 224: 112171.

[36] Yang L, Ye ZS, Lee CG, et al. A two-phase preventive maintenance policy considering imperfect repair and postponed replacement, European Journal of Operational Research, 2019, 274: 966-977.

[37] Wang J, Ma X, Zhao Y, et al. Condition-based maintenance management for two-stage continuous deterioration with two-dimensional inspection errors, Quality and Reliability Engineering International, 2024, DOI: 10.1002/qre.3613.

[38] Shang L, Liu B, Gao K, et al. Random Warranty and Replacement Models Customizing from the Perspective of Heterogeneity, Mathematics, 2023, 11(15): 3330.

[39] Cha J H, Finkelstein M, Levitin G. Optimal mission abort policy for partially repairable heterogeneous systems, European Journal of Operational Research, 2018, 271(3), 818–825.

[40] Zhang Z, Yang L. Postponed maintenance scheduling integrating state variation and environmental impact, Reliability Engineering & System Safety, 2020, 202: 107065.

[41] Zhao X, Chai X, Sun J, Qiu Q. Joint optimization of mission abort and component switching policies for multistate warm standby systems. Reliability Engineering & System Safety, 2021, 212: 107641.

[42] Qu L, Liao J, Gao K, et al. Joint Optimization of Production Lot Sizing and Preventive Maintenance Threshold Based on Nonlinear Degradation, Applied Sciences, 2022, 12(17): 8638.

[43] Wang J, Peng R, Qiu Q, et al. An inspection-based replacement planning in consideration of state-driven imperfect inspections, Reliability Engineering & System Safety, 2023, 232(6): 109064.

[44] Qiu Q, Cui L, Yang L. Maintenance Policies for Energy System Subject to Complex Failure Processes and Power Purchasing Agreement. Computers & Industrial Engineering, 2018, 119: 193-203.

[45] Shaked M, Shanthikumar J G. Stochastic orders. New York, NY: Springer New York, 2007.

[46] Chen N, Ye ZS, Xiang Y, et al. Condition-based maintenance using the inverse Gaussian degradation model. European Journal of Operational Research, 2015, 243(1): 190-199.

Research on Geometric Model Construction and Operating Feature Recognition Technology of Switchgear

X Kui[1], L Xin[2], C Peilong[3], Z Shijian[4], D Qichen[5]

[1]Guizhou Power Grid Co., Ltd. Electric Power Science Research Institute, China, 269536174@qq.com
[2]Guizhou Power Grid Co., Ltd. Electric Power Science Research Institute, No. 32 Jiefang Road, Nanming District, Guiyang City, Guizhou Province, China
[3]Guizhou Power Grid Co., Ltd. Electric Power Science Research Institute, No. 32 Jiefang Road, Nanming District, Guiyang City, Guizhou Province, China
[4]Guizhou Power Grid Co., Ltd. Electric Power Science Research Institute, No. 32 Jiefang Road, Nanming District, Guiyang City, Guizhou Province, China
[5]Guizhou Power Grid Co., Ltd. Electric Power Science Research Institute, No. 32 Jiefang Road, Nanming District, Guiyang City, Guizhou Province, China

Keywords: geometric model, humid air diffusion, operating characteristics, heat transfer model

Abstract - Substations play a crucial role in the power system, providing powerful technology and support for power transmission, distribution, and supply networks. This article constructs a geometric model by analyzing the internal structure and heating elements of the air switchgear. Based on the diffusion process of humid air from the cable trench to the switchgear, a heat transfer model for the switchgear is studied and established to predict its operating characteristics under different environmental conditions. This provides theoretical basis and practical guidance for the reliable operation and maintenance of air switchgear in substations.

1. Introduction

As indispensable and important equipment in the power system, the operation status of substations directly affects the safety and stability of the entire power system. With the continuous growth of electricity demand and the increasing complexity of the power system, the performance requirements for the most commonly used air switchgear in the power grid are also becoming higher and higher. However, the switchgear contains numerous heating elements such as conductors, joints, and contact points, which can cause temperature rise during operation due to factors such as resistance loss, eddy current loss, and hysteresis loss, thereby affecting the performance of equipment operation [1]. Therefore, studying and analyzing the temperature distribution inside the switchgear is of great significance for optimizing equipment design and improving operational efficiency.

In recent years, with the rapid development of computer technology and numerical simulation methods, the study of heat transfer in switchgear based on numerical simulation has gradually become a hot topic. By establishing accurate geometric models and heat transfer models, it is possible to effectively predict and analyze the temperature distribution and heat transfer process inside the switchgear. However, due to the complex internal structure of the switchgear, there are numerous small components and gaps. How to simplify the model reasonably and accurately reflect the actual working conditions is still a challenge.

This article constructs a geometric model by analyzing the internal structure and heating elements of the air switchgear. Based on the diffusion process of humid air from the cable trench to the switchgear, a heat transfer model for the switchgear is studied and established to predict its operating characteristics under different environmental conditions. This provides theoretical basis and practical guidance for the reliable operation and maintenance of air switchgear in substations.

2. Analysis of Structure and Heating Elements

The switchgear studied in this project is structurally complex and functionally clear electrical equipment, mainly composed of four core parts: bus-bar room, relay instrument room, cable room, and (relay) handcart room [2]. The overall three-dimensional structure is shown in Figure 1, with moderate dimensions of 1500 millimeters in length, 800 millimeters in width, and 2360 millimeters in height. This design not only meets the reasonable layout requirements of internal components, but also facilitates daily maintenance and management.

There are multiple heating elements inside the switchgear, including cables, bus-bars, branch bus-bars, contacts, and contact arms, which generate significant heat during equipment operation. In order to accurately evaluate the impact of these heating elements on the temperature distribution inside the switchgear, detailed modeling analysis is required.

Before modeling, the heating elements inside the switchgear were first sorted and calculated. The total heat generated by the contact and the contact arm is 240 watts, of which the heat generated by the contact head is 84 watts and the heat generated by the contact arm is 156 watts. The main bus-bar ABC has a heating capacity of 20 watts per line, with a total of 3 lines and a total of 60 watts; Each branch bus-bar ABC has a heating capacity of 10 watts, with a total of 3, totaling 30 watts; Each cable A, B, and C has a heating capacity of 20 watts, with a total of 3 cables and a total of 60 watts. The heat dissipation of these heating elements will directly affect the temperature field distribution inside the switchgear.

In terms of material settings, suitable materials were selected based on the functional requirements and operating environment of each component. Copper materials are used for conductive components such as bus-bars, branch bus-bars, contacts, handcart arms, and cables [3], while epoxy resin materials are used for insulation sleeves, contact boxes, current transformers, and handcart bases [4]. The cabinet shell is made of galvanized steel plate to ensure the durability and anti-corrosion performance of the equipment [5].

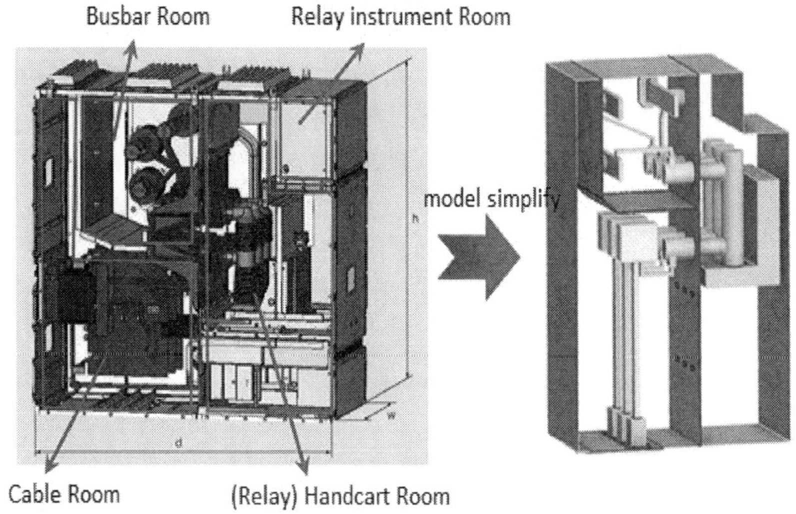

Figure 1. Simplified schematic diagram of switchgear structure

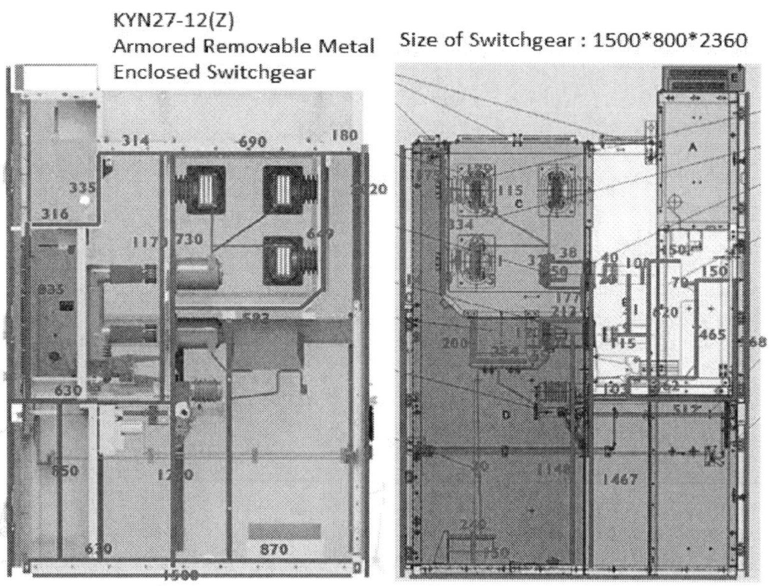

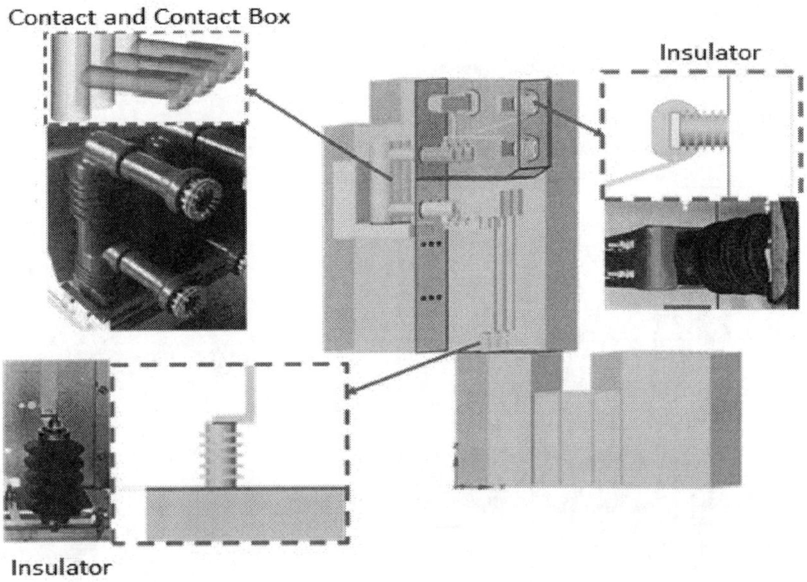

Figure 2. Internal structure and component structure of KYN27-12 (Z) switchgear

3. Geometric model construction

During the modeling process, it was considered that the switchgear contains numerous components and there are many small elements and gaps, but these small structures have little impact on the flow, heat transfer, and component transport processes inside the switchgear. Therefore, reasonable neglect was made during the modeling process. This study mainly focuses on components and structures that have a significant impact on heat transfer and fluid flow.

In order to facilitate calculations and improve computational efficiency, we have simplified the geometric structure of actual components to a certain extent. For example, simplifying irregular component shapes into regular geometries such as rectangular prisms, cylinders, etc. At the same time, we also considered the relative positions and connection methods between components to ensure the accuracy of the model. This simplification method not only reduces computational complexity, but also preserves the key features of the model, providing a reliable foundation for subsequent heat transfer analysis.

4. Modeling of Wet Air Diffusion Process

Specifically, the diffusion process of humid air from the cable trench to the switchgear was also considered during the modeling process (as shown in Figure 3). The cable trench was included in the model, and a narrow slit was set between the bottom of the cable compartment and the cable trench to simulate the diffusion of humid air from the slit into the cable compartment, thereby affecting the temperature and humidity environment inside the switchgear.

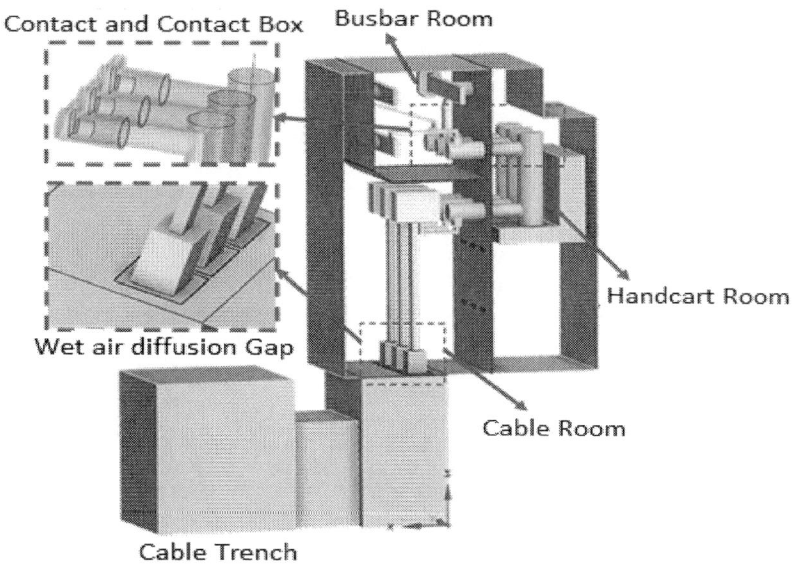

Figure 3. Wet air diffuses towards the switchgear through a narrow slit

The modeling of this process is crucial for accurately predicting the temperature and humidity distribution inside the switchgear. The diffusion of humid air not only affects the temperature field inside the switchgear, but may also cause condensation and other problems [6], thereby affecting the insulation performance and operational safety of the equipment. Therefore, we have carefully considered the diffusion path and rate of humid air in the model, as well as its impact on the internal environment of the switchgear.

By incorporating cable trenches and humid air diffusion processes into the model, we can more comprehensively simulate the actual operating environment of switchgear. This not only improves the accuracy of the model, but also provides the possibility for analyzing the operating characteristics of switchgear under different environmental conditions. For example, in the high humidity environment of Southwest China, the temperature and humidity changes of switchgear and other equipment can be evaluated for their impact on equipment performance, providing valuable references for the operation and maintenance of power grid equipment.

5. Model Validation and Application

This model validation comprehensively considers factors such as resistance loss, eddy current loss, and dielectric loss to simulate the temperature field distribution inside the switchgear. Research has shown that resistance loss is the main source of heat, especially in medium voltage switchgear where dielectric loss is relatively small and can be ignored [7]. In addition, eddy current losses account for a relatively high proportion of the total losses in switchgear, especially at the contact blades, where their impact is particularly significant. Therefore, optimization of eddy current losses should be emphasized in design [8].

By applying 1.5 times the current to the switchgear and waiting for the temperature rise to reach a steady state, the temperature at key measuring points was measured and compared with the predicted temperature by the model simulation. The comparison results are shown in Table 1.

Table 1. Experimental and Predicted Temperature Rise

Temperature Measurement Location	Predict Temperature Rise ℃	Experimental Temperature Rise ℃
Contact	35.5	36.3
Contact arms	35.3	37.3
Bus-bars	33.8	35.4
Branch Bus-bars	34.9	36
Cables	30.9	31.7

According to the experimental and predicted temperature rise tables, there is a difference between the predicted and actual experimental temperature rise values. The experimental temperature rise value is higher than the predicted temperature rise value, mainly because the actual contact resistance will change under the influence of temperature rise. During the prediction process, a large number of simplifications will be made inside the switchgear, which is different from the complex structure and heat dissipation inside the switchgear. In addition, the boundary conditions set are also different from the actual situation. Therefore, the predicted temperature results are different from the actual situation, but the error is also within an acceptable range. This indicates that the predicted and experimental results are basically consistent, and the heat transfer model can accurately predict the temperature rise of the switchgear under different working conditions.

6. Conclusion

This article analyzes the impact of the heat emitted by the heating elements inside the air switch cabinet on the temperature distribution inside the switch, and establishes an accurate and efficient heat transfer model for the switch cabinet by combining geometric models and modeling of the diffusion process of humid air. This model provides powerful guidance for the heat transfer analysis of switchgear, which can be used to optimize equipment design, predict operating characteristics, and improve operational safety. The research results indicate that considering the diffusion process of humid air is crucial for accurately predicting the temperature and humidity distribution inside the switchgear. This discovery provides new ideas for the design, operation, and maintenance of switchgear.

In addition, the modeling method presented in this article has universal applicability and can provide certain reference value for heat transfer modeling of other electrical equipment. Future research can further consider more influencing factors, such as air flow, radiative heat transfer, etc., to improve the accuracy and applicability of the model. Finally, by combining the research model with an intelligent monitoring system, real-time evaluation and prediction of the operation status of switchgear can be achieved, providing stronger guarantees for the safe and stable operation of the power system.

7. References

[1] S. Yi, L. Da jian, Z. Wei, and et al. "Analysis of Internal Heat Transfer Characteristics of High Voltage Switchgear Heating Fault," Guangxi Electric Power, vol. 44, no. 6, pp: 0064-0070, 2021.

[2] H. Xia, "Research on the Application of Electrical Installation Construction Technology in Construction Engineering," China Kitchen and Bath, vol. 23, no. 7, pp: 0061-0063, 2024.

[3] R. Zu cun, "Systematic Design and Manufacturing of High and Low Voltage Switchgear Equipment," Electrical Industry, no. 6, pp: 0022-0027, 2024.

[4] L. Jin, K. Xiaoxiao, D. Boxue, "Research progress on curing system regulation of insulation properties of bisphenol A epoxy resin/anhydride system," Journal of Electrical Engineering, vol. 19, no. 1, pp: 0358-0370, 2024.

[5] C. Wei, J. Xiaoyu, Z. Ziqiang, and et al. "Research on Salt Spray Corrosion Behavior and Mechanism of Hot Dip Galvanized Steel," Journal of Shaanxi University of Science and Technology, vol. 39, no. 4, pp: 0130-0135, 2021.

[6] R. Shuangzan, X. Jian, W. Hao, and et al. "Simulation study on temperature and humidity distribution of three-dimensional switchgear based on electromagnetic temperature humidity coupling," Smart Power, vol. 47, no. 9, pp: 0081-0085, 2019.

[7] S. Tao, Z. Lihua, L. Chen, and et al. "Research on temperature rise characteristics under contact fault of plum blossom contacts in medium voltage switchgear," High Voltage Apparatus, vol. 59, no. 5, pp: 0130-0138, 2023.

[8] W. Rui, W. Lijun, M. Xinyou, and et al. "Modeling and simulation study on temperature rise and its influencing factors of high current switchgear," High Voltage Apparatus, vol. 58, no. 5, pp: 0031-0040, 2022.

Optimal Checkpoint for Hardwareized Artificial Neural Networks

Kenichiro Naruse[1], Toshio Nakagawa[2]
[1]Faculty of Management & Information Sciences, Josai International University, Chiba, Japan, knaruse@jiu.ac.jp
[2]Department of Business Administration, Aichi Institute of Technology, Aichi, Japan, toshi-nakagawa@aitech.ac.jp

Keywords: Neural Networks, Reliability, Constant Task, Series System

Abstract - We propose artificial neural network(ANN) evaluation and checkpointing model with considering computing units reliability. ANN is an important essence of artificial intelligence. ANN builds up from several computing units like a neuron. If the computing unit in ANN occurs some error due to noises, hardware failure and so on, it will output some wrong result. To prevent such a matter, we need to make chekcpoint and recovery. Therefore, when we cannot make the error, we ignore some computing units, because all computing units need to work to output the result. We focus that the ANN doesn't need to work every computing unit depending on ANN weight and threshold. In this paper, we consider ANN computing units checkpoint model with all computing units working. Moreover we consider that resist some computing units faults depending on ANN weight and threshold.

1. Introduction

The concept of artificial intelligence has been devised, allowing computers to make judgments and give appropriate answers as if they had intelligence. In the past, attempts were made to make systems behave intelligently by accumulating information, such as with expert systems. However, computers at the time were unable to handle large amounts of information and data entry became a bottleneck, it is leading to failure. However, recently, artificial intelligence devised based on human neural networks seems to be working well, that's called an artificial neural network(ANN) [1–4]. Advances in artificial intelligence include using content on the Internet for data input, higher-performance CPUs, and higher capacity and lower prices for data storage. Furthermore, recent CPUs are equipped with neural processing units [5].

We explain supervised learning using neural networks(fig. 1). General or complex ANNs are implemented on a computer using programming. However, to use an ANN that specializes in a certain function, we consider using computational units connected by wires. In this paper, we consider the reliability of hardwareized ANN. We consider some damages to hardwareized ANN from these failures can be protected from failures by equipment redundancies and backup data [6–11].

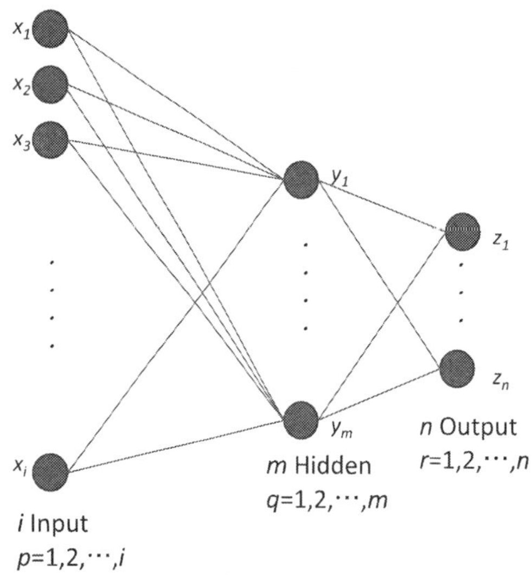

Figure 1: Neural network system

2. System Model

In a hardwareized ANN, an ANN is made by a number of cariculation units and it occurs failure by electrical noise, heating and so on. It might become faulty and lead to the wrong answer. ANN is made from input, hidden and output layers in Fig. 1.

We assume the ANN parameters as follows:(this variable definition cite from [3])

x_i is input to the i-th neuron in the input layer,

y_j is output from the j-th neuron in the hidden layer,

z_k is output from the k-th neuron in the output layer,

$w_p^{H_q}$ is weight from x_p to y_q $(p=1,2,\cdots i, q=1,2,\cdots,m)$,

$w_q^{O_r}$ is weight from y_q to z_r $(q=1,2,\cdots m, r=1,2,\cdots,n)$,

θ^{H_q} is threshold of hidden layer y_q $(q=1,2,\cdots m)$,

θ^{O_r} is threshold of output layer z_r $(r=1,2,\cdots n)$.

ANN learning method [3,4] are

1. A lot of data is prepared for learning and the correct answer.

2. Substitute the data and answer for x_p, y_q and z_r as simultaneous equations,

$$y_q = \sigma\left[\left(\sum_{q=1}^{i} w_p^{H_q} x_p\right) - \theta^{H_q}\right] \qquad (q = 1 \cdots m), \quad (1)$$

$$z_r = \sigma\left[\left(\sum_{r=1}^{j} w_q^{O_r} y_q\right) - \theta^{O_r}\right] \qquad (r = 1 \cdots n), \quad (2)$$

where $\sigma(x)$ is sigmoid function [3,4] given by

$$\sigma(x) = \frac{1}{1 + \mathrm{e}^{-x}}. \quad (3)$$

3. Solve the simultaneous equations for $w_p^{H_q}$, $w_q^{O_r}$, θ^{H_q} and θ^{O_r} in approximate, therefore the parameter values are desided for threshold and weight value.

Assuming that when the hardwareized ANN occurs any failure, it can recover from failure with a restart and reexecute from the first process.

3. Performance Analysis

Suppose that we have to execute a task with constant execution time $S(0 < S < \infty)$ of the process which does not include any overhead times, for example retryal and self-checking time. Then, we divide S equally into $N(N = 1, 2, \cdots)$ parts and create a selfcheck point at planned times $mT(m = 1, 2, \cdots N)$ where $S = NT$

To detect errors, we first provide self-checking neuron unit. When the self-checking neuron unit judges some errors have occurred, then the system needs a rollback operation to the newest checkpoint and a retry of the processes. The process completes when the process succeeds in all intervals.

Introducing a constant overhead C for the self-checking time, and it is assumed that some errors of one neuron unit occur at constant rate λ. i.e., the probability that any errors do not occur during $(0, t]$ is given by $\mathrm{e}^{-\lambda t}$. Thus, the probability of selfcheking with no error during $(0, t]$ is $\overline{F}(T) = \mathrm{e}^{-\lambda t}$ [12].

The mean execution time $L(q)$ of the process for one checkpoint interval $(0, T]$ is given by renewal equation:

$$L_1(1) = (T + C_1)\overline{F}(T) + [T + C_1 + L_1(1)]\, F(T), \quad (4)$$

and solving it,

$$L_1(1) = \frac{T + C_1}{\overline{F}(T)}. \quad (5)$$

Thus, the mean time to completing the process is

$$L_1(N) \equiv N L_1(1) = \frac{N\,(T + C_1)}{\overline{F}(T)}. \quad (6)$$

3.1 Series Model

Assuming that ANN is made from a number of $h = i+m+n(h > 0)$ neurons, and it needs all neurons to work without failure in one task. We assume that hardwareized neuron occurs some errors of one process at constant rate λ, i.e., the probability that any errors do not occur during $(0, t]$ is given by $\mathrm{e}^{-\lambda t}$ in a neuron. Thus, the probability that all neurons have no error during $(0, t]$ is $\overline{F}(T) = \mathrm{e}^{-h\lambda T}$.

From (6), the mean time to completion of the process is

$$L_1(N) = (S + NC_1)\mathrm{e}^{h\lambda S/N}. \quad (7)$$

We find optimal number N_1^* which minimizes $L_1(N)$ for a specified S. Evidently, $L_1(\infty) = \infty$ and

$$L_1(1) = (S + C_1)\mathrm{e}^{h\lambda S}. \quad (8)$$

Thus, there exists a finite number $N_1^*(1 \le N_1^* < \infty)$. Substituing $T = S/N$ in (6) and rewriting it by the function T,

$$L_1(T) = S\left(1 + \frac{C_1}{T}\right)\mathrm{e}^{h\lambda T} \qquad (0 < T \le S). \quad (9)$$

It is evident that $L_1(0) = \lim_{T \to 0} L_1(T) = \infty$ and $L_1(S)$ is given by (9). Thus there exists optimal $\widetilde{T}_1(0 < \widetilde{T}_1 \le S)$ which minimizes $L_1(T)$ in (9). Differenciating $L_1(T)$ with respect to T and setting it equal to zero,

$$T^2 + C_1 T - \frac{C_1}{h\lambda} = 0. \quad (10)$$

Solving (10) with T,

$$\widetilde{T}_1 = \frac{C_1}{2}\left(\sqrt{1 + \frac{4}{h\lambda C_1}} - 1\right). \quad (11)$$

Then, we have the following optimal interval number N_1^* [13].

i. If $\widetilde{T}_1 < S$, put $[S/\widetilde{T}_1] = N$, where $[x]$ denotes the greatest integer contained in x, and calculate $L_1(N)$ and $L_1(N+1)$ from (6). If $L_1(N) \le L_1(N+1)$ then $N_1^* = N$ and $T_1^* = S/N_1^*$, and conversely, if $L_1(N+1) < L_1(N)$ then $N_1^* = N + 1$.

ii. If $\widetilde{T}_1 \ge S$, it means that the system should make no checkpoint until time S, thus $N_1^* = 1$ and the mean time is given in (8).

We compute optimal number N_1^* to minimize $L_1(N)$ when $T = S/N$.

3.1.1 Numerical Example

Table 1 presents optimal N_1^* and the resulting execution times $L_1(N_1^*)$ when $S = 10.0$, $C_1 = 0.1$ and $\lambda = 0.050$ for h, N_1^* and $L_1(N_1^*)$.

For example, when $h = 5$, optimal N_1^* is 17 and $L_1(17)$ is 13.554. This means that the process needs to be divided 17 equally, and the mean time to complete the process is 13.554. Thus, the process increases 3.554 compare than original execution time S. This table indicate that h increases with N_1^* and $L_1(N_1^*)$.

Table 1: Optimal N_1^* and $L(N_1^*)$ when $S = 10.0$, $C_1 = 0.1$ and $\lambda = 0.05$.

h	N_1^*	$L_1(N_1^*)$
1	7	11.492
2	11	12.156
3	13	12.682
5	17	13.554
10	25	15.268
17	34	17.206
20	37	17.951
40	56	22.296

3.2 Modified Series Model

We have considered that all neurons need to work in ANN in Sec. 3.1. The mean resulting execution time is getting large with increasing neuron module in Table 1. We propose a model that tolerates a certain amount of failure depending on the neuron's weight as a modified series model. Because the small-weight neurons make a small signal to the next neurons.

We assume that the ANN allows a certain amount of failure for the weight. We propose the modified probability that input layers are $\exp(-i\lambda t)$, and the j-th hidden layers are $\exp[-\lambda t\sigma(A)]$ where

$$A = \sum_{p=1}^{i}\sum_{q=1}^{m} w_p^{H_q} - \sum_{q=1}^{m} \theta^{H_q},$$

and the k-th output layers are $\exp[-\lambda t\sigma(B)]$ where

$$B = \sum_{q=1}^{m}\sum_{r=1}^{n} w_q^{O_r} - \sum_{r=1}^{n} \theta^{O_r},$$

and $\sigma(x)$ is sigmoid function in (3).

From (6), the mean time to complete the process is

$$L_2(N) = (S + NC_1)\exp[i\lambda T + m\lambda T\sigma(A) + n\lambda T\sigma(B)]. \tag{12}$$

3.2.1 Numerical Example

Assuming the same assumption in Sec. 3.1 except ANN made from $i = 12$, $m = 3$, $n = 2$ neurons, and Tables 2, 3, 4,5 and 6 (this value cite from [3])

Thus, we have $\sum_{p=1}^{12}\sum_{q=1}^{3} w_p^{H_q} = 37.80$, $\sum_{q=1}^{3}\sum_{r=1}^{2} w_q^{O_r} = 36.88$, $\sum_{q=1}^{3}\theta^{H_q} = 22.35$ and $\sum_{r=1}^{2}\theta^{O_r} = 11.73$. We derive optimal number N_2^* and the resulting execution time $L_2(N_2^*)$ using (12).

Table 7 presents optimal N_2^* and the resulting execution times $L_2(N_2^*)$ when $S = 10.0$, $C_1 = 0.1$, $i = 12$, $j = 3$ and $k = 2$ for λ. For example, when $\lambda = 0.0050$, optimal N_2^* is 10 and $L_2(10)$ is 11.976. This means that the process needs to be divided 10 equally, and the mean time to complete the process is 11.976. Thus, the process increases 1.976 compare than original execution time S. And, N_2^* increase with λ.

Table 2: $w_p^{H_q}(p = 1, 2, \cdots, 12, q = 1, 2, 3)$.

p	$w_p^{H_1}$	$w_p^{H_2}$	$w_p^{H_3}$
1	0.26	0.05	2.92
2	0.00	4.97	0.00
3	0.92	0.04	2.13
4	0.00	0.57	0.00
5	2.51	0.00	5.24
6	0.03	0.37	0.00
7	0.00	0.68	0.00
8	6.52	0.03	0.06
9	0.00	0.40	0.02
10	4.75	0.01	0.02
11	0.00	5.00	0.00
12	0.26	0.02	0.03

Table 3: $w_q^{O_r}(q = 1, 2, 3, r = 1, 2)$.

q	$w_q^{O_1}$	$w_q^{O_2}$
1	0.00	14.75
2	11.57	0.00
3	0.05	10.51

Table 4: $\theta^{H_p}(p = 1, 2, 3)$.

p	θ^{H_p}
1	10.65
2	4.01
3	7.69

Table 5: $\theta^{O_r}(r = 1, 2)$.

r	θ^{H_r}
1	5.66
2	6.07

Table 6: A and B.

A	B
15.45	25.15

4. Conclusion

We have considered reliability of hardwarerized ANN as series system and discussed optimal checkpoint time, and compared and discussed the resulting execution time as series model and modified series model. We have given three numerical example and shown four figures. In the future, it is predicted that AI systems such as ANNs will be incorporated into even small systems. Especially, there may be cases where IoT and one bord computer are used. This model and results could be applied to those ANN systems with high performance.

Table 7: Optimal N_2^* and the resulting execution times $L_2(N_2^*)$ when $S = 10.0$, $C_1 = 0.1$, $i = 12$, $m = 3$, $n = 2$.

λ	N_2^*	$L_2(N_2^*)$
0.0010	4	10.852
0.0025	6	11.378
0.0050	10	11.976
0.0100	11	12.955
0.0250	11	16.335
0.0500	11	24.039

5. References

[1] K. Fukushima, Neocognitron: A self-organizing neural network model for a mechanism of pattern recognition unaffected by shift in position, Biological cybernetics 36 (4) (1980) 193–202.

[2] T. Dohi, S. Osaki, Software reliability assessment method using neural networks, Operations Research 44 (1999) 410–414.

[3] Y. Wakui, W. Sadami, Deep Learning for Beginners: Learn how AI works in an easy way, 2018.

[4] I. K. Sethi, A. K. Jain, Artificial neural networks and statistical pattern recognition: old and new connections, Vol. 11, Elsevier, 2014.

[5] Intel, Intel core ultra processors, https://www.intel.com/content/www/us/en/products/details/processors/core-ultra.html (2024).

[6] J. Thomas, G. Galligher, Improving backup system evaluations in information security risk assessments to combat ransomware, Computer and Information Science 11 (1) (2018) 14–25.

[7] C. Qian *et al.*, Optimal backup interval for a database system with full and periodic incremental backup., Journal of Computers. 5 (4) (2010) 557–564.

[8] S. Nakagawa *et al.*, Optimal archive copy interval for a file recovery with general fault latency time, International Journal of Reliability, Quality and Safety Engineering 06 (01) (1999) 91–100.

[9] M. Chen, M. Wang, C. Y. Cheng, Optimal random backup policies for a database system, International Journal of Reliability, Quality and Safety Engineering 21 (04) (2014) 1450017.

[10] S. Nakamura, X. Zhao, T. Nakagawa, Constant and random full backup models with incremental and differential backup schemes, International Journal of Reliability, Quality and Safety Engineering 24 (03) (2017) 1750015.

[11] K. Naruse, T. Nakagawa, S. Maeji, Optimal Checkpoint Intervals for Error Detection by Multiple Modular Redundancies, in: Advanced Reliability and Modelling II, 2006, pp. 293–300.

[12] S. Osaki, Applied Stochastic System Modeling, Springer, Berlin, 1992.

[13] T. Nakagawa, K. Yasui, H. Sandoh, Note on optimal partition problems in reliability models, Journal of Quality in Maintenance Engineering (10) (2004) 282–287.

Relationship between Frailty Classification of Older Adults and Residential Characteristics

Hibiki ADACHI, Masashi KUWANO, Yuka MINAMINO, Mio HOSOE

Graduate School of Sustainability Science, Tottori University
4-101, Minami, Koyama-cho, Tottori-shi, Tottori, 680-8552, Japan
Email: m25j6001c@edu.tottori-u.ac.jp
{kuwano, minamino, mhosoe}@tottori-u.ac.jp

Keywords: Healthy community development, Frailty, Categorical factor analysis, Cluster analysis, Decision tree analysis

Abstract

Support and intervention for the social participation of adults aged 75 years and older are crucial for their care and community revitalization. In addition, frailty prevention is essential to ensuring a healthy, long-lived community. In this study, we investigated 12 items related to frailty through a health assessment questionnaire for older adults in Tottori City to understand the relationship between their health conditions and residential environments. The 12 frailty-related items were classified into four health factors through categorical factor analysis, and older adults were classified into six types through cluster analysis. Decision tree analysis revealed that, in addition to age, the locations of lifestyle-related service stores, mass retailers, and general merchandise stores affect the health conditions of adults aged 75 years and older.

1. Background and objectives of the study

The growing population of older adults in Japan has resulted in increased social security benefits, such as pensions and medical care. Thus, preventive measures are required to mitigate illness and the need for care.

Frailty preventive measures have attracted attention for preventing an increase in the number of people who require care. Frailty is an intermediate state between the state of health (in good health) and the state of requiring care, and it affects an individual daily life [1] In other words, frailty is characterized by a decline in physical, mental, and social health. However, through appropriate intervention, one can recover from frailty to a state of health (in good health) [2]. Frailty can be prevented through individual health management. However, there are limited activities older adults can do to manage their health. Therefore, measures to promote the health of older adults throughout communities are needed. One such initiative is to develop residential environments that support a healthy lifestyle (e.g., older people can easily go out).

There are several advantages of healthy community development. However, only a few studies have quantitatively analyzed the impact of residential environments on the health conditions of older people.

It is necessary to understand the scientific basis for developing residential environments that support the health of adults aged 75 years and older. Therefore, to achieve healthy community development, the relationship between the health conditions of adults aged 75 years and older and the development of residential environments must be clarified.

In this study, we collected questionnaire data from adults aged 75 years and older who have not been certified as requiring long-term care. The older adults were classified into several categories according to their health conditions based on their responses to the questionnaire. Furthermore, we examined the relationship between their health conditions and the locations of facilities related to their daily lives.

2. Summary of the data used

The survey was conducted in Tottori City between November 30 and December 16, 2022. The survey subjects were 20,099 adults aged 75 years and older who live in Tottori City and have not been certified to require nursing care. The survey was conducted using a paper questionnaire, which was distributed and collected by mail. Among the survey subjects, only 13,842 responded (response rate: 68.9%).

An overview of the questionnaire is presented in Table 1. The questionnaire comprises 61 items, including basic items (4), Frailty items (12), Mind and body items (22), Going out behavior items (18) and Household and economic situation items (5).

Missing data processing was performed on the questionnaire data, during which samples with any unanswered items were deleted. Thus, the number of samples for subsequent analysis was reduced to 11,613.

Table 1. Summary of the survey data

Target Area	Tottori City, Tottori Prefecture, Japan
Target group	Adults aged 75 years and older who have not been certified to require nursing care
Number of subjects	20,099 persons
Valid response	11,613 (57.8% valid response rate)
Number of questions	61 items
Item content	Basic, Frailty, Mind and body, Going out behavior and Household and economic situation items

3. Relationship between the items related to frailty

3.1 Categorical Factor Analysis

The questionnaire data revealed the health conditions of older adults. In health screening conducted by municipalities and other organizations, an individual is categorized as a person at "high risk of frailty," a condition that indicates a need for long-term care, for their health condition to be accessed. To determine whether an individual falls into this category, Ishizaki et al. [3] established a criterion using a questionnaire for older adults developed by the Ministry of Health, Labor and Welfare in Japan. In particular, 12 items related to frailty were provided in the questionnaire.

Table 2 lists the 12 items related to frailty and their short forms used in this study. In general, if four or more of the 12 items are unhealthy, the individual is at high risk of frailty. However, when the 12 items are analyzed as data indicating only the risk of frailty, the distinctive features of the 12 items are largely lost. Considering the characteristics of the 12 items individually complicates the data and makes it difficult to understand trends. Therefore, we used the 12 items as much as possible, and the characteristics could be understood with a small amount of information. We reduced the amount of information via factor analysis. Notably, factor analysis can only be performed when all observed variables are continuous. Therefore, it is not applicable to binary variables (yes/no). Thus, we employed categorical factor analysis, which applies to binary observed variables. This type of analysis treats each observed variable on an ordinal scale [4]. The polychoric correlation coefficient is used to determine factor patterns and unique variance [5].

Table 2. Question items related to frailty and their short forms

Question items	short forms
Do you eat three meals a day?	Three meals a day
Do you have more difficulty eating hard foods than six months ago?	Difficult to eat
Do you sometimes choke on tea, soup, etc.?	Choke over
Did you change your weight by 2–3 kg in 6 months	Weight change
Do you think you walk slower than before?	Slowdown
Have you had any falls in the past year?	Falling down
Do you exercise, such as walking at least once a week?	Exercise regime
Do people around you tell you that you are forgetful, such as "always asking the same thing"?	Forgetfulness
Do you sometimes wonder what day it is today?	Unknown today
Do you go out at least once a week?	Outdoor habits
Do you usually socialize with family and friends?	Association
Is there someone close to you that you can talk to when you are not feeling well?	Consulting partners

3.2 Results of categorical factor analysis

As in factor analysis, the number of factors and the rotation method must be determined in categorical factor analysis. In this study, the Very Simple Structure criterion was used to determine the number of factors. The optimal number of factors was four; thus, it was adopted. The Promax rotation method was used to facilitate the interpretation of the factors.

The results of the categorical factor analysis are presented in Table 3. Each factor is defined as follows based on the factor loading of the observed variable.

Table 3. Factor loadings for each observed variable

Factor number	Factor 1	Factor 2	Factor 3	Factor 4
Factor Name	Physical ability	Socializing ability	Going out ability	Cognitive ability
Slowdown	0.58	−0.05	0.19	−0.05
Difficult to eat	0.55	−0.02	0.01	−0.02
Falling down	0.47	−0.04	0.02	0.08
Choke over	0.47	0.02	−0.14	0.11
Weight change	0.42	0.03	0.00	−0.04
Consulting partners	0.01	1.01	−0.22	−0.11
Association	−0.15	0.66	0.26	0.13
Three meals a day	0.18	0.26	0.08	0.02
Outdoor habits	−0.12	−0.04	0.80	0.14
Exercise regime	0.12	−0.02	0.59	−0.13
Unknown today	−0.03	0.08	−0.02	0.73
Forgetfulness	0.15	−0.12	0.03	0.63

Factor 1 has high values for "slowdown," "difficult to eat," "falling down," "choke over," and "weight change." Because these items are related to physical functions in daily life, Factor 1 is referred to as "Physical ability."

Factor 2 has high values for "consulting partners," "association," and "three meals a day," especially for "consulting partners" and "association." These items reflect the ability to relate to and interact with people daily. Therefore, Factor 2 is labeled "Socializing ability."

Factor 3 is referred to as "Going out ability" because of the high values of "outdoor habits" and "exercise regime," which are related to the ability to go out and be active in daily life.

Factor 4 is named "Cognitive ability" because of the high values of "unknown today" and "forgetfulness," which represent the ability to remember and retain things.

4. Classification of older adults according to health status

In the previous chapter, categorical factor analysis was used to categorize the information content of the 12 items questions about frailty into four factors. We then summarized the characteristics of the health conditions of older adults based on the four factors. We applied the k-means method to the factor scores of each sample for the four factors. The older adults were then classified into several groups based on their factor scores. The elbow method was used to determine the optimal number of clusters (six).

Figure 1 shows the group-by-group average factor scores for each factor when the number of clusters was set to six. The overall sample mean for each factor score is 0.

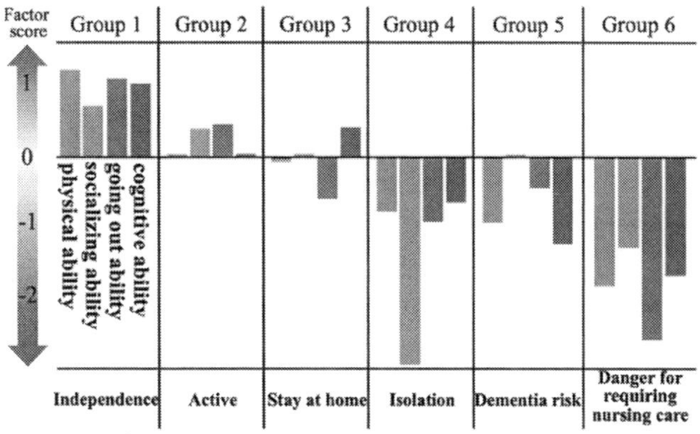

Figure 1. Mean factor scores for each factor.

Group 1 showed positive values for "physical ability," "socializing ability," "going out ability," and "cognitive ability," indicating that the samples belonging to Group 1 are healthy. Therefore, Group 1 is named "Type A: Independence."

Group 2 has positive values for the "socializing ability" and "going out ability" with high factor scores, indicating that the samples in Group 2 live active lives. Therefore, Group 2 is labeled "Type B: Active."

Group 3 has a high negative factor score for "going out ability." This indicates that samples belonging to Group 3 have few opportunities to go out and thus mostly stay home. Therefore, Group 3 is referred to as "Type C: Stay at home."

Group 4 samples have negative factor scores for "physical ability," "socializing ability," "going out ability," and "cognitive ability," with particularly large negative scores for "socializing ability." Thus, the samples belonging to Group 4 have little interaction with others and feel psychologically lonely. Therefore, Group 4 is named "Type D: Isolation."

Group 5 has large negative factor scores for "physical ability" and "cognitive ability." Thus, samples belonging to Group 5 are characterized by impaired judgment in their daily lives. Therefore, Group 5 is named "Type E: Dementia risk."

Group 6 has large negative scores for "physical ability," "socializing ability," "going out ability," and "cognitive ability." Thus, samples belonging to Group 6 have difficulties living alone. Therefore, Group 6 is named "Type F: Danger for requiring nursing care."

5. Relationship between health status and residential environment

Naturally, people's health deteriorates as they get older. Eventually, they fall into Type E or F. From the results of the non-hierarchical cluster analysis, Type C people have low "going out ability," and Type D patients have low "socializing ability." For older adults classified as Types C and D, improving their residential environments and promoting social interactions and physical activities may offer them the possibility to return to Type A or B. Therefore, we performed a decision tree analysis to analyze the relationship between the health conditions of older adults and residential environments for Types A–D.

The Classification and Regression Tree (CART) algorithm based on the within-node heterogeneity measure was used. In CART, the minimum sample size is 150, and the tree depth is 5 layers.

The variables are described in Table 4. The variables include personal attributes, such as age and gender. The number of 14 types of facilities, including food stores, clothing stores, and mass retailers, was used as residential environmental factors. Data on the residential environment were obtained from e-Stat [6] and building point data [7]. The explanatory variables representing the residential environment were aggregated according to the sample's place of residence. The range can be calculated by blocks, elementary school districts, and areas, and the number of facilities can be counted as number of facilities (items), number of facilities per person (items/person), and number of facilities per square kilometer (items/km^2). These are then combined and fed into the model.

Figure 2 shows the obtained decision tree diagram. The values shown in the square boxes are the percentages within the nodes of Types A–D.

Node 1 contains samples under the age of 78. Among the terminal nodes, the "Type A: Independence" samples appear the most.

Node 3 includes people aged between 78 and 82, and the number of lifestyle-related service stores per person in each block/district is less than 0.003. Furthermore, the number of general merchandise stores per square kilometer in each elementary school district is $55e^{-9}$ or more. Approximately 22.8% of the total samples meet the conditions for Node 3.

Node 8 is for samples aged 83 to 88, with the number of mass retailers per person in each town/district between 0.0021 and 0.0028. In addition, the samples are men. This node has the lowest proportion of "Type D: Isolation." The other end nodes can be considered similarly. Thus, the discussion is omitted to avoid redundancy.

Considering the above results, Figure 2 shows that areas with younger people and numerous general merchandise stores and lifestyle-related service stores (in other words, facilities related to daily life) have more "Type A: Independence" and "Type B: Active" samples. In addition, age items were confirmed in five of the 14 branches. Therefore, there is a tendency for younger people to be healthier. In a sample of people aged 83 to 88 and with a per capita number of mass retailers of less than 0.0028 in each town/district, men are more likely to be "Type C: Stay at home" and less likely to be "Type D: Isolation" than women.

Table 4. Variable groups used in decision tree analysis

Personal Attributes	Age, Gender
Residensial environment	Food retailers, Clothing retailers, General merchandise stores, Mass retailers, Hospitals, Infrastructure, Sports facilities, Supermarkets, Clinics, Restaurants, Pharmacies, Medical and welfare services stores, Rental service stores, Lifestyle-related service stores

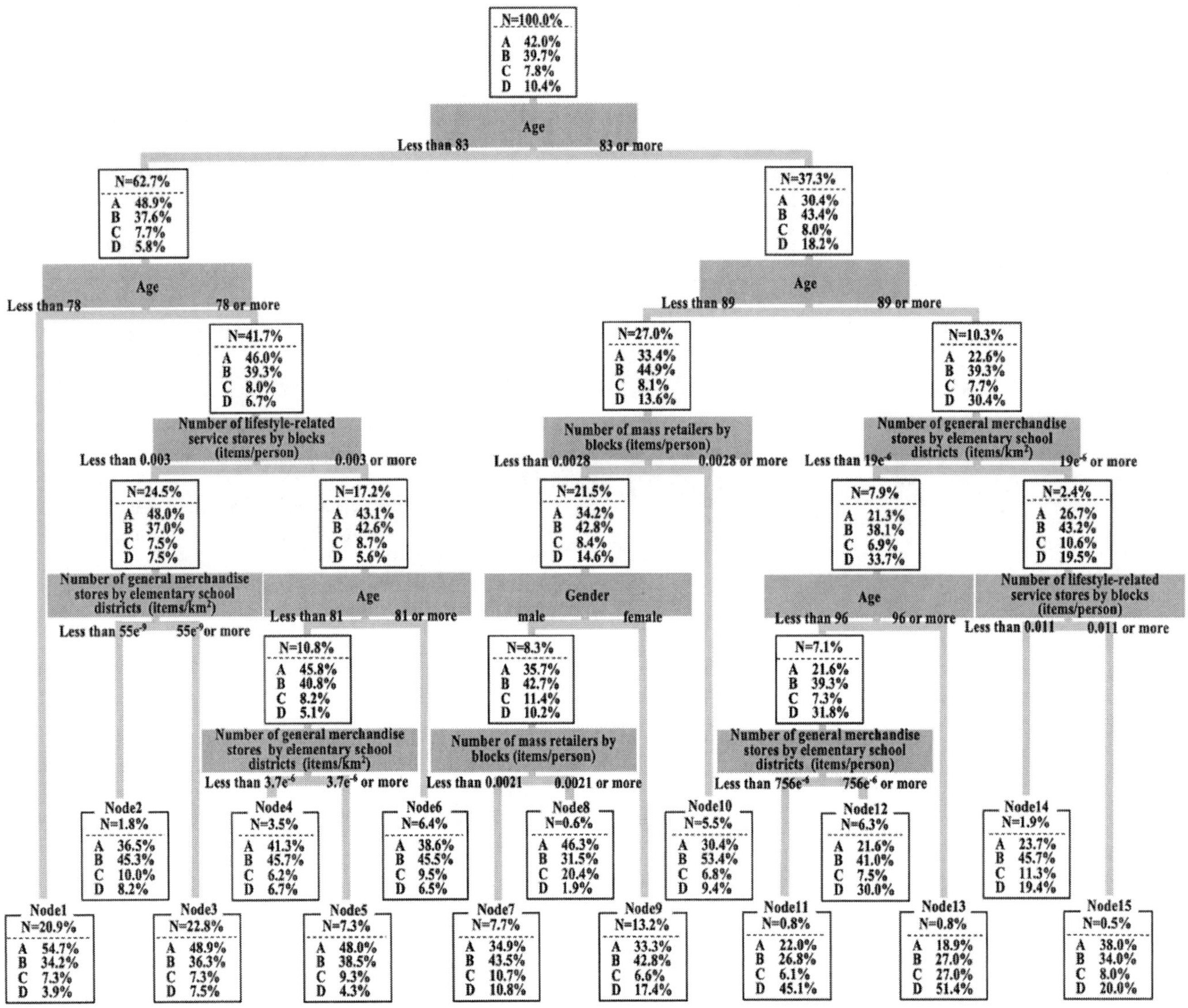

Figure 2. Classification results from decision tree analysis

6. Conclusion

In this study, questionnaire data on frailty and residential environment were analyzed to identify the health conditions of adults aged 75 years and older. In addition, the relationship between their health conditions and residential environments was clarified.

Specifically, categorical factor analysis was performed to classify the 12 frailty-related items into four factors: "physical ability," "socializing ability," "going out ability," and "cognitive ability." Based on cluster analysis, older adults were classified into six types: "Independence," "Active," "Stay at home," "Isolation," "Dementia risk," and "Danger for requiring nursing care." Finally, the relationship between health status and residential environment for the "Independence," "Active," "Stay at home," and "Isolation" classes of older adults was analyzed using a decision tree. The analysis revealed that personal attributes, such as age and gender, and the presence of lifestyle-related service stores, mass retailers, and general merchandise stores promote better health conditions among adults aged 75 years and older.

For adults aged 75 years and older to live independent and active lives, it is important to encourage their participation in local communities and activities. Future studies should analyze the relationship between health conditions and local communities and activities, as well as residential environments.

7. Acknowledgments

We thank Tottori City and the Tottori Prefectural Federation of National Health Insurance Associations for providing the data and advice for this study. This work was supported by JSPS KAKENSHI Grant Number JP23K26331.

8. References

[1] Mitsubishi Research Institute, "Medium and Long-Term Proposals for Social Security System Reform", https://www.mri.co.jp/knowledge/insight/policy/i5inlu000000bgh3-att/20240614pec.pdf (Confirmed on March 3, 2025)

[2] Lan D Cameron, Nicola Fairhall, Colleen Langron, Keri Lockwood, Noeline Monaghan, Chiristina Aggar, Catherine Sherrington, Stephen R Lord and Susan E Kurrle, "A multifactorial interdisciplinary intervention reduces frailty in older people: randomized trial", *BMC Medicine,* Vol. 11, 10 pages, 2013.

[3] Tatsuro Ishizaki, Yukie Masui, Takeshi Nakagawa, Yuko Yoshida, Yoshiko L. Ishioka, Noriko Hori, Hiroki Inagaki, Kae Ito, Madoka Ogawa, Mai Kabayama, Kei Kamide, Kazunori Ikebe, Yasumichi Arai and Yasuyuki Gondo, "Construct validity of a new health assessment questionnaire for the national screening program of older adults in Japan: The SONIC Study", *International Journal of Environmental Research and Public Health*, Vol. 19, No. 16, 10 pages, 2022.

[4] Yusuke Inagaki, "Reconsideration of the durable consumer goods as a determinant of status identification", *The study of sociology*, No. 101, pp. 85-114, 2018.

[5] Norie Obu, Minoru Kawamata, Satomi Shibazaki, Kazunori Kayaba and Osamu Hosoya, "Development of a self-evaluation scale for undergraduates in community - based interprofessional education-with cross-sectional and longitudinal data from three universities in the Kanto region -", *Japanese Journal of Health Education and Promotion*, Vol. 25, No. 3, pp. 168-79, 2017.

[6] General Contact Point for Government Statistics (e-stat), "Housing, Land and Statistics Survey", https://www.e-stat.go.jp (Confirmed on February 25, 2025)

[7] Zenrin Corporation, "Building Point Data", https://www.zenrin.co.jp/product/category/gis/contents/building-point/index.html (Confirmed on February 25, 2025)

Analysis of Loan Agreement using Deep Learning with a Regularization Term

Yutaka AZUMA, Masashi KUWANO, Yuka MINAMINO, and Mio HOSOE

Graduate School of Sustainability Science, Tottori-University
4-101, Minami, Koyama-cho, Tottori-shi, Tottori, 680-8552, Japan
Email: m24j6002x@edu.tottori-u.ac.jp
{kuwano, minamino, mhosoe}@tottori-u.ac.jp

Keywords: Deep Neural Network, LassoNet, Bank data

Abstract

Recent advances in information and communication technologies have resulted in the accumulation of vast amounts of data and the spread of machine learning methods. Deep learning (DL), which has attracted increasing attention among machine learning methods, is capable of highly accurate prediction; however, the black box nature of the computational process makes it difficult to interpret the prediction results. When using the results of DL-based analyses, an explanation of the rationale is required, and in recent years, transparency and accountability have become important requirements. In this study, we attempt to improve the interpretability of DL by selecting explanatory variables using a LassoNet model equipped with a variable extraction function. In an experiment, we predicted the probability of mortgage loan contracts using bank customer data comprising 344,384 samples and 141 variables. We also analyzed the relationship between the number of explanatory variables in the model and the prediction accuracy. By comparing the results of DL using only the important explanatory variables, we clarified the effect of selecting explanatory variables on the prediction accuracy.

1. Background and purpose

The spread and diversification of information and communication technology and the Internet of Things, as well as the promotion of data utilization by public agencies, have collectively fostered an environment in which large amounts of data, referred to as big data, can be collected efficiently. In addition, with the accumulation of big data, artificial intelligence (AI) technologies have been developed and their use has spread. Currently, AI and big data are utilized in various industries and for diverse purposes, and it is expected that they will become even more deeply permeated into society as effective problem-solving solutions in a wide range of fields. Among the various AI technologies, machine learning (ML) and deep learning (DL) methods have attracted considerable attention. DL extracts information one layer at a time over multiple layers. Its complex structure and internal computation enable complex pattern recognition from big data. Conventional ML requires an analyst to define the features to be learned; however, DL methods can automatically learn features from big data that are appropriate for the target prediction task [1]. DL methods have demonstrated superior performance in various fields, including image recognition, speech recognition, and natural language processing, enabling accurate predictions.

Research on DL is being conducted in various fields [2]; however, the black box problem has been identified in its application to social problems, e.g., healthcare decision-making and criminal risk assessment [3]. Neural network ML, including DL, is characterized by the fact that it does not present the regularities and models obtained from the learning results in a form that is easily understood by humans, and its learning process is a so-called black box. In other words, the computational process is so complex that humans cannot interpret why such decisions are made relative to the learning results, e.g., classification, prediction, and anomaly detection results. If decisions are made based on complex results that cannot be intuitively understood by humans, they can have a significant impact on people's lives and property. For example, it may lead to life-threatening errors in judgment in the medical field and it may lead to loss of property in the financial field. Improving model interpretability is particularly important in the marketing and medical fields, where decisions must be made based on a clear understanding of the features that influence the objective variables. Elucidating the features that influence the prediction results is also important from the perspective of countermeasures and policy considerations for the problem [4].

Generally, as the number of explanatory variables increases, the accuracy of the model increases. However, when the number of explanatory variables is increased, there are risks of overfitting and overtraining. In addition, when the number of explanatory variables increases, even if the reproducibility is high, the data collection costs increase and the model's generalizability deteriorates when applied to other data sets, e.g., future predictions, other regions, or other time periods. Thus, even with DL, models with fewer explanatory variables are more useful. From the perspective of model generalizability, it is important to consider the most significant explanatory variables and select only those variables when constructing models rather than including all available variables.

As a conventional and representative feature extraction method, sparse modeling has attracted attention and is used in a variety of engineering fields, e.g., information theory, signal processing, and ML [5]. The sparse modeling technique is employed to understand the structure of a large amount of complex data by extracting only the important items from many data items and represent them as an easy-to-understand model. Sparse modeling handles only small amounts of data, thereby reducing computational costs, and it can express complex data structures in an easy-to-understand manner. Kawasaki and Ueki

[6] applied four sparse modeling methods, including the Lasso method, to bank data to predict the success of telemarketing. The results demonstrated that the methods can reduce computational cost and improve interpretability by reducing unnecessary variables while maintaining the same level of accuracy as conventional regression-based prediction methods.

In this study, we employed LassoNet [7], which combines DL and feature extraction, to construct a predictive model that can extract explanatory variables that influence the prediction results from many explanatory variables. In addition, by applying only the extracted explanatory variables to DL and evaluating the prediction accuracy, we confirm whether the explanatory variables that influence the prediction results can be extracted. In a previous study, Xiaolu et al. [8] applied LassoNet to clinical data to predict the complications of acute coronary syndromes and select important features. As a result, several important features were extracted, including age, and their usefulness in terms of improving interpretability was demonstrated. In addition, Jiatong et al. [9] applied LassoNet to Chinese insurance data to identify features that affect individual depression and provide information about important features to decision makers and researchers by integrating the ranking of the features' importance and related results. However, there are few examples of LassoNet applications. As an empirical analysis of the model developed in this study, we applied LassoNet to a bank's customer data with many explanatory variables and numerous samples to identify the important explanatory variables that affect the prediction of an individual's probability of contracting a mortgage loan. The goal of this study was to examine whether it is possible to extract important features even when using data with numerous explanatory variables.

The remainder of this paper is structured as follows. Chapter 2 presents an overview of the dataset. Chapter 3 explains the construction of the LassoNet model. Chapter 4 describes the prediction results of mortgage contract probability using LassoNet, and Chapter 5 discusses the extracted important explanatory variables. Finally, Chapter 6 concludes with a discussion of the findings and suggestions for future research.

2. Overview of data

In this study, we used customer data from a bank in Japan. The cross-sectional data were obtained on July 31, 2022. The bank's customer data contain various customer attribute information, such as the account holder's age, deposit coefficient information, e.g., the total deposit balance, and other bank usage information for each customer. In this study, 141 variables in the five categories shown in Table 1 were used as the explanatory variables.

In this study, we focused the analysis on mortgage contracts. Newlyweds and households in their 30s and 40s who are raiding children are most likely to sign new mortgage contracts [10]. In fact, as shown in Fig. 1, in the data used in this study, the majority of mortgage loan holders are in the 30–40 age group. Thus, we focused on the data for this age group. We found that 5.76% of the samples in the 30–40 age group contracted a mortgage loan, which means that the number of people without a mortgage contract is very large compared with those who do have a contract, and the data are unbalanced. Thus, we adjusted the balance in our analysis. The details are discussed Section 3.2.

Table 1: Variables in bank customer data

Classification	Quantity	Items
Customer attribute information	76	Age, gender, etc.
Contract information	29	Safe-deposit box contracts, etc.
Performance information	25	Bonus transfer performance, etc.
Deposit coefficient information	5	Total deposit balance, Yen deposit balance, etc.
Loan coefficient information	6	Total loan amount, consumption balance, etc.

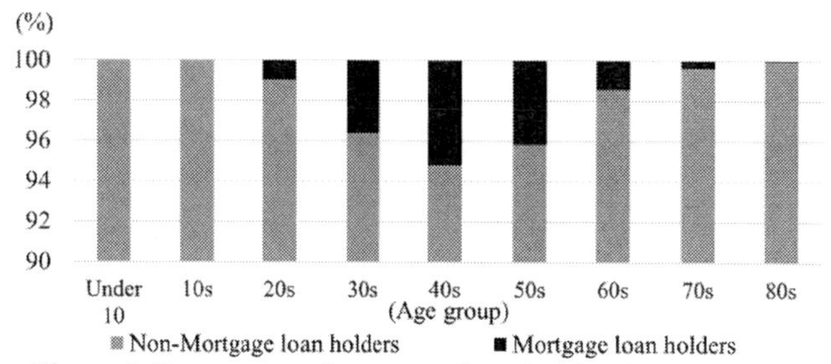

Figure 1: Percentage of mortgage loan holders by age group

3. Model construction and estimations

3.1 Analysis procedure

Fig. 2 illustrates the six-step analysis procedure employed in this study.

Step 1: A decision tree analysis was conducted to identify and exclude samples with extremely low mortgage contract probabilities. This preprocessing step reduced data noise and improved the efficiency of subsequent modeling.

Step 2: To address class imbalance, the majority class was clustered using the K-means method. Under-sampling was then performed within each cluster to construct a balanced dataset.

Step 3: A LassoNet model was constructed for predicting mortgage contract probabilities, with key hyperparameters such as learning rate and the number of layers tuned to optimize performance.

Step 4: The trained LassoNet model was applied to estimate the contract probability for each customer.

Step 5: Important explanatory variables were identified based on their adoption rates, defined as the frequency with which each variable was retained under increasing levels of regularization.

Step 6: To assess the effectiveness of feature selection, a DL model was trained using only the selected variables. Its prediction accuracy was then compared with that of a model trained on all explanatory variables.

3.2 Data preprocessing (STEP 1, 2)

We identified samples in the customer data that had not conducted transactions for a long period of time and samples that were unable to sign a mortgage loan contract due to income or other reasons. The prediction accuracy of the model is expected to increase by excluding samples with an extremely low probability of signing a contract. However, due to the large number of variables, it is difficult to establish effective criteria to exclude samples with a low likelihood of contracting. Thus, in

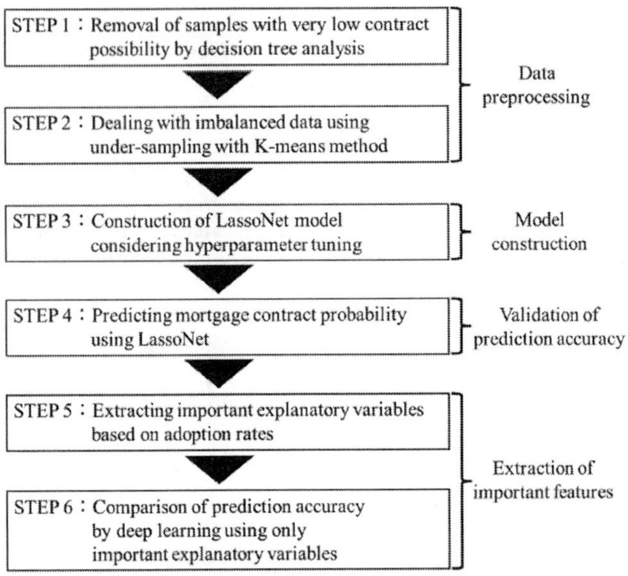

Figure 2: Analysis procedure

this study, we employed decision tree analysis [11] to analyze the attributes of samples with a low likelihood of contracting. Then, we excluded samples according to these criteria. As a result of the decision tree analysis, the number of samples determined to have no contracting potential was 4,742.

The 97,016 samples used in the analysis comprised 5,505 and 91,511 contracted and uncontracted samples, respectively. When ML is applied to imbalanced data in which the distribution of the sample classes is highly skewed, the resulting model tends to predict most samples as belonging to the majority class, which reduces classification performance for the minority class significantly. Wang et al. [12] stated that a major issue in detecting fraudulent transactions on online e-commerce platforms is the overwhelmingly low proportion of fraudulent transactions relative to the total number of transactions, which reduces model effectiveness considerably because a classifier that predicts "not fraudulent" for all purchase data are evaluated as having very high overall classification accuracy. In the current study, under-sampling, a method that samples from the majority class and adjusts the ratio of the number of samples to the minority class, was applied to eliminate the imbalance in the data. However, random sampling in the under-sampling process can destroy the distribution of explanatory variables in the majority class. Thus, we applied k-means clustering to the majority class in the training data and performed sampling from each cluster in proportion to its size. The results of the under-sampling process are shown in Table 2.

Table 2: Number of samples of the training data before and after under-sampling

Label	Training data before sampling	Training data after sampling
Number of samples	67,911	7,659
Number of contracts	3,831 (5.6%)	3,831 (49.9%)
Number of noncontracts	64,080 (94.4%)	3,828 (50.0%)

3.3 Model construction (STEP 3)

LassoNet [7] generalizes the Lasso linear regression model and extends the sparsity of Lasso to feedforward neural networks. To capture the nonlinear features, the linear and nonlinear components in the residuals of the neural network input and output values are optimized simultaneously. Here, if the regression coefficient of an explanatory variable in the linear component is nonzero, LassoNet allows the variable to be passed into the intermediate layers of the network. This design extends the sparsity of Lasso to the neural network, enabling feature selection within a deep learning framework.

Unlike other variable selection methods in neural networks, LassoNet employs an objective function with constraints and sparsity to combine variable selection and parameter learning. Equation (1) shows the objective function and constraint of the LassoNet model.

$$\min_{\theta,W} L(\theta,W) + \lambda\|\theta\|_1$$
$$subject\ to\ \left\|W_d^{(1)}\right\|_\infty \le M|\theta_d|, d = 1,\dots,D \qquad (1)$$

Here, $L(\theta,W)$ represents the residual neural network, where θ denotes the linear component parameters, and W represents the coefficients of the residual network. In addition, $W_d^{(1)}$ is the d-th component in the first layer of the residual network, M is the layer multiplier, and λ denotes the penalty term for the linear component. This objective function imposes an L1 regularization term on the residual between the input and output values via the residual neural network. The constraint condition indicates that the weight parameters W of the explanatory variables in each unit of the feedforward neural network are scaled by a feature of M.

In the LassoNet model constructed in this study, 141 variables (Table 1) were utilized as explanatory variables in the input layer, and the output was the probability that each sample will "contract" or "not contract." The samples to be analyzed were divided into training data (70%) and test data (30%). The threshold of the contract probability was set to 0.5, and the samples with an output probability equal to or greater than 0.5 were classified as "contract."

In addition to various parameters, e.g., as weights and biases, which were obtained automatically by calculating gradients using the error back propagation method, several hyperparameters must be adjusted manually, e.g., the number of intermediate layers, the learning rate, and the layer multipliers. In this study, three intermediate layers were set, and various hyperparameters, including the number of units in each of the other intermediate layers, were evaluated by trial and error with reference to the default values described in GitHub [13], and the combination that yielded the highest prediction accuracy was adopted. Table 3 shows the conditions of the LassoNet model constructed in this study.

In the LassoNet model, as the penalty term λ in Equation (1) increases, the coefficient of an explanatory variable that has little effect on the mortgage contract probability, i.e., the objective variable, becomes 0 and that explanatory variable is deleted. The value of λ is output when there is a change in the number of explanatory variables, and the process was terminated when the number of explanatory variables reached 0.

Table 3: Conditions of LassoNet model

Parameter	Value
Intermediate layers (Layer1, Layer2, Layer3)	152, 133, 254
Optimization algorithm	Adam
Activation function (intermediate layer)	ReLu
Activation function (output layer)	SoftMax
Batch size	92
Number of training epochs	200
Learning rate	0.001
Layer multiplier	10

4 Validation of prediction accuracy (STEP 4)

To verify the model's accuracy, we employed the recall value calculated from the actual measurement value and the predicted probabilities. Recall indicates the percentage of data that is predicted correctly as taking a mortgage loan out of the data that actually takes a mortgage loan.

Figs. 3 and 4 show the number of explanatory variables for λ and the recall results. As can be seen, when the value of λ was 0, all 141 variables were employed, and the recall value was approximately 0.86. The number of explanatory variables decreased as λ increased, and the recall value tended to decrease. When the λ value was less than 800, i.e., when the number of explanatory variables in the model was less than 25, the increase or decrease in the recall value becomes increasingly significant, which indicates that the model's accuracy became unstable with a small number of explanatory variables.

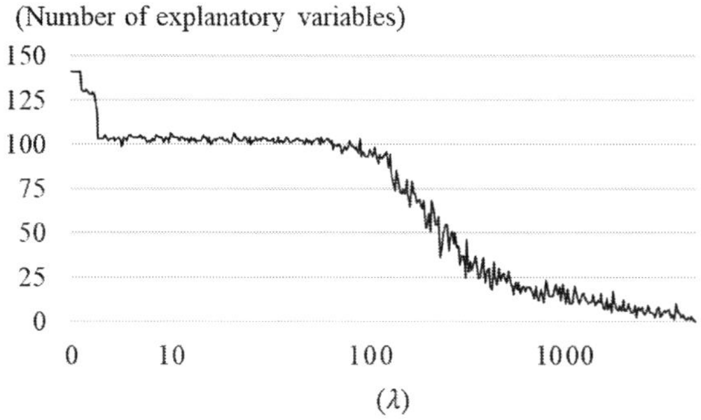

Figure 3: Number of explanatory variables for λ

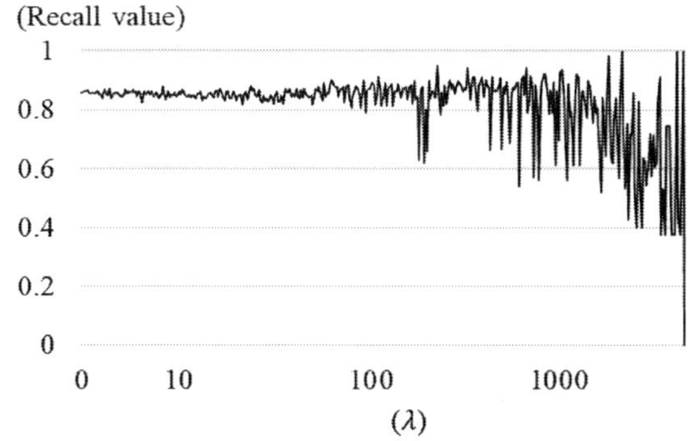

Figure 4: Recall value for λ

5 Extraction of important features (STEP 5, 6)

In this study, important explanatory variables were defined as those with a high adoption rate, calculated as the proportion of times a variable was not eliminated during the iterative increase of the regularization parameter λ in the LassoNet model. Note that these variables are considered to influence the prediction results significantly.

Fig. 5 shows the adoption rate and its rank for each explanatory variable, and Table 4 shows the top 25 variables in terms of the adoption rate for each explanatory variable. As shown in Fig. 5, the adoption rate of the top six variables exceeded 90%, which suggests that these six variables are important explanatory variables with a significant impact on the prediction. In contrast, the explanatory variables ranked 100 or higher exhibited a large decrease in the adoption rate; thus, they are unrelated to the prediction task. In addition, as shown in Table 4, for the "Water charge transfer payment record" and "Electricity charge transfer payment record" variables, we infer that many customers who sign a mortgage contract use the bank as their main bank and are more likely to use the bank's services and products. Furthermore, many of the explanatory variables

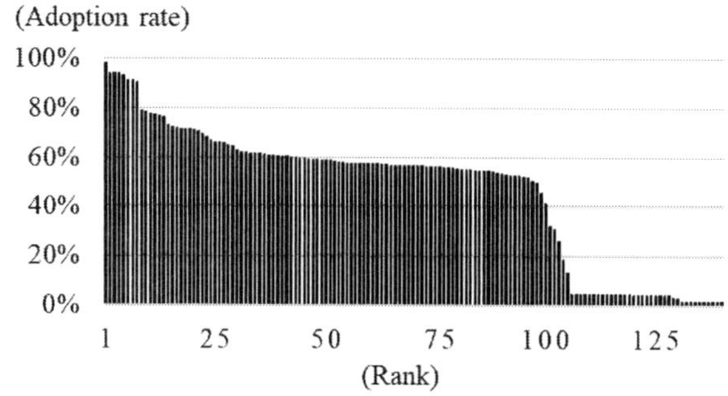

Figure 5: Percentage and rank of each explanatory variable

Table 4: Top 25 variables in terms of adoption rate for each explanatory variable

Explanatory variables	Adoption rate
Water charge transfer payment record	97.85%
Dummy for residents in the prefecture	94.09%
Consumer loan contract	93.01%
Savings account overdraft service contract	91.13%
Electricity charge transfer payment record	90.86%
Gender	90.32%
Amount of salary transfer (yen)	78.76%
Internet banking service contract	78.50%
Non-life insurance transfer payment contract	77.69%
Credit card transfer payment contract	76.88%
Telephone charge transfer payment contract	76.61%
Rating code_25	76.08%
Salary transfers record	73.12%
Rating debtor classification_10.0	72.31%
Water charge transfer payment contract	71.77%
Rating code_28	71.51%
NHK broadcasting fee transfer payment record	71.24%
Total credit line availability	71.24%
Utility bill transfer payment record	70.97%
Credit card transfers payment contract	70.43%
Total credit line	69.35%
Rating debtor classification_21.0	68.11%
Amount of pension transfer (yen)	66.67%
Gas charge transfer payment contract	65.86%
Bank credit transfer payment record	65.86%

exhibit an adoption rate of approximately 70%. These variables may be characterized by interaction effects when combined with other explanatory variables or by their influence on individuals with specific characteristics in the sample.

In this study, DL was performed using only the top 25 variables in terms of adoption rate, and the result demonstrated that the recall value was 0.83, which is not significantly less than the recall value of 0.86 obtained when all 141 variables were used. This result confirms that we extracted the important explanatory variables that affect the prediction results without reducing the prediction accuracy significantly.

6 Results and challenges

In this study, we verified the usefulness of variable extraction using the LassoNet model. As an empirical analysis, we utilized bank customer data to predict the probability of a mortgage contract. The explanatory variables that were repeatedly identified by the constructed model as having an influence on the objective variable were defined as important for the prediction task and extracted. By performing DL using only the extracted explanatory variables, there was no significant change in the recall value before and after extraction of the explanatory variables, which indicates that highly accurate predictions were possible when using only the extracted explanatory variables. In summary, the LassoNet model is useful in terms of interpretability and model generalizability because it can extract important explanatory variables while making predictions with high accuracy, and it is an analytical method that provides knowledge that can be utilized to acquire new customers.

We modeled the likelihood of contracting a mortgage using the cross-sectional data of customers at a certain point in time. However, while this analysis using cross-sectional data can elucidate correlations, it cannot identify causal relationships. Thus, the use of panel data from multiple time periods that continuously record customers' bank usage will be an important issue for future analysis of the characteristics of customers with a high likelihood of contracting a mortgage loan.

7 Acknowledgements

This study was conducted with data provided by a bank. We express our gratitude to the bank for providing the data. This work was supported by JSPS KAKENSHI Grant Numbers JP23K26331 and JP24K07948.

8 References

[1] Ministry of Internal Affairs and Communications, "White paper on information and communication in Japan", 2016. https://www.soumu.go.jp/johotsusintokei/whitepaper/ja/h28/pdf/n4200000.pdf (Confirmed on April 23, 2025)

[2] Hend A. Selmy, Hoda K. Mohamed, Walaa Medhat, "Big data analytics deep learning techniques and applications: A survey", Information Systems, Vol. 120, p. 102318, Feb 2024.

[3] Toshikazu Fukushima, Ryohei Fujimaki, Daisuke Okanohara, Masashi Sugiyama, "Outlook for big data and machine learning: Cutting-edge technological challenges and expanding applications", Journal of Information Processing and Management, Vol. 60, No. 8, pp. 543-554, Nov 2017.

[4] Christoph Molnar, "Interpretable machine learning: A guide for making black box models explainable", Independently published, 2024. https://christophm.github.io/interpretable-ml-book/ (Confirmed on April 23, 2025)

[5] Naoki Hayashi, Masaaki Nagahara, "Distributed sparse modeling for society 5.0: Big data analysis over multiagent networks", The Institute of Electronics, Information and Communication Engineers, Vol. 13, No. 2, pp. 95-107, Oct 2019.

[6] Yoshinori Kawasaki, Masao Ueki, "Sparse predictive modeling for bank telemarketing success using smooth-threshodl estimating equations", Journal of the Japanese Society of Computational Statistics, Vol. 28, No. 1, pp. 53-66, Dec 2015.

[7] Ismael Lemhadri, Feng Ruan, Louis Abraham, Robert Tibshirani, "LassoNet: A neural network with feature sparsity", Journal of Machine Learning Research, Vol. 22, No. 127, pp. 5633-5661, Dec 2021.

[8] Xiaolu Xu, Zitong Qi, Xiumei Han, Yuxing Wang, Ming Yu, Zhaohong Geng, "Combined-task deep network based on LassoNet feature selection for predicting the comorbidities of acute coronary syndrome", Computers in Biology and Medicine, Vol. 170, p. 107992, March 2024.

[9] Jiatong Han, Hao Li, Han Lin, Pingping Wu, Shidan Wang, Juan Tu, Jing Lu, "Depression prediction based on LassoNet-RNN model: A longitudinal study", Heliyon, Vol. 9, No. 10, p. e20684, Oct 2023.

[10] Japan Housing Finance Agency, "Survey of Flat 35 users in FY2023", 2024. https://www.jhf.go.jp/files/400370694.pdf (Confirmed on April 23, 2025)

[11] Leo Breiman, Jerome H. Friedman, Richard A. Olshen, Charles J. Stone, "Classification and Regression Trees", Wadsworth International Group, 1984.

[12] Shuo Wang, Leandro L. Minku, Xin Yao, "A systematic study of online class imbalance learning with concept drift", IEEE Transactions on Neural Networks and Learning Systems, Vol. 29, No. 10, pp. 4802-4821, Oct 2018.

[13] GitHub, "Welcome to LassoNet's documentation!", https://lasso-net.github.io//lassonet/api/ (Confirmed on April 23, 2025)

Numerical Evaluation of the Effectiveness of an Extended Warranty based on a Periodical Replacement Model

TAMURA Nobuyuki

Department of Industrial and Systems Engineering, Hosei University, Koganei-shi, Tokyo, Japan, tamura@hosei.ac.jp

Key Words: base warranty, extended warranty, periodical replacement, generalized Polya process, imperfect repair

Abstract - We consider a product with a base warranty provided by a manufacturer that is operated under a periodical replacement policy. Upon the occurrence of failures within the warranty, the product is repaired without cost to the customer and the failure process follows a generalized Polya process. After expiration of the base warranty, we may contract an extended warranty that the degree of repair and a loss due to failure are different from the case of the base warranty. To evaluate the effectiveness of the extended warranty, we derive expected cost rates with and without the extended warranty and perform numerical analysis for their comparison. As a result, we establish conditions on relative utilities for the extended warranty.

1 Introduction

In today's world, after-sales services are an important factor used to evaluate the competitiveness of business enterprises. Among these services, warranties have been widely employed to promote the quality of a manufacturer's repairable products. Indeed, offering an attractive warranty can serve as a significant advertising tool for manufacturers operating in an intensely competitive market. Since a warranty constitutes a potential expense for manufacturers, it can also be considered a negative factor adversely affecting the manufacturer's profit. The magnitude of this potential cost depends largely on the quality of the product and the length of the warranty period. Because of the significance and universalization, many kinds of mathematical techniques have been proposed, studied and applied for various problems concerned with warranty (see e.g. Blischke [2] and Murthy [23]).

Warranties are generally classified as base and extended warranties, and the former is attached with purchase of many products. On the other hand, extended warranties are options for the customer and the manufacturers want to earn an income through contraction of extended warranties. Thus, it is important to provide the usefulness of extended warranties from the perspective of economic aspects for customers to increase the contraction. However, compared with financial problems on base warranties, studies on cost models for extended warranties have not been so many.

Then, Gupta et al. [9], Yun et al. [29], Su et al. [26], Mitra [20], Afsahi et al. [1], Huang et al. [12], He et al. [10], Jung et al. [14], Hooti et al. [11], and Chang et al. [6] addressed a maintenance problem including an extended warranty. However, these studies do not pay attention to the influence of the degree of imperfect repair though an extended warranty. This means that they do not discuss whether a customer should contract an extended warranty after expiration of a base warranty or not. Different from the cases of extended warranties, many kinds of imperfect maintenance have been proposed and analyzed, and their applications to maintenance problems have been studied. The typical example is minimal repair that the failure rate of a repaired item is unchanged at the instant of the failure and Brown and Proschan [3] generalized minimal repair as imperfect repair. Afterwards, while Kijima [16], Lam [17], Finkelstein [8], Toledo et al. [27], Brown et al. [3], Cha [4] constructed the mathematical expression for an imperfect repair, these imperfect repairs do not necessarily have some sort of reciprocal relationship. Then, Lee et al. [18] proposed a cost model for a maintenance problem with a base warranty and applied the generalized Polya process studied by Cha [4] for an imperfect repair. However, this study did not include an extended warranty in the cost model.

In this study, we construct a cost model to measure the effect of an extended warranty after the expiration of a base warranty by using a block replacement policy. The difference whether an extended warranty is contracted or not is expressed by the degree of imperfect repair and a loss due to a failure. Then we suppose that the failure process follows a generalized Polya process. When a customer wants to decide an optimal time for preventive replacement after warranties, we provide conditions on the degree of an imperfect repair and the loss due to a failure through numerical analysis.

2 Cost Model

In this study, we construct a cost model based on a traditional block replacement policy for evaluating whether a customer contracts an extended warranty. Then, we derive two expected cost rates with and without an extended warranty as a measure for the comparison.

2.1 Notations

Here we introduce notations and symbols to explain the cost model.

T	:	lifetime of a new product
$f(t)$	:	probability density function (PDF) of a random variable T
$N_b(t)$	:	number of repairs of a product within a base warranty
$N_0(t)$	:	number of repairs of a product without an extended warranty after the expiration of a base warranty
$N_1(t)$	:	number of repairs within an extended warranty after the expiration of a base warranty
c_m	:	cost for repair
c_w	:	cost for contracting an extended warranty
c_d^0	:	loss due to a failure when an extended warranty is not contracted
c_d^1	:	loss due to a failure when an extended warranty is contracted
c_p	:	cost for purchasing a new product
w_b	:	base warranty duration
w_e	:	extended warranty duration
θ_b	:	degree of a repair within a base warranty
θ_0	:	degree of a repair after the expiration of a base or extended warranty
θ_1	:	degree of a repair within an extended warranty after the expiration of a base warranty
τ	:	preventive replacement time

Thus, we suppose that $F(t)$ is the CDF (cumulative distribution function) and $\lambda(t)$ is the failure rate for a random variable T.

2.2 Model Descriptions

A customer purchases a new product with a base warranty of period w_b at cost c_p from a manufacturer and operates it. Upon occurrence of a failure, the product undergoes a GPP (generalized Polya process) repair. Before explaining the GPP repair, we define the generalized Polya process. As preparation, we introduce a stochastic intensity λ_t of an orderly point process $\{N(t); t \geq 0\}$:

$$\lambda_t \equiv \lim_{\Delta t \to 0} \frac{\Pr\{N(t, t+\Delta t) = 1 \,|\, H_{t-}\}}{\Delta t} = \lim_{\Delta t \to 0} \frac{E[N(t, t+\Delta t) \,|\, H_{t-}]}{\Delta t},$$

where $N(t_1, t_2)$ $(t_1 < t_2)$ represents the number of events in $[t_1, t_2)$ and H_{t-} is the internal filtration of the orderly point process in $[0, t)$, that is,

$$H_{t-} \equiv \{N(u), 0 \leq u < t\}.$$

By using the stochastic intensity, the generalized Polya process can be defined as below.

Definition 2.1. *A counting process $\{N(t); t \geq 0\}$ is called the generalized Polya process (GPP) with the set of parameters $(\lambda(t), \alpha, \beta)$, if*

1. $N(0) = 0$,
2. $\lambda_t = (\alpha N(t-) + \beta)\lambda(t)$,

where $\alpha \geq 0$, $\beta \geq 0$.

Then, the GPP repair is defined as follow.

Definition 2.2. *For a product with the failure rate $\lambda(t)$, repair type is called the GPP repair with the parameter α if $\{N(t); t \geq 0\}$ is the GPP with the parameter set $(\lambda(t), \alpha, 1)$.*

If $\alpha = 0$ then the GPP reduces to the NHPP with the intensity function $\lambda(t)$, that is, the GPP repair coincides with the minimal repair. On the other hand, since the stochastic intensity increases with α, this means that the frequency of failures also increases and an imperfection of repair is expressed through the GPP repair. Similar to the previous studies concerned with warranty problems, the GPP with the parameter set $(\lambda(t), \theta_\bullet, 1)$ is applied to our model and $\theta_\bullet$, which is referred to the degree of repair, depends upon whether a warranty is contracted or not as θ_b, θ_0, and θ_1. Hereafter, we abbreviate the expression as the GPP repair with $\theta_\bullet$, if necessary. We assume that the time for repair is negligible, as a result, the number of failures constitutes the GPP.

At the instant that the contract of a base warranty expires, a customer can decide whether to contract an extended warranty or not. If a customer contracts an extended warranty of period w_e and operates the product, then the cost for repair is incurred by the manufacturer similar to the case of base warranty. After the expiration of the extended warranty, the customer operates the product without contraction of an extended warranty further, that is, the cost for repair is incurred by the customer, and stop operating at time τ_1 from the instant that the extended warranty is contracted and purchases a new product. Different from a base warranty, however, the degree of repair changes from θ_b to θ_1. While the cost for a base warranty is included in the price of a product, a customer chooses an appropriate extended warranty and spends the fee only. Since this indicates the details of their contracts may be different, we assume that the degrees of repair are different as θ_b and θ_1. If a customer does not contract an extended warranty and operates the product, then the cost for repair c_m is incurred not by the manufacturer but by the customer and the product undergoes the GPP repair with θ_0 upon the occurrence of a failure. After it elapsed τ_0 time units, the customer stops operating the product and purchases a new product. Then, whether an extended warranty is contracted or not has an influence on the loss due to a failure and the degree of repair, respectively. When a customer does not contract an extended warranty, the customer asks an external agent which is different from the manufacturer to repair the product upon the occurrence of failure. Thus, to consider that technical capability for repairing products differs, we introduce two non-identical degree of repair as θ_0 and θ_1. Similarly, to consider an ability for addressing failures of the manufacturer could be different from that of the external agent, we suppose that the losses due to failure differ as c_d^0 and c_d^1.

3 Formulation

3.1 Preparation

We derive two expected cost rates with and without an extended warranty as an objective function. As described in Section 2, we employ a periodical replacement policy with the GPP repair under a base and an extended warrantirs. In this study, we evaluate the two expected cost rates from the perspective of a customer. Also, since manufacturers decide warranty period based on the reliability of products and competitors, we suppose that w_b and w_e are given in advance. Thus, the decision variable of our model is an optimal time for preventive replacement.

Since $\{N_b(t); t \geq 0\}$, $\{N_0(t); t \geq 0\}$, and $\{N_1(t); t \geq 0\}$ follow the GPPs with θ_b, θ_1, and θ_1, respectively, we define

$$M_b(t) = E[N_b(t)],\ M_0(t) = E[N_0(t)],\ M_1(t) = E[N_1(t)],$$

which indicate the expected number of repairs within $(0, t]$.

Now the restarting property of the GPP is useful for the formulation of our problem. Thus, we provide an important proposition (See Cha [4], Cha and Finkelstein [5]).

Propotision 3.1. *(Cha [4])*
Let $\{N(t); t \geq 0\}$ be the GPP with the set of parameters $(\lambda(t), \alpha, \beta)$. At an arbitrary time $u > 0$, given $\{N(u-) = n, T_1 = t_1, T_2 = t_2, \cdots, T_n = t_n\}$, the conditional future process $\{N_u(t); t \geq 0\}$, where $N_u(t) \equiv N(u+t) - N(u)$, is also the GPP with the set of parameters $(\lambda(u+t), \alpha, \beta + n\alpha)$.

Also, for the GPP repair process $\{N(t); t \geq 0\}$ with the parameters $(\lambda(t), \alpha, 1)$, the expected number of GPP repairs in $(0, t]$ can be expressed as

$$E[N(t)] = \frac{1}{\alpha}\{\exp[\alpha\Lambda(t)] - 1\}, \tag{1}$$

where $\Lambda(t) = \int_0^t \lambda(s)ds$.

3.2 Expected cost rate without an extended warranty

Since the number of repairs follow the GPP with θ_b and a customer suffers the loss due to failures within a base warranty period, the expected loss is expressed as $c_d^1 M_b(t)$. When the customer does not contract an extended warranty at the expiration of the base warranty, whose period is w_b, the number of repairs follow the GPP with θ_0 and the loss due to failures and the cost for repair are incurred by the customer. Thus, the expected loss and cost in $[w_b, w_b + \tau)$ is expressed as

$$(c_d^0 + c_m)\{M_0(\tau + w_b) - M_0(w_b)\},$$

because the customer purchases a new product at $w_b + \tau$ with cost c_p.

Hence, the expected cost rate without an extended warranty $C_0(\tau)$ is expressed as

$$C_0(\tau) = \frac{c_d^1 M_b(w_b) + (c_d^0 + c_m)\{M_0(\tau + w_b) - M_0(w_b)\} + c_p}{w_b + \tau}, \tag{2}$$

and we define

$$C_0(\tau_0^*) \equiv \min\left[C_0(\tau)\right].$$

3.3 Expected cost rate with an extended warranty

Similar to the case without an extended warranty, the number of repairs within a base warranty follows the GPP with θ_b and the loss due to failures and the cost for repair are incurred by a customer. On the other hand, the customer contracts an extended warranty after the expiration of the base warranty with period w_b and the number of repairs follow the GPP with θ_1 instead of θ_0 without the extended warranty. However, the loss due to a failure is c_d^1 different from c_d^0. Thus, the expected loss and cost in $[w_b, w_b + w_e)$ is expressed as

$$(c_d^1 + c_m)\{M_1(w_b + w_e) - M_1(w_b)\}.$$

Also, after the expiration of the extended warranty, the customer operates and maintains the product without any warranty and replace it at τ.

Therefore, the expected cost rate with an extended warranty $C_1(\tau)$ is expressed as

$$\begin{aligned} C_1(\tau) = &\frac{1}{w_b + w_e + \tau}\left[c_d^1 M_b(w_b)\right. \\ &+ c_d^1\{M_1(w_e + w_b) - M_1(w_b)\} \\ &\left.+(c_d^0 + c_m)\{M_0(w_e + w_b + \tau) - M_0(w_e + w_b)\}\right], \end{aligned} \tag{3}$$

and we define

$$C_1(\tau_1^*) \equiv \min\left[C_1(\tau)\right].$$

4 Numerical Analysis

As described in Section 2, we suppose that whether a customer contracts an extended warranty affects the loss due to a failure and the degree of repair. Thus, we perform numerical experiments based on these combinations. In addition, we introduce a measure to evaluate the efficiency of an extended warranty by defining γ as

$$\gamma = \frac{M_1(w_b + w_e) - M_1(w_b)}{M_0(w_b + w_e) - M_0(w_b)}. \tag{4}$$

Eq.(4) means that the contraction of an extended warranty is more economical with increase of the efficiency γ compared with the maintenance policy without an extended warranty.

For numerical analysis, we suppose that the lifetime of a product follows the Weibull distributon with parameters

(α, β) and its CDF is given by

$$F(t) = 1 - \exp\left[-\alpha t^{\beta}\right] = 1 - \exp[-\Lambda(t)] = 1 - \exp\left[-\int_0^t \lambda(s)ds\right] \quad (t > 0).$$

And the basic parameters and costs are set as follows:

$$w_b = 1.0,\ w_e = 2.0, \theta_b = 0.0,\ \theta_1 = 0.1,$$
$$c_m = 1.5,\ c_p = 10.0,\ c_d^0 = 3.0,\ c_w = 1.0.$$

$\theta_b = 0.0$ means the minimal repair is conducted within a base warranty period.

These values are set except for the degrees of repair based on the information on personal computers (PCs) in use investigated by a research company in Japan. To agree with this situation, we set parameters α and β of the Weibull distribution whose expectation (mean lifetime) is $7-8$ (year), which is approximately the same as the expected period of use for PCs. Also, a base and extended warranty periods are also set based on the service of a maker that sells PCs in Japan.

4.1 Effect of the degree of repair

First, we investigate the effect of the degree of repair when an extended warranty is contracted. Thus, we suppose that $c_d^0 = c_d^1 = 3.0$ and change θ_0.

Table 1: Optimal policy when θ_0 changes under $\alpha = 0.1$ and $\beta = 1.1$

θ_0	t_0^*	$C_0(t_0^*)$	t_1^*	$C_1(t_1^*)$
0.5	13.428	1.658	11.709	1.695
1.0	8.755	2.116	6.885	2.157
1.5	6.678	2.491	4.737	2.523
2.0	5.449	2.821	3.463	2.832
2.5	4.618	**3.122**	2.597	**3.099**
3.0	4.011	3.122	2.597	3.099

Table 1 shows that it is better to contract an extended warranty when $\theta_0 = 2.5$. In this case, the efficiency changes from $\gamma = 1.525$ under $\theta_0 = 2.0$ to $\gamma = 1.709$ under $\theta = 2.5$.

Then, we make a hypothesis based on Table 1 that to contract an extended warranty is better under the approximately same efficiency and a different mean lifetime. To ascertain this hypothesis, we set $\alpha = 0.07$ and $\beta = 1.3$, and as a result, the mean lifetime is calculated as 7.142, which is close to the case of Table 1.

Table 2 tells us that it is better to contract an extended warranty when $\theta_0 = 3.0$ and $\theta_1 = 0.1$. Also, since we have the $\gamma = 1.721$ under $\theta_0 = 3.0$, the hypothesis seems to be appropriate to decide whether an extended warranty is contracted or not. However, we do not conclude that the hypothesis is correct under $\alpha = 0.04$ and $\beta = 1.5$, where the mean lifetime is 7.718, as Table 3, because an extended warranty does not become appropriate even if the efficiency is larger than that of the previous two examples.

Table 2: Optimal policy when θ_0 changes under $\alpha = 0.07$ and $\beta = 1.3$

θ_0	t_0^*	$C_0(t_0^*)$	t_1^*	$C_1(t_1^*)$
1.5	5.789	2.580	3.859	2.633
2.5	4.278	3.089	2.291	3.106
3.0	3.811	**3.310**	1.802	**3.295**
3.5	3.443	3.516	1.414	3.459
4.5	2.894	3.894	0.828	3.719

Table 3: Optimal policy when θ_0 changes under $\alpha = 0.04$ and $\beta = 1.5$

θ_0	t_0^*	$C_0(t_0^*)$	t_1^*	$C_1(t_1^*)$	γ
4.3	3.605	3.171	1.625	3.213	1.719
4.4	3.558	3.196	1.576	3.235	1.742
4.5	3.513	3.221	1.528	3.256	1.766
4.6	3.468	3.246	1.482	3.277	1.790
4.7	3.426	3.270	1.438	3.298	1.814

In Tables 1 and 2, the difference between t_0^* and t_1^* is approximately 2 in the three examples and it coincides with the extended warranty period. This means that the renewal cycles of the two maintenance policies are almost consistent.

4.2 Effect of the loss due to a failure

The results in Section 4.1 indicate that a customer cannot determine whether to contract an extended warranty based on the efficiency. In the next, we investigate the negative impact of the loss due to a failure without an extended warranty by changing c_d^0 when $\theta_b = 0.0$, $\theta_0 = \theta_1 = 0.1$, and $c_d^1 = 3.0$. Then, the efficiency is constant as $\gamma = 1.0$.

Table 4: Optimal policy when c_d^0 changes

Parameters	c_d^0	t_0*	$C_0(t_0^*)$	t_1^*	$C_1(t_1^*)$
$\alpha = 0.1$	5.5	25.249	1.536	23.301	1.537
$\beta = 1.1$	6.0	24.334	1.617	22.232	1.614
$\alpha = 0.07$	5.0	15.615	1.800	13.792	1.813
$\beta = 1.3$	5.5	14.997	1.898	13.057	1.897
$\alpha = 0.04$	7.0	11.076	2.096	9.118	2.101
$\beta = 1.5$	7.5	10.713	2.169	8.700	2.167

Table 4 shows that it is better to contract an extended warranty even if the efficiency is constant because the loss due to a failure without an extended warranty increases, in other words, this means that the comparative efficiency of an extended warranty increases. Also, we find that c_d^0/c_d^1 is different among the three mean lifetimes that are close. Thus, the effect of an extended warranty under the GPP repair could depend upon the shape of a failure rate under the GPP repair including the minimal repair.

Similar to the results in Section 4.1, we find that the difference between t_0^* and t_1^* is approximately 2 in the two examples even if the degree of repair is constant and the loss due to a failure changes.

4.3 Mixed effect of the degree of repair and the loss due to a failure

One can easily hypothesize that if the degree of repair and the loss due to a failure change simultaneously then an extended warranty should be appropriate under small efficiency. Similar to the previous two examples, we fix the values of c_d^1 and θ_1 as 3.0 and 0.1 and provide the efficiencies as well as the optimal solutions for comparison. Then we start the first numerical example from $\theta_0 = 0.15$ and $c_d^0 = 0.15$ since these values are larger by 50 percent than those with an extended warranty.

Table 5: Optimal policy when θ_0 and c_d^0 change under $\alpha = 0.1$ and $\beta = 1.1$

θ_0	c_d^0	t_0^*	$C_0(t_0^*)$	t_1^*	$C_1(t_1^*)$	γ
0.15	4.5	22.575	1.470	20.856	1.481	1.010
0.16	4.8	21.355	1.540	19.546	1.548	1.013
0.17	5.1	20.259	1.609	18.367	1.615	1.015
0.18	5.4	19.267	1.678	17.299	1.680	1.017
0.19	5.7	18.366	**1.747**	16.328	**1.745**	1.019
0.20	6.0	17.542	1.815	15.440	1.808	1.022

Table 5 shows that the efficiency for an appropriate extended warranty is smaller than the one in Table 1 since c_d^0 is also increased simultaneously.

Since the efficiency increases in Table 2 for the appropriate extended warranty, we set θ_0 and c_d^0 larger than the ones in Table 5 for the next numerical example under $\alpha = 0.07$ and $\beta = 1.3$.

Table 6: Optimal policy when θ_0 and c_d^0 change under $\alpha = 0.07$ and $\beta = 1.3$

θ_0	c_d^0	t_0^*	$C_0(t_0^*)$	t_1^*	$C_1(t_1^*)$	γ
1.1	3.6	6.551	2.472	4.620	2.511	1.201
1.5	3.9	5.421	2.787	3.440	2.803	1.294
1.9	4.2	4.747	**3.011**	2.732	**3.006**	1.395
2.3	4.5	4.227	3.214	2.203	3.184	1.505

Table 6 shows that while the efficiency is larger than the one in Table 5, it is smaller than that in Table 2, which changes the degree of repair only.

Table 7: Optimal policy when θ_0 and c_d^0 change under $\alpha = 0.04$ and $\beta = 1.5$

θ_0	c_d^0	t_0^*	$C_0(t_0^*)$	t_1^*	$C_1(t_1^*)$	γ
2.2	3.9	4.856	2.729	2.904	2.782	1.304
2.7	4.2	4.309	2.953	2.331	2.983	1.391
3.3	4.5	3.819	**3.193**	1.816	**3.188**	1.505

Similar to the results in Sections 4.1 and 4.2, the difference between t_0^* and t_1^* is approximately 2 in the three examples. Also, we obtain that to contract an extended warranty is appropriate, differently from the example that the degree of repair is only changed in Table 3.

5 Discussion

The numerical results that to contract an extended warranty is appropriate indicate that the difference between t_0^* and t_1^* is close to the extended warranty period, which is 2. Thus, we find that the renewal cycle under the optimal periodical replacement policy in our model does not depend upon whether a customer contracts an extended warranty or not.

Also, compared with the examples that the degree of repair changes only, the efficiency becomes smaller when the loss due to a failure is also reduced simultaneously. This result would agree with the intuition since the posive impact of an extended warranty on the cost becomes larger.

6 Conclusions

This research has constructed the periodical replacement policy with a base and extended warranties that the GPP repair is applied for occurrence of failures. To evaluate the effectiveness of an extended warranty, we consider the parameters of the GPP repair, which means the degree of repair, and the loss due to a failure as important factors depend upon whether a customer contracts an extended warranty or not. We have derived the expected cost rate for the two cases and conducted the numerical analysis for the comparison and evaluation. As a result, we showed that to contract an extended warranty is appropriate that the degree of repair and the loss due to a failure are relatively smaller than those without an extended warranty.

However, our model assumed that the parameters of the GPP change at the expiration of a base or extended warranty. This means that some kind of a preventive maintenance is conducted without any cost and the restarting property, which is Proposition 3.1, is not appropriately used for the modeling. However, to conduct a preventive maintenance is not a necessary condition for contracting an extended warranty, that is, the assumption that the parameters of the GPP changes is not realistic in many situations. Thus, to modify and analyze the model that uses the restarting property is the future work of this research. Also, it would be important to construct a cost model that a product is continuously monitored by a manufacturer during a base warranty because of recent techniques for remote monitoring.

References

[1] M. Afsahi and M. Shafiee, A stochastic simulation-optimization model for base-warranty and extended-warranty decision-making of user- and out-of-warranty products, *RESS*, Vol.197 (2020), 106722.

[2] W.R. Blischke and D.N.P. Murthy, Warranty Cost Analysis, Dekker (1994).

[3] M. Brown and F. Proschan, Imperfect repair, *Journal of Applied Probability*, Vol.20 (1983), pp.851-859.

[4] J.W. Cha, Characterization of the generalized Polya process and its applications, *Advances in Applied Probability*, Vol.46(2014), pp.1148-1171.

[5] J.H. Cha and M. Finkelstein, Point Processes for Reliability Analysis, Springer, 2018.

[6] W.L. Chang, J. Lin, Optimal maintenance policy and length of extended warranty within the life cycle of products, *Computers and Mathematics with Applications*, Vol.63 (2012), pp.144-150.

[7] Y. Chien, Optimal Periodic Replacement Policy for a GPP Repairable Product under the Free-Repair Warranty, *quality Technology and Quantitative Management*, Vol.16(2019), No.3, pp.347-354.

[8] M. Finkelstein, on the optimal degree of imperfect repair, *RESS*, Vol.138 (2015), pp.54-58.

[9] S.K. Gupta, I. Mukhopadhyay, A. Chatterjee, Two-dimensional extended warranty length design from incomplete warranty data based on a new price curve considering different maintenance, *Computers and Industrial Engineering*, Vol.170 (2022), 108323.

[10] Z. He, D. Wang, S. He, Y. Zhang, A. Dai, Two-dimensional extended warranty strategy, including maintenance level and purchase time: A win-win perspective, *Computers and Industrial Engineering*, Vol.141 (2020), 106294.

[11] F. Hooti, J. Ahmadi, M. Longobardi, Optimal extended warranty length with limited number of repairs in the warranty period, *RESS*, Vol.203 (2020), 10711.

[12] Y. Huang, C. Huang, J. Ho, A customized two-dimensional extended warranty with preventive maintenance, *EJOR*, Vol.257 (2017), pp.971-978.

[13] R. Jiang, A Novel Two-fold Sectional Approximation of Renewal Function and its Applications, *RESS*, Vol.193, 106624 (2020).

[14] K. Jung, M. Park, D. Park, Cost optimization model following extended renewing two-phase warranty, *Computers and Industrial Engineering*, Vol.79 (2015), pp.188-194.

[15] E. Kao and M. Smith, Computational Approximations of Renewal Process Relating to a Warranty Problem: The Case of Phase-type Lifetimes, *EJOR*, Vol.90, No.1, pp.156-170 (1996).

[16] M. Kijima, Some Results for Repairable systems with General Repair, *Journal of Applied Probability*, Vol.26, pp.89-102 (1989).

[17] Y. Lam, Geometric Processes and Replacement Problem, *Acta mathematicae Applicatae Sinica*, Vol.4, pp.366-377 (1988).

[18] H. Lee and J.H. Cha, New stochastic models for preventive maintenance and maintenance optimization, *EJOR*, Vo.255 (2016), pp.80-90.

[19] T. Li, S. He and Z. Zhao, Optimal Warranty Policy Design for Deteriorating Products with Random Failure Threshold, *Reliability Engineering and System Safety*, Vol.218, Part A, 108142 (2022).

[20] A. Mitra, Warranty parameters for extended two-dimensional warranties incorporating consumer preferences, *EJOR*, Vol.291 (2021), pp.525-535.

[21] T. Nakagawa, *Stochastic Processes with Application to Reliability Theory*, Springer (2011).

[22] Y. Pan and M.U. Thomas, Repair and Replacement Decisions for Warranted Products under Markov Deterioration, *IEEE Trans. Rel.*, Vol.59, No.2, pp.368-373 (2010).

[23] D.N.P. Murthy and W.R. Blischke, Warranty management and Product Manufacture, Springer (2006).

[24] M. Shafiee and S. Chukova, Maintenance Models in Warranty: a Literature Review, *EJOR* Vol.229, No.3, pp.561-572 (2013).

[25] L. Shang, S. Si, S. Sun and T. Jin, Optimal Warranty Design and Post-warranty Maintenance for Products Subject to Stochastic Degradation, *IISE Trans.*, Vol.50, No.10, pp.913-927 (2018).

[26] C. Su, X. Wang, A two-stage preventive maintenance optimization model incorporating two-dimensional extended warranty, *Reliability Engineering and System Safety*, Vol.155 (2016), pp.169–178.

[27] M. Toledo, M.A. Freitas, E.A. Colosimo, G.L. Gilardoni, ARA and ARI imperfect repair models: Estimation, goodness-of-fit and reliability prediction, *RESS*, Vol.140 (2015), pp.107-115.

[28] L. Wang, Y. Yang, H. Zhu and G. Liu, Optimal Condition-based Renewable Warranty Policy for Products with Three-stage Failure Process, *QTQM*, Vol.17, No.2, pp.216-233 (2020).

[29] W.Y. Yun, D.N.P. Murthy, N. Jack, Warranty servicing with imperfect repair, *International Journal of Production Economics*, Vol.111 (2008), pp.159-169.

A Trajectory-Learning-Driven Lifetime Prognosis Approach Capturing Nonlinear Degradation Heterogeneity

Jiaxuan Zhan[1], Binshi Wang[1], Fanping Wei[1*]

[1] School of Reliability and Systems Engineering, Beihang University, China

Keywords: Health prognosis, Degradation analysis, Failure risk evaluation, Adaptive trajectory learning, Stochastic process.

Abstract - Remaining useful life (RUL) prediction is crucial to supporting intelligent maintenance and health management of safety-critical products. Although advanced data-driven approaches such as deep neural networks are effective in processing high-dimensional non-linear health features, their application to field RUL prediction confronts with two challenges: (a) adaptivity of the lifetime parameter learning process is often restricted, and (b) prediction of multi-source uncertainties are almost analytically intractable. This paper addresses such challenges by devising a tractable, global adaptive model-data-interaction prognostic framework, where a non-linear stochastic degradation model governed by self-adaptive trajectory pattern is constructed to transfer historical health knowledge. In particular, a joint parameter learning framework is established under the structure of a multi-branch Bayesian network, such that to simultaneously learn: (a) degradation model parameters, and (b) network hyper-parameters. Additionally, the key control parameters of the degradation process are updated adaptively leveraging multi-dimensional sequential Bayesian learning. An efficient interpolation algorithm is further proposed to alleviate computation burden of RUL distributions. Case studies conducted on both turbofan engines degradation data and field train bearing vibration data demonstrate the superior model performance compared to existing methodologies.

1. Introduction

In recent years, remarkable progress has been made in machine learning for equipment fault diagnosis, remaining useful life prediction and health management [1-6]. In particular, deep neural networks (DNN) have received widespread attention due to their ability to extract high-dimensional nonlinear features from a large amount of monitoring data, such as restricted Boltzmann machines (RBM), recurrent neural networks (RNN), convolutional neural networks (CNN), etc [7-12]. These methods have been widely applied to remaining useful life (RUL) prediction, covering various fields such as train bearings, wind turbine gearboxes, lithium batteries, and aviation gyroscopes. Recently, prediction models based on graph neural networks (GNN) have also emerged, which improve prediction accuracy through cross-domain information fusion [13-17].

Despite the excellent performance of DNN-based methods, there are still two major challenges in practical applications [18, 19]. One is the insufficient generalization ability. Especially when dealing with data from new equipment or unseen data, the performance of the model may decline significantly [20-22][17]. This is because in practical scenarios, the training data often comes from a limited number of equipment that are not exactly the same, making it difficult for the model to adapt to new situations. The other is the insufficient uncertainty modeling [23-28]. Most DNN methods fail to effectively handle the sources of uncertainty in prediction, including the aleatoric uncertainty caused by sensor errors and noise, as well as the epistemic uncertainty due to insufficient model structure or data [29-35]. Ignoring these uncertainties may affect the robustness of predictions and the timeliness of maintenance decisions [36-40].

To address these issues, researchers have attempted to introduce uncertainty-aware mechanisms to improve prediction models [41-44]. For example, Kaplan et al. proposed a framework for quantifying uncertainty by evaluating the similarity between training and test data; Biggio et al. combined uncertainty modeling with deep Gaussian processes to enhance the adaptability to high-dimensional data[24]; Bayesian neural networks (BNN) have also been used for probabilistic modeling to capture multi-source uncertainties [45-50].

Another solution is to use stochastic process models to describe the degradation process of equipment. For example, the Wiener process is often used to model the degradation behavior with random properties. Model-driven methods of this kind can express aleatoric uncertainty through analytical functions and support online parameter updates to deal with equipment differences, thereby improving the generalization ability and the modeling of epistemic uncertainty. However, they usually lack the ability to learn complex degradation patterns from historical data and rely on predefined degradation trajectories, which may not perform well under dynamic operating conditions. To make up for this deficiency, some hybrid models have been proposed, such as the enhanced stochastic recurrent hybrid model (ESRHM) proposed by Lin et al. and the adaptive RUL prediction method (ARR) proposed by Kim et al.

In order to further improve the performance of remaining useful life (RUL) prediction, this paper proposes an easy-to-implement hybrid prognosis framework. This framework, through an adaptive multi-trajectory learning mechanism, uses a stochastic process that integrates data-driven evolutionary patterns and an adaptive drift term to model the potential degradation path. By learning multi-step future trajectories through a joint parameter training structure, it can extract hidden degradation features from global historical data, breaking through the limitations of traditional degradation models that rely on predefined trajectories.

Under this framework, there are mainly two calculation processes:

In the model training stage, a Bayesian network structure is constructed. A single DNN is used to simultaneously learn the degradation pattern and the noise level, and the variance is modeled as a new network branch.

In the RUL prediction stage, an interpolation approximation algorithm is proposed to generate virtual degradation paths. Compared with the traditional particle filter (PF), this algorithm does not require iterative simulation and can generate a complete path in one step, greatly improving the computational efficiency.

Empirical studies on the turbofan engine dataset show that the proposed method performs superiorly in terms of prediction accuracy and uncertainty quantification.

In summary, the main contributions of this paper include:

- Proposing an adaptive model-data collaborative prediction model that can not only capture the overall degradation trend but also adjust parameters adaptively according to changes in operating conditions.
- Designing an efficient interpolation algorithm that saves more computational resources and time compared with the particle filter.

The subsequent chapter arrangements are as follows: Section 2: Introduce the basic prognosis model. Section 3: Explain the life prediction method in detail. Section 4: Verify the effectiveness of the model through experiments. Section 5: Summarize the full text.

2. Model Framework

In this study, a hybrid adaptive model-data interactive intelligent prediction model is proposed. This model integrates the capabilities of global pattern learning and local adaptive parameter learning. Compared with traditional predefined degradation trajectory models, this model can more flexibly describe the evolution of unsteady and nonlinear degradation behaviors.

Specifically, the proposed prognosis framework includes the following three innovative technical modules, as indicated in Figure 1. :

Global DNN-driven evolutionary pattern: Through the deep neural network, the global degradation pattern is automatically learned from historical data to capture complex and dynamically changing degradation trends, instead of relying on predefined specific degradation paths.

Multi-source parameter estimation supported by joint training: A Bayesian network containing nodes related to specific degradation models is constructed to achieve rapid joint training of parameters and hyperparameters of stochastic processes and neural networks, avoiding the limitations brought by separate estimation.

Interpolation-based life prediction: In order to accelerate online RUL prediction and reduce the computational burden, an interpolation approximation algorithm is proposed. Compared with traditional particle filters, this method not only significantly reduces the computational load but also shows better performance in degeneracy control.

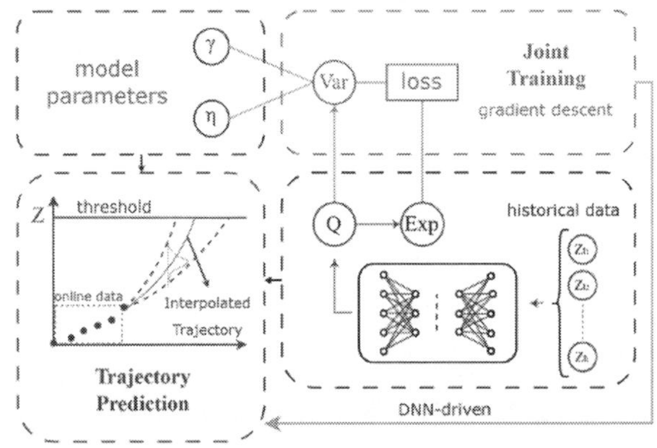

Figure 1. The prognostic framework.

2.1. Generalized Degradation Process

The degradation process of a product can be regarded as a continuous-time stochastic process $\{Z(t), t > t_0\}$, where $Z(t)$ represents the degradation level of the product at time t. When $Z(t)$ exceeds a pre-set threshold D, the product is considered to have failed. The evolution of the degradation process is controlled by a pattern term $Q(t;\Theta)$, where Θ is an unknown parameter. Since the future degradation state is not independent of the past degradation state, $Q(t;\Theta)$ can be expressed in the following form:

$$Q(t;\Theta) = f(Z_{t_i}, Z_{t_{i-1}}, Z_{t_{i-2}}, \cdots, Z_{t_0}, t;\Theta), t > t_i, \quad (1)$$

where t_i is the latest measurement point before t, Z_{t_i} is the observation value at t_i, and f is a nonlinear function parameterized by the unknown parameter Θ.

In this paper, a nonlinear stochastic process with adaptive drift and Brownian motion is used to characterize the degradation evolution. Therefore, the observation function at t is written as:

$$Z(t) = Z_{t_i} + \int_{t_i}^{t} \varphi(\tau) dQ(\tau;\Theta) + \int_{t_i}^{t} \eta(\tau) dB(\tau), t > t_i, \quad (2)$$

where $\varphi(t)$ is the drift term, $\eta(t)$ is the diffusion term, and $B(\cdot)$ represents a standard Brownian motion (BM).

It should be noted that $\eta(t)$ reflects the severity of the noise, and due to its stability, it can usually be simplified to $\eta(t) = \eta_B$. The drift term $\varphi(t)$ is a continuous and time-varying stochastic process, which is characterized by another general Wiener process, that is:

$$\varphi(t) = \varphi_{t_i} + \gamma\Lambda(t - t_i), \quad (3)$$

where γ is the diffusion parameter, and $\Lambda(\cdot)$ represents the standard BM.

According to the properties of the Brownian motion term, the entire term can be analytically represented by a Gaussian distribution. Equations (2) and (3) summarize three key influencing factors of the degradation trajectory: (a) the data-segmented evolution pattern $Q(\tau;\Theta)$, (b) the instantaneous degradation rate $\varphi(t)$ affected by random environmental disturbances, and (c) the unavoidable noise level η_B.

2.2. Joint Pattern Training

The model proposed in this study contains multiple parameters that need to be determined. These unknown model parameters can be divided into two categories:

(a) Explicit parameters of the stochastic degradation process, including the diffusion coefficient γ, the noise intensity η_B, and the initial drift term φ_{t_0};

(b) Implicit weight parameters of the DNN model, which can be regarded as internal nodes in the Bayesian network.

In traditional methods, these explicit parameters are usually treated as hyperparameters and need to be set based on experience. However, within the framework of this paper, by taking advantage of the good mathematical properties of Brownian motion (BM), we can establish the connection between the parameters of the stochastic process and the parameters of deep learning through maximum likelihood estimation (MLE), and then jointly estimate these two types of parameters. The specific calculation steps are described as follows.

In order to perform maximum likelihood estimation, we need to calculate the expectation and variance of the stochastic degradation process.

By utilizing the statistical properties of Brownian motion, the degradation quantity at any moment follows a normal distribution. Using the properties of expectation, the expectation can be expressed as:

$$\begin{aligned} E(Z(t)) &= E\left(Z_{t_i} + \int_{t_i}^{t} \varphi(\tau) dQ(\tau;\theta) + \eta_B B(t-t_i)\right) \\ &= Z_{t_i} + \int_{t_i}^{t} E(\varphi(\tau)) dQ(\tau;\theta) + 0 \\ &= Z_{t_i} + E(\varphi(t_i))(Q(t;\theta) - Q(t_i;\theta)). \end{aligned} \quad (4)$$

Since $Q(t;\theta)$ only affects the degradation trajectory after t_i, we can adjust the magnitude of $Q(t_i;\theta)$ to make $Z_{t_i} - E(\varphi(t_i))Q(t_i;\theta) = 0$. Similarly, we can scale $Q(t;\theta)$ by modifying θ so as to make $\varphi_{t_0} = 1$. Finally, we get $E(Z(t)) = Q(t;\theta)$.

The variance of the degradation process can be expressed as.

$$\begin{aligned} var(Z(t)) &= var\left(Z_{t_i} + \int_{t_i}^{t} \varphi(\tau) dQ(\tau;\theta) + \eta_B B(t-t_i)\right) \\ &= \gamma^2 \int_{t_i}^{t} (Q(t_i;\theta) - Q(\tau;\theta))^2 d\tau + \eta_B^2 (t-t_i). \end{aligned} \quad (5)$$

Through numerical calculation methods, the integration calculation process of the unknown function can be simplified into a calculation process of the existing data.

$$var(Z_{t_i}) \approx \frac{1}{3}\gamma^2 \Delta Q_i^2 \Delta t_i + \eta_B^2 \Delta t_i, \quad (6)$$

where, $\Delta Q_i = Q_{t_i} - Q_{t_{i-1}}$, $\Delta Z_i = Z_{t_i} - Z_{t_{i-1}}$, $\Delta t_i = t_i - t_{i-1}$.

Substitute the above expectation and variance formulas into the negative log-likelihood function, and we can obtain:

$$L \propto \frac{1}{n} \sum_{i=1}^{n} \left(\frac{\left(Z_{t_i} - Q(t_i;\Theta)\right)^2}{2var(Z_{t_i})} + \frac{1}{2} ln\left(var(Z_{t_i})\right) \right). \quad (7)$$

By using this function as the loss function, we can successfully relate the parameters of the stochastic process to the parameters of deep learning, and further transform the estimation problem of these two types of parameters into a machine learning problem.

3. RUL Calculation

Based on the model parameters and hyperparameters obtained through training, we can obtain the specific form of the degradation process. Then, we can use the degradation trajectory to predict the remaining useful life distribution, and its specific form is as follows:

$$Z(t) = \varphi_{t_i} Q(t;\theta) + B(\xi(t)), \quad (8)$$

Where $B(\cdot)$ represents the standard Brownian motion.

Since the degradation process has the characteristic of nonlinear evolution, it is very difficult to analytically solve the RUL distribution. Although the scale transformation method (ST) provides an approximate solution, the numerical stability is poor when the path is not smooth; although the particle filter (PF) has strong applicability, the computational cost is high and there is a "degeneracy" problem, and a complex resampling mechanism needs to be introduced to alleviate it.

For this reason, this paper adopts the Monte Carlo algorithm for numerical fitting, which can significantly reduce the computational overhead while ensuring the accuracy. Specifically, we construct the following alternative process:

$$\chi(t) = \varphi_{t_i} Q(t;\theta) + k\sqrt{\xi(t)}. \quad (9)$$

It can be seen that $\chi(t)$ has the same mean and variance as $Z(t)$ and is easy to sample. By finding the time point t_n that satisfies $\chi(t_n) = D$, the RUL distribution can be estimated.

4. Case Study

We conducted numerical experiments based on the NASA C-MAPSS turbofan engine degradation dataset. The entire dataset is divided into four subsets, namely FD001, FD002, FD003, and FD004, according to the operating conditions and engine serial numbers. Each subset contains multivariate time-series data from 21 sensors, and FD002 and FD004 also include different operation settings. The four subsets contain 100, 260, 100, and 248 samples respectively.

To verify the robustness of the model under different working conditions, we selected the FD002 subset for model parameter estimation and testing. Since the model in this paper models the degradation process in a univariate form, the multi-sensor data needs to be fused into a unified health index (HI). The HI is constructed through the "stacking" method, that is, the outputs of multiple regression models are combined to improve the prediction performance and alleviate the overfitting problem. Finally, the HI is comprehensively generated from these regression results and used as the input of the model.

4.1. Parameter Estimation

The parameters of the adaptive Wiener model and the adaptive DNN model are summarized in Table 2, including the initial drift rate φ_{t_0}, the diffusion coefficient γ^2, and the noise intensity η_B^2.

Table 1. Parameter Estimation

Approach	φ_{t_0}	γ^2	η_B^2
Adaptive Wiener	4.67e-3	1.16e-3	7.00e-6
Adaptive DNN	1	6.36e-4	6.41e-6

The φ_{t_0} estimated by the Wiener process is 4.67e−3, while the φ_{t_0} in the adaptive DNN is set to 1. γ^2 and η_B^2 represent epistemic uncertainty and aleatoric uncertainty respectively. As can be seen from Table 2, the aleatoric uncertainties of the two models are similar (η_B^2 is similar), and this type of uncertainty comes from uncontrollable random factors and is difficult to be completely eliminated.

In contrast, the epistemic uncertainty (i.e., model uncertainty) of the adaptive DNN is significantly lower than that of the adaptive Wiener model, which benefits from the ability of the DNN to learn features from historical data. Therefore, the overall uncertainty level is also effectively reduced.

4.2. Experimental Results

The experiments were mainly carried out on the FD002 test set. Table 3 summarizes the average values of indicators such as RMSE, PCIP (90% confidence interval coverage), and MPIW.

Table 2. Model Performance on FD002

Method	RMSE	PCIP	MPIW
Adaptive DNN	16.25	99.45	81.27
DNN	17.71	-	-
Bayesian-LSTM	25.90	-	-
Adaptive Wiener	43.22	99.45	122.22
Wiener	45.62	100.00	118.41

The results show that the adaptive DNN outperforms the adaptive Wiener model in all indicators. Compared with the non-adaptive DNN, the RMSE of the adaptive DNN is reduced from 17.71 to 16.25. This is because in FD002, the training and test data have similar degradation trends, so less adaptive adjustment is required, but it still brings performance improvement.

5. Conclusion

This study proposes an innovative hybrid life prediction framework. This framework learns the global degradation trajectory in a data-driven manner, and uses a deep neural network (DNN) to extract the evolutionary pattern from historical health data. It enables the joint training of model parameters and hyperparameters, and supports both global pattern learning and adaptive parameter updating, thus enhancing the robustness and flexibility of predictions. In addition, this framework can effectively capture various uncertainties. Experimental results show that compared with traditional non-adaptive DNN models and stochastic process models, it demonstrates superior performance on the turbofan engine degradation dataset.

Future work may consider introducing more types of stochastic process models and expanding it into a multivariate framework to enhance its application scope and accuracy.

6. Acknowledgement

This work is supported by the National Natural Science Foundation of China (Grant No. 72101010, 72431008), and the Basic Technical Research Project of China (Grant No. JSZL2018601B004).

7. References

[1] Khan S, Yairi T. A review on the application of deep learning in system health management, Mechanical Systems and Signal Processing, 2018, 107: 241-265.

[2] Li H, Zhang Z, Li T, et al. A review on physics-informed data-driven remaining useful life prediction: Challenges and opportunities, Mechanical Systems and Signal Processing, 2024, 209: 111120.

[3] Wang J, Peng R, Qiu Q, et al. An inspection-based replacement planning in consideration of state-driven imperfect inspections, Reliability Engineering & System Safety, 2023, 232(6): 109064.

[4] Ma X, Liu B, Yang L, et al. Reliability analysis and condition-based maintenance optimization for a warm standby cooling system, Reliability Engineering & System Safety, 2020, 193: 106588.

[5] Wang J, Ma X, Qiu Q, et al. A hybrid inspection-replacement policy for multi-stage degradation considering imperfect inspection with variable probabilities, 2023, 241: 109629.

[6] Liao L, Jin W, Pavel R. Enhanced restricted Boltzmann machine with prognosability regularization for prognostics and health assessment, IEEE Transactions on Industrial Electronics, 2016, 63(11): 7076-7083.

[7] Cheng Y, Zhu H, Wu J, et al. Machine health monitoring using adaptive kernel spectral clustering and deep long short-term memory recurrent neural networks, IEEE Transactions on Industrial Informatics, 2018, 15(2): 987-997.

[8] Peng W, Ye Z, Chen N. Bayesian deep-learning-based health prognostics toward prognostics uncertainty, IEEE Transactions on Industrial Electronics, 2019, 67(3): 2283-2293.

[9] Ma Y, Wang Z, Gao J, et al. A novel method for remaining useful life of solid-state lithium-ion battery based on improved CNN and health indicators derivation, Mechanical Systems and Signal Processing, 2024, 220: 111646.

[10] Liu R, Yang B, Hauptmann A. Simultaneous bearing fault recognition and remaining useful life prediction using joint-loss convolutional neural network, IEEE Transactions on Industrial Informatics, 2020, 16(1): 87-96.

[11] LeCun Y, Bengio Y, Hinton G. Deep learning, Nature, 2015, 521(7553): 436-444.

[12] Zhang Z, Yang L. State-Based Opportunistic Maintenance with Multifunctional Maintenance Windows, IEEE Transactions on Reliability, 2021, 70(4): 1481-1494.

[13] Zhang Z, Yang L. Postponed maintenance scheduling integrating state variation and environmental impact, Reliability Engineering & System Safety, 2020, 202: 107065.

[14] Wang J, Yang L, Ma X, et al. Joint optimization of multi-window maintenance and spare part provisioning policies for production systems, Reliability Engineering & System Safety, 2021, 216: 108006.

[15] Zhang Y, Li Y, Wang Y, et al. Adaptive spatio-temporal graph information fusion for remaining useful life prediction, IEEE Sensors Journal, 2021, 22(4): 3334-3347.

[16] Wang G, Zhang Y, Lu M, et al. Hierarchical graph neural network with adaptive cross-graph fusion for remaining useful life prediction, Measurement Science and Technology, 2023, 34(5): 055112.

[17] Zhang C, Bengio S, Hardt M, et al. Understanding deep learning (still) requires rethinking generalization, Communications of the ACM, 2021, 64(3): 107-115.

[18] Helton JC, Johnson JD, Oberkampf WL, et al. Representation of analysis results involving aleatory and epistemic uncertainty, International Journal of General Systems, 2010, 39(6): 605-646.

[19] Sankararaman S. Significance, interpretation, and quantification of uncertainty in prognostics and remaining useful life prediction, Mechanical Systems and Signal Processing, 2015, 52: 228-247.

[20] Kaplan L, Cerutti F, Sensoy M, et al. Uncertainty aware AI ML: why and how, arXiv preprint arXiv:1809.07882, 2018.

[21] Wei F, Tan L, Ma X, et al. A hybrid prognostic framework: Stochastic degradation process with adaptive trajectory learning to transfer historical health knowledge, Mechanical System & Signal Processing, 2025, 224: 112171.

[22] Yang L, Chen Y, Qiu Q, et al. Risk Control of Mission-Critical Systems: Abort Decision-Makings Integrating Health and Age Conditions, IEEE Transactions on Industrial Informatics, 2022, 18(10): 6887-6894.

[23] Shang L, Liu B, Qiu Q, et al. Three-dimensional warranty and post-warranty maintenance of products with monitored mission cycles, Reliability Engineering & System Safety, 2023, 239:109506.

[24] Biggio L, Wieland A, Chao MA, et al. Uncertainty-aware prognosis via deep Gaussian process, IEEE Access, 2021, 9: 123517-123527.

[25] Chen G, Liu M, Chen J. Frequency-temporal-logic-based bearing fault diagnosis and fault interpretation using Bayesian optimization with Bayesian neural networks, Mechanical Systems and Signal Processing, 2020, 145: 106951.

[26] Ge R, Zhai Q, Wang H, et al. Wiener degradation models with scale-mixture normal distributed measurement errors for RUL prediction, Mechanical Systems and Signal Processing, 2022, 173: 109029.

[27] Zhang Z, Si X, Hu C, et al. Degradation data analysis and remaining useful life estimation: A review on Wiener-process-based methods, European Journal of Operational Research, 2018, 271(3): 775-796.

[28] Shen L, Wang Y, Zhai Q, et al. Degradation modeling using stochastic processes with random initial degradation, IEEE Transactions on Reliability, 2018, 68(4): 1320-1329.

[29] Li N, Lei Y, Yan T, et al. A Wiener-process-model-based method for remaining useful life prediction considering unit-to-unit variability, IEEE Transactions on Industrial Electronics, 2018, 66(3): 2092-2101.

[30] Ma J, Cai L, Liao G, et al. A multi-phase Wiener process-based degradation model with imperfect maintenance activities, Reliability Engineering & System Safety, 2023, 232: 109075.

[31] Lin Y, Chang L, Guan L. Enhanced stochastic recurrent hybrid model for RUL predictions via semi-supervised learning, Reliability Engineering & System Safety, 2024, 248: 110167.

[32] Kim G, Choi J, Lim S. Using transformer and a reweighting technique to develop a remaining useful life estimation method for turbofan engines, Engineering Applications of Artificial Intelligence, 2024, 133: 108475.

[33] Si X. An adaptive prognostic approach via nonlinear degradation modeling: Application to battery data, IEEE Transactions on Industrial Electronics, 2015, 62(8): 5082-5096.

[34] Zhai Q, Ye Z. Robust degradation analysis with non-Gaussian measurement errors, IEEE Transactions on Instrumentation and Measurement, 2017, 66(11): 2803-2812.

[35] Yang L, Wei F, Qiu Q, et al. Controlling Mission Hazards through Integrated Abort and Spare Support Optimization, Risk Analysis, 2024, DOI: 10.1111/risa.17696.

[36] Yang L, Wei F, Qiu Q. Mission Risk Control via Joint Optimization of Sampling and Abort Decisions, Risk Analysis, 2024, 44(3): 666-685.

[37] Yang L, Zhou S, Ma X, et al. Group machinery intelligent maintenance: Adaptive health prediction and global dynamic maintenance decision-making, Reliability Engineering & System Safety, 2024: 110426.

[38] Wang J, Tang L, Ma X, et al. Prognosis-driven reliability analysis and replacement policy optimization for two-phase continuous degradation, Reliability Engineering & System Safety, 2023, 230:108909.

[39] Jia H, Peng R, Yang L, et al. Reliability evaluation of demand-based warm standby systems with capacity storage, Reliability Engineering & System Safety, 2022, 218: 108132.

[40] Yang L, Ye ZS, Lee CG, et al. A two-phase preventive maintenance policy considering imperfect repair and postponed replacement, European Journal of Operational Research, 2019, 274: 966-977.

[41] Yang L, Peng R, Li G, Lee CG. Operations management of wind farms integrating multiple impacts of wind conditions and resource constraints, Energy Conversion and Management, 2020, 205: 112162.

[42] Wu D, Han R, Ma Y, et al. A two-dimensional maintenance optimization framework balancing hazard risk and energy consumption rates, Computers & Industrial Engineering, 2022, 169, 108193.

[43] Chen Y, Ma X, Wei F, et al. Dynamic Scheduling of Intelligent Group Maintenance Planning under Usage Availability Constraint, Mathematics, 2022, 10 (15): 2730.

[44] Yang L, Sun Q, Ye Z. Designing mission abort strategies based on early-warning information: Application to UAV, IEEE Transactions on Industrial Informatics, 2020, 16 (1): 277-287.

[45] Chen Y, Wu T, Ma X, et al. System Maintenance Optimization Under Structural Dependency: A Dynamic Grouping Approach, IEEE Systems Journal, 2024, DOI: 10.1109/JSYST.2024.3422284.

[46] Wang J, Ma X, Zhao Y, et al. Condition-based maintenance management for two-stage continuous deterioration with two-dimensional inspection errors, Quality and Reliability Engineering International, 2024, DOI: 10.1002/qre.3613.

[47] Wei F, Wang J, Ma X, et al. An Optimal Opportunistic Maintenance Planning Integrating Discrete- and Continuous-State Information, Mathematics, 2023, 11(15): 3322.

[48] Shang L, Liu B, Gao K, et al. Random Warranty and Replacement Models Customizing from the Perspective of Heterogeneity, Mathematics, 2023, 11(15): 3330.

[49] Wang L, Song L, Qiu Q, et al. Warranty Cost Analysis for Multi-State Products Protected by Lemon Laws. Applied Sciences, 2023, 13(3): 1541.

[50] Qu L, Liao J, Gao K, et al. Joint Optimization of Production Lot Sizing and Preventive Maintenance Threshold Based on Nonlinear Degradation, Applied Sciences, 2022, 12(17): 8638.

Author Index

A

B

C

D

F

G

H

I

J

K

L

M

N

O

P

Q

S

T

W

X

Y

Z